Electronic Communications Systems

Fundamentals Through Advanced

Fourth Edition

Wayne Tomasi

DeVry Institute of Technology
Phoenix, Arizona

Prentice
Hall

Upper Saddle River, New Jersey
Columbus, Ohio

Library of Congress Cataloging-in-Publication Data

Tomasi, Wayne.
   Electronic communications systems: fundamentals through advanced / Wayne
Tomasi.—4th ed.
      p. cm.
   1. Telecommunication systems. I. Title.

TK5101 .T625 2001
621.382—dc21   00-020204

Vice President and Publisher: Dave Garza
Editor in Chief: Stephen Helba
Assistant Vice President and Publisher: Charles E. Stewart, Jr.
Associate Editor: Kate Linsner
Production Editor: Alexandrina Benedicto Wolf
Production/Editorial Coordination: Carlisle Publishers Services
Design Coordinator: Robin Chukes
Cover Designer: Tanya Burgess
Cover photo: Index Stock
Production Manager: Matthew Ottenweller
Marketing Manager: Barbara Rose

This book was set in Times Roman by Carlisle Communications, Ltd. and was printed and bound by
Von Hoffmann Press. The cover was printed by Von Hoffmann Press.

10 9 8 7 6 5 4 3
ISBN 0-13-022125-2

To Cheryl,
my best friend since high school
and my loving and faithful wife for the past 34 years

To our six children: Aaron, Pernell, Belinda, Loren, Tennille, and Marlis;
their wives, husbands, boyfriends, and girlfriends: Cathy, Kriket, Robin, Mark, and Brent;
and of course, my three grandchildren: Avery, Kyren, and Riley.

Preface

The purpose of this book is to introduce the reader to the basic concepts of conventional analog electronic communications systems and to expand the reader's knowledge to more modern digital, optical fiber, microwave, satellite, and cellular and PCS telephone communications systems. The book was written so that a reader with previous knowledge in basic electronic principles and an understanding of mathematics through the fundamental concepts of calculus will have little trouble understanding the topics presented. Within the text, there are numerous examples that emphasize the most important concepts. Questions and problems are included at the end of each chapter; answers to selected problems are provided at the end of the book.

Electronic Communications Systems: Fundamentals Through Advanced, Fourth Edition, provides a modern, comprehensive coverage of the field of electronic communications. The most important and extensive changes to this edition occur in the chapters that deal primarily with digital communications systems such as Chapters 12, 15, 16, 18, and 19. In addition, Chapter 20 is a new chapter, dedicated entirely to cellular and PCS telephone systems. The major new topics and enhancements incorporated into this edition, by chapter number, are as follows:

1. The introduction and several sections throughout this chapter, including the section on modulation and demodulation, have been rewritten and several figures have been modified. In addition, several new figures have been added along with sections on impulse noise and interference.
2. This chapter remains essentially the same as in the previous edition except for minor modifications to several figures.
3. This chapter remains essentially the same as in the previous edition except for the addition of new sections on AM envelopes produced by complex nonsinusoidal signals, quadrature amplitude modulation, and minor modifications to several figures.
4. The introduction and section on bandwidth improvement have been rewritten and several figures have been modified. In addition, new sections on noise limiters and blankers and alternate signal-to-noise measurements have been added.

5. New sections on single-sideband suppressed carrier and frequency-division multiplexing and double-sideband suppressed carrier and quadrature multiplexing have been added.

6. The introduction and several sections throughout this chapter, including deviation sensitivity, modulation index, frequency deviation, frequency and phase modulators, frequency up-conversion, and advantages and disadvantages of angle modulation, have been rewritten with more examples. Also, several figures have been modified and several new figures have been added to the chapter.

7. The sections on FM receivers, FM demodulators, and FM capture effect have been rewritten and several figures have been modified. The section on cellular telephone has been moved from this chapter to Chapter 20.

8. This chapter remains essentially the same as in the previous edition except for the addition of sections on microstrip and stripline.

9. Except for a few minor modifications, this chapter remains essentially the same as in the previous edition.

10. The introduction and several sections throughout this chapter, including the sections on antenna reciprocity, effective isotropic radiated power, captured power density, capture area and capture power, and antenna beamwidth, have been rewritten and several figures have been modified.

11. Optical fiber communications has been moved from Chapter 20 to here. The introduction and several sections throughout this chapter have been rewritten and several new sections have been added, including sections on light sources, optical power, optical sources, and link budget.

12. The sections on digital amplitude modulation, frequency shift keying, continuous-phase frequency shift keying, and M-ary encoding have been rewritten and a new section on trellis encoding has been added.

13. This chapter is essentially the same as in the previous edition except for the addition of a new section on CCITT modem recommendations.

14. This chapter remains essentially the same as in the previous edition.

15. The introduction and several sections throughout this chapter, including the sections on advantages and disadvantages of digital transmission and pulse code modulation, have been rewritten and a new section on PCM line speed has been added. Also, several figures have been modified.

16. The introduction and several sections throughout this chapter, including the sections on time-division multiplexing and T1 digital carrier systems, have been rewritten and new sections on extended superframe format and wavelength-division multiplexing have been added.

17. The introduction has been rewritten along with parts of several other sections, including the advantages and disadvantages of microwave communications, diversity, protection switching, fading, free-space path loss, and fade margin.

18. The introduction and several sections throughout this chapter have been rewritten, including the sections on history, satellite orbits, satellite elevation categories, satellite orbital patterns, geosynchronous satellites, antenna look angles, and footprints. New to this edition are sections on Kepler's laws, Clarke orbits, and limits of visibility.

19. Minor modifications have been made to the introduction and several other sections throughout this chapter. Significant changes and additions have occurred in the section on satellite radio navigation and Navstar GPS.

20. Sections from Chapter 7 of the previous edition have been rewritten and combined with several new sections to provide a comprehensive coverage of mobile telephone systems, including analog and digital cellular telephone (AMPS), the

CDMA personal communications system (PCS), and the Iridium personal communications satellite system (PCSS).

Appendix A has remained essentially the same as in the previous edition.

Acknowledgments

I would like to thank the following reviews for their valuable feedback: Micha Hohenberger, Temple University; Martin Knutilla, McHenry County College; Steven Schwarz, Queens College; Walter Thain, Southern Polytechnic State University; and Martin Weiss, University of Pittsburgh.

Contents

CHAPTER 4   AMPLITUDE MODULATION RECEPTION   140

CHAPTER 5   SINGLE-SIDEBAND COMMUNICATIONS SYSTEMS   189

Contents

CHAPTER 7   ANGLE MODULATION RECEIVERS, FM STEREO, AND TWO-WAY FM RADIO   275

CHAPTER 8   TRANSMISSION LINES   310

CHAPTER 10   ANTENNAS AND WAVEGUIDES   371

CHAPTER 12   DIGITAL COMMUNICATIONS

467

CHAPTER 17 MICROWAVE RADIO COMMUNICATIONS AND SYSTEM GAIN   761

CHAPTER 18 SATELLITE COMMUNICATIONS   793

CHAPTER 20   MOBILE TELEPHONE SERVICE 864

C H A P T E R 1

Introduction to Electronic Communications

INTRODUCTION

The fundamental purpose of an *electronic communications system* is to transfer *information* from one place to another. Thus, electronic communications can be summarized as the *transmission, reception,* and *processing* of information between two or more locations using electronic circuits. The original source information can be in *analog* (continuous) form, such as the human voice or music, or in *digital* (discrete) form, such as *binary-coded numbers* or *alphanumeric codes.* All forms of information, however, must be converted to *electromagnetic energy* before being propagated through an electronic communications system.

Samuel Morse developed the first electronic communications system in 1837. Morse used *electromagnetic induction* to transfer information in the form of dots, dashes, and spaces between a simple transmitter and receiver using a transmission line consisting of a length of metallic wire. He called his invention the *telegraph.* In 1876 Alexander Graham Bell and Thomas A. Watson were the first to successfully transfer human conversation over a crude metallic-wire communications system they called the *telephone.*

Guglielmo Marconi successfully transmitted the first *wireless* radio signals through Earth's atmosphere in 1894, and in 1908 Lee DeForest invented the triode vacuum tube which provided the first practical means of amplifying electrical signals. Commercial radio began in 1920 when radio stations began broadcasting *amplitude-modulated* (AM) signals, and in 1933, Major Edwin Howard Armstrong invented *frequency modulation* (FM). Commercial broadcasting of FM began in 1936.

Although the fundamental concepts and principles of electronic communications have changed little since their inception, the methods and circuits used to implement them have undergone considerable change. In recent years, *transistors* and *linear integrated circuits* have simplified the design of electronic communications circuits, thus allowing for miniaturization, improved performance and reliability, and reduced overall costs. In recent years, there has been an overwhelming need for more and more people to communicate

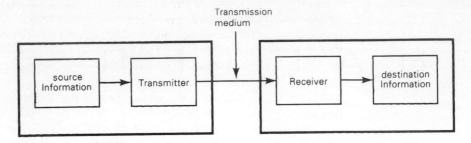

FIGURE 1-1 Simplified block diagram of an electronic communications system

with each other. This tremendous need has stimulated a monumental growth in the electronic communications industry. Modern electronic communications systems include *metallic cable* systems, *microwave* and *satellite radio* systems, and *optical fiber* systems.

ELECTRONIC COMMUNICATIONS SYSTEMS

Figure 1-1 shows a simplified block diagram for an electronic communications system, which includes a *transmitter*, a *transmission medium*, and a *receiver*. A transmitter is a collection of one or more electronic devices or circuits that converts the original source information to a signal that is more suitable for transmission over a given transmission medium. The transmission medium provides a means of transporting signals from a transmitter to a receiver and can be as simple as a pair of copper wires that propagate signals in the form of electric current flow. Information can also be converted to electromagnetic light waves and propagated over optical fiber cables constructed from glass or plastic, and free space can be used for transmission of electromagnetic radio waves over great distances or over terrain where it is difficult or expensive to install a physical cable. A receiver is a collection of electronic devices and circuits that accepts the transmitted signals from the transmission medium and converts them back to their original form.

MODULATION AND DEMODULATION

Because it is often impractical to propagate information signals over metallic or optical fiber cables or through Earth's atmosphere, it is often necessary to modulate the source information onto a higher-frequency analog signal called a *carrier*. In essence, the carrier signal carries the information through the system. The information signal *modulates* the carrier by changing either its amplitude, frequency, or phase. *Modulation* is simply the process of changing one or more properties of the carrier in proportion with the information signal.

The two basic types of electronic communications systems are *analog* and *digital*. An *analog communications system* is a system in which energy is transmitted and received in analog form (a continuously varying signal such as a sine wave). With analog communications systems, both the information and the carrier are analog signals.

The term *digital communications,* however, covers a broad range of communications techniques including *digital transmission* and *digital radio*. Digital transmission is a true digital system where digital pulses (discrete levels such as +5 V and ground) are transferred between two or more points in a communications system. With digital transmission there is no analog carrier and the original source information may be in digital or analog form. If it is in analog form, it must be converted to digital pulses prior to transmission and converted back to analog form at the receive end. Digital transmission systems require a physical facility between the transmitter and receiver such as a metallic wire or an optical fiber cable.

Digital radio is the transmittal of digitally modulated analog carriers between two or more points in a communications system. With digital radio, the modulating signal and the demodulated signal are digital pulses. The digital pulses could originate from a digital transmission system, from a digital source such as a computer, or be a binary encoded analog signal. In digital radio systems, the transmission medium may be a physical facility or free space (i.e., the Earth's atmosphere). Analog communications systems were the first to be developed; however, in recent years digital communications systems have become more popular.

Equation 1-1 is the general expression for a time-varying sine wave of voltage such as a high-frequency carrier signal. If the information signal is analog and the amplitude (V) of the carrier is varied proportional to the information signal, *amplitude modulation* (AM) is produced. If the frequency (f) is varied proportional to the information signal, *frequency modulation* (FM) is produced, and, if the phase (θ) is varied proportional to the information signal, *phase modulation* (PM) is produced.

If the information signal is digital and the amplitude (V) of the carrier is varied proportional to the information signal, a digitally modulated signal known as *amplitude shift keying* (ASK) is produced. If the frequency (f) is varied proportional to the information signal, *frequency shift keying* (FSK) is produced, and, if the phase (θ) is varied proportional to the information signal, *phase shift keying* (PSK) is produced. If both the amplitude and phase are varied proportional to the information signal, *quadrature amplitude modulation* (QAM) results. ASK, FSK, PSK, and QAM are forms of digital modulation and are described in detail in Chapter 12.

$$v(t) = V \sin(2\pi f t + \theta) \tag{1-1}$$

where $v(t)$ = time-varying sine wave of voltage
$\quad\quad V$ = peak amplitude (volts)
$\quad\quad f$ = frequency (hertz)
$\quad\quad \theta$ = phase shift (radians)

A summary of the various modulation techniques is shown below:

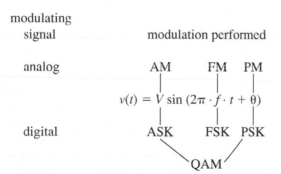

Modulation is performed in a transmitter by a circuit called a *modulator*. A carrier that has been acted upon by an information signal is called a *modulated wave* or *modulated signal*. *Demodulation* is the reverse process of modulation and converts the modulated carrier back to the original information (i.e., removes the information from the carrier). Demodulation is performed in a receiver by a circuit called a *demodulator*.

There are two reasons why modulation is necessary in electronic communications: (1) It is extremely difficult to radiate low-frequency signals from an antenna in the form of electromagnetic energy, and (2) information signals often occupy the same frequency band and, if signals from two or more sources are transmitted at the same time, they would

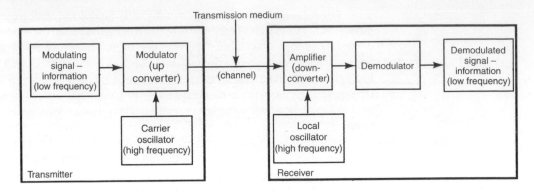

FIGURE 1-2 Communications system block diagram

interfere with each other. For example, all commercial FM stations broadcast voice and music signals that occupy the audio-frequency band from approximately 300 Hz to 15 kHz. To avoid interfering with each other, each station converts its information to a different frequency band or channel. The term *channel* is often used to refer to a specific band of frequencies allocated a particular service. A standard voice-band channel occupies approximately a 3-kHz bandwidth and is used for transmission of voice-quality signals; commercial AM broadcast channels occupy approximately a 10-kHz frequency band, and 30 MHz or more of bandwidth is required for microwave and satellite radio channels.

Figure 1-2 is the simplified block diagram for an electronic communications system showing the relationship among the modulating signal, the high-frequency carrier, and the modulated wave. The information signal (sometimes called the intelligence signal) combines with the carrier in the modulator to produce the modulated wave. The information can be in analog or digital form and the modulator can perform either analog or digital modulation. Information signals are *up-converted* from low frequencies to high frequencies in the transmitter and *down-converted* from high frequencies to low frequencies in the receiver. The process of converting a frequency or band of frequencies to another location in the total frequency spectrum is called *frequency translation*. Frequency translation is an intricate part of electronic communications because information signals may be up- and down-converted many times as they are transported through the system called a channel. The modulated signal is transported to the receiver over a transmission system. In the receiver the modulated signal is amplified, down-converted in frequency, then demodulated to reproduce the original source information.

THE ELECTROMAGNETIC SPECTRUM

The purpose of an electronic communications system is to communicate information between two or more locations commonly called *stations*. This is accomplished by converting the original information into electromagnetic energy and then transmitting it to one or more receive stations where it is converted back to its original form. Electromagnetic energy can propagate as a voltage or current along a metallic wire, as emitted radio waves through free space, or as light waves down an optical fiber. Electromagnetic energy is distributed throughout an almost infinite range of frequencies.

Frequency is simply the number of times a periodic motion, such as a sine wave of voltage or current, occurs in a given period of time. Each complete alternation of the waveform is called a *cycle*. The basic unit of frequency is hertz (Hz) and one hertz equals one cycle-per-second (1 Hz = 1 cps). In electronics it is common to use metric prefixes to represent higher frequencies. For example, kHz (kilohertz) is used for thousands of hertz and MHz (megahertz) is used for millions of hertz.

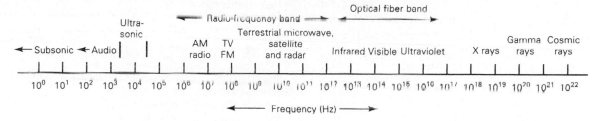

FIGURE 1-3 Electromagnetic frequency spectrum

Transmission Frequencies

The total *electromagnetic frequency spectrum* showing the approximate locations of various services is shown in Figure 1-3. The frequency spectrum extends from *subsonic* frequencies (a few hertz) to *cosmic rays* (10^{22} Hz).

The frequency spectrum is further divided into *subsections* or *bands*. Each band has a name and boundaries. In the United States, frequency assignments for *free-space radio propagation* are assigned by the *Federal Communications Commission* (FCC). For example, the commercial FM broadcast band has been assigned the 88-MHz to 108-MHz band. The exact frequencies assigned specific transmitters operating in the various classes of services are constantly being updated and altered to meet the nation's communications needs.

The total usable *radio-frequency* (RF) spectrum is divided into narrower frequency bands, which are given descriptive names and band numbers, and several of these bands are further broken down into various types of services. The *International Radio Consultative Committee's* (CCIR's) band designations are listed in Table 1-1. The CCIR band designations are summarized as follows:

Extremely low frequencies. Extremely low frequencies (ELFs) are signals in the 30-Hz to 300-Hz range and include ac power distribution signals (60 Hz) and low-frequency telemetry signals.

Voice frequencies. Voice frequencies (VFs) are signals in the 300-Hz to 3000-Hz range and include frequencies generally associated with human speech. Standard telephone channels have a 300-Hz to 3000-Hz bandwidth and are often called *voice-frequency* or *voice-band channels*.

Very low frequencies. Very low frequencies (VLFs) are signals in the 3-kHz to 30-kHz range, which include the upper end of the human hearing range. VLFs are used for some specialized government and military systems such as submarine communications.

Low frequencies. Low frequencies (LFs) are signals in the 30-kHz to 300-kHz range and are used primarily for marine and aeronautical navigation.

Medium frequencies. Medium frequencies (MFs) are signals in the 300-kHz to 3-MHz range and are used primarily for commercial AM radio broadcasting (535 kHz to 1605 kHz).

High frequencies. High frequencies (HFs) are signals in the 3-MHz to 30-MHz range and are often referred to as *short waves*. Most two-way radio communications use this range, and Voice of America and Radio Free Europe broadcast within the HF band. Amateur radio and citizens band (CB) radio also use signals in the HF range.

Very high frequencies. Very high frequencies (VHFs) are signals in the 30-MHz to 300-MHz range and are used for mobile radio, marine and aeronautical communications, commercial FM broadcasting (88 MHz to 108 MHz), and commercial television broadcasting of channels 2–13 (54 MHz to 216 MHz).

TABLE 1-1 CCIR Band Designations

Band Number	Frequency Range*	Designations
2	30 Hz–300 Hz	ELF (extremely low frequencies)
3	0.3 kHz–3 kHz	VF (voice frequencies)
4	3 kHz–30 kHz	VLF (very low frequencies)
5	30 kHz–300 kHz	LF (low frequencies)
6	0.3 MHz–3 MHz	MF (medium frequencies)
7	3 MHz–30 MHz	HF (high frequencies)
8	30 MHz–300 MHz	VHF (very high frequencies)
9	300 MHz–3 GHz	UHF (ultrahigh frequencies)
10	3 GHz–30 GHz	SHF (superhigh frequencies)
11	30 GHz–300 GHz	EHF (extremely high frequencies)
12	0.3 THz–3 THz	Infrared light
13	3 THz–30 THz	Infrared light
14	30 THz–300 THz	Infrared light
15	0.3 PHz–3 PHz	Visible light
16	3 PHz–30 PHz	Ultraviolet light
17	30 PHz–300 PHz	X rays
18	0.3 EHz–3 EHz	Gamma rays
19	3 EHz–30 EHz	Cosmic rays

*10^0, hertz (Hz); 10^3, kilohertz (kHz); 10^6, megahertz (MHz); 10^9 gigahertz (GHz); 10^{12}, terahertz (THz); 10^{15}, petahertz (PHz); 10^{18} exahertz (EHz)

Ultrahigh frequencies. Ultrahigh frequencies (UHFs) are signals in the 300-MHz to 3-GHz range and are used by commercial television broadcasting of channels 14–83, land mobile communications services, cellular telephones, certain radar and navigation systems, and microwave and satellite radio systems. Generally speaking, frequencies above 1 GHz are considered microwave frequencies, which includes the upper end of the UHF range.

Superhigh frequencies. Superhigh frequencies (SHFs) are signals in the 3-GHz to 30-GHz range and include the majority of the frequencies used for microwave and satellite radio communications systems.

Extremely high frequencies. Extremely high frequencies (EHFs) are signals in the 30-GHz to 300-GHz range and are seldom used for radio communications except in very sophisticated, expensive, and specialized applications.

Infrared. Infrared frequencies are signals in the 0.3-THz to 300-THz range and are not generally referred to as radio waves. Infrared refers to electromagnetic radiation generally associated with heat. Infrared signals are used in heat-seeking guidance systems, electronic photography, and astronomy.

Visible light. Visible light includes electromagnetic frequencies that fall within the visible range of humans (0.3 PHz to 3 PHz). Light wave communications is used with optical fiber systems, which in recent years have become a primary transmission medium for electronic communications systems.

Ultraviolet rays, X rays, gamma rays, and *cosmic rays* have little application to electronic communications and, therefore, will not be described.

When dealing with radio waves, it is common to use the units of wavelength rather than frequency. Wavelength is the length that one cycle of an electromagnetic wave occupies in space (i.e., the distance between similar points in a repetitive wave). Wavelength is inversely proportional to the frequency of the wave and directly proportional to the veloc-

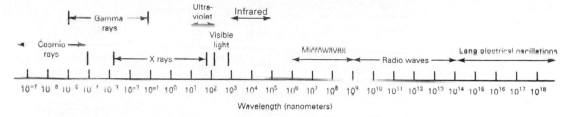

FIGURE 1-4 Electromagnetic wavelength spectrum

ity of propagation (the velocity of propagation of electromagnetic energy in free space is assumed to be the speed of light, 3×10^8 m/s). The relationship among frequency, velocity, and wavelength is expressed mathematically as

$$\text{wavelength} = \frac{\text{velocity}}{\text{frequency}}$$

$$\lambda = \frac{c}{f} \qquad (1\text{-}2a)$$

where λ = wavelength (meters per cycle)
c = velocity of light (300,000,000 meters per second)
f = frequency (hertz)

The total *electromagnetic wavelength* spectrum showing the various services within the band is shown in Figure 1-4.

Example 1-1

Determine the wavelength in meters for the following frequencies: 1 kHz, 100 kHz, and 10 MHz.

Solution   Substituting into Equation 1-2a,

$$\lambda = \frac{300,000,000}{1000} = 300,000 \text{ m}$$

$$\lambda = \frac{300,000,000}{100,000} = 3000 \text{ m}$$

$$\lambda = \frac{300,000,000}{10,000,000} = 30 \text{ m}$$

Equation 1-2b can be used to determine the wavelength in inches.

$$\lambda = \frac{c}{f} \qquad (1\text{-}2b)$$

where λ = wavelength (inches per cycle)
c = velocity of light (11.8×10^9 inches per second)
f = frequency (hertz)

Classification of Transmitters

For licensing purposes in the United States, radio transmitters are classified according to their bandwidth, modulation scheme, and type of information. The *emission classifications* are identified by a three-symbol code containing a combination of letters and numbers as shown in Table 1-2. The first symbol is a letter that designates the type of modulation of the main carrier. The second symbol is a number that identifies the type of emission, and the third symbol is another letter that describes the type of information being transmitted. For example, the designation A3E describes a double-sideband, full-carrier, amplitude-modulated signal carrying voice or music telephony information.

TABLE 1-2 FCC Emission Classifications

Symbol	Letter	Type of Modulation
First	Unmodulated	
	N	Unmodulated carrier
	Amplitude Modulation	
	A	Double-sideband, full carrier (DSBFC)
	B	Independent sideband, full carrier (ISBFC)
	C	Vestigial sideband, full carrier (VSB)
	H	Single-sideband, full carrier (SSBFC)
	J	Single-sideband, suppressed carrier (SSBSC)
	R	Single-sideband, reduced carrier (SSBRC)
	Angle Modulation	
	F	Frequency modulation (direct FM)
	G	Phase modulation (indirect FM)
	D	AM and FM simultaneously or sequenced
	Pulse Modulation	
	K	Pulse-amplitude modulation (PAM)
	L	Pulse-width modulation (PWM)
	M	Pulse-position modulation (PPM)
	P	Unmodulated pulses (binary data)
	Q	Angle modulated during pulses
	V	Any combination of pulse-modulation category
	W	Any combination of two or more of the above forms of modulation
	X	Cases not otherwise covered
Second	0	No modulating signal
	1	Digitally keyed carrier
	2	Digitally keyed tone
	3	Analog (sound or video)
	7	Two or more digital channels
	8	Two or more analog channels
	9	Analog and digital
Third	A	Telegraphy, manual
	B	Telegraphy, automatic (teletype)
	C	Facsimile
	D	Data, telemetry
	E	Telephony (sound broadcasting)
	F	Television (video broadcasting)
	N	No information transmitted
	W	Any combination of second letter

BANDWIDTH AND INFORMATION CAPACITY

The two most significant limitations on the performance of a communications system are *noise* and *bandwidth*. Noise is discussed later in this chapter. The bandwidth of an information signal is simply the difference between the highest and lowest frequencies contained in the information, and the bandwidth of a communications channel is the difference between the highest and lowest frequencies that the channel will allow to pass through it (i.e., its *passband*). The bandwidth of a communications channel must be large (wide) enough to pass all significant information frequencies. In other words, the bandwidth of the communications channel must be equal to or greater than the bandwidth of the information. For example, voice frequencies contain signals between 300 Hz and 3000 Hz. Therefore, a voice-frequency channel must have a bandwidth equal to or greater than 2700 Hz (300 Hz–3000 Hz). If a cable television transmission system has a passband from 500 kHz to 5000 kHz, it has a bandwidth of 4500 kHz. As a general rule, a communications channel cannot propagate a signal that contains a frequency that is changing at a rate greater than the bandwidth of the channel.

Information theory is a highly theoretical study of the efficient use of bandwidth to propagate information through electronic communications systems. Information theory can be used to determine the *information capacity* of a communications system. Information capacity is a measure of how much information can be transferred through a communications system in a given period of time. The amount of information that can be propagated through a transmission system is a function of system bandwidth and transmission time. In 1920, R. Hartley of Bell Telephone Laboratories developed the relationship among bandwidth, transmission time, and information capacity. Hartley's law simply states that the wider the bandwidth and the longer the time of transmission, the more information that can be conveyed through the system. Mathematically, Hartley's law is stated as

$$I \propto B \times t \tag{1-3}$$

where I = information capacity
           B = system bandwidth (hertz)
           t = transmission time (seconds)

Equation 1-3 shows that information capacity is a linear function and directly proportional to both system bandwidth and transmission time. If the bandwidth of a communications channel doubles, the amount of information it can carry also doubles. If the transmission time increases or decreases, there is a proportional change in the amount of information that can be transferred through the system.

In general, the more complex the information signal, the more bandwidth required to transport it in a given period of time. Approximately 3 kHz of bandwidth is required to transmit voice-quality telephone signals. In contrast 200 kHz of bandwidth is allocated for commercial FM transmission of high-fidelity music, and almost 6 MHz of bandwidth is required for broadcast-quality television signals.

In 1948, C. E. Shannon (also of Bell Telephone Laboratories) published a paper in the *Bell System Technical Journal* relating the information capacity of a communications channel in bits-per-second (bps) to bandwidth and signal-to-noise ratio. Mathematically stated, the *Shannon limit for information capacity* is

$$I = B \log_2\left(1 + \frac{S}{N}\right) \tag{1-4a}$$

or

$$I = 3.32 \, B \log_{10}\left(1 + \frac{S}{N}\right) \tag{1-4b}$$

where I = information capacity (bits per second)
           B = bandwidth (hertz)
           $\dfrac{S}{N}$ = signal-to-noise power ratio (unitless)

For a standard voice-band communications channel with a signal-to-noise power ratio of 1000 (30 dB) and a bandwidth of 2.7 kHz, the Shannon limit for information capacity is

$$I = 2700 \log_2 (1 + 1000)$$
$$= 26.9 \text{ kbps}$$

Shannon's formula is often misunderstood. The results of the preceding example indicate that 26.9 kbps can be transferred through a 2.7-kHz channel. This may be true, but it cannot be done with a binary system. To achieve an information transmission rate of 26.9 kbps through a 2.7-kHz channel, each symbol transmitted must contain more than one bit of information. Therefore, to achieve the Shannon limit for information capacity, digital transmission systems that have more than two output conditions (symbols) must be used.

Equation 1-4a can be rearranged and used to determine how much bandwidth is required to propagate a given amount of data through a system.

$$B = \frac{I}{\log_2\left(1 + \dfrac{S}{N}\right)}$$

(1-5)

where B = bandwidth (hertz)

I = information capacity (bits per second)

$\dfrac{S}{N}$ = signal-to-noise power ratio (unitless)

TRANSMISSION MODES

Electronic communications systems can be designed to handle transmission only in one direction, in both directions but in only one direction at a time, or in both directions at the same time. These are called *transmission modes*. Four transmission modes are possible: *simplex, half duplex, full duplex,* and *full/full duplex.*

Simplex (SX)

With simplex operation, transmissions can occur only in one direction. Simplex systems are sometimes called *one-way-only, receive-only,* or *transmit-only* systems. A location may be a transmitter or a receiver, but not both. An example of simplex transmission is commercial radio or television broadcasting; the radio station always transmits and you always receive.

Half Duplex (HDX)

With half-duplex operation, transmissions can occur in both directions, but not at the same time. Half-duplex systems are sometimes called *two-way-alternate, either-way,* or *over-and-out* systems. A location may be a transmitter and a receiver, but not both at the same time. Two-way radio systems that use *push-to-talk* (PTT) buttons to key their transmitters, such as citizens band and police band radio, are examples of half-duplex transmission.

Full Duplex (FDX)

With full-duplex operation, transmissions can occur in both directions at the same time. Full-duplex systems are sometimes called *two-way simultaneous, duplex,* or *both-way* lines. A location can transmit and receive simultaneously; however, the station it is transmitting to must also be the station it is receiving from. A standard telephone system is an example of full-duplex transmission.

Full/Full Duplex (F/FDX)

With full/full duplex operation, it is possible to transmit and receive simultaneously, but not necessarily between the same two locations (i.e., one station can transmit to a second station and receive from a third station at the same time). Full/full duplex transmissions are used almost exclusively with data communications circuits. The U.S. Postal Service is an example of full/full duplex operation.

CIRCUIT ARRANGEMENTS

Electronic communications circuits can be configured in several different ways. These configurations are called *circuit arrangements* and can include both two- and four-wire transmission.

Two-Wire Transmission

As the name implies, *two-wire transmission* involves two wires (one for the signal and one for a reference or ground) or a circuit configuration that is equivalent to only two wires. Two-wire circuits are ideally suited to simplex transmission, although they can be used for half- and full-duplex transmission. The telephone line between your home and the nearest telephone office is a two-wire circuit.

Figure 1-5 shows the block diagrams for two different two-wire circuit configurations. Figure 1-5a shows the simplest two-wire configuration, which is a passive circuit consisting of two wires connecting an information source through a transmitter to a destination at a receiver. The wires themselves are capable of two-way transmission, but the transmitter and receiver are not. To exchange information in the opposite direction, the locations of the transmitter and receiver would have to be switched. Therefore, this configuration is capable of only one-way transmission and provides no gain to the signal. To achieve half-duplex transmission with a two-wire circuit, a transmitter and receiver would be required at each location, and they would have to be connected to the same wire pair in a manner such that they do not interfere with each other.

Figure 1-5b shows an active two-wire circuit (i.e., one that provides gain). With this configuration, an amplifier is placed in the circuit between the transmitter and the receiver. The amplifier is a unidirectional device and, thus, limits transmissions to only one direction.

To achieve half- or full-duplex capabilities with a two-wire circuit, the information traveling in opposite directions would have to be altered in some way or by some method of converting the source to a destination and the destination to a source. Half- and full-duplex transmission can be accomplished with a two-wire circuit by using some form of modulation technique to *multiplex* or combine the two signals in such a way that they do not interfere with each other but can still be separated or converted back to their original form at the receiver. Both modulation and multiplexing are described in detail later in this book.

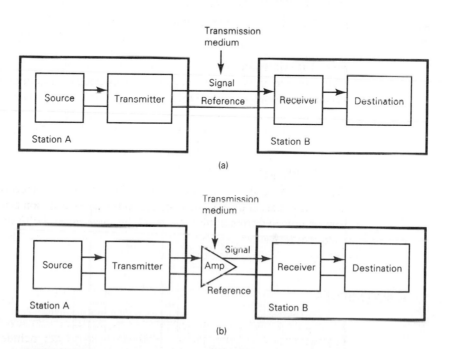

(a)

(b)

FIGURE 1-5 Two-wire circuit configurations: (a) passive; (b) active

Four-Wire Transmission

Four-wire transmission involves four wires (two for each direction, a signal and a reference ground) or a circuit configuration that is equivalent to four wires. Four-wire circuits are ideally suited to full-duplex transmission. Figure 1-6 shows the block diagram of an active four-wire system. As the figure shows, a four-wire circuit is equivalent to two two-wire circuits, one for each direction of transmission. With four-wire operation, the transmitter at one location is connected through a transmission medium to the receiver at the other location, and vice versa. However, the transmitters and receivers at a given location may be operated completely independently of each other.

There are several inherent advantages of four-wire circuits over two-wire circuits. For instance, four-wire circuits are considerably less noisy and provide more isolation between the two directions of transmission when either half- or full-duplex operation is used. However, two-wire circuits require less wire, less circuitry, and, thus, less money than their four-wire counterparts. The advantages and disadvantages of two- and four-wire circuits will become more apparent as you continue your studies in electronic communications.

Hybrids and Echo Suppressors

When a two-wire circuit is connected to a four-wire circuit, as in a long-distance telephone call, an interface circuit called a *hybrid* or *terminating set* is used to affect the interface. The hybrid set is used to match impedances and provide isolation between the two directions of signal flow.

Figure 1-7 shows the block diagram for a two-wire to four-wire hybrid network. The hybrid coil compensates for impedance variations in the two-wire portion of the circuit. The amplifiers and attenuators adjust the signal voltages to required levels, and the equalizers compensate for impairments in the transmission line that affect the frequency response of the transmitted signal, such as line inductance, capacitance, and resistance. Signals traveling west–east (W–E) enter the terminating set from the two-wire line where they are inductively coupled into the west-to-east transmitter section of the four-wire circuit. Signals received from the line are coupled into the east–west (E–W) receiver section of the four-wire circuit where they are applied to the center taps of the hybrid coils. If the impedances of the two-wire line and the balancing network are properly matched, all currents produced in the upper half of the hybrid by the E–W signal will be equal in magnitude but opposite in polarity. Therefore, the voltages induced in the secondaries will be 180° out of phase with each other and, thus, cancel. This prevents any portion of the received signal from being returned to the sender as an echo.

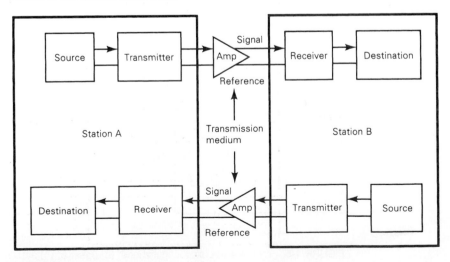

FIGURE 1-6 Active four-wire circuit

If the impedances of the two-wire line and the balancing network are not matched, the voltages induced in the secondaries of the hybrid coil will not completely cancel. This imbalance causes a portion of the received signal to be returned to the sender on the W–E portion of the four-wire circuit. The returned portion of the signal is heard as an echo by the talker and, if the round-trip delay of this signal exceeds approximately 45 ms, the echo can become quite annoying. To eliminate this echo, devices called *echo suppressors* are inserted at one end of the four-wire circuit. Figure 1-8 shows a simplified block diagram of an echo

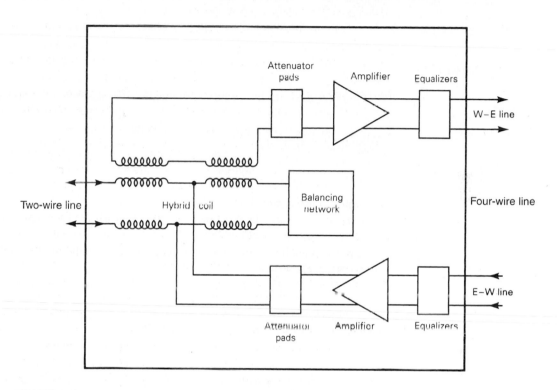

FIGURE 1-7 Two-wire to four-wire terminating set (hybrid)

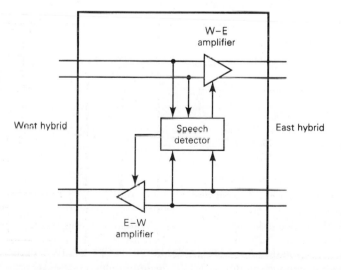

FIGURE 1-8 Echo suppressor

suppressor. The speech detector senses the presence and direction of the signal. It then enables the amplifier in the appropriate direction and disables the amplifier in the opposite direction, thus preventing the echo from returning to the speaker. If the conversation is changing direction rapidly, the people listening may be able to hear the echo suppressor turning on and off (every time an echo suppressor detects speech and is activated, the first instant of sound is removed from the message, giving the speech a choppy sound). With an echo suppressor in the circuit, transmissions cannot occur in both directions at the same time, thus limiting the circuit to half-duplex operation. Long-distance common carriers, such as AT&T, generally place echo suppressors in four-wire circuits that exceed 1500 electrical miles in length (the longer the circuit, the longer the round-trip time delay).

SIGNAL ANALYSIS

When designing electronic communications circuits, it is often necessary to analyze and predict the performance of the circuit based on the power distribution and frequency composition of the information signal. This is done with mathematical *signal analysis*. Although all signals in electronic communications are not single-frequency sine or cosine waves, many of them are, and the signals that are not can be represented by a combination of sine or cosine functions.

Sinusoidal Signals

In essence, signal analysis is the mathematical analysis of the frequency, bandwidth, and voltage level of a signal. Electrical signals are voltage—or current—time variations that can be represented by a series of sine or cosine waves. Mathematically, a single-frequency voltage or current waveform is

$$v(t) = V \sin(2\pi ft + \theta) \quad \text{or} \quad v(t) = V \cos(2\pi ft + \theta)$$
$$i(t) = I \sin(2\pi ft + \theta) \quad \text{or} \quad i(t) = I \cos(2\pi ft + \theta)$$

where
$v(t)$ = time-varying voltage sine wave
$i(t)$ = time-varying current sine wave
V = peak voltage (volts)
f = frequency (hertz)
θ = phase shift (radians)
I = peak current (amperes)
$2\pi f$ = ω angular velocity (radians per second)

Whether a sine or a cosine function is used to represent a signal is purely arbitrary and depends on which is chosen as the reference. However, it should be noted that $\sin \theta = \cos(\theta° - 90°)$. Therefore, the following relationships hold true:

$$v(t) = V \sin(2\pi ft + \theta) = V \cos(2\pi ft + \theta° - 90°)$$
$$v(t) = V \cos(2\pi ft + \theta) = V \sin(2\pi ft + \theta° + 90°)$$

The preceding formulas are for a single-frequency, repetitive waveform. Such a waveform is called a *periodic* wave because it repeats at a uniform rate (i.e., each successive cycle of the signal takes exactly the same length of time and has exactly the same amplitude variations as every other cycle; each cycle has exactly the same shape). A series of sine, cosine, or square waves are examples of periodic waves. Periodic waves can be analyzed in either the *time* or the *frequency domain*. In fact, it is often necessary when analyzing system performance to switch from the time domain to the frequency domain, and vice versa.

Time domain. A standard oscilloscope is a time-domain instrument. The display on the cathode ray tube (CRT) is an amplitude-versus-time representation of the input signal and is commonly called a *signal waveform*. Essentially, a signal waveform shows the shape and the instantaneous magnitude of the signal with respect to time but does not necessarily indicate its frequency content. With an oscilloscope, the vertical deflection is proportional to the amplitude of the total input signal, and the horizontal deflection is a function of time (sweep rate). Figure 1-9 shows the signal waveform for a single frequency sinusoidal signal with a peak amplitude of V volts and a frequency of f hertz.

Frequency domain. A spectrum analyzer is a frequency-domain instrument. Essentially, no waveform is displayed on the CRT. Instead, an amplitude-versus-frequency plot is shown (this is called a *frequency spectrum*). With a spectrum analyzer, the horizontal axis represents frequency and the vertical axis amplitude. Therefore, there is a vertical deflection for each frequency present at its input. Effectively, the input waveform is swept with a variable-frequency, high-Q bandpass filter whose center frequency is synchronized to the horizontal sweep rate of the CRT. Each frequency present in the input waveform produces a vertical line on the CRT (these are called *spectral components*). The vertical deflection (height) of each line is proportional to the amplitude of the frequency that it represents. A frequency-domain representation of a wave shows the frequency content, but does not necessarily indicate the shape of the waveform or the combined amplitude of all the input components at any specific time. Figure 1-10 shows the frequency spectrum for a single-frequency sinusoidal signal with a peak amplitude of V volts and a frequency of f hertz.

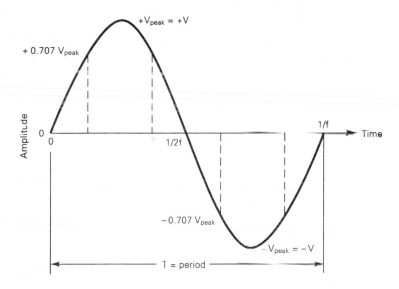

FIGURE 1-9 Time-domain representation (signal waveform) for a single-frequency sinusoidal wave

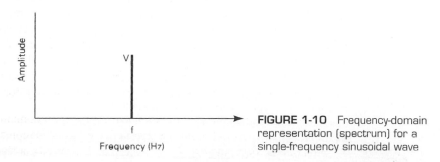

FIGURE 1-10 Frequency-domain representation (spectrum) for a single-frequency sinusoidal wave

Nonsinusoidal Periodic Waves (Complex Waves)

Essentially, any repetitive waveform that comprises more than one harmonically related sine or cosine wave is a *nonsinusoidal* or *complex periodic wave*. To analyze a complex periodic waveform, it is necessary to use a mathematical series developed in 1826 by the French physicist and mathematician Baron Jean Fourier. This series is appropriately called the *Fourier series*.

The Fourier series. The Fourier series is used in signal analysis to represent the sinusoidal components of a nonsinusoidal periodic waveform (i.e., to change a time-domain signal to a frequency-domain signal). In general, a Fourier series can be written for any periodic function as a series of terms that include trigonometric functions with the following mathematical expression:

$$f(t) = A_0 + A_1 \cos \alpha + A_2 \cos 2\alpha + A_3 \cos 3\alpha + \cdots + A_n \cos n\alpha$$
$$+ B_1 \sin \beta + B_2 \sin 2\beta + B_3 \sin 3\beta + \cdots + B_n \sin n\beta \qquad (1\text{-}6)$$

where $\alpha = \beta$.

Equation 1-6 states that the waveform $f(t)$ comprises an average (dc) value (A_0), a series of cosine functions in which each successive term has a frequency that is an integer multiple of the frequency of the first cosine term in the series, and a series of sine functions in which each successive term has a frequency that is an integer multiple of the frequency of the first sine term in the series. There are no restrictions on the values or relative values of the amplitudes for the sine or cosine terms. Equation 1-6 is stated in words as follows: Any *periodic waveform* is comprised of an average component and a series of harmonically related sine and cosine waves. A *harmonic* is an integral multiple of the fundamental frequency. The *fundamental frequency* is the *first harmonic* and is equal to the frequency (*repetition rate*) of the waveform. The second multiple of the fundamental is called the *second harmonic,* the third multiple is called the *third harmonic,* and so on. The fundamental frequency is the minimum frequency necessary to represent a waveform. Therefore, Equation 1-6 can be rewritten as

$$f(t) = \text{dc} + \text{fundamental} + \text{2nd harmonic} + \text{3rd harmonic} + \cdots + n\text{th harmonic}$$

Wave symmetry. Simply stated, *wave symmetry* describes the symmetry of a waveform in the time domain, that is, its relative position with respect to the horizontal (time) and vertical (amplitude) axes.

Even Symmetry. If a periodic voltage waveform is symmetric about the vertical (amplitude) axis, it is said to have *axes* or *mirror symmetry* and is called an *even function.* For all even functions, the *B* coefficients in Equation 1-6 are zero. Therefore, the signal simply contains a dc component and the cosine terms (note that a cosine wave is itself an even function). The sum of a series of even functions is an even function. Even functions satisfy the condition

$$f(t) = f(-t) \qquad (1\text{-}7)$$

Equation 1-7 states that the magnitude and polarity of the function at $+t$ is equal to the magnitude and polarity at $-t$. A waveform that contains only the even functions is shown in Figure 1-11a.

Odd Symmetry. If a periodic voltage waveform is symmetric about a line midway between the vertical and the negative horizontal axes (i.e., the axes in the second and fourth quadrants) and passing through the coordinate origin, it is said to have *point* or *skew* symmetry and is called an *odd function.* For all odd functions, the *A* coefficients in Equation 1-6 are zero. Therefore, the signal simply contains a dc component and the sine terms (note that a

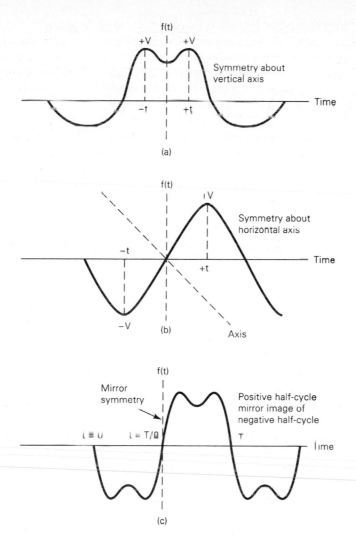

FIGURE 1-11 Wave symmetries: (a) even symmetry; (b) odd symmetry; (c) half-wave symmetry

sine wave is itself an odd function). The sum of a series of odd functions is an odd function. This form must be mirrored first in the Y-axis and then in the X-axis for superposition. Thus,

$$f(t) = -f(-t) \qquad (1\text{-}8)$$

Equation 1-8 states that the magnitude of the function at $+t$ is equal to the negative of the magnitude at $-t$ (i.e., equal in magnitude but opposite in sign). A periodic waveform that contains only the odd functions is shown in Figure 1-11b.

Half-Wave Symmetry. If a periodic voltage waveform is such that the waveform for the first half cycle ($t = 0$ to $t = T/2$) repeats itself except with the opposite sign for the second half cycle ($t = T/2$ to $t = T$), it is said to have *half-wave symmetry*. For all waveforms with half-wave symmetry, the even harmonics in the series for both the sine and co sine terms are zero. Therefore, half-wave functions satisfy the condition

$$f(t) = -f\left(\frac{T}{2} + t\right) \qquad (1\text{-}9)$$

TABLE 1-3 Fourier Series Summary

Waveform	Fourier Series

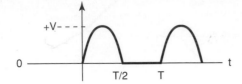

$$v(t) = \frac{V}{\pi} + \frac{V}{2} \sin \omega t - \frac{2V}{3\pi} \cos 2\omega t - \frac{2V}{15\pi} \cos 4\omega t + \cdots$$

$$v(t) = \frac{V}{\pi} + \frac{V}{2} \sin \omega t + \sum_{N=2}^{\infty} \frac{V[1 + (-1)^N]}{\pi(1 - N^2)} \cos N\omega t$$

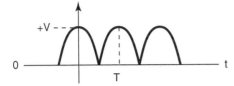

$$v(t) = \frac{2V}{\pi} + \frac{4V}{3\pi} \cos \omega t - \frac{4V}{15\pi} \cos 2\omega t + \cdots$$

$$v(t) = \frac{2V}{\pi} + \sum_{N=1}^{\infty} \frac{4V(-1)^N}{\pi[1 - (2N)^2]} \cos N\omega t$$

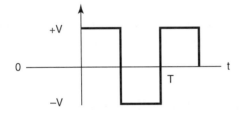

$$v(t) = \frac{4V}{\pi} \sin \omega t + \frac{4V}{3\pi} \sin 3\omega t + \cdots$$

$$v(t) = \sum_{N=\text{odd}}^{\infty} \frac{4V}{N\pi} \sin N\omega t$$

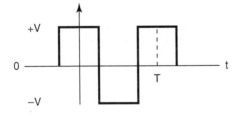

$$v(t) = \frac{4V}{\pi} \cos \omega t - \frac{4V}{3\pi} \cos 3\omega t + \frac{4V}{5\pi} \cos 5\omega t + \cdots$$

$$v(t) = \sum_{N=\text{odd}}^{\infty} \frac{V \sin N\pi/2}{N\pi/2} \cos N\omega t$$

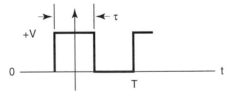

$$v(t) = \frac{V\tau}{T} + \sum_{N=1}^{\infty} \left(\frac{2V\tau}{T} \frac{\sin N\omega t/T}{N\pi t/T} \right) \cos N\pi t$$

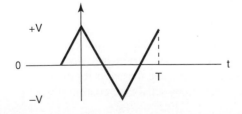

$$v(t) = \frac{8V}{\pi^2} \cos \omega t + \frac{8V}{(3\pi)^2} \cos 3\omega t + \frac{8V}{(5\pi)^2} \cos 5\omega t + \cdots$$

$$v(t) = \sum_{N=\text{odd}}^{\infty} \frac{8V}{(N\pi)^2} \cos N\omega t$$

A periodic waveform that exhibits half-wave symmetry is shown in Figure 1-11c. It should be noted that a waveform can have half-wave as well as either odd or even symmetry at the same time. The coefficients A_0, B_1 to B_n, and A_1 to A_n can be evaluated using the following integral formulas:

$$A_0 = \frac{1}{T} \int_0^T f(t)\, dt \qquad (1\text{-}10)$$

$$A_n = \frac{2}{T} \int_0^T f(t) \cos n\omega t\, dt \qquad (1\text{-}11)$$

$$B_n = \frac{2}{T} \int_0^T f(t) \sin n\omega t\, dt \qquad (1\text{-}12)$$

Solving Equations 1-10, 1-11, and 1-12 requires integral calculus, which is beyond the intent of this book. Therefore, in subsequent discussions, the appropriate solutions are given.

Table 1-3 is a summary of the Fourier series for several of the more common nonsinusoidal periodic waveforms.

Example 1-2

For the train of square waves shown in Figure 1-12,
(a) Determine the peak amplitudes and frequencies of the first five odd harmonics.
(b) Draw the frequency spectrum.
(c) Calculate the total instantaneous voltage for several times and sketch the time-domain waveform.

Solution (a) From inspection of the waveform in Figure 1-12, it can be seen that the average dc component is 0 V and the waveform has both odd and half wave symmetry. Evaluating Equations 1-10, 1-11, and 1-12 yields the following Fourier series for a square wave with odd symmetry.

$$v(t) = V_0 + \frac{4V}{\pi}\left[\sin \omega t + \frac{1}{3} \sin 3\omega t + \frac{1}{5} \sin 5\omega t + \frac{1}{7} \sin 7\omega t + \frac{1}{9} \sin 9\omega t + \ldots \right] \qquad (1\text{-}13a)$$

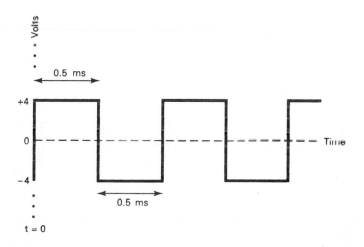

FIGURE 1-12 Waveform for Example 1-2

where $v(t)$ = time-varying voltage
        V_0 = average dc voltage (volts)
        V = peak amplitude of the square wave (volts)
        ω = $2\pi f$ (radians per second)
        T = period of the square wave (seconds)
        f = fundamental frequency of the square wave ($1/T$) (hertz)

The fundamental frequency of the square wave is

$$f = \frac{1}{T} = \frac{1}{1 \text{ ms}} = 1 \text{ kHz}$$

From Equation 1-13a, it can be seen that the frequency and amplitude of the nth odd harmonic can be determined from the following expressions:

$$f_n = n \times f \qquad\qquad\qquad\qquad\qquad\qquad\qquad\text{(1-13b)}$$

$$V_n = \frac{4V}{n\pi} \qquad n = \text{odd positive integer value} \qquad\text{(1-13c)}$$

where n = nth harmonic (odd harmonics only for a square wave)
        f = fundamental frequency of the square wave (hertz)
        V_n = peak amplitude of the nth harmonic (volts)
        f_n = frequency of the nth harmonic (hertz)
        V = peak amplitude of the square wave (volts)

Substituting $n = 1$ into Equations 1-13b and 1-13c gives

$$V_1 = \frac{4(4)}{\pi} = 5.09 \text{ V}_\text{p} \qquad f_1 = 1 \times 1000 = 1000 \text{ Hz}$$

Substituting $n = 3, 5, 7,$ and 9 into Equations 1-13b and 1-13c gives

n	Harmonic	Frequency (Hz)	Peak Voltage (V_p)
1	First	1000	5.09
3	Third	3000	1.69
5	Fifth	5000	1.02
7	Seventh	7000	0.73
9	Ninth	9000	0.57

(b) The frequency spectrum is shown in Figure 1-13.
(c) Substituting the results of the previous steps into Equation 1-13a gives

$$v(t) = 5.09 \sin[2\pi 1000t] + 1.69 \sin[2\pi 3000t] + 1.02 \sin[2\pi 5000t]$$
$$+ 0.73 \sin[2\pi 7000t] + 0.57 \sin[2\pi 9000t]$$

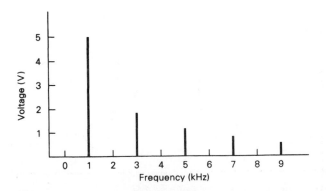

FIGURE 1-13 Frequency spectrum for Example 1-2

Solving for $v(t)$ at $t = 62.5$ μs gives

$$v(t) = 5.09 \sin[2\pi1000(62.5 \text{ μs})] + 1.69 \sin[2\pi3000(62.5 \text{ μs})]$$
$$+ 1.02 \sin[2\pi5000(62.5 \text{ μs})] + 0.73 \sin[2\pi7000(62.5 \text{ μs})]$$
$$+ 0.57 \sin[2\pi9000(62.5 \text{ μs})]$$
$$v(t) = 4.51 \text{ V}$$

Solving for $v(t)$ for several additional values of time gives the following table:

Time (μs)	$v(t)$ (volts peak)
0	0
62.5	4.51
125	3.96
250	4.26
375	3.96
437.5	4.51
500	0
562.5	−4.51
625	−3.96
750	−4.26
875	−3.96
937.5	−4.51
1000	0

The time-domain signal is derived by plotting the times and voltages calculated above on graph paper and is shown in Figure 1-14. Although the waveform shown is not an exact square wave, it does closely resemble one. To achieve a more accurate time-domain waveform, it would be necessary to solve for $v(t)$ for more values of time than are shown in this diagram.

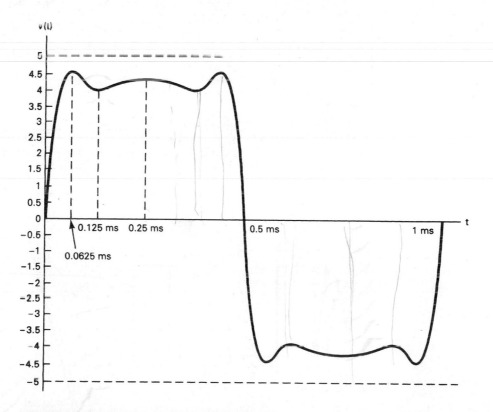

FIGURE 1-14 Time-domain signal for Example 1-2

Fourier Series for a Rectangular Waveform

When analyzing electronic communications circuits, it is often necessary to use *rectangular pulses*. A waveform showing a string of rectangular pulses is given in Figure 1-15. The *duty cycle* (DC) for the waveform is the ratio of the active time of the pulse to the period of the waveform. Mathematically, duty cycle is

$$DC = \frac{\tau}{T} \tag{1-14a}$$

$$DC(\%) = \frac{\tau}{T} \times 100 \tag{1-14b}$$

where   DC = duty cycle as a decimal
   DC(%) = duty cycle as a percent
    τ = pulse width of the rectangle wave (seconds)
    T = period of the rectangular wave (seconds)

  Regardless of the duty cycle, a rectangular waveform is made up of a series of harmonically related sine waves. However, the amplitude of the spectral components depends on the duty cycle. The Fourier series for a rectangular voltage waveform with even symmetry is

$$v(t) = \frac{V\tau}{T} + \frac{2V\tau}{T}\left[\frac{\sin x}{x}(\cos \omega t) + \frac{\sin 2x}{2x}(\cos 2\omega t) + \cdots + \frac{\sin nx}{nx}(\cos n\omega t)\right] \tag{1-15}$$

where $v(t)$ = time-varying voltage wave
   τ = pulse width of the rectangular wave (seconds)
   T = period of the rectangular wave (seconds)
   x = $\pi(\tau/T)$
   n = nth harmonic and can be any positive integer value
   V = peak pulse amplitude (volts)

From Equation 1-15, it can be seen that a rectangular waveform has a 0-Hz (dc) component equal to

$$V_0 = V \times \frac{\tau}{T} \quad \text{or} \quad V \times DC \tag{1-16}$$

where V_0 = dc voltage (volts)
   DC = duty cycle as a decimal
    τ = pulse width of rectangular wave (seconds)
    T = period of rectangular wave (seconds)

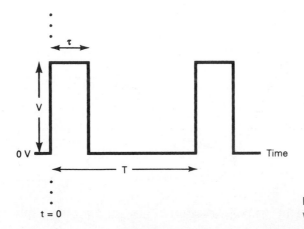

FIGURE 1-15 Rectangular pulse waveform

The narrower the pulse width is, the smaller the dc component will be. Also, from Equation 1-15, the amplitude of the nth harmonic is

$$V_n = \frac{2V\tau}{T} \times \frac{\sin nx}{nx} \qquad (1\text{-}17a)$$

or

$$V_n = \frac{2V\tau}{T} \times \frac{\sin[(n\pi\tau)/T]}{(n\pi\tau)/T} \qquad (1\text{-}17b)$$

where V_n = peak amplitude of the nth harmonic (volts)
   n = nth harmonic (any positive integer)
   π = 3.14159 radians
   V = peak amplitude of the rectangular wave (volts)
   τ = pulse width of the rectangular wave (seconds)
   T = period of the rectangular wave (seconds)

The $(\sin x)/x$ function is used to describe repetitive pulse waveforms. $\sin x$ is simply a sinusoidal waveform whose instantaneous amplitude depends on x and varies both positively and negatively between its peak amplitudes at a sinusoidal rate as x increases. With only x in the denominator, the denominator increases with x. Therefore, a $(\sin x)/x$ function is simply a damped sine wave in which each successive peak is smaller than the preceding one. A $(\sin x)/x$ function is shown in Figure 1-16.

Figure 1-17 shows the frequency spectrum for a rectangular pulse with a pulse width-to-period ratio of 0.1. It can be seen that the amplitudes of the harmonics follow a damped sinusoidal shape. At the frequency whose period equals $1/\tau$ (i.e., at frequency $10f$ hertz), there is a 0-V component. A second null occurs at $20f$ hertz (period = $2/\tau$), a third at $30f$ hertz (period = $3/\tau$), and so on. All spectrum components between 0 Hz and the first null frequency are considered in the first lobe of the frequency spectrum and are positive. All spectrum components between the first and second null frequencies are in the second lobe and are negative; components between the second and third nulls are in the third lobe and positive; and so on.

The following characteristics are true for all repetitive rectangular waveforms:

1. The dc component is equal to the pulse amplitude times the duty cycle.
2. There are 0-V components at frequency $1/\tau$ hertz and all integer multiples of that frequency providing $T = n\tau$, where n = any odd integer.
3. The amplitude-versus-frequency time envelope of the spectrum components take on the shape of a damped sine wave in which all spectrum components in odd-numbered lobes are positive and all spectrum components in even-numbered lobes are negative.

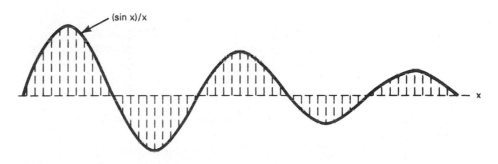

FIGURE 1-16 $(\sin x)/x$ function

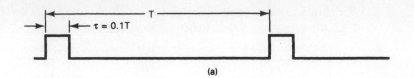

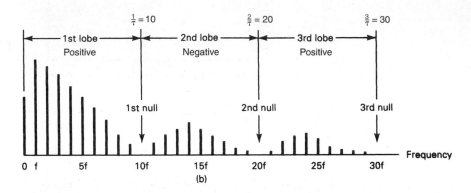

(b)

FIGURE 1-17 (sin x)/x function: (a) rectangular pulse waveform; (b) frequency spectrum

Example 1-3

For the pulse waveform shown in Figure 1-18,

(a) Determine the dc component.
(b) Determine the peak amplitudes of the first 10 harmonics.
(c) Plot the (sin x)/x function.
(d) Sketch the frequency spectrum.

Solution   (a) From Equation 1-16, the dc component is

$$V_0 = \frac{1(0.4 \text{ ms})}{2 \text{ ms}} = 0.2 \text{ V}$$

(b) The peak amplitudes of the first 10 harmonics are determined by substituting the values for τ, T, V, and n into Equation 1-17b, as follows:

$$V_n = 2(1)\left(\frac{0.4 \text{ ms}}{2 \text{ ms}}\right)\left\{\frac{\sin[(n\pi)(0.4 \text{ ms}/2 \text{ ms})]}{(n\pi)(0.4 \text{ ms}/2 \text{ ms})}\right\}$$

n	Frequency (Hz)	Amplitude (volts)
0	0	0.2 V dc
1	500	0.374 V_p
2	1000	0.303 V_p
3	1500	0.202 V_p
4	2000	0.094 V_p
5	2500	0.0 V
6	3000	-0.063 V_p
7	3500	-0.087 V_p
8	4000	-0.076 V_p
9	4500	-0.042 V_p
10	5000	0.0 V

(c) The (sin x)/x function is shown in Figure 1-19.
(d) The frequency spectrum is shown in Figure 1-20.

Although the frequency components in the even lobes are negative, it is customary to plot all voltages in the positive direction on the frequency spectrum.

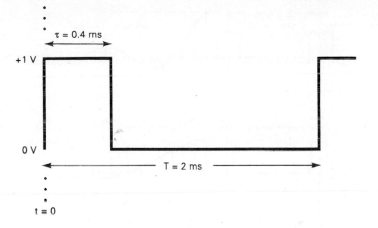

FIGURE 1-18 Pulse waveform for Example 1-3

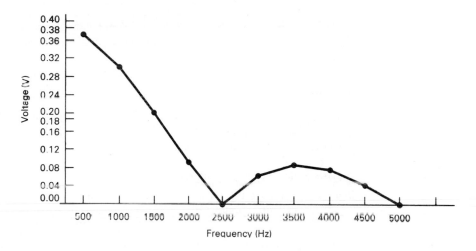

FIGURE 1-19 (sin *x*)/*x* function for Example 1-3

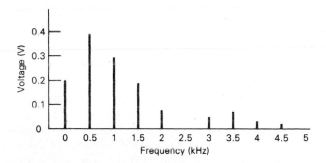

FIGURE 1-20 Frequency spectrum for Example 1-3

Figure 1-21 shows the effect that reducing the duty cycle (i.e., reducing the τ/T ratio) has on the frequency spectrum for a nonsinusoidal waveform. It can be seen that narrowing the pulse width produces a frequency spectrum with a more uniform amplitude. In fact, for infinitely narrow pulses, the frequency spectrum comprises an infinite number of harmonically related frequencies of equal amplitude. Such a spectrum is impossible to produce, let

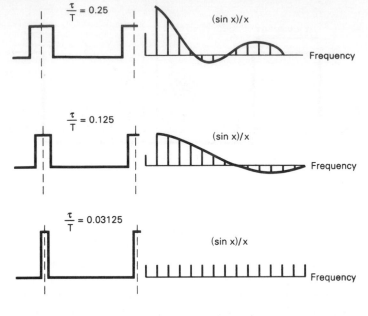

FIGURE 1-21 Effects of reducing the τ/T ratio (either decreasing τ or increasing T)

alone to propagate, which explains why it is difficult to produce extremely narrow pulses. Increasing the period of a rectangular waveform while keeping the pulse width constant has the same effect on the frequency spectrum.

Power and Energy Spectra

In the previous sections, we used the Fourier series to better understand the frequency- and time-domain representation of a complex signal. Both the frequency and time domain can be used to illustrate the relationship of signal voltages (magnitudes) with respect to either frequency or time for a time-varying signal.

However, there is another important application of the Fourier series. The goal of a communications channel is to transfer electromagnetic energy from a source to a destination. Thus, the relationship between the amount of energy transmitted and the amount received is an important consideration. Therefore, it is important that we examine the relationship between energy and power versus frequency.

Electrical power is the rate at which energy is dissipated, delivered, or used and is a function of the square of the voltage or current ($P = E^2/R$ or $P = I^2 \times R$). For power relationships, in the Fourier equation, $f(t)$ is replaced by $[f(t)]^2$. Figure 1-22 shows the power spectrum for a rectangular waveform with a 25% duty cycle. It resembles its voltage-versus-frequency spectrum except it has more lobes and a much larger primary lobe. Note also that all the lobes are positive, because there is no such thing as negative power.

From Figure 1-22, it can be seen that the power in a pulse is dispersed throughout a relatively wide frequency spectrum. However, note that most of that power is within the primary lobe. Consequently, if the bandwidth of a communications channel is sufficiently wide to pass only the frequencies within the primary lobe, it will transfer most of the energy contained in the pulse to the receiver.

Discrete and Fast Fourier Transforms

Many waveforms encountered in typical communications systems cannot be satisfactorily defined by mathematical expressions; however, their frequency-domain behavior is of primary interest. Often there is a need to obtain the frequency-domain behavior of signals that are be-

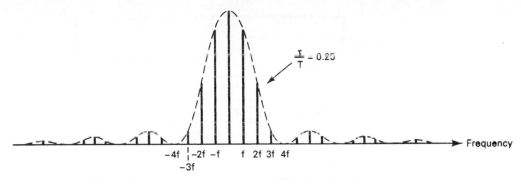

FIGURE 1-22 Power spectrum of a 25% duty cycle rectangular pulse

ing collected in the time domain (i.e., in real time). This is why the *discrete Fourier transform* was developed. With the discrete Fourier transform, a time-domain signal is sampled at discrete times. The samples are fed into a computer where an algorithm computes the transform. However, the computation time is proportional to n^2, where n is the number of samples. For any reasonable number of samples, the computation time is excessive. Consequently, in 1965 a new algorithm called the *fast Fourier transform* or FFT was developed by Cooley and Tukey. With the FFT the computing time is proportional to $n \log 2n$ rather than n^2. The FFT is now available as a subroutine in many scientific subroutine libraries at large computer centers.

Effects of Bandlimiting on Signals

All communications channels have a limited bandwidth and, therefore, have a limiting effect on signals that are propagated through them. We can consider a communications channel to be equivalent to an ideal *linear-phase filter* with a finite bandwidth. If a nonsinusoidal repetitive waveform passes through an ideal low-pass filter, the harmonic frequency components that are higher in frequency than the upper cutoff frequency of the filter are removed. Consequently, both the frequency content and shape of the waveform are changed. Figure 1-23a shows the time-domain waveform for the square wave used in Example 1-2. If this waveform is passed through a low-pass filter with an upper cutoff frequency of 8 kHz, frequencies above the eighth harmonic (9 kHz and above) are cut off, and the waveform shown in Figure 1-23b results. Figures 1-23c, d, and e show the waveforms produced when low-pass filters with upper cutoff frequencies of 6 kHz, 4 kHz, and 2 kHz are used, respectively.

It can be seen from Figure 1-23 that *bandlimiting* a signal changes the frequency content and, thus, the shape of its waveform and, if sufficient bandlimiting is imposed, the waveform eventually comprises only the fundamental frequency. In a communications system, bandlimiting reduces the information capacity of the system and, if excessive bandlimiting is imposed, a portion of the information signal can be removed from the composite waveform.

MIXING

Mixing is the process of combining two or more signals and is an essential process in electronic communications. In essence, there are two ways in which signals can be combined or mixed: linearly and nonlinearly.

Linear Summing

Linear summing occurs when two or more signals combine in a linear device, such as a passive network or a small-signal amplifier. The signals combine in such a way that no new frequencies are produced, and the combined waveform is simply the linear addition of the individual signals. In the audio recording industry, linear summing is sometimes called linear *mixing;* however, in radio communications, mixing almost always implies a nonlinear process.

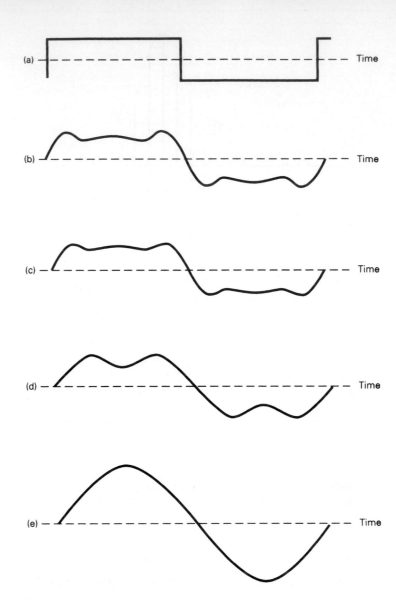

FIGURE 1-23 Bandlimiting signals: (a) 1-kHz square wave; (b) 1-kHz square wave bandlimited to 8 kHz; (c) 1-kHz square wave bandlimited to 6 kHz; (d) 1-kHz square wave bandlimited to 4 kHz; (e) 1-kHz square wave bandlimited to 2 kHz

Single-input frequency. Figure 1-24a shows the amplification of a single-input frequency by a linear amplifier. The output is simply the original input signal amplified by the gain of the amplifier (A). Figure 1-24b shows the output signal in the time domain, and Figure 1-24c shows the frequency domain. Mathematically, the output is

$$v_{\text{out}} = Av_{\text{in}} \qquad (1\text{-}18)$$

or
$$v_{\text{in}} = V_a \sin 2\pi f_a t$$

Thus,
$$v_{\text{out}} = AV_a \sin 2\pi f_a t$$

Multiple-input frequencies. Figure 1-25a shows two input frequencies combining in a small-signal amplifier. Each input signal is amplified by the gain (A). Therefore, the output is expressed mathematically as

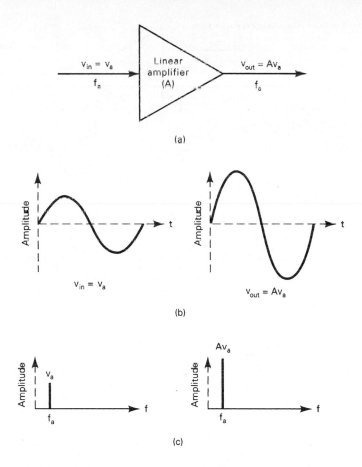

FIGURE 1-24 Linear amplification of a single-input frequency:
(a) linear amplification; (b) time domain; (c) frequency domain

$$v_{out} = Av_{in}$$

where
$$v_{in} = V_a \sin 2\pi f_a t + V_b \sin 2\pi f_b t$$

Therefore,
$$v_{out} = A(V_a \sin 2\pi f_a t + V_b \sin 2\pi f_b t) \qquad (1\text{-}19a)$$

or
$$v_{out} = A(V_a \sin 2\pi f_a t + AV_b \sin 2\pi f_b t) \qquad (1\text{-}19b)$$

v_{out} is simply a complex waveform containing both input frequencies and is equal to the algebraic sum of v_a and v_b. Figure 1-25b shows the linear summation of v_a and v_b in the time domain, and Figure 1-25c shows the linear summation in the frequency domain. If additional input frequencies are applied to the circuit, they are linearly summed with v_a and v_b. In high-fidelity audio systems, it is important that the output spectrum contain only the original input frequencies; therefore, linear operation is desired. However, in radio communications where modulation is essential, nonlinear mixing is often necessary.

Nonlinear Mixing

Nonlinear mixing occurs when two or more signals are combined in a nonlinear device such as a diode or large-signal amplifier. With nonlinear mixing, the input signals combine in a nonlinear fashion and produce additional frequency components.

Single-input frequency. Figure 1-26a shows the amplification of a single-frequency input signal by a nonlinear amplifier. The output from a nonlinear amplifier with

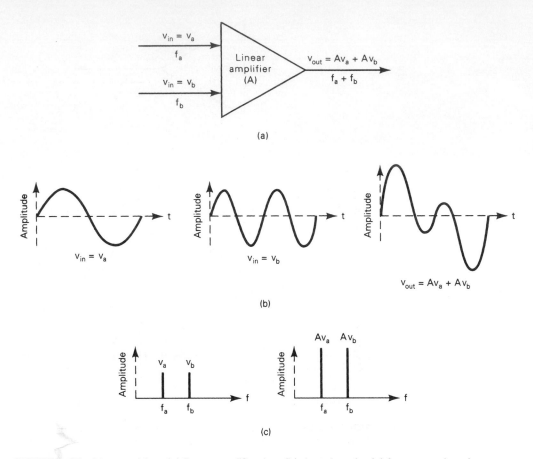

FIGURE 1-25 Linear mixing: (a) linear amplification; (b) time domain; (c) frequency domain

a single-frequency input signal is not a single sine or cosine wave. Mathematically, the output is in the infinite power series

$$v_{out} = Av_{in} + Bv_{in}^2 + Cv_{in}^3 \qquad \text{(1-20a)}$$

where $\qquad\qquad\qquad\qquad v_{in} = V_a \sin 2\pi f_a t$

Therefore, $\quad v_{out} = A(V_a \sin 2\pi f_a t) + B(V_a \sin 2\pi f_a t)^2 + C(V_a \sin 2\pi f_a t)^3 \qquad \text{(1-20b)}$

where $\quad Av_{in}$ = linear term or simply the input signal (f_a) amplified by the gain (A)
$\qquad\quad Bv_{in}^2$ = quadratic term that generates the second harmonic frequency ($2f_a$)
$\qquad\quad Cv_{in}^3$ = cubic term that generates the third harmonic frequency ($3f_a$)

v_{in}^n produces a frequency equal to n times f. For example, Bv_{in}^2 generates a frequency equal to $2f_a$. Cv_{in}^3 generates a frequency equal to $3f_a$, and so on. Integer multiples of a *base* frequency are called *harmonics*. As stated previously, the original input frequency (f_a) is the first harmonic or the fundamental frequency; $2f_a$ is the second harmonic; $3f_a$ the third, and so on. Figure 1-26b shows the output waveform in the time domain for a nonlinear amplifier with a single-input frequency. It can be seen that the output waveform is simply the summation of the input frequency and its higher harmonics (multiples of the fundamental frequency). Figure 1-26c shows the output spectrum in the frequency domain. Note that adjacent harmonics are separated in frequency by a value equal to the fundamental frequency, f_a.

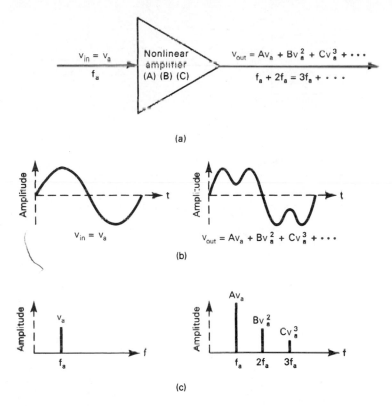

FIGURE 1-26 Nonlinear amplification of a single-input frequency:
(a) nonlinear amplification; (b) time domain; (c) frequency domain

Nonlinear amplification of a single frequency results in the generation of multiples or harmonics of that frequency. If the harmonics are undesired, it is called *harmonic distortion*. If the harmonics are desired, it is called *frequency multiplication*.

A JFET is a special-case nonlinear device that has characteristics that are approximately those of a square-law device. The output from a square-law device is

$$v_{\text{out}} = Bv_{\text{in}}^2 \tag{1-21}$$

The output from a square-law device with a single-input frequency is dc and the second harmonic. No additional harmonics are generated beyond the second. Therefore, less harmonic distortion is produced with a JFET than with a comparable BJT.

Multiple-input frequencies. Figure 1-27 shows the nonlinear amplification of two input frequencies by a large-signal (nonlinear) amplifier. Mathematically, the output of a large-signal amplifier with two input frequencies is

$$v_{\text{out}} = Av_{\text{in}} + Bv_{\text{in}}^2 + Cv_{\text{in}}^3$$

where

$$v_{\text{in}} = V_a \sin 2\pi f_a t + V_b \sin 2\pi f_b t$$

Therefore,

$$v_{\text{out}} = A(V_a \sin 2\pi f_a t + V_b \sin 2\pi f_b t) + B(V_a \sin 2\pi f_a t + V_b \sin 2\pi f_b t)^2$$
$$+ C(V_a \sin 2\pi f_a t + V_b \sin 2\pi f_b t)^3 + \cdots \tag{1-22a}$$

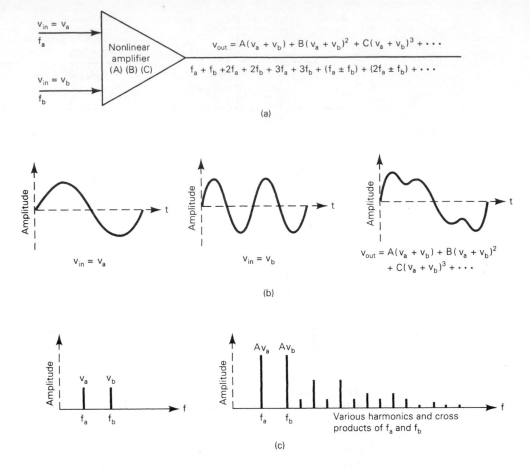

FIGURE 1-27 Nonlinear amplification of two sine waves: (a) nonlinear amplification; (b) time domain; (c) frequency domain

The preceding formula is an infinite series and there is no limit to the number of terms it can have. If the binomial theorem is applied to each higher-power term, the formula can be rearranged and written as

$$v_{\text{out}} = (Av_a' + Bv_a'^2 + Cv_a'^3 + \cdots) + (Av_b' + Bv_b'^2 + Cv_b'^3 + \cdots)$$
$$+ (2Bv_a'v_b' + 3Cv_a'^2v_b' + 3Cv_a'v_b'^2 + \cdots) \qquad (1\text{-}22b)$$

where $v_a' = V_a \sin 2\pi f_a t$

$v_b' = V_b \sin 2\pi f_b t$

The terms in the first set of parentheses generate harmonics of f_a ($2f_a$, $3f_a$, and so on). The terms in the second set of parentheses generate harmonics of f_b ($2f_b$, $3f_b$, and so on). The terms in the third set of parentheses generate the *cross products* ($f_a + f_b$, $f_a - f_b$, $2f_a + f_b$, $2f_a - f_b$, and so on). The cross products are produced from *intermodulation* among the two original frequencies and their harmonics. The cross products are the *sum* and *difference* frequencies; they are the sum and difference of the two original frequencies, the sums and differences of their harmonics, and the sums and differences of the original frequencies and all the harmonics. An infinite number of harmonic and cross-product frequencies are produced when two or more frequencies *mix* in a nonlinear device. If the cross products are undesired, it is called *intermodulation distortion*. If the cross products are desired, it is called *modulation*. Mathematically, the sum and difference frequencies are

$$\text{cross products} = mf_a \pm nf_b \qquad (1\text{-}23)$$

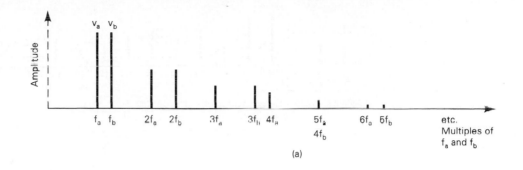

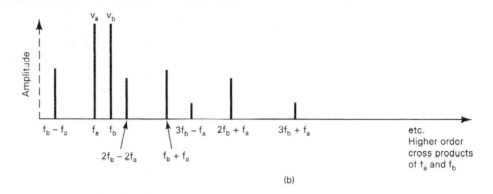

FIGURE 1-28 Output spectrum from a nonlinear amplifier with two input frequencies: (a) harmonic distortion; (b) intermodulation distortion

where m and n are positive integers between one and infinity. Figure 1-28 shows the output spectrum from a nonlinear amplifier with two input frequencies.

Intermodulation distortion is the generation of any unwanted cross-product frequency when two or more frequencies are mixed in a nonlinear device. Consequently, when two or more frequencies are amplified in a nonlinear device, both harmonic and intermodulation distortions are present in the output.

Example 1-4

For a nonlinear amplifier with two input frequencies, 5 kHz and 7 kHz,

(a) Determine the first three harmonics present in the output for each input frequency.
(b) Determine the cross products produced in the output for values of m and n of 1 and 2.
(c) Draw the output frequency spectrum for the harmonics and cross-product frequencies determined in steps (a) and (b).

Solution (a) The first three harmonics include the two original input frequencies of 5 kHz and 7 kHz; two times each of the original input frequencies, 10 kHz and 14 kHz; and three times each of the original input frequencies, 15 kHz and 21 kHz.

(b) The cross products for values of m and n of 1 and 2 are determined from Equation 1-23 and are summarized next.

m	n	Cross Products
1	1	7 kHz ± 5 kHz = 2 kHz and 12 kHz
1	2	7 kHz ± 10 kHz = 3 kHz and 17 kHz
2	1	14 kHz ± 5 kHz = 9 kHz and 19 kHz
2	2	14 kHz ± 10 kHz = 4 kHz and 24 kHz

(c) The output frequency spectrum is shown in Figure 1-29.

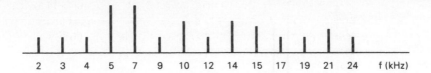

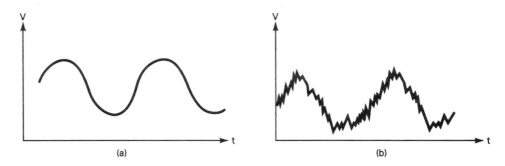

FIGURE 1-29 Output spectrum for Example 1-4

FIGURE 1-30 Effects of noise on a signal: (a) signal without noise; (b) signal with noise

NOISE ANALYSIS

Electrical noise is defined as any undesirable electrical energy that falls within the passband of the signal. For example, in audio recording any unwanted electrical signals that fall within the audio frequency band of 0 kHz to 15 kHz will interfere with the music and, therefore, are considered noise. Figure 1-30 shows the effect that noise has on an electrical signal. Figure 1-30a shows a sine wave without noise, and Figure 1-30b shows the same signal except in the presence of noise.

Noise can be divided into two general categories: *correlated* and *uncorrelated*. Correlation implies a relationship between the signal and the noise. Therefore, correlated noise exists only when a signal is present. Uncorrelated noise, on the other hand, is present all the time whether there is a signal or not.

Uncorrelated Noise

Uncorrelated noise is present regardless of whether there is a signal present or not. Uncorrelated noise can be further subdivided into two general categories: external and internal.

External noise. *External noise* is noise that is generated outside the device or circuit. The three primary sources of external noise are: atmospheric, extraterrestrial, and man-made.

Atmospheric Noise. *Atmospheric noise* is naturally occurring electrical disturbances that originate within Earth's atmosphere. Atmospheric noise is commonly called *static electricity* and is the familiar sputtering, crackling, and so on, often heard from a speaker when there is no signal present. The source of most static electricity is naturally occurring electrical conditions, such as lightning. Static electricity is often in the form of impulses that spread energy throughout a wide range of frequencies. The magnitude of this energy, however, is inversely proportional to its frequency. Consequently, at frequencies above 30 MHz, or so, atmospheric noise is relatively insignificant.

Extraterrestrial Noise. *Extraterrestrial noise* consists of electrical signals that originate from outside Earth's atmosphere and is, therefore, sometimes called *deep-space noise*. Extraterrestrial noise originates from the Milky Way, other galaxies, and the sun. Extraterrestrial noise is subdivided into two categories: solar and cosmic.

Solar noise is generated directly from the sun's heat. There are two parts to solar noise: a *quiet* condition when a relatively constant radiation intensity exists and *high intensity,* sporadic disturbances caused by *sun spot* activity and *solar flare-ups*. The magnitude of the sporadic noise caused by sun spot activity follows a cyclic pattern that repeats every 11 years.

Cosmic noise sources are continuously distributed throughout the galaxies. Because the sources of galactic noise are located much farther away than our sun, their noise intensity is relatively small. Cosmic noise is often called *black-body noise* and is distributed fairly evenly throughout the sky.

Man-Made Noise. *Man-made noise* is simply noise that is produced by mankind. The predominant sources of man-made noise are spark-producing mechanisms such as commutators in electric motors, automobile ignition systems, ac power-generating and switching equipment, and fluorescent lights. Man-made noise is impulsive in nature and contains a wide range of frequencies that are propagated through space in the same manner as radio waves. Man-made noise is most intense in the more densely populated metropolitan and industrial areas and is sometimes called *industrial noise*.

Internal noise. *Internal noise* is electrical interference generated within a device or circuit. There are three primary kinds of internally generated noise: shot, transit time, and thermal.

Shot Noise. *Shot noise* is caused by the random arrival of carriers (holes and electrons) at the output element of an electronic device, such as a diode, field-effect transistor, or bipolar transistor. Shot noise was first observed in the anode current of a vacuum-tube amplifier and was described mathematically by W. Schottky in 1918. The current carriers (for both ac and dc) are not moving in a continuous, steady flow because the distance they travel varies due to their random paths of motion. Shot noise is randomly varying and is superimposed onto any signal present. When amplified, shot noise sounds similar to metal pellets falling on a tin roof. Shot noise is sometimes called *transistor noise* and is additive with thermal noise.

Transit-Time Noise. Any modification to a stream of carriers as they pass from the input to the output of a device (such as from the emitter to the collector of a transistor) produces an irregular, random variation categorized as *transit-time noise*. When the time it takes for a carrier to propagate through a device is an appreciable part of the time of one cycle of the signal, the noise becomes noticeable. Transit-time noise in transistors is determined by carrier mobility, bias voltage, and transistor construction. Carriers traveling from emitter to collector suffer from emitter-time delays, base transit-time delays, and collector recombination-time and propagation-time delays. If transit delays are excessive at high frequencies, the device may add more noise than amplification to the signal.

Thermal Noise. *Thermal noise* is associated with the rapid and random movement of electrons within a conductor due to *thermal agitation*. This random movement was first noted by the English botanist Robert Brown. Brown first observed evidence for the moving-particle nature of matter in pollen grains. Random movement of electrons was first recognized in 1927 by J. B. Johnson of Bell Telephone Laboratories. Electrons within a conductor carry a unit negative charge, and the mean-square velocity of an electron is proportional to the absolute temperature. Consequently, each flight of an electron between collisions with molecules constitutes a short pulse of current that develops a small voltage across the resistive component of the conductor. Because this type of electron movement is totally random and in all directions, the average voltage in the substance due to this movement is 0 V dc. However, such a random movement does produce an ac component.

The ac component produced from thermal agitation has several names including *thermal noise* because it is temperature dependent, *Brownian noise* after its discoverer,

Johnson noise after the man who related Brownian particle movement of electron movement, and *white noise* because the random movement is at all frequencies. Hence, thermal noise is the random motion of free electrons within a conductor caused by thermal agitation.

Johnson proved that thermal noise power is proportional to the product of bandwidth and temperature. Mathematically, noise power is

$$N = KTB \qquad\qquad (1\text{-}24)$$

where N = noise power (watts)
  B = bandwidth (hertz)
  K = Boltzmann's proportionality constant (1.38×10^{-23} joules per kelvin)
  T = absolute temperature (kelvin) (room temperature = 17° C or 290 K)

To convert °C to kelvin, simply add 273°; thus, $T = °C + 273°$.

Example 1-5

Convert the following temperatures to kelvin: 100° C, 0° C, and −10° C

Solution The formula $T = °C + 273°$ is used to convert °C to kelvin.

$$T = 100°C + 273° = 373 \text{ K}$$
$$T = 0°C + 273° = 273 \text{ K}$$
$$T = -10°C + 273° = 263 \text{ K}$$

Noise power stated in dBm is a logarithmic function and equal to

$$N_{(dBm)} = 10 \log \frac{KTB}{0.001} \qquad\qquad (1\text{-}25)$$

Equations 1-24 and 1-25 show that at absolute zero (0 K or −273° C) there is no random molecular movement and the product *KTB* equals zero.

Example 1-6

Convert the following absolute power levels to dBm: 0.002 W, 0.0001 W, 10 mW, and 0.001 W.

Solution Absolute power levels are converted into dBm units by substituting into Equation 1-25.

$$10 \log \frac{0.002}{0.001} = 3 \text{ dBm}$$

$$10 \log \frac{0.0001}{0.001} = -10 \text{ dBm}$$

$$10 \log \frac{10 \text{ mW}}{0.001} = 10 \text{ dBm}$$

$$10 \log \frac{0.001}{0.001} = 0 \text{ dBm}$$

From Example 1-6, it can be seen that power levels above 1 mW yield positive dBm values, power levels below 1 mW yield negative dBm levels, and a power level of 1 mW is 0 dBm.

Rearranging Equation 1-25 gives:

$$N_{(dBm)} = 10 \log \frac{KT}{0.001} + 10 \log B \qquad\qquad (1\text{-}26)$$

and for a 1-Hz bandwidth at room temperature,

$$N_{(dBm)} = 10 \log \frac{(1.38 \times 10^{-23})(290)}{0.001} + 10 \log 1$$

$$= -174 \text{ dBm}$$

Thus, at room temperature, Equation 1-25 can be rewritten for any bandwidth as:

$$N_{(dBm)} = -174 \text{ dBm} + 10 \log B \tag{1-27}$$

Random noise results in a constant power density versus frequency, and Equation 1-24 indicates that the available power from a thermal noise source is proportional to bandwidth over any range of frequencies. This has been found to be true for frequencies from 0 Hz to the highest microwave frequencies used today. Thus, if the bandwidth is unlimited, it appears that the available power from a thermal noise source is also unlimited. This, of course, is not true, as it can be shown that at arbitrarily high frequencies thermal noise power eventually drops to zero. Because thermal noise is equally distributed throughout the frequency spectrum, a thermal noise source is sometimes called a *white noise source*, which is analogous to white light, which contains all visible-light frequencies. Therefore, the rms noise power measured at any frequency from a white noise source is equal to the rms noise power measured at any other frequency from the same noise source. Similarly, the total rms noise power measured in any fixed bandwidth is equal to the total rms noise power measured in an equal bandwidth anywhere else in the total noise spectrum. In other words, the rms white noise power present in the band from 1000 Hz to 2000 Hz is equal to the rms white noise power present in the band from 1,001,000 Hz to 1,002,000 Hz.

Thermal noise is random and continuous and occurs at all frequencies. Also, thermal noise is predictable, additive, and present in all devices. This is why thermal noise is the most significant of all noise sources.

Noise Voltage

Figure 1-31 shows the equivalent circuit for a thermal noise source where the internal resistance of the source (R_I) is in series with the rms noise voltage (V_N). For the worst-case condition and maximum transfer of noise power, the load resistance (R) is made equal to R_I. Thus, the noise voltage dropped across R is equal to half of the noise source $(V_R = V_N/2)$, and from Equation 1-24 the noise power (N) developed across the load resistor is equal to KTB. The mathematical expression for V_N is derived as follows:

$$N = KTB = \frac{(V_N/2)^2}{R} = \frac{V_N^2}{4R}$$

Thus,

$$V_N^2 = 4RKTB$$

and

$$V_N = \sqrt{4RKTB} \tag{1-28}$$

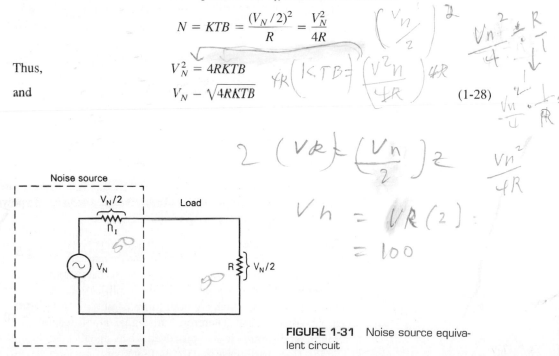

FIGURE 1-31 Noise source equivalent circuit

Example 1-7

For an electronic device operating at a temperature of 17° C with a bandwidth of 10 kHz, determine
(a) Thermal noise power in watts and dBm.
(b) Rms noise voltage for a 100-Ω internal resistance and a 100-Ω load resistance.

Solution   (a) The thermal noise power is found by substituting into Equation 1-24.

$$N = KTB \quad T \text{ (kelvin)} = 17°C + 273° = 290 \text{ K} \quad B = 1 \times 10^4 \text{ Hz}$$
$$= (1.38 \times 10^{-23})(290)(1 \times 10^4) = 4 \times 10^{-17} \text{ W}$$

Substituting, Equation 1-25 gives the noise power in dBm.

$$N_{(dBm)} = 10 \log \frac{[4 \times 10^{-17}]}{0.001} = -134 \text{ dBm}$$

or, substitute into Equation 1-27

$$N_{(dBm)} = -174 \text{ dBm} + 10 \text{ Log } 10,000$$
$$= -174 \text{ dBm} + 40 \text{ dB}$$
$$= -134 \text{ dBm}$$

(b) The rms noise voltage is found by substituting into Equation 1-28.

$$V_N = \sqrt{4RKTB} \quad \text{where } KTB = 4 \times 10^{-17}$$
$$= \sqrt{(4)(100)(4 \times 10^{-17})} = 0.1265 \ \mu V$$

Example 1-8

Convert the power level of 13 dBm to watts.

Solution   Power levels in dBm are converted to watts by rearranging Equation 1-25.

$$P_{(dBm)} = 10 \log \frac{P_{(watts)}}{0.001 \text{ W}}$$

$$13 \text{ dBm} = 10 \log \frac{P_{(watts)}}{0.001 \text{ W}}$$

Dividing both sides of the equation by 10 gives

$$\frac{13}{10} = \log \frac{P_{(watts)}}{0.001 \text{ W}}$$

$$1.3 = \log \frac{P_{(watts)}}{0.001 \text{ W}}$$

Taking the antilog of both sides of the equation clears the log function from the right member.

$$10^{1.3} = \left(\frac{P_{(watts)}}{0.001 \text{ W}} \right.$$

$$20 = \frac{P_{(watts)}}{0.001 \text{ W}}$$

Multiplying both sides of the equation by 0.001 gives

$$0.001(20) = P_{(watts)}$$
$$P_{(watts)} = 20 \text{ mW}$$

Correlated Noise

Correlated noise is noise that is correlated (mutually related) to the signal and cannot be present in a circuit unless there is an input signal—simply stated, no signal, no noise! Correlated noise is produced by nonlinear amplification and includes harmonic and intermodulation distortion, which are both forms of nonlinear distortion. All amplifiers are nonlinear to some extent. Therefore, all signal amplification produces nonlinear distortion. Nonlinear distortion is also produced when signals pass through nonlinear devices such as diodes. Correlated noise is a form of internal noise.

Harmonic distortion. *Harmonic distortion* is when unwanted harmonics of a signal are produced through nonlinear amplification (mixing). Harmonics are integer multiples of the original input signal. The original signal is the first harmonic and is called the *fundamental frequency*. Two times the original signal frequency is the second harmonic, three times is the third harmonic, and so forth. Amplitude distortion is another name for harmonic distortion.

There are various degrees of harmonic distortion. *Second order harmonic distortion is the ratio of the rms amplitude of the second harmonic frequency to the rms amplitude of the fundamental frequency.* *Third order harmonic distortion* is the ratio of the rms amplitude of the third harmonic to the rms amplitude of the fundamental frequency, and so on. *Total harmonic distortion* is the combined rms amplitude of the higher harmonics to the rms amplitude of the fundamental frequency. Mathematically total harmonic distortion (THD) is

$$\% \text{ THD} = \frac{v_{\text{higher}}}{v_{\text{fundamental}}} \times 100 \tag{1-29}$$

where $\% \text{ THD}$ = percent total harmonic distortion

v_{higher} = quadratic sum of the rms voltages of the harmonics above the fundamental frequency, $\sqrt{v_2^2 + v_3^2 + v_n^2}$

$v_{\text{fundamental}}$ = rms voltage of the fundamental frequency

Example 1-9

Determine

(a) Second, third, and twelfth harmonics for a 1-kHz repetitive wave.

(b) Percent second order, third order, and total harmonic distortion for a fundamental frequency with an amplitude of 8 Vrms, a second harmonic amplitude of 0.2 Vrms, and a third harmonic amplitude of 0.1 Vrms.

Solution   (a) Harmonic frequencies are simply integer multiples of the fundamental frequency.

$$\text{2nd harmonic} = 2 \times \text{fundamental} = 2 \times 1 \text{ kHz} = 2 \text{ kHz}$$
$$\text{3rd harmonic} = 3 \times \text{fundamental} = 3 \times 1 \text{ kHz} = 3 \text{ kHz}$$
$$\text{12th harmonic} = 12 \times \text{fundamental} = 12 \times 1 \text{ kHz} = 12 \text{ kHz}$$

(b)

$$\% \text{ 2nd order} = \frac{V_2}{V_1} \times 100 = \frac{0.2}{8} \times 100 = 2.5\%$$

$$\% \text{ 3rd order} = \frac{V_3}{V_1} \times 100 = \frac{0.1}{8} \times 100 = 1.25\%$$

$$\% \text{ THD} = \frac{\sqrt{(0.2)^2 + (0.1)^2}}{8} = 2.795\%$$

Intermodulation distortion. *Intermodulation distortion* is the generation of *unwanted sum* and *difference frequencies* when two or more signals are amplified in a nonlinear device, such as a large-signal amplifier. The emphasis here is on the word *unwanted*, because in communications circuits it is often desirable to mix two or more signals and produce sum and difference frequencies. The sum and difference frequencies are called *cross products*. Cross products are produced when harmonics as well as fundamental frequencies mix in a nonlinear device. For intermodulation distortion to occur, there must be two or more input signals. Mathematically, the sum and difference frequencies are

$$\text{cross products} = mf_1 \pm nf_2 \tag{1-30}$$

where f_1 and f_2 are fundamental frequencies where $f_1 > f_2$ and m and n are positive integers between one and infinity.

Example 1-10

For a nonlinear amplifier with two input frequencies, 3 kHz and 8 kHz, determine
(a) First three harmonics present in the output for each input frequency.
(b) Cross-product frequencies produced for values of m and n of 1 and 2.

Solution   (a) The first three harmonics include the two original frequencies, 3 kHz and 8 kHz; two times each of the original frequencies, 6 kHz and 16 kHz; and three times each of the original frequencies, 9 kHz and 24 kHz.
(b) The cross products for values of m and n of 1 and 2 are determined from Equation 1-30 and are summarized below.

m	n	Cross Products
1	1	8 kHz $\pm$ 3 kHz = 5 kHz and 11 kHz
1	2	8 kHz $\pm$ 6 kHz = 2 kHz and 14 kHz
2	1	16 kHz $\pm$ 3 kHz = 13 kHz and 19 kHz
2	2	16 kHz $\pm$ 6 kHz = 10 kHz and 22 kHz

Impulse Noise

Impulse noise is characterized by high-amplitude peaks of short duration in the total noise spectrum. As the name implies, impulse noise consists of sudden bursts of irregularly shaped pulses that generally last between a few microseconds and a fraction of a millisecond, depending on their amplitude and origin. The significance of impulse hits on voice communications is often more annoying than inhibitive as impulse hits produce a sharp, popping, or crackling sound. On data circuits, however, impulse noise can be devastating.

More impulse noise is encountered during transmission through mutual induction and electromagnetic radiation and is, therefore, generally considered a form of external noise. Common sources of impulse noise include transients produced from electromechanical switches (such as relays and solenoids); electric motors, appliances, and lights (especially fluorescent lights); power lines; automotive ignition systems; poor-quality solder joints; and lightning.

Interference

Interference is a form of external noise and, as the name implies, means "to disturb or detract from." Electrical interference is when information signals from one source produce frequencies that fall outside their allocated bandwidth and interfere with information signals from another source. Most interference occurs when harmonics or cross-product frequencies from one source fall into the passband of a neighboring channel. For example, CB radios transmit signals in the 27-MHz to 28-Mhz range. Their second harmonic frequencies (54–55 MHz) fall within the band allocated to VHF television (channel 3 in particular). If one person transmits on a CB radio and produces a high-amplitude second harmonic component, it could interfere with other people's television reception. Most interference occurs in the radio-frequency spectrum and is discussed in more detail in later chapters of this book.

Noise Summary

Table 1-4 summarizes the electrical noise sources described in this chapter.

Signal-to-Noise Power Ratio

Signal-to-noise power ratio (S/N) is the ratio of the signal power level to the noise power level. Mathematically, signal-to-noise power ratio is expressed as

$$\frac{\text{S}}{\text{N}} = \frac{P_s}{P_n} \qquad (1\text{-}31)$$

where P_s = signal power (watts)
   P_n = noise power (watts)

TABLE 1-4 Electrical Noise Sources

Correlated Noise (Internal)
   Nonlinear Distortion
      Harmonic Distortion
      Intermodulation Distortion
Uncorrelated Noise
   External
      Atmospheric
      Extraterrestrial
      Solar
      Cosmic
      Man-made
      Impulse
      Interference
   Internal
      Thermal
      Shot
      Transient-time

The signal-to-noise power ratio is often expressed as a logarithmic function with the decibel unit.

$$\frac{S}{N}(dB) = 10 \log \frac{P_s}{P_n} \tag{1-32}$$

Example 1-11

For an amplifier with an output signal power of 10 W and an output noise power of 0.01 W, determine the signal-to-noise power ratio.

Solution The signal-to-noise power ratio is found by substituting into Equation 1-31.

$$\frac{S}{N} = \frac{P_s}{P_n} = \frac{10}{0.01} = 1000$$

To express in dB, substitute into Equation 1-32

$$\frac{S}{N}(dB) = 10 \log \frac{P_s}{P_n} = 10 \log \frac{10}{0.01} = 30 \text{ dB} \tag{1-33}$$

Signal-to-noise power ratio can also be expressed in terms of voltages and resistances as shown below:

$$\frac{S}{N}(dB) = 10 \log \frac{\dfrac{V_s^2}{R_{in}}}{\dfrac{V_n^2}{R_{out}}} \tag{1-34}$$

where $\dfrac{S}{N}$ = signal-to-noise power ratio (decibels)

     R_{in} = input resistance (ohms)
   R_{out} = output resistance (ohms)
     V_s = signal voltage (volts)
     V_n = noise voltage (volts)

If the input and output resistances of the amplifier, receiver, or network being evaluated are equal, then Equation 1-34 reduces to;

$$\frac{S}{N}(dB) = 10 \log \left(\frac{V_s^2}{V_n^2}\right)$$

$$= 10 \log \left(\frac{V_s}{V_n}\right)^2$$

$$\frac{\text{S}}{\text{N}} \text{(dB)} = 20 \log \frac{V_s}{V_n} \qquad (1\text{-}35)$$

Example 1-12

For an amplifier with an output signal voltage of 4 V, an output noise voltage of 0.005 V, and input and output resistance of 50 Ω, determine the signal-to-noise power ratio.

Solution   The signal-to-noise power ratio is found by substituting into Equation 1-34.

$$\frac{\text{S}}{\text{N}} \text{(dB)} = 20 \log \frac{V_s}{V_n} = 20 \log \frac{4}{0.005} = 58.6 \text{ dB}$$

Noise Factor and Noise Figure

Noise factor (F) and *noise figure* (NF) are figures of merit used to indicate how much the signal-to-noise ratio deteriorates as a signal passes through a circuit or series of circuits. Noise factor is simply a ratio of input signal-to-noise power ratio to output signal-to-noise power ratio. In other words, it is a ratio of ratios. Mathematically, noise factor is

$$\text{F} = \frac{\text{input signal-to-noise power ratio}}{\text{output signal-to-noise power ratio}} \text{ (unitless ratio)} \qquad (1\text{-}36)$$

Noise figure is simply the noise factor stated in dB and is a parameter commonly used to indicate the quality of a receiver. Mathematically, noise figure is

$$\text{NF(dB)} = 10 \log \frac{\text{input signal-to-noise power ratio}}{\text{output signal-to-noise power ratio}} \qquad (1\text{-}37)$$

or $\text{NF(dB)} = 10 \log \text{F}$

In essence, noise figure indicates how much the signal-to-noise ratio deteriorates as a waveform propagates from the input to the output of a circuit. For example, an amplifier with a noise figure of 6 dB means that the signal-to-noise ratio at the output is 6 dB less than it was at the input. If a circuit is perfectly noiseless and adds no additional noise to the signal, the signal-to-noise ratio at the output will equal the signal-to-noise ratio at the input. For a perfect, noiseless circuit the noise factor is 1 and the noise figure is 0 dB.

An electronic circuit amplifies signals and noise within its passband equally well. Therefore, if the amplifier is ideal and noiseless, the input signal and noise are amplified the same, and the signal-to-noise ratio at the output will equal the signal-to-noise ratio at the input. In reality, however, amplifiers are not ideal. Therefore, the amplifier adds internally generated noise to the waveform, reducing the overall signal-to-noise ratio. The most predominant noise is thermal noise, which is generated in all electrical components. Therefore, all networks, amplifiers, and systems add noise to the signal and, thus, reduce the overall signal-to-noise ratio as the signal passes through them.

Figure 1-32a shows an ideal noiseless amplifier with a power gain (A_p), an input signal power level (S_i), and an input noise power level (N_i). The output signal level is simply $A_p S_i$, and the output noise level is $A_p N_i$. Therefore, the input and output S/N ratios are equal and are expressed mathematically as

$$\frac{S_{\text{out}}}{N_{\text{out}}} = \frac{A_p S_i}{A_p N_i} = \frac{S_i}{N_i}$$

where A_p equals amplifier power gain.

Figure 1-32b shows a nonideal amplifier that generates an internal noise (N_d). As with the ideal noiseless amplifier, both the input signal and noise are amplified by the circuit

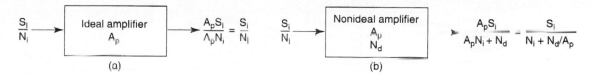

FIGURE 1-32 Noise figure: (a) ideal, noiseless amplifier; (b) amplifier with internally generated noise

gain. However, the circuit adds the internally generated noise to the waveform. Consequently, the output signal-to-noise ratio is less than the input signal-to-noise ratio by an amount proportional to N_d. Mathematically, the S/N ratio at the output of a nonideal amplifier is expressed mathematically as

$$\frac{S_{out}}{N_{out}} = \frac{A_p S_i}{A_p N_i + N_d} = \frac{S_i}{N_i + N_d/A_p}$$

where A_p = amplifer power gain
N_d = internal noise

Example 1-13

For a nonideal amplifier and the following parameters, determine
(a) Input S/N ratio (dB).
(b) Output S/N ratio (dB).
(c) Noise factor and noise figure.

Input signal power = 2×10^{-10} W

Input noise power = 2×10^{-18} W

Power gain = 1,000,000

Internal noise (N_d) = 6×10^{-12} W

Solution   (a) For the input signal and noise power levels given and substituting into Equation 1-33, the input S/N is

$$\frac{S}{N} = \frac{2 \times 10^{-10} \text{W}}{2 \times 10^{-18} \text{W}} = 100,000,000$$

$$10 \log (100,000,000) = 80 \text{ dB}$$

(b) The output noise power is the sum of the internal noise and the amplified input noise.

$$N_{out} = 1,000,000(2 \times 10^{-18}) + 6 \times 10^{-12} = 8 \times 10^{-12} \text{ W}$$

The output signal power is simply the product of the input power and the power gain.

$$P_{out} = 1,000,000(2 \times 10^{-10}) = 200 \text{ μW}$$

For the output signal and noise power levels calculated and substituting into Equation 1-33, the output S/N is

$$\frac{S}{N} = \frac{200 \times 10^{-6} \text{W}}{8 \times 10^{-12} \text{W}} = 25,000,000$$

$$10 \log (25,000,000) = 74 \text{ dB}$$

(c) The noise factor is found by substituting the results from steps (a) and (b) into Equation 1-36,

$$F = \frac{100,000,000}{25,000,000} = 4$$

and the noise figure is calculated from Equation 1-37,

$$NF = 10 \log 4 = 6 \text{ dB}$$

When two or more amplifiers are cascaded as shown in Figure 1-33, the total noise factor is the accumulation of the individual noise factors. *Friiss' formula* is used to calculate the total noise factor of several cascaded amplifiers. Mathematically, Friiss' formula is

$$F_T = F_1 + \frac{F_2 - 1}{A_1} + \frac{F_3 - 1}{A_1 A_2} + \frac{F_n - 1}{A_1 A_2 \cdots A_n} \qquad (1\text{-}38)$$

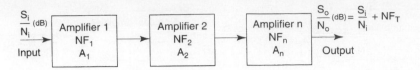

FIGURE 1-33 Noise figure of cascaded amplifiers

where F_T = total noise factor for n cascaded amplifiers
        F_1 = noise factor, amplifier 1
        F_2 = noise factor, amplifier 2
        F_3 = noise factor, amplifier 3
        F_n = noise factor, amplifier n
        A_1 = power gain, amplifier 1
        A_2 = power gain, amplifier 2
        A_n = power gain, amplifier n

Note that to use Friiss' formula, the noise figures must be converted to noise factors. The total noise figure is simply

$$NF_T(dB) = 10 \log F_T$$

Example 1-14

For three cascaded amplifier stages, each with noise figures of 3 dB and power gains of 10 dB, determine the total noise figure.

Solution   The noise figures must be converted to noise factors, then substituted into Equation 1-38 giving us a total noise factor of

$$F_T = F_1 + \frac{F_2 - 1}{A_1} + \frac{F_3 - 1}{A_1 A_2} + \frac{F_n - 1}{A_1 A_2 \cdots A_n}$$

$$= 2 + \frac{2 - 1}{10} + \frac{2 - 1}{100} = 2.11$$

Thus, the total noise figure is

$$NF_T = 10 \log 2.11 = 3.24 \text{ dB}$$

Several important observations can be made from Example 1-14. First, the overall noise figure of 3.24 dB was not significantly larger than the noise figure of the first stage (3 dB). From Equation 1-38 it can be seen that the first stage in a series of amplifiers, such as found in audio amplifiers and radio receivers, contributes the most to the overall noise figure. This is true as long as the gain of the first stage is sufficient to reduce the effects of the succeeding stages. For example, if A_1 and A_2 in Example 1-14 were only 3 dB, the overall noise figure would be 4.4 dB, a significant increase. Worse yet, if the first stage was passive and had a loss of 3 dB ($A = 0.5$), the overall noise figure would increase to 7.16 dB.

Figure 1-34 shows how signal-to-noise ratio can be reduced as a signal passes through a two-stage amplifier circuit. As the figure shows, both the input signal and input noise are amplified 10 dB in amplifier 1. Amplifier 1, however, adds an additional 1.5 dB of noise (i.e., a noise figure of 1.5 dB), thus reducing the signal-to-noise ratio at the output of amplifier 1 to 28.5 dB. Again, the signal and noise are both amplified by 10 dB in amplifier 2. Amplifier 2, however, adds 2.5 dB of additional noise (i.e., a noise figure of 2.5 dB), thus reducing the signal-to-noise ratio at the output of amplifier 2 to 26 dB. The overall reduction in the signal-to-noise ratio from the input of amplifier 1 to the output of amplifier 2 is 4 dB; thus, the total noise figure for the two amplifiers is 4 dB.

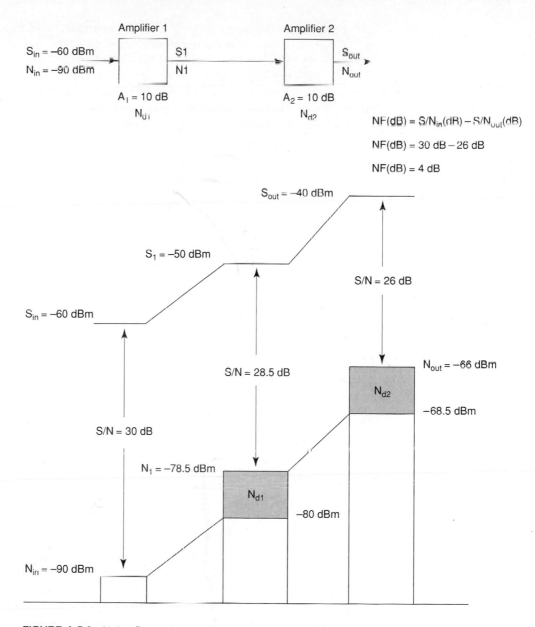

FIGURE 1-34   Noise figure degradation in cascaded amplifiers

Equivalent Noise Temperature

Because the noise produced from thermal agitation is directly proportional to temperature, thermal noise can be expressed in degrees as well as watts or dBm. Rearranging Equation 1-24 yields

$$T = \frac{N}{KB} \tag{1-39}$$

where T = environmental temperature (kelvin)
   N = noise power (watts)
   K = Boltzmann's constant (1.38×10^{-23} J/K)
   B = bandwidth (hertz)

Equivalent noise temperature (T_e) is a hypothetical value that cannot be directly measured. T_e is a convenient parameter often used rather than noise figure in low-noise, sophisticated VHF, UHF, microwave, and satellite radio receivers. T_e, as is noise factor, indicates the reduction in the signal-to-noise ratio a signal undergoes as it propagates through a receiver. The lower the equivalent noise temperature is, the better the quality of a receiver. A noise figure of 1 dB corresponds to an equivalent noise temperature of 75 K, and a noise figure of 6 dB corresponds to an equivalent noise temperature of 870 K. Typical values for T_e range from 20 K for cool receivers to 1000 K for noisy receivers. Mathematically, T_e at the input to a receiver is expressed as

$$T_e = T(F - 1) \tag{1-40}$$

where T_e = equivalent noise temperature (kelvin)
$\quad\quad\; T$ = environmental temperature (reference value of 290 K)
$\quad\quad\; F$ = noise factor (unitless)

Conversely, noise factor can be represented as a function of equivalent noise temperature with the following formula.

$$F = 1 + \frac{T_e}{T} \tag{1-41}$$

Example 1-15

Determine

(a) Noise figure for an equivalent noise temperature of 75 K (use 290 K for the reference temperature).
(b) Equivalent noise temperature for a noise figure of 6 dB.

Solution (a) Substituting into Equation 1-41 yields a noise factor of

$$F = 1 + \frac{T_e}{T} = 1 + \frac{75}{290} = 1.258$$

and noise figure is simply

$$NF = 10 \log(1.258) = 1 \text{ dB}$$

(b) Noise factor is found by rearranging Equation 1-37

$$F = \text{antilog}(NF/10) = \text{antilog}(6/10) = (10)^{0.6} = 4$$

Substituting into Equation 1-40 gives

$$T_e = T(F - 1) = 290(4 - 1) = 870 \text{ K}$$

QUESTIONS

1-1. Define *electronic communications*.

1-2. When was the first electronic communications system developed, who developed it, and what kind of a system was it?

1-3. When did *radio communications* begin?

1-4. What are the three primary components of a communications system?

1-5. What are the two basic types of *electronic communications systems?* analog digital

1-6. What organization assigns frequencies for free-space radio propagation in the United States?

1-7. Describe the following: *carrier signal, modulating signal,* and *modulated wave.*

1-8. Describe the terms *modulation* and *demodulation*.

1-9. What three properties of a sine wave can be varied and what type of modulation results from each of them?

1-10. List and describe two reasons why modulation is necessary in electronic communications.

1-11. Describe frequency *up-conversion* and where it is performed.

1-12. Describe frequency *down-conversion* and where it is performed.

1-13. List and describe the two most significant limitations on the performance of an electronic communications system.

1-14. What is the *information capacity* of a communications system?

1-15. Briefly describe the significance of *Hartley's law*.

1-16. Describe *signal analysis* as it pertains to electronic communications.

1-17. What is meant by the term *even symmetry*? What is another name for even symmetry?

1-18. What is meant by the term *odd symmetry*? What is another name for odd symmetry?

1-19. What is meant by the term *half-wave symmetry*?

1-20. Describe the term *duty cycle*.

1-21. Describe a $(\sin x)/x$ function.

1-22. Define *linear summing*.

1-23. Define *nonlinear mixing*.

1-24. Describe *electrical noise*.

1-25. What are the two general categories of electrical noise?

1-26. The phrase *no signal, no noise* describes which type of electrical interference?

1-27. List and describe which types of noise are considered *external noise*.

1-28. What is the predominant type of *internal noise*?

1-29. Describe the relationship among *thermal noise power, bandwidth*, and *temperature*.

1-30. Describe *white noise*.

1-31. List and describe the two types of *correlated noise*.

1-32. Describe *signal-to-noise power ratio*.

1-33. What is meant by the terms *noise factor* and *noise figure*?

1-34. Define *equivalent noise temperature*.

1-35. Describe a *harmonic*; a *cross-product frequency*.

PROBLEMS

1-1. What is the CCIR designation for the following frequency ranges:
(a) 3 kHz–30 kHz　(b) 0.3 MHz–3 MHz　(c) 3 GHz–30 GHz

1-2. What is the frequency range for the following CCIR designations:
(a) UHF　(b) ELF　(c) SHF

1-3. What is the effect on the information capacity of a communications channel when the allocated bandwidth doubles? Triples?

1-4. What is the effect on the information capacity of a communications channel when the allocated bandwidth halves and the transmission time doubles?

1-5. Convert the following temperatures to kelvin:
(a) 17° C　(b) 27° C　(c) −17° C　(d) −50° C

1-6. Convert the following thermal noise powers to dBm:
(a) 0.001 μW　(b) 1 pW　(c) 2×10^{-15} W　(d) 1.4×10^{-16} W

1-7. Convert the following thermal noise powers to watts:
(a) −150 dBm　(b) −100 dBm　(c) −120 dBm　(d) −174 dBm

1-8. Calculate the thermal noise power in both watts and dBm for the following amplifier bandwidths and temperatures:
(a) $B = 100$ Hz, $T = 17°$ C
(b) $B = 100$ kHz, $T = 100°$ C
(c) $B = 1$ MHz, $T = 500°$ C

1-9. For the train of square waves shown,
(a) Determine the amplitudes of the first five harmonics.
(b) Draw the frequency spectrum.
(c) Sketch the time-domain signal for frequency components up to the first five harmonics.

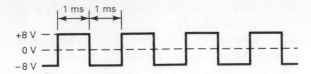

1-10. For the pulse waveform shown,
  (a) Determine the dc component.
  (b) Determine the peak amplitudes of the first five harmonics.
  (c) Plot the $(\sin x)/x$ function.
  (d) Sketch the frequency spectrum.

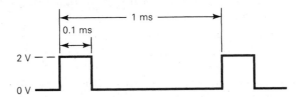

1-11. Describe the spectrum shown below. Determine the type of amplifier (linear or nonlinear) and the frequency content of the input signal.

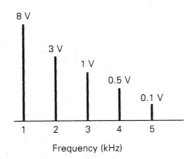

1-12. Repeat Problem 1-11 for the spectrum shown below:

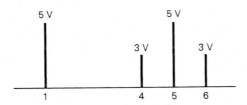

1-13. For a nonlinear amplifier with two input frequencies of 7 kHz and 4 kHz,
  (a) Determine the first three harmonics present in the output for each frequency.
  (b) Determine the cross-product frequencies produced in the output for values of *m* and *n* of 1 and 2.
  (c) Draw the output spectrum for the harmonics and cross-product frequencies determined in steps (a) and (b).

1-14. Determine the percent second order, third order, and total harmonic distortion for the output spectrum shown below.

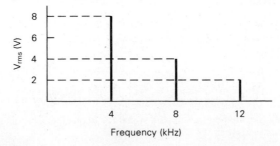

1-15. Determine the bandwidth necessary to produce 8×10^{-17} watts of thermal noise power at a temperature of 17° C.

1-16. Determine the thermal noise voltages for components operating at the following temperatures, bandwidths, and equivalent resistances:
   (a) $T = -50°$ C, $B = 50$ kHz, and $R = 50\ \Omega$
   (b) $T = 100°$ C, $B = 10$ kHz, and $R = 100\ \Omega$
   (c) $T = 50°$ C, $B = 500$ kHz, and $R = 72\ \Omega$

1-17. Determine the second, fifth, and fifteenth harmonics for a repetitive wave with a fundamental frequency of 2.5 kHz.

1-18. Determine the second, third, and total harmonic distortion for a repetitive wave with a fundamental frequency amplitude of 10 V_{rms}, a second harmonic amplitude of 0.2 V_{rms}, and a third harmonic amplitude of 0.1 V_{rms}.

1-19. For a nonlinear amplifier with sine wave input frequencies of 3 kHz and 5 kHz, determine the first three harmonics present in the output for each input frequency and the cross-product frequencies produced for values of m and n of 1 and 2.

1-20. Determine the power ratios in dB for the following input and output powers:
   (a) $P_{in} = 0.001$ W, $P_{out} = 0.01$ W
   (b) $P_{in} = 0.25$ W, $P_{out} = 0.5$ W
   (c) $P_{in} - 1$ W, $P_{out} = 0.5$ W
   (d) $P_{in} = 0.001$ W, $P_{out} = 0.001$ W
   (e) $P_{in} = 0.04$ W, $P_{out} = 0.16$ W
   (f) $P_{in} = 0.002$ W, $P_{out} = 0.0002$ W
   (g) $P_{in} = 0.01$ W, $P_{out} = 0.4$ W

1-21. Determine the voltage ratios in dB for the following input and output voltages (assume equal input and output resistance values):
   (a) $v_{in} = 0.001$ V, $v_{out} = 0.01$ V
   (b) $v_{in} = 0.1$ V, $v_{out} = 2$ V
   (c) $v_{in} = 0.5$ V, $v_{out} = 0.25$ V
   (d) $v_{in} = 1$ V, $v_{out} = 4$ V

1-22. Determine the overall noise factor and noise figure for three cascaded amplifiers with the following parameters:

$$A_1 - 10\ \text{dB}$$
$$A_2 = 10\ \text{dB}$$
$$A_3 = 20\ \text{dB}$$
$$NF_1 = 3\ \text{dB}$$
$$NF_2 = 6\ \text{dB}$$
$$NF_3 = 10\ \text{dB}$$

1-23. Determine the overall noise factor and noise figure for three cascaded amplifiers with the following parameters:

$$A_1 = 3\ \text{dB}$$
$$A_2 = 13\ \text{dB}$$
$$A_3 = 10\ \text{dB}$$
$$NF_1 = 10\ \text{dB}$$
$$NF_2 = 6\ \text{dB}$$
$$NF_3 = 10\ \text{dB}$$

1-24. If an amplifier has a bandwidth $B = 20$ kHz and a total noise power $N = 2 \times 10^{-17}$ W, determine the total noise power if the bandwidth increases to 40 kHz. Decreases to 10 kHz.

1-25. For an amplifier operating at a temperature of 27° C with a bandwidth of 20 kHz, determine
   (a) The total noise power in watts and dBm.
   (b) The rms noise voltage (V_N) for a 50-Ω internal resistance and a 50-Ω load resistor.

1-26. (a) Determine the noise power in watts and dBm for an amplifier operating at a temperature of 400° C with a 1-MHz bandwidth.

(b) Determine the decrease in noise power in decibels if the temperature decreased to 100° C.

(c) Determine the increase in noise power in decibels if the bandwidth doubled.

1-27. Determine the noise figure for an equivalent noise temperature of 1000 K (use 290 K for the reference temperature).

1-28. Determine the equivalent noise temperature for a noise figure of 10 dB.

1-29. Determine the noise figure for an amplifier with an input signal-to-noise ratio of 100 and an output signal-to-noise ratio of 50.

1-30. Determine the noise figure for an amplifier with an input signal-to-noise ratio of 30 dB and an output signal-to-noise ratio of 24 dB.

1-31. Calculate the input signal-to-noise ratio for an amplifier with an output signal-to-noise ratio of 16 dB and a noise figure of 5.4 dB.

1-32. Calculate the output signal-to-noise ratio for an amplifier with an input signal-to-noise ratio of 23 dB and a noise figure of 6.2 dB.

C H A P T E R 2

Signal Generation

INTRODUCTION

Modern electronic communications systems have many applications that require stable, repetitive waveforms (both sinusoidal and nonsinusoidal). In many of these applications, more than one frequency is required, and very often these frequencies must be synchronized to each other. Therefore, *signal generation, frequency synchronization,* and *frequency synthesis* are essential parts of an electronic communications system. The purpose of this chapter is to introduce the reader to the basic operation of oscillators, phase-locked loops, and frequency synthesizers and to show how these circuits are used for signal generation.

OSCILLATORS

The definition of *oscillate* is to fluctuate between two states or conditions. Therefore, to oscillate is to vibrate or change, and *oscillating* is the act of fluctuating from one state to another. An *oscillator* is a device that produces oscillations (i.e., generates a repetitive waveform). There are many applications for oscillators in electronic communications, such as high-frequency carrier supplies, pilot supplies, clocks, and timing circuits.

In electronic applications, an oscillator is a device or circuit that produces electrical oscillations. An electrical oscillation is a repetitive change in a voltage or current waveform. If an oscillator is *self-sustaining,* the changes in the waveform are *continuous* and *repetitive;* they occur at a periodic rate. A self-sustaining oscillator is also called a *free-running* oscillator. Oscillators that are not self-sustaining require an external input signal or *trigger* to produce a change in the output waveform. Oscillators that are not self-sustaining are called *triggered* or *one-shot* oscillators. The remainder of this chapter is restricted to explaining self-sustaining oscillators, which require no external input other than a dc supply voltage. Essentially, an oscillator converts a dc input voltage to an ac output voltage. The shape of the output waveform can be a sine wave, a square wave, a sawtooth wave, or any other waveform shape as long as it repeats at periodic intervals.

Feedback Oscillators

A *feedback oscillator* is an amplifier with a *feedback loop* (i.e., a path for energy to propagate from the output back to the input). Free-running oscillators are feedback oscillators. Once started, a feedback oscillator generates an ac output signal of which a small portion is fed back to the input, where it is amplified. The amplified input signal appears at the output and the process repeats; a *regenerative* process occurs in which the output is dependent on the input, and vice versa.

According to the *Barkhausen criterion,* for a feedback circuit to sustain oscillations, the net voltage gain around the feedback loop must be unity or greater, and the net phase shift around the loop must be a positive integer multiple of 360°.

There are four requirements for a feedback oscillator to work: *amplification, positive feedback, frequency determination,* and a *source* of electrical power.

1. *Amplification.* An oscillator circuit must include at least one active device and be capable of voltage amplification. In fact, at times it may be required to provide an infinite gain.
2. *Positive feedback.* An oscillator circuit must have a complete path for a portion of the output signal to be returned to the input. The feedback signal must be *regenerative,* which means it must have the correct phase and amplitude necessary to sustain oscillations. If the phase is incorrect or if the amplitude is insufficient, oscillations will cease. If the amplitude is excessive, the amplifier will saturate. *Regenerative feedback* is called *positive feedback,* where "positive" simply means that its phase aids the oscillation process and does not necessarily indicate a positive (+) or negative (−) polarity. *Degenerative feedback* is called *negative feedback* and supplies a feedback signal that inhibits oscillations from occurring.
3. *Frequency-determining components.* An oscillator must have frequency-determining components such as resistors, capacitors, inductors, or crystals to allow the frequency of operation to be set or changed.
4. *Power source.* An oscillator must have a source of electrical energy, such as a dc power supply.

Figure 2-1 shows an electrical model for a *feedback oscillator* circuit (i.e., a voltage amplifier with regenerative feedback). A feedback oscillator is a *closed-loop* circuit comprised of a voltage amplifier with an *open-loop voltage gain* (A_{ol}), a frequency-determining regenerative feedback path with a *feedback ratio* (β), and either a summer or a subtractor circuit. The open-loop voltage gain is the voltage gain of the amplifier with the feedback path open circuited. The *closed-loop voltage gain* (A_{cl}) is the overall voltage gain of the complete circuit with the feedback loop closed and is always less than the open-loop voltage gain. The feedback ratio is simply the transfer function of the feedback network (i.e., the ratio of its output to its input voltage). For a passive feedback network, the feedback ratio is always less than 1.

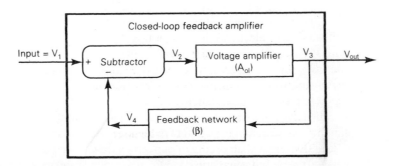

FIGURE 2-1 Model of an amplifier with feedback

From Figure 2-1, the following mathematical relationships are derived:

$$\frac{V_{out}}{V_{in}} = \frac{V_3}{V_1}$$

$$V_2 = V_1 - V_4$$

$$V_3 = A_{ol}V_2$$

$$A_{ol} = \frac{V_3}{V_2}$$

$$V_4 = \beta V_3$$

$$\beta = \frac{V_4}{V_3}$$

where
V_1 = external input voltage
V_2 = input voltage to the amplifier
V_3 = output voltage
V_4 = feedback voltage
A_{ol} = open-loop voltage gain
β = feedback ratio of the feedback network

Substituting for V_4 gives us $\qquad V_2 = V_1 - \beta V_3$

Thus, $\qquad\qquad\qquad V_3 = (V_1 - \beta V_3)A_{ol}$

and $\qquad\qquad\qquad V_3 = V_1 A_{ol} - V_3 \beta A_{ol}$

Rearranging and factoring yields

Thus, $\qquad\qquad\qquad \begin{aligned} V_3 + V_3\beta A_{ol} &= V_1 A_{ol} \\ V_3(1 + \beta A_{ol}) &= V_1 A_{ol} \end{aligned}$

and $\qquad\qquad\qquad \dfrac{V_{out}}{V_{in}} = \dfrac{V_3}{V_1} = \dfrac{A_{ol}}{1 + \beta A_{ol}} = A_{cl}$ $\qquad\qquad$ (2-1)

where A_{cl} is closed-loop voltage gain.

$A_{ol}/(1 + \beta A_{ol})$ is the standard formula used for the closed-loop voltage gain of an amplifier with feedback. If at any frequency βA_{ol} goes to -1, the denominator in Equation 2-1 goes to zero and V_{out}/V_{in} is infinity. When this happens, the circuit will oscillate and the external input may be removed.

For self-sustained oscillations to occur, a circuit must fulfill the four basic requirements for oscillation outlined previously, meet the criterion of Equation 2-1, and fit the basic feedback circuit model shown in Figure 2-1. Although oscillator action can be accomplished in many different ways, the most common configurations use *RC* phase shift networks, *LC* tank circuits, quartz crystals, or integrated-circuit chips. The type of oscillator used for a particular application depends on the following criteria:

1. Desired frequency of operation
2. Required frequency stability
3. Variable or fixed frequency operation
4. Distortion requirements or limitations
5. Desired output power
6. Physical size
7. Application (i.e., digital or analog)
8. Cost
9. Reliability and durability
10. Desired accuracy

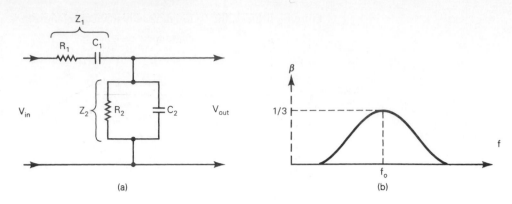

FIGURE 2-2 Lead–lag network: (a) circuit configuration; (b) input-versus-output transfer curve (β)

Untuned Oscillators

The Wien-bridge oscillator is an untuned RC phase shift oscillator that uses both positive and negative feedback. It is a relatively stable, low-frequency oscillator circuit that is easily tuned and commonly used in signal generators to produce frequencies between 5 Hz and 1 MHz. The Wien-bridge oscillator is the circuit that Hewlett and Packard used in their original signal generator design.

Figure 2-2a shows a simple lead–lag network. At the frequency of oscillation (f_o), $R = X_C$ and the signal undergoes a $-45°$ phase shift across Z_1 and a $+45°$ phase shift across Z_2. Consequently, at f_o, the total phase shift across the lead–lag network is exactly $0°$. At frequencies below the frequency of oscillation, the phase shift across the network leads and for frequencies above the phase shift lags. At extreme low frequencies, C_1 looks like an open circuit and there is no output. At extreme high frequencies, C_2 looks like a short circuit and there is no output.

A lead–lag network is a reactive voltage divider in which the input voltage is divided between Z_1 (the series combination of R_1 and C_1) and Z_2 (the parallel combination of R_2 and C_2). Therefore, the lead–lag network is frequency selective and the output voltage is maximum at f_o. The transfer function for the feedback network (β) equals $Z_2/(Z_1 + Z_2)$ and is maximum and equal to 1/3 at f_o. Figure 2-2b shows a plot of β versus frequency when $R_1 = R_2$ and $C_1 = C_2$. Thus, f_o is determined from the following expression:

$$f_o = \frac{1}{2\pi RC}$$

where $R = R_1 = R_2$
$C = C_1 = C_2$

Figure 2-3 shows a Wien-bridge oscillator. The lead–lag network and the resistive voltage divider make up a Wien bridge (hence, the name *Wien-bridge oscillator*). When the bridge is balanced, the difference voltage equals zero. The voltage divider provides negative or degenerative feedback that offsets the positive or regenerative feedback from the lead–lag network. The ratio of the resistors in the voltage divider is 2:1, which sets the noninverting voltage gain of amplifier A_1 to $R_f/R_i + 1 = 3$. Thus, at f_o, the signal at the output of A_1 is reduced by a factor of 3 as it passes through the lead–lag network (β = 1/3) and then amplified by 3 in amplifier A_1. Thus, at f_o, the loop voltage gain is equal to $A_{ol}β$ or $3 \times 1/3 = 1$.

To compensate for imbalances in the bridge and variations in component values due to heat, *automatic gain control* (AGC) is added to the circuit. A simple way of providing automatic gain is to replace R_i in Figure 2-3 with a variable resistance device such as a FET. The resistance of the FET is made inversely proportional to V_{out}. The circuit is designed such that, when V_{out} increases in amplitude, the resistance of the FET increases, and when

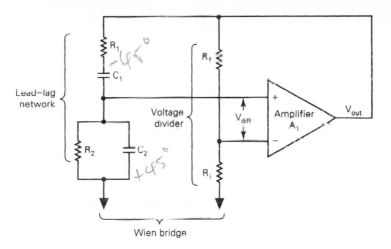

FIGURE 2-3 Wien-bridge oscillator

V_{out} decreases in amplitude, the resistance of the FET decreases. Therefore, the voltage gain of the amplifier automatically compensates for changes in amplitude in the output signal.

The operation of the circuit shown in Figure 2-3 is as follows. On initial power-up, noise (at all frequencies) appears at V_{out} and is fed back through the lead–lag network. Only noise at f_o passes through the lead–lag network with a 0° phase shift and a transfer ratio of 1/3. Consequently, only a single frequency (f_o) is fed back in phase, undergoes a loop voltage gain of 1, and produces self-sustained oscillations.

Tuned Oscillators

LC oscillators are oscillator circuits that utilize tuned *LC tank circuits* for the frequency-determining components. Tank-circuit operation involves an exchange of energy between *kinetic* and *potential*. Figure 2-4 illustrates *LC* tank-circuit operation As shown in Figure 2-4a, once current is injected into the circuit (time t_1), energy is exchanged between the inductor and capacitor, producing a corresponding ac output voltage (times t_2 to t_4). The output voltage waveform is shown in Figure 2-4b. The frequency of operation of an *LC* tank circuit is simply the resonant frequency of the parallel *LC* network, and the bandwidth is a function of the circuit *Q*. Mathematically, the resonant frequency of an *LC* tank circuit with a $Q \geq 10$ is closely approximated by

$$f_o = \frac{1}{2\pi\sqrt{(LC)}} \tag{2-2}$$

LC oscillators include the Hartley and Colpitts oscillators.

Hartley oscillator. Figure 2-5a shows the schematic diagram of a *Hartley oscillator*. The transistor amplifier (Q_1) provides the amplification necessary for a loop voltage gain of unity at the resonant frequency. The coupling capacitor (C_C) provides the path for regenerative feedback. L_{1a}, L_{1b}, and C_1 are the frequency-determining components, and V_{CC} is the dc supply voltage.

Figure 2-5b shows the dc equivalent circuit for the Hartley oscillator. C_C is a blocking capacitor that isolates the dc base bias voltage and prevents it from being shorted to ground through L_{1b}. C_2 is also a blocking capacitor that prevents the collector supply voltage from being shorted to ground through L_{1a}. The *radio-frequency choke* (RFC) is a dc short.

Figure 2-5c shows the ac equivalent circuit for the Hartley oscillator. C_C is a coupling capacitor for ac and provides a path for regenerative feedback from the tank circuit to the base of Q_1. C_2 couples ac signals from the collector of Q_1 to the tank circuit. The RFC looks open to ac, consequently isolating the dc power supply from ac oscillations.

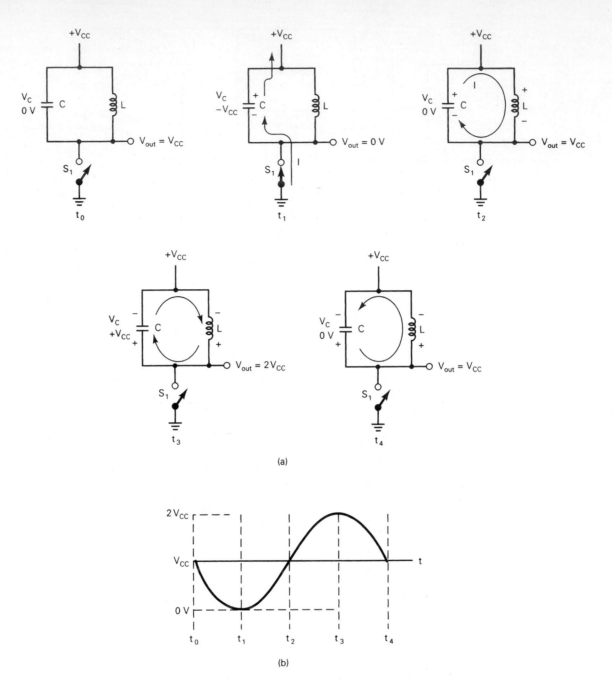

FIGURE 2-4 *LC* tank circuit: (a) oscillator action and flywheel effect; (b) output waveform

The Hartley oscillator operates as follows. On initial power-up, a multitude of frequencies appear at the collector of Q_1 and are coupled through C_2 into the tank circuit. The initial noise provides the energy necessary to charge C_1. Once C_1 is partially charged, oscillator action begins. The tank circuit will only oscillate efficiently at its resonant frequency. A portion of the oscillating tank circuit voltage is dropped across L_{1b} and fed back to the base of Q_1, where it is amplified. The amplified signal appears at the collector 180° out of phase with the base signal. An additional 180° of phase shift is realized across L_1; consequently, the signal fed back to the base of Q_1 is amplified and shifted in phase 360°. Thus, the circuit is regenerative and will sustain oscillations with no external input signal.

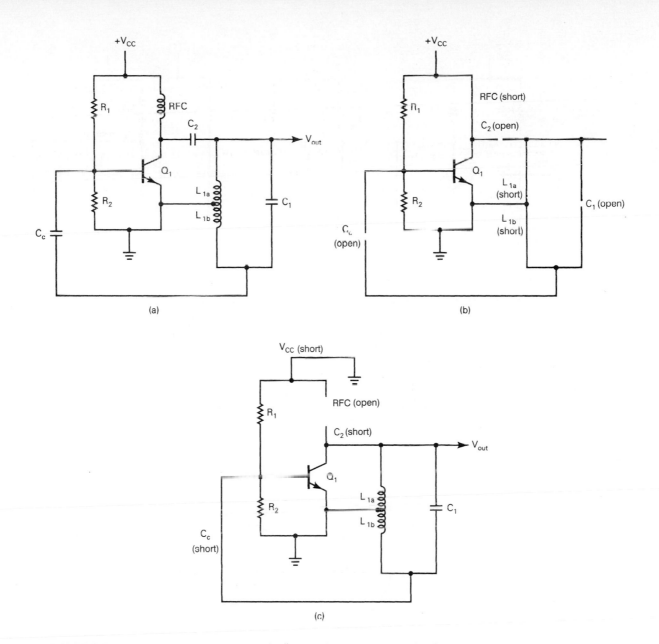

FIGURE 2 5 Hartley oscillator: (a) schematic diagram; (b) dc equivalent circuit; (c) ac equivalent circuit

The proportion of oscillating energy that is fed back to the base of Q_1 is determined by the ratio of L_{1b} to the total inductance ($L_{1a} + L_{1b}$). If insufficient energy is fed back, oscillations are damped. If excessive energy is fed back, the transistor saturates. Therefore, the position of the wiper on L_1 is adjusted until the amount of feedback energy is exactly what is required for a unity loop voltage gain and oscillations to continue.

The frequency of oscillation for the Hartley oscillator is closely approximated by the following formula:

$$f_o = \frac{1}{2\pi\sqrt{(LC)}} \qquad (2\text{-}3)$$

where $L = L_{1a} + L_{1b}$
$\quad\quad\quad C = C_1$

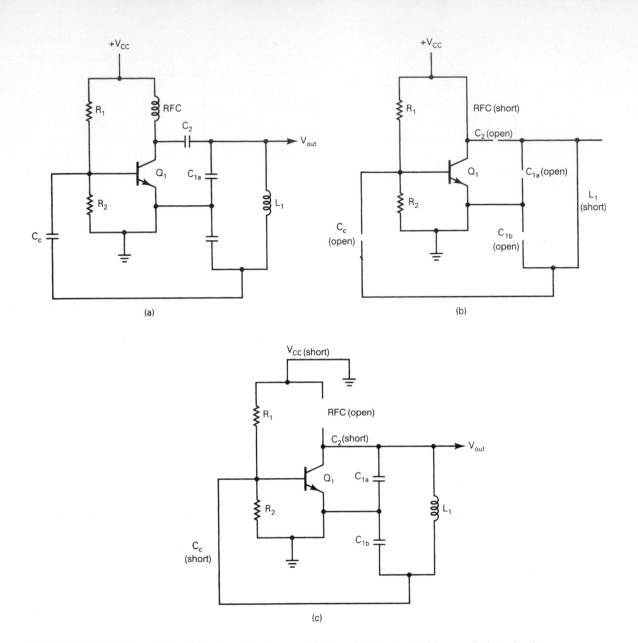

FIGURE 2-6 Colpitts oscillator: (a) schematic diagram; (b) dc equivalent circuit; (c) ac equivalent circuit

Colpitts oscillator. Figure 2-6a shows the schematic diagram of a *Colpitts oscillator.* The operation of a Colpitts oscillator is very similar to that of the Hartley except that a capacitive divider is used instead of a tapped coil. Q_1 provides the amplification, C_C provides the regenerative feedback path, L_1, C_{1a}, and C_{1b} are the frequency-determining components, and V_{CC} is the dc supply voltage.

Figure 2-6b shows the dc equivalent circuit for the Colpitts oscillator. C_2 is a blocking capacitor that prevents the collector supply voltage from appearing at the output. The RFC is again a dc short.

Figure 2-6c shows the ac equivalent circuit for the Colpitts oscillator. C_C is a coupling capacitor for ac and provides the feedback path for regenerative feedback from the tank circuit to the base of Q_1. The RFC is open to ac and decouples oscillations from the dc power supply.

The operation of the Colpitts oscillator is almost identical to that of the Hartley oscillator. On initial power-up, noise appears at the collector of Q_1 and supplies energy to the tank circuit, causing it to begin oscillating. C_{1a} and C_{1b} make up an ac voltage divider. The voltage dropped across C_{1b} is fed back to the base of Q_1 through C_C. There is a 180° phase shift from the base to the collector of Q_1 and an additional 180° phase shift across C_1. Consequently, the total phase shift is 360° and the feedback signal is regenerative. The ratio of C_{1a} to $C_{1a} + C_{1b}$ determines the amplitude of the feedback signal.

The frequency of oscillation of the Colpitts oscillator is closely approximated by the following formula:

$$f_o = \frac{1}{2\pi\sqrt{(LC)}} \qquad (2\text{-}4)$$

where $L = L_1$

$$C = \frac{(C_{1a}C_{1b})}{(C_{1a} + C_{1b})}$$

Clapp oscillator. A Clapp oscillator circuit is identical to the Colpitts oscillator shown in Figure 2-6a except with the addition of a small capacitor C_S placed in series with L_1. The capacitance of C_S is made smaller than C_{1a} or C_{1b}, thus providing a large reactance. Consequently, C_S has the most effect in determining the frequency of the tank circuit. The advantage of a Clapp oscillator is that C_{1a} and C_{1b} can be selected for an optimum feedback ratio while C_S can be variable and used for setting the frequency of oscillation. In some applications C_S incorporates a negative temperature coefficient that improves the oscillator's frequency stability.

Frequency Stability

Frequency stability is the ability of an oscillator to remain at a fixed frequency and is of primary importance in communications systems. Frequency stability is often stated as either short or long term. *Short-term stability* is affected predominantly by fluctuations in dc operating voltages, whereas *long-term stability* is a function of component aging and changes in the ambient temperature and humidity. In the *LC* tank-circuit and *RC* phase shift oscillators discussed previously, the frequency stability is inadequate for most radio communications applications, because *RC* phase shift oscillators are susceptible to both short- and long-term variations. In addition, the *Q*-factors of the *LC* tank circuits are relatively low, allowing the resonant tank circuit to oscillate over a wide range of frequencies.

Frequency stability is generally given as a percentage of change in frequency (tolerance) from the desired value. For example, an oscillator operating at 100 kHz with a ± 5% stability will operate at a frequency of 100 kHz ± 5 kHz or between 95 kHz and 105 kHz. Commercial FM broadcast stations must maintain their carrier frequencies to within ± 2 kHz of their assigned frequency, which is approximately a 0.002% tolerance. In commercial AM broadcasting, the maximum allowable shift in the carrier frequency is only ± 20 Hz.

Several factors affect the stability of an oscillator. The most obvious are those that directly affect the value of the frequency-determining components. These include changes in inductance, capacitance, and resistance values due to environmental variations in temperature and humidity and changes in the quiescent operating point of transistors and field-effect transistors. Stability is also affected by ac ripple in dc power supplies. The frequency stability of *RC* or *LC* oscillators can be greatly improved by regulating the dc power supply and minimizing the environmental variations. Also, special temperature-independent components can be used.

The FCC has established stringent regulations concerning the tolerances of radio-frequency carriers. Whenever the airway (free-space radio propagation) is used as the transmission medium, it is possible that transmissions from one source could interfere with transmissions from other sources if their transmit frequency or transmission bandwidths overlap. Therefore, it is important that all sources maintain their frequency of operation within a specified tolerance.

Crystal Oscillators

Crystal oscillators are feedback oscillator circuits in which the *LC* tank circuit is replaced with a crystal for the frequency-determining component. The crystal acts in a manner similar to the *LC* tank, except with several inherent advantages. Crystals are sometimes called crystal resonators and they are capable of producing precise, stable frequencies for frequency counters, electronic navigation systems, radio transmitters and receivers, televisions, videocassette recorders (VCRs), computer system clocks, and many other applications too numerous to list.

Crystallography is the study of the form, structure, properties, and classifications of crystals. Crystallography deals with lattices, bonding, and the behavior of slices of crystal material that have been cut at various angles with respect to the crystal's axes. The mechanical properties of crystal lattices allow them to exhibit the piezoelectric effect. Sections of crystals that have been cut and polished vibrate when alternating voltages are applied across their faces. The physical dimensions of a crystal, particularly its thickness and where and how it was cut, determine its electrical and mechanical properties.

Piezoelectric effect.   Simply stated, the *piezoelectric effect* occurs when oscillating mechanical stresses applied across a *crystal lattice structure* generate electrical oscillations, and vice versa. The stress can be in the form of squeezing (compression), stretching (tension), twisting (torsion), or shearing. If the stress is applied periodically, the output voltage will alternate. Conversely, when an alternating voltage is applied across a crystal at or near the natural resonant frequency of the crystal, the crystal will break into mechanical oscillations. This process is called *exciting* a crystal into *mechanical vibrations.* The mechanical vibrations are called *bulk acoustic waves* (BAWs) and are directly proportional to the amplitude of the applied voltage.

A number of natural crystal substances exhibit piezoelectric properties: *quartz, Rochelle salt,* and *tourmaline* and several manufactured substances such as ADP, EDT, and DKT. The piezoelectric effect is most pronounced in Rochelle salt, which is why it is the substance commonly used in crystal microphones. Synthetic quartz, however, is used more often for frequency control in oscillators because of its *permanence,* low *temperature coefficient,* and high *mechanical Q.*

Crystal cuts.   In nature, complete quartz crystals have a hexagonal cross section with pointed ends, as shown in Figure 2-7a. Three sets of axes are associated with a crystal: *optical, electrical,* and *mechanical.* The longitudinal axis joining points at the ends of the crystal is called the *optical* or *Z-axis.* Electrical stresses applied to the optical axis do not produce the piezoelectric effect. The *electrical* or *X-axis* passes diagonally through opposite corners of the hexagon. The axis that is perpendicular to the faces of the crystal is the *Y* or *mechanical axis.* Figure 2-7b shows the axes and the basic behavior of a quartz crystal.

If a thin flat section is cut from a crystal such that the flat sides are perpendicular to an electrical axis, mechanical stresses along the *Y*-axis will produce electrical charges on the flat sides. As the stress changes from compression to tension, and vice versa, the polarity of the charge is reversed. Conversely, if an alternating electrical charge is placed on the flat sides, a mechanical vibration is produced along the *Y*-axis. This is the piezoelectric effect and is also exhibited when mechanical forces are applied across the faces of a crystal cut with its flat sides perpendicular to the *Y*-axis. When a crystal wafer is cut parallel to the *Z*-axis with its faces perpendicular to the *X*-axis, it is called an *X*-cut crystal. When the faces are perpendicular to the *Y*-axis, it is called a *Y*-cut crystal. A variety of cuts can be obtained

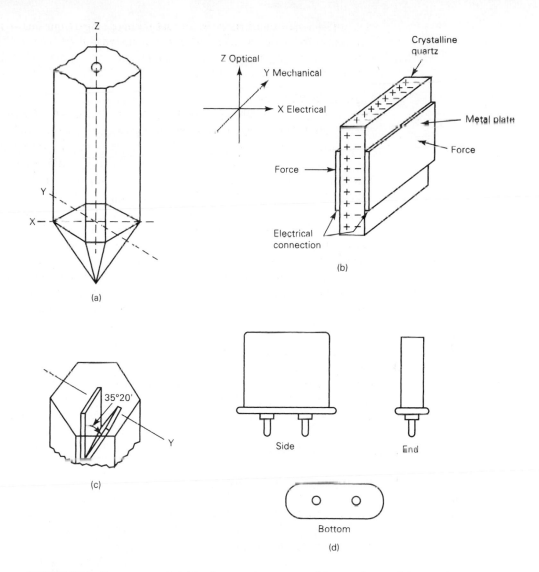

FIGURE 2-7 Quartz crystal: (a) basic crystal structure; (b) crystal axes; (c) crystal cuts; (d) crystal mountings

by rotating the plane of the cut around one or more axes. If the *Y* cut is made at a 35°20′ angle from the vertical axis (Figure 2-7c), an *AT* cut is obtained. Other types of crystal cuts include the *BT, CT, DT, ET, AC, GT, MT, NT,* and *JT* cuts. The *AT* cut is the most popular for high-frequency and very-high-frequency crystal resonators. The type, length, and thickness of a cut and the mode of vibration determine the natural resonant frequency of the crystal. Resonant frequencies for *AT*-cut crystals range from approximately 800 kHz up to approximately 30 MHz. *CT* and *DT* cuts exhibit low-frequency shear and are most useful in the 100-kHz to 500-kHz range. The *MT* cut vibrates longitudinally and is useful in the 50-kHz to 100-kHz range, and the *NT* cut has a useful range under 50 kHz.

Crystal *wafers* are generally mounted in *crystal holders,* which include the mounting and housing assemblies. A *crystal unit* refers to the holder and the crystal itself. Figure 2-7d shows a common crystal mounting. Because a crystal's stability is somewhat temperature dependent, a crystal unit may be mounted in an oven to maintain a constant operating temperature.

The relationship between a crystal's operating frequency and its thickness is expressed mathematically as

$$h = \frac{65.5}{f_n}$$

where h = crystal thickness (inches)
        f_n = crystal natural resonant frequency (hertz)

This formula indicates that for high-frequency oscillations the quartz wafer must be very thin. This makes it difficult to manufacture crystal oscillators with fundamental frequencies above approximately 30 MHz because the wafer becomes so thin that it is exceptionally fragile, and conventional cutting and polishing can only be accomplished at extreme costs. This problem can be alleviated by using chemical etching to achieve thinner slices. With this process, crystals with fundamental frequencies up to 350 MHz are possible.

Overtone crystal oscillator.   As previously stated, to increase the frequency of vibration of a quartz crystal, the quartz wafer is sliced thinner. This imposes an obvious physical limitation; the thinner the wafer, the more susceptible it is to damage and the less useful it becomes. Although the practical limit for fundamental-mode crystal oscillators is approximately 30 MHz, it is possible to operate the crystal in an overtone mode. In the overtone mode, harmonically related vibrations that occur simultaneously with the fundamental vibration are used. In the overtone mode, the oscillator is tuned to operate at the third, fifth, seventh, or even the ninth harmonic of the crystal's fundamental frequency. The harmonics are called overtones because they are not true harmonics. Manufacturers can process crystals such that one overtone is enhanced more than the others. Using an overtone mode increases the usable limit of standard crystal oscillators to approximately 200 MHz.

Temperature coefficient.   The natural resonant frequency of a crystal is influenced somewhat by its operating temperature. The ratio of the magnitude of frequency change (Δf) to a change in temperature (ΔC) is expressed in hertz change per megahertz of crystal operating frequency per degree Celsius (Hz/MHz/°C). The fractional change in frequency is often given in parts per million (ppm) per °C. For example, a temperature coefficient of $+20$ Hz/MHz/°C is the same as $+20$ ppm/°C. If the direction of the frequency change is the same as the temperature change (i.e., an increase in temperature causes an increase in frequency and a decrease in temperature causes a decrease in frequency), it is called a *positive temperature coefficient*. If the change in frequency is in the direction opposite to the temperature change (i.e., an increase in temperature causes a decrease in frequency and a decrease in temperature causes an increase in frequency), it is called a *negative temperature coefficient*. Mathematically, the relationship of the change in frequency of a crystal to a change in temperature is

$$\Delta f = k(f_n \times \Delta C) \tag{2-5}$$

where Δf = change in frequency (hertz)
        k = temperature coefficient (Hz/MHz/°C)
        f_n = natural crystal frequency (megahertz)
        ΔC = change in temperature (degrees Celsius)

and $f_o = f_n + \Delta f$ $\tag{2-6}$

where f_o is frequency of operation.

The temperature coefficient (k) of a crystal varies depending on the type of crystal cut and its operating temperature. For a range of temperatures from approximately $+20°$ C to $+50°$ C, both X- and Y-cut crystals have a temperature coefficient that is nearly constant. X-cut crystals are approximately 10 times more stable than Y-cut crystals. Typically, X-cut crystals have a temperature coefficient that ranges from -10 Hz/MHz/°C to -25 Hz/MHz/°C. Y-cut crystals have a temperature coefficient that ranges from approximately -25 Hz/MHz/°C to $+100$ Hz/MHz/°C.

Today, zero-coefficient (GT-cut) crystals are available that have temperature coefficients as low as -1 Hz/MHz/°C to $+1$ Hz/MHz/°C. The GT-cut crystal is almost a perfect zero-coefficient crystal from freezing to boiling, but is useful only at frequencies below a few hundred kilohertz.

Example 2-1

For a 10-MHz crystal with a temperature coefficient $k = +10$ Hz/MHz/°C, determine the frequency of operation if the temperature
(a) Increases 10° C.
(b) Decreases 5° C.

Solution   (a)   Substituting into Equations 2-5 and 2-6 gives us

$$\Delta f = k(f_n \times \Delta C)$$
$$= 10(10 \times 10) = 1 \text{ kHz}$$
$$f_o = f_n + \Delta f$$
$$= 10 \text{ MHz} + 1 \text{ kHz} = 10.001 \text{ MHz}$$

(b) Again, substituting into Equations 2-5 and 2-6 yields

$$\Delta f = 10[10 \times (-5)] = -500 \text{ Hz}$$
$$f_o = 10 \text{ MHz} + (-500 \text{ Hz})$$
$$= 9.9995 \text{ MHz}$$

Crystal equivalent circuit.   Figure 2-8a shows the electrical equivalent circuit for a crystal. Each electrical component is equivalent to a mechanical property of the crystal. C_2 is the actual capacitance formed between the electrodes of the crystal, with the crystal itself being the dielectric. C_1 is equivalent to the mechanical compliance of the crystal (also called the resilience or elasticity). L is equivalent to the mass of the crystal in vibration, and R is the mechanical friction loss. In a crystal, the mechanical *mass-to-friction ratio* (L/R) is quite high. Typical values of L range from 0.1 H to well over 100 H; consequently, Q-factors are quite high for crystals. Q-factors in the range from 10,000 to 100,000 and higher are not uncommon (as compared with Q-factors of 100 to 1000 for the discrete inductors used in LC tank circuits). This provides the high stability of crystal oscillators as compared to discrete LC tank circuit oscillators. Values for C_1 are typically less than 1 pF, and values for C_2 range between 4 pF and 40 pF.

Because there is a series and a parallel equivalent circuit for a crystal, there are also two equivalent impedances and two resonant frequencies: a series and a parallel. The series impedance is the combination of R, L, and C_1 (i.e., $Z_s = R \pm jX$, where $X = |X_L - X_C|$). The parallel impedance is approximately the impedance of L and C_2 [i.e., $Z_p = (X_L \times X_{C2})/(X_L + X_{C2})$]. At extreme low frequencies, the series impedance of L, C_1, and R is very high and capacitive ($-$). This is shown in Figure 2-8c. As the frequency is increased, a point is reached where $X_L = X_{C1}$. At this frequency (f_1), the series impedance is minimum, resistive, and equal to R. As the frequency is increased even further (f_2), the series impedance becomes high and inductive ($+$). The parallel combination of L and C_2 causes the crystal to act as a parallel resonant circuit (maximum impedance at resonance). The difference between f_1 and f_2 is usually quite small (typically about 1% of the crystal's natural frequency). A crystal can operate at either its series or parallel resonant frequency, depending on the

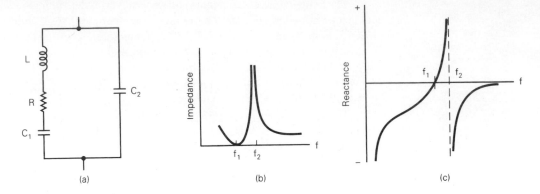

FIGURE 2-8 Crystal equivalent circuit: (a) equivalent circuit; (b) impedance curve; (c) reactance curve

circuit configuration in which it is used. The relative steepness of the impedance curve shown in Figure 2-8b also attributes to the stability and accuracy of a crystal. The series resonant frequency of a quartz crystal is simply

$$f_1 = \frac{1}{2\pi\sqrt{(LC_1)}}$$

and the parallel resonant frequency is

$$f_2 = \frac{1}{2\pi\sqrt{(LC)}}$$

where C is the series combination of C_1 and C_2.

Crystal oscillator circuits. Although there are many different crystal-based oscillator configurations, the most common are the discrete and integrated-circuit Pierce and the *RLC* half-bridge. If you need very good frequency stability and reasonably simple circuitry, the discrete Pierce is a good choice. If low cost and simple digital interfacing capabilities are of primary concern, an IC-based Pierce oscillator will suffice. However, for the best frequency stability, the *RLC* half-bridge is the best choice.

Discrete Pierce Oscillator. The discrete Pierce crystal oscillator has many advantages. Its operating frequency spans the full fundamental crystal range (1 kHz to approximately 30 MHz). It uses relatively simple circuitry requiring few components (most medium-frequency versions require only one transistor). The Pierce oscillator design develops a high output signal power while dissipating very little power in the crystal itself. Finally, the short-term frequency stability of the Pierce crystal oscillator is excellent (because the in-circuit loaded Q is almost as high as the crystal's internal Q). The only drawback to the Pierce oscillator is that it requires a high-gain amplifier (approximately 70). Consequently, you must use a single high-gain transistor or possibly even a multiple-stage amplifier.

Figure 2-9 shows a discrete 1-MHz Pierce oscillator circuit. Q_1 provides all the gain necessary for self-sustained oscillations to occur. R_1 and C_1 provide a 65° phase lag to the feedback signal. The crystal impedance is basically resistive with a small inductive component. This impedance combined with the reactance of C_2 provides an additional 115° of phase lag. The transistor inverts the signal (180° phase shift), giving the circuit the necessary 360° of total phase shift. Because the crystal's load is primarily nonresistive (mostly the series combination of C_1 and C_2), this type of oscillator provides very good short-term frequency stability. Unfortunately, C_1 and C_2 introduce substantial losses and, consequently, the transistor must have a relatively high voltage gain; this is an obvious drawback.

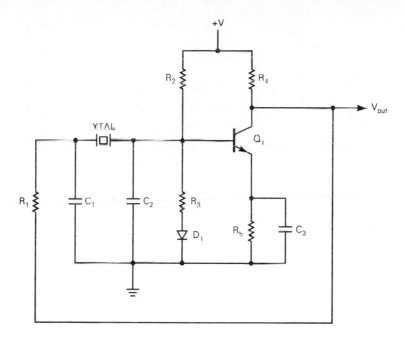

FIGURE 2-9 Discrete Pierce crystal oscillator

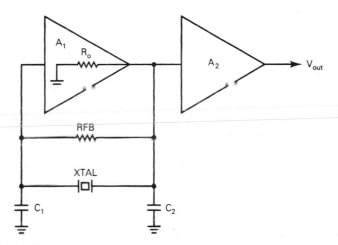

FIGURE 2-10 IC Pierce crystal oscillator

Integrated-Circuit Pierce Oscillator. Figure 2-10 shows an IC-based Pierce crystal oscillator. Although it provides less frequency stability, it can be implemented using simple digital IC design and reduces costs substantially over conventional discrete designs.

To ensure that oscillations begin, RFB dc biases inverting amplifier A_1's input and output for class A operation. A_2 converts the output of A_1 to a full rail-to-rail swing (cutoff to saturation), reducing the rise and fall times and buffering A_1's output. The output resistance of A_1 combines with C_2 to provide the RC phase lag needed. Complementary metal-oxide semiconductor (CMOS) versions operate up to approximately 2 MHz, and emitter-coupled logic (ECL) versions operate as high as 20 MHz.

RLC Half-Bridge Crystal Oscillator. Figure 2-11 shows the Meacham version of the *RLC* half-bridge crystal oscillator. The original Meacham oscillator was developed in the 1940s and used a full four-arm bridge and a negative-temperature-coefficient tungsten lamp. The circuit configuration shown in Figure 2-11 uses only a two-arm bridge and employs a

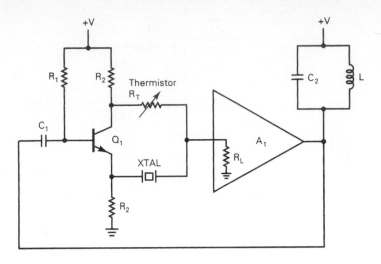

FIGURE 2-11 *RLC* half-bridge crystal oscillator

negative-temperature-coefficient thermistor. Q_1 serves as a phase splitter and provides two 180° out-of-phase signals. The crystal must operate at its series resonant frequency, so its internal impedance is resistive and quite small. When oscillations begin, the signal amplitude increases gradually, decreasing the thermistor resistance until the bridge almost nulls. The amplitude of the oscillations stabilizes and determines the final thermistor resistance. The *LC* tank circuit at the output is tuned to the crystal's series resonant frequency.

Crystal oscillator module. A *crystal oscillator module* consists of a crystal-controlled oscillator and a voltage-variable component such as a *varactor diode*. The entire oscillator circuit is contained in a single *metal can*. A simplified schematic diagram for a Colpitts crystal oscillator module is shown in Figure 2-12a. X_1 is a crystal itself and Q_1 is the active component for the amplifier. C_1 is a shunt capacitor that allows the crystal oscillator frequency to be varied over a narrow range of operating frequencies. VC_1 is a voltage-variable capacitor (*varicap* or *varactor diode*). A varactor diode is a specially constructed diode whose internal capacitance is enhanced when reverse biased, and by varying the reverse-bias voltage, the capacitance of the diode can be adjusted. A varactor diode has a special depletion layer between the *p*- and *n*-type materials that is constructed with various degrees and types of doping material (the term *graded junction* is often used when describing varactor diode fabrication). Figure 2-12b shows the capacitance versus reverse-bias voltage curves for a typical varactor diode. The capacitance of a varactor diode is approximated as

$$C_d = \frac{C}{\sqrt{(1 + 2|V_r|)}} \tag{2-7}$$

where C = diode capacitance with 0-V reverse bias (farads)
  $|V_r|$ = magnitude of diode reverse-bias voltage (volts)
  C_d = reverse-biased diode capacitance (farads)

The frequency at which the crystal oscillates can be adjusted slightly by changing the capacitance of VC_1 (i.e., changing the value of the reverse-bias voltage). The varactor diode, in conjunction with a temperature-compensating module, provides instant frequency compensation for variations caused by changes in temperature. The schematic diagram of a temperature-compensating module is shown in Figure 2-13. The compensation module includes a buffer amplifier (Q_1) and a temperature-compensating network (T_1). T_1 is a negative-temperature-coefficient thermistor. When the temperature falls below the thresh-

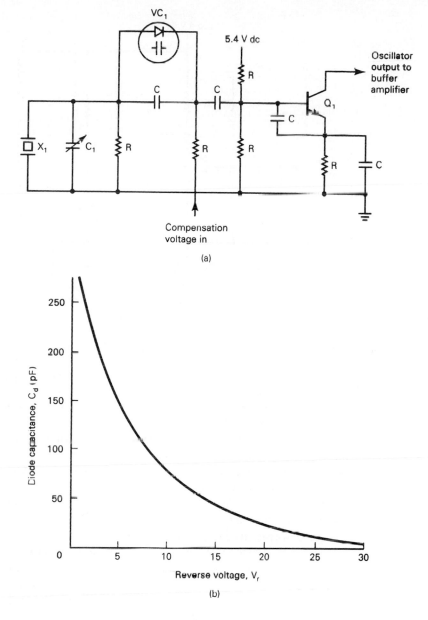

FIGURE 2-12 Crystal oscillator module: (a) schematic diagram; (b) varactor diode characteristics

old value of the thermistor, the compensation voltage increases. The compensation voltage is applied to the oscillator module, where it controls the capacitance of the varactor diode. Compensation modules are available that can compensate for u frequency stability of 0.0005% from −30° C to +80° C.

LARGE-SCALE INTEGRATION OSCILLATORS

In recent years the use of *large-scale integration* (LSI) integrated circuits for frequency and waveform generation has increased at a tremendous rate because integrated-circuit oscillators have excellent frequency stability and a wide tuning range and are easy to use. *Waveform* and *function generators* are used extensively in communications and telemetry

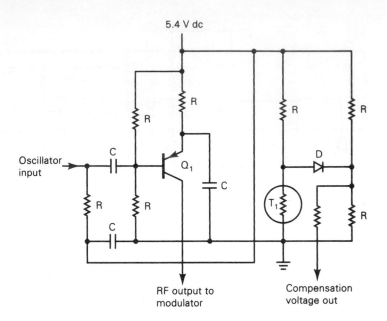

FIGURE 2-13 Compensation circuit

equipment, as well as in laboratories for test and calibration equipment. In many of these applications, commercial monolithic integrated-circuit oscillators and function generators are available that provide the circuit designer with a low-cost alternative to their nonintegrated-circuit counterparts.

The basic operations required for waveform generation and shaping are well suited to monolithic integrated-circuit technology. In fact, *monolithic linear integrated circuits* (LICs) have several inherent advantages over discrete circuits, such as the availability of a large number of active devices on a single chip and close matching and thermal tracking of component values. It is now possible to fabricate integrated-circuit waveform generators that provide a performance comparable to that of complex discrete generators at only a fraction of the cost.

LSI waveform generators currently available include function generators, timers, programmable timers, voltage-controlled oscillators, precision oscillators, and waveform generators.

Integrated-Circuit Waveform Generation

In its simplest form, a waveform generator is an oscillator circuit that generates well-defined, stable waveforms that can be externally modulated or swept over a given frequency range. A typical waveform generator consists of four basic sections: (1) an oscillator to generate the basic periodic waveform, (2) a waveshaper, (3) an optional AM modulator, and (4) an output buffer amplifier to isolate the oscillator from the load and provide the necessary drive current.

Figure 2-14 shows a simplified block diagram of an integrated-circuit waveform generator circuit showing the relationship among the four sections. Each section has been built separately in monolithic form for several years; therefore, fabrication of all four sections onto a single monolithic chip was a natural extension of a preexisting technology. The oscillator section generates the basic oscillator frequency and the waveshaper circuit converts the output from the oscillator to either a sine-, square-, triangular-, or ramp-shaped waveform. The modulator, when used, allows the circuit to produce amplitude-modulated signals, and the output buffer amplifier isolates the oscillator from its load and provides a convenient place to add dc levels to the output waveform. The sync output can be used either as a square-wave source or as a synchronizing pulse for external timing circuitry.

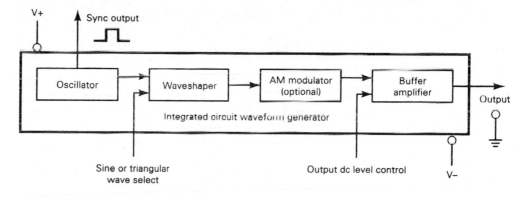

FIGURE 2-14 Integrated-circuit waveform generator

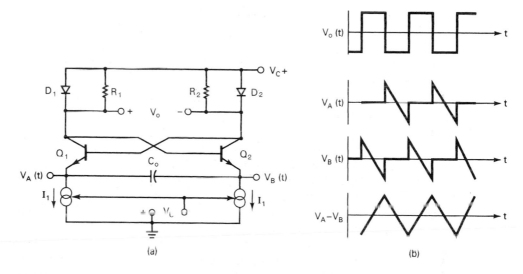

FIGURE 2-15 Simplified integrated-circuit waveform generator: (a) schematic diagram;
(b) waveforms

A typical IC oscillator circuit utilizes the constant-current charging and discharging of external timing capacitors. Figure 2-15a shows the simplified schematic diagram for such a waveform generator that uses an emitter-coupled multivibrator, which is capable of generating square waves as well as triangle and linear ramp waveforms. The circuit operates as follows. When transistor Q_1 and diode D_1 are conducting, transistor Q_2 and diode D_2 are off, and vice versa. This action alternately charges and discharges capacitor C_o from constant current source I_1. The voltage across D_1 and D_2 is a symmetrical square wave with a peak-to-peak amplitude of $2V_{BE}$. V_A is constant when Q_1 is on but becomes a linear ramp with a slope equal to $-I_1/C_o$ when Q_1 goes off. Output $V_B(t)$ is identical to $V_A(t)$, except it is delayed by a half-cycle. Differential output, $V_A(t) - V_B(t)$ is a triangle wave. Figure 2-15b shows the output voltage waveforms typically available.

Monolithic function generators.   The XR-2206 is a monolithic function generator integrated circuit manufactured by EXAR Corporation that is capable of producing high-quality sine, square, triangle, ramp, and pulse waveforms with both a high degree of stability and accuracy. The output waveforms from the XR-2206 can be both amplitude and frequency modulated by an external modulating signal, and the frequency of operation can be selected externally over a range from 0.01 Hz to more than 1 MHz. The XR-2206 is ideally suited to communications, instrumentation, and function generator applications requiring sinusoidal

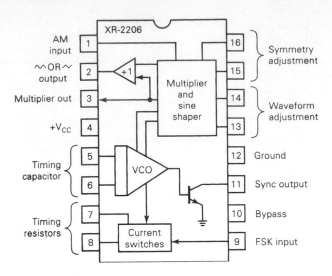

FIGURE 2-16 Block diagram for the XR-2206 monolithic function generator

tone, AM, or FM generation. The XR-2206 has a typical frequency stability of 20 ppm/°C and can be linearly swept over a 2000:1 frequency range with an external control voltage.

The block diagram for the XR-2206 is shown in Figure 2-16. The function generator is comprised of four functional blocks: a voltage-controlled oscillator (VCO), an analog multiplier and sineshaper, a unity-gain buffer amplifier, and a set of input current switches. A *voltage-controlled oscillator* is a free-running oscillator with a stable frequency of oscillation that depends on an external timing capacitance, timing resistance, and control voltage. The output from a VCO is a frequency, and its input is a bias or control signal that can be either a dc or an ac voltage. The VCO actually produces an output frequency that is proportional to an input current that is produced by a resistor from the timing terminals (either pin 7 or 8) to ground. The current switches route the current from one of the timing pins to the VCO. The current selected depends on the voltage level on the frequency shift keying input pin (pin 9). Therefore, two discrete output frequencies can be independently produced. If pin 9 is open circuited or connected to a bias voltage ≥ 2 V, the current passing through the resistor connected to pin 7 is selected. Similarly, if the voltage level at pin 9 is ≤ 1 V, the current passing through the resistor connected to pin 8 is selected. Thus, the output frequency can be keyed between f_1 and f_2 by simply changing the voltage on pin 9. The formulas for determining the two frequencies of operation are

$$f_1 = \frac{1}{R_1 C} \qquad f_2 = \frac{1}{R_2 C}$$

where R_1 = resistor connected to pin 7
R_2 = resistor connected to pin 8

The frequency of oscillation is proportional to the total timing current on either pin 7 or 8. Frequency varies linearly with current over a range of current values between 1 μA to 3 μA. The frequency can be controlled by applying a control voltage, V_C, to the selected timing pin, as shown in Figure 2-17. The frequency of oscillation is related to V_C by

$$f = \frac{1}{RC} \left[1 + \frac{R}{R_C} \frac{(1 - V_C)}{3} \right] \text{Hz} \tag{2-8}$$

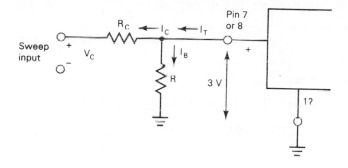

FIGURE 2-17 Circuit connection for control voltage frequency sweep of the XR-2206

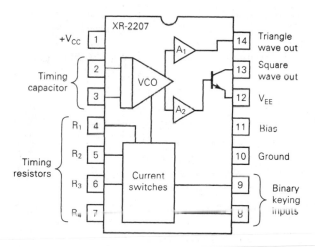

FIGURE 2-18 Block diagram for the XR-2207 monolithic voltage-controlled oscillator (VCO)

The voltage-to-frequency conversion gain K is given as

$$K = \frac{\Delta f}{\Delta V_C} = \frac{-0.32}{R_C C} \text{ Hz}/\text{V} \qquad (2\text{-}9)$$

Monolithic voltage-controlled oscillators. The XR-2207 is a monolithic voltage-controlled oscillator (VCO) integrated circuit featuring excellent frequency stability and a wide tuning range. The circuit provides simultaneous triangle- and square-wave outputs over a frequency range of from 0.01 Hz to 1 MHz. The XR-2207 is ideally suited for FM, FSK, and sweep or tone generation, as well as for phase-locked-loop applications. The XR-2207 has a typical frequency stability of 20 ppm/°C and can be linearly swept over a 1000:1 frequency range with an external control voltage. The duty cycle of the triangular- and square-wave outputs can be varied from 0.1% to 99.9%, generating stable pulse and saw-tooth waveforms.

The block diagram for the XR-2207 is shown in Figure 2-18. The circuit is a modified emitter-coupled multivibrator that utilizes four main functional blocks for frequency generation: a voltage-controlled oscillator (VCO), four current switches that are activated by binary keying inputs, and two buffer amplifiers. Two binary input pins (pins 8 and 9) determine which of the four timing currents are channeled to the VCO. These currents are set by resistors to ground from each of the four timing input terminals (pins 4 through 7). The

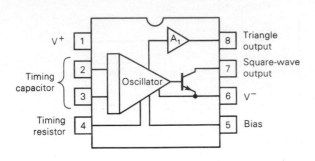

FIGURE 2-19 Block diagram for the XR-2209 monolithic precision oscillator

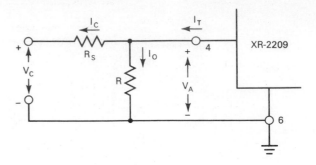

FIGURE 2-20 Circuit connection for control voltage frequency sweep of the XR-2209

triangular output buffer provides a low-impedance output (10 Ω typical), while the square-wave output is open collector.

Monolithic precision oscillators. The XR-2209 is a monolithic variable-frequency oscillator circuit featuring excellent temperature stability and a wide linear sweep range. The circuit provides simultaneous triangle- and square-wave outputs, and the frequency is set by an external RC product. The XR-2209 is ideally suited for frequency modulation, voltage-to-frequency conversion, and sweep or tone generation, as well as for phase-locked-loop applications when used in conjunction with an appropriate phase comparator.

The block diagram for the XR-2209 precision oscillator is shown in Figure 2-19. The oscillator is comprised of three functional blocks: a variable-frequency oscillator that generates the basic periodic waveforms and two buffer amplifiers for the triangular- and square-wave outputs. The oscillator frequency is set by an external capacitor and timing resistor. The XR-2209 is capable of operating over eight frequency decades from 0.01 Hz to 1 MHz. With no external sweep signal or bias voltage, the frequency of oscillation is simply equal to $1/RC$.

The frequency of operation for the XR-2209 is proportional to the timing current drawn from the timing pin. This current can be modulated by applying a control voltage, V_C, to the timing pin through series resistor R_S as shown in Figure 2-20. If V_C is negative with respect to the voltage on pin 4, an additional current, I_O, is drawn from the timing pin, causing the total input current to increase, thus increasing the frequency of oscillation. Conversely, if V_C is higher than the voltage on pin 4, the frequency of oscillation is decreased.

PHASE-LOCKED LOOPS

The *phase-locked loop* (PLL) is used extensively in electronic communications for performing modulation, demodulation, frequency generation, and frequency synthesis. PLLs are used in both transmitters and receivers with both analog and digital modulation and with the transmission of digital pulses. Phase-locked loops were first used in 1932 for synchronous detection of radio signals, instrumentation circuits, and space telemetry systems. However, for many years the use of PLLs was avoided because of their large size, necessary complexity, narrow bandwidth, and expense. With the advent of large-scale integration, PLLs now take up little space, are easy to use, and are more reliable. Therefore, PLLs have changed from a specialized design technique to a general-purpose, universal building block with numerous applications. Today, over a dozen different integrated-circuit PLL products are available from several IC manufacturers. Some of these are designated as general-purpose circuits suitable for a multitude of uses, while others are intended or optimized for special applications such as tone detection, stereo decoding, and frequency synthesis.

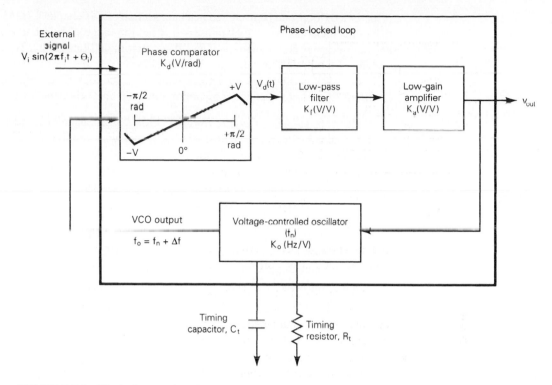

FIGURE 2-21 Block diagram for phase-locked loop

Essentially, a PLL is a closed-loop feedback control system in which the frequency of the feedback signal voltage is the parameter of interest rather than simply a voltage. The PLL provides frequency selective tuning and filtering without the need for coils or inductors. The basic phase-locked-loop circuit is shown in Figure 2-21 and consists of four primary blocks: a phase comparator (mixer), a low-pass filter, a low-gain amplifier (op-amp), and a voltage-controlled oscillator (VCO). With no external input signal, the output voltage, v_{out}, is equal to zero. The VCO operates at a set frequency called its *natural* or *free-running frequency* (f_n), which is set by external resistor (R_t) and capacitor (C_t). If an input signal is applied to the system, the phase comparator compares the phase and frequency of the input signal with the VCO natural frequency and generates an error voltage, $V_d(t)$, that is related to the phase and frequency difference between the two signals. This error voltage is then filtered, amplified, and applied to the input terminal of the VCO. If the input frequency, f_i, is sufficiently close to the VCO natural frequency, f_n, the feedback nature of the PLL causes the VCO to synchronize, or lock, to the incoming signal. Once in lock, the VCO frequency is identical to the input signal, except for a finite phase difference that is equal to the phase of the incoming signal minus the phase of the VCO output signal.

Lock and Capture Range

Two key parameters of PLLs that indicate their useful frequency range are lock and capture range.

Lock range. *Lock range* is defined as the range of frequencies in the vicinity of the VCO's natural frequency (f_n) over which the PLL can maintain lock with an input signal. This presumes that the PLL was initially locked onto the input signal. Lock range is also known as *tracking range*. It is the range of frequencies over which the PLL will accurately track or follow the input frequency. Lock range increases as the overall loop gain of the PLL is increased (loop gain is discussed in a later section of this chapter). *Hold-in range* is equal to half the lock range (i.e., lock range = 2 × hold-in range). The relationship between lock and hold-in range is shown in frequency diagram form in Figure 2-22. The lowest frequency that the PLL will track is called the *lower lock limit* (f_{ll}), and the highest frequency that the PLL will track is called the *upper lock limit* (f_{lu}). The lock range depends on the transfer functions (gains) of the phase comparator, low-gain amplifier, and VCO.

Capture range.   *Capture range* is defined as the band of frequencies in the vicinity of f_n where the PLL can establish or acquire lock with an input signal. The capture range is generally between 1.1 and 1.7 times the natural frequency of the VCO. Capture range is also known as *acquisition range*. Capture range is related to the bandwidth of the low-pass filter. The capture range of a PLL decreases as the bandwidth of the filter is reduced. *Pull-in range* is the peak capture range (i.e., capture range = 2 × pull-in range). Capture and pull-in ranges are shown in frequency diagram form in Figure 2-23. The lowest frequency the PLL can lock onto is called the *lower capture limit* (f_{cl}), and the highest frequency the PLL can lock onto is called the *upper capture limit* (f_{cu}).

The capture range is never greater than, and is almost always less than, the lock range. The relationship among capture, lock, hold-in, and pull-in range is shown in frequency diagram form in Figure 2-24. Note that lock range ≥ capture range and hold-in range ≥ pull-in range.

Voltage-Controlled Oscillator

A *voltage-controlled oscillator* (VCO) is an oscillator (more specifically, a free-running multivibrator) with a stable frequency of oscillation that depends on an external bias voltage. The output from a VCO is a frequency, and its input is a bias or control signal that may be a dc or ac voltage. When a dc or slowly changing ac voltage is applied to the VCO in-

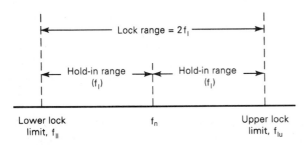

FIGURE 2-22 PLL lock range

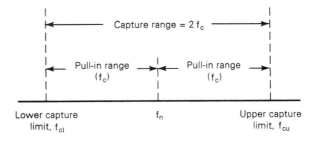

FIGURE 2-23 PLL capture range

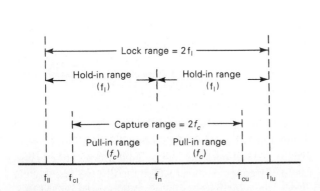

FIGURE 2-24 PLL capture and lock ranges

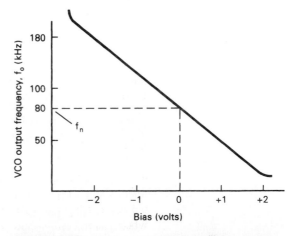

FIGURE 2-25 Voltage-controlled oscillator output frequency–versus–input bias voltage characteristics

put, the output frequency changes or deviates proportionally. Figure 2-25 shows a transfer curve (output frequency–versus–input bias voltage characteristics) for a typical VCO. The output frequency (f_o) with 0-V input bias is the VCO's natural frequency (f_n), which is determined by an external RC network, and the change in the output frequency caused by a change in the input voltage is called frequency deviation (Δf). Consequently, $f_o = f_n + \Delta f$, where f_o = VCO output frequency. For a symmetrical Δf, the natural frequency of the VCO should be centered within the linear portion of the input versus output curve. The transfer function for a VCO is

$$K_o = \frac{\Delta f}{\Delta V} \qquad (2\text{-}10)$$

where K_o = input versus output transfer function (hertz-per-volt)
       ΔV = change in the input control voltage (volts)
       Δf = change in the output frequency (hertz)

Phase Comparator

A phase comparator, sometimes called a *phase detector*, is a nonlinear device with two input signals: an externally generated frequency (f_i) and the VCO output frequency (f_o). The output from a phase comparator is the product of the two signals of frequencies f_i and f_o and, therefore, contains their sum and difference frequencies ($f_i \pm f_o$). The topic of mixing is analyzed in more detail later in this chapter. Figure 2-26a shows the schematic diagram for a simple phase comparator. v_o is applied simultaneously to the two halves of input transformer T_1. D_1, R_1, and C_1 make up a half-wave rectifier, as do D_2, R_2, and C_2 (note that $C_1 = C_2$ and $R_1 = R_2$). During the positive alternation of v_o, D_1 and D_2 are forward biased and *on*, charging C_1 and C_2 to equal values but with opposite polarities. Therefore, the average output voltage is $V_{out} = V_{C1} + (-V_{C2}) = 0$ V. This is shown in Figure 2-26b. During the negative half-cycle of v_o, D_1 and D_2 are reverse biased and *off*. Therefore, C_1 and C_2 discharge equally through R_1 and R_2, respectively, keeping the output voltage equal to 0 V. This is shown in Figure 2-26c. The two half-wave rectifiers produce equal-magnitude, opposite-polarity output voltages. Therefore, the output voltage due to v_o is constant and equal to 0 V. The corresponding input and output waveforms for a square-wave VCO signal are shown in Figure 2-26d.

    Circuit operation. When an external input signal [$v_{in} = V_i \sin(2\pi f_i t)$] is applied to the phase comparator, its voltage adds to v_o, causing C_1 and C_2 to charge and discharge, producing a proportional change in the output voltage. Figure 2-27a shows the unfiltered output waveform shaded when $f_o = f_i$ and v_o leads v_i by 90°. For the phase comparator to operate properly, v_o must be much larger than v_i. Therefore, D_1 and D_2 are switched *on* only during the positive alternation of v_o and are *off* during the negative alternation. During the first half of the *on* time, the voltage applied to $D_1 = v_o - v_i$, and the voltage applied to $D_2 = v_o + v_i$. Therefore, C_1 is discharging while C_2 is charging. During the second half of the *on* time, the voltage applied to $D_1 = v_o + v_i$, the voltage applied to $D_2 = v_o - v_i$, and C_1 is charging while C_2 is discharging. During the *off* time, C_1 and C_2 are neither charging nor discharging. For each complete cycle of v_o, C_1 and C_2 charge and discharge equally and the average output voltage remains at 0 V. Thus, the average value of V_{out} is 0 V when the input and VCO output signals are equal in frequency and 90° out of phase.

    Figure 2-27b shows the unfiltered output voltage waveform shaded when v_o leads v_i by 45°. v_i is positive for 75% of the *on* time and negative for the remaining 25%. As a result, the average output voltage for one cycle of v_o is positive and approximately equal to 0.3 V, where V is the peak input voltage. Figure 2-27c shows the unfiltered output waveform when v_o and v_i are in phase. During the entire *on* time, v_1 is positive. Consequently, the output voltage is positive and approximately equal to 0.636 V. Figures 2-27d and e show the unfiltered output waveform when v_o leads v_i by 135° and 180°, respectively. It can be seen that the output voltage goes negative when v_o leads v_i by more than 90° and reaches its maximum value when v_o leads v_i by 180°. In essence, a phase comparator rectifies v_i and integrates it to produce an output voltage that is proportional to the difference in phase between v_o and v_i.

Figure 2-28 shows the output voltage–versus–input phase difference characteristics for the phase comparator shown in Figure 2-26a. Figure 2-28a shows the curve for a square-

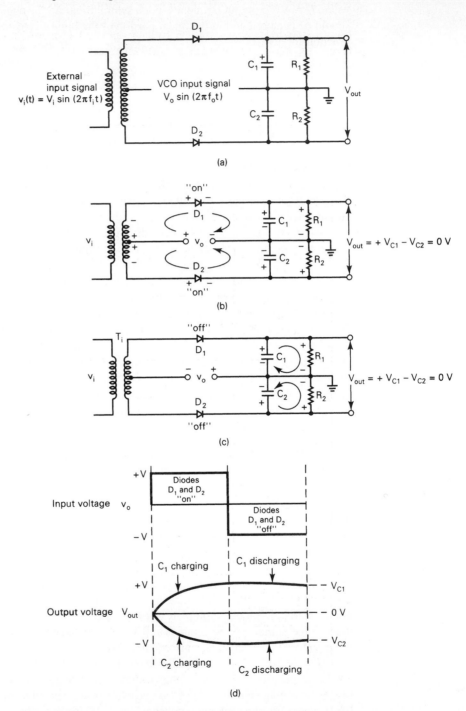

(a)

(b)

(c)

(d)

FIGURE 2-26 Phase comparator: (a) schematic diagram; (b) output voltage due to positive half-cycle of v_o; (c) output voltage due to negative half-cycle of v_o; (d) input and output voltage waveforms

wave phase comparator. The curve has a triangular shape with a negative slope from 0° to 180°. V_{out} is maximum positive when v_o and v_i are in phase, 0 V when v_o leads v_i by 90°, and maximum negative when v_o leads v_i by 180°. If v_o advances more than 180°, the output voltage become less negative, and if v_o lags behind v_i, the output voltage become less positive. Therefore, the maximum phase difference that the comparator can track is 90° ± 90° or from 0° to 180°. The phase comparator produces an output voltage that is proportional to the difference in phase between v_o and v_i. This phase difference is called the *phase error*. The phase error is expressed mathematically as

$$\theta_e = \theta_i - \theta_o \qquad (2\text{-}11)$$

where θ_e = phase error (radians)
   θ_o = phase of the VCO output signal voltage (radians)
   θ_i = phase of the external input signal voltage (radians)

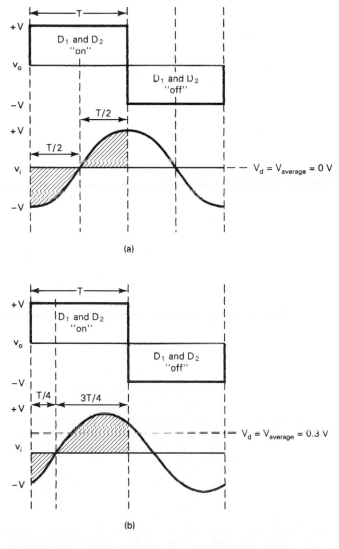

(a)

(b)

FIGURE 2-27   Phase comparator output voltage waveforms:
(a) v_o leads v_i by 90°; (b) v_o leads v_i by 45°; *(Continued)*

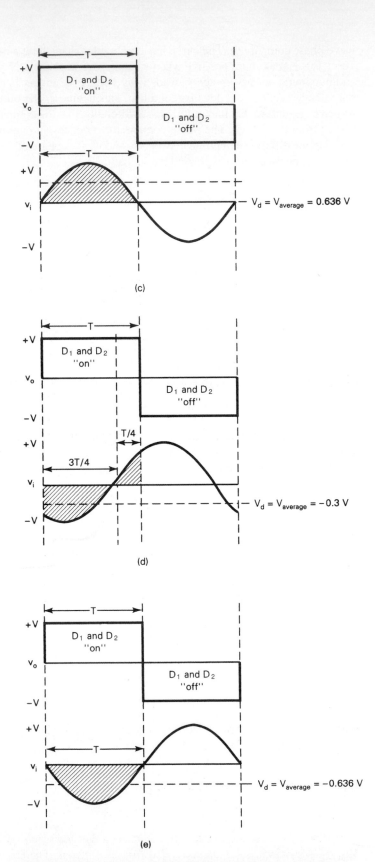

FIGURE 2-27 (Continued) (c) v_o and v_i in phase; (d) v_o leads v_i by 135°; (e) v_o leads v_i by 180°

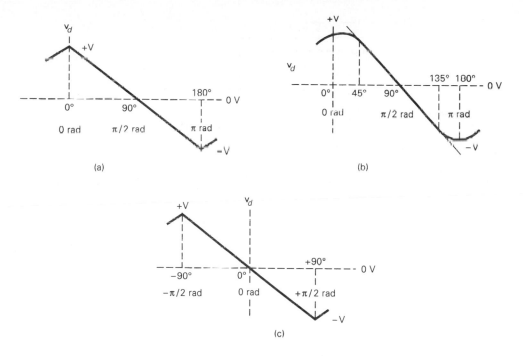

FIGURE 2-28 Phase comparator output voltage (V_d) versus phase difference (θ_e) characteristics: (a) square-wave inputs; (b) sinusoidal inputs; (c) square-wave inputs, phase bias reference

The output voltage from the phase comparator is linear for phase errors between 0° and 180° (0 to π radians). Therefore, the transfer function for a square-wave phase comparator for phase errors between 0° and 180° is given as

$$K_d = \frac{V_d}{\theta_e} = \frac{2v_i}{\pi} \qquad (2\text{-}12)$$

where K_d = transfer function or gain (volts per radian)
V_d = phase comparator output voltage (volts)
θ_e = phase error ($\theta_i - \theta_o$)(radians)
π = 3.14 radians
v_i = peak input signal voltage (volts)

    Figure 2-28b shows the output voltage–versus–input phase difference curve for an analog phase comparator with sinusoidal characteristics. The phase error versus output is nearly linear only from 45° to 135°. Therefore, the transfer function is given as

$$K_d = \frac{V_d}{\theta_e} \text{ volts per radian} \qquad (2\text{-}13a)$$

where K_d = transfer function or gain (volts per radian)
θ_e = phase error ($\theta_1 - \theta_o$) (radians)
V_d = phase comparator output voltage (volts)

Equation 2-13a can be rearranged to solve for V_d as follows:

$$V_d = K_d\theta \qquad (2\text{-}13b)$$

    From Figures 2-28a and b, it can be seen that the phase comparator output voltage $V_{out} = 0$ V when $f_o = f_i$ and v_o and v_i are 90° out of phase. Therefore, if the input frequency (f_i) is initially equal to the VCO's natural frequency (f_n), a 90° phase difference is required

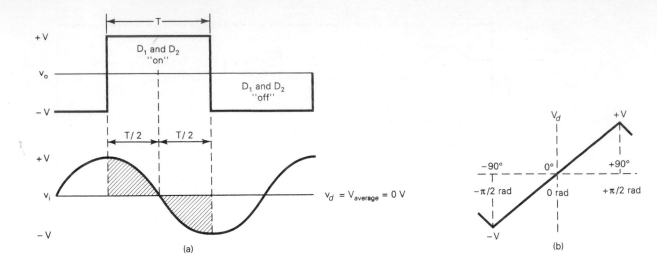

FIGURE 2-29 Phase comparator output voltage: (a) unfiltered output voltage waveform when v_i leads v_o by 90°; (b) output voltage–versus–phase difference characteristics

to keep the phase comparator output voltage at 0 V and the VCO output frequency equal to its natural frequency ($f_o = f_n$). This 90° phase difference is equivalent to a bias or offset phase. Generally, the phase bias is considered as the reference phase, which can be deviated $\pm \pi/2$ radians ($\pm 90°$). Therefore, V_{out} goes from its maximum positive value at $-\pi/2$ radians ($-90°$) and to its maximum negative value at $+\pi/2$ radians ($+90°$). Figure 2-28c shows the phase comparator output voltage–versus–phase error characteristics for square-wave inputs with the 90° phase bias as the reference.

Figure 2-29a shows the unfiltered output voltage waveform when v_i leads v_o by 90°. Note that the average value is 0 V (the same as when v_o led v_i by 90°). When frequency lock occurs, it is uncertain whether the VCO will lock onto the input frequency with a + or − 90° phase difference. Therefore, there is a 180° phase ambiguity in the phase of VCO output frequency. Figure 2-29b shows the output voltage–versus–phase difference characteristics for square-wave inputs when the VCO output frequency equals its natural frequency and it has locked onto the input signal with a −90° phase difference. Note that the opposite voltages occur for the opposite direction phase error, and the slope is positive rather than negative from $-\pi/2$ radians to $+\pi/2$ radians. When frequency lock occurs, the PLL produces a coherent frequency ($f_o = f_i$), but the phase of the incoming signal is uncertain (either f_o leads f_i by 90° $\pm \theta_e$, or vice versa).

Loop Operation

For the following explanations, refer to Figure 2-30.

Loop acquisition. An external input signal [$(V_i \sin(2\pi f_i t + \theta_i))$] enters the phase comparator and mixes with the VCO output signal (a square wave with fundamental frequency f_o). Initially, the two frequencies are not equal ($f_o \neq f_i$) and the loop is *unlocked*. Because the phase comparator is a nonlinear device, the input and VCO signals mix and generate cross-product frequencies (i.e., sum and difference frequencies). Therefore, the primary output frequencies from the phase comparator are the external input frequency (f_i), the VCO output frequency (f_o), and their sum ($f_i + f_o$) and difference ($f_i - f_o$) frequencies.

The low-pass filter (LPF) blocks the two original input frequencies and the sum frequency; thus, the input to the amplifier is simply the difference frequency ($f_i - f_o$), sometimes called the beat frequency. The beat frequency is amplified and then applied to the in-

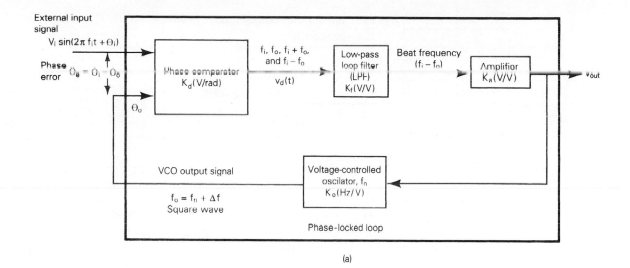

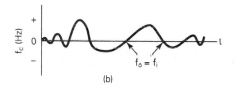

FIGURE 2-30 PLL operation: (a) block diagram; (b) beat frequency

put of the voltage-controlled oscillator, where it deviates the VCO by an amount proportional to its polarity and amplitude. As the VCO output frequency changes, the amplitude and frequency of the beat frequency change proportionately. Figure 2-30b shows the beat frequency produced when the VCO is swept by the difference frequency (f_d). After several cycles around the loop, the VCO output frequency equals the external input frequency and the loop is said to be locked. Once lock has occurred, the beat frequency at the output of the LPF is 0 Hz (a dc voltage), which is necessary to bias the VCO and keep it locked to the external input frequency. In essence, the phase comparator is a frequency comparator until frequency acquisition (zero beat) is achieved, then it becomes a phase comparator. Once the loop is locked, the difference in phase between the external input and VCO output frequencies is converted to a bias voltage (V_d) in the phase comparator, amplified, and then fed back to the VCO to hold lock. Therefore, it is necessary that a phase error be maintained between the external input signal and the VCO output signal. The change in the VCO frequency required to achieve lock and the time required to achieve lock (*acquisition* or *pull-in time*) for a PLL with no loop filter (loop filters are explained later in this chapter) is approximately equal to $5/K_v$ seconds, where K_v is the open-loop gain of the PLL. Once the loop is locked, any change in the input frequency is seen as a phase error, and the comparator produces a corresponding change in its output voltage, V_d. The change in voltage is amplified and fed back to the VCO to reestablish lock. Thus, the loop dynamically adjusts itself to follow input frequency changes.

Mathematically, the output from the phase comparator is (considering only the fundamental frequency for V_o and excluding the 90° phase bias)

$$V_d = [V \sin(2\pi f_o t + \theta_o) \times V \sin(2\pi f_i t + \theta_i)]$$

$$= \frac{V}{2} \cos(2\pi f_o t + \theta_o - 2\pi f_i t - \theta_i) - \frac{V}{2} \cos(2\pi f_o t + \theta_o + 2\pi f_i t - \theta_i)$$

where V_d = the phase detector output voltage (volts)

$V = V_oV_i$ (peak volts)

When $f_o = f_i$,

$$V_d = \frac{V}{2} \cos(\theta_i + \theta_o) \qquad (2\text{-}14)$$

$$= \frac{V}{2} \cos \theta_e$$

where $\theta_i + \theta_o = \theta_e$ (phase error). θ_e is the phase error required to change the VCO output frequency from f_n to f_i (a change $= \Delta f$) and is often called the *static phase error.*

Loop gain. The *loop gain* for a PLL is simply the product of the individual gains or transfer functions around the loop. In Figure 2-30, the open-loop gain is the product of the phase comparator gain, the low-pass filter gain, the amplifier gain, and the VCO gain. Mathematically, open-loop gain is

$$K_L = K_d K_f K_a K_o \qquad (2\text{-}15a)$$

where K_L = PLL open-loop gain (hertz per radian)

K_d = phase comparator gain (volts per radian)

K_f = low-pass filter gain (volts per volt)

K_a = amplifier gain (volts per volt)

K_o = VCO gain (hertz per volt)

and $\qquad K_L = \dfrac{(\text{volt})(\text{volt})(\text{volt})(\text{hertz})}{(\text{rad})(\text{volt})(\text{volt})(\text{volts})} = \dfrac{\text{hertz}}{\text{rad}}$

or PLL open-loop gain (K_v)in radian/second (s^{-1}) is

$$K_v = \frac{\text{cycles}/s}{\text{rad}} = \frac{\text{cycles}}{\text{rad-s}} \times \frac{2\pi \text{ rad}}{\text{cycle}} = 2\pi K_L \qquad (2\text{-}15b)$$

Expressed in decibels, this gives us

$$K_{v(\text{dB})} = 20 \log K_v \qquad (2\text{-}16)$$

From Equations 2-10, 2-13b, and 2-16, the following relationships are derived:

$$V_d = (\theta_e)(K_d) \text{ volts} \qquad (2\text{-}17)$$

$$V_{\text{out}} = (V_d)(K_f)(K_a) \text{ volts} \qquad (2\text{-}18)$$

$$\Delta f = (V_{\text{out}})(K_o) \text{ hertz} \qquad (2\text{-}19)$$

As previously stated, the hold-in range for a PLL is the range of input frequencies over which the PLL will remain locked. This presumes that the PLL was initially locked. The hold-in range is limited by the peak-to-peak swing in the phase comparator output voltage (ΔV_d) and depends on the phase comparator, amplifier, and VCO transfer functions. From Figure 2-28c it can be seen that the phase comparator output voltage (V_d) is corrective for $\pm\pi/2$ radians ($\pm90°$). Beyond these limits, the polarity of V_d reverses and actually chases the VCO frequency away from the external input frequency. Therefore, the maximum phase error (θ_e) that is allowed is $\pm\pi/2$ radians and the maximum phase comparator output voltage is

$$\pm V_{d(\text{max})} = [\theta_{e(\text{max})}](K_d) \qquad (2\text{-}20a)$$

$$= \pm\left(\frac{\pi}{2} \text{ rad}\right)(K_d) \qquad (2\text{-}20b)$$

where $\pm V_{d(\text{max})}$ = maximum peak change at the phase comparator output voltage

K_d = phase comparator transfer function

Consequently, the maximum change in the VCO output frequency is

$$\pm\Delta f_{max} = \pm\left(\frac{\pi}{2}\,rad\right)(K_d)(K_f)(K_a)(K_o) \tag{2-21}$$

where $\pm\Delta f_{max}$ is the hold-in range (maximum peak change in VCO output frequency).
Substituting K_v for $K_d K_f K_a K_o$ yields

$$\pm\Delta f_{max} = \pm\left(\frac{\pi}{2}\,rad\right)K_L \tag{2-22}$$

Example 2-2

For the PLL shown in Figure 2-30, a VCO natural frequency $f_n = 200$ kHz, an external input frequency $f_i = 210$ kHz, and the transfer functions $K_d = 0.2$ V/rad, $K_f = 1$, $K_a = 5$, and $K_o = 20$ kHz/V determine

(a) PLL open-loop gain in Hz/rad and rad/sec.
(b) Change in VCO frequency necessary to achieve lock (Δf).
(c) PLL output voltage (V_{out}).
(d) Phase detector output voltage (V_d).
(e) Static phase error (θ_e).
(f) Hold-in range (Δf_{max}).

Solution (a) From Equations 2-15a and 2-15b,

$$K_L = \frac{0.2\,V}{rad}\frac{1\,V}{V}\frac{5\,V}{V}\frac{20\,kHz}{V} = \frac{20\,kHz}{rad}$$

$$K_v = 2\pi K_L = \frac{20\,kHz}{rad} = \frac{20\,kilocycles}{rad\cdot s} \times \frac{2\pi\,rads}{cycle} = 125,600\,rad/sec$$

$$K_{v(dB)} = 20\log 125,600\,k = 102\,dB$$

(b) $\qquad\qquad \Delta f = f_i - f_n = 210\,kHz - 200\,kHz = 10\,kHz$

(c) Rearranging Equation 2-10 gives us

$$V_{out} = \frac{\Delta f}{K_o} = \frac{10\,kHz}{20\,kHz/V} = 0.5V$$

$$V_d = \frac{V_{out}}{(K_f)(K_a)} = \frac{0.5}{(1)(5)} = 0.1\,V$$

(d)
(e) Rearranging Equation 2-13b gives us

$$\theta_e = \frac{V_d}{K_d} = \frac{0.1\,V}{0.2\,V/rad} = 0.5\,rad \quad or \quad 28.65°$$

(f) Substituting into Equation 2-22 yields

$$\Delta f_{max} = \frac{(\pm\pi/2\,rad)(20\,kHz)}{rad} = +31.4\,kHz$$

Lock range is the range of frequencies over which the loop will stay locked onto the external input signal once lock has been established. Lock range is expressed in rad/s and is related to the open-loop gain K_v as

$$lock\ range = 2\Delta f_{max} = \pi K_L$$

where $K_L = (K_d)(K_f)(K_o)$ for a simple loop with a LPF, phase comparator, and VCO or $K_L = (K_d)(K_f)(K_a)(K_o)$ for a loop with an amplifier.

The lock range in radians per second is π times the dc loop voltage gain and is independent of the LPF response. The capture range depends on the lock range and on the LPF response, so it changes with the type of filter used and with the filter cutoff frequency. For a simple single-pole RC LPF, it is given by

$$capture\ range = \frac{2\sqrt{\Delta f_{max}}}{RC}$$

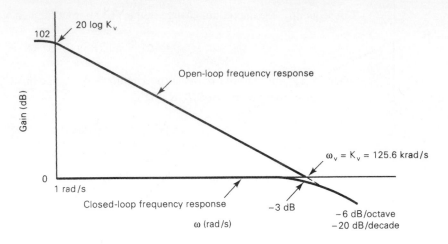

FIGURE 2-31 Frequency response for an uncompensated phase-locked loop

Closed-loop frequency response. The *closed-loop frequency response* for an *uncompensated* (unfiltered) PLL is shown in Figure 2-31. The open-loop gain of a PLL for a frequency of 1 rad/sec = K_v. The frequency response shown in Figure 2-31 is for the circuit and PLL parameters given in Example 2-2. It can be seen that the open-loop gain (K_v) at 1 rad/sec = 102 dB, and the open-loop gain equals 0 dB at the loop cutoff frequency (ω_v). Also, the closed-loop gain is unity up to ω_v, where it drops to −3 dB and continues to roll off at 6 dB/octave (20 dB/decade). Also, $\omega_v = K_v$ = 125.6 krad/s, which is the single-sided bandwidth of the uncompensated closed loop.

From Figure 2-31 it can be seen that the frequency response for an uncompensated PLL is identical to that of a single-pole (first-order) low-pass filter with a break frequency of ω_c = 1 rad/s. In essence, a PLL is a low-pass tracking filter that follows input frequency changes that fall within a bandwidth equal to $\pm K_v$.

If additional bandlimiting is required, a low-pass filter can be added between the phase comparator and amplifier as shown in Figure 2-30. This filter can be either a single- or multiple-pole filter. Figure 2-32 shows the loop frequency response for a simple single-pole *RC* filter with a cutoff frequency of ω_c = 100 rad/s. The frequency response follows that of Figure 2-31 up to the loop filter break frequency; then the response rolls off at 12 dB/octave (40 dB/decade). As a result, the compensated unity-gain frequency (ω_c') is reduced to approximately ± 3.5 krad/s.

Example 2-3

Plot the frequency response for a PLL with a loop gain of K_L = 15 kHz/rad (ω_v = 94.3 krad/s). On the same log paper, plot the response with the addition of a single-pole loop filter with a cutoff frequency ω_c = 1.59 Hz/rad (10 rad/s) and a two-pole loop filter with the same cutoff frequency.

Solution The specified frequency response curves are shown in Figure 2-33. It can be seen that with the single-pole filter the compensated loop response = ω_v' = 1 krad/s and with the two-pole filter, ω_v'' = 200 rad/s.

The bandwidth of the loop filter (or for that matter, whether a loop filter is needed) depends on the specific application.

Integrated-Circuit Precision Phase-Locked Loop

The XR-215 is an ultrastable monolithic phase-locked-loop system designed by EXAR Corporation for a wide variety of applications in both analog and digital communications systems. It is especially well suited for FM or FSK demodulation, frequency synthesis, and

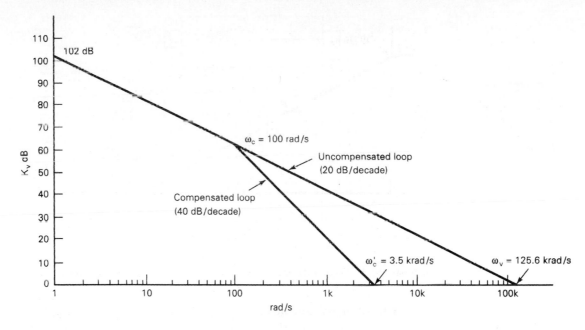

FIGURE 2-32 PLL frequency response for a single-pole RC filter

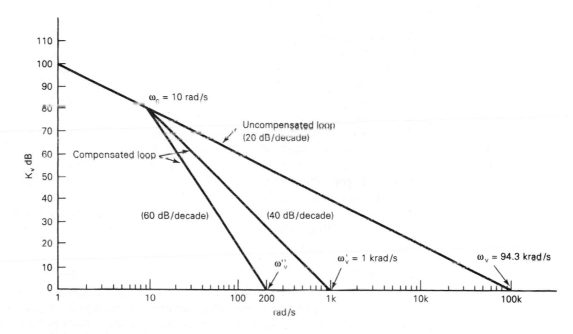

FIGURE 2-33 PLL frequency response for Example 2-3

tracking filter applications. The XR-215 can operate over a relatively wide frequency range from 0.5 Hz to 35 MHz and can accommodate analog input voltages between 300 μV and 3 V. The XR-215 can interface with conventional DTL, TTL, and ECL logic families.

The block diagram for the XR-215 is shown in Figure 2-34 and consists of three main sections: a balanced phase comparator, a highly stable voltage-controlled oscillator (VCO), and a high-speed operational amplifier (op-amp). The phase comparator outputs are internally connected to the VCO inputs and to the noninverting amplifier of the

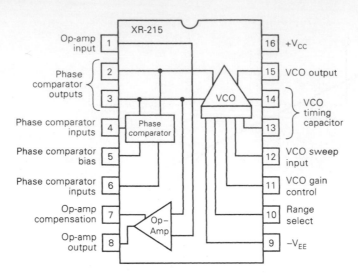

FIGURE 2-34 Block diagram for the XR-215 monolithic phase-locked loop

op-amp. A self-contained PLL system is formed by simply ac coupling the VCO output to either of the phase comparator inputs and adding a low-pass filter to the phase comparator output terminals.

The VCO section has frequency sweep, on-off keying, sync, and digital programming capabilities. Its frequency is highly stable and determined by a single external capacitor. The op-amp can be used for audio preamplification in FM detector applications or as a high-speed sense amplifier (or comparator) in FSK demodulation.

Phase comparator. One input to the phase comparator (pin 4) is connected to the external input signal, and the second input (pin 6) is ac coupled to the VCO output pin. The low-frequency ac (or dc) voltage across the phase comparator output pins (pins 2 and 3) is proportional to the phase difference between the two signals at the phase comparator inputs. The phase comparator outputs are internally connected to the VCO control terminals. One output (pin 3) is internally connected to the operational amplifier. The low-pass filter is achieved by connecting an *RC* network to the phase comparator outputs as shown in Figure 2-35. A typical transfer function (conversion gain) for the phase detector is 2 V/rad for input voltages $\geq$50 mV.

Voltage-controlled oscillator (VCO). The VCO free-running or natural frequency (f_n) is inversely proportional to the capacitance of a timing capacitor (C_o) connected between pins 13 and 14. The VCO produces an output signal with a voltage amplitude of approximately 2.5 V_{p-p} at pin 15 with a dc output level of approximately 2 V. The VCO can be swept over a broad range of output frequencies by applying an analog sweep voltage (V_s) to pin 12 as shown in Figure 2-36. Typical sweep characteristics are also shown. The frequency range of the XR-215 can be extended by connecting an external resistor between pins 9 and 10. The VCO output frequency is proportional to the sum of currents I_1 and I_2 flowing through two internal transistors. Current I_1 is set internally, whereas I_2 is set by an external resistor, R_x. Thus, for any value of C_o, the VCO free-running frequency can be expressed as

$$f_n = f\left(1 + \frac{0.6}{R_x}\right) \qquad (2\text{-}23)$$

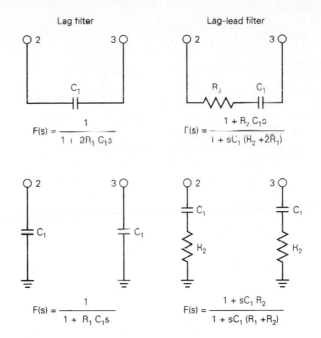

Lag filter

$$F(s) = \frac{1}{1 + 2R_1 C_1 s}$$

Lag-lead filter

$$F(s) = \frac{1 + R_2 C_1 s}{1 + sC_1 (R_2 + 2R_1)}$$

$$F(s) = \frac{1}{1 + R_1 C_1 s}$$

$$F(s) = \frac{1 + sC_1 R_2}{1 + sC_1 (R_1 + R_2)}$$

FIGURE 2-35   XR-215 low-pass filter connections

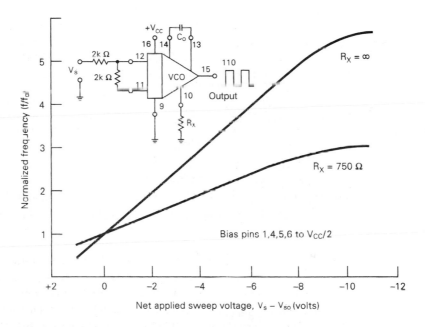

FIGURE 2-36   Typical frequency sweep characteristics as a function of applied sweep voltage

where f_n = VCO free-running frequency (hertz)

f = VCO output frequency with pin 10 open circuited (hertz)

R_x = external resistance (kilohms)

or

$$f_n = \frac{200}{C_o} \left(1 + \frac{0.6}{R_x} \right) \tag{2-24}$$

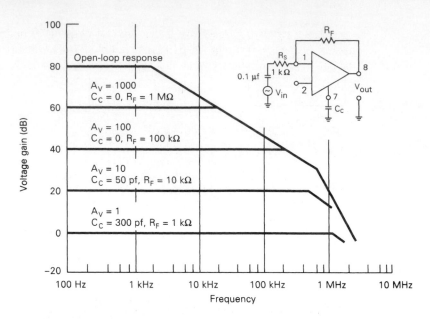

FIGURE 2-37   XR-215 Operational-amplifier frequency response

where C_o = external timing capacitor (microfarads)
         R_x = external resistance (kilohms)

The VCO voltage-to-frequency conversion gain (transfer function) is determined by the choice of timing capacitor C_o and gain control resistor R_o connected externally across pins 11 and 12. Mathematically, the transfer function is expressed as

$$K_o = \frac{700}{C_o R_o} \ (\text{rad}/\text{s})/\text{V} \tag{2-25}$$

where K_o = VCO conversion gain (radians per second per volt)
         C_o = capacitance (microfarads)
         R_o = resistance (kilohms)

Operational amplifier.   Pin 1 is the external connection to the inverting input of the operational amplifier section and is normally connected to pin 2 through a 10-kΩ resistor. The noninverting input is internally connected to one of the phase detector outputs. Pin 8 is used for the output terminal for FM or FSK demodulation. The amplifier voltage gain is determined by the resistance of feedback resistor R_f connected between pins 1 and 8. Typical frequency response characteristics for an amplifier are shown in Figure 2-37.

The voltage gain of the op-amp section is determined by feedback resistors R_f and R_p between pins (8 and 1) and (2 and 1), respectively, and stated mathematically as

$$A_v = \frac{-R_f}{R_s + R_p} \tag{2-26}$$

where A_v = voltage gain (volts per volt)
         R_f = feedback resistor (ohms)
         R_s = external resistor connected to pin 1 (ohms)
         R_p = internal 6-kΩ impedance at pin 1 (ohms)

Lock range. Lock range is the range of frequencies in the vicinity of the VCO's natural frequency over which the PLL can maintain lock with an external input signal. For the XR-215, if saturation or limiting does not occur, the lock range is equal to the open-loop gain or

$$\Delta\omega_L = K_v = (K_d)(K_o) \tag{2-27}$$

where $\Delta\omega_L$ = lock range (radians per second)
          K_v = open-loop gain (radians per second)
          K_d = phase detector conversion gain (volts per radian)
          K_o = VCO conversion gain (radians per second per volt)

Capture range. Capture range is the range of frequencies in the vicinity of the VCO's natural frequency where the PLL can establish or acquire lock with an input signal. For the XR-215, it can be approximated by a parametric equation of the form

$$\Delta\omega_C = \Delta\omega_L|F(j\Delta\omega_C)| \tag{2-28}$$

where $\Delta\omega_C$ = capture range (radians per second)
             $\Delta\omega_L$ = lock range (radians per second)
     $|F(j\Delta\omega_C)|$ = low-pass filter magnitude response at $\omega = \Delta\omega_C$

FREQUENCY SYNTHESIZERS

Synthesize means to form an entity by combining parts or elements. A *frequency synthesizer* is used to generate many output frequencies through the addition, subtraction, multiplication, and division of a smaller number of fixed frequency sources. Simply stated, a frequency synthesizer is a crystal-controlled variable-frequency generator. The objective of a synthesizer is twofold. It should produce as many frequencies as possible from a minimum number of sources, and each frequency should be as accurate and stable as every other frequency. The ideal frequency synthesizer can generate hundreds or even thousands of different frequencies from a single-crystal oscillator. A frequency synthesizer may be capable of simultaneously generating more than one output frequency, with each frequency being synchronous to a single reference or master oscillator frequency. Frequency synthesizers are used extensively in test and measurement equipment (audio and RF signal generators), tone-generating equipment (Touch-Tone), remote-control units (electronic tuners), multichannel communications systems (telephony), and music synthesizers.

Essentially, there are two methods of frequency synthesis: direct and indirect. With *direct frequency synthesis,* multiple output frequencies are generated by mixing the outputs from two or more crystal-controlled frequency sources or by dividing or multiplying the output frequency from a single-crystal oscillator. With *indirect frequency synthesis,* a feedback-controlled divider/multiplier (such as a PLL) is used to generate multiple output frequencies. Indirect frequency synthesis is slower and more susceptible to noise; however, it is less expensive and requires fewer and less complicated filters than direct frequency synthesis.

Direct Frequency Synthesizers

Multiple-crystal frequency synthesizer.   Figure 2-38 shows a block diagram for a *multiple-crystal frequency synthesizer* that uses nonlinear mixing (heterodyning) and filtering to produce 128 different frequencies from 20 crystals and two oscillator modules. For the crystal values shown, a range of frequencies from 510 kHz to 1790 kHz in 10-kHz steps is synthesized. A synthesizer such as this can be used to generate the carrier frequencies for the 106 AM broadcast-band stations (540 kHz to 1600 kHz). For the switch positions shown, the 160-kHz and 700-kHz oscillators are selected, and the outputs from the

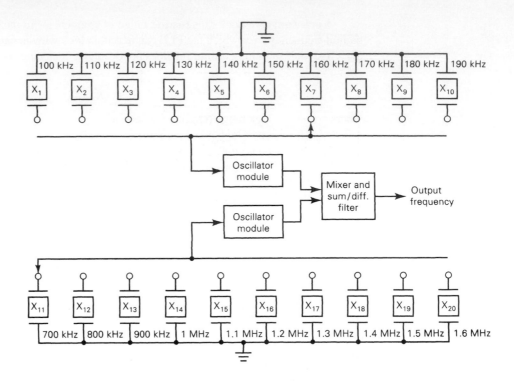

FIGURE 2-38 Multiple-crystal frequency synthesizer

balanced mixer are their sum and difference frequencies (700 kHz ± 160 kHz = 540 kHz and 860 kHz). The output filter is tuned to 540 kHz, which is the carrier frequency for channel 1. To generate the carrier frequency for channel 106, the 100-kHz crystal is selected with either the 1700-kHz (difference) or 1500-kHz (sum) crystal. The minimum frequency separation between output frequencies for a synthesizer is called *resolution*. The resolution for the synthesizer shown in Figure 2-38 is 10 kHz.

   Single-crystal frequency synthesizer.   Figure 2-39 shows a block diagram for a *single-crystal frequency synthesizer* that again uses frequency addition, subtraction, multiplication, and division to generate frequencies (in 1-Hz steps) from 1 Hz to 999,999 Hz. A 100-kHz crystal is the source for the master oscillator from which all frequencies are derived.

   The master oscillator frequency is a base frequency that is repeatedly divided by 10 to generate five additional subbase frequencies (10 kHz, 1 kHz, 100 Hz, 10 Hz, and 1 Hz). Each subbase frequency is fed to a separate harmonic generator (frequency multiplier), which consists of a nonlinear amplifier with a tunable filter. The filter is tunable to each of the first nine harmonics of its base frequency. Therefore, the possible output frequencies for harmonic generator 1 are 0 kHz to 900 kHz in 100-kHz steps; for harmonic generator 2, 10 kHz to 90 kHz in 10-kHz steps; and so on. The resolution for the synthesizer is determined by how many times the master crystal oscillator frequency is divided. For the synthesizer shown in Figure 2-39, the resolution is 1 Hz. The mixers used are balanced modulators with output filters that are tuned to the sum of the two input frequencies. For example, the harmonics selected in Table 2-1 produce a 246,313-Hz output frequency. Table 2-1 lists the selector switch positions for each harmonic generator and the input and output frequencies from each mixer. It can be seen that the five mixers simply sum the output frequencies from the six harmonic generators with three levels of mixing.

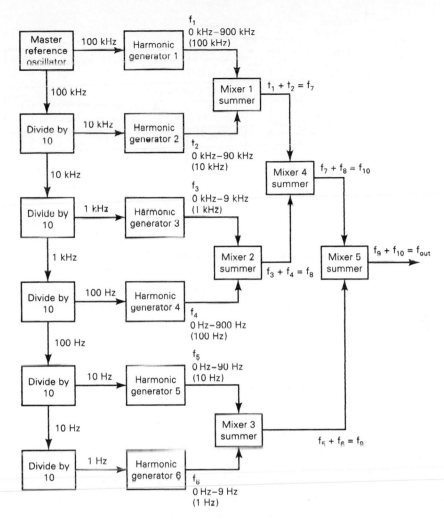

FIGURE 2-39 Single-crystal frequency synthesizer

TABLE 2-1 Switch Positions and Harmonics

Harmonic Generator	Selected Output Frequency	Mixer Output Frequency
1	200 kHz	mixer 1 out = 200 kHz + 40 kHz = 240 kHz
2	40 kHz	
3	6 kHz	mixer 2 out = 6 kHz + 0.3 kHz = 6.3 kHz
4	0.3 kHz	
5	10 Hz	mixer 3 out = 10 Hz + 3 Hz = 13 Hz
6	3 Hz	
		mixer 4 out = 240 kHz + 6.3 kHz = 246.3 kHz
		mixer 5 out = 246.3 kHz + 13 Hz = 246.313 kHz

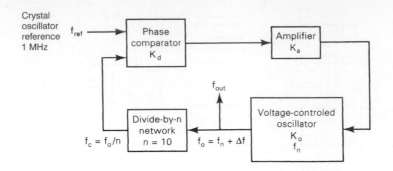

FIGURE 2-40 Single-loop PLL frequency synthesizer

Indirect Frequency Synthesizers

Phase-locked-loop frequency synthesizers.   In recent years, PLL frequency synthesizers have rapidly become the most popular method for frequency synthesis. Figure 2-40 shows a block diagram for a simple *single-loop* PLL frequency synthesizer. The stable frequency reference is a crystal-controlled oscillator. The range of frequencies generated and the resolution depend on the divider network and the open-loop gain. The frequency divider is a divide-by-*n* circuit, where *n* is any integer number. The simplest form of divider circuit is a programmable digital *up–down counter* with an output frequency of $f_c = f_o/n$, where f_o = the VCO output frequency. With this arrangement, once lock has occurred, $f_c = f_{ref}$, and the VCO and synthesizer output frequency $f_o = nf_{ref}$. Thus, the synthesizer is essentially a times-*n* frequency multiplier. The frequency divider reduces the open-loop gain by a factor of *n*. Consequently, the other circuits around the loop must have relatively high gains. The open-loop gain for the frequency synthesizer shown in Figure 2-40 is

$$K_v = \frac{(K_d)(K_a)(K_o)}{n} \tag{2-29a}$$

From Equation 2-29a, it can be seen that as *n* changes, the open-loop gain changes inversely proportionally. A way to remedy this problem is to program the amplifier gain as well as the divider ratio. Thus, the open-loop gain is

$$K_v = \frac{n(K_d)(K_a)(K_o)}{n} = (K_d)(K_a)(K_o) \tag{2-29b}$$

For the reference frequency and divider circuit shown in Figure 2-40, the range of output frequencies is

$$f_o = nf_{ref}$$
$$= f_{ref} \text{ to } 10f_{ref}$$
$$= 1 \text{ MHz to } 10 \text{ MHz}$$

Prescaled frequency synthesizer.   Figure 2-41 shows the block diagram for a frequency synthesizer that uses a phase-locked loop and a *prescaler* to achieve fractional division. Prescaling is also necessary for generating frequencies greater than 100 MHz because programmable counters are not available that operate efficiently at such high frequencies. The synthesizer in Figure 2-41 uses a *two-modulus* prescaler. The prescaler has two modes of operation. One mode provides an output for every input pulse (*P*), and the other mode provides an output for every $P + 1$ input pulse. Whenever the *m* register contains a nonzero number, the prescaler counts in the $P + 1$ mode. Consequently, once the *m* and *n* registers have been initially loaded, the prescaler will count down $(P + 1)$ *m* times

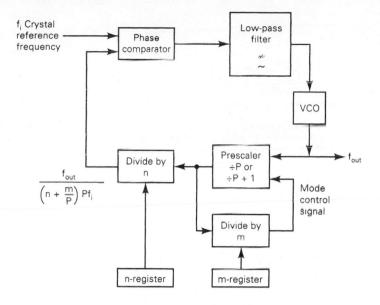

f_i Crystal reference frequency

Phase comparator

Low-pass filter

VCO

f_{out}

Prescaler ÷P or ÷P + 1

Mode control signal

Divide by n

$$\frac{f_{out}}{\left(n + \dfrac{m}{P}\right)Pf_i}$$

Divide by m

n-register

m-register

FIGURE 2-41 Frequency synthesizer using prescaling

until the m counter goes to zero, the prescaler operates in the P mode, and the n counter counts down $(n - m)$ times. At this time, both the m and n counters are reset to their initial values, which have been stored in the m and n registers, respectively, and the process repeats. Mathematically, the synthesizer output frequency f_o is

$$f_o = \left(n + \frac{m}{P}\right)Pf_i \tag{2-30}$$

Integrated-circuit prescalers.   Advanced ECL (emitter-coupled logic) integrated-circuit dual (divide by 128/129 or 64/65) and triple (divide by 64/65/72) modulus prescalers are now available that operate at frequencies from 1 Hz to 1.3 GHz. These integrated-circuit prescalers feature small size, low-voltage operation, low-current consumption, and simplicity. Integrated-circuit prescalers are ideally suited for cellular and cordless telephones, RF LANs (local area networks), test and measurement equipment, military radio systems, VHF/UHF mobile radios, and VHF/UHF handheld radios.

Figure 2-42 shows the block diagram for the NE/SA701 prescaler manufactured by Signetics Company. The NE701 is an advanced dual-modulus (divide by 128/129 or 64/65), low-power, ECL prescaler. It will operate with a minimum supply voltage of 2.5 V and has a maximum current drain of 2.8 mA, allowing application in battery-operated, low-power equipment. The maximum input signal frequency is 1.2 GHz for cellular and other land mobile applications. The circuit is implemented in ECL technology on the HS4+ process. The circuit is available in an 8-pin SO package.

The NE701 comprises a frequency divider implemented by using a divide by 4 or 5 synchronous prescaler followed by a fixed five-stage synchronous counter. The normal operating mode is for the SW (modulus set switch) input to be low and the MC (modulus control) input to be high, in which case it functions as a divide-by-128 counter. For divide-by-129 operation, the MC input is forced low, causing the prescaler to switch into divide-by-5 operation for the last cycle of the synchronous counter. Similarly, for divide-by-64/65, the NE701 will generate those respective moduli with the SW signal forced high, in which the fourth stage of the synchronous divider is bypassed. With SW open circuited, the divide-by-128/129 mode is selected, and with SW connected to V_{CC}, divide by 64/65 is selected.

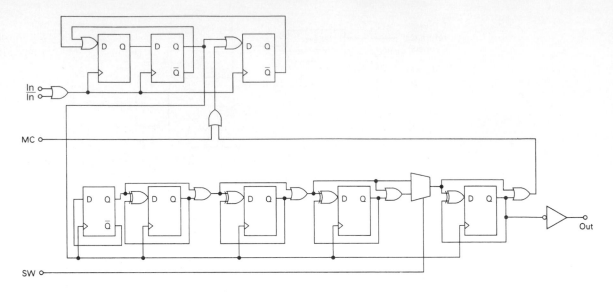

FIGURE 2-42 Block diagram of the NE/SA701 ECL prescaler

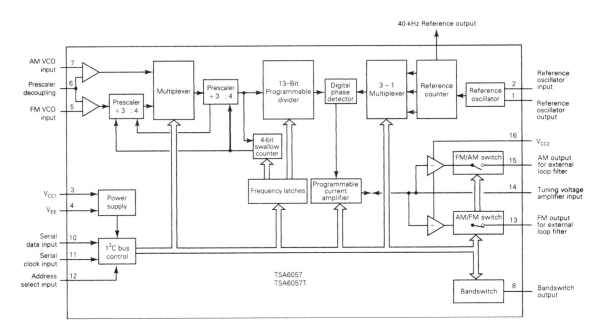

FIGURE 2-43 Block diagram of the TSA6057 radio-tuning PLL frequency synthesizer

Integrated-circuit radio-tuning PLL frequency synthesizer.   Figure 2-43 shows the block diagram for the Signetics TSA6057/T radio-tuning PLL frequency synthesizer. The TSA6057 is a bipolar, single-chip frequency synthesizer manufactured in SUBILO-N technology (components laterally separated by oxide). It performs all the tuning functions of a PLL radio-tuning system. The IC is designed for applications in all types of radio receivers and has the following features:

1. Separate input amplifiers for the AM and FM VCO signals
2. On-chip, high-input sensitivity AM (3:4) and FM (15:16) prescalers
3. High-speed tuning due to a powerful digital memory phase detector

4. On-chip high-performance, one-input (two-output) tuning voltage amplifier. One output is connected to the external AM loop filter and the other output to the external FM loop filter.

5. On-chip, two-level current amplifier that consists of a 5-μA and 450-μA current source. This allows adjustment of the loop gain, thus providing high-current, high-speed tuning, and low-current stable tuning.

6. One reference oscillator (4 MHz) for both AM and FM followed by a reference counter. The reference frequency can be 1 kHz, 10 kHz, or 25 kHz and is applied to the digital memory phase detector. The reference counter also outputs a 40-kHz reference frequency to pin 9 for cooperation with the FM/IF system.

7. Oscillator frequency ranges of 512 kHz to 30 MHz and 30 MHz to 150 MHz

QUESTIONS

2-1. Define *oscillate* and *oscillator*.

2-2. Describe the following terms: *self sustaining; repetitive; free-running; one-shot*.

2-3. Describe the regenerative process necessary for self-sustained oscillations to occur.

2-4. List and describe the four requirements for a *feedback oscillator* to work.

2-5. What is meant by the terms *positive* and *negative feedback?*

2-6. Define *open-* and *closed-loop gain*.

2-7. List the four most common oscillator configurations.

2-8. Describe the operation of a Wien-bridge oscillator.

2-9. Describe oscillator action for an *LC* tank circuit.

2-10. What is meant by a *damped oscillation?* What causes it to occur?

2-11. Describe the operation of a Hartley oscillator; a Colpitts oscillator.

2-12. Define *frequency stability*.

2-13. List several factors that affect the frequency stability of an oscillator.

2-14. Describe the *piezoelectric effect*.

2-15. What is meant by the term *crystal cut?* List and describe several crystal cuts and contrast their stabilities.

2-16. Describe how an overtone crystal oscillator works.

2-17. What is the advantage of an overtone crystal oscillator over a conventional crystal oscillator?

2-18. What is meant by *positive temperature coefficient? Negative temperature coefficient?*

2-19. What is meant by a *zero coefficient* crystal?

2-20. Sketch the electrical equivalent circuit for a crystal and describe the various components and their mechanical counterparts.

2-21. Which crystal oscillator configuration has the best stability?

2-22. Which crystal oscillator configuration is the least expensive and most adaptable to digital interfacing?

2-23. Describe a crystal oscillator module.

2-24. What is the predominant advantage of crystal oscillators over *LC* tank-circuit oscillators?

2-25. Describe the operation of a varactor diode.

2-26. Describe a phase-locked loop.

2-27. What types of LSI waveform generators are available?

2-28. Describe the basic operation of an integrated-circuit waveform generator.

2-29. List the advantages of a monolithic function generator.

2-30. List the advantages of a monolithic voltage-controlled oscillator.

2-31. Briefly describe the operation of a monolithic precision oscillator.

2-32. List the advantages of an integrated-circuit PLL over a discrete PLL.

2-33. Describe the operation of a voltage-controlled oscillator.

2-34. Describe the operation of a phase detector.

2-35. Describe how loop acquisition is accomplished with a PLL from an initial unlocked condition until frequency lock is achieved.

2-36. Define the following terms: *beat frequency; zero beat; acquisition time; open-loop gain.*

2-37. Contrast the following terms and show how they relate to each other: *capture range; pull-in range; closed-loop gain; hold-in range; tracking range; lock range.*

2-38. Define the following terms: *uncompensated PLL; loop cutoff frequency; tracking filter.*

2-39. Define *synthesize.* What is a frequency synthesizer?

2-40. Describe direct and indirect frequency synthesis.

2-41. What is meant by the resolution of a frequency synthesizer?

2-42. What are some advantages of integrated-circuit prescalers and frequency synthesizers over conventional nonintegrated-circuit equivalents?

PROBLEMS

2-1. For a 20-MHz crystal with a negative temperature coefficient of $k = -8$ Hz/MHz/°C, determine the frequency of operation for the following temperature changes:
 (a) Increase of 10° C
 (b) Increase of 20° C
 (c) Decrease of 20° C

2-2. For the Wien-bridge oscillator shown in Figure 2-3 and the following component values, determine the frequency of oscillation: $R_1 = R_2 = 1$ kΩ; $C_1 = C_2 = 100$ pF.

2-3. For the Hartley oscillator shown in Figure 2-5a and the following component values, determine the frequency of oscillation: $L_{1a} = L_{1b} = 50$ µH; $C_1 = 0.01$ µF.

2-4. For the Colpitts oscillator shown in Figure 2-6a, and the following component values, determine the frequency of oscillation: $C_{1a} = C_{1b} = 0.01$ µF; $L_1 = 100$ µH.

2-5. Determine the capacitance for a varactor diode with the following values: $C = 0.005$ µF; $V_r = -2$ V.

2-6. For the VCO input-versus-output characteristic curve shown, determine
 (a) Frequency of operation for a -2-V input signal.
 (b) Frequency deviation for a ±2-V_p input signal.
 (c) Transfer function, K_o, for the linear portion of the curve (-3 to $+3$ V).

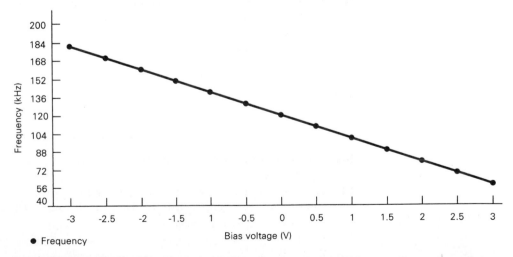

● Frequency

2-7. For the output voltage-versus-phase difference (θ_e) characteristic curve shown, determine
 (a) Output voltage for a $-45°$ phase difference.
 (b) Output voltage for a $+60°$ phase difference.

(c) Maximum peak output voltage.

(d) Transfer function, K_d.

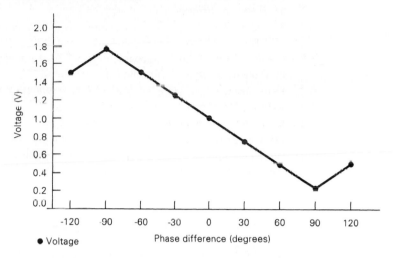

2-8. For the PLL shown in Figure 2-30, a VCO natural frequency of f_n = 150 kHz, an input frequency of f_i = 160 kHz, and the circuit gains K_d = 0.2 V/rad, K_f = 1, K_a = 4, and K_o = 15 kHz/V, determine

    (a) Open-loop gain, K_v

    (b) Δf

    (c) V_{out}

    (d) V_d

    (e) θ_e

    (f) Hold-in range, Δf_{max}

2-9. Plot the frequency response for a PLL with an open-loop gain of K_L = 20 kHz/rad. On the same log paper, plot the response with a single-pole loop filter with a cutoff frequency of ω_c = 100 rad/s and a two-pole filter with the same cutoff frequency.

2-10. Determine the change in frequency (Δf) for a VCO with a transfer function of K_o = 2.5 kHz/V and a dc input voltage change of ΔV = 0.8 V.

2-11. Determine the voltage at the output of a phase comparator with a transfer function of K_d = 0.5 V/rad and a phase error of θ_e = 0.75 rad.

2-12. Determine the hold-in range (Δf_{max}) for a PLL with an open-loop gain of K_v = 20 kHz/rad.

2-13. Determine the phase error necessary to produce a VCO frequency shift of Δf = 10 kHz for an open-loop gain of K_L = 40 kHz/rad.

2-14. Determine the output frequency from the multiple-crystal frequency synthesizer shown in Figure 2-38 if crystals X_8 and X_{18} are selected.

2-15. Determine the output frequency from the single-crystal frequency synthesizer shown in Figure 2-39 for the following harmonics.

Harmonic Generator	Harmonic	Harmonic Generator	Harmonic
1	6	4	1
2	4	5	2
3	7	6	6

2-16. Determine f_c for the PLL shown in Figure 2-40 for a natural frequency of f_n = 200 kHz, Δf = 0 Hz, and n = 20.

2-17. For a 10-MHz crystal with a negative temperature coefficient k = 12 Hz/MHz/°C, determine the frequency of operation for the following temperature changes:

    (a) Increase of 20° C

    (b) Decrease of 20° C

    (c) Increase of 10° C

2-18. For the Wien-bridge oscillator shown in Figure 2-3 and the following component values, determine the frequency of oscillation: $R_1 = R_2$ = 2 k; $C_1 = C_2$ = 1000 pF.

2-19. For the Wien-bridge oscillator shown in Figure 2-3 and the component values given in Problem 2-2, determine the phase shift across the lead–lag network for frequencies an octave above and below the frequency of oscillation.

2-20. For the Hartley oscillator shown in Figure 2-5a and the following component values, determine the frequency of oscillation: $L_{1a} = L_{1b} = 100$ μH; $C_1 = 0.001$ μF.

2-21. For the Colpitts oscillator shown in Figure 2-6a and the following component values, determine the frequency of oscillation: $C_{1a} = 0.0022$ μF, $C_{1b} = 0.022$ μF, and $L_1 = 3$ mH.

2-22. Determine the capacitance for a variactor diode with the following values: $C = 0.001$ μF and $v_r = -1.5$ V.

2-23. For the VCO input-versus-output characteristic curve shown below, determine
  (a) The frequency of operation for a -1.5 V input signal.
  (b) The frequency deviation for a 2 V_{p-p} input signal.
  (c) The transfer function, K_o for the linear portion of the curve (-2 V to $+2$ V).

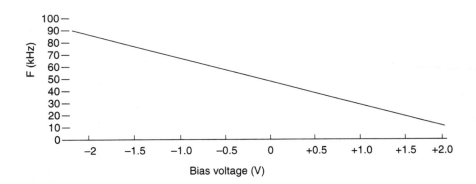

2-24. For the phase detector output voltage–versus–phase difference (θ_e) characteristic curve shown below, determine
  (a) The output voltage for a $-45°$ phase difference.
  (b) The output voltage for a $+60°$ phase difference.
  (c) The maximum peak output voltage.
  (d) The transfer function, K_d.

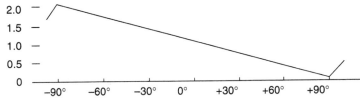

2-25. For the PLL shown in Figure 2-30a, a VCO natural frequency $f_n = 120$ kHz, an input frequency $f_i = 125$ kHz, and the following circuit gains $K_d = 0.2$ V/rad, $K_f = 1$, $K_a = 5$, and $K_o = 12$ kHz/V, determine
  (a) The open-loop gain, K_v **(d)** V_d
  (b) Δf **(e)** θ_e
  (c) V_{out} **(f)** The hold-in range, Δf_{max}

2-26. Plot the frequency response for a PLL with an open-loop gain K_v = 30 kHz/rad. On the same log paper, plot the response with a single-pole filter with a cutoff frequency ω_c = 200 rad/s and a two-pole filter with the same cutoff frequency.

2-27. Determine the change in frequency for a VCO with a transfer function K_o = 4 kHz/V and a dc input voltage change ΔV = 1.2 V_p.

2-28. Determine the voltage at the output of a phase comparator with a transfer function K_d = 0.4 V/rad and a phase error θ_e = 0.55 rad.

2-29. Determine the hold-in range for a PLL with an open-loop gain K_v = 25 kHz/rad.

2-30. Determine the phase error necessary to produce a VCO frequency shift of 20 kHz for an open-loop gain K_v = 50 kHz/rad.

CHAPTER 3

Amplitude Modulation Transmission

INTRODUCTION

Information signals are transported between a transmitter and a receiver over some form of transmission medium. However, the original information signals are seldom in a form that is suitable for transmission. Therefore, they must be transformed from their original form into a form that is more suitable for transmission. The process of impressing low-frequency information signals onto a high-frequency *carrier signal* is called *modulation. Demodulation* is the reverse process where the received signals are transformed back to their original form. The purpose of this chapter is to introduce the reader to the fundamental concepts of *amplitude modulation* (AM).

PRINCIPLES OF AMPLITUDE MODULATION

Amplitude modulation (AM) is the process of changing the amplitude of a relatively high frequency carrier signal in proportion with the instantaneous value of the modulating signal (information). Amplitude modulation is a relatively inexpensive, low-quality form of modulation that is used for commercial broadcasting of both audio and video signals. Amplitude modulation is also used for two-way mobile radio communications such as citizens band (CB) radio.

AM modulators are nonlinear devices with two inputs and one output. One input is a single, high-frequency carrier signal of constant amplitude and the second input is comprised of relatively low-frequency information signals which may be a single frequency or a complex waveform made up of many frequencies. Frequencies that are high enough to be efficiently radiated by an antenna and propagated through free space are commonly called *radio frequencies,* or simply RFs. In the modulator, the information acts on or modulates the RF carrier producing a modulated waveform. The information signal may be a single frequency or more likely consist of a range of frequencies. For example, typical voice-grade communications systems utilize a range of information frequencies between

300 Hz and 3000 Hz. The modulated output waveform from an AM modulator is often called an AM envelope.

The AM Envelope

Although there are several types of amplitude modulation, AM *double-sideband full carrier* (DSBFC) is probably the most commonly used. AM DSBFC is sometimes called *conventional* AM or simply AM. Figure 3-1 illustrates the relationship among the carrier $[V_c \sin(2\pi f_c t)]$, the modulating signal $[V_m \sin(2\pi f_m t)]$, and the modulated wave $[V_{am}(t)]$ for conventional AM. The figure shows how an AM waveform is produced when a single-frequency modulating signal acts on a high-frequency carrier signal. The output waveform contains all the frequencies that make up the AM signal and it is used to transport the information through the system. Therefore, the shape of the modulated wave is called the *AM envelope*. Note that with no modulating signal, the output waveform is simply the carrier signal. However, when a modulating signal is applied, the amplitude of the output wave varies in accordance with the modulating signal. Note that the repetition rate of the envelope is equal to the frequency of the modulating signal, and the shape of the envelope is identical to the shape of the modulating signal.

AM Frequency Spectrum and Bandwidth

An AM modulator is a nonlinear device. Therefore, nonlinear mixing occurs and the output envelope is a complex wave made up of a dc voltage, the carrier frequency, and the sum $(f_c + f_m)$ and difference $(f_c - f_m)$ frequencies (i.e., the cross products). The sum and difference frequencies are displaced from the carrier frequency by an amount equal to the modulating signal frequency. Therefore, an AM signal spectrum contains frequency components spaced f_m Hz on either side of the carrier. However, it should be noted that the modulated wave does not contain a frequency component that is equal to the modulating

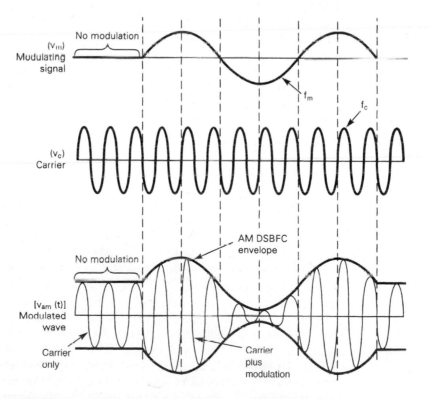

FIGURE 3-1 AM generation

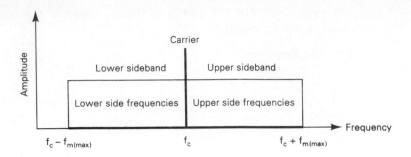

FIGURE 3-2 Frequency spectrum of an AM DSBFC wave

signal frequency. The effect of modulation is to translate the modulating signal in the frequency domain so that it is reflected symmetrically about the carrier frequency.

Figure 3-2 shows the frequency spectrum for an AM wave. The AM spectrum extends from $f_c - f_{m(max)}$ to $f_c + f_{m(max)}$, where f_c is the carrier frequency and $f_{m(max)}$ is the highest modulating signal frequency. The band of frequencies between $f_c - f_{m(max)}$ and f_c is called the *lower sideband* (LSB), and any frequency within this band is called a *lower side frequency* (LSF). The band of frequencies between f_c and $f_c + f_{m(max)}$ is called the *upper sideband* (USB), and any frequency within this band is called an *upper side frequency* (USF). Therefore, the bandwidth (B) of an AM DSBFC wave is equal to the difference between the highest upper side frequency and the lowest lower side frequency, or two times the highest modulating signal frequency (i.e., $B = 2f_{m(max)}$). For radio wave propagation, the carrier and all the frequencies within the upper and lower sidebands must be high enough to be sufficiently propagated through Earth's atmosphere.

Example 3-1

For an AM DSBFC modulator with a carrier frequency $f_c = 100$ kHz and a maximum modulating signal frequency $f_{m(max)} = 5$ kHz, determine

(a) Frequency limits for the upper and lower sidebands.

(b) Bandwidth.

(c) Upper and lower side frequencies produced when the modulating signal is a single-frequency 3-kHz tone.

(d) Draw the output frequency spectrum.

Solution (a) The lower sideband extends from the lowest possible lower side frequency to the carrier frequency or

$$\text{LSB} = [f_c - f_{m(max)}] \text{ to } f_c$$
$$= (100 - 5) \text{ kHz to } 100 \text{ kHz} = 95 \text{ kHz to } 100 \text{ kHz}$$

The upper sideband extends from the carrier frequency to the highest possible upper side frequency or

$$\text{USB} = f_c \text{ to } [f_c + f_{m(max)}]$$
$$= 100 \text{ kHz to } (100 + 5) \text{ kHz} = 100 \text{ kHz to } 105 \text{ kHz}$$

(b) The bandwidth is equal to the difference between the maximum upper side frequency and the minimum lower side frequency or

$$B = 2f_{m(max)}$$
$$= 2(5 \text{ kHz}) = 10 \text{ kHz}$$

(c) The upper side frequency is the sum of the carrier and modulating frequency or
$$f_{usf} = f_c + f_m = 100 \text{ kHz} + 3 \text{ kHz} = 103 \text{ kHz}$$

The lower side frequency is the difference between the carrier and the modulating frequency or
$$f_{lsf} = f_c - f_m = 100 \text{ kHz} - 3 \text{ kHz} = 97 \text{ kHz}$$

(d) The output frequency spectrum is shown in Figure 3-3.

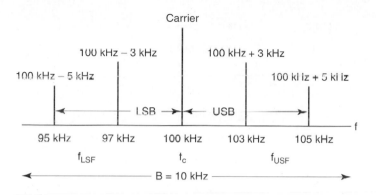

FIGURE 3-3 Output spectrum for Example 3-1

Phasor Representation of an Amplitude-Modulated Wave

For a single-frequency modulating signal, an AM envelope is produced from the vector addition of the carrier and the upper and lower side frequencies. The two side frequencies combine and produce a resultant component that combines with the carrier vector. Figure 3-4a shows this phasor addition. The phasors for the carrier and the upper and lower side frequencies all rotate in a counterclockwise direction. However, the upper side frequency rotates faster than the carrier ($\omega_{usf} > \omega_c$), and the lower side frequency rotates slower ($\omega_{lsf} < \omega_c$). Consequently, if the phasor for the carrier is held stationary, the phasor for the upper side frequency will continue to rotate in a counterclockwise direction relative to the carrier, and the phasor for the lower side frequency will rotate in a clockwise direction. The phasors for the carrier and the upper and lower side frequencies combine, sometimes in phase (adding) and sometimes out of phase (subtracting). For the waveform shown in Figure 3-4b, the maximum positive amplitude of the envelope occurs when the carrier and the upper and lower side frequencies are at their maximum positive values at the same time ($+V_{max} = V_c + V_{usf} + V_{lsf}$). The minimum positive amplitude of the envelope occurs when the carrier is at its maximum positive value at the same time that the upper and lower side frequencies are at their maximum negative values ($+V_{min} = V_c - V_{usf} - V_{lsf}$). The maximum negative amplitude occurs when the carrier and the upper and lower side frequencies are at their maximum negative values at the same time ($-V_{max} = -V_c - V_{usf} - V_{lsf}$). The minimum negative amplitude occurs when the carrier is at its maximum negative value at the same time that the upper and lower side frequencies are at their maximum positive values ($-V_{min} = -V_c + V_{usf} + V_{lsf}$).

Coefficient of Modulation and Percent Modulation

Coefficient of modulation is a term used to describe the amount of amplitude change (modulation) present in an AM waveform. *Percent modulation* is simply the coefficient of modulation stated as a percentage. More specifically, percent modulation gives the percentage change in the amplitude of the output wave when the carrier is acted on by a modulating signal. Mathematically, the modulation coefficient is

$$m = \frac{E_m}{E_c} \tag{3-1}$$

where m = modulation coefficient (unitless)

E_m = peak change in the amplitude of the output waveform voltage (volts)

E_c = peak amplitude of the unmodulated carrier voltage (volts)

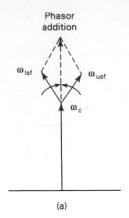

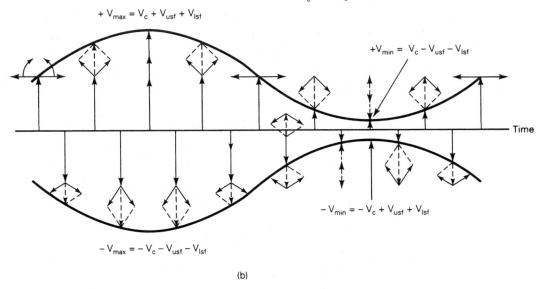

V_{usf} = voltage of the upper side frequency

V_{lsf} = voltage of the lower side frequency

V_c = voltage of the carrier

FIGURE 3-4 Phasor addition in an AM DSBFC envelope: (a) phasor addition of the carrier and the upper and lower side frequencies; (b) phasor addition producing an AM envelope

Equation 3-1 can be rearranged to solve for E_m and E_c as

$$E_m = mE_c \qquad (3\text{-}2)$$

and

$$E_c = \frac{E_m}{m} \qquad (3\text{-}3)$$

and percent modulation (M) is

$$M = \frac{E_m}{E_c} \times 100 \text{ or simply } m \times 100 \qquad (3\text{-}4)$$

The relationship among m, E_m, and E_c is shown in Figure 3-5.

If the modulating signal is a pure, single-frequency sine wave and the modulation process is symmetrical (i.e., the positive and negative excursions of the envelope's ampli-

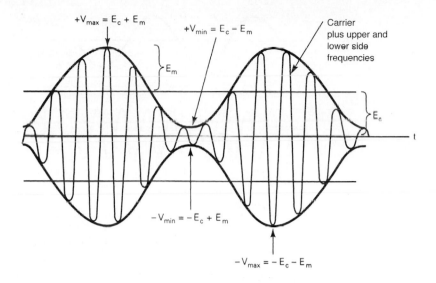

FIGURE 3-5 Modulation coefficient, E_m, and E_c

tude are equal), then percent modulation can be derived as follows (refer to Figure 3-5 for the following derivation):

$$E_m = \frac{1}{2}(V_{max} - V_{min}) \tag{3-5}$$

and

$$E_c = \frac{1}{2}(V_{max} + V_{min}) \tag{3-6}$$

Therefore,

$$M = \frac{1/2(V_{max} - V_{min})}{1/2(V_{max} + V_{min})} \times 100$$

$$= \frac{(V_{max} - V_{min})}{(V_{max} + V_{min})} \times 100 \tag{3-7}$$

where

$$V_{max} = E_c + E_m$$
$$V_{min} = E_c - E_m$$

The peak change in the amplitude of the output wave (E_m) is the sum of the voltages from the upper and lower side frequencies. Therefore, since $E_m = E_{usf} + E_{lsf}$ and $E_{usf} = E_{lsf}$, then

$$E_{usf} = E_{lsf} = \frac{E_m}{2} = \frac{1/2(V_{max} - V_{min})}{2} = \frac{1}{4}(V_{max} - V_{min}) \tag{3-8}$$

where E_{usf} = peak amplitude of the upper side frequency (volts)
E_{lsf} = peak amplitude of the lower side frequency (volts)

From Equation 3-1 it can be seen that the percent modulation goes to 100% when $E_m = E_c$. This condition is shown in Figure 3-6d. It can also be seen that at 100% modulation, the minimum amplitude of the envelope $V_{min} = 0$ V. Figure 3-6c shows a 50% modulated envelope; the peak change in the amplitude of the envelope is equal to one-half the amplitude of the unmodulated wave. The maximum percent modulation that can be imposed without causing excessive distortion is 100%. Sometimes percent modulation is expressed as the peak change in the voltage of the modulated wave with respect to the peak amplitude of the unmodulated carrier (i.e., percent change = $\Delta E_c/E_c \times 100$).

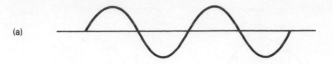

(a)

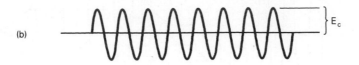

(b) $\}E_c$

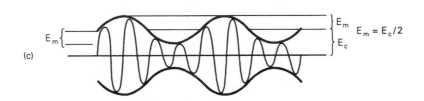

$E_m\{$ 　　　$\}\begin{matrix}E_m\\E_c\end{matrix}$ $E_m = E_c/2$

(c)

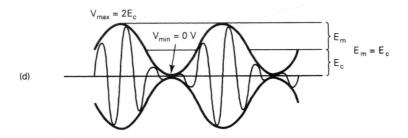

$V_{max} = 2E_c$

$V_{min} = 0\ V$

$\}\begin{matrix}E_m\\E_c\end{matrix}$ $E_m = E_c$

(d)

FIGURE 3-6 Percent modulation of an AM DSBFC envelope:
(a) modulating signal; (b) unmodulated carrier; (c) 50% modulated wave;
(d) 100% modulated wave

Example 3-2

For the AM waveform shown in Figure 3-7, determine
(a) Peak amplitude of the upper and lower side frequencies.
(b) Peak amplitude of the unmodulated carrier.
(c) Peak change in the amplitude of the envelope.
(d) Coefficient of modulation.
(e) Percent modulation.

Solution　(a) From Equation 3-8,

$$E_{usf} = E_{lsf} = \frac{1}{4}(18 - 2) = 4\ V$$

(b) From Equation 3-6,

$$E_c = \frac{1}{2}(18 + 2) = 10\ V$$

(c) From Equation 3-5,

$$E_m = \frac{1}{2}(18 - 2) = 8\ V$$

(d) From Equation 3-1,

$$m = \frac{8}{10} = 0.8$$

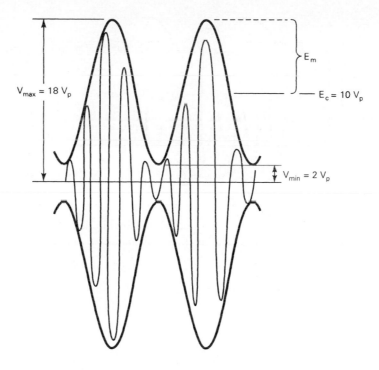

FIGURE 3-7 AM envelope for Example 3-2

(e) From Equation 3-4,

$$M = 0.8 \times 100 = 80\%$$

and from Equation 3-7,

$$M = \frac{18 - 2}{18 + 2} \times 100 = 80\%$$

AM Voltage Distribution

An unmodulated carrier can be described mathematically as

$$v_c(t) = E_c \sin(2\pi f_c t)$$

where $v_c(t)$ = time-varying voltage waveform for the carrier
E_c = peak carrier amplitude (volts)
f_c = carrier frequency (hertz)

In a previous section it was pointed out that the repetition rate of an AM envelope is equal to the frequency of the modulating signal, the amplitude of the AM wave varies proportional to the amplitude of the modulating signal, and the maximum amplitude of the modulated wave is equal to $E_c + E_m$. Therefore, the instantaneous amplitude of the modulated wave can be expressed as

$$v_{am}(t) = [E_c + E_m \sin(2\pi f_m t)][\sin(2\pi f_c t)] \qquad (3\text{-}9a)$$

where $[E_c + E_m \sin(2\pi f_m t)]$ = amplitude of the modulated wave
E_m = peak change in the amplitude of the envelope (volts)
f_m = frequency of the modulating signal (hertz)

If mE_c is substituted for E_m,

$$v_{am}(t) = [(E_c + mE_c \sin(2\pi f_m t)][\sin(2\pi f_c t)] \qquad (3\text{-}9b)$$

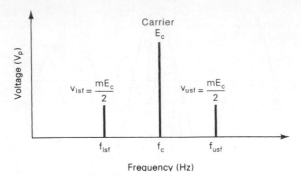

FIGURE 3-8 Voltage spectrum for an AM DSBFC wave

where $[E_c + mE_c \sin(2\pi f_m t)]$ equals the amplitude of the modulated wave.

Factoring E_c from Equation 3-9b and rearranging gives

$$v_{am}(t) = [1 + m\sin(2\pi f_m t)][E_c \sin(2\pi f_c t)] \qquad (3\text{-}9c)$$

where $[1 + m\sin(2\pi f_m t)]$ = constant + modulating signal
       $[E_c \sin(2\pi f_c t)]$ = unmodulated carrier

In Equation 3-9c, it can be seen that the modulating signal contains a constant component (1) and a sinusoidal component at the modulating signal frequency $[m\sin(2\pi f_m t)]$. The following analysis will show how the constant component produces the carrier component in the modulated wave and the sinusoidal component produces the side frequencies. Multiplying out Equation 3-9b or c yields

$$v_{am}(t) = E_c \sin(2\pi f_c t) + [mE_c \sin(2\pi f_m t)][\sin(2\pi f_c t)]$$

Therefore,

$$v_{am}(t) = E_c \sin(2\pi f_c t) - \frac{mE_c}{2}\cos[2\pi(f_c + f_m)t] + \frac{mE_c}{2}\cos[2\pi(f_c - f_m)t] \qquad (3\text{-}10)$$

where $E_c \sin(2\pi f_c t)$ = carrier signal (volts)
       $-(mE_c/2)\cos[2\pi(f_c + f_m)t]$ = upper side frequency signal (volts)
       $+(mE_c/2)\cos[2\pi(f_c - f_m)t]$ = lower side frequency signal (volts)

Several interesting characteristics about double-sideband full-carrier amplitude modulation can be pointed out from Equation 3-10. First, note that the amplitude of the carrier after modulation is the same as it was before modulation (E_c). Therefore, the amplitude of the carrier is unaffected by the modulation process. Second, the amplitude of the upper and lower side frequencies depends on both the carrier amplitude and the coefficient of modulation. For 100% modulation, $m = 1$ and the amplitudes of the upper and lower side frequencies are each equal to one-half the amplitude of the carrier ($E_c/2$). Therefore, at 100% modulation,

$$V_{(max)} = E_c + \frac{E_c}{2} + \frac{E_c}{2} = 2E_c$$

and

$$V_{(min)} = E_c - \frac{E_c}{2} - \frac{E_c}{2} = 0\ \text{V}$$

From the relationships shown above and using Equation 3-10, it is evident that, as long as we do not exceed 100% modulation, the maximum peak amplitude of an AM envelope $V_{(max)} = 2E_c$, and the minimum peak amplitude of an AM envelope $V_{(min)} = 0$ V. This relationship was shown in Figure 3-6d. Figure 3-8 shows the voltage spectrum for an AM DSBFC wave (note that all the voltages are given in peak values).

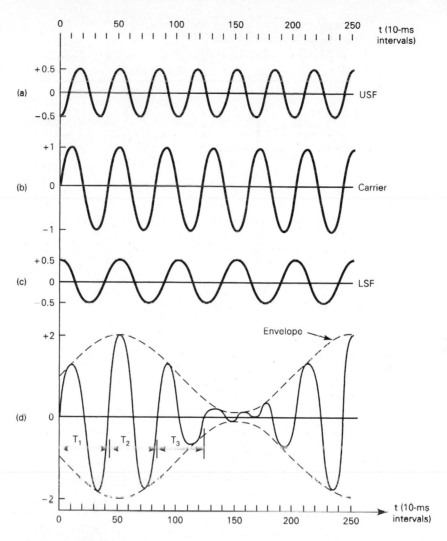

FIGURE 3-9 Generation of an AM DSBFC envelope shown in the time domain: (a) $-\frac{1}{2}\cos(2\pi30t)$; (b) $\sin(2\pi25t)$; (c) $+\frac{1}{2}\cos(2\pi20t)$; (d) summation of (a), (b), and (c)

Also, from Equation 3-10, the relative phase relationship between the carrier and the upper and lower side frequencies is evident. The carrier component is a + sine function, the upper side frequency a − cosine function, and the lower side frequency a + cosine function. Also, the envelope is a repetitive waveform. Thus, at the beginning of each cycle of the envelope, the carrier is 90° out of phase with both the upper and lower side frequencies, and the upper and lower side frequencies are 180° out of phase with each other. This phase relationship can be seen in Figure 3-9 for $f_c = 25$ Hz and $f_m = 5$ Hz.

Example 3-3

One input to a conventional AM modulator is a 500-kHz carrier with an amplitude of 20 V_p. The second input is a 10-kHz modulating signal that is of sufficient amplitude to cause a change in the output wave of ±7.5 V_p. Determine

(a) Upper and lower side frequencies.
(b) Modulation coefficient and percent modulation.
(c) Peak amplitude of the modulated carrier and the upper and lower side frequency voltages.
(d) Maximum and minimum amplitudes of the envelope.
(e) Expression for the modulated wave.

Then

(f) Draw the output spectrum.

(g) Sketch the output envelope.

Solution (a) The upper and lower side frequencies are simply the sum and difference frequencies, respectively.

$$f_{usf} = 500 \text{ kHz} + 10 \text{ kHz} = 510 \text{ kHz}$$
$$f_{lsf} = 500 \text{ kHz} - 10 \text{ kHz} = 490 \text{ kHz}$$

(b) The modulation coefficient is determined from Equation 3-1:

$$m = \frac{7.5}{20} = 0.375$$

Percent modulation is determined from Equation 3-4:
$$M = 100 \times 0.375 = 37.5\%$$

(c) The peak amplitude of the modulated carrier and the upper and lower side frequencies is

$$E_c(\text{modulated}) = E_c(\text{unmodulated}) = 20 \text{ V}_p$$

$$E_{usf} = E_{lsf} = \frac{mE_c}{2} = \frac{(0.375)(20)}{2} = 3.75 \text{ V}_p$$

(d) The maximum and minimum amplitudes of the envelope are determined as follows:

$$V_{(max)} = E_c + E_m = 20 + 7.5 = 27.5 \text{ V}_p$$
$$V_{(min)} = E_c - E_m = 20 - 7.5 = 12.5 \text{ V}_p$$

(e) The expression for the modulated wave follows the format of Equation 3-10.

$$v_{am}(t) = 20 \sin(2\pi 600kt) - 3.75 \cos(2\pi 510kt) + 3.75 \cos(2\pi 490kt)$$

(f) The output spectrum is shown in Figure 3-10.

(g) The modulated envelope is shown in Figure 3-11.

AM Time-Domain Analysis

Figure 3-9 shows how an AM DSBFC envelope is produced from the algebraic addition of the waveforms for the carrier and the upper and lower side frequencies. For simplicity, the following waveforms are used for the modulating and carrier input signals:

$$\text{carrier} = v_c(t) = E_c \sin(2\pi 25t) \qquad (3\text{-}11)$$

$$\text{modulating signal} = v_m(t) = E_m \sin(2\pi 5t) \qquad (3\text{-}12)$$

Substituting Equations 3-11 and 3-12 into Equation 3-10, the expression for the modulated wave is

$$v_{am}(t) = E_c \sin(2\pi 25t) - \frac{mE_c}{2}\cos(2\pi 30t) + \frac{mE_c}{2}\cos(2\pi 20t) \qquad (3\text{-}13)$$

where
$$E_c \sin(2\pi 25t) = \text{carrier (volts)}$$
$$-(mE_c/2)\cos(2\pi 30t) = \text{upper side frequency (volts)}$$
$$+(mE_c/2)\cos(2\pi 20t) = \text{lower side frequency (volts)}$$

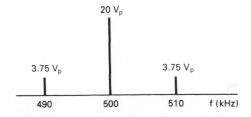

FIGURE 3-10 Output spectrum for Example 3-3

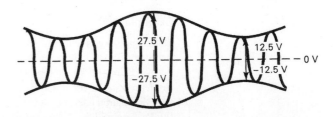

FIGURE 3-11 AM envelope for Example 3-3

Table 3-1 lists the values for the instantaneous voltages of the carrier, the upper and lower side frequency voltages, and the total modulated wave when values of t from 0 to 250 ms, in 10-ms intervals, are substituted into Equation 3-13. The unmodulated carrier voltage $E_c = 1$ V$_p$, and 100% modulation is achieved. The corresponding waveforms are shown in Figure 3-9. Note that the maximum envelope voltage is 2 V ($2E_c$) and the minimum envelope voltage is 0 V.

In Figure 3-9, note that the time between similar zero crossings within the envelope is constant (i.e., $T_1 = T_2 = T_3$, and so on). Also note that the amplitudes of successive peaks within the envelope are not equal. This indicates that a cycle within the envelope is not a pure sine wave and, thus, the modulated wave must be comprised of more than one frequency: the summation of the carrier and the upper and lower side frequencies. Figure 3-9 also shows that the amplitude of the carrier does not vary, but rather, the amplitude of the envelope varies in accordance with the modulating signal. This is accomplished by the addition of the upper and lower side frequencies to the carrier waveform.

AM Power Distribution

In any electrical circuit, the power dissipated is equal to the voltage squared, divided by the resistance. Thus, the average power dissipated in a load by an unmodulated carrier is equal to the rms carrier voltage squared, divided by the load resistance. Mathematically, power in an unmodulated carrier is

$$P_c = \frac{(0.707E_c)^2}{R}$$

$$= \frac{(E_c)^2}{2R} \tag{3-14}$$

TABLE 3-1 Instantaneous Voltages

USF, $-\frac{1}{2}\cos(2\pi30t)$	Carrier, $\sin(2\pi25t)$	LSF, $+\frac{1}{2}\cos(2\pi20t)$	Envelope, $v_{am}(t)$	Time, t(ms)
−0.5	0	+0.5	0	0
+0.155	+1	+0.155	+1.31	10
+0.405	0	−0.405	0	20
−0.405	−1	−0.405	−1.81	30
−0.155	0	+0.155	0	40
+0.5	+1	+0.5	2	50
−0.155	0	+0.155	0	60
−0.405	−1	−0.405	−1.81	70
+0.405	0	−0.405	0	80
+0.155	+1	+0.155	+1.31	90
−0.5	0	+0.5	0	100
+0.155	−1	+0.155	−0.69	110
+0.405	0	−0.405	0	120
−0.405	+1	−0.405	+0.19	130
−0.155	0	+0.155	0	140
+0.5	−1	+0.5	0	150
−0.155	0	+0.155	0	160
−0.405	+1	−0.405	+0.19	170
+0.405	0	−0.405	0	180
+0.155	−1	+0.155	−0.69	190
−0.5	0	+0.5	0	200
+0.155	+1	+0.155	+1.31	210
+0.405	0	−0.405	0	220
−0.405	−1	−0.405	−1.81	230
+0.405	0	−0.405	0	240
+0.155	+1	+0.155	+1.31	250

where P_c = carrier power (watts)
       E_c = peak carrier voltage (volts)
       R = load resistance (ohms)

The upper and lower sideband powers are expressed mathematically as

$$P_{usb} = P_{lsb} = \frac{(mE_c/2)^2}{2R}$$

where $mE_c/2$ is the peak voltage of the upper and lower side frequencies. Rearranging yields

$$P_{usb} = P_{lsb} = \frac{m^2 E_c^2}{8R} \tag{3-15a}$$

where P_{usb} = upper sideband power (watts)
       P_{lsb} = lower sideband power (watts)

Rearranging Equation 3-15a gives

$$P_{usb} = P_{lsb} = \frac{m^2}{4}\left(\frac{E_c^2}{2R}\right) \tag{3-15b}$$

Substituting Equation 3-14 into Equation 3-15b gives

$$P_{usb} = P_{lsb} = \frac{m^2 P_c}{4} \tag{3-16}$$

It is evident from Equation 3-16 that for a modulation coefficient $m = 0$ the power in the upper and lower sidebands is zero and the total transmitted power is simply the carrier power.

The total power in an amplitude-modulated wave is equal to the sum of the powers of the carrier, the upper sideband, and the lower sideband. Mathematically, the total power in an AM DSBFC envelope is

$$P_t = P_c + P_{usb} + P_{lsb} \tag{3-17}$$

where P_t = total power of an AM DSBFC envelope (watts)
       P_c = carrier power (watts)
    P_{usb} = upper sideband power (watts)
    P_{lsb} = lower sideband power (watts)

Substituting Equation 3-16 into Equation 3-17 yields

$$P_t = P_c + \frac{m^2 P_c}{4} + \frac{m^2 P_c}{4} \tag{3-18}$$

Combining terms gives

$$P_t = P_c + \frac{m^2 P_c}{2} \tag{3-19}$$

where $(m^2 P_c)/2$ is the total sideband power.
   Factoring P_c gives us

$$P_t = P_c\left(1 + \frac{m^2}{2}\right) \tag{3-20}$$

From the preceding analysis, it can be seen that the carrier power in the modulated wave is the same as the carrier power in the unmodulated wave. Thus, it is evident that the power of the carrier is unaffected by the modulation process. Also, because the total power

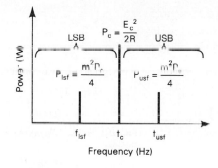

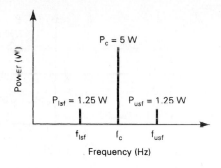

FIGURE 3-12 Power spectrum for an AM DSBFC wave with a single-frequency modulating signal

FIGURE 3-13 Power spectrum for Example 3-4d

in the AM wave is the sum of the carrier and sideband powers, the total power in an AM envelope increases with modulation (i.e., as m increases, P_t increases).

Figure 3-12 shows the power spectrum for an AM DSBFC wave. Note that with 100% modulation the maximum power in the upper or lower sideband is equal to only one-fourth the power in the carrier. Thus, the maximum total sideband power is equal to one-half the carrier power. One of the most significant disadvantages of AM DSBFC transmission is the fact that the information is contained in the sidebands although most of the power is wasted in the carrier. Actually, the power in the carrier is not totally wasted because it does allow for the use of relatively simple, inexpensive demodulator circuits in the receiver, which is the predominant advantage of AM DSBFC.

Example 3-4

For an AM DSBFC wave with a peak unmodulated carrier voltage $V_c = 10$ V$_p$, a load resistance $R_L = 10\ \Omega$, and a modulation coefficient $m = 1$, determine
(a) Powers of the carrier and the upper and lower sidebands.
(b) Total sideband power.
(c) Total power of the modulated wave.
Then
(d) Draw the power spectrum.
(e) Repeat steps (a) through (d) for a modulation index $m - 0.5$.

Solution (a) The carrier power is found by substituting into Equation 3-14:

$$P_c = \frac{10^2}{2(10)} = \frac{100}{20} = 5\ \text{W}$$

The upper and lower sideband power is found by substituting into Equation 3-16:

$$P_{usb} = P_{lsb} = \frac{(1^2)(5)}{4} = 1.25\ \text{W}$$

(b) The total sideband power is

$$P_{sbt} = \frac{m^2 P_c}{2} = \frac{(1^2)(5)}{2} = 2.5\ \text{W}$$

(c) The total power in the modulated wave is found by substituting into Equation 3-20:

$$P_t = 5\left[1 + \frac{(1)^2}{2}\right] = 7.5\ \text{W}$$

(d) The power spectrum is shown in Figure 3-13.

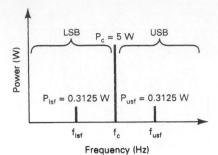

FIGURE 3-14 Power spectrum for Example 3-4

(e) The carrier power is found by substituting into Equation 3-14:

$$P_c = \frac{10^2}{2(10)} = \frac{100}{20} = 5 \text{ W}$$

The upper and lower sideband power is found by substituting into Equation 3-16:

$$P_{usb} = P_{lsb} = \frac{(0.5)^2(5)}{4} = 0.3125 \text{ W}$$

The total sideband power is

$$P_{sbt} = \frac{m^2 P_c}{2} = \frac{(0.5)^2(5)}{2} = 0.625 \text{ W}$$

The total power of the modulated wave is found by substituting into Equation 3-20:

$$P_t = 5\left[1 + \frac{(0.5)^2}{2}\right] = 5.625 \text{ W}$$

The power spectrum is shown in Figure 3-14.

From Example 3-4, it can be seen why it is important to use as high a percentage of modulation as possible while still being sure not to overmodulate. As the example shows, the carrier power remains the same as m changes. However, the sideband power was reduced dramatically when m decreased from 1 to 0.5. Because sideband power is proportional to the square of the modulation coefficient, a reduction in m of one-half results in a reduction in the sideband power of one-fourth (i.e., $0.5^2 = 0.25$). The relationship between modulation coefficient and power can sometimes be deceiving because the total transmitted power consists primarily of carrier power and is, therefore, not dramatically affected by changes in m. However, it should be noted that the power in the intelligence-carrying portion of the transmitted signal (i.e., the sidebands) is affected dramatically by changes in m. For this reason, AM DSBFC systems try to maintain a modulation coefficient between 0.9 and 0.95 (90% to 95% modulation) for the highest-amplitude intelligence signals.

AM Current Calculations

With amplitude modulation, it is very often necessary and sometimes desirable to measure the current of the carrier and modulated wave and then calculate the modulation index from these measurements. The measurements are made by simply metering the transmit antenna current with and without the presence of a modulating signal. The relationship between carrier current and the current of the modulated wave is

$$\frac{P_t}{P_c} = \frac{I_t^2 R}{I_c^2 R} = \frac{I_t^2}{I_c^2} = 1 + \frac{m^2}{2}$$

where
P_t = total transmit power (watts)
P_c = carrier power (watts)
I_t = total transmit current (ampere)
I_c = carrier current (ampere)
R = antenna resistance (ohms)

and
$$\frac{I_t}{I_c} = \sqrt{1 + \frac{m^2}{2}} \qquad (3\text{-}21a)$$

Thus,
$$I_t = I_c\sqrt{1 + \frac{m^2}{2}} \qquad (3\text{-}21b)$$

Modulation by a Complex Information Signal

In the previous sections of this chapter, frequency spectrum, bandwidth, coefficient of modulation, and voltage and power distribution for double-sideband full-carrier AM were analyzed for a single-frequency modulating signal. In practice, however, the modulating signal is very often a complex waveform made up of many sine waves with different amplitudes and frequencies. Consequently, a brief analysis will be given of the effects such a complex modulating signal would have on an AM waveform.

If a modulating signal contains two frequencies (f_{m1} and f_{m2}), the modulated wave will contain the carrier and two sets of side frequencies spaced symmetrically about the carrier. Such a wave can be written as

$$v_{am}(t) = \sin(2\pi f_c t) + \frac{1}{2}\cos[2\pi(f_c - f_{m1})t] - \frac{1}{2}\cos[2\pi(f_c + f_{m1})t]$$
$$+ \frac{1}{2}\cos[2\pi(f_c - f_{m2})t] - \frac{1}{2}\cos[2\pi(f_c + f_{m2})t]$$

When several frequencies simultaneously amplitude modulate a carrier, the combined coefficient of modulation is the square root of the quadratic sum of the individual modulation indexes as follows:

$$m_t = \sqrt{m_1^2 + m_2^2 + m_3^2 + m_n^2} \qquad (3\text{-}22)$$

where
m_t = total coefficient of modulation
$m_1, m_2, m_3, \text{ and } m_n$ = coefficients of modulation for input
signals 1, 2, 3, and n

The combined coefficient of modulation can be used to determine the total sideband and transmit powers as follows:

$$P_{usbt} + P_{lsbt} = \frac{P_c m_t^2}{4} \qquad (3\text{-}23)$$

and
$$P_{sbt}\frac{P_c m_t^2}{2} \qquad (3\text{-}24)$$

Thus,
$$P_t = P_c\left(1 + \frac{m_t^2}{2}\right) \qquad (3\text{-}25)$$

where
P_{usbt} = total upper sideband power (watts)
P_{lsbt} = total lower sideband power (watts)
P_{sbt} = total sideband power (watts)
P_t = total transmitted power (watts)

In an AM transmitter, care must be taken to ensure that the combined voltages of all the modulating signals do not overmodulate the carrier.

Example 3-5

For an AM DSBFC transmitter with an unmodulated carrier power $P_c = 100$ W that is modulated simultaneously by three modulating signals with coefficients of modulation $m_1 = 0.2$, $m_2 = 0.4$, and $m_3 = 0.5$, determine

(a) Total coefficient of modulation.
(b) Upper and lower sideband power.
(c) Total transmitted power.

Solution (a) The total coefficient of modulation is found by substituting into Equation 3-22.

$$m_t = \sqrt{0.2^2 + 0.4^2 + 0.5^2}$$
$$= \sqrt{0.04 + 0.16 + 0.25} = 0.67$$

(b) The total sideband power is found by substituting the results of step (a) into Equation 3-24.

$$P_{sbt} = \frac{(0.67^2)100}{2} = 22.445 \text{ W}$$

(c) The total transmitted power is found by substituting into Equation 3-25.

$$P_t = 100\left(1 + \frac{0.67^2}{2}\right) = 122.445 \text{ W}$$

AM MODULATOR CIRCUITS

The location in a transmitter where modulation occurs determines whether the circuit is a *low-* or *high-level transmitter.* With low-level modulation, the modulation takes place prior to the output element of the final stage of the transmitter, in other words, prior to the collector of the output transistor in a transistorized transmitter, prior to the drain of the output FET in a FET transmitter, or prior to the plate of the output tube in a vacuum-tube transmitter.

An advantage of low-level modulation is that less modulating signal power is required to achieve a high percentage of modulation. In high-level modulators, the modulation takes place in the final element of the final stage where the carrier signal is at its maximum amplitude and, thus, requires a much higher amplitude modulating signal to achieve a reasonable percent modulation. With high-level modulation, the final modulating signal amplifier must supply all the sideband power, which could be as much as 33% of the total transmit power. An obvious disadvantage of low-level modulation is in high-power applications when all the amplifiers that follow the modulator stage must be linear amplifiers, which is extremely inefficient.

Low-Level AM Modulator

A small signal, class A amplifier such as the one shown in Figure 3-15a can be used to perform amplitude modulation; however, the amplifier must have two inputs: one for the carrier signal and the second for the modulating signal. With no modulating signal present, the circuit operates as a linear class A amplifier and the output is simply the carrier amplified by the quiescent voltage gain. However, when a modulating signal is applied, the amplifier operates nonlinearly and signal multiplication as described by Equation 3-9a occurs. In Figure 3-15a the carrier is applied to the base and the modulating signal to the emitter. Therefore, this circuit configuration is called *emitter modulation.* The modulating signal varies the gain of the amplifier at a sinusoidal rate equal to the frequency of the modulating signal. The depth of modulation achieved is proportional to the amplitude of the modulating signal. The voltage gain for an emitter modulator is expressed mathematically as

$$A_v = A_q[1 + m \sin(2\pi f_m t)] \tag{3-26}$$

where A_v = amplifier voltage gain with modulation (unitless)
$\quad\quad A_q$ = amplifier quiescent (without modulation) voltage gain (unitless)

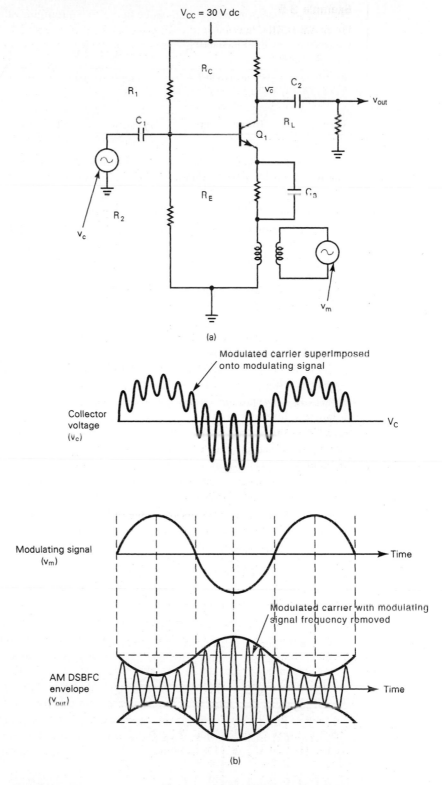

FIGURE 3-15 (a) Single transistor; emitter modulator; (b) output waveforms

$\text{Sin}(2\pi f_m t)$ goes from a maximum value of $+1$ to a minimum value of -1. Thus, Equation 3-26 reduces to

$$A_v = A_q(1 \pm m) \tag{3-27}$$

where m equals the modulation coefficient. At 100% modulation, $m = 1$ and Equation 3-27 reduces to

$$A_{v(\text{max})} = 2A_q$$
$$A_{v(\text{min})} = 0$$

Figure 3-15b shows the waveforms for the circuit shown in Figure 3-15a. The modulating signal is applied through isolation transformer T_1 to the emitter of Q_1 and the carrier is applied directly to the base. The modulating signal drives the circuit into both saturation and cutoff, thus producing the nonlinear amplification necessary for modulation to occur. The collector waveform includes the carrier and the upper and lower side frequencies as well as a component at the modulating signal frequency. Coupling capacitor C_2 removes the modulating signal frequency from the AM waveform, thus producing a symmetrical AM envelope at V_{out}.

With emitter modulation, the amplitude of the output signal depends on the amplitude of the input carrier and the voltage gain of the amplifier. The coefficient of modulation depends entirely on the amplitude of the modulating signal. The primary disadvantage of emitter modulation is the amplifier operates class A, which is extremely inefficient. Emitter modulators are also incapable of producing high-power output waveforms.

Example 3-6

For a low-level AM modulator similar to the one shown in Figure 3-15 with a modulation coefficient $m = 0.8$, a quiescent voltage gain $A_q = 100$, an input carrier frequency $f_c = 500$ kHz with an amplitude $V_c = 5$ mV, and a 1000-Hz modulating signal, determine

(a) Maximum and minimum voltage gains.
(b) Maximum and minimum amplitudes for V_{out}.
Then
(c) Sketch the output AM envelope.

Solution   (a)   Substituting into Equation 3-26,

$$A_{\text{max}} = 100(1 + 0.8) = 180$$
$$A_{\text{min}} = 100(1 - 0.8) = 20$$

(b) $$V_{\text{out(max)}} = 180(0.005) = 0.9 \text{ V}$$
$$V_{\text{out(min)}} = 20(0.005) = 0.1 \text{ V}$$

(c) The AM envelope is shown in Figure 3-16.

Medium-Power AM Modulator

Early medium- and high-power AM transmitters were limited to those that used vacuum tubes for the active devices. However, since the mid-1970s, solid-state transmitters have

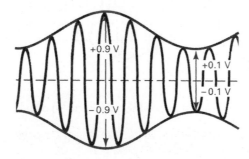

+0.9 V

+0.1 V

−0.1 V

−0.9 V

FIGURE 3-16   AM envelope for Example 3-6

been available with output powers as high as several thousand watts. This is accomplished by placing several final power amplifiers in parallel such that their output signals combine in phase and are, thus, additive.

Figure 3-17a shows the schematic diagram for a single-transistor medium-power AM modulator. The modulation takes place in the collector, which is the output element of the transistor. Therefore, if this is the final active stage of the transmitter (i.e., there are no amplifiers between it and the antenna), it is a high-level modulator.

To achieve high power efficiency, medium- and high-power AM modulators generally operate class C. Therefore, a practical efficiency of as high as 80% is possible. The circuit shown in Figure 3-17a is a class C amplifier with two inputs: a carrier (v_c) and a

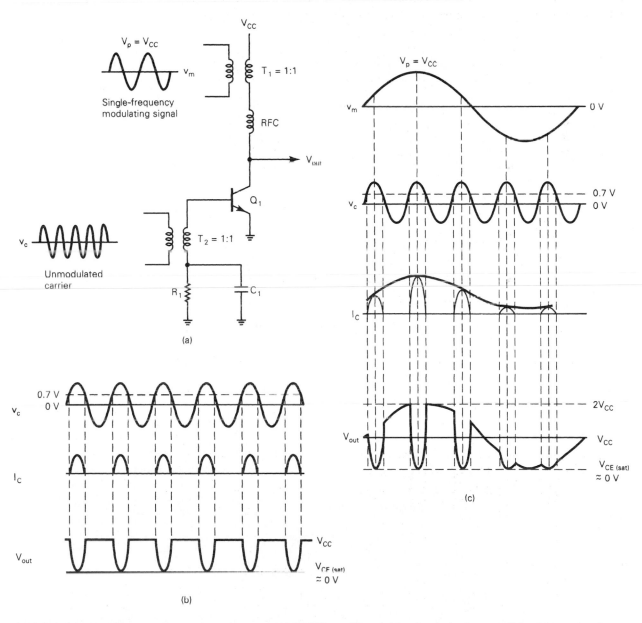

FIGURE 3-17 Simplified medium-power transistor AM DSBFC modulator: (a) schematic diagram; (b) collector waveforms with no modulating signal; (c) collector waveforms with a modulating signal

single-frequency modulating signal (v_m). Because the transistor is biased class C, it operates nonlinear and is capable of nonlinear mixing (modulation). This circuit is called a *collector modulator* because the modulating signal is applied directly to the collector. The RFC is a radio-frequency choke that acts as a short to dc and an open to high frequencies. Therefore, the RFC isolates the dc power supply from the high-frequency carrier and side frequencies, while still allowing the low-frequency intelligence signals to modulate the collector of Q_1.

Circuit operation. For the following explanation, refer to the circuit shown in Figure 3-17a and the waveforms shown in Figure 3-17b. When the amplitude of the carrier exceeds the barrier potential of the base–emitter junction (approximately 0.7 V for a silicon transistor), Q_1 turns on and collector current flows. When the amplitude of the carrier drops below 0.7 V, Q_1 turns off and collector current ceases. Consequently, Q_1 switches between saturation and cutoff controlled by the carrier signal, collector current flows for less than 180° of each carrier cycle, and class C operation is achieved. Each successive cycle of the carrier turns Q_1 on for an instant and allows current to flow for a short time, producing a negative-going waveform at the collector. The collector current and voltage waveforms are shown in Figure 3-17b. The collector voltage waveform resembles a repetitive half-wave rectified signal with a fundamental frequency equal to f_c.

When a modulating signal is applied to the collector in series with the dc supply voltage, it adds to and subtracts from V_{CC}. The waveforms shown in Figure 3-17c are produced when the maximum peak modulating signal amplitude equals V_{CC}. It can be seen that the out-

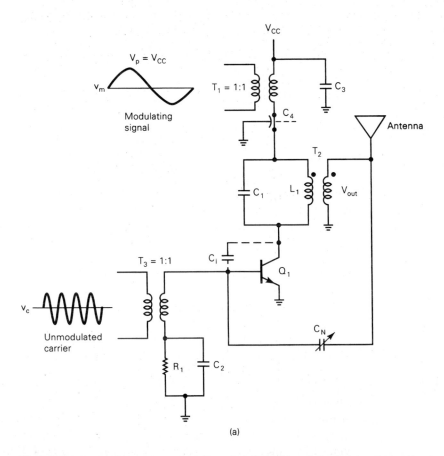

(a)

FIGURE 3-18 Medium-power transistor AM DSBFC modulator: (a) schematic diagram *(Continued)*

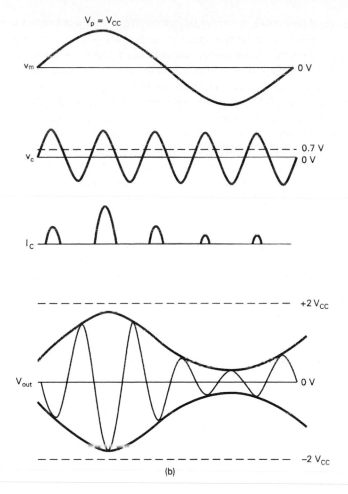

(b)

FIGURE 3-18 *(Continued)* (b) collector and output waveforms

put voltage waveform swings from a maximum value of $2V_{CC}$ to approximately 0 V [$V_{CE(\text{sat})}$]. The peak change in collector voltage is equal to V_{CC}. Again, the waveform resembles a half-wave rectified carrier superimposed onto a low-frequency ac intelligence signal.

Because Q_1 is operating nonlinear, the collector waveform contains the two original input frequencies (f_c and f_m) and their sum and difference frequencies ($f_c \pm f_m$). Because the output waveform also contains the higher-order harmonics and intermodulation components, it must be bandlimited to $f_c \pm f_m$ before being transmitted.

A more practical circuit for producing a medium-power AM DSBFC signal is shown in Figure 3-18a, with corresponding waveforms shown in Figure 3-18b. This circuit is also a collector modulator with a maximum peak modulating signal amplitude $V_{m(\text{max})} = V_{CC}$. Operation of this circuit is almost identical to the circuit shown in Figure 3-17a except for the addition of a tank circuit (C_1 and L_1) in the collector of Q_1. Because the transistor is operating between saturation and cutoff, collector current is not dependent on base drive voltage. The voltage developed across the tank circuit is determined by the ac component of the collector current and the impedance of the tank circuit at resonance, which depends on the quality factor (Q) of the coil. The waveforms for the modulating signal, carrier, and collector current are identical to those of the previous example. The output voltage is a symmetrical AM DSBFC signal with an average voltage of 0 V, a maximum positive peak amplitude equal to $2V_{CC}$, and a maximum negative peak amplitude equal to $-2V_{CC}$. The positive half-cycle of the output waveform is produced in the tank circuit by the *flywheel effect*. When Q_1 is conducting, C_1 charges to $V_{CC} + V_m$ (a maximum value of $2V_{CC}$) and, when Q_1 is off, C_1 discharges through L_1. When L_1 discharges, C_1 charges to a minimum value of $-2V_{CC}$. This produces the positive half-cycle of the AM envelope. The resonant frequency of the tank circuit is equal to the carrier frequency, and the bandwidth extends from $f_c - f_m$ to $f_c + f_m$. Consequently, the modulating signal, the harmonics, and all the higher-order cross products are removed from the waveform, leaving a symmetrical AM DSBFC wave. One hundred percent modulation occurs when the peak amplitude of the modulating signal equals V_{CC}.

Several components shown in Figure 3-18a have not been explained. R_1 is the bias resistor for Q_1. R_1 and C_2 form a clamper circuit that produces a reverse "self" bias and, in conjunction with the barrier potential of the transistor, determines the turn-on voltage for Q_1. Consequently, Q_1 can be biased to turn on only during the most positive peaks of the carrier voltage. This produces a narrow collector current waveform and enhances class C efficiency.

C_3 is a bypass capacitor that looks like a short to the modulating signal frequencies, preventing the information signals from entering the dc power supply. C_{bc} *is the base-to-collector junction capacitance of* Q_1. At radio frequencies, the relatively small junction capacitances within the transistor are insignificant. If the capacitive reactance of C_{bc} is significant, the collector signal may be returned to the base with sufficient amplitude to cause Q_1 to begin oscillating. Therefore, a signal of equal amplitude and frequency and 180° out of phase must be fed back to the base to cancel or *neutralize* the *interelectrode capacitance feedback*. C_N is a *neutralizing capacitor*. Its purpose is to provide a feedback path for a signal that is equal in amplitude and frequency but 180° out of phase with the signal fed back through C_{bc}. C_4 is a RF bypass capacitor. Its purpose is to isolate the dc power supply from radio frequencies. Its operation is quite similar; at the carrier frequency, C_4 looks like a short circuit, preventing the carrier from *leaking* into the power supply or the modulating signal circuitry and being distributed throughout the transmitter.

Simultaneous Base and Collector Modulation

Collector modulators produce a more symmetrical envelope than low-power emitter modulators, and collector modulators are more power efficient. However, collector modulators require a higher amplitude-modulating signal, and they cannot achieve a full saturation-to-cutoff output voltage swing, thus preventing 100% modulation from occurring. Therefore, to achieve symmetrical modulation, operate at maximum efficiency, develop a high output power, and require as little modulating signal drive power as possible, emitter and collector modulations are sometimes used simultaneously.

Circuit operation. Figure 3-19 shows an AM modulator that uses a combination of both base and collector modulations. The modulating signal is simultaneously fed into the collectors of the push–pull modulators (Q_2 and Q_3) and to the collector of the driver amplifier (Q_1). Collector modulation occurs in Q_1; thus, the carrier signal on the base of Q_2 and Q_3 has already been partially modulated and the modulating signal power can be reduced. Also, the modulators are not required to operate over their entire operating curve to achieve 100% modulation.

Linear Integrated-Circuit AM Modulators

Linear integrated-circuit function generators use a unique arrangement of transistors and FETs to perform signal multiplication, which is a characteristic that makes them ideally suited for generating AM waveforms. Integrated circuits, unlike their discrete counterparts, can precisely match current flow, amplifier voltage gain, and temperature variations. Linear integrated-circuit AM modulators also offer excellent frequency stability, symmetrical modu-

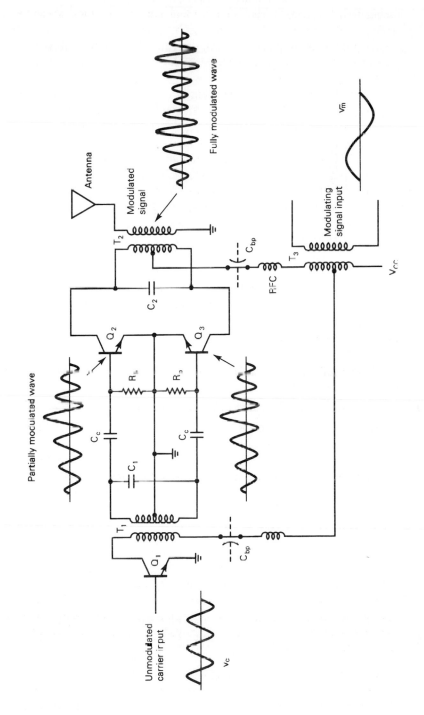

FIGURE 3-19 High-power AM DSBFC transistor modulator

lation characteristics, circuit miniaturization, fewer components, temperature immunity, and simplicity of design and troubleshooting. Their disadvantages include low output power, a relatively low usable frequency range, and susceptibility to fluctuations in the dc power supply.

The XR-2206 *monolithic function generator* is ideally suited for performing amplitude modulation. Figure 3-20a shows the block diagram for the XR-2206 and Figure 3-20b shows

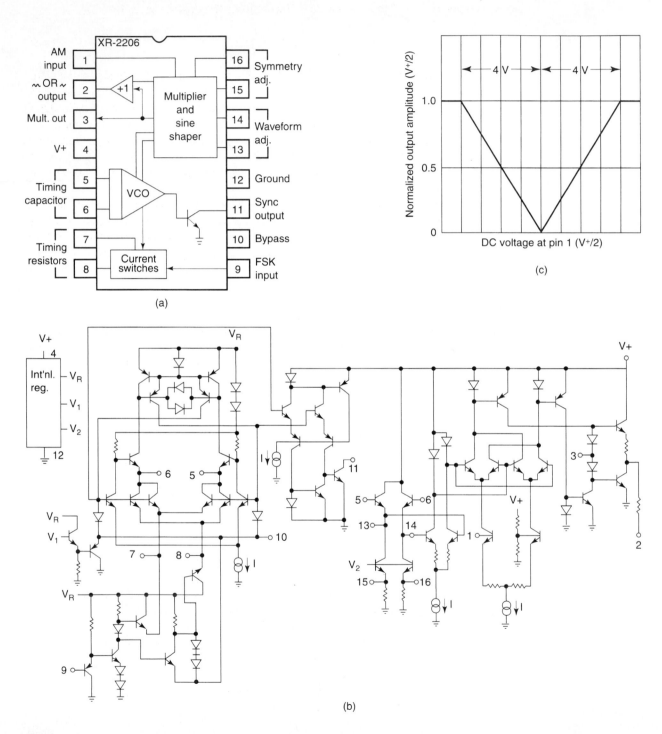

FIGURE 3-20   XR-2206: (a) Block diagram; (b) schematic diagram; (c) output voltage-versus-input voltage curve

the schematic diagram. The XR-2206 consists of four functional blocks: a voltage-controlled oscillator (VCO), an analog multiplier and sine shaper, a unity-gain buffer, and a set of current switches. The VCO frequency of oscillation f_c is determined by the external timing capacitor (C_1) between pins 5 and 6 and by timing resistor (R_1) connected between either pin 7 or 8 and ground. Whether pin 7 or 8 is selected is determined by the voltage level on pin 9. If pin 9 is open circuited or connected to an external voltage ≥ 32 V, pin 7 is selected. If the voltage on pin 9 is ≤ 1 V, pin 8 is selected. The oscillator frequency is given by

$$f_c = \frac{1}{R_1 C_1} \text{ Hz} \tag{3-28}$$

The output amplitude on pin 2 can be modulated by applying a dc bias and a modulating signal to pin 1. Figure 3-20c shows the normalized output amplitude-versus-dc bias. A normalized output of 1 corresponds to maximum output voltage, a normalized value of 0.5 corresponds to an output voltage equal to half the maximum value, and a normalized value of 0 corresponds to no output signal. As the figure shows, the output amplitude varies linearly with input bias for voltages within ± 4 volts of $V^+/2$. An input voltage equal to $V^+/2$ causes the output amplitude to go to 0 V and an input voltage either 4 V above or below $V^+/2$ produces maximum output amplitude.

Figure 3-21 shows the schematic diagram for a linear integrated-circuit AM modulator using the XR-2206. The VCO output frequency is the carrier signal. The modulating signal and bias voltage are applied to the internal multiplier (modulator) circuit through pin 1. The modulating signal mixes with the VCO signal producing an AM wave at V_{out}. The output wave is a symmetrical AM envelope containing the carrier and the upper and lower side frequencies.

Example 3-7

For an XR-2206 LIC modulator such as the one shown in Figure 3-21 with a power supply voltage V^+ = 12 V dc, a modulating signal amplitude $V_m = 2 \text{ V}_p$, a modulating signal frequency $f_m = 4$ kHz, a dc bias $V_{bias} = +4$ V dc, timing resistor $R_1 = 10$ kΩ, and timing capacitor $C_1 = 0.001$ μF; determine

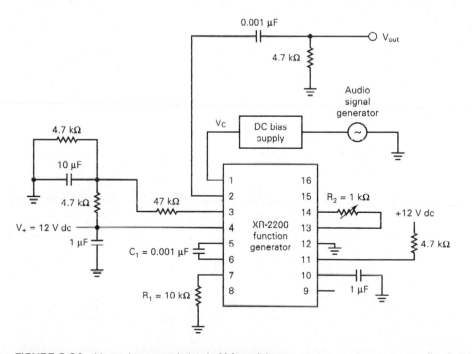

FIGURE 3-21 Linear integrated-circuit AM modulator

(a) Carrier frequency.

(b) Upper and lower side frequencies.

Then

(c) Sketch the output wave.

(d) From the output waveform, determine the coefficient of modulation and percent modulation.

Solution   (a) The carrier frequency is determined from Equation 3-28.

$$f_c = \frac{1}{(10 \text{ k}\Omega)(0.001 \text{ }\mu\text{F})} = 100 \text{ kHz}$$

(b) The upper and lower side frequencies are simply the sum and difference frequencies between the carrier and the modulating signal.

$$f_{usf} = 100 \text{ kHz} + 4 \text{ kHz} = 104 \text{ kHz}$$

$$f_{lsf} = 100 \text{ kHz} - 4 \text{ kHz} = 96 \text{ kHz}$$

(c) Figure 3-22 shows how an AM envelope is produced for the output voltage–versus–input voltage characteristics of the XR-2206.

(d) The percent modulation is determined from the AM envelope shown in Figure 3-22 using Equation 3-7.

$$V_{max} = 10 \text{ V}_p \qquad V_{min} = 0 \text{ V}$$

$$m = \frac{10 - 0}{10 + 0} = 1$$

$$M = 1 \times 100 = 100\%$$

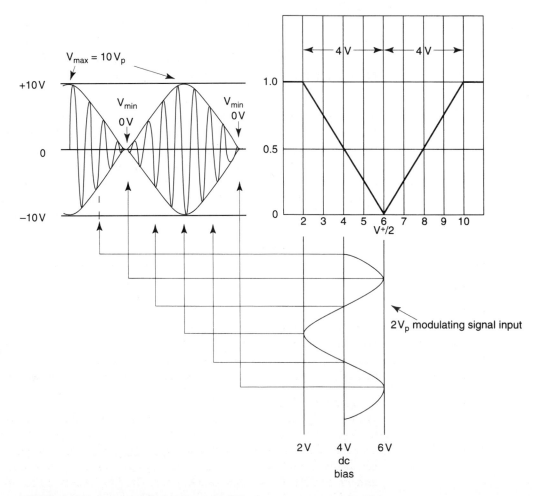

FIGURE 3-22 AM envelope for Example 3-7

Low-Level Transmitters

Figure 3-23 shows a block diagram for a low-level AM DSBFC transmitter. For voice or music transmission, the source of the modulating signal is generally an acoustical transducer, such as a microphone, a magnetic tape, a CD, or a phonograph record. The *preamplifier* is typically a sensitive, class A linear voltage amplifier with a high input impedance. The function of the preamplifier is to raise the amplitude of the source signal to a usable level while producing minimum nonlinear distortion and adding as little thermal noise as possible. The driver for the modulating signal is also a linear amplifier that simply amplifies the information signal to an adequate level to sufficiently drive the modulator. More than one drive amplifier may be required.

The RF *carrier oscillator* can be any of the oscillator configurations discussed in Chapter 2. The FCC has stringent requirements on transmitter accuracy and stability; therefore, crystal-controlled oscillators are the most common circuits used. The *buffer amplifier* is a low-gain, high-input impedance linear amplifier. Its function is to isolate the oscillator from the high-power amplifiers. The buffer provides a relatively constant load to the oscillator, which helps to reduce the occurrence and magnitude of short-term frequency variations. Emitter followers or integrated-circuit op-amps are often used for the buffer. The modulator can use either emitter or collector modulation. The intermediate and final power amplifiers are either linear class A or class B push–pull modulators. This is required with low level transmitters to maintain symmetry in the AM envelope. The antenna coupling network matches the output impedance of the final power amplifier to the transmission line and antenna.

Low-level transmitters such as the one shown in Figure 3-23 are used predominantly for low-power, low-capacity systems such as wireless intercoms, remote-control units, pagers, and short-range walkie-talkies.

High-Level Transmitters

Figure 3-24 shows the block diagram for a high-level AM DSBFC transmitter. The modulating signal is processed in the same manner as in the low-level transmitter except for the addition of a power amplifier. With high-level transmitters, the power of the modulating signal must be considerably higher than is necessary with low-level transmitters. This is because the carrier is at full power at the point in the transmitter where modulation occurs and, consequently, requires a high-amplitude modulating signal to produce 100% modulation.

The RF carrier oscillator, its associated buffer, and the carrier driver are also essentially the same circuits used in low-level transmitters. However, with high-level transmitters, the RF carrier undergoes additional power amplification prior to the modulator stage, and the final power amplifier is also the modulator. Consequently, the modulator is generally a drain-, plate-, or collector-modulated class C amplifier.

With high-level transmitters, the modulator circuit has three primary functions. It provides the circuitry necessary for modulation to occur (i.e., nonlinearity), it is the final power amplifier (class C for efficiency), and it is a frequency up-converter. An up-converter simply translates the low-frequency intelligence signals to radio frequency signals that can be efficiently radiated from an antenna and propagated through free space.

Trapezoidal Patterns

Trapezoidal patterns are used for observing the modulation characteristics of AM transmitters (i.e., coefficient of modulation and modulation symmetry). Although the modulation characteristics can be examined with an oscilloscope, a trapezoidal pattern is more easily and accurately interpreted. Figure 3-25 shows the basic test setup for producing a trapezoidal pattern on the CRT of a standard oscilloscope. The AM wave is applied to the vertical input of the oscilloscope, and the modulating signal is applied to the external horizontal input with

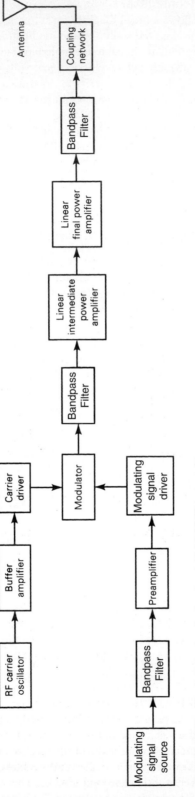

FIGURE 3-23 Block diagram of a low-level AM DSBFC transmitter

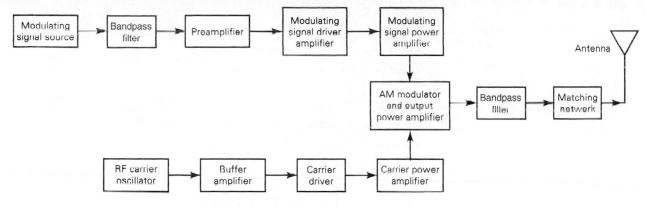

FIGURE 3-24 Block diagram of a high-level AM DSBFC transmitter

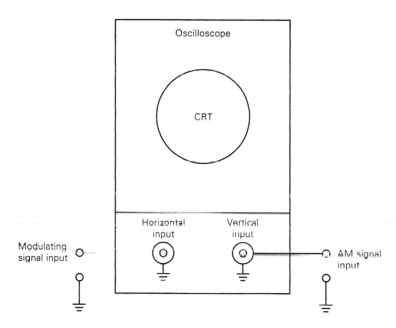

FIGURE 3-25 Test setup for displaying a trapezoidal pattern on an oscilloscope

the internal horizontal sweep disabled. Therefore, the horizontal sweep rate is determined by the modulating signal frequency, and the magnitude of the horizontal deflection is proportional to the amplitude of the modulating signal. The vertical deflection is totally dependent on the amplitude and rate of change of the modulated signal. In essence, the electron beam emitted from the cathode of the CRT is acted on simultaneously in both the horizontal and vertical planes.

Figure 3-26 shows how the modulated signal and the modulating signal produce a trapezoidal pattern. With an oscilloscope, when 0 V is applied to the external horizontal input, the electron beam is centered horizontally on the CRT. When a voltage other than 0 V is applied to the vertical or horizontal inputs, the beam will deflect vertically and horizontally, respectively. If we begin with both the modulated wave and the modulating signal at 0 V (t_0), the electron beam is located in the center of the CRT. As the modulating signal goes positive, the beam deflects to the right. At the same time the modulated signal is going positive, which deflects the beam upward. The beam continues to deflect to the right until the

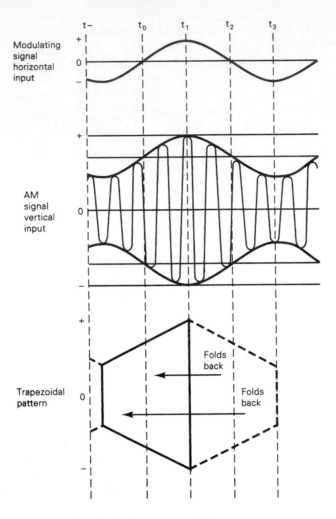

FIGURE 3-26 Producing a trapezoidal pattern

modulating signal reaches its maximum positive value (t_1). While the beam moves toward the right, it is also deflected up and down as the modulated signal alternately swings positive and negative. Notice that on each successive alternation the modulated signal reaches a higher magnitude than the previous alternation. Therefore, as the CRT beam is deflected to the right, its peak-to-peak vertical deflection increases with each successive cycle of the modulated signal. As the modulating signal becomes less positive, the beam is deflected to the left (toward the center of the CRT). At the same time, the modulated signal alternately swings positive and negative, deflecting the beam up and down, except now each successive alternation is lower in amplitude than the previous alternation. Consequently, as the beam moves horizontally toward the center of the CRT, the vertical deflection decreases. The modulating signal and the modulated signal pass through 0 V at the same time, and the beam is again in the center of the CRT (t_2). As the modulating signal goes negative, the beam is deflected to the left side of the CRT. At the same time, the modulated signal is decreasing in amplitude on each successive alternation. The modulating signal reaches its maximum negative value at the same time as the modulated signal reaches its minimum amplitude (t_3). The trapezoidal pattern shown between times t_1 and t_3 folds back on top of the pattern displayed during times $t-$ and t_1. Thus, a complete trapezoidal pattern is displayed on the screen after both the left-to-right and right-to-left horizontal sweeps are complete.

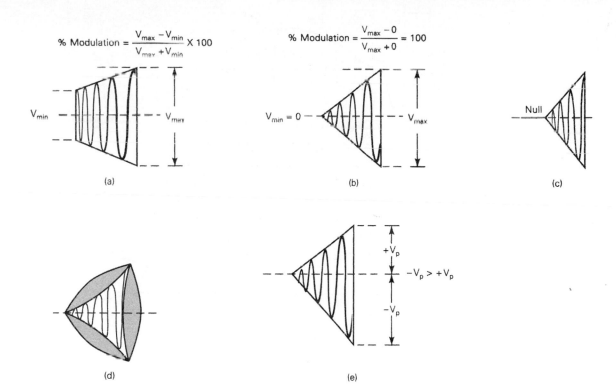

$$\% \text{ Modulation} = \frac{V_{max} - V_{min}}{V_{max} + V_{min}} \times 100$$

(a)

$$\% \text{ Modulation} = \frac{V_{max} - 0}{V_{max} + 0} = 100$$

(b)

V_{min} —— —— V_{max}

$V_{min} = 0$ —— —— V_{max}

Null

(c)

(d)

$+V_p$

$-V_p > +V_p$

$-V_p$

(e)

FIGURE 3-27 Trapezoidal patterns: (a) linear 50% AM modulation; (b) 100% AM modulation; (c) more than 100% AM modulation; (d) improper phase relationship; (e) nonsymmetrical AM envelope

If the modulation is symmetrical, the top half of the modulated signal is a mirror image of the bottom half, and a trapezoidal pattern such as the one shown in Figure 3-27a is produced. At 100% modulation, the minimum amplitude of the modulated signal is zero, and the trapezoidal pattern comes to a point at one end as shown in Figure 3-27b. If the modulation exceeds 100%, the pattern shown in Figure 3-27c is produced. The pattern shown in Figure 3-27a is a 50% modulated wave. If the modulating signal and the modulated signal are out of phase, a pattern similar to the one shown in Figure 3-27d is produced. If the magnitude of the positive and negative alternations of the modulated signal are not equal, the pattern shown in Figure 3-27e results. If the phase of the modulating signal is shifted 180° (inverted), the trapezoidal patterns would simply point in the opposite direction. As you can see, percent modulation and modulation symmetry are more easily observed with a trapezoidal pattern than with a standard oscilloscope display of the modulated signal.

Carrier Shift

Carrier shift is a term that is often misunderstood or misinterpreted. Carrier shift is sometimes called *upward* or *downward modulation* and has absolutely nothing to do with the frequency of the carrier. *Carrier shift* is a form of amplitude distortion introduced when the positive and negative alternations in the AM modulated signal are not equal (i.e., nonsymmetrical modulation). Carrier shift may be either positive or negative. If the positive alternation of the modulated signal has a larger amplitude than the negative alternation, positive carrier shift results. If the negative alternation is larger than the positive, negative carrier shift occurs.

Carrier shift is an indication of the average voltage of an AM modulated signal. If the positive and negative halves of the modulated signal are equal, the average voltage is 0 V. If the positive half is larger, the average voltage is positive, and if the negative half is larger, the average voltage is negative. Figure 3-28a shows a symmetrical AM envelope (no

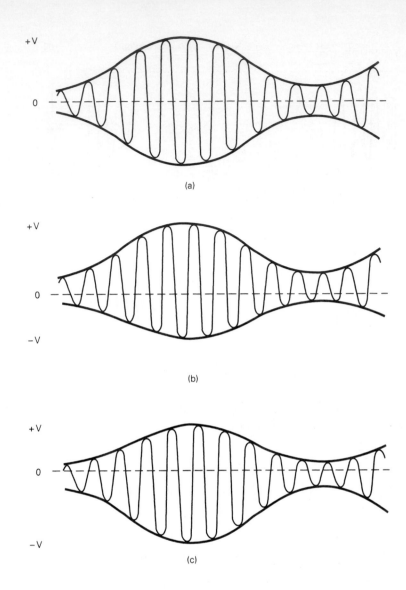

FIGURE 3-28 Carrier shift: (a) linear modulation; (b) positive carrier shift; (c) negative carrier shift

carrier shift); the average voltage is 0 V. Figures 3-28b and c show positive and negative carrier shifts, respectively.

AM Envelopes Produced By Complex Nonsinusoidal Signals

Nonsinusoidal signals are complex waveforms comprised of two or more frequencies. Complex repetitive waveforms are complex waves made up of two or more harmonically related sine waves and include square, rectangular, and triangular waves. Complex modulating signals can also contain two or more unrelated frequencies such as voice signals originating from different sources. When signals other than pure sine or cosine waves amplitude modulate a carrier, the modulated envelope contains upper and lower sideband frequencies commensurate with those contained in the modulating signal and, thus, the shape of the envelope resembles the shape of the original modulating waveform.

Figure 3-29 shows three complex modulating signals and their respective AM envelopes.

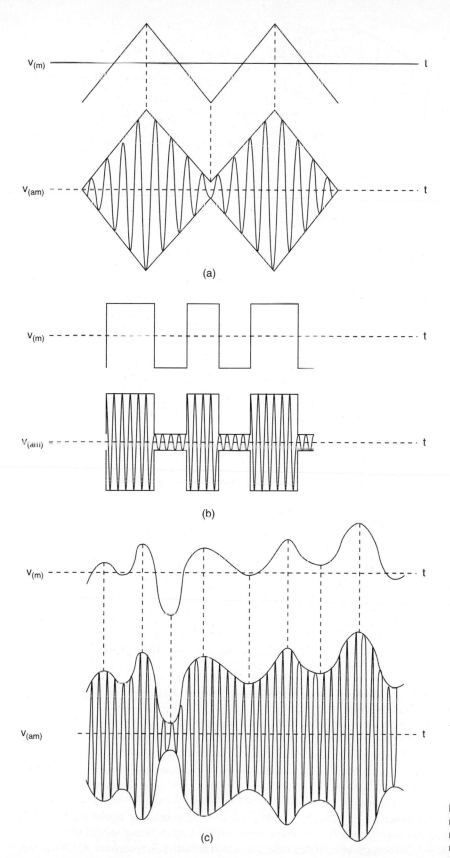

FIGURE 3-29 AM with complex modulating signal: (a) triangular wave modulation; (b) rectantular wave modulation; and (c) voice modulation

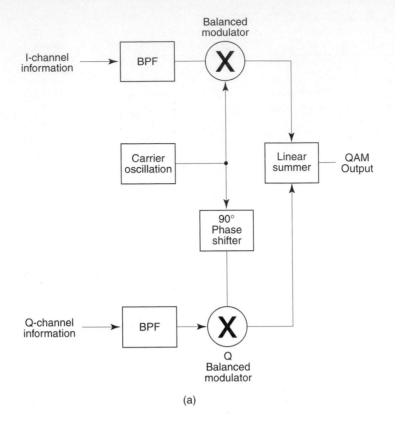

(a)

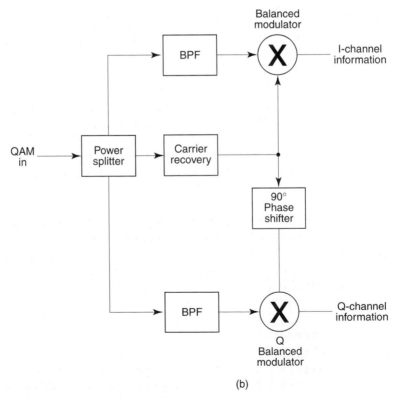

(b)

FIGURE 3-30 Quadrature AM: (a) modulator; (b) demodulator

QUADRATURE AMPLITUDE MODULATION

Quadrature amplitude modulation is a form of amplitude modulation where signals from two separate information sources (i.e., two channels) modulate the same carrier frequency at the same time without interfering with each other. The information sources modulate the same carrier after it has been separated into two carrier signals that are 90° out of phase with each other. This scheme is sometimes called *quadrature AM* (QUAM or QAM).

A simplified block diagram of a quadrature AM modulator is shown in Figure 3-30a. As the figure shows, there is a single carrier oscillator which produces an in-phase carrier to the *I*-modulator and then shifts the carrier 90° and supplies a second quadrature carrier to the *Q*-modulator. The outputs from the two modulators are linearly summed before undergoing additional stages of frequency up-conversion and power amplification.

Figure 3-30b shows a simplified block diagram for a quadrature AM demodulator. As the figure shows, demodulating quadrature AM signals requires a carrier recovery circuit to reproduce the original carrier frequency and phase and two balanced modulators to actually demodulate the signals. This is called *synchronous detection* and the process makes demodulating quadrature AM signals quite expensive when compared with conventional AM demodulator circuits. As you can see, quadrature AM is much more complex than conventional AM, costs more to implement, and produces approximately the same-quality demodulated signal. The primary advantage, however, of quadrature AM is conservation of bandwidth. Quadrature AM requires only half as much bandwidth as conventional AM, and two separate channels can modulate the same carrier. QAM is sometimes called *phase-division multiplexing* and was one of the modulation techniques considered for stereo broadcasting of AM signals. For now, quadrature AM is the modulation scheme used for encoding color signals in analog television broadcasting systems.

Today, quadrature AM is used almost exclusively for digital modulation of analog carriers in data modems to convey data through the public telephone network. Quadrature AM is also for digital satellite communications systems. Digital quadrature modulation and synchronous detection are topics covered in more detail in later chapters of this book.

QUESTIONS

3-1. Define *amplitude modulation.*

3-2. Describe the basic operation of an *AM modulator.*

3-3. What is meant by the term *RF?*

3-4. How many inputs are there to an *amplitude modulator?* What are they?

3-5. In an AM communications system, what is meant by the terms *modulating signal, carrier, modulated wave,* and *AM envelope?*

3-6. What is meant by the *repetition rate* of the AM envelope?

3-7. Describe *upper* and *lower sidebands* and the *upper* and *lower side frequencies.*

3-8. What is the relationship between the *modulating signal frequency* and the *bandwidth* in a *conventional AM system?*

3-9. Define *modulation coefficient* and *percent modulation.*

3-10. What is the highest modulation coefficient and percent modulation possible with a conventional AM system without causing excessive distortion?

3-11. For 100% modulation, what is the relationship between the voltage amplitudes of the side frequencies and the carrier?

3-12. Describe the meaning of the following expression:

$$v_{am}(t) = E_c \sin(2\pi f_c t) - \frac{mE_c}{2} \cos[2\pi(f_c + f_m)t] + \frac{mE_c}{2} \cos[2\pi(f_c - f_m)t]$$

3-13. Describe the meaning of each term in the following expression:

$$v_{am}(t) = 10 \sin(2\pi 500 kt) - 5 \cos(2\pi 515 kt) + 5 \cos(2\pi 485 kt)$$

3-14. What effect does modulation have on the amplitude of the carrier component of the modulated signal spectrum?

3-15. Describe the significance of the following formula:

$$P_t = P_c \left(1 + \frac{m^2}{2} \right)$$

3-16. What does *AM DSBFC* stand for?

3-17. Describe the relationship between the *carrier* and *sideband* powers in an AM DSBFC wave.

3-18. What is the predominant disadvantage of AM DSBFC?

3-19. What is the predominant advantage of AM DSBFC?

3-20. What is the primary disadvantage of low-level AM?

3-21. Why do any amplifiers that follow the modulator circuit in an AM DSBFC transmitter have to be linear?

3-22. Describe the differences between *low-* and *high-level modulators.*

3-23. List the advantages of low-level modulation; high-level modulation.

3-24. What are the advantages of using *linear-integrated circuit modulators* for AM?

3-25. What is the advantage of using a *trapezoidal pattern* to evaluate an AM envelope?

PROBLEMS

3-1. For an AM DSBFC modulator with a carrier frequency f_c = 100 kHz and a maximum modulating signal $f_{m(\text{max})}$ = 5 kHz, determine
  (a) Frequency limits for the upper and lower sidebands.
  (b) Bandwidth.
  (c) Upper and lower side frequencies produced when the modulating signal is a single-frequency 3-kHz tone.
  Then
  (d) Sketch the output frequency spectrum.

3-2. What is the maximum modulating signal frequency that can be used with an AM DSBFC system with a 20-kHz bandwidth?

3-3. If a modulated wave with an average voltage of 20 V_p changes in amplitude ±5 V, determine the minimum and maximum envelope amplitudes, the modulation coefficient, and the percent modulation.

3-4. Sketch the envelope for Problem 3-3 (label all pertinent voltages).

3-5. For a 30-V_p carrier amplitude, determine the maximum upper and lower side frequency amplitudes for an AM DSBFC envelope.

3-6. For a maximum positive envelope voltage of +12 V and a minimum positive envelope amplitude of +4 V, determine the modulation coefficient and percent modulation.

3-7. Sketch the envelope for Problem 3-6 (label all pertinent voltages).

3-8. For an AM DSBFC envelope with a $+V_{\text{max}}$ = 40 V and $+V_{\text{min}}$ = 10 V, determine
  (a) Unmodulated carrier amplitude.
  (b) Peak change in amplitude of the modulated wave.
  (c) Coefficient of modulation and percent modulation.

3-9. For an unmodulated carrier amplitude of 16 V_p and a modulation coefficient m = 0.4, determine the amplitudes of the modulated carrier and side frequencies.

3-10. Sketch the envelope for Problem 3-9 (label all pertinent voltages).

3-11. For the AM envelope shown below, determine
   (a) Peak amplitude of the upper and lower side frequencies.
   (b) Peak amplitude of the carrier.
   (c) Peak change in the amplitude of the envelope.
   (d) Modulation coefficient.
   (e) Percent modulation.

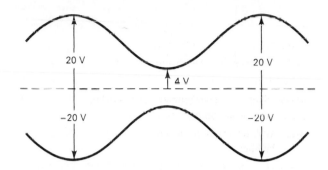

3-12. One input to an AM DSBFC modulator is an 800-kHz carrier with an amplitude of 40 V_p. The second input is a 25-kHz modulating signal whose amplitude is sufficient to produce a ± 10 V change in the amplitude of the envelope. Determine
   (a) Upper and lower side frequencies.
   (b) Modulation coefficient and percent modulation.
   (c) Maximum and minimum positive peak amplitudes of the envelope.
   Then
   (d) Draw the output frequency spectrum.
   (e) Draw the envelope (label all pertinent voltages).

3-13. For a modulation coefficient $m = 0.2$ and an unmodulated carrier power $P_c = 1000$ W, determine
   (a) Total sideband power.
   (b) Upper and lower sideband power.
   (c) Modulated carrier power.
   (d) Total transmitted power.

3-14. Determine the maximum upper, lower, and total sideband power for an unmodulated carrier power $P_c = 2000$ W.

3-15. Determine the maximum total transmitted power (P_t) for the AM system described in Problem 3-14.

3-16. For an AM DSBFC wave with an unmodulated carrier voltage of 25 V_p and a load resistance of 50 Ω, determine
   (a) Power in the unmodulated carrier.
   (b) Power of the modulated carrier, upper and lower sidebands, and total transmitted power for a modulation coefficient $m = 0.6$.

3-17. For a low-power transistor modulator with a modulation coefficient $m = 0.4$, a quiescent voltage gain $A_q = 80$, and an input carrier amplitude of 0.002 V; determine
   (a) Maximum and minimum voltage gains.
   (b) Maximum and minimum voltages for v_{out}.
   Then
   (c) Sketch the modulated envelope.

3-18. For the trapezoidal pattern shown below, determine
   (a) Modulation coefficient.
   (b) Percent modulation.
   (c) Carrier amplitude.
   (d) Upper and lower side frequency amplitudes.

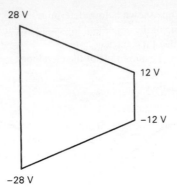

28 V

12 V

−12 V

−28 V

3-19. Sketch the approximate trapezoidal patterns for the following percent modulations and modulation conditions:

(a) 100%

(b) 50%

(c) >100%

(d) Improper phase relationship.

(e) Nonsymmetrical AM modulation.

3-20. For an AM modulator with a carrier frequency $f_c = 200$ kHz and a maximum modulating signal frequency $f_{m(max)} = 10$ kHz, determine

(a) Frequency limits for the upper and lower sidebands.

(b) Upper and lower side frequencies produced when the modulating signal is a single-frequency 7-kHz tone.

(c) Bandwidth necessary to pass the maximum modulating signal frequency.

Then

(d) Draw the output spectrum.

3-21. For an unmodulated carrier voltage of 10 V_p and a ± 4 V change in amplitude of the envelope, determine

(a) Modulation coefficient.

(b) Percent modulation.

3-22. For a maximum positive envelope voltage $V_{max} = +20$ V and a minimum positive envelope amplitude of +6 V, determine

(a) Modulation coefficient.

(b) Percent modulation.

(c) Carrier amplitude.

3-23. For an envelope with $+V_{max} = +30$ V_p and $+V_{min} = +10$ V_p, determine

(a) Unmodulated carrier amplitude.

(b) Modulated carrier amplitude.

(c) Peak change in the amplitude of the envelope.

(d) Modulation coefficient.

(e) Percent modulation.

3-24. Write the expression for an AM voltage wave with the following values:

Unmodulated carrier = 20 V_p

Modulation coefficient = 0.4

Modulating signal frequency = 5 kHz

Carrier frequency = 200 kHz

3-25. For an unmodulated carrier amplitude of 12 V_p and a modulation coefficient of 0.5, determine the following:

(a) Percent modulation.

(b) Peak voltages of the carrier and side frequencies.

(c) Maximum positive envelope voltage.

(d) Minimum positive envelope voltage.

3-26. Sketch the envelop for Problem 3-25.

3-27. For an AM envelope with a maximum peak voltage of 52 V and a minimum peak-to-peak voltage of 24 V, determine the following:
  (a) Percent modulation.
  (b) Peak voltages of the carrier and side frequencies.
  (c) Maximum positive envelope voltage.
  (d) Minimum positive envelope voltage.

3-28. One input to an AM DSBFC modulator is a 500-kHz carrier with a peak amplitude of 32 V. The second input is a 12 kHz modulating signal whose amplitude is sufficient to produce a $+14$ V$_p$ change in the amplitude of the envelope. Determine the following:
  (a) Upper and lower side frequencies.
  (b) Modulation coefficient and percent modulation.
  (c) Maximum and minimum amplitudes of the envelope.
  Then
  (d) Draw the output envelope.
  (e) Draw the output frequency spectrum.

3-29. For a modulation coefficient of 0.4 and a carrier power of 400 W, determine
  (a) Total sideband power.
  (b) Total transmitted power.

3-30. For an AM DSBFC wave with an unmodulated carrier voltage of 18 V$_p$ and a load resistance of 72 Ω, determine
  (a) Unmodulated carrier power.
  (b) Modulated carrier power.
  (c) Total sideband power.
  (d) Upper and lower sideband powers.
  (e) Total transmitted power.

3-31. For a low-power AM modulator with a modulation coefficient of 0.8, a quiescent gain of 90, and an input carrier amplitude of 10 mV$_p$, determine
  (a) Maximum and minimum voltage gains.
  (b) Maximum and minimum envelope voltages.
  Then
  (c) Sketch the AM envelope.

CHAPTER 4

Amplitude Modulation Reception

INTRODUCTION

AM demodulation is the reverse process of AM modulation. A conventional double-sideband AM receiver simply converts a received amplitude-modulated wave back to the original source information. To do this, a receiver must be capable of receiving, amplifying, and demodulating an AM wave. It must also be capable of bandlimiting the total radio-frequency spectrum to a specific desired band of frequencies. The selection process is called *tuning the receiver.*

To completely understand the demodulation process, first it is necessary to have a basic understanding of the terminology commonly used to describe radio receivers and their characteristics. Figure 4-1 shows a simplified block diagram of a typical AM receiver. The *RF section* is the first stage of the receiver and is therefore often called the *receiver front end.* The primary functions of the RF section are detecting, bandlimiting, and amplifying the received RF signals. The *mixer/converter section* is the next stage. This section down-converts the received RF frequencies to *intermediate frequencies* (IFs) which are simply frequencies that fall somewhere between the RF and information frequencies, hence the name *intermediate.* The primary functions of the *IF section* are amplification and selectivity. The *AM detector* demodulates the AM wave and converts it to the original information signal; and the *audio section* simply amplifies the recovered information.

RECEIVER PARAMETERS

There are several parameters commonly used to evaluate the ability of a receiver to successfully demodulate a radio signal. The most important parameters are selectivity and sensitivity, which are often used to compare the quality of one radio receiver to another.

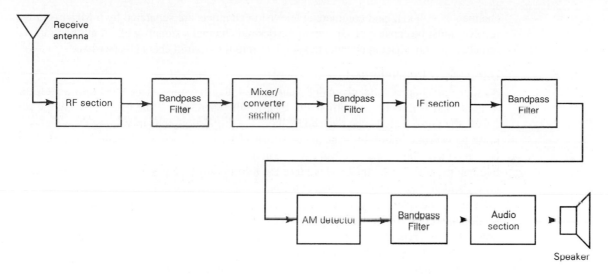

FIGURE 4-1 Simplified block diagram of an AM receiver

Selectivity

Selectivity is a receiver parameter that is used to measure the ability of the receiver to accept a given band of frequencies and reject all others. For example, with the commercial AM broadcast band, each station's transmitter is allocated a 10-kHz bandwidth. Therefore, for a receiver to select only those frequencies assigned a single channel, the receiver must limit its bandwidth to 10 kHz. If the passband is greater than 10 kHz, more than one channel may be received and demodulated simultaneously. If the passband of a receiver is less than 10 kHz, a portion of the modulating signal information for that channel is rejected or blocked from entering the demodulator and, consequently, lost.

There are several acceptable ways to describe the selectivity of a radio receiver. One common way is to simply give the bandwidth of the receiver at the −3 dB points. This bandwidth, however, is not necessarily a good means of determining how well the receiver will reject unwanted frequencies. Consequently, it is common to give the receiver bandwidth at two levels of attenuation. For example, −3 dB and −60 dB. The ratio of these two bandwidths is called the *shape factor* and is expressed mathematically as:

$$SF = \frac{B_{(-60\text{ dB})}}{B_{(-3\text{ dB})}} \tag{4-1}$$

where SF = shape factor (unitless)

    $B_{(-60\text{ dB})}$ = bandwidth 60 dB below maximum signal level

     $B_{(-3\text{ dB})}$ = bandwidth 3 dB below maximum signal level

Ideally, the bandwidth at the −3-dB and −60-dB points would be equal and the shape factor would be 1. This value, of course, is impossible to achieve in a practical circuit. A typical AM broadcast-band radio receiver might have a −3 dB bandwidth of 10 kHz and a −60-dB bandwidth of 20 kHz giving a shape factor of 2. More expensive and sophisticated satellite, microwave, and two-way radio receivers have shape factors closer to the ideal value of 1.

In today's overcrowded radio-frequency spectrum, the FCC makes adjacent channel assignments as close together as possible, with only 10-kHz separating commercial broadcast-band AM channels. Spacing for adjacent commercial broadcast-band FM channels is 200 kHz and commercial television channels are separated by 6 MHz. A radio receiver must be capable of separating the desired channel's signals without allowing interference from an adjacent channel to spill over into the desired channel's passband.

Bandwidth Improvement

As stated in Chapter 1 and given in Equation 1-24, thermal noise is the most prevalent form of noise and is directly proportional to bandwidth. Therefore, if the bandwidth can be reduced, the noise will also be reduced by the same proportion, thus increasing the signal-to-noise power ratio improving system performance. There is, of course, a system performance limitation as to how much the bandwidth can be reduced. The bottom line is that the circuit bandwidth must exceed the bandwidth of the information signal, otherwise the information power and/or the frequency content of the information signal will be reduced, effectively degrading system performance. When a signal propagates from the antenna through the RF section, mixer/converter section, and IF section, the bandwidth is reduced, thus reducing the noise. The theoretical problem is how much should the bandwidth be reduced and the practical problem is in the difficulty of constructing stable, narrow-band filters.

The input signal-to-noise ratio is calculated at a receiver input using the RF bandwidth for the noise power measurement. However, the RF bandwidth is generally wider than the bandwidth of the rest of the receiver (i.e., the IF bandwidth is narrower than the RF bandwidth for reasons that will be explained in subsequent sections of this chapter). Reducing the bandwidth is effectively equivalent to reducing (improving) the noise figure of the receiver. The noise reduction ratio achieved by reducing the bandwidth is called *bandwidth improvement* (BI) and is expressed mathematically as

$$BI = \frac{B_{RF}}{B_{IF}} \qquad (4\text{-}2)$$

where   BI = bandwidth improvement (unitless)
B_{RF} = RF bandwidth (hertz)
B_{IF} = IF bandwidth (hertz)

The corresponding reduction in the noise figure due to the reduction in bandwidth is called *noise figure improvement* and is expressed mathematically in dBas

$$NF_{improvement} = 10 \log BI \qquad (4\text{-}3)$$

Example 4-1

Determine the improvement in the noise figure for a receiver with an RF bandwidth equal to 200 kHz and an IF bandwidth equal to 10 kHz.

Solution   Bandwidth improvement is found by substituting into Equation 4-2:

$$BI = \frac{200 \text{ kHz}}{10 \text{ kHz}} = 20$$

and noise figure improvement is found by substituting into Equation 4-3:

$$NF_{improvement} = 10 \log 20 = 13 \text{ dB}$$

Sensitivity

The *sensitivity* of a receiver is the minimum RF signal level that can be detected at the input to the receiver and still produce a usable demodulated information signal. What constitutes a usable information signal is somewhat arbitrary. Generally, the signal-to-noise ratio and the power of the signal at the output of the audio section are used to determine the quality of a received signal and whether it is usable. For commercial AM broadcast band receivers, a 10-dB or more signal-to-noise ratio with 1/2 W (27 dBm) of power at the output of the audio section is considered to be usable. However, for broadband microwave receivers, a 40-dB or more signal-to-noise ratio with approximately 5 mW (7 dBm) of signal power is the minimum acceptable value. The sensitivity of a receiver is usually stated in microvolts of received signal. For example, a typical sensitivity for a commercial broadcast band AM receiver is 50 μV, and a two-way mobile radio receiver generally has a sensitivity between 0.1 μV and 10 μV. Receiver sensitivity is also called receiver *threshold*. The sensitivity of an AM receiver depends on the noise power present at the input to the receiver, the receiver's noise figure (an indication of the noise generated in the front end of the receiver), the sensitivity of the AM detector, and the bandwidth improvement factor of the receiver. The best way to improve the sensitivity of a receiver is to reduce the noise level. This can be accomplished by reducing either the temperature or the bandwidth of the receiver or improving the receiver's noise figure.

Dynamic Range

The *dynamic range* of a receiver is defined as the difference in decibels between the minimum input level necessary to discern a signal and the input level that will overdrive the receiver and produce distortion. In simple terms, dynamic range is the input power range over which the receiver is useful. The minimum receive level is a function of front-end noise, noise figure, and the desired signal quality. The input signal level that will produce overload distortion is a function of the net gain of the receiver (the total gain of all the stages in the receiver). The high-power limit of a receiver depends on whether it will operate with a single- or multiple-frequency input signal. If single-frequency operation is used, the *1-dB compression point* is generally used for the upper limit of usefulness. The 1-dB compression point is defined as the output power when the RF amplifier response is 1 dB less than the ideal linear-gain response. Figure 4-2 shows the linear gain and 1-dB compression point for a typical amplifier where the linear gain drops off just prior to saturation. The 1-dB compression point is often measured directly as the point where a 10-dB increase in input power results in a 9-dB increase in output power.

A dynamic range of 100 dB is considered about the highest possible. A low dynamic range can cause a desensitizing of the RF amplifiers and result in severe intermodulation distortion of the weaker input signals. Sensitivity measurements are discussed later in this chapter.

Fidelity

Fidelity is a measure of the ability of a communications system to produce, at the output of the receiver, an exact replica of the original source information. Any frequency, phase, or

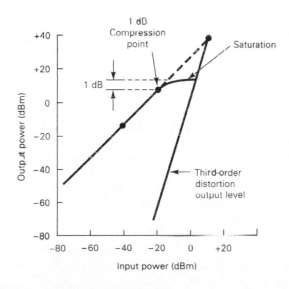

FIGURE 4-2 Linear gain, 1-dB compression point, and third-order intercept distortion for a typical amplifier

amplitude variations that are present in the demodulated waveform that were not in the original information signal are considered distortion.

Essentially, there are three forms of distortion that can deteriorate the fidelity of a communications system: *amplitude, frequency,* and *phase.* Phase distortion is not particularly important for voice transmission because the human ear is relatively insensitive to phase variations. However, phase distortion can be devastating to data transmission. The predominant cause of phase distortion is filtering (both wanted and unwanted). Frequencies at or near the break frequency of a filter undergo varying values of phase shift. Consequently, the cutoff frequency of a filter is often set beyond the minimum value necessary to pass the highest-frequency information signals (typically the upper cutoff frequency of a low-pass filter is approximately 1.3 times the minimum value). *Absolute phase shift* is the total phase shift encountered by a signal and can generally be tolerated as long as all frequencies undergo the same amount of phase delay. *Differential phase shift* occurs when different frequencies undergo different phase shifts and may have a detrimental effect on a complex waveform, especially if the information is encoded into the phase of the carrier as it is with phase shift keying modulation. If phase shift versus frequency is linear, delay is constant with frequency. If all frequencies are not delayed by the same amount of time, the frequency-versus-phase relationship of the received waveform is not consistent with the original source information and the recovered information is distorted.

Amplitude distortion occurs when the amplitude-versus-frequency characteristics of a signal at the output of a receiver differ from those of the original information signal. Amplitude distortion is the result of *nonuniform gain* in amplifiers and filters.

Frequency distortion occurs when frequencies are present in a received signal that were not present in the original source information. Frequency distortion is a result of harmonic and intermodulation distortion and is caused by nonlinear amplification. *Second-order products* ($2f_1, 2f_2, f_1 \pm f_2$, and so on) are usually only a problem in broadband systems because they generally fall outside the bandwidth of a narrowband system. However, *third-order products* often fall within the system bandwidth and produce a distortion called *third-order intercept distortion.* Third-order intercept distortion is a special case of intermodulation distortion and the predominant form of frequency distortion. Third-order intermodulation components are the cross-product frequencies produced when the second harmonic of one signal is added to the fundamental frequency of another signal (i.e., $2f_1 \pm f_2, f_1 \pm 2f_2$, and so on). Frequency distortion can be reduced by using a *square-law device,* such as a FET, in the front end of a receiver. Square-law devices have a unique advantage over BJTs in that they produce only second-order harmonic and intermodulation components. Figure 4-2 shows a typical third-order distortion characteristic as a function of amplifier input power and gain.

Insertion Loss

Insertion loss (IL) is a parameter associated with the frequencies that fall within the passband of a filter and is generally defined as the ratio of the power transferred to a load with a filter in the circuit to the power transferred to a load without the filter. Because filters are generally constructed from lossy components, such as resistors and imperfect capacitors, even signals that fall within the passband of a filter are attenuated (reduced in magnitude). Typical filter insertion losses are between a few tenths of a decibel to several decibels. In essence, insertion loss is simply the ratio of the output power of a filter to the input power for frequencies that fall within the filter's passband and is stated mathematically in decibels as

$$\text{IL}_{(\text{dB})} = 10 \log \frac{P_{\text{out}}}{P_{\text{in}}} \qquad (4\text{-}4)$$

TABLE 4-1 $[T = 17° C]$

NF (dB)	F (unitless)	T_e (°K)
0.8	1.2	58
1.17	1.31	90
1.5	1.41	119
2.0	1.58	168

Noise Temperature and Equivalent Noise Temperature

Because thermal noise is directly proportional to temperature, it stands to reason that noise can be expressed in degrees as well as watts or volts. Rearranging Equation 1-24 yields

$$T = \frac{N}{KB}$$ (4-5)

where T = environmental temperature (kelvin)
N = noise power (watts)
K = Boltzmann's constant (1.38×10^{-23} J/K)
B = bandwidth (hertz)

Equivalent noise temperature (T_e) is a hypothetical value that cannot be directly measured. T_e is a parameter that is often used in low-noise, sophisticated radio receivers rather than noise figure. T_e is an indication of the reduction in the signal-to-noise ratio as a signal propagates through a receiver. The lower the equivalent noise temperature, the better the quality of the receiver. Typical values for T_e range from 20° for *cool* receivers to 1000° for *noisy* receivers. Mathematically, T_e at the input to a receiver is expressed as

$$T_e = T(F - 1)$$ (4-6)

where T_e = equivalent noise temperature (kelvin)
T = environmental temperature (kelvin)
F = noise factor (unitless)

Table 4-1 lists several values of noise figure, noise factor, and equivalent noise temperature for an environmental temperature of 17° C (290° K).

AM RECEIVERS

There are two basic types of radio receivers: *coherent* and *noncoherent.* With a coherent or *synchronous* receiver, the frequencies generated in the receiver and used for demodulation are synchronized to oscillator frequencies generated in the transmitter (the receiver must have some means of recovering the received carrier and synchronizing to it). With noncoherent or *asynchronous* receivers, either no frequencies are generated in the receiver or the frequencies used for demodulation are completely independent from the transmitter's carrier frequency. *Noncoherent detection* is often called *envelope detection* because the information is recovered from the received waveform by detecting the shape of the modulated envelope. The receivers described in this chapter are noncoherent. Coherent receivers are described in Chapter 5.

Tuned Radio-Frequency Receiver

The *tuned radio-frequency* (TRF) *receiver* was one of the earliest types of AM receivers. TRF receivers are probably the simplest designed radio receiver available today; however, they have several shortcomings that limit their use to special applications. Figure 4-3 shows

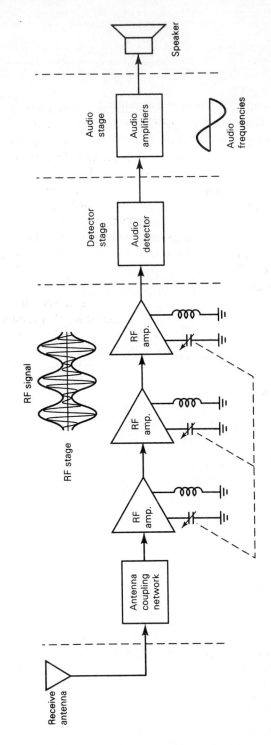

FIGURE 4-3 Noncoherent tuned radio frequency receiver block diagram

the block diagram of a three-stage TRF receiver that includes an RF stage, a detector stage, and an audio stage. Generally, two or three RF amplifiers are required to filter and amplify the received signal to a level sufficient to drive the detector stage. The detector converts RF signals directly to information, and the audio stage amplifies the information signals to a usable level.

Although TRF receivers are simple and have a relatively high sensitivity, they have three distinct disadvantages that limit their usefulness to single-channel, low-frequency applications. The primary disadvantage is their bandwidth is inconsistent and varies with center frequency when tuned over a wide range of input frequencies. This is caused by a phenomenon called the *skin effect*. At radio frequencies, current flow is limited to the outermost area of a conductor; thus, the higher the frequency, the smaller the effective area and the greater the resistance. Consequently, the *quality factor* ($Q = X_L/R$) of the tank circuits remains relatively constant over a wide range of frequencies causing the bandwidth (f/Q) to increase with frequency. As a result, the selectivity of the input filter changes over any appreciable range of input frequencies. If the bandwidth is set to the desired value for low-frequency RF signals, it will be excessive for high-frequency signals.

The second disadvantage of TRF receivers is instability due to the large number of RF amplifiers all tuned to the same center frequency. High-frequency, multistage amplifiers are susceptible to breaking into oscillations. This problem can be reduced somewhat by tuning each amplifier to a slightly different frequency, slightly above or below the desired center frequency. This technique is called *stagger tuning*. The third disadvantage of TRF receivers is their gains are not uniform over a very wide frequency range, due to the nonuniform L/C ratios of the transformer-coupled tank circuits in the RF amplifiers.

With the development of the *superheterodyne receiver*, TRF receivers are seldom used except for special-purpose, single-station receivers and therefore do not warrant further discussion.

Example 4-2

For an AM commercial broadcast-band receiver (535 kHz to 1605 kHz) with an input filter Q-factor of 54, determine the bandwidth at the low and high ends of the RF spectrum.

Solution The bandwidth at the low-frequency end of the AM spectrum is centered around a carrier frequency of 540 kHz and is

$$B = \frac{f}{Q} = \frac{540 \text{ kHz}}{54} = 10 \text{ kHz}$$

The bandwidth at the high-frequency end of the AM spectrum is centered around a carrier frequency of 1600 kHz and is

$$B = \frac{1600 \text{ kHz}}{54} = 29,630 \text{ Hz}$$

The −3-dB bandwidth at the low-frequency end of the AM spectrum is exactly 10 kHz, which is the desired value. However, the bandwidth at the high-frequency end is almost 30 kHz, which is three times the desired range. Consequently, when tuning for stations at the high end of the spectrum, three stations would be received simultaneously.

To achieve a bandwidth of 10 kHz at the high-frequency end of the spectrum, a Q of 160 is required (1600 kHz/10 kHz). With a Q of 160, the bandwidth at the low-frequency end is

$$B = \frac{540 \text{ kHz}}{160} = 3375 \text{ Hz}$$

which is obviously too selective because it would block approximately two-thirds of the information bandwidth.

Superheterodyne Receiver

The nonuniform selectivity of the TRF led to the development of the *superheterodyne receiver* near the end of World War I. Although the quality of the superheterodyne receiver

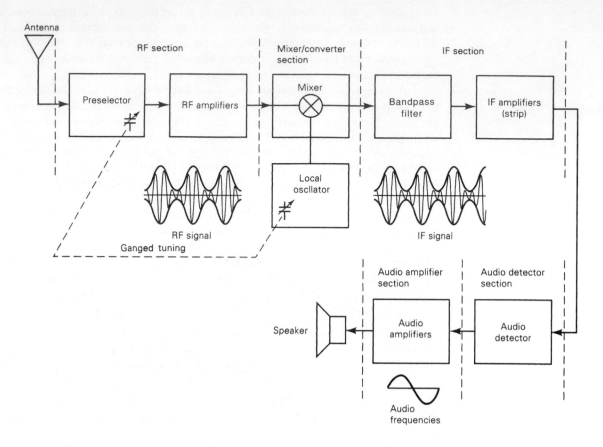

FIGURE 4-4 AM superheterodyne receiver block diagram

has improved greatly since its original design, its basic configuration has not changed much and it is still used today for a wide variety of radio communications services. The superheterodyne receiver has remained in use because its gain, selectivity, and sensitivity characteristics are superior to those of other receiver configurations.

Heterodyne means to mix two frequencies together in a nonlinear device or to translate one frequency to another using nonlinear mixing. A block diagram of a noncoherent superheterodyne receiver is shown in Figure 4-4. Essentially, there are five sections to a superheterodyne receiver: the RF section, the mixer/converter section, the IF section, the audio detector section, and the audio amplifier section.

RF section. The RF section generally consists of a preselector and an amplifier stage. They can be separate circuits or a single combined circuit. The preselector is a broad-tuned bandpass filter with an adjustable center frequency that is tuned to the desired carrier frequency. The primary purpose of the preselector is to provide enough initial bandlimiting to prevent a specific unwanted radio frequency, called the *image frequency,* from entering the receiver (image frequency is explained later in this section). The preselector also reduces the noise bandwidth of the receiver and provides the initial step toward reducing the overall receiver bandwidth to the minimum bandwidth required to pass the information signals. The RF amplifier determines the sensitivity of the receiver (i.e., sets the signal threshold). Also, because the RF amplifier is the first active device encountered by a received signal, it is the primary contributor of noise and, therefore, a predominant factor in determining the noise figure for the receiver. A receiver can have one or more RF amplifiers or it may not have any, depending on the desired sensitivity. Several advantages of including RF amplifiers in a receiver are as follows:

1. Greater gain, thus better sensitivity
2. Improved image-frequency rejection
3. Better signal-to-noise ratio
4. Better selectivity

Mixer/converter section. The mixer/converter section includes a radio-frequency oscillator stage (commonly called a *local oscillator*) and a mixer/converter stage (commonly called the *first detector*). The local oscillator can be any of the oscillator circuits discussed in Chapter 2, depending on the stability and accuracy desired. The mixer stage is a nonlinear device and its purpose is to convert radio frequencies to intermediate frequencies (RF-to-IF frequency translation). Heterodyning takes place in the mixer stage, and radio frequencies are down-converted to intermediate frequencies. Although the carrier and sideband frequencies are translated from RF to IF, the shape of the envelope remains the same and, therefore, the original information contained in the envelope remains unchanged. It is important to note that, although the carrier and upper and lower side frequencies change frequency, the bandwidth is unchanged by the heterodyning process. The most common intermediate frequency used in AM broadcast-band receivers is 455 kHz.

IF section. The IF section consists of a series of IF amplifiers and bandpass filters and is often called the *IF strip*. Most of the receiver gain and selectivity is achieved in the IF section. The IF center frequency and bandwidth are constant for all stations and are chosen so that their frequency is less than any of the RF signals to be received. The IF is always lower in frequency than the RF because it is easier and less expensive to construct high-gain, stable amplifiers for the low-frequency signals. Also, low-frequency IF amplifiers are less likely to oscillate than their RF counterparts. Therefore, it is not uncommon to see a receiver with five or six IF amplifiers and a single RF amplifier or possibly no RF amplification.

Detector section. The purpose of the detector section is to convert the IF signals back to the original source information. The detector is generally called an *audio detector* or the *second detector* in a broadcast-band receiver because the information signals are audio frequencies. The detector can be as simple as a single diode or as complex as a phase-locked loop or balanced demodulator.

Audio amplifier section. The audio section comprises several cascaded audio amplifiers and one or more speakers. The number of amplifiers used depends on the audio signal power desired.

Receiver operation. During the demodulation process in a superheterodyne receiver, the received signals undergo two or more frequency translations: First, the RF is converted to IF; then the IF is converted to the source information. The terms RF and IF are system dependent and are often misleading because they do not necessarily indicate a specific range of frequencies. For example, RF for the commercial AM broadcast band are frequencies between 535 kHz and 1605 kHz, and IF signals are frequencies between 450 kHz and 460 kHz. In commercial broadcast-band FM receivers, intermediate frequencies as high as 10.7 MHz are used, which are considerably higher than AM broadcast-band RF signals. Intermediate frequencies simply refer to frequencies that are used within a transmitter or receiver that fall somewhere between the radio frequencies and the original source information frequencies.

Frequency Conversion. *Frequency conversion* in the mixer/converter stage is identical to frequency conversion in the modulator stage of a transmitter except that in the receiver the frequencies are down-converted rather than up-converted. In the mixer/converter, RF signals are combined with the local oscillator frequency in a nonlinear device. The output of the mixer contains an infinite number of harmonic and cross-product frequencies, which include the sum and difference frequencies between the desired RF carrier and local oscillator frequencies. The IF filters are tuned to the difference frequencies. The local oscillator is designed such that its frequency of oscillation is always above or below the desired RF carrier by an amount equal to the IF center frequency. Therefore, the difference between the RF and the local oscillator frequency is always equal to the IF. The adjustment for the center frequency of the preselector and the adjustment for the local oscillator frequency are *gang tuned*. Gang tuning means that the two adjustments are mechanically tied together so that a single adjustment will change the center frequency of the preselector and, at the same time, change the local oscillator frequency. When the local oscillator frequency is tuned above the RF, it is called *high-side injection* or *high-beat injection*. When the local oscillator is tuned below the RF, it is called *low-side injection* or *low-beat injection*. In AM broadcast-band receivers, high-side injection is always used (the reason for this is explained later in this section). Mathematically, the local oscillator frequency is

For high-side injection: $\qquad\qquad f_{lo} = f_{RF} + f_{IF}$ (4-7a)

For low-side injection: $\qquad\qquad f_{lo} = f_{RF} - f_{IF}$ (4-7b)

where $\quad f_{lo}$ = local oscillator frequency (hertz)
$\qquad f_{RF}$ = radio frequency (hertz)
$\qquad f_{IF}$ = intermediate frequency (hertz)

Example 4-3

For an AM superheterodyne receiver that uses high-side injection and has a local oscillator frequency of 1355 kHz, determine the IF carrier, upper side frequency, and lower side frequency for an RF wave that is made up of a carrier and upper and lower side frequencies of 900 kHz, 905 kHz, and 895 kHz, respectively.

Solution Refer to Figure 4-5. Because high-side injection is used, the intermediate frequencies are the difference between the radio frequencies and the local oscillator frequency. Rearranging Equation 4-7a yields

$$f_{IF} = f_{lo} - f_{RF} = 1355 \text{ kHz} - 900 \text{ kHz} = 455 \text{ kHz}$$

The upper and lower intermediate frequencies are

$$f_{IF(usf)} = f_{lo} - f_{RF(lsf)} = 1355 \text{ kHz} - 895 \text{ kHz} = 460 \text{ kHz}$$
$$f_{IF(lsf)} = f_{lo} - f_{RF(usf)} = 1355 \text{ kHz} - 905 \text{ kHz} = 450 \text{ kHz}$$

Note that the side frequencies undergo a sideband reversal during the heterodyning process (i.e., the RF upper side frequency is translated to an IF lower side frequency, and the RF lower side frequency is translated to an IF upper side frequency). This is commonly called *sideband inversion*. Sideband inversion is not detrimental to conventional double-sideband AM because exactly the same information is contained in both sidebands.

Local Oscillator Tracking. *Tracking* is the ability of the local oscillator in a receiver to oscillate either above or below the selected radio frequency carrier by an amount equal to the intermediate frequency throughout the entire radio frequency band. With high-side injection, the local oscillator should track above the incoming RF carrier by a fixed frequency equal to $f_{RF} + f_{IF}$, and with low-side injection, the local oscillator should track below the RF carrier by a fixed frequency equal to $f_{RF} - f_{IF}$.

Figure 4-6a shows the schematic diagram of the preselector and local oscillator tuned circuit in a broadcast-band AM receiver. The broken lines connecting the two tuning capacitors indicate that they are *ganged* together (connected to a single tuning control). The tuned circuit in the preselector is tunable from a center frequency of 540 kHz to 1600 kHz

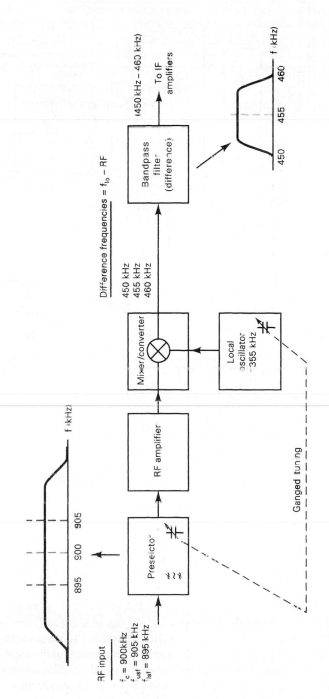

FIGURE 4-5 Figure for Example 4-3

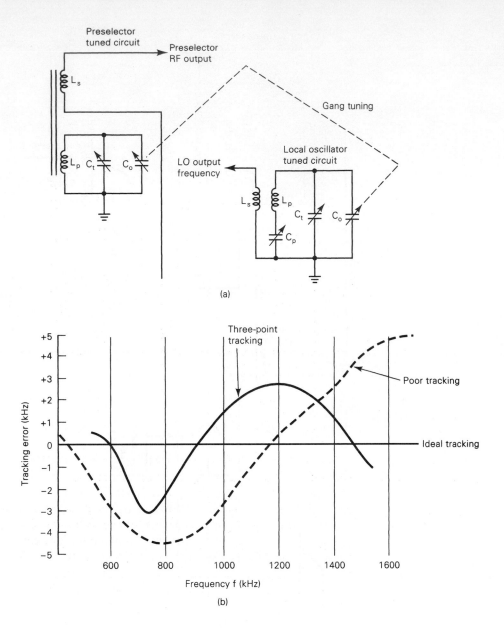

FIGURE 4-6 Receiver tracking: (a) preselector and local oscillator schematic; (b) tracking curve

(a ratio of 2.96 to 1), and the local oscillator is tunable from 995 kHz to 2055 kHz (a ratio of 2.06 to 1). Because the resonant frequency of a tuned circuit is inversely proportional to the square root of the capacitance, the capacitance in the preselector must change by a factor of 8.8, whereas, at the same time, the capacitance in the local oscillator must change by a factor of only 4.26. The local oscillator should oscillate 455 kHz above the preselector center frequency over the entire AM frequency band, and there should be a single tuning control. Fabricating such a circuit is difficult if not impossible. Therefore, perfect tracking over the entire AM band is unlikely to occur. The difference between the actual local oscillator frequency and the desired frequency is called *tracking error*. Typically, the tracking error is not uniform over the entire RF spectrum. A maximum tracking error of ±3 kHz is about the best that can be expected from a domestic AM broadcast-band receiver with a

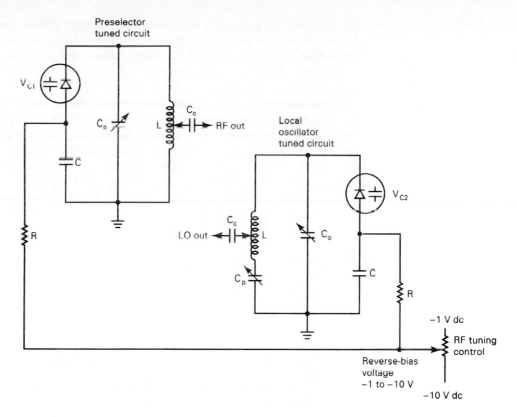

FIGURE 4-7 Electronic tuning

455-kHz intermediate frequency. Figure 4-6b shows a typical tracking curve. A tracking error of +3 kHz corresponds to an IF center frequency of 458 kHz, and a tracking error of −3 kHz corresponds to an IF center frequency of 452 kHz.

The tracking error is reduced by a technique called *three-point tracking*. The preselector and local oscillator each have a trimmer capacitor (C_t) in parallel with the primary tuning capacitor (C_o) that compensates for minor tracking errors at the high end of the AM spectrum. The local oscillator has an additional padder capacitor (C_p) in series with the tuning coil that compensates for minor tracking errors at the low end of the AM spectrum. With three-point tracking, the tracking error is adjusted to 0 Hz at approximately 600 kHz, 950 kHz, and 1500 kHz.

With low-side injection, the local oscillator would have to be tunable from 85 kHz to 1145 kHz (a ratio of 13.5 to 1). Consequently, the capacitance must change by a factor of 182. Standard variable capacitors seldom tune over more than a 10 to 1 range. This is why low-side injection is impractical for commercial AM broadcast-band receivers. With high-side injection, the local oscillator must be tunable from 995 kHz to 2055 kHz, which corresponds to a capacitance ratio of only 4.63 to 1.

Ganged capacitors are relatively large, expensive, and inaccurate, and they are somewhat difficult to compensate. Consequently, they are being replaced by solid-state electronically tuned circuits. Electronically tuned circuits are smaller, less expensive, more accurate, relatively immune to environmental changes, more easily compensated, and more easily adapted to digital remote control and push-button tuning than their mechanical counterparts. As with the crystal oscillator modules explained in Chapter 2, electronically tuned circuits use solid-state variable-capacitance diodes (varactor diodes). Figure 4-7 shows a schematic diagram for an electronically tuned preselector and local oscillator. The −1-V to −10-V reverse-biased voltage comes from a single tuning control. By changing the position of the wiper arm on a precision variable resistor, the dc reverse bias for the two tuning diodes (V_{C1} and V_{C2}) is changed. The diode capacitance and, consequently, the resonant frequency of the tuned circuit vary with the reverse bias. Three-point compensation with electronic tuning is accomplished the same as with mechanical tuning.

In a superheterodyne receiver, most of the receiver's selectivity is accomplished in the IF stage. For maximum noise reduction, the bandwidth of the IF filters is equal to the minimum bandwidth required to pass the information signal, which with double-sideband transmission is equal to two times the highest modulating signal frequency. For a maximum modulating signal frequency of 5 kHz, the minimum IF bandwidth with perfect tracking is 10 kHz. For a 455-kHz IF center frequency, a 450-kHz to 460-kHz passband is necessary. In reality, however, some RF carriers are tracked as much as ±3 kHz above or below 455 kHz. Therefore, the RF bandwidth must be expanded to allow the IF signals from the off-track stations to pass through the IF filters.

Example 4-4

For the tracking curve shown in Figure 4-8a, a 455-kHz IF center frequency, and a maximum modulating signal frequency of 5 kHz, determine the minimum IF bandwidth.

Solution A double-sideband AM signal with a maximum modulating signal frequency of 5 kHz would require 10 kHz of bandwidth. Thus, a receiver with a 455-kHz IF center frequency and ideal tracking would produce IF signals between 450 kHz and 460 kHz. The tracking curve shown in Figure 4-8a is for a receiver where perfect tracking occurs only for RF carrier frequencies of 600 kHz and 1000 kHz. The ideal IF passband is shown in Figure 4-8b.

The tracking curve in Figure 4-8a also shows that the maximum positive tracking error of −3 kHz occurs for a RF carrier frequency of 800 kHz and the maximum negative tracking error of +3

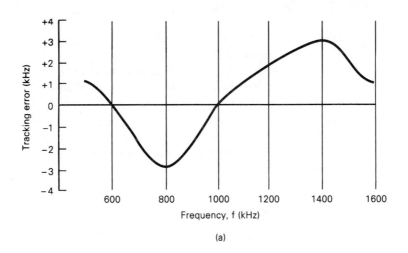

(a)

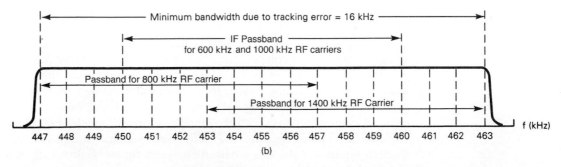

(b)

FIGURE 4-8 Tracking error for Example 4-4: (a) tracking curve; (b) bandpass characteristics

kHz occurs for a RF carrier frequency of 1400 kHz. Consequently, as shown in Figure 4-8b, the IF frequency spectrum produced for an 800-kHz carrier would extend from 447 kHz to 457 kHz and the IF frequency spectrum produced for a 1400-kHz carrier would extend from 453 kHz to 463 kHz.

Thus, the maximum intermediate frequency occurs for the RF carrier with the most positive tracking error (1400 kHz) and a 5-kHz modulating signal.

$$f_{\text{IF(max)}} = f_{\text{IF}} + \text{tracking error} + f_{m(\text{max})}$$
$$= 455 \text{ kHz} + 3 \text{ kHz} + 5 \text{ kHz} = 463 \text{ kHz}$$

The minimum intermediate frequency occurs for the RF carrier with the most negative tracking error (800 kHz) and a 5-kHz modulating signal.

$$f_{\text{IF(min)}} = f_{\text{IF}} + \text{tracking error} - f_{m(\text{max})}$$
$$= 455 \text{ kHz} + (-3 \text{ kHz}) - 5 \text{ kHz} = 447 \text{ kHz}$$

The minimum IF bandwidth necessary to pass the two sidebands is the difference between the maximum and minimum intermediate frequencies or

$$B_{\text{min}} = 463 \text{ kHz} - 447 \text{ kHz} = 16 \text{ kHz}$$

Figure 4-8b shows the IF bandpass characteristics for Example 4-4.

Image Frequency. An *image frequency* is any frequency other than the selected radio frequency carrier that, if allowed to enter a receiver and mix with the local oscillator, will produce a cross-product frequency that is equal to the intermediate frequency. An image frequency is equivalent to a second radio frequency that will produce an IF that will interfere with the IF from the desired radio frequency. Once an image frequency has been mixed down to IF, it cannot be filtered out or suppressed. If the selected RF carrier and its image frequency enter a receiver at the same time, they both mix with the local oscillator frequency and produce difference frequencies that are equal to the IF. Consequently, two different stations are received and demodulated simultaneously, producing two sets of information frequencies. For a radio frequency to produce a cross product equal to the IF, it must be displaced from the local oscillator frequency by a value equal to the IF. With high-side injection, the selected RF is below the local oscillator by an amount equal to the IF. Therefore, the image frequency is the radio frequency that is located in the IF frequency above the local oscillator. Mathematically, for high-side injection, the image frequency (f_{im}) is

$$f_{\text{im}} = f_{\text{lo}} + f_{\text{IF}} \tag{4-8a}$$

and, because the desired RF equals the local oscillator frequency minus the IF,

$$f_{\text{im}} = f_{\text{RF}} + 2f_{\text{IF}} \tag{4-8b}$$

Figure 4-9 shows the relative frequency spectrum for the RF, IF, local oscillator, and image frequencies for a superheterodyne receiver using high-side injection. Here we see that the higher the IF, the farther away in the frequency spectrum the image frequency is from the desired RF. Therefore, for better *image-frequency rejection,* a high intermediate frequency is preferred. However, the higher the IF, the more difficult it is to build stable

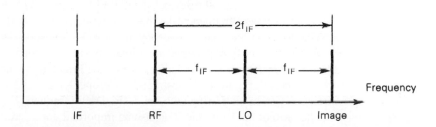

FIGURE 4-9 Image frequency

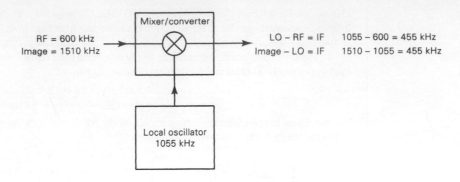

FIGURE 4-10 Frequency conversion for Example 4-5

amplifiers with high gain. Therefore, there is a trade-off when selecting the IF for a radio receiver between image-frequency rejection and IF gain and stability.

Image-Frequency Rejection Ratio. The *image-frequency rejection ratio* (IFRR) is a numerical measure of the ability of a preselector to reject the image frequency. For a single-tuned preselector, the ratio of its gain at the desired RF to the gain at the image frequency is the IFRR. Mathematically, IFRR is

$$\text{IFRR} = \sqrt{(1 + Q^2\rho^2)} \qquad (4\text{-}9a)$$

where $\rho = (f_{im}/f_{RF}) - (f_{RF}/f_{im})$.

$$\text{IFRR}_{(dB)} = 20 \log \text{IFRR} \qquad (4\text{-}9b)$$

If there is more than one tuned circuit in the front end of a receiver (perhaps a preselector filter and a separately tuned RF amplifier), the total IFRR is simply the product of the two ratios.

Example 4-5

For an AM broadcast-band superheterodyne receiver with IF, RF, and local oscillator frequencies of 455 kHz, 600 kHz, and 1055 kHz, respectively, refer to Figure 4-10 and determine
(a) Image frequency.
(b) IFRR for a preselector Q of 100.

Solution (a) From Equation 4-8a,

$$f_{im} = 1055 \text{ kHz} + 455 \text{ kHz} = 1510 \text{ kHz}$$

or from Equation 4-8b

$$f_{im} = 600 \text{ kHz} + 2(455 \text{ kHz}) = 1510 \text{ kHz}$$

(b) From Equations 4-9a and 4-9b,

$$\rho = \frac{1510 \text{ kHz}}{600 \text{ kHz}} - \frac{600 \text{ kHz}}{1510 \text{ kHz}} = 2.51 - 0.397 = 2.113$$

$$\text{IFRR} = \sqrt{1 + (100^2)(2.113^2)} = 212.15 \text{ or } 23.25 \text{ dB}$$

Once an image frequency has been down-converted to IF, it cannot be removed. Therefore, to reject the image frequency, it has to be blocked prior to the mixer/converter stage. Image-frequency rejection is the primary purpose for the RF preselector. If the bandwidth of the preselector is sufficiently narrow, the image frequency is prevented from entering the receiver. Figure 4-11 illustrates how proper RF and IF filtering can prevent an image frequency from interfering with the desired radio frequency.

The ratio of the RF to the IF is also an important consideration for image-frequency rejection. The closer the RF is to the IF, the closer the RF is to the image frequency.

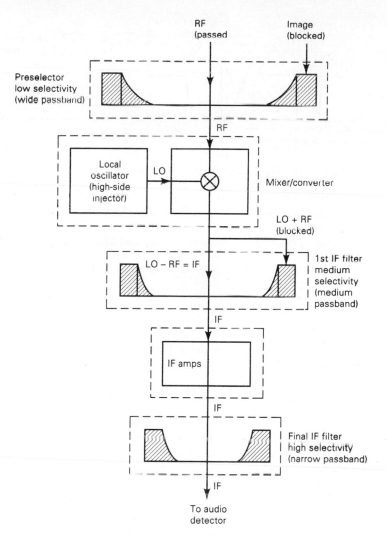

RF
(passed

Image
(blocked)

Preselector
low selectivity
(wide passband)

RF

Local
oscillator
(high-side
injector)

LO

Mixer/converter

LO + RF
(blocked)

LO – RF = IF

1st IF filter
medium
selectivity
(medium
passband)

IF

IF amps

IF

Final IF filter
high selectivity
(narrow passband)

IF

To audio
detector

FIGURE 4-11   Image-frequency rejection

Example 4-6

For a citizens band receiver using high-side injection with an RF carrier of 27 MHz and an IF center frequency of 455 kHz, determine

(a) Local oscillator frequency.
(b) Image frequency.
(c) IFRR for a preselector Q of 100.
(d) Preselector Q required to achieve the same IFRR as that achieved for an RF carrier of 600 kHz in Example 4-5.

Solution   (a) From Equation 4-7a,

$$f_{lo} = 27 \text{ MHz} + 455 \text{ kHz} = 27.455 \text{ MHz}$$

(b) From Equation 4-8a,

$$f_{im} = 27.455 \text{ MHz} + 455 \text{ kHz} = 27.91 \text{ MHz}$$

(c) From Equations 4-9a and 4-9b,

$$\text{IFRR} = 6.7 \text{ or } 16.5 \text{ dB}$$

(d) Rearranging Equation 4-9a,

$$Q = \frac{\sqrt{(\text{IFRR}^2 - 1)}}{\rho} = 3536$$

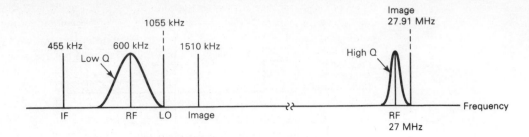

FIGURE 4-12 Frequency spectrum for Example 4-6

From Examples 4-5 and 4-6, it can be seen that the higher the RF carrier, the more difficult it is to prevent the image frequency from entering the receiver. For the same IFRR, the higher RF carriers require a much higher-quality preselector filter. This is illustrated in Figure 4-12.

From Examples 4-5 and 4-6, it can be seen that for a 455-kHz IF it is more difficult to prevent the image frequency from entering the receiver with high RF carrier frequencies than with low RF carrier frequencies. For the same IFRR, the higher RF carriers require a much more higher-quality preselector—in fact, in many cases unrealistic or unachievable values of Q. A simpler solution to the problem is to use higher IF frequencies when receiving higher RF carrier frequencies. For example, if a 5-MHz IF were used for the citizens band receiver in Example 4-6, the image frequency would be 37 MHz, which is sufficiently far away from the 27-MHz carrier to allow a preselector with a realistic Q to easily prevent the image frequency from entering the receiver.

Double Spotting. *Double spotting* occurs when a receiver picks up the same station at two nearby points on the receiver tuning dial. One point is the desired location and the other point is called the *spurious point*. Double spotting is caused by poor front-end selectivity or inadequate image-frequency rejection.

Double spotting is harmful because weak stations can be overshadowed by the reception of a nearby strong station at the spurious location in the frequency spectrum. Double spotting may be used to determine the intermediate frequency of an unknown receiver because the spurious point on the dial is precisely two times the IF center frequency below the correct receive frequency.

AM RECEIVER CIRCUITS

RF Amplifier Circuits

An RF amplifier is a high-gain, low-noise, tuned amplifier that, when used, is the first active stage encountered by the received signal. The primary purposes of an RF stage are selectivity, amplification, and sensitivity. Therefore, the following characteristics are desirable for RF amplifiers:

1. Low thermal noise
2. Low noise figure
3. Moderate to high gain
4. Low intermodulation and harmonic distortion (i.e., linear operation)
5. Moderate selectivity
6. High image-frequency rejection ratio

Two of the most important parameters for a receiver are amplification and noise figure, which both depend on the RF stage. An AM demodulator (or detector as it is sometimes called) detects amplitude variations in the modulated wave and converts them to amplitude changes in its output. Consequently, amplitude variations that were caused by noise are converted to erroneous fluctuations in the demodulator output, and the quality of the demodulated signal is degraded. The more gain that a signal experiences as it passes through a receiver, the more pronounced are the amplitude variations at the demodulator input, and the less noticeable are the variations caused by noise. The narrower the bandwidth is, the less noise propagated through the receiver and, consequently, the less noise demodulated by the detector. From Equation 1-28 ($V_N = \sqrt{4RKTB}$), noise voltage is directly proportional to the square root of the temperature, bandwidth, and equivalent noise resistance. Therefore, if these three parameters are minimized, the thermal noise is reduced. The temperature of an RF stage can be reduced by artificially cooling the front end of the receiver with air fans or even liquid helium in the more expensive receivers. The bandwidth is reduced by using tuned amplifiers and filters, and the equivalent noise resistance is reduced by using specially constructed solid-state components for the active devices. Noise figure is essentially a measure of the noise added by an amplifier. Therefore, the noise figure is improved (reduced) by reducing the amplifier's internal noise.

Intermodulation and harmonic distortion are both forms of nonlinear distortion that increase the magnitude of the noise figure by adding correlated noise to the total noise spectrum. The more linear an amplifier's operation is, the less nonlinear distortion produced, and the better the receiver's noise figure. The image-frequency reduction by the RF amplifier combines with the image-frequency reduction of the preselector to reduce the receiver input bandwidth sufficiently to help prevent the image frequency from entering the mixer/converter stage. Consequently, moderate selectivity is all that is required from the RF stage.

Figure 4-13 shows several commonly used RF amplifier circuits. Keep in mind that RF is a relative term and simply means that the frequency is high enough to be efficiently radiated by an antenna and propagated through free space as an electromagnetic wave. RF for the AM broadcast band is between 535 kHz and 1605 kHz, whereas RF for microwave radio is in excess of 1 GHz (1000 MHz). A common intermediate frequency used for FM broadcast-band receivers is 10.7 MHz, which is considerably higher than the radio frequencies associated with the AM broadcast band. RF is simply the radiated or received signal, and IF is an intermediate signal within a transmitter or receiver. Therefore, many of the considerations for RF amplifiers also apply to IF amplifiers, such as neutralization, filtering, and coupling.

Figure 4-13a shows a schematic diagram for a bipolar transistor RF amplifier. C_a, C_b, C_c, and L_1 form the coupling circuit from the antenna. Q_1 is class A biased to reduce nonlinear distortion. The collector circuit is transformer coupled to the mixer/converter through T_1, which is double tuned for more selectivity. C_x and C_y are RF bypass capacitors. Their symbols indicate that they are specially constructed *feedthrough* capacitors. Feedthrough capacitors offer less inductance, which prevents a portion of the signal from radiating from their leads. C_n is a *neutralization* capacitor. A portion of the collector signal is fed back to the base circuit to offset (or neutralize) the signal fed back through the transistor collector to base lead capacitance to prevent oscillations from occurring. C_f, in conjunction with C_n, form an ac voltage divider for the feedback signal. This neutralization configuration is called *off-ground* neutralization.

Figure 4-13b shows an RF amplifier using dual-gate field-effect transistors. This configuration uses DEMOS (depletion-enhancement metal-oxide semiconductor) FETs. The FETs feature high input impedance and low noise. A FET is a square-law device that generates only second-order harmonic and intermodulation distortion components, therefore producing less nonlinear distortion than a bipolar transistor. Q_1 is again biased class A for linear operation. T_1 is single tuned to the desired RF carrier frequency to enhance the receiver's selectivity and to improve the IFRR. L_5 is a radio frequency choke and, in conjunction with C_5, decouples RF signals from the dc power supply.

Figure 4-13c shows the schematic diagram for a special RF amplifier configuration called a *cascoded* amplifier. A cascoded amplifier offers higher gain and less noise than conventional cascaded amplifiers. The active devices can be either bipolar transistors or

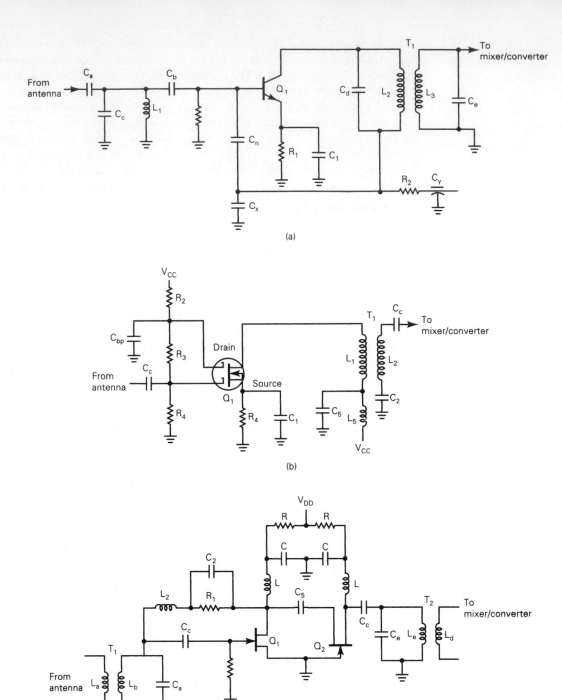

FIGURE 4-13 RF amplifier configurations: (a) bipolar transistor RF amplifier; (b) DEMOS-FET RF amplifier; (c) cascoded RF amplifier

FETs. Q_1 is a common-source amplifier whose output is impedance coupled to the source of Q_2. Because of the low input impedance of Q_2, Q_1 does not need to be neutralized; however, neutralization reduces the noise figure even further. Therefore, L_2, R_1, and C_2 provide the feedback path for neutralization. Q_2 is a common-gate amplifier and because of its low input impedance requires no neutralization.

Low-Noise Amplifiers

High-performance microwave receivers require a *low-noise amplifier* (LNA) as the input stage of the RF section to optimize their noise figure. Equation 1-38 showed that the first amplifier in a receiver is the most important in determining the receiver's noise figure. The first stage should have low noise and high gain. Unfortunately, this is difficult to achieve with a single amplifier stage; therefore, LNAs generally include two stages of amplification along with impedance-matching networks to enhance their performance. The first stage has moderate gain and minimum noise, and the second stage has high gain and moderate noise.

Low-noise RF amplifiers are biased class A and usually utilize silicon bipolar or field-effect transistors up to approximately 2 GHz and gallium arsenide FETs above this frequency. A special type of gallium arsenide FET most often used is the MESFET (MEsa Semiconductor FET). A MESFET is a FET with a metal–semiconductor junction at the gate of the device, called a Schottky barrier. Low noise amplifiers are discussed in more detail in a later chapter of this book.

Integrated-circuit RF amplifiers. The NE/SA5200 (Figure 4-14) is a wideband, unconditionally stable, low-power, dual-gain linear integrated-circuit RF amplifier manufactured by Signetics Corporation. The NE/SA5200 will operate from dc to approximately 1200 MHz and has a low noise figure. The NE/SA5200 has several inherent advantages over comparable discrete implementations; it needs no external biasing components, it occupies little space on a printed circuit board, and the high level of integration improves its reliability over discrete counterparts. The NE/SA5200 is also equipped with a power-down mode that helps reduce power consumption in applications where the amplifiers can be disabled.

The block diagram for the SA5200 is shown in Figure 4-14a, and a simplified schematic diagram is shown in Figure 4-14b. Note that the two wideband amplifiers are biased from the same bias generator. Each amplifier stage has a noise figure of about 3.6 dB and a gain of approximately 11 dB. Several stages of NE/SA5200 can be cascaded and used as an IF strip, and the enable pin can be used to improve the dynamic range of the receiver. For extremely high input levels, the amplifiers in the NE/SA5200 can be disabled. When disabled, the input signal is attenuated 13 dB, preventing receiver overload.

Mixer/Converter Circuits

The purpose of the mixer/converter stage is to down-convert the incoming radio frequencies to intermediate frequencies. This is accomplished by mixing the RF signals with the local oscillator frequency in a nonlinear device. In essence, this is heterodyning. A mixer is a nonlinear amplifier similar to a modulator, except that the output is tuned to the difference between the RF and local oscillator frequencies. Figure 4-15 shows a block diagram for a mixer/converter stage. The output of a balanced mixer is the product of the RF and local oscillator frequencies and is expressed mathematically as

$$V_{out} = (\sin 2\pi f_{RF} t)(\sin 2\pi f_{lo} t)$$

where
f_{RF} = incoming radio frequency (hertz)
f_{lo} = local oscillator frequency (hertz)

Therefore, using the trigonometric identity for the product of two sines, the output of a mixer is

$$V_{out} = \frac{1}{2} \cos[2\pi (f_{RF} - f_{lo})t] - \frac{1}{2} \cos[2\pi (f_{RF} + f_{lo})t]$$

The absolute value of the difference frequency ($|f_{RF} - f_{lo}|$) is the intermediate frequency.

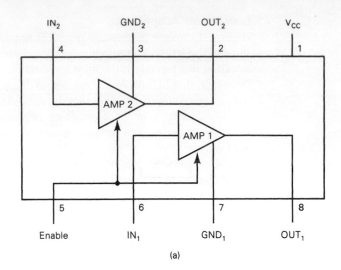

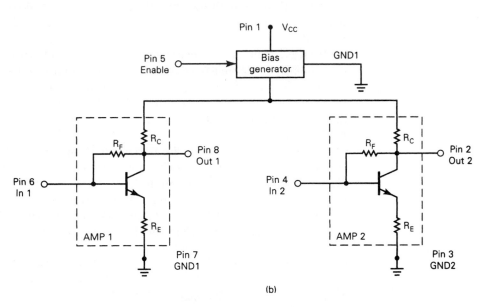

FIGURE 4-14 NE/SA5200 RF dual-gain stage: (a) block diagram; (b) simplified schematic diagram

Although any nonlinear device can be used for a mixer, a transistor or FET is generally preferred over a simple diode because it is also capable of amplification. However, because the actual output signal from a mixer is a cross-product frequency, there is a net loss to the signal. This loss is called *conversion loss* (or sometimes *conversion gain*) because a frequency conversion has occurred and, at the same time, the IF output signal is lower in amplitude than the RF input signal. The conversion loss is generally 6 dB (which corresponds to a conversion gain of -6 dB). The conversion gain is the difference between the level of the IF output with a RF input signal to the level of the IF output with an IF input signal.

Figure 4-16 shows the schematic diagrams for several common mixer/converter circuits. Figure 4-16a shows what is probably the simplest mixer circuit available (other than a single diode mixer) and is used exclusively for inexpensive AM broadcast-band receivers. Radio frequency signals from the antenna are filtered by the preselector tuned circuit (L_1 and C_1) and then transformer coupled to the base of Q_1. The active device for the mixer (Q_1)

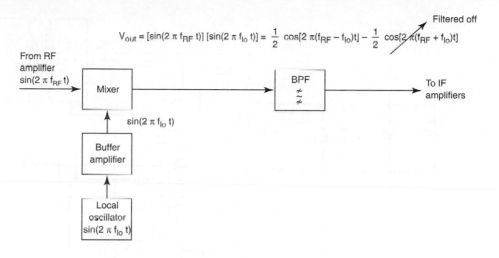

$$V_{out} = [\sin(2\,\pi\,f_{RF}\,t)]\,[\sin(2\,\pi\,f_{lo}\,t)] = \frac{1}{2}\,\cos[2\,\pi(f_{RF} - f_{lo})t] - \frac{1}{2}\,\cos[2\,\pi(f_{RF} + f_{lo})t]$$

FIGURE 4-15 Mixer/converter block diagram

also provides amplification for the local oscillator. This configuration is commonly called a *self-excited* mixer because the mixer excites itself by feeding energy back to the local oscillator tank circuit (C_2 and L_2) to sustain oscillations. When power is initially applied, Q_1 amplifies both the incoming RF signals and any noise present and supplies the oscillator tank circuit with enough energy to begin oscillator action. The local oscillator frequency is the resonant frequency of the tank circuit. A portion of the resonant tank-circuit energy is coupled through L_2 and L_5 to the emitter of Q_1. This signal drives Q_1 into its nonlinear operating region and, consequently, produces sum and difference frequencies at its collector. The difference frequency is the IF. The output tank circuit (L_3 and C_3) is tuned to the IF band. Therefore, the IF signal is transformer coupled to the input of the first IF amplifier. The process is regenerative as long as there is an incoming RF signal. The tuning capacitors in the RF and local oscillator tank circuits are ganged into a single tuning control. C_p and C_t are for three-point tracking. This configuration has poor selectivity and poor image-frequency rejection because there is no amplifier tuned to the RF signal frequency and, consequently, the only RF selectivity is in the preselector. In addition, there is essentially no RF gain, and the transistor nonlinearities produce harmonic and intermodulation components that may fall within the IF passband.

The mixer/converter circuit shown in Figure 4-16b is a *separately excited* mixer. Its operation is essentially the same as the self-excited mixer except that the local oscillator and the mixer have their own gain devices. The mixer itself is a FET, which has nonlinear characteristics that are better suited for IF conversion than those of a bipolar transistor. Feedback is from L_2 to L_3 of the transformer in the source of Q_1. This circuit is commonly used for high-frequency (HF) and very-high-frequency (VHF) receivers.

The mixer converter circuit shown in Figure 4-16c is a *single-diode* mixer. The concept is quite simple: the RF and local oscillator signals are coupled into the diode, which is a nonlinear device. Therefore, nonlinear mixing occurs and the sum and difference frequencies are produced. The output tank circuit (C_3 and L_3) is tuned to the difference (IF) frequency. A single-diode mixer is inefficient because it has a net loss. However, a diode mixer is commonly used for the audio detector in AM receivers and to produce the audio subcarrier in television receivers.

Figure 4-16d shows the schematic diagram for a *balanced diode* mixer. Balanced mixers are one of the most important circuits used in communications systems today. Balanced mixers are also called *balanced modulators, product modulators,* and *product*

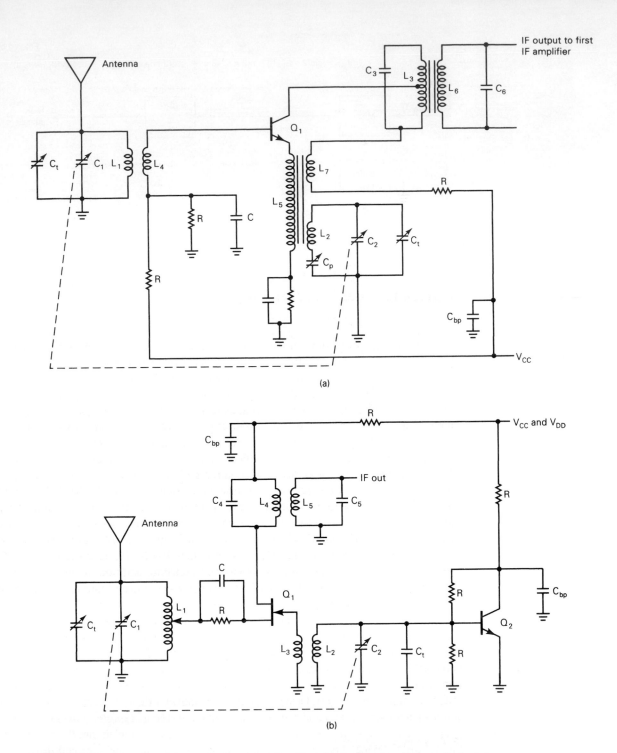

FIGURE 4-16 Mixer/converter circuits: (a) self-excited mixer; (b) separately excited mixer;
(*Continued*)

detectors. The phase detectors used in phase-locked loops and explained in Chapter 2 are balanced modulators. Balanced mixers are used extensively in both transmitters and receivers for AM, FM, and many of the digital modulation schemes, such as PSK and QAM. Balanced mixers have two inherent advantages over other types of mixers: noise reduction and carrier suppression.

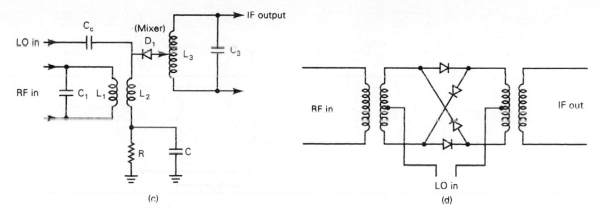

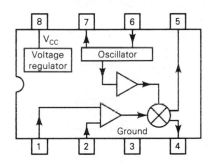

FIGURE 4-16 (*Continued*) (c) diode mixer; (d) balanced diode mixer

FIGURE 4-17 NE/SA602A double-balanced mixer and oscillator block diagram

Integrated-circuit mixer/oscillator. Figure 4-17 shows the block diagram for the Signetics NE/SA602A *double-balanced mixer and oscillator.* The NE/SA602A is a low-power VHF monolithic double-balanced mixer with input amplifier, on-board oscillator, and voltage regulator. It is intended to be used for high-performance, low-power communications systems; it is particularly well suited for *cellular radio* applications. The mixer is a *Gilbert cell* multiplier configuration, which typically provides 18 dB of gain at 45 MHz. A Gilbert cell is a differential amplifier that drives a balanced switching cell. The differential input stage provides gain and determines the noise figure and signal-handling performance of the system. The oscillator will operate up to 200 MHz and can be configured as a crystal or tuned LC tank-circuit oscillator of a buffer amplifier for an external oscillator. The noise figure for the NE/SA602A at 45 MHz is typically less than 5 dB. The gain, third-order intercept perform-ance, and low-power and noise characteristics make the NE/SA602A a superior choice for high-performance, battery-operated equipment. The input, RF mixer output, and oscillator ports can support a variety of input configurations. The RF inputs (pins 1 and 2) are biased internally and they are symmetrical. Figure 4-18 shows three typical input configurations: single-ended tuned input, balanced input, and single-ended untuned.

IF Amplifier Circuits

Intermediate frequency (IF) amplifiers are relatively high-gain tuned amplifiers that are very similar to RF amplifiers, except that IF amplifiers operate over a relatively narrow, fixed fre-quency band. Consequently, it is easy to design and build IF amplifiers that are stable, do not radiate, and are easily neutralized. Because IF amplifiers operate over a fixed frequency band, successive amplifiers can be inductively coupled with *double-tuned* circuits (with double-tuned circuits, both the primary and secondary sides of the transformer are tuned tank cir-cuits). Therefore, it is easier to achieve an optimum (low) shape factor and good selectivity.

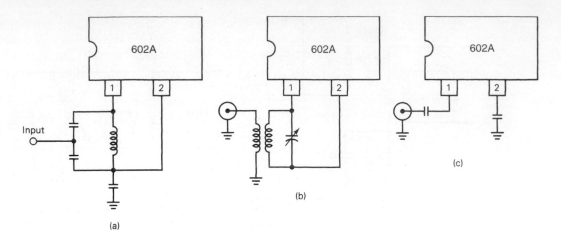

FIGURE 4-18 NE/SA602A. Typical input configurations: (a) single-ended tuned input; (b) balanced input; (c) single-ended untuned input

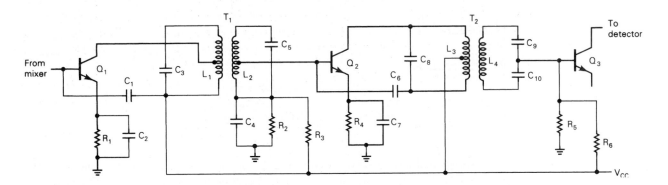

FIGURE 4-19 Three-stage IF section

Most of a receiver's gain and selectivity is achieved in the IF amplifier section. An IF stage generally has between two and five IF amplifiers. Figure 4-19 shows a schematic diagram for a three-stage IF section. T_1 and T_2 are double-tuned transformers; and L_1, L_2, and L_3 are tapped to reduce the effects of loading. The base of Q_3 is fed from the tapped capacitor pair, C_9 and C_{10}, for the same reason. C_1 and C_6 are neutralization capacitors.

Inductive coupling. *Inductive* or *transformer coupling* is the most common technique used for coupling IF amplifiers. With inductive coupling, voltage that is applied to the primary windings of a transformer is transferred to the secondary windings. The proportion of the primary voltage that is coupled across to the secondary depends on the number of turns in both the primary and secondary windings (the turns ratio), the amount of *magnetic flux* in the primary winding, the *coefficient of coupling,* and the speed at which the flux is changing (angular velocity). Mathematically, the magnitude of the voltage induced in the secondary windings is

$$E_s = \omega M I_p \qquad (4\text{-}10)$$

where E_s = voltage magnitude induced in the secondary winding (volts)
  ω = angular velocity of the primary voltage wave (radians per second)
  M = mutual inductance (henrys)
  I_p = primary current (amperes)

The ability of a coil to induce a voltage within its own windings is called *self-inductance* or simply *inductance* (L). When one coil induces a voltage through *magnetic induction* into another coil, the two coils are said to be *coupled* together. The ability of one coil to induce a voltage in another coil is called *mutual inductance* (M). Mutual inductance in a transformer is caused by the *magnetic lines of force (flux)* that are produced in the primary windings and cut through the secondary windings and is directly proportional to the coefficient of coupling. Coefficient of coupling is the ratio of the secondary flux to the primary flux and is expressed mathematically as

$$k = \frac{\phi_s}{\phi_p}$$

(4-11)

where k = coefficient of coupling (unitless)
ϕ_p = primary flux (webers)
ϕ_s = secondary flux (webers)

If all the flux produced in the primary windings cuts through the secondary windings, the coefficient of coupling is 1. If none of the primary flux cuts through the secondary windings, the coefficient of coupling is 0. A coefficient of coupling of 1 is nearly impossible to attain unless the two coils are wound around a common high-permeability iron core. Typically, the coefficient of coupling for standard IF transformers is much less than 1. The transfer of flux from the primary to the secondary windings is called *flux linkage* and is directly proportional to the coefficient of coupling. The mutual inductance of a transformer is directly proportional to the coefficient of coupling and the square root of the product of the primary and secondary inductances. Mathematically, mutual inductance is

$$M = k\sqrt{L_s L_p}$$

(4-12)

where M = mutual inductance (henrys)
L_s = inductance of the secondary winding (henrys)
L_p = inductance of the primary winding (henrys)
k = coefficient of coupling (unitless)

Transformer-coupled amplifiers are divided into two general categories: single and double tuned.

Single-Tuned Transformers.   Figure 4-20a shows a schematic diagram for a *single tuned inductively coupled amplifier.* This configuration is called *untuned primary–tuned secondary.* The primary side of T_1 is simply the inductance of the primary winding, whereas a capacitor is in parallel with the secondary winding, creating a tuned secondary. The transformer windings are not tapped because the loading effect of the FET is insignificant. Figure 4-20b shows the response curve for an untuned primary–tuned secondary transformer. E_s increases with frequency until the resonant frequency (f_o) of the secondary is reached; then E_s begins to decrease with further increases in frequency. The peaking of the response curve at the resonant frequency is caused by the reflected impedance. The impedance of the secondary is reflected back into the primary due to the mutual inductance between the two windings. For frequencies below resonance, the increase in ωM is greater than the decrease in I_p; therefore, E_s increases. For frequencies above resonance, the increase in ωM is less than the decrease in I_p; therefore, E_s decreases.

Figure 4-20c shows the effect of coupling on the response curve of an untuned primary–tuned secondary transformer. With *loose coupling* (low coefficient of coupling), the secondary voltage is relatively low and the bandwidth is narrow. As the degree of coupling increases (coefficient of coupling increases), the secondary induced voltage increases and the bandwidth widens. Therefore, for a high degree of selectivity, loose coupling is desired; however, signal amplitude is sacrificed. For high gain and a broad bandwidth, *tight*

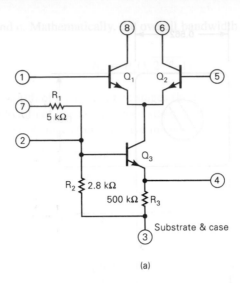

(a)

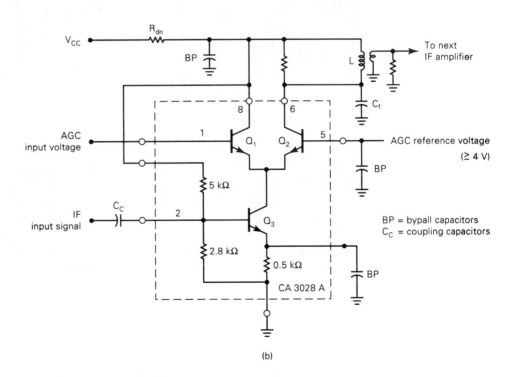

(b)

FIGURE 4-24 CA3028A linear integrated-circuit differential/cascoded amplifier: (a) schematic diagram; (b) cascoded amplifier configuration

AM Detector Circuits

The function of an AM detector is to demodulate the AM signal and recover or reproduce the original source information. The recovered signal should contain the same frequencies as the original information signal and have the same relative amplitude characteristics. The AM detector is sometimes called the *second detector*, with the mixer/converter being the first detector because it precedes the AM detector.

Peak detector. Figure 4-25a shows a schematic diagram for a simple noncoherent AM demodulator, which is commonly called a *peak detector*. Because a diode is a nonlin-

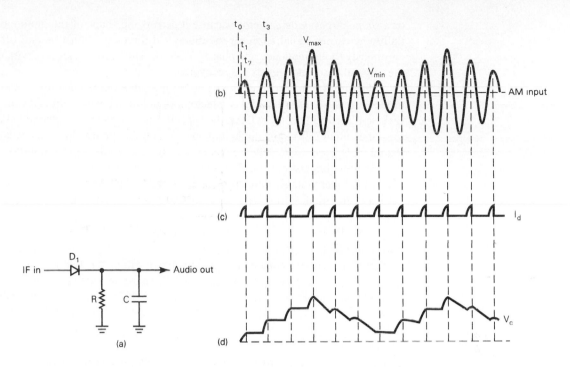

FIGURE 4-25 Peak detector: (a) schematic diagram; (b) AM input waveform; (c) diode current waveform; (d) output voltage waveform

ear device, nonlinear mixing occurs in D_1 when two or more signals are applied to its input. Therefore, the output contains the original input frequencies, their harmonics, and their cross products. If a 300-kHz carrier is amplitude modulated by a 2-kHz sine wave, the modulated wave is made up of a lower side frequency, carrier, and upper side frequency of 298 kHz, 300 kHz, and 302 kHz, respectively. If the resultant signal is the input to the AM detector shown in Figure 4-25a, the output will comprise the three input frequencies, the harmonics of all three frequencies, and the cross products of all possible combinations of the three frequencies and their harmonics. Mathematically, the output is

$$V_{\text{out}} = \text{input frequencies} + \text{harmonics} + \text{sums and differences}$$

Because the *RC* network is a low-pass filter, only the difference frequencies are passed on to the audio section. Therefore, the output is simply

$$V_{\text{out}} = 300 - 298 = 2 \text{ kHz}$$
$$= 302 - 300 = 2 \text{ kHz}$$
$$= 302 - 298 = 4 \text{ kHz}$$

Because of the relative amplitude characteristics of the upper and lower side frequencies and the carrier, the difference between the carrier frequency and either the upper or lower side frequency is the predominant output signal. Consequently, for practical purposes, the original modulating signal (2 kHz) is the only component that is contained in the output of the peak detector.

In the preceding analysis, the diode detector was analyzed as a simple mixer, which it is. Essentially, the difference between an AM modulator and an AM demodulator is that the output of a modulator is tuned to the sum frequencies (up-converter), whereas the output of a demodulator is tuned to the difference frequencies (down-converter). The demodulator circuit shown in Figure 4-25a is commonly called a *diode detector* because the nonlinear device is a diode, or a *peak detector* because it detects the peaks of the input envelope, or a *shape* or *envelope detector* because it detects the shape of the input envelope. Essentially, the carrier signal *captures* the diode and forces it to turn on and off (rectify) synchronously (both frequency and phase). Thus, the side frequencies mix with the carrier, and the original baseband signals are recovered.

Figures 4-25b, c, and d show a detector input voltage waveform, the corresponding diode current waveform, and the detector output voltage waveform. At time t_0 the diode is reverse biased and off ($i_d = 0$ A), the capacitor is completely discharged ($V_C = 0$ V), and, thus, the output is 0 V. The diode remains off until the input voltage exceeds the barrier potential of D_1 (approximately 0.3 V). When V_{in} reaches 0.3 V (t_1), the diode turns on and diode current begins to flow, charging the capacitor. The capacitor voltage remains 0.3 V below the input voltage until V_{in} reaches its peak value. When the input voltage begins to decrease, the diode turns off and i_d goes to 0 A (t_2). The capacitor begins to discharge through the resistor, but the RC time constant is made sufficiently long so that the capacitor cannot discharge as rapidly as V_{in} is decreasing. The diode remains off until the next input cycle, when V_{in} goes 0.3 V more positive than V_C (t_3). At this time the diode turns on, current flows, and the capacitor begins to charge again. It is relatively easy for the capacitor to charge to the new value because the RC charging time constant is R_dC, where R_d is the *on* resistance of the diode, which is quite small. This sequence repeats itself on each successive positive peak of V_{in}, and the capacitor voltage follows the positive peaks of V_{in} (hence, the name peak detector). The output waveform resembles the shape of the input envelope (hence, the name shape detector). The output waveform has a high-frequency ripple that is equal to the carrier frequency. This is due to the diode turning on during the positive peaks of the envelope. The ripple is easily removed by the audio amplifiers because the carrier frequency is much higher than the highest modulating signal frequency. The circuit shown in Figure 4-25 responds only to the positive peaks of V_{in} and, therefore, is called a *positive peak detector.* By simply turning the diode around, the circuit becomes a negative peak detector. The output voltage reaches its peak positive amplitude at the same time that the input envelope reaches its maximum positive value (V_{max}), and the output voltage goes to its minimum peak amplitude at the same time that the input voltage goes to its minimum value (V_{min}). For 100% modulation, V_{out} swings from 0 V to a value equal to $V_{max} - 0.3$ V.

Figure 4-26 shows the input and output waveforms for a peak detector with various percentages of modulation. With no modulation, a peak detector is simply a filtered half-wave rectifier and the output voltage is approximately equal to the peak input voltage minus the 0.3 V. As the percent modulation changes, the variations in the output voltage increase and decrease proportionately; the output waveform follows the shape of the AM

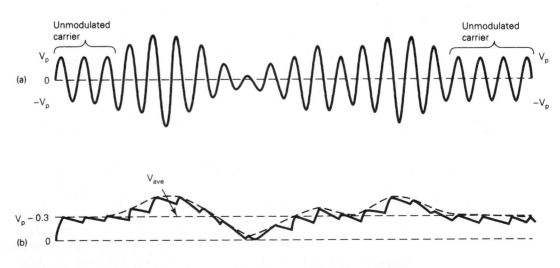

FIGURE 4-26 Positive peak detector: (a) input waveform; (b) output waveform

envelope. However, regardless of whether modulation is present, the average value of the output voltage is approximately equal to the peak value of the unmodulated carrier.

Detector distortion.   When successive positive peaks of the detector input waveform are increasing, it is important that the capacitor hold its charge between peaks (i.e., a relatively long RC time constant is necessary). However, when the positive peaks are decreasing in amplitude, it is important that the capacitor discharge between successive peaks to a value less than the next peak (a short RC time constant is necessary). Obviously, a trade-off between a long- and a short-time constant is in order. If the RC time constant is too short, the output waveform resembles a half-wave rectified signal. This is sometimes called *rectifier distortion* and is shown in Figure 4-27b. If the RC time constant is too long, the slope of the output waveform cannot follow the trailing slope of the envelope. This type of distortion is called *diagonal clipping* and is shown in Figure 4-27c.

The RC network following the diode in a peak detector is a low-pass filter. The slope of the envelope depends on both the modulating signal frequency and the modulation coefficient (m). Therefore, the maximum slope (fastest rate of change) occurs when the envelope is crossing its zero axis in the negative direction. The highest modulating signal frequency that can be demodulated by a peak detector without attenuation is given as

$$f_{m(\max)} = \frac{\sqrt{(1/m^2) - 1}}{2\pi RC} \tag{4-17a}$$

where $f_{m(\max)}$ = maximum modulating signal frequency (hertz)
m = modulation coefficient (unitless)
RC = time constant (seconds)

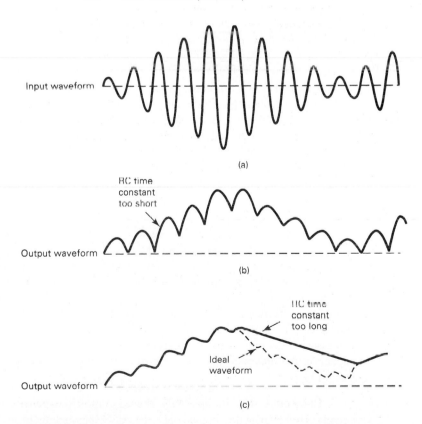

FIGURE 4-27 Detector distortion: (a) input envelope; (b) rectifier distortion; (c) diagonal clipping

For 100% modulation, the numerator in Equation 4-17a goes to zero, which essentially means that all modulating signal frequencies are attenuated as they are demodulated. Typically, the modulating signal amplitude in a transmitter is limited or compressed such that approximately 90% modulation is the maximum that can be achieved. For 70.7% modulation, Equation 4-17a reduces to

$$f_{m(\max)} = \frac{1}{2\pi RC} \tag{4-17b}$$

Equation 4-17b is commonly used when designing peak detectors to determine an approximate maximum modulating signal.

Automatic Gain Control Circuits

An *automatic gain control* (AGC) circuit compensates for minor variations in the received RF signal level. The AGC circuit automatically increases the receiver gain for weak RF input levels and automatically decreases the receiver gain when a strong RF signal is received. Weak signals can be buried in receiver noise and, consequently, be impossible to detect. An excessively strong signal can overdrive the RF and/or IF amplifiers and produce excessive nonlinear distortion and even saturation. There are several types of AGC, which include direct or simple AGC, delayed AGC, and forward AGC.

Simple AGC. Figure 4-28 shows a block diagram for an AM superheterodyne receiver with simple AGC. The automatic gain control circuit monitors the received signal level and sends a signal back to the RF and IF amplifiers to adjust their gain automatically. AGC is a form of degenerative or negative feedback. The purpose of AGC is to allow a receiver to detect and demodulate, equally well, signals that are transmitted from different stations whose output power and distance from the receiver vary. For example, an AM radio in a vehicle does not receive the same signal level from all the transmitting stations in the area or, for that matter, from a single station when the automobile is moving. The AGC circuit produces a voltage that adjusts the receiver gain and keeps the IF carrier power at the input to the AM detector at a relatively constant level. The AGC circuit is not a form of *automatic volume control* (AVC); AGC is independent of modulation and totally unaffected by normal changes in the modulating signal amplitude.

Figure 4-29 shows a schematic diagram for a simple AGC circuit. As you can see, an AGC circuit is essentially a peak detector. In fact, very often the AGC correction voltage is taken from the output of the audio detector. In Figure 4-26, it was shown that the dc voltage at the output of a peak detector is equal to the peak unmodulated carrier amplitude minus the barrier potential of the diode and is totally independent of the depth of modulation. If the carrier amplitude increases, the AGC voltage increases, and if the carrier amplitude decreases, the AGC voltage decreases. The circuit shown in Figure 4-29 is a negative peak detector and produces a negative voltage at its output. The greater the amplitude of the input carrier is, the more negative the output voltage. The negative voltage from the AGC detector is fed back to the IF stage where it controls the bias voltage on the base of Q_1. When the carrier amplitude increases, the voltage on the base of Q_1 becomes less positive, causing the emitter current to decrease. As a result, r'_e increases and the amplifier gain (r_c / r'_e) decreases, which in turn causes the carrier amplitude to decrease. When the carrier amplitude decreases, the AGC voltage becomes less negative, the emitter current increases, r'_e decreases, and the amplifier gain increases. Capacitor C_1 is an audio bypass capacitor that prevents changes in the AGC voltage due to modulation from affecting the gain of Q_1.

Delayed AGC. Simple AGC is used in most inexpensive broadcast-band radio receivers. However, with simple AGC, the AGC bias begins to increase as soon as the received signal level exceeds the thermal noise of the receiver. Consequently, the receiver be-

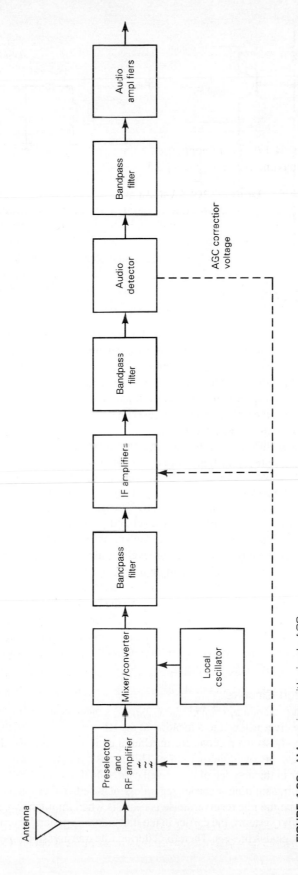

FIGURE 4-28 AM receiver with simple AGC

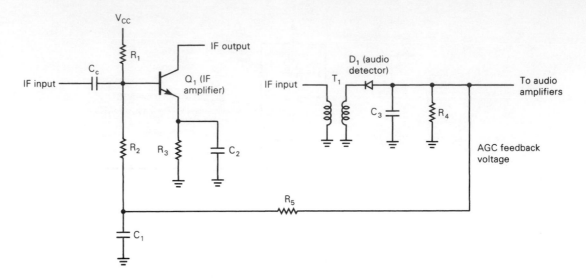

FIGURE 4-29 Simple AGC circuit

comes less sensitive (which is sometimes called *automatic desensing*). *Delayed AGC* prevents the AGC feedback voltage from reaching the RF or IF amplifiers until the RF level exceeds a predetermined magnitude. Once the carrier signal has exceeded the threshold level, the delayed AGC voltage is proportional to the carrier signal strength. Figure 4-30a shows the response characteristics for both simple and delayed AGC. It can be seen that with delayed AGC the receiver gain is unaffected until the AGC threshold level is exceeded, whereas with simple AGC the receiver gain is immediately affected. Delayed AGC is used with more sophisticated communications receivers. Figure 4-30b shows IF gain–versus–RF input signal level for both simple and delayed AGC.

Forward AGC.   An inherent problem with both simple and delayed AGC is the fact that they are both forms of *post-AGC* (after-the-fact) compensation. With post-AGC, the circuit that monitors the carrier level and provides the AGC correction voltage is located after the IF amplifiers; therefore, the simple fact that the AGC voltage changed indicates that it may be too late (the carrier level has already changed and propagated through the receiver). Therefore, neither simple nor delayed AGC can accurately compensate for rapid changes in the carrier amplitude. *Forward AGC* is similar to conventional AGC except that the receive signal is monitored closer to the front end of the receiver and the correction voltage is fed forward to the IF amplifiers. Consequently, when a change in signal level is detected, the change can be compensated for in succeeding stages. Figure 4-31 shows an AM superheterodyne receiver with forward AGC. For a more sophisticated method of accomplishing AGC, refer to Chapter 7, "Two-Way FM Radio Receivers."

Squelch Circuits

The purpose of a *squelch circuit* is to *quiet* a receiver in the absence of a received signal. If an AM receiver is tuned to a location in the RF spectrum where there is no RF signal, the AGC circuit adjusts the receiver for maximum gain. Consequently, the receiver amplifies and demodulates its own internal noise. This is the familiar crackling and sputtering heard on the speaker in the absence of a received carrier. In domestic AM systems, each station is continuously transmitting a carrier regardless of whether there is any modulation. Therefore, the only time the idle receiver noise is heard is when tuning between stations. However, in two-way radio systems, the carrier in the transmitter is generally turned off except when a modulating signal is present. Therefore, during idle transmission times, a receiver is simply ampli-

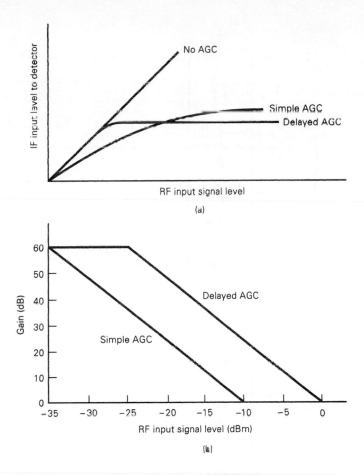

FIGURE 4-30 Automatic gain control (AGC): (a) response characteristics; (b) IF gain-versus-RF input signal level

fying and demodulating noise. A squelch circuit keeps the audio section of the receiver turned off or *muted* in the absence of a received signal (the receiver is squelched). A disadvantage of a squelch circuit is weak RF signals will not produce an audio output.

Figure 4-32 shows a schematic diagram for a typical squelch circuit. This squelch circuit uses the AGC voltage to monitor the received RF signal level. The greater the AGC voltage, the stronger the RF signal. When the AGC voltage drops below a preset level, the squelch circuit is activated and disables the audio section of the receiver. In Figure 4-32 it can be seen that the squelch detector uses a resistive voltage divider to monitor the AGC voltage. When the RF signal drops below the squelch threshold, Q_2 turns on and shuts off the audio amplifiers. When the RF signal level increases above the squelch threshold, the AGC voltage becomes more negative, turning off Q_2, and enabling the audio amplifiers. The squelch threshold level can be adjusted with R_3. A more sophisticated method of squelching a receiver is described in Chapter 7, "Two-Way FM Radio Receivers."

Noise Limiters and Blankers

Sporadic, high-amplitude noise transients of short duration, such as impulse noise, can often be removed using diode *limiters* or *clippers* in the audio section of a receiver. The limiting or clipping threshold level is normally established just above the maximum peak level of the audio signal. Therefore, the signal is virtually unaffected by them, but noise pulses will be limited to approximately the same level as the signal. Noise pulses are generally

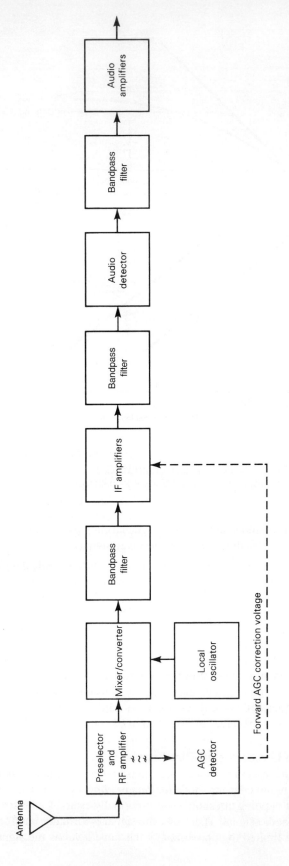

FIGURE 4-31 Forward AGC

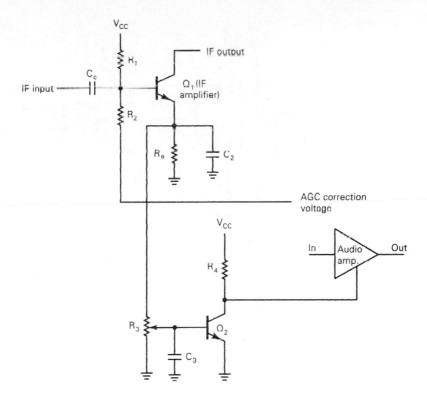

FIGURE 4-32 Squelch circuit

large amplitude, short duration signals; therefore, limiting them removes much of their energy and leaves them much less disturbing.

A *blanking circuit* is another circuit option commonly used for reducing the effects of high-amplitude noise pulses. In essence, a blanking circuit detects the occurrence of a high-amplitude, short duration noise spike, then mutes the receiver by shutting off a portion of the receiver for the duration of the pulse. For example, when a noise pulse is detected at the input to the IF amplifier section of a receiver, the blanking circuit shuts off the IF amplifiers for the duration of the pulse, thus quieting the receiver. Shutting off the IF amplifiers has proven more effective than shutting off the audio section, because the wider bandpass filters in the IF stage have a tendency of broadening the noise pulse.

Limiter and blanker circuits have little effect on white noise, however, because white noise power is generally much lower than the signal power level, and limiters and blankers only work when the noise surges to a level above that of the signal.

Alternate Signal-to-Noise Measurements

Sensitivity has little meaning unless it is accompanied by a signal-to-noise ratio and, because it is difficult to separate the signal from the noise and vice versa, sensitivity is often accompanied by a *signal plus noise-to-noise reading* (S+N)/N. The sensitivity of an AM receiver is generally given as the minimum signal level at the input of the receiver with 30% modulation necessary to produce at least 500 mW of audio output power with a 10-dB (S+N)/N ratio.

To measure (S+N)/N, an RF carrier modulated 30% by a 1-kHz tone is applied to the input of the receiver. Total audio power is measured at the output of the receiver which includes the audio signal and any noise present within the audio bandwidth. The modulation is then removed from the RF signal and the total audio power is again measured. This time, however,

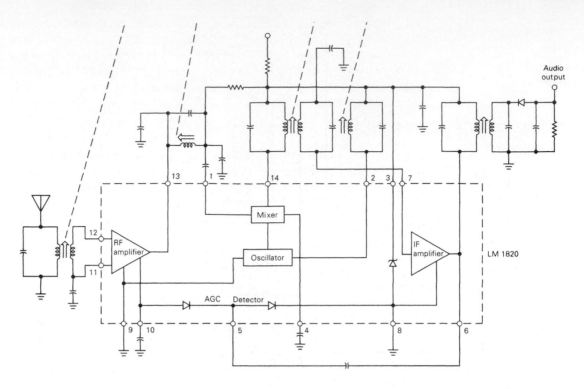

FIGURE 4-33 LM1820 linear integrated-circuit AM radio system

only noise signals are present. The purpose of leaving the carrier on rather than terminating the input to the receiver is the carrier is necessary to prevent the AGC circuit from detecting an absence of the carrier and turning the gain of the receiver up to maximum. The noise reading when the receiver is operating at maximum gain would amplify the internally generated noise well beyond its normal level, thus yielding a meaningless noise reading.

Another method of measuring signal strength relative to noise strength is called the *signal-to-notched noise* ratio. Again, an RF carrier modulated 30% by a 1-kHz tone is applied to the input of the receiver. Total audio power plus noise is measured at the output of the receiver. A narrowband 1-kHz notch filter is then inserted between the receiver output and the power meter and another power measurement is taken. Again, the power reading will include only noise. This time, however, the entire receiver operated under near-normal signal conditions because it was receiving and demodulating a modulated carrier. Signal-to-notched noise ratios are meaningful only if the notch filter has an extremely narrow bandwidth (a few hertz) and introduces 40 dB or more of attenuation to the signal.

Linear Integrated-Circuit AM Receivers

Linear integrated circuits are now available from several manufacturers that perform all receiver functions except RF and IF filtering and volume control on a single chip. Figure 4-33 shows the schematic diagram of an AM receiver that uses the National Semiconductor Corporation LM1820 linear integrated-circuit AM radio chip. The LM1820 has onboard RF amplifier, mixer, local oscillator, and IF amplifier stages. However, RF and IF selectivity is accomplished by adjusting tuning coils in externally connected tuned circuits or cans. Also, a LIC audio amplifier, such as the LM386, and a speaker are necessary to complete a functional receiver.

LIC AM radios are not widely used because the physical size reduction made possible by reducing the component count through integration is offset by the size of the external components necessary for providing bandlimiting and channel selection. Alternatives to *LC* tank circuits and IF cans, such as ceramic filters, may be integrable in the near future. Also, new receiver configurations (other than TRF or superheterodyne) may be possible in the future using phase-locked-loop technology. Phase-locked-loop receivers would need only two external components: a volume control and a station tuning control.

DOUBLE-CONVERSION AM RECEIVERS

For good image-frequency rejection, a relatively high intermediate frequency is desired. However, for high-gain selective amplifiers that are stable and easily neutralized, a low intermediate frequency is necessary. The solution is to use two intermediate frequencies. The *first IF* is a relatively high frequency for good image-frequency rejection, and the *second IF* is a relatively low frequency for easy amplification. Figure 4-34 shows a block diagram for a *double-conversion* AM receiver. The first IF is 10.625 MHz, which pushes the image frequency 21.25 MHz away from the desired RF. The first IF is immediately downconverted to 455 kHz and fed to a series of high-gain IF amplifiers. Figure 4-35 illustrates the filtering requirements for a double-conversion AM receiver.

NET RECEIVER GAIN

Thus far we have discussed RF gain, conversion gain, and IF gain. However, probably the most important gain is *net receiver gain*. The net receiver gain is simply the ratio of the demodulated signal level at the output of the receiver (audio) to the RF signal level at the input to the receiver, or the difference between the audio signal level in dBm and the RF signal level in dBm.

In essence, net receiver gain is the dB sum of all the gains in the receiver minus the dB sum of all the losses. Receiver losses typically include preselector loss, mixer loss (i.e., conversion gain), and detector losses. Gains include RF gain, IF gain, and audio-amplifier gain. Figure 4-36 shows the gains and losses found in a typical radio receiver.

Mathematically, net receiver gain is

$$G_{dB} = gains_{dB} - losses_{dB}$$

where   gains = RF amplifier gain + IF amplifier gain + audio-amplifier gain
          losses = preselector loss + mixer loss + detector loss

Example 4-8

For an AM receiver with a −80-dBm RF input signal level and the following gains and losses, determine the net receiver gain and the audio signal level.

Gains: RF amplifier = 33 dB, IF amplifier = 47 dB, audio amplifier = 25 dB
Losses: preselector loss = 3 dB, mixer loss = 6 dB, detector loss = 8 dB

Solution   The sum of the gains is

$$33 + 47 + 25 = 105 \text{ dB}$$

The sum of the losses is

$$3 + 6 + 8 = 17 \text{ dB}$$

Thus, net receiver gain

$$G = 105 - 17 = 88 \text{ dB}$$

and the audio signal level is

$$-80 \text{ dBm} + 88 \text{ dB} = 8 \text{ dBm}$$

It is important to note, however, that due to the effects of AGC, the IF and/or RF gain of a receiver could be stated as a maximum, minimum, or average value. For

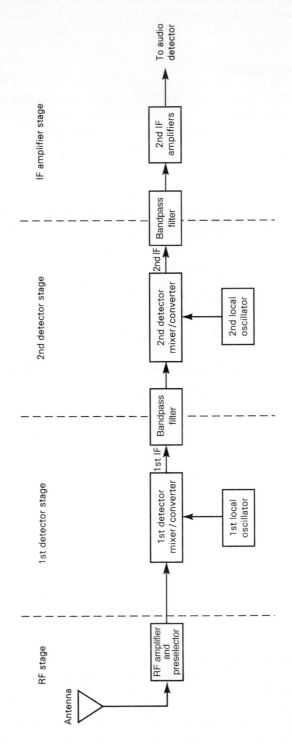

FIGURE 4-34 Double-conversion AM receiver

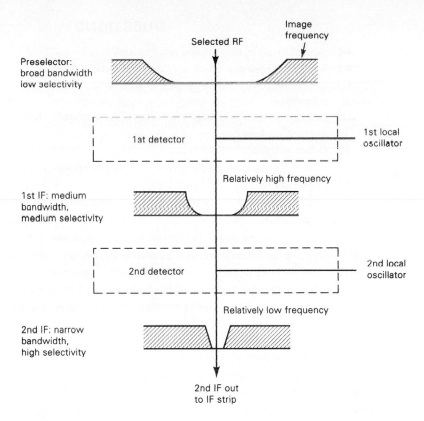

FIGURE 4-35 Filtering requirements for the double-conversion AM receiver shown in Figure 4-34

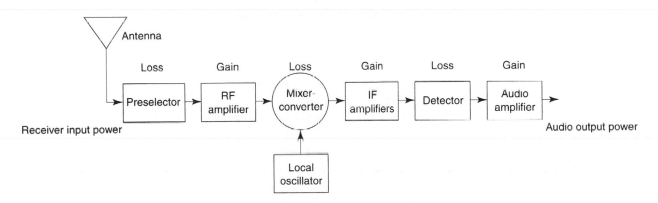

FIGURE 4-36 Receiver gains and losses

example, the IF gain for the receiver in Example 4-8 could vary due to AGC between 20 dB and 60 dB, depending on the input signal strength. Therefore, the net receiver gain could vary between a maximum value of 101 dB, a minimum value of 61 dB, with an average value of 81 dB.

Net receiver gain should not be confused with overall *system gain*. Net receiver gain includes only components within the receiver beginning at the input to the preselector. System gain includes all the gains and losses incurred by a signal as it propagates from the transmitter output stage to the output of the detector in the receiver and includes antenna gain and transmission line and propagation losses. System gain is discussed in detail in Chapter 17.

QUESTIONS

4-1. What is meant by the *front end* of a receiver?

4-2. What are the primary functions of the front end of a receiver?

4-3. Define *selectivity* and *shape factor*. What is the relationship between receiver noise and selectivity?

4-4. Describe *bandwidth improvement*. What is the relationship between bandwidth improvement and receiver noise?

4-5. Define *sensitivity*.

4-6. What is the relationship among receiver noise, bandwidth, and temperature?

4-7. Define *fidelity*.

4-8. List and describe the three types of distortion that reduce the fidelity of a receiver.

4-9. Define *insertion loss*.

4-10. Define *noise temperature* and *equivalent noise temperature*.

4-11. Describe the difference between a *coherent* and a *noncoherent* radio receiver.

4-12. Draw the block diagram for a TRF radio receiver and briefly describe its operation.

4-13. What are the three predominant disadvantages of a TRF receiver?

4-14. Draw the block diagram for an AM superheterodyne receiver and describe its operation and the primary functions of each stage.

4-15. Define *heterodyning*.

4-16. What is meant by the terms *high-* and *low-side injection?*

4-17. Define *local oscillator tracking* and *tracking error*.

4-18. Describe *three-point tracking*.

4-19. What is meant by *gang* tuning?

4-20. Define *image frequency*.

4-21. Define *image-frequency rejection ratio*.

4-22. List six characteristics that are desirable in an RF amplifier.

4-23. What advantage do FET RF amplifiers have over BJT RF amplifiers?

4-24. Define *neutralization*. Describe the neutralization process.

4-25. What is a *cascoded* amplifier?

4-26. Define *conversion gain*.

4-27. What is the advantage of a relatively high-frequency intermediate frequency; a relatively low-frequency intermediate frequency?

4-28. Define the following terms: *inductive coupling; self-inductance; mutual inductance; coefficient of coupling; critical coupling; optimum coupling*.

4-29. Describe *loose* coupling; *tight* coupling.

4-30. Describe the operation of a *peak detector*.

4-31. Describe *rectifier distortion* and its causes.

4-32. Describe *diagonal clipping* and its causes.

4-33. Describe the following terms: *simple AGC; delayed AGC; forward AGC*.

4-34. What is the purpose of a *squelch* circuit?

4-35. Explain the operation of a double-conversion superheterodyne receiver.

PROBLEMS

4-1. Determine the IF bandwidth necessary to achieve a bandwidth improvement of 16 dB for a radio receiver with an RF bandwidth of 320 kHz.

4-2. Determine the improvement in the noise figure for a receiver with an RF bandwidth equal to 40 kHz and IF bandwidth of 16 kHz.

4-3. Determine the equivalent noise temperature for an amplifier with a noise figure of 6 dB and an environmental temperature $T = 27°$ C.

4-4. For an AM commercial broadcast-band receiver with an input filter Q-factor of 85, determine the bandwidth at the low and high ends of the RF spectrum.

4-5. For an AM superheterodyne receiver using high-side injection with a local oscillator frequency of 1200 kHz, determine the IF carrier and upper and lower side frequencies for an RF envelope that is made up of a carrier and upper and lower side frequencies of 600 kHz, 604 kHz, and 596 kHz, respectively.

4-6. For a receiver with a ± 2.5-kHz tracking error, a 455-kHz IF, and a maximum modulating signal frequency $f_m = 6$ kHz, determine the minimum IF bandwidth.

4-7. For a receiver with IF, RF, and local oscillator frequencies of 455 kHz, 900 kHz, and 1355 kHz, respectively, determine
  (a) Image frequency.
  (b) IFRR for a preselector Q of 80.

4-8. For a citizens band receiver using high-side injection with an RF carrier of 27.04 MHz and a 10.645 MHz first IF, determine
  (a) Local oscillator frequency.
  (b) Image frequency.

4-9. For a three-stage double-tuned RF amplifier with an RF carrier equal to 800 kHz and a coefficient of coupling $k_{opt} = 0.025$, determine
  (a) Bandwidth for each individual stage.
  (b) Overall bandwidth for the three stages.

4-10. Determine the maximum modulating signal frequency for a peak detector with the following parameters: $C = 1000$ pF, $R = 10$ kΩ, and $m = 0.5$. Repeat the problem for $m = 0.707$.

4-11. Determine the bandwidth improvement for a radio receiver with an RF bandwidth of 60 kHz and an IF bandwidth of 15 kHz.

4-12. Determine the equivalent noise temperature for an amplifier with a noise figure $F = 8$ dB and an environmental temperature $T = 122°$ C.

4-13. For an AM commercial broadcast-band receiver with an input filter Q-factor of 60, determine the bandwidth at the low and high ends of the RF spectrum.

4-14. For an AM superheterodyne receiver using high-side injection with a local oscillator frequency of 1400 kHz, determine the IF carrier and upper and lower side frequencies for an RF envelope that is made up of a carrier and upper and lower side frequencies of 800 kHz, 806 kHz, and 794 kHz, respectively.

4-15. For a receiver with a ± 2800-Hz tracking error and a maximum modulating signal frequency $f_m = 4$ kHz, determine the minimum IF bandwidth.

4-16. For a receiver with IF, RF, and local oscillator frequencies of 455 kHz, 1100 kHz, and 1555 kHz, respectively, determine
  (a) Image frequency.
  (b) Image-frequency rejection ratio for a preselector $Q = 100$.
  (c) Image-frequency rejection ratio for a $Q = 50$.

4-17. For a citizens band receiver using high-side injection with an RF carrier of 27.04 MHz and a 10.645 MHz IF, determine
  (a) Local oscillator frequency.
  (b) Image frequency.

4-18. For a three-stage, double-tuned RF amplifier with an RF equal to 1000 kHz and a coefficient of coupling $k_{opt} = 0.01$, determine
  (a) Bandwidth for each individual stage.
  (b) Bandwidth for the three stages cascaded together.

4-19. Determine the maximum modulating signal frequency for a peak detector with the following parameters: $C = 1000$ pF, $R = 6.8$ kΩ, and $m = 0.5$. Repeat the problem for $m = 0.707$.

4-20. Determine the net receiver gain for an AM receiver with a RF input signal power of -87 dBm and an audio signal power of 10 dBm.

4-21. Determine the net receiver gain for an AM receiver with the following gains and losses:

Gains: RF amplifier = 30 dB, IF amplifier = 44 dB, audio amplifier = 24 dB

Losses: Preselector loss = 2 dB, mixer loss = 6 dB, detector loss = 8 dB

4-22. Determine the minimum RF input signal power necessary to produce an audio signal power of 10 dBm for the receiver described in Problem 4-21.

4-23. Determine the net receiver gain for an AM receiver with the following gains and losses:

Gains: RF amplifier = 33 dB, IF amplifier = 44 dB, audio amplifier = 22 dB

Losses: Preselector loss = 3.5 dB, mixer loss = 5 dB, detector loss = 9 dB

CHAPTER 5

Single-Sideband
Communications Systems

INTRODUCTION

Conventional AM double-sideband communications systems, such as those discussed in Chapters 3 and 4, have two inherent disadvantages. First, with conventional AM, carrier power constitutes two-thirds or more of the total transmitted power. This is a major drawback because the carrier contains no information; the sidebands contain the information. Second, conventional AM systems utilize twice as much bandwidth as needed with single-sideband systems. With double-sideband transmission, the information contained in the upper sideband is identical to the information contained in the lower sideband. Therefore, transmitting both sidebands is redundant. Consequently, conventional AM is both power and bandwidth inefficient, which are the two most predominant considerations when designing modern electronic communications systems.

The purpose of this chapter is to introduce the reader to several single-sideband AM systems and explain the advantages and disadvantages of choosing them over conventional double-sideband full-carrier AM.

The most prevalent use of single-sideband suppressed-carrier systems is with multi-channel communications systems employing frequency-division multiplexing (FDM) such as long-distance telephone systems. Frequency-division multiplexing is introduced later in this chapter, then discussed in more detail in Chapter 16.

SINGLE-SIDEBAND SYSTEMS

Single sideband was mathematically recognized and understood as early as 1914; however, not until 1923 was the first patent granted and a successful communications link established between England and the United States. There are many different types of *sideband* communications systems. Some of them conserve bandwidth, some conserve power, and some conserve both. Figure 5-1 compares the frequency spectra and relative power distributions for conventional AM and several of the more common single-sideband (SSB) systems.

189

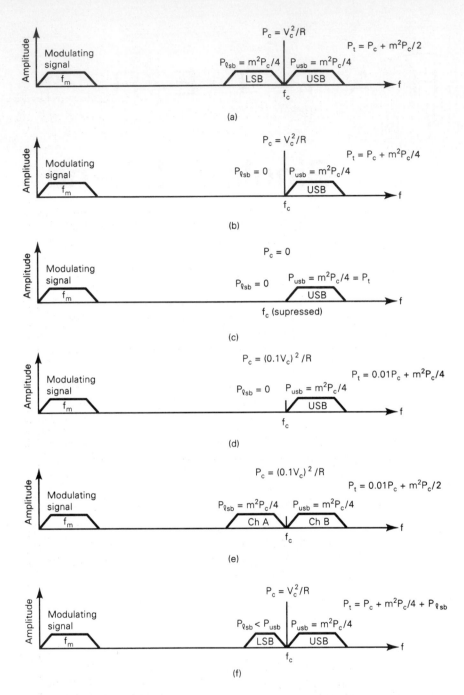

FIGURE 5-1 Single-sideband systems: (a) conventional DSBFC AM; (b) full-carrier single sideband; (c) suppressed-carrier single sideband; (d) reduced-carrier single sideband; (e) independent sideband; (f) vestigial sideband

AM Single-Sideband Full Carrier

AM *single-sideband full carrier* (SSBFC) is a form of amplitude modulation in which the carrier is transmitted at full power, but only one of the sidebands is transmitted. Therefore, SSBFC transmissions require only half as much bandwidth as conventional double-sideband AM. The frequency spectrum and relative power distribution for SSBFC are shown in Figure 5-1b. Note that with 100% modulation the carrier power (P_c) constitutes

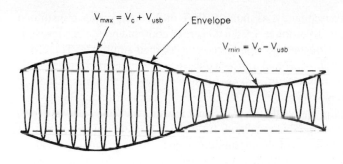

FIGURE 5-2   SSBFC waveform, 100% modulation

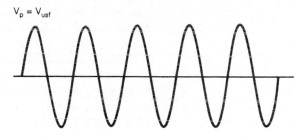

FIGURE 5-3   SSBSC waveform

four-fifths (80%) of the total transmitted power (P_t), and only one-fifth (20%) of the total power is in the sideband. For conventional double-sideband AM with 100% modulation, two-thirds (67%) of the total transmitted power is in the carrier and one-third (33%) is in the sidebands. Therefore, although SSBFC requires less total power, it actually utilizes a smaller percentage of that power for the information-carrying portion of the signal.

Figure 5-2 shows the waveform for a 100%-modulated SSBFC wave with a single-frequency modulating signal. The 100%-modulated single-sideband, full-carrier envelope looks identical to a 50%-modulated double-sideband, full-carrier envelope. Recall from Chapter 3 that the maximum positive and negative peaks of an AM DSBFC wave occur when the carrier and both sidebands reach their respective peaks at the same time, and the peak change in the envelope is equal to the sum of the amplitudes of the upper and lower side frequencies. With single-sideband transmission, there is only one sideband (either the upper or lower) to add to the carrier. Therefore, the peak change in the envelope is only half of what it is with double-sideband transmission. Consequently, with single-sideband full-carrier transmission, the demodulated signals have only half the amplitude of a double sideband demodulated wave. Thus, a trade-off is made. SSBFC requires less bandwidth than DSBFC but also produces a demodulated signal with a lower amplitude. However, when the bandwidth is halved, the total noise power is also halved (i.e., reduced by 3 dB); and if one sideband is removed, the power in the information portion of the wave is also halved. Consequently, the signal-to-noise ratios for single and double sideband are the same.

With SSBFC, the repetition rate of the envelope is equal to the frequency of the modulating signal, and the depth of modulation is proportional to the amplitude of the modulating signal. Therefore, as with double-sideband transmission, the information is contained in the envelope of the full-carrier modulated signal.

AM Single-Sideband Suppressed Carrier

AM *single-sideband suppressed carrier* (SSBSC) is a form of amplitude modulation in which the carrier is totally suppressed and one of the sidebands removed. Therefore, SSBSC requires half as much bandwidth as conventional double-sideband AM and considerably less transmitted power. The frequency spectrum and relative power distribution for SSBSC with upper sideband transmission are shown in Figure 5-1c. It can be seen that the sideband power makes up 100% of the total transmitted power. Figure 5-3 shows a SSBSC waveform for a single-frequency modulating signal. As you can see, the waveform is not an envelope; it is simply a sine wave at a single frequency equal to the carrier frequency plus the modulating-signal frequency or the carrier frequency minus the modulating-signal frequency, depending on which sideband is transmitted.

AM Single-Sideband Reduced Carrier

AM *single-sideband reduced carrier* (SSBRC) is a form of amplitude modulation in which one sideband is totally removed and the carrier voltage is reduced to approximately 10% of its unmodulated amplitude. Consequently, as much as 96% of the total power transmitted is in the unsuppressed sideband. To produce a reduced carrier component, the carrier is totally suppressed during modulation and then reinserted at a reduced amplitude. Therefore, SSBRC is sometimes called single-sideband *reinserted* carrier. The reinserted carrier is often called a pilot carrier and is reinserted for demodulation purposes, which is explained later in this chapter. The frequency spectrum and relative power distribution for SSBRC are shown in Figure 5-1d. The figure shows that the sideband power constitutes almost 100% of the transmitted power. As with double-sideband, full-carrier AM, the repetition rate of the envelope is equal to the frequency of the modulating signal. To demodulate a reduced carrier waveform with a conventional peak detector, the carrier must be separated, amplified, and then reinserted at a higher level in the receiver. Therefore, reduced-carrier transmission is sometimes called *exalted* carrier because the carrier is elevated in the receiver prior to demodulation. With exalted-carrier detection, the amplification of the carrier in the receiver must be sufficient to raise the level of the carrier to a value greater than that of the sideband signal. SSBRC requires half as much bandwidth as conventional AM and, because the carrier is transmitted at a reduced level, also conserves considerable power.

AM Independent Sideband

AM *independent sideband* (ISB) is a form of amplitude modulation in which a single carrier frequency is independently modulated by two different modulating signals. In essence, ISB is a form of double-sideband transmission in which the transmitter consists of two independent single-sideband suppressed-carrier modulators. One modulator produces only the upper sideband and the other produces only the lower sideband. The single-sideband output signals from the two modulators are combined to form a double-sideband signal in which the two sidebands are totally independent of each other except that they are symmetrical about a common carrier frequency. One sideband is positioned above the carrier in the frequency spectrum and one below. For demodulation purposes, the carrier is generally reinserted at a reduced level as with SSBRC transmission. Figure 5-1e shows the frequency spectrum and power distribution for ISB, and Figure 5-4 shows the transmitted waveform for two independent single-frequency information signals (f_{m1} and f_{m2}). The two information signals are equal in frequency; therefore, the waveform is identical to a double-sideband suppressed-carrier waveform except with a repetition rate equal to twice the modulating signal frequency. ISB conserves both transmit power and bandwidth as two information sources are transmitted within the same frequency spectrum as would be required by a single source using conventional double-sideband transmission. ISB is one technique that is used in the United States for stereo AM transmission. One channel (the left) is trans-

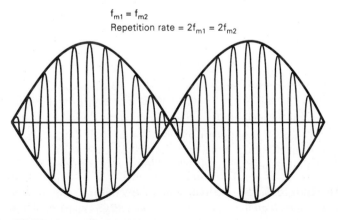

FIGURE 5-4 ISB waveform

mitted in the lower sideband, and the other channel (the right) is transmitted in the upper sideband.

AM Vestigial Sideband

AM *vestigial sideband* (VSB) is a form of amplitude modulation in which the carrier and one complete sideband are transmitted, but only part of the second sideband is transmitted. The carrier is transmitted at full power. In VSB, the lower modulating-signal frequencies are transmitted double sideband and the higher modulating-signal frequencies are transmitted single sideband. Consequently, the lower frequencies can appreciate the benefit of 100% modulation, whereas the higher frequencies cannot achieve more than the effect of 50% modulation. Consequently, the low-frequency modulating signals are emphasized and produce larger-amplitude signals in the demodulator than the high frequencies. The frequency spectrum and relative power distribution for VSB are shown in Figure 5-1f. Probably the most widely known VSB system is the picture portion of a commercial television broadcasting signal which is designated A5C by the FCC.

Comparison of Single-Sideband Transmission to Conventional AM

From the preceding discussion and Figure 5-1, it can be seen that bandwidth conservation and power efficiency are obvious advantages of single-sideband suppressed- and reduced-carrier transmission over conventional double-sideband full-carrier transmission (i.e., conventional AM). Single-sideband transmission requires only half as much bandwidth as double sideband, and suppressed- and reduced-carrier transmissions require considerably less total transmitted power than full-carrier AM.

The total power transmitted necessary to produce a given signal-to-noise ratio at the output of a receiver is a convenient and useful means of comparing the power requirement and relative performance of single-sideband to conventional AM systems. The signal-to-noise ratio determines the degree of intelligibility of a received signal.

Figure 5-5 summarizes the waveforms produced for a given modulating signal for three of the more common AM transmission systems: double-sideband full carrier (DSBFC,) double-sideband suppressed carrier (DSBSC), and single-sideband suppressed carrier (SSBSC). As the figure shows, the repetition rate of the DSBFC envelope is equal to the modulating signal frequency, the repetition rate of the DSBSC envelope is equal to twice the modulating signal frequency, and the SSBSC waveform is not an envelope at all but rather a single-frequency sinusoid equal in frequency to the unsuppressed sideband frequency (i.e., either the upper or lower side frequency).

A conventional AM wave with 100% modulation contains 1 unit of carrier power and 0.25 unit of power in each sideband for a total transmitted peak power of 1.5 units. A single-sideband transmitter rated at 0.5 unit of power will produce the same S/N ratio at the output of a receiver as 1.5 units of carrier plus sideband power from a double-sideband full-carrier signal. In other words, the same performance is achieved with SSBSC using only one-third as much transmitted power and half the bandwidth. Table 5-1 compares conventional AM to single-sideband suppressed carrier for a single-frequency modulating signal. *Peak envelope power* (PEP) is the rms power developed at the crest of the modulation envelope (i.e., when the modulating-signal frequency components are at their maximum amplitudes).

The voltage vectors for the power requirements stated are also shown. It can be seen that it requires 0.5 unit of voltage per sideband and 1 unit for the carrier with conventional AM for a total of 2 PEV (peak envelope volts) and only 0.707 PEV for single sideband. The RF envelopes are also shown, which correspond to the voltage and power relationships previously outlined. The demodulated signal at the output from a conventional AM receiver is proportional to the quadratic sum of the voltages from the upper and lower sideband signals, which equals 1 PEV unit. For single-sideband reception, the demodulated signal is $0.707 \times 1 = 0.707$ PEV. If the noise voltage for conventional AM is arbitrarily chosen as

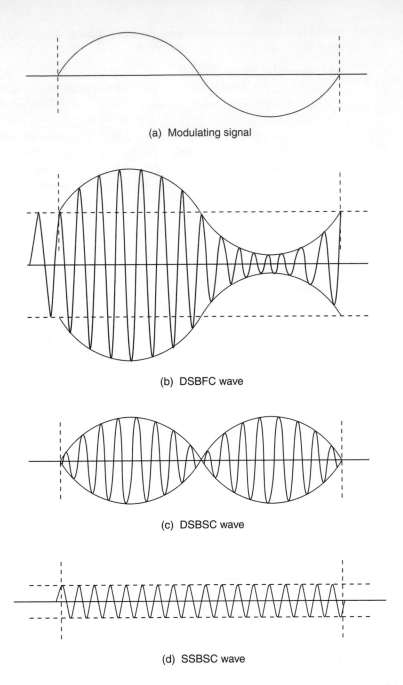

(a) Modulating signal

(b) DSBFC wave

(c) DSBSC wave

(d) SSBSC wave

FIGURE 5-5 Comparison of three common AM transmission systems; (a) modulating signal; (b) DSBFC wave; (c) DSBSC wave; and (d) SSBSC wave.

0.1 V/kHz, the noise voltage for single-sideband signal with half the bandwidth is 0.0707 V/kHz. Consequently, the S/N performance for SSBSC is equal to that of conventional AM.

Advantages of single-sideband transmission. Following are four predominant advantages of single-sideband suppressed- or reduced-carrier transmission over conventional double-sideband full-carrier transmission.

Power Conservation. Normally, with single-sideband transmission, only one sideband is transmitted and the carrier is either suppressed or reduced significantly. As a result,

TABLE 5-1 Conventional AM Versus Single Sideband

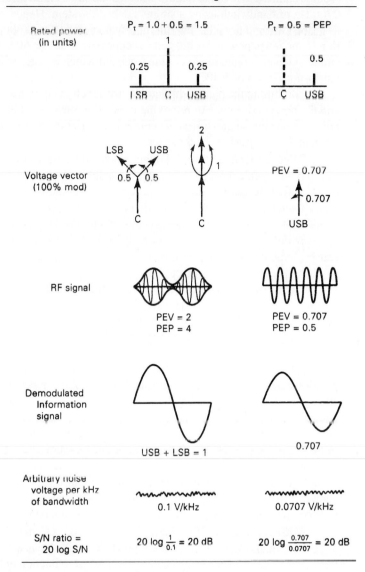

Rated power (in units)	$P_t = 1.0 + 0.5 = 1.5$	$P_t = 0.5 = PEP$
Voltage vector (100% mod)		$PEV = 0.707$
RF signal	$PEV = 2$ $PEP = 4$	$PEV = 0.707$ $PEP = 0.5$
Demodulated Information signal	$USB + LSB = 1$	0.707
Arbitrary noise voltage per kHz of bandwidth	0.1 V/kHz	0.0707 V/kHz
S/N ratio = 20 log S/N	$20 \log \frac{1}{0.1} = 20$ dB	$20 \log \frac{0.707}{0.0707} = 20$ dB

much less total transmitted power is necessary to produce essentially the same quality signal in the receiver as is achieved with double-sideband, full-carrier transmission. At least two-thirds of the power in a standard double-sideband, full-carrier AM signal is contained in the carrier, and the maximum power contained in either sideband is only one-sixth of the total power. Thus, eliminating the carrier would increase the power available for the sidebands by at least a factor of three providing a signal power advantage of 10 log (3) or approximately a 4.8 dB improvement in the signal-to-noise ratio.

Bandwidth Conservation. Single-sideband transmission requires half as much bandwidth as conventional AM double-sideband transmission. This advantage is especially important today with an already overcrowded radio-frequency spectrum. Eliminating one sideband actually reduces the required bandwidth by more than a factor of two, because most modulating signals, including audio signals, rarely extend all the way down to 0 Hz (dc). A more practical lower frequency limit for audio signals is 300 Hz; thus, a 3-kHz audio channel actually has a bandwidth of approximately 2700 Hz (300 Hz to 3000 Hz). Consequently, a 2700-Hz audio channel transmitted over a double-sideband AM system would require 6 kHz of bandwidth whereas the same audio information would require only 2700 Hz of bandwidth using a single-sideband system. Hence, the single-sideband system described appreciates a bandwidth improvement of 10 log (6000/2700) or a 3.5-dB reduction in the noise power. A safe, general approximation is a 50% reduction in bandwidth for single sideband compared to double sideband which equates to an improvement in the signal-to-noise ratio of 3 dB.

Combining the bandwidth improvement achieved by transmitting only one sideband and the power advantage of removing the carrier, the overall improvement in the signal-to-noise ratio using single-sideband suppressed carrier is approximately 7.8 dB (3 + 4.8) better than double-sideband full carrier.

Selective Fading. With double-sideband transmission, the two sidebands and carrier may propagate through the transmission media by different paths and, therefore, experience different transmission impairments. This condition is called *selective fading.* One type of selective fading is called *sideband fading.* With sideband fading, one sideband is significantly attenuated. This loss results in a reduced signal amplitude at the output of the receiver demodulator and, consequently, a 3-dB reduced signal-to-noise ratio. This loss causes some distortion but is not entirely detrimental to the signal because the two sidebands contain the same information.

The most common and most serious form of selective fading is *carrier-amplitude fading.* Reduction of the carrier level of a 100%-modulated wave will make the carrier voltage less than the vector sum of the two sidebands. Consequently, the envelope resembles an overmodulated envelope, causing severe distortion to the demodulated signal.

A third cause of selective fading is carrier or sideband phase shift. When the relative positions of the carrier and sideband vectors of the received signal change, a decided change in the shape of the envelope will occur, causing a severely distorted demodulated signal.

When only one sideband and either a reduced or totally suppressed carrier are transmitted, carrier phase shift and carrier fading cannot occur, and sideband fading only changes the amplitude and frequency response of the demodulated signal. These changes do not generally produce enough distortion to cause loss of intelligibility in the received signal. With single-sideband, transmission, it is not necessary to maintain a specific amplitude or phase relationship between the carrier and sideband signals.

Noise Reduction. Because a single-sideband system utilizes half as much bandwidth as conventional AM, the thermal noise power is reduced to half that of a double-sideband system. Taking into consideration both the bandwidth reduction and the immunity to selective fading, SSB systems enjoy approximately a 12-dB S/N ratio advantage over conventional AM (i.e., a conventional AM system must transmit a 12-dB more powerful signal to achieve the same performance as a comparable single-sideband system).

Disadvantages of single-sideband transmission. Following are two major disadvantages of single-sideband reduced- or suppressed-carrier transmission as compared to conventional double-sideband, full-carrier transmission.

Complex Receivers. Single-sideband systems require more complex and expensive receivers than conventional AM transmission, because most single-sideband transmissions include either a reduced or suppressed carrier; thus, envelope detection cannot be used unless the carrier is regenerated at an exalted level. Single-sideband receivers require a carrier recovery and synchronization circuit, such as a PLL frequency synthesizer, which adds to their cost, complexity, and size.

Tuning Difficulties. Single-sideband receivers require more complex and precise tuning than conventional AM receivers. This is undesirable for the average user. This disadvantage can be overcome by using more accurate, complex, and expensive tuning circuits.

MATHEMATICAL ANALYSIS OF SUPPRESSED-CARRIER AM

An AM modulator is a *product modulator;* the output signal is the product of the modulating signal and the carrier. In essence, the carrier is multiplied by the modulating signal. Equation 3-9c was given as

$$v_{am}(t) = [1 + m \sin(2\pi f_m t)] [E_c \sin(2\pi f_c t)]$$

where $1 + m \sin(2\pi f_m t) = $ constant + modulating signal
$E_c \sin(2\pi f_c t) = $ unmodulated carrier

If the constant component is removed from the modulating signal, then

$$v_{am}(t) = [m \sin(2\pi f_m t)] [E_c \sin(2\pi f_c t)]$$

Multiplying yields

$$v_{am}(t) = -\frac{mE_c}{2} \cos[2\pi(f_c + f_m)t] + \frac{mE_c}{2} \cos[2\pi(f_c - f_m)t]$$

where $-(mE_c/2) \cos[2\pi(f_c + f_m)t] = $ upper side frequency component
$+ (mE_c/2) \cos[2\pi(f_c - f_m)t] = $ lower side frequency component

From the preceding mathematical operation, it can be seen that, if the constant component is removed prior to performing the multiplication, the carrier component is removed from the modulated wave and the output signal is simply two cosine waves, one at the sum frequency ($f_c + f_m = f_{usf}$) and the other at the difference frequency ($f_c - f_m = f_{lsf}$). The carrier has been suppressed in the modulator. To convert to single sideband, simply remove either the sum or the difference frequency.

SINGLE-SIDEBAND GENERATION

In the preceding sections it was shown that with most single-sideband systems the carrier is either totally suppressed or reduced to only a fraction of its original value, and one sideband is removed. To remove the carrier from the modulated wave or to reduce its amplitude using conventional notch filters is extremely difficult, if not impossible, because the filters simply do not have sufficient Q-factors to remove the carrier without also removing a portion of the sideband. However, it was also shown that removing the constant component suppressed the carrier in the modulator itself. Consequently, modulator circuits that inherently remove the carrier during the modulation process have been developed. Such circuits are called *double-sideband suppressed-carrier (DSBSC) modulators.* It will be shown later in this chapter how one of the sidebands can be removed once the carrier has been suppressed.

A circuit that produces a double-sideband suppressed-carrier signal is a *balanced modulator.* The balanced modulator has rapidly become one of the most useful and widely used circuits in electronic communications. In addition to suppressed-carrier AM systems, balanced modulators are widely used in frequency and phase modulation systems as well as in digital modulation systems, such as phase shift keying and quadrature amplitude modulation.

Balanced Ring Modulator

Figures 5-6 and 5-7 show the schematic diagrams and waveforms for a *balanced ring modulator.* The schematic in Figure 5-6a is constructed with diodes and transformers. Semiconductor diodes are ideally suited for use in balanced modulator circuits because they are stable, require no external power source, have a long life, and require virtually no maintenance. The balanced ring modulator is sometimes called a *balanced lattice modulator* or simply *balanced modulator.* A balanced modulator has two inputs: a single-frequency

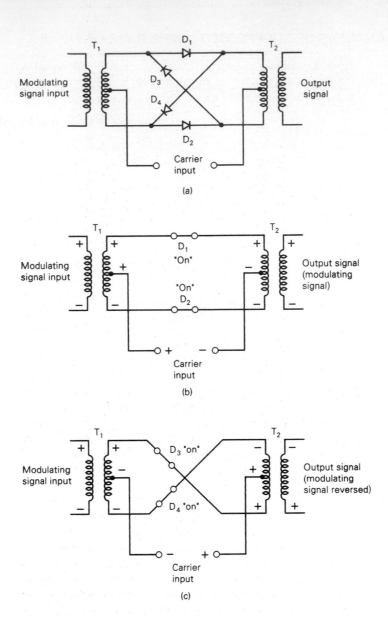

FIGURE 5-6 Balanced ring modulator: (a) schematic diagram; (b) D_1 and D_2 biased *on;* (c) D_3 and D_4 biased *on*

carrier and the modulating signal, which may be a single frequency or a complex waveform. For the balanced modulator to operate properly, the amplitude of the carrier must be sufficiently greater than the amplitude of the modulating signal (approximately six to seven times greater). This ensures that the carrier and not the modulating signal controls the on or off condition of the four diode switches (D_1 to D_4).

   Circuit operation.   Essentially, diodes D_1 to D_4 are electronic switches that control whether the modulating signal is passed from input transformer T_1 to output transformer T_2 as is or with a 180° phase shift. With the carrier polarity as shown in Figure 5-6b, diode switches D_1 and D_2 are forward biased and on, while diode switches D_3 and D_4 are reverse biased and off. Consequently, the modulating signal is transferred across the closed switches to T_2 without a phase reversal. When the polarity of the carrier reverses, as shown in Figure

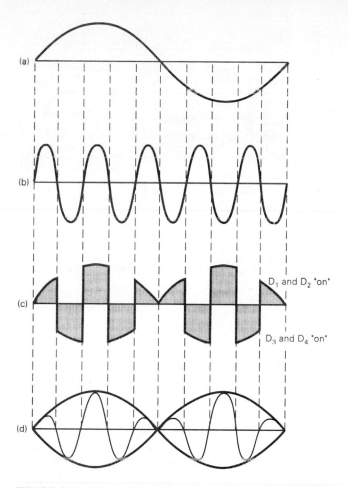

FIGURE 5-7 Balanced modulator waveforms: (a) modulating signal; (b) carrier signal; (c) output waveform before filtering; (d) output waveform after filtering

5-6c, diode switches D_1 and D_2 are reverse biased and off, while diode switches D_3 and D_4 are forward biased and on. Consequently, the modulating signal undergoes a 180° phase reversal before reaching T_2. Carrier current flows from its source to the center taps of T_1 and T_2, where it splits and goes in opposite directions through the upper and lower halves of the transformers. Thus, their magnetic fields cancel in the secondary windings of the transformer and the carrier is suppressed. If the diodes are not perfectly matched or if the transformers are not exactly center tapped, the circuit is out of balance and the carrier is not totally suppressed. It is virtually impossible to achieve perfect balance; thus, a small carrier component is always present in the output signal. This is commonly called *carrier leak.* The amount of carrier suppression is typically between 40 dB and 60 dB.

Figure 5-7 shows the input and output waveforms associated with a balanced modulator for a single-frequency modulating signal. It can be seen that D_1 and D_2 conduct only during the positive half-cycles of the carrier input signal, and D_3 and D_4 conduct only during the negative half-cycles. The output from a balanced modulator consists of a series of RF pulses whose repetition rate is determined by the RF carrier switching frequency, and amplitude is controlled by the level of the modulating signal. Consequently, the output waveform takes the shape of the modulating signal, except with alternating positive and negative polarities that correspond to the polarity of the carrier signal.

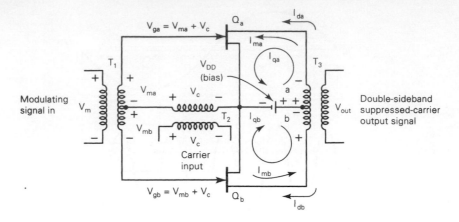

FIGURE 5-8 FET balanced modulator. For the polarities shown,

$$I_{ta} = I_{qa} + I_{da} + I_{ma}$$
$$I_{tb} = -I_{Qb} - I_{db} + I_{mb}$$
$$I_t = I_{ma} + I_{mb} = -2I_m$$

V_{OUT} is proportional to the modulating current (I_{ma} and I_{mb}).

FET Push–Pull Balanced Modulator

Figure 5-8 shows a schematic diagram for a balanced modulator that uses FETs rather than diodes for the nonlinear devices. A FET is a nonlinear device that exhibits square-law properties and produces only second-order cross-product frequencies. As is the diode balanced modulator, a FET modulator is a product modulator and produces only the sidebands at its output and suppresses the carrier. The FET balanced modulator is similar to a standard push–pull amplifier except that the modulator circuit has two inputs (the carrier and the modulating signal).

Circuit operation. The carrier is fed into the circuit in such a way that it is applied simultaneously and in phase to the gates of both FET amplifiers (Q_1 and Q_2). The carrier produces currents in both the top and bottom halves of output transformer T_3 that are equal in magnitude but 180° out of phase. Therefore, they cancel and no carrier component appears in the output waveform. The modulating signal is applied to the circuit in such a way that it is applied simultaneously to the gates of the two FETs 180° out of phase. The modulating signal causes an increase in the drain current in one FET and a decrease in the drain current in the other FET.

Figure 5-9 shows the phasor diagram for the currents produced in the output transformer of a FET balanced modulator. Figure 5-9a shows that the quiescent dc drain currents from Q_a and Q_b (I_{qa} and I_{qb}) pass through their respective halves of the primary winding of T_3 180° out of phase with each other. Figure 5-9a also shows that an increase in drain current due to the carrier signal (I_{da} and I_{db}) adds to the quiescent current in both halves of the transformer windings, producing currents (I_{qa} and I_{qb}) that are equal and simply the sum of the quiescent and carrier currents. I_{qa} and I_{qb} are equal but travel in opposite directions; consequently, they cancel each other. Figure 5-9b shows the phasor sum of the quiescent and carrier currents when the carrier currents travel in the opposite direction to the quiescent currents. The total currents in both halves of the windings are still equal in magnitude, but now they are equal to the difference between the quiescent and carrier currents. Figure 5-9c shows the phasor diagram when a current component is added due to a modulating signal. The modulating signal currents (I_{ma} and I_{mb}) produce in their respective halves of the output transformer currents that are in phase with each other. However, it can be seen that

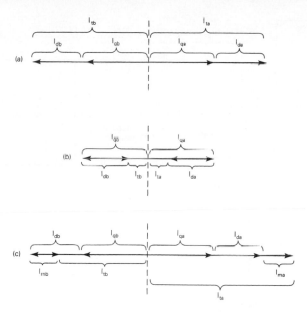

FIGURE 5-9 FET balanced modulator phasor diagrams: (a) in-phase sum of dc and carrier currents; (b) out-of-phase sum of dc and carrier currents; (c) sum of dc, carrier, and modulating-signal currents

in one-half of the windings the total current is equal to the difference between the dc and carrier currents and the modulating signal current, and in the other half of the winding, the total current is equal to the sum of the dc, carrier, and modulating signal currents. Thus, the dc and carrier currents cancel in the secondary windings, while the difference components add. The continuously changing carrier and modulating signal currents produce the cross-product frequencies.

The carrier and modulating signal polarities shown in Figure 5-8 produce an output current that is proportional to the carrier and modulating signal voltages. The carrier signal (V_c) produces a current in both FETs (I_{da} and I_{db}) that is in the same direction as the quiescent currents (I_{qa} and I_{qb}). The modulating signal (V_{ma} and V_{mb}) produces a current in $Q_a (I_{ma})$ that is in the same direction as I_{da} and I_{qa} and a current in $Q_b(I_{mb})$ that is in the opposite direction as I_{db} and I_{qb}. Therefore, the total current through the *a* side of T_3 is $I_{ta} = I_{da} + I_{qa} + I_{ma}$ and the total current through the *b* side of T_3 is $I_{tb} = -I_{db} - I_{qb} + I_{mb}$. Thus, the net current through the primary winding of T_3 is $I_{ta} + I_{tb} - I_{ma} + I_{mb}$. For a modulating signal with the opposite polarity, the drain current in Q_b will increase and in Q_a it will decrease. Ignoring the quiescent dc current (I_{qa} and I_{qb}), the drain current in one FET is the sum of the carrier and modulating signal currents ($I_d + I_m$), and the drain current in the other FET is the difference ($I_d - I_m$).

T_1 is an audio transformer whereas T_2 and T_3 are radio-frequency transformers. Therefore, any audio component that appears at the drain circuits of Q_1 and Q_2 is not passed on to the output. To achieve total carrier suppression, Q_a and Q_b must be perfectly matched and T_1 and T_3 must be exactly center tapped. As with the diode balanced modulators, the FET balanced modulator typically adds between 40 dB and 60 dB of attenuation to the carrier.

Balanced Bridge Modulator

Figure 5-10a shows the schematic diagram for a *balanced bridge modulator.* The operation of the bridge modulator, as the balanced ring modulator, is completely dependent on the switching action of diodes D_1 through D_4 under the influence of the carrier and modulating

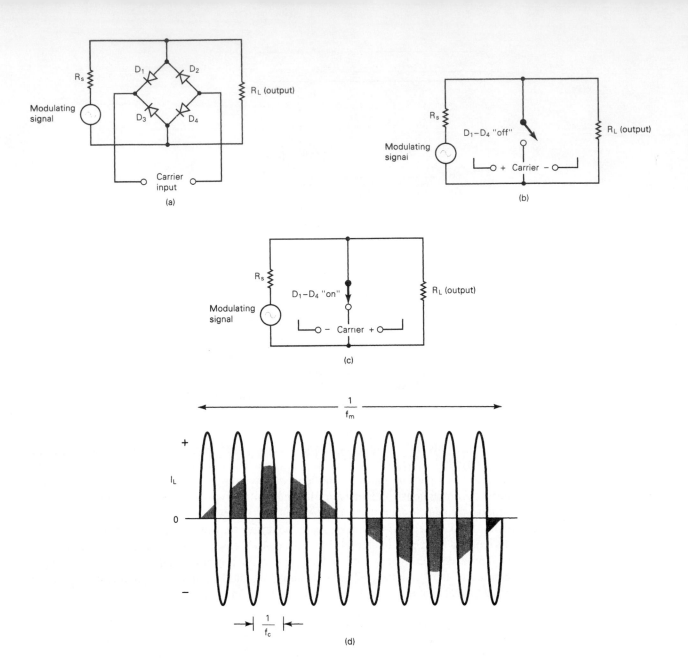

FIGURE 5-10 Balanced bridge modulator: (a) schematic diagram; (b) diodes biased *off;* (c) diodes biased *on;* (d) output waveform

signal voltages. Again, the carrier voltage controls the on or off condition of the diodes and, therefore, must be appreciably larger than the modulating signal voltage.

    Circuit operation.   For the carrier polarities shown in Figure 5-10b, all four diodes are reverse biased and off. Consequently, the audio signal voltage is transferred directly to the load resistor (R_L). Figure 5-10c shows the equivalent circuit for a carrier with the opposite polarity. All four diodes are forward biased and on, and the load resistor is bypassed (i.e., *shorted out*). As the carrier voltage changes from positive to negative, and vice versa, the output waveform contains a series of pulses that is comprised mainly of the upper and

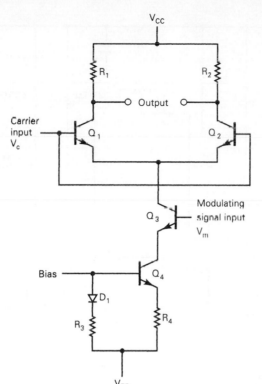

FIGURE 5-11 Differential amplifier schematic

lower sideband frequencies. The output waveform is shown in Figure 5-10d. The series of pulses is shown as the shaded area in the figure.

Linear Integrated-Circuit Balanced Modulators

Linear integrated-circuit (LIC) balanced modulators are available up to 100 MHz, such as the LM1496/1596, that can provide carrier suppression of 50 dB at 10 MHz and up to 65 dB at 500 kHz. The LM1496/1596 balanced modulator integrated circuit is a *double-balanced modulator/demodulator* that produces an output signal that is proportional to the product of its input signals. Integrated circuits are ideally suited for applications that require balanced operation.

Circuit operation. Figure 5-11 shows a simplified schematic diagram for a differential amplifier, which is the fundamental circuit of an LIC balanced modulator because of its excellent *common-mode rejection ratio* (typically 85 dB or more). When a carrier signal is applied to the base of Q_1, the emitter currents in both transistors will vary by the same amount. Because the emitter current for both Q_1 and Q_2 comes from a common constant-current source (Q_4), any increase in Q_1's emitter current results in a corresponding decrease in Q_2's emitter current, and vice versa. Similarly, when a carrier signal is applied to the base of Q_2, the emitter currents of Q_1 and Q_2 vary by the same magnitude, except in opposite directions. Consequently, if the same carrier signal is fed simultaneously to the bases of Q_1 and Q_2, the respective increases and decreases are equal and, thus, cancel. Therefore, the collector currents and output voltage remain unchanged. If a modulating signal is applied to the base of Q_3, it causes a corresponding increase or decrease (depending on its polarity) in the collector currents of Q_1 and Q_2. However, the carrier and modulating signal frequencies mix in the transistors and produce cross-product frequencies in the output. Therefore, the carrier and modulating signal frequencies are canceled in the balanced transistors, while the sum and difference frequencies appear in the output.

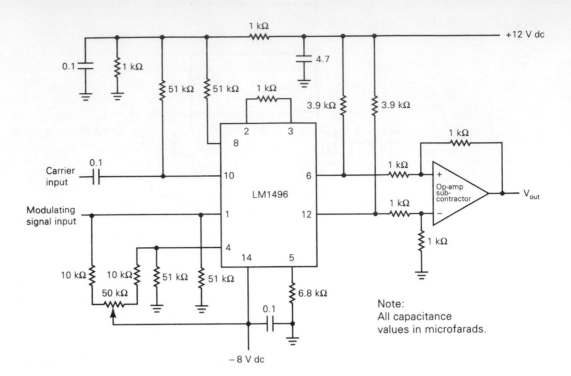

FIGURE 5-12 AM DSBSC modulator using the LM1496/1596 linear integrated circuit

Figure 5-12 shows the schematic diagram for a typical AM DSBSC modulator using the LM1496/1596 integrated circuit. The LM1496/1596 is a balanced modulator/demodulator for which the output is the product of its two inputs. The LM1496/1596 offers excellent carrier suppression (65 dB at 0.5 MHz), adjustable gain, balanced inputs and outputs, and a high common-mode rejection ratio (85 dB). When used as a product detector, the LM1496/1596 has a sensitivity of 3.0 μV and a dynamic range of 90 dB when operating at an intermediate frequency of 9 MHz.

The carrier signal is applied to pin 10, which, in conjunction with pin 8, provides an input to a quad cross-coupled differential output amplifier. This configuration is used to ensure that full-wave multiplication of the carrier and modulating signal occurs. The modulating signal is applied to pin 1, which, in conjunction with pin 4, provides a differential input to the current driving transistors for the output difference amplifier. The 50-kΩ potentiometer, in conjunction with V_{EE} (−8 V dc), is used to balance the bias currents for the difference amplifiers and null the carrier. Pins 6 and 12 are single-ended outputs that contain carrier and sideband components. When one of the outputs is inverted and added to the other, the carrier is suppressed and a double-sideband suppressed-carrier wave is produced. Such a process is accomplished in the op-amp subtractor. The subtractor inverts the signal at the inverting (−) input and adds it to the signal at the noninverting (+) input. Thus, a double-sideband suppressed-carrier wave appears at the output of the op-amp. The 6.8-kΩ resistor connected to pin 5 is a bias resistor for the internal constant-current supply.

The XR-2206 linear integrated-circuit AM DSBFC modulator described in Chapter 3 and shown in Figure 3-20a can also be used to produce a double-sideband suppressed-carrier wave by simply setting the dc bias to $V^+/2$ and limiting the modulating-signal amplitude to ± 4 V_p. As the modulating signal passes through its zero crossings, the phase of the carrier undergoes a 180° phase reversal. This property also makes the XR-2206 ideally suited as a phase shift modulator. The dynamic range of amplitude modulation for the XR-2206 is approximately 55 dB.

The transmitters used for single-sideband suppressed- and reduced-carrier transmission are identical except that the reinserted carrier transmitters have an additional circuit that adds a low-amplitude carrier to the single-sideband waveform after suppressed-carrier modulation has been performed and one of the sidebands has been removed. The reinserted carrier is called a *pilot carrier*. The circuit where the carrier is reinserted is called a *linear summer* if it is a resistive network and a *hybrid coil* if the SSB waveform and pilot carrier are inductively combined in a transformer bridge circuit. Three transmitter configurations are commonly used for single-sideband generation: the filter method, the phase shift method, and the so-called *third method*.

Single-Sideband Transmitter: Filter Method

Figure 5-13 shows a block diagram for a SSB transmitter that uses balanced modulators to suppress the unwanted carrier and filters to suppress the unwanted sideband. The figure shows a transmitter that uses three stages of frequency up-conversion. The modulating signal is an audio spectrum that extends from 0 kHz to 5 kHz. The modulating signal mixes with a low-frequency (LF) 100-kHz carrier in balanced modulator 1 to produce a double-sideband frequency spectrum centered around the suppressed 100-kHz IF carrier. Bandpass filter 1 (BPF 1) is tuned to a 5-kHz bandwidth centered around 102.5 kHz, which is the center of the upper sideband frequency spectrum. The pilot or reduced-amplitude carrier is added to the single-sideband waveform in the carrier reinsertion stage, which is simply a linear summer. The summer is a simple adder circuit that combines the 100-kHz pilot carrier with the 100-kHz to 105-kHz upper sideband frequency spectrum. Thus, the output of the summer is a SSBRC waveform. (If suppressed-carrier transmission is desired, the carrier pilot and summer circuit can be omitted.)

The low-frequency IF is converted to the final operating frequency band through a series of frequency translations. First, the SSBRC waveform is mixed in balanced modulator 2 with a 2-MHz medium-frequency (MF) carrier. The output is a double-sideband suppressed-carrier signal in which the upper and lower sidebands each contain the original SSBRC frequency spectrum. The upper and lower sidebands are separated by a 200-kHz frequency band that is void of information. The center frequency of BPF 2 is 2.1025 MHz with a 5-kHz bandwidth. Therefore, the output of BPF 2 is once again a single-sideband reduced-carrier waveform. Its frequency spectrum comprises a reduced 2.1-MHz second IF carrier and a 5-kHz-wide upper sideband. The output of BPF 2 is mixed with a 20-MHz high-frequency (HF) carrier in balanced modulator 3. The output is a double-sideband suppressed-carrier signal in which the upper and lower sidebands again each contain the original SSBRC frequency spectrum. The sidebands are separated by a 4.2-MHz frequency band that is void of information. BPF 3 is centered on 22.1025 MHz with a 5-kHz bandwidth. Therefore, the output of BPF 3 is once again a single-sideband waveform with a reduced 22.1-MHz RF carrier and a 5-kHz-wide upper sideband. The output waveform is amplified in the linear power amplifier and then transmitted.

In the transmitter just described, the original modulating-signal frequency spectrum was up-converted in three modulation steps to a final carrier frequency of 22.1 MHz and a single upper sideband that extended from the carrier to 22.105 MHz. After each up-conversion (frequency translation), the desired sideband is separated from the double-sideband spectrum with a BPF. The same final output spectrum can be produced with a single heterodyning process: one balanced modulator, one bandpass filter, and a single HF carrier supply. Figure 5-14a shows the block diagram and output frequency spectrum for a single-conversion transmitter. The output of the balanced modulator is a double-sideband frequency spectrum centered around a suppressed-carrier frequency of 22.1 MHz. To separate the 5-kHz-wide upper sideband from the composite frequency spectrum, a multiple-pole BPF with an extremely high Q is required. A BPF that meets this

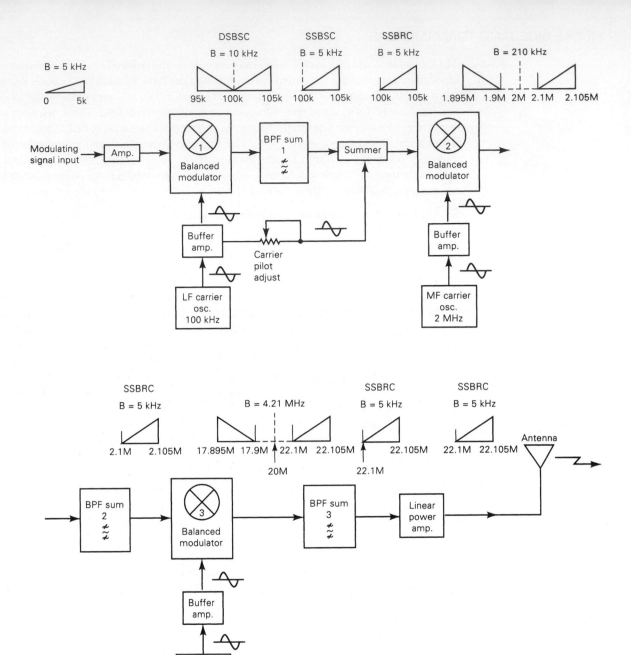

FIGURE 5-13 Single-sideband transmitter: filter method

criterion is in itself difficult to construct, but suppose that this were a multichannel transmitter and the carrier frequency were tunable; then the BPF must also be tunable. Constructing a tunable BPF in the megahertz frequency range with a passband of only 5 kHz is beyond economic and engineering feasibility. The only BPF in the transmitter shown in Figure 5-13 that has to separate sidebands that are immediately adjacent to each other is BPF 1. To construct a 5-kHz-wide, steep-skirted BPF at 100 kHz is a relatively simple

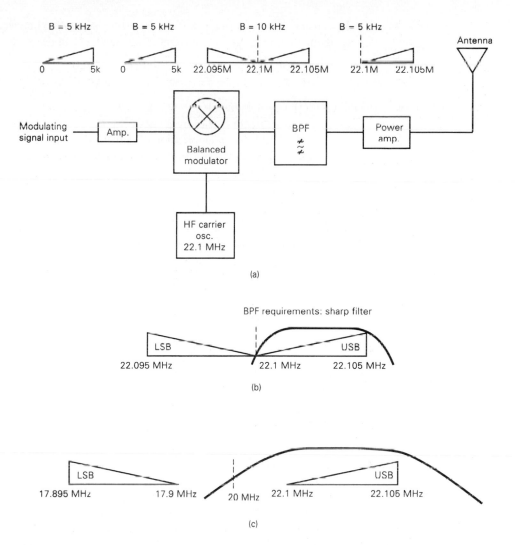

FIGURE 5-14 Single conversion SSBSC transmitter, filter method: (a) block diagram; (b) output spectrum and filtering requirements for a single-conversion transmitter; (c) output spectrum and filtering requirements for a three conversion transmitter

task, as only a moderate Q is required. The sidebands separated by BPF 2 are 200 kHz apart; thus, a low Q-filter with gradual roll-off characteristics can be used with no danger of passing any portion of the undesired sideband. BPF 3 separates sidebands that are 4.2 MHz apart. If multiple channels are used and the HF carrier is tunable, a single broadband filter can be used for BPF 3 with no danger of any portion of the undesired sideband leaking through the filter. For single-channel operation, the single conversion transmitter is the simplest design, but for multichannel operation, the three-conversion system is more practical. Figures 5-14b and c show the output spectrum and filtering requirements for both methods.

Single-sideband filters. It is evident that filters are an essential part of any electronic communications system and especially single-sideband systems. Transmitters as well as receivers have requirements for highly selective networks for limiting both the signal and noise frequency spectrums. The quality factor (Q) of a single-sideband filter depends on the carrier frequency, the frequency separation between sidebands, and the desired attenuation level of the unwanted sideband. Q can be expressed mathematically as

$$Q = \frac{f_c(\log^{-1} S/20)^{1/2}}{4\Delta f} \tag{5-1}$$

where
Q = quality factor
f_c = center or carrier frequency
S = dB level of suppression of unwanted sideband
Δf = frequency separation between the highest lower sideband frequency and the lowest upper sideband frequency

Example 5-1

Determine the quality factor (Q) necessary for a single-sideband filter with a 1-MHz carrier frequency, 80-dB unwanted sideband suppression, and the following frequency spectrum:

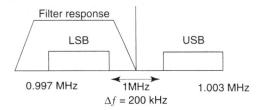

Solution Substituting into Equation 5-1 gives

$$Q = \frac{1 \text{ MHz}(\log^{-1} 80/20)^{1/2}}{4(200)} = 125{,}000$$

Conventional *LC* filters have relatively low Qs and are, therefore, not selective enough for most single-sideband applications. Therefore, filters used for single-sideband generation are usually constructed from either crystal or ceramic materials, mechanical filters, or surface acoustic wave (SAW) filters.

Crystal Filters. The *crystal lattice filter* is commonly used in single-sideband systems. The schematic diagram for a typical crystal lattice bandpass filter is shown in Figure 5-15a. The lattice comprises two sets of matched crystal pairs (X_1 and X_2, X_3 and X_4) connected between tuned input and output transformers T_1 and T_2. Crystals X_1 and X_2 are series connected, whereas X_3 and X_4 are connected in parallel. Each pair of crystals is matched in frequency within 10 Hz to 20 Hz. X_1 and X_2 are cut to operate at the filter lower cutoff frequency, and X_3 and X_4 are cut to operate at the upper cutoff frequency. The input and output transformers are tuned to the center of the desired passband, which tends to spread the difference between the series and parallel resonant frequencies. C_1 and C_2 are used to correct for any overspreading of frequency difference under matched crystal conditions.

The operation of the crystal filter is similar to the operation of a bridge circuit. When the reactances of the bridge arms are equal and have the same sign (either inductive or capacitive), the signals propagating through the two possible paths of the bridge cancel each other out. At the frequency where the reactances have equal magnitudes and opposite signs (one inductive and the other capacitive), the signal is propagated through the network with maximum amplitude.

Figure 5-15b shows a typical characteristic curve for a crystal lattice bandpass filter. Crystal filters are available with a Q as high as 100,000. The filter shown in Figure 5-15a is a single-element filter. However, for a crystal filter to adequately pass a specific band of frequencies and reject all others, at least two elements are necessary. Typical insertion losses for crystal filters are between 1.5 dB and 3 dB.

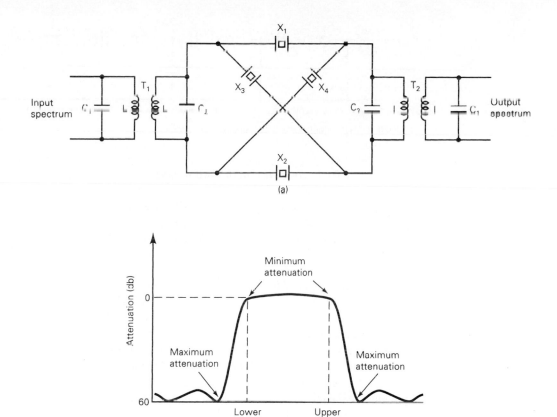

FIGURE 5-15 Crystal lattice filter. (a) schematic diagram; (b) characteristic curve

Ceramic Filters. *Ceramic filters* are made from lead zirconate-titanate, which exhibits the piezoelectric effect. Therefore, they operate quite similar to crystal filters except that ceramic filters do not have as high a Q-factor. Typical Q values for ceramic filters go up to about 2000. Ceramic filters are less expensive, smaller, and more rugged than their crystal lattice counterparts. However, ceramic filters have more loss. The insertion loss for ceramic filters is typically between 2 dB and 4 dB.

Ceramic filters typically come in one-element, three-terminal packages; two-element, eight-terminal packages; and four-element, fourteen-terminal packages. Ceramic filters feature small size, low profile, symmetrical selectivity characteristics, low spurious response, and excellent immunity to variations in environmental conditions with minimum variation in operating characteristics. However, certain precautions must be taken with ceramic filters, which include the following:

1. ***Impedance matching and load conditions.*** Ceramic filters differ from coils in that their impedance cannot readily be changed. When using ceramic filters, it is very important that impedances be properly matched.
2. ***Spurious signals.*** In practically all cases where ceramic filters are used, spurious signals are generated. To suppress these responses, impedance matching with IF transformers is the simplest and most effective way.
3. ***Matching coils.*** When difficulties arise in spurious response suppression or for improvement in selectivity or impedance matching in IF stages, use of an impedance matching coil is advised.

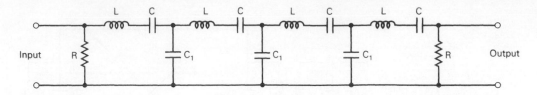

FIGURE 5-16 Mechanical filter equivalent circuit

4. *Error in wiring input and output connections.* Care must be taken when connecting the input and output terminals of a ceramic filter. Any error will cause waveform distortion and possibly frequency deviation of the signal.

5. *Use of two ceramic filters in cascade.* For best performance, a coil should be used between two ceramic filter units. When cost is a factor and a direct connection is necessary, a suitable capacitor or resistor can be used.

Mechanical Filters. A *mechanical filter* is a *mechanically resonant transducer.* It receives electrical energy, converts it to mechanical vibrations and then converts the vibrations back to electrical energy at its output. Essentially, four elements comprise a mechanical filter: an input transducer that converts the input electrical energy to mechanical vibrations, a series of mechanical resonant metal disks that vibrate at the desired resonant frequency, a coupling rod that couples the metal disks together, and an output transducer that converts the mechanical vibrations back to electrical energy. Figure 5-16 shows the electrical equivalent circuit for a mechanical filter. The series resonant circuits (*LC* combinations) represent the metal disks, coupling capacitor C_1 represents the coupling rod, and *R* represents the matching mechanical loads. The resonant frequency of the filter is determined by the series *LC* disks, and C_1 determines the bandwidth. Mechanical filters are more rugged than either ceramic or crystal filters and have comparable frequency-response characteristics. However, mechanical filters are larger and heavier and, therefore, are impractical for mobile communications equipment.

Surface Acoustic Wave Filters. *Surface acoustic wave (SAW) filters* were first developed in the 1960s but did not become commercially available until the 1970s. SAW filters use acoustic energy rather than electromechanical energy to provide excellent performance for precise bandpass filtering. In essence, SAW filters trap or guide acoustical waves along a surface. They can operate at center frequencies up to several gigahertz and bandwidths up to 50 MHz with more accuracy and reliability than their predecessor, the mechanical filter, and they do it at a lower cost. SAW filters have extremely steep roll-off characteristics and typically attenuate frequencies outside their passband between 30 dB and 50 dB more than the signals within their passband. SAW filters are used in both single- and multiple-conversion superheterodyne receivers for both RF and IF filters and in single-sideband systems for a multitude of filtering applications.

A SAW filter consists of transducers patterned from a thin aluminum film deposited on the surface of a semiconductor crystal material that exhibits the piezoelectric effect. This results in a physical deformation (rippling) on the surface of the substrate. These ripples vary at the frequency of the applied signal, but travel along the surface of the material at the speed of sound. With SAW filters, an oscillating electrical signal is applied across a small piece of semiconductor crystal that is part of a larger, flat surface, as shown in Figure 5-17a. The piezoelectric effect causes the crystal material to vibrate. These vibrations are in the form of acoustic energy that travels across the surface of the substrate until it reaches a second crystal at the opposite end, where the acoustic energy is converted back to electrical energy.

To provide filter action, a precisely spaced row of metallic *fingers* is deposited on the flat surface of the substrate, as shown in Figure 5-17b. The finger centers are spaced at ei-

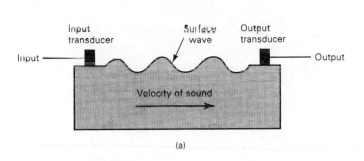
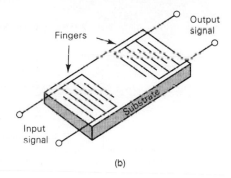

FIGURE 5-17   SAW filter: (a) surface wave; (b) metallic fingers

ther a half- or quarter-wavelength of the desired center frequency. As the acoustic waves travel across the surface of the substrate, they reflect back and forth as they impinge on the fingers. Depending on the acoustical wavelength and the spacing between the fingers, some of the reflected energy cancels and attenuates the incident wave energy (this is called *destructive interference*), while some of the energy aids (*constructive interference*). The exact frequencies of acoustical energy that are canceled depend on the spacing between the fingers. The bandwidth of the filter is determined by the thickness and number of fingers.

The basic SAW filter is *bidirectional*. That is, half the power is radiated toward the output transducer and the other half is radiated toward the end of the crystal substrate and is lost. By reciprocity, half the power is lost at the output transducer. Consequently, SAW filters have a relatively high insertion loss. This shortcoming can be overcome to a certain degree by using a more complex structure called a *unidirectional transducer*, which launches the acoustic wave in only one direction.

SAW filters are inherently very rugged and reliable. Because their operating frequencies and bandpass responses are set by the photolithographic process, they do not require complicated tuning operations nor do they become detuned over a period of time. The semiconductor wafer processing techniques used in manufacturing SAW filters permit large-volume production of economical and reproducible devices. Finally, their excellent performance capabilities are achieved with significantly reduced size and weight when compared to competing technologies.

The predominant disadvantage of SAW filters is their extremely high insertion loss, which is typically between 25 dB and 35 dB. For this reason, SAW filters cannot be used to filter low-level signals. SAW filters also exhibit a much longer delay time than their electronic counterparts (approximately 20,000 times as long). Consequently, SAW filters are sometimes used for *delay lines*.

Single-Sideband Transmitter: Phase Shift Method

With the phase shift method of single-sideband generation, the undesired sideband is canceled in the output of the modulator; therefore, sharp filtering is unnecessary. Figure 5-18 shows a block diagram for a SSB transmitter that uses the phase shift method to remove the upper sideband. Essentially, there are two separate double-sideband modulators (balanced modulators 1 and 2). The modulating signal and carrier are applied directly to one of the modulators and then both are shifted 90° and applied to the second modulator. The outputs from the two balanced modulators are double-sideband suppressed-carrier signals with the proper phase such that, when they are combined in a linear summer, the upper sideband is canceled.

Phasor representation.   The phasors shown in Figure 5-18 illustrate how the upper sideband is canceled by rotating both the carrier and the modulating signal 90° prior to

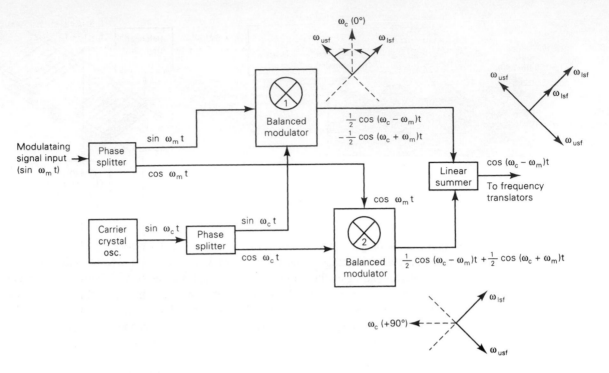

FIGURE 5-18 SSB transmitter: phase shift method

modulation. The output phase from balanced modulator 1 shows the relative position and direction of rotation of the upper (ω_{usf}) and lower (ω_{lsf}) side frequencies to the suppressed carrier (ω_c). The phasors at the output of balanced modulator 2 are essentially the same except that the phase of the carrier and the modulating signal are each rotated 90°. The output of the summer shows the sum of the phasors from the two balanced modulators. The two phasors for the lower sideband are in phase and additive, whereas the phasors for the upper sideband are 180° out of phase and, thus, cancel. Consequently, only the lower sideband appears at the output of the summer.

Mathematical analysis. In Figure 5-18 the input modulating signal ($\sin \omega_m t$) is fed directly to balanced modulator 1 and shifted 90° ($\cos \omega_m t$) and fed to balanced modulator 2. The low-frequency carrier ($\sin \omega_c t$) is also fed directly to balanced modulator 1 and shifted 90° ($\cos \omega_c t$) and fed to balanced modulator 2. The balanced modulators are product modulators and their outputs are expressed mathematically as

output from
balanced modulator 1 $= (\sin \omega_m t)(\sin \omega_c t)$

$$= \frac{1}{2}\cos(\omega_c - \omega_m)t - \frac{1}{2}\cos(\omega_c + \omega_m)t$$

output from
balanced modulator 2 $= (\cos \omega_m t)(\cos \omega_c t)$

$$= \frac{1}{2}\cos(\omega_c - \omega_m)t + \frac{1}{2}\cos(\omega_c + \omega_m)t$$

and the output from the linear summer is

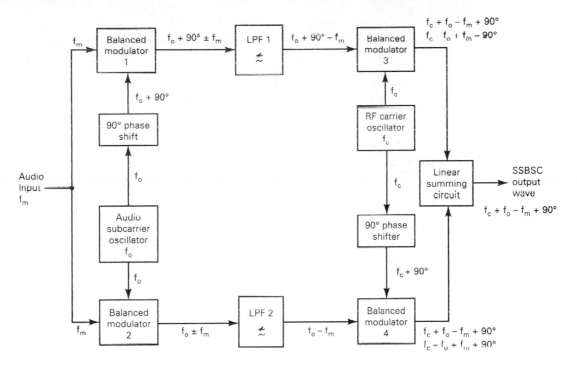

FIGURE 5-19 Single-sideband suppressed-carrier modulator: the "third method"

$$\frac{1}{2}\cos(\omega_c - \omega_m)t - \frac{1}{2}\cos(\omega_o + \omega_m)t$$

$$+ \frac{1}{2}\cos(\omega_c - \omega_m)t \quad | \quad \frac{1}{2}\cos(\omega_c + \omega_m)t$$

$$\overline{\cos(\omega_c - \omega_m)t \qquad \text{canceled}}$$

lower sideband
(difference signal)

Single-Sideband Transmitter: Third Method

The *third method* of single-sideband generation, developed by D. K. Weaver in the 1950s, is similar to the phase shift method in that it uses phase shifting and summing to cancel the undesired sideband. However, it has an advantage in that the information signal is initially modulated onto an audio *subcarrier,* thus eliminating the need for a *wideband* phase shifter (a phase shifter that has to shift a band of frequencies by the same amount, which is difficult to build in practice). The block diagram for a third-method SSB modulator is shown in Figure 5-19. Note that the inputs and outputs of the two phase shifters are single frequencies ($f_o, f_o + 90°, f_c$, and $f_c + 90°$). The input audio signals mix with the audio subcarrier in balanced modulators 1 and 2, which are supplied with quadrature (90° out of phase) subcarrier signals (f_o and $f_o + 90°$). The output from balanced modulator 2 contains the upper and lower sidebands ($f_o \pm f_m$), whereas the output from balanced modulator 1 contains the upper and lower sidebands, each shifted in phase 90° ($f_o \pm f_m + 90°$). The upper sidebands are removed by their respective low-pass filters, which have an upper cutoff frequency equal to that of the suppressed audio subcarrier. The output from LPF 1 ($f_o - f_m + 90°$) is mixed with the RF carrier (f_c) in balanced modulator 3, and the output from LPF 2 ($f_o - f_m$) is mixed with a 90° phase shifted RF carrier ($f_c + 90°$) in balanced modulator 4. The RF carriers are suppressed in balanced modulators 3 and 4. Therefore, the sum and difference output signals from balanced modulator 3, $(f_c + f_o - f_m + 90°) + (f_c - f_o + f_m - 90°)$, are combined in the linear summer with the sum and difference output signals from balanced modulator 4 $(f_c + f_o - f_m + 90°) + (f_c - f_o + f_m + 90°)$. The output from the summer is

$$(f_c + f_o - f_m + 90°) + (f_c - f_o + f_m - 90°)$$
$$+ (f_c + f_o - f_m + 90°) + (f_c - f_o + f_m + 90°)$$

$$\overline{\quad(f_c + f_o - f_m + 90°)\qquad\text{canceled}\quad}$$

The final RF output frequency is $f_c + f_o - f_m$, which is essentially the lower sideband of RF carrier $f_c + f_o$. The 90° offset phase is an absolute phase shift that all frequencies undergo and is, therefore, insignificant. If the RF upper sideband is desired, simply interchange the carrier inputs to balanced modulators 3 and 4, in which case the final RF carrier is $f_c - f_o$.

Independent Sideband Transmitter

Figure 5-20 shows a block diagram for an *independent sideband* (ISB) transmitter with three stages of modulation. The transmitter uses the filter method to produce two independent single-sideband channels (channel A and channel B). The two channels are combined; then a pilot carrier is reinserted. The composite ISB reduced-carrier waveform is up-converted to RF with two additional stages of frequency translation. There are two 5-kHz-wide information signals that originate from two independent sources. The channel A information signals modulate a 100-kHz LF carrier in balanced modulator A. The output from balanced modulator A passes through BPF A, which is tuned to the lower sideband (95 kHz to 100 kHz). The channel B information signals modulate the same 100-kHz LF carrier in balanced modulator B. The output from balanced modulator B passes through BPF B, which is tuned to the upper sideband (100 kHz to 105 kHz). The two single-sideband frequency spectrums are combined in a hybrid network to form a composite ISB suppressed-carrier spectrum (95 kHz to 105 kHz). The LF carrier (100 kHz) is reinserted in the linear summer to form an ISB reduced-carrier waveform. The ISB spectrum is mixed with a 2.7-MHz MF carrier in balanced modulator 3. The output from balanced modulator 3 passes through BPF 3 to produce an ISB reduced-carrier spectrum that extends from 2.795 MHz to 2.805 MHz with a reduced 2.8-MHz pilot carrier. Balanced modulator 4, BPF 4, and the HF carrier translate the MF spectrum to an RF band that extends from 27.795 MHz to 27.8 MHz (channel A) and 27.8 MHz to 27.805 MHz (channel B) with a 27.8-MHz reduced-amplitude carrier.

SINGLE-SIDEBAND RECEIVERS

Single-Sideband BFO Receiver

Figure 5-21 shows the block diagram for a simple noncoherent single-sideband *BFO receiver*. The selected radio-frequency spectrum is amplified and then mixed down to intermediate frequencies for further amplification and band reduction. The output from the IF amplifier stage is heterodyned (beat) with the output from a *beat frequency oscillator* (BFO). The BFO frequency is equal to the IF carrier frequency; thus, the difference between the IF and the BFO frequencies is the information signal. Demodulation is accomplished through several stages of mixing and filtering. The receiver is noncoherent because the RF local oscillator and BFO signals are not synchronized to each other or to the oscillators in the transmitter. Consequently, any difference between the transmit and receive local oscillator frequencies produces a frequency offset error in the demodulated information signal. For example, if the receive local oscillator is 100 Hz above its designated frequency and the BFO is 50 Hz above its designated frequency, the restored information is offset 150 Hz from its original frequency spectrum. Fifty hertz or more offset is distinguishable by a normal listener as a tonal variation.

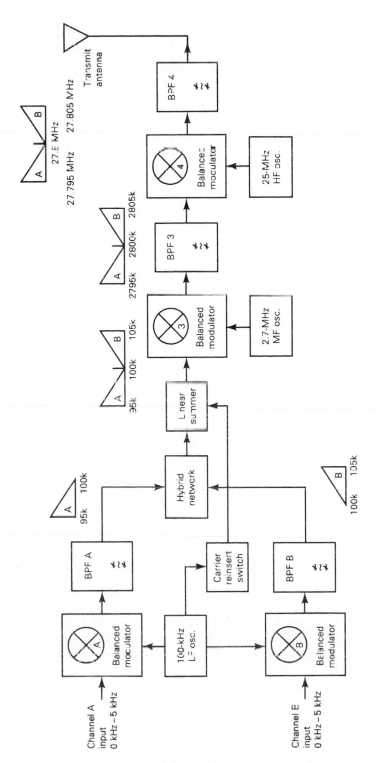

FIGURE 5-20 ISB transmitter: block diagram

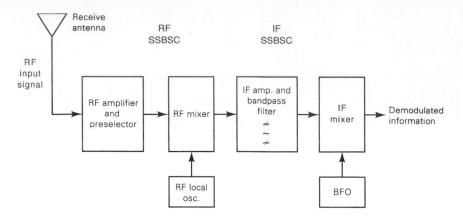

FIGURE 5-21 Noncoherent BFO SSB receiver

The RF mixer and second detector shown in Figure 5-21 are product detectors. As with the balanced modulators in the transmitter, their outputs are the product of their inputs. A product modulator and product detector are essentially the same circuit. The only difference is that the input to a product modulator is tuned to a low-frequency modulating signal and the output is tuned to a high-frequency carrier, whereas with a product detector, the input is tuned to a high-frequency modulated carrier and the output is tuned to a low-frequency information signal. With both the modulator and detector, the single-frequency carrier is the switching signal. In a receiver, the input signal, which is a suppressed or reduced RF carrier and one sideband, is mixed with the RF local oscillator frequency to produce an intermediate frequency. The output from the second product detector is the sum and difference frequencies between the IF and the beat frequency. The difference frequency band is the original input information.

Example 5-2

For the BFO receiver shown in Figure 5-21, a received RF frequency band of 30 MHz to 30.005 MHz, an RF local oscillator frequency of 20 MHz, an IF frequency band of 10 MHz to 10.005 MHz, and a BFO frequency of 10 MHz, determine

(a) Demodulated first IF frequency band and demodulated information frequency band.

(b) Demodulated information frequency band if the RF local oscillator frequency drifts down 0.001%.

Solution   (a) The IF output from the RF mixer is the difference between the received signal frequency and the RF local oscillator frequency or

$$f_{IF} = (30 \text{ MHz to } 30.005 \text{ MHz}) - 20 \text{ MHz} = 10 \text{ MHz to } 10.005 \text{ MHz}$$

The demodulated information signal spectrum is the difference between the intermediate frequency band and the BFO frequency or

$$f_m = (10 \text{ MHz to } 10.005 \text{ MHz}) - 10 \text{ MHz} = 0 \text{ kHz to } 5 \text{ kHz}$$

(b) A 0.001% drift would cause a decrease in the RF local oscillator frequency of

$$\Delta f = (0.00001)(20 \text{ MHz}) = 200 \text{ Hz}$$

Thus, the RF local oscillator frequency would drift down to 19.9998 Hz, and the output from the RF mixer is

$$f_{IF} = (30 \text{ MHz to } 30.005 \text{ MHz}) - 19.9998 \text{ MHz}$$
$$= 10.0002 \text{ MHz to } 10.0052 \text{ MHz}$$

The demodulated information signal spectrum is the difference between the intermediate frequency band and the BFO or

$$f_m = (10.0002 \text{ MHz to } 10.0052 \text{ MHz}) - 10 \text{ MHz}$$
$$= 200 \text{ Hz to } 5200 \text{ Hz}$$

The 0.001% drift in the RF local oscillator frequency caused a corresponding 200-Hz error in the demodulated information signal spectrum.

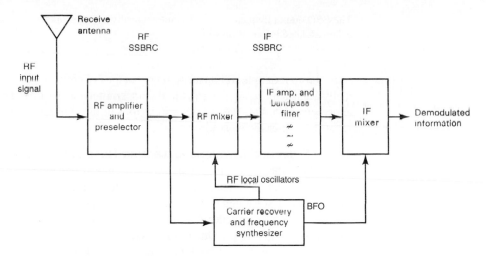

FIGURE 5-22 Coherent SSB BFO receiver

Coherent Single-Sideband BFO Receiver

Figure 5-22 shows a block diagram for a coherent single-sideband BFO receiver. This receiver is identical to the BFO receiver shown in Figure 5-21 except that the LO and BFO frequencies are synchronized to the carrier oscillators in the transmitter. The carrier *recovery circuit* is a narrowband PLL that tracks the pilot carrier in the composite SSBRC receiver signal and uses the recovered carrier to regenerate coherent local oscillator frequencies in the synthesizer. The synthesizer circuit produces a coherent RF local oscillator and BFO frequency. The carrier recovery circuit tracks the received pilot carrier. Therefore, minor changes in the carrier frequency in the transmitter are compensated for in the receiver, and the frequency offset error is eliminated. If the coherent receiver shown in Figure 5-22 had been used in Example 5-2, the RF local oscillator would not have been allowed to drift independently.

Example 5-3

For the coherent single-sideband BFO receiver shown in Figure 5-22, an RF reduced carrier frequency of 30 MHz with an upper sideband that extends from just above 30 MHz to 30.005 MHz, an RF local oscillator frequency of 20 MHz, an IF center frequency of 10 MHz, and a BFO output frequency of 10 MHz; determine

(a) Demodulated first IF frequency band and demodulated information frequency band

(b) Demodulated information frequency band if the reduced RF carrier input frequency drifted upward 60 Hz producing an RF carrier frequency of 30.0006 MHz and an upper sideband that extends to 30.00056 MHz.

Solution   (a)   The solution is identical to that provided in Example 5-2. The only difference is the method in which the RF local oscillator and BFO frequencies are produced. In the coherent receiver, the RF local oscillator and BFO frequencies are produced in the carrier recovery circuit and are, therefore, synchronized to the received RF carrier.

$$f_{IF} = (30 \text{ MHz to } 30.005 \text{ MHz}) - 20 \text{ MHz} = 10 \text{ MHz to } 10.005 \text{ MHz}$$

The demodulated information signal spectrum is simply the difference between the intermediate frequency band and the BFO frequency.

$$f_m = (10 \text{ MHz to } 10.005 \text{ MHz}) - 10 \text{ MHz} = 0 \text{ Hz to } 5 \text{ kHz}$$

(a) Because the RF local oscillator and BFO frequencies are synchronized to the received RF carrier signal, the RF local oscillator will shift proportionally with the change in the RF input signal. Therefore, the RF local oscillator frequency will automatically adjust to 20.0004 MHz producing an IF frequency spectrum of

$$f_{IF} = (30.0006 \text{ MHz to } 30.00056 \text{ MHz}) - 20.0004 \text{ MHz} = 10.0002 \text{ MHz to } 10.0052 \text{ MHz}$$

The BFO output frequency will also automatically adjust proportionally to 10.0002 MHz producing a demodulated information signal of

$$f_m = (10.0002 \text{ MHz to } 10.0052 \text{ MHz}) - 10.0002 \text{ MHz} = 0 \text{ Hz to } 5 \text{ kHz}$$

From Example 5-3 it can be seen that the coherent single-sideband receiver automatically adjusts to frequency drifts in the transmitted carrier frequency. Therefore, the coherent receiver is immune to carrier drift so long as the magnitude of the drift is within the limits of the carrier recovery circuit.

Single-Sideband Envelope Detection Receiver

Figure 5-23 shows the block diagram for a single-sideband receiver that uses synchronous carriers and envelope detection to demodulate the received signals. The reduced carrier pilot is detected, separated from the demodulated spectrum, and regenerated in the carrier recovery circuit. The regenerated pilot is divided and used as the stable frequency source for a frequency synthesizer, which supplies the receiver with frequency coherent local oscillators. The receive RF is mixed down to IF in the first detector. A regenerated IF carrier is added to the IF spectrum in the last linear summer, which produces a SSB full-carrier envelope. The envelope is demodulated in a conventional peak diode detector to produce the original information signal spectrum. This type of receiver is often called an exalted carrier receiver.

Multichannel Pilot Carrier Single-Sideband Receiver

Figure 5-24 shows a block diagram for a multichannel pilot carrier SSB receiver that uses a PLL carrier recovery circuit and a frequency synthesizer to produce coherent local and beat frequency oscillator frequencies. The RF input range extends from 4 MHz to 30 MHz, and the VCO natural frequency is coarsely adjusted with an external channel selector switch over a frequency range of 6 MHz to 32 MHz. The VCO frequency tracks above the incoming RF by 2 MHz, which is the first IF. A 1.8-MHz beat frequency sets the second IF to 200 kHz.

The VCO frequency is coarsely set with the channel selector switch and then mixed with the incoming RF signal in the first detector to produce a first IF difference frequency

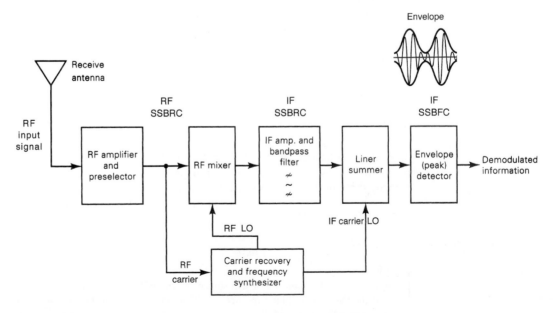

FIGURE 5-23 Single-sideband envelope detection receiver

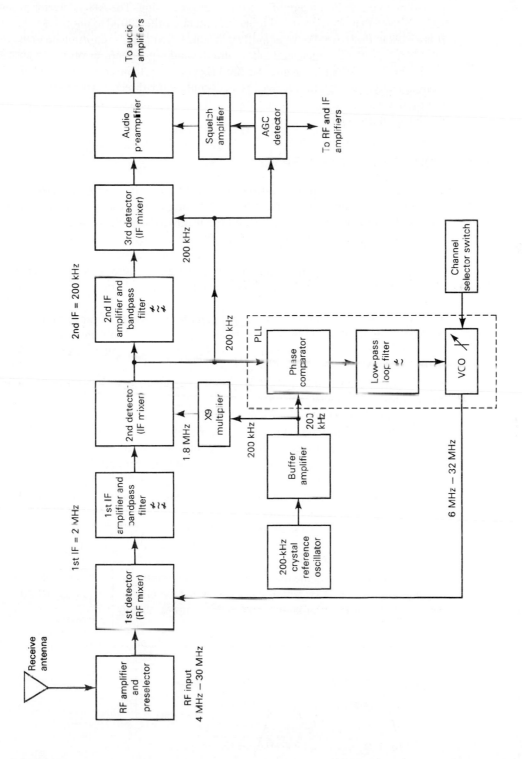

FIGURE 5-24 Multichannel pilot carrier SSB receiver

of 2 MHz. The first IF mixes with the 1.8-MHz beat frequency to produce a 200-kHz second IF. The PLL locks onto the 200-kHz pilot and produces a dc correction voltage that fine-tunes the VCO. The second IF is beat down to audio in the third detector, which is passed on to the audio preamplifier for further processing. The AGC detector produces an AGC voltage that is proportional to the amplitude of the 200-kHz pilot. The AGC voltage is fed back to the RF and/or IF amplifiers to adjust their gains proportionate to the received pilot level and to the squelch circuit to turn the audio preamplifier off in the absence of a received pilot. The PLL compares the 200-kHz pilot to a stable crystal-controlled reference. Consequently, although the receiver carrier supply is not directly synchronized to the transmit oscillators, the first and second IFs are, thus compensating for any frequency offset in the demodulated audio spectrum.

AMPLITUDE COMPANDORING SINGLE SIDEBAND

Amplitude compandoring single-sideband (ACSSB) systems provide narrowband voice communications for land-mobile services with nearly the quality achieved with FM systems and do it using less than one-third the bandwidth. With ACSSB, the audio signals are compressed before modulation by amplifying the higher-magnitude signals less than the lower-magnitude signals. After demodulation in the receiver, the audio signals are expanded by amplifying the higher-magnitude signals more than the lower-magnitude signals. A device that performs compression and expansion is called a *compandor* (*comp*ressor-exp*ander*).

Companding an information signal increases the dynamic range of a system by reducing the dynamic range of the information signals prior to transmission and then expanding them after demodulation. For example, when companding is used, information signals with an 80-dB dynamic range can be propagated through a communications system with only a 50-dB dynamic range. Companding slightly decreases the signal-to-noise ratios for the high-amplitude signals, while considerably increasing the signal-to-noise ratios of the low-amplitude signals.

ACSSB systems require that a pilot carrier signal be transmitted at a reduced amplitude along with the information signals. The pilot is used to synchronize the oscillators in the receiver and provides a signal for the AGC that monitors and adjusts the gain of the receiver and silences the receiver when no pilot is received.

ACSSB significantly reduces the dynamic range allowing the lower-level signals to be transmitted with greater power while remaining within the power ratings of the transmitter when higher-level signals are present. Consequently, the signal-to-noise ratio is significantly improved for the low-level signals while introducing an insignificant increase in the noise levels for the higher-level signals.

Figure 5-25 shows the relative location and amplitudes of the audio passband and pilot tone for an ACSSB system. It can be seen that the pilot is transmitted 10 dB below the maximum power level for signals within the audio passband.

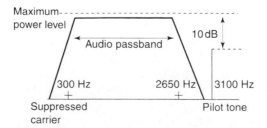

FIGURE 5-25 ACSSB signal

SINGLE-SIDEBAND SUPPRESSED CARRIER AND FREQUENCY-DIVISION MULTIPLEXING

Due to the bandwidth and power efficiencies inherent with single-sideband suppressed carrier, the most common application for it is in *frequency-division multiplexing* (FDM). *Multiplexing,* in general, is the process of combining transmissions from more than one source and transmitting them over a common facility such as a metallic or optical fiber cable or a radio-frequency channel. Frequency-division multiplexing is an analog method of combining two or more analog sources that originally occupied the same frequency band in such a manner that the channels do not interfere with each other. FDM is used extensively for combining many relatively narrowband sources into a single wideband channel, such as in public telephone systems.

With FDM, each narrowband channel is converted to a different location in the total frequency spectrum. The channels are essentially stacked on top of one another in the frequency domain. Figure 5-26 shows a simple FDM system where four, 5-kHz channels are frequency-division multiplexed into a single 20-kHz combined channel. As Figure 5-26a shows, channel 1 signals modulate a 100-kHz carrier in a balanced modulator, which inherently suppressed the 100-kHz carrier. The output of the balanced modulator is a double-sideband suppressed waveform with a bandwidth of 10 kHz. The DSBSC wave passes through a bandpass filter (BPF) where it is converted to a SSBSC signal. For this example, the lower sideband is blocked, thus the output of the BPF occupies the frequency band between 100 kHz and 105 kHz (a bandwidth of 5 kHz).

Channel 2 signals modulate a 105-kHz carrier in a balanced modulator again producing a DSBSC waveform which is converted to SSBSC by passing it through a bandpass filter tuned to pass only the upper sideband frequencies. Thus, the output from the BPF occupies a frequency band between 105 kHz and 110 kHz. The same process is used to convert signals from channel 3 and 4 to the frequency bands 110 kHz to 115 kHz and 115 kHz to 120 kHz, respectively. The combined frequency spectrum produced by combining the outputs from the four bandpass filters is shown in Figure 5-26b. As the figure shows, the total combined bandwidth is equal to 20 kHz and each channel occupies a different 5-kHz portion of the total 20-kHz bandwidth. In addition, all four carriers have been suppressed, enabling all the available power to be concentrated in the sideband signals.

Single-sideband suppressed-carrier transmission can be used to combine hundreds or even thousands of narrowband channels (such as voice or low-speed data circuits) into a single, composite wideband channel without the channels interfering with each other. For a more detailed description of frequency-division multiplexing, refer to Chapter 16.

DOUBLE-SIDEBAND SUPPRESSED CARRIER AND QUADRATURE MULTIPLEXING

Quadrature multiplexing (QM) is a multiplexing method that uses double-sideband suppressed-carrier transmission to combine two information sources into a single composite waveform which is then transmitted over a common facility without the two channels interfering with each other.

Figure 5-27 shows how two information sources are combined into a single communications channel using quadrature multiplexing. As the figure shows, each channel's information modulates the same carrier signal in balanced modulators. The primary difference between the two modulators is that the Q-channel carrier has been shifted in phase 90° from the 1-channel carrier. The two carriers are said to be *in quadrature* with each other. Thus, the output from the channel 1 modulator is the product of the information signals from source 1 $[v_{m1}(t)]$ and the in-phase carrier signal $[\sin(\omega_c t)]$. The output from the channel 2 modulator is the product of the information signals from source 2 $[v_{m2}(t)]$ and a

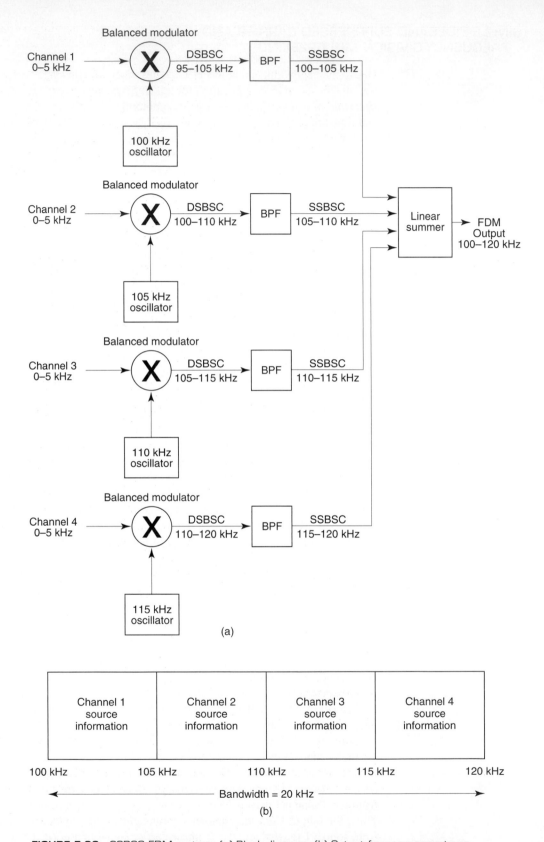

FIGURE 5-26 SSBSC FDM system: (a) Block diagram; (b) Output frequency spectrum

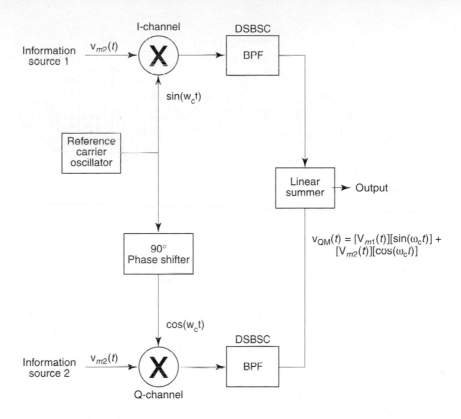

FIGURE 5-27 DSBSC QM System block diagram

carrier signal that has been shifted 90° in phase from the reference oscillator $[\cos(\omega_c t)]$. The outputs from the two bandpass filters are combined in a linear summer producing a composite waveform consisting of the two orthogonal (90°) double-sideband signals symmetrical about the same suppressed carrier, $v_{QM}(t) = [v_{m1}(t)][\sin(\omega_c t)] + [v_{m2}(t)][\cos(\omega_c t)]$. The two channels are thus separated in the phase domain. Quadrature multiplexing is typically used to multiplex information channels in data modems (Chapter 13) and to multiplex color signals in broadcast-band television (Chapter 11).

SINGLE-SIDEBAND MEASUREMENTS

Single-sideband transmitters are rated in peak envelope power (PEP) and peak envelope voltage (PEV), rather than simply rms power and voltage. For a single-frequency modulating signal, the modulated output signal with single-sideband suppressed-carrier transmission is not an envelope, but rather a continuous, single-frequency signal. A single frequency is not representative of a typical information signal. Therefore, for test purposes, a *two-frequency* test signal is used for the modulating signal for which the two tones have equal amplitudes. Figure 5-28a shows the waveform produced in a SSBSC modulator with a two-tone modulating signal. The waveform is the vector sum of the two equal-amplitude side frequencies and is similar to a conventional AM waveform except that the repetition rate is equal to the difference between the two modulating-signal frequencies. Figure 5-28b shows the envelope for a two-tone test signal when a low-amplitude pilot carrier is added. The envelope has basically the same shape except with the addition of a low-amplitude sine-wave ripple at the carrier frequency.

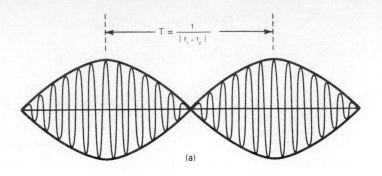

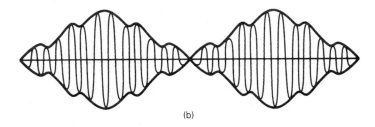

FIGURE 5-28 Two-tone SSB test signal: (a) without reinserted carrier; (b) with reinserted carrier

The envelope out of two-tone SSB is an important consideration because it is from this envelope that the output power for a SSB transmitter is determined. The PEP for a SSBSC transmitter is analogous to the total output power from a conventional double-sideband full-carrier transmitter. The rated PEP is the output power measured at the peak of the envelope when the input is a two-tone test signal and the two tones are equal in magnitude. With such an output signal, the actual power dissipated in the load is equal to half the PEP. Therefore, the voltage developed across the load is

$$e_{\text{total}} = \sqrt{E_1^2 + E_2^2}$$

where E_1 and E_2 are the rms voltages of the two test tones. Therefore,

$$\text{PEP} = \frac{(\sqrt{E_1^2 + E_2^2})^2}{R}$$

and because $E_1 = E_2$, $\qquad\qquad \text{PEP} = \dfrac{2E^2}{R}$ $\qquad\qquad\qquad\qquad$ (5-2)

However, the average power dissipated in the load is equal to the sum of the powers of the two tones:

$$P_{\text{ave}} = \frac{E_1^2}{2R} + \frac{E_2^2}{2R} = \frac{2E^2}{2R} = \frac{E^2}{R} \qquad\qquad\qquad (5\text{-}3)$$

which simplifies to $\qquad\qquad P_{\text{ave}} = \dfrac{\text{PEP}}{2}$ $\qquad\qquad\qquad\qquad\qquad$ (5-4)

Two equal-amplitude test tones are used for the test signal for the following reasons:

1. One tone produces a continuous single-frequency output that does not produce intermodulation.
2. A single-frequency output signal is not analogous to a normal information signal.

3. More than two tones make analysis impractical.
4. Two tones of equal amplitude place a more demanding requirement on the transmitter than is likely to occur during normal operation.

Example 5-4

For a two-tone test signal of 1.5 kHz and 3 kHz and a carrier frequency of 100 kHz, determine for a single-sideband suppressed-carrier transmission

(a) Output frequency spectrum if only the upper sideband is transmitted.

(b) For $E_1 = E_2 = 5$ V and a load resistance of 50 Ω, the PEP and average output power.

Solution   (a)   The output frequency spectrum contains the two upper side frequencies:

$$f_{usf1} = 100 \text{ kHz} + 1.5 \text{ kHz} = 101.5 \text{ kHz}$$

$$f_{usf2} = 100 \text{ kHz} + 3 \text{ kHz} = 103 \text{ kHz}$$

(b) Substituting into Equation 5-2 yields

$$PEP = \frac{2(0.707 \times 5)^2}{50} = 0.5 \text{ W}$$

Substituting into Equation 5-4 yields

$$P_{ave} = \frac{PEP}{2} = \frac{0.5}{2} = 0.25 \text{ W}$$

QUESTIONS

5-1. Describe AM SSBFC. Compare SSBFC to conventional AM.

5-2. Describe AM SSBSC. Compare SSBSC to conventional AM.

5-3. Describe AM SSBRC. Compare SSBRC to conventional AM.

5-4. What is a *pilot carrier?*

5-5. What is an *exalted* carrier?

5-6. Describe AM ISB. Compare ISB to conventional AM.

5-7. Describe AM VSB. Compare VSB to conventional AM.

5-8. Define *peak envelope power.*

5-9. Describe the operation of a balanced ring modulator.

5-10. What is a product modulator?

5-11. Describe the operation of a FET push–pull balanced modulator.

5-12. Describe the operation of a balanced bridge modulator.

5-13. What are the advantages of an LIC balanced modulator over a discrete circuit?

5-14. Describe the operation of a filter-type SSB transmitter.

5-15. Contrast crystal, ceramic, and mechanical filters.

5-16. Describe the operation of a phase-shift-type SSB transmitter.

5-17. Describe the operation of the "third type" of SSB transmitter.

5-18. Describe the operation of an independent sideband transmitter.

5-19. What is the difference between a product modulator and a product detector?

5-20. What is the difference between a coherent and a noncoherent receiver?

5-21. Describe the operation of a multichannel pilot carrier SSBRC receiver.

5-22. Why is a two-tone test signal used for making PEP measurements?

PROBLEMS

5-1. For the balanced ring modulator shown in Figure 5-6a, a carrier input frequency $f_c = 400$ kHz and a modulating-signal frequency range $f_m = 0$ kHz to 4 kHz; determine

(a) Output frequency spectrum.

(b) Output frequency for a single-frequency input $f_m = 2.8$ kHz.

5-2. For the LIC balanced modulator shown in Figure 5-12, a carrier input frequency of 200 kHz, and a modulating-signal frequency range $f_m = 0$ kHz to 3 kHz, determine

(a) Output frequency spectrum.

(b) Output frequency for a single-frequency input $f_m = 1.2$ kHz.

5-3. For the SSB transmitter shown in Figure 5-13, a low-frequency carrier of 100 kHz, a medium-frequency carrier of 4 MHz, a high-frequency carrier of 30 MHz, and a modulating-signal frequency range of 0 kHz to 4 kHz,

(a) Sketch the frequency spectrums for the following points: balanced modulator 1 out, BPF 1 out, summer out, balanced modulator 2 out, BPF 2 out, balanced modulator 3 out, and BPF 3 out.

(b) For a single-frequency input $f_m = 1.5$ kHz, determine the translated frequency for the following points: BPF 1 out, BPF 2 out, and BPF 3 out.

5-4. Repeat Problem 5-3, except change the low-frequency carrier to 500 kHz. Which transmitter has the more stringent filtering requirements?

5-5. For the SSB transmitter shown in Figure 5-14a, a modulating input frequency range of 0 kHz to 3 kHz, and a high-frequency carrier of 28 MHz,

(a) Sketch the output frequency spectrum.

(b) For a single-frequency modulating-signal input of 2.2 kHz, determine the output frequency.

5-6. Repeat Problem 5-5, except change the audio input frequency range to 300 Hz to 5000 Hz.

5-7. For the SSB transmitter shown in Figure 5-18, an input carrier frequency of 500 kHz, and a modulating-signal frequency range of 0 kHz to 4 kHz,

(a) Sketch the frequency spectrum at the output of the linear summer.

(b) For a single modulating-signal frequency of 3 kHz, determine the output frequency.

5-8. Repeat Problem 5-7, except change the input carrier frequency to 400 kHz and the modulating-signal frequency range to 300 Hz to 5000 Hz.

5-9. For the ISB transmitter shown in Figure 5-20, channel A input frequency range of 0 kHz to 4 kHz, channel B input frequency range of 0 kHz to 4 kHz, a low-frequency carrier of 200 kHz, a medium-frequency carrier of 4 MHz, and a high-frequency carrier of 32 MHz,

(a) Sketch the frequency spectrums for the following points: balanced modulator A out, BPF A out, balanced modulator B out, BPF B out, hybrid network out, linear summer out, balanced modulator 3 out, BPF 3 out, balanced modulator 4 out, and BPF 4 out.

(b) For an A-channel input frequency of 2.5 kHz and a B-channel input frequency of 3 kHz, determine the frequency components at the following points: BPF A out, BPF B out, BPF 3 out, and BPF 4 out.

5-10. Repeat Problem 5-9, except change the channel A input frequency range to 0 kHz to 10 kHz and the channel B input frequency range to 0 kHz to 6 kHz.

5-11. For the SSB receiver shown in Figure 5-21, a RF input frequency of 35.602 MHz, a RF local oscillator frequency of 25 MHz, and a 2-kHz modulating signal frequency, determine the IF and BFO frequencies.

5-12. For the multichannel pilot carrier SSB receiver shown in Figure 5-24, a crystal oscillator frequency of 300 kHz, a first IF frequency of 3.3 MHz, an RF input frequency of 23.303 MHz, and modulating signal frequency of 3 kHz, determine the following: VCO output frequency, multiplication factor, and second IF frequency.

5-13. For a two-tone test signal of 2 kHz and 3 kHz and a carrier frequency of 200 kHz,

(a) Determine the output frequency spectrum.

(b) For $E_1 = E_2 = 12$ V$_p$ and a load resistance $R_L = 50$ Ω, determine PEP and average power.

5-14. For the balanced ring modulator shown in Figure 5-6a, a carrier input frequency $f_c = 500$ kHz, and a modulating input signal frequency $f_m = 0$ kHz to 5 kHz, determine

(a) Output frequency range.

(b) Output frequency for a single input frequency $f_m = 3.4$ kHz.

5-15. For the LIC balanced modulator circuit shown in Figure 5-12, a carrier input frequency $f_c = 300$ kHz, and a modulating input signal frequency $f_m = 0$ kHz to 6 kHz, determine

    (a) Output frequency range.

    (b) Output frequency for a single-input frequency $f_m = 4.5$ kHz.

5-16. For the SSB transmitter shown in Figure 5-13, LF carrier frequency $f_{LF} = 120$ kHz, MF carrier frequency $f_{MF} = 3$ MHz, HF carrier frequency $f_{HF} = 28$ MHz, and an audio input frequency spectrum $f_m = 0$ kHz to 5 kHz,

    (a) Sketch the frequency spectrums for the following points: BPF 1 out, BPF 2 out, and BPF 3 out.

    (b) For a single-input frequency $f_m = 2.5$ kHz, determine the translated frequency at the following points: BPF 1 out, BPF 2 out, and BPF 3 out.

5-17. Repeat Problem 5-16 except change the LF carrier frequency to 500 kHz. Which transmitter has the more stringent filtering requirements?

5-18. For the SSB transmitter shown in Figure 5-14a, an audio input frequency $f_m = 0$ kHz to 4 kHz, and an HF carrier frequency $f_{HF} = 27$ MHz,

    (a) Sketch the output frequency spectrum.

    (b) For a single-frequency input signal $f_m = 1.8$ kHz, determine the output frequency.

5-19. Repeat Problem 5-18, except change the audio input frequency spectrum to $f_m = 300$ Hz to 4000 Hz.

5-20. For the SSB transmitter shown in Figure 5-18, a carrier frequency $f_c = 400$ kHz, and an input frequency spectrum $f_m = 0$ kHz to 5 kHz,

    (a) Sketch the frequency spectrum at the output of the linear summer.

    (b) For a single audio input frequency $f_m = 2.5$ kHz, determine the output frequency.

5-21. Repeat Problem 5-20, except change the carrier input frequency to 600 kHz and the input frequency spectrum to 300 Hz to 6000 Hz.

5-22. For the ISB transmitter shown in Figure 5-20, channel A input frequency $f_a = 0$ kHz to 5 kHz, channel B input frequency $f_b = 0$ kHz to 5 kHz, LF carrier frequency $f_{LF} = 180$ kHz, MF carrier frequency $f_{MF} = 3$ MHz, and HF carrier frequency $f_{HF} = 30$ MHz,

    (a) Sketch the frequency spectrums for the following points: BPF A out, BPF B out, BPF 3 out, and BPF 4 out.

    (b) For an A-channel input frequency $f_a = 2.5$ kHz and a B-channel input frequency $f_b = 2$ kHz, determine the frequency components at the following points: BPF A out, BPF B out, BPF 3 out, and BPF 4 out.

5-23. Repeat Problem 5-22, except change the channel A input frequency spectrum to 0 kHz to 8 kHz and the channel B input frequency spectrum to 0 kHz to 6 kHz.

5-24. For the SSB receiver shown in Figure 5-24, RF input frequency $f_{RF} = 36.803$ MHz, RF local oscillator frequency $f_{lo} = 26$ MHz, and a 3-kHz modulating-signal frequency, determine the following: BFO output frequency and detected information frequency.

5-25. For the multichannel pilot carrier SSB receiver shown in Figure 5-24, crystal oscillator frequency $f_{co} = 400$ kHz, first IF frequency $f_{IF} = 4.4$ MHz, RF input frequency $f_{RF} = 23.403$ MHz, and modulating-signal frequency $f_m = 3$ kHz; determine the following: VCO output frequency, multiplication factor, and second IF frequency.

5-26. For a two-tone test signal of 3 kHz and 4 kHz and a carrier frequency of 400 kHz, determine

    (a) Output frequency spectrum.

    (b) For E_1 and $E_2 = 20$ V$_p$ and a load resistor $R_L = 100$ Ω, determine the PEP and average power.

CHAPTER 6

Angle Modulation Transmission

INTRODUCTION

As previously stated, there are three properties of an analog signal that can be varied (modulated) by the information signal. Those properties are amplitude, frequency, and phase. Chapters 3, 4, and 5 described amplitude modulation. This chapter and Chapter 7 describe *frequency modulation* (FM) and *phase modulation* (PM), which are both forms of *angle modulation.* Unfortunately, both frequency and phase modulation are often referred to as simply FM, although there are actual distinctions between the two. Angle modulation has several advantages over amplitude modulation, such as noise reduction, improved system fidelity, and more efficient use of power. However, angle modulation also has several disadvantages when compared to AM including requiring a wider bandwidth and utilizing more complex circuits in both the transmitters and receivers.

Angle modulation was first introduced in 1931 as an alternative to amplitude modulation. It was suggested that an angle-modulated wave was less susceptible to noise than AM and, consequently, could improve the performance of radio communications. Major E. H. Armstrong (who also developed the superheterodyne receiver) developed the first successful FM radio system in 1936, and in July 1939 the first regularly scheduled broadcasting of FM signals began in Alpine, New Jersey. Today, angle modulation is used extensively for commercial radio broadcasting, television sound transmission, two-way mobile radio, cellular radio, and microwave and satellite communications systems.

The purposes of this chapter are to introduce the reader to the basic concepts of frequency and phase modulation and how they relate to each other, to show some of the common circuits used to produce angle-modulated waves, and to compare the performance of angle modulation to amplitude modulation.

ANGLE MODULATION

Angle modulation results whenever the phase angle (θ) of a sinusoidal wave is varied with respect to time. An angle-modulated wave is expressed mathematically as

$$m(t) = V_c \cos[\omega_c t + \theta(t)] \qquad\qquad (6\text{-}1)$$

where $m(t)$ = angle-modulated wave
   V_c = peak carrier amplitude (volts)
   ω_c — carrier radian frequency (i.e., angular velocity, $2\pi f_c$ radians per second)
   $\theta(t)$ = instantaneous phase deviation (radians)

With angle modulation, it is necessary that $\theta(t)$ be a prescribed function of the modulating signal. Therefore, if $v_m(t)$ is the modulating signal, the angle modulation is expressed mathematically as

$$\theta(t) = F[v_m(t)] \qquad\qquad (6\text{-}2)$$

where $v_m(t) = V_m \sin(\omega_m t)$
   ω_m — angular velocity of the modulating signal ($2\pi f_m$ radian per second)
   f_m = modulating signal frequency (hertz)
   V_m = peak amplitude of the modulating signal (volts)

In essence, the difference between frequency and phase modulation lies in which property of the carrier (the frequency or the phase) is directly varied by the modulating signal and which property is indirectly varied. Whenever the frequency of a carrier is varied, the phase is also varied, and vice versa. Therefore, FM and PM must both occur whenever either form of angle modulation is performed. If the frequency of the carrier is varied directly in accordance with the modulating signal, FM results. If the phase of the carrier is varied directly in accordance with the modulating signal, PM results. Therefore, direct FM is indirect PM and direct PM is indirect FM. Frequency and phase modulation can be defined as follows:

Direct frequency modulation *(FM)*: Varying the frequency of a constant-amplitude carrier directly proportional to the amplitude of the modulating signal at a rate equal to the frequency of the modulating signal.

Direct phase modulation *(PM)*: Varying the phase of a constant-amplitude carrier directly proportional to the amplitude of the modulating signal at a rate equal to the frequency of the modulating signal.

Figure 6-1 shows an angle-modulated signal [$m(t)$] in the frequency domain. The figure shows how the carrier frequency (f_c) is changed when acted on by a modulating signal [$v_m(t)$]. The magnitude and direction of the frequency shift (Δf) is proportional to the amplitude and polarity of the modulating signal (V_m), and the rate at which the frequency changes are occurring is equal to the frequency of the modulating signal (f_m). For this

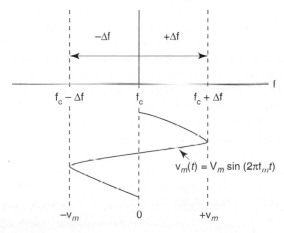

FIGURE 6-1 Angle-modulated wave in the frequency domain.

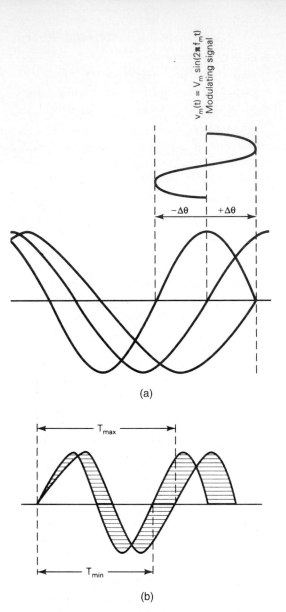

$v_m(t) = V_m \sin(2\pi f_m t)$
Modulating signal

$-\Delta\theta$ | $+\Delta\theta$

(a)

T_{max}

T_{min}

(b)

FIGURE 6-2 Angle modulation in the time domain: (a) phase changing with time; (b) frequency changing with time.

example, a positive modulating signal produces an increase in frequency and a negative modulating signal produces a decrease in frequency, although the opposite relationship could occur depending on the type of modulator circuit used.

Figure 6-2a shows in the time domain the waveform for a sinusoidal carrier for which angle modulation is occurring. As the figure shows, the phase (θ) of the carrier is changing proportional to the amplitude of the modulating signal [$v_m(t)$]. The relative angular displacement (shift) of the carrier phase in radians in respect to the reference phase is called *phase deviation* ($\Delta\theta$). The change in the carrier's phase produces a corresponding change in frequency. The relative displacement of the carrier frequency in hertz in respect to its unmodulated value is called *frequency deviation* (Δf). The magnitude of the frequency and phase deviation is proportional to the amplitude of the modulating signal (V_m), and the rate at which the changes are occurring is equal to the modulating signal frequency (f_m).

Figure 6-2b shows a sinusoidal carrier in which the frequency (f) is changed (*deviated*) over a period of time. The fat portion of the waveform corresponds to the peak-to-peak change in the period of the carrier (ΔT). The minimum period (T_{min}) corresponds to the maximum frequency (f_{max}), and the maximum period (T_{max}) corresponds to the minimum frequency (f_{min}). The peak-to-peak frequency deviation is determined by simply measuring the difference between the maximum and minimum frequencies ($\Delta f_{p-p} = 1/T_{min} - 1/T_{max}$).

Whenever the period (T) of a sinusoidal carrier changes, its frequency and phase also change, and if the changes are continuous, the wave is no longer a single frequency. It will be shown that the resultant angle-modulated waveform comprises the original unmodulated carrier frequency (often called the *carrier rests frequency*) and an infinite number of pairs of side frequencies are displaced on either side of the carrier by an integral multiple of the modulating-signal frequency.

Mathematical Analysis

The difference between FM and PM is more easily understood by defining the following four terms with reference to Equation 6-1: instantaneous phase deviation, instantaneous phase, instantaneous frequency deviation, and instantaneous frequency.

1. *Instantaneous phase deviation.* The *instantaneous phase deviation* is the instantaneous change in the phase of the carrier at a given instant of time and indicates how much the phase of the carrier is changing with respect to its reference phase. Instantaneous phase deviation is expressed mathematically as

$$\text{instantaneous phase deviation} = \theta(t) \quad \text{rad} \tag{6-3}$$

2. *Instantaneous phase.* The *instantaneous phase* is the precise phase of the carrier at a given instant of time and is expressed mathematically as

$$\text{instantaneous phase} = \omega_c t + \theta(t) \quad \text{rad} \tag{6-4}$$

where
$$\omega_c t = \text{carrier reference phase (radians)}$$
$$= [2\pi(\text{rad/cycle})][f_c(\text{cycles/s})][t\ (s)] = 2\pi f_c t(\text{rad})$$
$$f_c = \text{carrier frequency (hertz)}$$
$$\theta(t) = \text{instantaneous phase deviation (radians)}$$

3. *Instantaneous frequency deviation.* The *instantaneous frequency deviation* is the instantaneous change in the frequency of the carrier and is defined as the first time derivative of the instantaneous phase deviation. Therefore, the instantaneous phase deviation is the first integral of the instantaneous frequency deviation. In terms of Equation 6-3, the instantaneous frequency deviation is expressed mathematically as

$$\text{instantaneous frequency deviation} = \theta'(t)\ \text{rad/s} \tag{6-5}$$

or
$$= \frac{\theta'(t)\ \text{rad/s}}{2\pi\ \text{rad/cycle}} = \frac{\text{cycles}}{s} = \text{Hz}$$

The prime ($'$) is used to denote the first derivative with respect to time.

4. *Instantaneous frequency.* The *instantaneous frequency* is the precise frequency of the carrier at a given instant of time and is defined as the first time derivative of the instantaneous phase. In terms of Equation 6-4, the instantaneous frequency is expressed mathematically as

$$\text{instantaneous frequency} = \omega_i(t) = \frac{d}{dt}[\omega_c t + \theta(t)] \tag{6-6a}$$

$$= \omega_c + \theta'(t) \quad \text{rad/s} \tag{6-6b}$$

Substituting $2\pi f_c$ for ω_c gives

$$\text{instantaneous frequency} = f_i(t)$$

and

$$\omega_i(t) = \left(2\pi \frac{\text{rad}}{\text{cycle}}\right)\left(f_c \frac{\text{cycles}}{\text{s}}\right) + \theta'(t) = 2\pi f_c + \theta'(t) \quad \text{rad/s}$$

or

$$fi(t) = \frac{2\pi f_c + \theta(t) \text{ rad/s}}{2\pi \text{ rad/cycle}} = f_c + \frac{\theta'(t)}{2\pi} \frac{\text{cycles}}{\text{s}} = f_c + \frac{\theta'(t)}{2\pi} \quad \text{Hz} \tag{6-6c}$$

Deviation Sensitivity

Phase modulation can then be defined as angle modulation in which the instantaneous phase deviation, $\theta(t)$, is proportional to the amplitude of the modulating signal voltage and the instantaneous frequency deviation is proportional to the slope or first derivative of the modulating signal. Similarly, frequency modulation is angle modulation in which the instantaneous frequency deviation, $\theta'(t)$, is proportional to the amplitude of the modulating signal and the instantaneous phase deviation is proportional to the integral of the modulating-signal voltage.

For a modulating signal $v_m(t)$, the phase and frequency modulation are

$$\text{phase modulation} = \theta(t) = K v_m(t) \quad \text{rad} \tag{6-7}$$

$$\text{frequency modulation} = \theta'(t) = K_1 v_m(t) \quad \text{rad/s} \tag{6-8}$$

where K and K_1 are constants and are the *deviation sensitivities* of the phase and frequency modulators, respectively. The deviation sensitivities are the output-versus-input transfer functions for the modulators, which give the relationship between what output parameter changes in respect to specified changes in the input signal. For a frequency modulator, changes would occur in the output frequency in respect to changes in the amplitude of the input voltage. For a phase modulator, changes would occur in the phase of the output frequency in respect to changes in the amplitude of the input voltage.

The deviation sensitivity for a phase modulator is

$$K = \frac{\text{rad}}{\text{V}} \left(\frac{\Delta\theta}{\Delta V}\right)$$

and for a frequency modulator

$$K_1 = \frac{\text{rad/s}}{\text{V}} \quad \text{or} \quad \frac{\text{rad}}{\text{V} - \text{s}} \left(\frac{\Delta\omega}{\Delta V}\right)$$

Phase modulation is the first integral of the frequency modulation. Therefore, from Equations 6-7 and 6-8

$$\begin{aligned}
\text{phase modulation} = \theta(t) &= \int\theta'(t)\, dt \\
&= \int K_1 v_m(t)\, dt \\
&= K_1 \int v_m(t)\, dt \tag{6-9}
\end{aligned}$$

Therefore, substituting a modulating signal $v_m(t) = V_m \cos(\omega_m t)$ into Equation 6-1 yields,

For phase modulation,
$$\begin{aligned}
m(t) &= V_c \cos[\omega_c t + \theta(t)] \\
&= V_c \cos[\omega_c t + K V_m \cos(\omega_m t)] \tag{6-10}
\end{aligned}$$

For frequency modulation,
$$\begin{aligned}
m(t) &= V_c \cos[\omega_c t + \int\theta'(t)] \\
&= V_c \cos[\omega_c t + \int K_1 v_m(t)\, dt] \\
&= V_c \cos[\omega_c t + K_1 \int V_m \cos(\omega_m t)\, dt] \\
&= V_c \cos\left[\omega_c t + \frac{K_1 V_m}{\omega_m} \sin(\omega_m t)\right] \tag{6-11}
\end{aligned}$$

The preceding mathematical relationships are summarized in Table 6-1. Also, the expressions for the FM and PM waves that result when the modulating signal is a single-frequency sinusoidal wave are shown.

TABLE 6-1 Equations for Phase- and Frequency-Modulated Carriers

Type of Modulation	Modulating Signal	Angle-Modulated Wave, $m(t)$
(a) Phase	$v_m(t)$	$V_c \cos[\omega_c t + K v_m(t)]$
(b) Frequency	$v_m(t)$	$V_c \cos[\omega_c t + K_1 \int v_m(t)\, dt]$
(c) Phase	$V_m \cos(\omega_m t)$	$V_c \cos[\omega_c t + K V_m \cos(\omega_m t)]$
(d) Frequency	$V_m \cos(\omega_m t)$	$V_c \cos\left[\omega_c t + \dfrac{K_1 V_m}{\omega_m} \sin(\omega_m t)\right]$

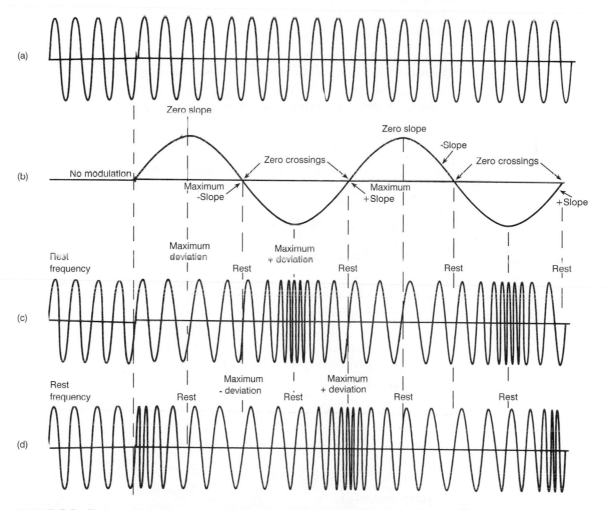

FIGURE 6-3 Phase and frequency modulation of a sine-wave carrier by a sine-wave signal: (a) unmodulated carrier; (b) modulating signal; (c) frequency-modulated wave; (d) phase-modulated wave.

FM and PM Waveforms

Figure 6-3 illustrates both frequency and phase modulation of a sinusoidal carrier by a single-frequency modulating signal. It can be seen that the FM and PM waveforms are identical except for their time relationship (phase). Thus, it is impossible to distinguish an FM waveform from a PM waveform without knowing the dynamic characteristics of the modulating signal. With FM, the maximum frequency deviation (change in the carrier frequency) occurs during the maximum positive and negative peaks of the modulating signal (i.e., the frequency deviation is proportional to the amplitude of the modulating signal). With PM, the maximum frequency deviation occurs during the zero crossings of the modulating signal (i.e., the frequency deviation is proportional to the slope or first derivative of the modulating signal). For both frequency and phase modulation, the rate at which the frequency changes occur is equal to the modulating-signal frequency.

Similarly, it is not apparent from Equation 6-1 whether an FM or PM wave is represented. It could be either. However, knowledge of the modulating signal will permit correct identification. If $\theta(t) = Kv_m(t)$, it is phase modulation, and if $\theta'(t) = K_1 v_m(t)$, it is frequency modulation. In other words, if the instantaneous frequency is directly proportional to the amplitude of the modulating signal, it is frequency modulation, and if the instantaneous phase is directly proportional to the amplitude of the modulating frequency, it is phase modulation.

Phase Deviation and Modulation Index

Comparing expressions (c) and (d) for the angle-modulated carrier in Table 6-1 shows that the expression for a carrier that is being phase or frequency modulated by a single-frequency modulating signal can be written in a general form by modifying Equation 6-1 as follows:

$$m(t) = V_c \cos[\omega_c t + m \cos(\omega_m t)] \qquad (6\text{-}12)$$

where $m \cos(\omega_m t)$ is the instantaneous phase deviation, $\theta(t)$. When the modulating signal is a single-frequency sinusoid, it is evident from Equation 6-12 that the phase angle of the carrier varies from its unmodulated value in a simple sinusoidal fashion.

In Equation 6-12, m represents the *peak phase deviation* in radians for a phase-modulated carrier. Peak phase deviation is called the *modulation index* (or sometimes *index of modulation*). One primary difference between frequency and phase modulation is the way in which the modulation index is defined. For PM, the modulation index is proportional to the amplitude of the modulating signal, independent of its frequency. The modulation index for a phase-modulated carrier is expressed mathematically as

$$m = KV_m \quad \text{(radians)} \qquad (6\text{-}13)$$

where m = modulation index and peak phase deviation ($\Delta\theta$, radians)
    K = deviation sensitivity (radians per volt)
    V_m = peak modulating-signal amplitude (volts)

thus, $m = K\left(\dfrac{\text{radians}}{\text{volt}}\right)V_m \text{ (volts)} = \text{radians}$

Therefore, for PM, Equation 6-1 can be rewritten as

$$m(t) = V_c \cos[\omega_c t + KV_m \cos(\omega_m t)] \qquad (6\text{-}14\text{a})$$

or $$m(t) = V_c \cos[\omega_c t + \Delta\theta \cos(\omega_m t)] \qquad (6\text{-}14\text{b})$$

or $$m(t) = V_c \cos[\omega_c t + m \cos(\omega_m t)] \qquad (6\text{-}14\text{c})$$

For a frequency-modulated carrier, the modulation index is directly proportional to the amplitude of the modulating signal and inversely proportional to the frequency of the modulating signal. Therefore, for FM, modulation index is expressed mathematically as

$$m = \frac{K_1 V_m}{\omega_m} \text{ (unitless)} \qquad (6\text{-}15)$$

where m = modulation index (unitless)
    K_1 = deviation sensitivity (radians per second per volt or radians per volts)

$$V_m = \text{peak modulating-signal amplitude (volts)}$$
$$\omega_m = \text{radian frequency (radians per second)}$$

thus,
$$m = \frac{K_1\left(\frac{\text{radians}}{\text{volt - s}}\right)V_m(\text{volt})}{\omega_m \text{ (radians/s)}} = \text{(unitless)}$$

From Equation 6-15 it can be seen that for FM the modulation index is a unitless ratio and is used only to describe the depth of modulation achieved for a modulating signal with a given peak amplitude and radian frequency.

Deviation sensitivity can be expressed in hertz per volt allowing Equation 6-15 to be written in a more practical form as

$$m = \frac{K_1 V_m}{f_m} \text{ (unitless)} \tag{6-16}$$

where m = modulation index (unitless)
K_1 = deviation sensitivity (cycles per second per volt or hertz per volt)
V_m = peak modulating-signal amplitude (volts)
f_m = cyclic frequency (hertz per second)

thus,
$$m = \frac{K_1\left(\frac{\text{hertz}}{\text{volt}}\right)V_m \text{ (volt)}}{f_m \text{ (hertz)}} = \text{(unitless)}$$

Frequency Deviation

Frequency deviation is the change in frequency that occurs in the carrier when it is acted on by a modulating-signal frequency. Frequency deviation is typically given as a peak frequency shift in hertz (Δf). The peak-to-peak frequency deviation ($2\Delta f$) is sometimes called *carrier swing*.

For an FM, the deviation sensitivity is often given in hertz per volt. Therefore, the peak frequency deviation is simply the product of the deviation sensitivity and the peak modulating-signal voltage and expressed mathematically as:

$$\Delta f = K_1 V_m \text{ (Hz)} \tag{6-17}$$

Equation 6-17 can be substituted into Equation 6-16 and the expression for the modulation index in FM can be rewritten as:

$$m = \frac{\Delta f \text{ (Hz)}}{f_m \text{ (Hz)}} \text{ (unitless)} \tag{6-18}$$

Therefore, for FM, Equation 6-1 can be rewritten as

$$m(t) = V_c \cos\left[\omega_c t + \frac{K_1 V_m}{f_m} \sin(\omega_m t)\right] \tag{6-19a}$$

or
$$m(t) = V_c \cos\left[\omega_c t + \frac{\Delta f}{f_m} \sin(\omega_m t)\right] \tag{6-19b}$$

or
$$m(t) = V_c \cos\left[\omega_c t + m \sin(\omega_m t)\right] \tag{6-19c}$$

From examination of Equations 6-15 and 6-16, it can be seen that the modulation indices for FM and PM relate to the modulating signal differently. With PM, both the modulation index and peak phase deviation are directly proportional to the amplitude of the modulating signal and unaffected by its frequency. With FM, however, both the

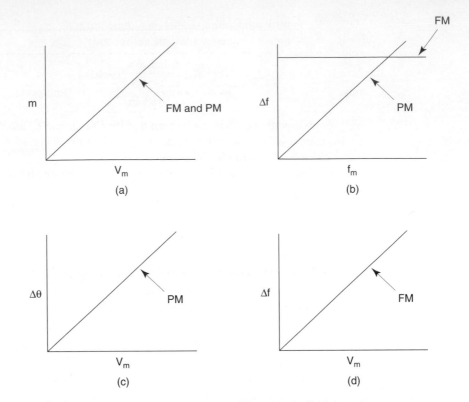

FIGURE 6-4 Relationship between modulation index, frequency deviation, and phase deviation in respect to modulations signal amplitude and frequency: (a) modulation index versus amplitude; (b) frequency deviation versus modulating frequency; (c) phase deviation versus amplitude; and (d) frequency deviation versus amplitude.

modulation index and frequency deviation are directly proportional to the amplitude of the modulating signal and the modulation index is inversely proportional to its frequency. Figure 6-4 graphically shows the relationship among modulation index and peak phase deviation for PM and the modulation index and peak frequency deviation for FM in respect to the modulating signal amplitude and frequency.

The preceding mathematical relationships are summarized in Table 6-2.

Example 6-1

(a) Determine the peak frequency deviation (Δf) and modulation index (m) for an FM modulator with a deviation sensitivity $K_1 = 5$ kHz/V and a modulating signal $v_m(t) = 2 \cos(2\pi 2000t)$.

(b) Determine the peak phase deviation (m) for a PM modulator with a deviation sensitivity $K = 2.5$ rad/V and a modulating signal $v_m(t) = 2 \cos(2\pi 2000t)$.

Solution   (a) The peak frequency deviation is simply the product of the deviation sensitivity and the peak amplitude of the modulating signal, or

$$\Delta f = \frac{5 \text{ kHz}}{\text{V}} \times 2 \text{ V} = 10 \text{ kHz}$$

The modulation index is determined by substituting into Equation 6-18.

$$m = \frac{10 \text{ kHz}}{2 \text{ kHz}} = 5$$

(b) The peak phase shift for a phase-modulated wave is the modulation index and is found by substituting into Equation 6-13.

$$m = \frac{2.5 \text{ rad}}{\text{V}} \times 2 \text{ V} = 5 \text{ rad}$$

TABLE 6-2 Angle Modulation Summary

	FM	PM
Modulated wave	$m(t) = V_c \cos\left[\omega_c t + \dfrac{K_1 V_m}{f_m} \sin(\omega_m t)\right]$	$m(t) = V_c \cos[\omega_c t + K V_m \cos(\omega_m t)]$
or	$m(t) = V_c \cos[\omega_c t + m \sin(\omega_m t)]$	$m(t) = V_c \cos[\omega_c t + m \cos(\omega_m t)]$
or	$m(t) = V_c \cos\left[\omega_c t + \dfrac{\Delta f}{f_m} \sin(\omega_m t)\right]$	$m(t) = V_c \cos[\omega_c t + \Delta\theta \cos(\omega_m t)]$
Deviation sensitivity	K_1 (Hz/V)	K (rad/V)
Deviation	$\Delta f = K_1 V_m$ (Hz)	$\Delta\theta = K V_m$ (rad)
Modulation index	$m = \dfrac{K_1 V_m}{f_m}$ (unitless)	$m = K V_m$ (rad)
or	$m = \dfrac{\Delta f}{f_m}$ (unitless)	$m = \Delta\theta$ (rad)
Modulating signal	$v_m(t) = V_m \sin(\omega_m t)$	$v_m(t) = V_m \cos(\omega_m t)$
Modulating frequency	$\omega_m = 2\pi f_m$ rad/s	$\omega_m = 2\pi f_m$ rad/s
or	$\omega_m/2\pi = f_m$ (Hz)	$\omega_m/2\pi = f_m$ (Hz)
Carrier signal	$V_c \cos(\omega_c t)$	$V_c \cos(\omega_c t)$
Carrier frequency	$\omega_c = 2\pi f_c$ (rad/s)	$\omega_c = 2\pi f_c$ (rad/s)
or	$\omega_c/2\pi = f_c$ (Hz)	$\omega_c/2\pi = f_c$ (Hz)

In Example 6-1, the modulation index for the frequency-modulated carrier was equal to the modulation index of the phase-modulated carrier (5). If the amplitude of the modulating signal is changed, the modulation index for both the frequency- and phase-modulated waves will change proportionally. However, if the frequency of the modulating signal changes, the modulation index for the frequency-modulated wave will change inversely proportional, while the modulation index of the phase-modulated wave is unaffected. Therefore, under identical conditions, FM and PM are indistinguishable for a single-frequency modulating signal; however, when the frequency of the modulating signal changes, the PM modulation index remains constant, whereas the FM modulation index increases as the modulating-signal frequency decreases, and vice versa.

Percent modulation. The percent modulation for an angle-modulated wave is determined in a different manner than it was with an amplitude-modulated wave. With angle modulation, percent modulation is simply the ratio of the frequency deviation actually produced to the maximum frequency deviation allowed by law stated in percent form. Mathematically, percent modulation is

$$\% \text{ modulation} = \frac{\Delta f_{(actual)}}{\Delta f_{(max)}} \times 100 \qquad (6\text{-}20)$$

For example, in the United States the Federal Communications Commission (FCC) limits the frequency deviation for commercial FM broadcast-band transmitters to ± 75 kHz. If a given modulating signal produces ± 50-kHz frequency deviation, the percent modulation is

$$\% \text{ modulation} = \frac{50 \text{ kHz}}{75 \text{ kHz}} \times 100 = 67\%$$

Phase and Frequency Modulators and Demodulators

A *phase modulator* is a circuit in which the carrier is varied in such a way that its instantaneous phase is proportional to the modulating signal. The unmodulated carrier is a single-frequency sinusoid and is commonly called the *rest* frequency. A *frequency modulator* (often called a *frequency deviator*) is a circuit in which the carrier is varied in such a way that its instantaneous phase is proportional to the integral of the modulating signal. Therefore, with a frequency modulator, if the modulating signal $v(t)$ is differentiated prior to being applied to the modulator, the instantaneous phase deviation is proportional to the integral of $v(t)$ or, in other words, proportional to $v(t)$ because $fv'(t) = v(t)$. Similarly, an FM modulator that is preceded by a differentiator produces an output wave in which the phase deviation is proportional to the modulating signal and is, therefore, equivalent to a phase modulator. Several other interesting equivalences are possible. For example, a frequency demodulator followed by an integrator is equivalent to a phase demodulator. Four commonly used equivalences are

1. PM modulator = differentiator followed by an FM modulator
2. PM demodulator = FM demodulator followed by an integrator
3. FM modulator = integrator followed by a PM modulator
4. FM demodulator = PM demodulator followed by a differentiator

Frequency Analysis of Angle-Modulated Waves

With angle modulation, the frequency components of the modulated wave are much more complexly related to the frequency components of the modulating signal than with amplitude modulation. In a frequency or phase modulator, a single-frequency modulating signal produces an infinite number of pairs of side frequencies and, thus, has an infinite bandwidth. Each side frequency is displaced from the carrier by an integral multiple of the modulating signal frequency. However, generally most of the side frequencies are negligibly small in amplitude and can be ignored.

Modulation by a single-frequency sinusoid. Frequency analysis of an angle-modulated wave by a single-frequency sinusoid produces a peak phase deviation of m radians, where m is the modulation index. Again, from Equation 6-12 and for a modulating frequency equal to ω_m, $m(t)$ is written as

$$m(t) = V_c \cos[\omega_c t + m \cos(\omega_m t)]$$

From Equation 6-12, the individual frequency components that make up the modulated wave are not obvious. However, *Bessel function identities* are available that may be applied directly. One such identity is

$$\cos(\alpha + m \cos \beta) = \sum_{n=-\infty}^{\infty} J_n(m) \cos\left(\alpha + n\beta + \frac{n\pi}{2}\right) \tag{6-21}$$

$J_n(m)$ is the Bessel function of the first kind of nth order with argument m. If Equation 6-21 is applied to Equation 6-13, $m(t)$ may be rewritten as

$$m(t) = V_c \sum_{n=-\infty}^{\infty} J_n(m) \cos\left(\omega_c t + n\omega_m t + \frac{n\pi}{2}\right) \tag{6-22}$$

Expanding Equation 6-22 for the first four terms yields

$$m(t) = V_c \left\{ J_0(m) \cos \omega_c t + J_1(m) \cos\left[(\omega_c + \omega_m)t + \frac{\pi}{2}\right] \right.$$

$$\left. -J_1(m) \cos\left[(\omega_c - \omega_m)t - \frac{\pi}{2}\right] + J_2(m) \cos[(\omega + 2\omega_m)t)] \right. \tag{6-23}$$

$$\left. + J_2(m) \cos[(\omega_c - 2\omega_m)t] + \ldots J_n(m) \ldots \right.$$

where $m(t)$ = angle-modulated wave

   m = modulation index

   V_c = peak amplitude of the unmodulated carrier

   $J_0(m)$ = carrier component

   $J_1(m)$ = first set of side frequencies displaced from the carrier by ω_m

   $J_2(m)$ = second set of side frequencies displaced from the carrier by $2\omega_m$

   $J_n(m)$ = nth set of side frequencies displaced from the carrier by $n\omega_m$

   Equations 6-22 and 6-23 show that with angle modulation a single-frequency modulating signal produces an infinite number of sets of side frequencies, each displaced from the carrier by an integral multiple of the modulating signal frequency. A sideband set includes an upper and a lower side frequency ($f_c \pm f_m$, $f_c \pm 2f_m$, $f_c \pm nf_m$, and so on). Successive sets of sidebands are called first-order sidebands, second-order sidebands, and so on, and their magnitudes are determined by the coefficients $J_1(m)$, $J_2(m)$, and so on, respectively.

   To solve for the amplitude of the side frequencies, J_n, Equation 6-23 can be converted to

$$J_n(m) = \left(\frac{m}{2}\right)^n \left[\frac{1}{n} - \frac{(m/2)^2}{1!(n+1)!} + \frac{(m/2)^4}{2!(n+2)!} - \frac{(m/2)^6}{3!(n+1)!} + \ldots \right] \qquad (6\text{-}24)$$

where   ! = factorial ($1 \times 2 \times 3 \times 4$, etc.)

   n = J or number of the side frequency

   m = modulation index

   Table 6-3 shows the Bessel functions of the first kind for several values of modulation index. We see that a modulation index of 0 (no modulation) produces zero side frequencies, and the larger the modulation index, the more sets of side frequencies produced. The values shown for J_n are relative to the amplitude of the unmodulated carrier. For example, $J_2 = 0.35$ indicates that the amplitude of the second set of side frequencies is equal to 35% of the unmodulated carrier amplitude (0.35 V_c). It can be seen that the amplitude of the higher-order side frequencies rapidly becomes insignificant as the modulation index decreases below unity. For larger values of m, the value of $J_n(m)$ starts to decrease rapidly as soon as $n = m$. As the modulation index increases from zero, the magnitude of the carrier $J_0(m)$ decreases. When m is equal to approximately 2.4, $J_0(m) = 0$ and the carrier component go to zero (this is called the *first carrier null*). This property is often used to determine the modulation index or set the deviation sensitivity of an FM modulator. The carrier reappears as m increases beyond 2.4. When m reaches approximately 5.4, the carrier component once again disappears (this is called the *second carrier null*). Further increases in the modulation index will produce additional carrier nulls at periodic intervals.

   Figure 6-5 shows the curves for the relative amplitudes of the carrier and several sets of side frequencies for values of m up to 10. It can be seen that the amplitudes of both the carrier and the side frequencies vary at a periodic rate that resembles a damped sine wave. The negative values for $J(m)$ simply indicate the relative phase of that side frequency set.

   In Table 6-3, only the significant side frequencies are listed. A side frequency is not considered significant unless it has an amplitude equal to or greater than 1% of the unmodulated carrier amplitude ($J_n \geq 0.01$). From Table 6-3 it can be seen that as m increases, the number of significant side frequencies increase. Consequently, the bandwidth of an angle-modulated wave is a function of the modulation index.

Example 6-2

For an FM modulator with a modulation index $m = 1$, a modulating signal $v_m(t) = V_m \sin(2\pi 1000t)$, and an unmodulated carrier $v_c(t) = 10 \sin(2\pi 500kt)$, determine

(a) Number of sets of significant side frequencies.

(b) Their amplitudes.

TABLE 6-3 Bessel Functions of the First Kind, $J_n(m)$

Modulation Index	Carrier					Side Frequency Pairs										
m	J_0	J_1	J_2	J_3	J_4	J_5	J_6	J_7	J_8	J_9	J_{10}	J_{11}	J_{12}	J_{13}	J_{14}
0.00	1.00	—	—	—	—	—	—	—	—	—	—	—	—	—	—
0.25	0.98	0.12	—	—	—	—	—	—	—	—	—	—	—	—	—
0.5	0.94	0.24	0.03	—	—	—	—	—	—	—	—	—	—	—	—
1.0	0.77	0.44	0.11	0.02	—	—	—	—	—	—	—	—	—	—	—
1.5	0.51	0.56	0.23	0.06	0.01	—	—	—	—	—	—	—	—	—	—
2.0	0.22	0.58	0.35	0.13	0.03	—	—	—	—	—	—	—	—	—	—
2.4	0	0.52	0.43	0.20	0.06	0.02	—	—	—	—	—	—	—	—	—
2.5	−0.05	0.50	0.45	0.22	0.07	0.02	0.01	—	—	—	—	—	—	—	—
3.0	−0.26	0.34	0.49	0.31	0.13	0.04	0.01	—	—	—	—	—	—	—	—
4.0	−0.40	−0.07	0.36	0.43	0.28	0.13	0.05	0.02	—	—	—	—	—	—	—
5.0	−0.18	−0.33	0.05	0.36	0.39	0.26	0.13	0.05	0.02	—	—	—	—	—	—
5.45	0	−0.34	−0.12	0.26	0.40	0.32	0.19	0.09	0.03	0.01	—	—	—	—	—
6.0	0.15	−0.28	−0.24	0.11	0.36	0.36	0.25	0.13	0.06	0.02	—	—	—	—	—
7.0	0.30	0.00	−0.30	−0.17	0.16	0.35	0.34	0.23	0.13	0.06	0.02	—	—	—	—
8.0	0.17	0.23	−0.11	−0.29	−0.10	0.19	0.34	0.32	0.22	0.13	0.06	0.03	—	—	—
8.65	0	0.27	0.06	−0.24	−0.23	0.03	0.26	0.34	0.28	0.18	0.10	0.05	0.02	—	—
9.0	−0.09	0.25	0.14	−0.18	−0.27	−0.06	0.20	0.33	0.31	0.21	0.12	0.06	0.03	0.01	—
10.0	−0.25	0.05	0.25	0.06	−0.22	−0.23	−0.01	0.22	0.32	0.29	0.21	0.12	0.06	0.03	0.01

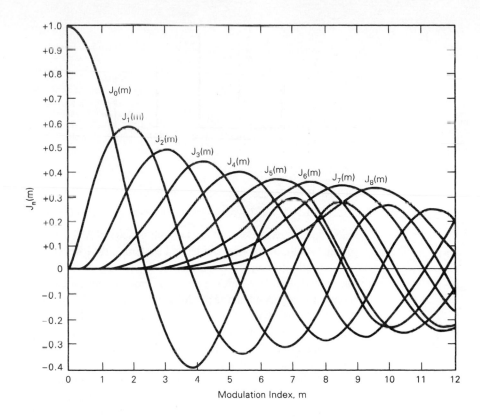

FIGURE 6-5 $J_n(m)$ versus m

Then

(c) Then draw the frequency spectrum showing their relative amplitudes.

Solution (a) From Table 6-3, a modulation index of 1 yields a reduced carrier component and three sets of significant side frequencies.

(b) The relative amplitudes of the carrier and side frequencies are

$$J_0 = 0.77(10) = 7.7 \text{ V}$$
$$J_1 = 0.44(10) = 4.4 \text{ V}$$
$$J_2 = 0.11(10) = 1.1 \text{ V}$$
$$J_3 = 0.02(10) = 0.2 \text{ V}$$

(c) The frequency spectrum is shown in Figure 6-6.

If the FM modulator used in Example 6-2 were replaced with a PM modulator and the same carrier and modulating signal frequencies were used, a peak phase deviation of 1 rad would produce exactly the same frequency spectrum.

Bandwidth Requirements for Angle-Modulated Waves

In 1922, J. R. Carson mathematically proved that for a given modulating-signal frequency a frequency-modulated wave cannot be accommodated in a narrower bandwidth than an amplitude-modulated wave. From the preceding discussion and Example 6-2, it can be seen that the bandwidth of an angle-modulated wave is a function of the modulating signal frequency and the modulation index. With angle modulation, multiple sets of sidebands are produced and, consequently, the bandwidth can be significantly wider than that of an amplitude-modulated wave with the same modulating signal. The modulator output waveform in Example 6-2 requires 6 kHz of bandwidth to pass the carrier and all the significant

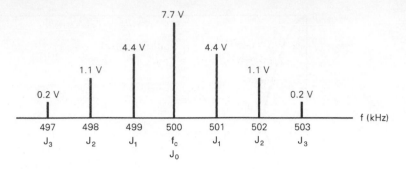

FIGURE 6-6 Frequency spectrum for Example 6-2

side frequencies. A conventional double-sideband AM modulator would require only 2 kHz of bandwidth, and a single-sideband system, only 1 kHz.

Angle-modulated waveforms are generally classified as either *low, medium,* or *high index.* For the low-index case, the modulation index is less than 1, and the high-index case occurs when the modulation index is greater than 10. Modulation indices greater than 1 and less than 10 are classified as medium index. From Table 6-3 it can be seen that with low-index angle modulation most of the signal information is carried by the first set of sidebands, and the minimum bandwidth required is approximately equal to twice the highest modulating-signal frequency. For this reason, low-index FM systems are sometimes called *narrowband FM.* For a high-index signal, a method of determining the bandwidth called the *quasi-stationary* approach may be used. With this approach, it is assumed that the modulating signal is changing very slowly. For example, for an FM modulator with a deviation sensitivity $K_1 = 2$ kHz/V and a 1-V_p modulating signal, the peak frequency deviation $\Delta f = 2000$ Hz. If the frequency of the modulating signal is very low, the bandwidth is determined by the peak-to-peak frequency deviation. Therefore, for large modulation indexes, the minimum bandwidth required to propagate a frequency-modulated wave is approximately equal to the peak-to-peak frequency deviation ($2\Delta f$).

Thus, for low-index modulation, the frequency spectrum resembles double-sideband AM and the minimum bandwidth is approximated by

$$B = 2f_m \quad \text{Hz} \tag{6-25}$$

and for high-index modulation, the minimum bandwidth is approximated by

$$B = 2\Delta f \quad \text{Hz} \tag{6-26}$$

The actual bandwidth required to pass all the significant sidebands for an angle-modulated wave is equal to two times the product of the highest modulating-signal frequency and the number of significant sidebands determined from the table of Bessel functions. Mathematically, the rule for determining the minimum bandwidth for an angle-modulated wave using the Bessel table is

$$B = 2(n \times f_m) \quad \text{Hz} \tag{6-27}$$

where n = number of significant sidebands

f_m = modulating-signal frequency (hertz)

In an unpublished memorandum dated August 28, 1939, Carson established a general rule to estimate the bandwidth for all angle-modulated systems regardless of the modulation index. This is called *Carson's rule.* Simply stated, Carson's rule approximates the bandwidth necessary to transmit an angle-modulated wave as twice the sum of the peak frequency deviation and the highest modulating-signal frequency. Mathematically stated, Carson's rule is

$$B = 2(\Delta f + f_m) \quad \text{Hz} \tag{6-28}$$

where Δf = peak frequency deviation (hertz)

          f_m = modulating-signal frequency (hertz)

For low modulation indices, f_m is much larger than Δf and Equation 6-28 reduces to Equation 6-25. For high modulation indices Δf is much larger than f_m and Equation 6-26 reduces to Equation 6-26.

     Carson's rule is an approximation and gives transmission bandwidths that are slightly narrower than the bandwidths determined using the Bessel table and Equation 6-27. Carson's rule defines a bandwidth that includes approximately 98% of the total power in the modulated wave. The actual bandwidth necessary is a function of the modulating signal waveform and the quality of transmission desired.

Example 6-3

For an FM modulator with a peak frequency deviation $\Delta f = 10$ kHz, a modulating-signal frequency $f_m = 10$ kHz, $V_c = 10$ V, and a 500-kHz carrier, determine

(a) Actual minimum bandwidth from the Bessel function table.

(b) Approximate minimum bandwidth using Carson's rule.

Then

(c) Plot the output frequency spectrum for the Bessel approximation.

Solution   (a) Substituting into Equation 6-18 yields

$$m = \frac{10 \text{ kHz}}{10 \text{ kHz}} = 1$$

From Table 6-3, a modulation index of 1 yields three sets of significant sidebands. Substituting into Equation 6-27, the bandwidth is

$$B = 2(3 \times 10 \text{ kHz}) = 60 \text{ kHz}$$

(b) Substituting into Equation 6-28, the minimum bandwidth is

$$B = 2(10 \text{ kHz} + 10 \text{ kHz}) = 40 \text{ kHz}$$

(c) The output frequency spectrum for the Bessel approximation is shown in Figure 6-7.

     From Example 6-3, it can be seen that there is a significant difference in the minimum bandwidth determined from Carson's rule and the minimum bandwidth determined from the Bessel table. The bandwidth from Carson's rule is less than the actual minimum bandwidth required to pass all the significant sideband sets as defined by the Bessel table. Therefore, a system that was designed using Carson's rule would have a narrower bandwidth and, thus, poorer performance than a system designed using the Bessel table. For modulation indexes above 5, Carson's rule is a close approximation to the actual bandwidth required.

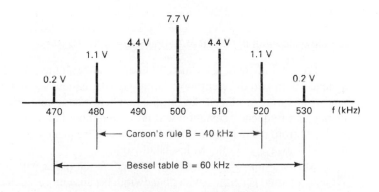

FIGURE 6-7   Frequency spectrum for Example 6-3

Deviation ratio. For a given FM system, the minimum bandwidth is greatest when the maximum frequency deviation is obtained with the maximum modulating-signal frequency (i.e., the highest modulating frequency occurs with the maximum amplitude allowed). By definition, *deviation ratio* (DR) is the *worst-case* modulation index and is equal to the maximum peak frequency deviation divided by the maximum modulating-signal frequency. The worst-case modulation index produces the widest output frequency spectrum. Mathematically, the deviation ratio is

$$DR = \frac{\Delta f_{(max)}}{f_{m(max)}} \tag{6-29}$$

where DR = deviation ratio (unitless)
$\Delta f_{(max)}$ = maximum peak frequency deviation (hertz)
$f_{m(max)}$ = maximum modulating-signal frequency (hertz)

For example, for the sound portion of a commercial TV broadcast-band station, the maximum frequency deviation set by the FCC is 50 kHz, and the maximum modulating-signal frequency is 15 kHz. Therefore, the deviation ratio for a television broadcast station is

$$DR = \frac{50 \text{ kHz}}{15 \text{ kHz}} = 3.33$$

This does not mean that whenever a modulation index of 3.33 occurs the widest bandwidth also occurs at the same time. It means that whenever a modulation index of 3.33 occurs for a maximum modulating-signal frequency the widest bandwidth occurs.

Example 6-4

(a) Determine the deviation ratio and bandwidth for the worst-case (widest-bandwidth) modulation index for an FM broadcast-band transmitter with a maximum frequency deviation of 75 kHz and a maximum modulating-signal frequency of 15 kHz.
(b) Determine the deviation ratio and maximum bandwidth for an equal modulation index with only half the peak frequency deviation and modulating-signal frequency.

Solution   (a)   The deviation ratio is found by substituting into Equation 6-29.

$$DR = \frac{75 \text{ kHz}}{15 \text{ kHz}} = 5$$

From Table 6-3, a modulation index of 5 produces eight significant sidebands. Substituting into Equation 6-27 yields

$$B = 2(8 \times 15,000) = 240 \text{ kHz}$$

(b) For a 37.5-kHz frequency deviation and a modulating-signal frequency f_m = 7.5 kHz, the modulation index is

$$m = \frac{37.5 \text{ kHz}}{7.5 \text{ kHz}} = 5$$

and the bandwidth is $B = 2(8 \times 7500) = 120 \text{ kHz}$

From Example 6-4, it can be seen that, although the same modulation index (5) was achieved with two different modulating-signal frequencies and amplitudes, two different bandwidths were produced. An infinite number of combinations of modulating-signal frequency and frequency deviation will produce a modulation index of 5. However, the case produced from the maximum modulating-signal frequency and maximum frequency deviation will always yield the widest bandwidth.

At first it may seem that a higher modulation index with a lower modulating-signal frequency would generate a wider bandwidth because more sideband sets are produced; but remember that the sidebands would be closer together. For example, a 1-kHz modulating signal that produces 10 kHz of frequency deviation has a modulation index of $m = 10$ and produces 14 significant sets of sidebands. However, the sidebands are only displaced from each other by 1 kHz, and, therefore, the total bandwidth is only 28,000 Hz [2(14 × 1000)].

With Carson's rule the same conditions produce the widest (worst-case) bandwidth. For the maximum frequency deviation and maximum modulating-signal frequency, the maximum bandwidth using Carson's rule for Example 6-4a is

$$B = 2[\Delta f_{(max)} + f_{m(max)}]$$
$$= 2(75 \text{ kHz} + 15 \text{ kHz})$$
$$= 180 \text{ kHz}$$

COMMERCIAL BROADCAST-BAND FM

The FCC has assigned the commercial FM broadcast service a 20-MHz band of frequencies that extends from 88 MHz to 108 MHz. The 20-MHz band is divided into 100, 200-kHz wide channels beginning at 88.1 MHz (i.e., 88.3 MHz, 88.5 MHz, and so on). To provide high-quality, reliable music, the maximum frequency deviation allowed is 75 kHz with a maximum modulating-signal frequency of 15 kHz.

Using Equation 6-27, the worst-case modulation index (i.e., the deviation ratio) for a commercial broadcast-band channel is 75 kHz/15 kHz = 5. Referring to the Bessel table, eight pairs of significant side frequencies are produced with a modulation index of 5. Therefore, from Equation 6-27, the minimum bandwidth necessary to pass all the significant side frequencies is $B = 2(8 \times 15 \text{ kHz}) = 240 \text{ kHz}$, which exceeds the allocated FCC bandwidth by 40 kHz. In essence this says that the highest side frequencies from one channel are allowed to spill over into adjacent channels producing an interference known as *adjacent channel interference*. This is generally not a problem, however, because the FCC has historically assigned only every other channel in a given geographic area. Therefore, a 200-kHz-wide guard band is usually on either side of each assigned channel. In addition, the seventh and eighth sets of side frequencies have little power in them, and it is also highly unlikely that maximum frequency deviation is ever obtained at the maximum modulating-signal frequency. Ironically, if you use Carson's approximation, the bandwidth for commercial broadcast-band channels is 2(75 kHz + 15 kHz) = 180 kHz, which is well within the band limits assigned by the FCC.

PHASOR REPRESENTATION OF AN ANGLE-MODULATED WAVE

As with amplitude modulation, an angle-modulated wave can be shown in phasor form. The phasor diagram for a low-index angle-modulated wave with a single-frequency modulating signal is shown in Figure 6-8. For this special case ($m < 1$), only the first set of sideband pairs is considered, and the phasor diagram closely resembles that of an AM wave except for a phase reversal of one of the side frequencies. The resultant vector has an amplitude that is close to unity at all times and a peak phase deviation of m radians. It is important to note that if the side frequencies from the higher-order terms were included the vector would have no amplitude variations. The dashed line shown in Figure 6-8e is the locus of the resultant formed by the carrier and the first set of side frequencies.

Figure 6-9 shows the phasor diagram for a high-index, angle-modulated wave with five sets of side frequencies (for simplicity only the vectors for the first two sets are shown). The resultant vector is the sum of the carrier component and the components of the significant side frequencies with their magnitudes adjusted according to the Bessel table. Each side frequency is shifted an additional 90° from the preceding side frequency. The locus of the resultant five-component approximation is curved and closely follows the signal locus. By definition, the locus is a segment of the circle with a radius equal to the amplitude of the unmodulated carrier. It should be noted that the resultant signal amplitude and, consequently, the signal power remain constant.

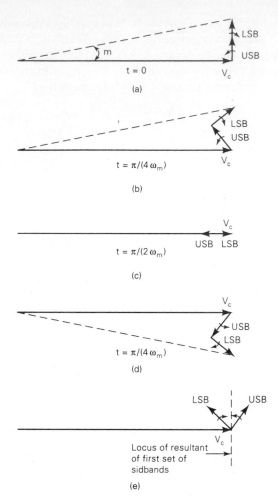

FIGURE 6-8 Angle modulation phasor representation, low modulation index

AVERAGE POWER OF AN ANGLE-MODULATED WAVE

One of the most important differences between angle modulation and amplitude modulation is the distribution of power in the modulated wave. Unlike AM, the total power in an angle-modulated wave is equal to the power of the unmodulated carrier (i.e., the sidebands do not add power to the composite modulated signal). Therefore, with angle modulation, the power that was originally in the unmodulated carrier is redistributed among the carrier and its sidebands. The average power of an angle-modulated wave is independent of the modulating signal, the modulation index, and the frequency deviation. It is equal to the average power of the unmodulated carrier, regardless of the depth of modulation. Mathematically, the average power in the unmodulated carrier is

$$P_c = \frac{V_c^2}{2R} \, \text{W}$$
(6-30)

where P_c = carrier power (watts)
        V_c = peak unmodulated carrier voltage (volts)
        R = load resistance (ohms)

The total instantaneous power in an angle-modulated carrier is

$$P_t = \frac{m(t)^2}{R} \, \text{W}$$
(6-31a)

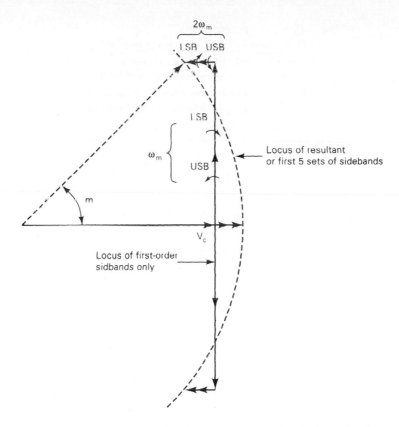

FIGURE 6-9 Angle modulation phasor representation, high modulation index

Substituting for $m(t)$ gives

$$P_t = \frac{V_c^2}{R} \cos^2[\omega_c t + \theta(t)] \qquad (6\text{-}31\text{b})$$

and expanding yields

$$= \frac{V_c^2}{R} \left\{ \frac{1}{2} + \frac{1}{2} \cos[2\omega_c t + 2\theta(t)] \right\} \qquad (6\text{-}31\text{c})$$

In Equation 6-31c, the second term consists of an infinite number of sinusoidal side frequency components about a frequency equal to twice the carrier frequency ($2\omega_c$). Consequently, the average value of the second term is zero, and the average power of the modulated wave reduces to

$$P_t = \frac{V_c^2}{2R} \text{ W} \qquad (6\text{-}32)$$

Note that Equations 6-30 and 6-32 are identical, so the average power of the modulated carrier must be equal to the average power of the unmodulated carrier. The modulated carrier power is the sum of the powers of the carrier and the side frequency components. Therefore, the total modulated wave power is

$$P_t = P_0 + P_1 + P_2 + P_3 + P_n \qquad (6\text{-}33\text{a})$$

$$P_t = \frac{V_c^2}{2R} + \frac{2(V_1)^2}{2R} + \frac{2(V_2)^2}{2R} + \frac{2(V_3)^2}{2R} + \frac{2(V_n)^2}{2R} \qquad (6\text{-}33\text{b})$$

where P_t = total power (watts)
 P_0 = modulated carrier power (watts)
 P_1 = power in the first set of sidebands (watts)
 P_2 = power in the second set of sidebands (watts)
 P_3 = power in the third set of sidebands (watts)
 P_n = power in the nth set of sidebands (watts)

Example 6-5

(a) Determine the unmodulated carrier power for the FM modulator and conditions given in Example 6-2 (assume a load resistance $R_L = 50\ \Omega$).

(b) Determine the total power in the angle-modulated wave.

Solution   (a) Substituting into Equation 6-30 yields

$$P_c = \frac{10^2}{2(50)} = 1\ \text{W}$$

(b) Substituting into Equation 6-33a gives us

$$P_t = \frac{7.7^2}{2(50)} + \frac{2(4.4)^2}{2(50)} + \frac{2(1.1)^2}{2(50)} + \frac{2(0.2)^2}{2(50)}$$

$$= 0.5929 + 0.3872 + 0.0242 + 0.0008 = 1.0051\ \text{W}$$

The results of (a) and (b) are not exactly equal because the values given in the Bessel table have been rounded off. However, the results are close enough to illustrate that the power in the modulated wave and the unmodulated carrier are equal.

NOISE AND ANGLE MODULATION

When thermal noise with a constant spectral density is added to an FM signal, it produces an unwanted deviation of the carrier frequency. The magnitude of this unwanted frequency deviation depends on the relative amplitude of the noise with respect to the carrier. When this unwanted carrier deviation is demodulated, it becomes noise if it has frequency components that fall within the information-frequency spectrum. The spectral shape of the demodulated noise depends on whether an FM or PM demodulator is used. The noise voltage at the output of a PM demodulator is constant with frequency, whereas the noise voltage at the output of an FM demodulator increases linearly with frequency. This is commonly called the FM *noise triangle* and is illustrated in Figure 6-10. It can be seen that the demodulated noise voltage is inherently higher for the higher-modulating-signal frequencies.

Phase Modulation Due to an Interfering Signal

Figure 6-11 shows phase modulation caused by a single-frequency noise signal. The noise component V_n is separated in frequency from the signal component V_c by frequency f_n. This

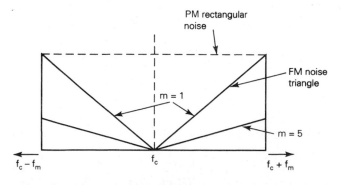

FIGURE 6-10 FM noise triangle

is shown in Figure 6-11b. Assuming that $V_c > V_n$, the peak phase deviation due to an interfering single-frequency sinusoid occurs when the signal and noise voltages are in quadrature and is approximated for small angles as

$$\Delta\theta_{\text{peak}} \simeq \frac{V_n}{V_c} \text{ rad} \qquad (6\text{-}34)$$

Figure 6-11c shows the effect of *limiting* the amplitude of the composite FM signal on noise. (Limiting is commonly used in angle-modulation receivers and is explained in Chapter 7.) It can be seen that the single-frequency noise signal has been transposed into a noise sideband pair each with amplitude $V_n/2$. These sidebands are coherent; therefore, the peak phase deviation is still V_n/V_c radians. However, the unwanted amplitude variations have been removed, which reduces the total power but does not reduce the interference in the demodulated signal due to the unwanted phase deviation.

Frequency Modulation Due to an Interfering Signal

From Equation 6-5, the instantaneous frequency deviation $\Delta f(t)$ is the first time derivative of the instantaneous phase deviation $\theta(t)$. When the carrier component is much larger than the interfering noise voltage, the instantaneous phase deviation is approximately

$$\theta(t) = \frac{V_n}{V_c} \sin(\omega_n t + \theta_n) \text{ rad} \qquad (6\text{-}35)$$

and, taking the first derivative, we obtain

$$\Delta\omega(t) = \frac{V_n}{V_c} \omega_n \cos(\omega_n t + \theta_n) \text{ rad /s} \qquad (6\text{-}36)$$

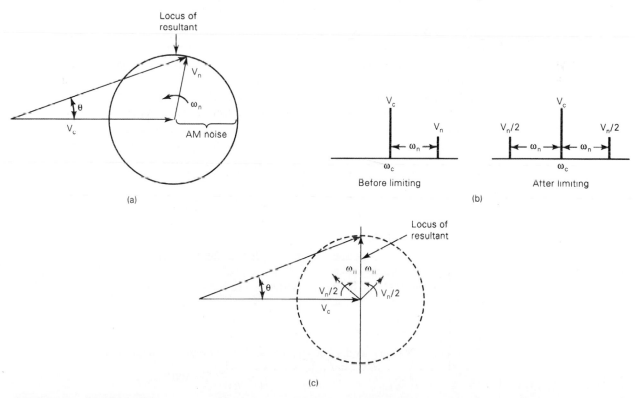

FIGURE 6-11   Interfering sinusoid of noise: (a) before limiting; (b) frequency spectrum; (c) after limiting

Therefore, the peak frequency deviation is

$$\Delta\omega_{\text{peak}} = \frac{V_n}{V_c}\,\omega_n\;\text{rad/s} \qquad (6\text{-}37)$$

$$\Delta f_{\text{peak}} = \frac{V_n}{V_c}\,f_n\;\text{Hz} \qquad (6\text{-}38)$$

Rearranging Equation 6-18, it can be seen that the peak frequency deviation (Δf) is a function of the modulating-signal frequency and the modulation index. Therefore, for a noise modulating frequency f_n, the peak frequency deviation is

$$\Delta f_{\text{peak}} = mf_n\quad\text{Hz} \qquad (6\text{-}39)$$

where m equals modulation index ($m \ll 1$).

From Equation 6-39, it can be seen that the farther the noise frequency is displaced from the carrier frequency, the larger the frequency deviation. Therefore, noise frequencies that produce components at the high end of the modulating-signal frequency spectrum produce more frequency deviation for the same phase deviation than frequencies that fall at the low end. FM demodulators generate an output voltage that is proportional to the frequency deviation and equal to the difference between the carrier frequency and the interfering signal frequency. Therefore, high-frequency noise components produce more demodulated noise than do low-frequency components.

The signal-to-noise ratio at the output of an FM demodulator due to unwanted frequency deviation from an interfering sinusoid is the ratio of the peak frequency deviation due to the information signal to the peak frequency deviation due to the interfering signal.

$$\frac{S}{N} = \frac{\Delta f_{\text{due to signal}}}{\Delta f_{\text{due to noise}}} \qquad (6\text{-}40)$$

Example 6-6

For an angle-modulated carrier $V_c = 6\cos(2\pi 110\text{ MHz }t)$ with 75-kHz frequency deviation due to the information signal and a single-frequency interfering signal $V_n = 0.3\cos(2\pi 109.985\text{ MHz }t)$, determine

(a) Frequency of the demodulated interference signal.
(b) Peak phase and frequency deviations due to the interfering signal.
(c) Voltage signal-to-noise ratio at the output of the demodulator.

Solution (a) The frequency of the noise interference is the difference between the carrier frequency and the frequency of the single-frequency interfering signal.

$$f_c - f_n = 110\text{ MHz} - 109.985\text{ MHz} = 15\text{ kHz}$$

(b) Substituting into Equation 6-34 yields

$$\Delta\theta_{\text{peak}} = \frac{0.3}{6} = 0.05\text{ rad}$$

Substituting into Equation 6-38 gives us

$$\Delta f_{\text{peak}} = \frac{0.3 \times 15\text{ kHz}}{6} = 750\text{ Hz}$$

(c) The voltage S/N ratio due to the interfering tone is the ratio of the carrier amplitude to the amplitude of the interfering signal, or

$$\frac{6}{0.3} = 20$$

The voltage S/N ratio after demodulation is found by substituting into Equation 6-40:

$$\frac{S}{N} = \frac{75\text{ kHz}}{750\text{ Hz}} = 100$$

Thus, there is a voltage signal-to-noise improvement of $100/20 = 5$ or $20\log 5 = 14$ dB.

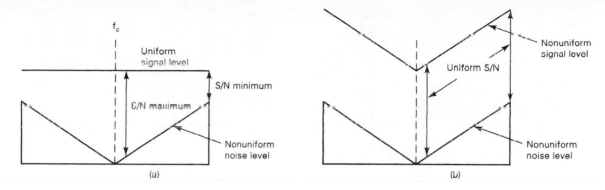

FIGURE 6-12 FM signal-to-noise: (a) without preemphasis; (b) with preemphasis

PREEMPHASIS AND DEEMPHASIS

The noise triangle shown in Figure 6-10 shows that, with FM, there is a nonuniform distribution of noise. Noise at the higher-modulating-signal frequencies is inherently greater in amplitude than noise at the lower frequencies. This includes both single-frequency interference and thermal noise. Therefore, for information signals with a uniform signal level, a nonuniform signal-to-noise ratio is produced, and the higher-modulating-signal frequencies have a lower signal-to-noise ratio than the lower frequencies. This is shown in Figure 6-12a. It can be seen that the S/N ratio is lower at the high-frequency ends of the triangle. To compensate for this, the high-frequency modulating signals are emphasized or boosted in amplitude in the transmitter prior to performing modulation. To compensate for this boost, the high-frequency signals are attenuated or deemphasized in the receiver after demodulation has been performed. Deemphasis is the reciprocal of preemphasis, and, therefore, a deemphasis network restores the original amplitude-versus-frequency characteristics to the information signals. In essence, the preemphasis network allows the high-frequency modulating signals to modulate the carrier at a higher level and, thus, cause more frequency deviation than their original amplitudes would have produced. The high-frequency signals are propagated through the system at an elevated level (increased frequency deviation), demodulated, and then restored to their original amplitude proportions. Figure 6-12b shows the effects of pre- and deemphasis on the signal-to-noise ratio. The figure shows that pre- and deemphasis produce a more uniform signal-to-noise ratio throughout the modulating-signal frequency spectrum.

A preemphasis network is a high-pass filter (i.e., a differentiator) and a deemphasis network is a low-pass filter (an integrator). Figure 6-13a shows the schematic diagrams for an active preemphasis network and a passive deemphasis network. Their corresponding frequency-response curves are shown in Figure 6-13b. A preemphasis network provides a constant increase in the amplitude of the modulating signal with an increase in frequency. With FM, approximately 12 dB of improvement in noise performance is achieved using pre- and deemphasis. The break frequency (the frequency where pre- and deemphasis begins) is determined by the RC or L/R time constant of the network. The break frequency occurs at the frequency where X_C or X_L equals R. Mathematically, the break frequency is

$$f_b = \frac{1}{2\pi RC} \tag{6-41a}$$

$$f_b = \frac{1}{2\pi L/R} \tag{6-41b}$$

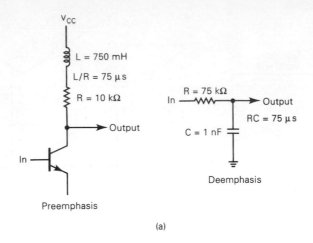

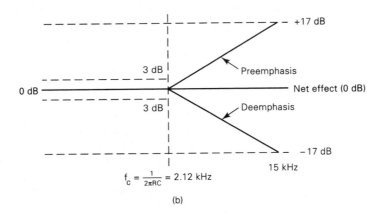

FIGURE 6-13 Preemphasis and deemphasis: (a) schematic diagrams; (b) attenuation curves

The networks shown in Figure 6-13 are for the FM broadcast band, which uses a 75-μs time constant. Therefore, the break frequency is approximately

$$f_b = \frac{1}{2\pi 75 \ \mu s} = 2.12 \ \text{kHz}$$

The FM transmission of the audio portion of commercial television broadcasting uses a 50-μs time constant.

As shown in Figure 6-13, an active rather than a passive preemphasis network is used, because a passive preemphasis network provides loss to all frequencies with more loss introduced at the lower modulating-signal frequencies. The result of using a passive network would be a decrease in the signal-to-noise ratio at the lower modulating-signal frequencies rather than an increase in the signal-to-noise ratio at the higher modulating-signal frequencies.

From the preceding explanation and Figure 6-13, it can be seen that the output amplitude from a preemphasis network increases with frequency for frequencies above the break frequency. Referring back to Equation 6-16, it can be seen that if changes in the frequency of the modulating signal (f_m) produce corresponding changes in its amplitude (V_m), the modulation index (m) remains constant with frequency. This, of course, is a characteristic of phase modulation. Consequently, with commercial broadcast-band modulators, frequencies below 2112 Hz produce frequency modulation and frequencies above 2112 Hz

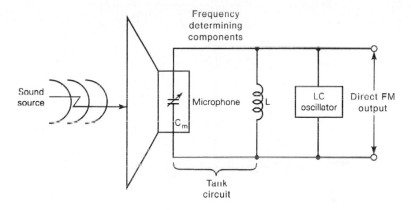

FIGURE 6-14 Simple direct FM modulator

produce phase modulation. Converting FM to PM is not the function of a preemphasis network, however, but rather a consequence.

FREQUENCY AND PHASE MODULATORS

In essence, the primary difference between frequency and phase modulators lies in whether the frequency or the phase of the carrier is directly changed by the modulating signal and which property is indirectly changed. When the frequency of the carrier oscillator is modulated by the information signal, direct FM (indirect PM) results. When the phase of the carrier signal is modulated by the information signal, direct PM (indirect FM) results.

The primary disadvantage of direct FM is that relatively unstable LC oscillators must be used to produce the carrier frequency which prohibits using crystal oscillators. Thus, direct FM requires the addition of some form of automatic frequency control circuitry to maintain the carrier frequency within the FCC's stringent frequency-stability requirements. The obvious advantage of direct FM is that relatively high-frequency deviations and modulation indices are easily obtained due to the fact that the oscillators are inherently unstable.

The primary advantage of direct PM is that the carrier oscillator is isolated from the actual modulator circuit and, therefore, can be an extremely stable source such as a crystal oscillator. The obvious disadvantage of direct PM is that crystal oscillators are inherently stable and, therefore, it is more difficult for them to achieve high phase deviations and modulation indices.

Direct FM Modulators

Direct FM is angle modulation in which the frequency of the carrier is varied (deviated) directly by the modulating signal. With direct FM, the instantaneous frequency deviation is directly proportional to the amplitude of the modulating signal. Figure 6-14 shows a schematic diagram for a simple (although highly impractical) direct FM generator. The tank circuit (L and C_m) is the frequency-determining section for a standard LC oscillator. The capacitor microphone is a transducer that converts acoustical energy to mechanical energy, which is used to vary the distance between the plates of C_m and, consequently, change its capacitance. As C_m is varied, the resonant frequency is varied. Thus, the oscillator output frequency varies directly with the external sound source. This is direct FM because the oscillator frequency is changed directly by the modulating signal, and the magnitude of the frequency change is proportional to the amplitude of the modulating-signal voltage. There are three common methods for producing direct frequency modulation: varactor diode modulators, FM reactance modulators, and linear integrated-circuit direct FM modulators.

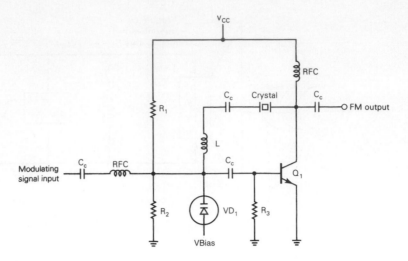

FIGURE 6-15 Varactor diode direct FM modulator

Varactor diode modulators.   Figure 6-15 shows the schematic diagram for a more practical direct FM generator that uses a varactor diode to deviate the frequency of a crystal oscillator. R_1 and R_2 develop a dc voltage that reverse biases varactor diode VD_1 and determines the rest frequency of the oscillator. The external modulating-signal voltage adds to and subtracts from the dc bias, which changes the capacitance of the diode and, thus, the frequency of oscillation (see Chapter 2 for more detailed description of varactor diodes). Positive alternations of the modulating signal increase the reverse bias on VD_1, which decreases its capacitance and increases the frequency of oscillation. Conversely, negative alternations of the modulating signal decrease the frequency of oscillation. Varactor diode FM modulators are extremely popular because they are simple to use and reliable and have the stability of a crystal oscillator. However, because a crystal is used, the peak frequency deviation is limited to relatively small values. Consequently, they are used primarily for low-index applications, such as two-way mobile radio.

Figure 6-16 shows a simplified schematic diagram for a voltage-controlled oscillator (VCO) FM generator. Again, a varactor diode is used to transform changes in the modulating-signal amplitude to changes in frequency. The center frequency for the oscillator is determined as follows

$$f_c = \frac{1}{2\pi\sqrt{LC}} \text{ Hz} \tag{6-42}$$

where f_c = carrier rest frequency (hertz)
   L = inductance of the primary winding of T_1 (henries)
   C = varactor diode capacitance (farads)

With a modulating signal applied, the frequency is

$$f = \frac{1}{2\pi\sqrt{L(C + \Delta C)}} \text{ Hz} \tag{6-43}$$

where f is the new frequency of oscillation and ΔC is the change in varactor diode capacitance due to the modulating signal. The change in frequency is

$$\Delta f = |f_c - f| \tag{6-44}$$

where Δf = peak frequency deviation (hertz)

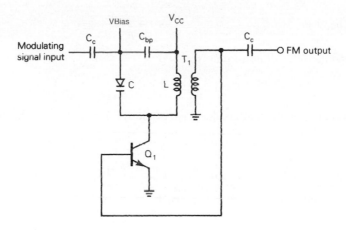

FIGURE 6-16 Varactor diode VCO FM modulator

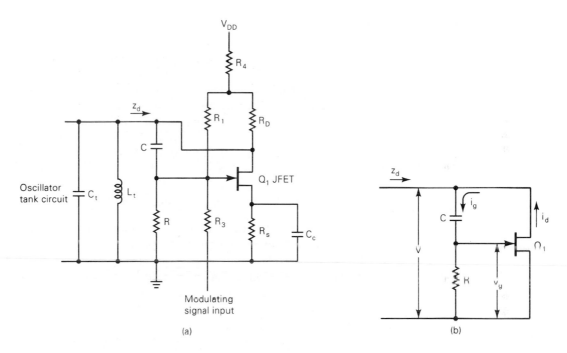

(a)

(b)

FIGURE 6-17 JFET reactance modulator: (a) schematic diagram; (b) ac equivalent circuit

FM reactance modulators. Figure 6-17a shows a schematic diagram for a reactance modulator using a JFET as the active device. This circuit configuration is called a reactance modulator because the JFET looks like a variable-reactance load to the LC tank circuit. The modulating signal varies the reactance of Q_1, which causes a corresponding change in the resonant frequency of the oscillator tank circuit.

Figure 6-17b shows the ac equivalent circuit. R_1, R_3, R_4, and R_C provide the dc bias for Q_1. R_E is bypassed by C_c and is, therefore, omitted from the ac equivalent circuit. Circuit operation is as follows. Assuming an ideal JFET (gate current $i_g = 0$),

$$v_g = i_g R$$

where

$$i_g = \frac{v}{R - jX_C}$$

Therefore,
$$v_g = \frac{v}{R - jX_C} \times R$$

and the JFET drain current is
$$i_d = g_m v_g = g_m \left(\frac{v}{R - jX_C} \right) \times R$$

where g_m is the transconductance of the JFET, and the impedance between the drain and ground is
$$z_d = \frac{v}{i_d}$$

Substituting and rearranging gives us
$$z_d = \frac{R - jX_C}{g_m R} = \frac{1}{g_m} \left(1 - \frac{jX_C}{R} \right)$$

Assuming that $R <<< X_C$, $\qquad z_d = -j \frac{X_C}{g_m R} = \frac{-j}{2\pi f_m g_m RC}$

$g_m RC$ is equivalent to a variable capacitance and is inversely proportional to resistance (R), the angular velocity of the modulating signal ($2\pi f_m$), and the transconductance (g_m) of Q_1, which varies with the gate-to-source voltage. When a modulating signal is applied to the bottom of R_3, the gate-to-source voltage is varied accordingly, causing a proportional change in g_m. As a result, the equivalent circuit impedance (z_d) is a function of the modulating signal. Therefore, the resonant frequency of the oscillator tank circuit is a function of the amplitude of the modulating signal, and the rate at which it changes is equal to f_m. Interchanging R and C causes the variable reactance to be inductive rather than capacitive, but does not affect the output FM waveform. The maximum frequency deviation obtained with a reactance modulator is approximately 5 kHz.

Linear integrated-circuit direct FM modulators. *Linear integrated-circuit voltage-controlled oscillators* and *function generators* can generate a direct FM output waveform that is relatively stable, accurate, and directly proportional to the input modulating signal. The primary disadvantage of using LIC VCOs and function generators for direct FM modulation is their low output power and the need for several additional external components for them to function, such as timing capacitors and resistors for frequency determination and power supply filters.

Figure 6-18 shows a simplified block diagram for a linear integrated-circuit monolithic function generator that can be used for direct FM generation. The VCO center frequency is determined by external resistor and capacitor (R and C). The input modulating signal [$v_m(t) = V_m \sin(2\pi f_m t)$] is applied directly to the input of the voltage-controlled oscillator where it deviates the carrier rest frequency (f_c) and produces an FM output signal.

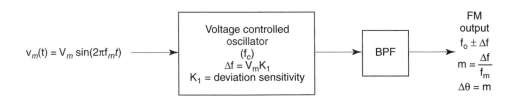

FIGURE 6-18 LIC Direct FM modulator—simplified block diagram.

The peak frequency deviation is determined by the product of the peak modulating-signal amplitude (V_m) and the deviation sensitivity of the VCO (K_1). The modulator output is

$$FM_{(out)} - f_c + \Delta f$$

where
f_c = carrier rest frequency (VCO's natural frequency – $1/RC$ hertz)
Δf = peak frequency deviation ($V_m K_1$ hertz)
K_1 = deviation sensitivity (hertz per volt)

Figure 6-19a shows the schematic diagram for the Motorola MC1376 monolithic FM transmitter. The MC1376 is a complete FM modulator on a single 8 pin DIP integrated-circuit chip. The MC1376 can operate with carrier frequencies between 1.4 MHz and 14 MHz and is intended to be used for producing direct FM waves for low-power applications such as cordless telephones. When the auxiliary transistor is connected to a 12-V supply voltage, output powers as high as 600 mW can be achieved. Figure 6-19b shows the

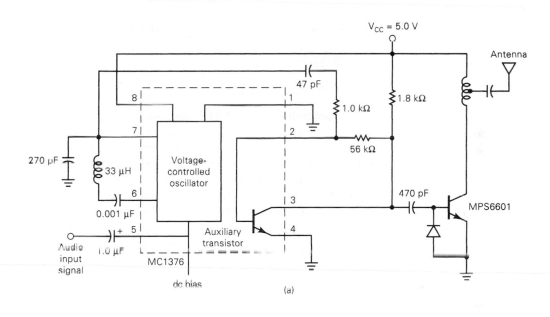

(a)

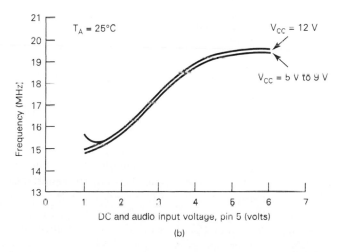

(b)

FIGURE 6-19 MC1376 FM transmitter LIC: (a) schematic diagram; (b) VCO output–versus–input frequency-response curve

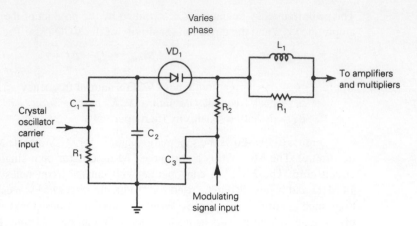

FIGURE 6-20 Direct PM modulator schematic diagram

output frequency–versus–input voltage curve for the internal VCO. As the figure shows, the curve is fairly linear between 2 V and 4 V and can produce a peak frequency deviation of nearly 150 kHz.

Direct PM Modulators

Varactor diode direct PM modulator. Direct PM (i.e., *indirect FM*) is angle modulation in which the frequency of the carrier is deviated indirectly by the modulating signal. Direct PM is accomplished by directly changing the phase of the carrier and is, therefore, a form of direct phase modulation. The instantaneous phase of the carrier is directly proportional to the modulating signal.

Figure 6-20 shows a schematic diagram for a direct PM modulator. The modulator comprises a varactor diode VD_1 in series with an inductive network (tunable coil L_1 and resistor R_1). The combined series–parallel network appears as a series resonant circuit to the output frequency from the crystal oscillator. A modulating signal is applied to VD_1, which changes its capacitance and, consequently, the phase angle of the impedance seen by the carrier varies, which results in a corresponding phase shift in the carrier. The phase shift is directly proportional to the amplitude of the modulating signal. An advantage of indirect FM is that a buffered crystal oscillator is used for the source of the carrier signal. Consequently, indirect FM transmitters are more frequency stable than their direct counterparts. A disadvantage is that the capacitance–versus–voltage characteristics of a varactor diode are nonlinear. In fact, they closely resemble a square-root function. Consequently, to minimize distortion in the modulated waveform, the amplitude of the modulating signal must be kept quite small, which limits the phase deviation to rather small values and its uses to low-index, narrowband applications.

Transistor direct PM modulator. Figure 6-21 shows the schematic diagram for a simple transistor direct PM modulator. The circuit is a standard class A common-emitter amplifier with two external inputs: a modulating-signal input $[v_m(t)]$ and an external carrier input $[v_c(t)]$. The quiescent operating conditions cause the transistor to act like a resistor from point x to ground. The transistor emitter-to-collector resistance (R_t) is part of a phase shifter consisting of C_1 in series with R_t and emitter resistor R_E. The output is taken across the series combination of R_t and R_E. If the circuit is designed such that at the carrier input frequency (f_c), the sum of R_t and R_E equals the capacitive reactance of C_1 (i.e., X_{C1}), the carrier input signal is shifted 45°.

When the modulating signal is applied, its voltage adds to and subtracts from the dc base bias, producing corresponding changes in the collector current. The changes in collector current dynamically change the transistor emitter-to-collector resistance, producing

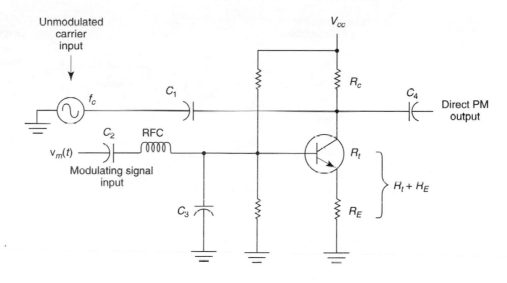

FIGURE 6-21   Transistor direct PM modulator

changes in the phase shift that the carrier undergoes as it passes through the phase shifting network. The phase shift is directly proportional to the amplitude of the modulating signal and occurs at a rate equal to the modulating-signal frequency. The higher the amplitude of the modulating input signal, the greater the change in emitter-to-collector resistance and the greater the phase shift.

Transistor phase shifters are capable of producing peak phase shifts as high as 0.375 radians (i.e., a modulation index of 0.375). With a modulating-signal frequency of 15 kHz, a modulation index of 0.375 corresponds to an indirect frequency shift of $15,000 \times 0.375 = 5625$ Hz.

FREQUENCY UP-CONVERSION

With FM and PM modulators, the carrier frequency at the output of the modulator is generally somewhat larger than the desired frequency of transmission. Therefore, with FM and PM transmitters, it is often necessary to up-convert the frequency of the modulated carrier after modulation has been performed. There are two basic methods of performing frequency up-conversion. One is by using a heterodyning process and the second method is through frequency multiplication. Figure 6-22 shows the two methods of performing frequency up-conversion.

Heterodyne Method of Frequency Up-Conversion

Figure 6-22a shows the heterodyne method of frequency up-conversion. With the heterodyne method, a relatively low-frequency, angle-modulated carrier along with its side frequencies are applied to one input of a balanced modulator. The second input is a relatively high-frequency, unmodulated RF carrier signal. In the balanced modulator the two inputs mix nonlinearly, producing sum and difference frequencies at its output. Sum and difference frequencies are also produced between the side frequencies of the modulated signal and the RF carrier. The bandpass filter (BPF) is tuned to the sum frequency with a passband wide enough to pass the carrier plus the upper and lower side frequencies. Thus, the BPF passes the sum of the modulated and the unmodulated carriers while the difference frequencies are blocked. The output from the bandpass filter is

$$f_{c(\text{out})} = f_{c(\text{in})} + f_{\text{RF}}$$

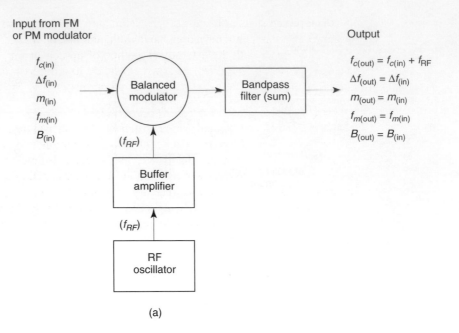

(a)

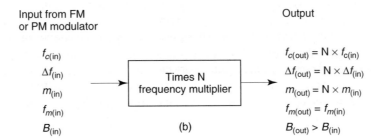

(b)

FIGURE 6-22 Frequency up-conversion: (a) heterodyne method; and (b) multiplication method

where $f_{c(\text{out})}$ = up-converted modulated signal
    $f_{c(\text{in})}$ = input modulated signal
    f_{RF} = RF carrier

   Since the side frequencies of the modulated carrier are unaffected by the heterodyning process, frequency deviation is also unaffected. Thus, the output of the BPF contains the original frequency deviation (both its magnitude Δf and rate of change f_m). The modulation index, phase deviation, and bandwidth are also unaffected by the heterodyne process. Therefore,

$$\Delta f_{(\text{out})} = \Delta f_{(\text{in})}$$
$$m_{(\text{out})} = m_{(\text{in})}$$
$$\Delta \theta_{(\text{out})} = \Delta \theta_{(\text{in})}$$
$$B_{(\text{out})} = B_{(\text{in})}$$
$$f_{m(\text{out})} = f_{m(\text{in})}$$

   If the bandpass filter at the output of the balanced modulator in Figure 6-22a were tuned to the difference frequency, frequency down-conversion would occur. As with frequency up-conversion, only the carrier frequency is affected. The modulation index, frequency deviation, phase deviation, bandwidth, and rate of change would be unchanged.

In essence, with the heterodyne method of up-conversion, a low-frequency modulated carrier can be either up- or down-converted to a different location in the frequency spectrum without changing its modulation properties.

Multiplication Method of Up-Conversion

Figure 6-22b shows the multiplication method of frequency up-conversion. With the multiplication method of frequency up-conversion, the modulation properties of a carrier can be increased at the same time that the carrier frequency is up-converted. With the multiplication method, the frequency of the modulated carrier is multiplied by a factor of N in the frequency multiplier. In addition, the frequency deviation is also multiplied. The rate of deviation, however, is unaffected by the multiplication process. Therefore, the output carrier frequency, frequency deviation, modulation index, and phase deviation at the output of the frequency multiplier are

$$f_{c(\text{out})} = Nf_{c(\text{in})}$$
$$\Delta f_{(\text{out})} = N\Delta f_{(\text{in})}$$
$$m_{(\text{out})} = Nm_{(\text{in})}$$
$$\Delta \theta_{(\text{out})} = N\Delta \theta_{(\text{in})}$$
$$f_{m(\text{out})} = f_{m(\text{in})}$$

N equals the multiplication factor.

Since the frequency deviation and modulation index are multiplied in the frequency multiplier, the number of side frequencies also increased, producing a corresponding increase in bandwidth. For modulation indices greater than 10 (i.e., high index modulation), Carson's rule can be applied and the bandwidth at the output of the multiplier can be approximated as

$$B(\text{out}) = N(2\Delta f)$$
$$= NB_{(\text{in})}$$

It is important to note, however, that the frequency deviation occurs at the modulating-signal frequency (f_m) which remains unchanged by the multiplication process. Therefore, the separation between adjacent side frequencies remains unchanged (i.e., $\pm f_m$, $\pm 2f_m$, $\pm 3f_m$, and so on).

In subsequent sections of this book, you will see that sometimes it is advantageous to use the heterodyne method of frequency up-conversion in FM and PM transmitters, sometimes it is advantageous to use the multiplication method, and sometimes both techniques are used in the same transmitter.

Example 6-7

For the carrier frequency and modulation properties listed, determine the carrier frequency and modulation properties at the output of

(a) A balanced modulator with a bandpass filter tuned to the sum frequency and an RF carrier input frequency of 99.5 MHz.
(b) A times 10 frequency multiplier.
$$\Delta f = 3 \text{ kHz}, f_m = 10 \text{ kHz}, m = 0.3, \text{ and } f_c = 500 \text{ kHz}$$

Solution (a) The output carrier frequency is simply the sum of the input modulated carrier and the RF carrier.

$$f_{c(\text{out})} = 0.5 \text{ MHz} + 99.5 \text{ MHz}$$
$$= 100 \text{ MHz}$$

The output modulation properties are identical to the input modulation properties.

$$\Delta f(\text{in}) = 3 \text{ kHz}, f_{m(\text{in})} = 10 \text{ kHz}, m = 0.3, \text{ and } f_{c(\text{in})} = 500 \text{ kHz}$$

(b) The output carrier frequency, frequency deviation, modulation index, and modulating frequency are simply

$$f_{c(\text{out})} = 10(500 \text{ kHz}) = 5 \text{ MHz}$$
$$\Delta f_{(\text{out})} = 10(3 \text{ kHz}) = 30 \text{ kHz}$$
$$m_{(\text{out})} = 10(0.3) = 3$$
$$f_{m(\text{out})} = 10 \text{ kHz}$$

DIRECT FM TRANSMITTERS

Direct FM transmitters produce an output waveform in which the frequency deviation is directly proportional to the modulating signal. Consequently, the carrier oscillator must be deviated directly. Therefore, for medium- and high-index FM systems, the oscillator cannot be a crystal because the frequency at which a crystal oscillates cannot be significantly varied. As a result, the stability of the oscillators in direct FM transmitters often cannot meet FCC specifications. To overcome this problem, *automatic frequency control* (AFC) is used. An AFC circuit compares the frequency of the noncrystal carrier oscillator to a crystal reference oscillator and then produces a correction voltage proportional to the difference between the two frequencies. The correction voltage is fed back to the carrier oscillator to automatically compensate for any drift that may have occurred.

Crosby Direct FM Transmitter

Figure 6-23 shows the block diagram for a commercial broadcast-band transmitter. This particular configuration is called a *Crosby direct FM transmitter* and includes an *AFC loop*. The frequency modulator can be either a reactance modulator or a voltage-controlled oscillator. The carrier rest frequency is the unmodulated output frequency from the master oscillator (f_c). For the transmitter shown in Figure 6-23, the center frequency of the master oscillator $f_c = 5.1$ MHz, which is multiplied by 18 in three steps ($3 \times 2 \times 3$) to produce a final transmit carrier frequency, $f_t = 91.8$ MHz. At this time, three aspects of frequency conversion should be noted. First, when the frequency of a frequency-modulated carrier is multiplied, its frequency and phase deviations are multiplied as well. Second, the rate at which the carrier is deviated (i.e., the modulating signal frequency, f_m) is unaffected by the mul-

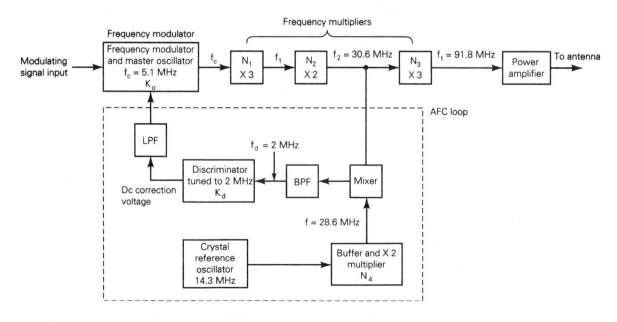

FIGURE 6-23 Crosby direct FM transmitter

tiplication process. Therefore, the modulation index is also multiplied. Third, when an angle-modulated carrier is heterodyned with another frequency in a nonlinear mixer, the carrier can be either up- or down-converted, depending on the passband of the output filter. However, the frequency deviation, phase deviation, and rate of change are unaffected by the heterodyning process. Therefore, for the transmitter shown in Figure 6-23, the frequency and phase deviations at the output of the modulator are also multiplied by 18. To achieve the maximum frequency deviation allowed FM broadcast-band stations at the antenna (75 kHz), the deviation at the output of the modulator must be

$$\Delta f = \frac{75 \text{ kHz}}{18} - 4166.7 \text{ Hz}$$

and the modulation index must be

$$m = \frac{4166.7 \text{ Hz}}{f_m}$$

For the maximum modulating-signal frequency allowed, $f_m = 15$ kHz,

$$m = \frac{4166.7 \text{ Hz}}{15,000 \text{ Hz}} = 0.2778$$

Thus, the modulation index at the antenna is

$$m = 0.2778(18) = 5$$

which is the deviation ratio for commercial FM broadcast transmitters with a 15-kHz modulating signal.

AFC loop.   The purpose of the *AFC loop* is to achieve near-crystal stability of the transmit carrier frequency without using a crystal in the carrier oscillator. With AFC, the carrier signal is mixed with the output signal from a crystal reference oscillator in a nonlinear device, down-converted in frequency, and then fed back to the input of a *frequency discriminator*. A frequency discriminator is a frequency-selective device whose output voltage is proportional to the difference between the input frequency and its resonant frequency (discriminator operation is explained in Chapter 7). For the transmitter shown in Figure 6-23, the output from the doubler $f_2 = 30.6$ MHz, which is mixed with a crystal-controlled reference frequency $f_r = 28.6$ MHz to produce a difference frequency $f_d = 2$ MHz. The discriminator is a relatively high-Q (narrowband) tuned circuit that reacts only to frequencies near its center frequency (2 MHz in this case). Therefore, the discriminator responds to long-term, low-frequency changes in the carrier center frequency due to master oscillator frequency drift and because low-pass filtering does not respond to the frequency deviation produced by the modulating signal. If the discriminator responded to the frequency deviation, the feedback loop would cancel the deviation and, thus, remove the modulation from the FM wave (this effect is called *wipe off*). The dc correction voltage is added to the modulating signal to automatically adjust the master oscillator's center frequency to compensate for the low-frequency drift.

Example 6-8

Use the transmitter model shown in Figure 6-23 to answer the following questions. For a total frequency multiplication of 20 and a transmit carrier frequency $f_t = 88.8$ MHz, determine

(a) Master oscillator center frequency.

(b) Frequency deviation at the output of the modulator for a frequency deviation of 75 kHz at the antenna.

(c) Deviation ratio at the output of the modulator for a maximum modulating-signal frequency $f_m = 15$ kHz.

(d) Deviation ratio at the antenna.

Solution (a)
$$f_c = \frac{f_t}{N_1 N_2 N_3} = \frac{88.8 \text{ MHz}}{20} = 4.43 \text{ MHz}$$

(b)
$$\Delta f = \frac{\Delta f_t}{N_1 N_2 N_3} = \frac{75 \text{ kHz}}{20} = 3750 \text{ Hz}$$

(c)
$$\text{DR} = \frac{\Delta f_{(max)}}{f_{m(max)}} = \frac{3750 \text{ Hz}}{15 \text{ kHz}} = 0.25$$

(d)
$$\text{DR} = 0.25 \times 20 = 5$$

Automatic frequency control. Because the Crosby transmitter uses either a VCO, a reactance oscillator, or a linear integrated-circuit oscillator to generate the carrier frequency, it is more susceptible to frequency drift due to temperature change, power supply fluctuations, and so on, than if it were a crystal oscillator. As stated in Chapter 2, the stability of an oscillator is often given in parts per million (ppm) per degree Celsius. For example, for the transmitter shown in Figure 6-23, an oscillator stability of ± 40 ppm could produce ± 204 Hz (5.1 MHz $\times$ ± 40 Hz/million) of frequency drift per degree Celsius at the output of the master oscillator. This would correspond to a ± 3672-Hz drift at the antenna ($18 \times \pm 204$), which far exceeds the ± 2-kHz maximum set by the FCC for commercial FM broadcasting. Although an AFC circuit does not totally eliminate frequency drift, it can substantially reduce it. Assuming a rock-stable crystal reference oscillator and a perfectly tuned discriminator, the frequency drift at the output of the second multiplier without feedback (i.e., open loop) is

$$\text{open-loop drift} = df_{o1} = N_1 N_2 df_c \tag{6-45}$$

where d denotes drift. The closed-loop drift is

$$\text{closed-loop drift} = df_{c1} = df_{o1} - N_1 N_2 k_d k_o df_{c1} \tag{6-46}$$

Therefore,
$$df_{c1} + N_1 N_2 k_d k_o df_{c1} = df_{o1}$$

and
$$df_{c1}(1 + N_1 N_2 k_d k_o) = df_{o1}$$

Thus,
$$df_{c1} = \frac{df_{o1}}{1 + N_1 N_2 k_d k_o} \tag{6-47}$$

where k_d = discriminator transfer function (volts per hertz)
k_o = master oscillator transfer function (hertz per volt)

From Equation 6-47 it can be seen that the frequency drift at the output of the second multiplier and, consequently, at the input to the discriminator is reduced by a factor of $1 + N_1 N_2 k_d k_o$ when the AFC loop is closed. The carrier frequency drift is multiplied by the AFC loop gain and fed back to the master oscillator as a correction voltage. The total frequency error cannot be canceled because then there would be no error voltage at the output of the discriminator to feed back to the master oscillator. In addition, Equations 6-45, 6-46, and 6-47 were derived assuming that the discriminator and crystal reference oscillator were perfectly stable, which of course they are not.

Example 6-9

Use the transmitter block diagram and values given in Figure 6-23 to answer the following questions. Determine the reduction in frequency drift at the antenna for a transmitter without AFC compared to a transmitter with AFC. Use a VCO stability = $+200$ ppm, k_o = 10 kHz/V, and k_d = 2 V/kHz.

Solution With the feedback loop open, the master oscillator output frequency is
$$f_c = 5.1 \text{ MHz} + (200 \text{ ppm} \times 5.1 \text{ MHz}) = 5,101,020 \text{ Hz}$$
and the frequency at the output of the second multiplier is
$$f_2 = N_1 N_2 f_c = (5,101,020)(6) = 30,606,120 \text{ Hz}$$

Thus, the frequency drift is

$$df_2 = 30{,}606{,}120 - 30{,}600{,}000 = 6120 \text{ Hz}$$

Therefore, the antenna transmit frequency is

$$f_t = 30{,}606{,}120(3) = 91.81836 \text{ MHz}$$

which is 18.36 kHz above the assigned frequency and well out of limits.

With the feedback loop closed, the frequency drift at the output of the second multiplier is reduced by a factor of $1 + N_1 N_2 k_d k_o$, or

$$1 + \frac{(2)(3)(10 \text{ kHz})}{\text{V}}\frac{2\text{V}}{\text{kHz}} = 121$$

Therefore,

$$df_2 = \frac{6120}{121} = 51 \text{ Hz}$$

Thus,

$$f_2 = 30{,}600{,}051 \text{ Hz}$$

and the antenna transmit frequency is

$$f_t = 30{,}600{,}051 \times 3 = 91{,}800{,}153 \text{ Hz}$$

The frequency drift at the antenna has been reduced from 18,360 Hz to 153 Hz, which is now well within the ± 2-kHz FCC requirements.

The preceding discussion and Example 6-9 assumed a perfectly stable crystal reference oscillator and a perfectly tuned discriminator. In actuality, both the discriminator and the reference oscillator are subject to drift, and the worst-case situation is when they both drift in the same direction as the master oscillator. The drift characteristics for a typical discriminator are on the order of ± 100 ppm. Perhaps now it can be seen why the output frequency from the second multiplier was mixed down to a relatively low frequency prior to being fed to the discriminator. For a discriminator tuned to 2 MHz with a stability of ± 200 ppm, the maximum discriminator drift is

$$df_d = \pm 100 \text{ ppm} \times 2 \text{ MHz} = \pm 200 \text{ Hz}$$

If the 30.6-MHz signal were fed directly into the discriminator, the maximum drift would be

$$df_d = \pm 100 \text{ ppm} \times 30.6 \text{ MHz} = \pm 3060 \text{ Hz}$$

Frequency drift due to discriminator instability is multiplied by the AFC open-loop gain. Therefore, the change in the second multiplier output frequency due to discriminator drift is

$$df_2 = df_d N_1 N_2 k_d k_o \tag{6-48}$$

Similarly, the crystal reference oscillator can drift and also contribute to the total frequency drift at the output of the second multiplier. The drift due to crystal instability is multiplied by 2 before entering the nonlinear mixer; therefore,

$$df_2 = N_4 df_o N_1 N_2 k_d k_o \tag{6-49}$$

and the maximum open-loop frequency drift at the output of the second multiplier is

$$df_{(\text{total})} = N_1 N_2 (df_c + k_o k_d f_d + k_o k_d N_4 df_o) \tag{6-50}$$

Phase-Locked-Loop Direct FM Transmitter

Figure 6-24 shows a *wideband* FM transmitter that uses a phase-locked loop to achieve crystal stability from a VCO master oscillator and, at the same time, generate a high-index, wideband FM output signal. The VCO output frequency is divided by N and fed back to the PLL phase comparator, where it is compared to a stable crystal reference frequency. The phase comparator generates a correction voltage that is proportional to the difference between the two frequencies. The correction voltage is added to the modulating signal and

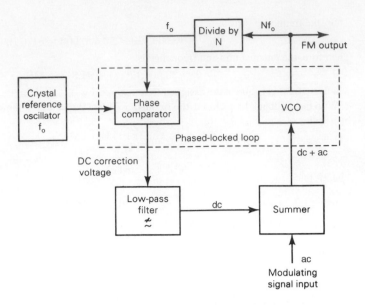

FIGURE 6-24   Phase-locked-loop FM transmitter

applied to the VCO input. The correction voltage adjusts the VCO center frequency to its proper value. Again, the low-pass filter prevents changes in the VCO output frequency due to the modulating signal from being converted to a voltage, fed back to the VCO, and wiping out the modulation. The low-pass filter also prevents the loop from locking onto a side frequency.

PM from FM.   An FM modulator preceded by a differentiator generates a PM waveform. If the transmitters shown in Figures 6-23 and 6-24 are preceded by a preemphasis network, which is a differentiator (high-pass filter), an interesting situation occurs. For a 75-μs time constant, the amplitude of frequencies above 2.12 kHz is emphasized through differentiation. Therefore, for modulating frequencies below 2.12 kHz, the output waveform is proportional to the modulating signal, and for frequencies above 2.12 kHz, the output waveform is proportional to the derivative of the input signal. In other words, frequency modulation occurs for frequencies below 2.12 kHz, and phase modulation occurs for frequencies above 2.12 kHz. Because the gain of a differentiator increases with frequency above the break frequency (2.12 kHz) and because the frequency deviation is proportional to the modulating-signal amplitude, the frequency deviation also increases with frequencies above 2.12 kHz. From Equation 6-18, it can be seen that if Δf and f_m increase proportionately, the modulation index remains constant, which is a characteristic of phase modulation.

INDIRECT FM TRANSMITTERS

Indirect FM transmitters produce an output waveform in which the phase deviation is directly proportional to the modulating signal. Consequently, the carrier oscillator is not directly deviated. Therefore, the carrier oscillator can be a crystal because the oscillator itself is not the modulator. As a result, the stability of the oscillators with indirect FM transmitters can meet FCC specifications without using an AFC circuit.

Armstrong Indirect FM Transmitter

With indirect FM, the modulating signal directly deviates the phase of the carrier, which indirectly changes the frequency. Figure 6-25 shows the block diagram for a wideband

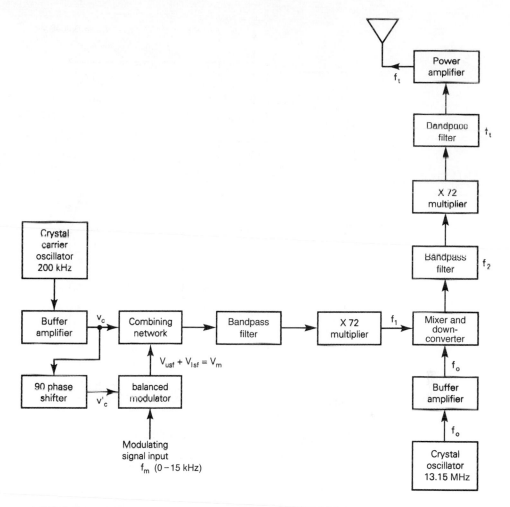

FIGURE 6-25   Armstrong indirect FM transmitter

Armstrong indirect FM transmitter. The carrier source is a crystal; therefore, the stability requirements for the carrier frequency set by the FCC can be achieved without using an AFC loop.

With an Armstrong transmitter, a relatively low-frequency subcarrier (f_c) is phase shifted 90° (f_c') and fed to a balanced modulator, where it is mixed with the input modulating signal (f_m). The output from the balanced modulator is a double-sideband, suppressed-carrier wave that is combined with the original carrier in a combining network to produce a low-index, phase-modulated waveform. Figure 6-26a shows the phasor for the original carrier (V_c), and Figure 6-26b shows the phasors for the side frequency components of the suppressed-carrier wave (V_{usf} and V_{lsf}). Because the suppressed-carrier voltage (V_c') is 90° out of phase with V_c, the upper and lower sidebands combine to produce a component (V_m) that is always in quadrature (at right angles) with V_c. Figures 6-24c through f show the progressive phasor addition of V_c, V_{usf}, and V_{lsf}. It can be seen that the output from the combining network is a signal whose phase is varied at a rate equal to f_m and whose magnitude is directly proportional to the magnitude of V_m. From Figure 6-26 it can be seen that the peak phase deviation (modulation index) can be calculated as follows:

$$\theta = m = \arctan \frac{V_m}{V_c} \tag{6-51a}$$

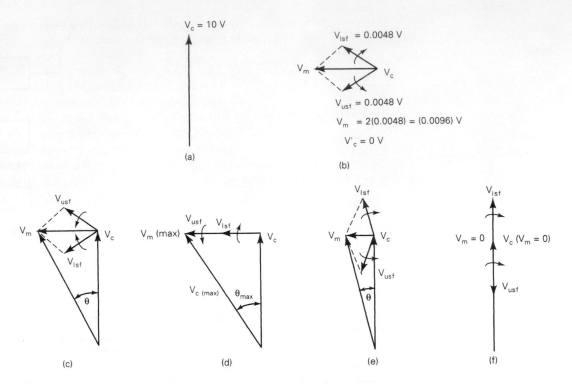

FIGURE 6-26 Phasor addition of V_C, V_{usf}, and V_{lsf}: (a) carrier phasor; (b) sideband phasors; (c)–(f) progressive phasor addition. Part (d) shows the peak phase shift.

For very small angles, the tangent of the angle is approximately equal to the angle; therefore,

$$\theta = m = \frac{V_m}{V_c} \tag{6-51b}$$

Example 6-10

For the Armstrong transmitter shown in Figure 6-25 and the phase-shifted carrier (V'_c), upper side frequency (V_{usf}), and lower side frequency (V_{lsf}) components shown in Figure 6-26, determine
(a) Peak carrier phase shift in both radians and degrees.
(b) Frequency deviation for a modulating-signal frequency $f_m = 15$ kHz.

Solution (a) The peak amplitude of the modulating component is

$$V_m = V_{usf} + V_{lsf}$$
$$= 0.0048 + 0.0048 = 0.0096$$

Peak phase deviation is the modulation index and can be determined by substituting into Equation 6-51a.

$$\theta = m = \arctan \frac{0.0096}{10} = 0.055°$$

$$= 0.055° \times \frac{\pi \text{ rad}}{180°} = 0.00096 \text{ rad}$$

(b) Rearranging Equation 6-18 gives us

$$\Delta f = m f_m = (0.00096)(15 \text{ kHz}) = 14.4 \text{ Hz}$$

From the phasor diagrams shown in Figure 6-26, it can be seen that the carrier amplitude is varied, which produces unwanted amplitude modulation in the output waveform, and $V_{c(max)}$ occurs when V_{usf} and V_{lsf} are in phase with each other and with V_c. The maximum phase deviation that can be produced with this type of modulator is approximately

1.67 milliradians. Therefore, from Equation 6-18 and a maximum modulating-signal frequency $f_{m(max)} = 15$ kHz, the maximum frequency deviation possible is

$$\Delta f_{max} = (0.00167)(15,000) = 25 \text{ Hz}$$

From the preceding discussion it is evident that the modulation index at the output of the combining network is insufficient to produce a wideband FM frequency spectrum and, therefore, must be multiplied considerably before being transmitted. For the transmitter shown in Figure 6-25, a 200-kHz phase-modulated subcarrier with a peak phase deviation $m = 0.00096$ rad only produces a frequency deviation of 14.4 Hz at the output of the combining network. To achieve 75-kHz frequency deviation at the antenna, the frequency must be multiplied by approximately 5208. However, this would produce a transmit carrier frequency at the antenna of

$$f_t = 5208 \times 200 \text{ kHz} = 1041.6 \text{ MHz}$$

which is well beyond the frequency limits for the commercial FM broadcast band. It is apparent that multiplication by itself is inadequate. Therefore, a combination of multiplying and mixing is necessary to develop the desired transmit carrier frequency with 75 kHz frequency deviation. The waveform at the output of the combining network is multiplied by 72, producing the following signal:

$$f_1 = 72 \times 200 \text{ kHz} = 14.4 \text{ MHz}$$
$$m = 72 \times 0.00096 = 0.06912 \text{ rad}$$
$$\Delta f = 72 \times 14.4 \text{ Hz} = 1036.8 \text{ Hz}$$

The output from the first multiplier is mixed with a 13.15-MHz crystal-controlled frequency (f_o) to produce a difference signal (f_2) with the following characteristics:

$$f_2 = 14.4 \text{ MHz} - 13.15 \text{ MHz} = 1.25 \text{ MHz (down-converted)}$$
$$m = 0.6912 \text{ rad (unchanged)}$$
$$\Delta f = 1036.8 \text{ Hz (unchanged)}$$

Note that only the carrier frequency is affected by the heterodyning process. The output from the mixer is once again multiplied by 72 to produce a transmit signal with the following characteristics:

$$f_t = 1.25 \text{ MHz} \times 72 - 90 \text{ MHz}$$
$$m = 0.06912 \times 72 = 4.98 \text{ rad}$$
$$\Delta f = 1036.8 \times 72 = 74,650 \text{ Hz}$$

In the preceding example with the use of both the multiplying and heterodyning processes, the carrier was increased by a factor of 450; at the same time, the frequency deviation and modulation index were increased by a factor of 5184.

With the Armstrong transmitter, the phase of the carrier is directly modulated in the combining network through summation, producing indirect frequency modulation. The magnitude of the phase deviation is directly proportional to the amplitude of the modulating signal but independent of its frequency. Therefore, the modulation index remains constant for all modulating-signal frequencies of a given amplitude. For example, for the transmitter shown in Figure 6-26, if the modulating-signal amplitude is held constant while its frequency is decreased to 5 kHz, the modulation index remains at 5, while the frequency deviation is reduced to $\Delta f = 5 \times 5000 = 25,000$ Hz.

FM from PM. A PM modulator preceded by an integrator produces an FM waveform. If the PM transmitter shown in Figure 6-25 is preceded by a low-pass filter (which is an integrator), FM results. The low-pass filter is simply a $1/f$ filter, which is commonly called a *predistorter* or *frequency correction network*.

FM versus PM

From a purely theoretical viewpoint, the difference between FM and PM is quite simple: The modulation index for FM is defined differently than for PM. With PM, the modulation index is directly proportional to the amplitude of the modulating signal and independent of its frequency. With FM, the modulation index is directly proportional to the amplitude of the modulating signal and inversely proportional to its frequency.

Considering FM as a form of phase modulation, the larger the frequency deviation is, the larger the phase deviation. Therefore, the latter depends, at least to a certain extent, on the amplitude of the modulating signal, just as with PM. With PM, the modulation index is proportional to the amplitude of the modulating signal voltage only, whereas with FM the modulation index is also inversely proportional to the modulating-signal frequency. If FM transmissions are received on a PM receiver, the bass frequencies would have considerably more phase deviation than a PM modulator would have given them. Because the output voltage from a PM demodulator is proportional to the phase deviation, the signal appears excessively bass-boosted. Alternatively (and this is the more practical situation), PM demodulated by an FM receiver produces an information signal in which the higher-frequency modulating signals are boosted.

ANGLE MODULATION VERSUS AMPLITUDE MODULATION

Advantages of Angle Modulation

Angle modulation has several inherent advantages over amplitude modulation.

Noise immunity. Probably the most significant advantage of angle modulation transmission (FM and PM) over amplitude modulation transmission is noise immunity. Most noise (including man-made noise) results in unwanted amplitude variations in the modulated wave (i.e., AM noise). FM and PM receivers include limiters that remove most of the AM noise from the received signal before the final demodulation process occurs—a process that cannot be used with AM receivers because the information is also contained in amplitude variations, and removing the noise would also remove the information.

Noise performance and signal-to-noise improvement. With the use of limiters, FM and PM demodulators can actually reduce the noise level and improve the signal-to-noise ratio during the demodulation process (a topic covered in more detail in Chapter 7). This is called FM thresholding. With AM, once the noise has contaminated the signal, it cannot be removed.

Capture effect. With FM and PM, a phenomenon known as the *capture effect* allows a receiver to differentiate between two signals received with the same frequency. Providing one signal at least twice as high in amplitude as the other, the receiver will capture the stronger signal and eliminate the weaker signal. With amplitude modulation, if two or more signals are received with the same frequency, both will be demodulated and produce audio signals. One may be larger in amplitude than the other, but both can be heard.

Power utilization and efficiency. With AM transmission (especially DSBFC), most of the transmitted power is contained in the carrier while the information is contained in the much lower–power sidebands. With angle modulation, the total power remains constant regardless if modulation is present. With AM, the carrier power remains constant with modulation and the sideband power simply adds to the carrier power. With angle modulation, power is taken from the carrier with modulation and redistributed in the sidebands, thus you might say, angle modulation puts most of its power in the information.

Disadvantages of Angle Modulation

Angle modulation also has several inherent disadvantages over amplitude modulation.

Bandwidth. High-quality angle modulation produces many side frequencies, thus necessitating a much wider bandwidth than is necessary for AM transmission. Narrowband FM utilizes a low modulation index and, consequently, produces only one set of sidebands. Those sidebands, however, contain an even more disproportionate percentage of the total power than a comparable AM system. For high-quality transmission, FM and PM require much more bandwidth than AM. Each station in the commercial AM radio band is assigned 10 kHz of bandwidth, whereas in the commercial FM broadcast band, 200 kHz is assigned each station.

Circuit complexity and cost. PM and FM modulators, demodulators, transmitters, and receivers are more complex to design and build than their AM counterparts. At one time, more complex meant more expensive. Today, however, with the advent of inexpensive, large-scale integration ICs, the cost of manufacturing FM and PM circuits is comparable to their AM counterparts.

QUESTIONS

6-1. Define *angle modulation.*

6-2. Define *direct FM* and *indirect FM.*

6-3. Define *direct PM* and *indirect PM.*

6-4. Define *frequency deviation* and *phase deviation.*

6-5. Define *instantaneous phase, instantaneous phase deviation, instantaneous frequency,* and *instantaneous frequency deviation.*

6-6. Define *deviation sensitivity* for a frequency modulator and for a phase modulator.

6-7. Describe the relationship between the instantaneous carrier frequency and the modulating signal for FM.

6-8. Describe the relationship between the instantaneous carrier phase and the modulating signal for PM.

6-9. Describe the relationship between frequency deviation and the amplitude and frequency of the modulating signal.

6-10. Define *carrier swing*

6-11. Define *modulation index* for FM and for PM.

6-12. Describe the relationship between modulation index and the modulating signal for FM; for PM.

6-13. Define percent modulation for angle-modulated signals.

6-14. Describe the difference between a direct frequency modulator and a direct phase modulator.

6-15. How can a frequency modulator be converted to a phase modulator; a phase modulator to a frequency modulator?

6-16. How many sets of sidebands are produced when a carrier is frequency modulated by a single input frequency?

6-17. What are the requirements for a side frequency to be considered significant?

6-18. Define a *low,* a *medium,* and a *high* modulation index.

6-19. Describe the significance of the *Bessel* table.

6-20. State *Carson's general rule* for determining the bandwidth for an angle-modulated wave.

6-21. Define *deviation ratio.*

6-22. Describe the relationship between the power in the unmodulated carrier and the power in the modulated wave for FM.

6-23. Describe the significance of the FM *noise triangle.*

6-24. What effect does *limiting* have on the composite FM waveform?

6-25. Define *preemphasis* and *deemphasis.*

6-26. Describe a preemphasis network; a deemphasis network.

6-27. Describe the basic operation of a varactor diode FM generator.

6-28. Describe the basic operation of a reactance FM modulator.

6-29. Describe the basic operation of a linear integrated-circuit FM modulator.

6-30. Draw the block diagram for a Crosby direct FM transmitter and describe its operation.

6-31. What is the purpose of an AFC loop? Why is one required for the Crosby transmitter?

6-32. Draw the block diagram for a phase-locked-loop FM transmitter and describe its operation.

6-33. Draw the block diagram for an Armstrong indirect FM transmitter and describe its operation.

6-34. Compare FM to PM.

PROBLEMS

6-1. If a frequency modulator produces 5 kHz of frequency deviation for a 10-V modulating signal, determine the deviation sensitivity. How much frequency deviation is produced for a 2-V modulating signal?

6-2. If a phase modulator produces 2 rad of phase deviation for a 5-V modulating signal, determine the deviation sensitivity. How much phase deviation would a 2-V modulating signal produce?

6-3. Determine (a) the peak frequency deviation, (b) the carrier swing, and (c) the modulation index for an FM modulator with deviation sensitivity $K_1 = 4$ kHz/V and a modulating signal $v_m(t) = 10 \sin(2\pi 2000t)$. What is the peak frequency deviation produced if the modulating signal were to double in amplitude?

6-4. Determine the peak phase deviation for a PM modulator with deviation sensitivity $K = 1.5$ rad/V and a modulating signal $v_m(t) = 2 \sin(2\pi 2000t)$. How much phase deviation is produced for a modulating signal with twice the amplitude?

6-5. Determine the percent modulation for a television broadcast station with a maximum frequency deviation $\Delta f = 50$ kHz when the modulating signal produces 40 kHz of frequency deviation at the antenna. How much deviation is required to reach 100% modulation of the carrier?

6-6. From the Bessel table, determine the number of sets of sidebands produced for the following modulation indices: 0.5, 1.0, 2.0, 5.0, and 10.0.

6-7. For an FM modulator with modulation index $m = 2$, modulating signal $v_m(t) = V_m \sin(2\pi 2000t)$, and an unmodulated carrier $v_c(t) = 8 \sin(2\pi 800kt)$,
(a) Determine the number of sets of significant sidebands.
(b) Determine their amplitudes.
(c) Draw the frequency spectrum showing the relative amplitudes of the side frequencies.
(d) Determine the bandwidth.
(e) Determine the bandwidth if the amplitude of the modulating signal increases by a factor of 2.5.

6-8. For an FM transmitter with 60-kHz carrier swing, determine the frequency deviation. If the amplitude of the modulating signal decreases by a factor of 2, determine the new frequency deviation.

6-9. For a given input signal, an FM broadcast-band transmitter has a frequency deviation $\Delta f = 20$ kHz. Determine the frequency deviation if the amplitude of the modulating signal increases by a factor of 2.5.

6-10. An FM transmitter has a rest frequency $f_c = 96$ MHz and a deviation sensitivity $K_1 = 4$ kHz/V. Determine the frequency deviation for a modulating signal $v_m(t) = 8 \sin(2\pi 2000t)$. Determine the modulation index.

6-11. Determine the deviation ratio and worst-case bandwidth for an FM signal with a maximum frequency deviation $\Delta f = 25$ kHz and a maximum modulating signal $f_{m(max)} = 12.5$ kHz.

6-12. For an FM modulator with 40-kHz frequency deviation and a modulating-signal frequency $f_m = 10$ kHz, determine the bandwidth using both the Bessel table and Carson's rule.

6-13. For an FM modulator with an unmodulated carrier amplitude $V_c = 20$ V, a modulation index $m = 1$, and a load resistance $R_L = 10\ \Omega$, determine the power in the modulated carrier and each side frequency, and sketch the power spectrum for the modulated wave.

6-14. For an angle-modulated carrier $v_c(t) = 2 \cos(2\pi 200\ \text{MHz}\ t)$ with 50 kHz of frequency deviation due to the modulating signal and a single-frequency interfering signal $V_n(t) = 0.5 \cos(2\pi 200.01\ \text{MHz}\ t)$, determine

(a) Frequency of the demodulated interference signal.

(b) Peak phase and frequency deviation due to the interfering signal.

(c) Signal-to-noise ratio at the output of the demodulator.

6-15. Determine the total peak phase deviation produced by a 5-kHz band of random noise with a peak voltage $V_n = 0.08$ V and a carrier $v_c(t) = 1.5 \sin(2\pi40 \text{ MHz } t)$.

6-16. For a Crosby direct FM transmitter similar to the one shown in Figure 6-23 with the following parameters, determine

(a) Frequency deviation at the output of the VCO and the power amplifier.

(b) Modulation index at the same two points.

(c) Bandwidth at the output of the power amplifier.

$N_1 = \times 3$

$N_2 = \times 3$

$N_3 = \times 2$

Crystal reference oscillator frequency = 13 MHz

Reference multiplier = $\times 3$

VCO deviation sensitivity $K_1 = 450$ Hz/V

Modulating signal $v_m(t) = 3 \sin(2\pi5 \times 10^3 t)$

VCO rest frequency $f_c = 4.5$ MHz

Discriminator resonant frequency $f_d = 1.5$ MHz

6-17. For an Armstrong indirect FM transmitter similar to the one shown in Figure 6-25 with the following parameters, determine

(a) Modulation index at the output of the combining network and the power amplifier.

(b) Frequency deviation at the same two points.

(c) Transmit carrier frequency.

Crystal carrier oscillator = 210 kHz

Crystal reference oscillator = 10.2 MHz

Sideband voltage $V_m = 0.018$ V

Carrier input voltage to combiner $V_c = 5$ V

First multiplier = $\times 40$

Second multiplier = $\times 50$

Modulating-signal frequency $f_m = 2$ kHz

6-18. If a frequency modulator produces 4 kHz of frequency deviation for a 10-V_p modulating signal, determine the deviation sensitivity.

6-19. If a phase modulator produces 1.5 rad of phase deviation for a 5-V_p modulating signal, determine the deviation sensitivity.

6-20. Determine (a) the peak frequency deviation, (b) the carrier swing, and (c) the modulation index for an FM modulator with a deviation sensitivity $K_1 = 3$ kHz/V and a modulating signal $v_m = 6 \sin(2\pi2000t)$.

6-21. Determine the peak phase deviation for a PM modulator with deviation sensitivity $K = 2$ rad/V and a modulating signal $v_m = 4 \sin(2\pi1000t)$.

6-22. Determine the percent modulation for a television broadcast station with a maximum frequency deviation $\Delta f = 50$ kHz when the modulating signal produces 30 kHz of frequency deviation.

6-23. From the Bessel table determine the number of side frequencies produced for the following modulation indices: 0.25, 0.5, 1.0, 2.0, 5.0, and 10.

6-24. For an FM modulator with modulation index $m = 5$, modulating signal $v_m = 2 \sin(2\pi5kt)$, and an unmodulated carrier frequency $f_c = 400$ kHz, determine

(a) Number of sets of significant sidebands.

(b) Sideband amplitudes.

Then (c) Draw the output frequency spectrum.

6-25. For an FM transmitter with an 80-kHz carrier swing, determine the frequency deviation. If the amplitude of the modulating signal decreases by a factor of 4, determine the new frequency deviation.

6-26. For a given input signal, an FM broadcast transmitter has a frequency deviation $\Delta f = 40$ kHz. Determine the frequency deviation if the amplitude of the modulating signal increases by a factor of 4.3.

6-27. An FM transmitter has a rest frequency $f_c = 94$ MHz and a deviation sensitivity $K_1 = 5$ kHz/V. Determine the frequency deviation for a modulating signal $v_m(t) = 4$ V_p.

6-28. Determine the deviation ratio and worst-case bandwidth for an FM system with a maximum frequency deviation of 40 kHz and a maximum modulating-signal frequency $f_m = 10$ kHz.

6-29. For an FM modulator with 50 kHz of frequency deviation and a modulating-signal frequency $f_m = 8$ kHz, determine the bandwidth using both the Bessel table and Carson's rule.

6-30. For an FM modulator with an unmodulated carrier voltage $v_c = 12$ V_p, a modulation index $m = 1$, and a load resistance $R_L = 12$ Ω, determine the power in the modulated carrier and each significant side frequency, and sketch the power spectrum for the modulated output wave.

6-31. For an angle-modulated carrier $v_c = 4 \cos(2\pi 300$ MHz $t)$ with 75 kHz of frequency deviation due to the modulating signal and a single-frequency interfering signal $v_n = 0.2 \cos(2\pi 300.015$ MHz $t)$, determine
  (a) Frequency of the demodulated interference signal.
  (b) Peak and rms phase and frequency deviation due to the interfering signal.
  (c) S/N ratio at the output of the FM demodulator.

6-32. Determine the total rms phase deviation produced by a 10-kHz band of random noise with a peak voltage $V_n = 0.04$ V and a carrier with a peak voltage $V_c = 4.5$ V_p.

6-33. For a Crosby direct FM transmitter similar to the one shown in Figure 6-23 with the following parameters, determine
  (a) Frequency deviation at the output of the VCO and the power amplifier.
  (b) Modulation index at the output of the VCO and the power amplifier.
  (c) Bandwidth at the output of the power amplifier.
  > $N_1 = \times 3$
  > $N_2 = \times 3$
  > $N_3 = \times 2$
  > Crystal reference oscillator frequency $= 13$ MHz
  > Reference multiplier $= \times 3$
  > VCO deviation sensitivity $k_1 = 250$ Hz/V
  > Modulating-signal peak amplitude $v_m = 4$ V_p
  > Modulating-signal frequency $f_m = 10$ kHz
  > VCO rest frequency $f_c = 4.3$ MHz
  > Discriminator resonant frequency $f_d = 1.5$ MHz

6-34. For an Armstrong indirect FM transmitter similar to the one shown in Figure 6-25 with the following parameters, determine
  (a) Modulation index at the output of the combining network and the power amplifier.
  (b) Frequency deviation at the same two points.
  (c) Transmit carrier frequency.
  > Crystal carrier oscillator $= 220$ kHz
  > Crystal reference oscillator $= 10.8$ MHz
  > Sideband voltage $V_m = 0.012$ V_p

CHAPTER 7

Angle Modulation Receivers, FM Stereo, and Two-Way FM Radio

INTRODUCTION

Receivers used for angle-modulated signals are very similar to those used for conventional AM or SSB reception, except for the method used to extract the audio information from the composite IF waveform. In FM receivers, the voltage at the output of the audio detector is directly proportional to the frequency deviation at its input. With PM receivers, the voltage at the output of the audio detector is directly proportional to the phase deviation at its input. Because frequency and phase modulation both occur with either angle modulation system, FM signals can be demodulated by PM receivers, and vice versa. Therefore, the circuits used to demodulate FM and PM signals are both described under the heading "FM Receivers."

With conventional AM, the modulating signal is impressed onto the carrier in the form of amplitude variations. However, noise introduced into the system also produces changes in the amplitude of the envelope. Therefore, the noise cannot be removed from the composite waveform without also removing a portion of the information signal. With angle modulation, the information is impressed onto the carrier in the form of frequency or phase variations. Therefore, with angle modulation receivers, amplitude variations caused by noise can be removed from the composite waveform simply by *limiting* (*clipping*) the peaks of the envelope prior to detection. With angle modulation, an improvement in the signal-to-noise ratio is achieved during the demodulation process; thus, system performance in the presence of noise can be improved by limiting. In essence, this is the major advantage of angle modulation over conventional AM.

The purposes of this chapter are to introduce the reader to the basic receiver configurations and circuits used for the reception and demodulation of FM and PM signals, and to describe how they function and how they differ from conventional AM or single-sideband receivers and circuits. In addition, several FM communications systems are described including FM stereo and two-way FM radio communications.

FM receivers, like their AM counterparts, are superheterodyne receivers. Figure 7-1 shows a simplified block diagram for a double-conversion superheterodyne FM receiver. As the figure shows, the FM receiver is similar to the AM receivers discussed in Chapter 4. The preselector, RF amplifier, first and second mixers, IF amplifier, and detector sections of an FM receiver perform almost identical functions as they did in AM receivers: The preselector rejects the image frequency, the RF amplifier establishes the signal-to-noise ratio and noise figure, the mixer/converter section down-converts RF to IF, the IF amplifiers provide most of the gain and selectivity of the receiver, and the detector removes the information from the modulated wave. Except for delayed AGC to prevent mixer saturation when strong RF signals are received, the AGC used with AM receivers is not used for FM receivers, because with FM transmission there is no information contained in the amplitude of the received signal. Because of the inherent noise suppression characteristics of FM receivers, RF amplifiers are also often not required with FM receivers.

With FM receivers, a constant amplitude IF signal into the demodulator is desirable. Consequently, FM receivers generally have much more IF gain than AM receivers. In fact, with FM receivers it is desirable that the final IF amplifier be saturated. The harmonics produced from overdriving the final IF amplifier are high enough that they are substantially reduced with bandpass filters that pass only the minimum bandwidth necessary to preserve the information signals. The final IF amplifier is specially designed for ideal saturation characteristics and is called a *limiter*, or sometimes *passband limiter* if the output is filtered.

The preselector, RF amplifiers, mixer/converter, and IF sections of an FM receiver operate essentially the same as they did in AM receivers; however, the audio detector stage used in FM receivers is quite different. The envelope (peak) detector common to AM receivers is replaced in FM receivers by a *limiter, frequency discriminator,* and *deemphasis network*. The frequency discriminator extracts the information from the modulated wave while the limiter circuit and deemphasis network contribute to an improvement in the signal-to-noise ratio that is achieved in the audio-demodulator stage of FM receivers.

For broadcast-band FM receivers, the first IF is a relatively high frequency (often 10.7 MHz) for good image-frequency rejection, and the second IF is a relatively low frequency (very often 455 kHz) that allows the IF amplifiers to have a relatively high gain and still not be susceptible to oscillating. With a first IF of 10.7 MHz, the image frequency for even the lowest frequency FM station (88.1 MHz) is 109.5 MHz, which is beyond the FM broadcast band.

FM DEMODULATORS

FM demodulators are frequency-dependent circuits designed to produce an output voltage that is proportional to the instantaneous frequency at its input. The overall transfer function for an FM demodulator is nonlinear, but when operated over its linear range is

$$K_d = \frac{V \,(\text{volts})}{f \,(\text{Hz})} \tag{7-1}$$

where K_d equals transfer function.

The output from an FM demodulator is expressed as

$$v_{\text{out}} \,(t) = K_d \Delta f \tag{7-2}$$

where $v_{\text{out}} \,(t)$ = demodulated output signal (volts)

         K_d = demodulator transfer function (volts per hertz)

         Δf = difference between the input frequency and the center frequency of the demodulator (hertz)

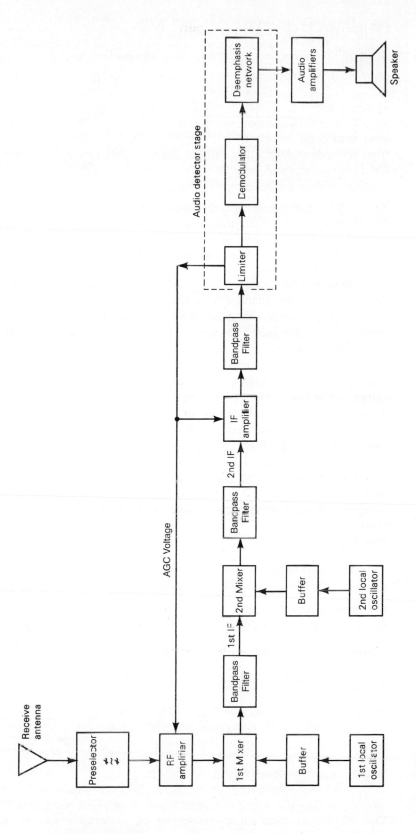

FIGURE 7-1 Double-conversion FM receiver block diagram

Example 7-1

For an FM demodulator circuit with a transfer function $K_d = 0.2$ V/kHz and an FM input signal with 20 kHz of peak frequency deviation, determine the peak output voltage.

Solution Substituting into Equation 7-2, the peak output voltage is

$$v_{out}(t) = \frac{0.2 \text{ V}}{\text{kHz}} \times 20 \text{ kHz}$$

$$= 4 \text{ V}_p$$

Several circuits are used for demodulating FM signals. The most common are the *slope detector, Foster-Seeley discriminator, ratio detector, PLL demodulator,* and *quadrature detector.* The slope detector, Foster-Seeley discriminator, and ratio detector are forms of *tuned-circuit frequency discriminators.*

Tuned-Circuit Frequency Discriminators

Tuned-circuit frequency discriminators convert FM to AM and then demodulate the AM envelope with conventional peak detectors. Also, most frequency discriminators require a 180° phase inverter, an adder circuit, and one or more frequency-dependent circuits.

Slope detector. Figure 7-2a shows the schematic diagram for a *single-ended slope detector,* which is the simplest form of tuned-circuit frequency discriminator. The single-ended slope detector has the most nonlinear voltage-versus-frequency characteristics and, therefore, is seldom used. However, its circuit operation is basic to all tuned-circuit frequency discriminators.

In Figure 7-2a, the tuned circuit (L_a and C_a) produces an output voltage that is proportional to the input frequency. The maximum output voltage occurs at the resonant frequency of the tank circuit (f_c), and its output decreases proportionately as the input frequency deviates above or below f_o. The circuit is designed so that the IF center frequency (f_c) falls in the center of the most linear portion of the voltage-versus-frequency curve, as shown in Figure 7-2b. When the intermediate frequency deviates above f_c, the output voltage increases; when the intermediate frequency deviates below f_c, the output voltage decreases. Therefore, the tuned circuit converts frequency variations to amplitude variations (FM-to-AM conversion). D_i, C_i, and R_i make up a simple peak detector that converts the amplitude variations to an output voltage that varies at a rate equal to that of the input frequency changes and whose amplitude is proportional to the magnitude of the frequency changes.

Balanced slope detector. Figure 7-3a shows the schematic diagram for a *balanced slope detector.* A single-ended slope detector is a tuned-circuit frequency discriminator, and

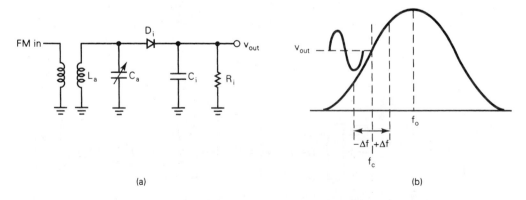

(a)

(b)

FIGURE 7-2 Slope detector: (a) schematic diagram; (b) voltage-versus-frequency curve

a balanced slope detector is simply two single-ended slope detectors connected in parallel and fed 180° out of phase. The phase inversion is accomplished by center tapping the tuned secondary windings of transformer T_1. In Figure 7-3a, the tuned circuits (L_a, C_a, and L_b, C_b) perform the FM-to-AM conversion, and the balanced peak detectors (D_1, C_1, R_1 and D_2, C_2, R_2) remove the information from the AM envelope. The top tuned circuit (L_a and C_a) is tuned to a frequency (f_a) that is above the IF center frequency (f_o) by approximately 1.33 $\times$ Δf (for the FM broadcast band this is approximately 1.33 $\times$ 75 kHz = 100 kHz). The lower tuned circuit (L_b and C_b) is tuned to a frequency (f_b) that is below the IF center frequency by an equal amount.

Circuit operation is quite simple. The output voltage from each tuned circuit is proportional to the input frequency, and each output is rectified by its respective peak detector. Therefore, the closer the input frequency is to the tank-circuit resonant frequency, the greater the tank-circuit output voltage. The IF center frequency falls exactly halfway between the resonant frequencies of the two tuned circuits. Therefore, at the IF center frequency, the output voltages from the two tuned circuits are equal in amplitude but opposite in polarity. Consequently, the rectified output voltage across R_1 and R_2, when added, produce a differential output voltage V_{out} = 0 V. When the IF deviates above resonance, the top tuned circuit produces a higher output voltage than the lower tank circuit and V_{out} goes positive. When the IF deviates below resonance, the output voltage from the lower tank circuit is larger than the output voltage from the upper tank circuit and V_{out} goes negative. The output-versus-frequency response curve is shown in Figure 7-3b.

Although the slope detector is probably the simplest FM detector, it has several inherent disadvantages, which include poor linearity, difficulty in tuning, and lack of provisions for limiting. Because limiting is not provided, a slope detector produces an output voltage that is proportional to amplitude, as well as frequency variations in the input signal, and, consequently, must be preceded by a separate limiter stage. A balanced slope detector is aligned by injecting a frequency equal to the IF center frequency and tuning C_a and C_b for 0 V at the output. Then, frequencies equal to f_a and f_b are alternately injected while C_a and C_b are tuned for maximum and equal output voltages with opposite polarities.

Foster-Seeley discriminator. A *Foster-Seeley discriminator* (sometimes called a *phase shift discriminator*) is a tuned-circuit frequency discriminator whose operation is very similar to that of the balanced slope detector. The schematic diagram for a Foster-Seeley discriminator is shown in Figure 7-4a. The capacitance value for C_c, C_1, and C_2 are chosen such that they are short circuits for the IF center frequency. Therefore, the right side of L_3 is at ac ground potential, and the IF signal (V_{in}) is fed directly (in phase) across L_3

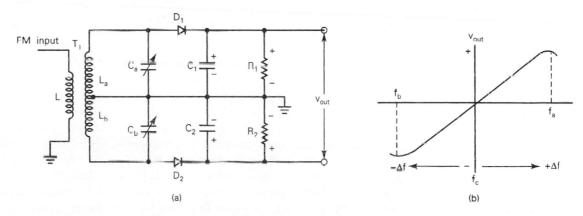

FIGURE 7-3 Balanced slope detector: (a) schematic diagram; (b) voltage-versus-frequency response curve

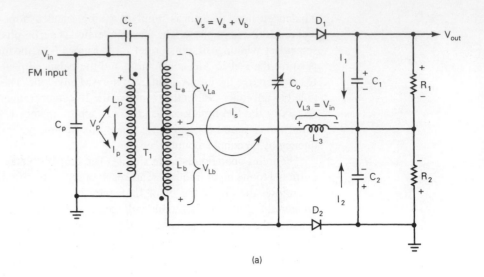

(a)

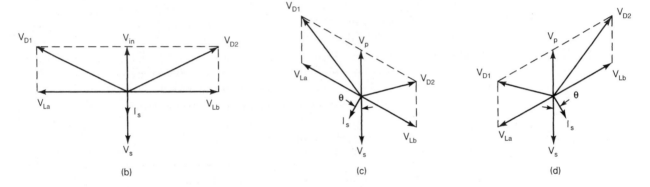

(b)   (c)   (d)

FIGURE 7-4 Foster-Seeley discriminator: (a) schematic diagram; (b) vector diagram, $f_{in} = f_o$; (c) vector diagram, $f_{in} > f_o$; (d) vector diagram, $f_{in} < f_o$

(V_{L3}). The incoming IF is inverted 180° by transformer T_1 and divided equally between L_a and L_b. At the resonant frequency of the secondary tank circuit (the IF center frequency), the secondary current (I_s) is in phase with the total secondary voltage (V_s) and 180° out of phase with V_{L3}. Also, due to loose coupling, the primary of T_1 acts as an inductor, and the primary current I_p is 90° out of phase with V_{in}, and, because magnetic induction depends on primary current, the voltage induced in the secondary is 90° out of phase with V_{in} (V_{L3}). Therefore, V_{La} and V_{Lb} are 180° out of phase with each other and in quadrature, or 90° out of phase with V_{L3}. The voltage across the top diode (V_{D1}) is the vector sum of V_{L3} and V_{La}, and the voltage across the bottom diode V_{D2} is the vector sum of V_{L3} and V_{Lb}. The corresponding vector diagrams are shown in Figure 7-4b. The figure shows that the voltages across D_1 and D_2 are equal. Therefore, at resonance, I_1 and I_2 are equal and C_1 and C_2 charge to equal magnitude voltages except with opposite polarities. Consequently, $V_{out} = V_{C1} - V_{C2} = 0$ V. When the IF goes above resonance ($X_L > X_C$), the secondary tank-circuit impedance becomes inductive, and the secondary current lags the secondary voltage by some angle θ, which is proportional to the magnitude of the frequency deviation. The corresponding phasor diagram is shown in Figure 7-4c. The figure shows that the vector sum of the voltage across D_1 is greater than the vector sum of the voltages across D_2. Consequently, C_1 charges while C_2 discharges and V_{out} goes positive. When the IF goes below

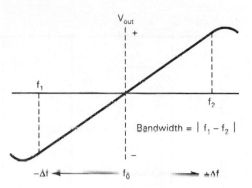

FIGURE 7-5 Discriminator voltage-versus-frequency response curve

resonance ($X_L < X_C$), the secondary current leads the secondary voltage by some angle θ, which is again proportional to the magnitude of the change in frequency. The corresponding phasors are shown in Figure 7-4d. It can be seen that the vector sum of the voltages across D_1 is now less than the vector sum of the voltages across D_2. Consequently, C_1 discharges while C_2 charges and V_{out} goes negative. A Foster-Seeley discriminator is tuned by injecting a frequency equal to the IF center frequency and tuning C_o for 0 volts out.

The preceding discussion and Figure 7-4 show that the output voltage from a Foster-Seeley discriminator is directly proportional to the magnitude and direction of the frequency deviation. Figure 7-5 shows a typical voltage-versus-frequency response curve for a Foster-Seeley discriminator. For obvious reasons, it is often called an *S-curve*. It can be seen that the output voltage-versus-frequency deviation curve is more linear than that of a slope detector, and because there is only one tank circuit, it is easier to tune. For distortionless demodulation, the frequency deviation should be restricted to the linear portion of the secondary tuned-circuit frequency response curve. As with the slope detector, a Foster-Seeley discriminator responds to amplitude as well as frequency variations and, therefore, must be preceded by a separate limiter circuit.

Ratio detector. The *ratio detector* has one major advantage over the slope detector and Foster-Seeley discriminator for FM demodulation: A ratio detector is relatively immune to amplitude variations in its input signal. Figure 7-6a shows the schematic diagram for a ratio detector. As with the Foster-Seeley discriminator, a ratio detector has a single tuned circuit in the transformer secondary. Therefore, the operation of a ratio detector is similar to that of the Foster-Seeley discriminator. In fact, the voltage vectors for D_1 and D_2 are identical to those of the Foster-Seeley discriminator circuit shown in Figure 7-4. However, with the ratio detector, one diode is reversed (D_2), and current (I_d) can flow around the outermost loop of the circuit. Therefore, after several cycles of the input signal, shunt capacitor C_s charges to approximately the peak voltage across the secondary winding of T_1. The reactance of C_s is low, and R_s simply provides a dc path for diode current. Therefore, the time constant for R_s and C_s is sufficiently long so that rapid changes in the amplitude of the input signal due to thermal noise or other interfering signals are shorted to ground and have no effect on the average voltage across C_s. Consequently, C_1 and C_2 charge and discharge proportional to frequency changes in the input signal and are relatively immune to amplitude variations. Also, the output voltage from a ratio detector is taken with respect to ground, and for the diode polarities shown in Figure 7-6a, the average output voltage is positive. At resonance, the output voltage is divided equally between C_1 and C_2 and redistributed as the input frequency is deviated above and below resonance. Therefore, changes in V_{out} are due to the changing ratio of the voltage across C_1 and C_2, while the total voltage is clamped by C_s.

Figure 7-6b shows the output frequency response curve for the ratio detector shown in Figure 7-6a. It can be seen that at resonance, V_{out} is not equal to 0 V but, rather, to one-half

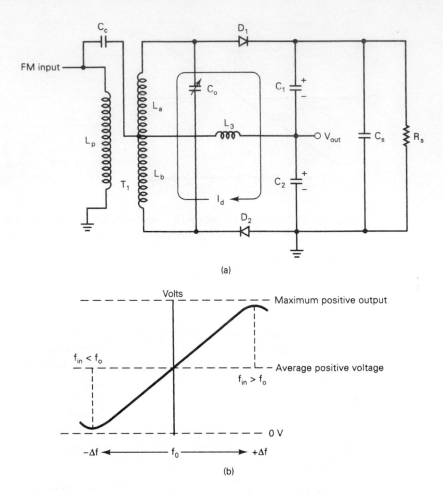

FIGURE 7-6   Ratio detector: (a) schematic diagram; (b) voltage-versus-frequency response curve

of the voltage across the secondary windings of T_1. Because a ratio detector is relatively immune to amplitude variations, it is often selected over a discriminator. However, a discriminator produces a more linear output voltage-versus-frequency response curve.

PHASE-LOCKED-LOOP FM DEMODULATOR

Since the development of LSI linear integrated circuits, FM demodulation can be accomplished quite simply with a phase-locked loop (PLL). Although the operation of a PLL is quite involved, the operation of a *PLL FM demodulator* is probably the simplest and easiest to understand. A PLL frequency demodulator requires no tuned circuits and automatically compensates for changes in the carrier frequency due to instability in the transmit oscillator. Figure 7-7a shows the simplified block diagram for a PLL FM demodulator.

In Chapter 2, a detailed description of PLL operation was given. It was shown that after frequency lock had occurred the VCO would track frequency changes in the input signal by maintaining a phase error at the input of the phase comparator. Therefore, if the PLL input is a deviated FM signal and the VCO natural frequency is equal to the IF center frequency, the correction voltage produced at the output of the phase comparator and fed back to the input of the VCO is proportional to the frequency deviation and is, thus, the demodulated information signal. If the IF amplitude is sufficiently limited prior to reaching the PLL and the loop is properly compensated, the PLL loop gain is constant and equal to K_v.

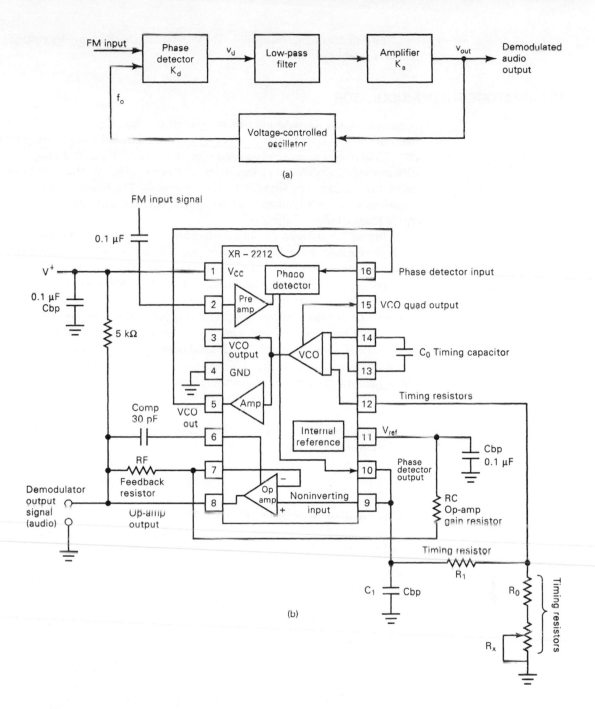

FIGURE 7-7 (a) Block diagram for a PLL FM demodulator; (b) PLL FM demodulator using the XR-2212 PLL

Therefore, the demodulated signal can be taken directly from the output of the internal buffer and is mathematically given as

$$V_{out} = \Delta f K_d K_a \tag{7-3}$$

Figure 7-7b shows a schematic diagram for an FM demodulator using the XR-2212. R_0 and C_0 are course adjustments for setting the VCO's free-running frequency. R_x is for fine tuning, and R_F and R_C set the internal op-amp voltage gain (K_a). The PLL closed-loop frequency response should be compensated to allow unattenuated demodulation of the entire information signal bandwidth. The PLL op-amp buffer provides voltage gain and current drive stability.

QUADRATURE FM DEMODULATOR

A *quadrature FM demodulator* (sometimes called a *coincidence detector*) extracts the original information signal from the composite IF waveform by multiplying two quadrature (90° out of phase) signals. A quadrature detector uses a 90° phase shifter, a single tuned circuit, and a product detector to demodulate FM signals. The 90° phase shifter produces a signal that is in quadrature with the received IF signals. The tuned circuit converts frequency variations to phase variations, and the product detector multiplies the received IF signals by the phase-shifted IF signal.

Figure 7-8 shows a simplified schematic diagram for an FM quadrature detector. C_i is a high-reactance capacitor that, when placed in series with tank circuit (R_o, L_o, and C_o), produces a 90° phase shift at the IF center frequency. The tank circuit is tuned to the IF center frequency and produces an additional phase shift (θ) that is proportional to the frequency deviation. The IF input signal (v_i) is multiplied by the quadrature signal (v_o) in the product detector and produces an output signal that is proportional to the frequency deviation. At the resonant frequency, the tank-circuit impedance is resistive. However, frequency variations in the IF signal produce an additional positive or negative phase shift. Therefore, the product detector output voltage is proportional to the phase difference between the two input signals and is expressed mathematically as

$$v_{\text{out}} = v_i v_o = [V_i \sin(\omega_i t + \theta)] [V_o \cos(\omega_o t)] \tag{7-4}$$

Substituting into the trigonometric identity for the product of a sine and a cosine wave of equal frequency gives us

$$v_{\text{out}} = \frac{V_i V_o}{2} [\sin (2\omega_i t + \theta) + \sin(\theta)] \tag{7-5}$$

The second harmonic ($2\omega_i$) is filtered out, leaving

$$v_{\text{out}} = \frac{V_i V_o}{2} \sin (\theta) \tag{7-6}$$

where $\theta = \tan^{-1} \rho Q$
$\rho = 2\pi f/f_o$ (fractional frequency deviation)
Q = tank-circuit quality factor

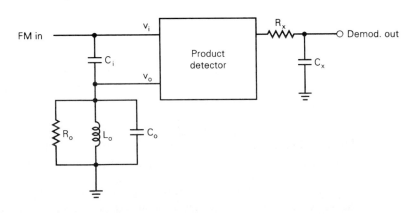

FIGURE 7-8 Quadrature FM demodulator

Probably the most important advantage of frequency modulation over amplitude modulation is the ability of FM receivers to suppress noise. Because most noise appears as amplitude variations in the modulated wave, AM demodulators cannot remove the noise without also removing some of the information. This is because the information is also contained in amplitude variations. With FM, however, the information is contained in frequency variations, allowing the unwanted amplitude variations to be removed with special circuits called *limiters.*

Amplitude Limiters and FM Thresholding

The vast majority of terrestrial FM radio communications systems use conventional noncoherent demodulation because most standard frequency discriminators use envelope detection to remove the intelligence from the FM waveform. Unfortunately, envelope detectors (including ratio detectors) will demodulate incidental amplitude variations as well as frequency variations. Transmission noise and interference add to the signal and produce unwanted amplitude variations. Also, frequency modulation is generally accompanied by small amounts of residual amplitude modulation. In the receiver, the unwanted AM and random noise interference are demodulated along with the signal and produce unwanted distortion in the recovered information signal. The noise is more prevalent at the peaks of the FM waveform and relatively insignificant during the zero crossings. A limiter is a circuit that produces a constant-amplitude output for all input signals above a prescribed minimum input level, which is often called the *threshold, quieting,* or *capture* level. Limiters are required in most FM receivers because many of the demodulators discussed earlier in this chapter demodulate amplitude as well as frequency variations. With amplitude limiters, the signal-to-noise ratio at the output of the demodulator (postdetection) can be improved by as much as 20 dB or more over the input (predetection) signal to noise.

Essentially, an amplitude limiter is an additional IF amplifier that is overdriven. Limiting begins when the IF signal is sufficiently large that it drives the amplifier alternately into saturation and cutoff. Figures 7-9a and 7-9b show the input and output waveforms for a typical limiter. In Figure 7-9b, it can be seen that for IF signals that are below threshold the AM noise is not reduced, and for IF signals above threshold there is a large reduction in the AM noise level. The purpose of the limiter is to remove all amplitude variations from the IF signal.

Figure 7-10a shows the limiter output when the noise is greater than the signal (i.e., the noise has captured the limiter). The irregular widths of the serrations are caused by noise impulses saturating the limiter. Figure 7-10b shows the limiter output when the signal is sufficiently greater than the noise (the signal has captured the limiter). The peaks of the signal have the limiter so far into saturation that the weaker noise is totally eliminated. The improvement in the S/N ratio is called *FM thresholding, FM quieting,* or the *FM capture effect.* Three criteria must be satisfied before FM thresholding can occur:

1. The predetection signal-to-noise ratio must be 10 dB or greater.
2. The IF signal must be sufficiently amplified to overdrive the limiter.
3. The signal must have a modulation index equal to or greater than unity ($m \geq 1$).

Figure 7-11 shows typical FM thresholding curves for low ($m = 1$) and medium ($m = 4$) index signals. The output voltage from an FM detector is proportional to m^2. Therefore, doubling m increases the S/N ratio by a factor of 4 (6 dB). The quieting ratio for $m = 1$ is an input S/N = 13 dB, and for $m = 4$, 22 dB. For S/N ratios below threshold, the receiver is said to be captured by the noise, and for S/N ratios above threshold, the receiver is said to be captured by the signal. Figure 7-11 shows that IF signals at the input to the limiter with 13 dB or more S/N undergo 17 dB of S/N improvement. FM

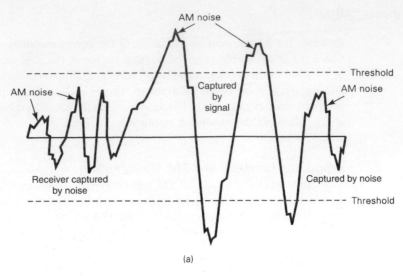

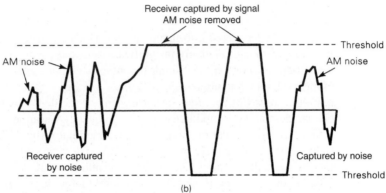

FIGURE 7-9 Amplitude limiter input and output waveforms; (a) input wave-form; (b) output waveform

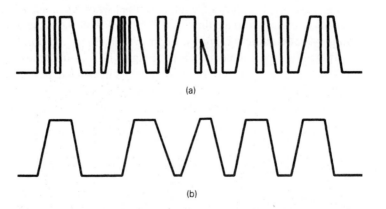

FIGURE 7-10 Limiter output: (a) captured by noise; (b) captured by signal

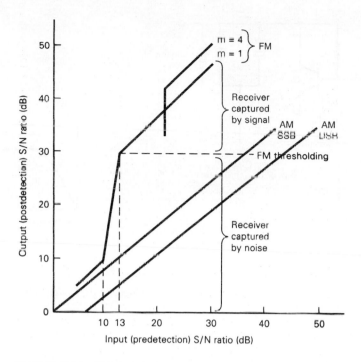

FIGURE 7-11 FM thresholding

quieting begins with an input S/N ratio of 10 dB, but does not produce the full 17-dB improvement until the input signal-to-noise ratio reaches 13 dB.

As shown in Figure 7-11, there is no signal-to-noise improvement with AM double-sideband or AM single-sideband transmission. With AM, the pre- and postdetection signal-to-noise ratios are essentially the same.

Limiter Circuits

Figure 7-12a shows a schematic diagram for a single-stage limiter circuit with a built-in output filter. This configuration is commonly called a *bandpass limiter/amplifier* (BPL). A BPL is essentially a class A biased tuned IF amplifier, and for limiting and FM quieting to occur, it requires an IF input signal sufficient enough to drive it into both saturation and cutoff. The output tank circuit is tuned to the IF center frequency. Filtering removes the harmonic and intermodulation distortion present in the rectangular pulses due to *hard limiting*. The effect of filtering is shown in Figure 7-13. If resistor R_2 were removed entirely, the amplifier would be biased for class C operation, which is also appropriate for this type of circuit, but requires more filtering. Figure 7-12b shows limiter action for the circuit shown in Figure 7-12a. For small signals (below the threshold voltage), no limiting occurs. When V_{in} reaches $V_{threshold}$, limiting begins, and for input amplitudes above V_{max}, there is actually a decrease in V_{out} with increases in V_{in}. This is because with high-input drive levels the collector current pulses are sufficiently narrow that they actually develop less tank-circuit power. The problem of over-driving the limiter can be rectified by incorporating AGC into the circuit.

FM Capture Effect

The inherent ability of FM to diminish the effects of interfering signals is called the *capture effect*. Unlike AM receivers, FM receivers have the ability to differentiate between two signals received at the same frequency. Therefore, if two stations are received simultaneously at the same or nearly the same frequency, the receiver locks onto the stronger station while suppressing the weaker station. Suppression of the weaker signal is accomplished in

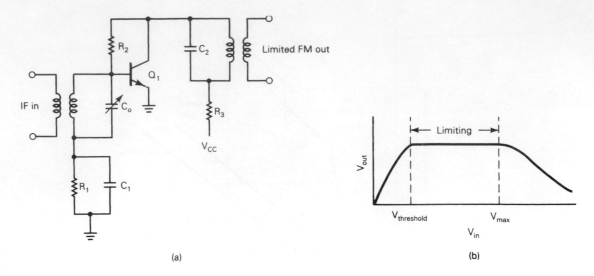

(a)

(b)

FIGURE 7-12 Single-stage tuned limiter: (a) schematic diagram; (b) limiter action

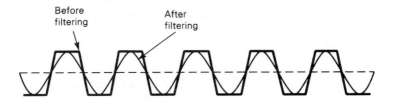

FIGURE 7-13 Filtered limiter output

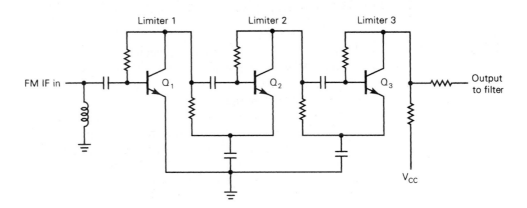

FIGURE 7-14 Three-stage cascaded limiter

amplitude limiters in the same manner that AM noise is suppressed. If two stations are received at approximately the same signal level, the receiver cannot sufficiently differentiate between them and may switch back and forth. The *capture ratio* of an FM receiver is the minimum dB difference in signal strength between two received signals necessary for the capture effect to suppress the weaker signal. Capture ratios of 1 dB are typical for high-quality FM receivers.

When two limiter stages are used, it is called *double limiting;* three stages, *triple limiting;* and so on. Figure 7-14 shows a three-stage *cascaded limiter* without a built-in filter. This

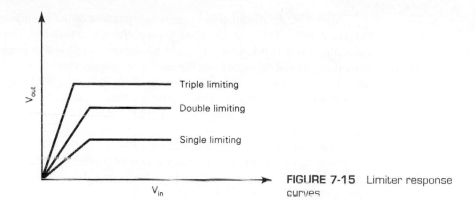

FIGURE 7-15 Limiter response curves

type of limiter circuit must be followed by either a ceramic or crystal filter to remove the non-linear distortion. The limiter shown has three RC coupled limiter stages that are dc series connected to reduce the current drain. Cascaded amplifiers combine several of the advantages of common-emitter and common-gate amplifiers. Cascading amplifiers also decrease the thresholding level and, thus, improve the quieting capabilities of the stage. The effects of double and triple limiting are shown in Figure 7-15. Because FM receivers have sufficient gain to saturate the limiters over a relatively large range of RF input signal levels, AGC is usually unnecessary. In fact, very often AGC actually degrades the performance of an FM receiver.

Example 7-2

For an FM receiver with a bandwidth B = 200 kHz, a power noise figure NF = 8 dB, and an input noise temperature T = 100 K, determine the minimum receive carrier power necessary to achieve a postdetection signal-to-noise ratio of 37 dB. Use the receiver block diagram shown in Figure 7-1 as the receiver model and the FM thresholding curve shown in Figure 7-11 for m = 1.

Solution From Figure 7-11, it can be seen that 17 dB of signal-to-noise improvement is evident in the detector, assuming the limiters are saturated and the input signal-to-noise is greater than 13 dB. Therefore, to achieve a postdetection signal-to-noise ratio of 37 dB, the predetection signal-to-noise ratio must be at least

$$37 \text{ dB} - 17 \text{ dB} = 20 \text{ dB}$$

Therefore, for an overall receiver noise figure equal to 8 dB, the S/N ratio at the input to the receiver must be at least

$$20 \text{ dB} + 8 \text{ dB} = 28 \text{ dB}$$

The receiver input noise power is

$$N_{(dBm)} = 10 \log \frac{KTB}{0.001} = 10 \log \frac{(1.38 \times 10^{-23})(100)(200,000)}{0.001} = -125.6 \text{ dBm}$$

Consequently, the minimum receiver signal power for a 28 dB S/N ratio is

$$S = -125.6 \text{ dBm} + 28 \text{ dB} = -97.6 \text{ dBm}$$

FREQUENCY VERSUS PHASE MODULATION

Although frequency and phase modulation are similar in many ways, they do have their differences and, consequently, there are advantages and disadvantages of both forms of angle modulation. At one time for large-scale applications, such as commercial broadcasting, FM was preferred because PM requires coherent demodulation, usually using a phase-locked loop. Frequency modulation, on the other hand, can be demodulated using noncoherent demodulators. Today, however, PLLs are probably less expensive than their noncoherent counterparts mainly because they come as integrated circuits and require no transformers or LC tank circuits.

With PM, the modulation index is independent of the modulating-signal frequency. Therefore, PM offers better signal-to-noise performance than FM, and PM does not require a preemphasis network. One important advantage of PM is that phase modulation is performed in a circuit separate from the carrier oscillator. Therefore, highly stable crystal oscillators can be used for the carrier source. With FM, the modulating signal is applied directly to the carrier oscillator, thus crystal oscillators cannot be used to produce the carrier signal. Therefore, FM modulators require AFC circuits to achieve the frequency stability required by the FCC.

One prominent advantage of FM over PM is that the VCOs used with FM can be directly modulated and produce outputs with high-frequency deviations and high modulation indices. PM modulators generally require frequency multipliers to increase the modulation index and frequency deviation to useful levels.

LINEAR INTEGRATED-CIRCUIT FM RECEIVERS

In recent years, several manufacturers of integrated circuits such as Signetics, RCA, and Motorola have developed reliable, low-power monolithic integrated circuits that perform virtually all the receiver functions for both AM and FM communications systems. These integrated circuits offer the advantages of being reliable, predictable, miniaturized, and easy to design with. The development of these integrated circuits is one of the primary reasons for the tremendous growth of both portable two-way FM and cellular radio communications systems that has occurred in the past few years.

Low-Power, Integrated-Circuit FM IF System

The NE/SA614A is an improved monolithic low-power FM IF system manufactured by Signetics Corporation. The NE/SA614A is a high-gain, high-frequency device that offers low-power consumption (3.3-mA typical current drain) and excellent input sensitivity (1.5 μV across its input pins) at 455 kHz. The NE/SA614A has an onboard temperature-compensated *received signal-strength indicator* (RSSI) with a logarithmic output and a dynamic range in excess of 90 dB. It has two audio outputs (one muted and one not). The NE/SA614A requires a low number of external components to function and meets cellular radio specifications. The NE/SA614A can be used for the following applications:

1. FM cellular radio
2. High-performance FM communications receivers
3. Intermediate frequency amplification and detection up to 25 MHz
4. RF signal-strength meter
5. Spectrum analyzer applications
6. Instrumentation circuits
7. Data transceivers

The block diagram for the NE/SA614A is shown in Figure 7-16. As the figure shows, the NE/SA614A includes two limiting intermediate-frequency amplifiers, an FM quadrature detector, an audio muting circuit, a logarithmic received signal-strength indicator (RSSI), and a voltage regulator. The NE/SA614A is an IF signal-processing system suitable for frequencies as high as 21.4 MHz.

IF amplifiers.   Figure 7-17 shows the equivalent circuit for the NE/SA614A. The IF amplifier section consists of two log-limiting amplifier stages. The first consists of two differential amplifiers with 39 dB of gain and a small-signal ac bandwidth of 41 MHz when driven from a 50-Ω source. The output of the first limiter is a low-impedance emitter follower with 1 kΩ of equivalent series resistance. The second limiting stage consists of three differential amplifiers with a total gain of 62 dB and a small-signal ac bandwidth of

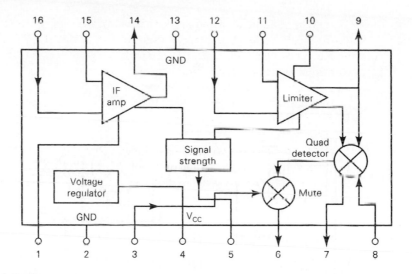

FIGURE 7-16 Block diagram for the Signetics NE/SA614A integrated-circuit, low-power FM IF system

28 MHz. The outputs of the final differential amplifier are buffered to the internal quadrature detector. One output is available to drive an external quadrature capacitor and *L/C* quadrature tank. Both limiting stages are dc biased with feedback. The buffered outputs of the final differential amplifier in each stage are fed back to the input of that stage through a 42-kΩ resistor. Because of the very high gain, wide bandwidth, and high input impedance of the limiters, the limiter stage is potentially unstable at IF frequencies above 455 kHz. The stability can be improved by reducing the gain. This is accomplished by adding attenuators between amplifier stages. The IF amplifiers also feature low phase shift (typically only a few degrees over a wide range of input frequencies).

Quadrature detector. Figure 7-18 shows the block diagram for the equivalent circuit for the quadrature detector in the NE/SA614A. A quadrature detector is a multiplier cell similar to a mixer stage, but instead of mixing two different frequencies, it mixes two signals with the same frequencies but with different phases. A constant-amplitude (amplitude-limited) signal is applied to the lower part of the multiplier. The same signal is applied single ended to an external capacitor connected to pin 9. There is a 90° phase shift across the plates of the capacitor. The phase shifted signal is applied to the upper port of the multiplier at pin 8. A quadrature tank (a parallel *LC* network) permits frequency selective phase shifting at the IF signal. The quadrature detector produces an output signal whose amplitude is proportional to the magnitude of the frequency deviation of the input FM signal.

Audio outputs. The NE/SA614A has two audio outputs. Both are PNP current-to-voltage converters with 55-kΩ nominal internal loads. The unmuted output is always active to permit the use of signaling tones such as for cellular radio. The other output can be muted with 70-dB typical attenuation. The two outputs have an internal 180° phase difference and, therefore, can be applied to the differential inputs of an op-amp amplifier or comparator. Once the threshold of the reference frequency has been established, the two output amplitudes will shift in opposite directions as the input frequency shifts.

RSSI. The received signal-strength indicator demonstrates a monotonic logarithmic output over a range of 90 dB. The signal-strength output is derived from the summed stage currents in the limiting amplifiers. It is essentially independent of the IF frequency. Thus, unfiltered signals at the limiter input, such as spurious products or regenerated signals, will

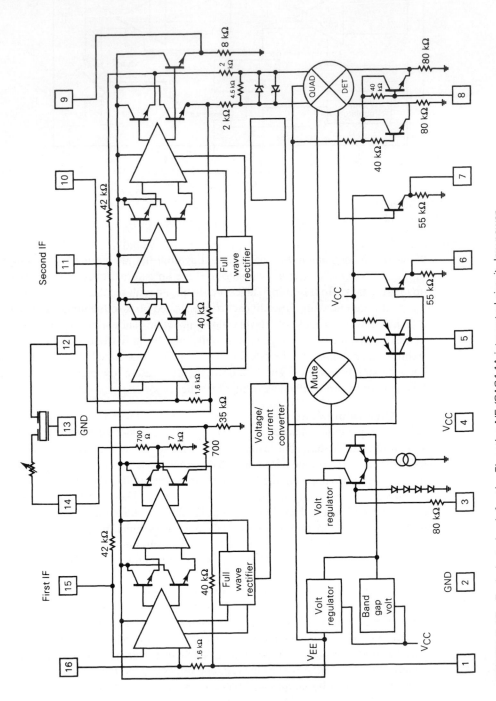

FIGURE 7-17 Equivalent circuit for the Signetics NE/SA614A integrated-circuit, low-power FM IF system

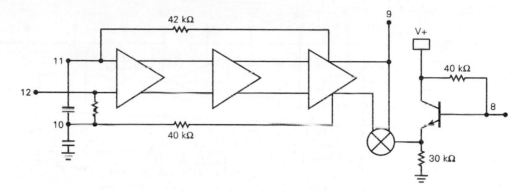

FIGURE 7-18 Quadrature detector block diagram

manifest themselves as an RSSI output. At low frequencies, the RSSI makes an excellent logarithmic ac voltmeter. The RSSI output is a current-to-voltage converter similar to the audio outputs.

Low-Voltage, High-Performance Mixer FM IF System

The NE/SA616 is a low-voltage, high-performance monolithic FM IF system similar to the NE/SA614A except with the addition of a mixer/oscillator circuit. The NE/SA616 will operate at frequencies up to 150 MHz and with as little as 2.7 V dc. The NE/SA616 features low power consumption, a mixer conversion power gain of 17 dB at 45 MHz, 102 dB of IF amplifier/limiter gain, and a 2-MHz IF amplifier/limiter small-signal ac bandwidth. The NE/SA616 can be used for the following applications:

1. Portable FM cellular radio
2. Cordless telephones
3. Wireless communications systems
4. RF signal-strength meter
5. Spectrum analyzer applications
6. Instrumentation circuits
7. Data transceivers
8. Log amps
9. Single-conversion VHF receivers

The block diagram for the NE/SA616 is shown in Figure 7-19. The NE/SA616 is similar to the NE/SA614A with the addition of a mixer and local oscillator stage. The input stage is a Gilbert cell mixer with an oscillator. Typical mixer characteristics include a noise figure of 6.2 dB, conversion gain of 17 dB, and input third-order intercept of −9 dBm. The oscillator will operate in excess of 200 MHz in an *LC* tank-circuit configuration. The output impedance of the mixer is a 1.5-kΩ resistor, permitting direct connection to a 455-kHz ceramic filter. The IF amplifier has 43 dB of gain and a 5.5-MHz bandwidth. The IF limiter has 60 dB of gain and a 4.5-MHz bandwidth. The quadrature detector also uses a Gilbert cell. One port of the cell is internally driven by the IF signal, and the other output of the IF is ac coupled to a tuned quadrature network, where it undergoes a 90° phase shift before being fed back to the other port of the Gilbert cell. The demodulator output of the quadrature detector drives an internal op-amp. The op amp can be configured as a unity-gain buffer, or for simultaneous gain, filtering, and second-order temperature compensation if needed.

Single-Chip FM Radio System

The TDA7000 is a monolithic integrated-circuit FM radio system manufactured by Signetics Corporation for monophonic FM portable radios. In essence, the TDA7000 is a complete FM

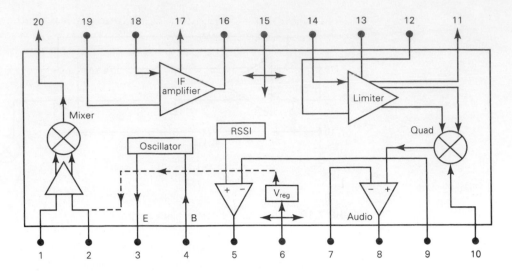

FIGURE 7-19 Block diagram for the Signetics NE/SA616 monolithic FM IF system

radio receiver on a single integrated-circuit chip. The TDA7000 features small size, lack of IF coils, easy assembly, and low power consumption. External to the IC is only one tunable *LC* tank circuit for the local oscillator, a few inexpensive ceramic plate capacitors, and one resistor. Using the TDA7000, a complete FM radio can be made small enough to fit inside a calculator, cigarette lighter, key-ring fob, or even a slim watch. The TDA7000 can also be used in equipment such as cordless telephones, radio-controlled models, paging systems, or the sound channel of a television receiver.

The block diagram for the TDA7000 is shown in Figure 7-20. The TDA7000 includes the following functional blocks: RF input stage, mixer, local oscillator, IF amplitude/limiter, phase demodulator, mute detector, and mute switch. The IC has an internal FLL (frequency-locked-loop) system with an intermediate frequency of 70 MHz. The FLL is used to reduce the total harmonic distortion (THD) by compressing the IF frequency swing (deviation). This is accomplished by using the audio output from the FM demodulator to shift the local oscillator frequency in opposition to the IF deviation. The principle is to compress 75 kHz of frequency deviation down to approximately 15 kHz. This limits the total harmonic distortion to 0.7% with ± 22.5-kHz deviation and to 2.3% with ± 75-kHz deviation. The IF selectivity is obtained with active *RC* Sallen-Key filters. The only function that needs alignment is the resonant circuit for the oscillator.

FM STEREO BROADCASTING

Until 1961, all commercial FM broadcast-band transmissions were *monophonic.* That is, a single 50-Hz to 15-kHz audio channel made up the entire voice and music information frequency spectrum. This single audio channel modulated a high-frequency carrier and was transmitted through a 200-kHz-bandwidth FM communications channel. With *mono* transmission, each speaker assembly at the receiver reproduces exactly the same information. It is possible to separate the information frequencies with special speakers, such as *woofers* for low frequencies and *tweeters* for high frequencies. However, it is impossible to separate monophonic sound *spatially.* The entire information signal sounds as though it is coming from the same direction (i.e., from a *point source,* there is no directivity to the sound). In 1961, the FCC authorized *stereophonic* transmission for the commercial FM broadcast band. With stereophonic transmission, the information signal is spatially divided into two 50-Hz to 15-kHz audio channels (a left and a right). Music that originated on the left side is repro-

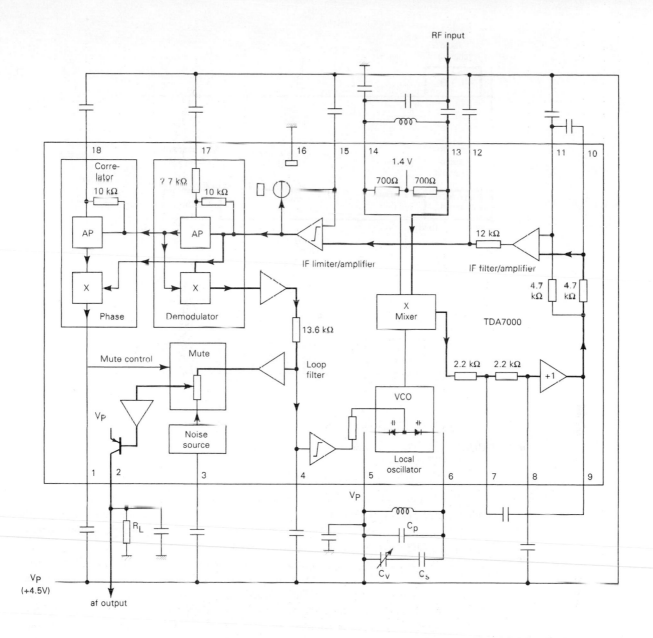

FIGURE 7-20 Block diagram for the Signetics TDA7000 integrated-circuit FM radio

duced only on the left speaker, and music that originated on the right side is reproduced only on the right speaker. Therefore, with stereophonic transmission, it is possible to reproduce music with a unique directivity and spatial dimension that before was possible only with live entertainment (i.e., from an *extended* source). Also, with stereo transmission, it is possible to separate music or sound by *tonal quality,* such as percussion, strings, horns, and so on.

A primary concern of the FCC before authorizing stereophonic transmission was its compatibility with monophonic receivers. Stereo transmission was not to affect mono reception. Also, monophonic receivers must be able to receive stereo transmission as monaural without any perceptible degradation in program quality. In addition, stereophonic receivers were to receive stereo programming with nearly perfect separation (40 dB or more) between the left and right channels.

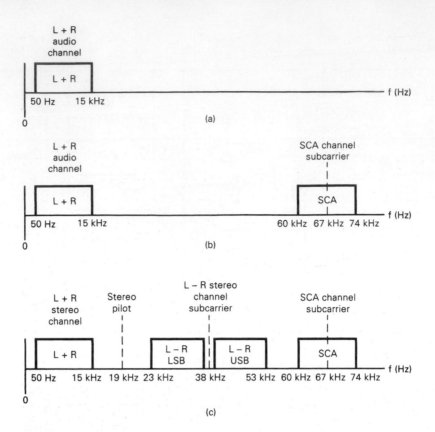

FIGURE 7-21 FM baseband spectrum: (a) prior to 1955; (b) prior to 1961; (c) since 1961

The original FM audio spectrum is shown in Figure 7-21a. The audio channel extended from 50 Hz to 15 kHz. In 1955, the FCC approved subcarrier transmission under the Subsidiary Communications Authorization (SCA). SCA is used to broadcast uninterrupted music to private subscribers, such as department stores, restaurants, and medical offices equipped with special SCA receivers. This is the music we sometimes cordially refer to as "elevator music." Originally, the SCA subcarrier ranged from 25 kHz to 75 kHz, but has since been standardized at 67 kHz. The subcarrier and its associated sidebands become part of the total signal that modulates the main carrier. At the receiver, the subcarrier is demodulated along with the primary channel, but cannot be heard because of its high frequency. The process of placing two or more independent channels next to each other in the frequency domain (stacking the channels), and then modulating a single high-frequency carrier with the combined signal is called *frequency division multiplexing* (FDM). With FM stereophonic broadcasting, three voice or music channels are frequency division multiplexed onto a single FM carrier. Figure 7-21b shows the total baseband frequency spectrum for FM broadcasting prior to 1961 (the composite baseband comprises the total modulating-signal spectrum). The primary audio channel remained at 50 Hz to 15 kHz, while an additional SCA channel is frequency translated to the 50-kHz to 74-kHz passband. The SCA subcarrier may be AM single- or double-sideband transmission or FM with a maximum modulating-signal frequency of 7 kHz. However, the SCA modulation of the main carrier is low-index narrowband FM and, consequently, is a much lower quality transmission than the primary FM channel. The total frequency deviation remained at 75 kHz with 90% (67.5 kHz) reserved for the primary channel and 10% (7.5 kHz) reserved for SCA.

Figure 7-21c shows the FM baseband frequency spectrum as it has been since 1961. It comprises the 50-Hz to 15-kHz stereo channel plus an additional stereo channel fre-

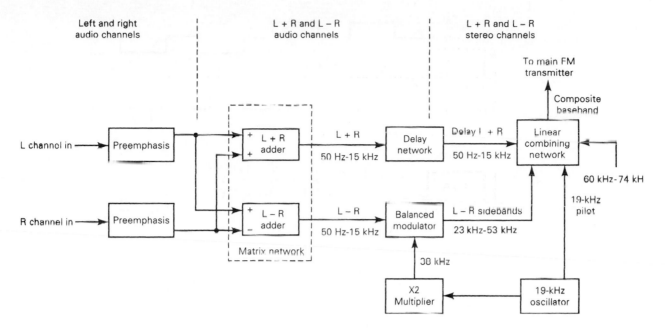

FIGURE 7-22 Stereo FM transmitter using frequency-division multiplexing

quency division multiplexed into a composite baseband signal with a 19-kHz pilot. The three channels are (1) the left (L) plus the right (R) audio channels (the L + R stereo channel), (2) the left plus the inverted right audio channels (the L − R stereo channel), and (3) the SCA subcarrier and its associated sidebands. The L + R stereo channel occupies the 0-kHz to 15-kHz passband (in essence, the unaltered L and R audio information combined). The L − R audio channel amplitude modulates a 38-kHz subcarrier and produces the L − R stereo channel, which is a double-sideband suppressed-carrier signal that occupies the 23-kHz to 53-kHz passband, used only for FM stereo transmission. SCA transmissions occupy the 60-kHz to 74-kHz frequency spectrum. The information contained in the L + R and L − R stereo channels is identical except for their phase. With this scheme, mono receivers can demodulate the total baseband spectrum, but only the 50-kHz to 15-kHz L + R audio channel is amplified and fed to all its speakers. Therefore, each speaker reproduces the total original sound spectrum. Stereophonic receivers must provide additional demodulation of the 23-kHz to 53-kHz L − R stereo channel, separate the left and right audio channels, and then feed them to their respective speakers. Again, the SCA subcarrier is demodulated by all FM receivers, although only those with special SCA equipment further demodulate the subcarrier to audio frequencies.

With stereo transmission, the maximum frequency deviation is still 75 kHz; 7.5 kHz (10%) is reserved for SCA transmission and another 7.5 kHz (10%) is reserved for a 19-kHz stereo pilot. This leaves 60 kHz of frequency deviation for the actual stereophonic transmission of the L + R and L − R stereo channels. However, the L + R and L − R stereo channels are not necessarily limited to 30-kHz frequency deviation each. A rather simple but unique technique is used to interleave the two channels such that at times either the L + R or the L − R stereo channel may deviate the main carrier 60 kHz by themselves. However, the total deviation will never exceed 60 kHz. This interleaving technique is explained later in this section.

FM Stereo Transmission

Figure 7-22 shows a simplified block diagram for a stereo FM transmitter. The L and R audio channels are combined in a matrix network to produce the L + R and L − R audio channels. The L − R audio channel modulates a 38-kHz subcarrier and produces a 23-kHz to

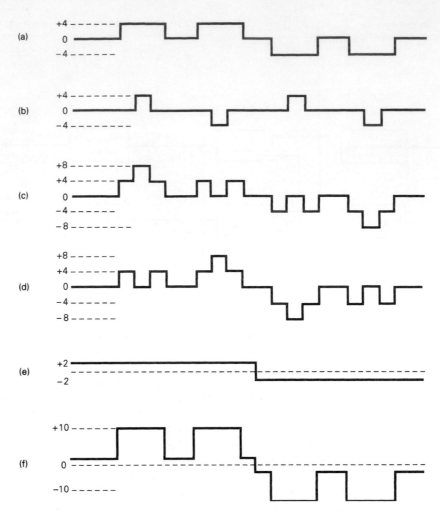

FIGURE 7-23 Development of the composite stereo signal for equal-amplitude L and R signals: (a) L audio signal; (b) R audio signal; (c) L + R stereo channel; (d) L − R stereo channel; (e) SCA + 19-kHz pilot; (f) composite baseband waveform

53-kHz L − R stereo channel. Because there is a time delay introduced in the L − R signal path as it propagates through the balanced modulator, the L + R stereo channel must be artificially delayed somewhat to maintain phase integrity with the L − R stereo channel for demodulation purposes. Also for demodulation purposes, a 19-kHz pilot is transmitted rather than the 38-kHz subcarrier because it is considerably more difficult to recover the 38-kHz subcarrier in the receiver. The composite baseband signal is fed to the FM transmitter, where it modulates the main carrier.

L + R and L − R channel interleaving. Figure 7-23 shows the development of the composite stereo signal for equal-amplitude L and R audio channel signals. For illustration purposes, rectangular waveforms are shown. Table 7-1 is a tabular summary of the individual and total signal voltages for Figure 7-23. Note that the L − R audio channel does not appear in the composite waveform. The L − R audio channel modulates the 38-kHz subcarrier to form the L − R stereo sidebands, which are part of the composite spectrum.

TABLE 7-1 Composite FM Voltages

L	R	L + R	L − R	SCA and Pilot	Total
0	0	0	0	2	2
4	0	4	4	2	10
0	4	4	−4	2	2
4	4	8	0	2	10
4	−4	0	8	2	10
−4	4	0	−8	−2	−10
−4	−4	−8	0	−2	−10

For the FM modulator in this example, it is assumed that 10 V of baseband signal will produce 75 kHz of frequency deviation of the main carrier, and the SCA and 19-kHz pilot polarities shown are for maximum frequency deviation. The L and R audio channels are each limited to a maximum value of 4 V; 1 V is for SCA, and 1 V is for the 19-kHz stereo pilot. Therefore, 8 V is left for the L + R and L − R stereo channels. Figure 7-23 shows the L, R, L + R, and L − R channels, the SCA and 19-kHz pilot, and the composite stereo waveform. It can be seen that the L + R and L − R stereo channels interleave and never produce more than 8 V of total amplitude and, therefore, never produce more than 60 kHz of frequency deviation. The total composite baseband never exceeds 10 V (75-kHz deviation).

Figure 7-24 shows the development of the composite stereo waveform for unequal values for the L and R signals. Again, it can be seen that the composite stereo waveform never exceeds 10 V or 75 kHz of frequency deviation. For the first set of waveforms, it appears that the sum of the L + R and L − R waveforms completely cancels. Actually, this is not true; it only appears that way because rectangular waveforms are used in this example.

FM Stereo Reception

FM stereo receivers are identical to standard FM receivers up to the output of the audio detector stage. The output of the discriminator is the total baseband spectrum that was shown in Figure 7-21c.

Figure 7-25 shows a simplified block diagram for an FM receiver that has both mono and stereo audio outputs. In the mono section of the signal processor, the L + R stereo channel, which contains all of the original information from both the L and R audio channels, is simply filtered, amplified, and then fed to both the L and R speakers. In the stereo section of the signal processor, the baseband signal is fed to a stereo demodulator where the L and R audio channels are separated and then fed to their respective speakers. The L + R and L − R stereo channels and the 19-kHz pilot are separated from the composite baseband signal with filters. The 19-kHz pilot is filtered with a high-Q bandpass filter, multiplied by 2, amplified, and then fed to the L − R demodulator. The L + R stereo channel is filtered off by a low-pass filter with an upper cutoff frequency of 15 kHz. The L − R double-sideband signal is separated with a broadly tuned bandpass filter and then mixed with the recovered 38-kHz carrier in a balanced modulator to produce the L − R audio information. The matrix network combines the L + R and L − R signals in such a way as to separate the L and R audio information signals, which are fed to their respective deemphasis networks and speakers.

Figure 7-26 shows the block diagram for a stereo matrix decoder. The L − R audio channel is added directly to the L + R audio channel. The output from the adder is

$$
\begin{array}{r}
L + R \\
+ (L - R) \\
\hline
2L
\end{array}
$$

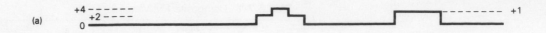

(a)

(b)

(c)

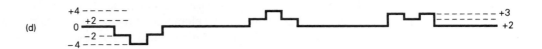

(d)

(e)

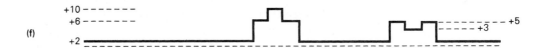

(f)

FIGURE 7-24 Development of the composite stereo signal for unequal amplitude L and R signals: (a) L audio signal; (b) R audio signal; (c) L + R stereo channel; (d) L − R stereo channel; (e) SCA + 19-kHz pilot; (f) composite baseband waveform

The L − R audio channel is inverted and then added to the L + R audio channel. The output from the adder is

$$
\begin{array}{r}
L + R \\
- (L - R) \\
\hline
2R
\end{array}
$$

stereo channel, which contains all the original information from both the L and R audio channels, is simply filtered, amplified, and then fed to both the L and R speakers. In the stereo section of the signal processor, the baseband signal is fed to a stereo demodulator where the L and R audio channels are separated and then fed to their respective speakers.

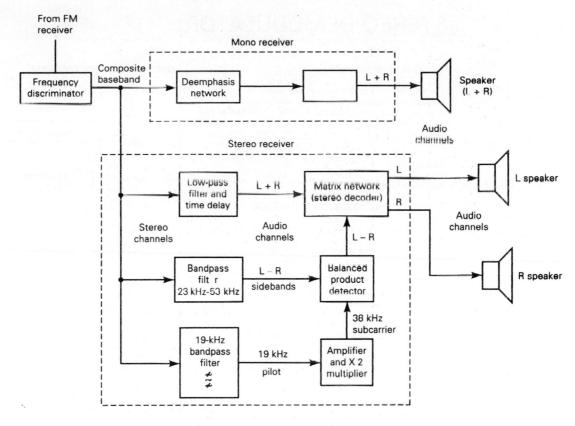

FIGURE 7-25 FM stereo and mono receiver

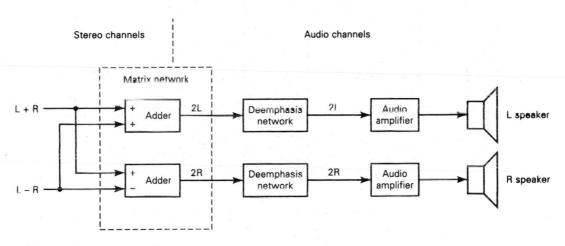

FIGURE 7-26 Stereo matrix network decoder

The L + R and L − R stereo channels and the 19-kHz pilot are separated from the composite baseband signal with filters. The 19-kHz pilot is filtered with a high Q bandpass filter, mulitiplied by 2, amplified, and then fed to the L − R demodulator. The L + R stereo channel is filtered off by a low-pass filter with an upper cutoff frequency of 15 kHz. The L − R double-sideband signal is separated with a broadly tuned bandpass filter and then

STEREO DEMODULATOR

FUNCTIONAL BLOCK DIAGRAM   March 1982

GENERAL DESCRIPTION

The XR-1310 is a unique FM stereo demodulator which uses phase-locked techniques to derive the right and left audio channels from the composite signal. Using a phase-locked loop to regenerate the 38 kHz subcarrier, it requires no external L-C tanks for tuning. Alignment is accomplished with a single potentiometer.

FEATURES

Requires No Inductors
Low External Part Count
Simple, Noncritical Tuning by Single Potentiometer Adjustment
Internal Stereo/Monaural Switch with 100 mA Lamp Driving Capability
Wide Dynamic Range: 600 mV (RMS) Maximum Composite Input Signal
Wide Supply Voltage Range: 8 to 14 Volts
Excellent Channel Separation
Low Distortion
Excellent SCA Rejection

ORDERING INFORMATION

Part Number	Package	Operating Temperature
XR-1310CP	Plastic	−40°C to +85°C

APPLICATIONS

FM Stereo Demodulation

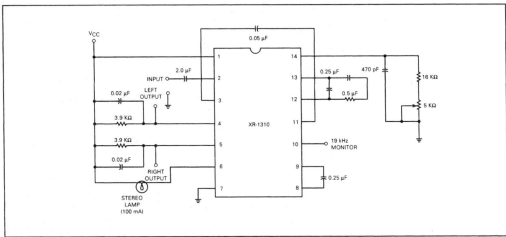

Figure 1. Typical Application

FIGURE 7-27   (*Continued*) XR-1310 stereo demodulator

mixed with the recovered 38-kHz carrier in a balanced modulator to produce the L – R audio information. The matrix network combines the L + R and L – R signals in such a way as to separate the L and R audio information signals, which are fed to their respective deemphasis networks and speakers.

    Large-scale integration stereo demodulator.   Figure 7-27 shows the specification sheet for the XR-1310 stereo demodulator/decoder. The XR-1310 is a monolithic FM stereo demodulator that uses phase-locked-loop techniques to derive the right and left audio channels from the composite stereo signal. The XR-1310 uses a phase-locked loop to lock onto the 19-kHz pilot and regenerate the 38-kHz subcarrier. The XR-1310 requires no external

ELECTRICAL CHARACTERISTICS

Test conditions: Unless otherwise noted; V_{CC}* = +12Vdc, T_A = +25°C, 560mV(RMS)(2.8Vp-p)standard multiplex composite signal with L or R channel only modulated at 1.0 kHz and with 100 mV (RMS) (10 % pilot level), using circuit of Figure 1.

PARAMETERS	MIN.	TYP.	MAX.	UNIT
Maximum Standard Composite Input Signal (0.5 % THD)	2.8			V (p-p)
Maximum Monural Input Signal (1.0 % THD)	2.8			V (p-p)
Input Impedance		50		kΩ
Stereo Channel Separation (50 Hz – 15 kHz)	30	40		dB
Audio Output Voltage (desired channel)		485		mV (rms)
Monaural Channel Balance (pilot tone "off")			1.5	dB
Total Harmonic Distortion		0.3		%
Ultrasonic Frequency Rejection 19 kHz	50	34.4		dB
38 kHz		45		
Inherent SCA Rejection (f = 67 kHz; 9.0 kHz beat note measured with 1.0 kHz modulation "off")		80		dB
Stereo Switch Level (19 kHz input for lamp "on")	13		20	mV (rms)
Hysteresis		6		dB
Capture Range (permissable tuning error of internal oscillator, reference circuit values of Figure 1)		±3.5		%
Operating Supply Voltage (loads reduced to 2.7 kΩ for 8.0-volt operation	8.0		14	V (dc)
Current Drain (lamp "off")		13		mA (dc)

*Symbols conform to JEDEC Engineering Bulletin No. 1 when applicable.

ABSOLUTE MAXIMUM RATINGS

(TA = +25°C unless otherwise noted)

Power Supply Voltage	14 V	Power Dissipation	625 mW
		(package limitation)	
		Derate above TA = +25°C	5.0 mW/°C
Lamp Current	75 mA	Operating Temperayure	–40 to +85°C
(nominal rating, 12 V lamp)		Range (Ambient)	
		Storage Temperature Range	–65 to +150°C

FIGURE 7-27 (Continued) XR-1310 stereo demodulator

LC tank circuits for tuning, and alignment is accomplished with a single potentiometer. The XR-1310 features simple noncritical tuning, excellent channel separation, low distortion, and a wide dynamic range.

TWO-WAY FM RADIO COMMUNICATIONS

Two-way FM radio communication is used extensively for *public safety* mobile communications, such as police and fire departments and emergency medical services. Three primary frequency bands are allocated by the FCC for two-way FM radio communications: 132 MHz to 174 MHz, 450 MHz to 470 MHz, and 806 MHz to 947 MHz. The maximum frequency deviation for two-way FM transmitters is typically 5 kHz, and the maximum modulating-signal frequency is 3 kHz. These values give a deviation ratio of 1.67 and a maximum Bessel bandwidth of approximately 24 kHz. However, the allocated FCC channel spacing is 30 kHz. Two-way FM radio is half-duplex, which supports two-way communications but not simultaneously; only one party can transmit at a time. Transmissions are initiated by closing a *push-to-talk* (PTT) switch, which turns on the transmitter and shuts off the receiver.

During idle conditions, the transmitter is shut off and the receiver is turned on to allow monitoring the radio channel for transmissions from other stations' transmitters.

Historical Perspective

Mobile radio was used as early as 1921 when the Detroit Police Department used a mobile radio system that operated at a frequency close to 2 MHz. In 1940, the FCC made available new frequencies for mobile radio in the 30-MHz to 40-MHz frequency band. However, not until researchers developed frequency modulation techniques to improve reception in the presence of electrical noise and signal fading did mobile radio become useful. The first commercial mobile telephone system in the United States was established in 1946 in St. Louis, Missouri, when the FCC allocated six 60-kHz mobile telephone channels in the 150-MHz frequency range. In 1947, a public mobile telephone system was established along the highway between New York City and Boston that operated in the 35-MHz to 40-MHz frequency range. In 1949, the FCC authorized 6 additional mobile channels to *radio common carriers,* which they defined as companies that do not provide public wireline telephone service but do interconnect to the public telephone network and provide equivalent *nonwireline* telephone service. The FCC later increased the number of channels from 6 to 11 by reducing the bandwidth to 30 kHz and spacing the new channels between the old ones. In 1950, the FCC added 12 new channels in the 450-MHz band.

Until 1964, mobile telephone systems operated only in the *manual mode;* a special mobile telephone operator handled every call to and from each *mobile unit.* In 1964, *automatic channel selection systems* were placed in service for mobile telephone systems. This eliminated the need for push-to-talk operation and allowed customers to *direct dial* their calls without the aid of an operator. *Automatic call completion* was extended to the 450-MHz band in 1969, and *improved mobile telephone systems* (IMTS) became the United States' standard mobile telephone service. Presently, there are more than 200,000 *mobile telephone service* (MTS) subscribers nationwide. MTS uses FM radio channels to establish communication links between mobile telephones and central *base station* transceivers, which are linked to the local telephone exchange via normal metallic telephone lines. Most MTS systems serve an area approximately 40 miles in diameter, and each channel operates similarly to a *party line.* Each channel may be assigned to several subscribers, but only one subscriber can use it at a time. If the preassigned channel is busy, the subscriber must wait until it is idle before either placing or receiving a call.

The growing demand for the overcrowded mobile telephone frequency spectrum prompted the FCC to issue Docket 18262, which inquired into a means for providing a higher frequency-spectrum efficiency. In 1971, AT&T submitted a proposal on the technical feasibility of providing efficient use of the mobile telephone frequency spectrum. AT&T's report, entitled *High Capacity Mobile Phone Service,* outlined the principles of cellular radio.

In April 1981, the FCC approved a licensing scheme for *cellular radio* markets. Each market services one *coverage area,* defined according to modified 1980 Census Bureau Standard Metropolitan Statistical Areas (SMSAs). In early 1982, the FCC approved a final plan for accepting cellular license applications beginning in June 1982 and a final round of applications by March 1983. The ensuing legal battles for cellular licenses between AT&T, MCI, GTE, and numerous other common carriers go well beyond the scope of this book.

Two-Way FM Radio Transmitter

The simplified block diagram for a *modular integrated-circuit* two-way indirect FM radio transmitter is shown in Figure 7-28. Indirect FM is generally used because direct FM transmitters do not have the frequency stability necessary to meet FCC standards without using AFC loops. The transmitter shown is a four-channel unit that operates in the 150-kHz to 174-MHz frequency band. The channel selector switch applies power to one of four crystal oscillator modules that operates at a frequency between 12.5 MHz and 14.5 MHz, de-

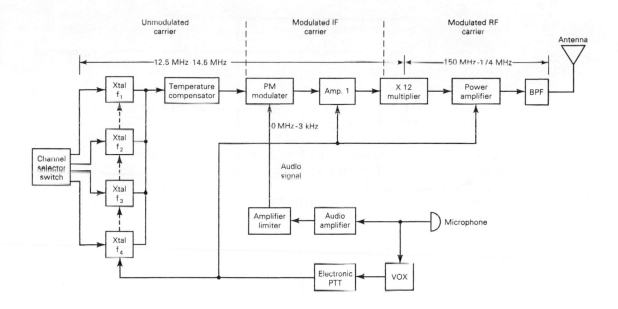

FIGURE 7-28   Two-way FM transmitter block diagram

pending on the final transmit carrier frequency. The oscillator frequency is temperature compensated by the compensation module to ensure a stability of ±0.0002%. The phase modulator uses a varactor diode that is modulated by the audio signal at the output of the audio limiter. The audio signal amplitude is limited to ensure that the transmitter is not overdeviated. The modulated IF carrier is amplified and then multiplied by 12 to produce the desired RF carrier frequency. The RF signal is further amplified and filtered prior to transmission. The *electronic push-to-talk* (PTT) is used rather than a simple mechanical switch to reduce the static noise associated with *contact bounce* in mechanical switches. Keying the PTT applies dc power to the selected transmit oscillator module and the RF power amplifiers.

Figure 7-29 shows the schematic diagram for a typical electronic PTT module. Keying the PTT switch grounds the base of Q_1, causing it to conduct and turn off Q_2. With Q_2 off, V_{CC} is applied to the transmitter and removed from the receiver. With the PTT switch released, Q_1 shuts off, removing V_{CC} from the transmitter, turning on Q_2, and applying V_{CC} to the receiver.

Transmitters equipped with VOX (*voice-operated transmitter*) are automatically keyed each time the operator speaks into the microphone, regardless of whether the PTT button is depressed. Transmitters equipped with VOX require an external microphone. The schematic diagram for a typical VOX module is shown in Figure 7-30. Audio signal power in the 400-Hz to 600-Hz passband is filtered and amplified by Q_1, Q_2, and Q_3. The output from Q_3 is rectified and used to turn on Q_4, which places a ground on the PTT circuit, enabling the transmitter and disabling the receiver. With no audio input signal, Q_4 is off and the PTT pin is open, disabling the transmitter and enabling the receiver.

Two-Way FM Radio Receiver

The block diagram for a typical two-way FM radio receiver is shown in Figure 7-31. The receiver shown is a four-channel integrated-circuit modular receiver with four separate crystal oscillator modules. Whenever the receiver is on, one of the four oscillator modules is activated, depending on the position of the channel selector switch. The oscillator frequency is temperature compensated and then multiplied by 9. The output from the

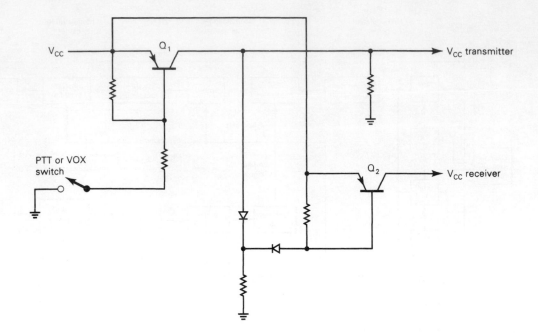

FIGURE 7-29 Electronic PTT schematic diagram

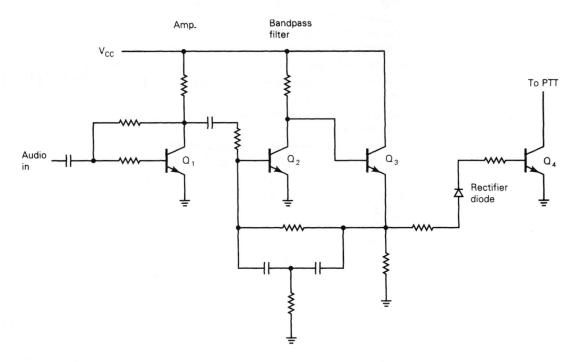

FIGURE 7-30 VOX schematic diagram

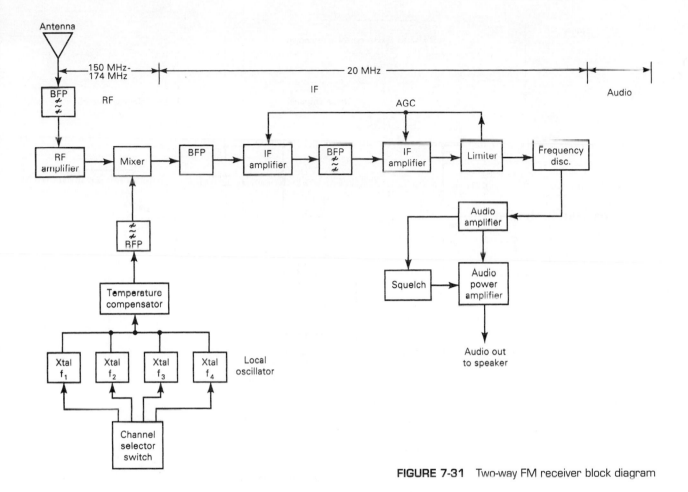

FIGURE 7-31 Two-way FM receiver block diagram

multiplier is applied to the mixer, where it heterodynes with the incoming RF signal to produce a 20-MHz intermediate frequency. This receiver uses low-side injection, and the crystal oscillator frequency is determined as follows:

$$\text{crystal frequency} = \frac{\text{RF frequency} - 20\ \text{MHz}}{9}$$

The IF signal is filtered, amplified, limited, and then applied to the frequency discriminator for demodulation. The discriminator output voltage is amplified and then applied to the speaker. A typical noise amplifier/squelch circuit is shown in Figure 7-32. The squelch circuit is keyed by out-of-band noise at the output of the audio amplifier. With no receive RF signal, AGC causes the gain of the IF amplifiers to increase to maximum, which increases the receiver noise in the 3-kHz to 5-kHz band. Whenever excessive noise is present, the audio amplifier is turned off and the receiver is quieted. The input bandpass filter passes the 3-kHz to 5-kHz noise signal, which is amplified and rectified. The rectified output voltage determines the off/on condition of squelch switch Q_3. When Q_3 is on, V_{CC} is applied to the audio amplifier. When Q_3 is off, V_{CC} is removed from the audio amplifier, quieting the receiver. R_x is a squelch sensitivity adjustment.

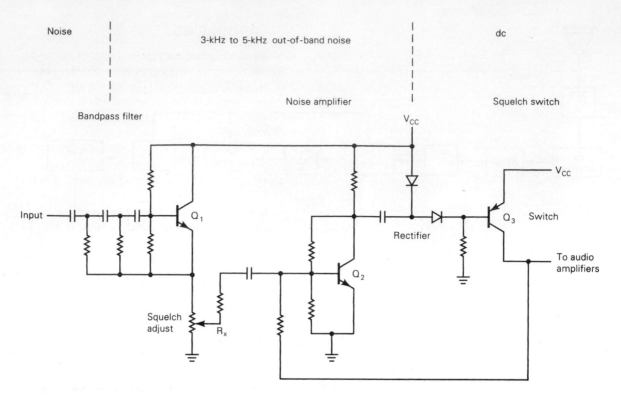

FIGURE 7-32 Squelch circuit

QUESTIONS

7-1. Describe the basic differences between AM and FM receivers.

7-2. Draw the schematic diagram for a *single-ended slope detector* and describe its operation.

7-3. Draw the schematic diagram for a *double-ended slope detector* and describe its operation.

7-4. Draw the schematic diagram for a *Foster-Seeley discriminator* and describe its operation.

7-5. Draw the schematic diagram for a *ratio detector* and describe its operation.

7-6. Describe the operation of a PLL FM demodulator.

7-7. Draw the schematic diagram for a *quadrature FM demodulator* and describe its operation.

7-8. Compare the advantages and disadvantages of the FM demodulator circuits discussed in Questions 7-1 through 7-7.

7-9. What is the purpose of a *limiter* in an FM receiver?

7-10. Describe *FM thresholding*.

7-11. Describe the operation of an FM *stereo transmitter;* an FM *stereo receiver.*

7-12. Draw the block diagram for a two-way FM radio transmitter and explain its operation.

7-13. Draw the block diagram for a two-way FM radio receiver and explain its operation.

7-14. Describe the operation of an electronic *push-to-talk circuit.*

7-15. Describe the operation of a *VOX circuit.*

7-16. Briefly explain how a composite *FM stereo* signal is produced.

7-17. What is meant by the term *interleaving* of L and R signals in stereo transmission?

7-18. What is the purpose of the 19-kHz *pilot* in FM stereo broadcasting?

7-19. What is the difference between *mobile radio* and *mobile telephone?*

PROBLEMS

7-1. Determine the minimum input S/N ratio required for a receiver with 15 dB of FM improvement, a noise figure NF = 4 dB, and a desired postdetection S/N = 33 dB.

7-2. For an FM receiver with a 100-kHz bandwidth, a noise figure NF = 6 dB, and an input noise temperature T = 200° C, determine the minimum receive carrier power to achieve a postdetection S/N = 40 dB. Use the receiver block diagram shown in Figure 7-1 as the receiver model and the FM thresholding curve shown in Figure 7-11.

7-3. For an FM receiver tuned to 92.75 MHz using high-side injection and a first IF of 10.7 MHz, determine the image frequency and the local oscillator frequency.

7-4. For an FM receiver with an input frequency deviation Δf = 40 kHz and a transfer ratio K = 0.01 V/kHz, determine V_{out}.

7-5. For the balanced slope detector shown in Figure 7-3a, a center frequency f_c = 20.4 MHz, and a maximum input frequency deviation Δf = 50 kHz, determine the upper and lower cutoff frequencies for the tuned circuit.

7-6. For the Foster-Seeley discriminator shown in Figure 7-4, V_{C1} = 1.2 V and V_{C2} = 0.8 V, determine V_{out}.

7-7. For the ratio detector shown in Figure 7-6, V_{C1} = 1.2 V and V_{C2} = 0.8 V, determine V_{out}.

7-8. For an FM demodulator with an FM improvement factor of 23 dB and an input S/N = 26 dB, determine the postdetection S/N.

7-9. From Figure 7-11, determine the approximate FM improvement factor for an input S/N = 10.5 dB and m = 1.

7-10. Determine the minimum input S/N ratio required for a receiver with 15 dB of FM improvement, a noise figure NF = 6 dB, and a desired postdetection signal-to-noise ratio = 38 dB.

7-11. For an FM receiver with 200-kHz bandwidth, a noise figure NF = 8 dB, and an input noise temperature T − 100° C, determine the minimum receive carrier power to achieve a postdetection S/N − 40 dB. Use the receiver block diagram shown in Figure 7-1 as the receiver model and the FM thresholding curve shown in Figure 7-11.

7-12. For an FM receiver tuned to 94.5 MHz using high-side injection and a first IF of 10.7 MHz, determine the image frequency and the local oscillator frequency.

7-13. For an FM receiver with an input frequency deviation Δf = 50 kHz and a transfer ratio K = 0.02 V/kHz, determine V_{out}.

7-14. For the balanced slope detector shown in Figure 7-3a, a center frequency f_c = 10.7 MHz and a maximum input frequency deviation Δf = 40 kHz, determine the upper and lower cutoff frequencies for the circuit.

7-15. For the Foster-Seeley discriminator shown in Figure 7-4, V_{C1} = 1.6 V and V_{C2} = 0.4 V, determine V_{out}.

7-16. For the ratio detector shown in Figure 7-6, V_{C1} = 1.6 V and determine V_{out}.

7-17. For an FM demodulator with an FM improvement factor equal to 18 dB and an input (predetection) signal-to-noise S_i/N_i = 32 dB, determine the postdetection S/N.

7-18. From Figure 7-11, determine the approximate FM improvement factor for an input S/N = 11 dB and m = 1.

C H A P T E R   8

Transmission Lines

INTRODUCTION

A *transmission line* is a *metallic conductor system* that is used to transfer electrical energy from one point to another. More specifically, a transmission line is two or more conductors separated by an insulator, such as a pair of wires or a system of wire pairs. A transmission line can be as short as a few inches or it can span several thousand miles. Transmission lines can be used to propagate dc or low-frequency ac (such as 60-cycle electrical power and audio signals); they can also be used to propagate very high frequencies (such as intermediate and radio-frequency signals). When propagating low-frequency signals, transmission-line behavior is rather simple and quite predictable; however, when propagating high-frequency signals, the characteristics of transmission lines become more involved and their behavior is somewhat peculiar to a student of lumped constant circuits and systems.

TRANSVERSE ELECTROMAGNETIC WAVES

Propagation of electrical power along a transmission line occurs in the form of *transverse electromagnetic* (TEM) *waves*. A wave is an *oscillatory motion*. The vibration of a particle excites similar vibrations in nearby particles. A TEM wave propagates primarily in the nonconductor (dielectric) that separates the two conductors of a transmission line. Therefore, a wave travels or propagates itself through a medium. For a transverse wave, the direction of displacement is perpendicular to the direction of propagation. A surface wave of water is a longitudinal wave. A wave in which the displacement is in the direction of propagation is called a *longitudinal wave*. Sound waves are longitudinal. An electromagnetic (EM) wave is produced by the acceleration of an electric charge. In a conductor, current and voltage are always accompanied by an electric (E) and a magnetic (H) field in the adjoining region of space. Figure 8-1a shows the spatial relationships between the E and H fields of an electromagnetic wave. Figure 8-1b shows the cross-sectional views of the E and H fields that surround a parallel two-wire and a coaxial line. It can be seen that the E and H fields are

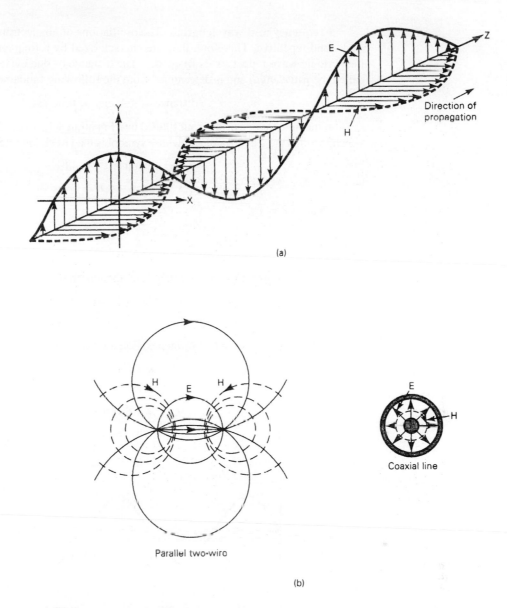

(a)

Parallel two-wire

Coaxial line

(b)

FIGURE 8-1 (a) Spatial and (b) cross-sectional views showing the relative displacement of the E and H fields on a transmission line

perpendicular to each other (at 90° angles) at all points. This is referred to as *space quadrature*. Electromagnetic waves that travel along a transmission line from the source toward the load are called *incident waves,* and those that travel from the load back toward the source are called *reflected waves.*

Characteristics of Electromagnetic Waves

Wave velocity. Waves travel at various speeds, depending on the type of wave and the characteristics of the propagation medium. Sound waves travel at approximately 1100 ft/s in the normal atmosphere. Electromagnetic waves travel much faster. In free space (a vacuum), TEM waves travel at the speed of light, c = 186,283 statute mi/s or 299,793,000 m/s, rounded off to 186,000 mi/s and 3×10^8 m/s. However, in air (such as Earth's atmosphere), TEM waves travel slightly more slowly, and along a transmission line, electromagnetic waves travel considerably more slowly.

Frequency and wavelength. The oscillations of an electromagnetic wave are periodic and repetitive. Therefore, they are characterized by a frequency. The rate at which the periodic wave repeats is its frequency. The distance of one cycle occurring in space is called the *wavelength* and is determined from the following fundamental equation:

$$\text{distance} = \text{velocity} \times \text{time} \qquad (8\text{-}1)$$

If the time for one cycle is substituted into Equation 8-1, we get the length of one cycle, which is called the wavelength and whose symbol is the Greek lowercase letter lambda (λ)

$$\lambda = \text{velocity} \times \text{period}$$
$$= v \times T$$

And, because $T = 1/f$,

$$\lambda = \frac{v}{f} \qquad (8\text{-}2)$$

For free-space propagation, $v = c$; therefore, the length of one cycle is

$$\lambda = \frac{c}{f} = \frac{3 \times 10^8 \, \text{m/s}}{f \, \text{cycles/s}} = \frac{\text{meters}}{\text{cycle}} \qquad (8\text{-}3\text{a})$$

To solve for wavelength in feet or inches, Equation 8-3a can be rewritten as

$$\lambda = \frac{11.8 \times 10^9 \, \text{in/s}}{f \, \text{cycles/s}} \quad \text{(inches)} \qquad (8\text{-}3\text{b})$$

$$\lambda = \frac{9.83 \times 10^8 \, \text{ft/s}}{f \, \text{cycles/s}} \quad \text{(feet)} \qquad (8\text{-}3\text{c})$$

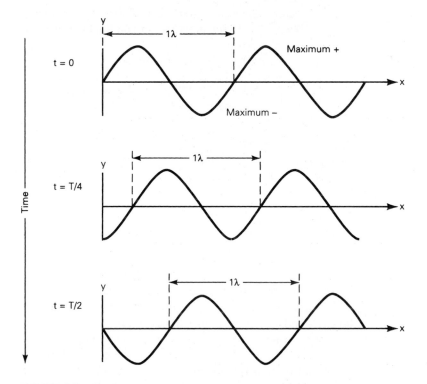

FIGURE 8-2 Displacement and velocity of a transverse wave as it propagates down a transmission line

Figure 8-2 shows a graph of the displacement and velocity of a transverse wave as it propagates along a transmission line from a source to a load. The horizontal (X) axis is distance and the vertical (Y) axis is displacement. One wavelength is the distance covered by one cycle of the wave. It can be seen that the wave moves to the right or propagates down the line with time. If a voltmeter is placed at any stationary point on the line, the voltage measured will fluctuate from zero to maximum positive, back to zero, to maximum negative, back to zero again, and then the cycle repeats.

TYPES OF TRANSMISSION LINES

Transmission lines can be generally classified as *balanced* or *unbalanced*. With two-wire balanced lines, both conductors carry current; one conductor carries the signal and the other is the return. This type of transmission is called *differential,* or *balanced,* signal transmission. The signal propagating down the wire is measured as the potential difference between the two wires. Figure 8-3 shows a balanced transmission system. Both conductors in a balanced line carry signal current, and the currents are equal in magnitude with respect to electrical ground but travel in opposite directions. Currents that flow in opposite directions in a balanced wire pair are called *metallic circuit currents.* Currents that flow in the same directions are called *longitudinal currents.* A balanced wire pair has the advantage that most noise interference (sometimes called *common-mode voltage*) is induced equally in both wires, producing longitudinal currents that cancel in the load. The cancelation of common-mode signals is called common-mode rejection (CMR). Common-mode rejection ratios (CMRR) of 40 dB to 70 dB are common.

Any pair of wires can operate in the balanced mode provided neither wire is at ground potential. This includes coaxial cable that has two center conductors and a shield. The shield is generally connected to ground to prevent static interference from penetrating the center conductors.

Figure 8-4 shows the result of metallic and longitudinal currents on a balanced transmission line. It can be seen that the longitudinal currents (often produced by static interference) cancel in the load.

With an unbalanced transmission line, one wire is at ground potential, whereas the other wire is at signal potential. This type of transmission is called *single-ended,* or *unbalanced,* signal transmission. With unbalanced signal transmission, the ground wire may also be the reference for other signal-carrying wires. If this is the case, the ground wire must go wherever any of the signal wires go. Sometimes this creates a problem because a length of wire has resistance, inductance, and capacitance and, therefore, a small potential difference may exist between any two points on the ground wire. Consequently, the ground wire is not a perfect reference point and is capable of having noise induced

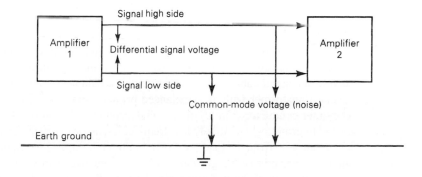

FIGURE 8-3 Differential, or balanced, transmission system

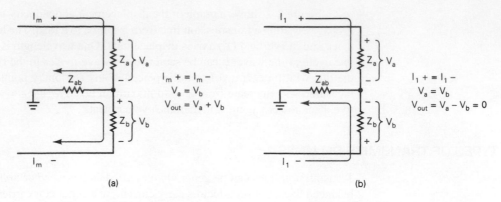

$$I_m += I_m -$$
$$V_a = V_b$$
$$V_{out} = V_a + V_b$$

$$I_1 += I_1 -$$
$$V_a = V_b$$
$$V_{out} = V_a - V_b = 0$$

(a)   (b)

FIGURE 8-4 Results of metallic and longitudinal currents on a balanced transmission line: (a) metallic currents due to signal voltages; (b) longitudinal currents due to noise voltages

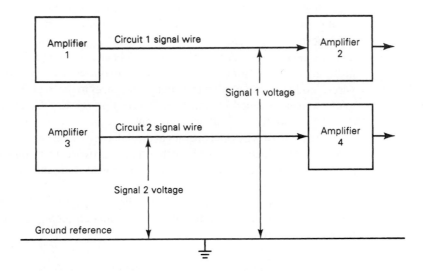

FIGURE 8-5 Single-ended, or unbalanced, transmission system

into it. A standard two-conductor coaxial cable is an unbalanced line. The second wire is the shield, which is generally connected to ground.

Figure 8-5 shows two unbalanced transmission systems. The potential difference on each signal wire is measured from that wire to ground. Balanced transmission lines can be connected to unbalanced lines, and vice versa, with special transformers called *baluns.*

Baluns

A circuit device used to connect a balanced transmission line to an unbalanced load is called a *balun* (balanced to unbalanced). Or more commonly, an unbalanced transmission line, such as a coaxial cable, can be connected to a balanced load, such as an antenna, using a special transformer with an unbalanced primary and a center-tapped secondary winding. The outer conductor (*shield*) of an unbalanced coaxial transmission line is generally connected to ground. At relatively low frequencies, an ordinary transformer can be used to isolate the ground from the load, as shown in Figure 8-6a. The balun must have an electrostatic shield connected to earth ground to minimize the effects of stray capacitances.

For relatively high frequencies, several different kinds of transmission-line baluns exist. The most common type is a *narrowband* balun, sometimes called a *choke, sleeve,* or

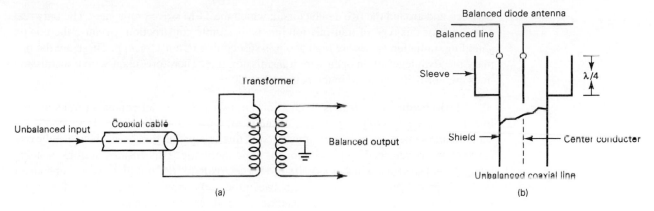

FIGURE 8-6   Baluns: (a) transformer balun; (b) bazooka balun

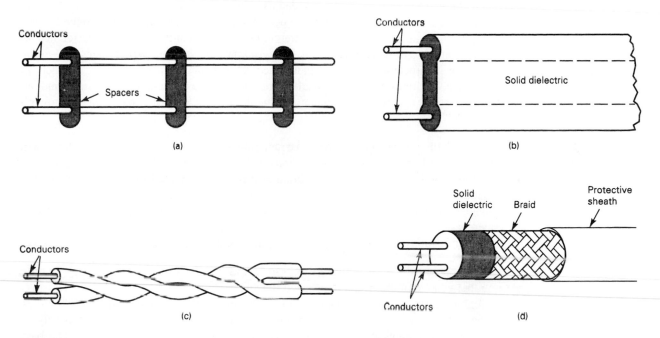

FIGURE 8-7   Transmission lines: (a) open wire; (b) twin lead; (c) twisted pair; (d) shielded pair

bazooka balun, which is shown in Figure 8-6b. A quarter-wavelength sleeve is placed around and connected to the outer conductor of a coaxial cable. Consequently, the impedance seen looking back into the transmission line is formed by the sleeve and the outer conductor and is equal to infinity (i.e., the outer conductor no longer has a zero impedance to ground). Thus, one wire of the balanced pair can be connected to the sleeve without short-circuiting the signal. The second conductor is connected to the inner conductor of the coaxial cable.

Parallel-Conductor Transmission Lines

Open-wire transmission line.   An *open-wire transmission line* is a *two wire parallel conductor;* it is shown in Figure 8-7a. It consists simply of two parallel wires, closely spaced and separated by air. Nonconductive spacers are placed at periodic intervals for support and to keep the distance between the conductors constant. The distance between the two conductors is generally between 2 inches and 6 inches. The dielectric is simply the air between and around the two conductors in which the TEM wave propagates. The only real advantage of this type of transmission line is its simple construction. Because there is no shielding, radiation losses are high and it is susceptible to noise pickup. These are the primary disadvantages of an open-wire transmission line. Therefore, open-wire transmission lines are normally operated in the balanced mode.

Twin lead. *Twin lead* is another form of two-wire parallel-conductor transmission line and is shown in Figure 8-7b. Twin lead is often called *ribbon cable*. Twin lead is essentially the same as an open-wire transmission line except that the spacers between the two conductors are replaced with a continuous solid dielectric. This ensures uniform spacing along the entire cable, which is a desirable characteristic for reasons that are explained later in the chapter. Typically, the distance between the two conductors is 5/16 inch for television transmission cable. Common dielectric materials are Teflon and polyethylene.

Twisted-pair cable. A *twisted-pair cable* is formed by twisting together two insulated conductors. Pairs are often stranded in *units,* and the units are then cabled into *cores.* The cores are covered with various types of *sheaths,* depending on their intended use. Neighboring pairs are twisted with different *pitch* (twist length) to reduce interference between pairs due to mutual induction. The *primary constants* of twisted-pair cable are its electrical parameters (resistance, inductance, capacitance, and conductance), which are subject to variations with the physical environment such as temperature, moisture, and mechanical stress and depend on manufacturing deviations. A twisted-pair cable is shown in Figure 8-7c.

Shielded-cable pair. To reduce radiation losses and interference, parallel two-wire transmission lines are often enclosed in a conductive metal *braid.* The braid is connected to ground and acts as a shield. The braid also prevents signals from radiating beyond its boundaries and keeps electromagnetic interference from reaching the signal conductors. A shielded-parallel wire pair is shown in Figure 8-7d. It consists of two parallel wire conductors separated by a solid dielectric material. The entire structure is enclosed in a braided conductive tube and then covered with a protective plastic coating.

Concentric or Coaxial Transmission Lines

Parallel-conductor transmission lines are suitable for low-frequency applications. However, at high frequencies, their radiation and dielectric losses, as well as their susceptibility to external interference, are excessive. Therefore, *coaxial conductors* are used extensively for high-frequency applications to reduce losses and to isolate transmission paths. The basic coaxial cable consists of a center conductor surrounded by a *concentric* (uniform distance from the center) *outer conductor.* At relatively high operating frequencies, the coaxial outer conductor provides excellent shielding against external interference. However, at lower operating frequencies, the use of shielding is usually not cost effective. Also, a coaxial cable's outer conductor is generally grounded, which limits its use to unbalanced applications.

Essentially, there are two types of coaxial cables: *rigid air-filled* or *solid flexible* lines. Figure 8-8a shows a rigid air coaxial line. It can be seen that the center conductor is surrounded coaxially by a tubular outer conductor and the insulating material is air. The outer conductor is physically isolated and separated from the center conductor by a spacer, which is generally made of Pyrex, polystyrene, or some other nonconductive material. Figure 8-8b shows a solid flexible coaxial cable. The outer conductor is braided, flexible, and coaxial to the center conductor. The insulating material is a solid nonconductive polyethylene material that provides both support and electrical isolation between the inner and outer conductors. The inner conductor is a flexible copper wire that can be either solid or hollow.

Rigid air-filled coaxial cables are relatively expensive to manufacture, and to minimize losses, the air insulator must be relatively free of moisture. Solid coaxial cables have

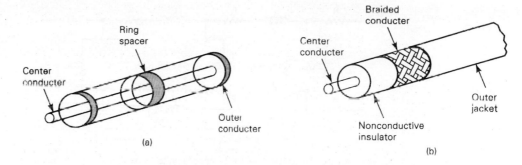

FIGURE 8-8 Concentric or coaxial transmission lines: (a) rigid air filled; (b) solid flexible line

lower losses and are easier to construct and to install and maintain. Both types of coaxial cables are relatively immune to external radiation, radiate little themselves, and can operate at higher frequencies than can their parallel-wire counterparts. The basic disadvantages of coaxial transmission lines is that they are expensive and must be used in the unbalanced mode.

TRANSMISSION-LINE EQUIVALENT CIRCUIT

Uniformly Distributed Lines

The characteristics of a transmission line are determined by its electrical properties, such as wire conductivity and insulator dielectric constant, and its physical properties, such as wire diameter and conductor spacing. These properties, in turn, determine the primary electrical constants: series dc resistance (R), series inductance (L), shunt capacitance (C), and shunt conductance (G). Resistance and inductance occur along the line, whereas capacitance and conductance occur between the two conductors. The primary constants are uniformly distributed throughout the length of the line and, therefore, are commonly called *distributed parameters*. To simplify analysis, distributed parameters are commonly *lumped together* per a given unit length to form an artificial electrical model of the line. For example, series resistance is generally given in ohms per unit length (i.e., ohms/meter).

Figure 8-9 shows the electrical equivalent circuit for a metallic two-wire transmission line showing the relative placement of the various lumped parameters. The conductance between the two wires is shown in reciprocal form and given as a shunt leakage resistance (R_s).

Transmission Characteristics

The transmission characteristics of a transmission line are called *secondary constants* and are determined from the four primary constants. The secondary constants are characteristic impedance and propagation constant.

    Characteristic impedance. For maximum power transfer from the source to the load (i.e., no reflected energy), a transmission line must be terminated in a purely resistive load equal to the *characteristic impedance* of the line. The characteristic impedance (Z_o) of a transmission line is a complex quantity that is expressed in ohms, is ideally independent of line length, and cannot be measured. Characteristic impedance (which is sometimes called *surge impedance*) is defined as the impedance seen looking into an infinitely long line or the impedance seen looking into a finite length of line that is terminated in a purely resistive load equal to the characteristic impedance of the line. A transmission line stores energy in its distributed inductance and capacitance. If the line is infinitely long, it can store energy indefinitely; energy from the source is entering the line and none is returned. Therefore, the line

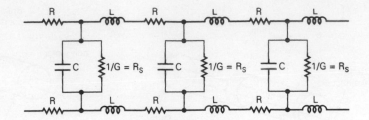

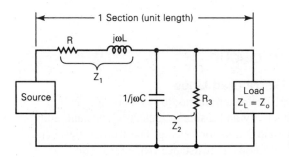

C = capacitance – two conductors separated
　　　by an insulator
R = resistance – opposition to current flow
L = self inductance
1/G = leakage resistance of dielectric
R_s = shunt leakage resistance

FIGURE 8-9 Two-wire parallel transmission line, electrical equivalent circuit

FIGURE 8-10 Equivalent circuit for a single section of transmission line terminated in a load equal to Z_o

acts as a resistor that dissipates all the energy. An infinite line can be simulated if a finite line is terminated in a purely resistive load equal to Z_o; all the energy that enters the line from the source is dissipated in the load (this assumes a totally lossless line).

Figure 8-10 shows a single section of a transmission line terminated in a load Z_L that is equal to Z_o. The impedance seen looking into a line of n such sections is determined from the following expression:

$$Z_o^2 = Z_1 Z_2 + \frac{Z_L^2}{n} \tag{8-4}$$

where n is the number of sections. For an infinite number of sections Z_L^2/n approaches 0 if

$$\lim \frac{Z_L^2}{n}\Big|_{n \to \infty} = 0$$

Then,
$$Z_o = \sqrt{Z_1 Z_2}$$

where
$$Z_1 = R + j\omega L$$

$$Y_2 = \frac{1}{Z_2} = \frac{1}{R_s} + \frac{1}{1/j\omega C}$$
$$= G + j\omega C$$

$$Z_2 = \frac{1}{G + j\omega C}$$

Therefore,
$$Z_o = \sqrt{(R + j\omega L)\frac{1}{G + j\omega C}}$$

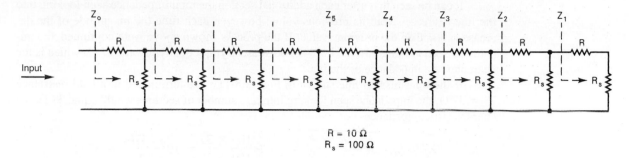

$R = 10\ \Omega$
$R_s = 100\ \Omega$

FIGURE 8-11 Characteristic impedance of a transmission line of infinite sections or terminated in load equal to Z_o

or

$$Z_o = \sqrt{\frac{R + j\omega L}{G + j\omega C}}$$

(8-5)

For extremely low frequencies, the resistances dominate and Equation 8-5 simplifies to

$$Z_o = \sqrt{\frac{R}{G}}$$

(8-6)

For extremely high frequencies, the inductance and capacitance dominate and Equation 8-5 simplifies to

$$Z_o = \sqrt{\frac{j\omega L}{j\omega C}} = \sqrt{\frac{L}{C}}$$

(8-7)

From Equation 8-7 it can be seen that for high frequencies the characteristic impedance of a transmission line approaches a constant, is independent of both frequency and length, and is determined solely by the distributed inductance and capacitance. It can also be seen that the phase angle is 0°. Therefore, Z_o looks purely resistive and all of the incident energy is absorbed by the line.

From a purely resistive approach, it can easily be seen that the impedance seen looking into a transmission line made up of an infinite number of sections approaches the characteristic impedance. This is shown in Figure 8-11. Again, for simplicity, only the series resistance R and the shunt resistance R_s are considered. The impedance seen looking into the last section of the line is simply the sum of R and R_s. Mathematically, Z_1 is

$$Z_1 = R + R_s = 10 + 100 = 110$$

Adding a second section, Z_2, gives

$$Z_2 = R + \frac{R_s Z_1}{R_s + Z_1} = 10 + \frac{100 \times 110}{100 + 110} = 10 + 52.38 = 62.38$$

and a third section, Z_3, is

$$Z_3 = R + \frac{R_s Z_2}{R_s + Z_2}$$

$$= 10 + \frac{100 \times 62.38}{100 + 62.38} = 10 + 38.42 = 48.32$$

A fourth section, Z_4, is

$$Z_4 = 10 + \frac{100 \times 48.32}{100 + 48.32} = 10 + 32.62 = 42.62$$

It can be seen that after each additional section the total impedance seen looking into the line decreases from its previous value; however, each time the magnitude of the decrease is less than the previous value. If the process shown above were continued, the impedance seen looking into the line will decrease asymptotically toward 37 Ω, which is the characteristic impedance of the line.

If the transmission line shown in Figure 8-11 were terminated in a load resistance $Z_L = 37\ \Omega$, the impedance seen looking into any number of sections would equal 37 Ω, the characteristic impedance. For a single section of line, Z_o is

$$Z_o = Z_1 = R + \frac{R_s \times Z_L}{R_s + Z_L} = 10 + \frac{100 \times 37}{100 + 37} = 10 + \frac{3700}{137} = 37\ \Omega$$

Adding a second section, Z_2, is

$$Z_o = Z_2 = R + \frac{R_s \times Z_1}{R_s + Z_1} = 10 + \frac{100 \times 37}{100 + 37} = 10 + \frac{3700}{137} = 37\ \Omega$$

Therefore, if this line were terminated into a load resistance $Z_L = 37\ \Omega$, $Z_o = 37\ \Omega$ no matter how many sections are included.

The characteristic impedance of a transmission line can also be determined using Ohm's law. When a source is connected to an infinitely long line and a voltage is applied, a current flows. Even though the load is open, the circuit is complete through the distributed constants of the line. The characteristic impedance is simply the ratio of source voltage (E_o) to line current (I_o). Mathematically, Z_o is

$$Z_o = \frac{E_o}{I_o} \tag{8-8}$$

The characteristic impedance of a two-wire parallel transmission line with an air dielectric can be determined from its physical dimensions (see Figure 8-12a) and the formula

$$Z_o = 276 \log \frac{D}{r} \tag{8-9}$$

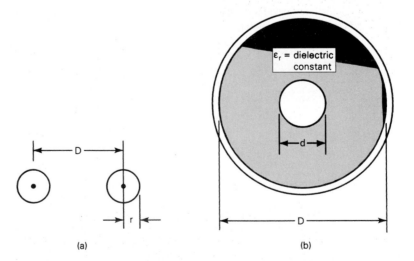

(a)   (b)

FIGURE 8-12 Physical dimensions of transmission lines: (a) two-wire parallel transmission line; (b) coaxial-cable transmission line

where D = distance between the centers of the two conductors (in)
       r = radius of the conductor (in)

and $D >> r$.

Example 8-1

Determine the characteristic impedance for an air dielectric two-wire parallel transmission line with a D/r ratio $= 12.22$.

Solution Substituting into Equation 8-9, we obtain

$$Z_o = 276 \log 12.22 = 300 \ \Omega$$

The characteristic impedance of a concentric coaxial cable can also be determined from its physical dimensions (see Figure 8-12b) and the formula

$$Z_o = \frac{138}{\sqrt{\epsilon_r}} \log \frac{D}{d} \tag{8-10}$$

where D = inside diameter of the outer conductor (in)
       d = outside diameter of the inner conductor (in)
       ϵ_r = dielectric constant (relative permativity) of the insulating material (unitless)

Example 8-2

Determine the characteristic impedance for an RG-59A coaxial cable with the following specifications: $L = 0.118 \ \mu H/ft$, $C = 21 \ pF/ft$, $d = 0.025$ in., $D = 0.15$ in., and $\epsilon = 2.23$.

Solution Substituting into Equation 8-8 yields

$$Z_o = \sqrt{\frac{L}{C}} = \sqrt{\frac{0.118 \times 10^{-6} H/ft}{21 \times 10^{-12} pF/ft}} = 75 \ \Omega$$

Substituting into Equation 8-10 gives us

$$Z_o = \frac{138}{\sqrt{2.23}} \log \frac{0.15 \ in.}{0.25 \ in.} = 71.9 \ \Omega$$

Transmission lines can be summarized thus far as follows:

1. The input impedance of an infinitely long line at radio frequencies is resistive and equal to Z_o.
2. Electromagnetic waves travel down the line without reflections; such a line is called *nonresonant*.
3. The ratio of voltage to current at any point along the line is equal to Z_o.
4. The incident voltage and current at any point along the line are in phase.
5. Line losses on a nonresonant line are minimum per unit length.
6. Any transmission line that is terminated in a purely resistive load equal to Z_o acts as if it were an infinite line.
   (a) $Z_i = Z_o$.
   (b) There are no reflected waves.
   (c) V and I are in phase.
   (d) There is maximum transfer of power from source to load.

Propagation constant. *Propagation constant* (sometimes called *propagation coefficient*) is used to express the attenuation (signal loss) and the phase shift per unit length of a transmission line. As a wave propagates down a transmission line, its amplitude decreases with distance traveled. The propagation constant is used to determine the reduction in voltage or current with distance as a TEM wave propagates down a transmission line. For an infinitely long line, all the incident power is dissipated in the resistance of the wire as the wave propagates down the line. Therefore, with an infinitely long line or a line that looks infinitely long, such as a finite line terminated in a matched load ($Z_o = Z_L$), no energy is returned or reflected back toward the source. Mathematically, the propagation constant is

$$\gamma = \alpha + j\beta \qquad (8\text{-}11a)$$

where $\quad$ γ = propagation constant
$\qquad$ α = attenuation coefficient (nepers per unit length)
$\qquad$ β = phase shift coefficient (radians per unit length)

The propagation constant is a complex quantity defined by

$$\gamma = \sqrt{(R + j\omega L)(G + j\omega C)} \qquad (8\text{-}11b)$$

Because a phase shift of 2π rad occurs over a distance of one wavelength,

$$\beta = \frac{2\pi}{\lambda} \qquad (8\text{-}12)$$

At intermediate and radio frequencies, $\omega L > R$ and $\omega C > G$; thus,

$$\alpha = \frac{R}{2Z_o} + \frac{GZ_o}{2} \qquad (8\text{-}13)$$

and $$\beta = \omega\sqrt{LC} \qquad (8\text{-}14)$$

The current and voltage distribution along a transmission line that is terminated in a load equal to its characteristic impedance (a matched line) are determined from the formulas

$$I = I_s e^{-l\gamma} \qquad (8\text{-}15)$$

$$V = V_s e^{-l\gamma} \qquad (8\text{-}16)$$

where $\quad$ I_s = current at the source end of the line (amps)
$\qquad$ V_s = voltage at the source end of the line (volts)
$\qquad$ γ = propagation constant
$\qquad$ l = distance from the source at which the current or voltage is determined

For a matched load $Z_L = Z_o$, and for a given length of cable l, the loss in signal voltage or current is the real part of γl, and the phase shift is the imaginary part.

TRANSMISSION-LINE WAVE PROPAGATION

Electromagnetic waves travel at the speed of light when propagating through a vacuum and nearly at the speed of light when propagating through air. However, in metallic transmission lines where the conductor is generally copper and the dielectric materials vary considerably with cable type, an electromagnetic wave travels much more slowly.

Velocity Factor

Velocity factor (sometimes called *velocity constant*) is defined simply as the ratio of the actual velocity of propagation through a given medium to the velocity of propagation through free space. Mathematically, the velocity factor is

$$V_f = \frac{V_p}{c} \qquad (8\text{-}17)$$

where $\quad$ V_f = velocity factor (unitless)
$\qquad$ V_p = actual velocity of propagation (meters per second)
$\qquad$ c = velocity of propagation through free space ($c = 3 \times 10^8$ m/s)

TABLE 8-1 Velocity Factors

Material	Velocity Factor
Air	0.95–0.975
Rubber	0.56–0.65
Polyethylene	0.66
Teflon	0.70
Teflon foam	0.82
Teflon pins	0.81
Teflon spiral	0.81

TABLE 8-2 Dielectric Constants

Material	Relative Dielectric Constant (ϵ_r)
Vacuum	1.0
Air	1.0006
Teflon	2.1
Polyethylene (PE)	2.27
Polystyrene	2.5
Paper, paraffined	2.5
Rubber	3.0
Polyvinyl chloride (PVC)	3.3
Mica	5.0
Glass	7.5

and
$$V_f \times c = V_p$$

The velocity at which an electromagnetic wave travels through a transmission line depends on the dielectric constant of the insulating material separating the two conductors. The velocity factor is closely approximated with the formula

$$V_f = \frac{1}{\sqrt{\epsilon_r}} \qquad (8\text{-}18)$$

where ϵ_r is the dielectric constant of a given material (the permittivity of the material relative to the permittivity of a vacuum—the ratio ϵ/ϵ_o).

Dielectric constant is simply the *relative permittivity* of a material. The relative dielectric constant of air is 1.0006. However, the dielectric constant of materials commonly used in transmission lines ranges from 1.2 to 2.8, giving velocity factors from 0.6 to 0.9. The velocity factors for several common transmission-line configurations are given in Table 8-1, and the dielectric constants for several insulating materials are listed in Table 8-2.

Dielectric constant depends on the type of material used. Inductors store magnetic energy and capacitors store electric energy. It takes a finite amount of time for an inductor or a capacitor to take on or give up energy. Therefore, the velocity at which an electromagnetic wave propagates along a transmission line varies with the inductance and capacitance of the cable. It can be shown that time $T = \sqrt{LC}$. Therefore, inductance, capacitance, and velocity of propagation are mathematically related by the formula

$$\text{velocity} \times \text{time} = \text{distance}$$

Therefore,
$$V_p = \frac{\text{distance}}{\text{time}} = \frac{D}{T} \qquad (8\text{-}19)$$

Substituting for time yields

$$V_p = \frac{D}{\sqrt{LC}}$$ (8-20)

If distance is normalized to 1 m, the velocity of propagation for a lossless line is

$$V_p = \frac{1 \text{ m}}{\sqrt{LC}} = \frac{1}{\sqrt{LC}} \text{ m/s}$$ (8-21)

where V_p = velocity of propagation (meters per second)

$\sqrt{LC}$ = seconds

Example 8-3

For a given length of RG8A/U coaxial cable with a distributed capacitance $C = 96.6$ pF/m, a distributed inductance $L = 241.56$ nH/m, and a relative dielectric constant $\epsilon_r = 2.3$, determine the velocity of propagation and the velocity factor.

Solution From Equation 8-21,

$$V_p = \frac{1}{\sqrt{96.6 \times 10^{-12} \times 241.56 \times 10^{-9}}} = 2.07 \times 10^8 \text{ m/s}$$

From Equation 8-17,

$$V_f = \frac{2.07 \times 10^8 \text{ m/s}}{3 \times 10^8 \text{ m/s}} = 0.69$$

From Equation 8-18,

$$V_f = \frac{1}{\sqrt{2.3}} = 0.66$$

Because wavelength is directly proportional to velocity and the velocity of propagation of a TEM wave varies with dielectric constant, the wavelength of a TEM wave also varies with dielectric constant. Therefore, for transmission media other than free space, Equation 8-3a can be rewritten as

$$\lambda = \frac{V_p}{f} = \frac{cV_f}{f} = \frac{c}{f\sqrt{\epsilon_r}}$$ (8-22)

Electrical Length of a Transmission Line

The length of a transmission line relative to the length of the wave propagating down it is an important consideration when analyzing transmission-line behavior. At low frequencies (long wavelengths), the voltage along the line remains relatively constant. However, for high frequencies, several wavelengths of the signal may be present on the line at the same time. Therefore, the voltage along the line may vary appreciably. Consequently, the length of a transmission line is often given in wavelengths rather than in linear dimensions. Transmission-line phenomena apply to long lines. Generally, a transmission line is defined as long if its length exceeds one-sixteenth of a wavelength; otherwise, it is considered short. A given length of transmission line may appear short at one frequency and long at another frequency. For example, a 10-m length of transmission line at 1000 Hz is short ($\lambda = 300,000$ m; 10 m is only a small fraction of a wavelength). However, the same line at 6 GHz is long ($\lambda = 5$ cm; the line is 200 wavelengths long). It will be apparent later in this chapter, in Chapter 9, and in Appendix A that electrical length is used extensively for transmission-line calculations and antenna design.

Delay Lines

In the previous section it was shown that the velocity of propagation of an electromagnetic wave depends on the media in which it is traveling. The velocity of an electromagnetic wave in free space (i.e., a vacuum) is the speed of light (3×10^8 m/s) and the velocity is slightly slower through the Earth's atmosphere (i.e., air). The velocity of propagation through a metallic transmission line is effected by the cable's electrical constants, inductance and capacitance. The velocity of propagation of a metallic transmission line is somewhat less than the velocity of propagation through either free space or the Earth's atmosphere.

Delay lines are transmission lines designed to intentionally introduce a time delay in the path of an electromagnetic wave. The amount of time delay is a function of the transmission line's inductance and capacitance. The inductance provides an opposition to changes in current as does the charge and discharge times of the capacitance. Delay time is calculated as follows:

$$t_d = LC \text{ (seconds)} \tag{8-23a}$$

where t_d = time delay (seconds)
L = inductance (henrys)
C = capacitance (farads)

If inductance and capacitance are given per unit length of transmission line (such as per foot or per meter), the time delay will also be per unit length (i.e., 1.5 ns/meter).

The time delay introduced by a length of coaxial cable is calculated with the following formula:

$$t_d = 1.016 \, \epsilon \tag{8-23b}$$

where ϵ is the dielectric constant of cable.

TRANSMISSION-LINE LOSSES

For analysis purposes, transmission lines are often considered totally lossless. In reality, however, there are several ways in which power is lost in a transmission line. They are conductor loss, radiation loss, dielectric heating loss, coupling loss, and corona.

Conductor Loss

Because current flows through a transmission line and the transmission line has a finite resistance, there is an inherent and unavoidable power loss. This is sometimes called *conductor* or *conductor heating loss* and is simply an I^2R loss. Because resistance is distributed throughout a transmission line, conductor loss is directly proportional to the square of the line length. Also, because power dissipation is directly proportional to the square of the current, conductor loss is inversely proportional to characteristic impedance. To reduce conductor loss, simply shorten the transmission line or use a larger-diameter wire (keep in mind that changing the wire diameter also changes the characteristic impedance and, consequently, the current).

Conductor loss depends somewhat on frequency because of an action called the *skin effect*. When current flows through an isolated round wire, the magnetic flux associated with it is in the form of concentric circles. This is shown in Figure 8-13. It can be seen that the flux density near the center of the conductor is greater than it is near the surface. Consequently, the lines of flux near the center of the conductor encircle the current and reduce the mobility of the encircled electrons. This is a form of self-inductance and causes the inductance near the center of the conductor to be greater than at the surface. Therefore, at radio frequencies, most of the current flows along the surface (outer skin) rather than near the center of the conductor. This is equivalent to reducing the cross-sectional area of the conductor and increasing the opposition to current flow (i.e., resistance). The additional opposition has a 0° phase angle and is, therefore, a resistance and not a reactance. Therefore, the ac resistance of the conductor is proportional to the square root of the frequency. The ratio of the ac resistance to the dc resistance of a conductor is called the *resistance ratio*. Above approximately 100 MHz, the center of a conductor can be completely removed and have absolutely no effect on the total conductor loss or EM wave propagation.

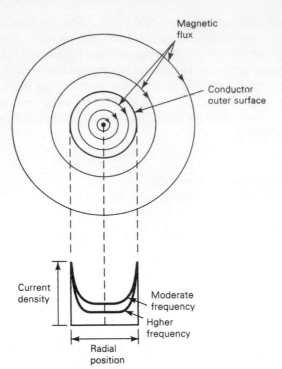

FIGURE 8-13 Isolated round conductor showing magnetic lines of flux, current distributions, and the skin effect

Conductor loss in transmission lines varies from as low as a fraction of a decibel per 100 m for rigid air dielectric coaxial cable to as high as 200 dB per 100 m for a solid dielectric flexible line.

Because both I^2R losses and dielectric losses are proportional to length, they are often lumped together and expressed in decibels of loss per unit length (i.e., dB/m).

Dielectric Heating Loss

A difference of potential between the two conductors of a transmission line causes *dielectric heating*. Heat is a form of energy and must be taken from the energy propagating down the line. For air dielectric lines, the heating loss is negligible. However, for solid lines, dielectric heating loss increases with frequency.

Radiation Loss

If the separation between conductors in a transmission line is an appreciable fraction of a wavelength, the electrostatic and electromagnetic fields that surround the conductor cause the line to act as if it were an antenna and transfer energy to any nearby conductive material. The amount of energy radiated depends on the dielectric material, the conductor spacing, and the length of the line. *Radiation losses* are reduced by properly shielding the cable. Therefore, coaxial cables have less radiation loss than do two-wire parallel lines. Radiation loss is also directly proportional to frequency.

Coupling Loss

Coupling loss occurs whenever a connection is made to or from a transmission line or when two separate pieces of transmission line are connected together. Mechanical connections are discontinuities (places where dissimilar materials meet). Discontinuities tend to heat up, radiate energy, and dissipate power.

Corona

Corona is a luminous discharge that occurs between the two conductors of a transmission line when the difference of potential between them exceeds the *breakdown* voltage of the dielectric insulator. Generally, once corona has occurred, the transmission line may be destroyed.

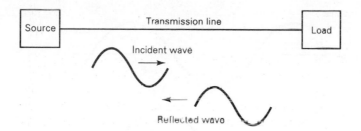

FIGURE 8-14 Source, load, transmission line, and their corresponding incident and reflected waves

INCIDENT AND REFLECTED WAVES

An ordinary transmission line is bidirectional; power can propagate equally well in both directions. Voltage that propagates from the source toward the load is called *incident voltage,* and voltage that propagates from the load toward the source is called *reflected voltage.* Similarly, there are incident and reflected currents. Consequently, incident power propagates toward the load, and reflected power propagates toward the source. Incident voltage and current are always in phase for a resistive characteristic impedance. For an infinitely long line, all the incident power is stored by the line and there is no reflected power. Also, if the line is terminated in a purely resistive load equal to the characteristic impedance of the line, the load absorbs all the incident power (this assumes a lossless line). For a more practical definition, reflected power is the portion of the incident power that was not absorbed by the load. Therefore, the reflected power can never exceed the incident power.

Resonant and Nonresonant Transmission Lines

A transmission line with no reflected power is called a *flat* or *nonresonant* line. A transmission line is nonresonant if it is of infinite length or if it is terminated with a resistive load equal in ohmic value to the characteristic impedance of the transmission line. On a flat line, the voltage and current are constant throughout its length, assuming no losses. When the load is not equal to the characteristic impedance of the line, some of the incident power is reflected back toward the source. If the load is either a short or an open circuit, all the incident power is reflected back toward the source. If the source were replaced with an open or a short and the line were lossless, energy present on the line would reflect back and forth (oscillate) between the source and load ends similar to the way energy is transferred back and forth between the capacitor and inductor in an *LC* tank circuit. This is called a *resonant* transmission line. In a resonant line, energy is alternately transferred between the magnetic and electric fields of the distributed inductance and capacitance of the line. Figure 8-14 shows a source, transmission line, and load with their corresponding incident and reflected waves.

Reflection Coefficient

The reflection coefficient (sometimes called the *coefficient of reflection*) is a vector quantity that represents the ratio of reflected voltage to incident voltage or reflected current to incident current. Mathematically, the reflection coefficient is gamma, Γ, defined by

$$\Gamma = \frac{E_r}{E_i} \text{ or } \frac{I_r}{I_i} \tag{8-24}$$

where Γ = reflection coefficient (unitless)
        E_i = incident voltage (volts)
        E_r = reflected voltage (volts)
        I_i = incident current (amps)
        I_r = reflected current (amps)

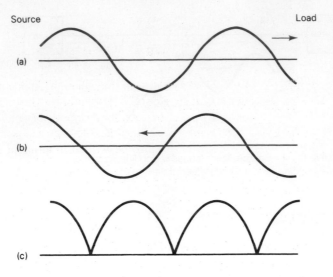

Source   Load

(a)

(b)

(c)

FIGURE 8-15 Developing a standing wave on a transmission line: (a) incident wave; (b) reflected wave; (c) standing wave

From Equation 8-24 it can be seen that the maximum and worst-case value for Γ is 1 ($E_r = E_i$), and the minimum value and ideal condition occur when $\Gamma = 0$ ($E_r = 0$).

STANDING WAVES

When $Z_o = Z_L$, all the incident power is absorbed by the load. This is called a *matched line*. When $Z_o \neq Z_L$, some of the incident power is absorbed by the load and some is returned (reflected) to the source. This is called an *unmatched* or *mismatched line*. With a mismatched line, there are two electromagnetic waves, traveling in opposite directions, present on the line at the same time (these waves are in fact called *traveling waves*). The two traveling waves set up an interference pattern known as a *standing wave*. This is shown in Figure 8-15. As the incident and reflected waves pass each other, stationary patterns of voltage and current are produced on the line. These stationary waves are called standing waves because they appear to remain in a fixed position on the line, varying only in amplitude. The standing wave has minima (nodes) separated by a half wavelength of the traveling waves and maxima (antinodes) also separated by a half wavelength.

Standing-Wave Ratio

The *standing-wave ratio* (SWR) is defined as the ratio of the maximum voltage to the minimum voltage or the maximum current to the minimum current of a standing wave on a transmission line. SWR is often called the *voltage standing-wave ratio* (VSWR). Essentially, SWR is a measure of the mismatch between the load impedance and the characteristic impedance of the transmission line. Mathematically, SWR is

$$\text{SWR} = \frac{V_{\max}}{V_{\min}} \text{ (unitless)} \qquad (8\text{-}25)$$

The voltage maxima ($V_{\max}$) occur when the incident and reflected waves are in phase (i.e., their maximum peaks pass the same point on the line with the same polarity), and the voltage minima ($V_{\min}$) occur when the incident and reflected waves are 180° out of phase. Mathematically, $V_{\max}$ and $V_{\min}$ are

$$V_{\max} = E_i + E_r \qquad (8\text{-}26a)$$

$$V_{\min} = E_i - E_r \qquad (8\text{-}26b)$$

Therefore, Equation 8-25 can be rewritten as

$$SWR = \frac{V_{max}}{V_{min}} = \frac{E_i + E_r}{E_i - E_r} \qquad (8\text{-}27)$$

From Equation 8-27, it can be seen that when the incident and reflected waves are equal in amplitude (a total mismatch) SWR = infinity. This is the worst-case condition. Also, from Equation 8-27, it can be seen that when there is no reflected wave ($E_r = 0$) SWR = E_i/E_i or 1. This condition occurs when $Z_o = Z_L$ and is the ideal situation.

The standing-wave ratio can also be written in terms of Γ. Rearranging Equation 8-25 yields

$$\Gamma E_i = E_r$$

Substituting into Equation 8-27 gives us

$$SWR = \frac{E_i + E_i\Gamma}{E_i - E_i\Gamma}$$

Factoring out E_i yields

$$SWR = \frac{E_i(1 + \Gamma)}{E_i(1 - \Gamma)} = \frac{1 + \Gamma}{1 - \Gamma} \qquad (8\text{-}28)$$

Cross multiplying gives

$$SWR(1 - \Gamma) = 1 + \Gamma$$
$$SWR - SWR\Gamma = 1 + \Gamma$$
$$SWR = 1 + \Gamma + (SWR)\Gamma$$
$$SWR - 1 = \Gamma(1 + SWR) \qquad (8\text{-}29)$$
$$\Gamma = \frac{SWR - 1}{SWR + 1} \qquad (8\text{-}30)$$

Example 8-4

For a transmission line with incident voltage $E_i = 5$ V and reflected voltage $E_r = 3$ V, determine
(a) Reflection coefficient.
(b) SWR.

Solution (a) Substituting into Equation 8-24 yields

$$\Gamma = \frac{E_r}{E_i} = \frac{3}{5} = 0.6$$

(b) Substituting into Equation 8-27 gives us

$$SWR = \frac{E_i + E_r}{E_i - E_r} = \frac{5 + 3}{5 - 3} = \frac{8}{2} = 4$$

Substituting into Equation 8-30, we obtain

$$\Gamma = \frac{4 - 1}{4 + 1} = \frac{3}{5} = 0.6$$

When the load is purely resistive, SWR can also be expressed as a ratio of the characteristic impedance to the load impedance, or vice versa. Mathematically, SWR is

$$SWR = \frac{Z_o}{Z_L} \text{ or } \frac{Z_L}{Z_o} \quad \text{(whichever gives an SWR greater than 1)} \qquad (8\text{-}31)$$

The numerator and denominator for Equation 8-31 are chosen such that the SWR is always a number greater than 1, to avoid confusion and comply with the convention established in Equation 8-27. From Equation 8-31 it can be seen that a load resistance $Z_L = 2Z_o$ gives the same SWR as a load resistance $Z_L = Z_o/2$; the degree of mismatch is the same.

The disadvantages of not having a matched (flat) transmission line can be summarized as follows:

1. One hundred percent of the source incident power does not reach the load.
2. The dielectric separating the two conductors can break down and cause corona as a result of the high-voltage standing-wave ratio.
3. Reflections and rereflections cause more power loss.
4. Reflections cause ghost images.
5. Mismatches cause noise interference.

Although it is highly unlikely that a transmission line will be terminated in a load that is either an open or a short circuit, these conditions are examined because they illustrate the worst-possible conditions that could occur and produce standing waves that are representative of less severe conditions.

Standing Waves on an Open Line

When incident waves of voltage and current reach an open termination, none of the power is absorbed; it is all reflected back toward the source. The incident voltage wave is reflected in exactly the same manner as if it were to continue down an infinitely long line. However, the incident current is reflected 180° reversed from how it would have continued if the line were not open. As the incident and reflected waves pass, standing waves are produced on the line. Figure 8-16 shows the voltage and current standing waves on a transmission line that is terminated in an open circuit. It can be seen that the voltage standing wave has a maximum value at the open end and a minimum value one-quarter wavelength from the open. The current standing wave has a minimum value at the open end and a maximum value one-quarter wavelength from the open. It stands to reason that maximum voltage occurs across an open and there is minimum current.

The characteristics of a transmission line terminated in an open can be summarized as follows:

1. The voltage incident wave is reflected back just as if it were to continue (i.e., no phase reversal).
2. The current incident wave is reflected back 180° from how it would have continued.
3. The sum of the incident and reflected current waveforms is minimum at the open.
4. The sum of the incident and reflected voltage waveforms is maximum at the open.

From Figure 8-16 it can also be seen that the voltage and current standing waves repeat every one-half wavelength. The impedance at the open end $Z = V_{max}/I_{min}$ and is maximum. The impedance one-quarter wavelength from the open $Z = V_{min}/I_{max}$ and is minimum. Therefore, one-quarter wavelength from the open an impedance inversion occurs and additional impedance inversions occur each one-quarter wavelength.

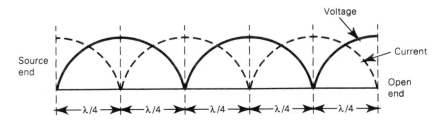

FIGURE 8-16 Voltage and current standing waves on a transmission line that is terminated in an open circuit

Figure 8-16 shows the development of a voltage standing wave on a transmission line that is terminated in an open circuit. Figure 8-17 shows an incident wave propagating down a transmission line toward the load. The wave is traveling at approximately the speed of light; however, for illustration purposes, the wave has been frozen at eighth-wavelength intervals. In Figure 8-17a it can be seen that the incident wave has not reached the open. Figure 8-17b shows the wave one time unit later (for this example, the wave travels one-eighth wavelength per time unit). As you can see, the wave has moved one-quarter wavelength

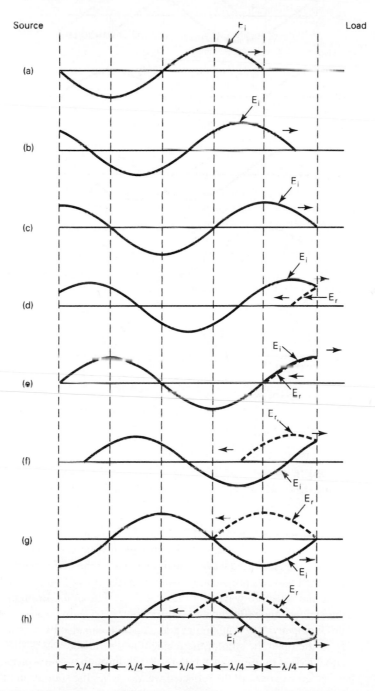

FIGURE 8-17 Incident and reflected waves on a transmission line terminated in an open circuit (*Continued*)

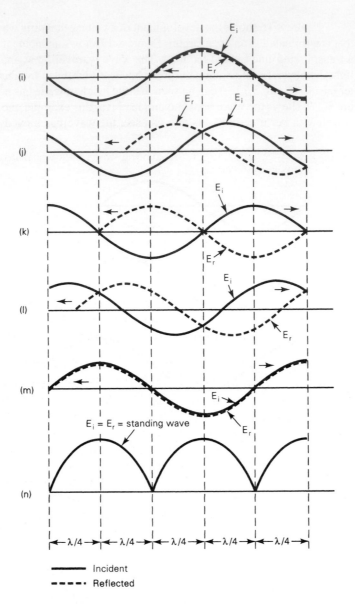

FIGURE 8-17 (Continued) Incident and reflected waves on a transmission line terminated in an open circuit

closer to the open. Figure 8-17c shows the wave just as it arrives at the open. Thus far, there has been no reflected wave and, consequently, no standing wave. Figure 8-17d shows the incident and reflected waves one time unit after the incident wave has reached the open; the reflected wave is propagating away from the open. Figures 8-17e, f, and g show the incident and reflected waves for the next three time units. In Figure 8-17e it can be seen that the incident and reflected waves are at their maximum positive values at the same time, thus producing a voltage maximum at the open. It can also be seen that one-quarter wavelength from the open the sum of the incident and reflected waves (the standing wave) is always equal to 0 V (a minimum). Figures 8-17h through m show propagation of the incident and reflected waves until the reflected wave reaches the source, and Figure 8-17n shows the resulting standing wave. It can be seen that the standing wave remains stationary (the voltage nodes and antinodes remain at the same points); however, the amplitude of the antinodes

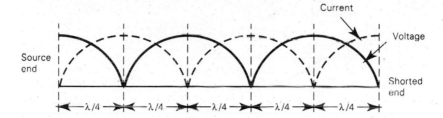

FIGURE 8-18 Voltage and current standing waves on a transmission line that is terminated in a short circuit

varies from maximum positive to zero to maximum negative and then repeats. For an open load, all the incident voltage is reflected ($E_r = E_i$); therefore, $V_{max} = E_i + E_r$ or $2E_i$. A similar illustration can be shown for a current standing wave (however, remember that the current reflects back with a 180° phase inversion).

Standing Waves on a Shorted Line

As with an open line, none of the incident power is absorbed by the load when a transmission line is terminated in a short circuit. However, with a shorted line, the incident voltage and current waves are reflected back in the opposite manner. The voltage wave is reflected 180° reversed from how it would have continued down an infinitely long line, and the current wave is reflected in exactly the same manner as if there were no short.

Figure 8-18 shows the voltage and current standing waves on a transmission line that is terminated in a short circuit. It can be seen that the voltage standing wave has a minimum value at the shorted end and a maximum value one-quarter wavelength from the short. The current standing wave has a maximum value at the short and a minimum value one-quarter wavelength back. The voltage and current standing waves repeat every one-quarter wavelength. Therefore, there is an impedance inversion every quarter-wavelength interval. The impedance at the short $Z = V_{min}/I_{max}$ = minimum, and one-quarter wavelength back $Z = V_{max}/I_{min}$ = maximum. Again, it stands to reason that a voltage minimum will occur across a short and there is maximum current.

The characteristics of a transmission line terminated in a short can be summarized as follows:

1. The voltage standing wave is reflected back 180° reversed from how it would have continued.
2. The current standing wave is reflected back the same as if it had continued.
3. The sum of the incident and reflected current waveforms is maximum at the short.
4. The sum of the incident and reflected voltage waveforms is zero at the short.

For a transmission line terminated in either a short or an open circuit, the reflection coefficient is 1 (the worst case) and the SWR is infinity (also the worst-case condition).

TRANSMISSION-LINE INPUT IMPEDANCE

In the preceding section it was shown that, when a transmission line is terminated in either a short or an open circuit, there is an *impedance inversion* every quarter-wavelength. For a lossless line, the impedance varies from infinity to zero. However, in a more practical situation where power losses occur, the amplitude of the reflected wave is always less than that of the incident wave except at the termination. Therefore, the impedance varies from some maximum to some minimum value, or vice versa, depending on whether the line is terminated in a short or an open. The input impedance for a lossless line seen looking into a transmission

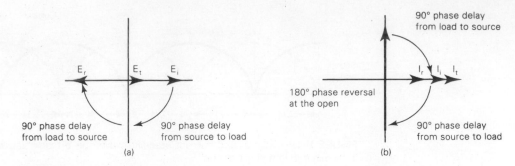

FIGURE 8-19 Voltage and current phase relationships for a quarter-wave line terminated in an open circuit: (a) voltage phase relationships; (b) current phase relationships

line that is terminated in a short or an open can be resistive, inductive, or capacitive, depending on the distance from the termination.

Phasor Analysis of Input Impedance: Open Line

Phasor diagrams are generally used to analyze the input impedance of a transmission line because they are relatively simple and give a pictorial representation of the voltage and current phase relationships. Voltage and current phase relations refer to variations in time. Figures 8-16, 8-17, and 8-18 show standing waves of voltage and current plotted versus distance and, therefore, are not indicative of true phase relationships. The succeeding sections use phasor diagrams to analyze the input impedance of several transmission-line configurations.

Quarter-wavelength transmission line. Figure 8-19a shows the phasor diagram for the voltage and Figure 8-19b shows the phasor diagram for the current at the input to a quarter-wave section of a transmission line terminated in an open circuit. I_i and V_i are the in-phase incident current and voltage waveforms, respectively, at the input (source) end of the line at a given instant in time. Any reflected voltage (E_r) present at the input of the line has traveled one-half wavelength (from the source to the open and back) and is, consequently, 180° behind the incident voltage. Therefore, the total voltage (E_t) at the input end is the sum of E_i and E_r. $E_t = E_i + E_r \underline{/-180°}$, and, assuming a small line loss, $E_t = E_i - E_r$. The reflected current is delayed 90° propagating from the source to the load and another 90° from the load back to the source. Also, the reflected current undergoes a 180° phase reversal at the open. The reflected current has effectively been delayed 360°. Therefore, when the reflected current reaches the source end, it is in phase with the incident current and the total current $I_t = I_i + I_r$. By examining Figure 8-19, it can be seen that E_t and I_t are in phase. Therefore, the input impedance seen looking into a transmission line one-quarter wavelength long that is terminated in an open circuit $Z_{in} = E_t \underline{/0°} / I_t \underline{/0°} = Z_{in} \underline{/0°}$. Z_{in} has a 0° phase angle, is resistive, and is minimum. Therefore, a quarter-wavelength transmission line terminated in an open circuit is equivalent to a series resonant LC circuit.

Figure 8-20 shows several voltage phasors for the incident and reflected waves on a transmission line that is terminated in an open circuit and how they produce a voltage standing wave.

Transmission line less than one-quarter wavelength long. Figure 8-21a shows the voltage phasor diagram and Figure 8-21b shows the current phasor diagram for a transmission line that is less than one-quarter wavelength long ($\lambda/4$) and terminated in an open circuit. Again, the incident current (I_i) and voltage (E_i) are in phase. The reflected voltage wave is delayed 45° traveling from the source to the load (a distance of one-eighth wavelength) and another 45° traveling from the load back to the source (an additional one-eighth wavelength). Therefore, when the reflected wave reaches the source end, it lags the incident wave by 90°. The total voltage at the source end is the vector sum of the incident and

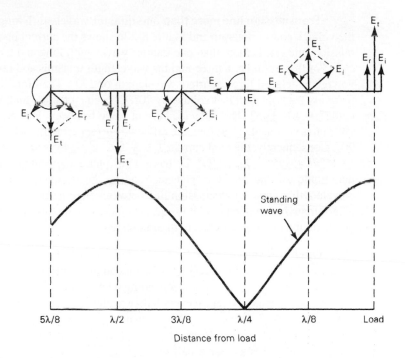

FIGURE 8-20 Vector addition of incident and reflected waves producing a standing wave

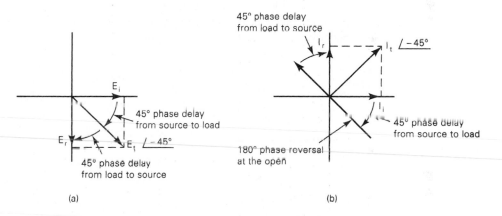

FIGURE 8-21 Voltage and current phase relationships for a transmission line less than one-quarter wavelength terminated in an open circuit: (a) voltage phase relationships; (b) current phase relationships

reflected waves. Thus, $E_t = \sqrt{E_i^2 + E_r^2} = E_t \angle{-45°}$. The reflected current wave is delayed 45° traveling from the source to the load and another 45° from the load back to the source (a total distance of one-quarter wavelength). In addition, the reflected current wave has undergone a 180° phase reversal at the open prior to being reflected. The reflected current wave has been delayed a total of 270°. Therefore, the reflected wave effectively leads the incident wave by 90°. The total current at the source end is the vector sum of the present and reflected waves. Thus, $I_t = \sqrt{I_i^2 + I_r^2} = I_t \angle{+45°}$. By examining Figure 8-21, it can be seen that E_t lags I_t by 90°. Therefore, $Z_{in} = E_t \angle{-45°} /I_t \angle{+45°} = Z_{in} \angle{-90°}$. Z_{in} has a $-90°$ phase angle and, therefore, is capacitive. Any transmission line that is less than one-quarter wavelength and terminated in an open circuit is equivalent to a capacitor. The amount of capacitance depends on the exact electrical length of the line.

Transmission line more than one-quarter wavelength long. Figure 8-22a shows the voltage phasor diagram and Figure 8-22b shows the current phasor diagram for a transmission line that is more than one-quarter wavelength long and terminated in an open circuit. For this example, a three-eighths wavelength transmission line is used. The reflected voltage is delayed three-quarters wavelength or 270°. Therefore, the reflected voltage effectively leads the incident voltage by 90°. Consequently, the total voltage $E_t 5 \text{ } \propto \overline{E_i^2 1 \text{ } E_r^2}$ $/+45° = E_t /+45°$. The reflected current wave has been delayed 270° and undergone an 180° phase reversal. Therefore, the reflected current effectively lags the incident current by 90°. Consequently, the total current $I_t 5 \text{ } \propto \overline{I_i^2 1 \text{ } I_r^2} /-45° = I_t /-45°$. Therefore, $Z_{in} 5 \text{ } E_t$ $/+45° /I_t /-45° = Z_{in} /+90°$. Z_{in} has a +90° phase angle and is, therefore, inductive. The magnitude of the input impedance equals the characteristic impedance at eighth-wavelength points. A transmission line between one-quarter and one-half wavelength that is terminated in an open circuit is equivalent to an inductor. The amount of inductance depends on the exact electrical length of the line.

Open transmission line as a circuit element. From the preceding discussion and Figures 8-19 through 8-22, it is obvious that an open transmission line can behave as a resistor, an inductor, or a capacitor, depending on its electrical length. Because standing-wave patterns on an open line repeat every half-wavelength interval, the input impedance also repeats. Figure 8-23 shows the variations in input impedance for an open transmission line of various electrical lengths. It can be seen that an open line is resistive and maximum at the open and at each successive half-wavelength interval, and resistive and minimum one-quarter wavelength from the open and at each successive half-wavelength interval. For electrical lengths less than one-quarter wavelength, the input impedance is capacitive and decreases with length. For electrical lengths between one-quarter and one-half wavelength, the input impedance is inductive and increases with length. The capacitance and inductance patterns also repeat every half-wavelength.

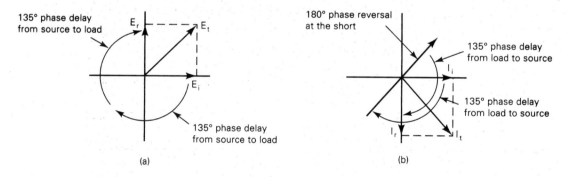

FIGURE 8-22 Voltage and current phase relationships for a transmission line more than one-quarter wavelength terminated in an open circuit: (a) voltage phase relationships; (b) current phase relationships

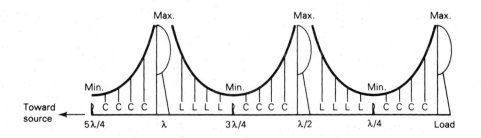

FIGURE 8-23 Input impedance variations for an open-circuited transmission line

Phasor Analysis of Input Impedance: Shorted Line

The following explanations use phasor diagrams to analyze shorted transmission lines in the same manner as with open lines. The difference is that with shorted transmission lines the voltage waveform is reflected back with a 180° phase reversal and the current waveform is reflected back as if there were no short.

Quarter-wavelength transmission line. The voltage and current phasor diagrams for a quarter-wavelength transmission line terminated in a short circuit are identical to those shown in Figure 8-19, except reversed. The incident and reflected voltages are in phase; therefore, $E_t = E_i + E_r$ and maximum. The incident and reflected currents are 180° out of phase; therefore, $I_t = I_i - I_r$ and minimum. $Z_{in} = E_i \angle 0° / I_t \angle 0° = Z_{in} / \angle 0°$ and maximum. Z_{in} has a 0° phase angle, is resistive, and is maximum. Therefore, a quarter-wavelength transmission line terminated in a short circuit is equivalent to a parallel *LC* circuit.

Transmission line less than one-quarter wavelength long. The voltage and current phasor diagrams for a transmission line less than one-quarter wavelength long and terminated in a short circuit are identical to those shown in Figure 8-21, except reversed. The voltage is reversed 180° at the short, and the current is reflected with the same phase as if it had continued. Therefore, the total voltage at the source end of the line leads the current by 90° and the line looks inductive.

Transmission line more than one-quarter wavelength long. The voltage and current phasor diagrams for a transmission line more than one-quarter wavelength long and terminated in a short circuit are identical to those shown in Figure 8-22, except reversed. The total voltage at the source end of the line lags the current by 90° and the line looks capacitive.

Shorted transmission line as a circuit element. From the preceding discussion it is obvious that a shorted transmission line can behave as if it were a resistor, an inductor, or a capacitor, depending on its electrical length. On a shorted transmission line, standing waves repeat every half-wavelength; therefore, the input impedance also repeats. Figure 8-24 shows the variations in input impedance of a shorted transmission line for various electrical lengths. It can be seen that a shorted line is resistive and minimum at the short and at each successive half wavelength interval, and resistive and maximum one-quarter wavelength from the short and at each successive half-wavelength interval. For electrical lengths less than one-quarter wavelength, the input impedance is inductive and increases with length. For electrical lengths between one-quarter and one-half wavelength, the input impedance is capacitive and decreases with length. The inductance and capacitance patterns also repeat every half-wavelength interval.

Transmission-line input impedance summary. Figure 8-25 summarizes the transmission-line configurations described in the preceding sections, their input impedance characteristics, and their equivalent *LC* circuits. It can be seen that both shorted and open sections of transmission lines can behave as resistors, inductors, or capacitors, depending on their electrical length.

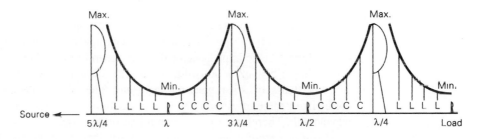

FIGURE 8-24 Input impedance variations for a short-circuited transmission line

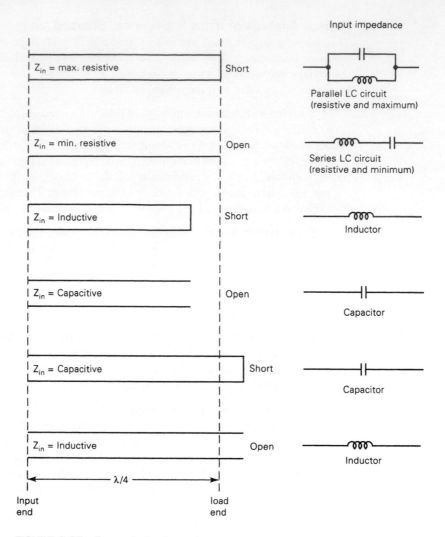

Input impedance

Z_{in} = max. resistive — Short — Parallel LC circuit (resistive and maximum)

Z_{in} = min. resistive — Open — Series LC circuit (resistive and minimum)

Z_{in} = Inductive — Short — Inductor

Z_{in} = Capacitive — Open — Capacitor

Z_{in} = Capacitive — Short — Capacitor

Z_{in} = Inductive — Open — Inductor

$\lambda/4$

Input end   load end

FIGURE 8-25 Transmission-line summary

Transmission-Line Impedance Matching

Power is transferred most efficiently to a load when there are no reflected waves, that is, when the load is purely resistive and equal to Z_o. Whenever the characteristic impedance of a transmission line and its load are not matched (equal), standing waves are present on the line and maximum power is not transferred to the load. Standing waves cause power loss, dielectric breakdown, noise, radiation, and *ghost signals.* Therefore, whenever possible a transmission line should be matched to its load. Two common transmission-line techniques are used to match a transmission line to a load having an impedance that is not equal to Z_o. They are quarter-wavelength transformer matching and stub matching.

     Quarter-wavelength transformer matching. *Quarter-wavelength transformers* are used to match transmission lines to purely resistive loads whose resistance is not equal to the characteristic impedance of the line. Keep in mind that a quarter-wavelength transformer is not actually a transformer, but rather a quarter-wavelength section of transmission line that acts as if it were a transformer. The input impedance to a transmission line varies from some maximum value to some minimum value, or vice versa, every quarter-wavelength. Therefore, a transmission line one-quarter wavelength long acts as a *step-up* or *step-down transformer,* depending on whether Z_L is greater than or less than Z_o. A

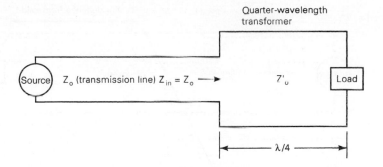

FIGURE 8-26 Quarter-wavelength transformer

quarter-wavelength transformer is not a broadband impedance-matching device; it is a quarter-wavelength at only a single frequency. The impedance transformations for a quarter-wavelength transmission line are as follows:

1. $R_L = Z_o$: The quarter-wavelength line acts as a transformer with a 1:1 turns ratio.
2. $R_L > Z_o$: The quarter-wavelength line acts as a step-down transformer.
3. $R_L < Z_o$: The quarter-wavelength line acts as a step-up transformer.

As with a transformer, a quarter-wavelength transformer is placed between a transmission line and its load. A quarter-wavelength transformer is simply a length of transmission line one-quarter wavelength long. Figure 8-26 shows how a quarter-wavelength transformer is used to match a transmission line to a purely resistive load. The characteristic impedance of the quarter-wavelength section is determined mathematically from the formula

$$Z_0' = \sqrt{Z_o Z_L} \tag{8-32}$$

where
Z_0' = characteristic impedance of a quarter-wavelength transformer
Z_o = characteristic impedance of the transmission line that is being matched
Z_L = load impedance

Example 8-5

Determine the physical length and characteristic impedance for a quarter-wavelength transformer that is used to match a section of RG-8A/U (Z_o = 50 Ω) to a 150-Ω resistive load. The frequency of operation is 150 MHz and the velocity factor V_f = 1.

Solution The physical length of the transformer depends on the wavelength of the signal. Substituting into Equation 8-2 yields

$$\lambda = \frac{c}{f} = \frac{3 \times 10^8 \text{ m/s}}{150 \text{ MHz}} = 2 \text{ m}$$

$$\frac{\lambda}{4} = \frac{2 \text{ m}}{4} = 0.5 \text{ m}$$

The characteristic impedance of the 0.5-m transformer is determined from Equation 8-32.

$$Z_o' = \sqrt{Z_o Z_L} = \sqrt{(50)(150)} = 86.6 \text{ Ω}$$

Stub matching. When a load is purely inductive or purely capacitive, it absorbs no energy. The reflection coefficient is 1 and the SWR is infinity. When the load is a complex impedance (which is usually the case), it is necessary to remove the reactive component to match the transmission line to the load. Transmission-line *stubs* are commonly used for this purpose. A transmission-line stub is simply a piece of additional transmission line that is placed across the primary line as close to the load as possible. The susceptance of the stub is used to tune out the susceptance of the load. With *stub matching,* either a shorted or an

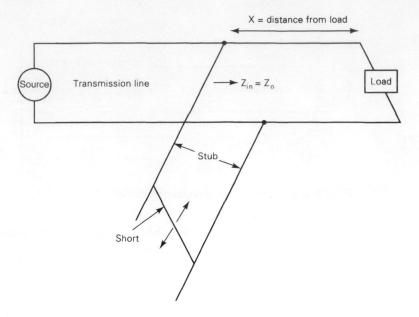

FIGURE 8-27 Shorted stub impedance matching

open stub can be used. However, shorted stubs are preferred because open stubs have a tendency to radiate, especially at the higher frequencies.

Figure 8-27 shows how a shorted stub is used to cancel the susceptance of the load and match the load resistance to the characteristic impedance of the transmission line. It has been shown how a shorted section of transmission line can look resistive, inductive, or capacitive, depending on its electrical length. A transmission line that is one-half wavelength or shorter can be used to tune out the reactive component of a load.

The process of matching a load to a transmission line with a shorted stub is as follows:

1. Locate a point as close to the load as possible where the conductive component of the input admittance is equal to the characteristic admittance of the transmission line.

$$Y_{in} = G - jB, \text{ where } G = \frac{1}{Z_o}$$

2. Attach the shorted stub to the point on the transmission line identified in step 1.
3. Depending on whether the reactive component at the point identified in step 1 is inductive or capacitive, the stub length is adjusted accordingly.

$$Y_{in} = G_o - jB + jB_{stub}$$
$$= G_o$$
if $$B = B_{stub}$$

For a more complete explanation of stub matching using the Smith chart, refer to Appendix A.

TIME-DOMAIN REFLECTOMETRY

Metallic cables, as with all components within an electronic communications system, can develop problems that inhibit their ability to perform as expected. Cable problems often create unique situations because cables often extend over large distances, sometimes as far

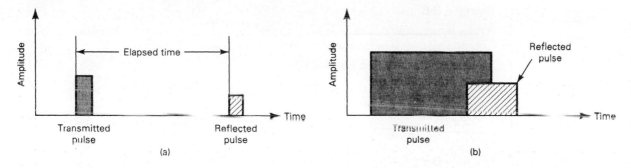

FIGURE 8-28 Time-domain reflectometry: (a) elapsed time; (b) transmitted pulse too long

as several thousand feet, or longer. Cable problems are often attributed to chemical erosion at cross-connect points and mechanical failure. When a problem occurs in a cable, it can be extremely time consuming and, consequently, quite expensive to determine the type and exact location of the problem.

A technique that can be used to locate an impairment in a metallic cable is called *time-domain reflectometry* (TDR). With TDR, transmission-line impairments can be pinpointed within several feet at distances of 10 miles. TDR makes use of the well-established theory that transmission-line impairments, such as shorts and opens, cause a portion of the incident signal to return to the source. How much of the transmitted signal returns depends on the type and magnitude of the impairment. The point in the line where the impairment is located represents a discontinuity to the signal. This discontinuity causes a portion of the transmitted signal to be reflected rather than continuing down the cable. If no energy is returned (i.e., the transmission line and load are perfectly matched), the line is either infinitely long or it is terminated in a resistive load with an impedance equal to the characteristic impedance of the line. TDR operates in a fashion similar to *radar*. A short duration pulse with a fast rise time is propagated down a cable; then the time for a portion of that signal to return to the source is measured. This return signal is sometimes called an *echo*. Knowing the velocity of propagation on the cable, the exact distance between the impairment and the source can be determined using the following mathematical relationships:

$$d = \frac{v \times t}{2} \tag{8-33}$$

where d = distance to the discontinuity (meters)
v = actual velocity (meters per second)
$v = k \times c$ (meters per second)
k = velocity factor (v/c) (unitless)
c = velocity in a vacuum (3×10^8 meters per second)
t = elapsed time (seconds)

The elapsed time is measured from the leading edge of the transmitted pulse to the reception of the reflected signal as shown in Figure 8-28a. It is important that the transmitted pulse be as narrow as possible. Otherwise, when the impairment is located close to the source, the reflected signal could return while the pulse is still being transmitted (Figure 8-28b), making it difficult to detect. For signals traveling at the speed of light (c), the velocity of propagation is 3×10^8 m/s or approximately 1 ns/ft. Consequently, a pulse width of several microseconds would limit the usefulness of TDR only to cable impairments that occurred several thousand feet or farther away. Producing an extremely narrow pulse was one of the limiting factors in the development of TDR for locating cable faults on short cables.

Example 8-6

A pulse is transmitted down a cable that has a velocity of propagation of 0.8 c. The reflected signal is received 1 μs later. How far down the cable is the impairment?

Solution Substituting into Equation 8-33,

$$d = \frac{(0.8\ c) \times 1\ \mu s}{2}$$

$$= \frac{0.8 \times (3 \times 10^8\ m/s) \times 1 \times 10^{-6}\ s}{2} = 120\ m$$

Example 8-7

Using TDR, a transmission-line impairment is located 3000 m from the source. For a velocity of propagation of 0.9 c, determine the time elapsed from the beginning of the pulse to the reception of the echo.

Solution Rearranging Equation 8-33 gives

$$t = \frac{2d}{v} = \frac{2d}{k \times c}$$

$$= \frac{2(3000\ m)}{0.9(3 \times 10^8\ m/s)} = 22.22\ \mu s$$

MICROSTRIP AND STRIPLINE TRANSMISSION LINES

At frequencies below about 300 MHz, the characteristics of open and shorted transmission lines such as those described earlier in this chapter have little relevance. Therefore, at low frequencies, standard transmission lines would be too long for practical use as reactive components or tuned circuits. For high-frequency (300 MHz to 3000 MHz) applications, however, special transmission lines constructed with copper patterns on a *printed circuit* (PC) board called *microstrip* and *stripline* have been developed to interconnect components on PC boards. Also, when the distance between the source and load ends of a transmission line is a few inches or less, standard coaxial cable transmission lines are impractical because the connectors, terminations, and cables themselves are simply too large.

Both microstrip and stripline use the traces (sometimes called *tracks*) on the PC board itself. The traces can be etched using the same processes as the other traces on the board; thus, they do not require any additional manufacturing processes. If the lines are etched onto the surface of the PC board only, they are called microstrip lines. When the lines are etched in the middle layer of a multilayer PC board, they are called striplines. Microstrip and stripline can be used to construct transmission lines, inductors, capacitors, tuned circuits, filters, phase shifters, and impedance matching devices.

Microstrip

Microstrip is simply a flat conductor separated from a ground plane by an insulating dielectric material. A simple single-track microstrip line is shown in Figure 8-29a. The ground plane serves as the circuit common point and must be at least 10 times wider than the top conductor and must be connected to ground. The microstrip is generally either one-quarter or one-half wavelength long at the frequency of operation and equivalent to an unbalanced transmission line. Shorted lines are usually preferred to open lines, because open lines have a greater tendency to radiate. Figure 8-29b shows a two-wire balanced microstrip transmission line.

As with any transmission line, the characteristic impedance of a microstrip line is dependent on its physical characteristics. Therefore, any characteristic impedance between 50 ohms and 200 ohms can be achieved with microstrip lines by simply changing its dimensions. The same is true for stripline. Unfortunately, every configuration of microstrip has

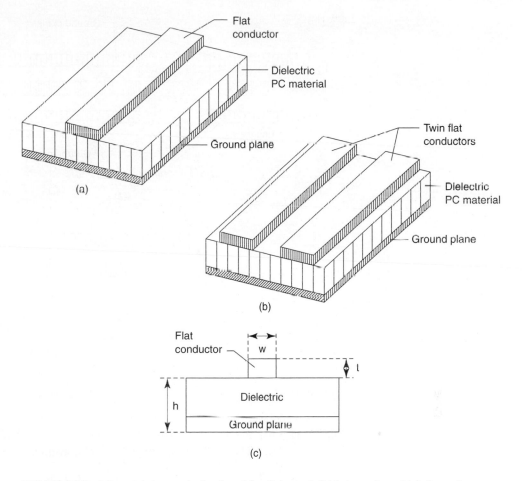

FIGURE 8-29 Microstrip transmission line: (a) unbalanced; (b) balanced; and (c) dimensions

its own unique formula. The formula for calculating the characteristic impedance of an unbalanced microstrip line such as the one shown in Figure 8-29c is

$$Z_o = \frac{87}{\sqrt{\epsilon + 1.41}} \ln\left(\frac{5.98h}{0.8w + t}\right) \qquad (8\text{-}34)$$

where Z_o = characteristic impedance (ohms)

ϵ = dielectric constant (FR-4 fiberglass ϵ = 4.5 and Teflon ϵ = 3)

w = width of copper trace*

t = thickness of copper trace*

h = distance between copper trace and the ground plane (i.e., thickness of dielectric)*

Stripline

Stripline is simply a flat conductor sandwiched between two ground planes, as shown in Figure 8-30. Although stripline is more difficult to manufacture than microstrip, it is less likely to radiate; thus losses in stripline are lower than with microstrip. Again, the length of

*The dimensions for w, t, and h can be any linear unit (inches, millimeters, etc.) so lonc as they all use the same unit.

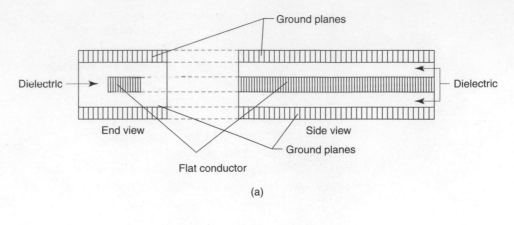

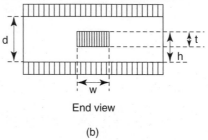

FIGURE 8-30 Stripline transmission line: (a) end and side views, and (b) dimensions

a stripline is either one-quarter or one-half wavelength and shorted lines are used more often than open lines. The characteristic impedance of a stripline configured as shown in Figure 8-30 is

$$Z_o = \frac{60}{\epsilon} \ln \left(\frac{4d}{0.67\pi w(0.8 + t/h)} \right) \tag{8-35}$$

where Z_o = characteristic impedance (ohms)
   ϵ = dielectric constant (FR-4 fiberglass ϵ = 4.5 and Teflon ϵ = 3)
   d = dielectric thickness*
   w = width of conducting copper trace*
   t = thickness of conducting copper trace*
   h = distance between copper trace and the ground plane*

QUESTIONS

8-1. Define *transmission line.*

8-2. Describe a transverse electromagnetic wave.

8-3. Define *wave velocity.*

8-4. Define *frequency* and *wavelength* for a transverse electromagnetic wave.

8-5. Describe balanced and unbalanced transmission lines.

8-6. Describe an open-wire transmission line.

8-7. Describe a twin-lead transmission line.

*The dimensions for *d, w, t,* and *h* can be any linear unit (inches, millimeters, etc.) so long as they all use the same unit.

8-8. Describe a twisted-pair transmission line.

8-9. Describe a shielded-cable transmission line.

8-10. Describe a concentric transmission line.

8-11. Describe the electrical and physical properties of a transmission line.

8-12. List and describe the four primary constants of a transmission line.

8-13. Define *characteristic impedance* for a transmission line.

8-14. What properties of a transmission line determine its characteristic impedance?

8-15. Define *propagation constant* for a transmission line.

8-16. Define *velocity factor* for a transmission line.

8-17. What properties of a transmission line determine its velocity factor?

8-18. What properties of a transmission line determine its dielectric constant?

8-19. Define *electrical length* for a transmission line.

8-20. List and describe five types of transmission-line losses.

8-21. Describe an incident wave; a reflected wave.

8-22. Describe a resonant transmission line; a nonresonant transmission line.

8-23. Define *reflection coefficient*.

8-24. Describe standing waves; standing-wave ratio.

8-25. Describe the standing waves present on an open transmission line.

8-26. Describe the standing waves present on a shorted transmission line.

8-27. Define *input impedance* for a transmission line.

8-28. Describe the behavior of a transmission line that is terminated in a short circuit that is greater than one-quarter wavelength long; less than one-quarter wavelength.

8-29. Describe the behavior of a transmission line that is terminated in an open circuit that is greater than one-quarter wavelength long; less than one-quarter wavelength long.

8-30. Describe the behavior of an open transmission line as a circuit element.

8-31. Describe the behavior of a shorted transmission line as a circuit element.

8-32. Describe the input impedance characteristics of a quarter-wavelength transmission line.

8-33. Describe the input impedance characteristics of a transmission line that is less than one-quarter wavelength long, greater than one-quarter wavelength long.

8-34. Describe quarter-wavelength transformer matching.

8-35. Describe how stub matching is accomplished.

8-36. Describe time-domain reflectometry.

PROBLEMS

8-1. Determine the wavelengths for electromagnetic waves in free space with the following frequencies: 1 kHz, 100 kHz, 1 MHz, and 1 GHz.

8-2. Determine the frequencies for electromagnetic waves in free space with the following wavelengths: 1 cm, 1 m, 10 m, 100 m, and 1000 m.

8-3. Determine the characteristic impedance for an air-dielectric transmission line with D/r ratio of 8.8.

8-4. Determine the characteristic impedance for an air-filled concentric transmission line with D/d ratio of 4.

8-5. Determine the characteristic impedance for a coaxial cable with inductance $L = 0.2$ μH/ft and capacitance $C = 16$ pF/ft.

8-6. For a given length of coaxial cable with distributed capacitance $C = 48.3$ pF/m and distributed inductance $L = 241.56$ nH/m, determine the velocity factor and velocity of propagation.

8-7. Determine the reflection coefficient for a transmission line with incident voltage $E_i = 0.2$ V and reflected voltage $E_r = 0.01$ V.

8-8. Determine the standing-wave ratio for the transmission line described in Problem 8-7.

8-9. Determine the SWR for a transmission line with maximum voltage standing-wave amplitude $V_{max} = 6$ V and minimum voltage standing-wave amplitude $V_{min} = 0.5$.

8-10. Determine the SWR for a 50-Ω transmission line that is terminated in a load resistance $Z_L = 75\ \Omega$.

8-11. Determine the SWR for a 75-Ω transmission line that is terminated in a load resistance $Z_L = 50\ \Omega$.

8-12. Determine the characteristic impedance for a quarter-wavelength transformer that is used to match a section of 75-Ω transmission line to a 100-Ω resistive load.

8-13. Using TDR, a pulse is transmitted down a cable with a velocity of propagation of 0.7 c. The reflected signal is received 1.2 μs later. How far down the cable is the impairment?

8-14. Using TDR, a transmission-line impairment is located 2500 m from the source. For a velocity of propagation of 0.95 c, determine the elapsed time from the beginning of the pulse to the reception of the echo.

8-15. Using TDR, a transmission-line impairment is located 100 m from the source. If the elapsed time from the beginning of the pulse to the reception of the echo is 833 ns, determine the velocity factor.

8-16. Determine the wavelengths for electromagnetic waves with the following frequencies: 5 kHz, 50 kHz, 500 kHz, and 5 MHz.

8-17. Determine the frequencies for electromagnetic waves with the following wavelengths: 5 cm, 50 cm, 5 m, 50 m.

8-18. Determine the characteristic impedance for an air-dielectric transmission line with a D/r ratio of 6.8.

8-19. Determine the characteristic impedance for an air-filled concentric transmission line with a D/d ratio of 6.

8-20. Determine the characteristic impedance for a coaxial cable with inductance $L = 0.15\ \mu$H/ft and capacitance $C = 20$ pF/ft.

8-21. For a given length of coaxial cable with distributed capacitance $C = 24.15$ pF/m and distributed inductance $L = 483.12$ nH/m, determine the velocity factor and velocity of propagation.

8-22. Determine the reflection coefficient for a transmission line with incident voltage $E_i = 0.4$ V and reflected voltage $E_r = 0.002$ V.

8-23. Determine the standing-wave ratio for the transmission line described in Problem 8-22.

8-24. Determine the SWR for a transmission line with a maximum voltage standing-wave amplitude $V_{max} = 8$ V and a minimum voltage standing-wave amplitude $V_{min} = 0.8$ V.

8-25. Determine the SWR for a 50-Ω transmission line that is terminated in a load resistance $Z_L = 60\ \Omega$.

8-26. Determine the SWR for a 60-Ω transmission line that is terminated in a load resistance $Z_L = 50\ \Omega$.

8-27. Determine the characteristic impedance for a quarter-wave transformer that is used to match a section of 50-Ω transmission line to a 60-Ω resistive load.

C H A P T E R 9

Electromagnetic Wave Propagation

INTRODUCTION

In Chapter 8 we explained transverse electromagnetic (TEM) waves and also described how metallic wires could be used as a transmission medium to transfer TEM waves from one point to another. However, very often in electronic communications systems, it is impractical or impossible to interconnect two pieces of equipment with a physical facility such as a metallic wire or cable. This is especially true when the equipment is separated by large spans of water, rugged mountains, or harsh desert terrain, or when communicating with satellite transponders orbiting 22,000 miles above Earth. Also, when the transmitters and receivers are mobile, as with two-way radio communications and mobile telephone, providing connections with metallic facilities is impossible. Therefore, free space or Earth's atmosphere is often used as a transmission medium.

Free-space propagation of electromagnetic waves is often called *radio-frequency* (RF) *propagation* or simply *radio propagation*. Although free space implies a vacuum, propagation through Earth's atmosphere is often referred to as free-space propagation and can often be treated as just that. The primary difference being that Earth's atmosphere introduces losses to the signal that are not encountered in a vacuum. TEM waves will propagate through any dielectric material, including air. TEM waves, however, do not propagate well through lossy conductors, such as sea water, because the electric fields cause currents to flow in the material that rapidly dissipate the wave's energy.

Radio waves are electromagnetic waves and, like light, propagate through free space in a straight line with a velocity of 300,000,000 meters per second. Other forms of electromagnetic waves include infrared, ultraviolet, X rays, and gamma rays. To propagate radio waves through Earth's atmosphere, it is necessary that the energy be radiated from the source, then the energy must be captured at the receive end. Radiating and capturing energy are antenna functions and are explained in Chapter 10, and the properties of electromagnetic waves were explained in Chapter 8. The purpose of this chapter is to describe the nature, behavior, and optical properties of radio waves propagating through Earth's atmosphere.

ELECTROMAGNETIC POLARIZATION

As explained in Chapter 8, an electromagnetic wave contains an electric field and a magnetic field at 90° to each other. The *polarization* of a plane electromagnetic wave is simply the orientation of the electric field vector in respect to the surface of the Earth (i.e., looking at the horizon). If the polarization remains constant, it is described as *linear polarization. Horizontal polarization* and *vertical polarization* are two forms of linear polarization. If the electric field is propagating parallel to the Earth's surface, the wave is said to be horizontally polarized. If the electric field is propagating perpendicular to the Earth's surface, the wave is said to be vertically polarized. If the polarization vector rotates 360° as the wave moves one wavelength through space and the field strength is equal at all angles of polarization, the wave is described as having *circular polarization*. When the field strength varies with changes in polarization, this is described as *elliptical polarization*. A rotating wave can turn in either direction. If the vector rotates in a clockwise direction, it is right-handed, and if the vector rotates in a counter-clockwise direction, it is considered left-handed.

RAYS AND WAVEFRONTS

Electromagnetic waves are invisible; therefore, they must be analyzed by indirect methods using schematic diagrams. The concepts of *rays* and *wavefronts* are aids to illustrating the effects of electromagnetic wave propagation through free space. A ray is a line drawn along the direction of propagation of an electromagnetic wave. Rays are used to show the relative direction of electromagnetic wave propagation; however, it does not necessarily represent the propagation of a single electromagnetic wave. Several rays are shown in Figure 9-1 (R_a, R_b, R_c, and so on). A wavefront shows a surface of constant phase of electromagnetic waves. A wavefront is formed when points of equal phase on rays propagated from the same source are joined together. Figure 9-1 shows a wavefront with a surface that is perpendicular to the direction of propagation (rectangle *ABCD*). When a surface is plane, its wavefront is perpendicular to the direction of propagation. The closer to the source, the more complicated the wavefront becomes.

Most wavefronts are more complicated than a simple plane wave. Figure 9-2 shows a point source, several rays propagating from it, and the corresponding wavefront. A *point source* is a single location from which rays propagate equally in all directions (an *isotropic source*). The wavefront generated from a point source is simply a sphere with radius R and its center located at the point of origin of the waves. In free space and a sufficient distance from the source, the rays within a small area of a spherical wavefront are nearly parallel. Therefore, the farther from a source, the more wave propagation appears as a plane wavefront.

ELECTROMAGNETIC RADIATION

Power Density and Field Intensity

Electromagnetic waves represent the flow of energy in the direction of propagation. The rate at which energy passes through a given surface area in free space is called *power den-*

FIGURE 9-1 Plane wave

sity. Therefore, power density is energy per unit time per unit of area and is usually given in watts per square meter. *Field intensity* is the intensity of the electric and magnetic fields of an electromagnetic wave propagating in free space. Electric field intensity is usually given in volts per meter and magnetic field intensity in ampere-turns per meter (At/m). Mathematically, power density is

$$\mathscr{P} = \mathscr{E}\mathscr{H} \quad \text{W/m}^2 \qquad (9\text{-}1)$$

where $\mathscr{P}$ = power density (watts per meter squared)
   $\mathscr{E}$ = rms electric field intensity (volts per meter)
   $\mathscr{H}$ = rms magnetic field intensity (ampere-turns per meter)

Characteristic Impedance of Free Space

The electric and magnetic field intensities of an electromagnetic wave in free space are related through the characteristic impedance (resistance) of free space. The characteristic impedance of a lossless transmission medium is equal to the square root of the ratio of its magnetic permeability to its electric permittivity. Mathematically, the characteristic impedance of free space (Z_s) is

$$Z_s = \sqrt{\frac{\mu_0}{\epsilon_0}} \qquad (9\text{-}2)$$

where Z_s = characteristic impedance of free space (ohms)
   μ_0 = magnetic permeability of free space (1.26×10^{-6} H/m)
   ϵ_0 = electric permittivity of free space (8.85×10^{-12} F/m)

Substituting into Equation 9-2, we have

$$Z_s = \sqrt{\frac{1.26 \times 10^{-6}}{8.85 \times 10^{-12}}} = 377 \ \Omega$$

Therefore, using Ohm's law, we obtain

$$\mathscr{P} = \frac{\mathscr{E}^2}{377} = 377\mathscr{H}^2 \quad \text{W/m}^2 \qquad (9\text{-}3)$$

$$\mathscr{H} = \frac{\mathscr{E}}{377} \quad \text{At/m} \qquad (9\text{-}4)$$

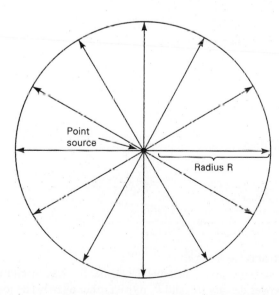

FIGURE 9-2   Wavefront from a point source

Point source

Radius R

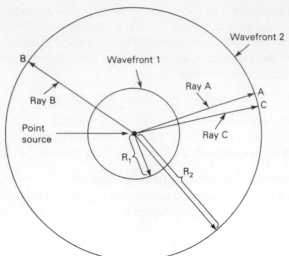

FIGURE 9-3 Spherical wavefront from an isotropic source

SPHERICAL WAVEFRONT AND THE INVERSE SQUARE LAW

Spherical Wavefront

Figure 9-3 shows a point source that radiates power at a constant rate uniformly in all directions. Such a source is called an *isotropic radiator*. A true isotropic radiator does not exist. However, it is closely approximated by an *omnidirectional antenna*. An isotropic radiator produces a spherical wavefront with radius R. All points distance R from the source lie on the surface of the sphere and have equal power densities. For example, in Figure 9-3 points A and B are an equal distance from the source. Therefore, the power densities at points A and B are equal. At any instant of time, the total power radiated, P_r watts, is uniformly distributed over the total surface of the sphere (this assumes a lossless transmission medium). Therefore, the power density at any point on the sphere is the total radiated power divided by the total area of the sphere. Mathematically, the power density at any point on the surface of a spherical wavefront is

$$\mathcal{P} = \frac{P_{rad}}{4\pi R^2} \tag{9-5}$$

where P_{rad} = total power radiated (watts)
           R = radius of the sphere (which is equal to the distance from any point on the surface of the sphere to the source)
   $4\pi R^2$ = area of the sphere

and for a distance R_a meters from the source, the power density is

$$\mathcal{P}_a = \frac{P_{rad}}{4\pi R_a^2}$$

Equating Equations 9-3 and 9-5 gives

$$\frac{P_{rad}}{4\pi R^2} = \frac{\mathcal{E}^2}{377}$$

Therefore, $$\mathcal{E}^2 = \frac{377 P_{rad}}{4\pi R^2} \quad \text{and} \quad \mathcal{E} = \frac{\sqrt{30 P_{rad}}}{R} \tag{9-6}$$

Inverse Square Law

From Equation 9-5 it can be seen that the farther the wavefront moves from the source, the smaller the power density (R_a and R_c move farther apart). The total power distributed over the surface of the sphere remains the same. However, because the area of the sphere increases in direct proportion to the distance from the source squared (i.e., the radius of the sphere squared), the power density is inversely proportional to the square of the distance from the source. This relationship is called the *inverse square law*. Therefore, the power density at any point on the surface of the outer sphere is

$$\mathcal{P}_2 = \frac{P_{rad}}{4\pi R_2^2}$$

and the power density at any point on the inner sphere is

$$\mathcal{P}_1 = \frac{P_{rad}}{4\pi R_1^2}$$

Therefore,

$$\frac{\mathcal{P}_2}{\mathcal{P}_1} = \frac{P_{rad}/4\pi R_2^2}{P_{rad}/4\pi R_1^2} = \frac{R_1^2}{R_2^2} = \left(\frac{R_1}{R_2}\right)^2 \qquad (9\text{-}7)$$

From Equation 9-7 it can be seen that as the distance from the source doubles the power density decreases by a factor of 2^2, or 4. When deriving the inverse square law of radiation (Equation 9-7), it was assumed that the source radiates isotropically, although it is not necessary; however, it is necessary that the velocity of propagation in all directions be uniform. Such a propagation medium is called an *isotropic medium*.

Example 9-1

For an isotropic antenna radiating 100 W of power, determine
(a) Power density 1000 m from the source.
(b) Power density 2000 m from the source.

Solution   (a)   Substituting into Equation 9-5 yields

$$\mathcal{P}_1 = \frac{100}{4\pi 1000^2} = 7.96 \; \mu W/m^2$$

(b) Again, substituting into Equation 9-5 gives

$$\mathcal{P}_2 = \frac{100}{4\pi 2000^2} = 1.99 \; \mu W/m^2$$

or, substituting into Equation 9-7, we have

$$\frac{\mathcal{P}_2}{\mathcal{P}_1} = \frac{1000^2}{2000^2} = 0.25$$

or $\mathcal{P}_2 = 7.96 \; \mu W/m^2 \, (0.25) = 1.99 \; \mu W/m^2$

WAVE ATTENUATION AND ABSORPTION

Free space is a vacuum, so no loss of energy occurs as a wave propagates through it. As waves propagate through free space, however, they spread out, resulting in a reduction in power density. This is called *attenuation* and occurs in free space as well as the Earth's atmosphere. Since Earth's atmosphere is not a vacuum, it contains particles that can absorb electromagnetic energy. This type of reduction of power is called *absorption loss* and does not occur in waves traveling outside our atmosphere.

Attenuation

The inverse square law for radiation mathematically describes the reduction in power density with distance from the source. As a wavefront moves away from the source, the continuous electromagnetic field that is radiated from that source spreads out. That is, the waves move farther away from each other and, consequently, the number of waves per unit area decreases. None of the radiated power is lost or dissipated because the wavefront is moving away from the source; the wave simply spreads out or disperses over a larger area, decreasing the power density. The reduction in power density with distance is equivalent to a power loss and is commonly called *wave attenuation*. Because the attenuation is due to the spherical spreading of the wave, it is sometimes called the *space attenuation* of the wave. Wave attenuation is generally expressed in terms of the common logarithm of the power density ratio (dB loss). Mathematically, wave attenuation (γ_a) is

$$\gamma_a = 10 \log \frac{\mathcal{P}_1}{\mathcal{P}_2} \tag{9-8}$$

The reduction in power density due to the inverse square law presumes free-space propagation (a vacuum or nearly a vacuum) and is called wave attenuation. The reduction in power density due to nonfree-space propagation is called *absorption.*

Absorption

Earth's atmosphere is not a vacuum. Rather, it is made up of atoms and molecules of various substances, such as gases, liquids, and solids. Some of these materials are capable of absorbing electromagnetic waves. As an electromagnetic wave propagates through Earth's atmosphere, energy is transferred from the wave to the atoms and molecules of the atmosphere. Wave absorption by the atmosphere is analogous to an I^2R power loss. Once absorbed, the energy is lost forever and causes an attenuation in the voltage and magnetic field intensities and a corresponding reduction in power density.

Absorption of radio frequencies in a normal atmosphere depends on frequency and is relatively insignificant below approximately 10 GHz. Figure 9-4 shows atmospheric absorption in decibels per kilometer due to oxygen and water vapor for radio frequencies above 10 GHz. It can be seen that certain frequencies are affected more or less by absorption, creating peaks and valleys in the curves. Wave attenuation due to absorption does not depend on distance from the radiating source, but rather the total distance that the wave propagates through the atmosphere. In other words, for a *homogeneous medium* (one with uniform properties throughout), the absorption experienced during the first mile of propagation is the same as for the last mile. Also, abnormal atmospheric conditions such as heavy rain or dense fog absorb more energy than a normal atmosphere. Atmospheric absorption (η) for a wave propagating from R_1 to R_2 is $\gamma(R_2 - R_1)$, where γ is the absorption coefficient. Therefore, wave attenuation depends on the ratio R_2/R_1, and wave absorption depends on the distance between R_1 and R_2. In a more practical situation (i.e., an *inhomogeneous*

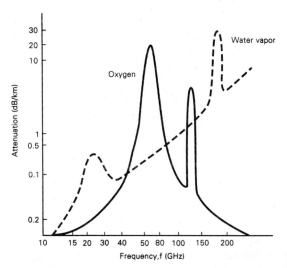

FIGURE 9-4 Atmospheric absorption of electromagnetic waves

medium), the absorption coefficient varies considerably with location, thus creating a difficult problem for radio systems engineers.

OPTICAL PROPERTIES OF RADIO WAVES

In Earth's atmosphere, ray–wavefront propagation may be altered from free-space behavior by *optical* effects such as *refraction, reflection, diffraction,* and *interference.* Using rather unscientific terminology, refraction can be thought of as *bending,* reflection as *bouncing,* diffraction as *scattering,* and interference as *colliding.* Refraction, reflection, diffraction, and interference are called optical properties because they were first observed in the science of optics, which is the behavior of light waves. Because light waves are high-frequency electromagnetic waves, it stands to reason that optical properties will also apply to radio wave propagation. Although optical principles can be analyzed completely by application of Maxwell's equations, this is necessarily complex. For most applications, *geometric ray tracing* can be substituted for analysis by Maxwell's equations.

Refraction

Electromagnetic *refraction* is the change in direction of a ray as it passes obliquely from one medium to another with different velocities of propagation. The velocity at which an electromagnetic wave propagates is inversely proportional to the density of the medium in which it is propagating. Therefore, refraction occurs whenever a radio wave passes from one medium into another medium of different density. Figure 9-5 shows refraction of a wavefront at a *plane* boundary between two media with different densities. For this example, medium 1 is less dense than medium 2 ($v_1 > v_2$). It can be seen that ray A enters the more dense medium before ray B. Therefore, ray B propagates more rapidly than ray A and travels distance B–B′ during the same time that ray A travels distance A–A′. Therefore, wavefront (A′B′) is *tilted* or bent in a downward direction. Because a ray is defined as being perpendicular to the wavefront at all points, the rays in Figure 9-5 have changed direction at the interface of the two media. Whenever a ray passes from a less dense to a more dense medium, it is effectively bent toward the *normal.* (The normal is simply an imaginary line drawn perpendicular to the interface at the point of incidence.) Conversely, whenever a ray passes from a more dense to a less dense medium, it is effectively bent away from

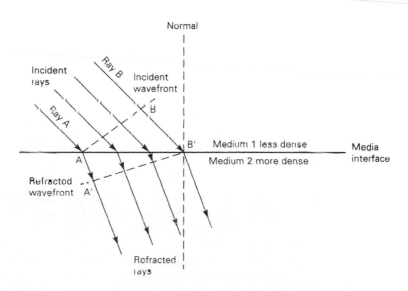

FIGURE 9-5 Refraction at a plane boundary between two media

the normal. The *angle of incidence* is the angle formed between the incident wave and the normal, and the *angle of refraction* is the angle formed between the refracted wave and the normal.

The amount of bending or refraction that occurs at the interface of two materials of different densities is quite predictable and depends on the *refractive index* (also called the *index of refraction*) of the two materials. The refractive index is simply the ratio of the velocity of propagation of a light ray in free space to the velocity of propagation of a light ray in a given material. Mathematically, the refractive index is

$$n = \frac{c}{v} \tag{9-9}$$

where n = refractive index (unitless)
   c = speed of light in free space (3×10^8 m/s)
   v = speed of light in a given material (meters per second)

The refractive index is also a function of frequency. However, the variation in most applications is insignificant and, therefore, is omitted from this discussion. How an electromagnetic wave reacts when it meets the interface of two transmissive materials that have different indexes of refraction can be explained with *Snell's law.* Snell's law simply states that

$$n_1 \sin \theta_1 = n_2 \sin \theta_2 \tag{9-10}$$

and
$$\frac{\sin \theta_1}{\sin \theta_2} = \frac{n_2}{n_1}$$

where n_1 = refractive index of material 1
   n_2 = refractive index of material 2
   θ_1 = angle of incidence (degrees)
   θ_2 = angle of refraction (degrees)

and because the refractive index of a material is equal to the square root of its dielectric constant,

$$\frac{\sin \theta_1}{\sin \theta_2} = \sqrt{\frac{\epsilon_{r2}}{\epsilon_{r1}}} \tag{9-11}$$

where ϵ_{r1} = dielectric constant of medium 1
   ϵ_{r2} = dielectric constant of medium 2

Refraction also occurs when a wavefront propagates in a medium that has a *density gradient* that is perpendicular to the direction of propagation (i.e., parallel to the wavefront). Figure 9-6 shows wavefront refraction in a transmission medium that has a gradual variation in its refractive index. The medium is more dense near the bottom and less dense at the top. Therefore, rays traveling near the top travel faster than rays near the bottom and, consequently, the wavefront tilts downward. The tilting occurs in a gradual fashion as the wave progresses, as shown.

Reflection

Reflect means to cast or turn back, and *reflection* is the act of reflecting. Electromagnetic reflection occurs when an incident wave strikes a boundary of two media and some or all of the incident power does not enter the second material. The waves that do not penetrate the second medium are reflected. Figure 9-7 shows electromagnetic wave reflection at a plane boundary between two media. Because all the reflected waves remain in medium 1, the velocities of the reflected and incident waves are equal. Consequently, the *angle of reflection* equals the *angle of incidence* ($\theta_i = \theta_r$). However the reflected voltage field intensity is less than the incident voltage field intensity. The ratio of the reflected to the incident

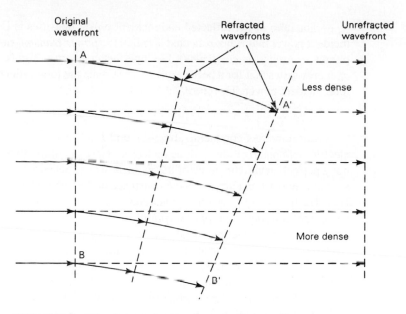

FIGURE 9-6   Wavefront refraction in a gradient medium

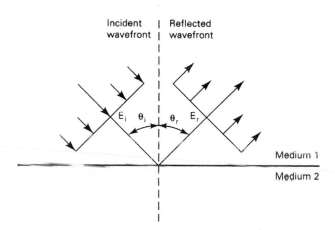

FIGURE 9-7   Electromagnetic reflection at a plane boundary
of two media

voltage intensities is called the *reflection coefficient*, Γ (sometimes called the *coefficient of reflection*). For a perfect conductor, $\Gamma = 1$. Γ is used to indicate both the relative amplitude of the incident and reflected fields and also the phase shift that occurs at the point of reflection. Mathematically, the reflection coefficient is

$$\Gamma = \frac{E_r e^{j\theta_r}}{E_i e^{j\theta_i}} = \frac{E_r}{E_i} = e^{j(\theta_r - \theta_i)} \qquad (9\text{-}12)$$

where Γ = reflection coefficient (unitless)
          E_i = incident voltage intensity (volts)
          E_r = reflected voltage intensity (volts)
          θ_i = incident phase (degrees)
          θ_r = reflected phase (degrees)

The ratio of the reflected and incident power densities is Γ. The portion of the total incident power that is not reflected is called the *power transmission coefficient* (*T*) (or simply the *transmission coefficient*). For a perfect conductor, *T* = 0. The *law of conservation of energy* states that for a perfect reflective surface the total reflected power must equal the total incident power. Therefore,

$$T + |\Gamma|^2 = 1 \tag{9-13}$$

For imperfect conductors, both $|\Gamma|^2$ and *T* are functions of the angle of incidence, the electric field polarization, and the dielectric constants of the two materials. If medium 2 is not a perfect conductor, some of the incident waves penetrate it and are absorbed. The absorbed waves set up currents in the resistance of the material and the energy is converted to heat. The fraction of power that penetrates medium 2 is called the *absorption coefficient* (or sometimes the *coefficient of absorption*).

When the reflecting surface is not plane (i.e., it is curved), the curvature of the reflected wave is different from that of the incident wave. When the wavefront of the incident wave is curved and the reflective surface is plane, the curvature of the reflected wavefront is the same as that of the incident wavefront.

Reflection also occurs when the reflective surface is *irregular* or *rough;* however, such a surface may destroy the shape of the wavefront. When an incident wavefront strikes an irregular surface, it is randomly scattered in many directions. Such a condition is called *diffuse reflection,* whereas reflection from a perfectly smooth surface is called *specular* (mirrorlike) *reflection.* Surfaces that fall between smooth and irregular are called *semirough surfaces.* Semirough surfaces cause a combination of diffuse and specular reflection. A semirough surface will not totally destroy the shape of the reflected wavefront. However, there is a reduction in the total power. The *Rayleigh criterion* states that a semirough surface will reflect as if it were a smooth surface whenever the cosine of the angle of incidence is greater than λ/8*d,* where *d* is the depth of the surface irregularity and λ is the wavelength of the incident wave. Reflection from a semirough surface is shown in Figure 9-8. Mathematically, Rayleigh's criterion is

$$\cos \theta_i > \frac{\lambda}{8d} \tag{9-14}$$

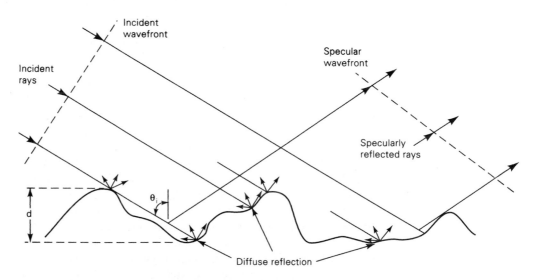

FIGURE 9-8 Reflection from a semirough surface

Diffraction

Diffraction is defined as the modulation or redistribution of energy within a wavefront when it passes near the edge of an *opaque* object. Diffraction is the phenomenon that allows light or radio waves to propagate (*peek*) around corners. The previous discussions of refraction and reflection assumed that the dimensions of the refracting and reflecting surfaces were large with respect to a wavelength of the signal. However, when a wavefront passes near an obstacle or discontinuity with dimensions comparable in size to a wavelength, simple geometric analysis cannot be used to explain the results and *Huygens's principle* (which is deduced from Maxwell's equations) is necessary.

Huygens's principle states that every point on a given spherical wavefront can be considered as a secondary point source of electromagnetic waves from which other secondary waves (wavelets) are radiated outward. Huygens's principle is illustrated in Figure 9-9. Normal wave propagation considering an infinite plane is shown in Figure 9-9a. Each secondary point source (p_1, p_2, and so on) radiates energy outward in all directions. However, the wavefront continues in its original direction rather than spreading out, because cancelation of the secondary wavelets occurs in all directions except straight forward. Therefore, the wavefront remains plane.

When a finite plane wavefront is considered, as in Figure 9-9b, cancelation in random directions is incomplete. Consequently, the wavefront spreads out or *scatters*. This scattering effect is called *diffraction*. Figure 9-9c shows diffraction around the edge of an obstacle. It can be seen that wavelet cancelation occurs only partially. Diffraction occurs around the edge of the obstacle, which allows secondary waves to "sneak" around the corner of the obstacle into what is called the *shadow zone*. This phenomenon can be observed when a door is opened into a dark room. Light rays diffract around the edge of the door and illuminate the area behind the door.

Interference

Interfere means to come into opposition, and *interference* is the act of interfering. Radio wave interference occurs when two or more electromagnetic waves combine in such a way that system performance is degraded. Refraction, reflection, and diffraction are categorized as geometric optics, which means that their behavior is analyzed primarily in terms of rays and wavefronts. Interference, on the other hand, is subject to the principle of *linear superposition* of electromagnetic waves and occurs whenever two or more waves simultaneously occupy the same point in space. The principle of linear superposition states that the total voltage intensity at a given point in space is the sum of the individual wave vectors. Certain types of propagation media have nonlinear properties; however, in an ordinary medium (such as air or Earth's atmosphere), linear superposition holds true.

Figure 9-10 shows the linear addition of two instantaneous voltage vectors whose phase angles differ by angle θ. It can be seen that the total voltage is not simply the sum of the two vector magnitudes, but rather the phasor addition of the two. With free-space propagation, a phase difference may exist simply because the *electromagnetic polarizations* of two waves differ. Depending on the phase angles of the two vectors, either addition or subtraction can occur. (This implies simply that the result may be more or less than either vector because the two electromagnetic waves can reinforce or cancel.)

Figure 9-11 shows interference between two electromagnetic waves in free space. It can be seen that at point X the two waves occupy the same area of space. However, wave B has traveled a different path than wave A, and, therefore, their relative phase angles may be different. If the difference in distance traveled is an odd integral multiple of one-half wavelength, reinforcement takes place. If the difference is an even integral multiple of one-half wavelength, total cancelation occurs. More likely the difference in distance falls somewhere between the two, and partial cancelation occurs. For frequencies below VHF, the relatively large wavelengths prevent interference from being a significant problem. However, with UHF and above, wave interference can be severe.

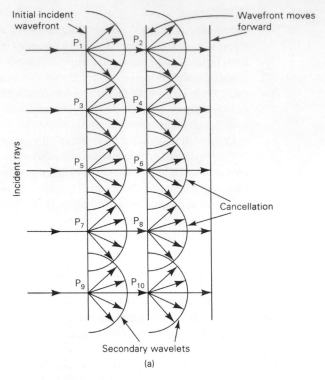

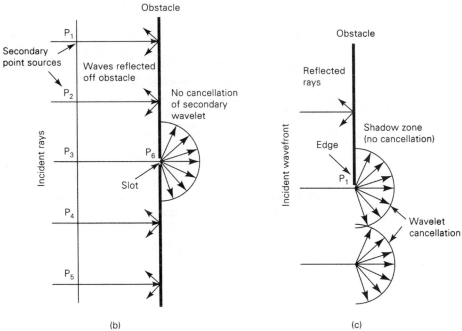

FIGURE 9-9 Electromagnetic wave diffraction: (a) Huygens's principle for a plane wavefront; (b) finite wavefront through a slot; (c) around an edge

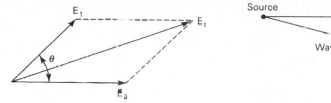

FIGURE 9-10 Linear addition of two vectors with differing phase angles

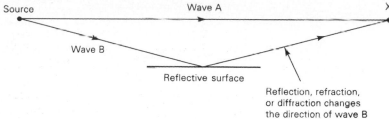

FIGURE 9-11 Electromagnetic wave interference

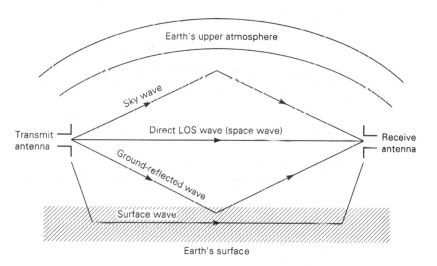

FIGURE 9-12 Normal modes of wave propagation

TERRESTRIAL PROPAGATION OF ELECTROMAGNETIC WAVES

Electromagnetic radio waves traveling within Earth's atmosphere are called *terrestrial waves,* and communications between two or more points on Earth is called *terrestrial radio communications.* Terrestrial waves are influenced by the atmosphere and Earth itself. In terrestrial radio communications, waves can be propagated in several ways, depending on the type of system and the environment. As previously explained, electromagnetic waves also travel in straight lines except when Earth and its atmosphere alter their path. Essentially, there are three ways of propagating electromagnetic waves within Earth's atmosphere: ground-wave, space-wave (which includes both direct and ground-reflected waves), and sky-wave propagation.

Figure 9-12 shows the normal modes of propagation between two radio antennas. Each of these modes exists in every radio system; however, some are negligible in certain frequency ranges or over a particular type of terrain. At frequencies below 1.5 MHz, ground waves provide the best coverage, because ground losses increase rapidly with frequency. Sky waves are used for high-frequency applications, and space waves are used for very high frequencies and above.

Ground-Wave Propagation

A *ground wave* is an electromagnetic wave that travels along the surface of Earth. Therefore, ground waves are sometimes called *surface waves.* Ground waves must be vertically polarized. This is because the electric field in a horizontally polarized wave would be parallel to Earth's surface, and such waves would be short-circuited by the conductivity of the

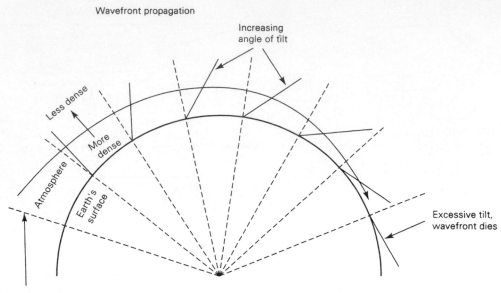

Wavefront propagation

Increasing
angle of tilt

Less dense

More dense

Atmosphere

Earth's surface

Excessive tilt,
wavefront dies

Wavefront perpendicular
to Earth's surface

FIGURE 9-13 Ground-wave propagation

ground. With ground waves, the changing electric field induces voltages in Earth's surface, which cause currents to flow that are very similar to those in a transmission line. Earth's surface also has resistance and dielectric losses. Therefore, ground waves are attenuated as they propagate. Ground waves propagate best over a surface that is a good conductor, such as salt water, and poorly over dry desert areas. Ground-wave losses increase rapidly with frequency. Therefore, ground-wave propagation is generally limited to frequencies below 2 MHz.

Figure 9-13 shows ground-wave propagation. Earth's atmosphere has a *gradient density* (i.e., the density decreases gradually with distance from Earth's surface), which causes the wavefront to tilt progressively forward. Therefore, the ground wave propagates around Earth, remaining close to its surface, and if enough power is transmitted, the wavefront could propagate beyond the horizon or even around the entire circumference of Earth. However, care must be taken when selecting the frequency and the terrain over which the ground wave will propagate to ensure that the wavefront does not tilt excessively and simply turn over, lie flat on the ground, and cease to propagate.

Ground-wave propagation is commonly used for ship-to-ship and ship-to-shore communications, for radio navigation, and for maritime mobile communications. Ground waves are used at frequencies as low as 15 kHz.

The disadvantages of ground-wave propagation are as follows:

1. Ground waves require a relatively high transmission power.
2. Ground waves are limited to very low, low, and medium frequencies (VLF, LF, and MF) requiring large antennas (the reason for this is explained in Chapter 11).
3. Ground losses vary considerably with surface material and composition.

The advantages of ground-wave propagation are as follows:

1. Given enough transmit power, ground waves can be used to communicate between any two locations in the world.
2. Ground waves are relatively unaffected by changing atmospheric conditions.

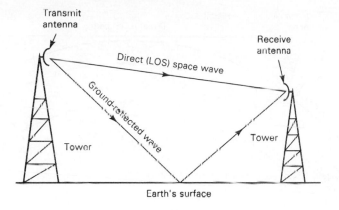

FIGURE 9-14 Space-wave propagation

Space-Wave Propagation

Space-wave propagation of electromagnetic energy includes radiated energy that travels in the lower few miles of Earth's atmosphere. Space waves include both direct and ground-reflected waves (see Figure 9-14). *Direct waves* travel essentially in a straight line between the transmit and receive antennas. Space-wave propagation with direct waves is commonly called *line-of-sight* (LOS) *transmission*. Therefore, direct space-wave propagation is limited by the curvature of the Earth. Ground-reflected waves are waves reflected by Earth's surface as they propagate between the transmit and receive antennas.

Figure 9-14 shows space-wave propagation between two antennas. It can be seen that the field intensity at the receive antenna depends on the distance between the two antennas (attenuation and absorption) and whether the direct and ground-reflected waves are in phase (interference).

The curvature of Earth presents a horizon to space-wave propagation commonly called the *radio horizon*. Due to atmospheric refraction, the radio horizon extends beyond the *optical horizon* for the common *standard atmosphere*. The radio horizon is approximately four-thirds that of the optical horizon. Refraction is caused by the troposphere, due to changes in its density, temperature, water-vapor content, and relative conductivity. The radio horizon can be lengthened simply by elevating the transmit or receive antennas (or both) above Earth's surface with towers or by placing them on top of mountains or high buildings.

Figure 9-15 shows the effect of antenna height on the radio horizon. The line-of-sight radio horizon for a single antenna is given as

$$d = \sqrt{2h} \qquad (9\text{-}15)$$

where d = distance to radio horizon (miles)
   h = antenna height above sea level (feet)

Therefore, for a transmit and receive antenna, the distance between the two antennas is

$$d = d_t + d_r$$

or   (9-16)

where d = total distance (miles)
   d_t = radio horizon for transmit antenna (miles)
   d_r = radio horizon for receive antenna (miles)
   h_t = transmit antenna height (feet)
   h_r = receive antenna height (feet)

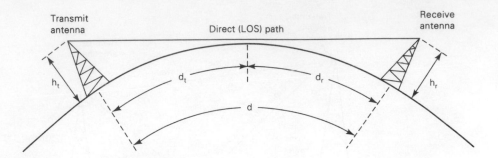

FIGURE 9-15 Space waves and radio horizon

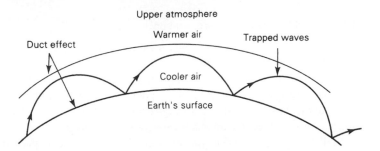

FIGURE 9-16 Duct propagation

The maximum distance between a transmitter and a receiver over average terrain can be approximated in metric units by the following equation:

$$d(\text{max}) = 17h_t + 17h_r \qquad (9\text{-}17)$$

where $d(\text{max})$ = maximum distance between transmitter and receiver (kilometers)
h_t = height of transmit antenna (meters)
h_r = height of receive antenna (meters)

From Equations 9-16 and 9-17, it can be seen that the space-wave propagation distance can be extended simply by increasing either the transmit or receive antenna height, or both.

Because the conditions in Earth's lower atmosphere are subject to change, the degree of refraction can vary with time. A special condition called *duct propagation* occurs when the density of the lower atmosphere is such that electromagnetic waves are trapped between it and Earth's surface. The layers of the atmosphere act as a duct, and an electromagnetic wave can propagate for great distances around the curvature of Earth within this duct. Duct propagation is shown in Figure 9-16.

Sky-Wave Propagation

Electromagnetic waves that are directed above the horizon level are called *sky waves.* Typically, sky waves are radiated in a direction that produces a relatively large angle with reference to Earth. Sky waves are radiated toward the sky, where they are either reflected or refracted back to Earth by the ionosphere. Because of this, sky-wave propagation is sometimes called ionospheric propagation. The ionosphere is the region of space located approximately 50 km to 400 km (30 mi to 250 mi) above Earth's surface. The ionosphere is the upper portion of Earth's atmosphere. Therefore, it absorbs large quantities of the sun's radiant energy, which ionizes the air molecules, creating free electrons. When a radio wave passes through the ionosphere, the electric field of the wave exerts a force on the free elec-

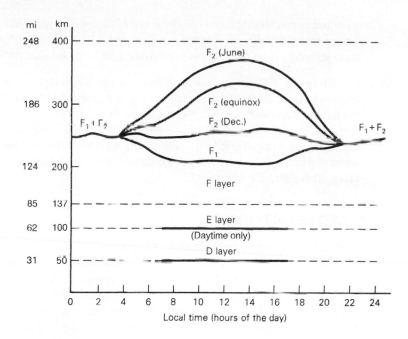

FIGURE 9-17 Ionospheric layers

trons, causing them to vibrate. The vibrating electrons decrease current, which is equivalent to reducing the dielectric constant. Reducing the dielectric constant increases the velocity of propagation and causes electromagnetic waves to bend away from the regions of high electron density toward regions of low electron density (i.e., increasing refraction). As the wave moves farther from Earth, ionization increases; however, there are fewer air molecules to ionize. Therefore, the upper atmosphere has a higher percentage of ionized molecules than in the lower atmosphere. The higher the ion density is, the more refraction. Also, due to the ionosphere's nonuniform composition and its temperature and density variations, it is *stratified*. Essentially, three layers comprise the ionosphere (the D, E, and F layers), which are shown in Figure 9-17. It can be seen that all three layers of the ionosphere vary in location and in *ionization density* with the time of day. They also fluctuate in a cyclic pattern throughout the year and according to the 11-year *sunspot cycle*. The ionosphere is most dense during times of maximum sunlight (during the daylight hours and in the summer).

D layer.   The *D layer* is the lowest layer of the ionosphere and is located approximately between 30 mi and 60 mi (50 km to 100 km) above Earth's surface. Because it is the layer farthest from the sun, there is little ionization. Therefore, the D layer has very little effect on the direction of propagation of radio waves. However, the ions in the D layer can absorb appreciable amounts of electromagnetic energy. The amount of ionization in the D layer depends on the altitude of the sun above the horizon. Therefore, it disappears at night. The D layer reflects VLF and LF waves and absorbs MF and HF waves. (See Table 1-1 for VLF, LF, MF, and HF frequency regions.)

E layer.   The *E layer* is located approximately between 60 mi and 85 mi (100 km to 140 km) above Earth's surface. The E layer is sometimes called the *Kennelly-Heaviside layer* after the two scientists who discovered it. The E layer has its maximum density at approximately 70 mi at noon, when the sun is at its highest point. As with the D layer, the E layer almost totally disappears at night. The E layer aids MF surface-wave propagation and reflects HF waves somewhat during the daytime. The upper portion of the E layer is sometimes considered separately and is called the sporadic E layer because it seems to come and go rather unpredictably. The sporadic E layer is caused by *solar flares* and *sunspot activity*. The sporadic E layer is a thin layer with a very high ionization density. When it appears, there generally is an unexpected improvement in long-distance radio transmission.

F layer.   The *F layer* is actually made up of two layers, the F_1 and F_2 layers. During the daytime, the F_1 layer is located between 85 mi and 155 mi (140 km to 250 km) above Earth's surface; the F_2 layer is located 85 mi to 185 mi (140 km to 300 km) above Earth's surface during the winter and 155 mi to 220 mi (250 km to 350 km) in the summer. During the night, the F_1 layer combines with the F_2 layer to form a single layer. The F_1 layer absorbs and attenuates some HF waves, although most of the waves pass through to the F_2 layer, where they are refracted back to Earth.

PROPAGATION TERMS AND DEFINITIONS

Critical Frequency and Critical Angle

Frequencies above the UHF range are virtually unaffected by the ionosphere because of their extremely short wavelengths. At these frequencies, the distances between ions are appreciably large and, consequently, the electromagnetic waves pass through them with little noticeable effect. Therefore, it stands to reason that there must be an upper frequency limit for sky-wave propagation. *Critical frequency* (f_c) is defined as the highest frequency that can be propagated directly upward and still be returned to Earth by the ionosphere. The critical frequency depends on the ionization density and, therefore, varies with the time of day and the season. If the vertical angle of radiation is decreased, frequencies at or above the critical frequency can still be refracted back to Earth's surface, because they will travel a longer distance in the ionosphere and, thus, have a longer time to be refracted. Therefore, critical frequency is used only as a point of reference for comparison purposes. However, every frequency has a maximum vertical angle at which it can be propagated and still be refracted back by the ionosphere. This angle is called the *critical angle*. The critical angle θ_c is shown in Figure 9-18.

A measurement technique called *ionospheric sounding* is sometimes used to determine the critical frequency. A signal is propagated straight up from the Earth's surface and gradually increased in frequency. At the lower frequencies, the signal will be completely

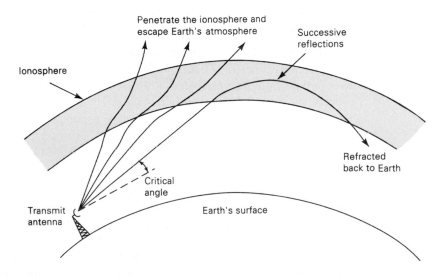

FIGURE 9-18 Critical angle

absorbed by the atmosphere. As the frequency is increased, however, it (or some portion of it) will be returned to Earth. At some frequency, however, the signal will pass through the Earth's atmosphere into outer space and not return to Earth. The highest frequency that will be returned to Earth in the vertical direction is the critical frequency.

Virtual Height

Virtual height is the height above Earth's surface from which a refracted wave appears to have been reflected. Figure 9-19 shows a wave that has been radiated from Earth's surface toward the ionosphere. The radiated wave is refracted back to Earth and follows path B. The actual maximum height that the wave reached is height h_a. However, path A shows the projected path that a reflected wave could have taken and still been returned to Earth at the same location. The maximum height that this hypothetical reflected wave would have reached is the virtual height (h_v).

Maximum Usable Frequency

The *maximum usable frequency* (MUF) is the highest frequency that can be used for sky-wave propagation between two specific points on Earth's surface. It stands to reason, then, that there are as many values possible for MUF as there are points on Earth and frequencies—an infinite number. MUF, as with the critical frequency, is a limiting frequency for sky-wave propagation. However, the maximum usable frequency is for a specific angle of incidence (the angle between the incident wave and the normal). Mathematically, MUF is

$$MUF = \frac{\text{critical frequency}}{\cos \theta} \qquad (9\text{-}18a)$$

$$= \text{critical frequency} \times \sec \theta \qquad (9\text{-}18b)$$

where θ is the angle of incidence.

Equation 9-18a is called the *secant law*. The secant law assumes a flat Earth and a flat reflecting layer, which, of course, can never exist. Therefore, MUF is used only for making preliminary calculations.

Due to the general instability of the ionosphere, the highest frequency used between two points is often selected lower than the MUF. It has been proven that operating at a frequency 85% of the MUF provides more reliable communications. This frequency is sometimes called the *optimum working frequency* (OWF).

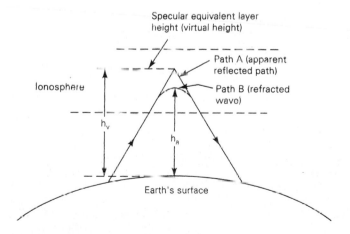

FIGURE 9-19 Virtual and actual height

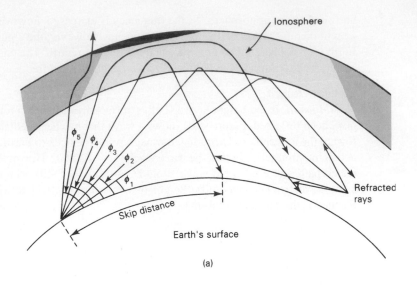

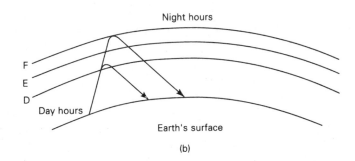

FIGURE 9-20 (a) Skip distance; (b) daytime-versus-nighttime propagation

Skip Distance

The *skip distance* (d_s) is the minimum distance from a transmit antenna that a sky wave of given frequency (which must be less than the MUF) will be returned to Earth. Figure 9-20a shows several rays with different elevation angles being radiated from the same point on Earth. It can be seen that the point where the wave is returned to Earth moves closer to the transmitter as the elevation angle (ϕ) is increased. Eventually, however, the angle of elevation is sufficiently high that the wave penetrates through the ionosphere and totally escapes Earth's atmosphere.

Figure 9-20b shows the effect on the skip distance of the disappearance of the D and E layers during nighttime. Effectively, the *ceiling* formed by the ionosphere is raised, allowing sky waves to travel higher before being refracted back to Earth. This effect explains how faraway radio stations are sometimes heard during the night that cannot be heard during daylight hours.

FREE-SPACE PATH LOSS

Free-space path loss is often defined as the loss incurred by an electromagnetic wave as it propagates in a straight line through a vacuum with no absorption or reflection of energy from nearby objects. This is a misstated and often misleading definition. Free-space path loss is a fabricated engineering quantity that evolved from manipulating communications system link budget equations into a particular format which includes transmit antenna gain, free-space path loss, and the effective area of the receiving antenna. No electromagnetic energy is actually lost—it merely spreads out as it propagates away from the source resulting in a lower power density at any given point a fixed distance from the source. Therefore, a more appropriate term for the phenomena is *spreading loss*. Spreading loss occurs simply because of the inverse-square law. The equation for free-space path loss is given as

$$L_p = \left(\frac{4\pi D}{\lambda}\right)^2 - \left(\frac{4\pi D}{c}\right)^2 \qquad (9\text{-}19)$$

where L_p = free-space path loss (unitless)
   D = distance (kilometers)
   f = frequency (hertz)
   λ = wavelength (meters)
   c = velocity of light in free space (3×10^8 meters per second)

Converting to dB yields

$$L_{p(dB)} = 20 \log \frac{4\pi f D}{c} = 20 \log \frac{4\pi}{c} + 20 \log f + 20 \log D$$

When the frequency is given in MHz and the distance in km,

$$L_{p(dB)} = 20 \log \frac{4\pi (10)^6 (10)^3}{3 \times 10^8} + 20 \log f_{(MHz)} + 20 \log D_{(km)} \qquad (9\text{-}20a)$$

$$= 32.4 + 20 \log f_{(MHz)} + 20 \log D_{(km)}$$

When the frequency is given in GHz and the distance in km,

$$L_{p(dB)} = 92.4 + 20 \log f_{(GHz)} + 20 \log D_{(km)} \qquad (9\text{-}20b)$$

Similar conversions can be made using distance in miles, frequency in kHz, and so on.

Example 9-2

For a carrier frequency of 6 GHz and a distance of 50 km, determine the free-space path loss.

Solution

$$L_p = 32.4 + 20 \log 6000 + 20 \log 50$$
$$= 32.4 + 75.6 + 34 = 142 \text{ dB}$$

or

$$L_p = 92.4 + 20 \log 6 + 20 \log 50$$
$$= 92.4 + 15.6 + 34 = 142 \text{ dB}$$

FADE MARGIN

Radio communications between remote locations, whether earth-to-earth or earth-to-satellite, require propagating electromagnetic signals through free space. As an electromagnetic wave propagates through Earth's atmosphere, the signal may experience intermittent losses in signal strength beyond the normal path loss. This loss can be attributed to several different phenomena and can include both short- and long-term effects. This variation in signal loss is called *fading* and can be attributed to weather disturbance, such as rainfall, snow, hail, and so forth; multiple transmission paths; and an irregular Earth surface. To accommodate temporary fading, an additional loss is added to the normal path loss. This loss is called *fade margin*.

Essentially, fade margin is a "fudge factor" included in the system gain equation that considers the nonideal and less predictable characteristics of radio wave propagation, such as *multipath propagation (multipath loss)* and *terrain sensitivity*. These characteristics cause temporary, abnormal atmospheric conditions that alter the free-space path loss and are usually detrimental to the overall system performance. Fade margin also considers system reliability objectives. Thus, fade margin is included in the system gain equation as a loss.

Solving the Barnett-Vignant reliability equations for a specified annual system availability for an unprotected, nondiversity system yields the following expression:

$$F_m = 30 \log D + 10 \log (6ABf) - 10 \log (1 - R) - 70 \qquad (9\text{-}21)$$

$$\underbrace{}_{\substack{\text{multipath} \\ \text{effect}}} \quad \underbrace{}_{\substack{\text{terrain} \\ \text{sensitivity}}} \quad \underbrace{}_{\substack{\text{reliability} \\ \text{objectives}}} \quad \underbrace{}_{\text{constant}}$$

where
F_m = fade margin (decibels)
D = distance (kilometers)
f = frequency (gigahertz)
R = reliability expressed as a decimal (i.e., 99.99% = 0.9999 reliability)
$1 - R$ = reliability objective for a one-way 400-km route
A = roughness factor
= 4 over water or a very smooth terrain
= 1 over an average terrain
= 0.25 over a very rough, mountainous terrain
B = factor to convert a worst-month probability to an annual probability
= 1 to convert an annual availability to a worst-month basis
= 0.5 for hot humid areas
= 0.25 for average inland areas
= 0.125 for very dry or mountainous areas

Example 9-3

Determine the fade margin for the following conditions: distance between sites, D = 40 km; frequency, f = 1.8 GHz; smooth terrain; humid climate; and a reliability objective 99.99%.

Solution Substituting into Equation 9-21 yields,

$$F_m = 30 \log 40 + 10 \log[(6)(4)(0.5)(1.8)] - 10 \log(1 - 0.9999) - 70$$
$$= 48.06 + 13.34 - (-40) - 70 = 31.4 \text{ dB}$$

QUESTIONS

9-1. Describe an electromagnetic ray; a wavefront.

9-2. Describe power density; voltage intensity.

9-3. Describe a spherical wavefront.

9-4. Explain the inverse square law.

9-5. Describe wave attenuation.

9-6. Describe wave absorption.

9-7. Describe refraction. Explain Snell's law for refraction.

9-8. Describe reflection.

9-9. Describe diffraction. Explain Huygens's principle.

9-10. Describe the composition of a good reflector.

9-11. Describe the atmospheric conditions that cause electromagnetic refraction.

9-12. Define *electromagnetic wave interference.*

9-13. Describe ground-wave propagation. List its advantages and disadvantages.

9-14. Describe space-wave propagation.

9-15. Explain why the radio horizon is at a greater distance than the optical horizon.

9-16. Describe the various layers of the ionosphere.

9-17. Describe sky-wave propagation.

9-18. Explain why ionospheric conditions vary with time of day, month of year, and so on.

9-19. Define *critical frequency; critical angle.*

9-20. Describe virtual height.

9-21. Define *maximum usable frequency.*

9-22. Define *skip distance* and give the reasons why it varies.

9-23. Describe path loss.

9-24. Describe fade margin.

9-25. Describe fading.

PROBLEMS

9-1. Determine the power density for a radiated power of 1000 W at distance of 20 km from an isotropic antenna.

9-2. Determine the power density for Problem 9-1 for a point that is 30 km from the antenna.

9-3. Describe the effects on power density if the distance from a transmit antenna is tripled.

9-4. Determine the radio horizon for a transmit antenna that is 100 ft high and a receiving antenna that is 50 ft high, and for antennas at 100 m and 50 m.

9-5. Determine the maximum usable frequency for a critical frequency of 10 MHz and an angle of incidence of 45°.

9-6. Determine the electric field intensity for the same point in Problem 9-1.

9-7. Determine the electric field intensity for the same point in Problem 9-2.

9-8. For a radiated power P_{rad} = 10 kW, determine the voltage intensity at a distance 20 km from the source.

9-9. Determine the change in power density when the distance from the source increases by a factor of 4.

9-10. If the distance from the source is reduced to one-half its value, what effect does this have on the power density?

9-11. The power density at a point from a source is 0.001 μW and the power density at another point is 0.00001 μW; determine the attenuation in decibels.

9-12. For a dielectric ratio $\sqrt{\epsilon_{r2} / \epsilon_{r1}}$ = 0.8 and an angle of incidence θ_i = 26°, determine the angle of refraction, θ_p

9-13. Determine the distance to the radio horizon for an antenna located 40 ft above sea level.

9-14. Determine the distance to the radio horizon for an antenna that is 40 ft above the top of a 4000-ft mountain peak.

9-15. Determine the maximum distance between identical antennas equidistant above sea level for Problem 9-13.

9-16. Determine the power density for a radiated power of 1200 W at distance of 50 km from an isotropic antenna.

9-17. Determine the power density for Problem 9-16 for a point 100 km from the same antenna.

9-18. Describe the effects on power density if the distance from a transmit antenna is reduced by a factor of 3

9-19. Determine the radio horizon for a transmit antenna that is 200 ft high and a receiving antenna that is 100 ft high, and for antennas at 200 m and 100 m.

9-20. Determine the maximum usable frequency for a critical frequency of 20 MHz and an angle of incidence of 35°.

9-21. Determine the voltage intensity for the same point in Problem 9-16.

9-22. Determine the voltage intensity for the same point in Problem 9-17.

9-23. Determine the change in power density when the distance from the source decreases by a factor of 8.

9-24. Determine the change in power density when the distance from the source increases by a factor of 8.

9-25. If the distance from the source is reduced to one-quarter its value, what effect does this have on the power density?

9-26. The power density at a point from a source is 0.002 μW and the power density at another point is 0.00002 μW, determine the attenuation in dB.

9-27. For a dielectric ratio of 0.4 and an angle of incidence $\theta_i = 18°$, determine the angle of refraction θ_r.

9-28. Determine the distance to the radio horizon for an antenna located 80 ft above sea level.

9-29. Determine the distance to the radio horizon for an antenna that is 80 ft above the top of a 5000-ft mountain.

9-30. Determine the maximum distance between identical antennas equidistant above sea level for Problem 9-29.

9-31. Determine the path loss for the following frequencies and distances:

f (MHz)	D (km)
400	0.5
800	0.6
3000	10
5000	5
8000	20
18,000	15

9-32. Determine the fade margin for a 30-km microwave hop. The RF frequency is 10 GHz, the terrain is water, and the reliability objective is 99.995%.

CHAPTER 10

Antennas and Waveguides

INTRODUCTION

An *antenna* is a metallic conductor system capable of radiating and capturing electromagnetic waves. Antennas are used to interface transmission lines to free space, free space to transmission lines, or both. In essence, a transmission line couples energy from a transmitter or a receiver to an antenna, which in turn couples the energy to the Earth's atmosphere and from the Earth's atmosphere to a transmission line. At the transmit end of a free-space radio communications system, an antenna converts electrical energy traveling along a transmission line into electromagnetic waves that are emitted into space. At the receive end, an antenna converts electromagnetic waves in space into electrical energy on a transmission line.

A *waveguide* is a special type of transmission line that consists of a conducting metallic tube through which high-frequency electromagnetic energy is propagated. A waveguide is used to efficiently interconnect high-frequency electromagnetic waves between an antenna and a transceiver.

BASIC ANTENNA OPERATION

Basic antenna operation is best understood by looking at the voltage standing-wave patterns on a transmission line, which are shown in Figure 10-1a. The transmission line is terminated in an open circuit, which represents an abrupt discontinuity to the incident voltage wave in the form of a phase reversal. The phase reversal results in some of the incident voltage being radiated, not reflected back toward the source. The radiated energy propagates away from the antenna in the form of transverse electromagnetic waves. The *radiation efficiency* of an open transmission line is extremely low. Radiation efficiency is the ratio of radiated to reflected energy. To radiate more energy, simply spread the conductors farther apart. Such an antenna is called a *dipole* (meaning two poles) and is shown in Figure 10-1b.

In Figure 10-1c, the conductors are spread out in a straight line to a total length of one-quarter wavelength. Such an antenna is called a basic *quarter-wave antenna* or a *vertical*

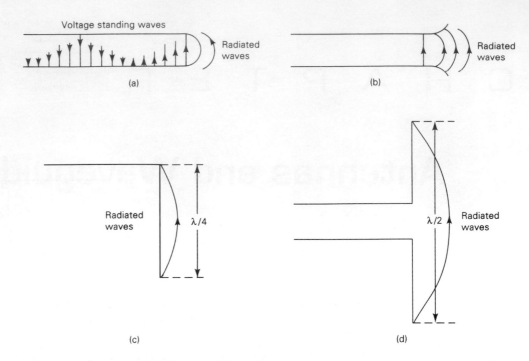

FIGURE 10-1 Radiation from a transmission line: (a) transmission-line radiation; (b) spreading conductors; (c) Marconi antenna; (d) Hertz antenna

monopole (sometimes called a Marconi antenna). A half-wave dipole is called a *Hertz antenna* and is shown in Figure 10-1d.

Antenna Equivalent Circuits

In radio communications systems, transmitters are connected to receivers through transmission lines, antennas, and free space. Electromagnetic waves are coupled from transmit to receive antennas through free space in a manner similar to the way energy is coupled from the primary to the secondary of a transformer. With antennas, however, the degree of coupling is much lower than with a transformer, and an electromagnetic wave is involved rather than just a magnetic wave. An antenna coupling system can be represented with a four-terminal network as shown in Figure 10-2a. Electromagnetic energy must be transferred from the transmitting antenna to free space then from free space to the receiving antenna. Figure 10-2b shows the equivalent circuit for a transmit antenna and Figure 10-2c shows the equivalent circuit for a receive antenna.

ANTENNA RECIPROCITY

A basic antenna is a *passive reciprocal device*—passive in that it cannot actually amplify a signal, at least not in the true sense of the word (however, you will see later in this chapter that an antenna can have gain). An antenna is a reciprocal device in that the transmit and receive characteristics and performance are identical (i.e., gain, directivity, frequency of operation, bandwidth, radiation resistance, efficiency, and so on).

Transmit antennas must be capable of handling high powers and, therefore, must be constructed with materials that can withstand high voltages and currents, such as metal tubing. Receive antennas, however, produce very small voltages and currents and can be constructed from small-diameter wire. In many radio communications systems, however, the same antenna is used for transmitting and receiving. If this is the case, the antenna must be

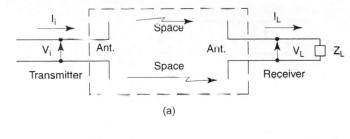

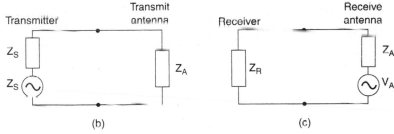

FIGURE 10-2 (a) Antenna as a four-terminal network; (b) transmit antenna equivalent circuit; (c) receive antenna equivalent circuit

constructed from heavy-duty materials. If one antenna is used for both transmitting and receiving, some means must be used to prevent the high-power transmit signals from being coupled into the relatively sensitive receiver. A special coupling device called a *diplexer* can be used to direct the transmit and receive signals and provide the necessary isolation.

Standard antennas have no active components (diodes, transistors, FETs, etc.); therefore, they are passive and reciprocal. In practice an active antenna does not exist. What is commonly called an active antenna is actually the combination of a passive antenna and a low-noise amplifier (LNA). Active antennas are nonreciprocal (i.e., they either transmit or receive but not both). It is important to note that active as well as passive antennas introduce power losses regardless of whether they are used for transmitting or receiving signals. Antenna gain is a misleading term that is explained in detail later in this chapter.

ANTENNA TERMINOLOGY AND DEFINITIONS

Antenna Coordinate System

The directional characteristics of an electromagnetic wave radiated or received by an antenna are generally described in terms of spherical coordinates as shown in Figure 10-3. Imagine the antenna placed in the center of the sphere and the distance to any point on the surface of the sphere can be defined in respect to the antenna by using the radius of the sphere d and angles θ and Φ. The x-y plane shown in the figure is referred to as the equatorial plane, and any plane at right angles to it is defined as a meridian plane.

Radiation Pattern

A *radiation pattern* is a *polar* diagram or graph representing field strengths or power densities at various angular positions relative to an antenna. If the radiation pattern is plotted in terms of electric field strength ($\mathcal{E}$) or power density ($\mathcal{P}$), it is called an *absolute* radiation pattern (i.e., variable distance, fixed power). If it plots field strength or power density with respect to the value at a reference point, it is called a *relative* radiation pattern (i.e., variable power, fixed distance). Figure 10-4a shows an absolute radiation pattern for an unspecified antenna. The pattern is plotted on *polar* coordinate paper with the heavy solid line representing points of equal power density (10 $\mu W/m^2$). The circular gradients indicate distance

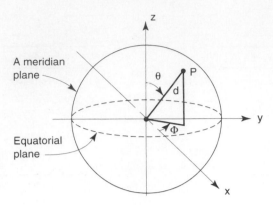

FIGURE 10-3 Spherical coordinates

in 2-km steps. It can be seen that maximum radiation is in a direction 90° from the reference. The power density 10 km from the antenna in a 90° direction is 10 μW/m^2. In a 45° direction, the point of equal power density is 5 km from the antenna; at 180°, only 4 km; and in a $-$90° direction, there is essentially no radiation.

In Figure 10-4a the primary beam is in a 90° direction and is called the *major lobe.* There can be more than one major lobe. There is also a *secondary* beam or *minor* lobe in a $-$180° direction. Normally, minor lobes represent undesired radiation or reception. Because the major lobe propagates and receives the most energy, that lobe is called the *front* lobe (the front of the antenna). Lobes adjacent to the front lobe are called *side* lobes (the 180° minor lobe is a side lobe), and lobes in a direction exactly opposite the front lobe are called *back* lobes (there is no back lobe shown on this pattern). The ratio of the front lobe power to the back lobe power is simply called the *front-to-back ratio,* and the ratio of the front lobe to a side lobe is called the *front-to-side ratio.* The line bisecting the major lobe, or pointing from the center of the antenna in the direction of maximum radiation, is called the *line of shoot,* or sometimes *point of shoot.*

Figure 10-4b shows a relative radiation pattern for an unspecified antenna. The heavy solid line represents points of equal distance from the antenna (10 km), and the circular gradients indicate power density in 1-μW/m^2 divisions. It can be seen that maximum radiation (5 μW/m^2) is in the direction of the reference (0°), and the antenna radiates the least power (1 μW/m^2) in a direction 180° from the reference. Consequently, the front-to-back ratio is 5:1 = 5. Generally, relative field strength and power density are plotted in decibels (dB), where dB = 20 log($\mathscr{E}/\mathscr{E}_{max}$) or 10 log($\mathscr{P}/\mathscr{P}_{max}$). Figure 10-4c shows a relative radiation pattern for power density in decibels. In a direction $\pm$45° from the reference, the power density is $-$3 dB (half-power) relative to the power density in the direction of maximum radiation (0°). Figure 10-4d shows a relative radiation pattern for power density for an omnidirectional antenna. An omnidirectional antenna radiates energy equally in all directions; therefore, the radiation pattern is simply a circle (actually, a sphere). Also, with an omnidirectional antenna, there are no front, back, or side lobes because radiation is equal in all directions.

The radiation patterns shown in Figure 10-4 are two dimensional. However, radiation from an actual antenna is three dimensional. Therefore, radiation patterns are taken in both the horizontal (from the top) and the vertical (from the side) planes. For the omnidirectional antenna shown in Figure 10-4d, the radiation patterns in the horizontal and vertical planes are circular and equal because the actual radiation pattern for an isotropic radiator is a sphere.

Recall from Chapter 9 that a true isotropic radiator radiates power at a constant rate uniformly in all directions. An ideal isotropic antenna also radiates all the power supplied to it. Isotropic radiators do not exist, however, and they are used only for analytical descriptions and comparisons.

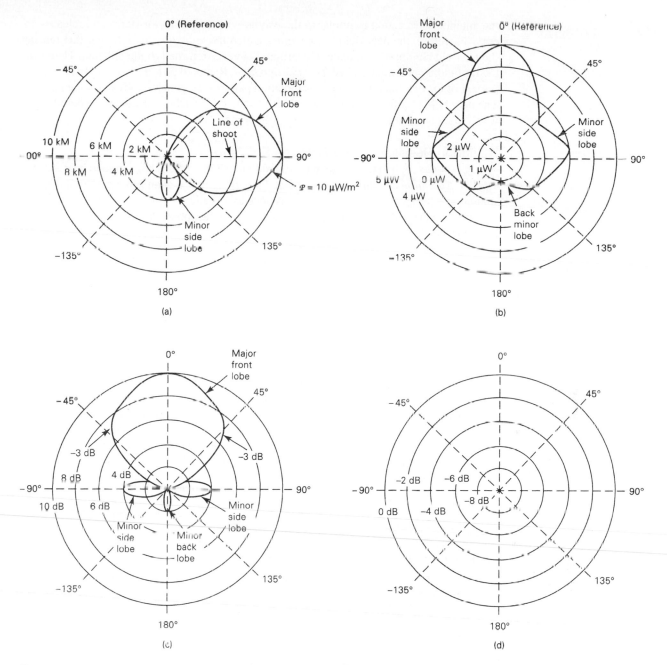

FIGURE 10-4 Radiation patterns: (a) absolute (fixed power) radiation pattern; (b) relative (fixed distance) radiation pattern; (c) relative (fixed distance) radiation pattern in decibels; and (d) relative (fixed distance) radiation pattern in decibels for an omnidirectional (point source) antenna

Near and Far Fields

The radiation field that is close to an antenna is not the same as the radiation field that is at a great distance. The term *near field* refers to the field pattern that is close to the antenna, and the term *far field* refers to the field pattern that is at great distance. During one-half of a cycle, power is radiated from an antenna where some of the power is stored temporarily in the near field. During the second half of the cycle, power in the near field is returned to the antenna. This action is similar to the way in which an inductor stores and releases energy. Therefore, the near field is sometimes called the *induction field*. Power that reaches the far field continues to radiate outward and is never returned to the antenna. Therefore, the far field is sometimes called the *radiation field*. Radiated power is usually the more important of the two; therefore, antenna radiation patterns are generally given for the far field. The near field is defined as the area within a distance D^2/λ from the antenna, where λ is the wavelength and D the antenna diameter in the same units.

Radiation Resistance and Antenna Efficiency

All the power supplied to an antenna is not radiated. Some of it is converted to heat and dissipated. *Radiation resistance* is somewhat "unreal" in that it cannot be measured directly. Radiation resistance is an ac antenna resistance and is equal to the ratio of the power radiated by the antenna to the square of the current at its feedpoint. Mathematically, radiation resistance is

$$R_r = \frac{P_{rad}}{i^2} \qquad (10\text{-}1)$$

where R_r = radiation resistance (ohms)
P_{rad} = power radiated by the antenna (watts)
i = antenna current at the feedpoint (ampere)

Radiation resistance is the resistance that, if it replaced the antenna, would dissipate exactly the same amount of power that the antenna radiates. The radiation resistance of an antenna as described in Equation 10-1 is in a sense a fictitious quantity because it is referenced to an arbitrary point on the antenna which would have different current values for different reference points. It is common practice, however, to refer the radiation resistance to the current maximum point or sometimes the current at the feed point, although in many cases the two points are one in the same. When referenced to the current maximum point, radiation resistance is sometimes called *loop radiation resistance,* because a current maximum is also called a current loop.

It seems apparent that radiation resistance is at times a rather nebulous concept as it is not always easily measured. It is a useful concept only when it is readily measurable and has no meaning for antennas in which there is no clearly defined current value to which it can be referenced.

Antenna efficiency is the ratio of the power radiated by an antenna to the sum of the power radiated and the power dissipated or the ratio of the power radiated by the antenna to the total input power. Mathematically, antenna efficiency is

$$\eta = \frac{P_{rad}}{P_{in}} \times 100 \qquad (10\text{-}2a)$$

where η = antenna efficiency (percentage)
P_{rad} = radiated power (watts)
P_{in} = input power (watts)

or

$$\eta = \frac{P_{rad}}{P_{rad} + P_d} \times 100 \qquad (10\text{-}2b)$$

where P_{rad} = power radiated by antenna (watts)
P_d = power dissipated in antenna (watts)

Figure 10-5 shows a simplified electrical equivalent circuit for an antenna. Some of the input power is dissipated in the effective resistance (ground resistance, corona, imper-

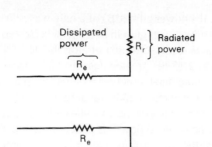

FIGURE 10-5 Simplified equivalent circuit of an antenna

fect dielectrics, eddy currents, and so on) and the remainder is radiated. The total antenna power is the sum of the dissipated and radiated powers. Therefore, in terms of resistance and current, antenna efficiency is

$$\eta = \frac{i^2 R_r}{i^2(R_r + R_e)} = \frac{R_r}{R_r + R_e} \tag{10-3}$$

where η = antenna efficiency
i = antenna current (ampere)
R_r = radiation resistance (ohms)
R_e = effective antenna resistance (ohms)

Directive Gain and Power Gain

The terms *directive gain* and *power gain* are often misunderstood and, consequently, misused. Directive gain is the ratio of the power density radiated in a particular direction to the power density radiated to the same point by a reference antenna, assuming both antennas are radiating the same amount of power. The relative power density radiation pattern for an antenna is actually a directive gain pattern if the power density reference is taken from a standard reference antenna, which is generally an isotropic antenna. The maximum directive gain is called *directivity*. Mathematically, directive gain is

$$D = \frac{\mathcal{P}}{\mathcal{P}_{ref}} \tag{10-4}$$

where D = directive gain (unitless)
D = power density at some point with a given antenna (watts per meter squared)
$\mathcal{P}_{ref}$ = power density a the same point with a reference antenna (watts per meter squared)

Power gain is the same as directive gain except that the total power fed to the antenna is used (i.e., antenna efficiency is taken into account). It is assumed that the given antenna and the reference antenna have the same input power and that the reference antenna is lossless ($\eta - 100\%$). Mathematically, power gain (A_p) is

$$A_p = D\eta \tag{10-5}$$

If an antenna is lossless, it radiates 100% of the input power and the power gain is equal to the directive gain. The power gain for an antenna is also given in decibels relative to some reference antenna. Therefore, power gain is

$$A_{P\,(dB)} = 10 \log \frac{\mathcal{P}\eta}{\mathcal{P}_{ref}} \tag{10-6}$$

For an isotropic reference, the power gain (dB) of a half-wave dipole is approximately 1.64 (2.15 dB). It is usual to state the power gain in decibels when referring to a λ/2 dipole (dBd). However, if reference is made to an isotropic radiator, the decibel figure is stated as dBi, or dB/isotropic radiator, and is 2.15 dB greater than if a half-wave dipole were used for the reference. It is important to note that the power radiated from an antenna can never exceed the input power. Therefore, the antenna does not actually amplify the input power. An antenna simply concentrates its radiated power in a particular direction. Therefore, points that are located in areas where the radiated power is concentrated realize an apparent gain relative to the power density at the same points had an isotropic antenna been used. If gain is realized in one direction, a corresponding reduction in power density (a loss) must be realized in another direction. The direction in which an antenna is "pointing" is always the direction of maximum radiation. Because an antenna is a reciprocal device, its radiation pattern is also its reception pattern. For maximum *captured* power, a receive antenna must be pointing in the direction from which reception is desired. Therefore, receive antennas have directivity and power gain just as transmit antennas do.

Effective Isotropic Radiated Power

Effective isotropic radiated power (EIRP) is defined as an equivalent transmit power and is expressed mathematically as

$$\text{EIRP} = P_{\text{rad}}D_t \text{ (watts)} \tag{10-7a}$$

where P_{rad} = total radiated power (watts)
              D_t = transmit antenna directive gain (unitless)

or $$\text{EIRP}_{(\text{dBm})} = 10 \log \frac{P_{\text{rad}}}{0.001} + 10 \log D_t \tag{10-7b}$$

or $$\text{EIRP}_{(\text{dBW})} = 10 \log (P_{\text{rad}}D_t) \tag{10-7c}$$

Equation 10-7a can be rewritten using antenna input power and power gain as

$$\text{EIRP} = P_{\text{in}}A_t \tag{10-7d}$$

where P_{in} = total antenna input power (watts)
              A_t = transmit antenna power gain (unitless)

or $$\text{EIRP}_{(\text{dBm})} = 10 \log \left(\frac{P_{\text{in}}A_t}{0.001} \right) \tag{10-7e}$$

$$\text{EIRP}_{(\text{dBW})} = 10 \log (P_{\text{in}}A_t) \tag{10-7f}$$

EIRP or simply ERP (effective radiated power) is the equivalent power that an isotropic antenna would have to radiate to achieve the same power density in the chosen direction at a given point as another antenna. For instance, if a given transit antenna has a power gain of 10, the power density a given distance from the antenna is 10 times greater than it would have been had the antenna been an isotropic radiator. An isotropic antenna would have to radiate 10 times as much power to achieve the same power density. Therefore, the given antenna effectively radiates 10 times as much power as an isotropic antenna with the same input power and efficiency.

To determine the power density at a given point distance R from a transmit antenna, Equation 9-5 can be expanded to include the transmit antenna gain and rewritten as

$$\mathcal{P} = \frac{P_{\text{in}}A_t}{4\pi R^2} \tag{10-8a}$$

or in terms of directive gain

$$\mathscr{P} = \frac{P_{rad}D_t}{4\pi R^2} \qquad (10\text{-}8b)$$

where $\mathscr{P}$ = power density (watts per meter squared)
P_{in} = transmit antenna input power (watts)
P_{rad} = power radiated from transmit antenna (watts)
A_t = transmit antenna power gain (unitless)
D_t = transmit antenna directive power gain (unitless)
R = distance from transmit antenna (meters)

Example 10-1

For a transmit antenna with a power gain $A_t = 10$ and an input power $P_{in} = 100$ W, determine
(a) EIRP in watts, dBm, and dBW.
(b) Power density at a point 10 km from the transmit antenna.
(c) Power density had an isotropic antenna been used with the same input power and efficiency.

Solution   (a) Substituting into Equations 10-7d, e, and f yields

$$EIRP = (100 \text{ W})(10)$$
$$= 1000 \text{ W}$$
$$EIRP_{(dBm)} = 10 \log \frac{1000}{0.001}$$
$$= 60 \text{ dBm}$$
$$EIRP_{(dBW)} = 10 \log 1000$$
$$= 30 \text{ dBW}$$

(b) Substituting into Equation 10-8a gives

$$\mathscr{P} = \frac{(100 \text{ W})(10)}{4\pi(10,000 \text{ m})^2}$$
$$= 0.796 \text{ } \mu\text{W/m}^2$$

(c) Substituting into Equation 9-5, we obtain

$$\mathscr{P} = \frac{(100 \text{ } W)}{4\pi(10,000 \text{ m})^2}$$
$$= 0.0796 \text{ } \mu\text{W/m}^2$$

It can be seen from Example 10-1 that the power density at a point 10 km from the transmit antenna is 10 times greater with the given antenna than it would be had an isotropic radiator been used. To achieve the same power density, the isotropic antenna would require an input power 10 times greater or 1000 W. The transmit antenna in the example effectively radiates the equivalent of 1000 W.

Example 10-2

For a transmit antenna with a radiation resistance $R_r = 72$ ohms, an effective antenna resistance $R_e = 8$ ohms, a directive gain $D = 20$, and an input power $P_{in} = 100$ W, determine
(a) Antenna efficiency.
(b) Antenna gain (absolute and dB).
(c) Radiated power in watts, dBm, and dBW.
(d) EIRP in watts, dBm, and dBW.

Solution   (a) Antenna efficiency is found by substituting into Equation 10-3

$$\eta = \frac{72}{72 + 8} \times 100$$
$$= 90\%$$

(b) Antenna gain is simply the product of the antenna's efficiency and directive gain

$$A = (0.9)(20)$$
$$= 18$$

and
$$A(\text{dB}) = 10 \log 18$$
$$= 12.55 \text{ dB}$$

(c) Radiated power is found by rearranging Equation 10-2a
$$P_{\text{rad}} = \eta P_{\text{in}}$$
$$= (0.9)(100 \text{ W})$$
$$= 90 \text{ W}$$
$$P_{\text{rad(dBm)}} = 10 \log \frac{90}{0.001}$$
$$= 49.54 \text{ dBm}$$
$$P_{\text{rad(dBW)}} = 10 \log 90$$
$$= 19.54 \text{ dBW}$$

(d) EIRP is found by substituting into Equations 10-7d, e, and f
$$\text{EIRP} = (100 \text{ W})(18)$$
$$= 1800 \text{ W}$$
$$\text{EIRP}_{\text{(dBm)}} = 10 \log \frac{1800}{0.001}$$
$$= 62.55 \text{ dBm}$$
$$\text{EIRP}_{\text{(dBW)}} = 10 \log 1800$$
$$= 32.55 \text{ dBW}$$

Captured Power Density

Antennas are reciprocal devices; thus, they have the same radiation resistance, efficiency, power gain, and directivity when used to receive electromagnetic waves as they have when transmitting electromagnetic waves. Consequently, the power density received or captured by an antenna is the product of the power density in the space immediately surrounding the receive antenna and the receive antenna's directive gain. Therefore, Equation 10-8a can be expanded to include the power gain of the receiver antenna and rewritten as

$$C = \frac{(P_{\text{in}})(A_t)(A_r)}{4\pi R^2} \qquad (10\text{-}9)$$

where C = captured power density (watts per meter squared)
P_{in} = transmit antenna input power (watts)
A_t = transmit antenna power gain (unitless)
A_r = receive antenna power gain (unitless)
R = distance between transmit and receive antennas (meters)

Captured power density is the power density (W/m^2) in space and a somewhat misleading quantity. What is more important is the actual power (in watts) that a receive antenna produces at its output terminals which, of course, depends on how much power is captured by the receive antenna and the antenna's efficiency.

Capture Area and Captured Power

Although a reciprocal relationship exists between transmitting and receiving antenna properties, it is often more useful to describe receiving properties in a slightly different way. Whereas power gain is the natural parameter for describing the increased power density of a transmitted signal due to the directional properties of the transmitting antenna, a related quantity called *capture area* is a more natural parameter for describing the reception properties of an antenna.

The *capture area* of an antenna is an *effective area* and can be described as follows. A transmit antenna radiates an electromagnetic wave that has a power density at the receive antenna's location in W/m^2. This is not the actual power received but rather the amount of power incident on, or passing through, each unit area of any imaginary surface that is per-power incident on, or passing through, each unit area of any imaginary surface that is perpendicular to the direction of propagation of the electromagnetic waves. A receiving antenna exposed to the electromagnetic field will have radio-frequency voltage and current induced in it, producing a corresponding radio-frequency power at the antenna's output terminals. In principle, the power available at the antenna's output terminals (in watts) is the *captured power*. The captured power can be delivered to a load such as a transmission line or a receiver's input circuitry. For the captured power to appear at the antenna's output terminals, the antenna must have captured power from a surface in space immediately surrounding the antenna.

Captured power is directly proportional to the received power density and the effective capture area of the receive antenna. As one might expect, the physical cross sectional area of an antenna and its effective capture area are not necessarily equal. In fact, sometimes antennas with physically small cross-sectional areas may have effective capture areas that are considerably larger than their physical areas. In these instances, it is as though the antenna is able to reach out and capture or absorb power from an area larger than its physical size.

There is an obvious relationship between an antenna's size and its ability to capture electromagnetic energy. This suggests that there must also be a connection between antenna gain and the antenna's receiving cross-sectional area. Mathematically, the two quantities are related as follows:

$$A_c = \frac{A_r \lambda^2}{4\pi} \tag{10-10}$$

where A_c = effective capture area (meters squared)
   λ = wavelength of receive signal (meters)
   A_r = receive antenna power gain (unitless)

Rearranging Equation 10-10 and solving for antenna gain gives us

$$A_r = \frac{A_c 4\pi}{\lambda^2} \tag{10-11}$$

The captured power is simply the product of the power density in the area surrounding the receive antenna and the receive antenna's capture area. Mathematically, captured power is

$$P_{cap} = \mathcal{P} A_c \tag{10-12}$$

where P_{cap} = captured power (watts)
   A_c = effective capture area (meters squared)
   $\mathcal{P}$ = captured power density (watts per meter squared)

Equations 10-8a and 10-10 can be substituted into Equation 10-12 yielding

$$P_{cap} = \frac{(P_{in}A_t)(A_r\lambda^2)}{16\pi^2 R^2} \tag{10-13}$$

where P_{cap} = captured power (watts)
   λ = wavelength of receive signal (meters)
   A_r = receive antenna power gain (unitless)
   A_t = transmit antenna power gain (unitless)
   R = distance between transmit and receive antennas (meters)
   P_{in} = transmit antenna input power (watts)

Example 10-3

For a receive power density of 10 μW/m^2 and a receive antenna with a capture area of 0.2 m^2, determine
(a) Captured power in watts.
(b) Captured power in dBm.

Solution   (a) Substituting into Equation 10-12 yields

$$P_{cap} = (10 \ \mu W/m^2)(0.2 m^2)$$

$$= 2 \ \mu W$$

(b)

$$P_{cap}(dBm) = 10 \log \frac{2 \ \mu W}{0.001 \ W}$$

$$= -27 \ dBm$$

Antenna Polarization

The *polarization* of an antenna refers simply to the orientation of the electric field radiated from it. An antenna may be *linearly* (generally, either horizontally or vertically polarized, assuming that the antenna elements lie in a horizontal or vertical plane), *elliptically,* or *circularly polarized.* If an antenna radiates a vertically polarized electromagnetic wave, the antenna is defined as vertically polarized; if an antenna radiates a horizontally polarized electromagnetic wave, the antenna is said to be horizontally polarized; if the radiated electric field rotates in an elliptical pattern, it is elliptically polarized; and if the electric field rotates in a circular pattern, it is circularly polarized. Figure 10-6 shows the various polarizations described.

Antenna Beamwidth

Antenna *beamwidth* is simply the angular separation between the two half-power (-3 dB) points on the major lobe of an antenna's plane radiation pattern, usually taken in one of the "principal" planes. The beamwidth for the antenna whose radiation pattern is shown in Figure 10-7 is the angle formed between points A, X, and B (angle θ). Points A and B are the half-power points (the power density at these points is one-half of what it is an equal dis-

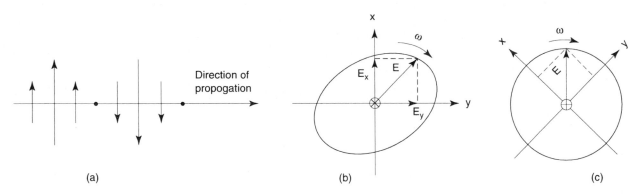

FIGURE 10-6   Antenna polarizations: (a) linear; (b) elliptical polarization; (c) circular polarization

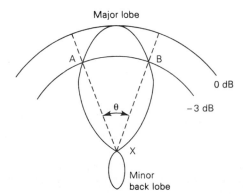

FIGURE 10-7   Antenna beamwidth

tance from the antenna in the direction of maximum radiation). Antenna beamwidth is sometimes called -3-dB beamwidth or half-power beamwidth.

Antenna gain is inversely proportional to beamwidth (i.e., the higher the gain of an antenna, the narrower the beamwidth). An omnidirectional (isotropic) antenna radiates equally well in all directions. Thus, it has a gain of unity and a beamwidth of 360°. Typical antennas have beamwidths between 30° and 60° and it is not uncommon for high-gain microwave antennas to have a beamwidth as low as 1°.

Antenna Bandwidth

Antenna *bandwidth* is vaguely defined as the frequency range over which antenna operation is "satisfactory." Bandwidth is normally taken as the difference between the half-power frequencies (difference between the highest and lowest frequencies of operation), but sometimes refers to variations in the antenna's input impedance. Antenna bandwidth is often expressed as a percentage of the antenna's optimum frequency of operation.

Example 10-4

Determine the percent bandwidth for an antenna with an optimum frequency of operation of 400 MHz and -3-dB frequencies of 380 MHz and 420 MHz.

Solution
$$\text{Bandwidth} = \frac{420 - 380}{400} \times 100$$
$$= 10\%$$

Antenna Input Impedance

Radiation from an antenna is a direct result of the flow of RF current. The current flows to the antenna through a transmission line, which is connected to a small gap between the conductors that make up the antenna. The point on the antenna where the transmission line is connected is called the antenna input terminal or simply the *feedpoint*. The feedpoint presents an ac load to the transmission line called the *antenna input impedance*. If the transmitter's output impedance and the antenna's input impedance are equal to the characteristic impedance of the transmission line, there will be no standing waves on the line, and maximum power is transferred to the antenna and radiated.

Antenna input impedance is simply the ratio of the antenna's input voltage to input current. Mathematically, input impedance is

$$Z_{\text{in}} = \frac{E_i}{I_i} \tag{10-14}$$

where
Z_{in} = antenna input impedance (ohms)
E_i = antenna input voltage (volts)
I_i = antenna input current (ampere)

Antenna input impedance is generally complex; however, if the feedpoint is at a current maximum and there is no reactive component, the input impedance is equal to the sum of the radiation resistance and the effective resistance.

BASIC ANTENNAS

Elementary Doublet

The simplest type of antenna is the *elementary doublet*. The elementary doublet is an electrically short dipole and is often referred to simply as a *short dipole, elementary dipole,* or *Hertzian dipole.* Electrically short means short compared with one-half wavelength but not necessarily one with a uniform current (generally, any dipole that is less than one-tenth wavelength long is considered electrically short). In reality, an elementary doublet cannot be achieved; however, the concept of a short dipole is useful in understanding more practical antennas.

An elementary doublet has uniform current throughout its length. However, the current is assumed to vary sinusoidally in time and at any instant is

$$i(t) = I \sin(2\pi f t + \theta)$$

where
$i(t)$ = instantaneous current (amperes)
I = peak amplitude of the RF current (amperes)
f = frequency (hertz)
t = instantaneous time (seconds)
θ = phase angle (radians)

With the aid of Maxwell's equations, it can be shown that the far (radiation) field is

$$\mathscr{E} = \frac{60\pi I l \sin \phi}{\lambda R} \qquad (10\text{-}15)$$

where
$\mathscr{E}$ = electric field intensity (volts per meter)
I = dipole current (amperes rms)
l = end-to-end length of the dipole (meters)
R = distance from the dipole (meters)
λ = wavelength (meters)
ϕ = angle between the axis of the antenna and the direction of radiation as shown in Figure 10-8a

Plotting Equation 10-15 gives the relative electric field intensity pattern for an elementary dipole, which is shown in Figure 10-8b. It can be seen that radiation is maximum at right angles to the dipole and falls off to zero at the ends.

The relative power density pattern can be derived from Equation 10-10 by substituting $\mathscr{P} = \mathscr{E}^2/120\pi$. Mathematically, we have

$$\mathscr{P} = \frac{30\pi I^2 l^2 \sin^2\phi}{\lambda^2 R^2} \qquad (10\text{-}16)$$

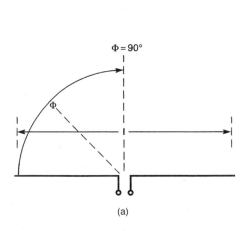

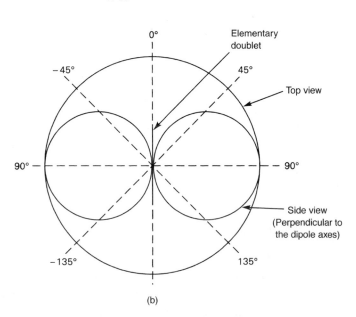

(a)   (b)

FIGURE 10-8 (a) Elementary doublet; (b) relative radiation pattern

Half-Wave Dipole

The linear half-wave dipole is one of the most widely used antennas at frequencies above 2 MHz. At frequencies below 2 MHz, the physical length of a half-wavelength antenna is prohibitive. The half-wave dipole is generally referred to as a *Hertz antenna* after Heinrich Hertz, who was the first to demonstrate the existence of electromagnetic waves.

A Hertz antenna is a *resonant* antenna. That is, it is a multiple of quarter-wavelengths long and open circuited at the far end. Standing waves of voltage and current exist along a resonant antenna. Figure 10-9 shows the idealized voltage and current distributions along a half-wave dipole. Each pole of the antenna looks as if it were an open quarter-wavelength section of transmission line. Thus, there is a voltage maximum and current minimum at the ends and a voltage minimum and current maximum in the middle. Consequently, assuming that the feedpoint is in the center of the antenna, the input impedance is E_{min}/I_{max} and a minimum value. The impedance at the ends of the antenna is E_{max}/I_{min} and a maximum value. Figure 10-10 shows the impedance curve for a center-fed half-wave dipole. The impedance varies from a maximum value at the ends of approximately 2500 Ω to a minimum value at the feedpoint of approximately 73 Ω (of which between 68 Ω and 70 Ω is the radiation resistance).

For an ideal antenna, the efficiency is 100%, directivity equals power gain, and the radiation resistance equals the input impedance (73), thus

$$D = A = \frac{120}{\text{radiation resistance}} \qquad (10\text{-}17)$$

$$\frac{120}{72}$$

$$= 1.667$$

and

$$10 \log 1.64 = 2.18 \text{ dB}$$

A wire radiator such as a half-wave dipole can be thought of as an infinite number of elementary doublets placed end to end. Therefore, the radiation pattern can be obtained by integrating Equation 10-15 over the length of the antenna. The free-space radiation pattern for a half-wave dipole depends on whether the antenna is placed horizontally or vertically with respect to Earth's surface. Figure 10-11a shows the vertical (from the side) radiation pattern for a vertically mounted half-wave dipole. Note that two major lobes radiate in opposite directions that are at right angles to the antenna. Also note that the lobes are not circles. Circular lobes are obtained only for the ideal case when the current is constant throughout the antenna's length, and this is unachievable in a practical antenna. Figure 10-11b shows the cross-sectional view. Note that the radiation pattern has a figure-eight pattern and resembles the shape of a doughnut. Maximum radiation is in a plane parallel to

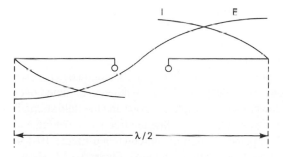

FIGURE 10-9 Idealized voltage and current distributions along a half-wave dipole

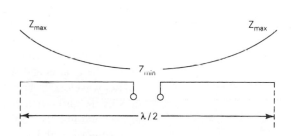

FIGURE 10-10 Impedance curve for a center-fed half-wave dipole

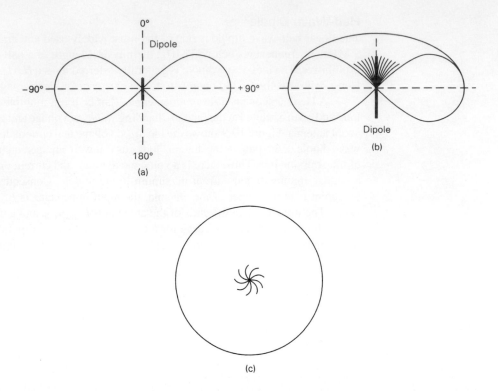

FIGURE 10-11 Half-wave dipole radiation patterns: (a) vertical (side) view of a vertically mounted dipole; (b) cross-sectional view; (c) horizontal (top) view

Earth's surface. The higher the angle of elevation is, the less the radiation, and for 90° there is no radiation. Figure 10-11c shows the horizontal (from the top) radiation pattern for a vertically mounted half-wave dipole. The pattern is circular because radiation is uniform in all directions perpendicular to the antenna.

Ground effects on a half-wave dipole. The radiation patterns shown in Figure 10-11 are for free-space conditions. In Earth's atmosphere, wave propagation is affected by antenna orientation, atmospheric absorption, and ground effects such as reflection. The effect of ground reflection for an ungrounded half-wave dipole is shown in Figure 10-12. The antenna is mounted an appreciable number of wavelengths (height h) above the surface of Earth. The field strength at any given point in space is the sum of the direct and ground-reflected waves. The ground-reflected wave appears to be radiating from an image antenna distance h below Earth's surface. This apparent antenna is a mirror image of the actual antenna. The ground-reflected wave is inverted 180° and travels a distance $2h \sin \theta$ farther than the direct wave to reach the same point in space (point P). The resulting radiation pattern is a summation of the radiations from the actual antenna and the mirror antenna. Note that this is the classical ray-tracing technique used in optics.

Figure 10-13 shows the vertical radiation patterns for a horizontally mounted half-wave dipole one-quarter and one-half wavelength above the ground. For an antenna mounted one-quarter wavelength above the ground, the lower lobe is completely gone and the field strength directly upward is doubled. Figure 10-13a shows in the dotted line the free-space pattern and in the solid line the vertical distribution in a plane through the antenna, and Figure 10-13b shows the vertical distribution in a plane at right angles to the antenna. Figure 10-13c shows the vertical radiation pattern for a horizontal dipole one-half wavelength above the ground. The figure shows that the pattern is now broken into two lobes, and the direction of maximum

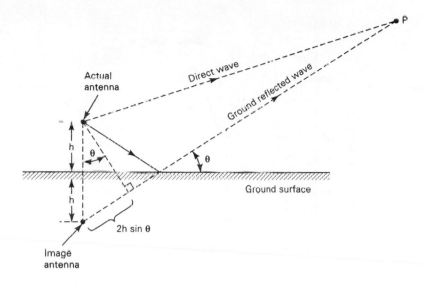

Actual antenna

Direct wave

Ground reflected wave

P

h

θ

θ

Ground surface

h

2h sin θ

Image antenna

FIGURE 10-12 Ground effects on a half-wave dipole

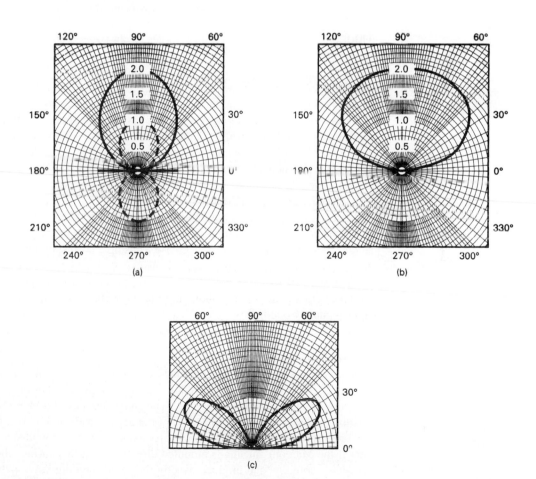

FIGURE 10-13 Vertical radiation pattern for a half-wave dipole. (a) In a plane through antenna;
(b) in a plane at right angles to antenna; (c) horizontal dipole one-half wavelength above ground

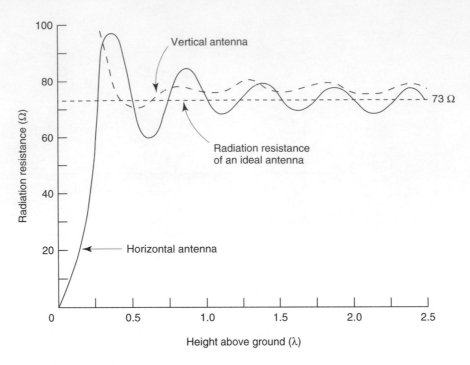

FIGURE 10-14 Radiation resistance versus height above ground

radiation (end view) is now at 30° to the horizontal instead of directly upward. There is no component along the ground for horizontal polarization because of the phase shift of the reflected component. Ground-reflected waves have similar effects on all antennas. The best way to eliminate or reduce the effect of ground reflected waves is to mount the antenna far enough above Earth's surface to obtain free-space conditions. However, in many applications, this is impossible. Ground reflections are sometimes desirable to get the desired elevation angle for the major lobe's maximum response.

The height of an ungrounded antenna above Earth's surface also affects the antenna's radiation resistance. This is due to the reflected waves cutting through or intercepting the antenna and altering its current. Depending on the phase of the ground-reflected wave, the antenna current can increase or decrease, causing a corresponding increase or decrease in the input impedance.

Figure 10-14 shows how the radiation resistance of vertical and horizontal half-wave dipoles varies with distance above the Earth's surface. As the figure shows, once beyond approximately one-half wavelength above ground, the effect of reflections is reduced dramatically and the radiation resistance remains relatively constant.

Grounded Antenna

A *monopole* (single pole) antenna one-quarter wavelength long, mounted vertically with the lower end either connected directly to ground or grounded through the antenna coupling network, is called a *Marconi antenna*. The characteristics of a Marconi antenna are similar to those of the Hertz antenna because of the ground-reflected waves. Figure 10-15a shows the voltage and current standing waves for a quarter-wave grounded antenna. It can be seen that if the Marconi antenna is mounted directly on Earth's surface the actual antenna and its *image* combine and produce exactly the same standing-wave patterns as those of the half-wave ungrounded (Hertz) antenna. Current maxima occur at the grounded ends, which causes high current flow through ground. To reduce power losses, the ground should be a good conductor, such as rich, loamy soil. If the ground is a poor conductor, such as sandy

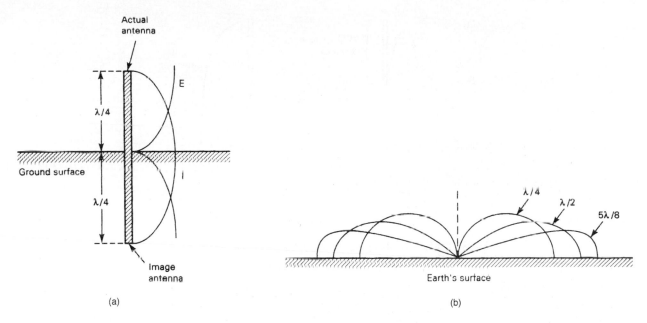

FIGURE 10-15 Quarter-wave grounded antenna: (a) voltage and current standing waves; (b) radiation pattern.

or rocky terrain, an artificial *ground plane* system made of heavy copper wires spread out radially below the antenna may be required. Another way of artificially improving the conductivity of the ground area below the antenna is with a *counterpoise*. A counterpoise is a wire structure placed below the antenna and erected above the ground. The counterpoise should be insulated from earth ground. A counterpoise is a form of capacitive ground system; capacitance is formed between the counterpoise and Earth's surface.

Figure 10-15b shows the radiation pattern for a quarter-wave grounded (Marconi) antenna. It can be seen that the lower half of each lobe is canceled by the ground-reflected waves. This is generally of no consequence because radiation in the horizontal direction is increased, thus increasing radiation along Earth's surface (ground waves) and improving area coverage. It can also be seen that increasing the antenna length improves horizontal radiation at the expense of sky-wave propagation. This is also shown in Figure 10-15b. Optimum horizontal radiation occurs for an antenna that is approximately five-eighths wavelength long. For a one-wavelength antenna, there is no ground-wave propagation.

A Marconi antenna has the obvious advantage over a Hertz antenna of being only half as long. The disadvantage of a Marconi antenna is that it must be located close to the ground.

ANTENNA LOADING

Thus far, we have considered antenna length in terms of wavelengths rather than physical dimensions. By the way, how long is a quarter-wavelength antenna? For a transmit frequency of 1 GHz, one-quarter wavelength is 0.075 m (2.95 in.). However, for a transmit frequency of 1 MHz, one-quarter wavelength is 75 m, and at 100 kHz, one-quarter wavelength is 750 m. It is obvious that the physical dimensions for low-frequency antennas are not practical, especially for mobile radio applications. However, it is possible to increase the electrical length of an antenna by a technique called *loading*. When an antenna is loaded, its physical length remains unchanged although its effective electrical length is increased. Several techniques are used for loading antennas.

Loading Coils

Figure 10-16a shows how a coil (inductor) added in series with a dipole antenna effectively increases the antenna's electrical length. Such a coil is appropriately called a *loading coil*.

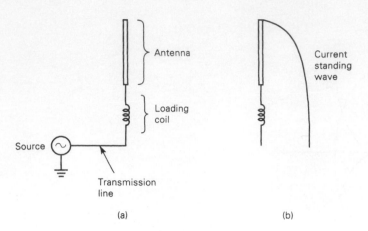

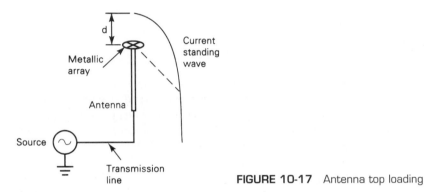

FIGURE 10-16 Loading coil: (a) antenna with loading coil; (b) current standing wave with loading coil

FIGURE 10-17 Antenna top loading

The loading coil effectively cancels out the capacitance component of the antenna input impedance. Thus, the antenna looks as if it were a resonant circuit, is resistive, and can now absorb 100% of the incident power. Figure 10-16b shows the current standing-wave patterns on an antenna with a loading coil. The loading coil is generally placed at the bottom of the antenna, allowing the antenna to be easily tuned to resonance. A loading coil effectively increases the radiation resistance of the antenna by approximately 5 Ω. Note also that the current standing wave has a maximum value at the coil, increasing power losses, creating a situation of possible corona, and effectively reducing the radiation efficiency of the antenna.

Top Loading

Loading coils have several shortcomings that can be avoided by using a technique called antenna *top loading*. With top loading, a metallic array that resembles a spoked wheel is placed on top of the antenna. The wheel increases the shunt capacitance to ground, reducing the overall antenna capacitance. Antenna top loading is shown in Figure 10-17. Notice that the current standing-wave pattern is pulled up along the antenna as though the antenna length had been increased distance *d,* placing the current maximum at the base. Top loading results in a considerable increase in the radiation resistance and radiation efficiency. It also reduces the voltage of the standing wave at the antenna base. Unfortunately, top loading is awkward for mobile applications.

The current loop of the standing wave can be raised even further (improving the radiation efficiency even more) if a *flat top* is added to the antenna. If a vertical antenna is

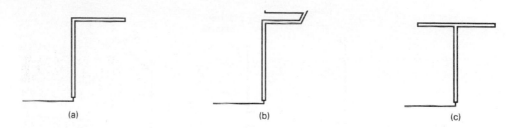

(a)   (b)   (c)

FIGURE 10-18   Flat-top antenna loading

folded over on top to form an L or T, as shown in Figure 10-18, the current loop will occur nearer the top of the radiator. If the flat top and vertical portions are each one-quarter wavelength long, the current maximum will occur at the top of the vertical radiator.

ANTENNA ARRAYS

An antenna *array* is formed when two or more antenna elements are combined to form a single antenna. An antenna element is an individual radiator such as a half- or quarter-wave dipole. The elements are physically placed in such a way that their radiation fields interact with each other, producing a total radiation pattern that is the vector sum of the individual fields. The purpose of an array is to increase the directivity of an antenna system and concentrate the radiated power within a smaller geographic area.

In essence, there are two types of antenna elements: *driven* and *parasitic* (nondriven). Driven elements are directly connected to the transmission line and receive power from or are driven by the source. Parasitic elements are not connected to the transmission line; they receive energy only through mutual induction with a driven element or another parasitic element. A parasitic element that is longer than the driven element from which it receives energy is called a *reflector.* A reflector effectively reduces the signal strength in its direction and increases it in the opposite direction. Therefore, it acts as if it were a concave mirror. This action occurs because the wave passing through the parasitic element induces a voltage that is reversed 180° with respect to the wave that induced it. The induced voltage produces an in-phase current and the element radiates (it actually reradiates the energy it just received). The reradiated energy sets up a field that cancels in one direction and reinforces in the other. A parasitic element that is shorter than its associated driven element is called a *director.* A director increases field strength in its direction and reduces it in the opposite direction. Therefore, it acts as if it were a convergent convex lens. This is shown in Figure 10-19.

Radiation directivity can be increased in either the horizontal or vertical plane, depending on the placement of the elements and whether they are driven. If not driven, the pattern depends on whether the elements are directors or reflectors. If driven, the pattern depends on the relative phase of the feeds.

Broadside Array

A *broadside array* is one of the simplest types of antenna arrays. It is made by simply placing several resonant dipoles of equal size (both length and diameter) in parallel with each other and in a straight line (collinear). All elements are fed in phase from the same source. As the name implies, a broadside array radiates at right angles to the plane of the array and radiates very little in the direction of the plane. Figure 10-20a shows a broadside array that is comprised of four driven half-wave elements separated by one-half wavelength. Therefore, the signal that is radiated from element 2 has traveled one-half wavelength farther than the signal radiated from element 1 (i.e., they are radiated 180° out of phase). Crisscrossing the transmission line produces an additional 180° phase shift. Therefore, the currents in all

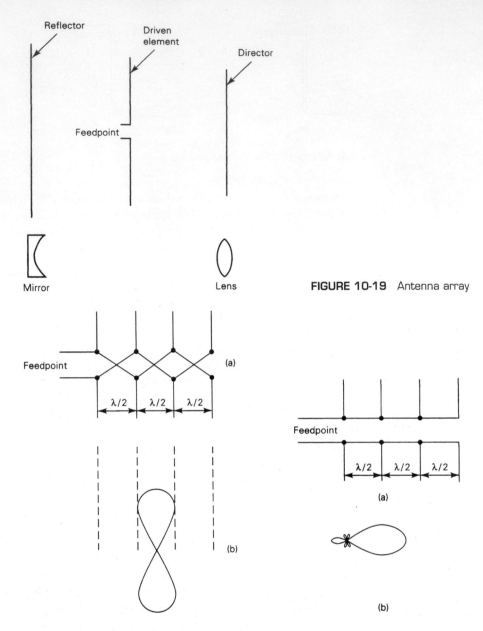

FIGURE 10-19 Antenna array

FIGURE 10-20 Broadside antenna: (a) broadside array; (b) radiation pattern

FIGURE 10-21 End-fire antenna: (a) end-fire array; (b) radiation pattern

the elements are in phase, and the radiated signals are in phase and additive in a plane at right angles to the plane of the array. Although the horizontal radiation pattern for each element by itself is omnidirectional, when combined, their fields produce a highly directive bidirectional radiation pattern (10-20b). Directivity can be increased even further by increasing the length of the array by adding more elements.

End-Fire Array

An *end-fire array* is essentially the same element configuration as the broadside array except that the transmission line is not crisscrossed between elements. As a result, the fields are additive in line with the plane of the array. Figure 10-21 shows an end-fire array and its resulting radiation pattern.

TABLE 10-1

Type	Power Gain (dB)	Beamwidth (°)	Front-to-Back Ratio (dB)
Isotropic radiator	0	360	0
Half-wave dipole	2.16	80	0
1 element (director or reflector)	7.16	52	15 or 20
2 elements (1 reflector + 1 director or 2 directors)	10.16	40	23
3 elements (1 reflector + 2 directors)	12.06	36	24
4 elements (1 reflector + 3 directors)	13.26	34	25
6 elements (1 reflector + 5 directors)	14.56	30	27
10 elements (1 reflector + 9 directors)	15.66	24	29.5

0.1 λ = director spacing
0.15 λ = reflector spacing
0.05 λ = length change per element

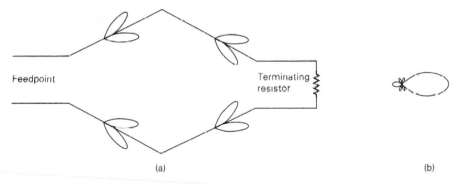

(a)   (b)

FIGURE 10-22 Rhombic antenna: (a) rhombic array; (b) radiation pattern

Table 10-1 shows the effects on the gain, beamwidth, and front-to-back ratio of a half-wave dipole by adding directors and reflectors.

Nonresonant Array: The Rhombic Antenna

The *rhombic antenna* is a nonresonant antenna that is capable of operating satisfactorily over a relatively wide bandwidth, making it ideally suited for HF transmission (range 3 MHz to 30 MHz). The rhombic antenna is made up of four nonresonant elements each several wavelengths long. The entire array is terminated in a resistor if unidirectional operation is desired. The most widely used arrangement for the rhombic antenna resembles a transmission line that has been pinched out in the middle; it is shown in Figure 10-22. The antenna is mounted horizontally and placed one-half wavelength or more above the ground. The exact height depends on the precise radiation pattern desired. Each set of elements acts as a transmission line terminated in its characteristic impedance; thus, waves are radiated only in the forward direction. The terminating resistor absorbs approximately one-third of the total antenna input power. Therefore, a rhombic antenna has a maximum efficiency of 67%. Gains of over 40 (16 dB) have been achieved with rhombic antennas.

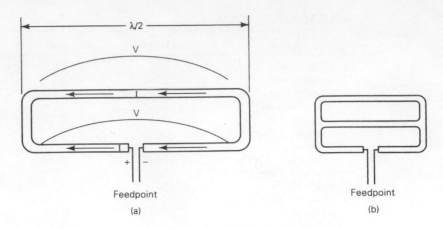

FIGURE 10-23 (a) Folded dipole; (b) three-element folded dipole

SPECIAL-PURPOSE ANTENNAS

Folded Dipole

A two-wire *folded dipole* and its associated voltage standing-wave pattern are shown in Figure 10-23a. The folded dipole is essentially a single antenna made up of two elements. One element is fed directly, whereas the other is conductively coupled at the ends. Each element is one-half wavelength long. However, because current can flow around corners, there is a full wavelength of current on the antenna. Therefore, for the same input power, the input current will be one-half that of the basic half-wave dipole and the input impedance is four times higher ($4 \times 72 = 288$). The input impedance of a folded dipole is equal to the half-wave impedance ($72 \ \Omega$) times the number of folded wires squared. For example, if there are three dipoles, as shown in Figure 10-23b, the input impedance is $3^2 \times 72 = 648 \ \Omega$. Another advantage of a folded dipole over a basic half-wave dipole is wider bandwidth. The bandwidth can be increased even further by making the dipole elements larger in diameter (such an antenna is appropriately called a *fat dipole*). However, fat dipoles have slightly different current distributions and input impedance characteristics than thin ones.

Yagi-Uda antenna. A widely used antenna that commonly uses a folded dipole as the driven element is the *Yagi-Uda antenna,* named after two Japanese scientists who invented it and described its operation. (The Yagi-Uda generally is called simply Yagi.) A Yagi antenna is a linear array consisting of a dipole and two or more parasitic elements: one reflector and one or more directors. A simple three-element Yagi is shown in Figure 10-24a. The driven element is a half-wavelength folded dipole. (This element is referred to as the driven element because it is connected to the transmission line; however, it is generally used for receiving only.) The reflector is a straight aluminum rod approximately 5% longer than the dipole, and the director is cut approximately 5% shorter than the driven element. The spacing between elements is generally between 0.1 and 0.2 wavelength. Figure 10-24b shows the radiation pattern for a Yagi antenna. The typical directivity for a Yagi is between 7 dB and 9 dB. The bandwidth of the Yagi can be increased by using more than one folded dipole, each cut to a slightly different length. Therefore, the Yagi antenna is commonly used for VHF television reception because of its wide bandwidth (the VHF TV band extends from 54 MHz to 216 MHz). Table 10-2 lists the element spacings for Yagi arrays with from two to eight elements.

Turnstile Antenna

A turnstile antenna is formed by placing two dipoles at right angles to each other, 90° out of phase as shown in Figure 10-25a. The radiation pattern shown in Figure 10-25b is the

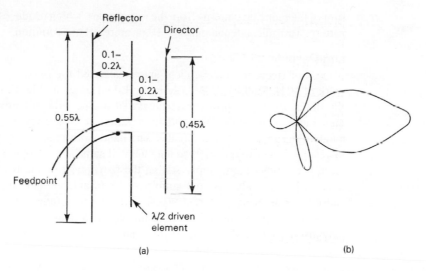

FIGURE 10-24   Yagi-Uda antenna: (a) three-element Yagi; (b) radiation pattern

TABLE 10-2   Element Spacing for Yagi Arrays (All units in wavelength, λ)

Element Spacing	Number of Elements						
	2	3	4	5	6	7	8
Reflector from driven element	0.19	0.19	0.19	0.18	0.18	0.18	0.18
Director 1 from driven element	—	0.17	0.16	0.16	0.16	0.16	0.15
Director 2 from director 1	—	—	0.16	0.18	0.20	0.21	0.22
Director 3 from director 2	—	—		0.20	0.25	0.30	0.30
Director 4 from director 3	—	—	—	—	0.28	0.28	0.29
Director 5 from director 4	—	—	—	—	—	0.30	0.30
Director 6 from director 5	—	—	—	—	—	—	0.35
Director 7 from director 6	—	—	—	—	—	—	—

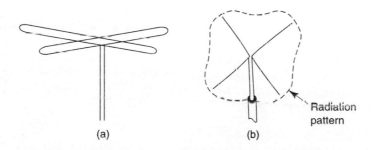

FIGURE 10-25   (a) Turnstile antenna; (b) radiation pattern

sum of the radiation patterns from the two dipoles, which produces a nearly omnidirectional pattern. Turnstile antenna gains of 10 or more dB are common.

Log-Periodic Antenna

A class of frequency-independent antennas called *log periodics* evolved from the initial work of V. H. Rumsey, J. D. Dyson, R. H. DuHamel, and D. E. Isbell at the University of Illinois in 1957. The primary advantage of log-periodic antennas is the independence of their radiation resistance and radiation pattern to frequency. Log-periodic antennas have bandwidth ratios of 10:1 or greater. The bandwidth ratio is the ratio of the highest to the lowest frequency over which an antenna will satisfactorily operate. The bandwidth ratio is often used rather than simply stating the percentage of the bandwidth to the center frequency. Log periodics are not simply a type of antenna but rather a class of antenna, because there are many different types, some that are quite unusual. Log-periodic antennas can be unidirectional or bidirectional and have a low-to-moderate directive gain. High gains may also be achieved by using them as an element in a more complicated array.

The physical structure of a log-periodic antenna is repetitive, which results in repetitive behavior in its electrical characteristics. In other words, the design of a log-periodic antenna consists of a basic geometric pattern that repeats, except with a different size pattern. A basic log-periodic dipole array is probably the closest that a log period comes to a conventional antenna; it is shown in Figure 10-26. It consists of several dipoles of different length and spacing that are fed from a single source at the small end. The transmission line is crisscrossed between the feedpoints of adjacent pairs of dipoles. The radiation pattern for a basic log-period antenna has maximum radiation outward from the small end. The lengths of the dipoles and their spacing are related in such a way that adjacent elements have a constant ratio to each other. Dipole lengths and spacings are related by the formula

$$\frac{R_2}{R_1} = \frac{R_3}{R_2} = \frac{R_4}{R_3} = \frac{1}{\tau} = \frac{L_2}{L_1} = \frac{L_3}{L_2} = \frac{L_4}{L_3} \tag{10-18}$$

or

$$\frac{1}{\tau} = \frac{R_n}{R_{n-1}} = \frac{L_n}{L_{n-1}}$$

where R = dipole spacing (inches)
  L = dipole length (inches)
  τ = design ratio (number less than 1)

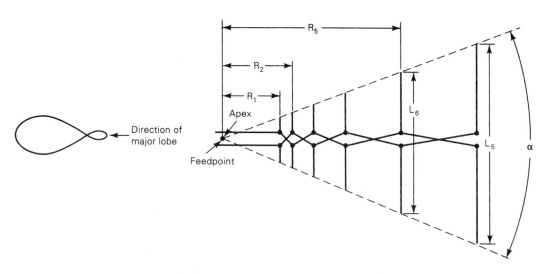

FIGURE 10-26 Log-periodic antenna

The ends of the dipoles lie along a straight line, and the angle where they meet is designated α. For a typical design, $\tau = 0.7$ and $\alpha = 30°$. With the preceding structural stipulations, the antenna input impedance varies repetitively when plotted as a function of frequency, and when plotted against the log of the frequency, varies periodically (hence the name "log periodic"). A typical plot of the input impedance is shown in Figure 10-27. Although the input impedance varies periodically, the variations are not necessarily sinusoidal. Also, the radiation pattern, directivity, power gain, and beamwidth undergo a similar variation with frequency.

The magnitude of a log-frequency period depends on the design ratio and, if two successive maxima occur at frequencies f_1 and f_2, they are related by the formula

$$\log f_2 - \log f_1 = \log \frac{f_2}{f_1} = \log \frac{1}{\tau} \qquad (10\text{-}19)$$

Therefore, the measured properties of a log-periodic antenna at frequency f will have identical properties at frequency τf, $\tau^2 f$, $\tau^3 f$, and so on. Log-periodic antennas, as are rhombic antennas, are used mainly for HF and VHF communications. However, log-periodic antennas do not have a terminating resistor and are, therefore, more efficient. Very often, TV antennas advertised as "high-gain" or "high-performance" antennas are log-period antennas.

Loop Antenna

The most fundamental *loop antenna* is simply a single-turn coil of wire that is significantly shorter than one wavelength and carries RF current. Such a loop is shown in Figure 10-28. If the radius (r) is small compared with a wavelength, current is essentially in phase throughout the loop. A loop can be thought of as many elemental dipoles connected together. Dipoles are straight; therefore, the loop is actually a polygon rather than circular. However, a circle can be approximated if the dipoles are assumed to be sufficiently short. The loop is surrounded by a magnetic field that is at right angles to the wire, and the directional pattern is independent of its exact shape. Generally, loops are circular; however, any

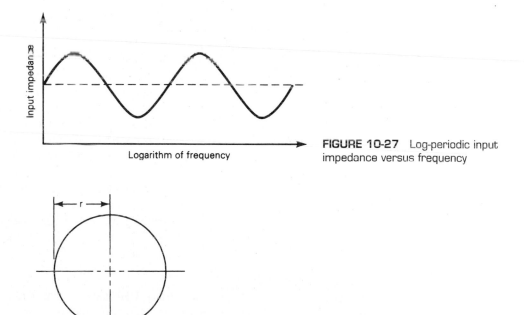

FIGURE 10-27 Log-periodic input impedance versus frequency

FIGURE 10-28 Loop antenna

shape will work. The radiation pattern for a loop antenna is essentially the same as that of a short horizontal dipole.

The radiation resistance for a small loop is

$$R_r = \frac{31{,}200A^2}{\lambda^4} \tag{10-20}$$

where A is the area of the loop. For very low frequency applications, loops are often made with more than one turn of wire. The radiation resistance of a multiturn loop is simply the radiation resistance for a single-turn loop times the number of turns squared. The polarization of a loop antenna, as that of an elemental dipole, is linear. However, a vertical loop is vertically polarized and a horizontal loop is horizontally polarized.

Small vertically polarized loops are very often used as direction-finding antennas. The direction of the received signal can be found by orienting the loop until a null or zero value is found. This is the direction of the received signal. Loops have an advantage over most other types of antennas in direction finding in that loops are generally much smaller and, therefore, more easily adapted to mobile communications applications.

Phased Array Antennas

A *phased array antenna* is a group of antennas or a group of antenna arrays that, when connected together, function as a single antenna whose beamwidth and direction (i.e., radiation pattern) can be changed electronically without having to physically move any of the individual antennas or antenna elements within the array. The primary advantage of phased array antennas is that they eliminate the need for mechanically rotating antenna elements. In essence, a phased array is an antenna whose radiation pattern can be electronically adjusted or changed. The primary application of phased arrays is in radar when radiation patterns must be capable of being rapidly changed to follow a moving object. However, governmental agencies that transmit extremely high-power signals to select remote locations all over the world, such as Voice of America, also use adjustable phased antenna arrays to direct their transmissions.

The basic principle of phased arrays is based on interference among electromagnetic waves in free space. When electromagnetic energies from different sources occupy the same space at the same time, they combine, sometimes constructively (aiding each other) and sometimes destructively (opposing each other).

There are two basic kinds of phased antenna arrays. In the first type, a single relatively high-power output device supplies transmit power to a large number of antennas through a set of power splitters and phase shifters. How much of the total transmit power goes to each antenna and the phase of the signal are determined by an intricate combination of adjustable attenuators and time delays. The amount of loss in the attenuators and the phase shift introduced in the time delays is controlled by a computer. The time delays pass the RF signal without distorting it, other than to provide a specific amount of time delay (phase shift). The second kind of phased antenna arrays uses approximately as many low-power variable output devices as there are radiating elements, and the phase relationship among the output signals is controlled with phase shifters. In both types of phased arrays, the radiation pattern is selected by changing the phase delay introduced by each phase shifter. Figure 10-29 shows a phased antenna array that uses several identical antenna elements, each with its own adjustable phase delay.

Helical Antenna

A *helical antenna* is a broadband VHF or UHF antenna that is ideally suited for applications for which radiating circular rather than horizontal or vertical polarized electromagnetic waves are required. A helical antenna can be used as a single-element antenna or stacked horizontally or vertically in an array to modify its radiation pattern by increasing the gain and decreasing the beamwidth of the primary lobe.

Variable phase waveforms

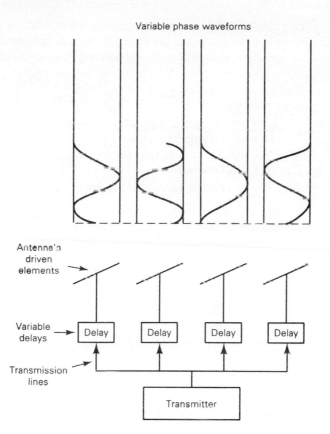

FIGURE 10-29 Phased array antenna

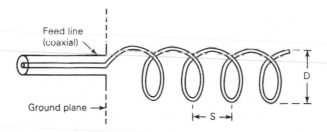

FIGURE 10-30 End-fire helical antenna

A basic end-fire helical antenna is shown in Figure 10-30. The driven element of the antenna consists of a loosely wound rigid helix with an axis length approximately equal to the product of the number of turns and the distance between turns (pitch). A helical antenna is mounted on a ground plane made up of either solid metal or a metal screen that resembles chicken wire. With a helical antenna, there are two modes of propagation: *normal* and *axial.* In the normal mode, electromagnetic radiation is in a direction at right angles to the axis of the helix. In the axial mode, radiation is in the axial direction and produces a broadband, relatively directional pattern. If the circumference of the helix is approximately equal to one wavelength, traveling waves propagate around the turns of the helix and radiate a circularly polarized wave. With the dimensions shown in Figure 10-30, frequencies within ±20% of the center frequency produce a directivity of almost 25 and a beamwidth of 90° between nulls.

The gain of a helical antenna depends on several factors, including the diameter of the helix, the number of turns in the helix, the pitch or spacing between turns, and the frequency of operation. Mathematically, the power gain of a helical antenna is

$$A_{p(\text{dB})} = 10 \log \left[15 \left(\frac{\pi D}{\lambda} \right)^2 \frac{(NS)}{\lambda} \right] \qquad (10\text{-}21)$$

where $A_{p(\text{dB})}$ = antenna power gain (dB)
        D = helix diameter (meters)
        N = number of turns (any positive integer)
        S = pitch (meters)
        λ = wavelength (meters per cycle)

Typically, a helical antenna will have between a minimum of 3 or 4 and a maximum of 20 turns and power gains between 15 dB and 20 dB. The 3-dB beamwidth of a helical antenna can be determined with the following mathematical expression:

$$\theta = \frac{52}{(\pi D / \lambda)(\sqrt{NS/\lambda})} \qquad (10\text{-}22)$$

where θ = beamwidth (degrees)
        D = helix diameter (meters)
        N = number of turns (any positive integer)
        S = pitch (meters)
        λ = wavelength (meters per cycle)

From Equations 10-21 and 10-22, it can be seen that, for a given helix diameter and pitch, the power gain increases proportionally to the number of turns and the beamwidth decreases. Helical antennas provide bandwidths anywhere between ±20% of the center frequency up to as much as a 2:1 span between the maximum and minimum operating frequencies.

UHF AND MICROWAVE ANTENNAS

Antennas used for UHF (0.3 GHz to 3 GHz) and microwave (1 GHz to 100 GHz) must be highly directive. An antenna has an apparent gain because it concentrates the radiated power in a narrow beam rather than sending it uniformly in all directions, and the beamwidth decreases with increases in antenna gain. The relationship among antenna area, gain, and beamwidth are shown in Figure 10-31. Microwave antennas ordinarily have half-power beamwidths on the order of 1° or less. A narrow beamwidth minimizes the effects of interference from outside sources and adjacent antennas. However, for line-of-site transmission, such as used with microwave radio, a narrow beamwidth imposes several limitations, such as mechanical stability and fading, which can lead to problems in antenna lineup.

All the electromagnetic energy emitted by a microwave antenna is not radiated in the direction of the *main lobe* (beam); some of it is concentrated in *minor lobes* called *side lobes,* which can be sources of interference into or from other microwave signal paths. Figure 10-32 shows the relationship between the main beam and the side lobes for a typical microwave antenna, such as a parabolic reflector.

Three important characteristics of microwave antennas are the front-to-back ratio, side-to-side coupling, and back-to-back coupling. The *front-to-back ratio* of an antenna is defined as the ratio of its maximum gain in the forward direction to its maximum gain in its backward direction. The front-to-back ratio of an antenna in an actual installation may be 20 dB or more below its isolated or free-space value because of foreground reflections from objects in or near the main transmission lobe. The front-to-back ratio of a microwave antenna is critical in radio system design because the transmit and receive antennas at repeater stations are often located opposite each other on the same structure (microwave ra-

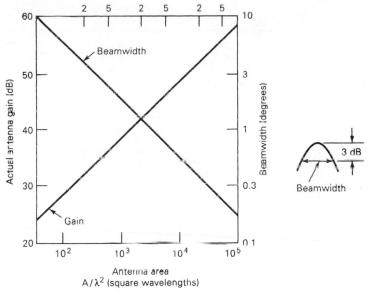

Note: Abscissa is actual antenna area, and actual
antenna gain is taken to be 3 dB below theoretical.

FIGURE 10-31   Antenna power gain and beamwidth relationship

dio systems and repeaters are discussed in more detail in Chapter 17). *Side-to-side* and *back-to-back coupling* express in decibels the coupling loss between antennas carrying transmitter output signals and nearby antennas carrying receiver input signals. Typically, transmitter output powers are 60 dB or higher in signal level than receiver input levels; accordingly, the coupling losses must be high to prevent a transmit signal from one antenna interfering with a receive signal of another antenna.

Highly directional (high gain) antennas are used with *point-to-point* microwave systems. By focusing the radio energy into a narrow beam that can be directed toward the receiving antenna, the transmitting antenna can increase the effective radiated power by several orders of magnitude over that of a nondirectional antenna. The receiving antenna, in a manner analogous to that of a telescope, can also increase the effective received power by a similar amount. The most common type of antenna used for microwave transmission and reception is the parabolic reflector.

Parabolic Reflector Antenna

Parabolic reflector antennas provide extremely high gain and directivity and are very popular for microwave radio and satellite communications links. A parabolic antenna consists of two main parts: a *parabolic reflector* and the active element called the *feed mechanism*. In essence, the feed mechanism houses the primary antenna (usually a dipole or a dipole array), which radiates electromagnetic waves toward the reflector. The reflector is a passive device that simply reflects the energy radiated by the feed mechanism into a concentrated, highly directional emission in which the individual waves are all in phase with each other (an in-phase wavefront).

Parabolic reflectors.   The parabolic reflector is probably the most basic component of a parabolic antenna. Parabolic reflectors resemble the shape of a plate or dish; therefore, they are sometimes called *parabolic dish* antennas or simply *dish* antennas. To understand how a parabolic reflector works, it is necessary to first understand the geometry of a *parabola.* A parabola is a plane curve that is expressed mathematically as $y = ax^2$ and defined as the locus of a point that moves so that its distance from another point (called the *focus*) added to its

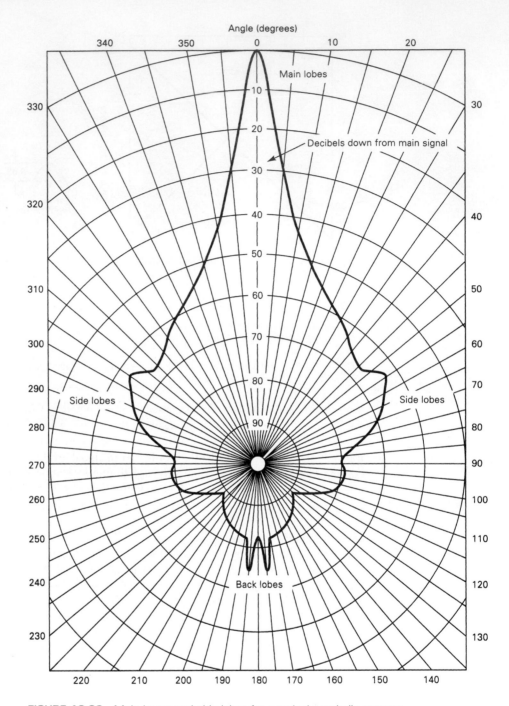

FIGURE 10-32 Main beam and side lobes for a typical parabolic antenna

distance from a straight line (called the *directrix*) is of constant length. Figure 10-33 shows the geometry of a parabola whose focus is at point *F* and whose axis is line *XY*.

For the parabola shown in Figure 10-33, the following relationships exist:

$$FA + AA' = FB + BB' = FC + CC' = k \quad \text{(a constant length)}$$

and FX = focal length of the parabola (meters)
       k = a constant for a given parabola (meters)
     WZ = directrix length (meters)

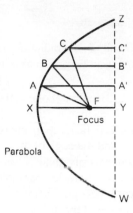

FIGURE 10-33 Geometry of a parabola

The ratio of the focal length to the diameter of the mouth of the parabola (*FX/WZ*) is called the *aperture ratio* or simply *aperture* of the parabola; the same term is used to describe camera lenses. A parabolic reflector is obtained when the parabola is revolved around the *XY* axis. The resulting curved surface dish is called a paraboloid. The reflector behind the bulb of a flashlight or the headlamp of an automobile has a paraboloid shape to concentrate the light in a particular direction.

A parabolic antenna consists of a paraboloid reflector illuminated with microwave energy radiated by a feed system located at the focus point. If electromagnetic energy is radiating toward the parabolic reflector from the focus, all radiated waves will travel the same distance by the time they reach the directrix, regardless from which point on the parabola they are reflected. Thus, all waves radiated toward the parabola from the focus will be in phase when they reach the directrix (line *WZ*). Consequently, radiation is concentrated along the *XY* axis, and cancellation takes place in all other directions. A paraboloid reflector used to receive electromagnetic energy exhibits exactly the same behavior. Thus, a parabolic antenna exhibits the *principle of reciprocity* and works equally well as a receive antenna for waves arriving from the *YY* direction (normal to the directrix). Rays received from all other directions are canceled at that point.

It is not necessary that the dish have a solid metal surface to efficiently reflect or receive the signals. The surface can be a mesh and still reflect or receive almost as much energy as a solid surface, provided the width of the openings is less than 0.1 wavelength. Using a mesh rather than a solid conductor considerably reduces the weight of the reflector. Mesh reflectors are also easier to adjust, are affected less by wind, and in general provide a much more stable structure.

Parabolic Antenna Beamwidth.   The three-dimensional radiation from a parabolic reflector has a main lobe that resembles the shape of a fat cigar in direction *XY* The approximate −3-dB beamwidth for a parabolic antenna in degrees is given as

$$\theta = \frac{70\lambda}{D}$$ (10-23a)

or

$$\theta = \frac{70c}{fD}$$ (10-23b)

where θ = beamwidth between half-power points (degrees)
λ = wavelength (meters)
$c = 3 \times 10^8$ meters per second
D = antenna mouth diameter (meters)
f = frequency (hertz)

and $$\phi_0 = 2\theta \qquad (10\text{-}24)$$

where ϕ_0 equals the beamwidth between nulls in the radiation pattern (degrees). Equations 10-23a and b and 10-24 are accurate when used for antennas with large apertures (i.e., narrow beamwidths).

Parabolic Antenna Efficiency (η). In a parabolic reflector, reflectance from the surface of the dish is not perfect. Therefore, a small portion of the signal radiated from the feed mechanism is absorbed at the dish surface. In addition, energy near the edge of the dish does not reflect but rather is diffracted around the edge of the dish. This is called *spillover* or *leakage*. Due to dimensional imperfections, only about 50% to 75% of the energy emitted from the feed mechanism is actually reflected by the paraboloid. Also, in a real antenna the feed mechanism is not a point source; it occupies a finite area in front of the reflector and actually obscures a small area in the center of the dish and causes a shadow area in front of the antenna that is incapable of either gathering or focusing energy. These imperfections contribute to a typical efficiency for a parabolic antenna of only about 55% ($\eta = 0.55$). That is, only 55% of the energy radiated by the feed mechanism actually propagates forward in a concentrated beam.

Parabolic Antenna Power Gain. For a transmit parabolic antenna, the power gain is approximated as

$$A_p = \eta\left(\frac{\pi D}{\lambda}\right)^2 \qquad (10\text{-}25a)$$

where A_p = power gain with respect to an isotropic antenna (unitless)
 D = mouth diameter of parabolic reflector (meters)
 η = antenna efficiency (antenna radiated power relative to the power radiated by the feed mechanism) (unitless)
 λ = wavelength (meters per cycle)

For a typical antenna efficiency of 55% ($\eta = 0.55$), Equation 10-25a reduces to

$$A_p = \frac{5.4D^2f^2}{c^2} \qquad (10\text{-}25b)$$

where c is the velocity of propagation (3×10^8 m/s). In decibel form

$$A_{p(\text{dB})} = 20\log f_{(\text{MHz})} + 20\log D_{(\text{m})} - 42.2 \qquad (10\text{-}25c)$$

where A_p = power gain with respect to an isotropic antenna (decibels)
 D = mouth diameter of parabolic reflector (meters)
 f = frequency (megahertz)
 42.2 = constant (decibels)

For an antenna efficiency of 100%, add 2.66 dB to the value computed with Equation 10-25c.

From Equations 10-25a, b, and c, it can be seen that the power gain of a parabolic antenna is inversely proportional to the wavelength squared. Consequently, the area (size) of the dish is an important factor when designing parabolic antennas. Very often, the area of the reflector itself is given in square wavelengths (sometimes called the *electrical* or *effective* area of the reflector). The larger the area is, the larger the ratio of the area to a wavelength, and the higher the power gain.

For a receive parabolic antenna, the surface of the reflector is again not completely illuminated, effectively reducing the area of the antenna. In a receiving parabolic antenna, the effective area is called the *capture area* and is always less than the actual mouth area.

The capture area can be calculated by comparing the power received with the power density of the signal being received. Capture area is expressed mathematically as

$$A_c = kA \tag{10-26}$$

where A_c = capture area (square meters)
       A = actual area (square meters)
       k = aperture efficiency, a constant that is dependent on the type of antenna used and configuration (approximately 0.55 for a paraboloid fed by a half-wave dipole)

Therefore, the power gain for a receive parabolic antenna is

$$A_p = \frac{4\pi A_c}{\lambda^2} = \frac{4\pi k A}{\lambda^2} \tag{10-27a}$$

Substituting the area of the mouth of a paraboloid into Equation 10-27a, the power gain of a parabolic receive antenna with an efficiency $\eta = 0.55$ can be closely approximated as

$$A_p = 5.4\left(\frac{D}{\lambda}\right)^2 \tag{10-27b}$$

where D = dish diameter (meters)
      λ = wavelength (meters per cycle)

In decibel form, $A_{p(dB)} = 10 \log\left[5.4\left(\frac{D}{\lambda}\right)^2\right]$ (10-27c)

The term k in Equation 10-26 is called *aperture efficiency* (or sometimes *illumination efficiency*). Aperture efficiency considers both the radiation pattern of the primary radiator and the effect introduced by the ratio of the focal length of the antenna to the reflector diameter (f/D). This ratio is called *aperture number.* Aperture number determines the angular aperture of the reflector, which indirectly determines how much of the primary radiation is reflected by the parabolic dish. Figure 10-34 illustrates radiation directions for parabolic reflectors (a) when the focal point is outside the reflector and (b) when the focal point is inside the reflector.

The transmit power gain calculated using Equation 10-25c and the receive antenna power gain calculated using Equation 10-27c will yield approximately the same results for a given antenna, thus proving the reciprocity of parabolic antennas.

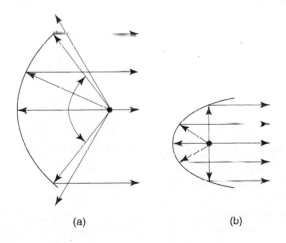

(a)   (b)

FIGURE 10-34 Radiation directions for parabolic reflectors: (a) focal point outside the reflector; (b) focal point inside the reflector

The radiation pattern shown in Figure 10-32 is typical for both transmit and receive parabolic antennas. The power gain within the main lobe is approximately 75 dB more than in the backward direction and almost 65 dB more than the maximum side lobe gain.

Example 10-5

For a 2-m diameter parabolic reflector with 10 W of power radiated by the feed mechanism operating at 6 GHz with a transmit antenna efficiency of 55% and an aperture efficiency of 55%, determine

(a) Beamwidth.
(b) Transmit power gain.
(c) Receive power gain.
(d) Effective isotropic radiated power (EIRP).

Solution (a) The beamwidth is found by substituting into Equation 10-23b.

$$\theta = \frac{70(3 \times 10^8)}{(6 \times 10^9)(2)} = 1.75°$$

(b) The transmit power gain is found by substituting into Equation 10-25c.

$$A_{p(\text{dB})} = 20 \log 6000 + 20 \log 2 - 42.2 = 39.4 \text{ dB}$$

(c) The receive power gain is found by substituting into Equation 10-27c.

$$\lambda = \frac{c(\text{m/s})}{\text{frequency (Hz)}} = \frac{3 \times 10^8}{6 \times 10^9} = 0.05 \text{ m/cycle}$$

$$A_{p(\text{dB})} = 10 \log\left[5.4\left(\frac{2}{0.05}\right)^2\right] = 39.4 \text{ dB}$$

(d) The EIRP is the product of the radiated power times the transmit antenna gain or, in decibels,

$$\text{EIRP} = A_{p(\text{dB})} + P_{\text{radiated(dBm)}}$$

$$= 39.4 + 10 \log \frac{10}{0.001}$$

$$= 39.4 \text{ dB} + 40 \text{ dBm} = 79.4 \text{ dBm}$$

Feed mechanisms.   The feed mechanism in a parabolic antenna actually radiates the electromagnetic energy and, therefore, is often called the *primary antenna*. The feed mechanism is of primary importance because its function is to radiate the energy toward the reflector. An ideal feed mechanism should direct all the energy toward the parabolic reflector and have no shadow effect. In practice, this is impossible to accomplish, although if care is taken when designing the feed mechanism, most of the energy can be radiated in the proper direction, and the shadow effect can be minimized. There are three primary types of feed mechanisms for parabolic antennas: center feed, horn feed, and Cassegrain feed.

Center Feed.   Figure 10-35 shows a diagram for a center-fed paraboloid reflector with an additional *spherical reflector.* The primary antenna is placed at the focus. Energy radiated toward the reflector is reflected outward in a concentrated beam. However, energy not reflected by the paraboloid spreads in all directions and has the tendency of disrupting the overall radiation pattern. The spherical reflector redirects such emissions back toward the parabolic reflector, where they are rereflected in the proper direction. Although the additional spherical reflector helps to concentrate more energy in the desired direction, it also has a tendency to block some of the initial reflections. Consequently, the good it accomplishes is somewhat offset by its own shadow effect, and its overall performance is only marginally better than without the additional spherical reflector.

Horn Feed.   Figure 10-36a shows a diagram for a parabolic reflector using a horn feed. With a horn-feed mechanism, the primary antenna is a small horn antenna rather than a simple dipole or dipole array. The horn is simply a flared piece of waveguide material that is placed at the focus and radiates a somewhat directional pattern toward the parabolic reflector. When a propagating electromagnetic field reaches the mouth of the horn, it continues to propagate in the same general direction, except that, in accordance with Huygens's

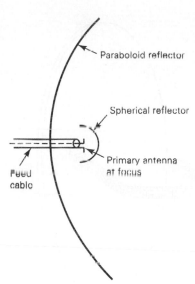

FIGURE 10-35 Parabolic antenna with a center feed

principle, it spreads laterally, and the wavefront eventually becomes spherical. The horn structure can have several different shapes, as shown in Figure 10-36b: sectoral (flaring only in one direction), pyramidal, or conical. As with the center feed, a horn feed presents somewhat of an obstruction to waves reflected from the parabolic dish.

The beamwidth of a horn in a plane containing the guide axis is inversely proportional to the horn mouth dimension in that plane. Approximate formulas for the half-power beamwidths of optimum-flare horns in the E and H planes are

$$\theta_E = \frac{56\lambda}{d_E} \tag{10-28a}$$

$$\theta_H = \frac{56\lambda}{d_H} \tag{10-28b}$$

where θ_E = half-power E-plane beamwidth (degrees)
   θ_H = half-power H-plane beamwidth (degrees)
   λ = wavelength (meters)
   d_E = E-plane mouth dimension (meters)
   d_H = H-plane mouth dimension (meters)

Cassegrain Feed. The Cassegrain feed is named after an eighteenth-century astronomer and evolved directly from astronomical optical telescopes. Figure 10-37 shows the basic geometry of a Cassegrain-feed mechanism. The primary radiating source is located in or just behind a small opening at the vertex of the paraboloid, rather than at the focus. The primary antenna is aimed at a small secondary reflector (*Cassegrain subreflector*) located between the vertex and the focus.

The rays emitted from the primary antenna are reflected from the Cassegrain subreflector and, then, illuminate the main parabolic reflector just as if they had originated at the focus. The rays are collimated by the parabolic reflector in the same way as with the center- and horn-feed mechanisms. The subreflector must have a hyperboloidal curvature to reflect the rays from the primary antenna in such a way as to function as a *virtual source* at the paraboloidal focus. The Cassegrain feed is commonly used for receiving extremely weak signals or when extremely long transmission lines or waveguide runs are required and it is necessary to place low-noise preamplifiers as close to the antenna as possible. With the Cassegrain feed, preamplifiers can be placed just before the feed mechanism and not be an obstruction to the reflected waves.

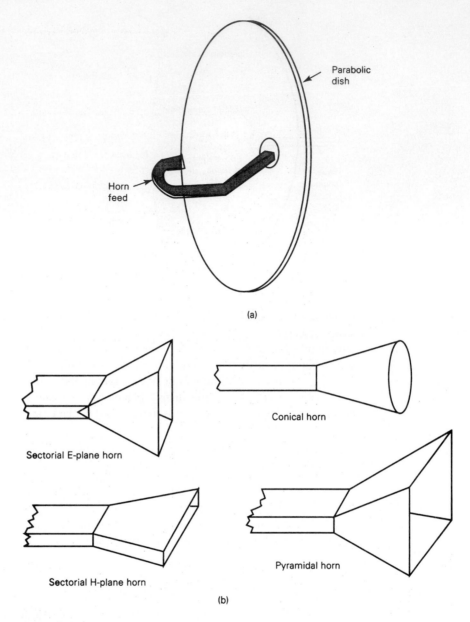

FIGURE 10-36 Parabolic antenna with a horn feed: (a) horn feed; (b) waveguide horn types

Conical Horn Antenna

A *conical horn* antenna consists of a cone that is truncated in a piece of circular waveguide as shown in Figure 10-38. The waveguide in turn connects the antenna to either the transmitter or the receiver. If the horn itself is used as the antenna, the *cone angle* θ (sometimes called the flare angle) is made approximately 50°. In this case, the length of the truncated cone determines the antenna gain. When a conical horn is used as the feed mechanism for a parabolic dish, the flare angle and length are adjusted for optimum illumination of the reflector. The simplest feed mechanism is when the mouth of the conical horn is located at the focal point of the reflector.

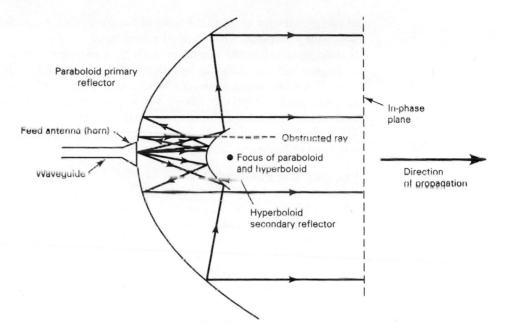

FIGURE 10-37   Parabolic antenna with a Cassegrain feed

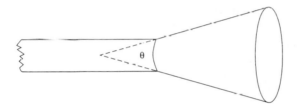

FIGURE 10-38   Conical horn antenna

WAVEGUIDES

Parallel-wire transmission lines, including coaxial cables, cannot effectively propagate electromagnetic energy above approximately 20 GHz, because of the attenuation caused by skin effect and radiation losses. In addition, parallel-wire transmission lines cannot be used to propagate signals with high powers because the high voltages associated with them cause the dielectric separating the two conductors to break down. Consequently, parallel-wire transmission lines are impractical for many UHF and microwave applications. There are several alternatives, including optical fiber cables and waveguides. Optical fibers are discussed in detail in Chapter 20.

In its simplest form, a *waveguide* is a hollow conductive tube, usually rectangular in cross section, but sometimes circular or elliptical. The dimensions of the cross section are selected such that electromagnetic waves can propagate within the interior of the guide (hence, the name waveguide). A waveguide does not conduct current in the true sense, but rather serves as a boundary that confines electromagnetic energy. The walls of the waveguide are conductors and, therefore, reflect electromagnetic energy from their surface. If the wall of the waveguide is a good conductor and very thin, little current flows in the interior walls and, consequently, very little power is dissipated. In a waveguide, conduction of energy does not occur in the walls of the waveguide, but rather through the dielectric within the waveguide, which is usually dehydrated air or inert gas. In essence, a waveguide is analogous to a metallic wire conductor with its interior removed. Electromagnetic energy propagates down a waveguide by reflecting back and forth in a zigzag pattern.

When discussing waveguide behavior, it is necessary to speak in terms of electromagnetic field concepts (i.e., electric and magnetic fields), rather than currents and voltages as for transmission lines. The cross-sectional area of a waveguide must be on the same order as the wavelength of the signal it is propagating. Therefore, waveguides are generally restricted to frequencies above 1 GHz.

Rectangular Waveguide

Rectangular waveguides are the most common form of waveguide. To understand how rectangular waveguides work, it is necessary to understand the basic behavior of waves reflecting from a conducting surface.

Electromagnetic energy is propagated through free space as transverse electromagnetic (TEM) waves with a magnetic field, an electric field, and a direction of propagation that are mutually perpendicular. For an electromagnetic wave to exist in a waveguide, it must satisfy Maxwell's equations through the guide. Maxwell's equations are necessarily complex and beyond the intent of this book. However, a limiting factor of Maxwell's equations is that a TEM wave cannot have a tangential component of the electric field at the walls of the waveguide. The wave cannot travel straight down a waveguide without reflecting off the sides, because the electric field would have to exist next to a conductive wall. If that happened, the electric field would be short-circuited by the walls themselves. To successfully propagate a TEM wave through a waveguide, the wave must propagate down the guide in a zigzag manner, with the electric field maximum in the center of the guide and zero at the surface of the walls.

In transmission lines, wave velocity is independent of frequency, and for air or vacuum dielectrics, the velocity is equal to the velocity in free space. However, in waveguides the velocity varies with frequency. In addition, it is necessary to distinguish between two different kinds of velocity: *phase velocity* and *group velocity.* Group velocity is the velocity at which a wave propagates, and the phase velocity is the velocity at which the wave changes phase.

Phase velocity and group velocity.   Phase velocity is the apparent velocity of a particular phase of the wave (for example, the crest or maximum electric intensity point). Phase velocity is the velocity with which a wave changes phase in a direction parallel to a conducting surface, such as the walls of a waveguide. Phase velocity is determined by measuring the wavelength of a particular frequency wave and, then, substituting it into the following formula:

$$v_{ph} = f\lambda \tag{10-29}$$

where v_{ph} = phase velocity (meters per second)
f = frequency (hertz)
λ = wavelength (meters per cycle)

Group velocity is the velocity of a group of waves (i.e., a pulse). Group velocity is the velocity at which information signals of any kind are propagated. It is also the velocity at which energy is propagated. Group velocity can be measured by determining the time it takes for a pulse to propagate a given length of waveguide. Group and phase velocities have the same value in free space and in parallel wire transmission lines. However, if these two velocities are measured at the same frequency in a waveguide, it will be found that, in general, the two velocities are not the same. At some frequencies they will be nearly equal and at other frequencies they can be considerably different.

The phase velocity is always equal to or greater than the group velocity, and their product is equal to the square of the free-space propagation velocity. Thus,

$$v_g v_{ph} = c^2 \qquad (10\text{-}30)$$

where v_{ph} = phase velocity (meters per second)
v_g = group velocity (meters per second)
$c = 3 \times 10^8$ meters per second

Phase velocity may exceed the velocity of light. A basic principle of physics states that no form of energy can travel at a greater velocity than light (electromagnetic waves) in free space. This principle is not violated because it is group velocity, not phase velocity, that represents the velocity of propagation of energy.

Because the phase velocity in a waveguide is greater than its velocity in free space, the wavelength for a given frequency will be greater in the waveguide than in free space. The relationship among free-space wavelength, guide wavelength, and the free-space velocity of electromagnetic waves is

$$\lambda_g = \lambda_o \frac{v_{ph}}{c} \qquad (10\text{-}31)$$

where λ_g = guide wavelength (meters per cycle)
λ_o = free-space wavelength (meters per cycle)
v_{ph} = phase velocity (meters per second)
c = free-space velocity of light (3×10^8 meters per second)

Cutoff frequency and cutoff wavelength. Unlike transmission lines that have a maximum frequency of operation, waveguides have a minimum frequency of operation called the *cutoff frequency*. The cutoff frequency is an absolute limiting frequency; frequencies below the cutoff frequency will not be propagated by the waveguide. Conversely, waveguides have a minimum wavelength that they can propagate called the *cutoff wavelength*. The cutoff wavelength is defined as the smallest free-space wavelength that is just unable to propagate in the waveguide. In other words, only frequencies with wavelengths less than the cutoff wavelength can propagate down the waveguide. The cutoff wavelength and frequency are determined by the cross-sectional dimensions of the waveguide.

The mathematical relationship between the guide wavelength at a particular frequency and the cutoff frequency is

$$\lambda_g = \frac{c}{\sqrt{f^2 - f_c^2}} \qquad (10\text{-}32)$$

where λ_g = guide wavelength (meters per cycle)
f = frequency of operation (hertz)
f_c = cutoff frequency (hertz)
c = free-space propagation velocity (3×10^8 meters per second)

Equation 10-32 can be rewritten in terms of the free-space wavelength as

$$\lambda_g = \frac{\lambda_o}{\sqrt{1 - (f_c/f)^2}} \qquad (10\text{-}33)$$

where λ_g = guide wavelength (meters per cycle)
λ_o = free-space wavelength (meters per cycle)
f = frequency of operation (hertz)
f_c = cutoff frequency (hertz)

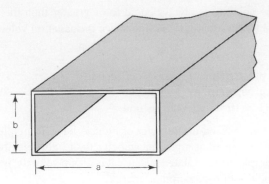

FIGURE 10-39 Cross-sectional view of a rectangular waveguide

Combining Equations 10-31 and 10-32 and rearranging gives

$$v_{ph} = \frac{c(\lambda_g)}{\lambda_o} = \frac{c}{\sqrt{1 - (f_c/f)^2}}$$

(10-34)

It is evident from Equation 10-34 that if f becomes less than f_c the phase velocity becomes imaginary, which means that the wave is not propagated. Also, it can be seen that, as the frequency of operation approaches the cutoff frequency, the phase velocity and the guide wavelength become infinite, and the group velocity goes to zero.

Figure 10-39 shows a cross-sectional view of a piece of rectangular waveguide with dimensions a and b (a is normally designated the wider of the two dimensions). Dimension a determines the cutoff frequency of the waveguide according to the following mathematical relationship:

$$f_c = \frac{c}{2a}$$

(10-35)

where f_c = cutoff frequency (hertz)
  a = cross-sectional length (meters)

or, in terms of wavelength

$$\lambda_c = 2a$$

(10-36)

where λ_c = cutoff wavelength (meters per cycle)
  a = cross-sectional length (meters)

Equations 10-35 and 10-36 indicate that cutoff occurs at the frequency for which the largest transverse dimension of the guide is exactly one-half of the free-space wavelength.

Figure 10-40 shows the top view of a section of rectangular waveguide and illustrates how electromagnetic waves propagate down the guide. For frequencies above the cutoff frequency (Figures 10-40a, b, and c), the waves propagate down the guide by reflecting back and forth between the wall at various angles. Figure 10-40d shows what happens to the electromagnetic wave at the cutoff frequency.

Example 10-6

For a rectangular waveguide with a wall separation of 3 cm and a desired frequency of operation of 6 GHz, determine

(a) Cutoff frequency.
(b) Cutoff wavelength.
(c) Group velocity.
(d) Phase velocity.

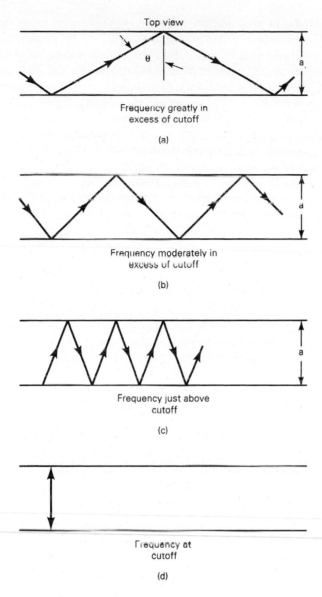

Top view

Frequency greatly in
excess of cutoff

(a)

Frequency moderately in
excess of cutoff

(b)

Frequency just above
cutoff

(c)

Frequency at
cutoff

(d)

FIGURE 10-40 Electromagnetic wave propagation in a
rectangular waveguide

Solution   (a) The cutoff frequency is determined by substituting into Equation 10-35.

$$f_c = \frac{3 \times 10^8 \text{ m/s}}{2(0.03 \text{ m})} = 5 \text{ GHz}$$

(b) The cutoff wavelength is determined by substituting into Equation 10-36.

$$\lambda_c = 2(3 \text{ cm}) = 6 \text{ cm}$$

(c) The phase velocity is found using Equation 10-34.

$$v_{ph} = \frac{3 \times 10^8}{\sqrt{1 - (5 \text{ GHz}/6 \text{ GHz})^2}} = 5.43 \times 10^8 \text{ m/s}$$

(d) The group velocity is found by rearranging Equation 10-30.

$$v_g = \frac{c^2}{v_{ph}} = \frac{(3 \times 10^8)^2}{5.43 \times 10^8} = 1.66 \times 10^8 \text{ m/s}$$

Modes of propagation. Electromagnetic waves travel down a waveguide in different configurations called propagation *modes*. In 1955, the Institute of Radio Engineers (IRE) published a set of standards. These standards designated the modes for rectangular waveguides as $TE_{m,n}$ for transverse-electric waves and $TM_{m,n}$ for transverse-magnetic waves. TE means that the electric field lines are everywhere transverse (i.e., perpendicular to the guide walls), and TM means that the magnetic field lines are everywhere transverse. In both cases, m and n are integers designating the number of half-wavelengths of intensity (electric or magnetic) that exist between each pair of walls. m is measured along the x-axis of the waveguide (the same axis the dimension a is measured on), and n is measured along the y-axis (the same as dimension b).

Figure 10-41 shows the electromagnetic field pattern for a $TE_{1,0}$ mode wave. The $TE_{1,0}$ mode is sometimes called the dominant mode because it is the most "natural" mode. A waveguide acts as a high-pass filter in that it passes only those frequencies above the minimum or cutoff frequency. At frequencies above the cutoff frequency, higher-order TE modes of propagation, with more complicated field configurations, are possible. However, it is undesirable to operate a waveguide at a frequency at which these higher modes can propagate. The next higher mode possible occurs when the free-space wavelength is equal to length a (i.e., at twice the cutoff frequency). Consequently, a rectangular waveguide is normally operated within the frequency range between f_c and $2f_c$. Allowing higher modes to propagate is undesirable because they do not couple well to the load and, thus, cause reflections to occur and standing waves to be created. The $TE_{1,0}$ mode is also desired because it allows for the smallest possible size waveguide for a given frequency of operation.

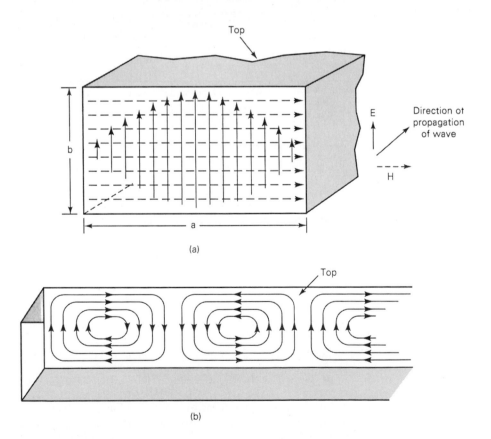

FIGURE 10-41 Electric and magnetic field vectors in a rectangular waveguide: (a) end view; (b) magnetic field configuration in a longitudinal section

In Figure 10-41a, the electric (E) field vectors are parallel to each other and perpendicular to the wide face of the guide. Their amplitude is greatest midway between the narrow walls and decreases to zero at the walls, in a cosinusoidal fashion. The magnetic (H) field vectors (shown by dashed lines) are also parallel to each other and perpendicular to the electric vectors. The magnetic intensity is constant in the vertical direction across the guide section. The wave is propagating in the longitudinal direction of the guide, perpendicular to the E and H vectors. Figure 10-41b shows the magnetic field configuration in a longitudinal section of waveguide for the $TE_{1,0}$ propagation mode.

Characteristic impedance. Waveguides have a characteristic impedance that is analogous to the characteristic impedance of parallel-wire transmission lines and closely related to the characteristic impedance of free space. The characteristic impedance of a waveguide has the same significance as the characteristic impedance of a transmission line, with respect to load matching, signal reflections, and standing waves. The characteristic impedance of a waveguide is expressed mathematically as

$$Z_o = \frac{377}{\sqrt{1 - (f_c/f)^2}} = 377\frac{\lambda_g}{\lambda_o} \qquad (10\text{-}37)$$

where Z_o = characteristic impedance (ohms)
   f_c = cutoff frequency (hertz)
   f = frequency of operation (hertz)

Z_o is generally greater than 377 Ω. In fact, at the cutoff frequency, Z_o becomes infinite, and at a frequency equal to twice the cutoff frequency ($2f_c$), Z_o = 435 Ω. Two waveguides with the same length a dimension but different length b dimensions will have the same value of cutoff frequency and the same value of characteristic impedance. However, if these two waveguides are connected together end to end and an electromagnetic wave is propagated down them, a discontinuity will occur at the junction point, and reflections will occur even though their impedances are matched.

Impedance matching. Reactive stubs are used in waveguides for impedance transforming and impedance matching just as they are in parallel-wire transmission lines. Short-circuited waveguide stubs are used with waveguides in the same manner that they are used in transmission lines.

Figure 10-42 shows how inductive and capacitive irises are installed in a rectangular waveguide to behave as if they were shunt susceptances. The irises consist of thin metallic

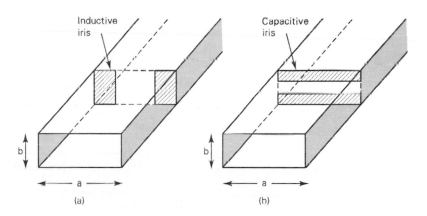

FIGURE 10-42 Waveguide impedance matching: (a) inductive iris; (b) capacitive iris

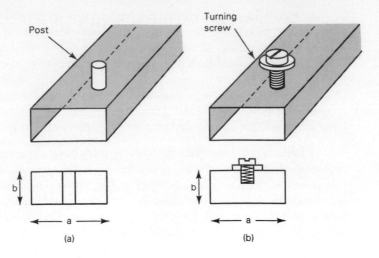

FIGURE 10-43 Waveguide impedance matching: (a) post; (b) tuning screw

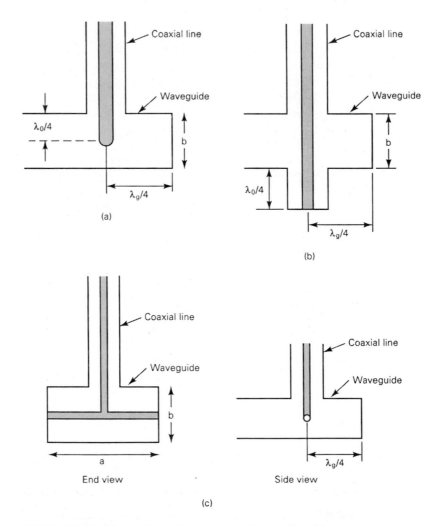

FIGURE 10-44 Transmission line-to-waveguide coupling: (a) quarter-wave probe coupler; (b) straight-through coupler; (c) cross-bar coupler

TABLE 10-3 Rectangular Waveguide Dimensions and Electrical Characteristics

Useful Frequency Range (GHz)	Outside Dimensions (mm)	Theoretical Average Attenuation (dB/m)	Theoretical Average (CW) Power Rating (kW)
1.12–1.70	169 × 86.6	0.0052	14,600
1.70–2.60	113 × 58.7	0.0097	6,400
2.60–3.95	76.2 × 38.1	0.019	2,700
3.95–5.85	50.8 × 25.4	0.036	1,700
5.85–8.20	38.1 × 19.1	0.058	635
8.20–12.40	25.4 × 12.7	0.110	245
12.40–18.00	17.8 × 9.9	0.176	140
18.0–26.5	12.7 × 6.4	0.37	51
26.5–40.0	9.1 × 5.6	0.58	27
40.0–60.0	6.8 × 4.4	0.95	13
60.0–90.0	5.1 × 3.6	1.50	5.1
90.0–140	4.0 (diam.)	2.60	2.2
140–220	4.0 (diam.)	5.20	0.9
220–325	4.0 (diam.)	8.80	0.4

plates placed perpendicular to the walls of the waveguide and joined to them at the edges, with an opening between them. When the opening is parallel to the narrow walls, the susceptance is inductive; when it is parallel to the wide walls, it is capacitive. The magnitude of the susceptance is proportional to the size of the opening.

A post placed across the narrowest dimension of the waveguide, as shown in Figure 10-43a, acts as an inductive shunt susceptance whose value depends on its diameter and its position in the transverse plane. Tuning screws, shown in Figure 10-43b, project partway across the narrow guide dimension, act as a capacitance, and may be adjusted.

Transmission line-to-waveguide coupling. Figure 10-44 shows several ways in which a waveguide and transmission line can be joined together. The couplers shown can be used as wave launchers at the input end of a waveguide or as wave receptors at the load end of the guide. The dimension labeled $\lambda_o/4$ and $\lambda_g/4$ are approximate. In practice, they are experimentally adjusted for best results.

Table 10-3 lists the frequency range, dimensions, and electrical characteristics for several common types of rectangular waveguide.

OTHER TYPES OF WAVEGUIDES

Circular Waveguide

Rectangular waveguides are by far the most common; however, circular waveguides are used in radar and microwave applications when it is necessary or advantageous to propagate both vertically and horizontally polarized waves in the same waveguide. Figure 10-45 shows two pieces of circular waveguide joined together by a rotation joint.

The behavior of electromagnetic waves in circular waveguides is the same as it is in rectangular waveguides. However, because of the different geometry, some of the calculations are performed in a slightly different manner.

The cutoff wavelength for circular waveguides is given as

$$\lambda_o = \frac{2\pi r}{kr} \tag{10-38}$$

where
λ_o = cutoff wavelength (meters per cycle)
r = internal radius of the waveguide (meters)
kr = solution of a Bessel function equation

Antennas and Waveguides

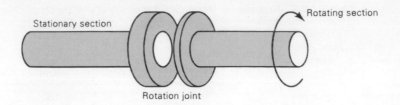

FIGURE 10-45 Circular waveguide with rotational joint

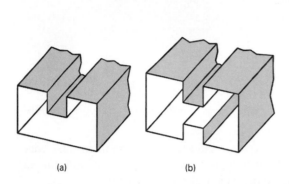

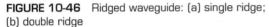

FIGURE 10-46 Ridged waveguide: (a) single ridge;
(b) double ridge

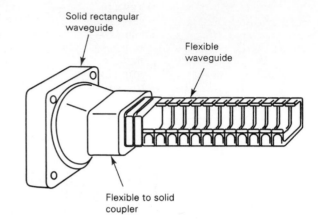

FIGURE 10-47 Flexible waveguide

Because the propagation mode with the largest cutoff wavelength is the one with the smallest value for kr (1.84), the $TE_{1,1}$ mode is dominant for circular waveguides. The cutoff wavelength for this mode reduces to

$$\lambda_o = 1.7d \qquad (10\text{-}39)$$

where d is the waveguide diameter (meters).

Circular waveguides are easier to manufacture than rectangular waveguides and easier to join together. However, circular waveguides have a much larger area than a corresponding rectangular waveguide used to carry the same signal. Another disadvantage of circular waveguides is that the plane of polarization may rotate while the wave is propagating down it (i.e., a horizontally polarized wave may become vertically polarized, and vice versa).

Ridged Waveguide

Figure 10-46 shows two types of ridged waveguide. A ridged waveguide is more expensive to manufacture than a standard rectangular waveguide; however, it also allows operation at lower frequencies for a given size. Consequently, smaller overall waveguide dimensions are possible using a ridged waveguide. A ridged waveguide has more loss per unit length than a rectangular waveguide. This characteristic combined with its increased cost limits its usefulness to specialized applications.

Flexible Waveguide

Figure 10-47 shows a length of flexible rectangular waveguide. A flexible waveguide consists of spiral-wound ribbons of brass or copper. The outside is covered with a soft dielectric coating (often rubber) to keep the waveguide air- and watertight. Short pieces of flexible waveguide are used in microwave systems when several transmitters and receivers are interconnected to a complex combining or separating unit. A flexible waveguide is also used extensively in microwave test equipment.

QUESTIONS

10-1. Define *antenna.*

10-2. Describe basic antenna operation using standing waves.

10-3. Describe a relative radiation pattern; an absolute radiation pattern.

10-4. Define *front-to-back ratio.*

10-5. Describe an omnidirectional antenna.

10-6. Define *near field* and *far field.*

10-7. Define *radiation resistance* and *antenna efficiency.*

10-8. Define and contrast *directive gain* and *power gain.*

10-9. What is the directivity for an isotropic antenna?

10-10. Define *effective isotropic radiated power.*

10-11. Define *antenna polarization.*

10-12. Define *antenna beamwidth.*

10-13. Define *antenna bandwidth.*

10-14. Define *antenna input impedance.* What factors contribute to an antenna's input impedance?

10-15. Describe the operation of an elementary doublet.

10-16. Describe the operation of a half-wave dipole.

10-17. Describe the effects of ground on a half-wave dipole.

10-18. Describe the operation of a grounded antenna.

10-19. What is meant by *antenna loading?*

10-20. Describe an antenna loading coil.

10-21. Describe antenna top loading.

10-22. Describe an antenna array.

10-23. What is meant by *driven element; parasitic element?*

10-24. Describe the radiation pattern for a broadside array; an end-fire array.

10-25. Define *nonresonant antenna.*

10-26. Describe the operation of the rhombic antenna.

10-27. Describe a folded dipole antenna.

10-28. Describe a Yagi-Uda antenna.

10-29. Describe a log-periodic antenna.

10-30. Describe the operation of a loop antenna.

10-31. Describe briefly how a *phased array antenna* works and what it is primarily used for.

10-32. Describe briefly how a *helical* antenna works.

10-33. Define the following terms: *main lobe, side lobes, side-to-side coupling,* and *back-to-back coupling.*

10-34. What are the two main parts of a *parabolic antenna?*

10-35. Describe briefly how a *parabolic reflector* works.

10-36. What is the purpose of the *feed mechanism* in a parabolic reflector antenna?

10-37. What is meant by the *capture area* of a parabolic antenna?

10-38. Describe how a *center-feed* mechanism works with a parabolic reflector.

10-39. Describe how a *horn-feed* mechanism works with a parabolic reflector.

10-40. Describe how a *Cassegrain feed* works with a parabolic reflector.

10-41. In its simplest form, what is a *waveguide?*

10-42. Describe *phase velocity; group velocity.*

10-43. Describe the *cutoff frequency* for a waveguide; *cutoff wavelength.*

10-44. What is meant by the TE mode of propagation? TM mode of propagation?

10-45. When is it advantageous to use a circular waveguide?

PROBLEMS

10-1. For an antenna with input power $P_{in} = 100$ W, rms current $I = 2$ A, and effective resistance $R_e = 2\ \Omega$, determine
   (a) Antenna's radiation resistance.
   (b) Antenna's efficiency.
   (c) Power radiated from the antenna, P_{rad}.

10-2. Determine the directivity in decibels for an antenna that produces power density $\mathcal{P} = 2\ \mu\text{W/m}^2$ at a point when a reference antenna produces $0.5\ \mu\text{W/m}^2$ at the same point.

10-3. Determine the power gain in decibels for an antenna with directive gain $\mathcal{D} = 40$ and efficiency $\eta = 65\%$.

10-4. Determine the effective isotropic radiated power for an antenna with power gain $A_p = 43$ dB and radiated power $P_{rad} = 200$ W.

10-5. Determine the effective isotropic radiated power for an antenna with directivity $\mathcal{D} = 33$ dB, efficiency $\eta = 82\%$, and input power $P_{in} = 100$ W.

10-6. Determine the power density at a point 20 km from an antenna that is radiating 1000 W and has power gain $A_p = 23$ dB.

10-7. Determine the power density at a point 30 km from an antenna that has input power $P_{in} = 40$ W, efficiency $\eta = 75\%$, and directivity $\mathcal{D} = 16$ dB.

10-8. Determine the power density captured by a receiving antenna for the following parameters: transmit antenna input $P_{in} = 50$ W; transmit antenna gain, $A_p = 30$ dB; distance between transmit and receive antennas, $d = 20$ km; receive antenna directive gain, $A_p = 26$ dB.

10-9. Determine the directivity (in decibels) for an antenna that produces a power density at a point that is 40 times greater than the power density at the same point when the reference antenna is used.

10-10. Determine the effective radiated power for an antenna with directivity $\mathcal{D} = 400$, efficiency $\eta = 0.60$, and input power $P_{in} = 50$ W.

10-11. Determine the efficiency for an antenna with radiation resistance $R_r = 18.8\ \Omega$, effective resistance $R_e = 0.4\ \Omega$, and directive gain $\mathcal{D} = 200$.

10-12. Determine the power gain A_p for Problem 10-11.

10-13. Determine the efficiency for an antenna with radiated power $P_{rad} = 44$ W, dissipated power $P_d = 0.8$ W, and directive gain $\mathcal{D} = 400$.

10-14. Determine power gain A_p for Problem 10-13.

10-15. Determine the power gain and beamwidth for an end-fire helical antenna with the following parameters: helix diameter = 0.1 m, number of turns = 10, pitch = 0.05 m, and frequency of operation = 500 MHz.

10-16. Determine the beamwidth and transmit and receive power gains of a parabolic antenna with the following parameters: dish diameter of 2.5 m, a frequency of operation of 4 GHz, and an efficiency of 55%.

10-17. For a rectangular waveguide with a wall separation of 2.5 cm and a desired frequency of operation of 7 GHz, determine
   (a) Cutoff frequency.
   (b) Cutoff wavelength.
   (c) Group velocity.
   (d) Phase velocity.

10-18. For an antenna with input power $P_{in} = 400$ W, rms current $i = 4$ A, and dc resistance $R_{dc} = 4\ \Omega$, determine
   (a) Antenna's radiation resistance.
   (b) Antenna's efficiency.
   (c) Power radiated from the antenna, P_{rad}.

10-19. Determine the directivity in decibels for an antenna that produces a power density $\mathcal{P} = 4\ \mu\text{W/m}^2$ at a point in space when a reference antenna produces $0.4\ \mu\text{W/m}^2$ at the same point.

10-20. Determine the power gain in decibels for an antenna with a directive gain $\mathcal{D} = 50$ dB and an efficiency of 75%.

10-21. Determine the effective isotropic radiated power for an antenna with a power gain $A_p = 26$ dB and a radiated power $P_{rad} = 400$ W.

10-22. Determine the effective isotropic radiated power for an antenna with a directivity $\mathcal{D} = 43$ dB, an efficiency of 75%, and an input power $P_{in} = 50$ W.

10-23. Determine the power density at a point 20 km from an antenna that is radiating 1200 W and has a power gain $A_p = 46$ dB.

10-24. Determine the power density at a point 50 km from an antenna that has an input power $P_{in} = 100$ W, an efficiency of 55%, and a directivity $\mathcal{D} = 23$ dB.

10-25. Determine the power captured by a receiving antenna for the following parameters:

Power radiated $P_{rad} = 100$ W

Transmit antenna directive gain $A_t = 40$ dB

Distance between transmit and receive antenna $d = 40$ km

Receive antenna directive gain $A_r = 23$ dB

10-26. Determine the directivity (in dB) for an antenna that produces a power density at a point that is 100 times greater than the power density at the same point when a reference antenna is used.

10-27. Determine the effective radiated power for an antenna with a directivity $\mathcal{D} = 300$, an efficiency = 80%, and an input power $P_{in} = 2500$ W.

10-28. Determine the efficiency for an antenna with radiation resistance $R_r = 22.2$ Ω, a dc resistance $R_{dc} = 2.8$ Ω, and a directive gain $\mathcal{D} = 40$ dB.

10-29. Determine the power gain, G, for Problem 10-28.

10-30. Determine the efficiency for an antenna with radiated power $P_{rad} = 65$ W, power dissipated $P_d = 5$ W, and a directive gain $\mathcal{D} = 200$.

10-31. Determine the power gain for Problem 10-30.

C H A P T E R   11

Optical Fiber Communications

INTRODUCTION

In essence, an *optical communications system* is an electronic communications system that uses light as the carrier of information. Propagating light waves through Earth's atmosphere, however, is difficult and impractical. Consequently, *optical fiber communications systems* use glass or plastic fibers to "contain" light waves and guide them in a manner similar to the way electromagnetic waves are guided through a waveguide. Optoelectronics is the branch of electronics that deals with the transmission of light through ultrapure fibers generally constructed from glass or plastic.

The *information-carrying capacity* of any electronic communications system is directly proportional to bandwidth. For comparison purposes, it is common to express the bandwidth of an analog communications system as a percentage of its carrier frequency. This is sometimes called the *bandwidth utilization ratio.* For instance, a VHF radio communications system operating at a carrier frequency of 100 MHz with 10-MHz bandwidth has a bandwidth utilization ratio of 10%. A microwave radio system operating at a carrier frequency of 10 GHz with a 10% bandwidth utilization ratio would have 1 GHz of bandwidth available. Obviously, the higher the carrier frequency, the more bandwidth available, and the greater the information-carrying capacity. Light frequencies used in optical fiber communications systems are between 1×10^{14} Hz and 4×10^{14} Hz (100,000 GHz to 400,000 GHz). A bandwidth utilization ratio of 10% would be a bandwidth between 10,000 GHz and 40,000 GHz.

HISTORY OF OPTICAL FIBERS

In 1880, Alexander Graham Bell experimented with an apparatus he called a *photophone.* The photophone was a device constructed from mirrors and selenium detectors that transmitted sound waves over a beam of light. The photophone was awkward, unreliable, and had no real practical application. Actually, visual light was a primary means of communicating long before electronic communications came about. Smoke signals and mirrors were used ages ago to convey short, simple messages. Bell's contraption, however, was the first attempt at using a beam of light for carrying information.

Transmission of light waves for any useful distance through Earth's atmosphere is impractical because water vapor, oxygen, and particulates in the air absorb and attenuate the signals at light frequencies. Consequently, the only practical type of optical communications system is one that uses a fiber guide. In 1930, J. L. Baird, an English scientist, and C. W. Hansell, a scientist from the United States, were granted patents for scanning and transmitting television images through uncoated fiber cables. A few years later a German scientist named H. Lamm successfully transmitted images through a single glass fiber. At that time, most people considered fiber optics more of a toy or a laboratory stunt and, consequently, it was not until the early 1950s that any substantial breakthrough was made in the field of fiber optics.

In 1951, A. C. S. van Heel of Holland and H. H. Hopkins and N. S. Kapany of England experimented with light transmission through *bundles* of fibers. Their studies led to the development of the *flexible fiberscope,* which is used extensively in the medical field. It was Kapany who coined the term "fiber optics" in 1956.

In 1958, Charles H. Townes, an American, and Arthur L. Schawlow, a Canadian, wrote a paper describing how it was possible to use stimulated emission for amplifying light waves (laser) as well as microwaves (maser). Two years later, Theodore H. Maiman, a scientist with Hughes Aircraft Company, built the first optical maser.

The *laser* (*l*ight *a*mplification by *s*timulated *e*mission of *r*adiation) was invented in 1960. The laser's relatively high output power, high frequency of operation, and capability of carrying an extremely wide bandwidth signal make it ideally suited for high-capacity communications systems. The invention of the laser greatly accelerated research efforts in fiber-optic communications, although it was not until 1967 that K. C. Kao and G. A. Bockham of the Standard Telecommunications Laboratory in England proposed a new communications medium using *cladded* fiber cables.

The fiber cables available in the 1960s were extremely *lossy* (more than 1000 dB/km), which limited optical transmissions to short distances. In 1970, Kapron, Keck, and Maurer of Corning Glass Works in Corning, New York, developed an optical fiber with losses less than 2 dB/km. That was the "big" breakthrough needed to permit practical fiber optics communications systems. Since 1970, fiber optics technology has grown exponentially. Recently, Bell Laboratories successfully transmitted 1 billion bps through a fiber cable for 600 mi without a regenerator.

In the late 1970s and early 1980s, the refinement of optical cables and the development of high-quality, affordable light sources and detectors opened the door to the development of high-quality, high-capacity, efficient, and affordable optical fiber communications systems. By the late 1980s, losses in optical fibers were reduced to as low as 0.16 dB/km, and in 1988 NEC Corporation set a new long-haul transmission record by transmitting 10 Gbits/s over 80.1 km of optical fiber. Also in 1988, the American National Standards Institute (ANSI) published the *Synchronous Optical Network* (*SONET*). By the mid-1990s optical voice and data networks were commonplace throughout the United States and much of the world.

OPTICAL FIBERS VERSUS METALLIC CABLE FACILITIES

Communications through glass or plastic fiber cables has several overwhelming advantages over communications using conventional *metallic* or *coaxial* cable facilities.

Advantages of Optical Fiber Systems

1. Greater information capacity: Optical fiber communications systems have a greater information capacity than metallic cables due to the inherently larger bandwidths available with optical frequencies. Optical fibers are available with bandwidths up to 10 GHz. Metallic cables exhibit capacitance between and inductance along their conductors causing them to act like low-pass filters, which limit their transmission frequencies, bandwidths, and information-carrying capacity. Modern optical fiber communications systems are capable of transmitting several gigabits per second over hundreds of miles allowing literally millions of individual voice and data channels to be combined and propagated over one optical fiber cable.

2. Immunity to crosstalk: Optical cables are immune to crosstalk between adjacent cables due to magnetic induction. Glass or plastic fibers are nonconductors of electricity and, therefore, do not have magnetic fields associated with them. In metallic cables, the primary cause of crosstalk is magnetic induction between conductors located physically close to each other.

3. Immunity to static interference: Optical cables are immune to static noise caused by electromagnetic interference (EMI) from lightning, electric motors, fluorescent lights, and other electrical noise sources. This immunity is also attributed to the fact that optical fibers are nonconductors of electricity and external electrical noise does not affect energy at light frequencies. Fiber cables do not radiate RF energy either and, therefore, cannot interfere with other communications systems. This characteristic makes optical fiber systems ideally suited for military applications where the effects of nuclear weapons (electromagnetic pulse interference-EMP) have a devastating effect on conventional electronic communications systems.

4. Environmental immunity: Optical cables are more resistant to environmental extremes than metallic cables. Optical cables also operate over wider temperature variations and fiber cables are less affected by corrosive liquids and gases.

5. Safety: Optical cables are safer and easier to install and maintain than metallic cables. Because glass and plastic fibers are nonconductors, there are no electrical currents or voltages associated with them. Optical fibers can be used around volatile liquids and gases without worrying about their causing explosions or fires. Optical fibers are smaller and much more lightweight than metallic cables. Consequently, they are easier to work with and much better suited to airborne applications. Fiber cables also require less storage space and are cheaper to transport.

6. Security: Optical fibers are more secure than metallic cables. It is virtually impossible to tap into a fiber cable without the user's knowledge, and optical cables cannot be detected with metal detectors unless they are reinforced with steel for strength. These are also qualities that make optical fibers attractive to military applications.

7. Longer lasting: Although it has not yet been proven, it is projected that fiber systems will last longer than metallic facilities. This assumption is based on the higher tolerances that fiber cables have to changes in environmental conditions and their immunity to corrosives.

8. Economics: The cost of optical fiber cables is approximately the same as metallic cables. Fiber cables have less loss, however, and therefore require fewer repeaters. Fewer repeaters equates to lower installation and overall system costs, and improved reliability.

Disadvantages of Optical Fiber Systems

1. Interfacing costs: Optical fiber systems are virtually useless by themselves. To be practical, they must be connected to standard electronic facilities which often requires expensive interfaces.

2. Strength: Optical fibers by themselves have a significantly lower tensile strength than coaxial cable. This can be improved by coating the fiber with standard Kevlar and a protective jacket of PVC.

3. Remote electrical power: Occasionally it is necessary to provide electrical power to remote interface or regenerating equipment. This cannot be accomplished with the optical cable so additional metallic cables must be included in the cable assembly.

4. Unproven: Optical fiber cable systems are relatively new and have not had sufficient time to prove their reliability.

5. Specialized tools, equipment, and training: Optical fibers require special tools to splice and repair cables and special test equipment to make routine measurements. Repairing fiber cables is also difficult and expensive and technicians working on optical fiber cables also require special skills and training.

ELECTROMAGNETIC SPECTRUM

The total electromagnetic frequency spectrum is shown in Figure 11-1. It can be seen that the frequency spectrum extends from the *subsonic* frequencies (a few hertz) to *cosmic rays* (10^{22} Hz). The light frequency spectrum can be divided into three general bands:

1. *Infrared:* band of light wavelengths that are too long to be seen by the human eye
2. *Visible:* band of light wavelengths to which the human eye will respond
3. *Ultraviolet:* band of light wavelengths that are too short to be seen by the human eye

When dealing with higher-frequency electromagnetic waves, such as light, it is common to use units of *wavelength* rather than frequency. Wavelength is the length of the wave that one cycle of an electromagnetic wave occupies in space. The length of a wavelength depends on the frequency of the wave and the velocity of light. Mathematically, wavelength is

$$\lambda = \frac{c}{f} \qquad (11\text{-}1)$$

where λ = wavelength (meters/cycle)
   c = velocity of light (300,000,000 meters per second)
   f = frequency (hertz)

With light frequencies, wavelength is often stated in *microns* (1 micron = 1 micrometer) or *nanometers* (1 nanometer = 10^{-9} meter or 0.001 micron). However, when describing the optical spectrum, the unit *angstrom* (Å) often has been used to express wavelength (1 Å = 10^{-10} meter or 0.0001 micron). Figure 11-2 shows the total electromagnetic wavelength spectrum.

OPTICAL FIBER COMMUNICATIONS SYSTEM BLOCK DIAGRAM

Figure 11-3 shows a simplified block diagram of an optical fiber communications link. The three primary building blocks of the link are the *transmitter,* the *receiver,* and the *fiber guide.*

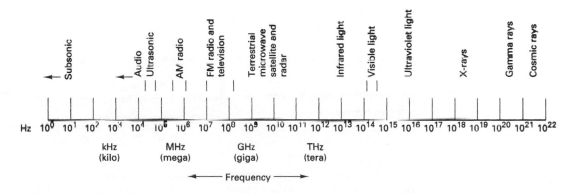

FIGURE 11-1 Electromagnetic frequency spectrum

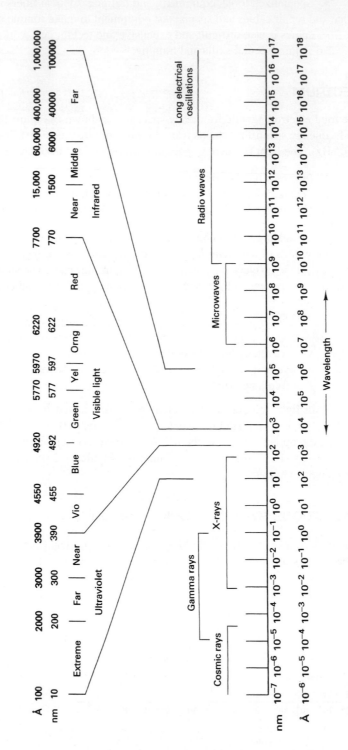

FIGURE 11-2 Electromagnetic wavelength spectrum

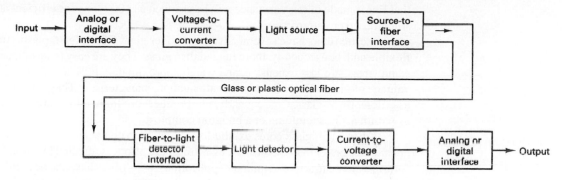

FIGURE 11-3 Simplified fiber optic communications link

The transmitter consists of an analog or digital interface, a voltage-to-current converter, a light source, and a source-to-fiber light coupler. The fiber guide is either an ultrapure glass or plastic cable. The receiver includes a fiber-to-light detector coupling device, a photo detector, a current-to-voltage converter, an amplifier, and an analog or digital interface.

In an optical fiber transmitter, the light source can be modulated by a digital or an analog signal. For analog modulation, the input interface matches impedances and limits the input signal amplitude. For digital modulation, the original source may already be in digital form or, if in analog form, it must be converted to a digital pulse stream. For the latter case, an analog-to-digital converter must be included in the interface.

The voltage-to-current converter serves as an electrical interface between the input circuitry and the light source. The light source is either a light-emitting diode (LED) or an injection laser diode (ILD). The amount of light emitted by either an LED or an ILD is proportional to the amount of drive current. Thus, the voltage-to-current converter converts an input signal voltage to a current that is used to drive the light source.

The source-to-fiber coupler (such as a lens) is a mechanical interface. Its function is to couple the light emitted by the source into the optical fiber cable. The optical fiber consists of a glass or plastic fiber core, a cladding, and a protective jacket. The fiber-to-light detector coupling device is also a mechanical coupler. Its function is to couple as much light as possible from the fiber cable into the light detector.

The light detector is very often either a PIN (*p*-type-*intrinsic*-*n*-type) diode or an APD (*a*valanche *photo*diode). Both the APD and the PIN diodes convert light energy to current. Consequently, a current-to-voltage converter is required. The current-to-voltage converter transforms changes in detector current to changes in output signal voltage.

The analog or digital interface at the receiver output is also an electrical interface. If analog modulation is used, the interface matches impedances and signal levels to the output circuitry. If digital modulation is used, the interface must include a digital-to-analog converter.

FIBER TYPES

Essentially, there are three varieties of optical fibers available today. All three varieties are constructed of either glass, plastic, or a combination of glass and plastic. The three varieties are

1. Plastic core and cladding
2. Glass core with plastic cladding (often called PCS fiber, plastic-clad silica)
3. Glass core and glass cladding (often called SCS, silica-clad silica)

Presently, Bell Laboratories is investigating the possibility of using a fourth variety that uses a *nonsilicate* substance, *zinc chloride*. Preliminary experiments have indicated that fibers made of this substance will be as much as 1000 times as efficient as glass—their silica-based counterpart.

Plastic fibers have several advantages over glass fibers. First, plastic fibers are more flexible and, consequently, more rugged than glass. They are easy to install, can better withstand stress, are less expensive, and weigh approximately 60% less than glass. The disadvantage of plastic fibers is their high attenuation characteristic: They do not propagate light as efficiently as glass. Consequently, plastic fibers are limited to relatively short runs, such as within a single building or a building complex.

Fibers with glass cores exhibit low attenuation characteristics; however, PCS fibers are slightly better than SCS fibers. PCS fibers are also less affected by radiation and, therefore, are more attractive to military applications. SCS fibers have the best propagation characteristics and they are easier to terminate than PCS fibers. Unfortunately, SCS cables are the least rugged, and they are more susceptible to increases in attenuation when exposed to radiation.

The selection of a fiber for a given application is a function of specific system requirements. There are always trade-offs based on the economics and logistics of a particular application.

Cable Construction

There are many different cable designs available today. Figure 11-4 shows examples of several fiber-optic cable configurations. Depending on the configuration, the cable may include a *core,* a *cladding,* a *protective tube, buffers, strength members,* and one or more *protective jackets.*

With the *loose* tube construction (shown in Figure 11-4a) each fiber is contained in a protective tube. Inside the protective tube, a polyurethane compound encapsules the fiber and prevents the intrusion of water. A phenomenon called *stress corrosion* or *static fatigue* can result if the glass fiber is exposed to long periods of high humidity. Silicon dioxide crystals interact with the moisture and cause bonds to break down, causing spontaneous fractures over a prolonged period. Some fiber cables have more than one protective coating to ensure that the fiber's characteristics do not alter if the fiber is exposed to extreme temperature changes. Surrounding the fiber's cladding is usually a coating of either lacquer, silicon, or acrylate that is typically applied to seal and preserve the fiber's strength and attenuation characteristics.

Figure 11-4b shows the construction of a *constrained* optical fiber cable. Surrounding the fiber cable are a primary and a secondary buffer. The buffer jackets provide protection for the fiber from external mechanical influences that could cause fiber breakage or excessive optical attenuation. Kevlar is a yarn-type material that increases the tensile strength of the cable. Again, an outer protective tube is filled with polyurethane, which prevents moisture from coming into contact with the fiber core.

Figure 11-4c shows a *multiple-strand* configuration. To increase the tensile strength, a steel central member and a layer of Mylar tape wrap are included in the package. Figure 11-4d shows a *ribbon* configuration, which is frequently seen in telephone systems using fiber optics. Figure 11-4e shows both the end and side views of a plastic-clad silica cable.

As mentioned, one disadvantage of optical fiber cables is their lack of tensile (pulling) strength which can be as low as a pound. For this reason, the fiber must be reinforced with strengthening material so that it can withstand mechanical stresses it will typically undergo when being pulled and jerked through underground and overhead ducts and hung on poles. Materials commonly used to strengthen and protect fibers from abrasion and environmental stress are steel, fiberglass, plastic, FR-PVC (flame-retardant polyvinyl chloride), Kevlar yarn, and paper. The type of cable construction used depends on the performance requirements of the system and both the economic and environmental constraints.

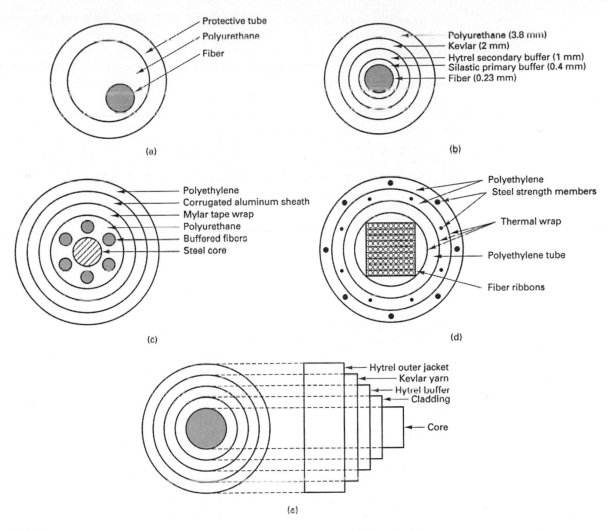

FIGURE 11-4 Fiber optic cable configurations: (a) loose tube construction; (b) constrained fiber; (c) multiple strands; (d) telephone cable; (e) plastic-clad silica cable

LIGHT PROPAGATION

The Physics of Light

Although the performance of optical fibers can be analyzed completely by application of Maxwell's equations, this is necessarily complex. For most practical applications, *geometric wave tracing* may be used instead of Maxwell's equations; ray tracing will yield sufficiently accurate results.

An atom has several energy levels or states, the lowest of which is the ground state. Any energy level above the ground state is called an *excited state*. If an atom in one energy level decays to a lower energy level, the loss of energy (in electron volts) is emitted as a photon. The energy of the photon is equal to the difference between the energy of the two energy levels. The process of decay from one energy level to another energy level is called *spontaneous decay* or *spontaneous emission*.

Atoms can be irradiated by a light source whose energy is equal to the difference between the ground level and an energy level. This can cause an electron to change from one energy level to another by absorbing light energy. The process of moving from one energy level to another is called *absorption*. When making the transition from one energy level to another, the atom absorbs a packet of energy called a *photon*. This process is similar to that of emission.

The energy absorbed or emitted (photon) is equal to the difference between the two energy levels. Mathematically,

$$E_2 - E_1 = E_p \qquad (11\text{-}2)$$

where E_p is the energy of the photon. Also,

$$E_p = hf \qquad (11\text{-}3)$$

where h = Planck's constant = 6.625×10^{-34} J-s
   f = frequency of light emitted (hertz)

Photon energy may also be expressed in terms of wavelength. Substituting Equation 11-1 into Equation 11-3 yields

$$E_p = hf \qquad (11\text{-}4)$$
$$= \frac{hc}{\lambda}$$

Velocity of Propagation

Electromagnetic energy, such as light, travels at approximately 300,000,000 m/s (186,000 miles per second) in free space. Also, the velocity of propagation is the same for all light frequencies in free space. However, it has been demonstrated that in materials more dense than free space, the velocity is reduced. When the velocity of an electromagnetic wave is reduced as it passes from one medium to another medium of a denser material, the light ray is *refracted* (bent) toward the normal. Also, in materials more dense than free space, all light frequencies do not propagate at the same velocity.

Refraction

Figure 11-5a shows how a light ray is refracted as it passes from a material of a given density into a less dense material. (Actually, the light ray is not bent, but rather, it changes direction at the interface.) Figure 11-5b shows how sunlight, which contains all light frequencies, is affected as it passes through a material more dense than free space. Refraction occurs at both air/glass interfaces. The violet wavelengths are refracted the most, and the red wavelengths are refracted the least. The spectral separation of white light in this manner is called *prismatic refraction*. It is this phenomenon that causes rainbows; water droplets in the atmosphere act as small prisms that split the white sunlight into the various wavelengths, creating a visible spectrum of color.

Refractive Index

The amount of bending or refraction that occurs at the interface of two materials of different densities is quite predictable and depends on the *refractive index* (also called *index of refraction*) of the two materials. The refractive index is simply the ratio of the velocity of propagation of a light ray in free space to the velocity of propagation of a light ray in a given material. Mathematically, the refractive index is

$$n = \frac{c}{v}$$

where c = speed of light in free space (300,000,000 meters per second)
   v = speed of light in a given material (meters per second)

Although the refractive index is also a function of frequency, the variation in most applications is insignificant and, therefore, omitted from this discussion. The indexes of refraction of several common materials are given in Table 11-1.

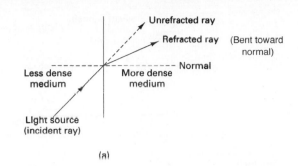

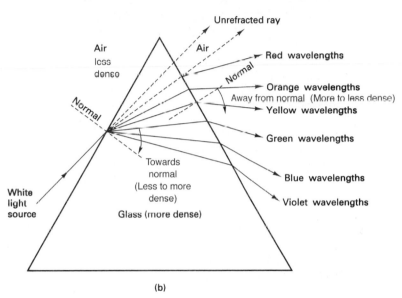

FIGURE 11-5 Refraction of light. (a) light refraction; (b) prismatic refraction

TABLE 11-1 Typical Indexes of Refraction

Medium	Index of Refraction*
Vacuum	1.0
Air	1.0003 ($\approx$1.0)
Water	1.33
Ethyl alcohol	1.36
Fused quartz	1.46
Glass fiber	1.5–1.9
Diamond	2.0–2.42
Silicon	3.4
Gallium-arsenide	3.6

Increasing density (with downward arrow beside the table)

as density increases, velocity of propagation decreases and the refractive index increases (i.e., refractive index is inversely proportional to velocity and directly proportional to density)

*Index of refraction is based on a wavelength of light emitted from a sodium flame (5890 Å).

How a light ray reacts when it meets the interface of two transmissive materials that have different indexes of refraction can be explained with Snell's law. Snell's law simply states

$$n_1 \sin \theta_1 = n_2 \sin \theta_2 \qquad (11\text{-}5)$$

where n_1 = refractive index of material 1 (unitless)
n_2 = refractive index of material 2 (unitless)
θ_1 = angle of incidence (degrees)
θ_2 = angle of refraction (degrees)

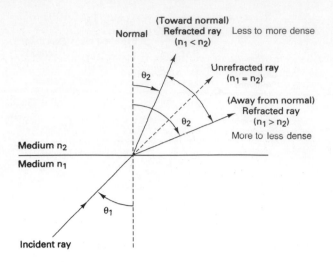

FIGURE 11-6 Refractive model for Snell's law.

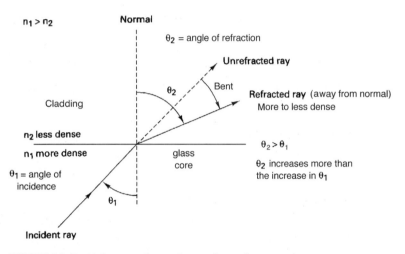

FIGURE 11-7 Light ray refracted away from the normal.

A refractive index model for Snell's law is shown in Figure 11-6. At the interface, the incident ray may be refracted toward the normal or away from it, depending on whether n_1 is less than or greater than n_2.

Figure 11-7 shows how a light ray is refracted as it travels from a more dense (higher refractive index) material into a less dense (lower refractive index) material. It can be seen that the light ray changes direction at the interface, and the angle of refraction is greater than the angle of incidence. Consequently, when a light ray enters a less dense material, the ray bends away from the normal. The normal is simply a line drawn perpendicular to the interface at the point where the incident ray strikes the interface. Similarly, when a light ray enters a more dense material, the ray bends toward the normal.

Example 11-1

In Figure 11-7, let medium 1 be glass and medium 2 be ethyl alcohol. For an angle of incidence of 30°, determine the angle of refraction.

Solution From Table 11-1,

$$n_1 \text{ (glass)} = 1.5$$
$$n_2 \text{ (ethyl alcohol)} = 1.36$$

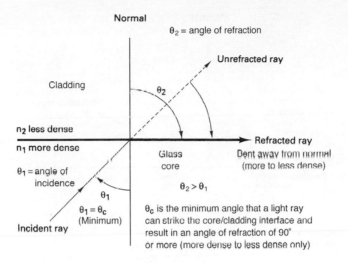

Normal

θ_2 = angle of refraction

Unrefracted ray

Cladding

θ_2

n_2 less dense

n_1 more dense

Refracted ray
Bent away from normal
(more to less dense)

Glass
core

θ_1 = angle of
incidence

$\theta_2 > \theta_1$

θ_1

$\theta_1 = \theta_c$
(Minimum)

Incident ray

θ_c is the minimum angle that a light ray
can strike the core/cladding interface and
result in an angle of refraction of 90°
or more (more dense to less dense only)

FIGURE 11-8 Critical angle refraction.

Rearranging Equation 11-5 and substituting for n_1, n_2, and θ_1 gives us

$$\frac{n_1}{n_2} \sin \theta_1 = \sin \theta_2$$

$$\frac{1.5}{1.36} \sin 30 = 0.5514 = \sin \theta_2$$

$$\theta_2 = \sin^{-1} 0.5514 = 33.47°$$

The result indicates that the light ray refracted (bent) or changed direction by 33.47° at the interface. Because the light was traveling from a more dense material into a less dense material, the ray bent away from the normal.

Critical Angle

Figure 11-8 shows a condition in which an *incident ray* is at an angle such that the angle of refraction is 90° and the refracted ray is along the interface. (It is important to note that the light ray is traveling from a medium of higher refractive index to a medium with a lower refractive index.) Again, using Snell's law,

$$\sin \theta_1 = \frac{n_2}{n_1} \sin \theta_2$$

With $\theta_2 = 90°$,

$$\sin \theta_1 = \frac{n_2}{n_1} (1) \qquad \text{or} \qquad \sin \theta_1 = \frac{n_2}{n_1}$$

and

$$\sin^{-1} \frac{n_2}{n_1} = \theta_1 = \theta_c \qquad (11\text{-}6)$$

where θ_c is the critical angle.

The *critical angle* is defined as the minimum angle of incidence at which a light ray may strike the interface of two media and result in an angle of refraction of 90° or greater. (This definition pertains only when the light ray is traveling from a more dense medium into a less dense medium.) If the angle of refraction is 90° or greater, the light ray is not allowed to penetrate the less dense material. Consequently, total reflection takes place at the interface, and the angle of reflection is equal to the angle of incidence. Figure 11-9 shows a comparison of the angle of refraction and the angle of reflection when the angle of incidence is less than or more than the critical angle.

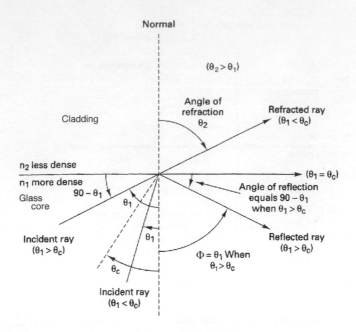

FIGURE 11-9 Angle of reflection and refraction

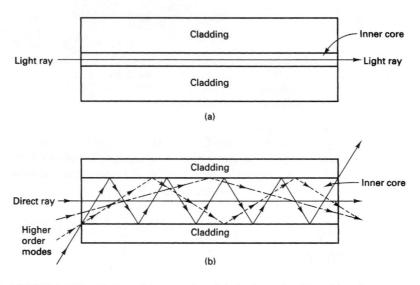

FIGURE 11-10 Modes of propagation: (a) single mode; (b) multimode

PROPAGATION OF LIGHT THROUGH AN OPTICAL FIBER

Light can be propagated down an optical fiber cable by either reflection or refraction. How the light is propagated depends on the *mode of propagation* and the *index profile* of the fiber.

Mode of Propagation

In fiber optics terminology, the word *mode* simply means path. If there is only one path for light to take down the cable, it is called *single mode*. If there is more than one path, it is called *multimode*. Figure 11-10 shows single and multimode propagation of light down an optical fiber.

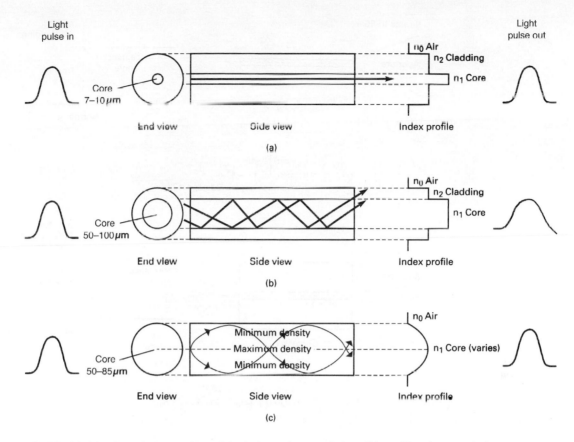

FIGURE 11-11 Core index profiles: (a) single-mode step index; (b) multimode step index; (c) multimode graded index

Index Profile

The index profile of an optical fiber is a graphical representation of the value of the refractive index across the fiber. The refractive index is plotted on the horizontal axis and the radial distance from the core axis is plotted on the vertical axis. Figure 11-11 shows the core index profiles of three types of fiber cables.

There are two basic types of index profiles: step and graded. A *step-index fiber* has a central core with a uniform refractive index. The core is surrounded by an outside cladding with a uniform refractive index less than that of the central core. From Figure 11-11 it can be seen that in a step-index fiber there is an abrupt change in the refractive index at the core/cladding interface. In a *graded-index fiber* there is no cladding, and the refractive index of the core is nonuniform; it is highest at the center and decreases gradually with distance toward the outer edge.

OPTICAL FIBER CONFIGURATIONS

Essentially, there are three types of optical fiber configurations: single-mode step index, multimode step index, and multimode graded index.

Single-Mode Step-Index Fiber

A *single-mode step-index fiber* has a central core that is sufficiently small so that there is essentially only one path that light may take as it propagates down the cable. This type of fiber is shown in Figure 11-12. In the simplest form of single-mode step-index fiber, the

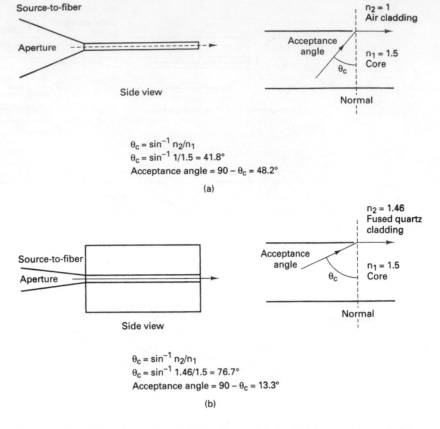

$$\theta_c = \sin^{-1} n_2/n_1$$
$$\theta_c = \sin^{-1} 1/1.5 = 41.8°$$
$$\text{Acceptance angle} = 90 - \theta_c = 48.2°$$

(a)

$$\theta_c = \sin^{-1} n_2/n_1$$
$$\theta_c = \sin^{-1} 1.46/1.5 = 76.7°$$
$$\text{Acceptance angle} = 90 - \theta_c = 13.3°$$

(b)

FIGURE 11-12 Single-mode step-index fibers: (a) air cladding; (b) glass cladding

outside cladding is simply air (Figure 11-12a). The refractive index of the glass core (n_1) is approximately 1.5, and the refractive index of the air cladding (n_0) is 1. The large difference in the refractive indexes results in a small critical angle (approximately 42°) at the glass/air interface. Consequently, the fiber will accept light from a wide aperture. This makes it relatively easy to couple light from a source into the cable. However, this type of fiber is typically very weak and of limited practical use.

A more practical type of single-mode step-index fiber is one that has a cladding other than air (Figure 11-12b). The refractive index of the cladding (n_2) is slightly less than that of the central core (n_1) and is uniform throughout the cladding. This type of cable is physically stronger than the air-clad fiber, but the critical angle is also much higher (approximately 77°). This results in a small acceptance angle and a narrow source-to-fiber aperture, making it much more difficult to couple light into the fiber from a light source.

With both types of single-mode step-index fibers, light is propagated down the fiber through reflection. Light rays that enter the fiber propagate straight down the core or, perhaps, are reflected once. Consequently, all light rays follow approximately the same path down the cable and take approximately the same amount of time to travel the length of the cable. This is one overwhelming advantage of single-mode step-index fibers and will be explained in more detail later in this chapter.

A single-mode optical fiber will transmit single mode for all wavelengths that are longer than the fiber's cutoff wavelength. The cutoff wavelength is calculated as follows:

$$\lambda_c = \frac{2\pi a n_1 \sqrt{2\Delta}}{2.405} \ (\mu m) \tag{11-7}$$

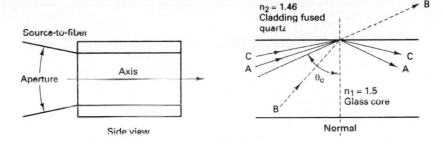

FIGURE 11-13 Multimode step-index fiber

where λ_c = cutoff wavelength (μm)
$\quad\quad\quad n_1$ = core index of refraction (unitless)
$\quad\quad\quad n_2$ = cladding index of refraction (unitless)
$\quad\quad\quad a$ = core radius (μm)

$$\Delta = \frac{n_1 - n_2}{n_1} \text{ (unitless)}$$

Example 11-2

For a 3-μm-diameter optical fiber with core and cladding indexes of refraction of 1.545 and 1.510, respectively; determine the cutoff wavelength.

$$\Delta = \frac{1.545 - 1.510}{1.545} = 0.023$$

$$a = \frac{3 \ \mu m}{2} = 1.5 \ \mu m$$

$$\lambda_c = \frac{(2\pi)(1.5 \ \mu m)(1.545)\sqrt{2(0.023)}}{2.405}$$

$$= 1.29 \ \mu m$$

Multimode Step-Index Fiber

A *multimode step-index fiber* is shown in Figure 11-13. It is similar to the single-mode configuration except that the center core is much larger. This type of fiber has a large light-to-fiber aperture and, consequently, allows more light to enter the cable. The light rays that strike the core/cladding interface at an angle greater than the critical angle (ray A) are propagated down the core in a zigzag fashion, continuously reflecting off the interface boundary. Light rays that strike the core/cladding interface at an angle less than the critical angle (ray B) enter the cladding and are lost. It can be seen that there are many paths that a light ray may follow as it propagates down the fiber. As a result, all light rays do not follow the same path and, consequently, do not take the same amount of time to travel the length of the fiber.

Multimode Graded-Index Fiber

A *multimode graded-index fiber* is shown in Figure 11-14. A multimode graded-index fiber is characterized by a central core that has a refractive index that is nonuniform; it is maximum at the center and decreases gradually toward the outer edge. Light is propagated down this type of fiber through refraction. As a light ray propagates diagonally across the core toward the center it is continually intersecting a less-dense-to-more-dense interface. Consequently, the light rays are constantly being refracted, which results in a continuous bending of the light rays. Light enters the fiber at many different angles. As they propagate down

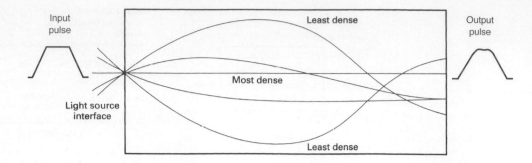

FIGURE 11-14 Multimode graded-index fiber

the fiber, the light rays that travel in the outermost area of the fiber travel a greater distance than the rays traveling near the center. Because the refractive index decreases with distance from the center and the velocity is inversely proportional to the refractive index, the light rays traveling farthest from the center propagate at a higher velocity. Consequently, they take approximately the same amount of time to travel the length of the fiber.

Comparison of the Three Types of Optical Fibers

Single-mode step-index fiber

Advantages

1. There is minimum dispersion. Because all rays propagating down the fiber take approximately the same path, they take approximately the same amount of time to travel down the cable. Consequently, a pulse of light entering the cable can be reproduced at the receiving end very accurately.
2. Because of the high accuracy in reproducing transmitted pulses at the receive end, larger bandwidths and higher information transmission rates are possible with single-mode step-index fibers than with the other types of fibers.

Disadvantages

1. Because the central core is very small, it is difficult to couple light into and out of this type of fiber. The source-to-fiber aperture is the smallest of all the fiber types.
2. Again, because of the small central core, a highly directive light source such as a laser is required to couple light into a single-mode step-index fiber.
3. Single-mode step-index fibers are expensive and difficult to manufacture.

Multimode step-index fiber

Advantages

1. Multimode step-index fibers are inexpensive and simple to manufacture.
2. It is easy to couple light into and out of multimode step-index fibers; they have a relatively large source-to-fiber aperture.

Disadvantages

1. Light rays take many different paths down the fiber, which results in large differences in their propagation times. Because of this, rays traveling down this type of fiber have a tendency to spread out. Consequently, a pulse of light propagating down a multimode step-index fiber is distorted more than with the other types of fibers.
2. The bandwidth and rate of information transfer possible with this type of cable are less than the other types.

Multimode graded-index fiber.   Essentially, there are no outstanding advantages or disadvantages of this type of fiber. Multimode graded-index fibers are easier to couple light into and out of than single-mode step-index fibers but more difficult than multimode

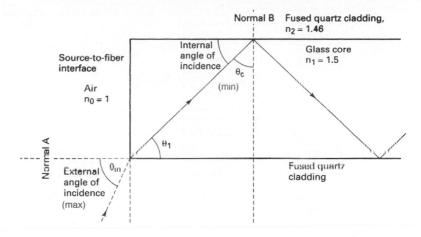

FIGURE 11-15 Ray propagation into and down an optical fiber cable

step-index fibers. Distortion due to multiple propagation paths is greater than in single-mode step-index fibers but less than in multimode step-index fibers. Graded-index fibers are easier to manufacture than single-mode step-index fibers but more difficult than multimode step-index fibers. The multimode graded-index fiber is considered an intermediate fiber compared with the other types.

ACCEPTANCE ANGLE AND ACCEPTANCE CONE

In previous discussions, the *source-to-fiber aperture* was mentioned several times, and the *critical* and *acceptance* angles at the point where a light ray strikes the core/cladding interface were explained. The following discussion deals with the light-gathering ability of the fiber, the ability to couple light from the source into the fiber cable.

Figure 11-15 shows the source end of a fiber cable. When light rays enter the fiber, they strike the air/glass interface at normal A. The refractive index of air is 1 and the refractive index of the glass core is 1.5. Consequently, the light entering at the air/glass interface propagates from a less dense medium into a more dense medium. Under these conditions and according to Snell's law, the light rays will refract toward the normal. This causes the light rays to change direction and propagate diagonally down the core at an angle (θ_c) that is different than the external angle of incidence at the air/glass interface (θ_{in}). For a ray of light to propagate down the cable, it must strike the internal core/cladding interface at an angle that is greater than the critical angle (θ_c).

Applying Snell's law to the external angle of incidence yields the following expression:

$$n_0 \sin \theta_{in} = n_1 \sin \theta_1 \tag{11-8}$$

and

$$\theta_1 = 90 - \theta_c$$

Thus,

$$\sin \theta_1 = \sin (90 - \theta_c) = \cos \theta_c \tag{11-9}$$

Substituting Equation 11-9 into Equation 11-8 yields the following expression:

$$n_0 \sin \theta_{in} = n_1 \cos \theta_c$$

Rearranging and solving for $\sin \theta_{in}$ gives us

$$\sin \theta_{in} = \frac{n_1}{n_0} \cos \theta_c \tag{11-10}$$

Figure 11-16 shows the geometric relationship of Equation 11-10.

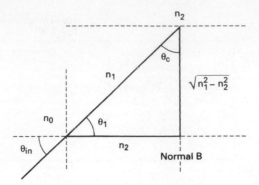

FIGURE 11-16 Geometric relationship of Equation 11-10

From Figure 11-16 and using the Pythagorean theorem, we obtain

$$\cos \theta_c = \frac{\sqrt{n_1^2 - n_2^2}}{n_1} \tag{11-11}$$

Substituting Equation 11-11 into Equation 11-10 yields

$$\sin \theta_{in} = \frac{n_1}{n_0} \frac{\sqrt{n_1^2 - n_2^2}}{n_1}$$

Reducing the equation gives

$$\sin \theta_{in} = \frac{\sqrt{n_1^2 - n_2^2}}{n_0} \tag{11-12}$$

and

$$\theta_{in} = \sin^{-1} \frac{\sqrt{n_1^2 - n_2^2}}{n_0} \tag{11-13}$$

Because light rays generally enter the fiber from an air medium, n_0 equals 1. This simplifies Equation 11-13 to

$$\theta_{in(max)} = \sin^{-1} \sqrt{n_1^2 - n_2^2} \tag{11-14}$$

θ_{in} is called the *acceptance angle* or *acceptance cone* half-angle. It defines the maximum angle in which external light rays may strike the air/fiber interface and still propagate down the fiber with a response that is no greater than 10 dB below the maximum value. Acceptance angle is shown in Figure 11-17a. Rotating the acceptance angle around the fiber axis describes the *acceptance cone* of the fiber input, shown in Figure 11-17b.

Numerical Aperture

Numerical aperture (NA) is closely related to acceptance angle and is the figure of merit commonly used to measure the magnitude of the acceptance angle. In essence, numerical aperture is used to describe the light-gathering or light-collecting ability of an optical fiber. The larger the magnitude of the numerical aperture, the greater the amount of external light the fiber will accept. For single or multimode fibers, numerical aperture is mathematically defined as the sine of the maximum angle a light ray entering the fiber can have in respect to the axis of the fiber and still propagate down the cable by internal reflection (i.e., the sine of the acceptance half-angle). Light rays entering the cable from outside the acceptance cone will enter the cladding and, therefore, will not propagate down the cable. Thus, for light entering the fiber from free space, numerical aperture is

$$NA = \sin \theta_{in} \tag{11-15}$$

and

$$NA = \sqrt{n_1^2 - n_2^2} \tag{11-16}$$

Also,

$$\sin^{-1} NA = \theta_{in} \tag{11-17}$$

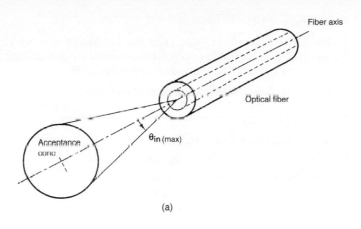

(a)

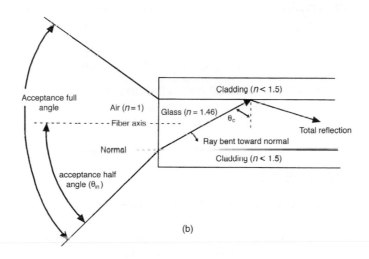

(b)

FIGURE 11-17 (a) Acceptance angle; (b) Acceptance cone

where   NA = numerical aperture (unitless)
        n_1 = refractive index of the glass core (unitless)
        n_2 = refractive index of the cladding (unitless)
        θ_{in} = acceptance angle (degrees)

A larger core diameter does not necessarily produce a larger numerical aperture; however, in practice, larger core fibers tend to have larger numerical apertures. Large-core fibers have numerical apertures of 0.3 or larger. Graded-index fibers generally have numerical apertures between 0.2 and 0.3, and single-mode fibers have numerical apertures between 0.1 to 0.15. The numerical aperture of single-mode fibers is generally not as important as it is for multimode fibers, because light leaving a fiber operating in the single mode does not spread out in the same way as it does from multimode fibers.

Numerical aperture can be calculated using Equation 11-15 but in practice it is generally measured by looking at the output of a fiber. Because the light-guiding properties of a fiber cable are symmetrical, light leaves a cable and spreads out over an angle equal to the acceptance angle.

Example 11-3

For this example refer to Figure 11-15. For a multimode step-index fiber with a glass core ($n_1 = 1.5$) and a fused quartz cladding ($n_2 = 1.46$), determine the critical angle (θ_c), acceptance angle (θ_{in}), and numerical aperture. The source-to-fiber medium is air.

Solution Substituting into Equation 11-6, we have

$$\theta_c = \sin^{-1}\frac{n_2}{n_1} = \sin^{-1}\frac{1.46}{1.5} = 76.7°$$

Substituting into Equation 11-14 yields

$$\theta_c = \sin^{-1}\sqrt{n_1^2 - n_2^2} = \sin^{-1}\sqrt{1.5^2 - 1.46^2} = 20.2°$$

Substituting into Equation 11-15 gives us

$$NA = \sin\theta_{in} = \sin 20.2 = 0.344$$

The maximum diameter a single-mode optical fiber can have is proportional to the wavelength of the light ray entering the cable and the numerical aperture of the fiber. Mathematically, the maximum radius of the core of a single-mode fiber is

$$r_{max} = \frac{0.383\,\lambda}{NA} \tag{11-18}$$

where r_{max} = maximum core radius (meters)
    NA = numerical aperture (unitless)
    λ = light ray wavelength (meters)

LOSSES IN OPTICAL FIBER CABLES

Power loss in an optical fiber cable is probably the most important characteristic of the cable. Power loss is often called *attenuation* and results in a reduction in the power of the light wave as it travels down the cable. Attenuation has several adverse effects on performance including reducing the system's bandwidth, information transmission rate, efficiency, and overall system capacity.

The standard formula used to express total power loss in a fiber cable is

$$A(\text{dB}) = 10\log\frac{P_{out}}{P_{in}} \tag{11-19}$$

where $A(\text{dB})$ = total reduction in power level (attenuation)
    P_{out} = cable output power (watts)
    P_{in} = cable input power (watts)

In general, multimode fibers tend to have higher attenuation loss than single-mode cables primarily due to the increased scattering of the light wave produced from the dopants. Table 11-2 shows output power as a percentage of input power for an optical fiber cable with several values of decibel loss. A 3-dB cable loss reduces the output power to 50% of the input power.

Although total power loss is of primary importance, attenuation in an optical cable is generally expressed in decibels of loss per unit length. Attenuation is expressed as a positive dB value because by definition it is a loss. Table 11-3 lists attenuation in dB/km for several types of fiber cables.

The optical power in watts measured at a given distance from a power source can be determined mathematically as

$$P = P_t \times 10^{-Al/10} \tag{11-20a}$$

TABLE 11-2 % Output Power-versus-Loss in dB

Loss (dB)	Output Power (%)
1	79
3	50
6	25
9	12.5
10	10
13	5
20	1
30	0.1
40	0.01
50	0.001

TABLE 11-3 Fiber Cable Attenuation

Cable Type	Core Diameter (μm)	Cladding Diameter (μm)	NA (unitless)	Attenuation (dB/km)
Single-mode	8	125	—	0.5 @ 1300 nm
	5	125	—	0.4 @ 1300 nm
Graded-index	50	125	0.2	4 @ 850 nm
	100	140	0.3	5 @ 850 nm
Step-index	200	380	0.27	6 @ 850 nm
	300	440	0.27	6 @ 850 nm
PCS	200	350	0.3	10 @ 790 nm
	400	550	0.3	10 @ 790 nm
Plastic	—	750	0.5	400 @ 650 nm
	—	1000	0.5	400 @ 650 nm

where P = measured power level (watts)
  P_t = transmit power level (watts)
  A = cable power loss (dB/km)
  l = cable length (km)

Likewise, the optical power in decibel units is

$$P(\text{dBm}) = P_{\text{in}}(\text{dBm}) - A(\text{dB}) \qquad (11\text{-}20\text{b})$$

where P = measured power level (dBm)
  P_{in} = transmit power (dBm)
  A = cable power loss (dB/km)

Example 11-4

For a single-mode optical cable with 0.25 dB/km loss, determine the optical power 100 km from a 0.1-m W source.

Solution Substituting into Equation 11-20a gives

$$P = 0.1 \text{ mW} \times 10^{-[(0.25)(100)/10]}$$
$$= 1 \times 10^{-4} \times 10^{-[(0.25)(100)/10]}$$
$$= [1 \times 10^{-4}][1 \times 10^{-2.5}]$$
$$= 0.316 \text{ μW}$$

and

$$P(\text{dBm}) = 10 \log \frac{0.316 \text{μW}}{0.001}$$
$$= -35 \text{ dBm}$$

or by substituting into Equation 11-20b

$$P(\text{dBm}) = 10 \log \frac{0.1 \text{ mW}}{0.001} - [(100 \text{ km})(0.25 \text{ dB/km})]$$
$$= -10 \text{ dBm} - 25 \text{ dB}$$
$$= -35 \text{ dBm}$$

Transmission losses in optical fiber cables are one of the most important characteristics of the fiber. Losses in the fiber result in a reduction in the light power and, thus, reduce the system bandwidth, information transmission rate, efficiency, and overall system capacity. The predominant fiber losses are as follows:

1. Absorption losses
2. Material or Rayleigh scattering losses
3. Chromatic or wavelength dispersion
4. Radiation losses
5. Modal dispersion
6. Coupling losses

Absorption Losses

Absorption loss in optical fibers is analogous to power dissipation in copper cables; impurities in the fiber absorb the light and convert it to heat. The ultrapure glass used to manufacture optical fibers is approximately 99.9999% pure. Still, absorption losses between 1 dB/km and 1000 dB/km are typical. Essentially, there are three factors that contribute to the absorption losses in optical fibers: ultraviolet absorption, infrared absorption, and ion resonance absorption.

Ultraviolet absorption.   Ultraviolet absorption is caused by valence electrons in the silica material from which fibers are manufactured. Light *ionizes* the valence electrons into conduction. The ionization is equivalent to a loss in the total light field and, consequently, contributes to the transmission losses of the fiber.

Infrared absorption.   Infrared absorption is a result of *photons* of light that are absorbed by the atoms of the glass core molecules. The absorbed photons are converted to random mechanical vibrations typical of heating.

Ion resonance absorption.   Ion resonance absorption is caused by OH^- ions in the material. The source of the OH^- ions is water molecules that have been trapped in the glass during the manufacturing process. Ion absorption is also caused by iron, copper, and chromium molecules.

Figure 11-18 shows typical losses in optical fiber cables due to ultraviolet, infrared, and ion resonance absorption.

Material or Rayleigh Scattering Losses

During the manufacturing process, glass is drawn into long fibers of very small diameter. During this process, the glass is in a plastic state (not liquid and not solid). The tension applied to the glass during this process causes the cooling glass to develop submicroscopic irregularities that are permanently formed in the fiber. When light rays that are propagating down a fiber strike one of these impurities, they are *diffracted*. Diffraction causes the light to disperse or spread out in many directions. Some of the diffracted light continues down the fiber and some of it escapes through the cladding. The light rays that escape represent a loss in light power. This is called *Rayleigh scattering loss*. Figure 11-19 graphically shows the relationship between wavelength and Rayleigh scattering loss.

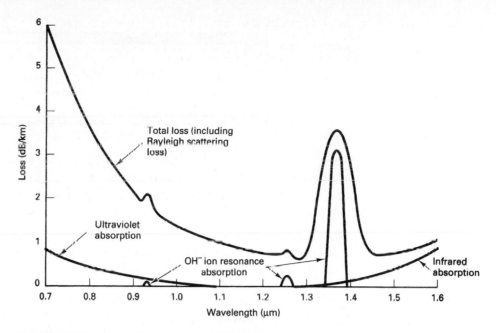

FIGURE 11-18 Absorption losses in optical fibers

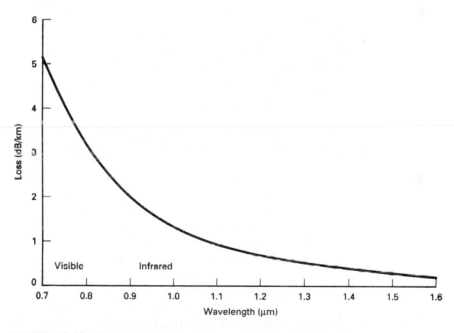

FIGURE 11-19 Rayleigh scattering loss as a function of wavelength

Chromatic or Wavelength Dispersion

As stated previously, the refractive index of a material is wavelength dependent. Light-emitting diodes (LEDs) emit light that contains a combination of wavelengths. Each wavelength within the composite light signal travels at a different velocity. Consequently, light rays that are simultaneously emitted from an LED and propagated down an optical fiber do not arrive at the far end of the fiber at the same time. This results in a distorted receive signal; the distortion is called *chromatic distortion*. Chromatic distortion can be eliminated by using a monochromatic source such as an injection laser diode (ILD). Chromatic or wavelength dispersion occurs only in fibers with a single mode of transmission.

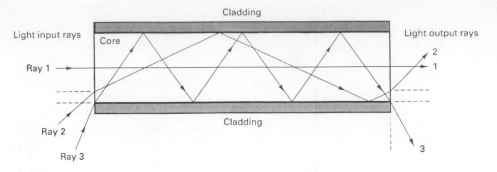

FIGURE 11-20 Light propagation down a multimode step-index fiber

Radiation Losses

Radiation losses are caused predominately by small bends and kinks in the fiber. Essentially, there are two types of bends: microbends and constant-radius bends. *Microbending* occurs as a result of differences in the thermal contraction rates between the core and cladding material. A microbend is a miniature bend or geometric imperfection along the axis of the fiber which represents a discontinuity in the fiber where Rayleigh scattering can occur. Microbending losses generally contribute less than 20% of the total attenuation in a fiber. *Constant-radius bends* are caused by excessive pressure and tension and generally occur when fibers are bent during handling or installation.

Modal Dispersion

Modal dispersion or *pulse spreading* is caused by the difference in the propagation times of light rays that take different paths down a fiber. Obviously, modal dispersion can occur only in multimode fibers. It can be reduced considerably by using graded-index fibers and almost entirely eliminated by using single-mode step-index fibers.

Modal dispersion can cause a pulse of light energy to spread out as it propagates down a fiber. If the pulse spreading is sufficiently severe, one pulse may fall back on top of the next pulse (this is an example of intersymbol interference). In a multimode step-index fiber, a light ray that propagates straight down the axis of the fiber takes the least amount of time to travel the length of the fiber. A light ray that strikes the core/cladding interface at the critical angle will undergo the largest number of internal reflections and, consequently, take the longest time to travel the length of the fiber.

For multimode propagation, dispersion is often expressed as a *bandwidth length product* (BLP) or *bandwidth distance product* (BDP). BLP indicates what signal frequencies can be propagated through a given distance of fiber cable and is expressed mathematically as the product of bandwidth (sometimes called *linewidth* with optical frequencies) and distance. Bandwidth length products are often expressed in MHz-km units.

Figure 11-20 shows three rays of light propagating down a multimode step-index fiber. The lowest-order mode (ray 1) travels in a path parallel to the axis of the fiber. The middle-order mode (ray 2) bounces several times at the interface before traveling the length of the fiber. The highest-order mode (ray 3) makes many trips back and forth across the fiber as it propagates the entire length. It can be seen that ray 3 travels a considerably longer distance than ray 1 as it propagates down the fiber. Consequently, if the three rays of light were emitted into the fiber at the same time and represented a pulse of light energy, the three rays would reach the far end of the fiber at different times and result in a spreading out of the light energy in respect to time. This is called modal dispersion and results in a stretched pulse that is also reduced in amplitude at the output of the fiber. All three rays of light propagate through the same material at the same velocity, but ray 3 must travel a longer distance and, consequently, takes a longer period of time to propagate down the fiber.

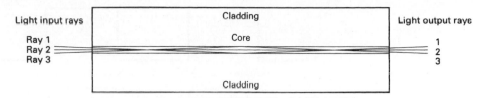

FIGURE 11-21 Light propagation down a single-mode step-index fiber

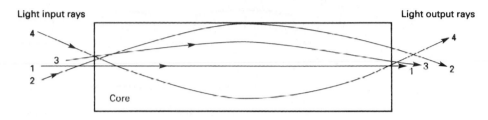

FIGURE 11-22 Light propagation down a multimode graded-index fiber

Figure 11-21 shows light rays propagating down a single-mode step-index fiber. Because the radial dimension of the fiber is sufficiently small, there is only a single path for each of the rays to follow as they propagate down the length of the fiber. Consequently, each ray of light travels the same distance in a given period of time and the light rays have exactly the same time relationship at the far end of the fiber as they had when they entered the cable. The result is no *modal dispersion* or *pulse stretching*.

Figure 11-22 shows light propagating down a multimode graded-index fiber. Three rays are shown traveling in three different modes. Each ray travels a different path but they all take approximately the same amount of time to propagate the length of fiber. This is because the refractive index of the fiber decreases with distance from the center, and the velocity at which a ray travels is inversely proportional to the refractive index. Consequently, the farther rays 2 and 3 travel from the center of the fiber, the faster they propagate.

Figure 11-23 shows the relative time/energy relationship of a pulse of light as it propagates down a fiber cable. It can be seen that as the pulse propagates down the fiber, the light rays that make up the pulse spread out in time, which causes a corresponding reduction in the pulse amplitude and stretching of the pulse width. This is called *pulse spreading* or *pulse-width dispersion* and causes errors in digital transmission. It can also be seen that as light energy from one pulse falls back in time, it will interfere with the next pulse causing intersymbol interference.

Figure 11-24a shows a unipolar return-to-zero (UPRZ) digital transmission. With UPRZ transmission (assuming a very narrow pulse) if light energy from pulse A were to fall back (*spread*) one bit time (t_b), it would interfere with pulse B and change what was a logic 0 to a logic 1. Figure 11-24b shows a unipolar nonreturn-to-zero (UPNRZ) digital transmission where each pulse is equal to the bit time. With UPNRZ transmission, if energy from pulse A were to fall back one-half of a bit time, it would interfere with pulse B. Consequently, UPRZ transmissions can tolerate twice as much delay or spread as UPNRZ transmissions.

The difference between the absolute delay times of the fastest and slowest rays of light propagating down a fiber of unit length is called the *pulse-spreading constant* (Δt) and is generally expressed in nanoseconds per kilometer (ns/km). The total pulse spread (ΔT) is then equal to the pulse-spreading constant (Δt) times the total fiber length (L). Mathematically, ΔT is

$$\Delta T_{(ns)} = \Delta t_{(ns/km)} \times L_{(km)} \tag{11-21}$$

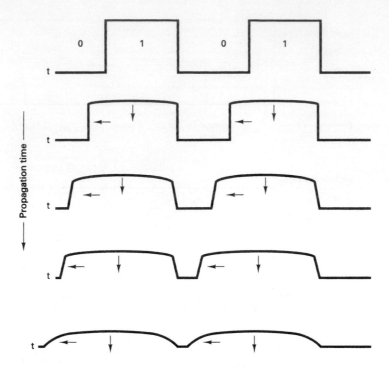

FIGURE 11-23 Pulse-width dispersion in an optical fiber cable

For UPRZ transmissions, the maximum data transmission rate in bits per second (bps) is expressed as

$$f_{b(\text{bps})} = \frac{1}{\Delta t \times L} \tag{11-22}$$

and for UPNRZ transmissions, the maximum transmission rate is

$$f_{b(\text{bps})} = \frac{1}{2\,\Delta t \times L} \tag{11-23}$$

Example 11-5

For an optical fiber 10 km long with a pulse-spreading constant of 5 ns/km, determine the maximum digital transmission rates for
(a) Return-to-zero.
(b) Nonreturn-to-zero transmissions.

Solution (a) Substituting into Equation 11-22 yields

$$f_b = \frac{1}{5\ \text{ns/km} \times 10\ \text{km}} = 20\ \text{Mbps}$$

(b) Substituting into Equation 11-23 yields

$$f_b = \frac{1}{(2 \times 5\ \text{ns/km}) \times 10\ \text{km}} = 10\ \text{Mbps}$$

The results indicate that the digital transmission rate possible for this optical fiber is twice as high (20 Mbps versus 10 Mbps) for UPRZ as for UPNRZ transmission.

Coupling Losses

In fiber cables coupling losses can occur at any of the following three types of optical junctions: light source-to-fiber connections, fiber-to-fiber connections, and fiber-to-photodetector

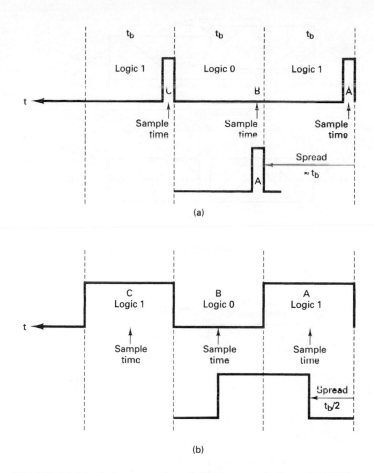

FIGURE 11-24 Pulse spreading of digital transmissions: (a) UPRZ; (b) UPNRZ

connections. Junction losses are most often caused by one of the following alignment problems: lateral misalignment, gap misalignment, angular misalignment, and imperfect surface finishes. These impairments are shown in Figure 11-25.

Lateral misalignment. This is shown in Figure 11-25a and is the lateral or axial displacement between two pieces of adjoining fiber cables. The amount of loss can be from a couple of tenths of a decibel to several decibels. This loss is generally negligible if the fiber axes are aligned to within 5% of the smaller fiber's diameter.

Gap misalignment. This is shown in Figure 11-25b and is sometimes called *end separation*. When *splices* are made in optical fibers, the fibers should actually touch. The farther apart the fibers are, the greater the loss of light. If two fibers are joined with a connector, the ends should not touch, because the two ends rubbing against each other in the connector could cause damage to either or both fibers.

Angular misalignment. This is shown in Figure 11-25c and is sometimes called *angular displacement*. If the angular displacement is less than 2°, the loss will be less than 0.5 dB.

Imperfect surface finish. This is shown in Figure 11-25d. The ends of the two adjoining fibers should be highly polished and fit together squarely. If the fiber ends are less than 3° off from perpendicular, the losses will be less than 0.5 dB.

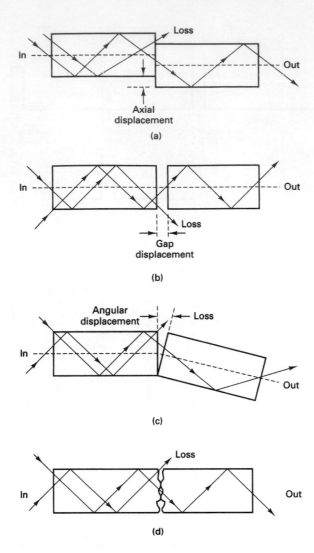

FIGURE 11-25 Fiber alignment impairments: (a) lateral misalignment; (b) gap displacement; (c) angular misalignment; (d) surface finish

LIGHT SOURCES

The range of light frequencies detectable by the human eye occupies a very narrow segment of the total electromagnetic frequency spectrum. For example, blue light occupies the higher wavelengths of visible light and red hues occupy the lower wavelengths. Figure 11-26 shows the light wavelength distribution produced from a tungsten lamp and the range of wavelengths perceivable by the human eye. As the figure shows, the human eye can detect only those lightwaves between approximately 380 nm and 780 nm. Furthermore, light consists of many shades of colors which are directly related to the heat of the energy being radiated. Figure 11-26 also shows that more visible light is produced as the temperature of the lamp is increased.

Light sources used for optical fiber systems must be at wavelengths efficiently propagated by the optical fiber. In addition, the range of wavelengths must be considered, because the wider the range, the more likely the chance that chromatic dispersion will occur. Light sources must also produce sufficient power to allow the light to propagate through

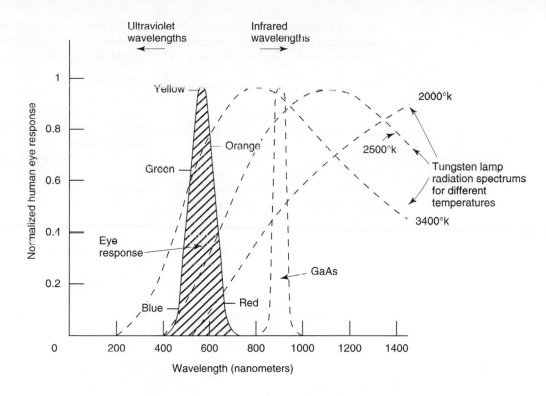

FIGURE 11-26 Tungsten lamp radiation and human eye response.

the fiber without causing nonlinear distortion in the fiber itself or in the receiver. Lastly, the light source must be constructed so that its output can be efficiently coupling into the fiber.

Optical Power

Light intensity is a rather complex concept that can be expressed in either *photometric* or *radiometric* terms. Photometry is the science of measuring only light waves that are visible to the human eye. Radiometry, on the other hand, measures light throughout the entire electromagnetic spectrum. In photometric terms, light intensity is generally described in terms of luminous *flux density* and measured in lumens per unit area. Radiometric terms, however, are often more useful to the engineer and technologist. In radiometric terms, *optical power* measures the rate at which electromagnetic waves transfer light energy. In simple terms, optical power is described as the flow of light energy past a given point in a specified time. Optical power is expressed mathematically as

$$Power = \frac{d(\text{energy})}{d(\text{time})}$$

or

$$P = \frac{dQ}{dt} \text{ (watts)} \tag{11-24}$$

where P = optical power (watts)
  dQ = instantaneous charge (joules)
  dt = instantaneous change in time (seconds)

Optical power is sometimes called *radiant flux* (ϕ), which is equivalent to joules per second, and is the same power that is measured electrically or thermally in watts. Radiometric terms are generally used with light sources with output powers ranging from tens of microwatts to more than 100 milliwatts. Optical power is generally stated in decibels relative to a defined power level such as 1 mW (dBm) or 1 μW (dBμ). Mathematically stated,

$$dBm = 10 \log \frac{P(\text{watts})}{0.001 \text{ watt}} \qquad (11\text{-}25)$$

and

$$dB\mu = 10 \log \frac{P(\text{watts})}{0.000001 \text{ watt}} \qquad (11\text{-}26)$$

Example 11-6

Determine the optical power in dBm and dBμ for power levels of
(a) 10 mW, (b) 0.1 mW, and (c) 20 μW.

Solution   (a)   Substituting into Equations 11-25 and 11-26 gives

$$dBm = 10 \log \frac{10 \text{ mW}}{1 \text{ mW}} = 10 \text{ dBm}$$

$$dB\mu = 10 \log \frac{10 \text{ mW}}{1 \text{ μW}} = 40 \text{ dB}\mu$$

(b) Substituting into Equations 11-25 and 11-26 gives

$$dBm = 10 \log \frac{0.1 \text{ mW}}{1 \text{ mW}} = -10 \text{ dBm}$$

$$dB\mu = 10 \log \frac{0.1 \text{ mW}}{1 \text{ μW}} = 20 \text{ dB}\mu$$

(c) Substituting into Equations 11-25 and 11-26 gives

$$dBm = 10 \log \frac{20 \text{ μW}}{1 \text{ mW}} = -17 \text{ dBm}$$

$$dB\mu = 10 \log \frac{20 \text{ μW}}{1 \text{ μW}} = 13 \text{ dB}\mu$$

OPTICAL SOURCES

Essentially, there are only two devices commonly used to generate light for optical fiber communications systems: light-emitting diodes (LEDs) and injection laser diodes (ILDs). Both devices are constructed from semiconductor materials and have advantages and disadvantages. Standard LEDs have spectral widths of 30 nm to 50 nm while injection lasers have spectral widths of only 1 nm to 3 nm (1 nm corresponds to a frequency of about 178 GHz). Therefore, a 1320 nm light source with a spectral *linewidth* of 0.0056 nm has a frequency bandwidth of approximately 1 GHz. Linewidth is the wavelength equivalent of bandwidth.

Selection of one light-emitting device over the other is determined by system economic and performance requirements. The higher cost of laser diodes is offset by higher performance, whereas light-emitting diodes typically have a lower cost and a correspondingly lower performance.

Light-Emitting Diodes

A *light-emitting diode* (LED) is a *p-n junction diode,* usually made from a semiconductor material such as aluminum-gallium-arsenide (AlGaAs) or gallium-arsenide-phosphide (GaAsP). LEDs emit light by spontaneous emission—light is emitted as a result of the recombination of electrons and holes. When forward biased, minority carriers are injected across the *p-n* junction. Once across the junction, these minority carriers recombine with majority carriers and give up energy in the form of light. This process is essentially the same

TABLE 11-4 Semiconductor
Material Wavelengths

Material	Wavelength (nm)
AlGaInP	630–680
GaInP	670
GaAlAs	620–895
GaAs	904
InGaAs	980
InGaAsP	1100–1650
InGaAsSb	1700–4400

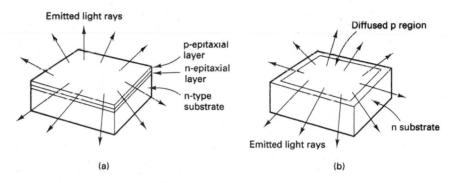

FIGURE 11-27 Homojunction LED structures: (a) silicon-doped gallium arsenide; (b) planar diffused

as in a conventional semiconductor diode except that in LEDs certain semiconductor materials and dopants are chosen such that the process is radiative; that is, a photon is produced. A photon is a quantum of electromagnetic wave energy. Photons are particles that travel at the speed of light but at rest have no mass. In conventional semiconductor diodes (germanium and silicon, for example), the process is primarily nonradiative and no photons are generated. The energy gap of the material used to construct an LED determines the color of light it emits and whether the light emitted by it is visible to the human eye.

To produce LEDs, semiconductors are formed from materials with atoms having either three or five valence electrons (known as Group III and Group IV atoms, respectively, because of their location in the periodic table of elements). To produce light wavelengths in the 800-nm range, LEDs are constructed from Group III atoms such as gallium (Ga) and aluminum (Al) and a Group IV atom such as arsenide (As). The junction formed is commonly abbreviated GaAlAs for gallium-aluminum-arsenide. For longer wavelengths, gallium is combined with the Group III atom indium (In) and arsenide is combined with the Group V atom phosphate (P) which forms a gallium-indium-arsenide-phosphate (GaInAsP) junction. Table 11-4 lists some of the common semiconductor materials used in LED construction and their respective output wavelengths.

Homojunction LEDs. A *p-n* junction made from two different mixtures of the same types of atoms is called a homojunction structure. The simplest LED structures are homojunction and epitaxially grown, or single-diffused semiconductor devices such as the two shown in Figure 11-27. *Epitaxially grown* LEDs are generally constructed of silicon-doped gallium-arsenide (Figure 11-27a). A typical wavelength of light emitted from this construction is 940 nm, and a typical output power is approximately 2 mW (3 dBm) at 100 mA of forward current. Light waves from homojunction sources do not produce a very useful light for an optical fiber. Light is emitted in all directions equally; therefore, only a small amount of

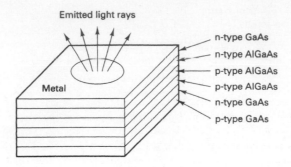

Emitted light rays

n-type GaAs
n-type AlGaAs
p-type AlGaAs
p-type AlGaAs
n-type GaAs
p-type GaAs

Metal

FIGURE 11-28 Planar heterojunction LED

the total light produced is coupled into the fiber. In addition, the ratio of electricity converted to light is very low. Homojunction devices are often called *surface emitters*.

Planar diffused homojunction LEDs (Figure 11-27b) output approximately 500 μW at a wavelength of 900 nm. The primary disadvantage of homojunction LEDs is the nondirectionality of their light emission, which makes them a poor choice as a light source for optical fiber systems.

Heterojunction LEDs. Heterojunction LEDs are made from a *p*-type semiconductor material of one set of atoms and an *n*-type semiconductor material from another set. Heterojunction devices are layered (usually two) such that the concentration effect is enhanced. This produces a device that confines the electron and hole carriers and the light to a much smaller area. The junction is generally manufactured on a substrate backing material and then sandwiched between metal contacts which are used to connect the device to a source of electricity.

With heterojunction devices, light is emitted from the edge of the material and are therefore often called *edge emitters*. A *planar heterojunction LED* (Figure 11-28) is quite similar to the epitaxially grown LED except that the geometry is designed such that the forward current is concentrated to a very small area of the active layer.

Heterojunction devices have the following advantages over homojunction devices.

1. The increase in current density generates a more brilliant light spot.
2. The smaller emitting area makes it easier to couple its emitted light into a fiber.
3. The small effective area has a smaller capacitance, which allows the planar heterojunction LED to be used at higher speeds.

Figure 11-29 shows the typical electrical characteristics for a low-cost infrared light-emitting diode. Figure 11-29a shows the output power versus forward current. From the figure, it can be seen that the output power varies linearly over a wide range of input current [0.5 mW (−3 dBm) at 20 mA to 3.4 mW (5.3 dBm) at 140 mA]. Figure 11-29b shows output power versus temperature. It can be seen that the output power varies inversely with temperature between a temperature range of −40 °C to 80 °C. Figure 11-29c shows relative output power in respect to output wavelength. For this particular example, the maximum output power is achieved at an output wavelength of 825 nm.

Burrus etched-well surface-emitting LED. For the more practical applications, such as telecommunications, data rates in excess of 100 Mbps are required. For these applications, the etched-well LED was developed. Burrus and Dawson of Bell Laboratories developed the etched-well LED. It is a surface-emitting LED and is shown in Figure 11-30. The Burrus etched-well LED emits light in many directions. The etched well helps concentrate the emitted light to a very small area. Also, domed lenses can be placed over the emitting surface to direct the light into a smaller area. These devices are more efficient than the standard surface emitters and they allow more power to be coupled into the optical fiber, but they are also more difficult and expensive to manufacture.

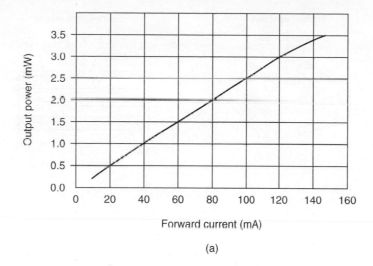

(a)

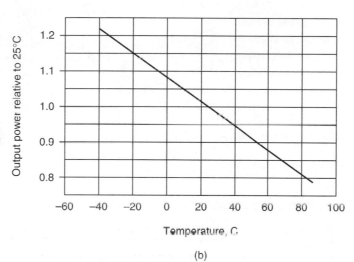

(b)

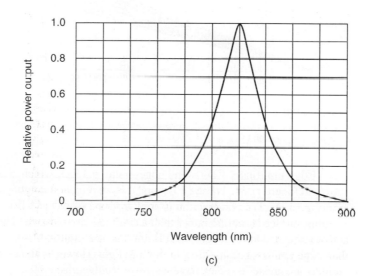

(c)

FIGURE 11-29 Typical LED electrical characteristics: (a) output power-versus-forward current; (b) output power-versus-temperature; and (c) output power-versus-output wavelength.

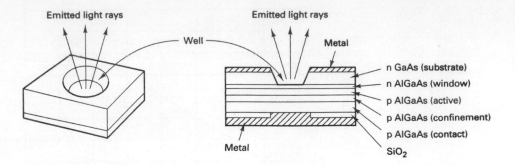

FIGURE 11-30 Burrus etched-well surface-emitting LED

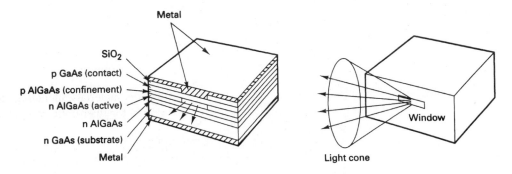

FIGURE 11-31 Edge-emitting LED

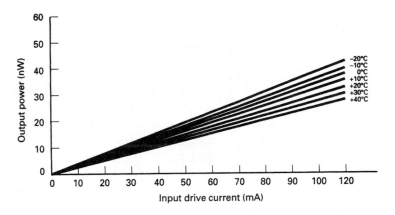

FIGURE 11-32 Output power versus forward current and operating temperature for an LED

Edge-emitting LED. The edge-emitting LED, which was developed by RCA, is shown in Figure 11-31. These LEDs emit a more directional light pattern than do the surface-emitting LEDs. The construction is similar to the planar and Burrus diodes except that the emitting surface is a stripe rather than a confined circular area. The light is emitted from an active stripe and forms an elliptical beam. Surface-emitting LEDs are more commonly used than edge emitters because they emit more light. However, the coupling losses with surface emitters are greater and they have narrower bandwidths.

The *radiant* light power emitted from an LED is a linear function of the forward current passing through the device (Figure 11-32). It can also be seen that the optical output power of an LED is, in part, a function of the operating temperature.

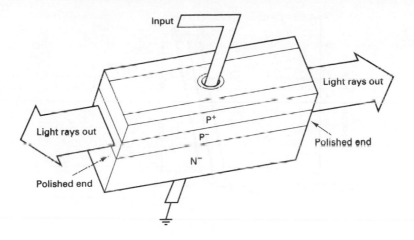

FIGURE 11-33 Injection laser diode construction

Injection Laser Diode

Lasers are constructed from many different materials, including gases, liquids, and solids, although the type of laser used most often for fiber-optic communications is the semiconductor laser.

The *injection laser diode* (ILD) is similar to the LED. In fact, below a certain threshold current, an ILD acts similarly to an LED. Above the threshold current, an ILD oscillates; lasing occurs. As current passes through a forward-biased *p-n* junction diode, light is emitted by spontaneous emission at a frequency determined by the energy gap of the semiconductor material. When a particular current level is reached, the number of minority carriers and photons produced on either side of the *p-n* junction reaches a level where they begin to collide with already excited minority carriers. This causes an increase in the ionization energy level and makes the carriers unstable. When this happens, a typical carrier recombines with an opposite type of carrier at an energy level that is above its normal before-collision value. In the process, two photons are created; one is stimulated by another. Essentially, a gain in the number of photons is realized. For this to happen, a large forward current that can provide many carriers (holes and electrons) is required.

The construction of an ILD is similar to that of an LED (Figure 11-33) except that the ends are highly polished. The mirrorlike ends trap the photons in the active region and, as they reflect back and forth, stimulate free electrons to recombine with holes at a higher-than-normal energy level. This process is called *lasing*.

The radiant output light power of a typical ILD is shown in Figure 11-34. It can be seen that very little output power is realized until the threshold current is reached; then lasing occurs. After lasing begins, the optical output power increases dramatically, with small increases in drive current. It can also be seen that the magnitude of the optical output power of the ILD is more dependent on operating temperature than is the LED.

Figure 11-35 shows the light radiation patterns typical of an LED and an ILD. Because light is radiated out the end of an ILD in a narrow concentrated beam, it has a more direct radiation pattern.

Advantages of ILDs

1. Because ILDs have a more direct radiation pattern, it is easier to couple their light into an optical fiber. This reduces the coupling losses and allows smaller fibers to be used.

2. The radiant output power from an ILD is greater than that for an LED. A typical output power for an ILD is 5 mW (7 dBm) and 0.5 mW (−3 dBm) for LEDs. This allows ILDs to provide a higher drive power and to be used for systems that operate over longer distances.

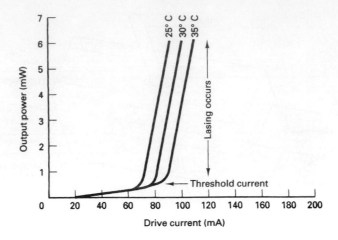

FIGURE 11-34 Output power versus forward current and temperature for an ILD

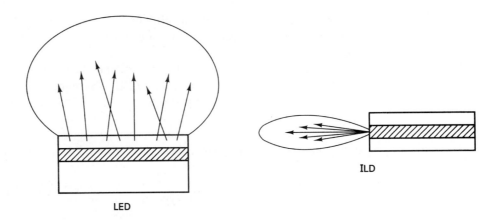

FIGURE 11-35 LED and ILD radiation patterns

3. ILDs can be used at higher bit rates than can LEDs.

4. ILDs generate monochromatic light, which reduces chromatic or wavelength dispersion.

Disadvantages of ILDs

1. ILDs are typically on the order of 10 times more expensive than LEDs.

2. Because ILDs operate at higher powers, they typically have a much shorter lifetime than LEDs.

3. ILDs are more temperature dependent than LEDs.

LIGHT DETECTORS

There are two devices commonly used to detect light energy in fiber-optic communications receivers: PIN (*p*-type-*i*ntrinsic-*n*-type) diodes and APD (*a*valanche *p*hoto*d*iodes).

PIN Diodes

A *PIN diode* is a *depletion-layer photodiode* and is probably the most common device used as a light detector in fiber-optic communications systems. Figure 11-36 shows the basic construction of a PIN diode. A very lightly doped (almost pure or intrinsic) layer of *n*-type semi-

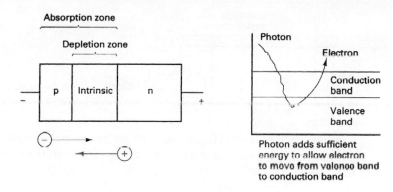

FIGURE 11-36 PIN photodiode construction

conductor material is sandwiched between the junction of the two heavily doped n- and p-type contact areas. Light enters the device through a very small window and falls on the carrier-void intrinsic material. The intrinsic material is made thick enough so that most of the photons that enter the device are absorbed by this layer. Essentially, the PIN photodiode operates just the opposite of an LED. Most of the photons are absorbed by electrons in the valence band of the intrinsic material. When the photons are absorbed, they add sufficient energy to generate carriers in the depletion region and allow current to flow through the device.

Photoelectric effect.   Light entering through the window of a PIN diode is absorbed by the intrinsic material and adds enough energy to cause electronics to move from the valence band into the conduction band. The increase in the number of electrons that move into the conduction band is matched by an increase in the number of holes in the valence band. To cause current to flow in a photodiode, light of sufficient energy must be absorbed to give valence electrons enough energy to jump the energy gap. The energy gap for silicon is 1.12 eV (electron volts). Mathematically, the operation is as follows.

For silicon, the energy gap (E_g) equals 1.12 eV:

$$1 \text{ eV} = 1.6 \times 10^{-19} \text{ J}$$

Thus, the energy gap for silicon is

$$E_g = (1.12 \text{ eV})\left(1.6 \times 10^{-19} \frac{\text{J}}{\text{eV}}\right) = 1.792 \times 10^{-19} \text{ J}$$

and   energy $(E) = hf$ (11-27)

where h = Planck's constant = 6.6256×10^{-34} J/Hz
          f = frequency (hertz)

Rearranging and solving for f yields

$$f = \frac{E}{h} \qquad\qquad (11\text{-}28)$$

For a silicon photodiode,

$$f = \frac{1.792 \times 10^{-19} \text{ J}}{6.6256 \times 10^{-34} \text{ J/Hz}} = 2.705 \times 10^{14} \text{ Hz}$$

Converting to wavelength yields

$$\lambda = \frac{c}{f} = \frac{3 \times 10^8 \text{ m/s}}{2.705 \times 10^{14} \text{ Hz}} = 1109 \text{ nm/cycle}$$

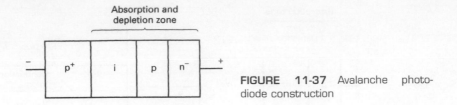

FIGURE 11-37 Avalanche photo-diode construction

Consequently, light wavelengths of 1109 nm or shorter, or light frequencies of 2.705×10^{14} Hz or higher, are required to cause enough electrons to jump the energy gap of a silicon photodiode.

Avalanche Photodiodes

Figure 11-37 shows the basic construction of an *avalanche photodiode* (APD). An APD is a *pipn* structure. Light enters the diode and is absorbed by the thin, heavily doped *n*-layer. A high electric field intensity developed across the *i-p-n* junction by reverse bias causes impact ionization to occur. During impact ionization, a carrier can gain sufficient energy to ionize other bound electrons. These ionized carriers, in turn, cause more ionizations to occur. The process continues as in an avalanche and is, effectively, equivalent to an internal gain or carrier multiplication. Consequently, APDs are more sensitive than PIN diodes and require less additional amplification. The disadvantages of APDs are relatively long transit times and additional internally generated noise due to the avalanche multiplication factor.

Characteristics of Light Detectors

The most important characteristics of light detectors are

   1. *Responsivity.* Responsivity is a measure of the conversion efficiency of a photodetector. It is the ratio of the output current of a photodiode to the input optical power and has the unit of amperes/watt. Responsivity is generally given for a particular wavelength or frequency.
   2. *Dark current.* Dark current is the leakage current that flows through a photodiode with no light input. Dark current is caused by thermally generated carriers in the diode.
   3. *Transit time.* Transit time is the time it takes a light-induced carrier to travel across the depletion region. This parameter determines the maximum bit rate possible with a particular photodiode.
   4. *Spectral response.* Spectral response is the range of wavelength values that can be used for a given photodiode. Generally, relative spectral response is graphed as a function of wavelength or frequency. Figure 11-38 is an illustrative example of a spectral response curve. It can be seen that this particular photodiode more efficiently absorbs energy in the range 800 nm to 820 nm.
   5. *Light sensitivity.* In essence, light sensitivity is the minimum optical power a light detector can receive and still produce a usable electrical output signal. Light sensitivity is generally given for a particular wavelength in either dBm or dBμ.

LASERS

Laser technology deals with the concentration of light into very small, powerful beams. The acronym was chosen when technology shifted from microwaves to light waves.

   The first laser was developed by Theodore H. Maiman, a scientist who worked for Hughes Aircraft Company in California. Maiman directed a beam of light into ruby crystals with a xenon flashlamp and measured emitted radiation from the ruby. He discovered that when the emitted radiation increased beyond threshold it caused emitted radiation to become extremely intense and highly directional. Uranium lasers were developed in 1960

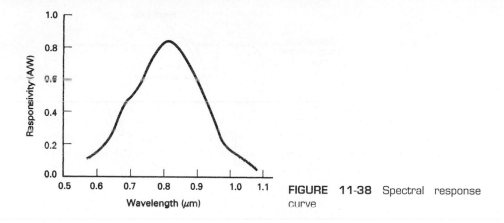

FIGURE 11-38 Spectral response curve

along with other rare-earth materials. Also in 1960, A. Javin of Bell Laboratories developed the helium laser. Semiconductor lasers (injection laser diodes) were manufactured in 1962 by General Electric, IBM, and Lincoln Laboratories.

Laser Types

Basically, there are four types of lasers: gas, liquid, solid, and semiconductor.

1. *Gas lasers.* Gas lasers use a mixture of helium and neon enclosed in a glass tube. A flow of coherent (one frequency) light waves is emitted through the output coupler when an electric current is discharged into the gas. The continuous light-wave output is monochromatic (one color).

2. *Liquid lasers.* Liquid lasers use organic dyes enclosed in a glass tube for an active medium. Dye is circulated into the tube with a pump. A powerful pulse of light excites the organic dye.

3. *Solid lasers.* Solid lasers use a solid, cylindrical crystal, such as ruby, for the active medium. Each end of the ruby is polished and parallel. The ruby is excited by a tungsten lamp tied to an alternating-current power supply. The output from the laser is a continuous wave.

4. *Semiconductor lasers.* Semiconductor lasers are made from semiconductor *p-n* junctions and are commonly called *injection laser diodes* (ILDs). The excitation mechanism is a direct-current power supply that controls the amount of current to the active medium. The output light from an ILD is easily modulated, making it very useful in many electronic communications applications.

Laser Characteristics

All types of lasers have several common characteristics: (1) They all use an active material to convert energy into laser light, (2) a pumping source to provide power or energy, (3) optics to direct the beam through the active material to be amplified, (4) optics to direct the beam into a narrow powerful cone of divergence, (5) a feedback mechanism to provide continuous operation, and (6) an output coupler to transmit power out of the laser.

The radiation of a laser is extremely intense and directional. When focused into a fine hairlike beam, it can concentrate all its power into the narrow beam. If the beam of light were allowed to diverge, it would lose most of its power.

Laser Construction

Figure 11-39 shows the construction of a basic laser. A power source is connected to a flashtube that is coiled around a glass tube that holds the active medium. One end of the glass tube is a polished mirror face for 100% internal reflection. The flashtube is energized by a trigger pulse and produces a high-level burst of light (similar to a flashbulb). The flash

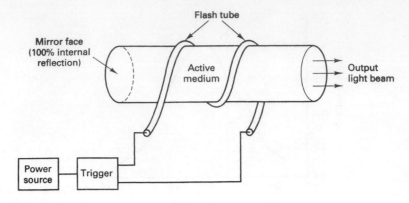

FIGURE 11-39 Laser construction

causes the chromium atoms within the active crystalline structure to become excited. The process of pumping raises the level of the chromium atoms from ground state to an excited energy state. The ions then decay, falling to an intermediate energy level. When the population of ions in the intermediate level is greater than the ground state, a population inversion occurs. The population inversion causes laser action (lasing) to occur. After a period of time, the excited chromium atoms will fall to the ground energy level. At this time, photons are emitted. A photon is a packet of radiant energy. The emitted photons strike atoms and two other photons are emitted (hence, the term "stimulated emission"). The frequency of the energy determines the strength of the photons; higher frequencies cause greater strength photons.

OPTICAL FIBER SYSTEM LINK BUDGET

As with any communications system, optical fiber systems consist of a source and a destination, which are separated by numerous components and devices that introduce various amounts of loss or gain to the signal as it propagates through the system. Figure 11-40 shows two typical optical fiber communications system configurations. Figure 11-40a shows a repeaterless system where the source and destination are interconnected through one or more sections of optical cable. With a repeaterless system, there are no amplifiers or regenerators between the source and destination.

Figure 11-40b shows an optical fiber system that includes a repeater that either amplifies or regenerates the signal. Repeatered systems are obviously used when the source and destination are separated by great distances.

Link budgets are generally calculated between a light source and a light detector; therefore, for our example, we look at a link budget for a repeaterless system. A repeaterless system consists of a light source such as an LED or ILD and a light detector such as an APD connected by optical fiber and connectors. Therefore, the link budget consists of a light power source, a light detector, and various cable and connector losses. Losses typical to optical fiber links include the following:

1. *Cable losses.* Cable losses depend on cable length, material, and material purity. They are generally given in dB/km and can vary between a few tenths of a dB to several dB per km.
2. *Connector losses.* Mechanical connectors are sometimes used to connect two sections of cable. If the mechanical connection is not perfect, light energy can escape,

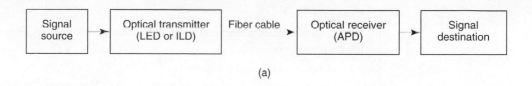

(a)

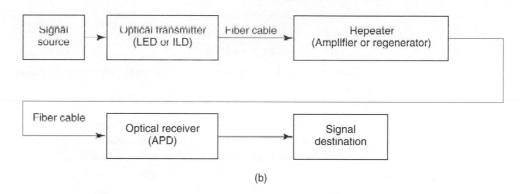

(b)

FIGURE 11-40 Optical fiber communications systems (a) without repeaters and (b) with repeaters.

resulting in a reduction in optical power. Connector losses typically vary between a few tenths of a dB to as much as 2 dB for each connector.

3. *Source-to-cable interface loss.* The mechanical interface used to house the light source and attach it to the cable is seldom perfect. Therefore, a small percentage of optical power is not coupled into the cable, representing a power loss to the system of several tenths of a dB.

4. *Cable-to-light detector interface loss.* The mechanical interface used to house the light detector and attach it to the cable is also not perfect and, therefore, prevents a small percentage of the power leaving the cable from entering the light detector. This, of course, represents a loss to the system usually of a few tenths of a dB.

5. *Splicing loss.* If more than one continuous section of cable is required, cable sections can be fused together (spliced). Because the splices are not perfect, losses ranging from a couple tenths of a dB to several dB can be introduced to the signal.

6. *Cable bends.* When an optical cable is bent at too large an angle, the internal characteristics of the cable can change dramatically. If the changes are severe, total reflections for some of the light rays may no longer be achieved, resulting in refraction. Light refracted at the core/cladding interface enters the cladding, resulting in a net loss to the signal of a few tenths of a dB to several dB.

As with any link or system budget, the useful power available in the receiver depends on transmit power and link losses. Mathematically, receive power is represented as

$$P_r = P_t - \text{losses} \qquad (11\text{-}29)$$

where
$\quad P_r = $ power received (dBm)
$\quad P_t = $ power transmitted (dBm)
$\quad \text{losses} = $ sum of all losses (dB)

Example 11-7

Determine the optical power received in dBm and watts for a 20-km optical fiber link with the following parameters:

> LED output power of 30 mW
>
> Four, 5-km sections of optical cable each with a loss of 0.5 dB/km
>
> Three cable-to-cable connectors with a loss of 2 dB each
>
> No cable splices
>
> Light source-to-fiber interface loss of 1.9 dB
>
> Fiber-to-light detector loss of 2.1 dB
>
> No losses due to cable bends

Solution The LED output power is converted to dBm using Equation 11-25

$$P_{out} = 10 \log \frac{30 \text{ mW}}{1 \text{ mW}}$$

$$= 14.8 \text{ dBm}$$

The cable loss is simply the product of the total cable length in km and the loss in dB/km. Four, 5-km sections of cable is a total cable length of 20 km; therefore,

$$\text{total cable loss} = 20 \text{ km} \times 0.5 \text{ dB/km}$$

$$= 10 \text{ dB}$$

Cable connector loss is simply the product of the loss in dB per connector and the number of connectors. The maximum number of connectors is always one less than the number of sections of cable. Four sections of cable would then require three connectors; therefore,

$$\text{total connector loss} = 3 \text{ connectors} \times 2 \text{ dB/connector}$$

$$= 6 \text{ dB}$$

The light source-to-cable and cable-to-light detector losses were given as 1.9 dB and 2.1 dB, respectively. Therefore,

$$\text{total loss} = \text{cable loss} + \text{connector loss} + \text{light source-to-cable loss} + \text{cable-to-light detector loss}$$

$$= 10 \text{ dB} + 6 \text{ dB} + 1.9 \text{ dB} + 2.1 \text{ dB}$$

$$= 20 \text{ dB}$$

The receive power is determined by substituting into Equation 11-29

$$P_r = 14.8 \text{ dBm} - 20 \text{ dB}$$

$$= -5.2 \text{ dBm}$$

$$= 0.302 \text{ mW}$$

QUESTIONS

11-1. Define a fiber-optic system.

11-2. What is the relationship between information capacity and bandwidth?

11-3. What development in 1951 was a substantial breakthrough in the field of fiber optics? In 1960? In 1970?

11-4. Contrast the advantages and disadvantages of fiber-optic cables and metallic cables.

11-5. Outline the primary building blocks of a fiber-optic system.

11-6. Contrast glass and plastic fiber cables.

11-7. Briefly describe the construction of a fiber-optic cable.

11-8. Define the following terms: *velocity of propagation, refraction,* and *refractive index.*

11-9. State Snell's law for refraction and outline its significance in fiber-optic cables.

11-10. Define *critical angle.*

11-11. Describe what is meant by *mode of operation;* by *index profile.*

11-12. Describe a step-index fiber cable; a graded-index cable.

11-13. Contrast the advantages and disadvantages of step-index, graded-index, single-mode propagation, and multimode propagation.

11-14. Why is single-mode propagation impossible with graded-index fibers?

11-15. Describe the source-to-fiber aperture.

11-16. What are the *acceptance angle* and the *acceptance cone* for a fiber cable?

11-17. Define *numerical aperture.*

11-18. List and briefly describe the losses associated with fiber cables.

11-19. What is *pulse spreading?*

11-20. Define *pulse spreading constant.*

11-21. List and briefly describe the various coupling losses.

11-22. Briefly describe the operation of a light-emitting diode.

11-23. What are the two primary types of LEDs?

11-24. Briefly describe the operation of an injection laser diode.

11-25. What is lasing?

11-26. Contrast the advantages and disadvantages of ILDs and LEDs.

11-27. Briefly describe the function of a photodiode.

11-28. Describe the photoelectric effect.

11-29. Explain the difference between a PIN diode and an APD.

11-30. List and describe the primary characteristics of light detectors.

PROBLEMS

11-1. Determine the wavelengths in nanometers and angstroms for the following light frequencies.
   (a) 3.45×10^{14} Hz
   (b) 3.62×10^{14} Hz
   (c) 3.21×10^{14} Hz

11-2. Determine the light frequency for the following wavelengths.
   (a) 670 nm
   (b) 7800 Å
   (c) 710 nm

11-3. For a glass ($n = 1.5$)/quartz ($n = 1.38$) interface and an angle of incidence of 35°, determine the angle of refraction.

11-4. Determine the critical angle for the fiber described in Problem 11-3.

11-5. Determine the acceptance angle for the cable described in Problem 11-3.

11-6. Determine the numerical aperture for the cable described in Problem 11-3.

11-7. Determine the maximum bit rate for RZ and NRZ encoding for the following pulse-spreading constants and cable lengths.
   (a) $\Delta t = 10$ ns/m, $L = 100$ m
   (b) $\Delta t = 20$ ns/m, $L = 1000$ m
   (c) $\Delta t = 2000$ ns/km, $L = 2$ km

11-8. Determine the lowest light frequency that can be detected by a photodiode with an energy gap $= 1.2$ eV.

11-9. Determine the wavelengths in nanometers and angstroms for the following light frequencies:
   (a) 3.8×10^{14} Hz
   (b) 3.2×10^{14} Hz
   (c) 3.5×10^{14} Hz

11-10. Determine the light frequencies for the following wavelengths:
   (a) 650 nm
   (b) 7200 Å
   (c) 690 nm

11-11. For a glass ($n = 1.5$)/quartz ($n = 1.41$) interface and an angle of incidence of 38°, determine the angle of refraction.

11-12. Determine the critical angle for the fiber described in Problem 11-11.

11-13. Determine the acceptance angle for the cable described in Problem 11-11.

11-14. Determine the numerical aperture for the cable described in Problem 11-11.

11-15. Determine the maximum bit rate for RZ and NRZ encoding for the following pulse-spreading constants and cable lengths.
 (a) $\Delta t = 14$ ns/m, $L = 200$ m
 (b) $\Delta t = 10$ ns/m, $L = 50$ m
 (c) $\Delta t = 20$ ns/m, $L = 200$ m

11-16. Determine the lowest light frequency that can be detected by a photodiode with an energy gap = 1.25 eV.

11-17. Determine the optical power received in dBm and watts for a 24-km optical fiber link with the following parameters:

  LED output power of 20 mW

  Six, 4-km sections of optical cable each with a loss of 0.6 dB/km

  Three cable-to-cable connectors with a loss of 2.1 dB each

  No cable splices

  Light source–to–fiber interface loss of 2.2 dB

  Fiber-to-light detector loss of 1.8 dB

  No losses due to cable bends

C H A P T E R 12

Digital Communications

INTRODUCTION

In essence, electronic communications is the transmission, reception, and processing of *information* with the use of electronic circuits. Information is defined as knowledge or intelligence communicated or received. Figure 12-1 shows a simplified block diagram of an electronic communications system, which comprises three primary sections: a *source,* a *destination,* and a *transmission medium.* Information is propagated through a communications system in the form of symbols that can be *analog* (proportional), such as the human voice, video picture information, or music, or *digital* (discrete), such as binary-coded numbers, alpha/numeric codes, graphic symbols, microprocessor op-codes, or database information. However, very often the source information is unsuitable for transmission in its original form and must be converted to a more suitable form prior to transmission. For example, with digital communications systems, analog information is converted to digital form prior to transmission, and with analog communications systems, digital data are converted to analog signals prior to transmission.

Traditional electronic communications systems that use conventional analog modulation techniques, such as *amplitude modulation* (AM), *frequency modulation* (FM), and *phase modulation* (PM), are rapidly being replaced with more modern digital communications systems which offer several outstanding advantages over traditional analog systems: ease of processing, ease of multiplexing, and noise immunity.

Digital communications, however, is a rather ambiguous term that could mean entirely different things to different people. In the context of this book, digital communications systems include systems where relatively high-frequency analog carriers are modulated by relatively low-frequency digital information signals and systems involving the transmission of digital pulses.

FIGURE 12-1 Simplified block diagram for an electronic communications system

DIGITAL COMMUNICATIONS

The term *digital communications* covers a broad area of communications techniques, including *digital transmission* and *digital radio*. Digital transmission is the transmittal of digital pulses between two or more points in a communications system. Digital radio is the transmittal of digitally modulated analog carriers between two or more points in a communications system. Digital transmission systems require a physical facility between the transmitter and receiver, such as a metallic wire pair, a coaxial cable, or an optical fiber cable. In digital radio systems, the transmission medium could be free space, Earth's atmosphere, or a physical facility such as a metallic or optical fiber cable.

Figure 12-2 shows simplified block diagrams of both a digital transmission system and a digital radio system. In a digital transmission system, the original source information may be in digital or analog form. If it is in analog form, it must be converted to digital pulses prior to transmission and converted back to analog form at the receive end. In a digital radio system, the modulating input signal and the demodulated output signal are digital pulses. The digital pulses could originate from a digital transmission system, from a digital source such as a mainframe computer, or from the binary encoding of an analog signal.

SHANNON LIMIT FOR INFORMATION CAPACITY

The *information capacity* of a communications system represents the number of independent symbols that can be carried through the system in a given unit of time. The most basic symbol is the *binary digit* (bit). Therefore, it is often convenient to express the information capacity of a system in *bits per second* (bps). In 1928, R. Hartley of Bell Telephone Laboratories developed a useful relationship among bandwidth, transmission time, and information capacity. Simply stated, *Hartley's law* is

$$I \propto B \times T \tag{12-1a}$$

where I = information capacity (bits per second)
   B = bandwidth (hertz)
   T = transmission time (seconds)

From Equation 12-1a it can be seen that the information capacity is a linear function of bandwidth and transmission time and is directly proportional to both. If either the bandwidth or the transmission time is changed, a directly proportional change in information capacity will occur.

In 1948, C. E. Shannon (also of Bell Telephone Laboratories) published a paper in the *Bell System Technical Journal* relating the information capacity of a communications channel to bandwidth and signal-to-noise ratio. Mathematically stated, the *Shannon limit for information capacity* is

$$I = B \log_2\left(1 + \frac{S}{N}\right) \tag{12-1b}$$

or
$$I = 3.32\, B \log_{10}\left(1 + \frac{S}{N}\right) \tag{12-1c}$$

where I = information capacity (bits per second)
   B = bandwidth (hertz)
   $\dfrac{S}{N}$ = signal-to-noise power ratio (unitless)

For a standard voice-band communications channel with a signal-to-noise power ratio of 1000 (30 dB) and a bandwidth of 2.7 kHz, the Shannon limit for information capacity is

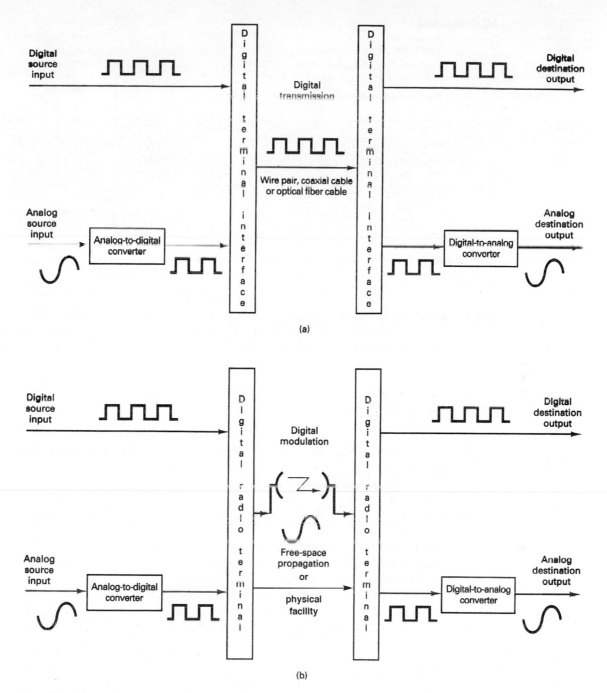

FIGURE 12-2 Digital communications systems: (a) digital transmission; (b) digital radio

$$I = 2700 \log_2 (1 + 1000)$$
$$= 26.9 \text{ kbps}$$

Shannon's formula is often misunderstood. The results of the preceding example indicate that 26.9 kbps can be transferred through a 2.7-kHz channel. This may be true, but it cannot be done with a binary system. To achieve an information transmission rate of 26.9 kbps through a 2.7-kHz channel, each symbol transmitted must contain more than one bit of information. Therefore, to achieve the Shannon limit for information capacity, digital

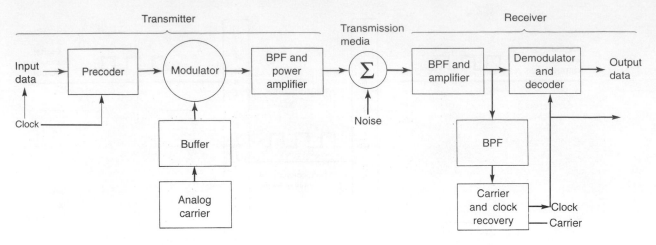

FIGURE 12-3 Simplified block diagram of a digital radio system

transmission systems that have more than two output conditions (symbols) must be used. Several such systems are described in the following chapters. These systems include both analog and digital modulation techniques and the transmission of both digital and analog signals.

DIGITAL RADIO

The property that distinguishes a digital radio system from a conventional AM, FM, or PM radio system is the nature of the modulating signal. Both digital and analog radio systems use analog carriers; however, with analog modulation, the modulating signal is analog, and with digital modulation, the modulating signal is digital. Keep in mind, however, that with both analog and digital modulation, the original source information could have been either analog or digital.

Figure 12-3 shows a simplified block diagram for a digital radio system. In the transmitter, the precoder performs level conversion then encodes or groups the incoming data into a control word that modulates the analog carrier. The modulated carrier is shaped (filtered), amplified, then transmitted through the transmission medium to the receiver. In the receiver, the incoming signal is filtered, amplified, and then applied to the demodulator circuit which reproduces the original source information. Clock and carrier-recovery circuits remove carrier and clock timing information from the incoming modulated signal.

DIGITAL AMPLITUDE MODULATION

The simplest digital modulation technique is *digital amplitude modulation,* which is simply double-sideband, full-carrier amplitude modulation where the input modulating signal is a binary waveform. Mathematically, digital amplitude modulation by a binary signal is

$$v_{am}(t) = [1 + v_m(t)] \left[\frac{A}{2} \cos(\omega_c t) \right] \qquad (12\text{-}2)$$

where $v_{am}(t)$ = digital amplitude-modulated wave
         $A/2$ = unmodulated carrier amplitude (volts)
       $v_m(t)$ = modulating binary signal (volts)
         ω_c = carrier radian frequency (radians per second)

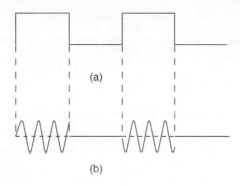

(a)

(b)

FIGURE 12-4 Digital amplitude modulation: (a) input binary; (b) output OOK waveform

In Equation 12-2, the modulating signal $[v_m(t)]$ is a normalized binary waveform, where $+1$ V = logic 1 and -1 V = logic 0. Therefore for a logic 1 input, $v_m(t) = +1$ and Equation 12-2 reduces to

$$v_{am}(t) = [1 + 1]\left[\frac{A}{2}\cos(\omega_c t)\right]$$
$$= A\cos(\omega_c t)$$

and for a logic 0 input, $v_m(t) = -1$ and Equation 12-2 reduces to

$$v_{am}(t) = [1 - 1]\left[\frac{A}{2}\cos(\omega_c t)\right]$$
$$= 0$$

Thus, for 100% modulation $v_{am}(t)$ is either $A\cos(\omega_c t)$ or 0. Hence, the carrier is either "on" or "off," which is why digital amplitude modulation is commonly referred to as *on-off keying* (OOK) modulation. Digital amplitude modulation is sometimes called *continuous wave* (CW), because when the carrier is being transmitted (i.e., on) it has a constant amplitude, constant frequency, and constant phase.

Figure 12-4 shows the input and output waveforms for a digital amplitude modulation transmitter. An OOK waveform can be demodulated either coherently or noncoherently with little difference in performance. The use of amplitude-modulated analog carriers to transport digital information is a relatively low-quality, low-cost type of digital radio and is, therefore, seldom used in high-capacity, high-performance communications systems.

FREQUENCY SHIFT KEYING

Frequency shift keying (FSK) is another relatively simple, low-performance type of digital modulation. Binary FSK is a form of constant-amplitude angle modulation similar to conventional frequency modulation (FM) except that the modulating signal is a binary signal that varies between two discrete voltage levels rather than a continuously changing analog waveform. The general expression for binary FSK is

$$v_{fsk}(t) = V_c \cos\{2\pi[f_c + v_m(t)\Delta f]t\} \qquad (12\text{-}3)$$

where $v_{fsk}(t)$ = binary FSK waveform
V_c = peak carrier amplitude (volts)
f_c = carrier center frequency (hertz)
Δf = peak frequency deviation (hertz)
$v_m(t)$ = binary input modulating signal (± 1)

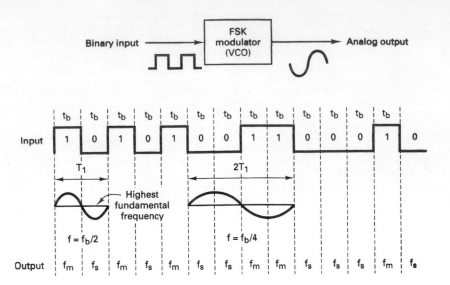

FIGURE 12-5 Binary FSK input and output waveforms

In Equation 12-3, the peak shift in the carrier frequency Δf is proportional to the amplitude and polarity of the binary input signal. The modulating signal $[v_m(t)]$ is a normalized binary waveform where a logic $1 = +1$ and a logic $0 = -1$. Thus, for a logic 1 input, $v_m(t) = +1$ and Equation 12-3 can be rewritten as

$$v_{fsk}(t) = V_c \cos[2\pi(f_c + \Delta f)t]$$

For a logic 0 input, $v_m(t) = -1$ and Equation 12-3 becomes

$$v_{fsk}(t) = V_c \cos[2\pi(f_c - \Delta f)t]$$

With binary FSK, the carrier frequency is shifted (deviated) by the binary input signal. As the binary input signal changes from a logic 0 to a logic 1, and vice versa, the output frequency shifts between two frequencies: a *mark* or logic 1 frequency (f_m) and a space or logic 0 frequency (f_s). The mark and space frequencies are separated from the carrier frequency by the peak frequency deviation (i.e., $f_c \pm \Delta f$). It is important to note, however, that the mark and space frequencies are arbitrarily assigned, depending on system design.

Figure 12-5 shows a binary input signal and FSK output waveform for an FSK modulator. As the figure shows, as the binary input changes from a logic 1 to a logic 0 and vice versa, the FSK output frequency changes from a mark frequency (f_m) to a space frequency (f_s) and vice versa. In Figure 12-5, the mark frequency is the higher frequency $(f_c + \Delta f)$ and the space frequency is the lower frequency $(f_c - \Delta f)$.

FSK Bit Rate and Baud

With binary FSK, there is a change in the output frequency each time the logic condition of the binary input signal changes. Consequently, the output rate of change is equal to the input rate of change. In digital modulation, the rate of change at the input to the modulator is called the *bit rate* (f_b) and has the unit of bits per second (bps). The rate of change at the output of the modulator is called *baud,* after J. M. E. Baudot.

Baud is often misunderstood and commonly confused with bit rate. Baud is a rate of change and is equal to the reciprocal of the time of one output signaling element. With FSK, the time of an output signaling element is the minimum time either the mark or space frequency is outputted, which is equal to the time of a single bit (t_b). As shown in Figure 12-5, the output changes from a mark frequency to a space frequency and vice versa at the same rate that the input condition changes from logic 1 to a logic 0 and vice versa. It is also

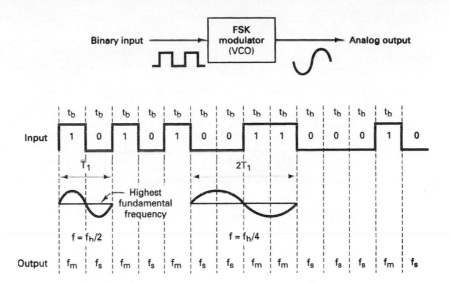

FIGURE 12-6   FSK modulator; t_b, time of one bit = $1/f_b$; f_m, mark frequency; f_s, space frequency; T_1, period of shortest cycle; $1/T_1$, fundamental frequency of binary square wave; f_b, input bit rate (bps)

evident that the minimum time that a mark or space frequency can be outputted equals the time of one bit. Therefore, with binary FSK, the time of a signaling element and the time of a bit are equal; thus, the input and output rates of change are equal and the bit rate and baud must also be equal.

FSK Transmitter

Figure 12-6 shows a simplified binary FSK transmitter which is very similar to a conventional FM modulator, and is very often a voltage-controlled oscillator (VCO). The carrier rest (or center) frequency is chosen such that it falls halfway between the mark and space frequencies. A logic 1 input shifts the VCO output to the mark frequency, and a logic 0 input shifts the VCO output to the space frequency. Consequently, as the binary input signal changes back and forth between logic 1 and logic 0 conditions, the VCO output shifts or deviates back and forth between the mark and space frequencies.

In a binary FSK modulator, Δf is the peak frequency deviation of the carrier and is equal to the difference between the carrier rest frequency and either the mark or space frequency (or half the difference between the carrier rest frequency) and either the mark or space frequency (or half the difference between the mark and space frequencies). A VCO-FSK modulator can be operated in the sweep mode where the peak frequency deviation is simply the product of the binary input voltage and the deviation sensitivity of the VCO. With the sweep mode of modulation, the frequency deviation is expressed mathematically as

$$\Delta f = v_m(t)k_l \tag{12-4}$$

where Δf = peak frequency deviation (hertz)
   $v_m(t)$ = peak binary modulating-signal voltage (volts)
   k_l = deviation sensitivity (hertz per volt)

With binary FSK, the amplitude of the input signal can only be one of two values, one for a logic 1 condition and one for a logic 0 condition. Therefore, the peak frequency deviation is constant and always at its maximum value. Frequency deviation is simply plus or minus the peak voltage of the binary signal times the deviation sensitivity of the VCO. Since the peak voltage is the same for a logic 1 as it is for a logic 0, the magnitude of the frequency deviation is also the same for a logic 1 as it is for a logic 0.

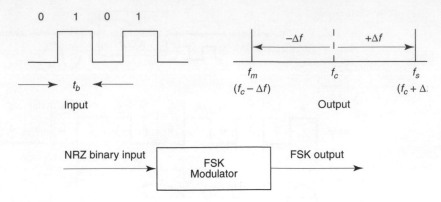

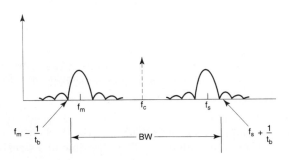

FIGURE 12-7 FSK frequency deviation

FIGURE 12-8 FSK frequency spectrum

Bandwidth Considerations of FSK

The output of a FSK modulator is related to the binary input as shown in Figure 12-7 where a logic 0 corresponds to space frequency f_s, a logic 1 corresponds to the mark frequency f_m, and f_c is the carrier frequency. The peak frequency deviation is given as

$$\Delta f = \frac{|f_m - f_s|}{2} \qquad (12\text{-}5)$$

where Δf = peak frequency deviation (hertz)
f_m = mark frequency (hertz)
f_s = space frequency (hertz)

From Figure 12-7, it can be seen that FSK consists of two pulsed sinusoidal waves of frequency f_m and f_s. Pulsed sinusoidal waves have frequency spectrums that are *sin x/x* functions. Therefore, we can represent the output spectrum for a FSK signal as shown in Figure 12-8. Assuming that the peaks of the power spectrum contain the bulk of the energy, the minimum bandwidth necessary to pass a FSK signal can be approximated as

$$B = |(f_s + f_b) - (f_m - f_b)|$$
$$= (|f_s - f_m|) + 2f_b \qquad (12\text{-}6)$$

and since $|f_s - f_m|$ equals $2\Delta f$, the minimum bandwidth can be approximated as

$$B = 2\Delta f + 2f_b$$
$$= 2(\Delta f + f_b) \qquad (12\text{-}7)$$

where B = minimum bandwidth (hertz)
Δf = minimum peak frequency deviation (hertz)
f_m = mark frequency (hertz)
f_s = space frequency (hertz)

Example 12-1

Determine (a) the peak frequency deviation, (b) the minimum bandwidth, and (c) baud for an FSK signal with a mark frequency of 49 kHz, a space frequency of 51 kHz, and an input bit rate of 2 kbps.

Solution (a) The peak frequency deviation is found by substituting into Equation 12-5

$$\Delta f_c = \frac{|49 \text{ kHz} - 51 \text{ kHz}|}{2} = 1 \text{ kHz}$$

(b) The minimum bandwidth is found by substituting into Equation 12-7

$$B = 2(1000 + 2000)$$
$$= 6 \text{ kHz}$$

(c) With FSK, the baud is equal to the bit rate, 2000.

It might be noted how closely Equation 12-7 resembles Carson's rule for determining the approximate bandwidth of a medium index FM wave. The only difference in the two equations is for FSK the bit rate f_b is substituted for the modulating-signal frequency f_m.

Bessel functions can also be used to determine the approximate minimum bandwidth for a FSK wave. As shown in Figure 12-6, the fastest rate of change in a nonreturn-to-zero (NRZ) binary signal occurs when alternating 1s and 0s are occurring (i.e., a square wave). Since it takes a high and a low to produce a cycle, the highest fundamental frequency contained in a square wave equals the repetition rate of the square wave which with a binary signal is equal to half the bit rate. Therefore,

$$f_a = f_b/2 \tag{12-8}$$

where f_a = highest fundamental frequency of the binary modulating signal (hertz)
$f_b/2$ = bit rate (bits per second)

The formula used for modulation index in FM is also valid for FSK, thus

$$h = \frac{\Delta f}{f_a} \quad \text{(unitless)} \tag{12-9a}$$

where h = FM modulation index called the h-factor in FSK
f_a = fundamental frequency of the binary modulating signal (hertz)
Δf = peak frequency deviation (hertz)

The worst-case modulation index (deviation ratio) is that which yields the widest bandwidth. The worst-case or widest bandwidth occurs when both the frequency deviation and the modulating-signal frequency are at their maximum values. As described earlier, the peak frequency deviation in FSK is constant and always at its maximum value and the highest fundamental frequency is equal to half the incoming bit rate. Thus,

$$h = \frac{\frac{|f_m - f_s|}{2}}{\frac{f_b}{2}} \quad \text{(unitless)} \tag{12-9b}$$

or
$$h = \frac{|f_m - f_s|}{f_b} \tag{12-10}$$

where h = h-factor (unitless)
f_m = mark frequency (hertz)
f_s = space frequency (hertz)
f_b = bit rate (bits per second)

Example 12-2

Using a Bessel table, determine the minimum bandwidth for the same FSK signal described in Example 12-1 with a mark frequency of 49 kHz, a space frequency of 51 kHz, and an input bit rate of 2 kbps.

Solution The modulation index is found by substituting into Equation 12-10

or

$$h = \frac{|49\ kHz - 51\ kHz|}{2\ kbps}$$

$$= \frac{2\ kHz}{2\ kbps}$$

$$= 1$$

From a Bessel table, three sets of significant sidebands are produced for a modulation index of one. Therefore, the bandwidth can be determined as follows:

$$B = 2(3 \times 1000)$$

$$= 6000\ Hz$$

The bandwidth determined in Example 12-2 using the Bessel table is identical to the bandwidth determined in Example 12-1.

FSK Receiver

FSK demodulation is quite simple with a circuit such as the one shown in Figure 12-9. The FSK input signal is simultaneously applied to the inputs of both bandpass filters (BPFs) through a power splitter. The respective filter passes only the mark or only the space frequency on to its respective envelope detector. The envelope detectors, in turn, indicate the total power in each passband and the comparator responds to the largest of the two powers. This type of FSK detection is referred to as noncoherent detection; there is no frequency involved in the demodulation process that is synchronized either in phase, frequency, or both with the incoming FSK signal.

Figure 12-10 shows the block diagram for a coherent FSK receiver. The incoming FSK signal is multiplied by a recovered carrier signal that has the exact same frequency and phase as the transmitter reference. However, the two transmitted frequencies (the mark and space

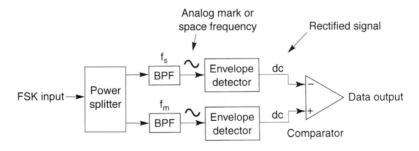

FIGURE 12-9 Noncoherent FSK demodulator

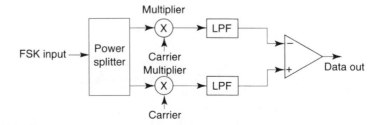

FIGURE 12-10 Coherent FSK demodulator

frequencies) are not generally continuous; it is not practical to reproduce a local reference that is coherent with both of them. Consequently, coherent FSK detection is seldom used.

The most common circuit used for demodulating binary FSK signals is the *phase-locked loop* (PLL), which is shown in block diagram form in Figure 12-11. A PLL-FSK demodulator works similarly to a PLL-FM demodulator. As the input to the PLL shifts between the mark and space frequencies, the *dc error voltage* at the output of the phase comparator follows the frequency shift. Because there are only two input frequencies (mark and space), there are also only two output error voltages. One represents a logic 1 and the other a logic 0. Therefore, the output is a two-level (binary) representation of the FSK input. Generally, the natural frequency of the PLL is made equal to the center frequency of the FSK modulator. As a result, the changes in the dc error voltage follow the changes in the analog input frequency and are symmetrical around 0 V.

Binary FSK has a poorer error performance than PSK or QAM and, consequently, is seldom used for high-performance digital radio systems. Its use is restricted to low-performance, low-cost, asynchronous data modems that are used for data communications over analog, voice-band telephone lines (see Chapter 13).

Continuous-Phase Frequency Shift Keying

Continuous-phase frequency shift keying (CP-FSK) is binary FSK except the mark and space frequencies are synchronized with the input binary bit rate. Synchronous simply implies that there is a precise time relationship between the two; it does not mean they are equal. With CP-FSK, the mark and space frequencies are selected such that they are separated from the center frequency by an exact odd multiple of one-half the bit rate [f_m and f_s = $n(f_b/2)$, where n = any odd integer]. This ensures a smooth phase transition in the analog output signal when it changes from a mark to a space frequency, or vice versa. Figure 12-12 shows a noncontinuous FSK waveform. It can be seen that when the input changes from a logic 1 to a logic 0, and vice versa, there is an abrupt phase discontinuity in the

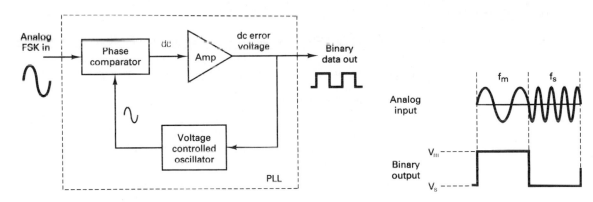

FIGURE 12-11 PLL-FSK demodulator

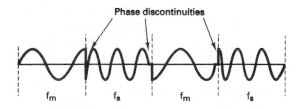

FIGURE 12-12 Noncontinuous FSK waveform

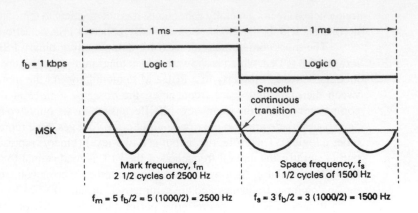

$f_m = 5\ f_b/2 = 5\ (1000/2) = 2500\ \text{Hz}$ $f_s = 3\ f_b/2 = 3\ (1000/2) = 1500\ \text{Hz}$

FIGURE 12-13 Continuous-phase MSK waveform

analog signal. When this occurs, the demodulator has trouble following the frequency shift; consequently, an error may occur.

Figure 12-13 shows a continuous phase FSK waveform. Notice that when the output frequency changes, it is a smooth, continuous transition. Consequently, there are no phase discontinuities. CP-FSK has a better bit-error performance than conventional binary FSK for a given signal-to-noise ratio. The disadvantage of CP-FSK is that it requires synchronization circuits and is, therefore, more expensive to implement.

If the difference between the mark and space frequencies is one-half the bit rate (i.e., $f_s - f_m = 0.5\ f_b$), the modulation index $h = 0.5$. When this is the case, there is a minimum difference between the mark and space frequencies. This particular form of CP-FSK is called *minimum-shift keying* (MSK).

PHASE SHIFT KEYING

Phase shift keying (PSK) is another form of angle-modulated, constant-amplitude digital modulation. PSK is similar to conventional phase modulation except that with PSK the input signal is a binary digital signal and a limited number of output phases are possible.

Binary Phase Shift Keying

With *binary phase shift keying* (BPSK), two output phases are possible for a single carrier frequency ("binary" meaning "2"). One output phase represents a logic 1 and the other a logic 0. As the input digital signal changes state, the phase of the output carrier shifts between two angles that are 180° out of phase. Other names for BPSK are *phase reversal keying* (PRK) and *biphase modulation*. BPSK is a form of suppressed-carrier, square-wave modulation of a continuous wave (CW) signal.

    BPSK transmitter. Figure 12-14 shows a simplified block diagram of a BPSK transmitter. The balanced modulator acts as a phase reversing switch. Depending on the logic condition of the digital input, the carrier is transferred to the output either in phase or 180° out of phase with the reference carrier oscillator.

Figure 12-15a shows the schematic diagram of a balanced ring modulator. The balanced modulator has two inputs: a carrier that is in phase with the reference oscillator and the binary digital data. For the balanced modulator to operate properly, the digital input voltage must be much greater than the peak carrier voltage. This ensures that the digital input controls the on/off state of diodes D1–D4. If the binary input is a logic 1 (positive voltage), diodes D1 and D2 are forward biased and on, while diodes D3 and D4 are reverse bi-

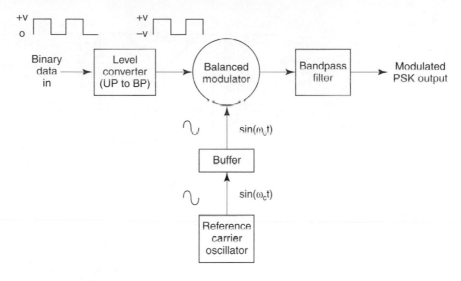

FIGURE 12-14 BPSK transmitter

ased and off (Figure 12-15b). With the polarities shown, the carrier voltage is developed across transformer T2 in phase with the carrier voltage across T1. Consequently, the output signal is in phase with the reference oscillator.

If the binary input is a logic 0 (negative voltage), diodes D1 and D2 are reverse biased and off, while diodes D3 and D4 are forward biased and on (Figure 12-15c). As a result, the carrier voltage is developed across transformer T2 180° out of phase with the carrier voltage across T1. Consequently, the output signal is 180° out of phase with the reference oscillator. Figure 12-16 shows the truth table, phasor diagram, and constellation diagram for a BPSK modulator. A *constellation diagram,* which is sometimes called a *signal state-space diagram,* is similar to a phasor diagram except that the entire phasor is not drawn. In a constellation diagram, only the relative positions of the peaks of the phasors are shown.

Bandwidth considerations of BPSK. A balanced modulator is a *product modulator;* the output signal is the product of the two input signals. In a BPSK modulator, the carrier input signal is multiplied by the binary data. If $+1$ V is assigned to a logic 1 and -1 V is assigned to a logic 0, the input carrier ($\sin \omega_c t$) is multiplied by either a $+$ or -1. Consequently, the output signal is either $+1 \sin \omega_c t$ or $-1 \sin \omega_c t$; the first represents a signal that is *in phase* with the reference oscillator, the latter a signal that is 180° out of phase with the reference oscillator. Each time the input logic condition changes, the output phase changes. Consequently, for BPSK, the output rate of change (baud) is equal to the input rate of change (bps), and the widest output bandwidth occurs when the input binary data are an alternating 1/0 sequence. The fundamental frequency (f_a) of an alternative 1/0 bit sequence is equal to one-half of the bit rate ($f_b/2$). Mathematically, the output of a BPSK modulator is proportional to

$$\text{BPSK output} = [\sin(2\pi f_a t)] \times [\sin(2\pi f_c t)] \qquad (12\text{-}11)$$

where f_a = maximum fundamental frequency of binary input (hertz)
f_c = reference carrier frequency (hertz)

solving for the trig identity for the product of two sine functions

$$\frac{1}{2}\cos[2\pi(f_c - f_a)t] - \frac{1}{2}\cos[2\pi(f_c + f_a)t]$$

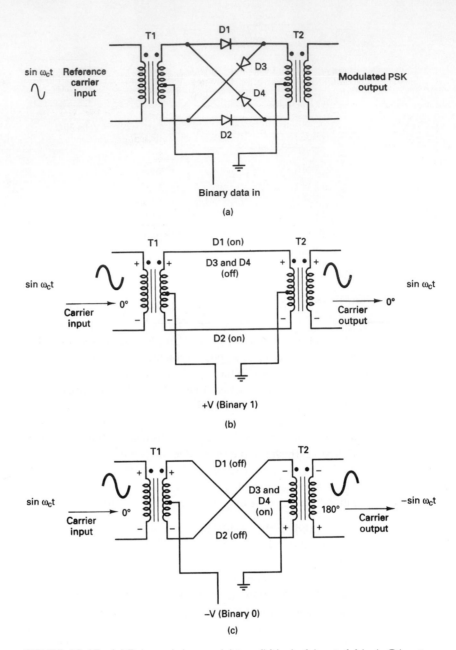

FIGURE 12-15 (a) Balanced ring modulator; (b) logic 1 input; (c) logic 0 input

Thus, the minimum double-sided Nyquist bandwidth (F_N) is

$$
\begin{array}{ccc}
f_c + f_a & & f_c + f_a \\
\underline{-(f_c + f_a)} & \text{or} & \underline{-f_c + f_a} \\
& & 2f_a
\end{array}
$$

and because $f_a = f_b/2$ where f_b = input bit rate,

$$
B = \frac{2f_b}{2} = f_b
$$

where B is the minimum double-sided Nyquist bandwidth.

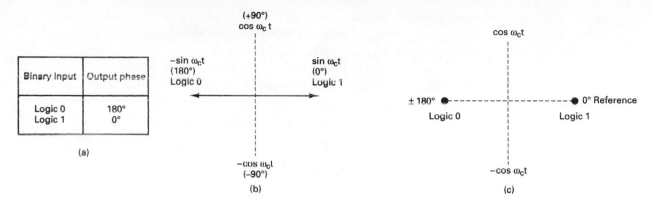

Binary Input	Output phase
Logic 0	180°
Logic 1	0°

(a)

(b)

(c)

FIGURE 12-16 BPSK modulator: (a) truth table; (b) phasor diagram; (c) constellation diagram

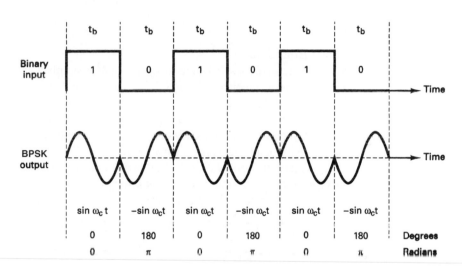

FIGURE 12-17 Output phase-versus-time relationship for a BPSK modulator

Figure 12-17 shows the output phase-versus-time relationship for a BPSK waveform. The output spectrum from a BPSK modulator is simply a double-sideband, suppressed-carrier signal where the upper and lower side frequencies are separated from the carrier frequency by a value equal to one-half the bit rate. Consequently, the minimum bandwidth (f_N) required to pass the worst-case BPSK output signal is equal to the input bit rate.

Example 12-3

For a BPSK modulator with a carrier frequency of 70 MHz and an input bit rate of 10 Mbps, determine the maximum and minimum upper and lower side frequencies, draw the output spectrum, determine the minimum Nyquist bandwidth, and calculate the baud.

Solution   Substituting into Equation 12-11 yields

$$\text{output} = (\sin \omega_a t)(\sin \omega_c t)$$
$$= [\sin 2\pi(5 \text{ MHz})t][\sin 2\pi(70 \text{ MHz})t]$$
$$= \underbrace{\frac{1}{2} \cos 2\pi(70 \text{ MHz} - 5 \text{ MHz})t}_{\text{lower side frequency}} - \underbrace{\frac{1}{2} \cos 2\pi(70 \text{ MHz} + 5 \text{ MHz})t}_{\text{upper side frequency}}$$

Minimum lower side frequency (LSF):
$$\text{LSF} = 70\text{ MHz} - 5\text{ MHz} = 65\text{ MHz}$$
Maximum upper side frequency (USF):
$$\text{USF} = 70\text{ MHz} + 5\text{ MHz} = 75\text{ MHz}$$
Therefore, the output spectrum for the worst-case binary input conditions is as follows:

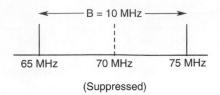

(Suppressed)

The minimum Nyquist bandwidth (f_N) is
$$f_N = 75\text{ MHz} - 65\text{ MHz} = 10\text{ MHz}$$
and the baud $= f_b$ or 10 megabaud.

M-ary Encoding

M-*ary* is a term derived from the word *binary*. *M* is simply a digit that represents the number of conditions or combinations possible for a given number of binary variables. The two types of digital modulation techniques discussed thus far (binary FSK and BPSK) are binary systems; they encode single bits and there are only two output conditions possible. FSK outputs either a logic 1 or mark frequency or a logic 0 or space frequency, and BPSK outputs either a logic 1 phase or a logic 0 phase. Binary FSK and BPSK are *M*-ary systems where $M = 2$.

With digital modulation, it is often advantageous to encode at a level higher than binary (sometimes referred to as *beyond binary* or *higher than binary*). For example, a PSK system with four possible output phases is an *M*-ary system where $M = 4$. If there are eight possible output phases, $M = 8$, and so on. The number of output conditions is expressed mathematically as

$$N = \log_2 M \tag{12-12}$$

where N = number of bits encoded
  M = number of output conditions possible with N bits

For example, with binary FSK each input bit acts independently on the carrier, producing one of two possible output frequencies. Thus,

$$N = \log_2 2$$
$$2^N = 2$$

converting to logs and solving for N

$$\log 2^N = \log 2$$
$$N \log 2 = \log 2$$
$$N = \frac{\log 2}{\log 2}$$
$$N = 1$$

With BPSK, each input bit also independently acts on the carrier, therefore, $N = 1$.

If two bits are inputted, encoded together, and then allowed to simultaneously modulate a carrier, the number of output conditions is

$$M = 2^2$$
$$= 4$$

The number of output conditions possible for several values of N is shown in the following table.

N	M
1	2
2	4
3	8
4	16
5	32

The minimum bandwidth necessary to pass M-ary digitally modulated carriers other than FSK (i.e., PSK or QAM) can be expressed mathematically as

$$B = \frac{f_b}{\log_2 M} \tag{12-13a}$$

where B = minimum bandwidth (hertz)
f_b = input bit rate (bits per second)
M = number of output states (unitless)

If N is substituted for $\log_2 M$, Equation 12-13a reduces to

$$B = \frac{f_b}{N} \tag{12-13b}$$

where N is the number of NRZ bits encoded.

Therefore, for M-ary PSK or QAM the absolute minimum system bandwidth is equal to the input bit rate divided by the number of bits encoded or grouped together.

BPSK receiver.   Figure 12-18 shows the block diagram of a BPSK receiver. The input signal may be $+\sin \omega_c t$ or $-\sin \omega_c t$. The coherent carrier recovery circuit detects and regenerates a carrier signal that is both frequency and phase coherent with the original transmit carrier. The balanced modulator is a product detector; the output is the product of the two inputs (the BPSK signal and the recovered carrier). The low-pass filter (LPF) separates the recovered binary data from the complex demodulated signal. Mathematically, the demodulation process is as follows.

For a BPSK input signal of $+\sin \omega_c t$ (logic 1), the output of the balanced modulator is

$$\text{output} = (\sin \omega_c t)(\sin \omega_c t) = \sin^2 \omega_c t \tag{12-14}$$

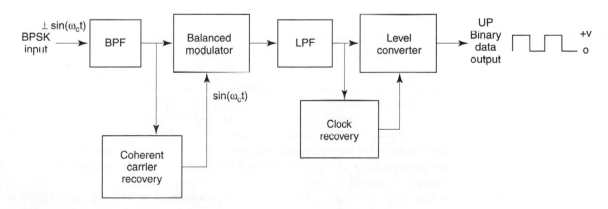

FIGURE 12-18

or

$$\sin^2 \omega_c t = \frac{1}{2}(1 - \cos 2\omega_c t) = \frac{1}{2} - \frac{1}{2} \overset{\text{(filtered out)}}{\cos 2 \omega_c t}$$

leaving

$$\text{output} = +\frac{1}{2}V = \text{logic 1}$$

It can be seen that the output of the balanced modulator contains a positive voltage $[+(1/2)V]$ and a cosine wave at twice the carrier frequency ($2\omega_c$) The LPF has a cutoff frequency much lower than $2\omega_c$ and, thus, blocks the second harmonic of the carrier and passes only the positive constant component. A positive voltage represents a demodulated logic 1.

For a BPSK input signal of $-\sin \omega_c t$ (logic 0), the output of the balanced modulator is

$$\text{output} = (-\sin \omega_c t)(\sin \omega_c t) = -\sin^2 \omega_c t$$

or

$$-\sin^2 \omega_c t = -\frac{1}{2}(1 - \cos 2\omega_c t) = -\frac{1}{2} + \frac{1}{2} \overset{\text{(filtered out)}}{\cos 2 \omega_c t}$$

leaving

$$\text{output} = -\frac{1}{2}V = \text{logic 0}$$

The output of the balanced modulator contains a negative voltage $[-(1/2)V]$ and a cosine wave at twice the carrier frequency ($2\omega_c$). Again, the LPF blocks the second harmonic of the carrier and passes only the negative constant component. A negative voltage represents a demodulated logic 0.

Quaternary Phase Shift Keying

Quaternary phase shift keying (QPSK), or *quadrature PSK* as it is sometimes called, is another form of angle-modulated, constant-amplitude digital modulation. QPSK is an *M*-ary encoding technique where $M = 4$ (hence, the name "quaternary," meaning "4"). With QPSK four output phases are possible for a single carrier frequency. Because there are four different output phases, there must be four different input conditions. Because the digital input to a QPSK modulator is a binary (base 2) signal, to produce four different input conditions, it takes more than a single input bit. With two bits, there are four possible conditions: 00, 01, 10, and 11. Therefore, with QPSK, the binary input data are combined into groups of two bits called *dibits*. Each dibit code generates one of the four possible output phases. Therefore, for each two-bit dibit clocked into the modulator, a single output change occurs. Therefore, the rate of change at the output (baud rate) is one-half of the input bit rate.

QPSK transmitter. A block diagram of a QPSK modulator is shown in Figure 12-19. Two bits (a dibit) are clocked into the bit splitter. After both bits have been serially inputted, they are simultaneously parallel outputted. One bit is directed to the I channel and the other to the Q channel. The I bit modulates a carrier that is in phase with the reference oscillator (hence, the name "I" for "in phase" channel), and the Q bit modulates a carrier that is 90° out of phase or in quadrature with the reference carrier (hence, the name "Q" for "quadrature" channel).

It can be seen that once a dibit has been split into the I and Q channels, the operation is the same as in a BPSK modulator. Essentially, a QPSK modulator is two BPSK modulators combined in parallel. Again, for a logic $1 = +1$ V and a logic $0 = -1$ V, two phases are possible at the output of the I balanced modulator ($+\sin \omega_c t$ and $-\sin \omega_c t$), and two phases are possible at the output of the Q balanced modulator ($+\cos \omega_c t$ and $-\cos \omega_c t$). When the linear summer combines the two quadrature (90° out of phase) signals, there are four possible resultant phasors given by these expressions: $+\sin \omega_c t + \cos \omega_c t$, $+\sin \omega_c t - \cos \omega_c t$, $-\sin \omega_c t + \cos \omega_c t$, and $-\sin \omega_c t - \cos \omega_c t$.

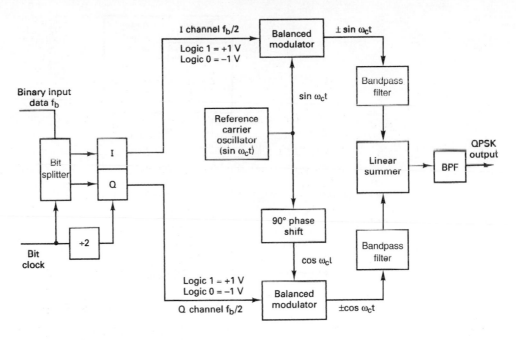

FIGURE 12-19 QPSK modulator

Example 12-4

For the QPSK modulator shown in Figure 12-19, construct the truth table, phasor diagram, and constellation diagram.

Solution For a binary data input of Q = 0 and I = 0, the two inputs to the I balanced modulator are −1 and $\sin \omega_c t$, and the two inputs to the Q balanced modulator are −1 and $\cos \omega_c t$. Consequently, the outputs are

$$\text{I balanced modulator} = (-1)(\sin \omega_c t) = -1 \sin \omega_c t$$

$$\text{Q balanced modulator} = (-1)(\cos \omega_c t) = -1 \cos \omega_c t$$

and the output of the linear summer is

$$-1 \cos \omega_c t - 1 \sin \omega_c t = 1.414 \sin(\omega_c t - 135°)$$

For the remaining dibit codes (01, 10, and 11), the procedure is the same. The results are shown in Figure 12-20a.

In Figures 12-20b and 20c it can be seen that with QPSK each of the four possible output phasors has exactly the same amplitude. Therefore, the binary information must be encoded entirely in the phase of the output signal. This constant amplitude characteristic is the most important characteristic of PSK that distinguishes it from QAM, which is explained later in this chapter. Also, from Figure 12-20b it can be seen that the angular separation between any two adjacent phasors in QPSK is 90°. Therefore, a QPSK signal can undergo almost a +45° or −45° shift in phase during transmission and still retain the correct encoded information when demodulated at the receiver. Figure 12-21 shows the output phase-versus-time relationship for a QPSK modulator.

Bandwidth considerations of QPSK. With QPSK, because the input data are divided into two channels, the bit rate in either the I or the Q channel is equal to one-half of the input data rate ($f_b/2$). (Essentially, the bit splitter stretches the I and Q bits to twice their input bit length.) Consequently, the highest fundamental frequency present at the data input to the I or the Q balanced modulator is equal to one-fourth of the input data rate (one-half of $f_b/2$ = $f_b/4$). As a result, the output of the I and Q balanced modulators requires a minimum double-sided Nyquist bandwidth equal to one-half of the incoming bit rate (f_N = twice $f_b/4$ = $f_b/2$).

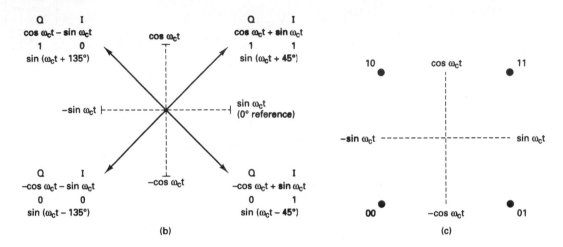

Binary input		QPSK output phase
Q	I	
0	0	−135°
0	1	−45°
1	0	+135°
1	1	+45°

(a)

(b)

(c)

FIGURE 12-20 QPSK modulator: (a) truth table; (b) phasor diagram; (c) constellation diagram

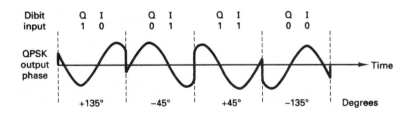

FIGURE 12-21 Output phase-versus-time relationship for a QPSK modulator

Thus, with QPSK, a bandwidth compression is realized (the minimum bandwidth is less than the incoming bit rate). Also, because the QPSK output signal does not change phase until two bits (a dibit) have been clocked into the bit splitter, the fastest output rate of change (baud) is also equal to one-half of the input bit rate. As with BPSK, the minimum bandwidth and the baud are equal. This relationship is shown in Figure 12-22.

In Figure 12-22 it can be seen that the worse-case input condition to the I or Q balanced modulator is an alternative 1/0 pattern, which occurs when the binary input data has a 1100 repetitive pattern. One cycle of the fastest binary transition (a 1/0 sequence) in the I or Q channel takes the same time as four input data bits. Consequently, the highest fundamental frequency at the input and fastest rate of change at the output of the balanced modulators is equal to one-fourth of the binary input bit rate.

The output of the balanced modulators can be expressed mathematically as

$$output = (\sin \omega_a t)(\sin \omega_c t)$$

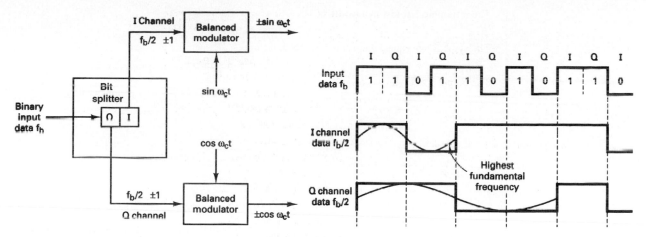

FIGURE 12-22 Bandwidth considerations of a QPSK modulator

where
$$\omega_a t = 2\pi \frac{f_b}{4} t \quad \text{and} \quad \omega_c t = 2\pi f_c t$$

$$\underbrace{\phantom{\omega_a t = 2\pi \frac{f_b}{4} t}}_{\substack{\text{modulating} \\ \text{phase}}} \qquad \underbrace{}_{\substack{\text{unmodulated} \\ \text{carrier phase}}}$$

Thus,
$$\text{output} = \left(\sin 2\pi \frac{f_b}{4} t\right)(\sin 2\pi f_c t)$$

$$\frac{1}{2}\cos 2\pi\left(f_c - \frac{f_b}{4}\right)t - \frac{1}{2}\cos 2\pi\left(f_c + \frac{f_b}{4}\right)t$$

The output frequency spectrum extends from $f_c + f_b/4$ to $f_c - f_b/4$ and the minimum bandwidth (f_N) is

$$\left(f_c + \frac{f_b}{4}\right) - \left(f_c - \frac{f_b}{4}\right) = \frac{2f_b}{4} = \frac{f_b}{2}$$

Example 12-5

For a QPSK modulator with an input data rate (f_b) equal to 10 Mbps and a carrier frequency of 70 MHz, determine the minimum double-sided Nyquist bandwidth (f_N) and the baud. Also, compare the results with those achieved with the BPSK modulator in Example 12-3. Use the QPSK block diagram shown in Figure 12-19 as the modulator model.

Solution The bit rate in both the I and Q channels is equal to one-half of the transmission bit rate or

$$f_{bQ} = f_{bI} = \frac{f_b}{2} = \frac{10 \text{ Mbps}}{2} = 5 \text{ Mbps}$$

The highest fundamental frequency presented to either balanced modulator is

$$f_a = \frac{f_{bQ}}{2} \text{ or } \frac{f_{bI}}{2} = \frac{5 \text{ Mbps}}{2} = 2.5 \text{ MHz}$$

The output wave from each balanced modulator is

$$(\sin 2\pi f_a t)(\sin 2\pi f_c t)$$

$$\frac{1}{2}\cos 2\pi(f_c - f_a)t - \frac{1}{2}\cos 2\pi(f_c + f_a)t$$

$$\frac{1}{2}\cos 2\pi[(70 - 2.5) \text{ MHz}]t - \frac{1}{2}\cos 2\pi[(70 + 2.5) \text{ MHz}]t$$

$$\frac{1}{2}\cos 2\pi(67.5 \text{ MHz})t - \frac{1}{2}\cos 2\pi(72.5 \text{ MHz})t$$

The minimum Nyquist bandwidth is

$$f_N = (72.5 - 67.5) \text{ MHz} = 5 \text{ MHz}$$

The symbol rate equals the bandwidth; thus,

$$\text{symbol rate} = 5 \text{ megabaud}$$

The output spectrum is as follows:

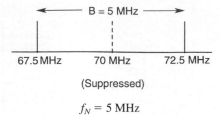

(Suppressed)

$$f_N = 5 \text{ MHz}$$

It can be seen that for the same input bit rate the minimum bandwidth required to pass the output of the QPSK modulator is equal to one-half of that required for the BPSK modulator in Example 12-3. Also, the baud rate for the QPSK modulator is one-half that of the BPSK modulator.

The minimum bandwidth for the QPSK system described in Example 12-5 can also be determined by simply substituting into Equation 12-13b

$$B = \frac{10 \text{ Mbps}}{2}$$

$$= 5 \text{ MHz}$$

QPSK receiver. The block diagram of a QPSK receiver is shown in Figure 12-23. The power splitter directs the input QPSK signal to the I and Q product detectors and the carrier recovery circuit. The carrier recovery circuit reproduces the original transmit carrier oscillator signal. The recovered carrier must be frequency and phase coherent with the transmit reference carrier. The QPSK signal is demodulated in the I and Q product detectors, which generate the original I and Q data bits. The outputs of the product detectors are fed to the bit combining circuit, where they are converted from parallel I and Q data channels to a single binary output data stream.

The incoming QPSK signal may be any one of the four possible output phases shown in Figure 12-20. To illustrate the demodulation process, let the incoming QPSK signal be $-\sin \omega_c t + \cos \omega_c t$. Mathematically, the demodulation process is as follows.

The receive QPSK signal ($-\sin \omega_c t + \cos \omega_c t$) is one of the inputs to the I product detector. The other input is the recovered carrier ($\sin \omega_c t$). The output of the I product detector is

$$I = \underbrace{(-\sin \omega_c t) + \cos \omega_c t)}_{\text{QPSK input signal}} \underbrace{(\sin \omega_c t)}_{\text{carrier}}$$

$$= (-\sin \omega_c t)(\sin \omega_c t) + (\cos \omega_c t)(\sin \omega_c t)$$

$$= -\sin^2 \omega_c t + (\cos \omega_c t)(\sin \omega_c t)$$

$$= -\frac{1}{2}(1 - \cos 2\omega_c t) + \frac{1}{2}\sin(\omega_c + \omega_c)t + \frac{1}{2}\sin(\omega_c - \omega_c)t$$

$$I = -\frac{1}{2} + \frac{1}{2}\cos 2\omega_c t + \overset{\text{(filtered out)}}{\overset{\nearrow}{\frac{1}{2}\sin 2\omega_c t}} + \overset{\text{(equals 0)}}{\overset{\nearrow}{\frac{1}{2}\sin 0}}$$

$$= -\frac{1}{2}\text{ V (logic 0)}$$

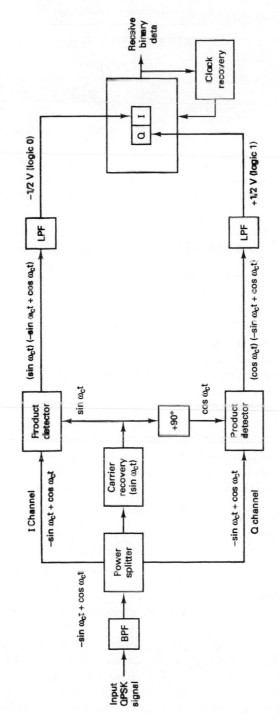

FIGURE 12-23 QPSK receiver

Again, the receive QPSK signal $(-\sin \omega_c t + \cos \omega_c t)$ is one of the inputs to the Q product detector. The other input is the recovered carrier shifted 90° in phase $(\cos \omega_c t)$. The output of the Q product detector is

$$Q = \underbrace{(-\sin \omega_c t + \cos \omega_c t)}_{\text{QPSK input signal}}\underbrace{(\cos \omega_c t)}_{\text{carrier}}$$

$$= \cos^2 \omega_c t - (\sin \omega_c t)(\cos \omega_c t)$$

$$= \frac{1}{2}(1 + \cos 2\omega_c t) - \frac{1}{2}\sin(\omega_c + \omega_c)t - \frac{1}{2}\sin(\omega_c - \omega_c)t$$

$$Q = \frac{1}{2} + \frac{1}{2}\underset{\text{(filtered out)}}{\cos 2\omega_c t} - \frac{1}{2}\underset{\text{(equals 0)}}{\sin 2\omega_c t} - \frac{1}{2}\sin 0$$

$$= \frac{1}{2} \text{ V (logic 1)}$$

The demodulated I and Q bits (0 and 1, respectively) correspond to the constellation diagram and truth table for the QPSK modulator shown in Figure 12-20.

Offset QPSK. *Offset QPSK* (OQPSK) is a modified form of QPSK where the bit waveforms on the I and Q channels are offset or shifted in phase from each other by one-half of a bit time.

Figure 12-24 shows a simplified block diagram, the bit sequence alignment, and the constellation diagram for a OQPSK modulator. Because changes in the I channel occur at the midpoints of the Q channel bits, and vice versa, there is never more than a single bit change in the dibit code, and therefore, there is never more than a 90° shift in the output phase. In conventional QPSK, a change in the input dibit from 00 to 11 or 01 to 10 causes a corresponding 180° shift in the output phase. Therefore, an advantage of OQPSK is the limited phase shift that must be imparted during modulation. A disadvantage of OQPSK is that changes in the output phase occur at twice the data rate in either the I or Q channels. Consequently, with OQPSK the baud and minimum bandwidth are twice that of conventional QPSK for a given transmission bit rate. OQPSK is sometimes called OKQPSK (*offset-keyed QPSK*).

Eight-Phase PSK
Eight-phase PSK (8-PSK) is an *M*-ary encoding technique where $M = 8$. With an 8-PSK modulator, there are eight possible output phases. To encode eight different phases, the incoming bits are considered in groups of three bits, called *tribits* $(2^3 = 8)$.

8-PSK transmitter. A block diagram of an 8-PSK modulator is shown in Figure 12-25. The incoming serial bit stream enters the bit splitter, where it is converted to a parallel, three-channel output (the I or in-phase channel, the Q or in-quadrature channel, and the C or control channel). Consequently, the bit rate in each of the three channels is $f_b/3$. The bits in the I and C channels enter the I channel 2-to-4-level converter, and the bits in the Q and $\overline{C}$ channels enter the Q channel 2-to-4-level converter. Essentially, the 2-to-4-level converters are parallel-input *digital-to-analog converters* (DACs). With two input bits, four output voltages are possible. The algorithm for the DACs is quite simple. The I or Q bit determines the polarity of the output analog signal (logic $1 = +V$ and logic $0 = -V$), whereas the C or $\overline{C}$ bit determines the magnitude (logic $1 = 1.307$ V and logic $0 = 0.541$ V). Consequently, with two magnitudes and two polarities, four different output conditions are possible.

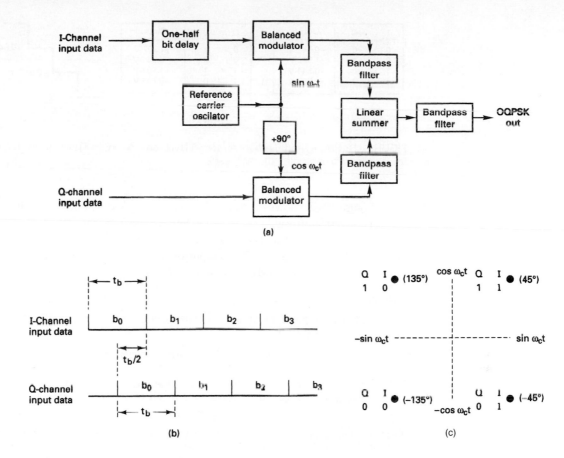

(a)

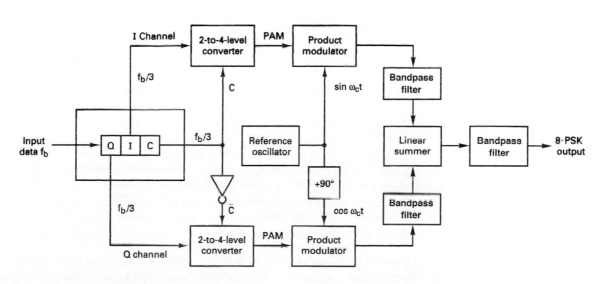

(b)   (c)

FIGURE 12-24 Offset keyed (OQPSK): (a) block diagram; (b) bit alignment; (c) constellation diagram

FIGURE 12-25 8-PSK modulator

I	C	Output
0	0	−0.541 V
0	1	−1.307 V
1	0	+0.541 V
1	1	+1.307 V

Q	$\bar{C}$	Output
0	1	−1.307 V
0	0	−0.541 V
1	1	+1.307 V
1	0	+0.541 V

(c)

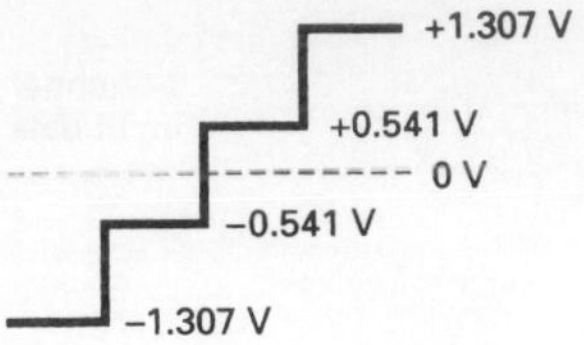

+1.307 V
+0.541 V
0 V
−0.541 V
−1.307 V

(a) (b) (c)

FIGURE 12-26 I- and Q-channel 2-to-4-level converters: (a) I-channel truth table; (b) Q-channel truth table; (c) PAM levels

Figure 12-26 shows the truth table and corresponding output conditions for the 2-to-4-level converters. Because the C and $\bar{C}$ bits can never be the same logic state, the outputs from the I and Q 2-to-4-level converters can never have the same magnitude, although they can have the same polarity. The output of a 2-to-4-level converter is an *M*-ary, *pulse-amplitude-modulated* (PAM) signal where $M = 4$.

Example 12-6

For a tribit input of Q = 0, I = 0, and C = 0 (000), determine the output phase for the 8-PSK modulator shown in Figure 12-25.

Solution The inputs to the I channel 2-to-4-level converter are I = 0 and C = 0. From Figure 12-26 the output is −0.541 V. The inputs to the Q channel 2-to-4-level converter are Q = 0 and $\bar{C} = 1$. Again from Figure 12-26, the output is −1.307 V.

Thus, the two inputs to the I channel product modulators are −0.541 and sin $\omega_c t$. The output is

$$I = (-0.541)(\sin \omega_c t) = -0.541 \sin \omega_c t$$

The two inputs to the Q channel product modulator are −1.307 V and cos $\omega_c t$. The output is

$$Q = (-1.307)(\cos \omega_c t) = -1.307 \cos \omega_c t$$

The outputs of the I and Q channel product modulators are combined in the linear summer and produce a modulated output of

$$\text{summer output} = -0.541 \sin \omega_c t - 1.307 \cos \omega_c t$$
$$= 1.41 \sin(\omega_c t - 112.5°)$$

For the remaining tribit codes (001, 010, 011, 100, 101, 110, and 111), the procedure is the same. The results are shown in Figure 12-27.

From Figure 12-27 it can be seen that the angular separation between any two adjacent phasors is 45°, half what it is with QPSK. Therefore, an 8-PSK signal can undergo almost a ±22.5° phase shift during transmission and still retain its integrity. Also, each phasor is of equal magnitude; the tribit condition (actual information) is again contained only in the phase of the signal. The PAM levels of 1.307 and 0.541 are relative values. Any levels may be used as long as their ratio is 0.541/1.307 and their arc tangent is equal to 22.5°. For example, if their values were doubled to 2.614 and 1.082, the resulting phase angles would not change, although the magnitude of the phasor would increase proportionally.

It should also be noted that the tribit code between any two adjacent phases changes by only one bit. This type of code is called the *Gray code* or, sometimes, the *maximum distance code*. This code is used to reduce the number of transmission errors. If a signal were to undergo a phase shift during transmission, it would most likely be shifted to an adjacent phasor. Using the Gray code results in only a single bit being received in error.

Figure 12-28 shows the output phase-versus-time relationship of an 8-PSK modulator.

Bandwidth considerations of 8-PSK. With 8-PSK, because the data are divided into three channels, the bit rate in the I, Q, or C channel is equal to one-third of the binary input data rate ($f_b/3$). (The bit splitter stretches the I, Q, and C bits to three times their in-

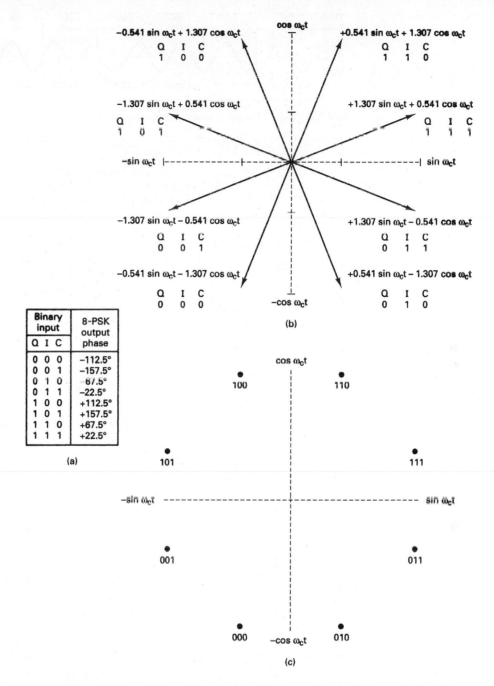

Binary input			8-PSK output phase
Q	I	C	
0	0	0	−112.5°
0	0	1	−157.5°
0	1	0	−67.5°
0	1	1	−22.5°
1	0	0	+112.5°
1	0	1	+157.5°
1	1	0	+67.5°
1	1	1	+22.5°

(a)

(b)

(c)

FIGURE 12-27 8-PSK modulator: (a) truth table; (b) phasor diagram; (c) constellation diagram

put bit length.) Because the I, Q, and C bits are outputted simultaneously and in parallel, the 2-to-4-level converters also see a change in their inputs (and consequently their outputs) at a rate equal to $f_b/3$.

Figure 12-29 shows the bit timing relationship between the binary input data; the I, Q, and C channel data; and the I and Q PAM signals. It can be seen that the highest fundamental frequency in the I, Q, or C channel is equal to one-sixth the bit rate of the binary

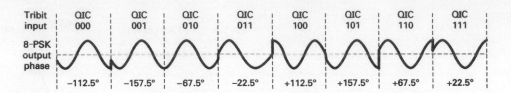

Tribit input	QIC 000	QIC 001	QIC 010	QIC 011	QIC 100	QIC 101	QIC 110	QIC 111

8-PSK output phase

−112.5°   −157.5°   −67.5°   −22.5°   +112.5°   +157.5°   +67.5°   +22.5°

FIGURE 12-28 Output phase-versus-time relationship for an 8-PSK modulator

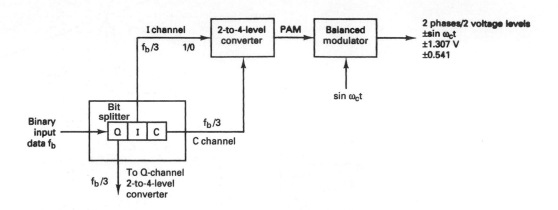

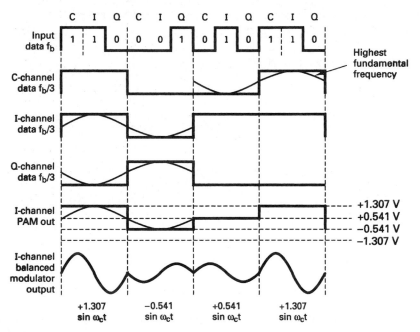

FIGURE 12-29 Bandwidth considerations of an 8-PSK modulator

input (one cycle in the I, Q, or C channel takes the same amount of time as six input bits). Also the highest fundamental frequency in either PAM signal is equal to one-sixth of the binary input bit rate.

With an 8-PSK modulator, there is one change in phase at the output for every three data input bits. Consequently, the baud for 8-PSK equals $f_b/3$, the same as the minimum bandwidth. Again, the balanced modulators are product modulators; their outputs are the product of the carrier and the PAM signal. Mathematically, the output of the balanced modulators is

$$\theta = (X \sin \omega_a t)(\sin \omega_c t)$$

where $\qquad \underbrace{\omega_a t = 2\pi \dfrac{f_b}{6} t}_{\text{modulating signal}} \quad$ and $\quad \underbrace{\omega_c t = 2\pi f_c t}_{\text{carrier}}$

and $\qquad\qquad\qquad X = \pm 1.307 \text{ or } \pm 0.541$

Thus, $\qquad\qquad \theta = \left(X \sin 2\pi \dfrac{f_b}{6} t \right)(\sin 2\pi f_c t)$

$$= \dfrac{X}{2} \cos 2\pi \left(f_c - \dfrac{f_b}{6} \right) t - \dfrac{X}{2} \cos 2\pi \left(f_c + \dfrac{f_b}{6} \right) t$$

The output frequency spectrum extends from $f_c + f_b/6$ to $f_c - f_b/6$ and the minimum bandwidth (f_N) is

$$\left(f_c + \dfrac{f_b}{6} \right) - \left(f_c - \dfrac{f_b}{6} \right) = \dfrac{2f_b}{6} = \dfrac{f_b}{3}$$

Example 12-7

For an 8 PSK modulator with an input data rate (f_b) equal to 10 Mbps and a carrier frequency of 70 MHz, determine the minimum double-sided Nyquist bandwidth (f_N) and the baud. Also, compare the results with those achieved with the BPSK and QPSK modulators in Examples 12-3 and 12-5. Use the 8-PSK block diagram shown in Figure 12-25 as the modulator model.

Solution The bit rate in the I, Q, and C channels is equal to one-third of the input bit rate, or

$$f_{bC} = f_{bQ} = f_{bI} = \dfrac{10 \text{ Mbps}}{3} = 3.33 \text{ Mbps}$$

Therefore, the fastest rate of change and highest fundamental frequency presented to either balanced modulator is

$$f_a = \dfrac{f_{bC}}{2} \text{ or } \dfrac{f_{bQ}}{2} \text{ or } \dfrac{f_{bI}}{2} = \dfrac{3.33 \text{ Mbps}}{2} = 1.667 \text{ Mbps}$$

The output wave from the balance modulators is

$$(\sin 2\pi f_a t)(\sin 2\pi f_c t)$$

$$\dfrac{1}{2} \cos 2\pi (f_c - f_a)t - \dfrac{1}{2} \cos 2\pi (f_c + f_a)t$$

$$\dfrac{1}{2} \cos 2\pi[(70 - 1.667) \text{ MHz}]t - \dfrac{1}{2} \cos 2\pi[(70 + 1.667) \text{ MHz}]t$$

$$\dfrac{1}{2} \cos 2\pi(68.333 \text{ MHz})t - \dfrac{1}{2} \cos 2\pi(71.667 \text{ MHz})t$$

The minimum Nyquist bandwidth is

$$f_N = (71.667 - 68.333) \text{ MHz} = 3.333 \text{ MHz}$$

The minimum bandwidth for the 8-PSK can also be determined by simply substituting into Equation 12-13b

$$B = \dfrac{10 \text{ Mbps}}{3}$$

$$= 3.33 \text{ MHz}$$

Again, the baud equals the bandwidth; thus,

$$\text{baud} = 3.333 \text{ megabaud}$$

The output spectrum is as follows:

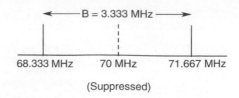

$$f_N = 3.333 \text{ MHz}$$

It can be seen that for the same input bit rate the minimum bandwidth required to pass the output of an 8-PSK modulator is equal to one-third that of the BPSK modulator in Example 12-3 and 50% less than that required for the QPSK modulator in Example 12-5. Also, in each case the baud has been reduced by the same proportions.

8-PSK receiver. Figure 12-30 shows a block diagram of an 8-PSK receiver. The power splitter directs the input 8-PSK signal to the I and Q product detectors and the carrier recovery circuit. The carrier recovery circuit reproduces the original reference oscillator signal. The incoming 8-PSK signal is mixed with the recovered carrier in the I product detector and with a quadrature carrier in the Q product detector. The outputs of the product detectors are 4-level PAM signals that are fed to the 4-to-2-level *analog-to-digital converters* (ADCs). The outputs from the I channel 4-to-2-level converter are the I and C bits, whereas the outputs from the Q channel 4-to-2-level converter are the Q and $\overline{C}$ bits. The parallel-to-serial logic circuit converts the I/C and Q/$\overline{C}$ bit pairs to serial I, Q, and C output data streams.

Sixteen-Phase PSK

Sixteen-phase PSK (16-PSK) is an *M*-ary encoding technique where $M = 16$; there are 16 different output phases possible. A 16-PSK modulator acts on the incoming data in groups of four bits ($2^4 = 16$), called *quadbits*. The output phase does not change until four bits have been inputted into the modulator. Therefore, the output rate of change (baud) and the minimum bandwidth are equal to one-fourth of the incoming bit rate ($f_b/4$). The truth table and constellation diagram for a 16-PSK transmitter are shown in Figure 12-31.

With 16-PSK, the angular separation between adjacent output phases is only 22.5°. Therefore, a 16-PSK signal can undergo almost a ±11.25° phase shift during transmission and still retain its integrity. Because of this, 16-PSK is highly susceptible to phase impairments introduced in the transmission medium and is, therefore, seldom used.

QUADRATURE AMPLITUDE MODULATION

Quadrature amplitude modulation (QAM) is a form of digital modulation where the digital information is contained in both the amplitude and phase of the transmitted carrier.

Eight QAM

Eight QAM (8-QAM) is an *M*-ary encoding technique where $M = 8$. Unlike 8-PSK, the output signal from an 8-QAM modulator is not a constant-amplitude signal.

8-QAM transmitter. Figure 12-32a shows the block diagram of an 8-QAM transmitter. As you can see, the only difference between the 8-QAM transmitter and the 8-PSK transmitter shown in Figure 12-25 is the omission of the inverter between the C channel and the Q product modulator. As with 8-PSK, the incoming data are divided into groups of three bits (tribits): the I, Q, and C bit streams, each with a bit rate equal to one-third of the

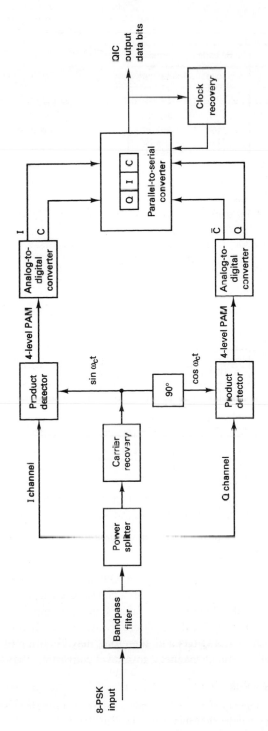

FIGURE 12-30 8-PSK receiver

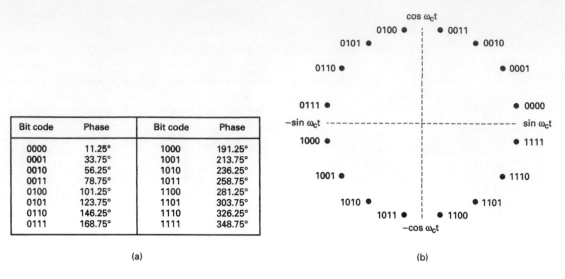

Bit code	Phase	Bit code	Phase
0000	11.25°	1000	191.25°
0001	33.75°	1001	213.75°
0010	56.25°	1010	236.25°
0011	78.75°	1011	258.75°
0100	101.25°	1100	281.25°
0101	123.75°	1101	303.75°
0110	146.25°	1110	326.25°
0111	168.75°	1111	348.75°

(a)

(b)

FIGURE 12-31 16-PSK: (a) truth table; (b) constellation diagram

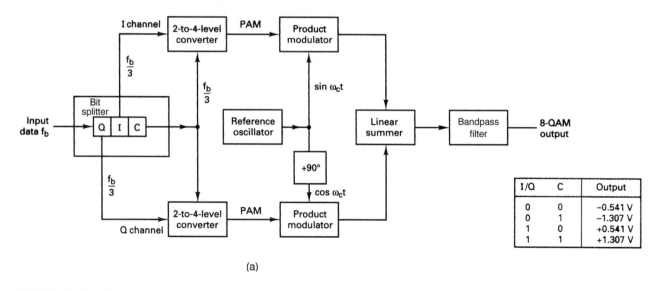

(a)

I/Q	C	Output
0	0	−0.541 V
0	1	−1.307 V
1	0	+0.541 V
1	1	+1.307 V

FIGURE 12-32 8-QAM transmitter: (a) block diagram; (b) truth table 2-4 level converters

incoming data rate. Again, the I and Q bits determine the polarity of the PAM signal at the output of the 2-to-4-level converters, and the C channel determines the magnitude. Because the C bit is fed uninverted to both the I and Q channel 2-to-4-level converters, the magnitudes of the I and Q PAM signals are always equal. Their polarities depend on the logic condition of the I and Q bits and, therefore, may be different. Figure 12-32b shows the truth table for the I and Q channel 2-to-4-level converters; they are identical.

Example 12-8

For a tribit input of Q = 0, I = 0, and C = 0 (000), determine the output amplitude and phase for the 8-QAM transmitter shown in Figure 12-32a.

Solution The inputs to the I channel 2-to-4-level converter are I = 0 and C = 0. From Figure 12-32b the output is −0.541 V. The inputs to the Q channel 2-to-4-level converter are Q = 0 and C = 0. Again from Figure 12-32b, the output is −0.541 V.

Thus, the two inputs to the I channel product modulator are -0.541 and $\sin \omega_c t$. The output is

$$I = (-0.541)(\sin \omega_c t) = -0.541 \sin \omega_c t$$

The two inputs to the Q channel product modulator are -0.541 and $\cos \omega_c t$. The output is

$$Q = (-0.541)(\cos \omega_c t) = -0.541 \cos \omega_c t$$

The outputs from the I and Q channel product modulators are combined in the linear summer and produce a modulated output of

$$\text{summer output} = -0.541 \sin \omega_c t - 0.541 \cos \omega_c t$$
$$= 0.765 \sin(\omega_c t - 135°)$$

For the remaining tribit codes (001, 010, 011, 100, 101, 110, and 111), the procedure is the same. The results are shown in Figure 12-33.

Figure 12-34 shows the output phase-versus-time relationship for an 8-QAM modulator. Note that there are two output amplitudes and only four phases are possible.

Bandwidth considerations of 8-QAM. In 8-QAM, the bit rate in the I and Q channels is one-third of the input binary rate, the same as in 8-PSK. As a result, the highest fundamental modulating frequency and fastest output rate of change in 8-QAM are the same as with 8-PSK. Therefore, the minimum bandwidth required for 8-QAM is $f_b/3$, the same as in 8-PSK.

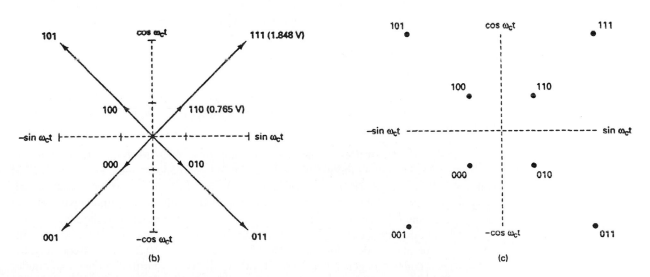

Binary input			8-QAM output	
Q	I	C	Amplitude	Phase
0	0	0	0.765 V	−135°
0	0	1	1.848 V	−135°
0	1	0	0.765 V	−45°
0	1	1	1.848 V	−45°
1	0	0	0.765 V	+135°
1	0	1	1.848 V	+135°
1	1	0	0.765 V	+45°
1	1	1	1.848 V	+45°

(a)

(b)

(c)

FIGURE 12-33 8-QAM modulator: (a) truth table; (b) phasor diagram; (c) constellation diagram

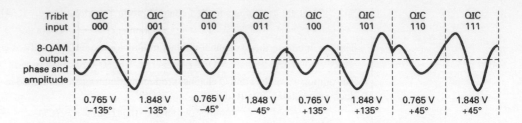

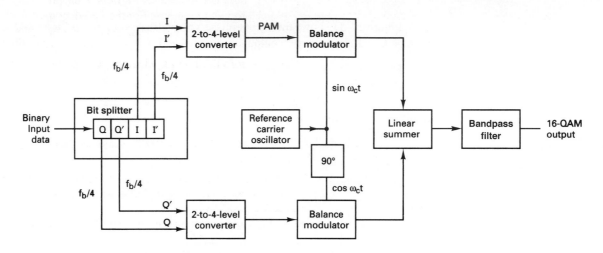

FIGURE 12-34 Output phase and amplitude-versus-time relationship for 8-QAM

FIGURE 12-35 16-QAM transmitter block diagram

8-QAM receiver. An 8-QAM receiver is almost identical to the 8-PSK receiver shown in Figure 12-30. The differences are the PAM levels at the output of the product detectors and the binary signals at the output of the analog-to-digital converters. Because there are two transmit amplitudes possible with 8-QAM that are different from those achievable with 8-PSK, the four demodulated PAM levels in 8-QAM are different from those in 8-PSK. Therefore, the conversion factor for the analog-to-digital converters must also be different. Also, with 8-QAM the binary output signals from the I channel analog-to-digital converter are the I and C bits, and the binary output signals from the Q channel analog-to-digital converter are the Q and C bits.

Sixteen QAM

As with the 16-PSK, 16-QAM is an *M*-ary system where $M = 16$. The input data are acted on in groups of four ($2^4 = 16$). As with 8-QAM, both the phase and amplitude of the transmit carrier are varied.

16-QAM transmitter. The block diagram for a 16-QAM transmitter is shown in Figure 12-35. The input binary data are divided into four channels: the I, I′, Q, and Q′. The bit rate in each channel is equal to one-fourth of the input bit rate ($f_b/4$). Four bits are serially clocked into the bit splitter; then they are outputted simultaneously and in parallel with the I, I′, Q, and Q′ channels. The I and Q bits determine the polarity at the output of the 2-to-4-level converters (a logic 1 = positive and a logic 0 = negative). The I′ and Q′ bits determine the magnitude (a logic 1 = 0.821 V and a logic 0 = 0.22 V). Consequently, the 2-to-4-level converters generate a 4-level PAM signal. Two polarities and two magnitudes are possible at the output of each 2-to-4-level converter. They are ±0.22 V and ±0.821 V.

I	I′	Output		Q	Q′	Output
0	0	−0.22 V		0	0	−0.22 V
0	1	−0.821 V		0	1	−0.821 V
1	0	+0.22 V		1	0	+0.22 V
1	1	+0.821 V		1	1	+0.821 V
		(a)				(b)

FIGURE 12-36 Truth tables for the I- and Q-channel 2-to-4-level converters: (a) I channel; (b) Q channel

The PAM signals modulate the in-phase and quadrature carriers in the product modulators. Four outputs are possible for each product modulator. For the I product modulator they are $+0.821 \sin \omega_c t$, $-0.821 \sin \omega_c t$, $+0.22 \sin \omega_c t$, and $-0.22 \sin \omega_c t$. For the Q product modulator they are $+0.821 \cos \omega_c t$, $+0.22 \cos \omega_c t$, $-0.821 \cos \omega_c t$, and $-0.22 \cos \omega_c t$. The linear summer combines the outputs from the I and Q channel product modulators and produces the 16 output conditions necessary for 16-QAM. Figure 12-36 shows the truth table for the I and Q channel 2-to-4-level converters.

Example 12-9

For a quadbit input of $I = 0$, $I' = 0$, $Q = 0$, and $Q' = 0$ (0000), determine the output amplitude and phase for the 16-QAM modulator shown in Figure 12-35.

Solution The inputs to the I channel 2-to-4-level converter are $I = 0$ and $I' = 0$. From Figure 12-36 the output is −0.22 V. The inputs to the Q channel 2-to-4-level converter are $Q = 0$ and $Q' = 0$. Again from Figure 12-36, the output is −0.22 V.

Thus, the two inputs to the I channel product modulator are −0.22 V and $\sin \omega_c t$. The output is

$$I = (-0.22)(\sin \omega_c t) = -0.22 \sin \omega_c t$$

The two inputs to the Q channel product modulator are −0.22 V and $\cos \omega_c t$. The output is

$$Q = (-0.22)(\cos \omega_c t) = -0.22 \cos \omega_c t$$

The outputs from the I and Q channel product modulators are combined in the linear summer and produce a modulated output of

$$\text{summer output} = -0.22 \sin \omega_c t - 0.22 \cos \omega_c t$$
$$- 0.311 \sin(\omega_c t - 135°)$$

For the remaining quadbit codes the procedure is the same. The results are shown in Figure 12-37.

Bandwidth considerations of 16-QAM. With 16-QAM, because the input data are divided into four channels, the bit rate in the I, I′, Q, or Q′ channel is equal to one-fourth of the binary input data rate $(f_b/4)$. (The bit splitter stretches the I, I′, Q, and Q′ bits to four times their input bit length.) Also, because the I, I′, Q, and Q′ bits are outputted simultaneously and in parallel, the 2-to-4-level converters see a change in their inputs and outputs at a rate equal to one-fourth of the input data rate.

Figure 12-38 shows the bit timing relationship between the binary input data; the I, I′, Q, and Q′ channel data; and the I PAM signal. It can be seen that the highest fundamental frequency in the I, I′, Q, or Q′ channel is equal to one-eighth of the bit rate of the binary input data (one cycle in the I, I′, Q, or Q′ channel takes the same amount of time as eight input bits). Also, the highest fundamental frequency of either PAM signal is equal to one-eighth of the binary input bit rate.

With a 16-QAM modulator, there is one change in the output signal (either its phase, amplitude, or both) for every four input data bits. Consequently, the baud equals $f_b/4$, the same as the minimum bandwidth.

Again, the balanced modulators are product modulators and their outputs can be represented mathematically as

$$\text{output} = (X \sin \omega_a t)(\sin \omega_c t) \tag{12-15}$$

Binary input				16-QAM output	
Q	Q'	I	I'		
0	0	0	0	0.311 V	−135°
0	0	0	1	0.850 V	−165°
0	0	1	0	0.311 V	−45°
0	0	1	1	0.850 V	−15°
0	1	0	0	0.850 V	−105°
0	1	0	1	1.161 V	−135°
0	1	1	0	0.850 V	−75°
0	1	1	1	1.161 V	−45°
1	0	0	0	0.311 V	135°
1	0	0	1	0.850 V	165°
1	0	1	0	0.311 V	45°
1	0	1	1	0.850 V	15°
1	1	0	0	0.850 V	105°
1	1	0	1	1.161 V	135°
1	1	1	0	0.850 V	75°
1	1	1	1	1.161 V	45°

(a)

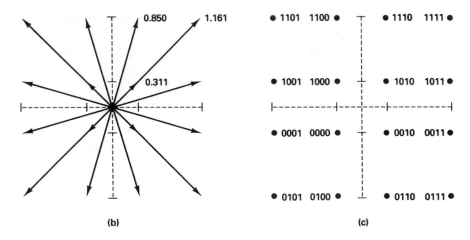

(b)   (c)

FIGURE 12-37 16-QAM modulator: (a) truth table; (b) phasor diagram; (c) constellation diagram

where

$$\underbrace{\omega_a t = 2\pi \frac{f_b}{8} t}_{\substack{\text{modulating-signal} \\ \text{phase}}} \quad \text{and} \quad \underbrace{\omega_c t = 2\pi f_c t}_{\text{carrier phase}}$$

and

$$X = \pm 0.22 \quad \text{or} \quad \pm 0.821$$

Thus,

$$\text{output} = \left(X \sin 2\pi \frac{f_b}{8} t \right)(\sin 2\pi f_c t)$$

$$= \frac{X}{2} \cos 2\pi \left(f_c - \frac{f_b}{8} \right) t = \frac{X}{2} \cos 2\pi \left(f_c + \frac{f_b}{8} \right) t$$

The output frequency spectrum extends from $f_c + f_b/8$ to $f_c − f_b/8$ and the minimum bandwidth (f_N) is

$$\left(f_c + \frac{f_b}{8} \right) - \left(f_c - \frac{f_b}{8} \right) = \frac{2f_b}{8} = \frac{f_b}{4}$$

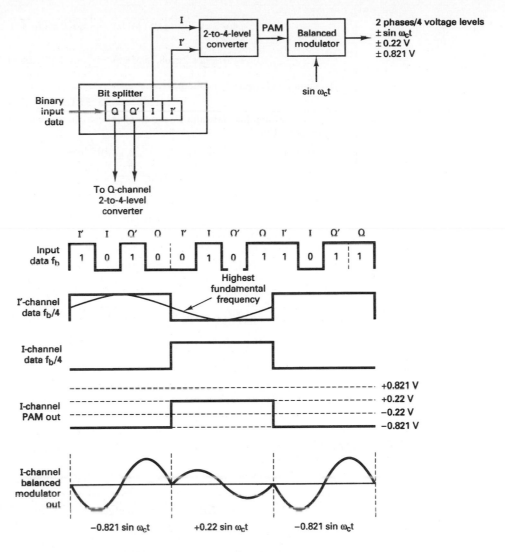

FIGURE 12-38   Bandwidth considerations of a 16-QAM modulator

Example 12-10

For a 16-QAM modulator with an input data rate (f_b) equal to 10 Mbps and a carrier frequency of 70 MHz, determine the minimum double-sided Nyquist frequency (f_N) and the baud. Also, compare the results with those achieved with the BPSK, QPSK, and 8-PSK modulators in Examples 12-3, 12-5, and 12-7. Use the 16-QAM block diagram shown in Figure 12-35 as the modulator model.

Solution   The bit rate in the I, I′, Q, and Q′ channels is equal to one-fourth of the input bit rate or

$$f_{bI} = f_{bI'} = f_{bQ} = f_{bQ'} = \frac{f_b}{4} = \frac{10 \text{ Mbps}}{4} = 2.5 \text{ Mbps}$$

Therefore, the fastest rate of change and highest fundamental frequency presented to either balanced modulator is

$$f_a = \frac{f_{bI}}{2} \text{ or } \frac{f_{bI'}}{2} \text{ or } \frac{f_{bQ}}{2} \text{ or } \frac{f_{bQ'}}{2} = \frac{2.5 \text{ Mbps}}{2} = 1.25 \text{ MHz}$$

The output wave from the balanced modulator is

$$(\sin 2\pi f_a t)(\sin 2\pi f_c t)$$

$$\frac{1}{2} \cos 2\pi (f_c - f_a)t - \frac{1}{2} \cos 2\pi (f_c + f_a)t$$

$$\frac{1}{2}\cos 2\pi[(70 - 1.25)\text{ MHz}]t - \frac{1}{2}\cos 2\pi[(70 + 1.25)\text{ MHz}]t$$

$$\frac{1}{2}\cos 2\pi(68.75\text{ MHz})t - \frac{1}{2}\cos 2\pi(71.25\text{ MHz})t$$

The minimum Nyquist bandwidth is

$$f_N = (71.25 - 68.75)\text{ MHz} = 2.5\text{ MHz}$$

The minimum bandwidth for the 16-QAM can also be determined by simply substituting into Equation 12-13b

$$B = \frac{10\text{ Mbps}}{4}$$
$$= 2.5\text{ MHz}$$

The symbol rate equals the bandwidth; thus,

$$\text{symbol rate} = 2.5\text{ megabaud}$$

The output spectrum is as follows:

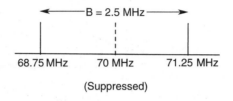

$$f_N = 2.5\text{ MHz}$$

For the same input bit rate, the minimum bandwidth required to pass the output of a 16-QAM modulator is equal to one-fourth that of the BPSK modulator, one-half that of QPSK, and 25% less than with 8-PSK. For each modulation technique, the baud is also reduced by the same proportions.

BANDWIDTH EFFICIENCY

Bandwidth efficiency (or *information density* as it is sometimes called) is often used to compare the performance of one digital modulation technique to another. In essence, it is the ratio of the transmission bit rate to the minimum bandwidth required for a particular modulation scheme. Bandwidth efficiency generally is normalized to a 1-Hz bandwidth and, thus, indicates the number of bits that can be propagated through a medium for each hertz of bandwidth. Mathematically, bandwidth efficiency is

$$\text{BW efficiency} = \frac{\text{transmission rate (bps)}}{\text{minimum bandwidth (Hz)}} \qquad (12\text{-}16)$$

$$= \frac{\text{bits/second}}{\text{hertz}} = \frac{\text{bits/second}}{\text{cycles/second}} = \frac{\text{bits}}{\text{cycle}}$$

Example 12-11

Determine the bandwidth efficiencies for the following modulation schemes: BPSK, QPSK, 8-PSK, and 16-QAM.

Solution Recall from Examples 12-3, 12-5, 12-7, and 12-10 the minimum bandwidths required to propagate a 10-Mbps transmission rate with the following modulation schemes:

Modulation Scheme	Minimum Bandwidth (MHz)
BPSK	10
QPSK	5
8-PSK	3.33
16-QAM	2.5

TABLE 12-1 Digital Modulation Summary

Modulation	Encoding	Bandwidth (Hz)	Baud	Bandwidth Efficiency (bps/Hz)
FSK	Single bit	$\geq f_b$	f_b	≤ 1
BPSK	Single bit	f_b	f_b	1
QPSK	Dibit	$f_b/2$	$f_b/2$	2
8-PSK	Tribit	$f_b/3$	$f_b/3$	3
8-QAM	Tribit	$f_b/3$	$f_b/3$	3
16-PSK	Quadbit	$f_b/4$	$f_b/4$	4
16-QAM	Quadbit	$f_b/4$	$f_b/4$	4

Substituting into Equation 12-16, the bandwidth efficiencies are determined as follows:

$$\text{BPSK: BW efficiency} = \frac{10 \text{ Mbps}}{10 \text{ MHz}} = \frac{1 \text{ bps}}{\text{Hz}} = \frac{1 \text{ bit}}{\text{cycle}}$$

$$\text{QPSK: BW efficiency} = \frac{10 \text{ Mbps}}{5 \text{ MHz}} = \frac{2 \text{ bps}}{\text{Hz}} = \frac{2 \text{ bits}}{\text{cycle}}$$

$$\text{8-PSK: BW efficiency} = \frac{10 \text{ Mbps}}{3.33 \text{ MHz}} = \frac{3 \text{ bps}}{\text{Hz}} = \frac{3 \text{ bits}}{\text{cycle}}$$

$$\text{16-QAM: BW efficiency} = \frac{10 \text{ Mbps}}{2.5 \text{ MHz}} = \frac{4 \text{ bps}}{\text{Hz}} = \frac{4 \text{ bits}}{\text{cycle}}$$

The results indicate that BPSK is the least efficient and 16-QAM is the most efficient. 16-QAM requires one-fourth as much bandwidth as BPSK for the same input bit rate.

The various forms of FSK, PSK, and QAM are summarized in Table 12-1.

CARRIER RECOVERY

Carrier recovery is the process of extracting a phase-coherent reference carrier from a receiver signal. This is sometimes called *phase referencing.*

In the phase modulation techniques described thus far, the binary data were encoded as a precise phase of the transmitted carrier. (This is referred to as *absolute phase encoding.*) Depending on the encoding method, the angular separation between adjacent phasors varied between 30° and 180°. To correctly demodulate the data, a phase-coherent carrier was recovered and compared with the received carrier in a product detector. To determine the absolute phase of the received carrier, it is necessary to produce a carrier at the receiver that is phase coherent with the transmit reference oscillator. This is the function of the carrier recovery circuit.

With PSK and QAM, the carrier is suppressed in the balanced modulators and, therefore, is not transmitted. Consequently, at the receiver the carrier cannot simply be tracked with a standard phase-locked loop. With suppressed-carrier systems, such as PSK and QAM, sophisticated methods of carrier recovery are required such as a *squaring loop,* a *Costas loop,* or a *remodulator.*

Squaring Loop

A common method of achieving carrier recovery for BPSK is the *squaring loop.* Figure 12-39 shows the block diagram of a squaring loop. The received BPSK waveform is filtered and then squared. The filtering reduces the spectral width of the received noise. The squaring circuit removes the modulation and generates the second harmonic of the carrier frequency. This harmonic is phase tracked by the PLL. The VCO output frequency from the PLL then is divided by 2 and used as the phase reference for the product detectors.

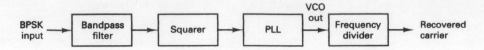

FIGURE 12-39   Squaring loop carrier recovery circuit for a BPSK receiver

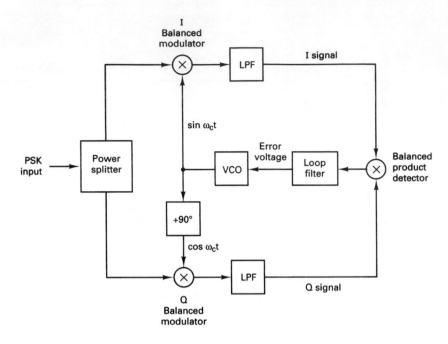

FIGURE 12-40   Costas loop carrier recovery circuit

With BPSK, only two output phases are possible: $+\sin \omega_c t$ and $-\sin \omega_c t$. Mathematically, the operation of the squaring circuit can be described as follows. For a receive signal of $+\sin \omega_c t$ the output of the squaring circuit is

$$\text{output} = (+\sin \omega_c t)(+\sin \omega_c t) = +\sin^2 \omega_c t$$

$$= \frac{1}{2}(1 - \cos 2\omega_c t) = \underset{\text{(filtered out)}}{\frac{1}{2}} - \underset{}{\frac{1}{2}\cos 2\omega_c t}$$

For a received signal of $-\sin \omega_c t$ the output of the squaring circuit is

$$\text{output} = (-\sin \omega_c t)(-\sin \omega_c t) = +\sin^2 \omega_c t$$

$$= \frac{1}{2}(1 - \cos 2\omega_c t) = \underset{\text{(filtered out)}}{\frac{1}{2}} - \underset{}{\frac{1}{2}\cos 2\omega_c t}$$

It can be seen that in both cases the output from the squaring circuit contained a constant voltage ($+1/2$ V) and a signal at twice the carrier frequency ($\cos 2\omega_c t$). The constant voltage is removed by filtering, leaving only $\cos 2\omega_c t$.

Costas Loop

A second method of carrier recovery is the Costas, or quadrature, loop shown in Figure 12-40. The Costas loop produces the same results as a squaring circuit followed by an ordinary PLL in place of the BPF. This recovery scheme uses two parallel tracking loops

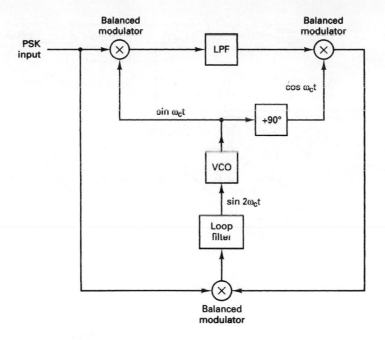

FIGURE 12-41 Remodulator loop carrier recovery circuit

(I and Q) simultaneously to derive the product of the I and Q components of the signal that drives the VCO. The in-phase (I) loop uses the VCO as in a PLL, and the quadrature (Q) loop uses a 90° shifted VCO signal. Once the frequency of the VCO is equal to the suppressed-carrier frequency, the product of the I and Q signals will produce an error voltage proportional to any phase error in the VCO. The error voltage controls the phase and, thus, the frequency of the VCO.

Remodulator

A third method of achieving recovery of a phase and frequency coherent carrier is the remodulator, shown in Figure 12-41. The remodulator produces a loop error voltage that is proportional to twice the phase error between the incoming signal and the VCO signal. The remodulator has a faster acquisition time than either the squaring or the Costas loops.

Carrier recovery circuits for higher-than-binary encoding techniques are similar to BPSK except that circuits that raise the receive signal to the fourth, eighth, and higher powers are used.

DIFFERENTIAL PHASE SHIFT KEYING

Differential phase shift keying (DPSK) is an alternative form of digital modulation where the binary input information is contained in the difference between two successive signaling elements rather than the absolute phase. With DPSK it is not necessary to recover a phase-coherent carrier. Instead, a received signaling element is delayed by one signaling element time slot and then compared with the next received signaling element. The difference in the phase of the two signaling elements determines the logic condition of the data.

Differential BPSK

DBPSK transmitter. Figure 12-42a shows a simplified block diagram of a *differential binary phase shift keying* (DBPSK) transmitter. An incoming information bit is XNORed with the preceding bit prior to entering the BPSK modulator (balanced modulator). For the

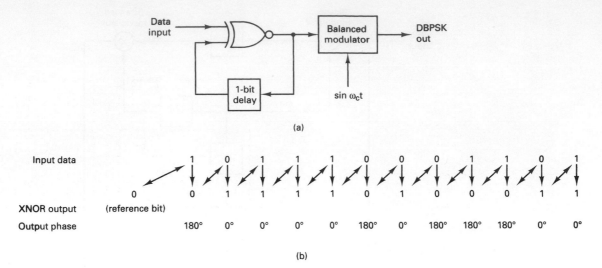

(a)

Input data		1	0	1	1	1	0	0	0	1	1	0	1
	0												
XNOR output	(reference bit)	0	1	1	1	1	0	1	0	0	0	1	1
Output phase		180°	0°	0°	0°	0°	180°	0°	180°	180°	180°	0°	0°

(b)

FIGURE 12-42 DBPSK modulator: (a) block diagram; (b) timing diagram

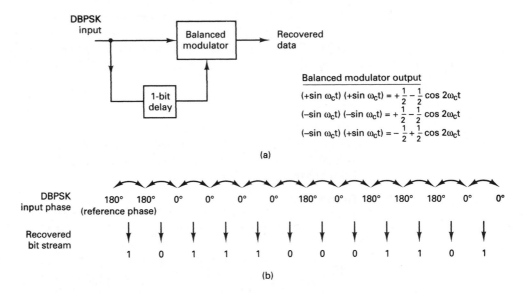

(a)

DBPSK input phase	180°	180°	0°	0°	0°	0°	180°	0°	180°	180°	180°	0°	0°
	(reference phase)												
Recovered bit stream		1	0	1	1	1	0	0	0	1	1	0	1

(b)

FIGURE 12-43 DBPSK demodulator: (a) block diagram; (b) timing sequence

first data bit, there is no preceding bit with which to compare it. Therefore, an initial reference bit is assumed. Figure 12-42b shows the relationship between the input data, the XNOR output data, and the phase at the output of the balanced modulator. If the initial reference bit is assumed a logic 1, the output from the XNOR circuit is simply the complement of that shown.

In Figure 12-42b the first data bit is XNORed with the reference bit. If they are the same, the XNOR output is a logic 1; if they are different, the XNOR output is a logic 0. The balanced modulator operates the same as a conventional BPSK modulator; a logic 1 produces $+\sin \omega_c t$ at the output and a logic 0 produces $-\sin \omega_c t$ at the output.

DBPSK receiver.   Figure 12-43 shows the block diagram and timing sequence for a DBPSK receiver. The received signal is delayed by one bit time, then compared with the next signaling element in the balanced modulator. If they are the same, a logic 1 (+ voltage) is generated. If they are different, a logic 0 (− voltage) is generated. If the reference phase is incorrectly assumed, only the first demodulated bit is in error. Differential encod-

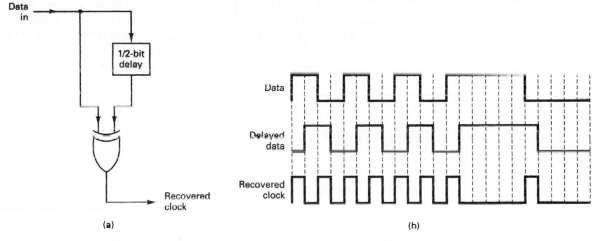

FIGURE 12-44 (a) Clock recovery circuit; (b) timing diagram

ing can be implemented with higher-than-binary digital modulation schemes, although the differential algorithms are much more complicated than for DBPSK.

The primary advantage of DBPSK is the simplicity with which it can be implemented. With DBPSK, no carrier recovery circuit is needed. A disadvantage of DBPSK is that it requires between 1 dB and 3 dB more signal-to-noise ratio to achieve the same bit error rate as that of absolute PSK.

CLOCK RECOVERY

As with any digital system, digital radio requires precise timing or clock synchronization between the transmit and the receive circuitry. Because of this, it is necessary to regenerate clocks at the receiver that are synchronous with those at the transmitter.

Figure 12-44a shows a simple circuit that is commonly used to recover clocking information from the received data. The recovered data are delayed by one-half a bit time and then compared with the original data in an XOR circuit. The frequency of the clock that is recovered with this method is equal to the received data rate (f_b). Figure 12-44b shows the relationship between the data and the recovered clock timing. From Figure 12-44b it can be seen that as long as the receive data contains a substantial number of transitions (1/0 sequences), the recovered clock is maintained. If the receive data were to undergo an extended period of successive 1s or 0s, the recovered clock would be lost. To prevent this from occurring, the data are scrambled at the transmit end and descrambled at the receive end. Scrambling introduces transitions (pulses) into the binary signal using a prescribed algorithm, and the descrambler uses the same algorithm to remove the transitions.

PROBABILITY OF ERROR AND BIT ERROR RATE

Probability of error $P(e)$ and *bit error rate* (BER) are often used interchangeably, although in practice they do have slightly different meanings. $P(e)$ is a theoretical (mathematical) expectation of the bit error rate for a given system. BER is an empirical (historical) record of a system's actual bit error performance. For example, if a system has a $P(e)$ of 10^{-5}, this means that mathematically, you can expect one bit error in every 100,000 bits transmitted ($1/10^5 = 1/100,000$). If a system has a BER of 10^{-5}, this means that in the past there was one bit error for every 100,000 bits transmitted. A bit error rate is measured, then compared with the expected probability of error to evaluate a system's performance.

Probability of error is a function of the *carrier-to-noise power ratio* (or more specifically, the average *energy per bit-to-noise power density ratio*) and the number of possible encoding conditions used (*M*-ary). Carrier-to-noise power ratio is the ratio of the average carrier power (the combined power of the carrier and its associated sidebands) to the *thermal noise power*. Carrier power can be stated in watts or dBm, where

$$C_{(dBm)} = 10 \log \frac{C_{(watts)}}{0.001} \qquad (12\text{-}17)$$

Thermal noise power is expressed mathematically as

$$N = KTB \quad \text{(watts)} \qquad (12\text{-}18a)$$

where N = thermal noise power (watts)
K = Boltzmann's proportionality constant (1.38×10^{-23} joules per kelvin)
T = temperature (kelvin: 0 K = $-273°$ C, room temperature = 290 K)
B = bandwidth (hertz)

Stated in dBm, $$N_{(dBm)} = 10 \log \frac{KTB}{0.001} \qquad (12\text{-}18b)$$

Mathematically, the carrier-to-noise power ratio is

$$\frac{C}{N} = \frac{C}{KTB} \text{ (unitless ratio)} \qquad (12\text{-}19a)$$

where C = carrier power (watts)
N = noise power (watts)

Stated in dB, $$\frac{C}{N} \text{(dB)} = 10 \log \frac{C}{N} \qquad (12\text{-}19b)$$

$$= C_{(dBm)} - N_{(dBm)}$$

Energy per bit is simply the energy of a single bit of information. Mathematically, energy per bit is

$$E_b = CT_b \text{ (J/bit)} \qquad (12\text{-}20a)$$

where E_b = energy of a single bit (joules per bit)
T_b = time of a single bit (seconds)
C = carrier power (watts)

Stated in dBJ, $$E_{b(dBJ)} = 10 \log E_b \qquad (12\text{-}20b)$$

and because $T_b = 1/f_b$, where f_b is the bit rate in bits per second, E_b can be rewritten as

$$E_b = \frac{C}{f_b} \text{ (J/bit)} \qquad (12\text{-}20c)$$

Stated in dBJ, $$E_{b(dBJ)} = 10 \log \frac{C}{f_b} \qquad (12\text{-}20d)$$

$$= 10 \log C - 10 \log f_b \qquad (12\text{-}20e)$$

Noise power density is the thermal noise power normalized to a 1-Hz bandwidth (i.e., the noise power present in a 1-Hz bandwidth). Mathematically, noise power density is

$$N_0 = \frac{N}{B} \text{ (W/Hz)} \qquad (12\text{-}21a)$$

where N_0 = noise power density (watts per hertz)
$\quad\quad\quad$ N = thermal noise power (watts)
$\quad\quad\quad$ B = bandwidth (hertz)

Stated in dBm, $\quad\quad\quad\quad\quad N_{0(dBm)} = 10 \log \dfrac{N}{0.001} - 10 \log B$ $\quad\quad\quad$ (12-21b)

$$= N_{(dBm)} - 10 \log B \quad\quad\quad (12\text{-}21c)$$

Combining Equations 12-18a and 12-21a yields

$$N_0 = \frac{KTB}{B} = KT \text{ (W/Hz)} \quad\quad\quad (12\text{-}21d)$$

Stated in dBm,

$$N_{0(dBm)} = 10 \log \frac{K}{0.001} + 10 \log T \quad\quad\quad (12\text{-}21e)$$

Energy per bit-to-noise power density ratio is used to compare two or more digital modulation systems that use different transmission rates (bit rates), modulation schemes (FSK, PSK, QAM), or encoding techniques (*M*-ary). The energy per bit-to-noise power density ratio is simply the ratio of the energy of a single bit to the noise power present in 1 Hz of bandwidth. Thus, E_b/N_0 normalizes all multiphase modulation schemes to a common noise bandwidth allowing for a simpler and more accurate comparison of their error performance. Mathematically, E_b/N_0 is

$$\frac{E_b}{N_0} = \frac{C/f_b}{N/B} = \frac{CB}{Nf_b} \quad\quad\quad (12\text{-}22a)$$

where E_bN_0 is the energy per bit-to-noise power density ratio. Rearranging Equation 12-22a yields the following expression:

$$\frac{E_b}{N_0} = \frac{C}{N} \times \frac{B}{f_b} \quad\quad\quad (12\text{-}22b)$$

where E_b/N_0 = energy per bit-to-noise power density ratio
$\quad\quad\quad$ C/N = carrier-to-noise power ratio
$\quad\quad\quad$ B/f_b = noise bandwidth-to-bit rate ratio

Stated in dB, $\quad\quad\quad\quad \dfrac{E_b}{N_0} \text{ (dB)} = 10 \log \dfrac{C}{N} + 10 \log \dfrac{B}{f_b}$ $\quad\quad\quad$ (12-22c)

or $\quad\quad\quad\quad\quad\quad\quad\quad\quad = 10 \log E_b - 10 \log N_0$ $\quad\quad\quad$ (12-22d)

From Equation 12-22b it can be seen that the E_b/N_0 ratio is simply the product of the carrier-to-noise power ratio and the noise bandwidth-to-bit rate ratio. Also, from Equation 12-22b, it can be seen that when the bandwidth equals the bit rate, $E_b/N_0 = C/N$.

In general, the minimum carrier-to-noise power ratio required for QAM systems is less than that required for comparable PSK systems, Also, the higher the level of encoding used (the higher the value of *M*), the higher the minimum carrier-to-noise power ratio. In Chapter 18, several examples are shown for determining the minimum carrier-to-noise power and energy per bit-to-noise density ratios for a given *M*-ary system and desired $P(e)$.

Example 12-12

For a QPSK system and the given parameters, determine
(a) Carrier power in dBm.
(b) Noise power in dBm.
(c) Noise power density in dBm.
(d) Energy per bit in dBJ.

(e) Carrier-to-noise power ratio in dB.

(f) E_b/N_0 ratio.

$$C = 10^{-12} \text{W} \qquad f_b = 60 \text{ kbps}$$
$$N = 1.2 \times 10^{-14} \text{W} \qquad B = 120 \text{ kHz}$$

Solution (a) The carrier power in dBm is determined by substituting into Equation 12-17.

$$C = 10 \log \frac{10^{-12}}{0.001} = -90 \text{ dBm}$$

(b) The noise power in dBm is determined by substituting into Equation 12-18b.

$$N = 10 \log \frac{1.2 \times 10^{-14}}{0.001} = -109.2 \text{ dBm}$$

(c) The noise power density is determined by substituting into Equation 12-21c.

$$N_0 = -109.2 \text{ dBm} - 10 \log 120 \text{ kHz} = -160 \text{ dBm}$$

(d) The energy per bit is determined by substituting into Equation 12-20d.

$$E_b = 10 \log \frac{10^{-12}}{60 \text{ kbps}} = -167.8 \text{ dBJ}$$

(e) The carrier-to-noise power ratio is determined by substituting into Equation 12-19b.

$$\frac{C}{N} = 10 \log \frac{10^{-12}}{1.2 \times 10^{-14}} = 19.2 \text{ dB}$$

(f) The energy per bit-to-noise density ratio is determined by substituting into Equation 12-22c.

$$\frac{E_b}{N_0} = 19.2 + 10 \log \frac{120 \text{ kHz}}{60 \text{ kbps}} = 22.2 \text{ dB}$$

PSK Error Performance

The bit error performance for the various multiphase digital modulation systems is directly related to the distance between points on a signal state-space diagram. For example, on the signal state-space diagram for BPSK shown in Figure 12-45a, it can be seen that the two signal points (logic 1 and logic 0) have maximum separation (*d*) for a given power level (*D*). In essence, one BPSK signal state is the exact negative of the other. As the figure shows, a noise vector (V_N), when combined with the signal vector (V_S), effectively shifts the phase of the signaling element (V_{SE}) alpha degrees. If the phase shift exceeds $\pm 90°$, the signal element is shifted beyond the threshold points into the error region. For BPSK, it would require a noise vector of sufficient amplitude and phase to produce more than a $\pm 90°$ phase shift in the signaling element to produce an error. For PSK systems, the general formula for the threshold points is

$$\text{TP} = \pm \frac{\pi}{M} \tag{12-23}$$

where *M* is the number of signal states.

The phase relationship between signaling elements for BPSK (i.e., 180° out of phase) is the optimum signaling format, referred to as *antipodal signaling,* and occurs only when two binary signal levels are allowed and when one signal is the exact negative of the other. Because no other bit-by-bit signaling scheme is any better, antipodal performance is often used as a reference for comparison.

The error performance of the other multiphase PSK systems can be compared with that of BPSK simply by determining the relative decrease in error distance between points on a signal state-space diagram. For PSK, the general formula for the maximum distance between signaling points is given by

$$\sin \theta = \sin \frac{360°}{2M} = \frac{d/2}{D} \tag{12-24}$$

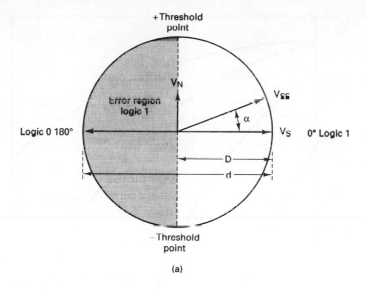

(a)

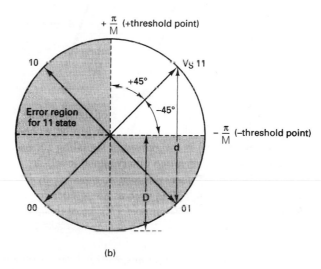

(b)

FIGURE 12-45 PSK error region: (a) BPSK; (b) QPSK

where d = error distance
    M = number of phases
    D = peak signal amplitude

Rearranging Equation 12-24 and solving for d yields

$$d = \left(2 \sin \frac{180°}{M}\right) \times D \qquad (12\text{-}25)$$

Figure 12-45b shows the signal state-space diagram for QPSK. From Figure 12-45b and Equation 12-24 it can be seen that QPSK can tolerate only a $\pm45°$ phase shift. From Equation 12-23, the maximum phase shift for 8-PSK and 16-PSK is $\pm22.5°$ and $\pm11.5°$, respectively. Consequently, the higher levels of modulation (i.e., the greater the value of M) require a greater energy per bit-to-noise power density ratio to reduce the effect of noise interference. Hence, the higher the level of modulation, the smaller the angular separation between signal points and the smaller the error distance.

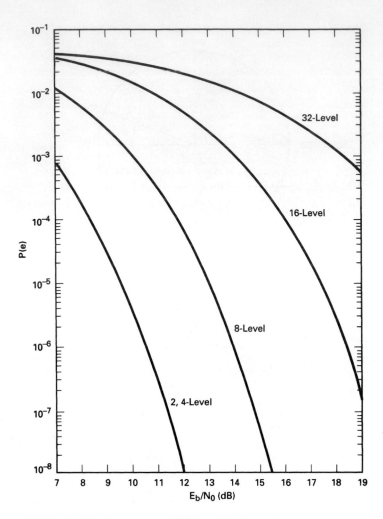

FIGURE 12-46 Error rates of PSK modulation systems

The general expression for the bit error probability of an *M*-phase PSK system is

$$P(e) = \frac{1}{\log_2 M} \, \text{erf} \, (z) \qquad (12\text{-}26)$$

where   erf = error function
$$z = \sin(\pi/M)(\sqrt{\log_2 M})(\sqrt{E_b/N_0})$$

By substituting into Equation 12-26 it can be shown that QPSK provides the same error performance as BPSK. This is because the 3-dB reduction in error distance for QPSK is offset by the 3-dB decrease in its bandwidth (in addition to the error distance, the relative widths of the noise bandwidths must also be considered). Thus, both systems provide optimum performance. Figure 12-46 shows the error performance for 2-, 4-, 8-, 16-, and 32-PSK systems as a function of E_b/N_0.

Example 12-13

Determine the minimum bandwidth required to achieve a $P(e)$ of 10^{-7} for an 8-PSK system operating at 10 Mbps with a carrier-to-noise power ratio of 11.7 dB.

Solution From Figure 12-46, the minimum E_b/N_0 ratio to achieve a $P(e)$ of 10^{-7} for an 8-PSK system is 14.7 dB. The minimum bandwidth is found by rearranging Equation 12-22b.

$$\frac{B}{f_b} = \frac{E_b}{N_0} - \frac{C}{N}$$
$$= 14.7 \text{ dB} - 11.7 \text{ dB} = 3 \text{ dB}$$
$$\frac{B}{f_b} = \text{antilog } 3 = 2$$
$$B = 2 \times 10 \text{ Mbps} = 20 \text{ MHz}$$

QAM Error Performance

For a large number of signal points (i.e., M-ary systems greater than 4), QAM outperforms PSK. This is because the distance between signaling points in a PSK system is smaller than the distance between points in a comparable QAM system. The general expression for the distance between adjacent signaling points for a QAM system with L levels on each axis is

$$d = \frac{\sqrt{2}}{L-1} \times D \tag{12-27}$$

where d = error distance
   L = number of levels on each axis
   D = peak signal amplitude

In comparing Equation 12-25 to Equation 12-27, it can be seen that QAM systems have an advantage over PSK systems with the same peak signal power level.

The general expression for the bit error probability of an L-level QAM system is

$$P(e) = \frac{1}{\log_2 L}\left(\frac{L-1}{L}\right)\text{erfc}(z) \tag{12-28}$$

where erfc(z) is the complementary error function.

$$z = \frac{\sqrt{\log_2 L}}{L-1}\sqrt{\frac{E_b}{N_0}}$$

Figure 12-47 shows the error performance for 4-, 16-, 32-, and 64-QAM systems as a function of E_b/N_0.

Table 12-2 lists the minimum carrier-to-noise power ratios and energy per bit-to-noise power density ratios required for a probability of error 10^{-6} for several PSK and QAM modulation schemes.

Example 12-14

Which system requires the highest E_b/N_0 ratio for a probability of error of 10^{-6}, a four-level QAM system or an 8-PSK system?

TABLE 12-2 Performance Comparison of Various Digital Modulation Schemes (BER = 10^{-6})

Modulation Technique	C/N Ratio (dB)	E_b/N_0 Ratio (dB)
BPSK	10.6	10.6
QPSK	13.6	10.6
4-QAM	13.6	10.6
8-QAM	17.6	10.6
8-PSK	18.5	14
16-PSK	24.3	18.3
16-QAM	20.5	14.5
32-QAM	24.4	17.4
64-QAM	26.6	18.8

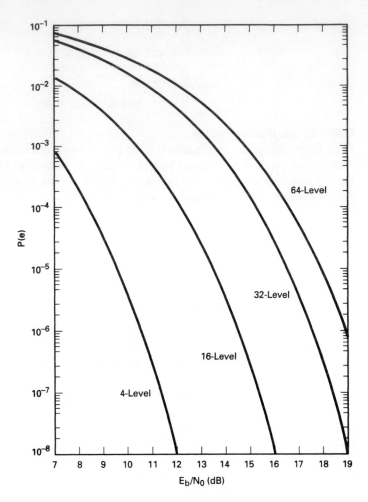

FIGURE 12-47 Error rates of QAM modulation systems

Solution From Figure 12-47, the minimum E_b/N_0 ratio required for a four-level QAM system is 10.6 dB. From Figure 12-46, the minimum E_b/N_0 ratio required for an 8-PSK system is 14 dB. Therefore, to achieve a $P(e)$ of 10^{-6}, a four-level QAM system would require 3.4 dB less E_b/N_0 ratio.

FSK Error Performance

The error probability for FSK systems is evaluated in a somewhat different manner than PSK and QAM. There are essentially only two types of FSK systems: noncoherent (asynchronous) and coherent (synchronous). With noncoherent FSK, the transmitter and receiver are not frequency or phase synchronized. With coherent FSK, local receiver reference signals are in frequency and phase lock with the transmitted signals. The probability of error for noncoherent FSK is

$$P(e) = \frac{1}{2}\exp\left(-\frac{E_b}{2N_0}\right) \tag{12-29}$$

The probability of error for coherent FSK is

$$P(e) = \text{erfc}\sqrt{\frac{E_b}{N_0}} \tag{12-30}$$

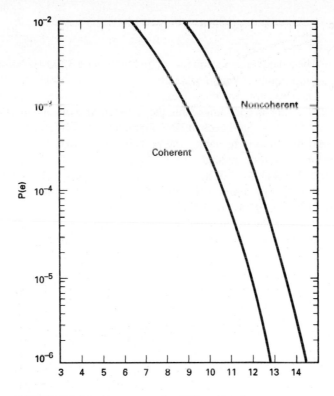

FIGURE 12-48 Error rates for FSK modulation systems

Figure 12-48 shows probability of error curves for both coherent and noncoherent FSK for several values of E_b/N_0. From Equations 12-29 and 12-30 it can be determined that the probability of error for noncoherent FSK is greater than that of coherent FSK for equal energy per bit-to-noise power density ratios.

TRELLIS ENCODING

Achieving data transmission rates in excess of 9600 bps over standard voice-band telephone channels obviously requires an encoding scheme well beyond the quadbits used with 16-PSK or 16-QAM (i.e., M must be significantly greater than 16). As might be expected, higher encoding schemes require higher signal-to-noise (S/N) ratios. Using the Shannon limit for information capacity (Equation 12-1c), a data transmission rate of 28.8 kbps using a communications channel with 3200 Hz of bandwidth requires a signal-to-noise ratio of

$$I(\text{bps}) = (3.32 \times B) \log(1 + S/N)$$

therefore,
$$28.8 \text{ kbps} = (3.32)(3200) \log(1 + S/N)$$

$$28,800 = 10,624 \log(1 + S/N)$$

$$\frac{28,800}{10,624} = \log(1 + S/N)$$

$$2.71 = \log(1 + S/N)$$

thus,
$$10^{2.71} = 1 + S/N$$

$$513 = 1 + S/N$$

$$512 = S/N$$

$$\text{in dB,} \qquad S/N_{(dB)} = 10 \log 512$$
$$= 27 \text{ dB}$$

Similarly, a data transmission rate of 56 kbps over a 3200-Hz bandwidth channel would require a minimum S/N ratio of 53 dB.

Data transmission rates in excess of 56 kbps can be achieved over standard telephone channels using an encoding technique called *trellis code modulation* (TCM). TCM was developed by Dr. Ungerboeck at IBM Zuerich Research Laboratory. TCM combines encoding and modulation to reduce the probability of error, thus improving the bit error performance. The fundamental idea behind TCM is introducing controlled redundancy which reduces the likelihood of transmission errors. What sets TCM apart from standard encoding schemes is the introduction of redundancy by doubling the number of signal points in a given PSK or QAM constellation.

Trellis code modulation is sometimes thought of as a magical method of increasing transmission bit rates over communications systems using QAM or PSK with fixed bandwidths. Few people fully understand it, as modem manufacturers do not seem willing to share information on TCM concepts. Therefore, the following explanation is not intended to fully describe the process of TCM, but rather to introduce the topic and give the reader a basic understanding of how TCM works and the advantage it has over conventional digital modulation techniques.

M-ary QAM and PSK utilize a signal set of $2^N = M$ where N equals the number of bits encoded into M different conditions. Therefore, $N = 2$ produces a standard PSK constellation with four signal points (i.e., QPSK) as shown in Figure 12-49a. Using TCM, the number of signal points increases to two times M possible symbols for the same factor-of-M reduction in bandwidth while transmitting each signal during the same time interval. TCM-encoded QPSK is shown in Figure 12-49b.

Trellis coding also defines the manner in which signal-state transitions are allowed to occur, and transitions that do not follow this pattern are interpreted in the receiver as transmission errors. Therefore, TCM can improve error performance by restricting the manner

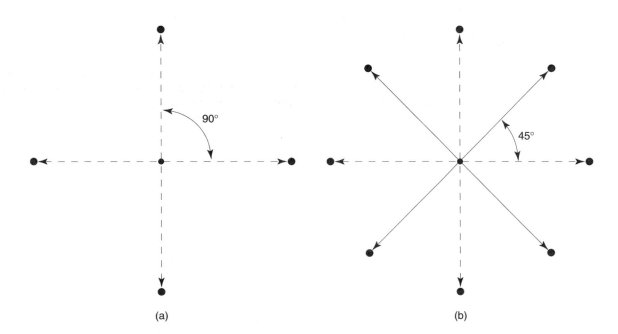

(a)   (b)

FIGURE 12-49 QPSK constellations: (a) standard encoding format; (b) trellis encoding format

in which signals are allowed to transition. For values of N greater than 2, QAM is the modulation scheme of choice for TCM; however, for simplification purposes the following explanation uses PSK as it is easier to illustrate.

Figure 12-50 shows a TCM scheme using two-state 8-PSK, which is essentially two QPSK constellations offset by 45°. One four-state constellation is labeled 0-4-2-6 and the other is labeled 1-5-3-7. For this explanation, the signal point labels 0 through 7 are not meant to represent the actual data conditions but rather to simply indicate a convenient method of labeling the various signal points. Each digit represents one of four signal points permitted within each of the two QPSK constellations. When in the 0-4-2-6 constellation and a 0 or 4 is transmitted, the system remains in the same constellation. However, when either a 2 or 6 is transmitted, the system switches to the 1-5-3-7 constellation. Once in the 1-5-3-7 constellation and a 3 or 7 is transmitted, the system remains in the same constellation and if a 1 or 5 is transmitted the system switches to the 0-4-2-6 constellation. Remember that each symbol represents two bits so the system undergoes a 45° phase shift whenever it switches between the two constellations. A complete error analysis of standard QPSK compared with TCM QPSK would reveal a coding gain for TCM of 2-to-1 1 or 3 dB. Table 12-3 lists the coding gains achieved for TCM coding schemes with several different trellis states.

The maximum data rate achievable using a given bandwidth can be determined by rearranging Equation 12-13b.

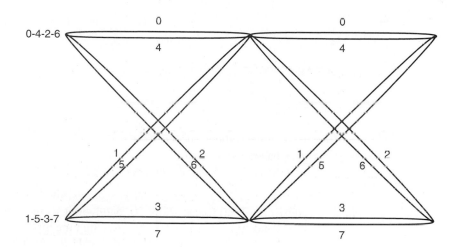

FIGURE 12-50 8-PSK TCM constellations

TABLE 12-3 Trellis Coding Gain

Number of Trellis States	Coding Gain (dB)
2	3.0
4	5.5
8	6.0
16	6.5
32	7.1
64	7.3
128	7.3
256	7.4

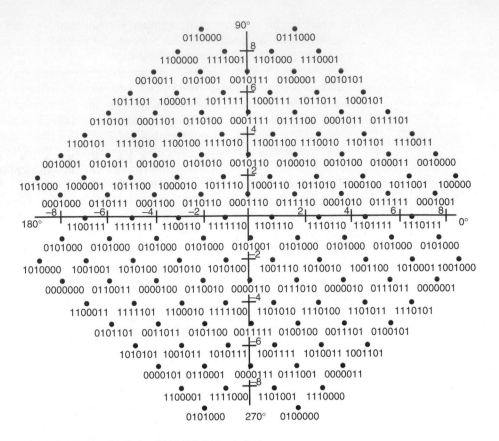

FIGURE 12-51 32-Point QAM TCM constellation

$$N \times B = f_b$$

where N = number of bits encoded (bits)

            B = bandwidth (hertz)

            f_b = transmission bit rate (bits per second)

Remember that with *M*-ary QAM or PSK systems, the baud equals the minimum required bandwidth. Therefore, a 3200-Hz bandwidth using a nine-bit trellis code produces a 3200 baud signal with each baud carrying nine bits. Therefore, the transmission rate f_b = 9 × 3200 = 28.8 kbps.

TCM is thought of as a coding scheme that improves on standard QAM. The first TCM system used a five-bit code which included four QAM bits (a quadbit) and a fifth bit used to help decode the quadbit. Transmitting five bits within a single signaling element requires producing 32 discernible signals. Figure 12-51 shows a 32-point QAM constellation that uses four amplitudes and eight phases to produce the 32 discrete signal states.

A 3200 baud signal using nine-bit TCM encoding produces 512 different codes. The nine data bits plus a redundant bit for TCM encoding requires a 960-point constellation. Figure 12-52 illustrates one-fourth of the 960-point superconstellation showing 240 signal points. The full superconstellation can be obtained by rotating the 240 points shown by 0°, 90°, 180°, and 270°.

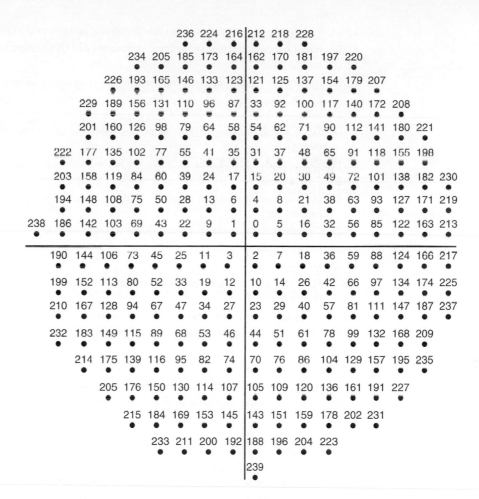

FIGURE 12-52 One-fourth of a 960-Point QAM TCM constellation

QUESTIONS

12-1. Explain *digital transmission* and *digital radio.*

12-2. Define *information capacity.*

12-3. What are the three most predominant modulation schemes used in digital radio systems?

12-4. Explain the relationship between bits per second and baud for an FSK system.

12-5. Define the following terms for FSK modulation: *frequency deviation, modulation index,* and *deviation ratio.*

12-6. Explain the relationship between (a) the minimum bandwidth required for an FSK system and the bit rate, and (b) the mark and space frequencies.

12-7. What is the difference between standard FSK and MSK? What is the advantage of MSK?

12-8. Define *PSK.*

12-9. Explain the relationship between bits per second and baud for a BPSK system.

12-10. What is a constellation diagram, and how is it used with PSK?

12-11. Explain the relationship between the minimum bandwidth required for a BPSK system and the bit rate.

12-12. Explain *M*-ary.

12-13. Explain the relationship between bits per second and baud for a QPSK system.

12-14. Explain the significance of the I and Q channels in a QPSK modulator.

12-15. Define *dibit*.

12-16. Explain the relationship between the minimum bandwidth required for a QPSK system and the bit rate.

12-17. What is a coherent demodulator?

12-18. What advantage does OQPSK have over conventional QPSK? What is a disadvantage of OQPSK?

12-19. Explain the relationship between bits per second and baud for an 8-PSK system.

12-20. Define *tribit*.

12-21. Explain the relationship between the minimum bandwidth required for an 8-PSK system and the bit rate.

12-22. Explain the relationship between bits per second and baud for a 16-PSK system.

12-23. Define *quadbit*.

12-24. Define *QAM*.

12-25. Explain the relationship between the minimum bandwidth required for a 16-QAM system and the bit rate.

12-26. What is the difference between PSK and QAM?

12-27. Define *bandwidth efficiency*.

12-28. Define *carrier recovery*.

12-29. Explain the differences between absolute PSK and differential PSK.

12-30. What is the purpose of a clock recovery circuit? When is it used?

12-31. What is the difference between probability of error and bit error rate?

PROBLEMS

12-1. Determine the bandwidth and baud for an FSK signal with a mark frequency of 32 kHz, a space frequency of 24 kHz, and a bit rate of 4 kbps.

12-2. Determine the maximum bit rate for an FSK signal with a mark frequency of 48 kHz, a space frequency of 52 kHz, and an available bandwidth of 10 kHz.

12-3. Determine the bandwidth and baud for an FSK signal with a mark frequency of 99 kHz, a space frequency of 101 kHz, and a bit rate of 10 kbps.

12-4. Determine the maximum bit rate for an FSK signal with a mark frequency of 102 kHz, a space frequency of 104 kHz, and an available bandwidth of 8 kHz.

12-5. Determine the minimum bandwidth and baud for a BPSK modulator with a carrier frequency of 40 MHz, and an input bit rate of 500 kbps. Sketch the output spectrum.

12-6. For the QPSK modulator shown in Figure 12-19, change the $+90°$ phase-shift network to $-90°$ and sketch the new constellation diagram.

12-7. For the QPSK demodulator shown in Figure 12-23, determine the I and Q bits for an input signal of $\sin \omega_c t - \cos \omega_c t$.

12-8. For an 8-PSK modulator with an input data rate (f_b) equal to 20 Mbps and a carrier frequency of 100 MHz, determine the minimum double-sided Nyquist bandwidth (f_N) and the baud. Sketch the output spectrum.

12-9. For the 8-PSK modulator shown in Figure 12-25, change the reference oscillator to $\cos \omega_c t$ and sketch the new constellation diagram.

12-10. For a 16-QAM modulator with an input bit rate (f_b) equal to 20 Mbps and a carrier frequency of 100 MHz, determine the minimum double-sided Nyquist bandwidth (f_N) and the baud. Sketch the output spectrum.

12-11. For the 16-QAM modulator shown in Figure 12-35, change the reference oscillator to $\cos \omega_c t$ and determine the output expressions for the following I, I', Q, and Q' input conditions: 0000, 1111, 1010, and 0101.

12-12. Determine the bandwidth efficiency for the following modulators.

    (a) QPSK, f_b = 10 Mbps

    (b) 8-PSK, f_b = 21 Mbps

    (c) 16-QAM, f_b = 20 Mbps

12-13. For the DBPSK modulator shown in Figure 12-42a, determine the output phase sequence for the following input bit sequence: 00110011010101 (assume that the reference bit = 1).

12-14. For a QPSK system and the given parameters, determine

    (a) Carrier power in dBm.

    (b) Noise power in dBm.

    (c) Noise power density in dBm.

    (d) Energy per bit in dBJ.

    (e) Carrier-to-noise power ratio.

    (f) E_b/N_0 ratio.

$$C = 10^{-13}\text{W} \qquad f_b = 30 \text{ kbps}$$
$$N = 0.06 \times 10^{-15}\text{W} \qquad B = 60 \text{ kHz}$$

12-15. Determine the minimum bandwidth required to achieve a $P(e)$ of 10^{-6} for an 8-PSK system operating at 20 Mbps with a carrier-to-noise power ratio of 11 dB.

12-16. Determine the minimum bandwidth and baud for a BPSK modulator with a carrier frequency of 80 MHz and an input bit rate f_b = 1 Mbps. Sketch the output spectrum.

12-17. For the QPSK modulator shown in Figure 12-19, change the reference oscillator to cos $\omega_c t$ and sketch the new constellation diagram.

12-18. For the QPSK demodulator shown in Figure 12-23, determine the I and Q bits for an input signal $-\sin \omega_c t + \cos \omega_c t$.

12-19. For an 8-PSK modulator with an input bit rate f_b = 10 Mbps and a carrier frequency f_c = 80 MHz, determine the minimum Nyquist bandwidth and the baud. Sketch the output spectrum.

12-20. For the 8-PSK modulator shown in Figure 12-25, change the +90° phase-shift network to a −90° phase shifter and sketch the new constellation diagram.

12-21. For a 16-QAM modulator with an input bit rate f_b = 10 Mbps and a carrier frequency f_c = 60 MHz, determine the minimum double-sided Nyquist frequency and the baud. Sketch the output spectrum.

12-22. For the 16-QAM modulator shown in Figure 12-35, change the 90° phase shift network to a −90° phase shifter and determine the output expressions for the following I, I', Q, and Q' input conditions: 0000, 1111, 1010, and 0101.

12-23. Determine the bandwidth efficiency for the following modulators:

    (a) QPSK, f_b = 20 Mbps

    (b) 8-PSK, f_b = 28 Mbps

    (c) 16-PSK, f_b = 40 Mbps

12-24. For the DBPSK modulator shown in Figure 12-42, determine the output phase sequence for the following input bit sequence: 11001100101010 (assume that the reference bit is a logic 1).

C H A P T E R 13

Data Communications

INTRODUCTION

In the *data communications* world, *data* generally are defined as information that is stored in digital form. The word *data* is plural; a single unit of data is called a *datum. Data communications* is the process of transferring digital *information* (usually in binary form) between two or more points. Information is defined as knowledge or intelligence. Information that has been processed, organized, and stored is called data. Data can be alphabetic, numeric, or symbolic in nature and consist of any one or a combination of the following: binary-coded alpha/numeric symbols, microprocessor op-codes, control codes, user addresses, program data, or data base information. At both the source and destination, data are in digital form; however, during transmission, data may be in digital or analog form.

A data communications network can be as simple as two personal computers connected through a public telecommunications network, or it can comprise a complex network of one or more mainframe computers and hundreds (or even thousands) of remote terminals, personal computers, and work stations. Today, data communications networks are used to interconnect virtually all kinds of digital computing equipment such as automatic teller machines (ATMs) to bank computers; personal computers to information highways, such as the Internet; and work stations to mainframe computers. Data communications networks are also used for airline and hotel reservation systems and for mass media and news networks such as the Associated Press (AP) or United Press International (UPI). The list of applications for data communications networks goes on almost indefinitely.

HISTORY OF DATA COMMUNICATIONS

It is highly likely that data communications began long before recorded time in the form of smoke signals or tom-tom drums, although it is improbable that these signals were binary coded. If we limit the scope of data communications to methods that use electrical signals to transmit binary-coded information, then data communications began in 1837 with the invention of the *telegraph* and the development of the *Morse code* by Samuel F. B. Morse. With telegraph, dots and dashes (analogous to binary 1s and 0s) are transmitted across a wire using electromechanical induction. Various combinations of these dots and dashes were used to represent binary codes for letters, numbers, and punctuation. Actually, the first telegraph was invented in England by Sir Charles Wheatstone and Sir William Cooke, but their contraption required six different wires for a single telegraph line. In 1840, Morse secured an American patent for the telegraph and in 1844 the first telegraph line was established between Baltimore and Washington, D.C. In 1849, the first slow-speed telegraph printer was invented, but it was not until 1860 that high-speed (15 bps) printers were available. In 1850, the Western Union Telegraph Company was formed in Rochester, New York, for the purpose of carrying coded messages from one person to another.

In 1874, Emile Baudot invented a telegraph *multiplexer,* which allowed signals from up to six different telegraph machines to be transmitted simultaneously over a single wire. The telephone was invented in 1876 by Alexander Graham Bell and, consequently, very little new evolved in telegraph until 1899, when Marconi succeeded in sending radio telegraph messages. Telegraph was the only means of sending information across large spans of water until 1920, when the first commercial radio stations were installed.

Bell Laboratories developed the first special-purpose computer in 1940 using electromechanical relays. The first general-purpose computer was an automatic sequence-controlled calculator developed jointly by Harvard University and International Business Machines (IBM) Corporation. The UNIVAC computer, built in 1951 by Remington Rand Corporation (now Sperry Rand), was the first mass-produced electronic computer. Since 1951, the number of mainframe computers, small business computers, personal computers, and computer terminals has increased exponentially, creating a situation where more and more people have the need to exchange digital information with each other. Consequently, the need for data communications has also increased exponentially.

Until 1968, the AT&T operating tariff allowed only equipment furnished by AT&T to be connected to AT&T lines. In 1968, a landmark Supreme Court decision, the Carterfone decision, allowed non-Bell companies to interconnect to the vast AT&T communications network. This decision started the *interconnect industry,* which has led to competitive data communications offerings by a large number of independent companies.

STANDARDS ORGANIZATIONS FOR DATA COMMUNICATIONS

During the past decade, the data communications industry has grown at an astronomical rate. Consequently, the need to provide communications between dissimilar computer systems has also increased. Thus, to ensure an orderly transfer of information between two or more data communications systems using different equipment with different needs, a consortium of organizations, manufacturers, and users meet on a regular basis to establish guidelines and standards. It is the intent that all data communications users comply with these standards. Several of the organizations are described below.

International Standards Organization (ISO). The ISO is the international organization for standardization. The ISO creates the sets of rules and standards for graphics, document exchange, and related technologies. The ISO is responsible for endorsing and coordinating the work of the other standards organizations.

Consultative Committee for International Telephony and Telegraphy (CCITT). The membership of the CCITT consists of government authorities and representatives from many countries. The CCITT is now the standards organization for the United Nations and develops the recommended sets of rules and standards for telephone and telegraph communications. The CCITT has developed three sets of specifications: the

V series for modem interfacing, the X series for data communications, and the I and Q series for Integrated Services Digital Network (ISDN).

American National Standards Institute (ANSI). ANSI is the official standards agency for the United States and is the U.S. voting representative for ISO.

Institute of Electrical and Electronics Engineers (IEEE). The IEEE is a U.S. professional organization of electronics, computer, and communications engineers.

Electronic Industries Association (EIA). The EIA is a U.S. organization that establishes and recommends industrial standards. The EIA is responsible for developing the RS (recommended standard) series of standards for data and telecommunications.

Standards Council of Canada (SCC). The SCC is the official standards agency for Canada with similar responsibilities to those of ANSI.

DATA COMMUNICATIONS CIRCUITS

Figure 13-1 shows a simplified block diagram of a data communications network. As the figure shows, there is a source of digital information (primary station), a transmission medium (facility), and a destination (*secondary* station). The *primary* (or host) location is very often a mainframe computer with its own set of local terminals and peripheral equipment. For simplicity, there is only one secondary (or remote) station shown on the figure. The secondary stations are the users of the network. How many secondary stations there are and how they are interconnected to each other and the host station vary considerably depending on the system and its applications. There are many different types of transmission media, including free-space radio transmission (terrestrial and satellite microwave), metallic cable facilities (both digital and analog systems), and optical fiber cables (light wave propagation).

Data terminal equipment (DTE) is a general term that describes the interface equipment used at the stations to adapt the digital signals from the computers and terminals to a form more suitable for transmission. Essentially, any piece of equipment between the mainframe computer and the modem or the station equipment and its modem is classified as data terminal equipment. *Data communications equipment* (DCE) is a general term that describes the equipment that converts digital signals to analog signals and interfaces the data terminal equipment to the analog transmission medium. In essence, a DCE is a *modem* (*mod*ulator/*dem*odulator). A modem converts binary digital signals to analog signals such as FSK, PSK, and QAM, and vice versa.

Serial and Parallel Data Transmission

Binary information can be transmitted either in parallel or serially. Figure 13-2a shows how the binary code 0110 is transmitted from location A to location B in parallel. As the figure shows, each bit position (A_0 to A_3) has its own transmission line. Consequently, all four bits can be transmitted simultaneously during the time of a single clock pulse (T). This type of transmission is called *parallel-by-bit* or *serial-by-character.*

Figure 13-2b shows how the same binary code is transmitted serially. As the figure shows, there is a single transmission line and, thus, only one bit can be transmitted at a time. Consequently, it requires four clock pulses ($4T$) to transmit the entire word. This type of transmission is often called *serial-by-bit.*

Obviously, the principal trade-off between parallel and serial transmission is speed versus simplicity. Data transmission can be accomplished much more quickly using parallel transmission; however, parallel transmission requires more lines between the source and destination. As a general rule, parallel transmission is used for short-distance communications, and within a computer; and serial transmission is used for long-distance communications.

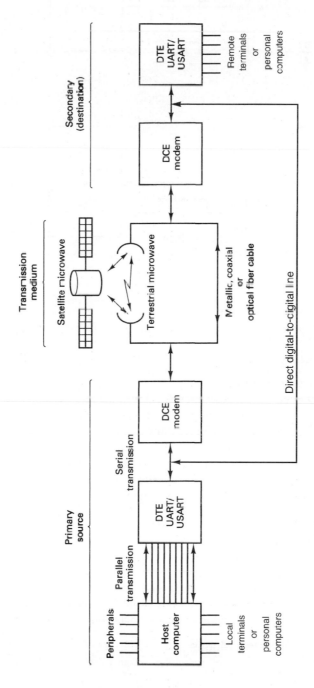

FIGURE 13-1 Simplified block diagram of a data communications network

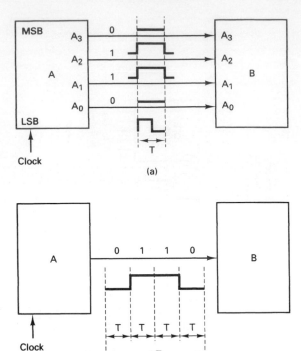

FIGURE 13-2 Data transmission: (a) parallel; (b) serial

Configurations

Data communications circuits can be categorized generally as either two-point or multi-point. A *two-point* configuration involves only two locations or stations, whereas a *multi-point* configuration involves three or more stations. A two-point circuit can involve the transfer of information between a mainframe computer and a remote computer terminal, two mainframe computers, or two remote computer terminals. A multipoint circuit is generally used to interconnect a single mainframe computer (*host*) to many remote computer terminals, although any combination of three or more computers or computer terminals constitutes a multipoint circuit.

Topologies

The topology or architecture of a data communications circuit identifies how the various locations within the network are interconnected. The most common topologies used are the *point to point,* the *star,* the *bus* or *multidrop,* the *ring* or *loop,* and the *mesh.* These are multipoint configurations except the point to point. Figure 13-3 shows the various circuit configurations and topologies used for data communications networks.

Transmission Modes

Essentially, there are four modes of transmission for data communications circuits: *simplex, half duplex, full duplex,* and *full/full duplex.*

   Simplex.   With simplex operation, data transmission is unidirectional; information can be sent only in one direction. Simplex lines are also called *receive-only, transmit-only,* or *one-way-only* lines. Commercial television and radio systems are examples of simplex transmission.

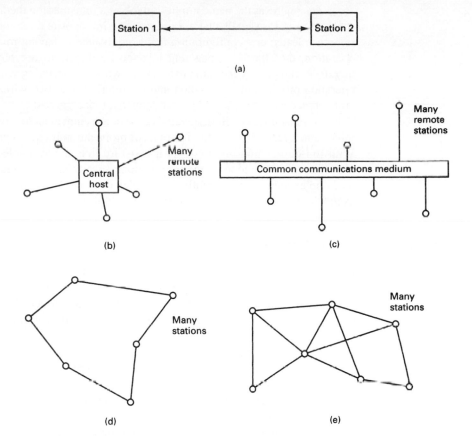

FIGURE 13-3 Data network topologies: (a) point to point; (b) star; (c) bus or multidrop; (d) ring or loop; (e) mesh

Half duplex (HDX).   In the half-duplex mode, data transmission is possible in both directions, but not at the same time. Half-duplex lines are also called two-way alternate or either-way lines. Citizens band (CB) radio is an example of half-duplex transmission.

Full duplex (FDX).   In the full-duplex mode, transmissions are possible in both directions simultaneously, but they must be between the same two stations. Full-duplex lines are also called two-way-simultaneous, *duplex,* or both-way lines. A standard telephone system is an example of full-duplex transmission.

Full/full duplex (F/FDX).   In the full/full duplex mode, transmission is possible in both directions at the same time but not between the same two stations (i.e., one station is transmitting to a second station and receiving from a third station at the same time). F/FDX is possible only on multipoint circuits. The U.S. postal system is an example of full/full duplex transmission.

Two-Wire Versus Four-Wire Operation

Two-wire, as the name implies, involves a transmission medium that either uses two wires (a signal and a reference lead) or a configuration that is equivalent to having only two wires. With two-wire operation, simplex, half-, or full-duplex transmission is possible. For full-duplex operation, the signals propagating in opposite directions must occupy different bandwidths; otherwise, they will mix linearly and interfere with each other.

Four-wire, as the name implies, involves a transmission medium that uses four wires (two are used for signals that are propagating in opposite directions and two are used for reference leads) or a configuration that is equivalent to having four wires. With four-wire operation, the signals propagating in opposite directions are physically separated and, therefore, can occupy the same bandwidths without interfering with each other. Four-wire operation provides more isolation and is preferred over two-wire, although four-wire requires twice as many wires and, consequently, twice the cost.

A transmitter and its associated receiver are equivalent to a two-wire circuit. A transmitter and a receiver for both directions of propagation is equivalent to a four-wire circuit. With full-duplex transmission over a two-wire line, the available bandwidth must be divided in half, thus reducing the information capacity in either direction to one-half of the half-duplex value. Consequently, full-duplex operation over two-wire lines requires twice as much time to transfer the same amount of information.

DATA COMMUNICATIONS CODES

Data communications codes are prescribed bit sequences used for encoding characters and symbols. Consequently, data communications codes are often called *character sets, character codes, symbol codes,* or *character languages.* In essence, there are only three types of characters used in data communications codes: *data link control characters,* which are used to facilitate the orderly flow of data from a source to a destination; *graphic control characters,* which involve the syntax or presentation of the data at the receive terminal; and *alpha/numeric* characters, which are used to represent the various symbols used for letters, numbers, and punctuation in the English language.

The first data communications code that saw widespread usage was the Morse code. The Morse code used three unequal-length symbols (dot, dash, and space) to encode alpha/numeric characters, punctuation marks, and an interrogation word.

The Morse code is inadequate for use in modern digital computer equipment because all characters do not have the same number of symbols or take the same length of time to send, and each Morse code operator transmits code at a different rate. Morse code also has an insufficient selection of graphic and data link control characters to facilitate the transmission and presentation of the data typically used in contemporary computer applications.

The three most common character sets presently used for character encoding are the Baudot code, the American Standard Code for Information Interchange (ASCII), and the Extended Binary-Coded Decimal Interchange Code (EBCDIC).

Baudot Code

The *Baudot code* (sometimes called the *Telex code*) was the first fixed-length character code. The Baudot code was developed by a French postal engineer, Thomas Murray, in 1875 and named after Emile Baudot, an early pioneer in telegraph printing. The Baudot code is a five-bit character code that is used primarily for low-speed teletype equipment such as the TWX/Telex system. With a five-bit code there are only 2^5 or 32 combinations possible, which is insufficient to represent the 26 letters of the alphabet, the 10 digits, and the various punctuation marks and control characters. Therefore, the Baudot code uses *figure* shift and *letter* shift characters to expand its capabilities to 58 characters. The latest version of the Baudot code is recommended by the CCITT as the International Alphabet No. 2. The Baudot code is still used by Western Union Company for the TWX and Telex teletype systems. The AP and UPI news services for years used the Baudot code for sending news information around the world. The most recent version of the Baudot code is shown in Table 13-1.

TABLE 13-1 Baudot Code

Character Shift		Binary Code				
Letter	Figure	Bit: 4	3	2	1	0
A	—	1	1	0	0	0
B	?	1	0	0	1	1
C	:	0	1	1	1	0
D	$	1	0	0	1	0
E	3	1	0	0	0	0
F	!	1	0	1	1	0
G	&	0	1	0	1	1
H	#	0	0	1	0	1
I	8	0	1	1	0	0
J	'	1	1	0	1	0
K	(	1	1	1	1	0
L	)	0	1	0	0	1
M	.	0	0	1	1	1
N	,	0	0	1	1	0
O	9	0	0	0	1	1
P	0	0	1	1	0	1
Q	1	1	1	1	0	1
R	4	0	1	0	1	0
S	bel	1	0	1	0	0
T	5	0	0	0	0	1
U	7	1	1	1	0	0
V	;	0	1	1	1	1
W	2	1	1	0	0	1
X	/	1	0	1	1	1
Y	6	1	0	1	0	1
Z	"	1	0	0	0	1
Figure shift		1	1	1	1	1
Letter shift		1	1	0	1	1
Space		0	0	1	0	0
Line feed (LF)		0	1	0	0	0
Blank (null)		0	0	0	0	0

ASCII Code

In 1963, in an effort to standardize data communications codes, the United States adopted the Bell System model 33 teletype code as the United States of America Standard Code for Information Interchange (USASCII), better known simply as ASCII-63. Since its adoption, ASCII has generically progressed through the 1965, 1967, and 1977 versions, with the 1977 version being recommended by the CCITT as the International Alphabet No. 5. ASCII is a seven-bit character set, which has 2^7 or 128 combinations. With ASCII, the least significant bit (LSB) is designated b_0 and the most significant bit (MSB) is designated b_6. b_7 is not part of the ASCII code but is generally reserved for the parity bit, which is explained later in this chapter. Actually, with any character set, all bits are equally significant because the code does not represent a weighted binary number. It is common with character codes to refer to bits by their order; b_0 is the zero-order bit, b_1 is the first-order bit, b_7 is the seventh-order bit, and so on. With serial transmission, the bit transmitted first is called the LSB. With ASCII, the low order bit (b_0) is the LSB and is transmitted first. ASCII is probably the code most often used today. The 1977 version of the ASCII code is shown in Table 13-2.

TABLE 13-2 ASCII-77 Code—Odd Parity

	Binary Code								Hex		Binary Code								Hex
Bit:	7	6	5	4	3	2	1	0		Bit:	7	6	5	4	3	2	1	0	
NUL	1	0	0	0	0	0	0	0	00	@	0	1	0	0	0	0	0	0	40
SOH	0	0	0	0	0	0	0	1	01	A	1	1	0	0	0	0	0	1	41
STX	0	0	0	0	0	0	1	0	02	B	1	1	0	0	0	0	1	0	42
ETX	1	0	0	0	0	0	1	1	03	C	0	1	0	0	0	0	1	1	43
EOT	0	0	0	0	0	1	0	0	04	D	1	1	0	0	0	1	0	0	44
ENQ	1	0	0	0	0	1	0	1	05	E	0	1	0	0	0	1	0	1	45
ACK	1	0	0	0	0	1	1	0	06	F	0	1	0	0	0	1	1	0	46
BEL	0	0	0	0	0	1	1	1	07	G	1	1	0	0	0	1	1	1	47
BS	0	0	0	0	1	0	0	0	08	H	1	1	0	0	1	0	0	0	48
HT	1	0	0	0	1	0	0	1	09	I	0	1	0	0	1	0	0	1	49
NL	1	0	0	0	1	0	1	0	0A	J	0	1	0	0	1	0	1	0	4A
VT	0	0	0	0	1	0	1	1	0B	K	1	1	0	0	1	0	1	1	4B
FF	1	0	0	0	1	1	0	0	0C	L	0	1	0	0	1	1	0	0	4C
CR	0	0	0	0	1	1	0	1	0D	M	1	1	0	0	1	1	0	1	4D
SO	0	0	0	0	1	1	1	0	0E	N	1	1	0	0	1	1	1	0	4E
SI	1	0	0	0	1	1	1	1	0F	O	0	1	0	0	1	1	1	1	4F
DLE	0	0	0	1	0	0	0	0	10	P	1	1	0	1	0	0	0	0	50
DC1	0	0	0	1	0	0	0	1	11	Q	0	1	0	1	0	0	0	1	51
DC2	1	0	0	1	0	0	1	0	12	R	0	1	0	1	0	0	1	0	52
DC3	0	0	0	1	0	0	1	1	13	S	1	1	0	1	0	0	1	1	53
DC4	1	0	0	1	0	1	0	0	14	T	0	1	0	1	0	1	0	0	54
NAK	0	0	0	1	0	1	0	1	15	U	1	1	0	1	0	1	0	1	55
SYN	0	0	0	1	0	1	1	0	16	V	1	1	0	1	0	1	1	0	56
ETB	1	0	0	1	0	1	1	1	17	W	0	1	0	1	0	1	1	1	57
CAN	1	0	0	1	1	0	0	0	18	X	0	1	0	1	1	0	0	0	58
EM	0	0	0	1	1	0	0	1	19	Y	1	1	0	1	1	0	0	1	59
SUB	0	0	0	1	1	0	1	0	1A	Z	1	1	0	1	1	0	1	0	5A
ESC	1	0	0	1	1	0	1	1	1B	[	0	1	0	1	1	0	1	1	5B
FS	0	0	0	1	1	1	0	0	1C	\	1	1	0	1	1	1	0	0	5C
GS	1	0	0	1	1	1	0	1	1D	]	0	1	0	1	1	1	0	1	5D
RS	1	0	0	1	1	1	1	0	1E	∧	0	1	0	1	1	1	1	0	5E
US	0	0	0	1	1	1	1	1	1F	-	1	1	0	1	1	1	1	1	5F
SP	0	0	1	0	0	0	0	0	20	`	1	1	1	0	0	0	0	0	60
!	1	0	1	0	0	0	0	1	21	a	0	1	1	0	0	0	0	1	61
"	1	0	1	0	0	0	1	0	22	b	0	1	1	0	0	0	1	0	62
#	0	0	1	0	0	0	1	1	23	c	1	1	1	0	0	0	1	1	63
$	1	0	1	0	0	1	0	0	24	d	0	1	1	0	0	1	0	0	64
%	0	0	1	0	0	1	0	1	25	e	1	1	1	0	0	1	0	1	65
&	0	0	1	0	0	1	1	0	26	f	1	1	1	0	0	1	1	0	66
'	1	0	1	0	0	1	1	1	27	g	0	1	1	0	0	1	1	1	67
(	1	0	1	0	1	0	0	0	28	h	0	1	1	0	1	0	0	0	68
)	0	0	1	0	1	0	0	1	29	i	1	1	1	0	1	0	0	1	69
*	0	0	1	0	1	0	1	0	2A	j	1	1	1	0	1	0	1	0	6A
+	1	0	1	0	1	0	1	1	2B	k	0	1	1	0	1	0	1	1	6B
,	0	0	1	0	1	1	0	0	2C	l	1	1	1	0	1	1	0	0	6C
-	1	0	1	0	1	1	0	1	2D	m	0	1	1	0	1	1	0	1	6D
.	1	0	1	0	1	1	1	0	2E	n	0	1	1	0	1	1	1	0	6E
/	0	0	1	0	1	1	1	1	2F	o	1	1	1	0	1	1	1	1	6F
0	1	0	1	1	0	0	0	0	30	p	0	1	1	1	0	0	0	0	70
1	0	0	1	1	0	0	0	1	31	q	1	1	1	1	0	0	0	1	71
2	0	0	1	1	0	0	1	0	32	r	1	1	1	1	0	0	1	0	72
3	1	0	1	1	0	0	1	1	33	s	0	1	1	1	0	0	1	1	73
4	0	0	1	1	0	1	0	0	34	t	1	1	1	1	0	1	0	0	74
5	1	0	1	1	0	1	0	1	35	u	0	1	1	1	0	1	0	1	75
6	1	0	1	1	0	1	1	0	36	v	0	1	1	1	0	1	1	0	76
7	0	0	1	1	0	1	1	1	37	w	1	1	1	1	0	1	1	1	77
8	0	0	1	1	1	0	0	0	38	x	1	1	1	1	1	0	0	0	78

(continued)

TABLE 13-2 [*Continued*]

	Binary Code								Hex	Bit:	Binary Code								Hex
Bit:	7	6	5	4	3	2	1	0			7	6	5	4	3	2	1	0	
9	1	0	1	1	1	0	0	1	39	y	0	1	1	1	1	0	0	1	79
:	1	0	1	1	1	0	1	0	3A	z	0	1	1	1	1	0	1	0	7A
;	0	0	1	1	1	0	1	1	3B	{	1	1	1	1	1	0	1	1	7B
<	1	0	1	1	1	1	0	0	3C	|	0	1	1	1	1	1	0	0	7C
=	0	0	1	1	1	1	0	1	3D	}	1	1	1	1	1	1	0	1	7D
>	0	0	1	1	1	1	1	0	3E	~	1	1	1	1	1	1	1	0	7E
?	1	0	1	1	1	1	1	1	3F	DEL	0	1	1	1	1	1	1	1	7F

NUL = null	VT = vertical tab	SYN = synchronous
SOH = start of heading	FF = form feed	ETB = end of transmission block
STX = start of text	CR = carriage return	CAN = cancel
ETX = end of text	SO = shift-out	SUB = substitute
EOT = end of transmission	SI = shift-in	ESC = escape
ENQ = enquiry	DLE = data link escape	FS = field separator
ACK = acknowledge	DC1 = device control 1	GS = group separator
BEL = bell	DC2 = device control 2	RS = record separator
BS = back space	DC3 = device control 3	US = unit separator
HT = horizontal tab	DC4 = device control 4	SP = space
NL = new line	NAK = negative acknowledge	DEL = delete

00   1   00   28028   555555555   2

(a)

Start margin	Data character	Check characters	Stop characters	Stop margin

(b)

FIGURE 13-4 [a] Bar code; [b] bar code structure

EBCDIC Code

EBCDIC is an eight-bit character code developed by IBM. With eight bits, 2^8 or 256 combinations are possible, making EBCDIC the most powerful character set. Note that with EBCDIC the LSB is designated b_7 and the MSB is designated b_0. Therefore, with EBCDIC, the high-order bit (b_7) is transmitted first and the low-order bit (b_0) is transmitted last. The EBCDIC code does not facilitate the use of a parity bit.

Bar Codes

Bar codes are those omnipresent black and white striped stickers that seem to be showing up on almost every consumer item found in nearly every store in the United States and most of the rest of the modern world. The bar code is a series of black bars separated by white spaces. The widths of the bars along with their reflective abilities represent binary 1s and 0s that identify the cost of the item. In addition, bar codes may contain information regarding inventory management and control, security access, shipping and receiving, production counting, document and order processing, automatic billing, and many other applications. A typical bar code is shown in Figure 13-4a.

Figure 13-4b shows the layout of the fields found on a typical bar code. The start field consists of a unique sequence of bars and spaces used to identify the beginning of the data field. The data characters correspond to the bar code symbology or format used. Serial data encoded in the data character field are extracted from the card with an optical scanner. The

TABLE 13-3 Code 39 Character Set

Character	Binary Word	Bars	Spaces	Check Character Value
0	000110100	00110	0100	0
1	100100001	10001	0100	1
2	001100001	01001	0100	2
3	101100000	11000	0100	3
4	000110001	00101	0100	4
5	100110000	10100	0100	5
6	001110000	01100	0100	6
7	000100101	00011	0100	7
8	100100100	10010	0100	8
9	001100100	01010	0100	9
A	100001001	10001	0010	10
B	001001001	01001	0010	11
C	101001000	11000	0010	12
D	000011001	00101	0010	13
E	100011000	10100	0010	14
F	001011000	01100	0010	15
G	000001101	00011	0010	16
H	100001100	10010	0010	17
I	001001100	01010	0010	18
J	000011100	00110	0010	19
K	100000011	10001	0001	20
L	001000011	01001	0001	21
M	101000010	11000	0001	22
N	000010011	00101	0001	23
O	100010010	10100	0001	24
P	001010010	01100	0001	25
Q	000000111	00011	0001	26
R	100000110	10010	0001	27
S	001000110	01010	0001	28
T	000010110	00110	0001	29
U	110000001	10001	1000	30
V	011000001	01001	1000	31
W	111000000	11000	1000	32
X	010010001	00101	1000	33
Y	110010000	10100	1000	34
Z	011010000	01100	1000	35
–	010000101	00011	1000	36
.	110000100	10010	1000	37
(space)	011000100	01010	1000	38
*	010010100	00110	1000	—
$	010101000	00000	1110	39
/	010100010	00000	1101	40
+	010001010	00000	1011	41
%	000101010	00000	0111	42

scanner reproduces logic conditions that correspond to the difference in reflectivity of the printed bars and underlying white spaces. To read the information, simply scan over the printed bar with a smooth, uniform motion. A photodetector in the scanner senses the reflected light and converts it to electrical signals (1s and 0s) for decoding.

There are numerous bar code formats available using codes that vary from numeric symbols only to the full ASCII code. One of the most common codes was developed in 1974 and is referred to as simply *Code 39*. Code 39 (also called *Code 3 of 9* or *3 of 9 Code*) uses an alpha/numeric code similar to ASCII and is shown in Table 13-3. Code 39 consists of 36 unique codes representing the 10 digits and 24 uppercase letters. There are seven additional codes used for special characters, and an exclusive start/stop character coded as an asterisk (*).

Each character contains nine elements (bars and spaces). The logic condition (1 or 0) of each element is encoded by varying the width of the bar or space. A wide element, whether it is a bar or a space, represents a logic 1 and a narrow element represents a logic 0. A 3:1 width ratio is used to distinguish 1s from 0s (i.e., a bar or space representing a logic 1 is three times wider than a bar or space representing a logic 0).

Three of the nine elements in Code 39 must be logic 1s and the remaining six must be logic 0s. In addition, of the three logic 1s, two must be bars and one a space. Each character begins and ends with a black bar with alternating white bars in between. All characters are separated with an intercharacter space. Codes that use intercharacter spaces are classified as codes whose characters are separated by gaps. Gaps are generally one element wide.

The Code 39 format includes two optional check characters for error detection. Each character has a check character value assigned to it. The value of the characters within a message are summed then divided by a constant. The remainder is rounded off to one or two decimal places then converted to a Code 39 character and appended to the end of the character field. For example, if a data field contained the message "CODE 39," the check character(s) would be determined as follows:

Message	C	O	D	E	space	3	9
Check value	12	24	13	14	38	3	9

Sum of check values = 113

Dividing by constant 43 gives 113/43 = 2 remainder 27

Final message: CODE 39R

where R equals check character value for 27.

ERROR CONTROL

A data communications circuit can be as short as a few feet or as long as several thousand miles, and the transmission medium can be as simple as a piece of wire or as complex as a microwave, satellite, or optical fiber system. Therefore, due to the nonideal transmission characteristics that are associated with any communications system, it is inevitable that errors will occur and that it is necessary to develop and implement procedures for error control. Error control can be divided into two general categories: error detection and error correction.

Error Detection

Error detection is simply the process of monitoring the received data and determining when a transmission error has occurred. Error detection techniques do not identify which bit (or bits) is in error, only that an error has occurred. The purpose of error detection is not to prevent errors from occurring but to prevent undetected errors from occurring. How a system reacts to transmission errors is system dependent and varies considerably. The most common error detection techniques used for data communications circuits are redundancy, echoplex, exact-count encoding, parity, checksum, vertical and horizontal redundancy checking, and cyclic redundancy checking.

Redundancy.   *Redundancy* involves transmitting each character twice. If the same character is not received twice in succession, a transmission error has occurred. The same concept can be used for messages. If the same sequence of characters is not received twice in succession, in exactly the same order, a transmission error has occurred.

Echoplex.   Echoplex is a relatively simple type of error detection scheme that is used almost exclusively in data communications systems where human operators are used to enter data manually from a keyboard. Echoplex requires full-duplex operation where each character is transmitted immediately after it has been typed into the transmit

TABLE 13-4 ARQ Exact-Count Code

	Binary Code							Character	
Bit:	1	2	3	4	5	6	7	Letter	Figure
	0	0	0	1	1	1	0	Letter shift	
	0	1	0	0	1	1	0	Figure shift	
	0	0	1	1	0	1	0	A	-
	0	0	1	1	0	0	1	B	?
	1	0	0	1	1	0	0	C	:
	0	0	1	1	1	0	0	D	(WRU)
	0	1	1	1	0	0	0	E	3
	0	0	1	0	0	1	1	F	%
	1	1	0	0	0	0	1	G	@
	1	0	1	0	0	1	0	H	£
	1	1	1	0	0	0	0	I	8
	0	1	0	0	0	1	1	J	(bell)
	0	0	0	1	0	1	1	K	(
	1	1	0	0	0	1	0	L	)
	1	0	1	0	0	0	1	M	.
	1	0	1	0	1	0	0	N	'
	1	0	0	0	1	1	0	O	9
	1	0	0	1	0	1	0	P	0
	0	0	0	1	1	0	1	Q	1
	1	1	0	0	1	0	0	R	4
	0	1	0	1	0	1	0	S	'
	1	0	0	0	1	0	1	T	5
	0	1	1	0	0	1	0	U	7
	1	0	0	1	0	0	1	V	=
	0	1	0	0	1	0	1	W	2
	0	0	1	0	1	1	0	X	/
	0	0	1	0	1	0	1	Y	6
	0	1	1	0	0	0	1	Z	+
	0	0	0	0	1	1	1	(blank)	
	1	1	0	1	0	0	0	(space)	
	1	0	1	1	0	0	0	(line feed)	
	1	0	0	0	0	1	1	(carriage return)	

terminal. At the receive terminal, once a character has been received, it is immediately transmitted back to the originating terminal where it appears on that terminal's screen. When the character appears on the screen, the operator has verification that that character has been received at the destination terminal. If a transmission error has occurred, the wrong character will be displayed on the transmit terminal's screen. When this occurs, the operator can send a backspace and remove the erroneous character then retype the correct character.

Echoplex is a simple concept requiring relatively simple circuitry. One disadvantage of echoplex, however, occurs when a transmitted character has been received correctly, then a transmission error occurs while it is being sent back to the originator. This would necessitate an unnecessary retransmission. Another disadvantage of echoplex is it relies on human operators to detect and correct transmission errors. Echoplex also requires a full-duplex circuit when useful information is actually only being sent in one direction.

Exact-count encoding. With *exact-count encoding,* the number of 1s in each character is the same. An example of an exact-count encoding scheme is the ARQ code shown in Table 13-4. Within the ARQ code, each character has three 1s, and, therefore, a simple

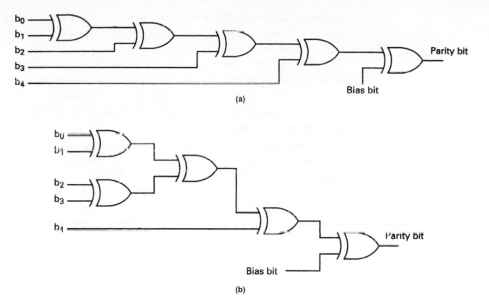

FIGURE 13-5 Parity generators: (a) serial; (b) parallel. 1 = odd parity; 2 = even parity

count of the number of 1s received in each character can determine if a transmission error has occurred.

Parity. *Parity* is probably the simplest error detection scheme used for data communications systems and is used with both vertical and horizontal redundancy checking. With parity, a single bit (called a *parity bit*) is added to each character to force the total number of 1s in the character, including the parity bit, to be either an odd number (odd parity) or an even number (even parity). For example, the ASCII code for the letter C is 43 hex or P1000011 binary, with the P bit representing the parity bit. There are three 1s in the code, not counting the parity bit. If odd parity is used, the P bit is made a 0, keeping the total number of 1s at three, an odd number. If even parity is used, the P bit is made a 1 and the total number of 1s is four, an even number.

Taking a closer look at parity, it can be seen that the parity bit is independent of the number of 0s in the code and unaffected by pairs of 1s. For the letter C, if all the 0 bits are dropped, the code is P1———11. For odd parity, the P bit is still a 0 and for even parity, the P bit is still a 1. If pairs of 1s are also excluded, the code is either P1———, P———1, or P———1—. Again, for odd parity the P bit is a 0, and for even parity the P bit is a 1.

The definition of parity is *equivalence* or *equality*. A logic gate that will determine when all its inputs are equal is the XOR gate. With an XOR gate, if all the inputs are equal (either all 0s or all 1s), the output is a 0. If all inputs are not equal, the output is a 1. Figure 13-5 shows two circuits that are commonly used to generate a parity bit. Essentially, both circuits go through a comparison process eliminating 0s and pairs of 1s. The circuit shown in Figure 13-5a uses *sequential (serial)* comparison, whereas the circuit shown in Figure 13-5b uses *combinational (parallel)* comparison. With the sequential parity generator b_0 is XORed with b_1, the result is XORed with b_2, and so on. The result of the last XOR operation is compared with a *bias* bit. If even parity is desired, the bias bit is made a logic 0. If odd parity is desired, the bias bit is made a logic 1. The output of the circuit is the parity bit, which is appended to the character code. With the parallel parity generator, comparisons are made in layers or levels. Pairs of bits (b_0 and b_1, b_2 and b_3, etc.) are XORed. The results of the first-level XOR gates are then XORed together. The process continues until only one bit is left, which is XORed with the bias bit. Again, if even parity is desired, the bias bit is made a logic 0 and if odd parity is desired, the bias bit is made a logic 1.

The circuits shown in Figure 13-5 can also be used for the parity checker in the receiver. A parity checker uses the same procedure as a parity generator except that the logic condition of the final comparison is used to determine if a parity violation has occurred (for odd parity a 1 indicates an error and a 0 indicates no error; for even parity, a 1 indicates an error and a 0 indicates no error).

The primary advantage of parity is its simplicity. The disadvantage is that when an even number of bits are received in error, the parity checker will not detect it (i.e., if the logic conditions of two bits are changed, the parity remains the same). Consequently, parity, over a long period of time, will detect only 50% of the transmission errors (this assumes an equal probability that an even or an odd number of bits could be in error).

Checksum. *Checksum* is an extremely simple method of error detection. A checksum is simply the least significant byte of the arithmetic sum of the binary data being transmitted. While data are being transmitted, each character is added (summed) with the accumulated sum of the previously transmitted characters. When the end of the message is reached, the adder has accumulated the sum of all the characters included in the message just sent. The least significant byte of the sum is appended to the end of the message and transmitted. The receive terminal replicates the summing operation and determines its own sum and checksum character. The least significant byte of the receiver's sum is compared with the checksum appended to the end of the message. If they are the same, most likely no transmission error has occurred. If they are different, a transmission error has definitely occurred. When an error is detected, a retransmission of the entire message is called for.

Vertical and horizontal redundancy checking. *Vertical redundancy checking* (VRC) is an error detection scheme that uses parity to determine if a transmission error has occurred within a character. Therefore, VRC is sometimes called *character parity*. With VRC, each character has a parity bit added to it prior to transmission. It may use even or odd parity. The example shown under the topic "Parity" involving the ASCII character "C" is an example of how VRC is used.

Horizontal or *longitudinal redundancy checking* (HRC or LRC) is an error detection scheme that uses parity to determine if a transmission error has occurred in a message and is, therefore, sometimes called *message parity*. With LRC, each bit position has a parity bit. In other words, b_0 from each character in the message is XORed with b_0 from all of the other characters in the message. Similarly, b_1, b_2, and so on, are XORed with their respective bits from all the other characters in the message. Essentially, LRC is the result of XORing the "characters" that comprise a message, whereas VRC is the XORing of the bits within a single character. With LRC, only even parity is used.

The LRC bit sequence is computed in the transmitter prior to sending the data, then transmitted as though it were the last character of the message. At the receiver, the LRC is recomputed from the data and the recomputed LRC is compared with the LRC transmitted with the message. If they are the same, it is assumed that no transmission errors have occurred. If they are different, a transmission error must have occurred.

Example 13-1 shows how VRC and LRC are determined.

Example 13-1

Determine the VRC and LRC for the following ASCII-encoded message: THE CAT. Use odd parity for VRC and even parity for LRC.

Solution

Character		T	H	E	sp	C	A	T	LRC
Hex		54	48	45	20	43	41	54	2F
ASCII code									
LSB	b_0	0	0	1	0	1	1	0	1
	b_1	0	0	0	0	1	0	0	1
	b_2	1	0	1	0	0	0	1	1
	b_3	0	1	0	0	0	0	0	1
	b_4	1	0	0	0	0	0	1	0
	b_5	0	0	0	1	0	0	0	1
MSB	b_6	1	1	1	0	1	1	1	0
VRC	b_7	0	1	0	0	0	1	0	0

The LRC is 2FH or 00101111 binary. In ASCII, this is the character /.

The VRC bit for each character is computed in the vertical direction, and the LRC bits are computed in the horizontal direction. This is the same scheme that was used with early teletype paper tapes and keypunch cards and has subsequently been carried over to present-day data communications applications.

The group of characters that comprise the message (i.e., THE CAT) is often called a *block* of data. Therefore, the bit sequence for the LRC is often called a *block check character* (BCC) or a *block check sequence* (BCS). BCS is more appropriate because the LRC has no function as a character (i.e., it is not an alpha/numeric, graphic, or data link control character); the LRC is simply a *sequence of bits* used for error detection.

Historically, LRC detects between 95% and 98% of all transmission errors. LRC will not detect transmission errors when an even number of characters have an error in the same bit position. For example, if b_4 in two different characters is in error, the LRC is still valid even though multiple transmission errors have occurred.

If VRC and LRC are used simultaneously, the only time an error would go undetected is when an even number of bits in an even number of characters were in error and the same bit positions in each character are in error, which is highly unlikely to happen. VRC does not identify which bit is in error in a character, and LRC does not identify which character has an error in it. However, for single-bit errors, VRC used together with LRC will identify which bit is in error. Otherwise, VRC and LRC only identify that an error has occurred.

Cyclic redundancy checking. Probably the most reliable scheme for error detection is *cyclic redundancy checking* (CRC). With CRC, approximately 99.95% of all transmission errors are detected. CRC is generally used with eight-bit codes such as EBCDIC or seven-bit codes when parity is not used.

In the United States, the most common CRC code is CRC-16, which is identical to the international standard, CCITT V.41. With CRC-16, 16 bits are used for the BCS. Essentially, the CRC character is the remainder of a division process. A data message polynominal $G(x)$ is divided by a generator polynomial function $P(x)$, the quotient is discarded, and the remainder is truncated to 16 bits and added to the message as the BCS. With CRC generation, however, the division is not accomplished with a standard arithmetic division process. Instead of using straight subtraction, the remainder is derived from an XOR operation. In the receiver, the received data stream including the BCS are

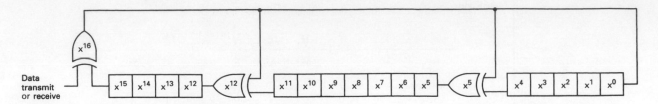

FIGURE 13-6 CRC-16 generating circuit (CCITT V.41)

divided by the same generating function $P(x)$. If no transmission errors have occurred, the remainder will be zero.

The generating polynomial for CRC-16 is

$$P(x) = x^{16} + x^{12} + x^5 + x^0$$

where $x^0 = 1$.

The number of bits in the CRC code is equal to the highest exponent of the generating polynomial. The exponents identify the bit positions that contain a 1. Therefore, b_{16}, b_{12}, b_5, and b_0 are 1s and all other bit positions are 0s.

Figure 13-6 shows the block diagram for a circuit that will generate a CRC-16 BCS for the CCITT V.41 standard. Note that for each bit position of the generating polynomial where there is a 1 an XOR gate is placed except for x^0.

Example 13-2

Determine the BCS for the following data and CRC generating polynomials:

$$\text{data } G(x) = x^7 + x^5 + x^4 + x^2 + x^1 + x^0 \quad \text{or} \quad 10110111$$
$$\text{CRC } P(x) = x^5 + x^4 + x^1 + x^0 \text{ or } 110011$$

Solution First $G(x)$ is multiplied by the number of bits in the CRC code, 5.

$$x^5(x^7 + x^5 + x^4 + x^2 + x^1 + x^0) = x^{12} + x^{10} + x^9 + x^7 + x^6 + x^5$$
$$= 1011011100000$$

Then divide the result by $P(x)$.

```
                                  11010111
               110011  | 1011011100000
                         110011
                         111101
                         110011
                          111010
                          110011
                          100100
                          110011
                           101110
                           110011
                            111010
                            110011
                            01001  =  CRC
```

The CRC is appended to the data to give the following transmitted data stream:

$$\begin{array}{cc} G(x) & \text{CRC} \\ 10110111 & 01001 \end{array}$$

At the receiver, the transmitted data are again divided by $P(x)$.

```
                                    11010111
              110011 ⌐ 1011011101001
                       110011
                       111101
                       110011
                        111010
                        110011
                         100110
                         110011
                          101010
                          110011
                           110011
                           110011
                           000000        Remainder = 0
                                         No error occurred
```

Error Correction

Essentially, there are three methods of error correction: symbol substitution, retransmission, and forward error correction.

Symbol substitution.   *Symbol substitution* was designed to be used in a human environment—when there is a human being at the receive terminal to analyze the received data and make decisions on its integrity. With symbol substitution, if a character is received in error, rather than revert to a higher level of error correction or display the incorrect character, a unique character that is undefined by the character code, such as a reverse question mark (ʕ), is substituted for the bad character. If the character in error cannot be discerned by the operator, retransmission is called for (i.e., symbol substitution is a form of selective retransmission). For example, if the message "Name" had an error in the first character, it would be displayed as " ʕame." An operator can discern the correct message by inspection, and retransmission is unnecessary. However, if the message "$ ʕ,000.00" were received, an operator could not determine the correct character, and retransmission is required.

Retransmission.   *Retransmission,* as the name implies, is resending a message when it is received in error and the receive terminal automatically calls for retransmission of the entire message. Retransmission is often called ARQ, which is an old radio communications term that means *automatic request for retransmission.* ARQ is probably the most reliable method of error correction, although it is not always the most efficient. Impairments on transmission media occur in bursts. If short messages are used, the likelihood that an impairment will occur during a transmission is small. However, short messages require more acknowledgments and line turnarounds than do long messages. Acknowledgments and line turnarounds for error control are forms of *overhead* (characters other than data that must be transmitted). With long messages, less turnaround time is needed, although the likelihood that a transmission error will occur is higher than for short messages. It can be shown statistically that message blocks between 256 and 512 characters are of optimum size when using ARQ for error correction.

Forward error correction.   *Forward error correction* (FEC) is the only error correction scheme that actually detects and corrects transmission errors at the receive end without calling for retransmission.

With FEC, bits are added to the message prior to transmission. A popular error-correcting code is the *Hamming code,* developed by R. W. Hamming at Bell Laboratories. The number of bits in the Hamming code is dependent on the number of bits in the data character. The number of Hamming bits that must be added to a character is determined from the following expression:

$$2^n \geq m + n + 1 \tag{13-1}$$

where n = number of Hamming bits
       m = number of bits in the data character

Example 13-3

For a 12-bit data string of 101100010010, determine the number of Hamming bits required, arbitrarily place the Hamming bits into the data string, determine the condition of each Hamming bit, assume an arbitrary single-bit transmission error, and prove that the Hamming code will detect the error.

Solution   Substituting into Equation 13-1, the number of Hamming bits is

$$2^n \geq m + n + 1$$

For $n = 4$, $2^4 = 16 \geq m + n + 1 = 12 + 4 + 1 = 17$

$16 < 17$; therefore, four Hamming bits are insufficient.

For $n = 5$, $2^5 = 32 \geq m + n + 1 = 12 + 5 + 1 = 18$

$32 > 18$; therefore, five Hamming bits are sufficient to meet the criterion of Equation 13-1. Therefore, a total of $12 + 5 = 17$ bits make up the data stream.

Arbitrarily place five Hamming bits into the data stream:

```
17 16 15 14 13 12 11 10 9 8 7 6 5 4 3 2 1
 H  1  0  1  H  1  0  0 H H 0 1 0 H 0 1 0
```

To determine the logic condition of the Hamming bits, express all bit positions that contain a 1 as a five-bit binary number and XOR them together.

Bit position	Binary number
2	00010
6	00110
XOR	00100
12	01100
XOR	01000
14	01110
XOR	00110
16	10000
XOR	10110 = Hamming code

$$b_{17} = 1, b_{13} = 0, b_9 = 1, b_8 = 1, b_4 = 0$$

The 17-bit encoded data stream becomes

```
 H       H      H H       H
 1 1 0 1 0 1 0 0 1 1 0 1 0 0 0 1 0
```

Assume that during transmission, an error occurs in bit position 14. The received data stream is

```
 1 1 0 0 0 1 0 0 1 1 0 1 0 0 0 1 0
```

At the receiver, to determine the bit position in error, extract the Hamming bits and XOR them with the binary code for each data bit position that contains a 1.

Bit position	Binary number
Hamming code	10110
2	00010
XOR	10100
6	00110
XOR	10010
12	01100
XOR	11110
16	10000
XOR	01110 = binary 14

Bit position 14 was received in error. To fix the error, simply complement bit 14.

The Hamming code described here will detect only single-bit errors. It cannot be used to identify multiple-bit errors or errors in the Hamming bits themselves. The Hamming code, as with all FEC codes, requires the addition of bits to the data, consequently, lengthening the transmitted message. The purpose of FEC codes is to reduce or eliminate the wasted time of retransmissions. However, the addition of the FEC bits to each message wastes transmission time in itself. Obviously, a trade-off is made between ARQ and FEC and system requirements determine which method is best suited to a particular system. FEC is often used for simplex transmissions to many receivers when acknowledgments are impractical.

SYNCHRONIZATION

Synchronize means to coincide or agree in time. In data communications, there are four types of synchronization that must be achieved: bit or clock synchronization, modem or carrier synchronization, character synchronization, and message synchronization. The clock and carrier recovery circuits discussed in Chapter 12 accomplish bit and carrier synchronization, and message synchronization is discussed in Chapter 14.

Character Synchronization
Clock synchronization ensures that the transmitter and receiver agree on a precise time slot for the occurrence of a bit. When a continuous string of data is received, it is necessary to identify which bits belong to which characters and which bit is the least significant data bit, the parity bit, and the stop bit. In essence, this is character synchronization: identifying the beginning and the end of a character code. In data communication circuits, there are two formats used to achieve character synchronization: asynchronous and synchronous.

Asynchronous data format. With *asynchronous data,* each character is framed between a *start* and a *stop* bit. Figure 13-7 shows the format used to frame a character for asynchronous data transmission. The first bit transmitted is the start bit and is always a logic 0. The character code bits are transmitted next beginning with the LSB and continuing through the MSB. The parity bit (if used) is transmitted directly after the MSB of the character. The last bit transmitted is the stop bit, which is always a logic 1. There can be either 1, 1.5, or 2 stop bits.

Stop bit (1, 1.5, 2)	Parity bit		Data bits (5–7)							Start bit
1	1	1/0	b6 MSB	b5	b4	b3	b2	b1	b0 LSB	0

FIGURE 13-7 Asynchronous data format

A logic 0 is used for the start bit because an idle condition (no data transmission) on a data communications circuit is identified by the transmission of continuous 1s (these are often called *idle line 1s*). Therefore, the start bit of the first character is identified by a high-to-low transition in the received data, and the bit that immediately follows the start bit is the LSB of the character code. All stop bits are logic 1s, which guarantees a high-to-low transition at the beginning of each character. After the start bit is detected, the data and parity bits are clocked into the receiver. If data are transmitted in real time (i.e., as an operator types data into the computer terminal), the number of idle line 1s between each character will vary. During this *dead time,* the receiver will simply wait for the occurrence of another start bit before clocking in the next character.

Example 13-4

For the following string of asynchronous ASCII-encoded data, identify each character (assume even parity and two stop bits).

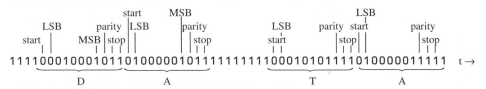

Synchronous data format. With *synchronous data,* rather than frame each character independently with start and stop bits, a unique synchronizing character called a SYN character is transmitted at the beginning of each message. For example, with ASCII code, the SYN character is 16H. The receiver disregards incoming data until it receives the SYN character, then it clocks in the next eight bits and interprets them as a character. The character that is used to signify the end of a transmission varies with the type of protocol used and what kind of transmission it is. Message-terminating characters are discussed in Chapter 14.

With asynchronous data, it is not necessary that the transmit and receive clocks be continuously synchronized. It is only necessary that they operate at approximately the same rate and be synchronized at the beginning of each character. This was the purpose of the start bit, to establish a time reference for character synchronization. With synchronous data, the transmit and receive clocks must be synchronized because character synchronization occurs only once at the beginning of the message.

Example 13-5

For the following string of synchronous ASCII-encoded data, identify each character (assume odd parity).

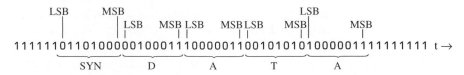

With asynchronous data, each character has two or three bits added to each character (one start bit and one or two stop bits). These bits are additional overhead and, thus, reduce the efficiency of the transmission (i.e., the ratio of information bits to total transmitted bits).

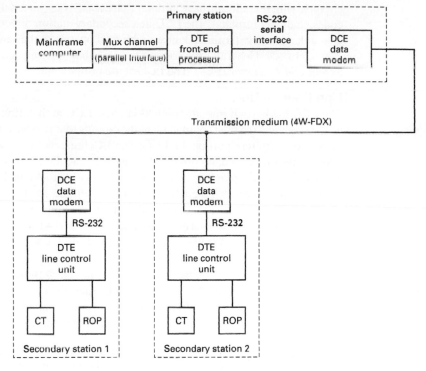

FIGURE 13-8 Multipoint data communications circuit block diagram

Synchronous data have two SYN characters (16 bits of overhead) added to each message. Therefore, asynchronous data are more efficient for short messages, and synchronous data are more efficient for long messages.

DATA COMMUNICATIONS HARDWARE

Figure 13-8 shows the block diagram of a multipoint data communications circuit that uses a bus topology. This arrangement is one of the most common configurations used for data communications circuits. At one station there is a mainframe computer and at each of the other two stations there is a *cluster* of computer terminals. The hardware and associated circuitry that connect the host computer to the remote computer terminals is called a *data communications link.* The station with the mainframe is called the *host* or *primary* and the other stations are called *secondaries* or simply *remotes.* An arrangement such as this is called a *centralized network;* there is one centrally located station (the host) with the responsibility of ensuring an orderly flow of data between the remote stations and itself. Data flow is controlled by an applications program that is stored at the primary station.

At the primary station there is a mainframe computer, a *line control unit* (LCU), and a *data modem* (or simply *modem*). At each secondary station there is a modem, an LCU, and terminal equipment such as computer terminals and printers. The mainframe is the host of the network and is where the application program is stored for each circuit it serves. For simplicity, Figure 13-8 shows only one circuit served by the primary, although there can be many different circuits served by one mainframe computer. The primary station has the capability of storing, processing, or retransmitting the data it receives from the secondary stations. The primary also stores software for data base management.

The LCU at the primary station is more complicated than the LCUs at the secondary stations. The LCU at the primary station directs data traffic to and from many different circuits, which could all have different characteristics (i.e., different bit rates, character codes, and data formats). The LCU at a secondary station directs data traffic between one data link and a few terminal devices, which all operate at the same speed and use the same character code. Generally speaking, if the LCU has software associated with it, it is called a *front-end processor* (FEP). The LCU at the primary station is usually an FEP.

Line Control Unit

The LCU has several important functions. The LCU at the primary station serves as an interface between the host computer and the circuits that it serves. Each circuit served is connected to a different port on the LCU. The LCU directs the flow of input and output data between the different data communications links and their respective applications program. The LCU performs parallel-to-serial and serial-to-parallel conversion of data. The mux interface channel between the mainframe computer and the LCU transfers data in parallel. Data transfers between the modem and the LCU are done serially. The LCU also houses the circuitry that performs error detection and correction. Also, data link control (DLC) characters are inserted and deleted in the LCU. Data link control characters are explained in Chapter 14.

The LCU operates on the data when it is in digital form and, therefore, is called *data terminal equipment* (DTE). Within the LCU, there is a single integrated circuit that performs several of the LCU's functions. This circuit is called a UART when asynchronous transmission is used and a USRT when synchronous transmission is used.

Universal asynchronous receiver/transmitter (UART). The UART is used for asynchronous transmission of data between the DTE and the DCE. Asynchronous transmission means that an asynchronous data format is used and there is no clocking information transferred between the DTE and the DCE. The primary functions of the UART are

1. To perform serial-to-parallel and parallel-to-serial conversion of data
2. To perform error detection by inserting and checking parity bits
3. To insert and detect start and stop bits

Functionally, the UART is divided into two sections: the transmitter and the receiver. Figure 13-9a shows a simplified block diagram of a UART transmitter.

Prior to transferring data in either direction, a *control* word must be programmed into the UART control register to indicate the nature of the data, such as the number of data bits; if parity is used, and if so, whether it is even or odd; and the number of stop bits. Essentially, the start bit is the only bit that is not optional; there is always only one start bit and it must be a logic 0. Figure 13-9b shows how to program the control word for the various functions. In the UART, the control word is used to set up the data-, parity-, and stop-bit steering logic circuit.

UART Transmitter. The operation of the UART transmitter section is really quite simple. The UART sends a transmit buffer empty (TBMT) signal to the DTE to indicate that it is ready to receive data. When the DTE senses an active condition on TBMT, it sends a parallel data character to the transmit data lines (TD_0–TD_7) and strobes them into the transmit buffer register with the transmit data strobe signal ($\overline{TDS}$). The contents of the transmit buffer register are transferred to the transmit shift register when the transmit end-of-character (TEOC) signal goes active (the TEOC signal simply tells the buffer register when the shift register is empty and available to receive data). The data pass through the steering logic circuit, where they pick up the appropriate start, stop, and parity bits. After data have been loaded into the transmit shift register, they are serially outputted on the transmit serial output (TSO) pin with a bit rate equal to the transmit clock (TCP) frequency. While the data in the transmit shift register are sequentially clocked out, the DTE loads the next character into the buffer register. The process continues until the DTE has transferred all its data. The preceding sequence is shown in Figure 13-10.

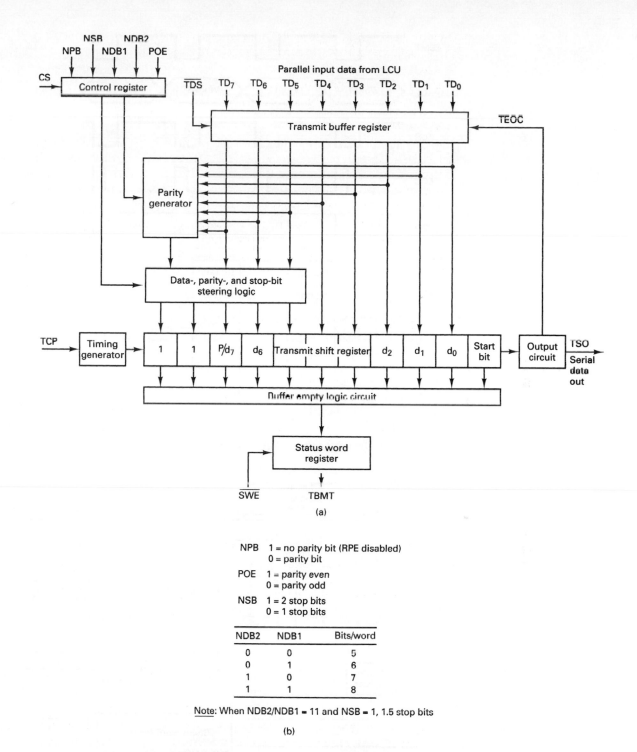

FIGURE 13-9 UART transmitter: (a) simplified block diagram; (b) control word

UART Receiver. A simplified block diagram of a UART receiver is shown in Figure 13-11. The number of stop bits, data bits, and the parity-bit information for the UART receiver is determined by the same control word that is used by the transmitter (i.e., the type of parity, the number of stop bits, and the number of data bits used for the UART receiver must be the same as that used for the UART transmitter).

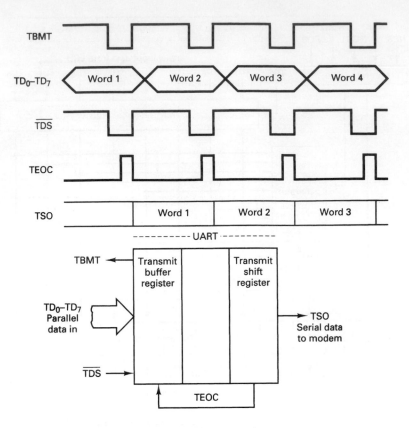

FIGURE 13-10 Timing diagram: UART transmitter

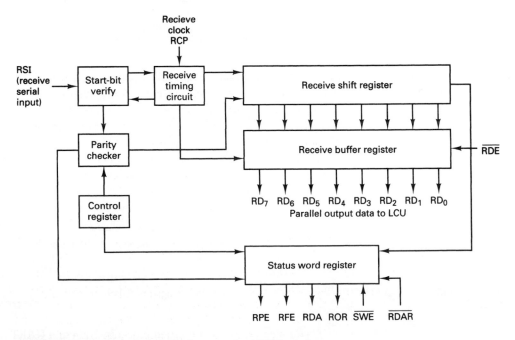

FIGURE 13-11 Simplified block diagram of a UART receiver

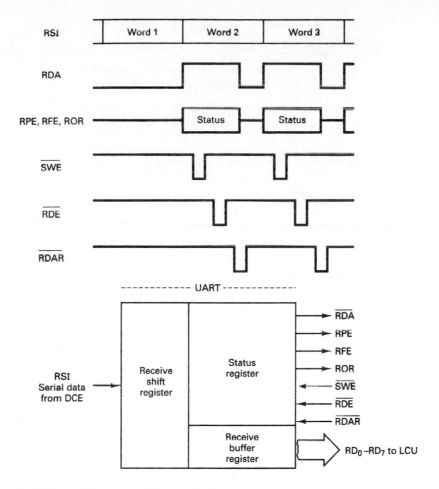

FIGURE 13-12 Timing diagram: UART receiver

The UART receiver ignores idle time line 1s. When a valid start bit is detected by the start bit verification circuit, the data character is serially clocked into the receive shift register. If parity is used, the parity bit is checked in the parity check circuit. After one complete data character is loaded into the shift register, the character is transferred in parallel into the buffer register and the receive data available (RDA) flag is set in the status word register. To read the status register, the DTE monitors status word enable ($\overline{\text{SWE}}$) and, if it is active, reads the character from the buffer register by placing an active condition on the receive data enable (RDE) pin. After reading the data, the DTE places an active signal on the receive data available reset ($\overline{\text{RDAR}}$) pin, which resets the RDA pin. Meanwhile, the next character is received and clocked into the receive shift register and the process is repeated until all the data have been received. The preceding sequence is shown in Figure 13-12.

The status word register is also used for diagnostic information. The receive parity error (RPE) flag is set when a received character has a parity error in it. The receive framing error (RFE) flag is set when a character is received without any or an improper number of stop bits. The receive overrun (ROR) flag is set when a character in the buffer register is written over with another character (i.e., the DTE failed to service an active condition on RDA before the next character was received by the shift register).

The receive clock for the UART (RCP) is 16 times higher than the receive data rate. This allows the start-bit verification circuit to determine if a high-to-low transition in the received data is actually a valid start bit and not simply a negative-going noise spike.

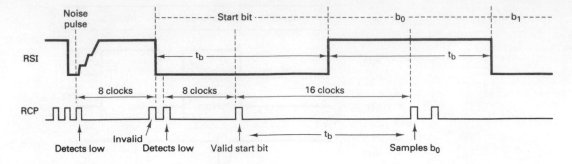

FIGURE 13-13 Start-bit verification

Figure 13-13 shows how this is accomplished. The incoming idle line 1s (continuous high condition) are sampled at a rate 16 times the actual bit rate. This ensures that a high-to-low transition is detected with 1/16 of a bit time after it occurs. Once a low is detected, the verification circuit counts off seven clock pulses, then resamples the data. If it is still low, it is assumed that a valid start bit has been detected. If it has reverted to the high condition, it is assumed that the high-to-low transition was simply a noise pulse and, therefore, is ignored. Once a valid start bit has been detected and verified, the verification circuit samples the incoming data once every 16 clock cycles, which is equal to the data rate. Sampling at 16 times the bit rate also establishes the sample time to within 1/16 of a bit time from the center of a bit.

Universal synchronous receiver/transmitter (USRT). The USRT is used for synchronous data transmission between the DTE and the DCE. Synchronous transmission means that there is clocking information transferred between the USRT and the modem and each transmission begins with a unique SYN character. The primary functions of the USRT are

1. To perform serial-to-parallel and parallel-to-serial conversion of data
2. To perform error detection by inserting and checking parity bits
3. To insert and detect SYN characters

The block diagram of the USRT is shown in Figure 13-14a. The USRT operates very similarly to the UART, and, therefore, only the differences are explained. With the USRT, start and stop bits are not allowed. Instead, unique SYN characters are loaded into the transmit and receive SYN registers prior to transferring data. The programming information for the control word is shown in Figure 13-14b.

USRT Transmitter. The transmit clock signal (TCP) is set at the desired bit rate and the desired SYN character is loaded from the parallel input pins (DB_0–DB_7) into the transmit SYN register by pulsing transmit SYN strobe (TSS). Data are loaded into the transmit data register from DB_0–DB_7 by pulsing the transmit data strobe (TDS). The next character transmitted is extracted from the transmit data register provided that the TDS pulse occurs during the presently transmitted character. If TDS is not pulsed, the next transmitted character is extracted from the transmit SYN register and the SYN character transmitted (SCT) signal is set. The transmit buffer empty (TBMT) signal is used to request the next character from the DTE. The serial output data appears on the transmit serial output (TSO) pin.

USRT Receiver. The receive clock signal (RCP) is set at the desired bit rate and the desired SYN character is loaded into the receive SYN register from DB_0–DB_7 by pulsing receive SYN strobe (RSS). On a high-to-low transition of the receiver rest input (RR), the receiver is placed in the search (bit phase) mode. In the search mode, serially received data are examined on a bit-by-bit basis until a SYN character is found. After each bit is clocked

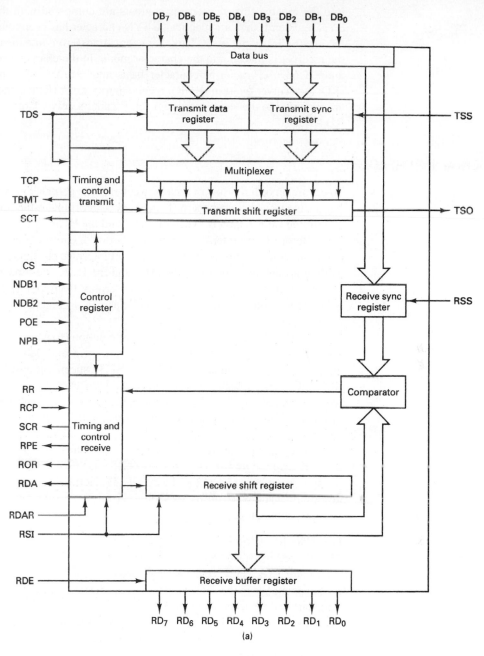

FIGURE 13-14 USRT transceiver: (a) block diagram; (b) control word

NPB 1 = no parity bit (RPE disabled)
0 = parity bit

POE 1 = parity even
0 = parity odd

NDB2	NDB1	Bits/word
0	0	5
0	1	6
1	0	7
1	1	8

(b)

into the receive shift register, its contents are compared with the contents of the receive SYN register. If they are identical, a SYN character has been found and the SYN character receive (SCR) output is set. This character is transferred into the receive buffer register and the receiver is placed into the character mode. In the character mode, receive data are examined on a character-by-character basis and receiver flags for receive data available (RDA), receiver overrun (ROR), receive parity error (RPE), and SYN character received are provided to the status word register. Parallel receive data are outputted to the DTE on RD_0–RD_7.

SERIAL INTERFACES

To ensure an orderly flow of data between the line control unit and the modem, a *serial interface* is placed between them. This interface coordinates the flow of data, control signals, and timing information between the DTE and the DCE.

Before serial interfaces were standardized, every company that manufactured data communications equipment used a different interface configuration. More specifically, the cabling arrangement between the DTE and the DCE, the type and size of the connectors used, and the voltage levels varied considerably from vender to vender. To interconnect equipment manufactured by different companies, special level converters, cables, and connectors had to be built.

In 1962 the Electronic Industries Association (EIA), in an effort to standardize interface equipment between data terminal equipment and data communications equipment, agreed on a set of standards called the RS-232 specifications. In 1969, the third revision, RS-232C, was published and remained the industrial standard until 1987 when RS-232D was introduced. The RS-232D version of the interface is compatible with the C version. The primary difference between the two versions is the addition of three test circuits in the D version.

The RS-232 specifications identify the mechanical, electrical, functional, and procedural description for the interface between the DTE and DCE. The RS-232 interface is similar to the combined CCITT standards V.28 (electrical specifications) and V.24 (functional description) and is designed for serial transmission of data up to 20 kbps for a distance of approximately 50 ft.

RS-232 Interface

The RS-232 interface specifies a 25-wire cable with a DB25P/DB25S-compatible connector. Figure 13-15 shows the electrical characteristics of the RS-232 interface. The terminal load capacitance of the cable is specified as 2500 pF, which includes cable capacitance. The impedance at the terminating end must be between 3000 Ω and 7000 Ω, and the output impedance is specified as greater than 300 Ω. With these electrical specifications and for a maximum bit rate of 20,000 bps, the nominal maximum length of the RS-232 interface is approximately 50 ft.

Although the RS-232 interface is simply a cable and two connectors, the standard also specifies limitations on the voltage levels that the DTE and DCE can output onto or receive from the cable. In both the DTE and DCE, there are circuits that convert their internal logic levels to RS-232 values. For example, a DTE uses TTL logic and is interfaced to a DCE that uses ECL logic; they are not compatible. Voltage-leveling circuits convert the internal voltage values of the DTE and DCE to RS-232 values. If both the DCE and DTE output and input RS-232 levels, they are electrically compatible regardless of which logic family they use internally. A leveler is called a *driver* if it outputs a signal voltage to the cable and a *terminator* if it accepts a signal voltage from the cable. Table 13-5 lists the voltage limits for both drivers and terminators. Note that the data lines use negative logic and the control lines use positive logic.

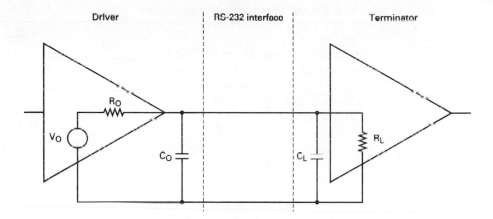

FIGURE 13-15 RS-232 electrical specifications

TABLE 13-5 RS-232 Voltage Specifications (V dc)

	Data Pins		Control Pins	
	Logic 1	Logic 0	Enable "On"	Disable "Off"
Driver	−5 to −15	+5 to +15	+5 to +15	−5 to −15
Terminator	−3 to −25	+3 to +25	+3 to +25	−3 to −25

From Table 13-5 it can be seen that the limits for a driver are more inclusive than those for a terminator. The driver can output any voltage between +5 V and +15 V or −5 V and −15 V dc, and a terminator will accept any voltage between +3 V and +25 V and −3 V and −25 V dc. The difference in the voltage levels between a driver and a terminator is called *noise margin*. The noise margin reduces the susceptibility of the interface to noise transients on the cable. Typical voltages used for data and control signals are +7 V dc and +10 V dc.

The pins on the RS-232 interface cable are functionally categorized as either ground, data, control (handshaking), or timing pins. All the pins are unidirectional (signals are propagated only from the DTE to the DCE, or vice versa). Table 13-6 lists the 25 pins of the RS-232 interface, their designations, and the direction of signal propagation (i.e., either toward the DTE or toward the DCE). The RS-232 specifications designate the ground, data, control, and timing pins as A, B, C, and D, respectively. These are nondescriptive designations. It is more practical and useful to use acronyms to designate the pins that reflect the pin functions. Table 13-6 lists the CCITT and EIA designations and the nomenclature more commonly used by industry in the United States.

EIA RS-232 pin functions. Twenty of the 25 pins of the RS-232 interface are designated for specific purposes or functions. Pins 9, 10, 11, and 18 are unassigned; pins 1 and 7 are grounds; pins 2, 3, 14, and 16 are data pins; pins 15, 17, and 24 are timing pins; and all the other assigned pins are reserved for control or handshaking signals. There are two full-duplex data channels available with the RS-232 interface; one channel is for primary data (actual information) and the second channel is for secondary data (diagnostic information and handshaking signals). The functions of the 25 pins are summarized below.

Pin 1: Protective ground. This pin is frame ground and is used for protection against electrical shock. Pin 1 should be connected to the third-wire ground of the ac electrical system at one end of the cable (either at the DTE or the DCE, but not at both ends).

TABLE 13-6 EIA RS-232 Pin Designations

Pin Number	EIA Nomenclature	Common Acronyms	Direction
1	Protective ground (AA)	GWG	None
2	Transmitted data (BA)	TD, SD	DTE to DCE
3	Received data (BB)	RD	DCE to DTE
4	Request to send (CA)	RS, RTS	DTE to DCE
5	Clear to send (CB)	CS, CTS	DCE to DTE
6	Data set ready (CC)	DSR, MR	DCE to DTE
7	Signal ground (AB)	GND	None
8	Received line signal detect (CF)	RLSD, CD	DCE to DTE
9	Unassigned		
10	Unassigned		
11	Unassigned		
12	Secondary received line signal detect (SCF)	SRLSD	DCE to DTE
13	Secondary clear to send (SCB)	SCS	DCE to DTE
14	Secondary transmitted data (SBA)	STD	DTE to DCE
15	Transmission signal element timing (DB)	SCT	DCE to DTE
16	Secondary received data (SBB)	SRD	DCE to DTE
17	Receiver signal element timing (DD)	SCR	DCE to DTE
18	Local loopback	LL	DTE to DCE
19	Secondary request to send (SCA)	SRS	DTE to DCE
20	Data terminal ready (CD)	DTR	DTE or DCE
21	Signal quality detector (CG), or	SQD	DCE to DTE
	Remote loopback	RL	DTE to DCE
22	Ring indicator (CE)	RI	DCE to DTE
23	Data signal rate selector (CH)	DSRS	DTE to DCE
24	Transmit signal element timing (DA)	SCTE	DTE to DCE
25	Test mode	TM	DCE to DTE

Pin 2: Transmit data (TD). Serial data on the primary channel from the DTE to the DCE are transmitted on this pin. TD is enabled by an active condition on the CS pin.

Pin 3: Received data (RD). Serial data on the primary channel are transferred from the DCE to the DTE on this pin. RD is enabled by an active condition on the RLSD pin.

Pin 4: Request to send (RS). The DTE bids for the primary communications channel from the DCE on this pin. An active condition on RS turns on the modem's analog carrier. The analog carrier is modulated by a unique bit pattern called a training sequence that is used to initialize the communications channel and synchronize the receive modem. RS cannot go active unless pin 6 (DSR) is active.

Pin 5: Clear to send (CS). This signal is a handshake from the DCE to the DTE in response to an active condition on request to send. CS enables the TD pin.

Pin 6: Data set ready (DSR). On this pin the DCE indicates the availability of the communications channel. DSR is active as long as the DCE is connected to the communications channel (i.e., the modem or the communications channel is not being tested or is not in the voice mode).

Pin 7: Signal ground. The pin is the signal reference for all the data, control, and timing pins. Usually, this pin is strapped to frame ground (pin 1).

Pin 8: Receive line signal detect (RLSD). The DCE uses this pin to signal the DTE when the DCE is receiving an analog carrier on the primary data channel. RLSD enables the RD pin.

Pin 9: Unassigned.

Pin 10: Unassigned.

Pin 11: Equalizer mode (non-EIA). This circuit is used by the data set to notify the DTE when the data set begins self-adjusting because error performance is poor. When RLSD is on and this circuit is off, the data set is retraining and the probability of error in the data on RD is high. When RLSD is on and this circuit is on, the modem is trained and the probability of error on RD is small.

Pin 12: Secondary receive line signal detect (SRLSD). This pin is active when the DCE is receiving an analog carrier on the secondary channel. SRLSD enables the SRD pin.

Pin 13: Secondary clear to send (SCS). This pin is used by the DCE to send a handshake to the DTE in response to an active condition on the secondary request to send pin. SCS enables the STD pin.

Pin 14: Secondary transmit data (STD). Diagnostic data are transferred from the DTE to the DCE on this pin. STD is enabled by an active condition on the SCS pin.

New synch (non-EIA). The use of this circuit is optional and is intended for use with a data set at the primary of a multipoint dedicated network. When the primary is in a polling operation, rapid resynchronization of the receiver to many remote transmitters is required. The receiver clock normally maintains the timing information of the previous message for some interval after the message has ended. This may interfere with resynchronization on the receipt of the next message. An on condition should be applied to this circuit by the DTE for at least 1 ms but no longer than the intermessage interval to squelch the existing timing information in the modem after the message has been received.

Pin 15: Transmission signal element timing (SCT). Transmit clocking signals are sent from the DCE to the DTE on this pin.

Pin 16: Secondary received data (SRD). Diagnostic data are transferred from the DCE to the DTE on this pin. SRD is enabled by an active condition on the SCS pin.

Pin 17: Receive signal element timing (SCR). Receive clocking signals are sent from the DCE to the DTE on this pin. The clock frequency is equal to the bit rate of the primary data channel.

Pin 18: Local loopback (LL). Control signal from the DTE to the DCE placing the DCE (modem) into a loopback condition. A local loopback disconnects the transmitted analog signal from the communications line and connects it directly to the receiver, which enables the local terminal to perform troubleshooting tests on the modem.

Pin 19: Secondary request to send (SRS). The DTE bids for the secondary communications channel from the DCE on this pin.

Pin 20: Data terminal ready (DTR). The DTE sends information to the DCE on this pin concerning the availability of the data terminal equipment (i.e., access to the mainframe at the primary station or status of the computer terminal at the secondary station). DTR is used primarily with dial-up data communications circuits to handshake with RI.

Pin 21: Signal quality detector (SQD). The DCE sends signals to the DTE on this pin that reflect the quality of the received analog carrier.

Remote loopback (RL). Control signal from the DTE to the DCE that places the DCE (modem) into a remote loopback condition. A remote loopback connects the receive data pin on the modem to its transmit data pin allowing the distant end terminal to perform troubleshooting tests on the modem.

Pin 22: Ring indicator (RI). This pin is used with dial-up lines for the DCE to signal the DTE that there is an incoming call.

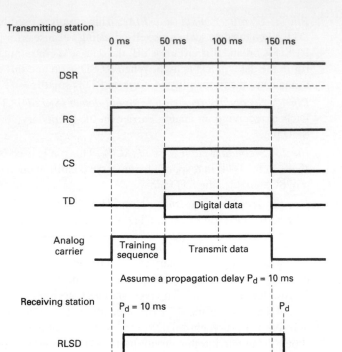

FIGURE 13-16 Timing diagram: basic operation of the RS-232 interface

Pin 23: Data signal rate selector (DSRS). The DTE uses this pin to select the transmission bit rate (clock frequency) of the DCE.

Pin 24: Transmit signal element timing (SCTE). Transmit clocking signals are sent from the DTE to the DCE on this pin when the master clock oscillator is located in the DTE.

Pin 25: Test mode (TM). Control signal from the DCE to the DTE that is enabled whenever either a local or remote loopback test is being performed.

Pins 1 through 8 are used with both asynchronous and synchronous modems. Pins 15, 17, and 24 are used for only synchronous modems. Pins 12, 13, 14, 16, and 19 are used only when the DCE is equipped with a secondary channel. Pins 19 and 22 are used exclusively for dial-up telephone connections.

The basic operation of the RS-232 interface is shown in Figure 13-16 and described as follows. When the DTE has primary data to send, it enables request to send ($t = 0$ ms). After a predetermined time delay (50 ms), CS goes active. During the RS/CS delay, the modem is outputting an analog carrier that is modulated by a unique bit pattern called a *training sequence.* The training sequence is used to initialize the communications line and synchronize the carrier and clock recovery circuits in the receive modem. After the RS/CS delay, TD is enabled and the DTE begins to transmit data. After the receive DTE detects an analog carrier, RD is enabled. When the transmission is complete ($t = 150$ ms), RS goes low, turning off the analog carrier and shutting off CS.

TABLE 13-7 RS-530 Pin Designations

Signal Name	Pin Number(s)
Shield	1
Transmitted data[a]	2, 14
Received data[a]	3, 16
Request to send[a]	4, 19
Clear to send[a]	5, 13
DCE ready[a]	6, 22
DTE ready[a]	20, 23
Signal ground	7
Received line signal detect[a]	8, 10
Transmit signal element timing (DCE source)[a]	15, 12
Receiver signal element timing (DCE source)[a]	17, 9
Local loopback[b]	18
Remote loopback[b]	21
Transmit signal element timing (DTE source)[a]	24, 11
Test mode[b]	25

[a]Category I circuits (RS-422A)
[b]Category II circuits (RS-423A)

RS-449 and RS-530 Interface Standards

Contemporary data rates have exceeded the capabilities of the RS-232 interface. Therefore, in 1977 the EIA introduced the RS-449 specification with the intention of replacing the RS-232 interface. The RS-449 interface uses a 37-pin connector that provides more functions, faster data transmission rates, and greater distance capabilities. However, the industry never embraced the RS-449 standard and it came and went virtually unnoticed by most of the data communications industry. Consequently, in 1987 the EIA introduced the RS-530 standard, which was intended to operate at data rates from 20 kbps to 2 Mbps using the same 25-pin, DB-25 connector used by the RS-232 interface. Table 13-7 lists the 25 pins for the RS-530 interface and their designations.

The RS-530 interface, however, does not include electrical specifications. Instead the electrical specifications used with the RS-530 are specified by either the RS-422A or RS-423A standard. The RS-422A standard specifies a balanced interface cable that will operate at bit rates up to 10 Mbps and span distances up to 1200 m. This does not mean, however, that 10 Mbps can be transmitted 1200 m. At 10 Mbps the maximum distance is approximately 15 m, and 90 kbps is the maximum bit rate that can be transmitted 1200 m. The RS-423A standard specifies an unbalanced interface cable that will operate at a maximum line speed of 100 kbps and span a maximum distance of 90 m.

Figure 13-17 shows the *balanced* digital interface circuit for the RS-422A, and Figure 13-18 shows the *unbalanced* digital interface circuit for the RS-423A.

A balanced interface, such as the RS-422A, transfers information to a *balanced transmission line.* With a balanced transmission line, both conductors carry current except the current in the two wires travel in opposite directions. With a bidirectional *unbalanced* line, one wire is at ground potential and the currents in the two wires may be different. Currents that flow in opposite directions in a balanced wire pair are called *metallic circuit* currents. Currents that flow in the same direction are called *longitudinal* currents. A balanced pair has the advantage that most noise interference is induced equally in both wires, producing longitudinal currents that cancel in the load. Figure 13-19 shows the results of metallic and longitudinal currents on a balanced transmission line. It can be seen that longitudinal currents (generally produced by static interference) cancel in the load. Balanced transmission lines can be connected to unbalanced loads, and vice versa, with special transformers called *baluns* (*bal*anced to *un*balanced).

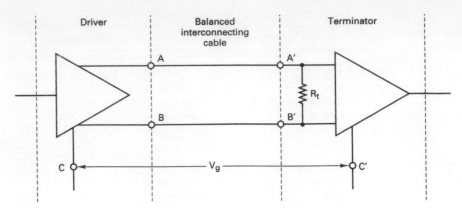

FIGURE 13-17 RS-422A interface circuit, R_t, optional cable termination resistance; V_g, ground potential difference; A, B, driver interface points; A′, B′, terminator interface points; C, driver circuit ground; C′, terminator circuit ground; A-B, balanced driver output; A′-B′, balanced terminator input

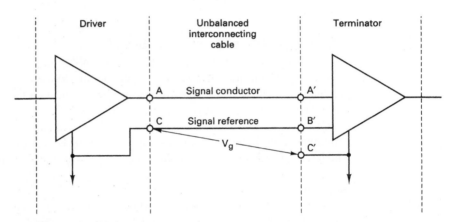

FIGURE 13-18 RS-423A interface circuit. A, C, driver interface; A′, B′, terminator interface; V_g, ground potential difference; C, driver circuit ground; C′, terminator circuit ground

The RS-232 and RS-530 standards provide specifications for answering calls, but not for dialing. The EIA has a different standard, RS-366, for automatic calling units. The principal use of RS-366 is for dial backup of private-line data circuits and for automatic dialing of remote terminals.

CCITT X.21

In 1976, the CCITT introduced the X.21 recommendation, which includes the specifications for placing and receiving calls and for sending and receiving data using full-duplex synchronous transmission. The X.21 recommendation presumes a direct digital connection to a digital telephone network. Thus, all data transmissions must be synchronous, and the data communications equipment will need to provide both bit and character synchronization. The minimum data rate used for X.21 is 64 kbps because this is the bit rate currently used to encode voice in digital form on the telephone network.

The X.21 specifies only six signals, which are listed in Table 13-8. Data are transmitted toward the modem on the transmit line, and the modem returns data on the receive line. The control and indication lines are control channels for the two transmission directions. The signal element timing line carries the bit timing signal (clock) and the byte

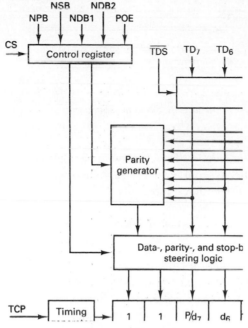

FIGURE 13-19 Results of metallic and longitudinal currents on a balanced transmission line: (a) metallic currents due to signal voltages; (b) longitudinal currents due to noise voltages

TABLE 13-8 CCITT X.21 Pin Designations

Interchange Circuit	Name	Direction
G	Signal ground	*
GA	DTE common return	DTE to DCE
T	Transmit	DTE to DCE
R	Receive	DCE to DTE
C	Control	DTE to DCE
I	Indication	DCE to DTE
S	Signal element timing	DCE to DTE
B	Byte timing	DCE to DTE

*See X.24 Recommendations

timing line carries the character synchronization information. The electrical specifications for X.21 are listed either in recommendation X.26 (balanced) or recommendation X.27 (unbalanced).

The major advantage of the X.21 standard over the RS-232 and RS-530 standards is that X.21 signals are encoded in serial digital form, which sets the stage for providing spe cial new services in computer communications.

PARALLEL INTERFACES

Parallel interfaces transfer data between two devices eight or more bits at a time. That is, one entire data word is transmitted (received) at a time as opposed to one bit at a time as with serial interfaces. Parallel transmission is sometimes referred to as *serial-by-word* transmission. One obvious advantage of parallel transmission is data are transmitted much faster than with serial transmission. This, of course, is because there is a transmission path for each bit of the word. For example, a system utilizing eight-bit words would have eight separate communications channels between the transmitter and receiver. Another advantage of parallel transmission is most computer terminals and peripheral equipment process

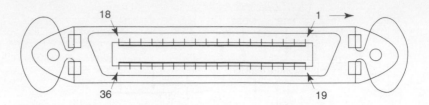

FIGURE 13-20 Printer interface and pin alignment

data internally in parallel. Therefore, with parallel interfaces there is no need to convert data from parallel to serial or vice versa. A disadvantage of parallel transmission is higher costs for transmission lines, especially when there are long distances between the transmitter and receiver. Therefore, parallel interfaces are commonly used to transfer data between two or more devices that are located in close proximity to each other, such as a computer and a printer.

Centronics Parallel Interface

The *Centronics parallel interface* was originally designed to be used for transferring data between a microcomputer and a printer. Centronics was one of the original companies to design printers especially for desktop computers. Before the advent of the Centronics interface, most printers used 20-mA loops for RS-232 interfaces. Centronics simplified the interface by designing an interface that accepted data in the same format used internally by most computers (i.e., eight-bit words transferred in parallel using TTL logic). The Centronics parallel interface soon became the de facto standard and, today, is the most common interface used for interfacing personal computers to printers and other peripheral devices. Printers manufactured by companies other than Centronics sometimes use different names for some of the control lines and the minimum timing of some of the control signals may vary slightly. However, it is safe to say that almost any printer with a Centronics port will work with almost any computer with a Centronics port.

Figure 13-20 shows a Centronics printer interface and pin alignment. The connector is a 36-pin Amphenol connector, which is sometimes called a *champ connector*. When interfacing an IBM-compatible personal computer to a Centronics printer, the Centronics interface uses a DB-25 connector at the computer end and several of the interface lines are omitted. Table 13-9 lists the pin assignments, names, abbreviations, active conditions, types, and directions of propagation for signals on the Centronics printer interface. The pins are divided into three categories: data, control, and status. Also note that all the data lines and several of the control and status lines have unique return lines. In addition there are several ground pins and one +5 V dc line. Figure 13-21 shows how the data, control, and status lines interface a computer to a printer using the Centronics parallel interface.

Data lines.   Pins 2 through 9 of the Centronics parallel interface are eight parallel data circuits that may be labeled d_0–d_7 or d_1–d_8 with either d_0 or d_1 as the least significant bit. All of the data lines are unidirectional (computer to printer) and each line has a dedicated return line. Characters are transmitted from the computer to the printer in the form of either seven-bit ASCII (possibly including an eighth bit, the parity bit) or in the form of eight-bit extended ASCII or EBCDIC characters.

Control lines.   The Centronics interface utilizes four unidirectional control lines that convey control information from the computer to the printer. The first control signal, the *strobe* ($\overline{\text{STB}}$) line, is a negative-edge-triggered signal outputted by the computer that directs the printer to accept data from the interface's data lines. The strobe signal is used for handshaking between the computer and printer.

TABLE 13-9 Centronics Printer Interface Lines

Pin Number	Return Pin	Signal	Abbreviation	Active	Type	Direction
1	19	Strobe	$\overline{STB}$	Low	Control	To printer
2	20	Data bit 0	d_0		Data	To printer
3	21	Data bit 1	d_1		Data	To printer
4	22	Data bit 2	d_2		Data	To printer
5	23	Data bit 3	d_3		Data	To printer
6	24	Data bit 4	d_4		Data	To printer
7	25	Data bit 5	d_5		Data	To printer
8	26	Data bit 6	d_6		Data	To printer
9	27	Data bit 7	d_7		Data	To printer
10	28	Acknowledge	$\overline{ACK}$	Low	Status	To computer
11	29	Busy	BUSY	High	Status	To computer
12		Paper out	PO	High	Status	To computer
13		Select	SLCT	High	Status	To computer
14		Auto feed	$\overline{AF}$	Low	Control	To printer
15		Unused	—	—	—	—
16		Signal ground	SG	—	—	—
17		Frame ground	FG	—	—	—
18		+5 V	—	—	—	—
31	30	Prime	$\overline{PRIME}$	Low	Control	To printer
32		Error	$\overline{ERROR}$	Low	Status	To computer
33		Signal ground	SG	—	—	—
34		Unused	—	—	—	—
35		Unused	—	—	—	—
36		Select in	$\overline{SLCTIN}$	Low	Control	To printer

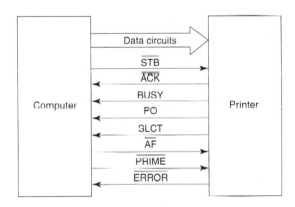

FIGURE 13-21 Control, data, and status lines for Centronics parallel interface

The *auto feed* ($\overline{AF}$) control line is an active-low signal that dictates whether the printer automatically performs a line feed function after it receives a carriage return character from the computer. Normally, the carriage return character only causes the print head to return to the left side of the paper, and a separate line feed character causes the paper to advance to the next line. The auto feed line allows one signal to perform both functions. If the computer holds $\overline{AF}$ low, the printer responds to the carriage return character by performing a carriage return and a line feed.

The *prime* ($\overline{PRIME}$) control line (sometimes called *initialize*) is an active-low signal outputted by the computer to clear the printer's memory, including the printer programming and the print buffer. After detecting an active condition on the prime line, the printer returns to the condition it was in when it was first turned on. The prime control line may be used to abort a printing job while it is still in progress.

The fourth control line is called *select* ($\overline{\text{SLCTIN}}$). The select control line is seldom used. When used, the printer must see a low signal on the $\overline{\text{SLCTIN}}$ line before it will accept data from the computer. Many printers have an internal override switch that permanently places a ground on the $\overline{\text{SLCTIN}}$ line.

Status lines. All of the status lines are unidirectional and convey information from the printer to the computer. The status lines are used by the printer to tell the computer what the printer is doing. For example, the *acknowledge* ($\overline{\text{ACK}}$) status line is an active-low response made by the printer after receiving an active $\overline{\text{STB}}$ signal from the computer. The printer uses $\overline{\text{ACK}}$ to signal the computer that it has processed the last byte of data that it received over the interface data lines and that the printer is ready for another character.

The *busy* status line is an active-high control signal that goes high anytime the printer is busy and unable to accept data from the computer. There are four conditions that can cause the printer to be busy:

1. The printer is inputting data from the data lines or the printer's data buffer is full and unable to accept any more data.
2. The printer is printing or otherwise processing data.
3. The printer is turned off or otherwise *off line.* Many printers have an off-line switch that prevents them from receiving or printing data.
4. The printer's $\overline{\text{ERROR}}$ line is low.

The *paper out* (PO) control line is self-explanatory; it goes active whenever the printer is out of paper. Whenever PO is activated, the $\overline{\text{ERROR}}$ line is also activated.

The *select* (SLCT) control line is an active-high status line that simply indicates whether the printer is selected. The printer holds SLCT high whenever it is on line and low whenever it is off line. The $\overline{\text{ERROR}}$ status line is an active-low signal that is used to indicate a printer problem. The printer holds $\overline{\text{ERROR}}$ high during normal operation. The following conditions can cause $\overline{\text{ERROR}}$ to go active:

1. The printer is off line.
2. The printer is out of paper.
3. There is some other undefined problem with the printer preventing it from operating properly.

Miscellaneous lines. Pins 20 through 27 on the Centronics parallel interface are return signal lines for data pins d_0 through d_7, respectively. Pins 19, 28, 29, and 30 are the return paths for the $\overline{\text{STB}}$, $\overline{\text{ACK}}$, BUSY, and $\overline{\text{PRIME}}$ lines. Pins 16 and 33 are signal ground lines that serve as a common return path for lines that do not have their own dedicated return lines. Pin 17 is frame ground (FG), which electrically connects the chassis of the computer and the printer to reduce the possibility of electrical shock. Pin 18 is used to provide the +5 V dc power supply from the computer to the printer. The +5 V dc is used to power the printer's status circuits when the printer is turned off, but it is not designed to provide power for the printer's overall operation. Pin 18 is generally not used.

Interfacing. The Centronics interface was originally designed to use a 36-pin connector. The earliest personal computers, however, used 25-pin DB connectors for their printer port. Consequently, eleven pins had to be omitted from the interface. Today, printer cables generally come with an Amphenol 36-pin connector on the printer end of the cable and the DB-25 connector on the computer end.

Table 13-10 shows the pin assignments for both the Amphenol 36-pin connector and the adapted DB-25 connector. As the table shows, the unused Centronics pins have been omitted and only four of the individual return paths (grounds) for data signals are used.

TABLE 13-10 Connecting a Centronics Cable to a DB-25 Connector

Amphenol Connector	Signal	DB-25 Connector
1	Strobe	1
2	Data bit 0	2
3	Data bit 1	3
4	Data bit 2	4
5	Data bit 3	5
6	Data bit 4	6
7	Data bit 5	7
8	Data bit 6	8
9	Data bit 7	9
10	Acknowledge	10
11	Busy	11
12	Paper out	12
13	Select	13
14	Auto feed	14
15	Unused	Not connected
16	Signal ground	Not connected
17	Frame ground	Not connected
18	+5 V	Not connected
19	Strobe return	19
20	Data bit 0 return	Not connected
21	Data bit 1 return	20
22	Data bit 2 return	Not connected
23	Data bit 3 return	21
24	Data bit 4 return	Not connected
25	Data bit 5 return	22
26	Data bit 6 return	Not connected
27	Data bit 7 return	23
28	Acknowledge return	Not connected
29	Busy return	24
30	Prime return	25
31	Prime	16
32	Error	15
33	Signal ground	18
34	Unused	Not connected
35	Unused	Not connected
36	Select in	17

Also, signal and frame ground, the acknowledge signal return path, and the +5 V dc supply are not connected. Because printers are relatively slow devices, the personal computer version of the Centronics interface is more than adequate for sending data to a printer.

IEEE 488 Bus

The IEEE 488 bus uses eight bidirectional data lines connected in parallel to interface up to 15 remote devices (usually computer-controlled pieces of test equipment). Because the various pieces of equipment interfaced with the IEEE 488 are located in proximity with each other, the interface was designed for a maximum distance between adjacent devices of less than 7 ft, and the maximum length of the entire bus is about 65 ft. Devices are connected to the bus by a 24-pin ribbon connector. Table 13-11 summarizes the characteristics of the IEEE 488 bus.

With the IEEE 488 bus, the *controller* determines which device can transmit data and which devices are receivers. The controller selects a single device to send data over the bus. The selected device is called the talker and there can be only one talker at a time. Any number of receivers (called listeners) can be selected at a time. Devices not programmed as talkers, listeners, or controllers are placed in the *standby mode*. The characteristics of the four types of devices are summarized in Table 13-12. The controller can change the function of

TABLE 13-11 IEEE 488 Bus Characteristics

Logic levels	TTL
Data lines	8, bidirectional
Maximum number of devices	15
Distance between adjacent devices	2 m maximum
Maximum total length	20 m
Connector	24-pin ribbon
Maximum speed with open-collector drivers	250 kbps
Maximum speed with tristate drivers	1 Mbps

TABLE 13-12 IEEE 488 Devices

Device	Function
Controller	In charge of bus. Specifies which devices are programmed as the talker, as listeners, or are in the standby mode. There can be only one controller at a time.
Talker	Sends data over the bus to the listeners. There can be only one talker at a time.
Listeners	Receive data from the talker. There can be many listeners.
Standby	All devices that are not programmed as a controller, talker, or listener are in the standby mode.

the devices under its supervision. For example, the talker can be reprogrammed as a listener and a different device designated as the new talker. The controller can even relinquish control of the bus and designate another device as the controller. In this case, the former controller becomes either a talker, a listener, or placed in the standby mode.

Operating modes.   The IEEE bus has only two modes of operation: *command* and *data*. The interface is switched between the two modes by the controller using the *attention* ($\overline{\text{ATN}}$) bus management control line. When the controller puts $\overline{\text{ATN}}$ low, all devices connected to the interface switch to the command mode. When the controller makes $\overline{\text{ATN}}$ high, all devices are switched to the data mode.

When in the command mode, the controller can program other devices connected to the interface. For example, the controller could use the command mode to program the frequency of a function generator or the voltage range for a digital voltmeter. The controller could also program a device to operate as either a talker or listener. Each device connected to the interface has a unique address. In the command mode, the controller directs commands to a specific device by sending that device's address over the data bus. When in the command mode, all information that passes over the data bus is either a command or an address. When in the data mode, the only information allowed to pass over the data bus is data sent from the talker to the listener(s).

IEEE 488 interface lines.   Table 13-13 lists the pin assignments for the IEEE 488 interface. In essence, there are three groups of circuits (lines): data circuits, handshake circuits (sometimes called *byte transfer lines*), and interface management circuits.

Data Circuits.   There are eight bidirectional data lines numbered DI01 through DI08 with DI08 being the most significant. The purpose of the data lines is to carry eight-bit parallel data from the talker to the listener(s) or to carry addresses and commands from the controller to the other devices connected to the interface.

Handshake Circuits.   The IEEE 448 bus uses three handshaking circuits: not ready for data ($\overline{\text{NRFD}}$), data not accepted ($\overline{\text{NDAC}}$), and data valid ($\overline{\text{DAV}}$). The function of the handshaking circuits is to coordinate the transfer of data from the talker to the listener(s). $\overline{\text{NRFD}}$ is an active-low control signal that the listener outputs when it is not ready to accept data from the data circuits. The $\overline{\text{NRFD}}$ output pins of the devices are wire-ORed together

TABLE 13-13 Pin Assignment of the IEEE 488 Interface

Pin	Line Name	Abbreviation	Type
1	Data bit 1 (LSB)	DIO1	Data
2	Data bit 2	DIO2	Data
3	Data bit 3	DIO3	Data
4	Data bit 4	DIO4	Data
5	End or identify	$\overline{\text{EOI}}$	Interface mgt.
6	Data available	$\overline{\text{DAV}}$	Handshake
7	Not ready for data	$\overline{\text{NRFD}}$	Handshake
8	Not data accepted	$\overline{\text{NDAC}}$	Handshake
9	Interface clear	$\overline{\text{IFC}}$	Interface mgt.
10	Service request	$\overline{\text{SRQ}}$	Interface mgt.
11	Attention	$\overline{\text{ATN}}$	Interface mgt.
12	Shield (earth ground)		
13	Data bit 5	DIO5	Data
14	Data bit 6	DIO6	Data
15	Data bit 7	DIO7	Data
16	Data bit 8 (MSB)	DIO8	Data
17	Remote enable	$\overline{\text{REN}}$	Interface mgt.
18	Ground return for DAV		
19	Ground return for NRFD		
20	Ground return for NDAC		
21	Ground return for IFC		
22	Ground return for SRQ		
23	Ground return for ATN		
24	Signal ground		

so that any listener connected to the bus can pull the $\overline{\text{NRFD}}$ line low. If there is more than one listener, the wire-OR configuration ensures that the $\overline{\text{NRFD}}$ line remains low as long as the slowest listener is not ready to receive data.

The not data accepted ($\overline{\text{NDAC}}$) circuit is an active-low signal that is controlled by the listener(s). $\overline{\text{NDAC}}$ signals the talker that the listeners have not accepted data yet and that the talker should continue holding the data on the bus. $\overline{\text{NDAC}}$ is also wire ORed to all the devices on the interface so that any listener can hold the line low until the slowest listener has accepted the data from the interface bus.

The data available ($\overline{\text{DAV}}$) line is an active-low control line used by the talker in the data mode or by the controller in the command mode to signal the other devices on the bus that there is either a data byte, address, or command to be read from the data bus.

Interface Management Circuits. The IEEE 488 bus has five interface management circuits that control certain operations of the devices connected to the interface and manage the flow of information among those devices.

1. *Attention ($\overline{\text{ATN}}$).* The controller uses $\overline{\text{ATN}}$ to switch the bus between the data and command modes. When $\overline{\text{ATN}}$ is high, the interface is in the data mode, and the talker can send data over the data bus to the listeners. When ATN is low, the IEEE interface is in the command mode, at which time the controller can send only addresses and commands over the data bus.

2. *Interface clear ($\overline{\text{IFC}}$).* When the controller activates $\overline{\text{IFC}}$, all devices connected to the interface suspend operations and the bus is placed in the idle state, at which time no communications can take place. $\overline{\text{IFC}}$ functions similar to a reset line.

3. *Remote enable ($\overline{\text{REN}}$).* $\overline{\text{REN}}$ is an active-low signal used by the controller to switch the devices connected to the interface between local and remote operation. When $\overline{\text{REN}}$ is activated, all devices are placed into remote operation and operate under the command of the controller. When $\overline{\text{REN}}$ is high (inactive) all devices

(usually pieces of test equipment) are under local control and respond only to the control knobs on their own front panels, thus allowing operators to control them directly without having to program them through a computer.

4. *Service request ($\overline{SRQ}$).* Any device connected to the interface can activate $\overline{SRQ}$ to interrupt the normal operation of the interface and signal the controller that it requires attention. When the controller senses an active $\overline{SRQ}$ signal, it determines which device requested the service and why by placing the interface in the command mode and polling each device individually. When the controller addresses the device that activated the $\overline{SRQ}$, that device responds by sending codes over the data bus that disclose the action that the controller should take.

5. *End or identify ($\overline{EOI}$).* The $\overline{EOI}$ circuit has two purposes. When in the data mode, the talker has control of $\overline{EOI}$ and activates it when it sends its last byte of data in a particular message. When in the command mode, the controller can activate $\overline{EOI}$ to perform a group poll to obtain information from several devices at the same time.

THE TELEPHONE NETWORK

In its simplest form, data communication is the transmittal of digital information between two DTEs. The DTEs may be separated by a few feet or several thousand miles. At the present time, there is an insufficient number of transmission media to carry digital information from source to destination in digital form. Therefore, the most convenient alternative is to use the existing public telephone network (PTN) as the transmission medium for data communications circuits. Unfortunately, the PTN was designed (and most of it constructed) long before the advent of large-scale data communications. The PTN was intended to be used for transferring voice telephone communications signals, not digital data. Therefore, to use the PTN for data communications, the data must be converted to a form more suitable for transmission over analog carrier systems.

The following explanation is limited to telecommunications using the PTN. *Telco* includes all of the telephone companies that make up the PTN. Telco offers two general categories of service: *direct distance dialing* (DDD) and *private line.* DDD originally included only those switches and facilities required to complete a long-distance telephone call without the assistance of a Telco operator. The DDD now includes the entire public switched network, that is, any service associated with a telephone number. Private-line services are dedicated to a single user.

DDD Network

The DDD network, commonly referred to as the *dial-up* or *switched network,* imposes several limitations that must be overcome before it can be used for data communications. A basic understanding of the electrical operation of the telephone network would be helpful. The DDD network can be divided into four main sections: instruments, dial switches, local loops, and trunk circuits. An *instrument* is the device used to originate and receive signals, such as a telephone set (telset). The instrument is often referred to as *station equipment* and the location of the instrument as the *station.* A *dial switch* is a programmed matrix that provides a temporary signal path. A *local loop* is the dedicated transmission path between an instrument and the nearest dial switch. A *trunk circuit* is a transmission path between two dial switches. The dial switches are located in Telco central offices and are categorized as local, tandem, or toll. A *local* dial switch serves a limited area. The size of the area is determined by how many telephone numbers are required or desired in a given geographical area. Telco designates these areas as branch area exchanges. A branch exchange is a dial switch. The *subscriber* is the operator or user of the instrument: If you have a home telephone, you are a subscriber. A subscriber is the customer of Telco: the person placing the

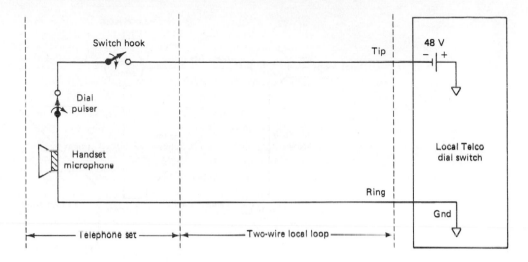

FIGURE 13-22 Simplified two-wire loop showing telset hookup to a local dial switch (loop start operation)

call. Telco refers to this person as either the talker or the listener, depending on his or her role at a particular time during a conversation.

A telephone number consists of seven digits. The first three digits make up the prefix and the last four constitute the extension number. Each prefix can accommodate 10,000 telephone numbers (0000 to 9999). The capacity of a dial switch is determined by how many prefixes it serves. The local dial switch provides a two-wire cable (local loop) for each telephone number it serves (Figure 13-22). One wire is designated the *tip* and the other the *ring*. The station end of the loop is terminated in a telephone set. The dial switch applies −48 V dc on the tip and a ground on the ring of each loop. This dc voltage is used for supervisory signaling and to provide a talk battery for the telset microphone. On-hook, off-hook, and dial pulsing are examples of supervisory signaling.

When a subscriber goes off-hook (lifts the handset off the teleset cradle), a switch hook is released, completing a dc short between the tip and the ring of the loop through the telset microphone. The dial switch senses a dc current in the loop and recognizes this as an off-hook condition. This procedure is referred to as a *loop start operation:* The loop is completed to indicate an off-hook condition. The dial switch responds with an audible dial tone. On hearing the dial tone, the subscriber dials the destination telephone number. The originating and destination telephone numbers are referred to as the *calling* and the *called numbers,* respectively.

Dialing is accomplished with switch closures (dial pulses) or touch-tone signaling. Dial pulsing is the interruption of the dc loop current by a telset dialing mechanism. Eight tone oscillators are contained in each telset equipped with a touch-tone pad. In touch-tone signaling, depending on the digit depressed, the telset outputs two of the eight tone frequencies.

After the entire called number has been dialed, the dial switch searches for a signal path through the switching matrix to the loop associated with the number called. Once the dial switch identifies a signal path and locates the destination loop, it tests the loop for an off-hook (busy) condition. If the destination loop is busy, the dial switch signals the calling loop with a busy signal. A station busy signal is a 60-ppm buzz. If the destination loop is on-hook (idle), the dial switch applies a 20-Hz 110-V ac ringing signal to it. A typical ringing cycle is 2 seconds on, 4 seconds off. When the destination telephone is answered (goes off-hook), the dial switch terminates the ringing signal and completes the transmission path between the two loops through the matrix. The signal path through the dial switch will be

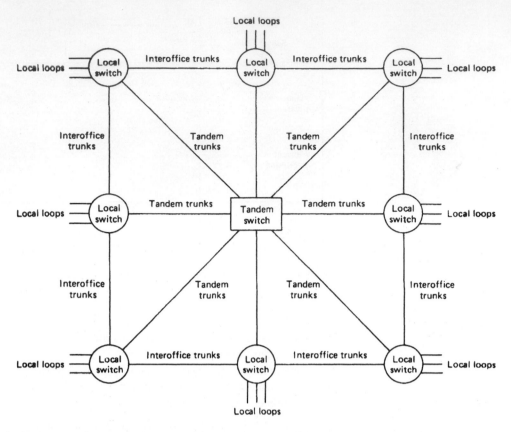

FIGURE 13-23 Community telephone system showing the use of a tandem switch to facilitate interzone calling

maintained as long as both loops remain closed. When either instrument goes on-hook, the signal path is interrupted.

What if the calling and the called telephone numbers are not served by the same dial switch? Generally, a community is served by only one local telephone company. The community is divided into zones; each zone is served by a different dial switch. The number of zones established in a given community is determined by the number of stations served and their density. If a subscriber in one zone wishes to call a station in another zone, a minimum of two dial switches are required. The calling station receives off-hook supervision and dial pulses are outputted as previously described. The dial switch in the calling zone recognizes that the prefix of the destination telephone number is served by a different dial switch. There are two ways that the serving dial switch can complete the call. It can locate a direct trunk (interoffice) circuit to the dial switch in the destination zone or it can route the call through a tandem switch. A *tandem switch* is a switcher's switch. It is a switching matrix used to interconnect dial switches. Trunk circuits that terminate in tandem switches are called *tandem trunks*. Normally, direct trunk circuits are provided only between adjacent zones. If a call must pass through more than one zone, a tandem switch must be used (Figure 13-23). If no direct trunks between the originating and the terminating dial switches exist and a common tandem switch is not available, the call is classified as a *toll call* and cannot be completed as dialed. Toll calls involve an additional charge and the dialed number must be preceded by a "1."

The telephone number prefix identifies which particular dial switch serves a station. With three digits, 1000 (000 to 999) prefixes can be generated for dial switches. A single

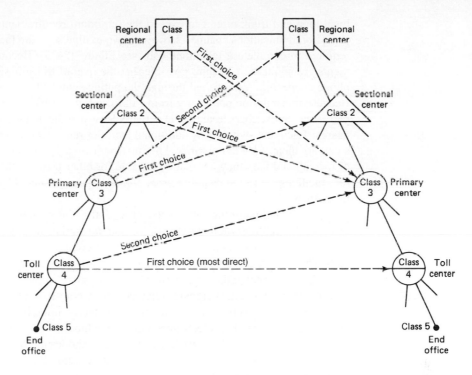

FIGURE 13-24 Public telephone switching hierarchy showing some possible route choices to complete a toll call between two end offices

metropolitan exchange alone may serve 20 to 30 prefixes. In the United States, there are over 20,000 local dial switches. It is obvious that further encoding is required to differentiate between the same prefix and extension in two different parts of the country. In the United States, an additional three-digit area code is assigned to each telephone number. The area code precedes the prefix but needs to be included only when calls are destined outside the area of the originating station. When a dialed telephone number is preceded by a "1," it is routed from the local dial switch to a toll switch by way of a *toll-connecting trunk.* Telco's present toll-switching plan includes five ranks or classes of switching centers. From highest to lowest classification, they are the regional center, sectional center, primary center, toll center, and end office. Local dial switches are classified as end (central) offices. All toll switches are capable of functioning as tandem switches to other toll switches.

The Telco switching plan includes a switching hierarchy that allows a certain degree of route selection when establishing a long-distance call (Figure 13-24). The choice is not offered the subscriber, but rather, the toll switches, using software translation, select the best route available at the time the call is made. The best route is not necessarily the shortest route. It is the route requiring the fewest number of dial switches. If a call cannot be completed because the necessary trunk circuits are not available, the local dial switch signals the calling station with an equipment busy signal. An equipment busy signal is similar to a station busy signal except that it repeats at a 120-ppm rate. The worst-case condition encountered when completing a long-distance call is when seven tandem toll (intertoll) trunks are required. Based on Telco statistics, the probability of this occurring is 1 in 100,000. Because software translations in the automatic switching machines permit the use of alternate routes, and each route includes many different trunk circuits, the probability of using the same facilities on identical calls is unlikely. This is an obvious disadvantage when using the PTN for data transmission because inconsistencies in the transmission parameters are introduced from call to call. Telco guarantees the transmission parameters of each local loop and trunk circuit to exceed the minimum requirements of a basic voice-grade (VG) communications channel. However, two to nine separate facilities in tandem may be required to complete a telephone call (see Figure 13-25). Because transmission impairments are additive, it is quite possible that the overall transmission parameters of a telephone connection, established through the public switched network, may be substandard. Because transmission paths vary from call to call, it is difficult to compensate for line impairments. Subscribers to the DDD network lease a dedicated loop from their station to the nearest Telco dial switch. Any additional facilities required for the subscribers to complete a call are theirs only temporarily. The subscriber uses these facilities only for the duration of the call and then they are made available for other users of the network. These temporary facilities are called *common usage trunks*—they are shared by all of the subscribers of the network.

The switching transients associated with the dial switches are another disadvantage of using the public switched network for data transmission. The older dial switches were electromechanical machines. Mechanical relay contacts were used to establish a signal path. The contact closures in the switching machines induced static interference that bled into adjacent signal paths. The static electricity caused impulse noise that produced transmission errors in the data signals. Telco is rapidly converting to *Electronic Switching Systems* (ESS). ESS machines are by no means perfectly quiet, but they are a tremendous improvement over the older electromechanical machines.

For a toll call to be completed, the dialed phone number must be transferred from switch to switch. Ultimately, the switching matrix at the destination end office requires the prefix and extension numbers to establish the final connection. The transmission paths between switching machines are very often carrier systems: microwave links, coaxial cables, or digital T-carriers. Microwave links and coaxial cables use analog carriers and are ac coupled. Therefore, the traditional dc supervisory and dial pulsing techniques cannot be used. An alternate method of transferring supervisory signals using a *single-frequency* (SF) *tone*

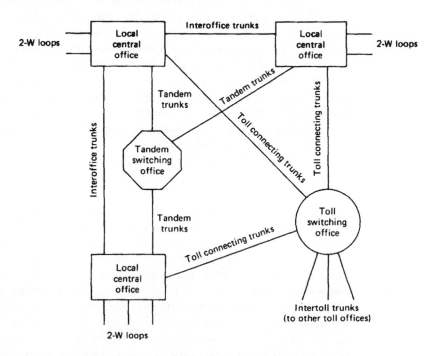

FIGURE 13-25 Typical switching layout showing relationship between local, tandem, and toll switches in the public telephone network

has been devised. An idle trunk circuit has a 2600-Hz SF tone present in both directions. An off-hook indication at either end is indicated by the removal of the SF tone. The receiving switch acknowledges the off-hook indication by removing the SF in the opposite direction. Two methods are available for dial pulsing. The SF tone can be pulsed on and off to represent the dialed number, or a signaling method called *multifrequency* (MF) *signaling* can be used. MF is a 2-of-6 code similar to touch tone; however, the MF tone frequencies are higher and are transmitted at a faster rate. Touch tone and MF are not compatible. Digital T-carriers use a completely different method for transferring supervisory information.

Private-Line Service

In addition to subscriptions to the public switched telephone network, Telco offers a comprehensive assortment of private-line services. Private-line subscribers lease those facilities required for a complete circuit. These facilities are hard-wired together in the Telco offices and are available only to one subscriber. Private-line circuits are *dedicated, private, leased* facilities. A dedicated circuit can be designed to meet voice-grade requirements from station to station—the end-to-end transmission parameters are fixed at the time the circuit is installed and will remain relatively constant. Circuit impairments will also remain relatively constant and can be compensated for by the subscriber. Private-line circuits afford several advantages over conventional dial-up circuits:

1. Availability
2. Improved performance
3. Greater reliability
4. Lower cost

Because private-line circuits are leased on a 24-hour basis, they are always available to the subscriber. Because the transmission parameters on a private-line circuit are guaranteed end to end, the overall performance is improved and a more reliable communications link is established. Heavy-usage private-line circuits are more economical than dial-ups; however, dial-ups are more cost effective for a person using the lines only a small percentage of the time.

Private-line circuit arrangements differ from dial-ups only in the fact that their circuits are permanently connected and dial switches and common-usage trunks are unnecessary. The terms "local loop" and "trunk" have a slightly different meaning to private-line subscribers. On a private-line circuit, a local loop is a transmission path between an instrument and the nearest Telco office; a trunk circuit is a transmission path between two Telco offices (see Figure 13-26). The only change in the definition is the substitution of "Telco office" for "dial switch."

Examples of private-line offerings are

1. Foreign exchange (FX)
2. Full data (FD)
3. Full period (FP)
4. Digital data service (DDS)

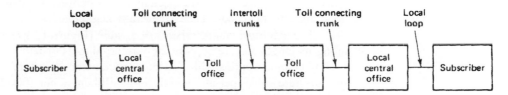

FIGURE 13-26 Simplified private-line circuit layout showing dedicated loops and trunks with hard-wired cross-connects in each Telco office (two-point circuit)

FX circuits differ from conventional DDD subscriptions only in the fact that subscribers, instead of leasing a dedicated loop to the nearest dial switch, lease a loop to a dial switch of their choice. This facilitates toll-free interzone calling to specific zones. FD circuits are four-wire, dedicated data circuits capable of full-duplex operation at a data rate of 9600 bps (bits per second). A local bank's system of automatic teller machines is an example of an FD circuit. FP circuits are four-wire, dedicated voice circuits. The hoot-and-holler (yell-down) circuits used by auto dismantlers (previously called "junkyards") to locate used auto parts is an example of an FP circuit.

THE TELEPHONE CIRCUIT

A *telephone circuit* consists of two or more facilities, interconnected in tandem, to provide a transmission path between a source and a destination. The interconnects may be temporary, as in a dial-up circuit, or permanent private-line circuits. The facilities may be cable pairs or carrier systems, and the information may be transferred on a coaxial, metallic, microwave, optic fiber, or satellite communications system. The information transferred is called the *message* and the circuit used is called the *message channel*. Telco offers a wide assortment of message channels ranging from a basic 4-kHz voice-band circuit to wideband (30-MHz) microwave channels that are capable of transferring high-resolution video signals. The following discussion will be limited to a basic voice-band circuit. In Telco terminology, the word *message* originally denoted speech information. This definition has been extended to include any standard voice-frequency signal. Thus, a message channel may include the transmission of speech, supervisory signaling, or voice-band data.

The Local Loop

The local loop is the only Telco facility required by all voice-band data circuits. It is the primary cause of attenuation distortion and phase distortion. A local loop is a metallic transmission line (cable pair), consisting of two insulated conductors twisted together. The insulating material may be wood pulp or polyethylene plastic; the wire conductor is usually copper and, in some instances, aluminum. Wire pairs are stranded together into units. Adjacent wire pairs within a unit are twisted with different pitch (twist length). This reduces the undesired effects of inductive coupling between pairs and helps to eliminate crosstalk. Units are cabled together into cores and then placed inside a plastic sheath. Depending on the insulating material used, sheaths contain between 6 and 900 pairs of wire. Sheaths are connected together and strung between distribution frames within Telco central offices and junction boxes located in manholes, back alleys, or telephone equipment rooms within large building complexes. The length of a subscriber loop depends on the station location relative to a local central telephone office.

The transmission characteristics of a cable pair depend on the wire diameter, conductor spacing, dielectric constant of the insulator, and the conductivity of the wire. These physical properties, in turn, determine the inductance, resistance, capacitance, and conductance of the line. The resistance and inductance are distributed along the length of the wire, whereas the conductance and capacitance exist between the two wires. If the insulation is good, the effect of conductance is generally negligible.

The electrical characteristics of a cable (Figure 13-27) are uniformly distributed along its length and are appropriately referred to as *distributed parameters*. Because it is cumbersome working with distributed parameters, it is common practice to lump them into discrete values per unit length (i.e., millihenrys per 1000 ft). The amount of attenuation and phase delay experienced by a signal propagating down a line is a function of the *frequency* of the signal and the *electrical characteristics* of the cable pair. Figure

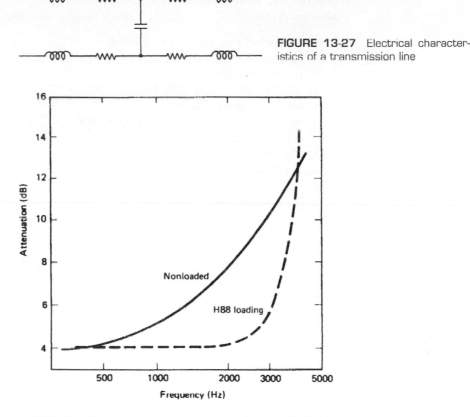

FIGURE 13-27 Electrical characteristics of a transmission line

FIGURE 13-28 Frequency versus attenuation for 12,000 ft of 26-gauge wire

13-28 illustrates the effect of frequency on attenuation for a given length of line. On this unloaded wire, a 3000-Hz signal suffers 6 dB more attenuation than a 500-Hz signal on the same line. The cable acts as a low-pass filter for the signal. Extensive studies of attenuation on cable pairs have shown that a reduction in attenuation can be achieved if inductors are added in series with the wire. This is called *loading*. Loaded cable is identified by the addition of the letters H, D, or B and an inductance value to the wire gauge number. H, D, and B indicate that the loading coils are separated by 6000 ft, 4500 ft, and 3000 ft, respectively. Generally, the amount of series inductance added is either 44 mH, 88 mH, or 135 mH. A cable pair with the designation 26H88 is made of 26-gauge wire with 88 mH of series inductance added every 6000 ft. If a loaded cable is used, a 3000-Hz signal will suffer only 1.5 dB more loss than a 500-Hz signal. Note that the loss-versus-frequency characteristics for a loaded cable are relatively flat up to approximately 2000 Hz.

The low-pass filter characteristics of a cable also affect the phase distortion-versus-frequency characteristics of a signal. The amount of *phase distortion* is proportional to the *length* and *gauge* of the wire. Loading a cable also affects the phase characteristics of a line. The telephone company must often add gain and delay equalizers to a circuit in order to achieve the minimum requirements. Equalizers introduce discontinuities or ripples in the bandpass characteristics of a circuit. Automatic equalizers in modems are sensitive to this condition and, very often, an overequalized circuit causes as many problems to a data signal as an underequalized circuit.

Transmission Parameters

Transmission parameters are divided into three broad categories:

1. Bandwidth parameters, which include
   (a) Attenuation distortion
   (b) Envelope delay distortion
2. Interface parameters, which include
   (a) Terminal impedance
   (b) In-band and out-of-band signal power
   (c) Test signal power
   (d) Ground isolation
3. Facility parameters, which include
   (a) Noise measurements
   (b) Frequency and phase distortion
   (c) Amplitude distortion
   (d) Nonlinear distortion

Bandwidth parameters. The only transmission parameters with limits specified by the Federal Communications Commission (FCC) are attenuation distortion and envelope delay. *Attenuation distortion* is the difference in circuit gain experienced at a particular frequency with respect to the circuit gain of a reference frequency. This characteristic is also called *frequency response, differential gain,* and *1004-Hz deviation. Envelope delay* is an indirect method of evaluating the phase delay characteristics of a circuit. FCC tariff number 260 specifies the limits for attenuation distortion and envelope delay distortion. The limits are prescribed by line conditioning requirements. Through line conditioning, the attenuation and delay characteristics of a circuit are artificially altered to meet prescribed limits. Line conditioning is available only to private-line subscribers for an additional monthly charge. The basic voice-band, 3002 channel satisfies the minimum line conditioning requirements.

Telco offers two types of line conditioning: C type and D type. *C-type conditioning* specifies the maximum limits for attenuation distortion and envelope delay distortion. *D-type conditioning* sets the minimum requirement for signal-to-noise ratio (S/N) and deals with nonlinear distortion.

D-type conditioning is referred to as high-performance conditioning and has two categories, D1 and D2. Limits imposed by D1 and D2 conditioning are identical. D1 conditioning is available for two-point circuits, and D2 conditioning is available for multipoint arrangements. D-type conditioned circuits must meet the following specifications:

1. Signal-to-C-notched noise: ≥ 28 dB
2. Nonlinear distortion
   (a) Signal-to-second order: ≥ 35 dB
   (b) Signal-to-third order: ≥ 40 dB

D-type conditioning is mandatory when the data transmission rate is 9600 bps. If a facility is assigned by Telco for use as a 9600-bps circuit, and it does not meet the minimum requirements of D-type conditioning, it is so identified by Telco data technical support personnel and never considered for that purpose again. A different facility is sought. A circuit cannot be upgraded to meet D-type conditioning requirements by adding corrective devices.

C-type conditioning pertains to line impairments for which compensation can be made, to a certain degree, by filters and equalizers. This is accomplished with Telco-provided equipment. When a circuit is turned up for service with a particular C-type conditioning, it must meet the minimum requirements for that type of conditioning. The subscriber may include devices within the station equipment that compensate for minor long-term variations in the bandwidth requirements.

TABLE 13-14 C-Type Bandwidth Parameter Limits

Channel Conditioning	Attenuation Distortion (Frequency Response) Relative to 1004 Hz		Envelope Delay Distortion	
	Frequency Range (Hz)	Variation (dB)	Frequency Range (Hz)	Variation (µs)
Basic	500–2500	+2 to −8	800–2600	1750
	300–3000	+3 to −12		
C1	1000–2400	+1 to −3	1000–2400	1000
	300–2700	+2 to −6	800–2600	1750
	300–3000	+3 to −12		
C2	500–2800	+1 to −3	1000–2600	500
	300–3000	+2 to −6	600–2600	1500
			500–2800	3000
C3 (access line)	500–2800	+.5 to −1.5	1000–2600	110
	300–3000	+.8 to −3	600–2600	300
			500–2800	650
C3 (trunk)	500–2800	+.5 to −1	1000–2600	80
	300–3000	−.8 to −2	600–2600	260
			500–2800	500
C4	500–3000	+2 to −3	1000–2600	300
	300–3200	+2 to −6	800–2800	500
			600–3000	1500
			500–3000	3000
C5	500–2800	+.5 to −1.5	1000–2600	100
	300–3000	+1 to −3	600–2600	300
			500–2800	600

There are five classifications of C-type conditioning.

1. C1 and C2 pertain to two-point and multipoint circuits.
2. C4 pertains to two-point circuits and multipoint arrangements that have a maximum of four station locations.
3. C5 specifications pertain only to two-point circuits.
4. C3 conditioning is for access lines and trunk circuits associated with private-switched networks.

Private-switched networks are telephone systems dedicated to a single customer, usually with a large number of stations. An example is a large corporation with offices and complexes at different geographical locations with an on-premises private branch exchange (PBX) at each location. A PBX is a low-capacity dial switch where the subscribers are generally limited to stations within the same building complex. Common-usage access lines and trunk circuits are required to interconnect the PBXs. They are common only to the subscribers of the private network and not to the entire public telephone network.

Table 13-14 shows the various limits prescribed by the different types of C-type conditioning on attenuation distortion and envelope delay. Figures 13-29 through 13-33 show a graphic presentation of several of the bandwidth parameter limits.

Attenuation Distortion and C-Type Conditioning. The attenuation distortion limits for a basic 3002 channel require the circuit gain at any frequency between 500 Hz and 2500 Hz to be not greater than 2 dB above the circuit gain at 1004 Hz and not more than 3 dB below the circuit gain at 1004 Hz (Figure 13-29). For attenuation distortion, the circuit gain at 1004 Hz is always used as the reference. Also, within the frequency bands from 300 Hz to 499 Hz and from 2501 Hz to 3000 Hz, the circuit gain cannot be greater than 3 dB above or more than 12 dB below the gain at 1004 Hz.

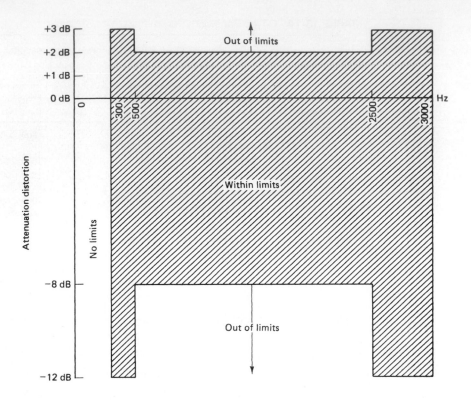

FIGURE 13-29 Graphic presentation of the limits for attenuation distortion in a basic 3002 channel

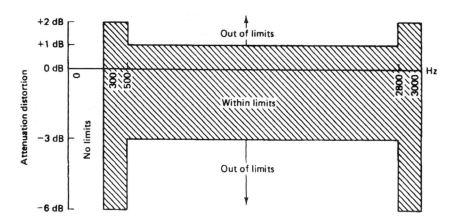

FIGURE 13-30 Graphic presentation of the limits for attenuation distortion on a channel with C2 conditioning

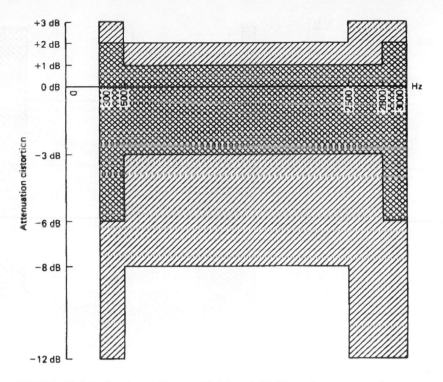

FIGURE 13-31 Overlay of Figures 13-29 and 13-30 to demonstrate the more stringent requirements imposed by C2 conditioning

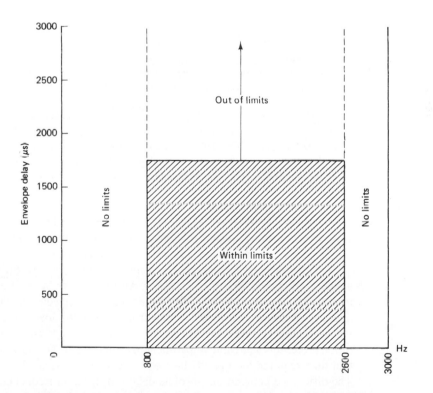

FIGURE 13-32 Graphic presentation of the limits for envelope delay in a basic 3002 channel

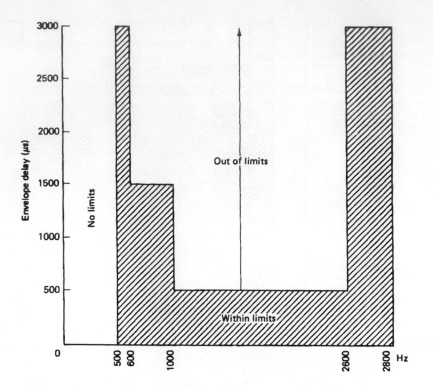

FIGURE 13-33 Graphic presentation of the limits for envelope delay on a channel with C2 conditioning

Example 13-6

A 1004-Hz test tone is transmitted at 0 dBm and received at −16 dBm. The circuit gain is −16 dB (this is actually a loss of 16 dB—negative dB values are negative gains, or losses). Frequencies from 500 Hz to 2500 Hz must be received at a minimum level of −24 dBm and at a maximum level of −14 dBm. Frequencies within the bands of 300 Hz to 499 Hz and 2501 Hz to 3000 Hz must be received at signal-strength levels between −13 dBm and −28 dBm, inclusive. If the same transmission levels were applied to a circuit with C2 conditioning, frequencies between 500 Hz and 2800 Hz must be received at signal levels ranging from −15 dBm to −19 dBm. Frequencies within the bands of 300 Hz to 499 Hz and 2801 Hz to 3000 Hz must be received at signal levels ranging from −14 dBm to −22 dBm. Table 13-14 shows that the higher the classification of conditioning imposed on a circuit, the flatter the frequency response, therefore, a better-quality circuit.

Envelope Delay. A linear phase-versus-frequency relationship is a requirement for error-free data transmission. This relationship is difficult to measure because of the difficulty in establishing a phase reference. Envelope delay is an alternate method of evaluating the phase-versus-frequency relationship of a circuit.

The time delay encountered by a signal as it propagates from source to destination is called *propagation time* or *phase delay*. All frequencies in the usable voice band (300 Hz to 3000 Hz) do not experience the same time delay in a circuit. Therefore, a complex frequency spectrum, such as the output from a modem, does not possess the same phase-versus-frequency characteristics when it is received as when it was transmitted. This condition represents a possible impairment to a data signal. The *absolute phase delay* is the actual time required for a particular frequency to be propagated from source to destination. The difference between the absolute delays of different frequencies is phase distortion. A graph of phase delay versus frequency for a typical circuit is nonlinear.

By definition, envelope delay is the first derivative of phase with respect to frequency:

$$\text{envelope delay} = \frac{d\phi(\omega)}{d\omega}$$

In actuality, envelope delay only closely approximates $d\phi(\omega)/d\omega$. Envelope delay measurements do not evaluate true phase-versus-frequency characteristics, but rather the phase of a wave that is the resultant of a narrow band of frequencies. It is a common misconception to confuse true phase distortion (also called delay distortion) with envelope delay distortion (EDD). *Envelope delay* is the time required to propagate a change in an AM envelope through a transmission medium. To measure envelope delay, a narrowband amplitude-modulated carrier, whose frequency is varied over the usable voice band, is transmitted. (The AM modulation rate is typically between 25 Hz and 100 Hz.) At the receiver, phase variations of the low-frequency envelopes are measured. The phase difference at the different carrier frequencies is *envelope delay distortion*. The carrier frequency that produces the minimum envelope delay is established as the reference and is normalized to zero. Therefore, EDD measurements yield only positive values and indicate the relative envelope delays of the various carrier frequencies with respect to the reference frequency. The reference frequency of a typical voice-band circuit is approximately 1800 Hz.

EDD measurements do not yield true phase delays, nor do they determine the relative relationships between true phase delays. EDD measurements are used to determine a close approximation of the relative phase delay characteristics of a circuit.

The EDD limit of a basic 3002 channel is 1750 μs between 800 Hz and 2600 Hz, as shown in Table 13-14. This indicates that the maximum difference in envelope delay between any two carrier frequencies in this range cannot exceed 1750 μs.

Example 13-7

An EDD test on a basic 3002 channel indicated that an 1800-Hz carrier experienced the minimum absolute delay of 400 μs. Therefore, it is the reference. The absolute envelope delay experienced by any frequency within the 800-Hz to 2600-Hz band cannot exceed 2150 (400 + 1750) μs.

The absolute time delay encountered by a signal between any two points in the continental United States will never exceed 100 ms, which is not sufficient to cause any problems. Consequently, relative rather than absolute values of envelope delay are measured. For the previous example, as long as EDD tests yielded relative values less than +1750 μs, the circuit is within limits.

Interface parameters.   The two primary considerations of the interface parameters are

1. Electrical protection of the telephone network and its personnel
2. Standardization of design arrangements

These considerations are summarized below. Station equipment impedances should be 600 Ω resistive over the usable voice band, and the station equipment should be isolated from ground by a minimum of 20 MΩ dc and 50 kΩ ac. The basic voice-grade telephone circuit is a 3002 channel; it has a usable bandwidth of 300 Hz to 3000 Hz. The circuit gain at 3000 Hz is 3 dB below the specified in-band signal power. The gain at 4 kHz must be at least 15 dB below the gain at 3 kHz. The maximum transmitted signal power for a private-line circuit is 0 dBm. The transmitted signal power for dial-up circuits is established for each loop so that the signal is received at the central Telco office at −12 dBm.

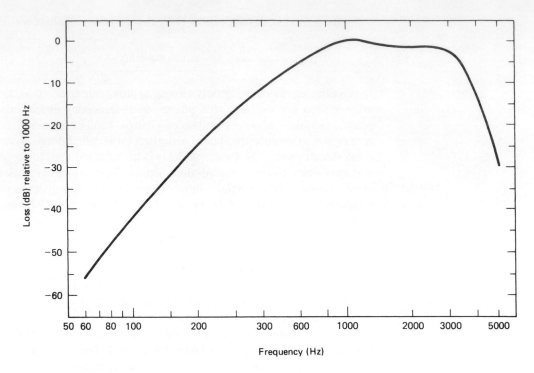

FIGURE 13-34 C-message weighting curve

Facility parameters. Facility parameters represent potential impairments to a data signal. These impairments are caused by Telco equipment and the limits specified pertain to all voice-band circuits regardless of conditioning.

1004-Hz Variation. Telco has established 1004 Hz as the standard test-tone frequency. The frequency 1004 Hz was selected because of its relative location in the passband of a standard voice-band circuit. The purpose of this test tone is to simulate the combined signal power of a standard voice-band transmission. The 1004-Hz channel loss for a private-line circuit is 16 dB. A 1004-Hz test tone applied to the transmit local loop at 0 dBm should appear at the output of the destination loop at −16 dBm. Long-term variations in the gain of the transmission facilities should not exceed ±4 dB; the received signal power must be within the limits of −12 dBm to 220 dBm.

Noise. Noise can be generally defined as any undesired energy present in the usable passband of a communication channel. The noise is either correlated or uncorrelated. *Correlation* implies a relationship between the signal and the noise. Uncorrelated noise is energy present in the absence of a signal such as thermal noise. Correlated noise is unwanted energy that is present as a direct result of the signal, such as nonlinear distortion.

Noise Weighting. Signal interference by noise is categorized in terms of annoyance or intelligibility. Noise may be annoying to the listener but not to the degree that the conversation cannot be understood. Western Electric Company conducted experiments in which groups of listeners were asked to rate the annoyance caused by 14 different audible frequencies between 180 Hz and 3500 Hz. These frequencies were presented to the listeners on a standard 500-type telephone (the old black dialer that Grandma had). The listeners first compared the annoyance of each frequency to the annoyance of a reference frequency of 1000 Hz in the absence of speech power. Then the same experiments were repeated with speech present. The results of the two tests were averaged and smoothed to produce the *C-message weighting curve.* This curve is shown in Figure 13-34.

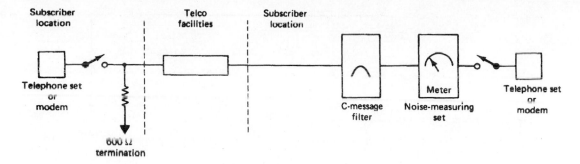

FIGURE 13-35 Terminated C-message noise test

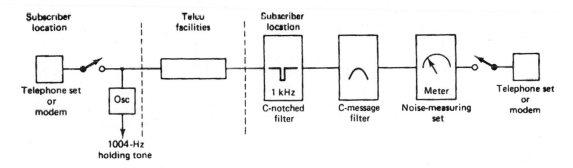

FIGURE 13-36 C-notched noise test

C-message noise is significant because it indicates the passband characteristics that should be considered when conducting noise tests on voice-band communications circuits. The frequencies from 600 Hz to 3000 Hz proved to be the most annoying and, as the frequency decreased below 600 Hz, the annoyance factor also decreased. Because of these results, C-message filters were developed that have a response similar to the C-message weighting curve. These filters increase the attenuation of the noise power at frequencies below 600 Hz and above 3000 Hz, but they have a relatively flat response to noise power within the 600-Hz to 3000-Hz passband. This response makes the measured strength of the noise frequencies proportional to the amount of annoyance they produce. These filters are inserted in noise-measuring sets at a point just before where the noise power is measured. The noise-measuring set then evaluates the noise in a manner similar to the human ear. The human ear cannot appreciate the true rms power of sound if the duration of the sound is 200 ms or less. Therefore, a noise-measuring set for voice circuits includes a 200-ms time constant that prevents them from reacting to short bursts of noise power. What significance does C-message weighting have on data circuits? Typical voice-band data modems exhibit an output frequency spectrum that concentrates most of the transmitted signal power in the 600-Hz to 3000-Hz band. Because a C-message filter has a relatively flat frequency response over this range, noise measurements with this type of filter are valid for data applications also.

C-Message Noise. C-message noise measurements determine the average continuous rms noise power. This noise is commonly referred to as background, white, thermal, or Gaussian noise. This noise is inherently present in a circuit due to the electrical makeup of the circuit. Because white noise is additive, its magnitude is dependent, in part, on the electrical length of the circuit. C-message noise measurements are the terminated rms power readings at the receive end of a circuit with the transmit end terminated in the characteristic impedance of the telephone line (see Figure 13-35). There is a disadvantage in

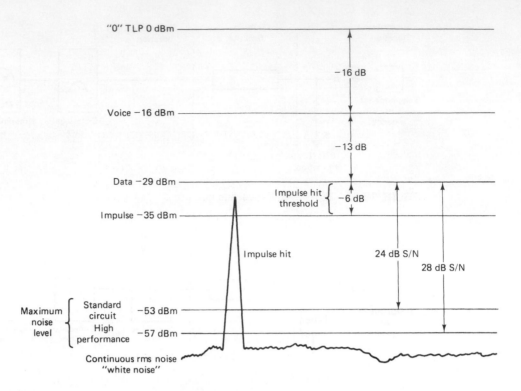

FIGURE 13-37 C-notched and impulse noise

measuring noise this way. The overall circuit characteristics, in the absence of a signal, are not necessarily the same as when a signal is present. The use of companders and automatic gain devices in the circuit causes this difference. Companders are devices that exhibit frequency-dependent gain characteristics (companders are explained in detail in Chapter 15). For this reason C-notched noise measurements were developed.

C-notched noise measurements differ from standard C-message noise measurements only in the fact that a holding tone (usually 1004 Hz or 2804 Hz) is applied to the transmit end of the circuit during the test. The holding tone ensures that the circuit operation simulates a loaded voice or data transmission. "Loaded" is a communications term that indicates the presence of a signal power comparable to the power of an actual message transmission. The holding tone is filtered (notched out) in the noise-measuring set prior to the C-message filter. The bandpass characteristics of the notch filter are such that only the holding tone is removed. The noise power in the usable passband is measured with a standard C-message noise-measuring set. This test (Figure 13-36) ensures that the noise readings obtained actually reflect the loaded circuit characteristics of a normal voice-band transmission.

The physical makeup of a private-line data circuit may require the use of several trunk circuits in tandem. Each individual trunk may be an analog, digital, companded, or a non-companded facility. Various combinations of these facilities may be used to configure a circuit. Telco has established realistic C-notched noise requirements for each type of facility for various trunk lengths. These requirements assist Telco in evaluating the performance of a facility and in expediting trouble-isolation procedures. A subscriber to the telephone network need only be concerned with the overall (end-to-end) C-notched noise requirement. Standard private-line data circuits, operating at less than 9600 bps, require a minimum

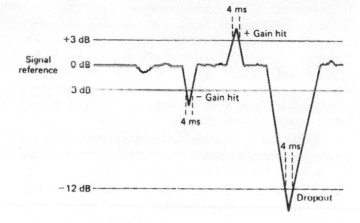

FIGURE 13-38 Gain hits and dropouts

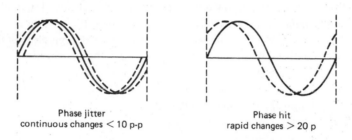

Phase jitter
continuous changes < 10 p-p

Phase hit
rapid changes > 20 p

FIGURE 13-39 Phase distortion

signal-to-C-notched noise ratio of 24 dB. Data circuits operating at 9600 bps require a high-performance line with a minimum signal to C notched noise ratio of 28 dB.

Impulse Noise.   *Impulse noise* is characterized by high-amplitude peaks (impulses) of short duration in the total noise spectrum. The significance of impulse noise hits on data transmission has been a controversial topic. Telco has accepted the fact that the absolute magnitude of the impulse hit is not as important as the magnitude of the hit relative to the signal amplitude. Empirically, it has been determined that an impulse hit will not produce transmission errors in a data signal unless it comes within 6 dB of the signal level (see Figure 13-37). Hit counters are designed to register a maximum of seven counts per second. This produces a "dead" time of 143 ms between counts when additional impulse hits are not registered. Contemporary high-speed data formats transfer data in block form and whether one hit or many occur during a single block is unimportant. Any error within a block necessitates retransmission of the entire block. Counting additional impulses during the time of a single block does not correlate well with data transmission performance.

Impulse tests are performed by placing a 2804-Hz holding tone on the circuit to ensure loaded circuit characteristics. The counter records the number of hits in a prescribed time interval (usually 15 minutes). An impulse hit is typically less than 4 ms and never more than 10 ms in duration. Telco's limit for recordable impulse hits is 15 within a 15-minute time interval. This does not limit the number of hits to one per minute but rather limits the average to one per minute.

Gain Hits and Dropouts.   A *gain hit* is a sudden, random change in the gain of a circuit. Gain hits are classified as temporary variations in the gain exceeding ±3 dB, lasting more than 4 ms, and returning to the original value within 200 ms. The primary cause of a gain hit is that of transients caused by switching radio facilities in the normal course of a day. Atmospheric fades produce the necessity for switching radio facilities. A *dropout* is a decrease in circuit gain of more than 12 dB that lasts longer than 4 ms. Dropouts are characteristics of a temporary open-circuit condition and are caused by deep radio fades or Telco maintenance activities. Dropouts occur at a rate of approximately one per hour. Gain hits and dropouts (see Figure 13-38) are detected by monitoring the receive level of a 1004-Hz test tone.

Phase Hits. *Phase hits* (see Figure 13-39) are sudden, random changes in the phase of a transmitted signal. Phase hits are classified as temporary variations in the phase of a signal that last longer than 4 ms. Generally, phase hits are not recorded unless they exceed $\pm 20°$ peak. Phase hits, as gain hits, are caused by transients produced when radio facilities are switched.

Phase Jitter. *Phase jitter* (see Figure 13-39) is a form of incidental phase modulation—a continuous, uncontrolled variation in the zero crossings of a signal. Generally, a phase jitter occurs at less than a 300-Hz rate, and its primary cause is a low-frequency ac ripple in Telco power plant supplies. The number of power supplies required in a circuit is directly proportional to the number of trunk circuits and Telco offices that make up a message channel. Each trunk facility has a separate phase jitter specification. The maximum end-to-end phase jitter allowed is 10° peak-to-peak regardless of the number of radio links, cable facilities, or digital carrier spans used in the circuit. Limiting the number of trunk circuits is a primary design consideration for a data circuit. Phase jitter is measured by observing the zero crossings of a 1004-Hz test tone.

Single-Frequency Interference. *Single-frequency interference* is the presence of one or more continuous, unwanted tones within a message channel. The tones are called spurious tones and are often caused by crosstalk or cross modulation between different channels in a carrier system. Spurious tones are measured by terminating the transmit end of a circuit, then searching through the channel spectrum with a frequency-selective voltmeter or observing the channel passband with a spectrum analyzer. Spurious tones can produce the same undesired circuit behavior as white noise.

Frequency Shifts. Analog carrier systems used by the telephone companies operate single-sideband suppressed carrier (SSBSC) and, therefore, require coherent demodulation. In *coherent demodulation,* the frequency of the suppressed carrier must be recovered and reproduced exactly by the receiver. If this is not done, the demodulated signal will be offset in frequency by the difference between the transmit and the receive carrier frequencies. Frequency shift is measured by transmitting a 1004-Hz test tone and then measuring the frequency of the tone at the receiver.

Phase Intercept Distortion. *Phase intercept distortion* occurs in coherent SSBSC systems when the received carrier is not reinserted with the exact phase relationship to the received signal as the transmit carrier possessed. This impairment causes a constant phase shift to all frequencies. This impairment is of little concern with data modems that use frequency shift keying, differential phase-shift keying, or quadrature amplitude modulation. Because these are the more common methods of modulation, the telephone company has not set any limits on phase intercept distortion.

Nonlinear Distortion. Nonlinear distortion is an example of correlated noise. The noise caused by nonlinear distortion is in the form of additional tones present because of the nonlinear amplification of a signal—no signal, no noise! Nonlinear distortion produces distorted sine waves. Two classifications of nonlinear distortion are

1. *Harmonic distortion*—unwanted multiples of the transmitted frequencies
2. *Intermodulation distortion*—cross products (sums and differences) of the input frequencies

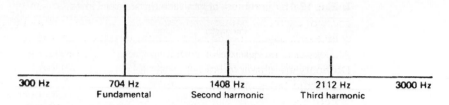

300 Hz	704 Hz	1408 Hz	2112 Hz	3000 Hz
	Fundamental	Second harmonic	Third harmonic	

FIGURE 13-40 Harmonic distortion

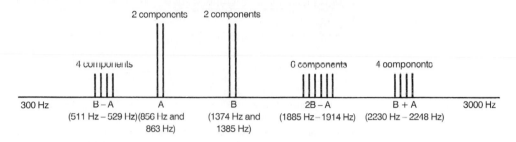

FIGURE 13-41 Nonlinear distortion

Harmonic and intermodulation distortion, if of sufficient amplitude, can cause a data signal to be destroyed. The degree of circuit nonlinearity can be measured using either harmonic or intermodulation distortion tests.

Harmonic distortion is measured by applying a single-frequency test tone to a data channel. At the receive end, the power of the fundamental, second, and third harmonic frequencies is measured. Harmonic distortion is classified as second, third, nth order or as total harmonic distortion. Generally, harmonics above the third extend beyond the passband of a voice-band channel and are of insufficient amplitude to be important. The actual amount of nonlinearity in a circuit is determined by comparing the power of the fundamental with the combined powers of the second and third harmonics. Harmonic distortion tests use a single-frequency (704-Hz) source (see Figure 13-40); therefore, no cross-product frequencies are produced.

Although simple harmonic distortion tests provide an accurate measurement of the nonlinear characteristics of an analog message channel, they are inadequate for digital (T-carrier) facilities. For this reason, a more refined method was developed that uses a multifrequency test-tone signal. Four test frequencies are used (see Figure 13-41): two designated the A band (A1 = 856 Hz, A2 = 863 Hz), and two designated the B band (B1 = 1374 Hz, B2 = 1385 Hz). The four frequencies are transmitted with equal power, and the total combined power is equal to that of a composite data signal. The nonlinear amplification of the circuit produces multiples of each frequency and also their cross products. For reasons beyond the scope of this text, the following second- and third-order products were selected for measurement: B + A, B − A, and 2B − A. The combined signal power of the four A and B band frequencies is compared with the second-order products and, then, compared with the third-order products. Harmonic and intermodulation distortion tests do not directly determine the amount of interference caused by nonlinear circuit gain. They serve as a figure of merit only when evaluating circuit parameters.

Peak-to-Average Ratio.   The difficulties encountered in measuring true phase distortion or envelope delay distortion led to the development of peak-to-average ratio (PAR) tests. A signal containing a series of distinctly shaped pulses with a high peak-to-average ratio (hence, the name) is transmitted. Delay distortion in a circuit has a tendency to spread

TABLE 13-15 Summary of Interface Parameter Limits

Parameter	Limit
1. Recommended impedance of terminal equipment	600 Ω resistive ± 10%
2. Recommended isolation to ground of terminal equipment	At least 20 MΩ dc At least 50 kΩ ac At least 1500 V rms breakdown voltage at 60 Hz
3. Data transmit signal power	0 dBm (3-s average)
4. In-band transmitted signal power	2450-Hz to 2750-Hz band should not exceed signal power in 800-Hz to 2450-Hz band
5. Out-of-band transmitted signal power *Above voice band:*	
(a) 3995 Hz–4005 Hz	At least 18 dB below maximum allowed in-band signal power
(b) 4 kHz–10 kHz band	Less than −16 dBm
(c) 10 kHz–25 kHz band	Less than −24 dBm
(d) 25 kHz–40 kHz band	Less than −36 dBm
(e) Above 40 kHz	Less than −50 dBm

Below voice band:
- (f) Rms current per conductor as specified by Telco, but never greater than 0.35 A.
- (g) Magnitude of peak conductor-to-ground voltage not to exceed 70 V.
- (h) Conductor-to-conductor voltage shall be such that conductor-to-ground voltage is not exceeded. For an underground signal source, the conductor-to-conductor limit is the same as the conductor-to-ground limit.
- (i) Total weighted rms voltage in band from 50 Hz to 300 Hz, not to exceed 100 V. Weighting factors for each frequency component (f) are: $f^2/10^4$ for f between 50 Hz and 100 Hz, and $f^{3.3}/10^{6.6}$ for f between 101 Hz and 300 Hz.

6. Maximum test signal power: same as transmitted data power.

the pulses and reduce the peak-to-average ratio. The received peak-to-average ratio is converted to a number between 0 and 100. The higher the number, the less the phase distortion. Peak-to-average tests do not indicate the exact amount of phase distortion present in a circuit; they only provide a figure of merit that can indicate the presence of a problem. Peak-to-average tests are less sensitive to attenuation distortion than envelope delay distortion tests and are easier to accomplish.

Tables 13-15 and 13-16 summarize the interface parameter limits and facility parameter limits discussed in this chapter.

Abbreviations associated with signal- and noise-level measurements

1. *dB (decibel).* Experiments indicate that a listener cannot give a reliable estimate of the loudness of a sound, but he can distinguish the difference in loudness between two sounds. The ear's sensitivity to a change in sound power follows a logarithmic rather than a linear scale, and the dB has become the unit of this change.

$$\text{dB} = 20 \log \frac{V_1}{V_2} \qquad \text{dB} = 20 \log \frac{I_1}{I_2} \qquad \text{dB} = 10 \log \frac{P_1}{P_2}$$

If the larger value is assigned to the numerator, the dB value will be positive. dB yields a relative value—the relative size of the numerator compared with the denominator.

2. *dBm*
   - (a) dBm is the dB in reference to 1 mW.
   - (b) dBm is a measure of absolute power.
   - (c) A 10-dBm signal is equal to 10 mW.
   - (d) A 20-dBm signal is equal to 100 mW.

TABLE 13-16 Summary of Facility Parameter Limits

Parameter	Limit		
1. 1004-Hz loss variation	Not more than ±4 dB long term		
2. C-message noise	Maximum rms noise at modem receiver (nominal −16 dBm point)		
Facility miles		*dBm*	*dBrncO*
0–50		−61	32
51–100		−59	34
101–400		−58	35
401–1000		−55	38
1001–1500		−54	39
1501–2500		−52	41
2501–4000		−50	43
4001–8000		−47	46
8001–16,000		−44	49
3. C-notched noise	(minimum values)		
(a) Standard voice-band channel	24-dB signal-to-C-notched noise		
(b) High-performance line	28-dB signal-to-C-notched noise		
4. Single-frequency interference	At least 3 dB below C-message noise limits		
5. Impulse noise			
Threshold with respect to	*Maximum counts above threshold*		
1004-Hz holding tone	*allowed in 15 minutes*		
0 dB	15		
+4 dB	9		
+8 dB	5		
6. Frequency shift	±5 Hz end to end		
7. Phase intercept distortion	No limits		
8. Phase jitter	No more than 10° peak to peak (end-to-end requirement)		
9. Nonlinear distortion			
(D-conditioned circuits only)			
Signal-to-second order	At least 35 dB		
Signal-to-third order	At least 40 dB		
10. Peak-average ratio	Reading of 50 minimum end to end with standard PAR meter		
11. Phase hits	8 or less in any 15-minute period greater than +20° peak		
12. Gain hits	8 or less in any 15-minute period greater than ±3 dB		
13. Dropouts	2 or less in any 15-minute period greater than 12 dB		

3. *TLP (transmission level point).* Knowing the signal power at any point in a system is relatively worthless. A signal at a particular point can be 10 dBm. Is this good or bad? This could be answered if it is known what the signal strength should be at that point. The TLP does just that. The reference for TLP is 0 dBm. A −15 dBm TLP indicates that, at this specified point, the signal should be −15 dBm. A 0 TLP is a TLP where the signal power should be 0 dBm. The TLP says nothing about the signal itself.

4. *dBmO.* dBmO is a power measurement adjusted to 0 dBm that indicates what the power would be if it were measured at 0 TLP. This value compares the actual signal at a point with what that signal should be at that point (TLP). A +4-dBm signal measured at a −16 dBm TLP is +20 dBmO. It is 20 dB stronger than the reference. A −2-dBm signal measured at a 10 dBm TLP is equal to 18 dBmO.

5. *rn (reference noise).* This value is the dB value used as noise reference. This value is *always* −90 dBm or 1 pW. This value is taken as the reference because the signal value at any point should never be less than this.

6. *dBrnc.* This is the dB value of noise with respect to reference noise with C-message weighting. The larger this value is, the worse the condition because of a larger amount of noise.

7. *dBrncO*. This is the amount of noise corrected to 0 TLP. The amount of noise at a point does not really indicate how detrimental its effect is on a given signal. 0.3 dBm of noise with a 20-dBm signal is insignificant; however, the same amount of noise with a 0.3-dBm signal strength may completely obscure the signal. Noise of 34 dBrnc at +7 dBm TLP yields a value of 27 dBrncO. dBrncO relates noise power reading (dBrnc) to 0 TLP. This unit establishes a common reference point throughout the system.

8. *DLP (data level point)*. This parameter is equivalent to the TLP as far as its function is concerned. It is used as a reference for data transmission. TLP is used as a reference for voice transmission. Whatever the TLP is, the DLP is always 13 dB below that value for the same point. If the TLP is -12 dBm, the DLP is -25 dBm for that same point. For example,

Noise $= -72$ dBm (noise, in all cases, will mean C-message noise)

Signal $= -27$ dBm at -24 dBm TLP

Find:

Signal _____ dBmO	answer -3
Noise _____ dBrnc	answer $+18$
Noise _____ dBrncO	answer $+42$
S/N_____ dB	answer $+45$

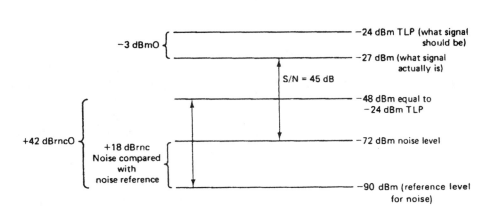

9. *dBrn*. This value is used only when there is excessive low-frequency noise and that noise is exceeding the levels specified in the interface parameters. Its value is measured with a device that has a 3-kHz flat filter (instead of a C-message filter) (see Figure 13-42). In normal circuits, dBrn is typically 1.5 dB above what would be read with a C-message filter.

DATA MODEMS

The primary purpose of a *data modem* is to interface computers, computer networks, and other digital terminal equipment to analog communication lines and radio channels. Often the analog communications lines are part of the public telephone network. Modems are also used when computers are too far apart to be interconnected using standard computer cables. The word *modem* is a contraction derived from the words *mo*dulator and *dem*modulator. In a modem transmitter, digital signals modulate an analog carrier, and in a receiving modem, analog signals are demodulated and converted into digital signals. A modem is sometimes called a DCE (data communications equipment), a data set, a dataphone, or simply a modem.

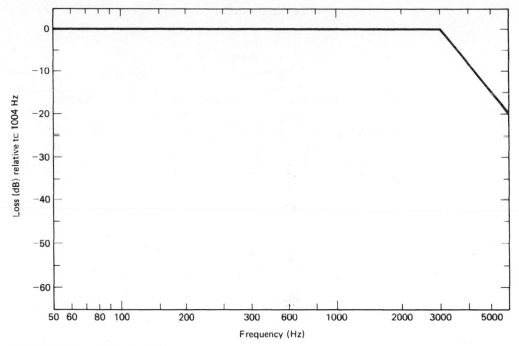

FIGURE 13-42 3-kHz flat filter

In essence, a modem is simply a repeater that converts electrical signals from a digital form to analog form and vice versa. A modem is physically located between a piece of digital computer equipment and an analog communications channel. At the transmit end of the data communications system, a modem accepts discrete digital pulses (which are usually in binary form) from a serial digital interface (such as the RS-232) and converts them to continuously changing analog signals. The analog signals are then outputted onto an analog communications channel where they are transferred through the system to a distant destination. At the destination or receive end of a data communications system, a modem accepts analog signals from the communications channel and converts them to digital pulses. The digital pulses are then outputted onto a serial digital interface.

Modems are generally classified as either asynchronous or synchronous and use one of the following modulation techniques: amplitude shift keying (ASK), frequency shift keying (FSK), phase shift keying (PSK), or quadrature amplitude modulation (QAM). With synchronous modems, clocking information is recovered in the receiver, but with asynchronous modems it is not. Asynchronous modems generally use ASK or FSK and are restricted to relatively low-speed applications (generally below 2.4 kbps). Synchronous modems use PSK and QAM and are used for medium- and high-speed applications (up to 57.6 kbps).

Asynchronous Modems

At one time, the Bell System dominated the modem market. Consequently, the operating parameters for the various Bell modems are the standards from which modern international standards specified by the CCITT have evolved. The CCITT is now called the International Standards Union—Telecommunication Standardization Sector (ITU-TS).

Asynchronous modems are used primarily for low-speed data circuits. There are several standard modem designs commonly used for low-speed asynchronous data transmission. For half-duplex operation using the two-wire public telephone network or full-duplex operation over four-wire, dedicated private-line circuits, the Bell System 202T/S modem or

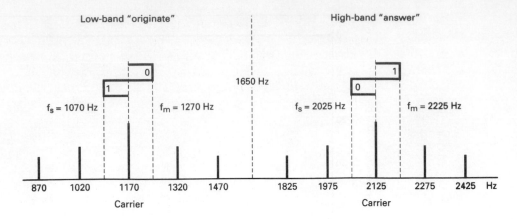

FIGURE 13-43 Output spectrum for a 103 modem. Carrier frequency: low band = 1170, high band = 2125; input data = 300 bps alternating 1/0 sequence

equivalent is a popular standard. The 202T standard specifies four-wire, full-duplex operation and the 202S standard specifies two-wire, half-duplex operation.

The 202T modem is an asynchronous transceiver utilizing frequency shift keying. It uses a 1700-Hz carrier that can be shifted at a maximum rate of 1200 times a second. When a logic 1 (mark) is applied to the modulator, the carrier is shifted down 500 Hz, to 1200 Hz. When a logic 0 (space) is applied, the carrier is shifted up 500 Hz, to 2200 Hz. Consequently, as the data input signal alternates between 1 and 0, the carrier is shifted back and forth between 1200 and 2200 Hz, respectively. This process can be related to conventional frequency modulation. The difference between the mark and space frequencies (1200 Hz to 2200 Hz) is the peak-to-peak frequency deviation, and the rate of change of the digital input signal (bit rate) is equal to twice the frequency of the modulating signal. Therefore, for the worst-case situation, the 1700-Hz carrier is frequency modulated by a 1200-Hz square wave.

To operate full duplex with a two-wire dial-up circuit, it is necessary to divide the usable bandwidth of a voice-band circuit in half, creating two equal-capacity data channels. A popular modem that does this is the Bell System 103 or equivalent. The 103 modem is capable of full-duplex operation over a two-wire line at bit rates up to 300 bps. With the 103 modem, there are two data channels each with separate mark and space frequencies. One channel is the *low-band channel* and occupies a passband from 300 Hz to 1650 Hz. The second channel is the *high-band channel* and occupies a passband from 1650 Hz to 3000 Hz. The mark and space frequencies for the low-band channel are 1270 Hz and 1070 Hz, respectively. The mark and space frequencies for the high-band channel are 2225 Hz and 2025 Hz, respectively. The frequency spectrum for a 103 modem is shown in Figure 13-43. The high- and low-band data channels occupy different frequency bands and, therefore, can use the same two-wire facility without interfering with each other. This is called *frequency-division multiplexing* and is explained in detail in Chapter 17.

The low-band channel is commonly called the *originate channel* and the high-band channel is called the *answer channel*. It is standard procedure on a dial-up circuit for the station that originates the call to transmit on the low-band frequencies and receive on the high-band frequencies, and the station that answers the call to transmit on the high-band frequencies and receive on the low-band frequencies.

Synchronous Modems
Synchronous modems are used for medium- and high-speed data transmission and use either PSK or QAM modulation. With synchronous modems the transmit clock, together with the data, digitally modulate an analog carrier. The modulated carrier is transmitted to the

receive modem, where a coherent carrier is recovered and used to demodulate the data. The transmit clock is recovered from the data and used to clock the received data into the DTE. Because of the clock and carrier recovery circuits, a synchronous modem is more complicated and, thus, more expensive than its asynchronous counterpart.

PSK modulation is used for medium-speed (2400 bps to 4800 bps) synchronous modems. More specifically, QPSK is used with 2400-bps modems and 8-PSK is used with 4800-bps modems. QPSK has a bandwidth efficiency of 2 bps/Hz; therefore, the baud rate and minimum bandwidth for a 2400-bps synchronous modem are 1200 baud and 1200 Hz. The standard 2400-bps synchronous modem is the Bell System 201C or equivalent. The 201C uses a 1600-Hz carrier and has an output spectrum that extends from 1000 Hz to 2200 Hz. 8-PSK has a bandwidth efficiency of 3 bps/Hz; therefore, the baud rate and minimum bandwidth for 4800-bps synchronous modems are 1600 baud and 1600 Hz. The standard 4800-bps synchronous modem is the Bell System 208A or equivalent. The 208A also uses a 1600-Hz carrier but has an output spectrum that extends from 800 Hz to 2400 Hz. Both the 201C and 208A are full-duplex modems designed to be used with four-wire private-line circuits. The 201C and 208A can operate over two-wire dial-up circuits but only in the simplex mode. There are half-duplex two-wire versions of both models: the 201B and 208B.

High-speed synchronous modems operate at 9600 bps and use 16-QAM modulation. 16-QAM has a bandwidth efficiency of 4 bps/Hz; therefore, the baud rate and minimum bandwidth for 9600-bps synchronous modems are 2400 baud and 2400 Hz. The standard 9600-bps modem is the Bell System 209A or equivalent. The 209A uses a 1650-Hz carrier and has an output spectrum that extends from 450 Hz to 2850 Hz. The Bell System 209A is a four-wire synchronous modem designed to be used on full-duplex private line circuits. The 209B is the two-wire version designed for half-duplex dial-up circuits.

Normally, an asynchronous data format is used with asynchronous modems and a synchronous data format is used with synchronous modems. However, asynchronous data are occasionally used with synchronous modems; this is called *isochronous transmission.* Synchronous data are never used with asynchronous modems.

Table 13-17 summarizes the standard Bell System modems.

Modem Synchronization

During the RTS/CTS delay, the transmit modem outputs a special, internally generated bit pattern called the *training sequence.* This bit pattern is used to synchronize (train) the receive modem. Depending on the type of modulation, transmission bit rate, and the complexity of the modem, the training sequence accomplishes one or more of the following functions in the receive modem:

1. Verify continuity (activate RLSD).
2. Initialize the descrambler circuits. (These circuits are used for clock recovery explained later in this section.)
3. Initialize the automatic equalizer. (These circuits compensate for telephone line impairments—explained later in this section.)
4. Synchronize the transmitter and receiver carrier oscillators.
5. Synchronize the transmitter and receiver clock oscillators.
6. Disable any echo suppressors in the circuit.
7. Establish the gain of any AGC amplifiers in the circuit.

Low-Speed Modems

Because low-speed modems are generally asynchronous and use noncoherent FSK, the transmit carrier and clock frequencies need not be recovered by the receive modem. Therefore, scrambler and descrambler circuits are unnecessary. The pre- and postequalization

TABLE 13-17 Bell System Modem Summary

Bell System Designation	Line Facility	Operating Mode	Wires	Synchronization	Modulation	Bit Rate (bps)
103	Dial-up	FDM/FDX	2	Async	FSK	300
113A/B	Dial-up	FDM/FDX	2	Async	FSK	300
201B	Dial-up	HDX	2	Sync	QPSK	2400
201C	Leased	FDX	4	Sync	QPSK	2400
202S	Dial-up	HDX	2	Async	FSK	1200
202T	Leased	FDX	4	Async	FSK	1800
208A	Leased	FDX	4	Sync	8-PSK	4800
208B	Dial-up	HDX	2	Sync	8-PSK	4800
209A	Leased	FDX	4	Sync	16-QAM	9600
209B	Dial-up	HDX	2	Sync	16-QAM	9600
212A	Dial-up	HDX	2	Async	FSK	600
212B	Leased	FDX	4	Sync	QPSK	1200

Dial-up—public telephone network
Leased—private-line circuit
FDM—frequency-division multiplexed
FDX—full-duplex
HDX—half-duplex
FSK—frequency shift keying
QPSK—quadrature phase shift keying
8-PSK—8-phase shift keying
16-QAM—16 quadrature-amplitude modulation

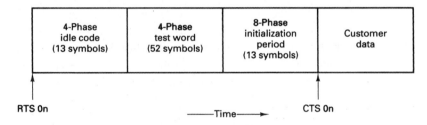

FIGURE 13-44 Training sequence for a 208 modem

circuits, if used, are generally manual and do not require initialization. The special bit pattern transmitted during the RTS/CTS delay is usually a constant string of 1s (idle line 1s) and is used to verify continuity, set the gain of the AGC amplifiers, and disable any echo suppressors in dial-up applications.

Medium- and High-Speed Modems

Medium- and high-speed modems are used where transmission rates of 2400 bps or more are required. To transmit at these higher bit rates, PSK or QAM modulation is used, which requires the receiver carrier oscillators to be at least frequency coherent (and possibly phase coherent). Because these modems are synchronous, clock timing recovery by the receive modem must be achieved. These modems contain *scrambler* and *descrambler circuits* and *adaptive (automatic) equalizers.*

Training. The type of modulation and encoding technique used determines the number of bits required and, therefore, the duration of the training sequence. The 208 modem is a synchronous, 4800-bps modem that uses 8-DPSK. The training sequence for this modem is shown in Figure 13-44. Each symbol represents three bits (one tribit) and is 0.625 ms in duration. The four-phase idle code sequences through four of the eight possible phase shifts. This

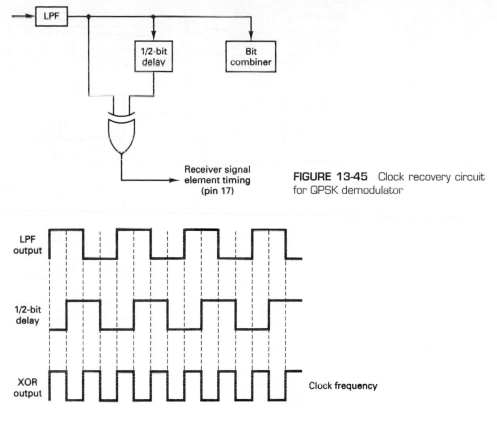

FIGURE 13-45 Clock recovery circuit for QPSK demodulator

FIGURE 13-46 Clock recovery from I (or Q) channel of a QPSK demodulator

allows the receiver to recover the carrier and the clock timing information rapidly. The four-phase test word allows the adaptive equalizer in the receive modem to adjust to its final setting. The eight-phase initialization period prepares the descrambler circuits for eight-phase operation. The entire training sequence (234 bits) requires 48.75 ms for transmission.

Clock recovery.   Although timing (clock) synchronization is first established during the training sequence, it must be maintained for the duration of the transmission. The clocking information can be extracted from either the I or the Q channel, or from the output of the bit combiner. If an alternating 1/0 pattern is assumed at the output of the LPF (Figure 13-45) a clock frequency at the bit rate of the I (or Q) channel can be recovered. The waveforms associated with Figure 13-45 are shown in Figure 13-46.

This clocking information is used to phase-lock loop the receive clock oscillator onto the transmitter clock frequency. To recover clocking information by this method successfully, there must be sufficient transitions in the received data stream. That these transitions will automatically occur cannot be assumed. In a QPSK system, an alternating 1/0 pattern applied to the transmit modulator produces a sequence of all 1s in the I or Q channel, and a sequence of all 0s in the opposite channel. A prolonged sequence of all 1s or all 0s applied to the transmit modulator would not provide any transitions in either the I, Q, or the composite received data stream. Restrictions could be placed on the customer's protocol and message format to prevent an undesirable bit sequence from occurring, but this is a poor solution to the problem.

Scramblers and descramblers.   A better method is to scramble the customer's data before the data modulate the carrier. The receiver circuitry must contain the corresponding descrambling algorithm to recover the original bit sequence before data are sent

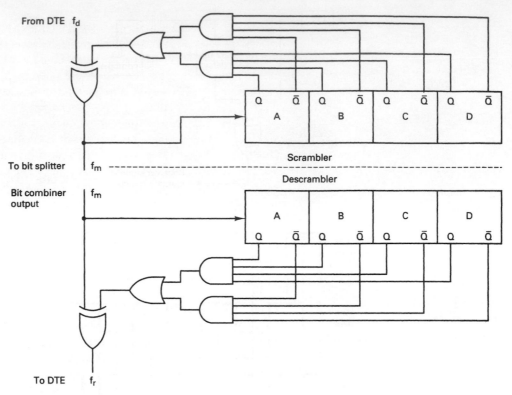

FIGURE 13-47 Scrambler and descrambler circuits

to the DTE. The purpose of a scrambler is not simply to randomize the transmitted bit sequence, but to detect the occurrence of an undesirable bit sequence and convert it to a more acceptable pattern.

A block diagram of a scrambler and descrambler circuit is shown in Figure 13-47. These circuits are incomplete because an additional gate would be required to detect a varying sequence that would create an all 1 or all 0 sequence in a modulator channel after the bits were split.

The scrambler circuit is inserted prior to the bit splitter in the QPSK modulator and the descrambler is inserted after the bit combiner in the QPSK demodulator. In general, the output of the scrambler or descrambler OR gate is A B C D + A′ B′ C′ D′.

$$f_m = f_d \oplus (A\,B\,C\,D + A'\,B'\,C'\,D') \qquad \text{top XOR gate}$$
$$f_r = f_m \oplus (A\,B\,C\,D + A'\,B'\,C'\,D') \qquad \text{bottom XOR gate}$$

Substituting for f_m in the second equation, we have

$$f_r = f_d \oplus (A\,B\,C\,D + A'\,B'\,C'\,D') \oplus (A\,B\,C\,D + A'\,B'\,C'\,D')$$

Because any identity XORed with itself yields 0,

$$f_r = f_d \oplus 0$$
$$f_r = f_d$$

This simply shows that the original transmitted data (f_d) will be fully recovered by the receiver.

The output of either OR gate will be a 1 if the four-bit register contains either all 1s or all 0s. Neither of these is a desirable sequence. If the OR gate output is a 1, f_m will be the complement (opposite) of f_d, or f_r will be the complement of f_m. The intent is to create transitions in a prolonged bit stream of either all 1s or all 0s. If the output of the OR gate is a 0, neither of these undesired conditions exists and $f_m = f_d$ or $f_r = f_m$: The data pass through the XOR gate unchanged. If the other logic gates (AND, OR, NAND, NOR) were used either alone or in combination in place of the XOR gates, the necessary transitions could be created in the scrambler circuit, but the original data could not be recovered in the descrambler circuit. If a long string of all 1s or all 0s is applied to the scrambler circuit, this circuit will introduce transitions; however, there may be times when the scrambler creates an undesired sequence. The XOR output is always either a 1 or a 0. No matter what the output of the OR gate, a value of f_d may be found to produce a 1 or a 0 at the XOR output. If either value for f_d was equiprobable, the scrambler circuit would be unnecessary. If the four-bit register contains all 1s, if $f_d = 1$, we would like to see it inverted. However, if $f_d = 0$, we would prefer to pass it through the XOR gate unchanged. The scrambler circuit for this situation inverts the 0 and extends the output string of 1s. It is beyond the intended scope of this book to delve deeply into all parameters involved in scrambler design. Let it be enough to say that scramblers will cure more problems than they create.

Equalizers. *Equalization* is the compensation for the phase delay distortion and amplitude distortion of a telephone line. One form of equalization is C-type conditioning. Additional equalization may be performed by the modems. *Compromise equalizers* are contained in the transmit section of the modem and they provide *preequalization*. They shape the transmitted signal by altering its delay and gain characteristics before it reaches the telephone line. It is an attempt to compensate for impairments anticipated in the bandwidth parameters of the line. When a modem is installed, the compromise equalizers are manually adjusted to provide the best *bit error rate* (BER). Typically, compromise equalizer settings affect

1. Amplitude only
2. Delay only
3. Amplitude and delay
4. Neither amplitude nor delay

The settings above may be applied to either the high- or low-voice-band frequencies or symmetrically to both at the same time. Once a compromise equalizer setting has been selected, it can only be changed manually. The setting that achieves the best BER is dependent on the electrical length of the circuit and the type of facilities that comprise it. *Adaptive equalizers* are located in the receiver section of the modem and provide *postequalization* to the received analog signal. Adaptive equalizers automatically adjust their gain and delay characteristics to compensate for telephone line impairments. An adaptive equalizer may determine the quality of the received signal within its own circuitry or it may acquire this information from the demodulator or descrambler circuits. Whichever the case, the adaptive equalizer may continuously vary its settings to achieve the best overall bandwidth characteristics for the circuit.

Modem Control—The AT Command Set

First-generation modems are often called *dumb modems* because they consisted of little more than a modulator and demodulator. Modems were originally designed to be used primarily on private-line data circuits, which made it awkward to use them on dial-up telephone circuits. Operators at both ends of the circuit were required to perform almost all the functions necessary to initiate, complete, and terminate a call. *Intelligent (smart)* modems were introduced in the early 1970s. Smart modems have built-in microprocessors that performed routine functions such as automatic answering, call initiating and dialing, busy signal recognition, and error correction. Smart modems are often controlled by other larger computers through a system of commands. The most common system of modem commands is the *AT command set,* which is also known as the *Hayes command set.* Hayes Microcomputer Products originally developed the AT command set for its own line of modems, but other manufacturers soon

TABLE 13-18 AT Command Set (Partial List)

Character(s)	Command
AT	Attention
A	Answer an incoming call
DT	Dial using DTMF tones
DP	Dial using pulse dialing
E0	Do not echo transmitted data to terminal screen
E1	Echo transmitted data to terminal screen
F0	Half-duplex communications
F1	Full-duplex communications
H	Go on-hook (hang up)
O	Switch from command to on-line mode
Z	Reset modem
+++	Escape code; switch from on-line to command mode

adopted the system and it rapidly became the de facto standard in the United States. Table 13-18 lists some of the most common AT commands.

AT command mode. All modem commands in the AT command set begin with the ASCII characters AT (ATtention). Whenever a modem is not communicating directly with another modem, it is in the *command mode*. In the command mode, the modem monitors information sent to it through the DTE by the local terminal looking for the ASCII characters AT. After detecting the AT sequence, the modem interprets the characters that immediately follow the AT as commands. For example, the ASCII character T is the command to use tones rather than dial pulses, and the ASCII character D is the command to dial. For example to dial the telephone number 1-(602)461-7777 the character sequence would be: ATDT16024617777.

AT on-line mode. Once communications have been established with a remote modem, the local modem switches to the *on-line mode*. In the on-line mode, a modem becomes transparent and interprets characters received from the DTE, including AT characters, as data. The local modem simply accepts the characters and allows them to modulate its carrier before sending them to a remote location. The local terminal can switch the modem from the on-line mode to the command mode, by momentarily pausing the transmission of data, sending three consecutive plus signs (+++), then pausing again. This sequence is called an *escape code*. In response to the escape code, the modem switches to the command mode and begins monitoring data for the ASCII AT command code.

CCITT Modem Recommendations

Since the late 1980s, the CCITT, which is part of the International Telecommunications Union (ITU) headquartered in Geneva, Switzerland, has developed transmission standards for data modems outside of the United States. The CCITT specifications are known as the V-series, which include a number indicating the standard (V.21, V.23, etc.). Sometimes the V-series is followed by the French word *bis,* meaning "second," and thus the standard is a revision of an earlier standard. If the standard includes the French word *terbo,* meaning "third," the bis standard also has been modified. CCITT standards V.21, V.23, and V.26 describe modem specifications similar to the Bell System 103, 202, and 201 modems, respectively. V.22 describes modem specifications similar to the Bell System 212A; and V.29 outlines specifications similar to the Bell System 209. Table 13-19 lists some of the CCITT modems and recommendations.

CCITT Modem Recommendation V.29

The CCITT V.29 specification is the first internationally accepted standard for a 9600-bps data transmission rate. The V.29 standard is intended to provide synchronous data

TABLE 13-19 CCITT V-Series Modem Standards

CCITT Designation	Specification
V.1	Defines binary 0/1 data bits as space/mark line conditions
V.2	Limits output power levels of modems used on telephone lines
V.4	Sequence of bits within a transmitted character
V.5	Standard synchronous signaling rates for dial-up telephone lines
V.6	Standard synchronous signaling rates for private leased communications lines
V.7	List of modem terminology in English, Spanish, and French
V.10	Unbalanced high-speed electrical interface specifications (similar to RS-423)
V.11	Balanced high-speed electrical interface specifications (similar to RS-422)
V.13	Simulated carrier control for full-duplex modem operating in the half-duplex mode
V.14	Asynchronous-to-synchronous conversion
V.15	Acoustical couplers
V.16	Electrocardiogram transmission over telephone lines
V.17	Application-specific modulation scheme for Group III fax (provides two-wire, half duplex trellis-coded transmission at 7.2 kbps, 9.6 kbps, 12 kbps, and 14.4 kbps).
V.19	Low-speed parallel data transmission using DTMF modems
V.20	Parallel data transmission modems
V.21	0-to-300 bps full-duplex two-wire modems similar to Bell System 103
V.22	1200/600 bps full-duplex modems for switched or dedicated lines
V.22bis	1200/2400 bps two-wire modems for switched or dedicated lines
V.23	1200/75 bps modems (host transmits 1200 bps and terminal transmits 75 bps). V.23 also supports 600 bps in the high channel speed. V.23 is similar to Bell System 202. V.23 is used in Europe to support some videotext applications.
V.24	Known in the United States as RS-232. V.24 defines only the functions of the interface circuits where as RS-232 also defines the electrical characteristics of the connectors.
V.25	Automatic answering equipment and parallel automatic dialing similar to Bell System 801 (defines the 2100-Hz answer tone that modems send)
V.25bis	Serial automatic calling and answering—CCITT equivalent to the Hayes AT command set used in the United States
V.26	2400-bps four-wire modems identical to Bell System 201 for four-wire leased lines
V.26bis	2400/1200 bps half-duplex modems similar to Bell System 201 for two-wire switched lines
V.26terbo	2400/1200 bps full-duplex modems for switched lines using echo canceling
V.27	4800 bps four-wire modems for four-wire leased lines. Similar to Bell System 208 with manual equalization
V.27bis	4800/2400 bps four-wire modems same as V.27 except with automatic equalization
V.28	Electrical characteristics for V.24
V.29	9600-bps four-wire full-duplex modems similar to Bell System 209 for leased lines.
V.31	Older electrical characteristics rarely used today
V.31bis	V.31 using optocouplers
V.32	9600/4800 bps full-duplex modems for switched or leased facilities
V.32bis	4.8-kbps, 7.2-kbps, 9.6-kbps, 12-kbps, and 14.4-kbps modems and rapid rate regeneration for full-duplex leased lines
V.32terbo	Same as V.32bis except with the addition of adaptive speed leveling which boosts transmission rates to as high as 21.6 kbps
V.33	12.2 kbps and 14.4 kbps for four-wire leased communications lines
V.34	(V. fast) 28.8-kbps data rates without compression
V.34+	Enhanced specifications of V.34
V.35	48-kbps four-wire modems (no longer used)
V.36	48-kbps four-wire full-duplex modems
V.37	72-kbps four-wire full-duplex modems
V.40	Method teletypes use to indicate parity errors
V.41	An older obsolete error-control scheme
V.42	Error-correcting procedures for modems using asynchronous-to-synchronous conversion (V.22, B.22bis, V.26terbo, V.32, and V.32bis, and LAP M protocol)
V.42bis	Lempel-Ziv-based data compression scheme used with V.42 LAP M
V.50	Standard limits for transmission quality for modems
V.51	Maintenance of international data circuits

TABLE 13-19 (*Continued*)

CCITT Destination	Specification
V.52	Apparatus for measuring distortion and error rates for data transmission
V.53	Impairment limits for data circuits
V.54	Loop test devices for modems
V.55	Impulse noise-measuring equipment
V.56	Comparative testing of modems
V.57	Comprehensive test set for high-speed data transmission
V.100	Interconnection between public data networks and public switched telephone networks
V.110	ISDN terminal adaption
V.120	ISDN terminal adaption with statistical multiplexing
V.230	General data communications interface, ISO layer 1

transmission over four-wire leased lines. V.29 uses 16-QAM modulation of a 1700-Hz carrier frequency. Data are clocked into the modem in groups of four bits called quadbits, resulting in a 2400-baud transmission rate. Occasionally, V.29-compatible modems are used in the half-duplex mode over two-wire switched telephone lines. Pseudo full-duplex operation can be achieved over the two-wire lines using a method called *ping-pong*. With ping-pong, data sent to the modem at each end of the circuit by their respective DTE are buffered and automatically exchanged over the data link by rapidly turning the carriers on and off in succession.

Pseudo full-duplex operation over a two-wire line can also be accomplished using *statistical duplexing*. Statistical duplexing utilizes a 300-bps reverse data channel. The reverse channel allows a data operator to enter keyboard data while simultaneously receiving a file from the distant modem. By monitoring the data buffers inside the modem, the direction of data transmission can be determined and the high- and low-speed channels can be reversed.

CCITT Modem Recommendation V.32

The CCITT V.32 specification provides for a 9600-bps data transmission rate with true full-duplex operation over four-wire leased private lines or two-wire switched telephone lines. V.32 also provides for data rates of 2400 bps and 4800 bps. V.32 specifies QAM with a carrier frequency of 1800 Hz. V.32 is similar to V.29, except with V.32 the advanced coding technique *trellis encoding* is specified (see Chapter 12). Trellis encoding produces a superior signal-to-noise ratio by dividing the incoming data stream into groups of five bits called *quintbits* (*M*-ary, where $M = 2^5 = 32$). The constellation diagram for 32-state trellis encoding was developed by Dr. Ungerboeck at IBM Zuerich Research Laboratory and combines coding and modulation to improve bit error performance. The basic idea behind trellis encoding is to introduce controlled redundancy which reduces channel error rates by doubling the number of signal points on the QAM constellation. The trellis encoding constellation used with V.32 is shown in Figure 13-48.

Full-duplex operation over two-wire switched telephone lines is achieved with V.32 using a technique called *echo cancellation*. Echo cancellation involves adding an inverted replica of the transmitted signal to the received signal. This allows the data transmitted from each modem to simultaneously use the same carrier frequency, modulation scheme, and bandwidth.

CCITT Modem Recommendation V.32bis and V.32terbo

CCITT recommendation V.32bis was introduced in 1991 and created a new benchmark for the data modem industry by allowing transmission bit rates of 14.4 kbps over standard voice-band telephone channels. V.32bis uses a 64-point signal constellation with each signaling condition representing six bits of data. The constellation diagram for V.32 is shown in Figure 13-49. The transmission bit rate for V.32 is 6 bits/code × 2400 codes/second = 14,400 bps. The signaling rate (baud) is 2400.

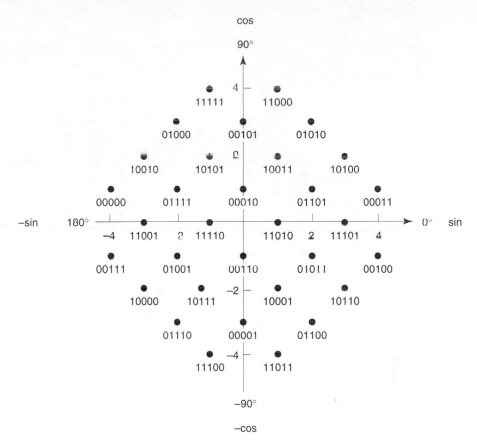

FIGURE 13-48 V.32 constellation diagram using Trellis encoding

V.32bis also includes automatic *fall forward* and *fall back* features which allow the modem to change its transmission rate to accommodate changes in the quality of the communications line. The fall back feature slowly reduces the transmission bit rate to 12.2 kbps, 9.6 kbps, or 4.8 kbps if the quality of the communications line degrades. The fall forward feature gives the modem the ability to return to the higher transmission rate when the quality of the communications channel improves. V.32bis support Group III fax, which is the transmission standard that outlines the connection procedures used between two fax machines or fax modems. V.32bis also specifies the data compression procedure used during transmissions.

In August 1993, U.S. robotics introduced V.32terbo. V.32terbo includes all the features of V.32bis plus a proprietary technology called *adaptive speed leveling*. V.32terbo includes two categories of new features: increased data rates and enhanced fax abilities. V.32terbo also outlines the new 19.2-kbps data transmission rate developed by AT&T.

CCITT Modem Recommendation V.33
CCITT specification V.33 is intended for modems that operate over dedicated two-point, private-line four-wire circuits. V.33 uses trellis coding and is similar to V.32 except a V.33 signaling element includes six information bits and one redundant bit resulting in a data transmission rate of 14.4 kbps, 2400 baud, and an 1800-Hz carrier. The 128-point constellation used with V.33 is shown in Figure 13-49.

CCITT Modem Recommendation V.42 and V.42bis
In 1988, the ITU adopted the V.42 standard *error-correcting procedures for DCEs* (modems). V.42 specifications address asynchronous-to-synchronous transmission conversions and

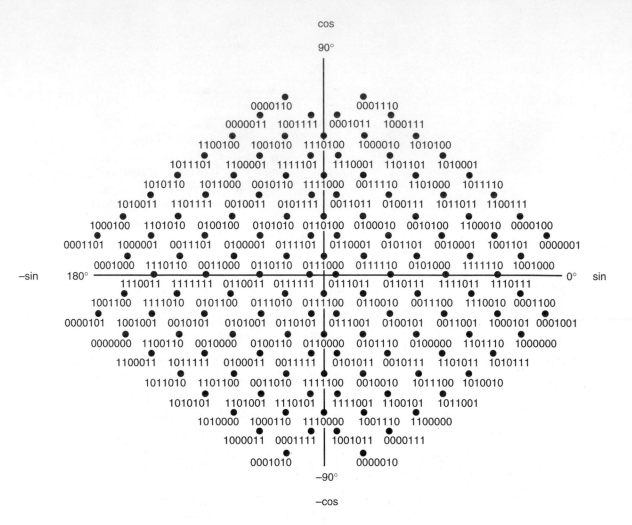

FIGURE 13-49 V.33 signal constellation diagram using Trellis encoding

error control which includes both detection and correction. V.42's primary purpose specifies a relatively new modem protocol called Link Access Procedures for Modems (LAP M). LAP M is almost identical to the packet-switching protocol used with the X.25 standard.

V.42bis is a specification designed to enhance the error-correcting capabilities of modems that implement the V.42 standard. Modems employing data compression schemes have proven to significantly surpass the data throughput performance of the predecessors. The V.42bis standard is capable of achieving somewhere between 3-to-1 and 4-to-1 compression ratios for ASCII-coded text. The compression algorithm specified is British Telecom's BTLZ. Throughput rates of up to 56 kbps can be achieved using V.42bis data compression.

CCITT Modem Recommendation V.32 (V.fast)

Officially adopted in 1994, V.fast is considered the next generation in data transmission. Data rates of 28.8 kbps without compression are possible using V.34. Using current data compression techniques, V.fast modems will be able to transmit data at two to three times current data rates. V.32 automatically adapts to changes in transmission-line characteristics and dynamically adjusts data rates either up or down depending on the quality of the communication channel.

V.34 innovations include:

1. Nonlinear coding which offsets the adverse effects of system nonlinearities that produce harmonic and intermodulation distortion and amplitude proportional noise.
2. Multidimensional coding and constellation shaping, which enhance data immunity to channel noise.
3. Reduced complexity in decoders found in receivers.
4. Precoding of data for more of the available bandwidth of the communications channel to be used by improving transmission of data in the outer limits of the channel where amplitude, frequency, and phase distortion are at their worst.
5. Line probing which is a technique that receive modems use to rapidly determine the best correction to compensate for transmission-line impairments.

CCITT Modem Recommendation V.34+

V.34+ is an enhanced standard adopted by the ITU in 1996. V.34+ adds 31.2 kbps and 33.6 kbps to the V.34 specification. Theoretically, V.34+ adds 17% to the transmission rate; however, it is not significant enough to warrant serious consideration at this time.

QUESTIONS

13-1. Define *data communications*.

13-2. What was the significance of the Carterfone decision?

13-3. Explain the difference between a two-point and a multipoint circuit.

13-4. What is a data communications topology?

13-5. Define the four transmission modes for data communications circuits?

13-6. Which of the four transmission modes can be used only with multipoint circuits?

13-7. Explain the differences between two-wire and four-wire circuits.

13-8. What is a data communications code? What are some of the other names for data communications codes?

13-9. What are the three types of characters used in data communications codes?

13-10. Which data communications code is the most powerful? Why?

13-11. What are the two general categories of error control? What is the difference between them?

13-12. Explain the following error detection techniques: redundancy, exact-count encoding, parity, vertical redundancy checking, longitudinal redundancy checking, and cyclic redundancy checking.

13-13. Which error detection technique is the simplest?

13-14. Which error detection technique is the most reliable?

13-15. Explain the following error correction techniques: symbol substitution, retransmission, and forward error correction.

13-16. Which error correction technique is designed to be used in a human environment?

13-17. Which error correction technique is the most reliable?

13-18. Define *character synchronization*.

13-19. Describe the asynchronous data format.

13-20. Describe the synchronous data format.

13-21. Which data format is best suited to long messages? Why?

13-22. What is a cluster?

13-23. Describe the functions of a control unit.

13-24. What is the purpose of the data modem?

13-25. What are the primary functions of the UART?

13-26. What is the maximum number of bits that can make up a single character with a UART?

13-27. What do the status signals RPE, RFE, and ROR indicate?

13-28. Why does the receive clock for a UART operate 16 times faster than the receive bit rate?

13-29. What are the major differences between a UART and a USRT?

13-30. What is the purpose of the serial interface?

13-31. What is the most prominent serial interface in the United States?

13-32. Why did the EIA establish the RS-232 interface?

13-33. What is the nominal maximum length for the RS-232 interface?

13-34. What are the four general classifications of pins on the RS-232 interface?

13-35. What is the maximum positive voltage that a driver will output?

13-36. Which classification of pins uses negative logic?

13-37. What is the primary difference between the RS-449A interface and the RS-232 interface?

13-38. Higher bit rates are possible with a *(balanced, unbalanced)* interface cable.

13-39. Who provides the most commonly used transmission medium for data communications circuits? Why?

13-40. Explain the differences between DDD circuits and private-line circuits.

13-41. Define the following terms: *local loop, trunk, common usage,* and *dial switch.*

13-42. What is a DCE?

13-43. What is the primary difference between a synchronous and an asynchronous modem?

13-44. What is necessary for full-duplex operation using a two-wire circuit?

13-45. What do *originate* and *answer mode* mean?

13-46. What modulation scheme is used for low-speed applications? For medium-speed applications? For high-speed applications?

13-47. Why are synchronous modems required for medium- and high-speed applications?

13-48. Higher frequencies generally suffer greater attenuation than lower frequencies when traveling through a given cable of a fixed length.   (T, F)

13-49. A loaded telephone cable identification number indicates three characteristics of that cable. What are they?

13-50. A metallic cable acts as what type of filter?

13-51. A cable is loaded by adding _____ in series with the wire.

13-52. 1004-Hz deviation is another name for envelope delay.   (T, F)

13-53. Dial-up lines may be conditioned.   (T, F)

13-54. What type of line has minimum conditioning?

13-55. D-type conditioning may be achieved by adding inductors in series to the line.   (T, F)

13-56. D-type conditioning is mandatory if the transmission rate is _____ bps.

13-57. Which frequency is used as the reference for attenuation distortion measurements when determining the type of conditioning?

13-58. Which frequency is used as the reference for envelope delay measurements when determining the type of conditioning?

13-59. All frequencies take the same time to propagate down a particular cable of fixed length.   (T, F)

13-60. In determining the amount of phase distortion, *(relative, absolute)* phase delay is the more important parameter.

13-61. A C4 conditioned line must meet *(more, less)* stringent requirements than a C2 conditioned line.

13-62. Phase distortion is caused by the fact that it takes different frequencies different times to propagate down a line.   (T, F)

13-63. Phase distortion is synonymous with delay distortion.   (T, F)

13-64. Delay distortion is synonymous with EDD.   (T, F)

13-65. The maximum allowed transmitted signal power for a dial-up circuit is always 2 mW. (T, F)

13-66. The maximum allowed transmitted signal power for a private-line circuit is _____ mW.

13-67. All voice-band frequencies suffer the same attenuation when passing through a C-message filter.   (T, F)

13-68. C-message filters are used in circuits to improve the signal-to-noise ratio.   (T, F)

13-69. What is the difference in measuring C-message noise and C-notched noise?

13-70. For a private line, what is the minimum signal-to-C-notched noise for
   (a) Transmission at less than 9600 bps?
   (b) 9600-bps transmission?

13-71. Empirical determinations are the results of mathematical proofs of theory.   (T, F)

13-72. Three impulse hits on a message block would necessitate a different action than a single impulse hit on the same block.   (T, F)

13-73. What is the difference between a gain hit and an impulse hit?

13-74. Name two types of nonlinear distortion.

13-75. What unit of measurement indicates the actual signal strength relative to what the signal strength should be?

13-76. What is the magnitude of noise, in dBm, that is used as the reference?

13-77. What is the unit of noise measurement that is corrected to 0 TLP?

13-78. Data transmission relates a signal strength to a DLP that is always _____ dB below the TLP?

13-79. What is the noise unit that is used to measure low-frequency noise?

PROBLEMS

13-1. Determine the LRC and VRC for the following message (use even parity for LRC and odd parity for VRC).

   D A T A sp C O M M U N I C A T I O N S

13-2. Determine the BCS for the following data- and CRC-generating polynomials.

$$G(x) = x^7 + x^4 + x^2 + x^0 = 1\ 0\ 0\ 1\ 0\ 1\ 0\ 1$$
$$P(x) = x^3 + x^4 + x^1 + x^0 = 1\ 1\ 0\ 0\ 1\ 1$$

13-3. How many Hamming bits are required for a single ASCII character?

13-4. Determine the Hamming bits for the ASCII character "B." Insert the Hamming bits into every other location starting at the left.

13-5. Determine the LRC and VRC for the following message (use even parity for LRC and odd parity for VRC).

```
P S S S                    E B P
A Y Y T A S C I I sp C O D E T C A
D N N X                    X C D
```

13-6. Determine the BSC for the following data- and CRC-generating polynomials:
$$G(x) = x^8 + x^5 + x^2 + x^0$$
$$P(x) = x^5 + x^4 + x^1 + x^0$$

13-7. How many Hamming bits are required for an ASCII character (1 start bit, 7 data bits, 1 parity bit, and 2 stop bits; 11 total bits)?

13-8. Determine the Hamming bits for the ASCII character "C" (use odd parity and two stop bits). Insert the Hamming bits into every other location starting at the right.

13-9. A cable is identified as 16D44. This indicates that _____ -mH inductors have been added in series every _____ feet to a _____-gauge wire.

13-10. A 1800-Hz signal takes 2 ms to propagate down a line. A 600-Hz signal takes 2.5 ms to travel down the same line. What is the absolute phase delay of the 600-Hz signal? What is the relative phase delay of this same signal?

13-11. A line has C4 conditioning. A 1004-Hz signal is received at −10 dBm and the propagation delay for a 1800-Hz signal is 5 ms. A signal frequency of 400 Hz can take no more than

_____ ms to travel down this line and its received signal strength must be between _____ dBm and _____ dBm.

13-12. Draw a graphic representation for attenuation distortion and envelope delay distortion for a channel with C4 conditioning.

13-13. Frequencies of 250 Hz and 1 kHz are applied to a C-message filter. Their difference in amplitude would be (_greater, the same, less_) at the output than at the input.

13-14. Dedicated lines are used to transmit data at 4800 bps. The received signal level is 500 μW. What is the maximum amount of C-notched noise allowed to satisfy D-type conditioning?

13-15. A C-message noise measurement taken at a -22 dBm TLP indicates -72 dBm of noise. A test tone is measured at the same TLP at -25 dBm. Determine the following levels.
  (a) Signal power relative to TLP (dBmO)
  (b) C-message noise relative to reference noise (dBrn)
  (c) C-message noise relative to reference noise adjusted to a 0 TLP (dBrncO)
  (d) Signal-to-noise ratio (dB)

13-16. A C-message noise measurement taken at -20 dBm TLP indicates a corrected reading of 43 dBrncO. A test tone at data level (O DLP)l is used to determine a signal-to-noise ratio of 30 dB. Determine the following levels.
  (a) Signal power relative to TLP (dBmO)
  (b) C-message noise relative to reference noise (dBrnc)
  (c) Actual test tone signal power level (dBm)
  (d) Actual C-message noise power level (dBm)

13-17. A test tone signal power of -62 dBm is measured at a -61 dBm TLP. The C-message noise is measured at the same TLP at -10 dBrnc. Determine the following levels.
  (a) C-message noise relative to reference noise at O TLP (dBrncO)
  (b) Actual C-message noise power level (dBm)
  (c) Signal power relative to TLP (dBmO)
  (d) Signal-to-noise ratio (dB)

C H A P T E R　14

Data Communications Protocols and Network Configurations

INTRODUCTION

The primary goal of *network architecture* is to give the users of the network the tools necessary for setting up the network and for performing data flow control. A network architecture outlines the way in which a data communications network is arranged or structured and generally includes the concept of *levels* or *layers* within the architecture. Each layer within the network consists of specific *protocols* or rules for communicating that perform a given set of functions.

Protocols are arrangements between people or processes. In essence, a protocol is a set of customs or regulations dealing with formality or precedence, such as diplomatic or military protocol. A *data communications network protocol* is a set of rules governing the orderly exchange of data within the network.

As stated previously, the function of a line control unit is to control the flow of data between the applications program and the remote terminals. Therefore, there must be a set of rules that govern how an LCU reacts to or initiates different types of transmissions. This set of rules is called a *data link protocol*. Essentially, a data link protocol is a set of procedures, including precise character sequences, that ensure an orderly exchange of data between two LCUs.

In a data communications circuit, the station that is presently transmitting is called the *master* and the receiving station is called the *slave*. In a centralized network, the primary station controls when each secondary station can transmit. When a secondary station is transmitting, it is the master and the primary station is now the slave. The role of master is temporary, and which station is master is delegated by the primary. Initially, the primary is master. The primary station solicits each secondary station, in turn, by *polling* it. A poll is an invitation from the primary to a secondary to transmit a message. Secondaries cannot poll a primary. When a primary polls a secondary, the primary is initiating a *line turnaround;* the polled secondary has been designated the master and must respond. If the primary *selects* a secondary, the secondary is identified as a receiver. A selection is an interrogation by the primary of a secondary to determine the secondary's status (i.e., ready to receive or not ready to receive a message). Secondary stations cannot select the primary. Transmissions from the primary go to all the secondaries; it is up to the secondary stations to individually decode each transmission and determine if it is intended for them. When a secondary transmits, it sends only to the primary.

Data link protocols are generally categorized as either asynchronous or synchronous. As a rule, asynchronous protocols use an asynchronous data format and asynchronous modems, whereas synchronous protocols use a synchronous data format and synchronous modems.

OPEN SYSTEMS INTERCONNECTION

The term *open systems interconnection* (OSI) is the name for a set of standards for communications among computers. The primary purpose of OSI standards is to serve as a structural guideline for exchanging information between computers, terminals, and networks. The OSI is endorsed by both the ISO and CCITT, which have worked together to establish a set of ISO standards and CCITT recommendations that are essentially identical. In 1983, the ISO and CCITT adopted a seven-layer communication architecture reference model. Each layer consists of specific protocols for communicating.

The ISO Protocol Hierarchy

The ISO–Open Systems Interconnection Seven-Layer Model is shown in Figure 14-1. This hierarchy was developed to facilitate the intercommunications of data processing equipment by separating network responsibilities into seven distinct layers. The basic concept of layering responsibilities is that each layer adds value to services provided by the sets of lower layers. In this way, the highest level is offered the full set of services needed to run a distributed data application.

There are several advantages to using a layered architecture for the OSI model. The different layers allow different computers to communicate at different levels. In addition,

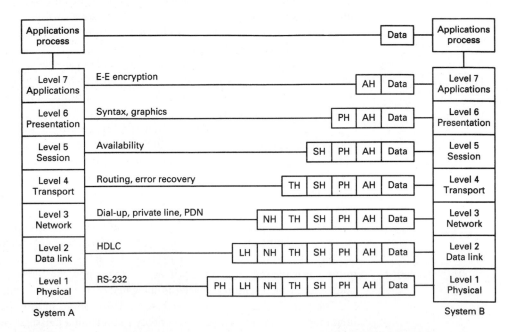

FIGURE 14-1 ISO international protocol hierarchy. AH, applications header; PH, presentation header; SH, session header; TH, transport header; NH, network header; LH, link header; PH, physical header

as technological advances occur, it is easier to modify one layer's protocol without having to modify all other layers. Each layer is essentially independent of every other layer. Therefore, many of the functions found in the lower layers have been removed entirely from software tasks and replaced with hardware. Some examples of these functions are shown in Figure 14-1. The primary disadvantage of the seven-layer architecture is the tremendous amount of overhead required in adding headers to the information being transmitted through the various layers. In fact, if all seven levels are addressed, less than 15% of the transmitted message is source information; the rest is overhead. The result of adding headers to each layer is illustrated in Figure 14-1.

Levels 4, 5, 6, and 7 allow for two host computers to communicate directly. The three bottom layers are concerned with the actual mechanics of moving data (at the bit level) from one machine to another. The basic services provided by each layer of the hierarchy are summarized below.

1. *Physical layer.* The physical layer is the lowest level of the hierarchy and specifies the physical, electrical, functional, and procedural standards for accessing the data communications network. Definitions such as maximum and minimum voltage levels and circuit impedances are made at the physical layer. The specifications outlined by the physical layer are similar to those specified by the EIA RS-232 serial interface standard.

2. *Data link layer.* The data link layer is responsible for communications between primary and secondary nodes within the network. The data link layer provides a means to activate, maintain, and deactivate the data link. The data link layer provides the final framing of the information envelope, facilitates the orderly flow of data between nodes, and allows for error detection and correction. Examples of data link protocols are IBM's bisynchronous communications (Bisync) and synchronous data link control (SDLC).

3. *Network layer.* The network layer determines which network configuration (dialup, leased, or packet) is most appropriate for the function provided by the network. The network layer also defines the mechanism in which messages are broken into data packets and routed from a sending node to a receiving node within a communications network.

4. *Transport layer.* The transport layer controls the end-to-end integrity of the message, which includes message routing, segmenting, and error recovery. The transport layer is the highest layer in terms of communications. Layers above the transport layer are not concerned with technological aspects of the network. The upper three layers address the applications aspects of the network, where the lower three layers address the message transfer. Thus, the transport layer acts as the interface between the network and the session layers.

5. *Session layer.* The session layer is responsible for network availability (i.e., buffer storage and processor capacity). Session responsibilities include network log-on and log-off procedures and user authentication. A session is a temporary condition that exists when data are actually in the process of being transferred and does not include procedures such as call establishment, setup, or disconnect procedures. The session layer determines the type of dialogue available (i.e., simplex, half duplex, or full duplex).

6. *Presentation layer.* The presentation layer addresses any code or syntax conversion necessary to present the data to the network in a common format for communications. Presentation functions include data file formatting, encoding (ASCII, EBCDIC, etc.), encryption and decryption of messages, dialogue procedures, data compression, synchronization, interruption, and termination. The presentation layer performs code and character set translation and determines the display mechanism for messages.

7. *Application layer.* The application layer is the highest layer in the hierarchy and is analogous to the general manager of the network. The application layer controls the sequence of activities within an application and also the sequence of events between the computer application and the user of another application. The application layer communicates directly with the user's application program.

DATA TRANSMISSION MODES

Data transmission modes describe how human-operated terminals transmit alpha/numeric data characters to host computers. Basically, there are only two transmission modes available: character and block.

Character Mode

When operating in the character mode, character codes are transmitted to the host computer immediately after a key has been depressed by an operator. The character is sent asynchronously because transmissions are not synchronized with the speed of the operator's keystrokes. When an operator is not typing, the terminal is in the *idle state*. Data characters transmitted from the host to the remote terminal are displayed on the screen at the current position of the cursor. Nondata characters (Bel, CR, LF, etc.) are acted on accordingly.

Block Mode

In the block mode of data transmission, characters are not transmitted immediately as they are typed. Instead, the operator enters characters into their terminals where they are stored in buffers and displayed on the screen. When the operator is ready to transmit the information displayed on the screen, he depresses the ENTER or RETURN key, which transmits all data characters entered into the local terminal. The assortment of characters transmitted as a group is called a *block* of data. The format used within the block depends on the system protocol selected. Most modern, smart terminals are capable of operating in either the character or block mode. The character mode of transmission is more common when terminals are communicating directly to the host through a direct communications connection, such as a dial-up telephone line. The block mode of transmission is more appropriate for multidrop data communications circuits operating in a polling environment.

ASYNCHRONOUS PROTOCOLS

Two of the most commonly used asynchronous data protocols are Western Electric's *selective calling system* (8A1/8B1) and IBM's *asynchronous data link protocol* (83B). In essence, these two protocols are the same set of procedures.

Asynchronous protocols are *character oriented.* That is, unique data link control characters such as end of transmission (EOT) and start of text (STX), no matter where they occur in a transmission, warrant the same action or perform the same function. For example, the end-of-transmission character used with ASCII is 04H. No matter when 04H is received by a secondary, the LCU is cleared and placed in the line monitor mode. Consequently, care must be taken to ensure that the bit sequences for data link control characters do not occur within a message unless they are intended to perform their designated data link functions. Vertical redundancy checking (parity) is the only type of error detection used with asynchronous protocols, and symbol substitution and ARQ (retransmission) are used for error correction. With asynchronous protocols, each secondary station is generally limited to a single terminal/printer pair. This station arrangement is called a *stand alone.* With the stand-alone configuration, all messages transmitted from or received on the terminal CRT are also written on the printer. Thus, the printer simply generates a hard copy of all transmissions.

In addition to the line monitoring mode, a remote station can be in any one of three operating modes: *transmit, receive,* and *local.* A secondary station is in the transmit mode whenever it has been designed master. In the transmit mode, the secondary can send formatted messages or acknowledgments. A secondary is in the receive mode whenever it has been selected by the primary. In the receive mode, the secondary can receive formatted messages from the primary. For a terminal operator to enter information into his or her computer terminal, the terminal must be in the local mode. A terminal can be placed in the local mode through software commands sent from the primary or the operator can do it manually from the keyboard.

The polling sequence for most asynchronous protocols is quite simple and usually encompasses sending one or two data link control characters, then a *station polling address.* A typical polling sequence is

```
E  D
O  C  A
T  3
```

The EOT character is the *clearing* character and always precedes the polling sequence. EOT places all the secondaries in the line monitor mode. When in the line monitor mode, a secondary station listens to the line for its polling or selection address. When DC3 immediately follows EOT, it indicates that the next character is a station polling address. For this example, the station polling address is the single ASCII character "A." Station A has been designated the master and must respond with either a formatted message or an acknowledgment. There are two acknowledgment sequences that may be transmitted in response to a poll. They are listed below with their functions.

Acknowledgment	Function
\ A C K	No message to transmit, ready to receive
\ \	No message to transmit, not ready to receive

The selection sequence, which is very similar to the polling sequence, is

```
E
O  X  Y
T
```

Again, the EOT character is transmitted first to ensure that all the secondary stations are in the line monitor mode. Following the EOT is a two-character selection address "X Y." Station XY has been selected by the primary and designated as a receiver. Once selected, a secondary station must respond with one of three acknowledgment sequences indicating its status. They are listed below with their functions.

Acknowledgment	Function
\ A C K	Ready to receive
\ \	Not ready to receive, terminal in local, or printer out of paper
* *	Not ready to receive, have a formatted message to transmit

More than one station can be selected simultaneously with *group* or *broadcast* addresses. Group addresses are used when the primary desires to select more than one but not all of the remote stations. There is a single broadcast address that is used to select simultaneously all the remote stations. With asynchronous protocols, acknowledgment procedures for group and broadcast selections are somewhat involved and for this reason are seldom used.

Messages transmitted from the primary and secondary use exactly the same data format. The format is as follows:

```
S                    E
T  message  data  O
X                    T
```

The preceding format is used by the secondary to transmit data to the primary in response to a poll. The STX and EOT characters frame the message. STX precedes the data and indicates that the message begins with the character that immediately follows it. The EOT character signals the end of the message and relinquishes the role of master to the primary. The same format is used when the primary transmits a message except that the STX and EOT characters have an additional function. The STX is a *blinding* character. Upon receipt of the STX character, all previously unselected stations are "blinded," which means that they ignore all transmissions except EOT. Consequently, the subsequent message transmitted by the primary is received only by the previously selected station. The unselected secondaries remain blinded until they receive an EOT character, at which time they will return to the line monitor mode and again listen to the line for their polling or selection addresses. STX and EOT are not part of the message; they are data link control characters and are inserted and deleted by the LCU.

Sometimes it is necessary or desirable to transmit coded data, in addition to the message, that are used only for data link management, such as date, time of message, message number, message priority, routing information, and so on. This bookkeeping information is not part of the message; it is overhead and is transmitted as *heading* information. To identify the heading, the message begins with a start-of-heading character (SOH). SOH is transmitted first, followed by the heading information, STX, then the message. The entire sequence is terminated with an EOT character. When a heading is included, STX terminates the heading and also indicates the beginning of the message. The format for transmitting heading information together with message data is

```
S               S                     E
0  heading  T  message data  0
H               X                     T
```

SYNCHRONOUS PROTOCOLS

With synchronous protocols, a secondary station can have more than a single terminal/printer pair. The group of devices is commonly called a *cluster*. A single LCU can serve a cluster with as many as 50 devices (terminals and printers). Synchronous protocols can be either character or bit oriented. The most commonly used character-oriented synchronous protocol is IBM's 3270 binary synchronous communications (BSC or bisync), and the most popular bit-oriented protocol (BOP) is IBM's synchronous data link control (SDLC).

IBM's Bisync Protocol

With bisync, each transmission is preceded by a unique SYN character: 16H for ASCII and 32H for EBCDIC. The SYN character places the receive USRT in the character or byte mode and prepares it to receive data in eight-bit groupings. With bisync, SYN characters are always transmitted in pairs (hence, the name *bisync*). Figure 14-2 shows the logic diagram for an even parity ASCII SYN character detection circuit. Received data are shifted serially through the detection circuit and monitored in groups of 16 bits looking for the occurrence of two successive SYN characters. When two successive SYN characters are detected the SYNC output signal goes active.

If eight successive bits are received in the middle of a message that are equivalent to a SYN character, they are ignored. For example, the characters A and b have the following hex and binary codes:

```
A = 41H = 0 1 0 0 0 0 0 1
b = 62H - 0 1 1 0 0 0 1 0
```

If the ASCII characters A and b occur successively during a message or heading, the following bit sequence occurs:

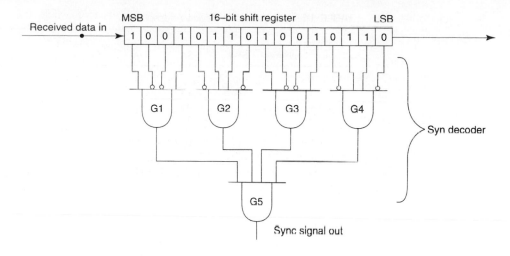

FIGURE 14-2   Bisync detector circuit

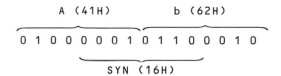

As you can see, it appears that a SYN character has been transmitted when actually it has not. To avoid this situation, SYN characters are always transmitted in pairs, and consequently, if only one is received, it is ignored. The likelihood of two false SYN characters occurring one immediately after the other is remote.

With synchronous protocols, the concepts of polling, selecting, and acknowledging are identical to those used with asynchronous protocols, except with bisync, group and broadcast selections are not allowed. There are two polling formats used with bisync: general and specific. The format for a general poll is

```
P S S E P S S S     E P
A Y Y O A Y Y P P " " N A
D N N T D N N A A     Q D
```

The PAD character at the beginning of the sequence is called a *leading* pad and is either a 55H or an AAH (01010101 or 10101010 binary). As you can see, a leading pad is simply a string of alternating 1s and 0s. The purpose of the leading pad is to ensure that transitions occur in the data prior to the actual message. The transitions are needed for clock recovery in the receive modem to maintain bit synchronization. Next, there are two SYN characters to establish character synchronization. The EOT character is again used as a clearing character and places all the secondary stations into the line monitor mode. The PAD character immediately following the second SYN character is simply a string of successive logic 1s that is used for a time fill, giving each of the secondary stations time to clear. The number of 1s transmitted during this time fill may not be a multiple of eight bits. Consequently, the two SYN characters are repeated to reestablish character synchronization. The SPA is not an ASCII or EBCDIC character. The letters SPA stand for *station polling address*. Each secondary station has a unique SPA. Two SPAs are transmitted for the purpose of error detection (redundancy). A secondary will not respond to a poll unless its SPA appears twice. The two quotation marks signify that the poll is for any device at that station that is in the send mode. If two or more devices are in the send mode when a general poll is received, the LCU determines which device's message is transmitted. The enquiry (ENQ) character is sometimes called a *format* or *line turnaround character,* because

TABLE 14-1 Station and Device Addresses

Station or Device Number	SPA	SSA	DA	Station or Device Number	SPA	SSA	DA
0	sp	-	sp	16	&	0	&
1	A	/	A	17	J	1	J
2	B	S	B	18	K	2	K
3	C	T	C	19	L	3	L
4	D	U	D	20	M	4	M
5	E	V	E	21	N	5	N
6	F	W	F	22	O	6	O
7	G	X	G	23	P	7	P
8	H	Y	H	24	Q	8	Q
9	I	Z	I	25	R	9	R
10	[	|	[	26	]	:	]
11	.	,	.	27	$	#	$
12	<	%	<	28	*	@	*
13	(	—	(	29	)	`	)
14	+	>	+	30	;	=	;
15	!	?	!	31	∧	"	∧

it completes the polling format and initiates a line turnaround (i.e., the secondary station identified by the SPA is designated master and must respond).

The PAD character at the end of the polling sequence is called a *trailing* pad and is simply a 7FH (DEL or delete character). The purpose of the trailing pad is to ensure that the RLSD signal in the receive modem is held active long enough for the entire received message to be demodulated. If the carrier were shut off immediately at the end of the message, RLSD would go inactive and disable the receive data pin. If the last character of the message were not completely demodulated, the end of it would be cut off.

The format for a specific poll is

```
P S S E P S S S       E P
A Y Y O A Y Y P P D D N A
D N N T D N N A A A A Q D
```

The character sequence for a specific poll is similar to that of a general poll except that the two DAs (*device addresses*) are substituted for the two quotation marks. With a specific poll, both the station and device addresses are included. Therefore, a specific poll is an invitation for a specific device at a given station to transmit its message. Again, two DAs are transmitted for redundancy error detection.

The character sequence for a selection is

```
P S S E P S S S       E P
A Y Y O A Y Y S S D D N A
D N N T D N N A A A A Q D
```

The sequence for a selection is similar to that of a specific poll except that two SSA characters are substituted for the two SPAs. SSA stands for "station select address." All selections are specific; they are for a specific device (device DA). Table 14-1 lists the SPAs, SSAs, and DAs for a network that can have a maximum of 32 stations and the LCU at each station can serve a 32-device cluster.

Example 14-1

Determine the character sequences for

(a) A general poll for station 8.
(b) A specific poll for device 6 at station 8.
(c) A selection of device 6 at station 8.

Solution   (a)   From Table 14-1 the SPA for station 8 is H; therefore, the sequence for a general poll is

```
P S S E P S S       E P
A Y Y O A Y Y H H " " N A
D N N T D N N       Q D
```

(b) From Table 14-1 the DA for device 6 is F; therefore, the sequence for a specific poll is

```
P S S E P S S       E P
A Y Y O A Y Y H H F F N A
D N N T D N N       Q D
```

(c) From Table 14-1 the SSA for station 8 is Y; therefore, the sequence for a selection is

```
P S S E P S S       E P
A Y Y O A Y Y Y Y F F N A
D N N T D N N       Q D
```

With bisync, there are only two ways in which a secondary can respond to a poll: with a formatted message or with a *handshake*. A handshake is simply a response from the secondary that indicates it has no formatted messages to transmit (i.e., a handshake is a negative acknowledgment to a poll). The character sequence for a handshake is

```
P S S E P
A Y Y O A
D N N T D
```

A secondary can respond to a selection with either a positive or a negative acknowledgment. A positive acknowledgment to a selection indicates that the device selected is ready to receive. The character sequence for a positive acknowledgment is

```
P S S D   P
A Y Y L 0 A
D N N E   D
```

A negative acknowledgment to a selection indicates that the device selected is not ready to receive. A negative acknowledgment is called a *reverse interrupt* (RVI). The character sequence for a RVI is

```
P S S D   P
A Y Y L < A
D N N E   D
```

With bisync, formatted messages are sent from a secondary to the primary in response to a poll and sent from the primary to a secondary after the secondary has been selected. Formatted messages use the following format:

```
P S S S               S         E B P
A Y Y 0 heading T message T C A
D N N H               X         X C D
```

Note: If CRC-16 is used for error detection, there are two block check characters.

Longitudinal redundancy checking (LRC) is used for error detection with ASCII-coded messages, and cyclic redundancy checking (CRC) is used for EBCDIC. The BCC is computed beginning with the first character after SOH and continues through and includes ETX. (If there is no heading, the BCC is computed beginning with the first character after STX.) With synchronous protocols, data are transmitted in blocks. Blocks of data are generally limited to 256 characters. ETX is used to terminate the last block of a message. ETB is used for multiple block messages to terminate all message blocks except the last one. The last block of a message is always terminated with ETX. All BCCs must be acknowledged by the receiving station. A positive acknowledgment indicates that the BCC was good and a negative acknowledgment means that the BCC was bad. A negative acknowledgment is an automatic request for retransmission. The character sequences for positive and negative acknowledgments are as follows:

Positive acknowledgment

```
P S S D   P       P S S D   P
A Y Y L 0 A  or   A Y Y L 1 A
D N N E   D       D N N E   D
   even-numbered      odd-numbered
      blocks             blocks
```

Negative acknowledgment

```
P S S N P
A Y Y A A
D N N K D
```

Transparency.   It is possible that a device that is attached to one of the ports of a station LCU is not a computer terminal or a printer—for example, a microprocessor-controlled monitor system that is used to monitor environmental conditions (temperature, humidity, etc.) or a security alarm system. If so, the data transferred between it and the applications program are not ASCII- or EBCDIC-encoded characters; they are microprocessor op-codes or binary-encoded data. Consequently, it is possible that an eight-bit sequence could occur in the message that is equivalent to a data link control character. For example, if the binary code 00000011 (03H) occurred in a message, the LCU would misinterpret it as the ASCII code for ETX. Consequently, the receive LCU would prematurely terminate the message and interpret the next eight-bit sequence as a BCC. To prevent this from occurring, the LCU is made *transparent* to the data. With bisync, a *data link escape* character (DLE) is used to achieve transparency. To place an LCU in the transparent mode, STX is preceded by a DLE. This causes the LCU to transfer the data to the selected device without searching through the message for data link control characters. To come out of the transparent mode, DLE ETX is transmitted. To transmit a DLE as part of the text, it must be preceded by DLE (i.e., DLE DLE). Actually, there are only five characters that it is necessary to precede with DLE:

1. *DLE STX*. Places the receive LCU into the transparent mode.
2. *DLE ETX*. Used to terminate the last block of transparent text and take the LCU out of the transparent mode.
3. *DLE ETB*. Used to terminate blocks of transparent text other than the final block.
4. *DLE ITB*. Used to terminate blocks of transparent text other than the final block when ITB is used for a block-terminating character.
5. *DLE SYN*. Used only with transparent messages that are more than 1 s long. With bisync, two SYN characters are inserted in the text entry to ensure that the receive LCU does not lose character synchronization. In a multipoint circuit with a polling environment, it is highly unlikely that any blocks of data would exceed 1 s in duration. SYN character insertion is used almost exclusively for two-point circuits.

Synchronous Data Link Communications

Synchronous data link communications (SDLC) is a synchronous *bit-oriented* protocol developed by IBM. A bit-oriented protocol (BOP) is a discipline for serial-by-bit information transfer over a data communication channel. With a BOP, data link control information is transferred and interpreted on a bit-by-bit basis rather than with unique data link control characters. SDLC can transfer data either simplex, half duplex, or full duplex. With a BOP, there is a single control field that performs essentially all the data link control functions.

F Flag 01111110	A Address	C Control	I Information	FCS Frame check sequence	F Flag 01111110
0 bits	8 bits	8 bits	Variable must be multiple of 8 bits	16 bits CRC-16	8 bits

←——— Span of CRC accumulation ——→

←——————————— Span of zero insertion ———————————→

FIGURE 14-3 SDLC frame format

The character language used with SDLC is EBCDIC and data are transferred in groups called *frames*. Frames are generally limited to 256 characters in length. There are two types of stations in SDLC: primary stations and secondary stations. The *primary station* controls data exchange on the communications channel and issues *commands*. The *secondary station* receives commands and returns *responses* to the primary.

There are three transmission states with SDLC: transient, idle, and active. The *transient state* exists before and after the initial transmission and after each line turnaround. An *idle state* is presumed after 15 or more consecutive 1s have been received. The *active state* exists whenever either the primary or a secondary station is transmitting information or control signals.

Figure 14-3 shows the frame format used with SDLC. The frames sent from the primary and the frames sent from a secondary use exactly the same format. There are five fields used with SDLC: the flag field, the address field, the control field, the text or information field, and the frame check field.

Information field. All information transmitted in an SDLC frame must be in the information field (I field), and the number of bits in the I field must be a multiple of 8. An I field is not allowed with all SDLC frames. The types of frames that allow an I field are discussed later.

Flag field. There are two flag fields per frame: the beginning flag and the ending flag. The flags are used for the *delimiting sequence* and to achieve character synchronization. The delimiting sequence sets the limits of the frame (i.e., when the frame begins and when it ends). The flag is used with SDLC in the same manner that SYN characters are used with bisync—to achieve character synchronization. The sequence for a flag is 7EH, 01111110 binary, or the EBCDIC character "=." There are several variations of how flags are used. They are

1. One beginning and one ending flag for each frame.

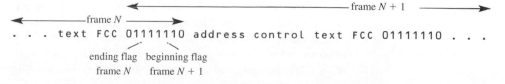

2. The ending flag from one frame can be used for the beginning flag for the next frame.

3. The last zero of an ending flag is also the first zero of the beginning flag of the next frame.

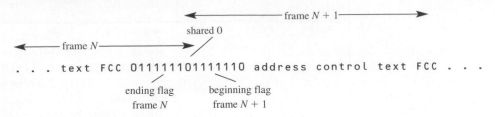

4. Flags are transmitted in lieu of idle line 1s.

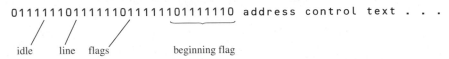

Address field. The address field has eight bits; thus, 256 addresses are possible with SDLC. The address 00H (00000000) is called the *null* or *void address* and is never assigned to a secondary. The null address is used for network testing. The address FFH (11111111) is the *broadcast address* and is common to all secondaries. The remaining 254 addresses can be used as *unique* station addresses or as *group* addresses. In frames sent from the primary, the address field contains the address of the destination station (a secondary). In frames sent from a secondary, the address field contains the address of that secondary. Therefore, the address is always that of a secondary. The primary station has no address because all transmissions from secondary stations go to the primary.

Control field. The control field is an eight-bit field that identifies the type of frame it is. The control field is used for polling, confirming previously received information frames, and several other data link management functions. There are three frame formats used with SDLC: *information, supervisory,* and *unnumbered.*

Information Frame. With an information frame there must be an information field. Information frames are used for transmitting sequenced information. The bit pattern for the control field of an information frame is

Bit:	b_0	b_1	b_2	b_3	b_4	b_5	b_6	b_7
Function:	←	nr	→	P or F $\overline{P}$ or $\overline{F}$	←	ns	→	0

An information frame is identified by a 0 in the least-significant bit position (b_7 with EBCDIC code). Bits b_4, b_5, and b_6 are used for numbering transmitted frames (ns = number sent). With three bits, the binary numbers 000 through 111 (0–7) can be represented. The first frame transmitted is designated frame 000, the second frame 001, and so on up to frame 111 (the eighth frame); then, the count cycles back to 000 and repeats.

Bits b_0, b_1, and b_2 are used to confirm correctly received information frames (nr = number received) and to automatically request retransmission of incorrectly received information frames. The nr is the number of the next frame that the transmitting station expects to receive, or the number of the next frame that the receiving station will transmit. The nr confirms received frames through nr − 1. Frame nr − 1 is the last frame received without a transmission error. Any transmitted I frame not confirmed must be retransmitted. Together, the ns and nr bits are used for error correction (ARQ). The primary must keep track of an ns and nr for each secondary. Each secondary must keep track of only its ns and nr. After all frames have been confirmed, the primary's ns must agree with the secondary's nr, and vice versa. For the example shown next, the primary and secondary stations begin with their ns and nr counters reset to 000. The primary sends three numbered information frames (ns = 0, 1, and 2). At the same time the primary sends nr = 0 because the next frame it expects to receive is frame 0, which is the secondary's present ns. The secondary responds with two information frames (ns = 0 and 1). The secondary received all three frames from the primary without any errors, so the nr transmitted in the secondary's control field is 3 (which is the number of the next frame that the primary will send). The primary now sends information frames 3 and 4 with an nr = 2. The nr = 2 confirms the correct reception of frames 0 and 1. The secondary responds with frames ns = 2, 3, and 4 with an nr = 4. The nr = 4 confirms reception of only frame 3 from the primary (nr 1). Consequently, the primary must retransmit frame 4. Frame 4 is retransmitted together with four additional frames (ns = 5, 6, 7, and 0). The primary's nr = 5, which confirms frames 2, 3, and 4 from the secondary. Finally, the secondary sends information frame 5 with an nr = 1. The nr = 1 confirms frames 4, 5, 6, 7, and 0 from the primary. At this point, all the frames transmitted have been confirmed except frame 5 from the secondary.

Primary's ns:	0 1 2		3 4		4 5 6 7 0	
Primary's nr:	0 0 0		2 2		5 5 5 5 5	
Secondary's ns:		0 1		2 3 4		5
Secondary's nr:		3 3		4 4 4		1

With SDLC, a station can never send more than seven numbered frames without receiving a confirmation. For example, if the primary sent eight frames (ns = 0, 1, 2, 3, 4, 5, 6, and 7) and the secondary responded with an nr = 0, it is ambiguous which frames are being confirmed. Does nr = 0 mean that all eight frames were received correctly, or that frame 0 had an error in it and all eight frames must be retransmitted? (With SDLC, all previously transmitted frames beginning with frame nr 1 must be retransmitted.)

Bit b_3 is the *poll* (P) or *not-a-poll* ($\overline{P}$) bit when sent from the primary and the *final* (F) or *not-a-final* ($\overline{F}$) bit when sent by a secondary. In a frame sent by the primary, if the primary desires to poll the secondary, the P bit is set (1). If the primary does not wish to poll the secondary, the P bit is reset (0). A secondary cannot transmit unless it receives a frame addressed to it with the P bit set. In a frame sent from a secondary, if it is the last (final) frame of the message, the F bit is set (1). If it is not the final frame, the F bit is reset (0). With I frames, the primary can select a secondary station, send formatted information, confirm previously received I frames, and poll with a single transmission.

Example 14-2

Determine the bit pattern for the control field of a frame sent from the primary to a secondary station for the following conditions: primary is sending information frame 3, it is a poll, and the primary is confirming the correct reception of frames 2, 3, and 4 from the secondary.

Solution

$b_7 = 0$ because it is an information frame.
b_4, b_5, and b_6 are 011 (binary 3 for ns = 3).
$b_3 = 1$, it is a polling frame.
b_0, b_1, and b_2 are 101 (binary 5 for nr = 5).
control field = B6H.

b_0	b_1	b_2	b_3	b_4	b_5	b_6	b_7
1	0	1	1	0	1	1	0

Supervisory Frame. An information field is not allowed with a supervisory frame. Consequently, supervisory frames cannot be used to transfer information; they are used to assist in the transfer of information. Supervisory frames are used to confirm previously received information frames, convey ready or busy conditions, and to report frame numbering errors. The bit pattern for the control field of a supervisory frame is

Bit:	b_0	b_1	b_2	b_3	b_4	b_5	b_6	b_7
Function:	←	nr	→	P or F $\overline{P}$ or $\overline{F}$	X	X	0	1

A supervisory frame is identified by a 01 in bit positions b_6 and b_7, respectively, of the control field. With the supervisory format, bit b_3 is again the poll/not-a-poll or final/not-a-final bit and b_0, b_1, and b_2 are the nr bits. However, with a supervisory format, b_4 and b_5 are used to indicate either the receive status of the station transmitting the frame or to request transmission or retransmission of sequenced information frames. With two bits, there are four combinations possible. The four combinations and their functions are as follows:

b_4	b_5	Receiver Status
0	0	Ready to receive (RR)
0	1	Ready not to receive (RNR)
1	0	Reject (REJ)
1	1	Not used with SDLC

When the primary sends a supervisory frame with the P bit set and a status of ready to receive, it is equivalent to a general poll with bisync. Supervisory frames are used by the primary for polling and for confirming previously received information frames when there is no information to send. A secondary uses the supervisory format for confirming previously received information frames and for reporting its receive status to the primary. If a secondary sends a supervisory frame with RNR status, the primary cannot send it numbered information frames until that status is cleared. RNR is cleared when a secondary sends an information frame with the F bit = 1 or an RR or REJ frame with the F bit = 0. The REJ command/response is used to confirm information frames through nr − 1 and to request retransmission of numbered information frames beginning with the frame number identified in the REJ frame. An information field is prohibited with a supervisory frame and the REJ command/response is used only with full-duplex operation.

Example 14-3

Determine the bit pattern for the control field of a supervisory frame sent from a secondary station to the primary for the following conditions: the secondary is ready to receive, it is the final frame, and the secondary station is confirming frames 3, 4, and 5.

Solution

b_6 and b_7 = 01 because it is a supervisory frame.
b_4 and b_5 = 00 (ready to receive).
b_3 = 1 (it is the final frame).
b_0, b_1 and b_2 = 110 (binary 6 for nr = 6).
control field = D1H

b_0	b_1	b_2	b_3	b_4	b_5	b_6	b_7
1	1	0	1	0	0	0	1

Unnumbered Frame. An unnumbered frame is identified by making bits b_6 and b_7 in the control field 11. The bit pattern for the control field of an unnumbered frame is

Bit:	b_0	b_1	b_2	b_3	b_4	b_5	b_6	b_7
Function:	X	X	X	P or F $\overline{P}$ or $\overline{F}$	X	X	1	1

TABLE 14-2 Unnumbered Commands and Responses

Binary Configuration b₀		b₇	Acronym	Command	Response	I Field Prohibited	Resets ns and nr
000	P/F	0011	UI	Yes	Yes	No	No
000	F	0111	RIM	No	Yes	Yes	No
000	P	0111	SIM	Yes	No	Yes	Yes
100	P	0011	SNRM	Yes	No	Yes	Yes
000	F	1111	DM	No	Yes	Yes	No
010	P	0011	DISC	Yes	No	Yes	No
011	F	0011	UA	No	Yes	Yes	No
100	F	0111	FRMR	No	Yes	No	No
111	F	1111	BCN	No	Yes	Yes	No
110	P/F	0111	CFGR	Yes	Yes	No	No
010	F	0011	RD	No	Yes	Yes	No
101	P/F	1111	XID	Yes	Yes	No	No
001	P	0011	UP	Yes	No	Yes	No
111	P/F	0011	TEST	Yes	Yes	No	No

With an unnumbered frame, bit b_3 is again either the $P/\overline{P}$ or $F/\overline{F}$ bit. Bits b_0, b_1, b_2, b_4, and b_5 are used for various unnumbered commands and responses. With five bits available, 32 unnumbered commands/responses are possible. The control field in an unnumbered frame sent by the primary is a command. The control field in an unnumbered frame sent by a secondary is a response. With unnumbered frames, there are no ns or nr bits. Therefore, numbered information frames cannot be sent or confirmed with the unnumbered format. Unnumbered frames are used to send network control and status information. Two examples of control functions are (1) placing secondary stations on-line and off-line and (2) LCU initialization. Table 14-2 lists several of the more commonly used unnumbered commands and responses. An information field is prohibited with all the unnumbered commands/responses except UI, FRMR, CFGR, TEST, and XID.

A secondary station must be in one of three modes: the initialization mode, the normal response mode, or the normal disconnect mode. The procedures for the *initialization mode* are system specified and vary considerably. A secondary in the *normal response mode* cannot initiate unsolicited transmissions; it can transmit only in response to a frame received with the P bit set. When in the *normal disconnect mode,* a secondary is off-line. In this mode, a secondary can receive only a TEST, XID, CFGR, SNRM, or SIM command from the primary and can respond only if the P bit is set.

The unnumbered commands and responses are summarized below.

Unnumbered information (UI). UI is a command/response that is used to send unnumbered information. Unnumbered information transmitted in the I field is not confirmed.

Set initialization mode (SIM). SIM is a command that places the secondary station into the initialization mode. The initialization procedure is system specified and varies from a simple self-test of the station controller to executing a complete IPL (initial program logic) program. SIM resets the ns and nr counters at the primary and secondary stations. A secondary is expected to respond to a SIM command with a UA response.

Request initialization mode (RIM). RIM is a response sent by a secondary station to request the primary to send an SIM command.

Set normal response mode (SNRM). SNRM is a command that places a secondary station in the normal response mode (NRM). A secondary station cannot send or receive numbered information frames unless it is in the normal response mode. Essentially, SNRM places a secondary station on-line. SNRM resets the ns and nr counters at the primary and secondary stations. UA is the normal response to an SNRM command. Unsolicited responses are not allowed when the secondary is in the NRM. A secondary remains in the NRM until it receives a DISC or SIM command.

Disconnect mode (DM). DM is a response that is sent from a secondary station if the primary attempts to send numbered information frames to it when the secondary is in the normal disconnect mode.

Request disconnect (RD). RD is a response sent when a secondary wishes to be placed in the disconnect mode.

Disconnect (DISC). DISC is a command that places a secondary station in the normal disconnect mode (NDM). A secondary cannot send or receive numbered information frames when it is in the normal disconnect mode. When in the normal disconnect mode, a secondary can receive only an SIM or SNRM command and can transmit only a DM response. The expected response to a DISC command is UA.

Unnumbered acknowledgment (UA). UA is an affirmative response that indicates compliance to a SIM, SNRM, or DISC command. UA is also used to acknowledge unnumbered information frames.

Frame reject (FRMR). FRMR is for reporting procedural errors. The FRMR sequence is a response transmitted when the secondary has received an invalid frame from the primary. A received frame may be invalid for any one of the following reasons:

1. The control field contains an invalid or unassigned command.
2. The amount of data in the information field exceeds the buffer space at the secondary.
3. An information field is received in a frame that does not allow information.
4. The nr received is incongruous with the secondary's ns. For example, if the secondary transmitted ns frames 2, 3, and 4 and then the primary responded with an nr of 7.

A secondary cannot release itself from the FRMR condition, nor does it act on the frame that caused the condition. The secondary repeats the FRMR response until it receives one of the following *mode-setting* commands: SNRM, DISC, or SIM. The information field for a FRMR response always contains three bytes (24 bits) and has the following format:

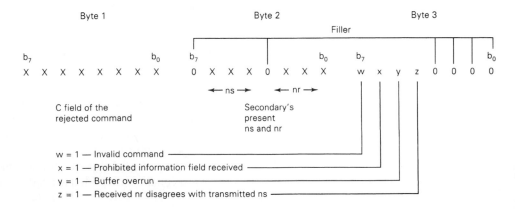

TEST. Test is a command that can be sent in any mode to solicit a TEST response. If an information field is included with the command, the secondary returns it with the response. The TEST command/response is exchanged for link testing purposes.

Exchange station identification (XID). As a command, XID solicits the identification of the secondary station. An information field can be included in the frame to convey the identification data of either the primary or secondary station. For dial-up circuits, it is often necessary that the secondary station identify itself before the primary will exchange information frames with it, although XID is not restricted to only dial-up data circuits.

Frame check sequence field. The FCS field contains the error detection mechanism for SDLC. The FCS is equivalent to the BCC used with bisync. SDLC uses CRC-16 and the following generating polynomial:

$$x^{16} + x^{12} + x^5 + x^1$$

SDLC Loop Operation

An SDLC *loop* is operated in the half-duplex mode. The primary difference between the loop and bus configurations is that in a loop, all transmissions travel in the same direction on the communications channel. In a loop configuration, only one station transmits at a time. The primary transmits first, then each secondary station responds sequentially. In an SDLC loop, the transmit port of the primary station controller is connected to one or more secondary stations in a serial fashion; then the loop is terminated back at the receive port of the primary. Figure 14-4 shows an SDLC loop configuration.

In an SDLC loop, the primary transmits frames that are addressed to any or all of the secondary stations. Each frame transmitted by the primary contains an address of the secondary station to which that frame is directed. Each secondary station, in turn, decodes the address field of every frame, then serves as a repeater for all stations that are down-loop from it. If a secondary detects a frame with its address, it accepts the frame, then passes it onto the next down-loop station. All frames transmitted by the primary are returned to the primary. When the primary has completed transmitting, it follows the last flag with eight consecutive 0s. A flag followed by eight consecutive 0s is called a *turnaround* sequence, which signals the end of the primary's transmission. Immediately following the turnaround sequence, the primary transmits continuous 1s, which generates a *go-ahead* sequence (01111111). A secondary cannot transmit until it has received a frame addressed to it with the P bit set, a turnaround sequence, and then a go-ahead sequence. Once the primary has begun transmitting 1s, it goes into the receive mode.

The first down-loop secondary station that has received a frame addressed to it with the P bit set, changes the seventh 1 bit in the go-ahead sequence to a 0, thus creating a flag. That flag becomes the beginning flag of the secondary's response frame or frames. After the secondary has transmitted its last frame, it again becomes a repeater for the idle line 1s from the primary. These idle line 1s again become the go-ahead sequence for the next secondary station. The next down loop station that has received a frame addressed to it with the P bit set detects the turnaround sequence, any frames transmitted from up-loop secondaries, and then, the go-ahead sequence. Each secondary station inserts its response frames immediately after the last repeated frame. The cycle is completed when the primary receives its own turnaround sequence, a series of response frames, and then, the go-ahead sequence.

Configure command/response. The configure command/response (CFGR) is an unnumbered command/response that is used only in a loop configuration. CFGR contains a one-byte *function descriptor* (essentially a subcommand) in the information field. A CFGR command is acknowledged with a CFGR response. If the low-order bit of the function descriptor is set, a specified function is initiated. If it is reset, the specified function is cleared. There are six subcommands that can appear in the configure command's function field.

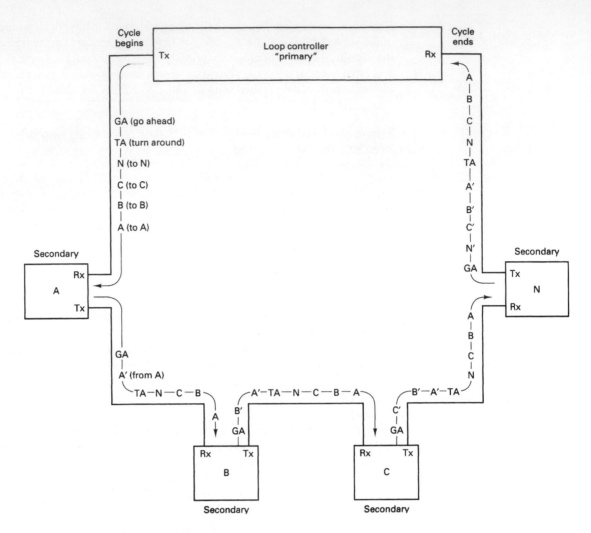

FIGURE 14-4 SDLC loop configuration

1. *Clear—00000000.* A clear subcommand causes all previously set functions to be cleared by the secondary. The secondary's response to a clear subcommand is another clear subcommand, 00000000.

2. *Beacon test (BCN)—0000000X.* The beacon test causes the secondary receiving it to turn on or turn off its carrier. If the X bit is set, the secondary suppresses transmission of the carrier. If the X bit is reset, the secondary resumes transmission of the carrier. The beacon test is used to isolate an open-loop problem. Also, whenever a secondary detects the loss of a receive carrier, it automatically begins to transmit its beacon response. The secondary will continue transmitting the beacon until the loop resumes normal status.

3. *Monitor mode—0000010X.* The monitor command causes the addressed secondary to place itself into a monitor (receive-only) mode. Once in the monitor mode, a secondary cannot transmit until it receives a monitor mode clear (00000100) or a clear (00000000) subcommand.

4. *Wrap—0000100X.* The wrap command causes the secondary station to loop its transmissions directly to its receiver input. The wrap command places the secondary effectively off-line for the duration of the test. A secondary station does not send the results of a wrap test to the primary.

5. *Self-test—0000101X.* The self-test subcommand causes the addressed secondary to initiate a series of internal diagnostic tests. When the tests are completed, the secondary will respond. If the P bit in the configure command is set, the secondary will respond following completion of the self-test at its earliest opportunity. If the P bit is reset, the secondary will respond following completion of the test to the next poll-type frame it receives. All other transmissions are ignored by the secondary while it is performing the self-tests. The secondary indicates the results of the self-test by setting or resetting the low-order bit (X) of its self-test response. A 1 indicates that the tests were unsuccessful, and a 0 indicates that they were successful.

6. *Modified link test—0000110X.* If the modified link test function is set (X bit set), the secondary station will respond to a TEST command with a TEST response that has an information field containing the first byte of the TEST command information field repeated n times. The number n is system implementation dependent. If the X bit is reset, the secondary station will respond to a TEST command, with or without an information field, with a TEST response with a zero-length information field. The modified link test is an optional subcommand and is only used to provide an alternative form of link test to that previously described for the TEST command.

Transparency

The transparency mechanism used with SDLC is called *zero-bit insertion* or *zero stuffing.* The flag bit sequence (01111110) can occur in a frame where this pattern is not intended to be a flag. For example, any time that 7EH occurs in the address, control, information, or FCS field it would be interpreted as a flag and disrupt character synchronization. Therefore, 7EH must be prohibited from occurring except when it is intended to be a flag. To prevent a 7EH sequence from occurring, a zero is automatically inserted after any occurrence of five consecutive 1s except in a designated flag sequence (i.e., flags are not zero inserted). When five consecutive 1s are received and the next bit is a 0, the 0 is deleted or removed. If the next bit is a 1, it must be a valid flag. An example of zero insertion/deletion is shown below.

Original frame bits at the transmit station:

01111110	01101111	11010011	1110001100110101	01111110
flag	address	control	FCS	flag

After zero insertion but prior to transmission:

01111110	01101111	101010011	1110000011 00110101	01111110
flag	address	control	FCS	flag

⬆ inserted zeros ⬆

After zero deletion at the receive end:

01111110	01101111	11010011	1110001100110101	01111110
flag	address	control	FCS	flag

Message Abort

Message abort is used to prematurely terminate a frame. Generally, this is only done to accommodate high-priority messages such as emergency link recovery procedures, and so on. A message abort is any occurrence of 7 to 14 consecutive 1s. Zeros are not inserted in an abort sequence. A message abort terminates an existing frame and immediately begins the higher-priority frame. If more than 14 consecutive 1s occur in succession, it is considered an idle line condition. Therefore, 15 or more successive 1s place the circuit into the idle state.

Invert-On-Zero Encoding

A binary synchronous transmission such as SDLC is time synchronized to enable identification of sequential binary digits. Synchronous data communications assumes that bit or

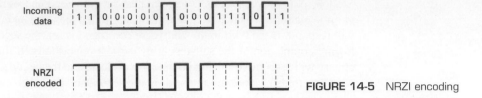

FIGURE 14-5 NRZI encoding

clock synchronization is provided by either the DCE or the DTE. With synchronous transmissions, a receiver samples incoming data at the same rate that they were transmitted. Although minor variations in timing can exist, synchronous modems provide received data clock recovery and dynamically adjusted sample timing to keep sample times midway between bits. For a DTE or a DCE to recover the clock, it is necessary that transitions occur in the data. *Invert-on-zero coding* is an encoding scheme that guarantees at least one transition in the data for every seven bits transmitted. Invert-on-zero coding is also called NRZI (*nonreturn-to-zero inverted*).

With NRZI encoding, the data are encoded in the transmitter, then decoded in the receiver. Figure 14-5 shows an example of NRZI encoding. The encoded waveform is unchanged by ones in the NRZI encoder. However, 0s invert the encoded transmission level. Consequently, consecutive 0s generate an alternating high/low sequence. With SDLC, there can never be more than six 1s in succession (a flag). Therefore, a high-to-low transition is guaranteed to occur at least once for every seven bits transmitted except during a message abort or an idle line condition. In a NRZI decoder, whenever a high/low transition occurs in the received data, a 0 is generated. The absence of a transition simply generates a 1. In Figure 14-5, a high level is assumed prior to encoding the incoming data.

NRZI encoding was intended to be used with asynchronous modems that do not have clock recovery capabilities. Consequently, the DTE must provide time synchronization, which is aided by using NRZI-encoded data. Synchronous modems have built in scramblers and descramblers that ensure that transitions occur in the data, and, thus, NRZI encoding is unnecessary. The NRZI encoder/decoder is placed between the DTE and the DCE.

High-Level Data Link Control

In 1975, the International Standards Organization (ISO) defined several sets of substandards that, when combined, are called *high-level data link control* (HDLC). Since HDLC is a superset of SDLC, only the added capabilities are explained.

HDLC comprises three standards (subdivisions) that, when combined, outline the frame structure, control standards, and class of operation for a bit-oriented data link control (DLC).

ISO 3309–1976(E). This standard defines the frame structure, delimiting, sequence, and transparency mechanism used with HDLC. These are essentially the same as with SDLC except that HDLC has extended addressing capabilities and checks the FCS in a slightly different manner. The delimiting sequence used with HDLC is identical to SDLC: a 01111110 sequence.

HDLC can use either the *basic* eight-bit address field or an *extended* addressing format. With extended addressing the address field may be extended recursively. If b_0 in the address byte is a logic 1, the seven remaining bits are the secondary's address (the ISO defines the low-order bit as b_0, whereas SDLC designates the high-order bit as b_0). If b_0 is a logic 0, the next byte is also part of the address. If b_0 of the second byte is a 0, a third address byte follows, and so on, until an address byte with a logic 1 for the low-order bit is encountered. Essentially, there are seven bits unavailable in each address byte for address encoding. An example of a three-byte extended addressing scheme is shown, b_0 in the first two bytes of the address field are 0s, indicating that additional address bytes follow and b_0 in the third address byte is a logic 1, which terminates the address field.

```
       b_0 = 0          b_0 = 0         b_0 = 1
         |                |               |
01111110    0XXXXXXX    0XXXXXXX    1XXXXXXX . . .
  flag          three-byte address field       control field, etc.
```

HDLC uses CRC-16 with a generating polynomial specified by CCITT V.41. At the transmit station, the CRC is computed such that if it is included in the FCS computation at the receive end, the remainder for an errorless transmission is always F0BBH.

ISO 4335–1979(E).   This standard defines the elements of procedure for HDLC. The control field, information field, and supervisory format have increased capabilities over SDLC.

Control Field.   With HDLC, the control field can be extended to 16 bits. Seven bits are for the ns and 7 bits are for the nr. Therefore, with the extended control format, there can be a maximum of 127 outstanding (unconfirmed) frames at any given time.

Information Field.   HDLC permits any number of bits in the information field of an information command or response (SDLC is limited to eight-bit bytes). With HDLC any number of bits may be used for a character in the I field as long as all characters have the same number of bits.

Supervisory Format.   With HDLC, the supervisory format includes a fourth status condition: selective reject (SREJ). SREJ is identified by an 11 in bit position b_4 and b_5 of a supervisory control field. With a SREJ, a single frame can be rejected. An SREJ calls for the retransmission of only the frame identified by nr, whereas an REJ calls for the retransmission of all frames beginning with nr. For example, the primary sends I frames ns = 2, 3, 4, and 5. Frame 3 was received in error. An REJ would call for a retransmission of frames 3, 4, and 5; an SREJ would call for the retransmission of only frame 3. SREJ can be used to call for the retransmission of any number of frames except that only one is identified at a time.

Operational Modes.   HDLC has two operational modes not specified in SDLC: asynchronous response mode and asynchronous disconnect mode.

1. *Asynchronous response mode (ARM).* With the ARM, secondary stations are allowed to send unsolicited responses. To transmit, a secondary does not need to have received a frame from the primary with the P bit set. However, if a secondary receives a frame with the P bit set, it must respond with a frame with the F bit set.
2. *Asynchronous disconnect mode (ADM).* An ADM is identical to the normal disconnect mode except that the secondary can initiate a DM or RIM response at any time.

ISO 7809–1985(E).   This standard combines previous standards 6159(E) (unbalanced) and 6256(E) (balanced) and outlines the class of operation necessary to establish the link-level protocol.

Unbalanced Operation.   This class of operation is logically equivalent to a multipoint private-line circuit with a polling environment. There is a single primary station responsible for central control of the network. Data transmission may be either half or full duplex.

Balanced Operation.   This class of operation is logically equivalent to a two-point private-line circuit. Each station has equal data link responsibilities, and channel access is through contention using the asynchronous response mode. Data transmission may be half or full duplex.

A *public data network* (PDN) is a switched data communications network similar to the public telephone network except that a PDN is designed for transferring data only. Public data networks combine the concepts of both *value-added networks* (VANs) and *packet-switching networks.*

Value-Added Network

A value-added network "adds value" to the services or facilities provided by a common carrier to provide new types of communication services. Examples of added values are error control, enhanced connection reliability, dynamic routing, failure protection, logical multiplexing, and data format conversions. A VAN comprises an organization that leases communications lines from common carriers such as AT&T and MCI and adds new types of communications services to those lines. Examples of value-added networks are GTE Telnet, DATAPAC, TRANSPAC, and Tymnet Inc.

Packet-Switching Network

Packet switching involves dividing data messages into small bundles of information and transmitting them through communications networks to their intended destinations using computer-controlled switches. Three common switching techniques are used with public data networks: *circuit switching, message switching,* and *packet switching.*

Circuit switching. Circuit switching is used for making a standard telephone call on the public telephone network. The call is established, information is transferred, and then, the call is disconnected. The time required to establish the call is called the *setup* time. Once the call has been established, the circuits interconnected by the network switches are allocated to a single user for the duration of the call. After a call has been established, information is transferred in *real time.* When a call is terminated, the circuits and switches are once again available for another user. Because there are a limited number of circuits and switching paths available, *blocking* can occur. Blocking is the inability to complete a call because there are no facilities or switching paths available between the source and destination locations. When circuit switching is used for data transfer, the terminal equipment at the source and destination must be compatible; they must use compatible modems and the same bit rate, character set, and protocol.

A circuit switch is a *transparent* switch. The switch is transparent to the data; it does nothing more than interconnect the source and destination terminal equipment. A circuit switch adds no value to the circuit.

Message switching. Message switching is a form of *store-and-forward* network. Data, including source and destination identification codes, are transmitted into the network and stored in a switch. Each switch within the network has message storage capabilities. The network transfers the data from switch to switch when it is convenient to do so. Consequently, data are not transferred in real time; there can be a delay at each switch. With message switching, blocking cannot occur. However, the delay time from message transmission to reception varies from call to call and can be quite long (possibly as long as 24 hours). With message switching, once the information has entered the network, it is converted to a more suitable format for transmission through the network. At the receive end, the data are converted to a format compatible with the receiving data terminal equipment. Therefore, with message switching, the source and destination data terminal equipment do not need to be compatible. Message switching is more efficient than circuit switching because data that enter the network during busy times can be held and transmitted later when the load has decreased.

A message switch is a *transactional* switch because it does more than simply transfer the data from the source to the destination. A message switch can store data or change

TABLE 14-3 Switching Technique Summary

Circuit Switching	Message Switching	Packet Switching
Dedicated transmission path	No dedicated transmission path	No dedicated transmission path
Continuous transmission of data	Transmission of messages	Transmission of packets
Operates in real time	Not real time	Near real time
Messages not stored	Messages stored	Messages held for short time
Path established for entire message	Route established for each message	Route established for each packet
Call setup delay	Message transmission delay	Packet transmission delay
Busy signal if called party busy	No busy signal	No busy signal
Blocking may occur	Blocking cannot occur	Blocking cannot occur
User responsible for message-loss protection	Network responsible for lost messages	Network may be responsible for each packet but not for entire message
No speed or code conversion	Speed and code conversion	Speed and code conversion
Fixed bandwidth transmission (i.e., fixed information capacity)	Dynamic use of bandwidth	Dynamic use of bandwidth
No overhead bits after initial setup delay	Overhead bits in each message	Overhead bits in each packet

its format and bit rate, then convert the data back to their original form or an entirely different form at the receive end. Message switching multiplexes data from different sources onto a common facility.

Packet switching. With packet switching, data are divided into smaller segments, called *packets,* prior to transmission through the network. Because a packet can be held in memory at a switch for a short period of time, packet switching is sometimes called a *hold-and-forward* network. With packet switching, a message is divided into packets and each packet can take a different path through the network. Consequently, all packets do not necessarily arrive at the receive end at the same time or in the same order in which they were transmitted. Because packets are small, the hold time is generally quite short and message transfer is near real time and blocking cannot occur. However, packet-switching networks require complex and expensive switching arrangements and complicated protocols. A packet switch is also a transactional switch. Circuit, message, and packet-switching techniques are summarized in Table 14-3.

CCITT X.1 International User Class of Service
The CCITT X.1 standard divides the various classes of service into three basic modes of transmission for a public data network. The three modes are: *start/stop, synchronous,* and *packet.*

Start/stop mode. With the start/stop mode, data are transferred from the source to the network and from the network to the destination in an asynchronous data format (i.e., each character is framed within a start and stop bit). Call control signaling is done in International Alphabet No. 5 (ASCII-77). Two common protocols used for start/stop transmission are IBM's 83B protocol and AT&T's 8A1/B1 selective calling arrangement.

Synchronous mode. With the synchronous mode, data are transferred from the source to the network and from the network to the destination in a synchronous data format (i.e., each message is preceded by a unique synchronizing character). Call control signaling is identical to that used with private-line data circuits and common protocols used for synchronous transmission are IBM's 3270 bisync, Burrough's BASIC, and UNIVAC's UNISCOPE.

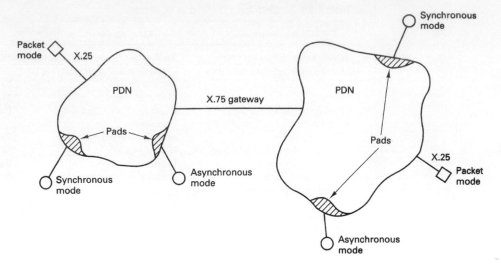

FIGURE 14-6 Public data network

Packet mode. With the packet mode, data are transferred from the source to the network and from the network to the destination in a frame format. The ISO HDLC frame format is the standard data link protocol used with the packet mode. Within the network, data are divided into smaller packets and transferred in accordance with the CCITT X.25 user-to-network interface protocol.

Figure 14-6 illustrates a typical layout for a public data network showing each of the three modes of operation. The packet assembler/disassembler (PAD) interfaces user data to X.25 format when the user's data are in either the asynchronous or synchronous mode of operation. A PAD is unnecessary when the user is operating in the packet mode. X.75 is recommended by the CCITT for the gateway protocol. A gateway is used to interface two public data networks.

CCITT X.25 USER-TO-NETWORK INTERFACE PROTOCOL

In 1976, the CCITT designated the X.25 user interface as the international standard for packet network access. Keep in mind that X.25 is strictly a *user-to-network* interface and addresses only the physical, data link, and network layers in the ISO seven-layer model. X.25 uses existing standards when possible. For example, X.25 specifies X.21, X.26, and X.27 standards as the physical interface, which correspond to EIA RS-232, RS-423A, and RS-422A standards, respectively. X.25 defines HDLC as the international standard for the data link layer and the American National Standards Institute (ANSI) 3.66 *Advanced Data Communications Control Procedures* (ADCCP) as the U.S. standard. ANSI 3.66 and ISO HDLC were designed for private-line data circuits with a polling environment. Consequently, the addressing and control procedures outlined by them are not appropriate for packet data networks. ANSI 3.66 and HDLC were selected for the data link layer because of their frame format, delimiting sequence, transparency mechanism, and error detection method.

At the link level, the protocol specified by X.25 is a subset of HDLC, referred to as *Link Access Procedure Balanced* (LAPB). LAPB provides for two-way, full-duplex communications between DTE and DCE at the packet network gateway. Only the address of the DTE or DCE may appear in the address field of a LAPB frame. The address field refers to a link address, not a network address. The network address of the destination terminal is embedded in the packet header, which is part of the information field.

TABLE 14-4 LAPB Commands

Command Name	Bit Number			
	8 7 6	5	4 3 2	1
1 (information)	nr	P	ns	0
RR (receiver ready)	nr	P	0 0 0	1
RNR (receiver not ready)	nr	P	0 1 0	1
REJ (reject)	nr	P	1 0 0	1
SABM (set asynchronous balanced mode)	0 0 1	P	1 1 1	1
DISC (disconnect)	0 1 0	P	0 0 1	1

TABLE 14-5 LAPB Responses

Command Name	Bit Number			
	8 7 6	5	4 3 2	1
RR (receiver ready)	nr	F	0 0 0	1
RNR (receiver not ready)	nr	F	0 1 0	1
REJ (reject)	nr	F	1 0 0	1
UA (unnumbered acknowledgment)	0 1 1	F	0 0 1	1
DM (disconnect mode)	0 0 0	F	1 1 1	1
FRMR (frame rejected)	1 0 0	F	0 1 1	1

Tables 14-4 and 14-5 show the commands and responses, respectively, for an LAPB frame. During LAPB operation, most frames are commands. A response frame is compelled only when a command frame is received containing a poll (P-bit) = 1. SABM/UA is a command/response pair used to initialize all counters and timers at the beginning of a session. Similarly, DISC/DM is a command/response pair used at the end of a session. FRMR is a response to any illegal command for which there is no indication of transmission errors according to the frame check sequence field.

Information (I) commands are used to transmit packets. Packets are never sent as responses. Packets are acknowledged using ns and nr just as they were in SDLC. RR is sent by a station when it needs to respond (acknowledge) something, but has no information packets to send. A response to an information command could be RR with F = 1. This procedure is called *checkpointing*.

REJ is another way of requesting transmission of frames. RNR is used for the flow control to indicate a busy condition and prevents further transmissions until cleared with an RR.

The network layer of X.25 specifies three switching services offered in a switched data network: permanent virtual circuit, virtual call, and datagram.

Permanent Virtual Circuit

A *permanent virtual circuit* (PVC) is logically equivalent to a two-point dedicated private-line circuit except slower. A PVC is slower because a hard-wired, end-to-end connection is not provided. The first time a connection is requested, the appropriate switches and circuits must be established through the network to provide the interconnection. A PVC identifies the routing between two predetermined subscribers of the network that is used for all subsequent messages. With a PVC, a source and destination address are unnecessary because the two users are fixed.

Virtual Call

A *virtual call* (VC) is logically equivalent to making a telephone call through the DDD network except no direct end-to-end connection is made. A VC is a one-to-many arrangement.

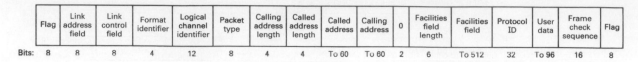

Flag	Link address field	Link control field	Format identifier	Logical channel identifier	Packet type	Calling address length	Called address length	Called address	Calling address	0	Facilities field length	Facilities field	Protocol ID	User data	Frame check sequence	Flag
Bits: 8	8	8	4	12	8	4	4	To 60	To 60	2	6	To 512	32	To 96	16	8

FIGURE 14-7 Call request packet format

Any VC subscriber can access any other VC subscriber through a network of switches and communication channels. Virtual calls are temporary virtual connections that use common usage equipment and circuits. The source must provide its address and the address of the destination before a VC can be completed.

Datagram

A *datagram* (DG) is, at best, vaguely defined by X.25 and, until it is completely outlined, has very limited usefulness. With a DG, users send small packets of data into the network. Each packet is self-contained and travels through the network independent of other packets of the same message by whatever means available. The network does not acknowledge packets nor does it guarantee successful transmission. However, if a message will fit into a single packet, a DG is somewhat reliable. This is called a *single-packet-per-segment* protocol.

X.25 Packet Format

A virtual call is the most efficient service offered for a packet network. There are two packet formats used with virtual calls: a call request packet and a data transfer packet.

Call request packet. Figure 14-7 shows the field format for a call request packet. The delimiting sequence is 01111110 (an HDLC flag), and the error detection/correction mechanism is CRC-16 with ARQ. The link address field and the control field have little use and, therefore, are seldom used with packet networks. The rest of the fields are defined in sequence.

Format Identifier. The format identifier identifies whether the packet is a new call request or a previously established call. The format identifier also identifies the packet numbering sequence (either 0–7 or 0–127).

Logical Channel Identifier (LCI). The LCI is a 12-bit binary number that identifies the source and destination users for a given virtual call. After a source user has gained access to the network and has identified the destination user, they are assigned an LCI. In subsequent packets, the source and destination addresses are unnecessary; only the LCI is needed. When two users disconnect, the LCI is relinquished and can be reassigned to new users. There are 4096 LCIs available. Therefore, there may be as many as 4096 virtual calls established at any given time.

Packet Type. This field is used to identify the function and the content of the packet (new request, call clear, call reset, etc.).

Calling Address Length. This four-bit field gives the number of digits (in binary) that appear in the calling address field. With four bits, up to 15 digits can be specified.

Called Address Length. This field is the same as the calling address field except that it identifies the number of digits that appear in the called address field.

Called Address. This field contains the destination address. Up to 15 BCD digits (60 bits) can be assigned to a destination user.

Calling Address. This field is the same as the called address field except that it contains up to 15 BCD digits that can be assigned to a source user.

Facilities Length Field. This field identifies (in binary) the number of eight-bit octets present in the facilities field.

Flag	Link address field	Link control field	Format identifier	Logical channel identifier	Send packet sequence number P(s)	0	Receive packet sequence number P(r)	0	User data	Frame check sequence	Flag
Bits: 8	8	8	4	12	3/7	5/1	3/7	5/1	To 1024	16	8

FIGURE 14-8 Data transfer packet format

Facilities Field. This field contains up to 512 bits of optional network facility information, such as reverse billing information, closed user groups, and whether it is a simplex transmit or simplex receive connection.

Protocol Identifier. This 32-bit field is reserved for the subscriber to insert user-level protocol functions such as log-on procedures and user identification practices.

User Data Field. Up to 96 bits of user data can be transmitted with a call request packet. These are unnumbered data that are not confirmed. This field is generally used for user passwords.

Data transfer packet. Figure 14-8 shows the field format for a data transfer packet. A data transfer packet is similar to a call request packet except that a data transfer packet has considerably less overhead and can accommodate a much larger user data field. The data transfer packet contains a send-and-receive packet sequence field that was not included with the call request format.

The flag, link address, link control, format identifier, LCI, and FCS fields are identical to those used with the call request packet. The send and receive packet sequence fields are described as follows.

Send Packet Sequence Field. The P(s) field is used in the same manner that the ns and nr sequences are used with SDLC and HDLC. P(s) is analogous to ns, and P(r) is analogous to nr. Each successive data transfer packet is assigned the next P(s) number in sequence. The P(s) can be a 14- or 7-bit binary number and, thus, number packets from either 0–7 or 0–127. The numbering sequence is identified in the format identifier. The send packet field always contains eight bits and the unused bits are reset.

Receive Packet Sequence Field. P(r) is used to confirm received packets and call for retransmission of packets received in error (ARQ). The I field in a data transfer packet can have considerably more source information than an I field in a call request packet.

The X Series of Recommended Standards

X.25 is part of the X series of CCITT-recommended standards for public data networks. The X series is classified into two categories: X.1 through X.39, which deal with services and facilities, terminals, and interfaces; and X.40 through X.199, which deal with network architecture, transmission, signaling, switching, maintenance, and administrative arrangements. Table 14-6 lists the most important X standards with their titles and descriptions.

Asynchronous Transfer Mode

Asynchronous transfer mode (ATM) is a communications standard that uses a high-speed form of packet-switching network as the transmission media. ATM was developed as part of the *Broadband Integrated Services Digital Network* (BISDN), which is described later in this chapter. ATM is intended to utilize the *Synchronous Optical Network* (SONET), also discussed later in this chapter, to accommodate the specialized data communications needs of corporate private networks. Some experts claim that ATM may eventually replace both private leased T1 digital carrier systems and on-premise switching equipment. Conventional electronic switching (ESS) machines currently utilize a central processor to establish switching paths and route traffic through a network. ATM switches, however, will include self-routing procedures where individual *cells* containing subscriber data will route their

TABLE 14-6 CCITT X Series Standards

X.1	International user classes of service in public data networks. Assigns numerical class designations to different terminal speeds and types.
X.2	International user services and facilities in public data networks. Specifies essential and additional services and facilities.
X.3	Packet assembly/disassembly facility (PAD) in a public data network. Describes the packet assembler/disassembler, which normally is used at a network gateway to allow connection of a start/stop terminal to a packet network.
X.20bis	Use on public data networks of DTE designed for interfacing to asynchronous full-duplex V-series modems. Allows use of V.24/V.28 (essentially the same as EIA RS-232).
X.21bis	Use on public data networks of DTE designed for interfacing to synchronous full-duplex V-series modems. Allows use of V.24/V.28 (essentially the same as EIA RS-232) or V.35.
X.25	Interface between DTE and DCE for terminals operating in the packet mode on public data networks. Defines the architecture of three levels of protocols existing in the serial interface cable between a packet-mode terminal and a gateway to a packet network.
X.28	DTE/DCE interface for a start/stop mode DTE accessing the PAD in a public data network situated in the same country. Defines the architecture of protocols existing in a serial interface cable between a start/stop terminal and an X.3 PAD.
X.29	Procedures for the exchange of control information and user data between a PAD and a packet mode DTE or another PAD. Defines the architecture of protocols behind the X.3 PAD, either between two PADs or between a PAD and a packet-mode terminal on the other side of the network.
X.75	Terminal and transit call control procedures and data transfer system on international circuits between packet-switched data networks. Defines the architecture of protocols between two public packet networks.
X.121	International numbering plan for public data networks. Defines a numbering plan including code assignments for each nation.

own way through the ATM switching network in real time using their own address instead of relying on an external process to establish the switching path (a cell is a short, fixed-length packet of data).

ATM uses *virtual channels* (VCs) and *virtual paths* (VPs) to route cells through a network. In essence, a virtual channel is merely a connection between a source and a destination location, which may entail establishing several ATM links between local switching centers. With ATM, all communications occur on the virtual channel, which preserves cell sequence. On the other hand, a virtual path is a group of virtual channels connected between two points that could comprise several ATM links.

An ATM cell contains all of the network information needed to relay individual cells from node to node over a preestablished ATM connection. Figure 14-9 shows the ATM cell structure, which is 53 bytes long, which includes a 5-byte header field and a 48-byte information field. The information field consists entirely of user data. Individual cells can be mixed together and routed to their destination through the telecommunications network. The header field is for networking purposes and contains all of the address and control information necessary for address and flow control.

ATM header field. Figure 14-10 shows the structure of the 5-byte ATM header field, which includes the following: generic flow control field, virtual path identifier, virtual channel identifier, payload type identifier, cell loss priority, and header error control.

Generic Flow Control Field (GFC). The GFC field uses the first four bits of the first byte of the header field. The GFC controls the flow of traffic across the user network interface (UNI) and into the network.

Virtual Path Identifier (VPI) and Virtual Channel Identifier (VCI). The 24 bits immediately following the GFC are used for the ATM address.

Payload Type Identifier (PT). The first three bits of the second half of byte 4 specify the type of message (payload) in cell. With three bits, there are eight different types of

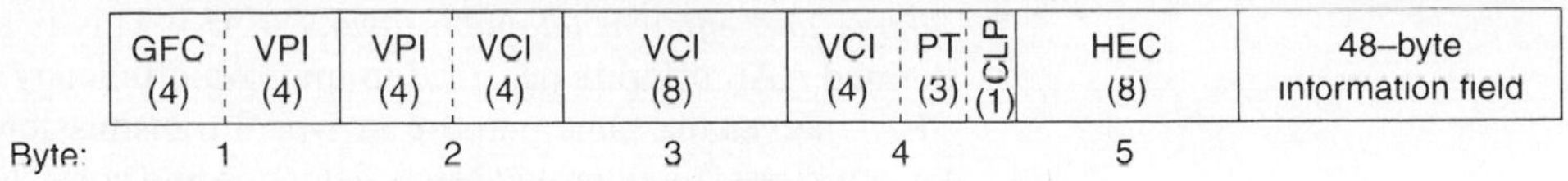

GFC (4)	VPI (4)	VPI (4)	VCI (4)	VCI (8)	VCI (4)	PT (3)	CLP (1)	HEC (8)	48–byte information field

Byte: 1   2   3   4   5

FIGURE 14-9 ATM five-byte header field structure

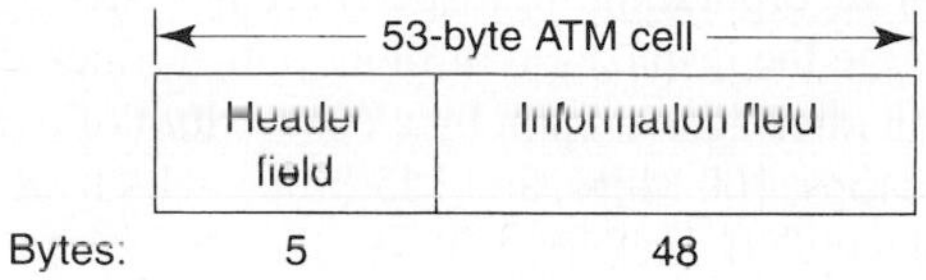

|←———— 53-byte ATM cell ————→|

Header field	Information field

Bytes: 5   48   **FIGURE 14-10** ATM cell structure

payloads possible. At the present time, however, types 0–3 are used for identifying the type of user data, types 4 and 5 indicate management information, and types 6 and 7 are reserved for future use.

Cell Loss Priority (CLP). The last bit of byte 4 is used to indicate whether a cell is eligible to be discarded by the network during congested traffic periods. The CLP bit is set by the user or cleared by the user. If set, the network may discard the cell during times of heavy use.

Header Error Control (HEC). The last byte of the header field is for error control and is used to detect and correct single-bit errors that occur in the header field only; the HEC does not serve as an entire cell check character. The value placed in the HEC is computed from the four previous bytes of the header field. The HEC provides some protection against the delivery of cells to the wrong destination address.

ATM information field. The 48-byte information field is reserved for user data. Insertion of data into the information field of a cell is a function of the upper half of layer two of the ISO-OSI seven-layer protocol hierarchy. This layer is specifically called the ATM Adaptation Layer (AAL). The AAL gives ATM the versatility necessary to facilitate, in a single format, a wide variety of different types of services ranging from continuous processes signals, such as voice transmission, to messages carrying highly fragmented bursts of data such as those produced from local area networks. Because most user data occupy more than 48 bytes, the AAL divides information into 48-byte segments and places them into a series of segments. The five types of AALs are

1. *Constant bit rate (CBR).* CBR information fields are designed to accommodate PCM-TDM traffic, which allows the ATM network to emulate voice or DSN services.
2. *Variable bit rate (VBR) timing-sensitive services.* This type of AAL is currently undefined; however, it is reserved for future data services requiring transfer of timing information between terminal points as well as data (i.e., packet video).
3. *Connection-oriented VBR data transfer.* Type 3 information fields transfer VBR data such as impulsive data generated at irregular intervals between two subscribers over a preestablished data link. The data link is established by network signaling procedures that are very similar to those used by the public-switched telephone network. This type of service is intended for large, long-duration data transfers, such as file transfers or file backups.
4. *Connectionless VBR data transfer.* This AAL type provides for transmission of VBR data that does not have a preestablished connection. Type 4 information fields are intended to be used for short, highly bursty type transmissions, such as those generated from a local area network.

5. *Simple and efficient adaption layer (SEAL).* This is a relatively new and well-defined AAL offering designed to improve efficiency over type 3 transmissions. SEAL serves the same purpose as type 3 transmissions and assumes that higher layer processes will provide error detection and correction. The SEAL format simplifies sublayers of the AAL by filling all 48 bytes of the information field with user data.

It is hoped that incorporating high-speed ATM systems into data communications networks will encourage the installation of more optical fiber systems in the very near future. The transmission rates agreed upon by a consortium of over 120 firms, known as the ATM Forum, are 45 Mbps, 100 Mbps, and 155 Mbps, which are the same rates used by the Synchronous Optical Network (SONET) OC-3 rate. The ATM Forum was founded in 1991 by Adaptive, Cisco, Northern Telcom, and Sprint. Current ATM transmission rates go up to 622 Mbps.

Synchronous Optical Network

The American National Standards Institute (ANSI) published a standard called Synchronous Optical Network (SONET) in 1988 and entitled it ANSI T1.105. Since then, the CCITT has incorporated the SONET standard into their Synchronous Digital Hierarchy (SDH) recommendations. SONET has since emerged as a vanguard in telecommunications technologies. SONET's major goal is to standardize optical fiber network equipment, thus allowing for internetworking optical communications systems from a variety of different vendors. It is believed that SONET possesses sufficient flexibility to allow it to eventually be used as the underlying transport layer for BISDN and ATM cells.

SONET signal hierarchy and bit rates. SONET defined their *optical carrier hierarchy* and their equivalent electrical *synchronous transport signals* (STSs) for an optical fiber-based transmission system. Table 14-7 lists the standard transmission bit rates used with SONET.

The 51.84-Mbps STS-1 rate is the fundamental line rate from which all the other SONET optical bit rates are derived. As the table shows, higher bit rates are integer multiples of the OC-1 rate. For STS-*N,* the only values of *N* allowed are 1, 3, 9, 12, 18, 24, 36, and 48. The current standard does not provide for future bit rates in excess of $N = 256$.

SONET frame format. The transport mechanism adopted by SONET uses a synchronous binary bit stream made up of groups of bytes organized into a frame structure, which includes user data. The basic 51.84-Mbps STS-1 frame format is shown in Figure 14-11. It can be seen that the frame format is best described as a 9-row by 90-column matrix representing individual bytes of synchronous data. Data are transmitted byte by byte

TABLE 14-7 SONET Transmission Rates

Optical Carrier	Synchronous Transport Signal	Line Rate (Mbps)
OC-1*	STS-1	51.84
OC-3*	STS-3	155.52
OC-9	STS-9	466.56
OC-12*	STS-12	622.08
OC-18	STS-18	933.12
OC-24	STS-24	1244.16
OC-36	STS-36	1866.24
OC-48*	STS-48	2488.32

*Popular SONET physical layer interface

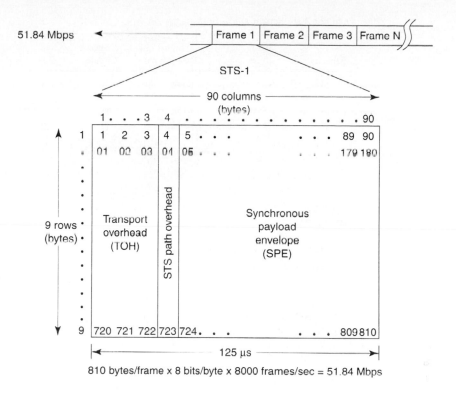

FIGURE 14-11 SONET STS-1 frame format

beginning with byte 1, then continuing from left to right and top to bottom for a total of 810 bytes (9 × 90) or 6480 bits (810 × 8). The transmission bit rate is

$$bps = \frac{bits}{time} = \frac{6480 \text{ bits}}{125 \text{ }\mu s} = 51.84 \text{ Mbps}$$

STS-1 frames are divided into two general areas: the *transport overhead* (TOH) and the *synchronous payload envelope* (SPE). The TOH occupies the first three columns of the 90-column matrix. The remaining 87 columns comprise the SPE. The initial SPE column is called the STS *path overhead*, which contains payload-specific data and does not change as the SPE travels through the network. The remaining 86 columns in the SPE carry the payload or network traffic.

The TOH portion of the STS-1 frame is used for alarm monitoring, bit error monitoring, and other data communications overhead necessary to ensure reliable transmission of the synchronous payload envelope between nodes within the synchronous network. The SPE is designed to transport user data through the synchronous network from source to destination. The SPE is assembled and disassembled only once on its route through the network, regardless of how many times it changes transport systems. In most cases, however, the SPE is assembled where it enters the network and disassembled where it exits.

The *payload* is the revenue-producing traffic transported through the SONET network. Once assembled, the payload can be routed through the network to its destination. STS-1 payload has the capacity to transport the various types of digital signals listed in Table 14-8.

The 86 columns of the SPE designed to carry payload are arranged in accordance with standard mapping rules, which are a function of the data service subscribing to the network (DS1, DS2, etc.). The specific arrangement used for a given service is called a *virtual tributary* (VT). SONET facilitates various-size VTs. For example, VT1.5 is a frame comprised

TABLE 14-8 STS-1 Payload Capacity

Capacity	Signal Type	Signal Rate (Mbps)	Voice Circuits	T1s
28	DS1	1.544	24	1
21	CEPT1	2.048	30	—
14	DS1C	3.152	48	2
7	DS2	6.312	96	4
1	DS3	44.736	672	28

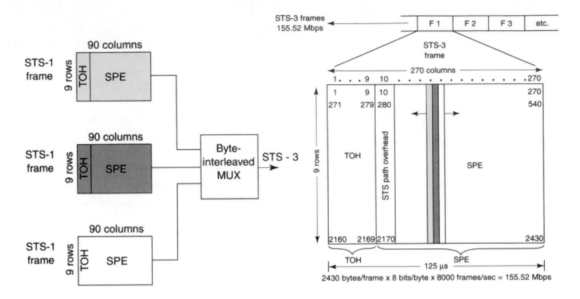

FIGURE 14-12 SONET STS-3 byte-interleaved multiplexing

of 27 bytes formatted in three columns of nine bytes each. With a 125 μs frame time (i.e., 8 kHz rate), the bytes provide a transport capacity of 1.728 Mbps, which will accommodate mapping a DS1 compatible signal that has a rate of 1.544 Mbps. Twenty-eight VT1.5s may be multiplexed into the STS-1 SPE.

SONET multiplexing. SONET utilizes a multiplexing technique called byte-interleaved multiplexing to achieve higher levels of synchronous transport. By using byte-interleave multiplexing, N STS-1 circuits can be multiplexed into a single STS-*N* circuit. Figure 14-12 shows how three STS-1 frames are multiplexed into a single STS-3 frame. The STS-3 frame has 270 columns and nine rows for a total byte capacity of 2430 bytes. Because the STS-3 frame is also transmitted in 125 μs, the transmission rate is three times that of a single STS-1 frame or 155.52 Mbps. Note in Figure 14-12 that the byte-interleaved process produces a matrix with multiplexed rows and columns. The first 9 columns of the STS-3 frame comprise the TOHs from the three STS-1 signals, and the remaining 261 columns are occupied by the SPEs of the three STS-1 signals.

INTEGRATED SERVICES DIGITAL NETWORK

Introduction to ISDN

The data and telephone communications industry is continually changing to meet the demands of contemporary telephone, video, and computer communications systems. Today, more and more people have a need to communicate with each other than ever before. In order to meet these needs, old standards are being updated and new standards are being developed and implemented almost on a daily basis.

The *Integrated Services Digital Network* (ISDN) is a proposed network designed by the major telephone companies in conjunction with the CCITT with the intent of providing worldwide telecommunications support of voice, data, video, and facsimile information within the same network (in essence, ISDN is the integrating of a wide range of services into a single multipurpose network). ISDN is a network that proposes to interconnect an unlimited number of independent users through a common communications network.

To date only a small number of ISDN facilities have been developed; however, the telephone industry is presently implementing an ISDN system so that in the near future, subscribers will access the ISDN system using existing public telephone and data networks. The basic principles and evolution of ISDN have been outlined by the Consultative Committee for International Telephony and Telegraphy (CCITT) in its recommendation CCITT 1.120 (1984). CCITT 1.120 lists the following principles and evolution of ISDN:

Principles of ISDN

1. The main feature of the ISDN concept is to support a wide range of voice (telephone) and nonvoice (digital data) applications in the same network using a limited number of standardized facilities.

2. ISDNs support a wide variety of applications including both switched and non-switched (dedicated) connections. Switched connections include both circuit- and packet-switched connections and their concatenations.

3. Whenever practical, new services introduced into an ISDN should be compatible with 64-kbps switched digital connections. The 64-kbps digital connection is the basic building block of ISDN.

4. An ISDN will contain intelligence for the purpose of providing service features, maintenance, and network management functions. In other words, ISDN is expected to provide services beyond the simple setting up of switched circuit calls.

5. A layered protocol structure should be used to specify the access procedures to an ISDN and can be mapped into the open system interconnection (OSI) model. Standards already developed for OSI related applications can be used for ISDN, such as X.25 level 3 for access to packet-switching services.

6. It is recognized that ISDNs may be implemented in a variety of configurations according to specific national situations. This accommodates both single-source or competitive national policy.

Evolution of ISDNs

1. ISDNs will be based on the concepts developed for telephone ISDNs and may evolve by progressively incorporating additional functions and network features including those of any other dedicated networks such as circuit and packet switching for data so as to provide for existing and new services.

2. The transition from an existing network to a comprehensive ISDN may require a period of time extending over one or more decades. During this period, arrangements must be developed for the internetworking of services on ISDNs and services on other networks.

3. In the evolution toward an ISDN, digital end-to-end connectivity will be obtained via plant and equipment used in existing networks, such as digital transmission, time division multiplex, and/or space-division multiplex switching. Existing relevant recommendations for these constituent elements of an ISDN are contained in the appropriate series of recommendations of CCITT and CCIR.

4. In the early stages of the evolution of ISDNs, some interim user-network arrangements may need to be adopted in certain countries to facilitate early penetration of digital service capabilities.

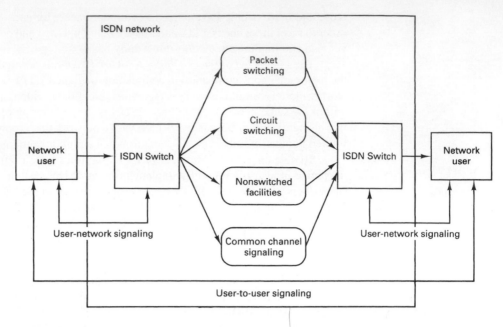

FIGURE 14-13 Architecture for ISDN functions

5. An evolving ISDN may also include at later stages switched connections at bit rates higher and lower than 64 kbps.

ISDN Architecture

A block diagram indicating the proposed architecture for ISDN functions is shown in Figure 14-13. The ISDN is designed to support an entirely new physical connection for the user, a digital subscriber loop, and a variety of transmission services.

A *common physical interface* will be defined to provide a DTE-DCE interface connection. A single interface will be used for telephones, computer terminals, and video equipment. Therefore, various protocols will be required to allow control information to be exchanged between the user's device and the ISDN. There are three basic types of channels available with ISDN. They are

B channel: 64 kbps

D channel: 16 or 64 kbps

H channel: 384, 1536, or 1920 kbps

ISDN standards specify that residential users of the network (i.e., the subscribers) be provided a *basic access* consisting of three full-duplex, time-division multiplexed digital channels, two operating at 64 kbps (designated the B channels, for *bearer*) and one at 16 kbps (designated the D channel, for *data*). The B and D bit rates were selected to be compatible with existing DS1–DS4 digital carrier systems. The D channel is used for carrying signaling information and for exchanging network control information. One B channel is used for digitally encoded voice and the other for applications such as data transmission, PCM-encoded digitized voice, and videotex. The 2B + D service is sometimes called the *basic rate interface* (BRI). BRI systems require bandwidths that can accommodate two 64-kbps B channels and one 16-kbps D channel plus framing, synchronization, and other overhead bits for a total bit rate of 192 kbps. The H channels are used to provide higher bit rates for special services such as fast facsimile, video, high-speed data, and high-quality audio.

There is another service called the *primary service, primary access,* or *primary rate interface* (PRI) that will provide multiple 64-kbps channels intended to be used by the

TABLE 14-9 Projected ISDN Services

Service	Transmission Rate	Channel
Telephone	64 kbps	BC
System alarms	100 bps	D
Utility company metering	100 bps	D
Energy management	100 bps	D
Video	2.4–64 kbps	BP
Electronic mail	4.8–64 kbps	BP
Facsimile	4.8–64 kbps	BC
Slow scan television	64 kbps	BC

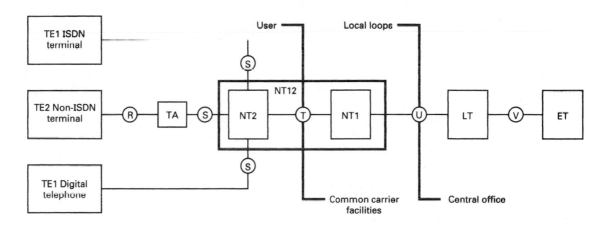

FIGURE 14-14 ISDN connections and reference points

higher volume subscribers to the network. In the United States, Canada, Japan, and Korea, the primary rate interface consists of twenty-three 64-kbps B channels and one 64-kbps D channel (23B + D) for a combined bit rate of 1.544 Mbps. In Europe, the primary rate interface uses thirty 64-kbps B channels and one 64-kbps D channel for a combined bit rate of 2.048 Mbps.

It is intended that ISDN provide a circuit-switched B channel with the existing telephone system; however, packet-switched B channels for data transmission at nonstandard rates would have to be created.

The subscriber's loop, as with the twisted pair cable used with a common telephone, provides the physical signal path from the subscriber's equipment to the ISDN central office. The subscriber loop must be capable of supporting full-duplex digital transmission for both basic and primary data rates. Ideally, as the network grows, optical fiber cables will replace the metallic cables.

Table 14-9 lists the services proposed to be used by ISDN subscribers. BC designates a circuit-switched B channel, BP designates a packed-switched B channel, and D designates a D channel.

ISDN System Connections and Interface Units

ISDN subscriber units and interfaces are defined by their function and reference within the network. Figure 14-14 shows how users may be connected to an ISDN. As the figure shows, subscribers must access the network through one of two different types of entry devices, *terminal equipment type 1* (TE1) and *terminal equipment type 2* (TE2). TE1 equipment supports standard ISDN interfaces and, therefore, requires no protocol translation. Data enters the network and are immediately configured into ISDN protocol format. TE2 equipment is classified as non-ISDN; thus, computer terminals are connected to the system through physical interfaces such as the RS-232 and host computers with X.25. Translation between non-ISDN data protocol and ISDN protocol is performed in a device called a *terminal adapter* (TA). Terminal adapters convert the user's data into the 64 kbps ISDN channel B or the 16 kbps channel D format, and X.25 packets are converted to ISDN packet formats. If any additional signaling is required, it is added by the terminal adapter. The terminal adapters can also support traditional analog telephones and facsimile signals by using a 3.1-kHz audio service channel. The analog signals are digitized and put into ISDN format before entering the network.

User data at points designated as *reference point S (system)* are presently in ISDN format and provide the 2B + D data at 192 kbps. These reference points separate user terminal equipment from network-related system functions. *Reference point T (terminal)* locations correspond to a minimal ISDN network termination at the user's location. These reference points separate the network provider's equipment from the user's equipment. *Reference point R (rate)* provides an interface between non-ISDN compatible user equipment and the terminal adapters. *Network termination* 1 (NT1) provides the functions associated with the physical interface between the user and the common carrier and are designated by the letter *T* (these functions correspond to OSI layer 1). The NT1 is a boundary to the network and may be controlled by the ISDN provider. The NTI performs line maintenance functions and supports multiple channels at the physical level (e.g., 2B + D). Data from these channels are time-division multiplexed together. Network terminal 2 devices are intelligent and can perform *concentration* and switching functions (functionally up through OSI level 3). NT2 terminations can also be used to terminate several S-point connections and provide local switching functions and two-wire to four-wire and four-wire to two-wire conversions. *U-reference points* refer to interfaces between the common carrier subscriber loop and the *central office switch*. A *U loop* is the media interface point between an NT1 and the central office. Network termination 1,2 (NT12) constitutes one piece of equipment that combines the functions of NT1 and NT2. U loops are terminated at the central office by a *line termination* (LT) unit, which provides physical layer interface functions between the central office and the loop lines. The LT unit is connected to an *exchange termination* (ET) at *reference point* V. An ET routes data to an outgoing channel or central office user.

There are several types of transmission channels in addition to the B and D types described in the previous section. They include the following:

> *HO channel.* This interface supports multiple 384-kbps HO channels. These structures are 3HO + D and 4HO + D for the 1.544-Mbps interface and 5HO + D for the 2.048-Mbps interface.
>
> *H11 channel.* This interface consists of one 1.536-Mbps H11 channel (twenty-four 64-kbps channels).
>
> *H12 channel.* European version of H11 that uses 30 channels for a combined data rate of 1.92 Mbps.
>
> *E channel.* Packet switched using 64 kbps (similar to the standard D channel).

ISDN Protocols

Standards developed for ISDN include protocols that allow interaction between ISDN users and the network itself and also for interaction between one ISDN user and another. In addition, it is desirable to fit the new ISDN protocols into the OSI framework. Figure 14-15 shows the relationships between OSI and ISDN. In essence, ISDN is not concerned with OSI layers 4–7. These layers are for end-to-end exchange of information between the network users.

Layer 1 specifies the physical interface for both basic and primary access to the network. B and D channels are time-division multiplexed onto the same interface; consequently, the same standards apply to both types of channels. However, the protocols of layers 2 and 3 differ for the two channels. The protocol used by ISDN for the data link layer

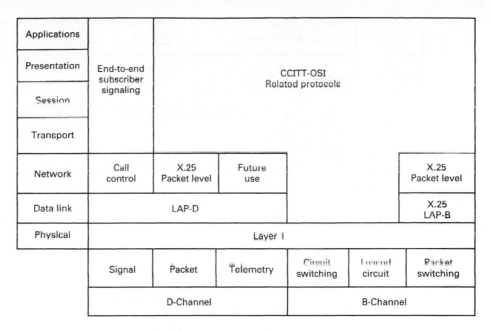

Applications					
Presentation	End-to-end subscriber signaling	CCITT-OSI Related protocols			
Session					
Transport					
Network	Call control	X.25 Packet level	Future use		X.25 Packet level
Data link	LAP-D				X.25 LAP-B
Physical	Layer I				

Signal	Packet	Telemetry	Circuit switching	Leased circuit	Packet switching
D-Channel			B-Channel		

FIGURE 14-15 Structured relationships between OSI and ISDN user network

is very similar to the HDLC format discussed earlier in this chapter and is called *Link Access Protocol for D-Channels* (LAP-D) and *Link Access Protocol for B-Channels* (LAP-B). CCITT standards Q920 and Q921 give the details of these specifications.

LAP-D services. All data transmissions on the LAP-D channel are between the subscriber equipment and an ISDN switching element. LAP-D provides two types of services: *unacknowledged* and *acknowledged information transfer*. The unacknowledged information transfer provides for the transfer of data frames with no acknowledgment. This service supports both point-to-point or broadcast transmission, but neither guarantees successful transmission of data, nor informs the sender if the transmission fails. Unacknowledged information transfer does not provide any type of data flow control or error-control mechanism. Error detection is used to detect and discard any damaged frames. Transmission of unacknowledged information transfer simply provides a means of transferring data quickly and is useful for services such as sending alarm messages.

The acknowledged information transfer service is much more commonly used. This service is similar to the services offered by LAP-B. With acknowledged information transfer, a logical connection is established between two subscribers prior to the transfer of any data. Then data are transferred in sequentially numbered frames that are acknowledged either individually or in groups. Both error and flow control are included in this service. This type of service is sometimes referred to as multiple-frame operation.

LAP-D format. With LAP-D protocol, subscriber information as well as protocol control information and parameters are transmitted in frames. The basic LAP-D frame is identical to that of HDLC except for the address field. The LAP-D frame format is shown in Figure 14-16. As shown, the frame begins with the transmission of a flag field, followed by the address field. The flag field delimits the frame at both ends with a hex 7E (binary 01111110). LAP-D has to contend with two types of multiplexing: subscriber site multiplexing where there may be multiple devices sharing the same physical interface and within each user device where there may be multiple forms of traffic multiplexed together (such as packet-switched data and control signaling).

Beginning flag	Address field		Control field	Information field	Frame check sequence	Ending flag
7E 01111110	C/R SAPI 0 X XXXXXX	TEI 1 XXXXXXX	Control word	Data	CRC-16	7E 01111110
1-byte	1-byte	1-byte	1-2 bytes	1-128 or 0-260 bytes	2-bytes	1-byte

SAPI = Service point identifier
TEI = Terminal endpoint identifier
CRC = Cyclic redundancy check
C/R = Command/response

FIGURE 14-16 ISDN LAP-D format

TABLE 14-10 TEI Assignments

TEI	User Type
0–63	Nonautomatic TEI assignment subscriber equipment
64–126	Automatic TEI assignment subscriber equipment
127	Used during automatic TEI assignment

TABLE 14-11 SAPI Assignments

SAPI	Related Layer 3 or Management Function
0	Call control procedures
1	Reserved for packet-mode transmissions using I.451 call control procedures
16	Packet-mode transmissions using X.25 level 3
63	Layer 2 management and control procedures
all others	Reserved for future uses

To accommodate the two forms of multiplexing, LAP-D uses a two-part address field that consists of a *terminal endpoint identifier* (TEI) and a *service point identifier* (SAPI). Typically each subscriber is assigned a unique TEI. It is also possible for a single device to have more than one TEI, such as for a terminal concentrator. TEI assignments can be made automatically when the equipment is first turned up, or manually by the subscriber. The SAPI identifies a layer 3 subscriber of LAP-D. Only four SAPI identifiers are currently in use. A SAPI of 0 is used for call-control procedures for managing B channel circuits, a SAPI of 1 is used for packet-mode transmissions using I.451 control procedures (such as subscriber-to-subscriber signaling), a SAPI of 16 is reserved for packet-mode transmissions on the D channel using X.25 level 3, and a SAPI of 63 is used for the exchange of layer 2 management and control information. The TEI and SAPI assignments are given in Tables 14-10 and 14-11, respectively. The TEI and SAPI can be used together to uniquely identify a logical connection. When used in this manner, the combination of TEI and SAPI is referred to as a *data link connection identifier* (DLCI).

An additional bit, called the *command/response* (C/R) bit, is used to identify the frame as a command (logic 0 for traffic from terminals and logic 1 for traffic from the network) or a response message (opposite logic condition).

The control field identifies the type of frame and keeps track of the frame sequence the same as with SDLC and HDLC. Information, supervisory, and unnumbered control fields are also the same as with SDLC and HDLC with these exceptions. The set normal response unnumbered frame is replaced with a set asynchronous balanced-mode extended frame, which functions in a similar manner and establishes a data link for acknowledged data transfers of information frames. An additional unnumbered frame, *transfer ID* (XID), is also included to allow stations to identify themselves for line management purposes.

The information field is allowed only with information frames and certain special unnumbered frames. The information field can contain any sequence of bits so long as they consist of an integral multiple of eight (octets). The information field is variable within system-defined specifications; however, for both control signaling and packet information, the maximum length is 260 octets.

The frame check sequence (FCS) is a CRC CCITT code used for error detection of all bits within the frame except the flags.

LAP-B frames are similar to LAP-D although XID and unnumbered information (UI) frames are not used. Also, with LAP-B the frames are limited to 3-bit modulo 8 numbers (0–7) where LAP-D uses 7-bit modulo 128 numbers (0–127).

Broadband ISDN

Broadband ISDN (BISDN) is defined by the CCITT as a service that provides transmission channels capable of supporting transmission rates greater than the primary data rate. With BISDN, services requiring data rates of a magnitude beyond those provided by ISDN, such as video transmission, will become available. With the advent of BISDN, the original concept of ISDN is being referred to as *narrowband* ISDN.

In 1988, the CCITT first recommended as part of its I-series recommendations relating to BISDN: I.113, *Vocabulary of terms for broadband aspects of ISDN,* and I.121, *Broadband aspects of ISDN.* These two documents are a consensus concerning the aspects of the future of BISDN. They outline preliminary descriptions of future standards and development work.

The new BISDN standards are based upon the concept of an *asynchronous transfer mode* (ATM), which will incorporate optical fiber cable as the transmission medium for data transmission. The BISDN specifications set a maximum length of 1 km per cable length but is making provisions for repeated interface extensions. The expected data rates on the optical fiber cables will be either 11 Mbps, 155 Mbps, or 600 Mbps, depending on the specific application and the location of the fiber cable within the network.

CCITT classifies the services that could be provided by BISDN as interactive and distribution services. *Interactive services* include those in which there is a two-way exchange of information (excluding control signaling) between two subscribers or between a subscriber and a service provider. *Distribution services* are those in which information transfer is primarily from service provider to subscriber. On the other hand, *conversational services* will provide a means for bidirectional end-to-end data transmission, in real time, between two subscribers or between a subscriber and a service provider.

The authors of BISDN composed specifications that require the new services meet both existing ISDN interface specifications and the new BISDN needs. A standard ISDN terminal and a *broadband terminal interface* (BTI) will be serviced by the *subscriber's premise network* (SPN), which will multiplex incoming data and transfer them to the *broadband node.* The broadband node is called a *broadband network termination* (BNT), which codes the data information into smaller packets used by the BISDN network. Data transmission within the BISDN network can be asymmetric (i.e., access on to and off of the network may be accomplished at different transmission rates, depending on system requirements).

Asynchronous transfer mode. The asynchronous transfer mode (ATM) is a means by which data can enter and exit the BISDN network in an asynchronous (time independent) fashion. ATM uses labeled channels that are transferable at fixed data rates. The data rates can be anywhere from 16 kbps up to the maximum rate of the system. Once data has entered the network, they are transferred into fixed time slots called *cells.* A cell is identified by a *label* in the *cell header.* The format for a cell header is shown in Figure 14-17. The *virtual channel identifier* indicates the node source and packet destination. The

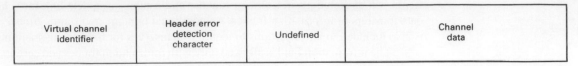

Virtual channel identifier	Header error detection character	Undefined	Channel data

FIGURE 14-17 ATM cell header format

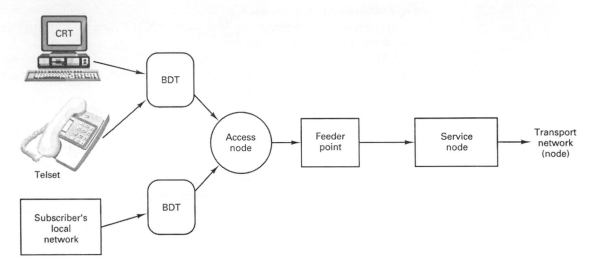

FIGURE 14-18 BISDN access

channel is virtual, rather than specific, which allows the actual physical routing of the packet and network entry and exit times to be determined by network availability and access rights. Immediately after the virtual channel identifier is the *header error detection character,* which may be a CRC character or any other form of error detection. The CRC is for the header label only and separate error detection methods are used for the actual data field. The next section of the header cell is unidentified and is reserved for future use.

BISDN configuration. Figure 14-18 shows how access to the BISDN network is accomplished. Each peripheral device is interfaced to the *access node* of a BISDN network through a *broadband distant terminal* (BDT). The BDT is responsible for the electrical-to-optical conversion, multiplexing of peripherals, and maintenance of the subscriber's local system. Access nodes concentrate several BDTs into high-speed optical fiber lines directed through a *feeder point* into a *service node.* Most of the control functions for system access are managed by the service node, such as call processing, administrative functions, and switching and maintenance functions. The functional modules are interconnected in a star configuration and include switching, administrative, gateway, and maintenance modules. The interconnection of the function modules is shown in Figure 14-19. The central control hub acts as the end user interface for control signaling and data traffic maintenance. In essence, it oversees the operation of the modules.

Subscriber terminals near the central office may bypass the access nodes entirely and be directly connected to the BISDN network through a service node. BISDN networks that use optical fiber cables can utilize much wider bandwidths and, consequently, have higher transmission rates and offer more channel-handling capacity than ISDN systems.

Broadband channel rates. The CCITT has published preliminary definitions of new broadband channel rates that will be added to the existing ISDN narrowband channel rates. The new channel rates are

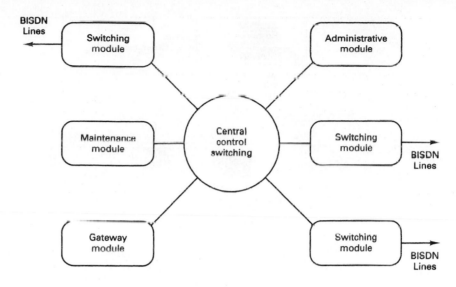

FIGURE 14-19 BISDN functional module interconnections

1. H21: 32.768 Mbps
2. H22: 43 Mbps to 45 Mbps
3. H4: 132 Mbps to 138.24 Mbps

The H21 and H22 data rates are intended to be used for full-motion video transmission for video conferencing, video telephone, and video messaging. The H4 data rate is intended for bulk data transfer of text, facsimile, and enhanced video information. The H21 data rate is equivalent to 512 64-kbps channels. The H22 and H4 data rates must be multiples of the basic 64 kbps transmission rate.

LOCAL AREA NETWORKS

Studies have indicated that most (80%) of the communications among data terminals and other data equipment occurs within a relatively small local environment. A *local area network* (LAN) provides the most economical and effective means of handling local data communication needs. A local area network is typically a privately owned data communications system in which the users share resources, including software. LANs provide two-way communications between a large variety of data communications terminals within a limited geographical area such as within the same room, building, or building complex. Most LANs link equipment that is within a few miles of each other.

Figure 14-20 shows how several PCs could be connected to a LAN to share common resources such as a modem, printer, or server. The server may be a more powerful computer than the other PCs sharing the network or it may simply have more disk storage space. The server "serves" information to the other PCs on the network in the form of software and data information files. A PC server is analogous to a mainframe computer, except on a much smaller scale.

LANs allow for a room full or more of computers to share common resources such as printers and modems. The average PC uses these devices only a small percentage of the time, so there is no need to dedicate individual printers and modems to each PC. To print a document or file, a PC simply sends the information over the network to the server. The server organizes and prioritizes the documents, then sends them, one document at a time, to the common usage printer. Meanwhile, the PCs are free to continue performing other

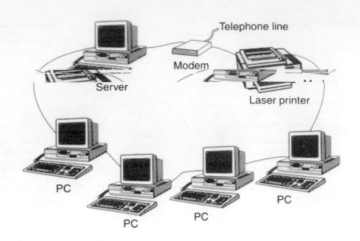

FIGURE 14-20 Typical local area network component configuration

useful tasks. When a PC needs a modem, the network establishes a *virtual connection* between the modem and the PC. The network is transparent to the virtual connection, which allows the PC to communicate with the modem as if they were connected directly to each other.

LANS allow people to send and receive messages and documents through the network much quicker than they could be sent through a paper mail system. *Electronic mail* (e-mail) is a communications system that allows users to send messages to each other through their computers. Electronic mail enables any PC on the network to send or receive information from any other PC on the network as long as the PCs and the server use the same or compatible software. Electronic mail can also be used to interconnect users on different networks in different cities, states, countries, or even continents. To send an e-mail message, a user at one PC sends its address and message along with the destination address to the server. The server effectively "relays" the message to the destination PC if they are subscribers to the same network. If the destination PC is busy or not available for whatever reason, the server stores the message and resends it later. The server is the only computer that has to keep track of the location and address of all the other PCs on the network. To send e-mail to subscribers of other networks, the server relays the message to the server on the destination user's network, which in turn relays the mail to the destination PC. Electronic mail can be used to send text information (letters) as well as program files, graphics, audio, and even video. This is referred to as multimedia communications.

LANs are used extensively to interconnect a wide range of data services including the following:

Data terminals
Laser printers
Graphic plotters
Large-volume disk and tape storage devices
Facsimile machines
Personal computers
Mainframe computers
Data modems
Data bases
Word processors

Public switched telephone networks

Digital carrier systems (T-carriers)

Electronic mail servers

Local Area Network System Considerations

The capabilities of a local area network are established primarily by three factors: *topology, transmission medium,* and *access control protocol.* Together these three factors determine the type of data, rate of transmission, efficiency, and applications that a network can effectively support.

LAN topologies. The topology or physical architecture of a LAN identifies how the stations (terminals, printers, modems, etc.) are interconnected. The transmission media used with LANs include metallic *twisted-wire pairs, coaxial cable,* and *optical fiber cables.* Presently, most LANs use coaxial cable; however, optical fiber cable systems are being installed in many new networks. Fiber systems can operate at higher transmission bit rates and have a larger capacity to transfer information than coaxial cables.

The most common LAN topologies are the star, bus, bus tree, and ring, which are illustrated in Figure 14-21.

Star Topology. The preeminent feature of the star topology is that each station is radially linked to a *central node* through a direct point-to-point connection as shown in Figure 14-21a. With a star configuration, a transmission from one station enters the central node where it is retransmitted on all of the outgoing links. Therefore, although the circuit arrangement physically resembles a star, it is logically configured as a bus (i.e., transmissions from any station are received by all other stations).

Central nodes offer a convenient location for system or station troubleshooting because all traffic between outlying nodes must flow through the central node. The central node is sometimes referred to as *central control, star coupler,* or *central switch* and typically is a computer. The star configuration is best adapted to applications where most of the communications occur between the central node and outlying nodes. The star arrangement is also well suited to systems where there is a large demand to communicate with only a few of the remote terminals. Time-sharing systems are generally configured with a star topology. A star configuration is also well suited for word processing and data base management applications.

Star couplers can be implemented either passively or actively. When passive couplers are used with a metallic transmission medium, transformers in the coupler provide an electromagnetic linkage through the coupler, which passes incoming signals on to outgoing links. If optical fiber cables are used for the transmission media, coupling can be achieved by fusing fibers together. With active couplers, digital circuitry in the central node acts as a repeater. Incoming data are simply regenerated and repeated on to all outgoing lines.

One disadvantage of a star topology is that the network is only as reliable as the central node. When the central node fails, the system fails. If one or more outlying nodes fail, however, the rest of the users can continue to use the remainder of the network. When failure of any single entity within a network is critical to the point that it will disrupt service on the entire network, that entity is referred to as a *critical resource.* Thus, the central node in a star configuration is a critical resource.

Bus Topology. In essence, the bus topology is a multipoint or multidrop circuit configuration where individual nodes are interconnected by a common, shared communications channel as shown in Figure 14-21b. With the bus topology, all stations connect, using appropriate interfacing hardware, directly to a common linear transmission medium, generally referred to as a bus. In a bus configuration, network control is not centralized to a particular node. In fact, the most distinguishing feature of a bus LAN is that control is distributed among all the nodes connected to the LAN. Data transmissions on a bus network are

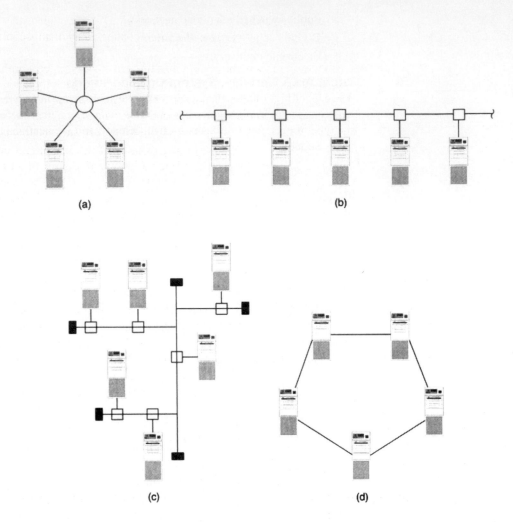

FIGURE 14-21   LAN topologies: (a) star; (b) bus; (c) tree bus; (d) ring or loop

usually in the form of small packets containing user addresses and data. When one station desires to transmit data to another station, it monitors the bus first to determine if it is currently being used. If no other stations are communicating over the network (i.e., the network is clear), the monitoring station can commence to transmit its data. When one station begins transmitting, all other stations become receivers. Each receiver must monitor all transmission on the network and determine which are intended for them. When a station identifies its address on a received data message, it acts upon it or it ignores that transmission.

One advantage of a bus topology is no special routing or circuit switching is required and, therefore, it is not necessary to store and retransmit messages intended for other nodes. This advantage eliminates a considerable amount of message identification overhead and processing time. However, with heavy usage systems, there is a high likelihood that more than one station may desire to transmit at the same time. When transmissions from two or more stations occur simultaneously, a data collision occurs, disrupting data communications on the entire network. Obviously, a priority contention scheme is necessary to handle data collision. Such a priority scheme is called *carrier sense, multiple access with collision detect* (CSMA/CD) which is discussed in a later section of this chapter.

Because network control is not centralized in a bus configuration, a node failure will not disrupt data flow on the entire LAN. The critical resource in this case is not a node but instead the bus itself. A failure anywhere along the bus opens the network and, depending on the versatility of the communications channel, may disrupt communication on the entire network.

The addition of new nodes on a bus can sometimes be a problem because gaining access to the bus cable may be a cumbersome task, especially if it is enclosed within a wall, floor, or ceiling. One means of reducing installation problems is to add secondary buses to the primary communications channel. By branching off into other bases, a multiple bus structure called a *tree bus* is formed. Figure 14-21c shows a tree bus configuration.

Ring Topology. With a ring topology, adjacent stations are interconnected by repeaters in a closed-loop configuration as shown in Figure 14-21d. Each node participates as a repeater between two adjacent links within the ring. The repeaters are relatively simple devices capable of receiving data from one link and retransmitting them on a second link. Messages, usually in packet form, are propagated in the simplex mode (one-way only) from node to node around the ring until it has circled the entire loop and returned to the originating node where it is verified that the data in the returned message are identical to the data originally transmitted. Hence, the network configuration serves as an inherent error-detection mechanism. The destination station(s) can acknowledge reception of the data by setting or clearing appropriate bits within the control segment of the message packet. Packets contain both source and destination address fields as well as additional network control information and user data. Each node examines incoming data packets, copying packets designated for them, and acting as a repeater for all data packets by retransmitting them (bit by bit) to the next down-line repeater. A repeater should neither alter the content of received packets nor change the transmission rate.

Virtually any physical transmission medium can be used with the ring topology. Twisted-wire pairs offer low cost but severely limited transmission rates. Coaxial cables provide greater capacity than twisted-wire pairs at practically the same cost. The highest data rates, however, are achieved with optical fiber cables, except at a substantially higher installation cost.

LAN transmission formats. Two transmission techniques or formats are used with local area networks, baseband and broadband, to multiplex transmissions from a multitude of stations onto a single transmission medium.

Baseband Transmission Format. Baseband transmission formats are defined as transmission formats that use digital signaling. In addition, baseband formats use the transmission medium as a single-channel device. Only one station can transmit at a time and all stations must transmit and receive the same types of signals (encoding schemes, bit rates, etc.). Baseband transmission formats time-division multiplex signals onto the transmission medium. All stations can use the media but only one at a time. The entire frequency spectrum (bandwidth) is used by (or at least made available to) whichever station is presently transmitting. With a baseband format, transmissions are bidirectional. A signal inserted at any point on the transmission medium propagates in both directions to the ends, where it is absorbed. Digital signaling requires a bus topology because digital signals cannot be easily propagated through the splitters and joiners necessary in a tree bus topology. Because of transmission line losses, baseband LANs are limited to a distance of no more than a couple miles.

Broadband Transmission Formats. Broadband transmission formats use the connecting media as a multichannel device. Each channel occupies a different frequency band within the total allocated bandwidth (i.e., frequency-division multiplexing). Consequently, each channel can contain different modulation and encoding schemes and operate at different transmission rates. A broadband network permits voice, digital data, and video to be transmitted simultaneously over the same transmission medium. However, broadband systems are unidirectional and require RF modems, amplifiers, and more complicated transceivers than baseband systems. For this reason baseband systems are more prevalent.

TABLE 14-12 Baseband Versus Broadband Transmission Formats

Baseband	Broadband
Uses digital signaling	Analog signaling requiring RF modems and amplifiers
Entire bandwidth used by each transmission—no FDM	FDM possible; i.e., multiple data channels (video, audio, data, etc.)
Bidirectional	Unidirectional
Bus topology	Bus or tree bus topology
Maximum length approximately 1500 m	Maximum length up to tens of kilometers
Advantages	
Less expensive	High capacity
Simpler technology	Multiple traffic types
Easier and quicker to install	More flexible circuit configurations, larger area covered
Disadvantages	
Single channel	RF modem and amplifiers required
Limited capacity	Complex installation and maintenance
Grounding problems	Double propagation delay
Limited distance	

Circuit components used with broadband LANs easily facilitate splitting and joining operations; consequently, both bus and tree bus topologies are allowed. Broadband systems can span much greater distances than baseband systems. Distances of up to tens of miles are possible.

The layout for a baseband system is much less complex than a broadband system and, therefore, easier and less expensive to implement. The primary disadvantages of baseband are its limited capacity and length. Broadband systems can carry a wide variety of different kinds of signals on a number of channels. By incorporating amplifiers, broadband can span much greater distances than baseband. Table 14-12 summarizes baseband and broadband transmission formats.

LAN access control methodologies. In a practical local area network, it is very likely that more than one user may wish to use the network media at any given time. For a medium to be shared by various users, a means of controlling access is necessary. Media-sharing methods are known as access methodologies. Network access methodologies describe how users access the communications channel in a local area network. The first LANs were developed by computer manufacturers; they were expensive and worked only with certain types of computers with a limited number of software programs. LANs also required a high degree of technical knowledge and expertise to install and maintain. In 1980, the IEEE, in an effort to resolve problems with local area networks, formed the 802 Local Area Network Standards Committee. In 1983, the committee established several recommended standards for LANs. The two most prominent standards are IEEE Standard 802.3, which addresses an access method for bus topologies called *carrier sense, multiple access with collision detection* (CSMA/CD), and IEEE Standard 802.5, which describes an access method for ring topologies called *token passing*.

Carrier Sense, Multiple Access with Collision Detection. CSMA/CD is an access method used primarily with LANs configured in a bus topology. CSMA/CD uses the basic philosophy that, "If you have something to say, say it. If there's a problem, we'll work it out later." With CSMA/CD, any station (node) can send a message to any other station (or stations) as long as the transmission medium is free of transmissions from other stations. Stations monitor (listen to) the line to determine if the line is busy. If a station has a message to transmit but the line is busy, it waits for an idle condition before transmitting its message. If two stations transmit at the same time, a *collision* occurs. When this happens, the station first sensing the collision sends a special jamming signal to all other stations on the network. All stations then cease transmitting (*back off*) and wait a random period of time before attempting a retransmission. The random delay time for each station is different and, therefore, allows for prioritizing the stations on the network. If successive collisions occur, the back-off period for each station is doubled.

With CSMA/CD, stations must contend for the network. A station is not guaranteed access to the network. To detect the occurrence of a collision, a station must be capable of transmitting and receiving simultaneously. CSMA/CD is used by most LANs configured in a bus topology. *Ethernet* is an example of a LAN that uses CSMA/CD and is described later in this chapter.

Another factor that could possibly cause collisions with CSMA/CD is *propagation delay*. Propagation delay is the time it takes a signal to travel from a source to a destination. Due to propagation delay, it is possible for the line to appear idle when, in fact, another station is transmitting a signal that has not yet reached the monitoring station.

Token Passing. *Token passing* is a network access method used primarily with LANs configured in a ring topology using either baseband or broadband transmission formats. When using *token passing* access, nodes do not contend for the right to transmit data. With token passing, a specific packet of data, called a *token,* is circulated around the ring from station to station, always in the same direction. The token is generated by a designated station known as the *active monitor.* Before a station is allowed to transmit, it must first possess the token. Each station, in turn, acquires the token and examines the data frame to determine if it is carrying a packet addressed to it. If the frame contains a packet with the receiving station's address, it copies the packet into memory, appends any messages it has to send to the token, then relinquishes the token by retransmitting all data packets and the token to the next node on the network. With token passing, each station has equal access to the transmission medium. As with CSMA/CD, each transmitted packet contains source and destination address fields. Successful delivery of a data frame is confirmed by the destination station by setting *frame status flags,* then forwarding the frame around the ring to the original transmitting station. The packet then is removed from the frame before transmitting the token. A token cannot be used twice, and there is a time limitation on how long a token can be held. This prevents one station from disrupting data transmissions on the network by holding the token until it has a packet to transmit. When a station does not possess the token, it can only receive and transfer other packets destined to other stations.

Some 16-Mbps token ring networks use a modified form of token passing methodology where the token is relinquished as soon as a data frame has been transmitted instead of waiting until the transmitted data frame has been returned. This is known as an *early token release mechanism.*

TOKEN PASSING RING

Olaf Soderblum is given credit for developing the first *token passing ring* network architecture in 1969. IBM, however, became the driving force behind the standardization and adoption of the token ring, and a prototype developed by IBM in Zurich, Switzerland, served as a model for the IEEE Token Ring Standard 802.5. IEEE 802.5 does not include a specification for a transmission rate (bps) for token rings although IBM has specified token ring networks that operate at both 4 Mbps and 16 Mbps.

Figure 14-22a shows the token layout for the IEEE 802.5 specified frame. The token consists of three *octets* where an octet is eight bits of data. The words *octet* and *byte* are often used interchangeably as the difference between them is rather subtle and subject to opinion. A byte is sometimes thought of as an eight-bit word that represents a particular

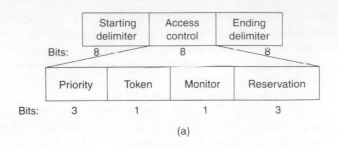

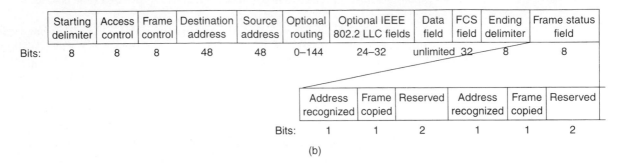

FIGURE 14-22 IEEE 802.5 Token and MAC sublayer frame layout: (a) token frame layout; (b) MAC sublayer frame layout

character, number, or function, whereas an octet is merely eight bits of data, which could represent digitized voice, video, image, or other digital information or possibly even be broken down into smaller groupings. On the other hand, a byte of data is sometimes thought of as simply any meaningful grouping of bits regardless of length. The basic functions of the fields within IEEE 802.5 token and sublayer frames are briefly summarized below.

Starting delimiter field. The starting delimiter field alerts receive stations on a token passing ring that a frame is approaching. Both the token and MAC sublayer frames begin with a starting delimiter.

Access control field. The access control field distinguishes between tokens and MAC (media access control) sublayer frames. If the token (T) bit is cleared, the received frame is a free token and the access control field is immediately followed by an ending delimiter. The receive station can obtain the token by setting the token bit. The starting delimiter field plus the access control field with the T-bit set form the first two fields of the IEEE 802.5 MAC sublayer data frame (shown in Figure 14-22b), allowing the station to append address information, data, and the remaining fields in the data frame layout, then transmit the frame onto the network.

The monitor (M) bit in the access control field is used by the station designated as the active token monitor to manage error conditions such as no token circulating and persistent busy token. The monitor station detects a lost-token condition by using a timeout greater than the time necessary for the longest frame to traverse the complete ring. If no token is detected during this time, it is assumed to be lost. To recover, the monitor station purges the ring of any residual data and releases a free token. To detect a circulating busy token, the monitor station sets a monitor bit to a logic 1 on any passing busy token. If it detects a busy token with the M-bit already set, it knows that the originating station failed to purge its packet. The monitor station then changes the busy token to a free token.

The three priority (P) bits within the access control field are used to prioritize stations waiting to transmit onto the network. There are eight levels of priority. The three reservation (R) bits are used to reserve future tokens. A station having a higher priority than the current busy token can reserve the next free token for its priority level as the busy token passes by. After the current transmitting station has completed its transmission, it issues a free token at the higher priority level. Stations with a lower priority level cannot seize the token, thus, allowing it to pass on to the requesting station of equal or higher priority.

Frame control field. If the received frame contained a set T-bit in the access control field, then the frame is the MAC sublayer data frame and the next field is the frame control field, which indicates whether the frame contains data or is a special network management frame.

Source and destination address fields. The source and destination address fields each contain six octets that identify the sending and receiving stations, respectively.

Routing information field (RIF). The routing information field is optional and used with devices called source routing bridges, which are used to link multiple token ring LANs. The RIF can be up to 18 octets long.

IEEE 802.2 logical link control (LLC) fields. The LLC fields contain three or four optional octets for the destination service access point (DSAP) field, source service access point (SSAP) field, and control field. The DSAP and SSAP fields are used to identify the types of protocols embedded within the data field. Service access point codes are assigned by the IEEE to identify particular protocols. For example, the SAP code EO identifies a Novell protocol and a SAP code of 06 identifies a TCP/IP protocol.

Data field. The data field contains embedded upper-level protocol data if the frame is a data frame, and network management information if the frame is a network management frame. The length of the data field is unlimited as long as the transmitting station does not exceed the timing limit that a station can possess a token. For example, a 10-ms time limit places a practical limit on the length of the data field in a 4-Mbps token ring network of approximately 4500 bytes and of 16,000 to 18,000 bytes on a 16-Mbps network.

Frame check sequence (FCS) field. IEEE 802.5 specifies a 32-bit cyclic redundancy check identical to that used with IEEE 802.3.

Ending delimiter field. The ending delimiter field notifies the receiving station when the end of a frame has arrived and also whether the frame is an intermediate frame with more related data immediately following. The ending delimiter can also indicate that a station other than the source or destination stations has detected an error in a frame. When an error is detected, the frame should be ignored and returned around the ring to the source station for removal.

Frame status field. The frame status field contains eight bits that are used to let the source station know if the frame was successfully delivered. If the destination station recognizes its address, the address recognize bits are set. If the frame was successfully copied into the destination station's memory, the frame copied bits are set. There are two address recognize and frame copied bits for redundancy because this field is not checked by the FCS field.

In addition to the functions described in the previous sections, the station designated as the active monitor for the network must perform the following tasks:

Remove frames that have not been removed by the sending station.

Regenerate lost or damaged tokens.

Provide a special 24-bit buffer if the physical length of the ring is not long enough to provide enough time delay (latency) to hold the 24-bit token.

Control the master system clock.

Ensure that there is only one station designated as the active monitor.

Slotted Ring

The *slotted ring* is a variation of the token passing ring. With the slotted ring, a finite number of contiguous time slots arc circulated around the ring. Each slot is of fixed size and contains positions in the slot for source and destination addresses and packet data. A *busy/not busy* bit is included at the beginning of each circulating slot to indicate whether that slot is available. A slot is either *full* or *empty,* depending on the logic condition of the busy/not busy bit (logic 0 − empty, logic 1 = full). If a station (node) wishes to transmit data, it must find an empty time slot. The transmitting station inserts its data into the empty slot in the appropriate place, sets the busy bit, then passes the slot on to the next station. When a station identifies its address in a received packet, it copies the data into its buffers and resets the busy bit to indicate that slot is now empty and available for subsequent nodes to use.

Token Bus

Token passing is occasionally used in a bus or tree topology. In such a configuration, stations on the bus must form a logical ring. However, because the physical layout of a bus does not conform to a ring format, some kind of orderly and logical sequence has to be devised to pass the token from node to node. The token, with its destination address, is passed around the bus in a virtual ring configuration. That is, each station receives and transmits to predetermined stations as though they were up or down link from them. Again, a control packet, known as a token, regulates the right of access. When a station receives the token, it is granted control of the transmission medium for a predetermined time slot. The station may transmit one or more packets and may poll other stations or receive packets. When a station is done with the packet or when the prescribed time is over, the station passes the token on to the next logical station. Nontoken stations are allowed on the bus; however, they can only respond to polls from other stations or requests for acknowledgment.

ETHERNET

Ethernet is a baseband data transmission system designed by Xerox Corporation in the middle 1970s. A man named Robert Metcalfe, who later became the founder of 3COM Corporation, generally is considered to be the original inventor of Ethernet. By 1980, Xerox joined forces with Intel Corporation and Digital Equipment Corporation (DEC) in an attempt to make Ethernet an industry standard. In 1981 a version of Ethernet called DIX 1.0 or Ethernet I was developed. Ethernet I was replaced in 1982 by DIX 2.0 or Ethernet II, which remains the current standard. By 1983, the consortium had developed and introduced a single-chip controller for Ethernet. Later, Mostek Corporation, working with DEC and Advanced Micro Devices, announced a two-chip set for this purpose—one chip in the local area network controller for Ethernet (LANCE) and the second as a serial interface adapter. After adding safety and signaling features, the IEEE Standards Committee adopted Ethernet and published the initial Ethernet standard known as 10BASE-5. The term "10BASE-5" refers to the specifications for the physical layer and data link layers of the ISO network hierarchy. The "10" means that this adaption of Ethernet operates at 10 Mbps, and the word "BASE" means the LAN carries baseband data (i.e., no carrier). The "5" indicates that the maximum end-to-end network length is 500 m unless a repeater is used to amplify the signals. Ethernet uses CSMA/CD to access the network.

The combined ANSI/IEEE 802.3 subcommittee has defined alternative transmission media to the 10BASE-5 system. Today, there are four Ethernet specifications: 10BASE-5 (Thick Ethernet), 10BASE-2 (Thinwire Ethernet), 1BASE-5 (StarLAN), and 10BASE-T (Twisted-Pair Ethernet). Currently, efforts are underway to develop methods of transporting Ethernet signals on optical fiber cables [10BASE-FL (FOIRL)—fiber-optic interrepeater link], over radio-frequency broadcasts (both terrestrial and satellite), and on infrared

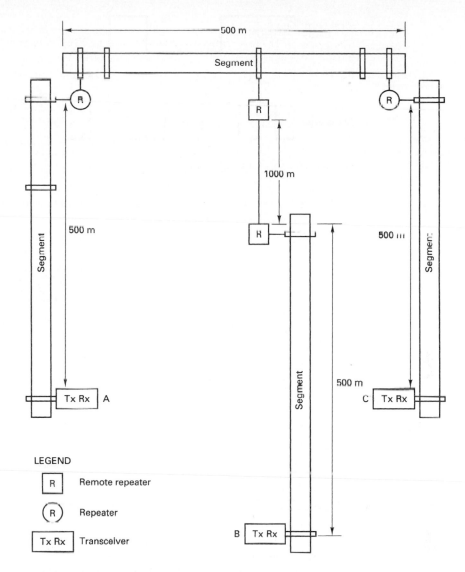

FIGURE 14-23 Ethernet 10BASE-5 network configuration

light systems at transmission rates in excess of 100 Mbps. The 1BASE-5 Ethernet system has never received widespread acceptance by industry due to its slow transmission rate; therefore, it will not be discussed.

10BASE-5 Ethernet

10BASE-5 is the original Ethernet system that specifies a "thick" 50-Ω, double-shielded coaxial cable for a transmission medium. Hence, this version of Ethernet is sometimes called *Thicknet* or *Thick Ethernet*. Because of its inflexible nature, 10BASE-5 Ethernet is also sometimes called "frozen yellow garden hose." The 10BASE-5 system uses a multidrop bus topology as shown in Figure 14-23. The 10BASE-5 system supports up to 100 nodes per segment with a minimum node separation of 2.5 m. Three additional 500-m segments can be added, provided a repeater is used to amplify the signals and pass them from one segment to another. Thus, the maximum system length is extended to 1500 m, as shown between points A and C in Figure 14-23. Remote repeaters can be used with a maximum distance of 1000 m between them, thus extending the maximum end-to-end length to

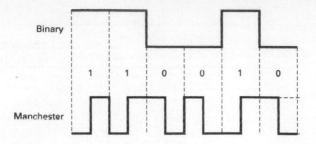

FIGURE 14-24 Manchester code

2.5 km. In Figure 14-23, if the center and right segments were interchanged, there would be a 2.5-km separation between points A and B. However, there must always be only one signal path between any two stations. 10BASE-5 Ethernet uses a device called *media access unit* (MAU) to connect terminals to the cable. Each connection is called a *tap* and the cable that connects a MAU to its terminal is called a *drop*. Within each MAU, a transceiver transfers the electrical signals between the drop and the coaxial transmission medium.

The baseband protocol for 10BASE-5 supports a 10-Mbps transmission rate that uses a signaling technique known as *Manchester encoding*. Manchester encoding is used when a system clock is not provided on a separate line. With Manchester encoding, each bit cell is divided into two parts: the first half contains the complement of the bit value and the second half contains the actual bit value. Thus, a low-to-high transition in the middle of a bit cell represents a logic 1 and a high-to-low transition represents a logic 0. The Manchester encoding format is shown in Figure 14-24. This coding format ensures that a signal transition occurs in every bit cell, enhancing clock recovery. This technique of recovering a clock from the serial data stream is sometimes called *self-clocking*. The Manchester format also ensures that the encoded bit stream will be high 50% of the time and low 50% of the time, thus reducing the charge developed across the inherent capacitance of the transmission.

10BASE-2 Ethernet

10BASE-5 Ethernet uses 50-Ω RG-11 coaxial cable, which is thick enough to give it a high noise immunity, thus making it well suited to laboratory and industrial applications. The RG-11 cable is expensive to install. Consequently, the initial costs of implementing a 10BASE-5 Ethernet system are too high for many small businesses. In an effort to reduce the cost, International Computer Ltd., Hewlett-Packard, and 3COM Corporation developed an Ethernet variation that uses thinner, less expensive 50-Ω RG-58 coaxial cable. RG-58 is similar to the cable used to carry television signals. It is less expensive to purchase and install than RG-11. In 1985, the IEEE 803.2 Standards Committee adopted the new version of Ethernet and gave it the name 10BASE-2. 10BASE-2 Ethernet is sometimes referred to as *CheaperNet* or *Thinwire Ethernet*. 10BASE-2 Ethernet allows a maximum segment length of 185 m with a maximum of 30 nodes per segment, which is sufficient for most office applications. 10BASE-2 Ethernet also eliminates the MAU. The transceiver is located inside the terminal and a simple BNC-T connector connects the Ethernet network interface card (NIC) directly to the coaxial cable. This eliminates the expensive transceiver cable and the need to tap or drill into the coaxial cable. CheaperNet is most popular in PC-based LAN applications.

10BASE-T Ethernet

10BASE-T Ethernet is another popular Ethernet transmission standard commonly used with PC-based LAN environments, utilizing a star topology. The "T" stands for *unshielded twisted-pair wire,* or simply UTP. The 10BASE-T system was developed to allow Ethernet to utilize existing voice-grade telephone wiring to carry Ethernet signals. Standard modular RJ-45 and RJ-11 telephone jacks and four-pair UTP telephone wire are specified in the

Preamble	Destination address	Source address	Type	Data unit	Frame check sequence
Bytes: 8	6	6	2	46–1500	4

(a)

Preamble	Start frame delimiter	Destination address	Source address	Length	Logical link control IEEE 802.2 data	Frame check sequence	End of frame delimiter
Bytes: 7	1	2–6	2–6	2	46–1500	4	9.6 μs

(b)

FIGURE 14-25 (a) Ethernet frame layout; (b) IEEE 802.3 frame layout

standard for interconnecting nodes to the LAN. The RJ-45 connector plugs directly into the *network interface card* located in the PC. 10BASE-T operates at a transmission rate of 10 Mbps and uses the standard CSMA/CD protocol; however, it uses a *concentrator* to distribute the transmission media to the end users, essentially converting a number of point-to-point connections into a single LAN. The concentrator is basically an intelligent "hub" or multipoint repeater that expands the 10BASE-5 star topology.

Nodes are added to the network through a port. When a node is turned on, its transceiver sends a DC current over the twisted pair to the hub. The hub senses the current and enables the port, thus connecting the node to the network. The port remains connected as long as the node continues to supply DC current to the hub. If the node is turned off, or, if an open or short circuit condition arises in the twisted pair between the node and the hub, the DC current stops and the hub disconnects the port while the remainder of the LAN continues to operate status quo.

Ethernet Data Format

In actuality, Ethernet II and IEEE standard 802.3 are not identical, although the term *Ethernet* is generally used to refer to any IEEE 802.3–compliant network. Ethernet and IEEE 802.3 both specify that data are transmitted from one station to another in blocks called frames. The frame formats for both the IEEE 802.3 standard and Ethernet are shown in Figure 14-25 and described as follows.

Ethernet II frame layout

Preamble. The preamble consists of 8 bytes (64 bits) of alternating 1s and 0s. The purpose of the preamble is to establish clock synchronization. The last two bits of the preamble are reserved for the start frame delimiter.

Start frame delimiter. The start frame delimiter is simply a series of two logic 1s appended to the end of the preamble whose purpose is to mark the end of the preamble and the beginning of the data frame.

Destination address. The source and destination addresses and the field type make up the frame header. The destination address consists of six bytes (48 bits) and is the address of the node or nodes that have been designated to receive the frame. The address can be a unique, group, or broadcast address and is determined by the following bit combinations:

bit 0=0.   If bit 0 is a 0, the address is interpreted as a unique address intended for only one station.

bit 0=1.   If bit 0 is a 1, the address is interpreted as a multicast (group) address. All stations that have been preassigned with this group address will accept the frame.

bit 0–47.   If all bits in the destination field are 1s, this identifies a broadcast address and all nodes have been identified as receivers of this frame.

Source address. The source address consists of six bytes (48 bits) that correspond to the address of the station sending the frame.

Type field. Ethernet does not use the 16-bit type field. It is placed in the frame so it can be used for higher layers of the OSI protocol hierarchy.

Data field. The data field contains the information and can be between 46 bytes and 1500 bytes long. The data field is transparent. Data link control characters and zero-bit stuffing are not used. Transparency is achieved by counting back from the FCS character.

Frame check sequence field. The CRC field contains 32 bits for error detection and is computed from the header and data fields.

IEEE 802.3 standard frame layout

Preamble. The preamble consists of seven bytes to establish clock synchronization. The last byte of the preamble is used for the start frame delimiter.

Start frame delimiter. The start frame delimiter is simply a series of two logic 1s appended to the end of the preamble whose purpose is to mark the end of the preamble and the beginning of the data frame.

Destination and source addresses. The destination and source addresses are defined the same as with Ethernet II.

Length field. The 2-byte length field in the IEEE 802.3 frame replaces the type field in the Ethernet frame. The length field indicates the length of the variable-length logical link control (LLC) data field, which contains all upper-layered embedded protocols.

Logical link control (LLC). The LLC field contains the information and can be between 46 bytes and 1500 bytes long. The LLC field defined in IEEE 802.3 is identical to the LLC field defined for token ring networks.

Frame check sequence field. The CRC field is defined the same as with Ethernet II.

End of frame delimiter. The end frame delimiter is a period of time (9.6 μs) in which no bits are transmitted. With Manchester encoding, a void in transitions longer than 1-bit time indicates the end of the frame.

System Operation

Transmission. The data link control for Ethernet is CSMA/CD. Stations acquire access to the transmission system through contention. They are not polled, nor do they have specific time slots for transmission. A station wishing to transmit first determines if another station is currently using the transmission system. The controller accomplishes this through the transceiver by sensing the presence of a carrier on the line. The controller may be a hardware or a software function, depending on the complexity of the station.

The presence of a carrier is denoted by the signal transitions on the line produced by the Manchester code. If a carrier is detected, the station defers transmission until the line is quiet. After the required delay, the station sends digital data to the controller. The controller converts these data to Manchester code, inserts the CRC, adds the preamble, and places the packet on-line. The transmission of the entire packet is not yet assured. A different station may also have detected the quiet line and started to transmit its own packet. The first station monitors the line for a period called the *collision window* or the *collision interval*. This interval is a function of the end-to-end propagation delay of the line. This delay, including the delay caused by any repeaters, measured in distance, cannot exceed 2.5 km. If a data collision has not occurred in this interval, the station is said to have line acquisition and will continue to transmit the entire packet. Should a collision be detected, both of the transmitting stations will immediately abort their transmissions for a random period of time and then attempt retransmission. A data collision may be detected by the transceiver by comparing the received signal with the transmitted signal. To make this comparison, a station must still be transmitting its packet while a previously transmitted signal has propagated to the end of the line and back. This dictates that a packet be of some minimum size. If a collision is detected, it is the controller that must take the necessary action. The controller-transceiver interface contains a line for notification of Collision Presence (10-MHz square wave). The remaining three lines of this interface are the Transmit Data, Receive Data, and power for the transceiver. Because a collision is manifested in some form of phase violation, the controller alone may detect a collision. In Ethernet, data collision is detected mainly by the transceiver. When feasible, this is supplemented by a collision detection facility in the controller. To ensure that all stations are aware of the collision, a *collision enforcement consensus procedure* is invoked. When the controller detects a collision, it transmits four to six bytes of random data. These bytes are called the *jam sequence*. If a collision has occurred, the station's random waiting time before retransmission is determined from a *binary exponential back-off algorithm*. The time slot is usually set to be slightly longer than the round-trip transmission time of the channel. The time of the wait delay is randomly selected from this interval.

Example 14-4

Transmission time slot = time of 512 bits

$$\text{Maximum time of the interval} = \frac{512 \text{ bits}}{10 \text{ Mbps}} = 51.2 \ \mu s$$

Time delay interval $= 0$ to $51.2 \ \mu s$

For each succeeding collision encountered by the same packet, the time interval is doubled until a maximum interval is reached. The maximum interval is given as $2^{10} \times$ transmission time slot. After 15 unsuccessful attempts at transmitting a packet have been made, no further attempts are made and the error is reported to the station. This is the major drawback of Ethernet—it cannot guarantee packet delivery at a time of heavy transmission load.

Reception. The line is monitored until the station's address is detected. The controller strips the preamble, checks the CRC, and converts the Manchester code back to digital format. If the packet contains any errors, it is discarded. The end of the packet is recognized by the absence of a carrier on the transmission line. This means that no transitions were detected for the period of 75 ns to 125 ns since the center of the last bit cell. The decoding is accomplished through a phase-locked loop. The phase-locked loop is initialized by the known pattern of the preamble.

Table 14-13 shows a comparison of IEEE standard 802.3 and Ethernet 10BASE-5, 10BASE-2, and 10BASE-T physical specifications.

FIBER DISTRIBUTED DATA INTERFACE

First-generation LAN standards, such as Ethernet and token ring, do not have the bandwidth necessary to handle the high transmission rates required to communicate multiplexed high-capacity systems carrying digitized sound, still pictures, and compressed video, especially over long distances. Consequently, in 1984 the American National Standards Institute (ANSI) published a set of standards (X3T9.5) called *Fiber Data Distributed Interface* (FDDI). FDDI specifies standards for a ring topology using optical fiber cables with transmission rates up to 100 Mbps that allow for distances up to 2 km between stations. FDDI is not an IEEE standard; however, it does support IEEE 802.2 logical link control protocols, offering a transparent interoperability to layers 3 through 7 of IEEE-compliant protocols.

TABLE 14-13 Comparison of IEEE Standard 802.3 Physical Specifications for Ethernet 10BASE-5, 10BASE-2, and 10BASE-T

	10BASE-5 (Ethernet)	10BASE-2 (CheapNet)	10BASE-T (UTP)
Access control	CSMA/CD	CSMA/CD	CSMA/CD
Topology	Bus	Bus	Star
Message protocol	Variable packet size	Variable packet size	Variable packet size
Signaling rate	10 Mbps	10 Mbps	10 Mbps
Signaling type	Baseband	Baseband	Baseband
Cable type	IEEE 802.3 thick double-shielded coax	RG-58 coax	UTP level 3 or level 4 telephone cable
Cable impedance	50 Ω	50 Ω	NA
Minimum node separation	2.5 m	0.5 m	NA
Maximum segment length	500 m	185 m	100 m (PC to hub)
Maximum nodes per segment	100	30	1024 (per network)
Maximum number of segments	5	2	NA
Maximum station separation	2500 m	925 m	NA

In addition to wider bandwidths and higher operating speeds, FDDI also has a higher degree of reliability and security than Ethernet and token rings. The higher degree of reliability can be attributed to the transmission medium. Optical fibers are immune to both electromagnetic interference (EMI) and radio frequency interference (RFI). FDDI's physical topology lends itself to a more reliable system because FDDI is comprised of two separate rings: a primary and a backup ring. The topology used with FDDI is a double (dual-counter rotating) ring configuration as shown in Figure 14-26. One of the rings is designated the *primary ring* and the other the *secondary ring.* Data propagates around the two rings in opposite directions. Under normal operating conditions, only the primary ring carries data; the secondary ring is reserved as a backup and used only if the primary ring fails. As with the IEEE 802 standard, FDDI uses token passing for its access method. There are several differences between the two, however, that are intended to allow FDDI to take advantage of its high-speed ring to maximize efficiency.

FDDI Nodes

FDDI LANs can have up to 500 nodes separated by 2 km, and the entire media can extend for a total distance of up to 200 km (125 miles), if repeaters are used at least every 2 km. FDDI can use two types of nodes: *single attach* and *dual attach,* as shown in Figure 14-26. As shown in the figure, dual-attach nodes are stations that are connected to both the primary and the secondary rings of the FDDI LAN. Single-attach nodes are connected to the primary ring only through an access device similar to an Ethernet hub called a *concentrator.* Single-attach stations cannot use the secondary ring as a backup if the primary ring fails. Thus, if the connection between the concentrator and the primary ring fails or is broken, all single-attach stations are disconnected from the network. Dual-attach stations must have two optical transmitters and two optical receivers, which obviously makes them more expensive. Consequently, in many FDDI networks only the most critical nodes, such as the network server, are dual attached.

As with Ethernet and token ring hubs, FDDI concentrators are able to sense when one of the single-attach nodes has the power shut off or is disconnected. When this happens, the concentrator disconnects the disabled node from the network. The concentrator also has the ability to completely bypass defective single-attach nodes to restore continuity to the remainder of the primary ring.

Figure 14-27 illustrates the self-healing feature of an FDDI network. Whenever there is a break in the cable, the dual-attach nodes on either side of the break connect the primary

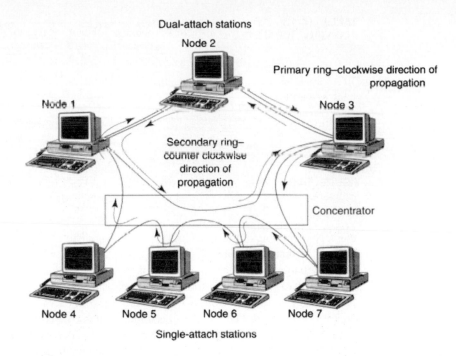

Dual-attach stations

Node 2

Primary ring—clockwise direction of propagation

Node 1

Node 3

Secondary ring— counter clockwise direction of propagation

Concentrator

Node 4   Node 5   Node 6   Node 7

Single-attach stations

FIGURE 14-26   FDDI LAN circuit configuration

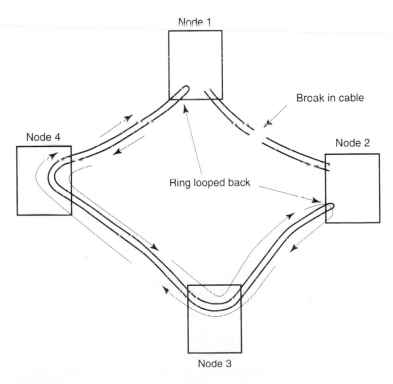

Node 1

Break in cable

Node 4

Node 2

Ring looped back

Node 3

FIGURE 14-27   FDDI self-healing feature

Data Communications Protocols and Network Configurations

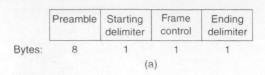

Preamble	Starting delimiter	Frame control	Ending delimiter
Bytes: 8	1	1	1

(a)

	Preamble	Starting delimiter	Frame control	Destination address	Source address	DATA up to	Frame check sequence	Ending delimiter	Frame status
Bytes:	8	1	1	6	6	4500	4 (32 bit CRC)	.5 (4 bits)	1.5 (12 bits)

(b)

FIGURE 14-28 Token and data frame layouts: (a) FDDI token layout; (b) FDDI data frame structure

and secondary rings to form a single, longer ring. The ability of an FDDI network to re-configure around cable and circuit defects by establishing what is called a *ring-wrap,* makes it more reliable than either Ethernet or token ring networks.

FDDI uses a modified form of token passing for its access methodology. The FDDI methodology is different from IEEE standard 802.5 in two aspects. First, due to the greater lengths possible with FDDI LANs, it is impractical to convert free tokens to busy tokens and allow one station to monopolize the network until it receives confirmation that its last message was successfully received by the destination station. Instead of simply changing the logic condition of the T-bit in the access control byte, FDDI physically removes the token from the ring and transmits a full data frame. After completing transmission, a new token is released. Collisions are avoided as only one station can possess the free token at a time.

The second aspect that is different with FDDI is that numerous successive messages can be sent by a single station before it must relinquish the token. Recall that IEEE 802.5 allows only one message per token per user. Frames transmitted in a continuous stream are called synchronous frames and are prioritized according to a methodology known as *synchronous bandwidth allocation* (SBA). Figure 14-28 shows the layout for an FDDI token and an FDDI data frame structure.

FDDI Network Using Twisted-Pair Metallic Transmission Lines

FDDI was originally designed to be used with an optical fiber transmission line rather than copper wires. Optical fiber cables can support higher data transmission rates, are much more immune to noise interference, and do not radiate electromagnetic energy as do their metallic counterparts. However, the transducers used with optical fiber cables that convert light energy to electrical energy (photodetectors) and vice versa (light-emitting diodes) are relatively expensive and can add several hundred dollars to the cost of each node in the FDDI network.

To reduce the initial cost of an FDDI network, ANSI published a version of the FDDI standard that specifies twisted-pair metallic wire rather than an optical fiber cable. The standard specifies a transmission rate of 100 Mbps using the same protocol as the optical fiber version of FDDI. Because most standard telephone cable cannot support a 100-Mbps data rate, special *data-grade* cable must be installed. Even with the more expensive cable, however, metallic FDDI networks are still less expensive than optical cable systems.

Fibre Channel

Although high-speed network standards, such as FDDI, provide relatively inexpensive, reliable digital communications at data rates up to 100 Mbps, many commercial, educational, industrial, and scientific environments are still investigating systems that support even higher data rates. Hewlett-Packard Co., IBM, and Sun Microsystems Computer Corp.

recently announced the *Fibre Channel Systems Initiative* as an incentive to accelerate development of an affordable, high-speed interconnection standard for workstations and peripherals using optical fiber communications channels. The ANSI X3T9.3 *Fibre Channel Standard* is designed to facilitate data transmission rates in excess of 1 Gbps for distances up to 10 km using an optical fiber transmission medium.

The Fibre data channel specifies a matrix of switches, called a *fabric*, that performs network switching functions that are similar to those used with a standard telephone system. Computer systems attach to the fabric using dedicated transmit and receive lines designed to function as point-to-point, bidirectional serial communications channels. Network switches are capable of routing incoming data signals to any output port.

100BASE-T Ethernet

The 100BASE-T Ethernet includes a family of fast Ethernet standards offering 100-Mbps data transmission rates using CSMA/CD access methodology. Proposed IEEE Standard 802.3u details operation of the 100BASE-T network. There are three media-specific physical layer standards for 100BASE-T: 100BASE-TX, 100BASE-T4, and 100BASE-FX.

1. 100BASE-TX is the most common of the three standards and the one with the most technology available. The 100BASE-TX specifies 100-Mbps data transmission rates over two pair of Category 5 UTP (unshielded twisted pair) or two pair of Type 1 STP (shielded twisted pair).
2. 100BASE-T4 is a physical layer standard specifying 100-Mbps data rates over four pair of Category 3, 4, or 5 UTP.
3. 100BASE-FX is a physical layer standard specifying 100-Mbps data rates over optical fiber cables.

QUESTIONS

14-1. Define *data communications protocol.*

14-2. What is a master station? A slave station?

14-3. Define *polling* and *selecting.*

14-4. What is the difference between a synchronous and an asynchronous protocol?

14-5. What is the difference between a character-oriented protocol and a bit-oriented protocol?

14-6. Define the three operating modes used with data communications circuits.

14-7. What is the function of the clearing character?

14-8. What is a unique address? A group address? A broadcast address?

14-9. What does a negative acknowledgment to a poll indicate?

14-10. What is the purpose of a heading?

14-11. Why is IBM's 3270 synchronous protocol called "bisync"?

14-12. Why are SYN characters always transmitted in pairs?

14-13. What is an SPA? An SSA? A DA?

14-14. What is the purpose of a leading pad? A trailing pad?

14-15. What is the difference between a general poll and a specific poll?

14-16. What is a handshake?

14-17. (*Primary, secondary*) stations transmit polls.

14-18. What does a negative acknowledgment to a poll indicate?

14-19. What is a positive acknowledgment to a poll?

14-20. What is the difference between ETX, ETB, and ITB?

14-21. What character is used to terminate a heading and begin a block of text?

14-22. What is transparency? When is it necessary? Why?

14-23. What is the difference between a command and a response with SDLC?

14-24. What are the three transmission states used with SDLC? Explain them.

14-25. What are the five fields used with an SDLC frame? Briefly explain each.

14-26. What is the delimiting sequence used with SDLC?

14-27. What is the null address in SDLC? When is it used?

14-28. What are the three frame formats used with SDLC? Explain what each format is used for.

14-29. How is an information frame identified in SDLC? A supervisory frame? An unnumbered frame?

14-30. What are the purposes of the nr and ns sequences in SDLC?

14-31. With SDLC, when is the P bit set? The F bit?

14-32. What is the maximum number of unconfirmed frames that can be outstanding at any one time with SDLC? Why?

14-33. With SDLC, which frame formats can have an information field?

14-34. With SDLC, which frame formats can be used to confirm previously received frames?

14-35. What command/response is used for reporting procedural errors with SDLC?

14-36. Explain the three modes in SDLC that a secondary station can be in.

14-37. When is the configure command/response used with SDLC?

14-38. What is a go-ahead sequence? A turnaround sequence?

14-39. What is the transparency mechanism used with SDLC?

14-40. What is a message abort? When is it transmitted?

14-41. Explain invert-on-zero encoding. Why is it used?

14-42. What supervisory condition exists with HDLC that is not included with SDLC?

14-43. What is the delimiting sequence used with HDLC? The transparency mechanism?

14-44. Explain extended addressing as it is used with HDLC.

14-45. What is the difference between the basic control format and the extended control format with HDLC?

14-46. What is the difference in the information fields used with SDLC and HDLC?

14-47. What operational modes are included with HDLC that are not included with SDLC?

14-48. What is a public data network?

14-49. Describe a value-added network.

14-50. Explain the differences in circuit-, message-, and packet-switching techniques.

14-51. What is blocking? With which switching techniques is blocking possible?

14-52. What is a transparent switch? A transactional switch?

14-53. What is a packet?

14-54. What is the difference between a store-and-forward and a hold-and-forward network?

14-55. Explain the three modes of transmission for public data networks.

14-56. What is the user-to-network protocol designated by CCITT?

14-57. What is the user-to-network protocol designated by ANSI?

14-58. Which layers of the ISO protocol hierarchy are addressed by X.25?

14-59. Explain the following terms: *permanent virtual circuit, virtual call,* and *datagram.*

14-60. Why was HDLC selected as the link-level protocol for X.25?

14-61. Briefly explain the fields that comprise an X.25 call request packet.

14-62. Describe a local area network.

14-63. What is the connecting medium used with local area networks?

14-64. Explain the two transmission formats used with local area networks.

14-65. Explain CSMA/CD.

14-66. Explain token passing.

14-67. Describe what an ISDN is and who proposed its concept.

14-68. What are the primary principles of ISDN?

14-69. What are the evolutions of ISDN?

14-70. Describe the proposed architecture for ISDN.

14-71. Describe an ISDN D channel. An ISDN B channel.

14-72. Describe the following ISDN terms: *terminal equipment 1; terminal equipment 2; terminal adapter; reference point S; reference point T; reference point R; network termination 1; network termination 2; network termination 1,2; line termination unit; exchange termination;* and *reference point V.*

14-73. Describe the ISDN LAP-D format.

14-74. What are the differences between the ISDN LAP-D and LAP-B formats?

14-75. What is an ISDN service point identifier and when is it used?

14-76. What is an ISDN terminal endpoint identifier and when is it used?

14-77. Describe the basic concepts of BISDN and how it differs from narrowband ISDN.

14-78. What is meant by the asynchronous transfer mode?

14-79. What are the proposed new BISDN channel data rates?

14-80. What is the transmission media used with the asynchronous transfer mode communications standard?

14-81. Describe virtual channels and virtual paths as they are used with ATM.

14-82. Identify and explain the various subfields used with an ATM header field.

14-83. Identify and explain the various subfields used within an ATM information field.

14-84. What is the primary transmission media used with SONET?

14-85. Describe the frame format used with SONET.

14-86. What multiplexing technique is used with SONET to achieve higher levels of synchronous transport?

14-87. Describe the topologies commonly used with LANs.

14-88. List and describe the transmission formats used with LANs.

14-89. List and describe the access control methodologies used with LANs.

14-90. Describe the various fields and sublayer frames used with a token passing ring network.

14-91. Describe the operation of a slotted ring LAN.

14-92. What is Ethernet?

14-93. Briefly describe the following Ethernet systems: 10BASE-5, 10BASE-2, and 10BASE-T.

14-94. Identify and explain the various sections of an Ethernet II frame layout.

PROBLEMS

14-1. Determine the hex code for the control field in an SDLC frame for the following conditions: information frame, poll, transmitting frame 4, and confirming reception of frames 2, 3, and 4.

14-2. Determine the hex code for the control field in an SDLC frame for the following conditions: supervisory frame, ready to receive, final, confirming reception of frames 6, 7, and 0.

14-3. Insert 0s into the following SDLC data stream.

111 001 000 011 111 111 100 111 110 100 111 101 011 111 111 111 001 011

14-4. Delete 0s from the following SDLC data stream.

010 111 110 100 011 011 111 011 101 110 101 111 101 011 100 011 111 00

14-5. Sketch the NRZI waveform for the following data stream (start with a high condition).

1 0 0 1 1 1 0 0 1 0 1 0

14-6. Determine the hex code for the control field in an SDLC frame for the following conditions: information frame, not a poll, transmitting frame number 5, and confirming the reception of frames 0, 1, 2, and 3.

14-7. Determine the hex code for the control field in an SDLC frame for the following conditions: supervisory frame, not ready to receive, not a final, confirming reception of frames 7, 0, 1, and 2.

14-8. Insert 0s into the following SDLC data stream.

011011111101100001111100101110001011111111011111001

14-9. Delete 0s from the following SDLC data stream.

00101111100111110111110110001000111101110101100010 1

14-10. Sketch the NRZI levels for the following data stream (start with a high condition).

1 1 0 1 0 0 0 1 1 0 1

CHAPTER 15

Digital Transmission

INTRODUCTION

As stated in earlier chapters, *digital transmission* is the transmittal of digital signals between two or more points in a communications system. The signals can be binary or any other form of discrete-level digital pulses. The original source information may be in digital form or it could be analog signals that have been converted to digital pulses prior to transmission and then converted back to analog signals in the receiver. With digital transmission systems, a physical facility such as a metallic wire, a coaxial cable, or an optical fiber link is required to interconnect the various points within the system. The pulses are contained in and propagate down the facility.

Advantages of Digital Transmission

1. The primary advantage of digital transmission over analog transmission is noise immunity. Digital pulses are less susceptible than analog signals to variations caused by noise. With digital transmission, it is not necessary to evaluate the amplitude, frequency, and phase characteristics as precisely as it is with analog transmission. Instead, the received pulses are evaluated during a precise sample interval, and a simple determination is made whether the pulse is above or below a certain threshold level. The exact amplitude, frequency, or phase of the received signal is not important.

2. Digital signals are better suited to processing and multiplexing than analog signals. Digital signal processing (DSP) is the processing of analog signals using digital methods. Signal processing includes filtering, equalizing, and phase shifting. Digital pulses can be stored easier than analog signals. Also, the transmission rate of a digital system can be changed easily to adapt to different environments and to interface with different types of equipment.

3. Digital transmission systems are more noise resistant than their analog counterparts. Digital systems use signal regeneration rather than signal amplification. Noise produced in electronic amplifier circuits is additive; therefore, the signal-to-noise ratio deteriorates each time an analog signal is amplified. Consequently, the total distance analog signals can be transported is limited by the number of amplifiers. Digital regenerators, however, sample the noisy input signal, then reproduce an entirely new digital signal with the same signal-to-noise ratio as the original transmitted signal. Digital signals can, therefore, be transported longer distances than analog signals.

4. Digital signals are simpler to measure and evaluate. Therefore, it is easier to compare the performance of alternate digital systems with unequal signaling and information capacities than it is with comparable analog systems.

5. Digital systems are better suited to evaluate error performance. Transmission errors in digital signals can be detected and corrected more easily and more accurately than is possible with analog systems.

Disadvantages of Digital Transmission

1. The transmission of digitally encoded analog signals requires significantly more bandwidth than simply transmitting the original analog signal. Bandwidth is important because it is costly and often quite limited.

2. Analog signals must be converted to digital codes prior to transmission and converted back to analog form at the receiver, thus necessitating additional encoding and decoding circuitry.

3. Digital transmission requires precise time synchronization between transmit and receiver clocks. Therefore, digital systems require expensive clock recovery circuits in all receivers.

4. Digital transmission systems are incompatible with older analog transmission facilities.

PULSE MODULATION

Pulse modulation includes many different methods of converting information into pulse form for transferring pulses from a source to a destination. The four predominant methods are *pulse width modulation* (PWM), *pulse position modulation* (PPM), *pulse amplitude modulation* (PAM), and *pulse code modulation* (PCM). The four most common methods of pulse modulation are summarized below and shown in Figure 15-1.

1. *PWM.* This method is sometimes called pulse duration modulation (PDM) or pulse length modulation (PLM). The pulse width (active portion of the duty cycle) is proportional to the amplitude of the analog signal.

2. *PPM.* The position of a constant-width pulse within a prescribed time slot is varied according to the amplitude of the analog signal.

3. *PAM.* The amplitude of a constant-width, constant-position pulse is varied according to the amplitude of the analog signal.

4. *PCM.* The analog signal is sampled and converted to a fixed-length, serial binary number for transmission. The binary number varies according to the amplitude of the analog signal.

PAM is used as an intermediate form of modulation with PSK, QAM, and PCM, although it is seldom used by itself. PWM and PPM are used in special-purpose communications systems (usually for the military) but are seldom used for commercial systems. PCM is by far the most prevalent method of pulse modulation and, consequently, will be the topic of discussion for the remainder of this chapter.

PULSE CODE MODULATION

Pulse code modulation (PCM) was developed by AT&T in 1937 at their Paris laboratories. Alex H. Reeves is credited with its invention. Although the merits of PCM were recognized

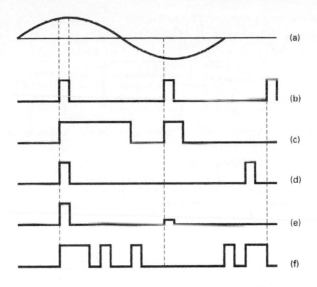

FIGURE 15-1 Pulse modulation: (a) analog signal;
(b) sample pulse; (c) PWM; (d) PPM; (e) PAM; (f) PCM

early in its development, it was not until the mid-1960s with the advent of solid-state electronics that PCM became prevalent. In the United States today, PCM is the preferred method of communication within the public switched telephone network.

Pulse code modulation is the only one of the digitally encoded modulation techniques shown in Figure 15-1 that is used for digital transmission. The term "pulse code modulation" is somewhat of a misnomer as it is not really a modulation form, but rather a form of source coding. With PCM, the pulses are of fixed length and fixed amplitude. PCM is a binary system where a pulse or lack of a pulse within a prescribed time slot represents either a logic 1 or a logic 0 condition. PWM, PPM, and PAM are digital but seldom binary, as a pulse does not represent a single binary digit (bit).

Figure 15-2 shows a simplified block diagram of a single-channel, *simplex* (one-way only) PCM system. The bandpass filter limits the frequency of the input analog signal to the standard voice-band frequency range of 300 Hz to 3000 Hz. The *sample-and-hold* circuit periodically samples the analog input signal and converts those samples to a multilevel PAM signal. The *analog-to-digital converter* (ADC) converts the PAM samples to parallel PCM codes, which are converted to serial data in the *parallel-to-serial* converter then outputted onto the transmission line. The transmission line repeaters periodically regenerate the PCM codes.

In the receiver, the *serial-to-parallel converter* converts serial data from the transmission line to parallel PCM codes. The *digital-to-analog converter* (DAC) converts the parallel PCM code to multilevel PAM signals. The *hold* circuit and *low-pass filter* convert the PAM signal back to its original analog form.

Figure 15-2 also shows several clocks and sample pulses that will be explained in later sections of this chapter. An integrated circuit that performs the PCM encoding and decoding functions is called a *codec* (coder/decoder) and is detailed in Chapter 16.

PCM Sampling

The function of a sampling circuit in a PCM transmitter is to periodically sample the continually changing analog input signal and convert those samples to a series of pulses that can more easily be converted to binary PCM code. For the ADC to accurately convert a signal to a binary code, the signal must be relatively constant. If not, before the ADC can complete the conversion, the input would change and the ADC would be continually attempting to follow the analog changes and may never stabilize on any PCM code.

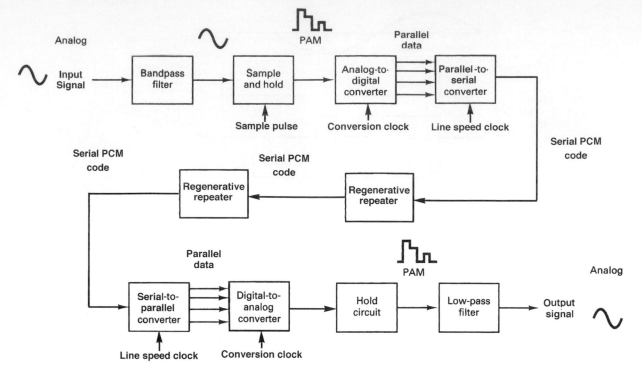

FIGURE 15-2 Simplified block diagram of a single-channel, simplex PCM transmission system

There are two basic techniques used to perform the sample-and-hold function: natural and flat-top sampling. *Natural sampling* is shown in Figure 15-3. Natural sampling is when the tops of the sampled analog waveform retain their natural shape. In Figure 15-3a, the FET analog switch simply grounds the input waveform when the sample pulse is high. When the sample pulse is low, however, the input signal is allowed to pass unaltered through the output amplifier to the input of the analog-to-digital converter. The waveform for a naturally sampled signal resembles a series of equally spaced pulses with rounded tops, as shown in Figure 15-3b.

With natural sampling, the frequency spectrum of the sampled output is different from that of an ideal sample. The amplitude of the frequency components produced from narrow, finite-width pulses decreases for the higher harmonics in a (sin x)/x manner. This alters the information frequency spectrum requiring the use of frequency equalizers (compensation filters) before recovery by a low-pass filter.

The most common method used for sampling voice signals in PCM systems is *flat-top sampling,* which is accomplished in a *sample-and-hold circuit.* The purpose of a sample-and-hold circuit is to periodically sample the continually changing analog input signal and convert those samples to a series of constant-amplitude PAM levels. Flat-top sampling alters the frequency spectrum and introduces an error called *aperture error,* which prevents the recovery circuit in the PCM receiver from exactly reproducing the original analog signal. The magnitude of error depends on how much the analog signal changes while the sample is being taken.

Figure 15-4a shows the schematic diagram of a sample-and-hold circuit. The FET acts as a simple analog switch. When turned on, Q_1 provides a low-impedance path to deposit the analog sample voltage across capacitor C_1. The time that Q_1 is on is called the *aperture* or *acquisition time.* Essentially, C_1 is the hold circuit. When Q_1 is off, C_1 does not have a complete path to discharge through and, therefore, stores the sampled voltage. The

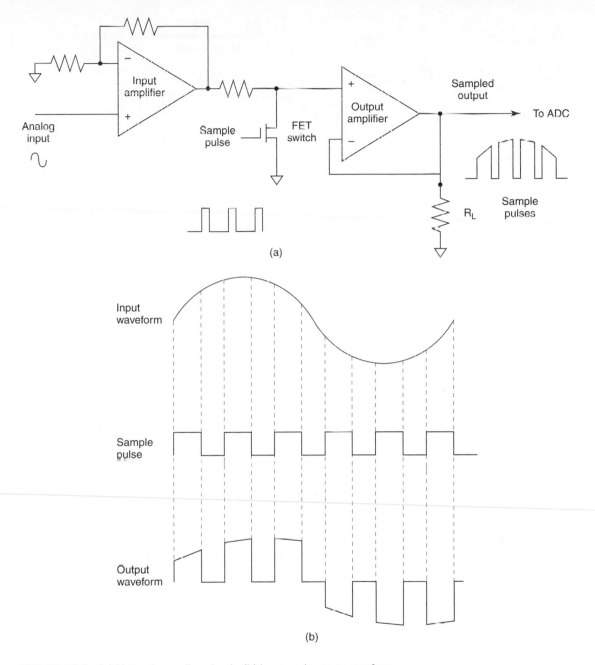

FIGURE 15-3 (a) Natural sampling circuit; (b) input and output waveforms

storage time of the capacitor is called the A/D *conversion time,* because it is during this time that the ADC converts the sample voltage to a PCM code. The acquisition time should be very short to ensure that a minimum change occurs in the analog signal while it is being deposited across C_1. If the input to the ADC is changing while it is performing the conversion, *aperture distortion* results. Thus, by having a short aperture time and keeping the input to the ADC relatively constant, the sample-and-hold circuit can reduce aperture distortion. Flat-top sampling introduces less aperture distortion than natural sampling and requires a slower analog-to-digital converter.

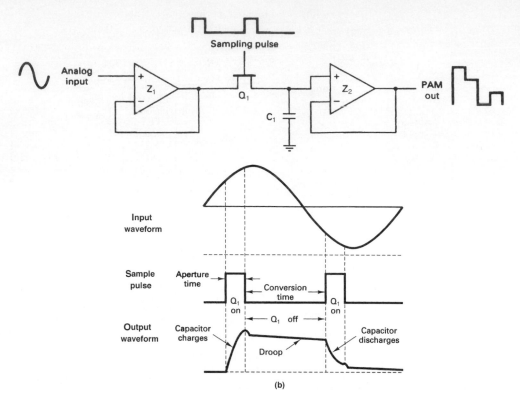

FIGURE 15-4 (a) Sample-and-hold circuit; (b) input and output waveforms

Figure 15-4b shows the input analog signal, the sampling pulse, and the waveform developed across C_1. It is important that the output impedance of voltage follower Z_1 and the on resistance of Q_1 be as small as possible. This ensures that the RC charging time constant of the capacitor is kept very short, allowing the capacitor to charge or discharge rapidly during the short acquisition time. The rapid drop in the capacitor voltage immediately following each sample pulse is due to the redistribution of the charge across C_1. The interelectrode capacitance between the gate and drain of the FET is placed in series with C_1 when the FET is off, thus acting as a capacitive voltage-divider network. Also, note the gradual discharge across the capacitor during the conversion time. This is called *droop* and is caused by the capacitor discharging through its own leakage resistance and the input impedance of voltage follower Z_2. Therefore, it is important that the input impedance of Z_2 and the leakage resistance of C_1 be as high as possible. Essentially, voltage followers Z_1 and Z_2 isolate the sample-and-hold circuit (Q_1 and C_1) from the input and output circuitry.

Example 15-1

For the sample-and-hold circuit shown in Figure 15-4b, determine the largest-value capacitor that can be used. Use an output impedance for Z_1 of 10 Ω, an on resistance for Q_1 of 10 Ω, an acquisition time of 10 μs, a maximum peak-to-peak input voltage of 10 V, a maximum output current from Z_1 of 10 mA, and an accuracy of 1%.

Solution The expression for the current through a capacitor is

$$i = C \frac{dv}{dt}$$

Rearranging and solving for C yields

$$C = i \frac{dt}{dv}$$

where C = maximum capacitance (farads)

            i = maximum output current from Z_1, 10 mA

         dv = maximum change in voltage across C_1, which equals 10 V

         dt = charge time, which equals the aperture time, 10 μs

Therefore,
$$C_{max} = \frac{(10 \text{ mA})(10 \text{ μs})}{10 \text{ V}} = 10 \text{ nF}$$

The charge time constant for C when Q_1 is on is
$$\tau = RC$$

where τ = one charge time constant (seconds)

         R = output impedance of Z_1 plus the on resistance of Q_1 (ohms)

         C = capacitance value of C_1 (farads)

Rearranging and solving for C gives us

$$C_{max} = \frac{\tau}{R}$$

The charge time of capacitor C_1 is also dependent on the accuracy desired from the device. The percent accuracy and its required RC time constant are summarized as follows:

Accuracy (%)	Charge Time
10	2.3τ
1	4.6τ
0.1	6.9τ
0.01	9.2τ

For an accuracy of 1%,
$$C = \frac{10 \text{ μs}}{4.6(20)} = 108.7 \text{ nF}$$

To satisfy the output current limitations of Z_1, a maximum capacitance of 10 nF was required. To satisfy the accuracy requirements, 108.7 nF was required. To satisfy both requirements, the smaller-value capacitor must be used. Therefore, C_1 can be no larger than 10 nF.

Sampling Rate

The Nyquist sampling theorem establishes the *minimum sampling rate* (f_s) that can be used for a given PCM system. For a sample to be reproduced accurately at the receiver, each cycle of the analog input signal (f_a) must be sampled at least twice. Consequently, the minimum sampling rate is equal to twice the highest audio input frequency. If f_s is less than two times f_a, distortion will result. The distortion is called *aliasing* or *foldover distortion*. Mathematically, the minimum Nyquist sample rate is

$$f_s \geq 2f_a \tag{15-1}$$

where f_s = minimum Nyquist sample rate (hertz)

         f_a = highest frequency to be sampled (hertz)

Essentially, a sample-and-hold circuit is an AM modulator. The switch is a nonlinear device that has two inputs: the sampling pulse and the input analog signal. Consequently, *nonlinear mixing* (*heterodyning*) occurs between these two signals. Figure 15-5a shows the frequency-domain representation of the output spectrum from a sample-and-hold circuit. The output includes the two original inputs (the audio and the fundamental frequency of the sampling pulse), their sum and difference frequencies ($f_s \pm f_a$), all the harmonics of f_s and f_a ($2f_s$, $2f_a$, $3f_s$, $3f_a$, etc), and their associated cross products ($2f_s \pm f_a$, $3f_s \pm f_a$, etc.).

Because the sampling pulse is a repetitive waveform, it is made up of a series of harmonically related sine waves. Each of these sine waves is amplitude modulated by the

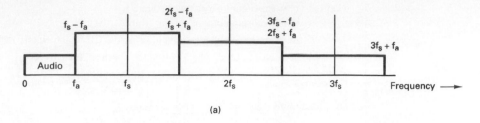

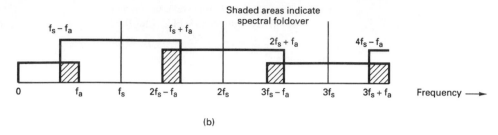

FIGURE 15-5 Output spectrum for a sample-and-hold circuit: (a) no aliasing; (b) aliasing distortion

analog signal and produces sum and difference frequencies symmetrical around each of the harmonics of f_s. Each sum and difference frequency generated is separated from its respective center frequency by f_a. As long as f_s is at least twice f_a, none of the side frequencies from one harmonic will spill into the sidebands of another harmonic and aliasing does not occur. Figure 15-5b shows the results when an analog input frequency greater than $f_s/2$ modulates f_s. The side frequencies from one harmonic fold over into the sideband of another harmonic. The frequency that folds over is an alias of the input signal (hence, the names "aliasing" or "foldover distortion"). If an alias side frequency from the first harmonic folds over into the audio spectrum, it cannot be removed through filtering or any other technique.

Example 15-2

For a PCM system with a maximum audio input frequency of 4 kHz, determine the minimum sample rate and the alias frequency produced if a 5-kHz audio signal were allowed to enter the sample-and-hold circuit.

Solution Using Nyquist's sampling theorem (Equation 15-1), we have

$$f_s \geq 2f_a \quad \text{therefore,} \quad f_s \geq 8 \text{ kHz}$$

If a 5-kHz audio frequency entered the sample-and-hold circuit, the output spectrum shown in Figure 15-6 is produced. It can be seen that the 5-kHz signal produces an alias frequency of 3 kHz that has been introduced into the original audio spectrum.

The input bandpass filter shown in Figure 15-2 is called an *antialiasing* or *antifoldover filter.* Its upper cutoff frequency is chosen such that no frequency greater than one-half of the sampling rate is allowed to enter the sample-and-hold circuit, thus eliminating the possibility of foldover distortion occurring.

With PCM, the analog input signal is sampled, then converted to a serial binary code. The binary code is transmitted to the receiver, where it is converted back to the original analog signal. The binary codes used for PCM are *n*-bit codes, where *n* may be any positive integer greater than 1. The codes currently used for PCM are *sign-magnitude codes,* where the *most significant bit* (MSB) is the sign bit and the remaining bits are used for magnitude. Table 15-1 shows an *n*-bit PCM code where *n* equals 3. The most significant bit is used to represent the sign of the sample (logic 1 = positive and logic 0 = negative). The two remaining bits represent the magnitude. With two magnitude bits, there are four codes possi-

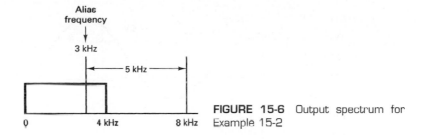

Alias
frequency

3 kHz

|← 5 kHz →|

0   4 kHz   8 kHz

FIGURE 15-6 Output spectrum for Example 15-2

TABLE 15-1 3 Bit PCM Code

Sign	Magnitude		Level	Decimal
1	1	1		+3
1	1	0		+2
1	0	1		+1
1	0	0		+0
0	0	0		−0
0	0	1		−1
0	1	0		−2
0	1	1		−3

ble for positive numbers and four codes possible for negative numbers. Consequently, there is a total of eight possible codes ($2^3 = 8$).

Folded Binary Code

The PCM code shown in Table 15-1 is called a *folded binary code.* Except for the sign bit, the codes on the bottom half of the table are a mirror image of the codes on the top half. (If the negative codes were folded over on top of the positive codes, they would match perfectly.) Also, with folded binary there are two codes assigned to zero volts, 100 (+0) and 000 (−0). For this example, the magnitude of the minimum step size is 1 V. Therefore, the maximum voltage that may be encoded with this scheme is +3 V (111) or −3 V (011). If the magnitude of a sample exceeds the highest quantization interval, *overload distortion* (also called *peak limiting*) occurs. Assigning PCM codes to absolute magnitudes is called *quantizing.* The magnitude of the minimum step size is called *resolution,* which is equal in magnitude to the voltage of the least significant bit (V_{lsb} or the magnitude of the minimum step size of the ADC). The resolution is the minimum voltage other than 0 V that can be decoded by the DAC at the receiver. The smaller the magnitude of the minimum step size, the better (smaller) the resolution and the more accurately the quantization interval will resemble the actual analog sample.

In Table 15-1, each three-bit code has a range of input voltages that will be converted to that code. For example, any voltage between +0.5 and +1.5 will be converted to the code 101. Any voltage between +1.5 and +2.5 will be encoded as 110. Each code has a *quantization range* equal to + or − one-half the resolution except the codes for +0 V and −0 V. The 0-V codes each have an input range equal to only one-half the resolution, but because there are two 0-V codes, the range for 0 V is also + or − one-half the resolution. Consequently, the maximum input voltage to the system is equal to the voltage of the highest magnitude code plus one-half of the voltage of the least significant bit.

Figure 15-7 shows an analog input signal, the sampling pulse, the corresponding PAM signal, and the PCM code. The analog signal is sampled three times. The first sample occurs at t_1 when the analog voltage is exactly +2 V. The PCM code that corresponds to sample 1 is 110. Sample 2 occurs at time t_2 when the analog voltage is −1 V. The corresponding PCM code is 001. To determine the PCM code for a particular sample, simply

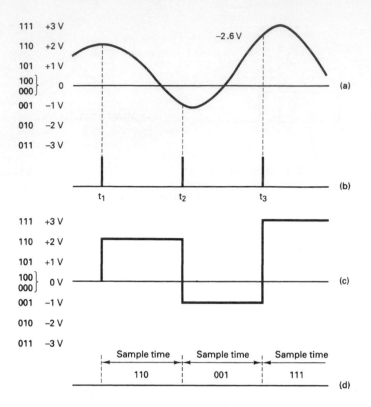

FIGURE 15-7 (a) Analog input signal; (b) sample pulse; (c) PAM signal; (d) PCM code

divide the voltage of the sample by the resolution, convert it to an *n*-bit binary code, and add the sign bit to it. For sample 1, the sign bit is 1, indicating a positive voltage. The magnitude code (10) corresponds to a binary 2. Two times 1 V equals 2 V, the magnitude of the sample.

Sample 3 occurs at time t_3. The voltage at this time is approximately +2.6 V. The folded PCM code for +2.6 V is 2.6/1 = 2.6. There is no code for this magnitude. If successive approximation ADCs are used, the magnitude of the sample is rounded off to the nearest valid code (111 or +3 V for this example). This results in an error when the code is converted back to analog by the DAC at the receive end. This error is called *quantization error* (Q_e). The quantization error is equivalent to additive white noise (it alters the signal amplitude). Similar to noise, the quantization error may add to or subtract from the actual signal. Consequently, quantization error is also called *quantization noise* (Q_n) and its maximum magnitude is one-half the voltage of the minimum step size ($V_{lsb}/2$). For this example, $Q_e = 1$ V/2 or 0.5 V.

Figure 15-8 shows the input-versus-output transfer function for a linear analog-to-digital converter (sometimes called a linear quantizer). As the figure shows for a linear analog input signal (i.e., a ramp), the quantized signal is a staircase. Thus, as shown in Figure 15-8c, the maximum quantization error is the same for any magnitude input signal.

Figure 15-9 shows the same analog input signal used in Figure 15-7 being sampled at a faster rate. As the figure shows, reducing the time between samples (i.e., increasing the sample rate) produces a PAM signal that more closely resembles the original analog input signal. However, it should also be noted that increasing the sample rate does not reduce the quantization error of the samples.

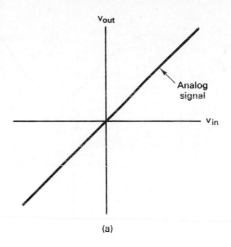

(a)

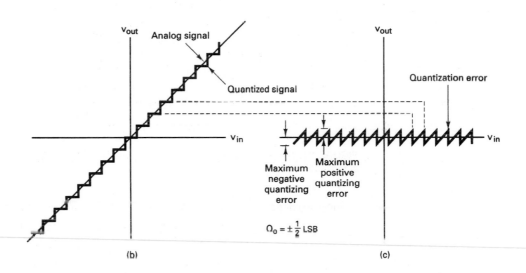

(b)   (c)

FIGURE 15-8 Linear input-versus-output transfer curve: (a) linear transfer function; (b) quantization; (c) Q_e

Dynamic Range

The number of PCM bits transmitted per sample is determined by several variables, which include maximum allowable input amplitude, resolution, and dynamic range. *Dynamic range* (DR) is the ratio of the largest possible magnitude to the smallest possible magnitude that can be decoded by the DAC. Mathematically, dynamic range is

$$DR = \frac{V_{max}}{V_{min}} \tag{15-2}$$

where V_{min} is equal to the resolution and V_{max} is the maximum voltage magnitude that can be decoded by the DACs. Thus,

$$DR = \frac{V_{max}}{\text{resolution}}$$

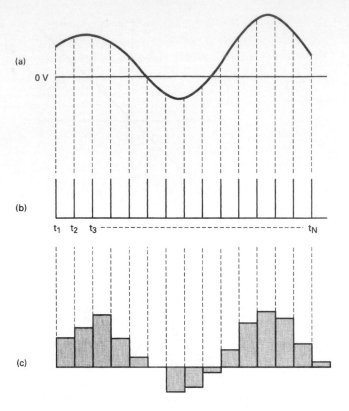

FIGURE 15-9 PAM: (a) input signal; (b) sample pulse; (c) PAM signal

For the system shown in Table 15-1,

$$DR = \frac{3 \text{ V}}{1 \text{ V}} = 3$$

It is common to represent dynamic range in decibels; therefore,

$$DR = 20 \log \frac{V_{max}}{V_{min}} = 20 \log \frac{3}{1} = 9.54 \text{ dB}$$

A dynamic range of 3 indicates that the ratio of the largest to the smallest decoded signal voltage is 3.

If a smaller resolution is desired, such as 0.5 V, to maintain a dynamic range of 3, the maximum allowable input voltage must be reduced by the same factor; one-half.

$$DR = \frac{1.5}{0.5} = 3$$

Therefore, V_{max} is reduced by a factor of 2 and the dynamic range is independent of resolution. If the resolution were reduced by a factor of 2 (0.25 V), to maintain the same maximum input amplitude, the dynamic range must double:

$$DR = \frac{1.5}{0.25} = 6$$

The number of bits used for a PCM code depends on the dynamic range. With a two-bit PCM code, the minimum decodable magnitude has a binary code of 01. The maximum magnitude is 11. The ratio of the maximum binary code to the minimum binary code is 3, the same as the dynamic range. Because the minimum binary code is always 1, DR is simply the maximum binary number for a system. Consequently, to determine the number of bits required for a PCM code, the following mathematical relationship is used.

$$2^n - 1 \geq DR$$

and for a minimum value of n,

$$2^n - 1 = DR \tag{15-3a}$$

where n = number of PCM bits, excluding sign bit
          DR = absolute value of dynamic range

Why $2^n - 1$? One PCM code is used for 0 V, which is not considered for dynamic range. Therefore,

$$2^n = DR + 1 \tag{15-3b}$$

To solve for n, convert to logs,

$$\log 2^n = \log(DR + 1)$$
$$n \log 2 = \log(DR + 1)$$
$$n = \frac{\log(3 + 1)}{\log 2} = \frac{0.602}{0.301} = 2$$

For a dynamic range of 3, a PCM code with two bits is required. Dynamic range can be represented in decibels as

$$DR_{(dB)} = 20 \log \frac{V_{max}}{V_{min}} \tag{15-4a}$$

or

$$= 20 \log (2^n - 1) \tag{15-4b}$$

where n is the number of PCM bits. For large values of n, dynamic range is approximately

$$DR_{(dB)} \approx 20 \log (2^n)$$
$$\approx 20n \log (2)$$

thus,

$$\approx 6n \tag{15-5}$$

Equation 15-5 means that there is approximately 6 dB per bit dynamic range for a linearly encoded PCM system. Table 15-2 summarizes dynamic range for a PCM code of n bits for values of n up to 16.

Example 15-3

A PCM system has the following parameters: a maximum analog input frequency of 4 kHz, a maximum decoded voltage at the receiver of ± 2.55 V, and a minimum dynamic range of 46 dB. Determine the following: minimum sample rate, minimum number of bits used in the PCM code, resolution, and quantization error.

Solution   Substituting into Equation 15-1, the minimum sample rate is

$$f_s = 2f_a - 2(4 \text{ kHz}) = 8 \text{ kHz}$$

To determine the absolute value of the dynamic range, substitute into Equation 15-4a:

$$46 \text{ dB} = 20 \log \frac{V_{max}}{V_{min}}$$

$$2.3 = \log \frac{V_{max}}{V_{min}}$$

$$10^{2.3} = \frac{V_{max}}{V_{min}} = DR$$

$$199.5 = DR$$

TABLE 15-2 Dynamic Range versus Number of PCM Bits

Number of Bits in PCM Code (n)	Number of Levels Possible ($M = 2^n$)	Dynamic Range (dB)
0	1	0
1	2	6.02
2	4	12
3	8	18.1
4	16	24.1
5	32	30.1
6	64	36.1
7	128	42.1
8	256	48.2
9	512	54.2
10	1024	60.2
11	2048	66.2
12	4096	72.2
13	8192	78.3
14	16,384	84.3
15	32,768	90.3
16	65,536	96.3

Substitute into Equation 15-4b and solve for *n:*

$$n = \frac{\log(199.5 + 1)}{\log 2} = 7.63$$

The closest whole number greater than 7.63 is 8; therefore, eight bits must be used for the magnitude.

Because the input amplitude range is ± 2.55 V, one additional bit, the sign bit, is required. Therefore, the total number of PCM bits is nine and the total number of PCM codes is 2^9 or 512. (There are 255 positive codes, 255 negative codes, and 2 zero codes.)

To determine the actual dynamic range, substitute into Equation 15-4b:

$$DR = 20 \log 255 = 48.13 \text{ dB}$$

To determine the resolution, divide the maximum + or − magnitude by the number of positive or negative nonzero PCM codes.

$$\text{resolution} = \frac{V_{max}}{2^n - 1} = \frac{2.55}{2^8 - 1} = \frac{2.55}{256 - 1} = 0.01 \text{ V}$$

The maximum quantization error is

$$Q_e \frac{\text{resolution}}{2} = \frac{0.01}{2} = 0.005 \text{ V}$$

Coding Efficiency

Coding efficiency is a numerical indication of how efficiently a PCM code is utilized. Coding efficiency is the ratio of the minimum number of bits required to achieve a certain dynamic range to the actual number of PCM bits used. Mathematically, coding efficiency is

$$\text{coding efficiency} = \frac{\text{minimum number of bits (including sign bit)}}{\text{actual number of bits (including sign bit)}} \times 100 \quad (15\text{-}6)$$

The coding efficiency for Example 15-3 is

$$\text{coding efficiency} = \frac{8.63}{9} \times 100 = 95.89\%$$

Signal-to-Quantization Noise Ratio

The three-bit PCM coding scheme described in the preceding section is a linear code. That is, the magnitude change between any two successive codes is the same. Consequently, the magnitude of their quantization error is also the same. The maximum quantization noise is the voltage of the least significant bit divided by 2. Therefore, the worst possible *signal voltage–to–quantization noise voltage ratio* (SQR) occurs when the input signal is at its minimum amplitude (101 or 001). Mathematically, the worst-case voltage SQR is

$$SQR = \frac{\text{minimum voltage}}{\text{quantization noise voltage}} = \frac{V_{lsb}}{V_{lsb}/2} - 2$$

For a maximum amplitude input signal of 3V (either 111 or 011), the maximum quantization noise is also the voltage of the least significant bit divided by 2. Therefore, the voltage SQR for a maximum input signal condition is

$$SQR = \frac{\text{maximum voltage}}{\text{quantization noise voltage}} = \frac{V_{max}}{V_{ls/2}} = \frac{3}{0.5} = 6$$

From the preceding example it can be seen that even though the magnitude of error remains constant throughout the entire PCM code, the percentage of error does not; it decreases as the magnitude or the input signal increases. As a result, the SQR is not constant.

The preceding expression for SQR is for voltage and presumes the maximum quantization error and a constant-amplitude analog signal; therefore, it is of little practical use and is shown only for comparison purposes. In reality and as shown in Figure 15-7, the difference between the PAM waveform and the analog input waveform varies in magnitude. Therefore, the signal-to-quantization noise ratio is not constant. Generally, the quantization error or distortion caused by digitizing an analog sample is expressed as an average signal power–to–average noise power ratio. For linear PCM codes (all quantization intervals have equal magnitudes), the signal power-to-quantizing noise power ratio (also called *signal-to-distortion ratio* or *signal-to-noise ratio*) is determined as follows:

$$SQR_{(dB)} = 10 \log \frac{v^2/R}{(q^2/12)/R}$$

where
R = resistance (ohm)
v = rms signal voltage (volts)
q = quantization interval (volts)
v^2/R = average signal power (watts)
$(q^2/12)/R$ = average quantization noise power (watts)

If the resistances are assumed to be equal,

$$SQR_{(dB)} = 10 \log \frac{v^2}{q^2/12} \tag{15-7a}$$

$$= 10.8 + 20 \log \frac{v}{q} \tag{15-7b}$$

Linear Versus Nonlinear PCM Codes

Early PCM systems used *linear codes* (i.e., the magnitude change between any two successive steps is uniform). With linear encoding, the accuracy (resolution) for the higher-amplitude analog signals is the same as for the lower-amplitude signals, and the SQR for the lower-amplitude signals is less than for the higher-amplitude signals. With voice transmission, low-amplitude signals are more likely to occur than large-amplitude signals. Therefore, if there were more codes for the lower amplitudes, it would increase the accuracy where the accuracy is needed. As a result, there would be fewer codes available for the higher amplitudes, which would increase the quantization error for the larger-amplitude signals (thus, decreasing the SQR). Such a coding technique is called *nonlinear* or *nonuniform encoding*. With nonlinear encoding, the step size increases with the amplitude of the input signal. Figure 15-10 shows the step outputs from a linear and a nonlinear ADC.

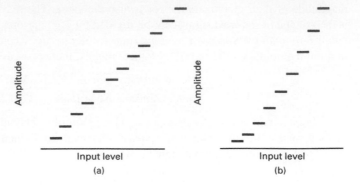

FIGURE 15-10 (a) Linear versus; (b) nonlinear encoding

Note, with nonlinear encoding, there are more codes at the bottom of the scale than there are at the top, thus increasing the accuracy for the smaller signals. Also note that the distance between successive codes is greater for the higher-amplitude signals, thus increasing the quantization error and reducing the SQR. Also, because the ratio of V_{max} to V_{min} is increased with nonlinear encoding, the dynamic range is larger than with a uniform code. It is evident that nonlinear encoding is a compromise; SQR is sacrificed for the high-amplitude signals to achieve more accuracy for the low-amplitude signals and to achieve a larger dynamic range. It is difficult to fabricate nonlinear ADCs; consequently, alternative methods of achieving the same results have been devised and are discussed later in this chapter.

Idle Channel Noise

During times when there is no analog input signal, the only input to the PAM sampler is random, thermal noise. This noise is called *idle channel noise* and is converted to a PAM sample just as if it were a signal. Consequently, even input noise is quantized by the ADC. Figure 15-11 shows a way to reduce idle channel noise by a method called *midtread quantization.* With midtread quantizing, the first quantization interval is made larger in amplitude than the rest of the steps. Consequently, input noise can be quite large and still be quantized as a positive or negative zero code. As a result, the noise is suppressed during the encoding process.

In the PCM codes described thus far, the lowest-magnitude positive and negative codes have the same voltage range as all the other codes (+ or − one-half the resolution). This is called *midrise quantization.* Figure 15-11 contrasts the idle channel noise transmitted with a midrise PCM code to the idle channel noise transmitted when midtread quantization is used. The advantage of midtread quantization is less idle channel noise. The disadvantage is a larger possible magnitude for Q_e in the lowest quantization interval.

With a folded binary PCM code, residual noise that fluctuates slightly above and below 0 V is converted to either a + or − zero PCM code and, consequently, is eliminated. In systems that do not use the two 0-V assignments, the residual noise could cause the PCM encoder to alternate between the zero code and the minimum + or − code. Consequently, the decoder would reproduce the encoded noise. With a folded binary code, most of the residual noise is inherently eliminated by the encoder.

Coding Methods

There are several coding methods used to quantize PAM signals into 2^n levels. These methods are classified according to whether the coding operation proceeds a level at a time, a digit at a time, or a word at a time.

Level-at-a-time coding. This type of coding compares the PAM signal to a ramp waveform while a binary counter is being advanced at a uniform rate. When the ramp wave-

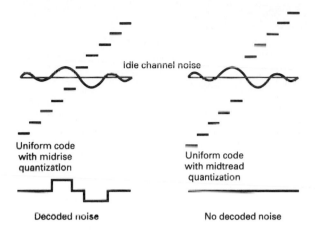

FIGURE 15-11 Idle channel noise

form equals or exceeds the PAM sample, the counter contains the PCM code. This type of coding requires a very fast clock if the number of bits in the PCM code is large. Level-at-a-time coding also requires that 2^n sequential decisions be made for each PCM code generated. Therefore, level-at-a-time coding is generally limited to low-speed applications. Nonuniform coding is achieved by using a nonlinear function as the reference ramp.

Digit-at-a-time coding. This type of coding determines each digit of the PCM code sequentially. Digit-at-a-time coding is analogous to a balance where known reference weights are used to determine an unknown weight. Digit-at-a-time coders provide a compromise between speed and complexity. One common kind of digit-at-a-time coder, called a *feedback coder,* uses a successive approximation register (SAR). With this type of coder, the entire PCM code word is determined simultaneously.

Word-at-a-time coding. Word-at-a-time coders are flash encoders and are more complex; however, they are more suitable for high-speed applications. One common type of word-at-a-time coder uses multiple threshold circuits. Logic circuits sense the highest threshold circuit sensed by the PAM input signal and produce the approximate PCM code. This method is again impractical for large values of n.

Companding

Companding is the process of *compressing,* then *expanding.* With companded systems, the higher-amplitude analog signals are compressed (amplified less than the lower-amplitude signals) prior to transmission, then expanded (amplified more than the smaller-amplitude signals) at the receiver.

Figure 15-12 illustrates the process of companding. An input signal with a dynamic range of 50 dB is compressed to 25 dB for transmission, then expanded to 50 dB at the receiver. With PCM, companding may be accomplished through analog or digital techniques. Early PCM systems used analog companding, whereas more modern systems use digital companding.

Analog Companding

Historically, analog compression was implemented using specially designed diodes inserted in the analog signal path in the PCM transmitter prior to the sample-and-hold circuit. Analog expansion was also implemented with diodes that were placed just after the receive low-pass filter. Figure 15-13 shows the basic process of analog companding. In the transmitter, the analog signal is compressed, sampled, then converted to a linear PCM code. In

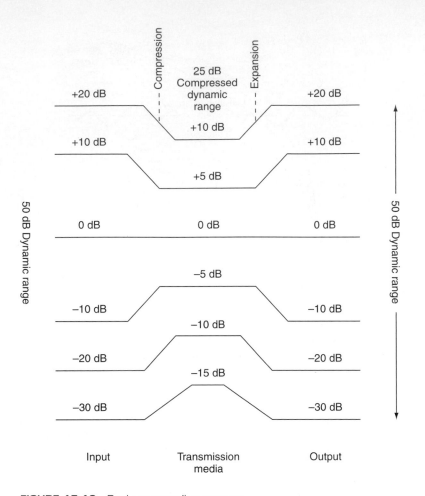

FIGURE 15-12 Basic companding process

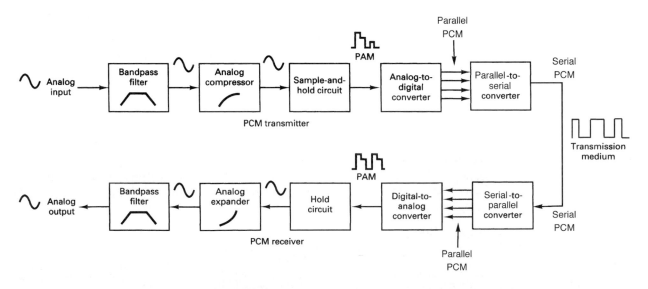

FIGURE 15-13 PCM system with analog companding

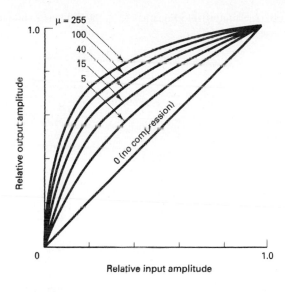

FIGURE 15-14 μ-law compression characteristics

the receiver, the PCM code is converted to a PAM signal, filtered, then expanded back to its original input amplitude characteristics.

Different signal distributions require different companding characteristics. For instance, voice signals require relatively constant SQR performance over a wide dynamic range, which means that the distortion must be proportional to signal amplitude for any input signal level. This requires a logarithmic compression ratio. A truly logarithmic assignment code requires an infinite dynamic range and an infinite number of PCM codes, which is impossible. There are two methods of analog companding currently being used that closely approximate a logarithmic function and are often called *log-PCM* codes. They are μ-*law* and A-*law companding.*

μ-law companding. In the United States and Japan, μ-law companding is used. The compression characteristic for μ-law is

$$V_{out} = \frac{V_{max} \times \ln(1 + \mu V_{in}/V_{max})}{\ln(1 + \mu)} \tag{15-8}$$

where V_{max} = maximum uncompressed analog input amplitude (volts)
  V_{in} = amplitude of the input signal at a particular instant of time (volts)
  μ = parameter used to define the amount of compression (unitless)
  V_{out} = compressed output amplitude (volts)

Figure 15-14 shows the compression for several values of μ. Note that the higher the μ, the more compression. Also note that for a μ = 0, the curve is linear (no compression).

The parameter μ determines the range of signal power in which the SQR is relatively constant. Voice transmission requires a minimum dynamic range of 40 dB and a seven-bit PCM code. For a relatively constant SQR and a 40-dB dynamic range, μ = 100 or larger is required. The early Bell System digital transmission systems used a seven-bit PCM code with μ = 100. The most recent digital transmission systems use eight-bit PCM codes and μ = 255.

Example 15-4

For a compressor with a μ = 255, determine

(a) The voltage gain for the following relative values of V_{in}: V_{max}, $0.75V_{max}$, $0.5V_{max}$, and $0.25V_{max}$.
(b) The compressed output voltage for a maximum input voltage of 4 V.
(c) Input and output dynamic ranges and compression.

Solution (a) Substituting into Equation 15-8, the following voltage gains are achieved for the various input magnitudes.

V_{in}	Compressed voltage gain
V_{max}	1.00
0.75 V_{max}	1.26
0.50 V_{max}	1.75
0.25 V_{max}	3.00

(b) Using the compressed voltage gains determined in step a,

V_{in}	V_{out}
$V_{max} = 4$	4.00
0.75 $V_{max} = 3$	3.78
0.50 $V_{max} = 2$	3.50
0.25 $V_{max} = 1$	3.00

(c) Dynamic range is calculated by substituting into Equation 15-4a.

$$\text{input dynamic range} = 20 \log \frac{4}{1} = 12 \text{ dB}$$

$$\text{output dynamic range} = 20 \log \frac{4}{3} = 2.5 \text{ dB}$$

$$\text{compression} = \text{input dynamic range} - \text{output dynamic range}$$
$$= 12 \text{ dB} - 2.5 \text{ dB} = 9.5 \text{ dB}$$

A-law companding. In Europe, the CCITT has established A-law companding to be used to approximate true logarithmic companding. For an intended dynamic range, A-law companding has a slightly flatter SQR than μ-law. A-law companding, however, is inferior to μ-law in terms of small-signal quality (idle channel noise). The compression characteristic for A-law companding is

$$V_{out} = V_{max} \frac{A V_{in} / V_{max}}{1 + \ln A} \qquad 0 \le \frac{V_{in}}{V_{max}} \le \frac{1}{A} \qquad (15\text{-}9\text{a})$$

$$= V_{max} \frac{1 + \ln(A V_{in}/V_{max})}{1 + \ln A} \qquad \frac{1}{A} \le \frac{V_{in}}{V_{max}} \le 1 \qquad (15\text{-}9\text{b})$$

Digital Companding

Digital companding involves compression at the transmit end after the input sample has been converted to a linear PCM code and expansion at the receive end prior to PCM decoding. Figure 15-15 shows the block diagram of a digitally companded PCM system.

With digital companding, the analog signal is first sampled and converted to a linear code, then the linear code is digitally compressed. At the receive end, the compressed PCM code is received, expanded, then decoded. The most recent digitally compressed PCM systems use a 12-bit linear code and an 8-bit compressed code. This companding process closely resembles a $\mu = 255$ analog compression curve by approximating the curve with a set of eight straight-line *segments* (segments 0 through 7). The slope of each successive segment is exactly one-half that of the previous segment. Figure 15-16 shows the 12-bit-to-8-bit digital compression curve for positive values only. The curve for negative values is identical except the inverse. Although there are 16 segments (eight positive and eight neg-

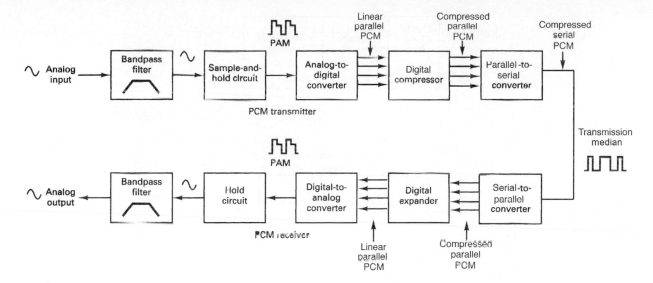

FIGURE 15-15 Digitally companded PCM system

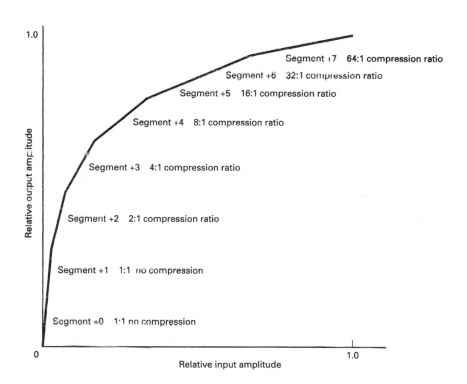

FIGURE 15-16 μ255 compression characteristics (positive values only)

ative), this scheme is often called *13-segment compression*, because the curve for segments +0, +1, −0, and −1 is a straight line with a constant slope and is often considered as one segment.

The digital companding algorithm for a 12-bit-linear-to-8-bit-compressed code is actually quite simple. The 8-bit compressed code consists of a sign bit, a 3-bit segment identifier, and a 4-bit magnitude code that identifies the *quantization interval* within the specified segment (see Figure 15-17a).

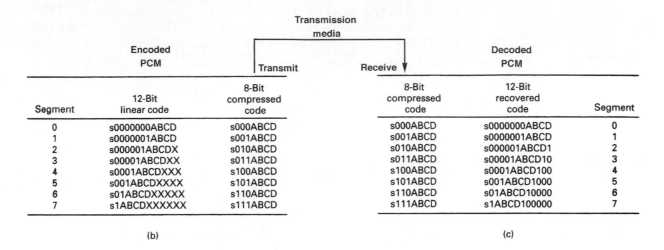

Sign bit 1 = + 0 = −	3-Bit segment identifier	4-Bit quantization interval A B C D
	000 to 111	0000 to 1111

(a)

Transmission
media

Transmit | Receive

	Encoded PCM			Decoded PCM	
Segment	12-Bit linear code	8-Bit compressed code	8-Bit compressed code	12-Bit recovered code	Segment
0	s0000000ABCD	s000ABCD	s000ABCD	s0000000ABCD	0
1	s0000001ABCD	s001ABCD	s001ABCD	s0000001ABCD	1
2	s000001ABCDX	s010ABCD	s010ABCD	s000001ABCD1	2
3	s00001ABCDXX	s011ABCD	s011ABCD	s00001ABCD10	3
4	s0001ABCDXXX	s100ABCD	s100ABCD	s0001ABCD100	4
5	s001ABCDXXXX	s101ABCD	s101ABCD	s001ABCD1000	5
6	s01ABCDXXXXX	s110ABCD	s110ABCD	s01ABCD10000	6
7	s1ABCDXXXXXX	s111ABCD	s111ABCD	s1ABCD100000	7

(b) | (c)

FIGURE 15-17 12-bit-to-8-bit digital companding: (a) 8-bit μ255 compressed code format; (b) μ255 encoding table; (c) μ255 decoding table

In the μ255 encoding table shown in Figure 15-17b, the bit positions designated with an X are truncated during compression and are consequently lost. Bits designated A, B, C, and D are transmitted as is. The sign bit is also transmitted as is. Note that for segments 0 and 1, the original 12 bits are duplicated exactly at the output of the decoder (Figure 15-17c), whereas for segment 7, only the most significant six bits are recovered. With 11 magnitude bits, there are 2048 possible codes. There are 16 codes in segment 0 and in segment 1. In segment 2, there are 32 codes; segment 3 has 64. Each successive segment beginning with segment 3 has twice as many codes as the previous segment. In each of the eight segments, only sixteen 12-bit codes can be recovered. Consequently, in segments 0 and 1, there is no compression (of the 16 possible codes, all 16 can be recovered). In segment 2, there is a compression ratio of 2:1 (32 possible transmit codes and 16 possible recovered codes). In segment 3, there is a 4:1 compression ratio (64 possible transmit codes and 16 possible recovered codes). The compression ratio doubles with each successive segment. The compression ratio in segment 7 is 1024/16 or 64:1.

The compression process is as follows. The analog signal is sampled and converted to a linear 12-bit sign-magnitude code. The sign bit is transferred directly to the 8-bit code. The segment is determined by counting the number of leading 0s in the 11-bit magnitude portion of the code beginning with the MSB. Subtract the number of leading 0s (not to exceed 7) from 7. The result is the segment number, which is converted to a 3-bit binary number and substituted into the 8-bit code as the segment identifier. The four magnitude bits (A, B, C, and D) are the quantization interval and are substituted into the least significant four bits of the 8-bit compressed code.

Essentially, segments 2 through 7 are subdivided into smaller subsegments. Each segment has 16 subsegments, which correspond to the 16 conditions possible for bits A, B, C, and D (0000 1111). In segment 2 there are two codes per subsegment. In segment 3 there are four. The number of codes per subsegment doubles with each subsequent segment. Consequently, in segment 7, each subsegment has 64 codes. Figure 15-18 shows the breakdown of segments versus subsegments for segments 2, 5, and 7. Note that in each subsegment, all 12-bit codes, once compressed and expanded, yield a single 12-bit code. This is shown in Figure 15-18.

From Figures 15-17 and 15-18, it can be seen that the most significant of the truncated bits is reinserted at the decoder as a 1. The remaining truncated bits are reinserted as 0s. This ensures that the maximum magnitude of error introduced by the compression and expansion process is minimized. Essentially, the decoder guesses what the truncated bits were prior to encoding. The most logical guess is halfway between the minimum- and maximum-magnitude

Segment	12-Bit linear code		12-Bit expanded code	Subsegment
7	s11111111111 ⋯⋯⋯⋯⋯ s11111000000	64 : 1	s11111100000	15
7	s11110111111 ⋯⋯⋯⋯⋯ s11110000000	64 : 1	s11110100000	14
7	s11101111111 ⋯⋯⋯⋯⋯ s11101000000	64 : 1	s11101100000	13
7	s11100111111 ⋯⋯⋯⋯⋯ s11100000000	64 : 1	s11100100000	12
7	s11011111111 ⋯⋯⋯⋯⋯ s11011000000	64 : 1	s11011100000	11
7	s11010111111 ⋯⋯⋯⋯⋯ s11010000000	64 : 1	s11010100000	10
7	s11001111111 ⋯⋯⋯⋯⋯ s11001000000	64 : 1	s11001100000	9
7	s11000111111 ⋯⋯⋯⋯⋯ s11000000000	64 : 1	s11000100000	8
7	s10111111111 ⋯⋯⋯⋯⋯ s10111000000	64 : 1	s10111100000	7
7	s10110111111 ⋯⋯⋯⋯⋯ s10110000000	64 : 1	s10110100000	6
7	s10101111111 ⋯⋯⋯⋯⋯ s10101000000	64 : 1	s10101100000	5
7	s10100111111 ⋯⋯⋯⋯⋯ s10100000000	64 : 1	s10100100000	4
7	s10011111111 ⋯⋯⋯⋯⋯ s10011000000	64 : 1	s10011100000	3
7	s10010111111 ⋯⋯⋯⋯⋯ s10010000000	64 : 1	s10010100000	2
7	s10001111111 ⋯⋯⋯⋯⋯ s10001000000	64 : 1	s10001100000	1
7	s10000111111 ⋯⋯⋯⋯⋯ s10000000000	64 : 1	s10000100000	0
	s1ABCD-------			

(a)

FIGURE 15-18 12-bit segments divided into subsegments: (a) segment 7; (b) segment 5 (*Continued*)

Segment	12-Bit linear code		12-Bit expanded code	Subsegment
5	s00111111111 ... s00111110000	16 : 1	s00111111000	15
5	s00111101111 ... s00111100000	16 : 1	s00111101000	14
5	s00111011111 ... s00111010000	16 : 1	s00111011000	13
5	s00111001111 ... s00111000000	16 : 1	s001110010000	12
5	s00110111111 ... s00110110000	16 : 1	s00110111000	11
5	s00110101111 ... s00110100000	16 : 1	s00110101000	10
5	s00110011111 ... s00110010000	16 : 1	s00110011000	9
5	s00110001111 ... s00110000000	16 : 1	s00110001000	8
5	s00101111111 ... s00101110000	16 : 1	s00101111000	7
5	s00101101111 ... s00101100000	16 : 1	s00101101000	6
5	s00101011111 ... s00101010000	16 : 1	s00101011000	5
5	s00101001111 ... s00101000000	16 : 1	s00101001000	4
5	s00100111111 ... s00100110000	16 : 1	s00100111000	3
5	s00100101111 ... s00100100000	16 : 1	s00100101000	2
5	s00100011111 ... s00100010000	16 : 1	s00100011000	1
5	s00100001111 ... s00100000000	16 : 1	s00100001000	0
	s001ABCD----			

(b)

FIGURE 15-18 (Continued) (b) segment 5

codes. For example, in segment 5, the five least significant bits are truncated during compression. At the receiver, the decoder must determine what those bits were. The possibilities are any code between 00000 and 11111. The logical guess is 10000, approximately half the maximum magnitude. Consequently, the maximum compression error is slightly more than one-half the magnitude of that segment.

Example 15-5

Determine the 12-bit linear code, the 8-bit compressed code, and the recovered 12-bit code for a resolution of 0.01 V and analog sample voltages of
(a) 0.05 V
(b) 0.32 V
(c) 10.23 V

Solution (a) To determine the 12-bit linear code for 0.05 V, simply divide the sample voltage by the resolution and convert the result to a 12-bit sign-magnitude binary number.

Segment	12-Bit linear code		12-Bit expanded code	Subsegment
2	s00000111111 .... s00000111110	} 2 : 1	s00000111111	15
2	s00000111101 .... s00000111100	} 2 : 1	s00000111101	14
2	s00000111011 .... s00000111010	} 2 : 1	s00000111011	13
2	s00000111001 .... s00000111000	} 2 : 1	s00000111001	12
2	s00000110111 .... s00000110110	} 2 : 1	s00000110111	11
2	s00000110101 .... s00000110100	} 2 : 1	s00000110101	10
2	s00000110011 .... s00000110010	} 2 : 1	s00000110011	9
2	s00000110001 .... s00000110000	} 2 : 1	s00000110001	8
2	s00000101111 .... s00000101110	} 2 : 1	s00000101111	7
2	s00000101101 .... s00000101100	} 2 : 1	s00000101101	6
2	s00000101011 .... s00000101010	} 2 : 1	s00000101011	5
2	s00000101001 .... s00000101000	} 2 : 1	s00000101001	4
2	s000000100111 .... s00000100110	} 2 : 1	s00000100111	3
2	s00000100101 .... s00000100100	} 2 : 1	s00000100101	2
2	s00000100011 .... s00000100010	} 2 : 1	s00000100011	1
2	s00000100001 .... s00000100000	} 2 : 1	s00000100001	0
	s000001ABCD-			

(c)

FIGURE 15-18 (Continued) (c) segment 2

12-bit linear code:

$$\frac{0.05\ V}{0.01\ V} = 5 = \begin{matrix} & & & & & & & & & A & B & C & D \\ 1 & 0 & 0 & 0 & 0 & 0 & 0 & 0 & 0 & 1 & 0 & 1 \\ s & & & & & & & & & & & \end{matrix}$$

s ——————— magnitude ———————
(11-bit binary number)

8-bit compressed code:

```
1 0 0 0 0 0 0 0 0 1 0 1
s    (7 − 7 = 0 or 000)  A  B  C  D
1         0 0 0      0 1 0 1
↑
sign bit      unit        quantization
(+)        identifier      interval
          (segment 0)         (5)
```

12-bit recovered code:

```
1               0 0 0   0 1 0 1
s   (7 − 0 = 7 leading 0s)   A   B   C   D
1 0 0 0 0 0 0 0 0 1 0 1
↑
```

sign bit   segment identifier   quantization
            determines the   interval
            number of leading
            0s

As you can see, the recovered 12-bit code is exactly the same as the original 12-bit linear code. This is true for all codes in segments 0 and 1. Consequently, there is no compression error in these two segments.

(b) For the 0.32-V sample,

12-bit linear code:

$$\frac{0.32 \text{ V}}{0.01 \text{ V}} = 32 = \begin{matrix} 1 & 0\ 0\ 0\ 0\ 0\ 1\ 0\ 0\ 0\ 0\ 0 \\ s & \text{————— magnitude —————} \end{matrix}$$

8-bit compressed code:

```
1 0 0 0 0 1       0 0 0 0 0
s     (7 − 5 = 2 or 010)   A   B   C   D   X
1             0 1 0       0 0 0 0 ↑
(+)          (segment 2)           truncated
```

12-bit recovered code:

```
1               0 1 0       0 0 0 0
s   (7 − 2 = 5 leading 0s)   A   B   C   D   X
1 0 0 0 0 0 1       0 0 0 0 1
            ↑                   ↑
        inserted            inserted
```

Note the two inserted 1s in the decoded 12-bit code. The least significant bit is determined from the decoding table in Figure 15-17. The stuffed 1 in bit position 6 was dropped during the 12-bit-to-8-bit conversion. Transmission of this bit is redundant because if it were not a 1, the sample would not be in segment 2. Consequently, in all segments except 0, a 1 is automatically inserted after the reinserted zeros. For this sample, there is an error in the received voltage equal to the resolution, 0.01 V. In segment 2, for every two 12-bit codes possible, there is only one recovered 12-bit code. Thus, a coding compression of 2:1 is realized.

(c) To determine the codes for 10.23 V, the process is the same.

12-bit linear code:

```
1   0   1 1 1 1   1 1 1 1
↑       ↑   ‾‾‾‾    ‾‾‾‾
sign        ABCD    truncated
        dropped
        (7 − 1 = 6)
```

8-bit compressed code:

```
1       1 1 0   1 1 1 1
↑       ‾‾‾‾‾   ‾‾‾‾‾
sign    segment   A B C D
          6
```

12-bit recovered code:

```
1   0   1   1 1 1 1   1 0 0 0 0
↑       ↑    ‾‾‾‾       ↑
sign    |    ABCD    inserted
     inserted
```

The difference between the original 12-bit code and the recovered 12-bit code is

$$
\begin{array}{r}
1011 \quad 1111 \quad 1111 \\
-1011 \quad 1111 \quad 0000 \\
\hline
0000 \quad 0000 \quad 1111 = 15(0.01) = 0.15 \text{ V}
\end{array}
$$

Percentage Error

For comparison purposes, the following formula is used for computing the *percentage of error* introduced by digital compression:

$$
\% \ \text{error} = \frac{|\text{Tx voltage} - \text{Rx voltage}|}{\text{Rx voltage}} \times 100 \tag{15-10}
$$

Example 15-6

The maximum percentage of error will occur for the smallest number in the lowest subsegment within any given segment. Because there is no compression error in segments 0 and 1, for segment 3 the maximum % error is computed as follows:

Transmit 12-bit code: s 00001000000
Receive 12-bit code: s 00001000010
Magnitude of error: 00000000010

$$
\% \ \text{error} = \frac{|1000000 - 1000010|}{1000010} \times 100
$$

$$
= \frac{|64 - 66|}{66} \times 100 = 3.03\%
$$

For segment 7:

Transmit 12-bit code: s 10000000000
Receive 12-bit code: s 10000100000
Magnitude of error: 00000100000

$$
\% \ \text{error} = \frac{|10000000000 - 10000100000|}{10000100000} \times 100
$$

$$
= \frac{|1024 - 1056|}{1056} \times 100 = 3.03\%
$$

Although the magnitude of error is higher for segment 7, the percentage of error is the same. The maximum percentage of error is the same for segments 3 through 7, and consequently, the SQR degradation is the same for each segment.

Although there are several ways in which the 12-bit-to-8-bit compression and the 8-bit-to-12-bit expansion can be accomplished with hardware, the simplest and most economical method is with a look-up table in ROM (read-only memory).

Essentially every function performed by a PCM encoder and decoder is now accomplished with a single integrated-circuit chip called a *codec*. Most of the more recently developed codecs include an antialiasing (bandpass) filter, a sample-and-hold circuit, and an analog-to-digital converter in the transmit section and a digital-to-analog converter, a sample-and-hold circuit, and a bandpass filter in the receive section. The operation of a codec is detailed in Chapter 16.

Vocoders

The PCM coding and decoding processes described in the preceding sections were concerned primarily with reproducing waveforms as accurately as possible. The precise nature of the waveform was unimportant as long as it occupied the voice-band frequency range. When digitizing speech signals only, special voice encoders/decoders called *vocoders* are often used. To achieve acceptable speech communications, the short-term power spectrum of the speech information is all that must be preserved. The human ear is relatively insensitive to the phase relationship between individual frequency components within a voice waveform. Therefore, vocoders are designed to reproduce only the short-term power spectrum, and the decoded time waveforms often only vaguely resemble the original input signal. Vocoders cannot be used in applications where analog signals other than voice are present, such as output signals from voice-band data modems. Vocoders typically produce *unnatural* sounding speech and, therefore, are generally used for recorded information such as "wrong number" messages, encrypted voice for transmission over analog telephone circuits, computer output signals, and educational games.

The purpose of a vocoder is to encode the minimum amount of speech information necessary to reproduce a perceptible message with fewer bits than those needed by a conventional encoder/decoder. Vocoders are used primarily in limited bandwidth applications. Essentially, there are three vocoding techniques available: the *channel vocoder,* the *formant vocoder,* and the *linear predictive coder.*

Channel vocoders. The first channel vocoder was developed by Homer Dudley in 1928. Dudley's vocoder compressed conventional speech waveforms into an analog signal with a total bandwidth of approximately 300 Hz. Present-day digital vocoders operate at less than 2 kbps. Digital channel vocoders use bandpass filters to separate the speech waveform into narrower *subbands.* Each subband is full-wave rectified, filtered, then digitally encoded. The encoded signal is transmitted to the destination receiver, where it is decoded. Generally speaking, the quality of the signal at the output of a vocoder is quite poor. However, some of the more advanced channel vocoders operate at 2400 bps and can produce a highly intelligible, although slightly synthetic sounding speech.

Formant vocoders. A formant vocoder takes advantage of the fact that the short-term spectral density of typical speech signals seldom distributes uniformly across the entire voice-band spectrum (300 Hz to 3000 Hz). Instead, the spectral power of most speech energy concentrates at three or four peak frequencies called *formants.* A formant vocoder simply determines the location of these peaks and encodes and transmits only the information with the most significant short-term components. Therefore, formant vocoders can operate at lower bit rates and, thus, require narrower bandwidths. Formant vocoders sometimes have trouble tracking changes in the formants. However, once the formants have been identified, a formant vocoder can transfer intelligible speech at less than 1000 bps.

Linear predictive coders. A linear predictive coder extracts the most significant portions of speech information directly from the time waveform rather than from the frequency spectrum as with the channel and formant vocoders. A linear predictive coder produces a time-varying model of the *vocal tract excitation* and transfer function directly from the speech waveform. At the receive end, a *synthesizer* reproduces the speech by passing the specified excitation through a mathematical model of the vocal tract. Linear predictive coders provide more natural sounding speech than either the channel or formant vocoder. Linear predictive coders typically encode and transmit speech at between 1.2 kbps and 2.4 kbps.

PCM Line Speed

Line speed is simply the rate at which serial PCM bits are clocked out of the transmitter onto the transmission line or the rate at which serial PCM bits are clocked off the transmission line into the receiver. Line speed is directly proportional to the sample rate and the number of bits in the compressed PCM code. Mathematically,

$$\text{line speed} = \frac{\text{samples}}{\text{second}} \times \frac{\text{bits}}{\text{sample}} \qquad (15\text{-}11)$$

where line speed is the transmission bit rate (bps). For example, a single-channel PCM system with a sample rate $f_s = 8000$ samples/second and an eight-bit compressed PCM code would require the following:

$$\text{line speed} = \frac{8000 \text{ samples}}{\text{second}} \times \frac{8 \text{ bits}}{\text{sample}}$$

$$= 64,000 \text{ bps}$$

DELTA MODULATION PCM

Delta modulation uses a single-bit PCM code to achieve digital transmission of analog signals. With conventional PCM, each code is a binary representation of both the sign and magnitude of a particular sample. Therefore, multiple-bit codes are required to represent the many values that the sample can be. With delta modulation, rather than transmit a coded representation of the sample, only a single bit is transmitted, which simply indicates whether that sample is larger or smaller than the previous sample. The algorithm for a delta modulation system is quite simple. If the current sample is smaller than the previous sample, a logic 0 is transmitted. If the current sample is larger than the previous sample, a logic 1 is transmitted.

Delta Modulation Transmitter

Figure 15-19 shows a block diagram of a delta modulation transmitter. The input analog is sampled and converted to a PAM signal, which is compared with the output of the DAC. The output of the DAC is a voltage equal to the regenerated magnitude of the previous sample, which was stored in the up–down counter as a binary number. The up–down counter is incremented or decremented depending on whether the previous sample is larger or smaller than the current sample. The up–down counter is clocked at a rate equal to the sample rate. Therefore, the up–down counter is updated after each comparison.

Figure 15-20 shows the ideal operation of a delta modulation encoder. Initially, the up–down counter is zeroed and the DAC is outputting 0 V. The first sample is taken, converted to a PAM signal, and compared with zero volts. The output of the comparator is a logic 1 condition (+V), indicating that the current sample is larger in amplitude than the previous sample. On the next clock pulse, the up–down counter is incremented to a count of 1. The DAC now outputs a voltage equal to the magnitude of the minimum step size (resolution). The steps change value at a rate equal to the clock frequency (sample rate). Consequently, with the input signal shown, the up–down counter follows the input analog

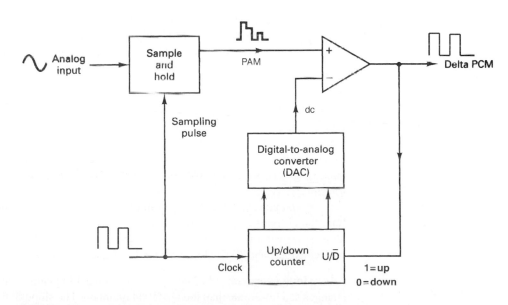

FIGURE 15-19 Delta modulation transmitter

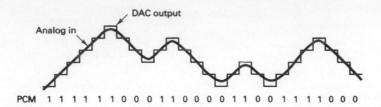

PCM 1 1 1 1 1 1 0 0 0 1 1 0 0 0 0 1 1 0 0 1 1 1 1 0 0 0

FIGURE 15-20 Ideal operation of a delta modulation encoder

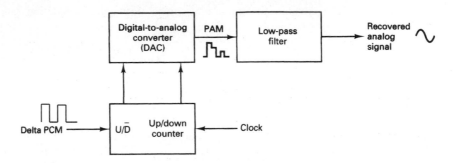

FIGURE 15-21 Delta modulation receiver

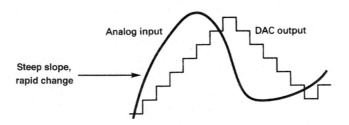

FIGURE 15-22 Slope overload distortion

signal up until the output of the DAC exceeds the analog sample; then the up/down-counter will begin counting down until the output of the DAC drops below the sample amplitude. In the idealized situation (shown in Figure 15-20), the DAC output follows the input signal. Each time the up–down counter is incremented, a logic 1 is transmitted, and each time the up–down counter is decremented, a logic 0 is transmitted.

Delta Modulation Receiver

Figure 15-21 shows the block diagram of a delta modulation receiver. As you can see, the receiver is almost identical to the transmitter except for the comparator. As the logic 1s and 0s are received, the up–down counter is incremented or decremented accordingly. Consequently, the output of the DAC in the decoder is identical to the output of the DAC in the transmitter.

With delta modulation, each sample requires the transmission of only one bit; therefore, the bit rates associated with delta modulation are lower than conventional PCM systems. However, there are two problems associated with delta modulation that do not occur with conventional PCM: slope overload and granular noise.

Slope overload. Figure 15-22 shows what happens when the analog input signal changes at a faster rate than the DAC can maintain. The slope of the analog signal is greater

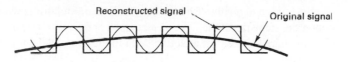

FIGURE 15-23 Granular noise

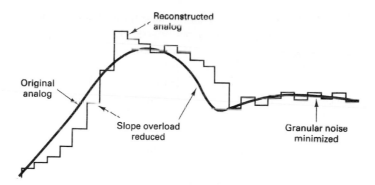

FIGURE 15-24 Adaptive delta modulation

than the delta modulator can maintain, and is called *slope overload*. Increasing the clock frequency reduces the probability of slope overload occurring. Another way to prevent slope overload is to increase the magnitude of the minimum step size.

Granular noise. Figure 15-23 contrasts the original and reconstructed signals associated with a delta modulation system. It can be seen that when the original analog input signal has a relatively constant amplitude, the reconstructed signal has variations that were not present in the original signal. This is called *granular noise*. Granular noise in delta modulation is analogous to quantization noise in conventional PCM.

Granular noise can be reduced by decreasing the step size. Therefore, to reduce the granular noise, a small resolution is needed; and to reduce the possibility of slope overload occurring, a large resolution is required. Obviously, a compromise is necessary.

Granular noise is more prevalent in analog signals that have gradual slopes and whose amplitudes vary only a small amount. Slope overload is more prevalent in analog signals that have steep slopes or whose amplitudes vary rapidly.

ADAPTIVE DELTA MODULATION PCM

Adaptive delta modulation is a delta modulation system where the step size of the DAC is automatically varied depending on the amplitude characteristics of the analog input signal. Figure 15-24 shows how an adaptive delta modulator works. When the output of the transmitter is a string of consecutive 1s or 0s, this indicates that the slope of the DAC output is less than the slope of the analog signal in either the positive or negative direction. Essentially, the DAC has lost track of exactly where the analog samples are and the possibility of slope overload occurring is high. With an adaptive delta modulator, after a predetermined number of consecutive 1s or 0s, the step size is automatically increased. After the next sample, if the DAC output amplitude is still below the sample amplitude, the next step is increased even further until eventually the DAC catches up with the analog signal. When an alternative sequence of 1s and 0s is occurring, this indicates that the possibility of granular noise occurring is high. Consequently, the DAC will automatically revert to its minimum step size and, thus, reduce the magnitude of the noise error.

A common algorithm for an adaptive delta modulator is when three consecutive 1s or 0s occur, the step size of the DAC is increased or decreased by a factor of 1.5. Various other algorithms may be used for adaptive delta modulators, depending on particular system requirements.

DIFFERENTIAL PULSE CODE MODULATION

In a typical PCM-encoded speech waveform, there are often successive samples taken in which there is little difference between the amplitudes of the two samples. This necessitates transmitting several identical PCM codes, which is redundant. Differential pulse code modulation (DPCM) is designed specifically to take advantage of the sample-to-sample redundancies in typical speech waveforms. With DPCM, the difference in the amplitude of two successive samples is transmitted rather than the actual sample. Because the range of sample differences is typically less than the range of individual samples, fewer bits are required for DPCM than conventional PCM.

Figure 15-25 shows a simplified block diagram of a DPCM transmitter. The analog input signal is bandlimited to one-half of the sample rate, then compared with the preceding accumulated signal level in the differentiator. The output of the differentiation is the difference between the two signals. The difference is PCM encoded and transmitted. The A/D converter operates the same as in a conventional PCM system, except that it typically uses fewer bits per sample.

Figure 15-26 shows a simplified block diagram of a DPCM receiver. Each received sample is converted back to analog, stored, and then summed with the next sample received. In the receiver shown in Figure 15-26 the integration is performed on the analog signals, although it could also be performed digitally.

PULSE TRANSMISSION

All digital carrier systems involve the transmission of pulses through a medium with a finite bandwidth. A highly selective system would require a large number of filter sections, which is impractical. Therefore, practical digital systems generally utilize filters with bandwidths that are approximately 30% or more in excess of the ideal Nyquist bandwidth. Figure 15-27a shows the typical output waveform from a *bandlimited* communications channel when a narrow pulse is applied to its input. The figure shows that bandlimiting a pulse causes the energy from the pulse to be spread over a significantly longer time in the form

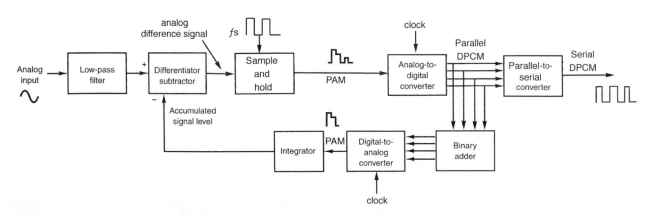

FIGURE 15-25 DPCM transmitter

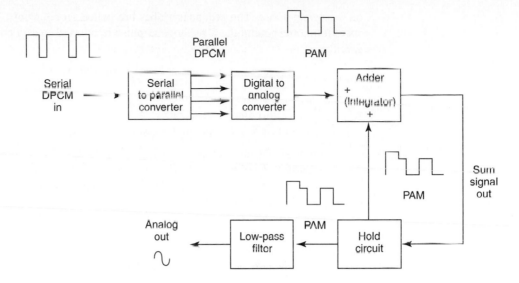

FIGURE 15-26 DPCM receiver

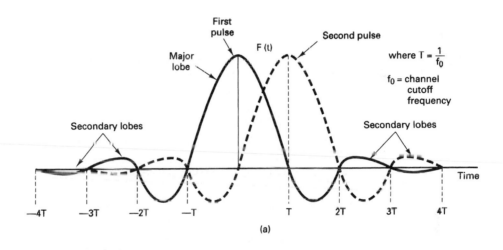

(a)

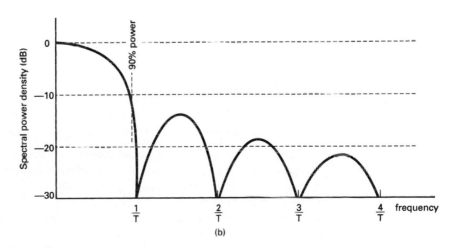

(b)

FIGURE 15-27 Pulse response: (a) typical pulse response of a bandlimited filter; (b) spectrum of square pulse with duration 1/T

of *secondary lobes*. The secondary lobes are called *ringing tails*. The output frequency spectrum corresponding to a rectangular pulse is referred to as a (sin *x*)/*x* response and is given as

$$f(\omega) = (T)\frac{\sin(\omega T/2)}{\omega T/2} \qquad (15\text{-}12)$$

where $\omega = 2\pi f$ (radians)
T = pulse width (seconds)

Figure 15-27b shows the distribution of the total spectrum power. It can be seen that approximately 90% of the signal power is contained within the first *spectral null* (i.e., $f = 1/T$). Therefore, the signal can be confined to a bandwidth $B = 1/T$ and still pass most of the energy from the original waveform. In theory, only the amplitude at the middle of each pulse interval needs to be preserved. Therefore, if the bandwidth is confined to $B = 1/2T$, the maximum signaling rate achievable through a low-pass filter with a specified bandwidth without causing excessive distortion is given as the Nyquist rate and is equal to twice the bandwidth. Mathematically, the Nyquist rate is

$$R = 2B \qquad (15\text{-}13)$$

where R = signaling rate = $1/T$
B = specified bandwidth

Intersymbol Interference

Figure 15-28 shows the input signal to an ideal minimum bandwidth, low-pass filter. The input signal is a random, binary nonreturn-to-zero (NRZ) sequence. Figure 15-28b shows the output of a low-pass filter that does not introduce any phase or amplitude distortion. Note that the output signal reaches its full value for each transmitted pulse at precisely the center of each sampling interval. However, if the low-pass filter is imperfect (which in reality it will be), the output response will more closely resemble that shown in Figure 15-28c. At the sampling instants (i.e., the center of the pulses), the signal does not always attain the maximum value. The ringing tails of several pulses have *overlapped,* thus interfering with the *major pulse lobe.* Assuming no time delays through the system, energy in the form of spurious responses from the third and fourth impulses from one pulse appears during the sampling instant ($T = 0$) of another pulse. This interference is commonly called *intersymbol interference* or simply ISI. ISI is an important consideration in the transmission of pulses over circuits with a limited bandwidth and a nonlinear phase response. Simply stated, rectangular pulses will not remain rectangular in less than an infinite bandwidth. The narrower the bandwidth, the more rounded the pulses. If the phase distortion is excessive, the pulse will *tilt* and, consequently, affect the next pulse. When pulses from more than one source are multiplexed together, the amplitude, frequency, and phase responses become even more critical. ISI causes *crosstalk* between channels that occupy adjacent time slots in a time-division-multiplexed carrier system. Special filters called *equalizers* are inserted in the transmission path to "equalize" the distortion for all frequencies, creating a uniform transmission medium and reducing transmission impairments. The four primary causes of ISI are

1. *Timing inaccuracies.* In digital transmission systems, transmitter timing inaccuracies cause intersymbol interference if the rate of transmission does not conform to the *ringing frequency* designed into the communications channel. Generally, timing inaccuracies of this type are insignificant. Because receiver clocking information is derived from the received signals, which are contaminated with noise, inaccurate sample timing is more likely to occur in receivers than in transmitters.

2. *Insufficient bandwidth.* Timing errors are less likely to occur if the transmission rate is well below the channel bandwidth (i.e., the Nyquist bandwidth is significantly be-

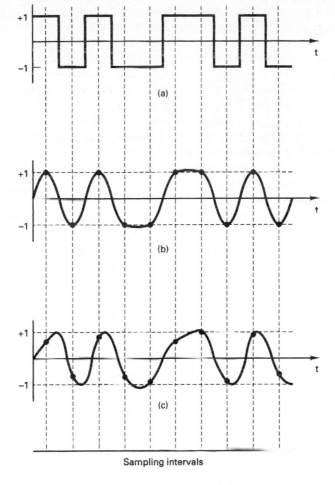

Sampling intervals

FIGURE 15-28 Pulse response: (a) NRZ input signal; (b) output from a perfect filter; (c) output from an imperfect filter

low the channel bandwidth). As the bandwidth of a communications channel is reduced, the ringing frequency is reduced and intersymbol interference is more likely to occur.

3. *Amplitude distortion.* Filters are placed in a communications channel to bandlimit signals and reduce or eliminate predicted noise and interference. Filters are also used to produce a specific pulse response. However, the frequency response of a channel cannot always be predicted absolutely. When the frequency characteristics of a communications channel depart from the normal or expected values, *pulse distortion* results. Pulse distortion occurs when the peaks of pulses are reduced, causing improper ringing frequencies in the time domain. Compensation for such impairments is called amplitude equalization.

4. *Phase distortion.* A pulse is simply the superposition of a series of harmonically related sine waves with specific amplitude and phase relationships. Therefore, if the relative phase relations of the individual sine waves are altered, phase distortion occurs. Phase distortion occurs when frequency components undergo different amounts of time delay while propagating through the transmission medium. Special delay equalizers are placed in the transmission path to compensate for the varying delays, thus reducing the phase distortion. Phase equalizers can be manually adjusted or designed to automatically adjust themselves to varying transmission characteristics.

Eye Patterns

The performance of a digital transmission system depends, in part, on the ability of a repeater to regenerate the original pulses. Similarly, the quality of the regeneration process depends on the decision circuit within the repeater and the quality of the signal at the input to the decision circuit. Therefore, the performance of a digital transmission system can be measured by displaying the received signal on an oscilloscope and triggering the time base at the data rate. Thus, all waveform combinations are superimposed over adjacent signaling intervals. Such a display is called an *eye pattern* or *eye diagram*. An eye pattern is a convenient technique for determining the effects of the degradations introduced into the pulses as they travel to the regenerator. The test setup to display an eye pattern is shown in Figure 15-29. The received pulse stream is fed to the vertical input of the oscilloscope, and the symbol clock is fed to the external trigger input, while the sweep rate is set approximately equal to the symbol rate.

Figure 15-30 shows an eye pattern generated by a symmetrical waveform for *ternary* signals in which the individual pulses at the input to the regenerator have a cosine-squared shape. In an *m*-level system, there will be $m - 1$ separate eyes. The horizontal lines labeled $+1, 0$, and -1 correspond to the ideal received amplitudes. The vertical lines, separated by the signaling interval, *T*, correspond to the ideal *decision times*. The decision levels for the

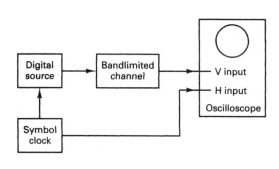

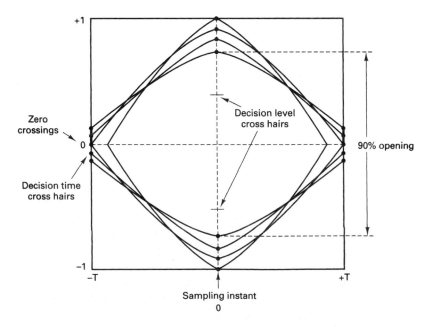

FIGURE 15-29 Eye diagram measurement setup

FIGURE 15-30 Eye diagram

regenerator are represented by *crosshairs*. The vertical hairs represents the decision time, whereas the horizontal hairs represents the decision level. The eye pattern shows the quality of shaping and timing and discloses any noise and errors that might be present in the line equalization. The eye opening (the area in the middle of the eye pattern) defines a boundary within which no waveform *trajectories* can exist under any code-pattern condition. The eye opening is a function of the number of code levels and the intersymbol interference caused by the ringing tails of any preceding or succeeding pulses. To regenerate the pulse sequence without error, the eye must be open (i.e., a decision area must exist), and the decision crosshairs must be within the open area. The effect of pulse degradation is a reduction in the size of the ideal eye. In Figure 15-30 it can be seen that at the center of the eye (i.e., the sampling instant) the opening is about 90%, indicating only minor ISI degradation due to filtering imperfections. The small degradation is due to the nonideal Nyquist amplitude and phase characteristics of the transmission system. Mathematically, the ISI degradation is

$$\text{ISI} = 20 \log \frac{h}{H} \qquad (15\text{-}14)$$

where H = ideal vertical opening (cm)

   h = degraded vertical opening (cm)

For the eye diagram shown in Figure 15-30,

$$20 \log \frac{90}{100} = 0.915 \text{ dB} \quad \text{(ISI degradation)}$$

In Figure 15-30 it can also be seen that the overlapping signal pattern does not cross the horizontal zero line at exact integer multiples of the symbol clock. This is an impairment known as *data transition jitter*. This jitter has an effect on the symbol timing (clock) recovery circuit and, if excessive, may significantly degrade the performance of cascaded regenerative sections.

SIGNAL POWER IN BINARY DIGITAL SIGNALS

Because binary digital signals can originate from literally scores of different types of data sources, it is impossible to predict which patterns or sequences of bits are most likely to occur over a given period of time in a given system. Thus, for signal analysis purposes, it is generally assumed that there is an equal probability of the occurrence of a 1 and a 0. Therefore, power can be averaged over an entire message duration and the signal can be modeled as a continuous sequence of alternating 1s and 0s as shown in Figure 15-31. Figure 15-31a shows a stream of rectangularly shaped pulses with a pulse width-to-pulse duration ratio τ/T less than 0.5, and Figure 15-31b shows a stream of square wave pulses with a τ/T ratio of 0.5.

The normalized $(R - 1)$ average power is derived for signal $f(t)$ from

$$\overline{P} = \lim_{T \to x} \frac{1}{T} \int_{-T/2}^{T/2} [f(t)]^2 \, dt \qquad (15\text{-}15)$$

where T is the period of integration. If $f(t)$ is a periodic signal with period T_0, then Equation 15-15 reduces to

$$\overline{P} = \frac{1}{T_0} \int_{-T_0/2}^{T_0/2} [v(t)]^2 \, dt \qquad (15\text{-}16)$$

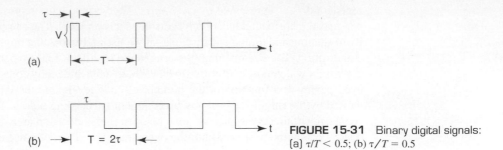

FIGURE 15-31 Binary digital signals: [a] $\tau/T < 0.5$; (b) $\tau/T = 0.5$

If rectangular pulses of amplitude V with a τ/T ratio of 0.5 begin at $t = 0$, then

$$v(t) = \begin{cases} V & 0 \le t \le \tau \\ 0 & \tau < t \le T \end{cases} \tag{15-17}$$

Thus, from Equation 15-16,

$$\overline{P} = \frac{1}{T_0}\int_0^T (V)^2 dt = \frac{1}{T_0} V^2 t|_0^\tau \tag{15-18}$$

$$= \frac{\tau}{T_0} V^2$$

and

$$\overline{P} = \left(\frac{\tau}{T}\right)\frac{V^2}{R}$$

Because the effective rms value of a periodic wave is found from $P = (V_{rms})^2/R$, the rms voltage for a rectangular pulse is

$$V_{rms} = \sqrt{\frac{\tau}{T}} V \tag{15-19}$$

Because $\overline{P} = (V_{rms})^2/R$, $\overline{P} = (\sqrt{\tau/T}\, V)^2/R = (\tau V^2)/(TR)$.

With the square wave shown in Figure 15-31, $\tau/T = 0.5$, therefore, $\overline{P} = V^2/2R$. Thus, the rms voltage for the square wave is the same as for sine waves, $V_{rms} = V/\sqrt{2}$.

QUESTIONS

15-1. Contrast the advantages and disadvantages of digital transmission.

15-2. What are the four most common methods of pulse modulation?

15-3. Which method listed in Question 15-2 is the only form of pulse modulation that is used in a digital transmission system? Explain.

15-4. What is the purpose of the sample-and-hold circuit?

15-5. Define *aperture* and *acquisition time*.

15-6. What is the difference between natural and flat-top sampling?

15-7. Define *droop*. What causes it?

15-8. What is the Nyquist sampling rate?

15-9. Define and state the causes of foldover distortion.

15-10. Explain the difference between a magnitude-only code and a sign-magnitude code.

15-11. Explain overload distortion.

15-12. Explain quantizing.

15-13. What is quantization range? Quantization error?

15-14. Define *dynamic range.*

15-15. Explain the relationship between dynamic range, resolution, and the number of bits in a PCM code.

15-16. Explain coding efficiency.

15-17. What is SQR? What is the relationship between SQR, resolution, dynamic range, and the number of bits in a PCM code?

15-18. Contrast linear and nonlinear PCM codes.

15-19. Explain idle channel noise.

15-20. Contrast midtread and midrise quantization.

15-21. Define *companding.*

15-22. What does the parameter μ determine?

15-23. Briefly explain the process of digital companding.

15-24. What is the effect of digital compression on SQR, resolution, quantization interval, and quantization noise?

15-25. Contrast delta modulation PCM and standard PCM.

15-26. Define *slope overload* and *granular noise.*

15-27. What is the difference between adaptive delta modulation and conventional delta modulation?

15-28. Contrast differential and conventional PCM.

PROBLEMS

15-1. Determine the Nyquist sample rate for a maximum analog input frequency of
  (a) 4 kHz
  (b) 10 kHz

15-2. For the sample-and-hold circuit shown in Figure 15-4a, determine the largest-value capacitor that can be used. Use the following parameters: an output impedance for $Z_1 = 20\ \Omega$, an on resistance of Q_1 of $20\ \Omega$, an acquisition time of $10\ \mu s$, a maximum output current from Z_1 of 20 mA, and an accuracy of 1%

15-3. For a sample rate of 20 kHz, determine the maximum analog input frequency.

15-4. Determine the alias frequency for a 14-kHz sample rate and an analog input frequency of 8 kHz.

15-5. Determine the dynamic range for a 10-bit sign-magnitude PCM code.

15-6. Determine the minimum number of bits required in a PCM code for a dynamic range of 80 dB. What is the coding efficiency?

15-7. For a resolution of 0.04 V, determine the voltages for the following linear 7-bit sign-magnitude PCM codes.
  (a) 0 1 1 0 1 0 1
  (b) 0 0 0 0 0 1 1
  (c) 1 0 0 0 0 0 1
  (d) 0 1 1 1 1 1 1
  (e) 1 0 0 0 0 0 0

15-8. Determine the SQR for a 2-v_{rms} signal and a quantization interval of 0.2 V.

15-9. Determine the resolution and quantization error for an 8-bit linear sign-magnitude PCM code for a maximum decoded voltage of 1.27 V.

15-10. A 12-bit linear PCM code is digitally compressed into 8 bits. The resolution = 0.03 V. Determine the following for an analog input voltage of 1.465 V
  (a) 12-bit linear PCM code
  (b) 8-bit compressed code
  (c) Decoded 12-bit code
  (d) Decoded voltage
  (e) Percentage error

15-11. For a 12-bit linear PCM code with a resolution of 0.02 V, determine the voltage range that would be converted to the following PCM codes.

    (a) 1 0 0 0 0 0 0 0 0 0 0 1
    (b) 0 0 0 0 0 0 0 0 0 0 0 0
    (c) 1 1 0 0 0 0 0 0 0 0 0 0
    (d) 0 1 0 0 0 0 0 0 0 0 0 0
    (e) 1 0 0 1 0 0 0 0 0 0 0 1
    (f) 1 0 1 0 1 0 1 0 1 0 1 0

15-12. For each of the following 12-bit linear PCM codes, determine the 8-bit compressed code to which they would be converted.
    (a) 1 0 0 0 0 0 0 0 1 0 0 0
    (b) 1 0 0 0 0 0 0 0 1 0 0 1
    (c) 1 0 0 0 0 0 0 1 0 0 0 0
    (d) 0 0 0 0 0 0 1 0 0 0 0 0
    (e) 0 1 0 0 0 0 0 0 0 0 0 0
    (f) 0 1 0 0 0 0 1 0 0 0 0 0

15-13. Determine the Nyquist sampling rate for the following maximum analog input frequencies: 2 kHz, 5 kHz, 12 kHz, and 20 kHz.

15-14. For the sample-and-hold circuit shown in Figure 15-3, determine the largest-value capacitor that can be used for the following parameters: Z_1 output impedance = 15 Ω, an on resistance of Q_1 of 15 Ω, an acquisition time of 12 μs, a maximum output current from Z_1 of 10 mA, an accuracy of 0.1%, and a maximum change in voltage dv = 10 V.

15-15. Determine the maximum analog input frequency for the following Nyquist sample rates: 2.5 kHz, 4 kHz, 9 kHz, and 11 kHz.

15-16. Determine the alias frequency for the following sample rates and analog input frequencies

f_a (kHz)	f_s (kHz)
3	4
5	8
6	8
5	7

15-17. Determine the dynamic range in dB for the following n-bit linear sign-magnitude PCM codes: n = 7, 8, 12, and 14.

15-18. Determine the minimum number of bits required for PCM codes with the following dynamic ranges, and determine the coding efficiencies: DR = 24 dB, 48 dB, and 72 dB.

15-19. For the following values of μ, V_{max}, and V_{in}, determine the compressor gain.

μ	V_{max} (V)	V_{in} (V)
255	1	0.75
100	1	0.75
255	2	0.5

15-20. For the following resolutions, determine the range of the 8-bit sign-magnitude PCM codes.

Code	Resolution (V)
10111000	0.1
00111000	0.1
11111111	0.05
00011100	0.02
00110101	0.02
11100000	0.02
00000111	0.02

15-21. Determine the SQR for the following input signal and quantization noise magnitudes.

V_s	V_n (V)
1 v_{rms}	0.01
2 v_{rms}	0.02
3 v_{rms}	0.01
4 v_{rms}	0.2

15-22. Determine the resolution and quantization noise for an 8-bit linear sign-magnitude PCM code for the following maximum decoded voltages: $V_{\text{max}} = 3.06 \ V_p$, 3.57 V_p, 4.08 V_p, and 4.59 V_p.

15-23. A 12-bit linear sign-magnitude PCM code is digitally compressed into 8 bits. For a resolution of 0.016 V, determine the following quantities for the indicated input voltages: 12-bit linear PCM code, 8-bit compressed code, decoded 12-bit code, decoded voltage, and percentage error. $V_{\text{in}} = -6.592$ V, $+12.992$ V, and -3.36 V.

15-24. For the 12-bit linear PCM codes given, determine the voltage range that would be converted to them.

12-Bit Linear Code	Resolution (V)
100011110010	0.12
000001000000	0.10
000111111000	0.14
111111110000	0.12

15-25. For the following 12-bit linear PCM codes, determine the 8-bit compressed code to which they would be converted.

12-Bit Linear Code
100011110010
000001000000
000111111000
111111110010
000000100000

15-26. For the following 8-bit compressed codes, determine the expanded 12-bit code.

8-Bit Code
11001010
00010010
10101010
01010101
11110000
11011011

C H A P T E R 16

Multiplexing

INTRODUCTION

Multiplexing is the transmission of information (in any form) from more than one source to more than one destination over the same transmission medium (facility). Although transmissions occur on the same facility, they do not necessarily occur at the same time. The transmission medium may be a metallic wire pair, a coaxial cable, a PCS mobile telephone, a terrestrial microwave radio system, a satellite microwave system, or an optical fiber cable.

There are several domains in which multiplexing can be accomplished including space, phase, time, frequency, and wavelength. *Space-division multiplexing* (SDM) is a rather unsophisticated form of multiplexing which simply constitutes propagating signals from different sources on different cables that are contained within the same trench. The trench is considered to be the transmission medium. QPSK is a form of *phase-division multiplexing* (PDM) where two data channels (the I and Q) modulated the same carrier frequency that has been shifted 90° in phase. Thus, the I-channel bits modulate a sine wave carrier while the Q-channel bits modulate a cosine wave carrier. After modulation has occurred, the I- and Q-channel carriers are linearly combined and propagated at the same time over the same transmission medium which can be a cable or free space.

The three most predominant methods of multiplexing signals are time-division multiplexing (TDM), frequency-division multiplexing (FDM), and the more recently developed wavelength-division multiplexing (WDM). The remainder of this chapter will be dedicated to time-, frequency-, and wavelength-division multiplexing.

TIME-DIVISION MULTIPLEXING

With time-division multiplexing (TDM), transmissions from multiple sources occur on the same facility but not at the same time. Transmissions from various sources are *interleaved* in the time domain. The most common type of modulation used with TDM systems is PCM. With a PCM-TDM system, two or more voice-band channels are sampled, converted to PCM codes, and then time-division multiplexed onto a single metallic cable pair or an optical fiber cable.

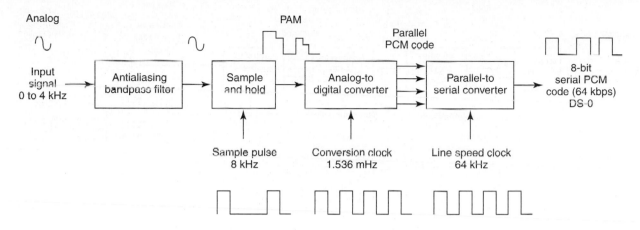

FIGURE 16-1 Single-channel (DS-0-level) PCM transmission system

The fundamental building block for any TDM system begins with a DS-0 channel (digital signal—level 0). Figure 16-1 shows the simplified block diagram for a DS-0 single-channel PCM system. As the figure shows, DS-0 channels use an 8-kHz sample rate and an eight-bit PCM code which produces a 64-kbps PCM signal at its output.

$$\frac{8000 \text{ samples}}{\text{second}} \times \frac{8 \text{ bits}}{\text{sample}} = 64 \text{ kbps}$$

Figure 16-2a shows the simplified block diagram for a multiplexed PCM-TDM carrier system made of two DS-0 channels. Each input channel is alternately sampled at an 8-kHz rate and converted to PCM code. While the PCM code for channel 1 is being transmitted, channel 2 is sampled and converted to PCM code. While the PCM code from channel 2 is being transmitted, the next sample is taken from channel 1 and converted to PCM code. This process continues and samples are taken alternately from each channel, converted to PCM code, and transmitted. The multiplexer is simply an electronically controlled digital switch with two inputs and one output. Channel 1 and channel 2 are alternately selected and connected to the multiplexer output. The time it takes to transmit one sample from each channel is called the *frame time*. The frame time is equal to the reciprocal of the sample rate ($1/f_s$ or $1/8000 = 125$ μs). Figure 16-2b shows the TDM frame allocation for a two-channel PCM system with an 8-kHz sample rate.

The PCM code for each channel occupies a fixed time slot (epoch) within the total TDM frame. With a two channel system, one sample is taken from each channel during each frame and the time allocated to transmit the PCM bits from each channel is equal to one-half the total frame time. Therefore, eight bits from each channel must be transmitted during each frame (a total of 16 bits per frame). Thus, the line speed at the output of the multiplexer is

$$\frac{2 \text{ channels}}{\text{frame}} \times \frac{8000 \text{ frames}}{\text{second}} \times \frac{8 \text{ bits}}{\text{channel}} = 128 \text{ kbps}$$

Although each channel is producing and transmitting only 64 kbps, the bits must be clocked out onto the line at a128-kHz rate to allow eight bits from each channel to be transmitted in each 125-μs time slot.

T1 DIGITAL CARRIER SYSTEM

A digital carrier system is a communications system that uses digital pulses, rather than analog signals, to encode information. Figure 16-3a shows the block diagram for the Bell

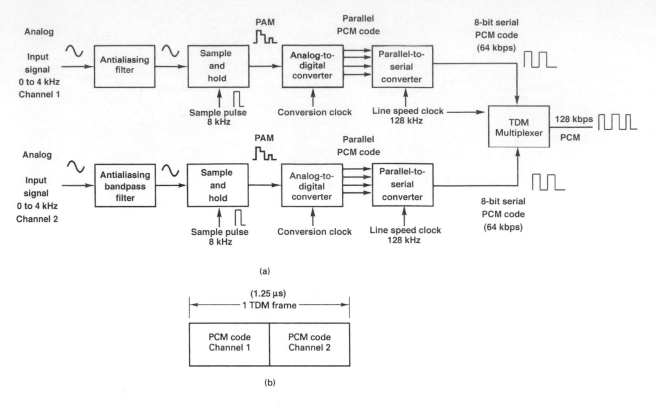

FIGURE 16-2 Two-channel PCM-TDM system: (a) block diagram; (b) TDM frame

System T1 digital carrier system (equivalent to the GTE 9002B system). The Bell System T1 carrier system is the North American telephone standard and recognized by the CCITT as CCITT Recommendation G.733. A T1 carrier time-division multiplexes PCM-encoded samples from 24 voice-band channels for transmission over a single metallic wire pair or optical fiber transmission line. Each voice-band channel has a bandwidth of approximately 300 Hz to 3000 Hz. Again, the multiplexer is simply a digital switch, except now it has 24 inputs and a single output. The PCM outputs from the 24 voice-band channels are sequentially selected and connected through the multiplexer to the transmission line.

Simply time-division multiplexing 24 voice-band channels does not in itself constitute a T1 carrier system. At this point, the output of the multiplexer is simply a multiplexed first-level digital signal (DS—level 1). The system does not become a T1 carrier until it is line encoded and placed on special conditioned cables called *T1 lines*. This is explained in more detail later in this chapter.

With a T1 carrier system, D-type (digital) channel banks perform the sampling, encoding, and multiplexing of 24 voice-band channels. Each channel contains an eight-bit PCM code and is sampled 8000 times a second. Therefore, one 64-kbps PCM-encoded sample is transmitted for each voice-band channel during each frame. The transmit line speed is calculated as follows:

$$\frac{24 \text{ channels}}{\text{frame}} \times \frac{8 \text{ bits}}{\text{channel}} = 192 \text{ bits per frame}$$

thus,

$$\frac{192 \text{ bits}}{\text{frame}} \times \frac{8000 \text{ frames}}{\text{second}} = 1.536 \text{ Mbps}$$

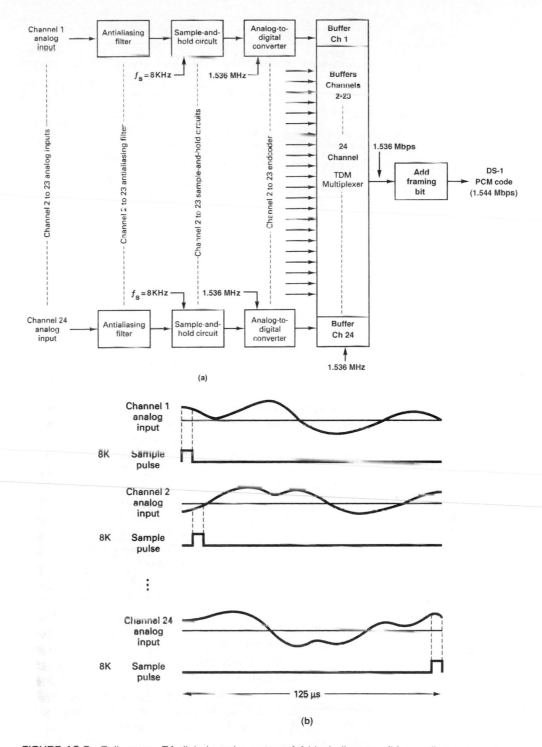

FIGURE 16-3 Bell system T1 digital carrier system: (a) block diagram; (b) sampling sequence

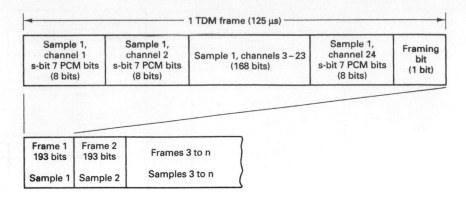

FIGURE 16-4 T1 carrier system frame and sample alignment using D1A channel banks

Later, an additional bit (the *framing bit*) is added to the transmit signal of each frame. The framing bit occurs once per frame (8000-bps rate) and is recovered in the receiver circuitry where it is used to maintain frame and sample synchronization between the TDM transmitter and receiver. As a result, each frame contains 193 bits, and the line speed for a T1 digital carrier system is

$$\frac{193 \text{ bits}}{\text{frame}} \times \frac{8000 \text{ frames}}{\text{second}} = 1.544 \text{ Mbps}$$

It is important to note that each channel is sampled at the same rate but not necessarily at the same time. Figure 16-3b shows the channel sampling sequence for a 24-channel T1 digital carrier system. As the figure shows, each channel is sampled once each frame but not at the same time. Each channel's sample is offset from the previous channel's sample by 1/24th of the total frame time.

D-Type Channel Banks

The early T1 carrier systems were equipped with D1A channel banks that use a seven-bit magnitude-only PCM code with analog companding and $\mu = 100$. A later version of the D1 channel bank (D1D) used an eight-bit sign-magnitude PCM code. With D1D channel banks an eighth bit (the s bit) is added to each PCM code word for the purpose of *signaling* (supervision: on-hook, off-hook, dial pulsing, and so on). Consequently, the signaling rate for D1D channel banks is 8 kbps. Also, with D1D channel banks, the framing bit sequence is simply an alternating 1/0 pattern. Figure 16-4 shows the frame and sample alignment for the T1 carrier system using D1D channel banks.

Generically, the T1 carrier system has progressed through the D2, D3, D4, D5, and D6 channel banks. D4, D5, and D6 use a digitally companded, eight-bit sign-magnitude compressed PCM code with $\mu = 255$. In the D1 channel bank, the compression and expansion characteristics were implemented in circuitry separate from the encoder and decoder. The D2, D3, D4, and D5 channel banks incorporate the companding functions directly in the encoders and decoders. Although the D2 and D3 channel banks are functionally similar, the D3 channel banks were the first to incorporate separate customized LSI integrated circuits (codecs) for each voice-band channel. With D1, D2, and D3 channel banks, common equipment performs the encoding and decoding functions. Consequently, a single equipment malfunction constitutes a total system failure.

D1A channel banks use a magnitude-only code; consequently, an error in the most significant bit (MSB) of a channel sample always produces a decoded error equal to one-half the total quantization range (V_{max}). Because D1D, D2, D3, D4, and D5 channel banks use a sign-magnitude code, an error in the MSB (sign bit) causes a decoded error equal to

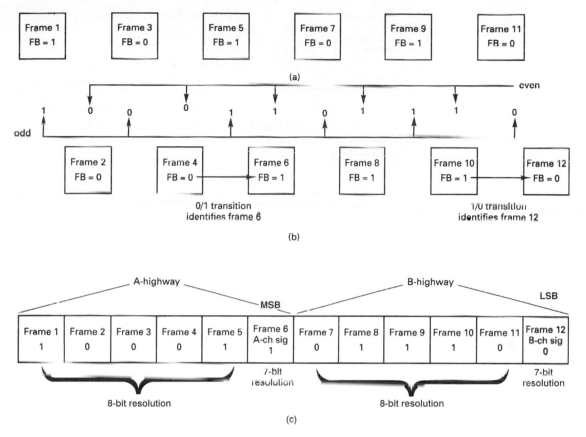

FIGURE 16-5 Framing bit sequence or the T1 superframe format using D2 or D3 channel banks: (a) frame synchronizing bits (odd-numbered frames), (b) signaling frame alignment bits (even-numbered frames); (c) composite frame alignment

twice the sample magnitude (from +V to −V, or vice versa). The worst-case error is equal to twice the total quantization range. However, maximum amplitude samples occur rarely, and most errors with D1D, D2, D3, D4, and D5 coding are less than one-half the coding range. On the average, the error performance with a sign-magnitude code is better than with a magnitude-only code.

Superframe Format

The 8-kbps signaling rate used with D1 channel banks is excessive for voice transmission. Therefore, with D2 and D3 channel banks, a signaling bit is substituted only into the least significant bit (LSB) of every sixth frame. Therefore, five of every six frames have 8-bit resolution, while one of every six frames (the signaling frame) has only 7-bit resolution. Consequently, the signaling rate on each channel is 1.333 kbps (8000 bps/6), and the effective number of bits per sample is actually 7 5/6 bits and not eight.

Because only every sixth frame includes a signaling bit, it is necessary that all the frames be numbered so that the receiver knows when to extract the signaling information. Also, because the signaling is accomplished with a two-bit binary word, it is necessary to identify the MSB and LSB of the signaling word. Consequently, the *superframe* format shown in Figure 16-5 was devised. Within each superframe are 12 consecutively numbered frames (1–12). The signaling bits are substituted in frames 6 and 12, the MSB into frame 6 and the LSB into frame 12. Frames 1–6 are called the A-highway, with frame 6 designated as the A-channel signaling frame. Frames 7–12 are called the B-highway, with frame 12 designated as the B-channel signaling frame. Therefore, in addition to identifying the signaling frames, the sixth and twelfth frames must be positively identified.

To identify frames 6 and 12, a different framing bit sequence is used for the odd- and even-numbered frames. The odd frames (frames 1, 3, 5, 7, 9, and 11) have an alternating 1/0 pattern, and the even frames (frames 2, 4, 6, 8, 10, and 12) have a 0 0 1 1 1 0 repetitive pattern. As a result, the combined bit pattern for the framing bits is a 1 0 0 0 1 1 0 1 1 1 0 0 repetitive pattern. The odd-numbered frames are used for frame and sample synchronization, and the even-numbered frames are used to identify the A- and B-channel signaling frames (6 and 12). Frame 6 is identified by a 0/1 transition in the framing bit between frames 4 and 6. Frame 12 is identified by a 1/0 transition in the framing bit between frames 10 and 12.

Figure 16-6 shows the frame, sample, and signaling alignment for the T1 carrier system using D2 or D3 channel banks.

In addition to *multiframe alignment* bits and PCM sample bits, certain time slots are used to indicate alarm conditions. For example, in the case of a transmit power supply failure, a common equipment failure, or loss of multiframe alignment, the second bit in each channel is made a 0 until the alarm condition has cleared. Also, the framing bit in frame 12 is complemented whenever multiframe alignment is lost (this is assumed whenever frame alignment is lost). In addition, there are special framing conditions that must be avoided in order to maintain clock and bit synchronization at the receive demultiplexing equipment. These special conditions are explained later in this chapter.

Figure 16-7a shows the framing bit circuitry for the 24-channel T1 carrier system using either D2 or D3 channel banks (DS-1). Note that the bit rate at the output of the TDM multiplex is 1.536 Mbps and the bit rate at the output of the 193-bit shift register is 1.544 Mbps. The difference (8 kbps) is due to the addition of the framing bit in the shift register.

D4 channel banks time-division multiplex 48 voice-band channels and operate at a transmission rate of 3.152 Mbps. This is slightly more than twice the line speed for 24-channel D1, D2, or D3 channel banks, because with D4 channel banks, rather than transmitting a single framing bit with each frame, a 10-bit frame synchronization pattern is used. Consequently, the total number of bits in a D4 (DS-1C) TDM frame is

$$\frac{8 \text{ bits}}{\text{channel}} \times \frac{48 \text{ channels}}{\text{frame}} = \frac{384 \text{ bits}}{\text{frame}} + \frac{10 \text{ syn bits}}{\text{frame}} = \frac{394 \text{ bits}}{\text{frame}}$$

and the line speed is

$$\text{line speed} = \frac{394 \text{ bits}}{\text{frame}} \times \frac{8000 \text{ frames}}{\text{second}} = 3.152 \text{ Mbps}$$

The framing for the DS-1 (T1) system or the framing pattern for the DS-1C (T1C) time-division multiplexed carrier systems is added to the multiplexed digital signal at the output of the multiplexer. The framing bit circuitry used for the 48-channel DS-1C (T1) digital carrier system using D4 channel banks is shown in Figure 16-7b.

Extended Superframe Format

Another framing format recently developed for new designs of T1 carrier systems is the *extended superframe*. The extended superframe format consists of 24 frames (3 ms) totaling 4632 bits of which 24 are framing bits. The framing bit occurs once every 193 bits. Only 6 of the 24 framing bits, however, are used for frame synchronization. The frame synchronization bits occur in frames 4, 8, 12, 16, 20, and 24 and have a bit sequence of 0 0 1 0 1 1. Another 6 of the framing bits are used for a CRC-6 error detection code which is simply a short version of CRC-16. The CRC-6 bits occur in frames 1, 5, 9, 13, 17, and 21. The 12 remaining framing bits provide for a management channel called the *facilities data link* (FDL). FDL bits function in a manner similar to data link control characters in HDLC. FDL bits occur in frames 2, 3, 6, 7, 10, 11, 14, 15, 18, 19, 22, and 23. The extended superframe framing bit pattern is summarized in Table 16-1.

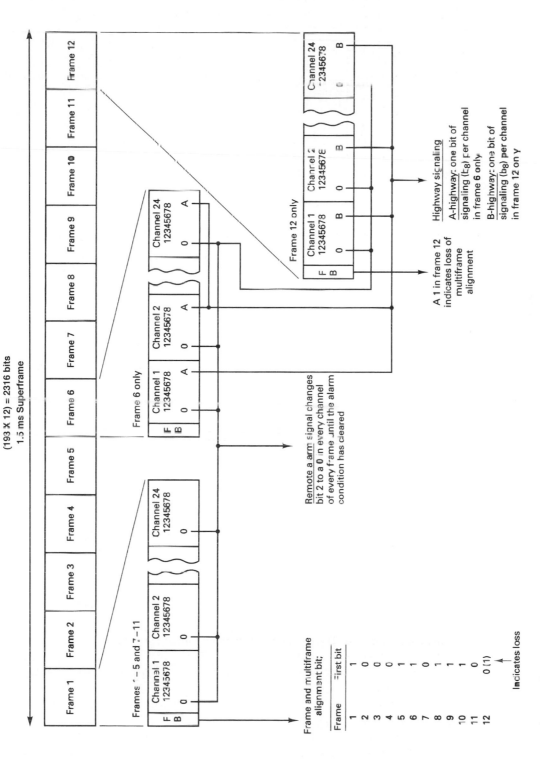

FIGURE 16-6 T1 carrier frame, sample, and signaling alignment for D2 and D3 channel banks

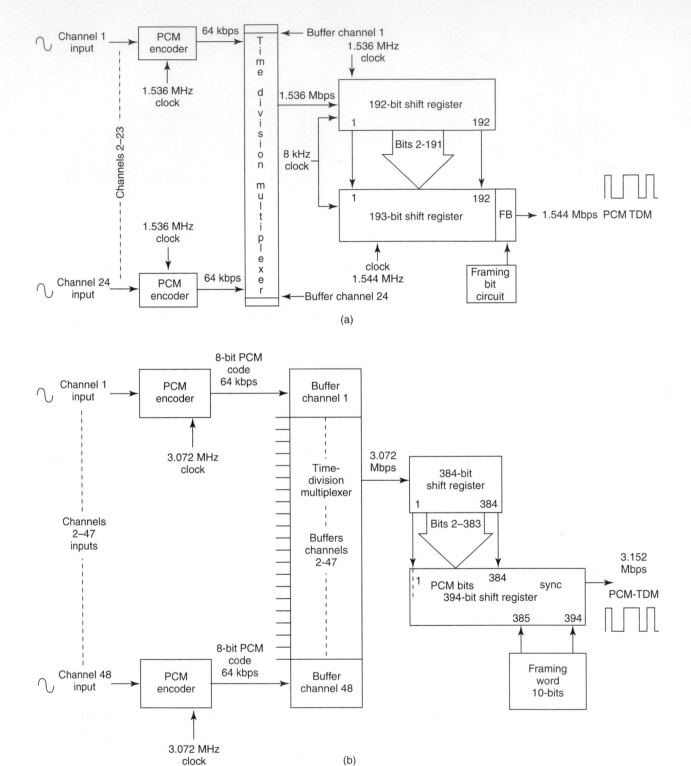

FIGURE 16-7 Framing bit circuitry T1 carrier system: (a) DS-1; (b) DS-1C

TABLE 16-1 Extended Superframe Format.

Frame Number	Framing Bit	Frame Number	Framing Bit
1	C	13	C
2	F	14	F
3	F	15	F
4	S=0	16	S=0
5	C	17	C
6	F	18	F
7	F	19	F
8	S=0	20	S=1
9	C	21	C
10	F	22	F
11	F	23	F
12	S=1	24	S=1

The extended superframe format supports a four-bit signaling word with signaling bits provided in the second least significant bit of every channel during every sixth frame. The signaling bit in frame 6 is called the A bit, the signaling bit in frame 12 is called the B bit, the signaling bit in frame 18 is called the C bit, and the signaling bit in frame 24 is called the D bit.

CCITT TIME-DIVISION MULTIPLEXED CARRIER SYSTEM

Figure 16-8 shows the frame alignment for the CCITT (Comité Consultatif International Téléphonique et Télégraphique) European standard PCM-TDM system. With the CCITT system, a 125-μs frame is divided into 32 equal time slots. Time slot 0 is used for a frame alignment pattern and for an alarm channel. Time slot 17 is used for a common signaling channel. The signaling for all the voice-band channels is accomplished on the common signaling channel. Consequently, 30 voice-band channels are time-division multiplexed into each CCITT frame.

With the CCITT standard, each time slot has eight bits. Consequently, the total number of bits per frame is

$$\frac{8 \text{ bits}}{\text{time slot}} \times \frac{32 \text{ time slots}}{\text{frame}} = \frac{256 \text{ bits}}{\text{frame}}$$

and the line speed is

$$\text{line speed} = \frac{256 \text{ bits}}{\text{frame}} \times \frac{8000 \text{ frames}}{\text{second}} = 2.048 \text{ Mbps}$$

CODECS

A *codec* is a large-scale integration (LSI) chip designed for use in the telecommunications industry for *private branch exchanges* (PBXs), central office switches, digital handsets, voice store-and-forward systems, and digital echo suppressors. Essentially, the codec is applicable for any purpose that requires the digitizing of analog signals, such as in a PCM-TDM carrier system.

Codec is a generic term that refers to the *co*ding functions performed by a device that converts analog signals to digital codes and digital codes to analog signals. Recently developed codecs are called *combo* chips, because they combine codec and filter functions in the

Time slot 0	Time slot 1	Time slots 2–16	Time slot 17	Time slots 18–30	Time slot 31
Framing and alarm channel	Voice channel 1	Voice channels 2–15	Common signaling channel	Voice channels 16–29	Voice channel 30
8 bits	8 bits	112 bits	8 bits	112 bits	8 bits

(a)

Time slot 17

	Bits	
Frame	1234	5678
0	0000	xyxx
1	ch 1	ch 16
2	ch 2	ch 17
3	ch 3	ch 18
4	ch 4	ch 19
5	ch 5	ch 20
6	ch 6	ch 21
7	ch 7	ch 22
8	ch 8	ch 23
9	ch 9	ch 24
10	ch 10	ch 25
11	ch 11	ch 26
12	ch 12	ch 27
13	ch 13	ch 28
14	ch 14	ch 29
15	ch 15	ch 30

16 frames equal one multiframe; 500 multiframes are transmitted each second

x = spare
y = loss of multiframe alignment if a 1

4 bits per channel are transmitted once every 16 frames, resulting in a 500 word per second (2000 bps) signaling rate for each channel

(b)

FIGURE 16-8 CCITT TDM frame alignment and common signaling channel alignment: (a) CCITT TDM frame (125 μs, 256 bits, 2.048 Mbps); (b) common signaling channel

same LSI package. The input/output filter performs the following functions: bandlimiting, noise rejection, antialiasing, and reconstruction of analog audio waveforms after decoding. The codec performs the following functions: analog sampling, encoding/decoding (analog-to-digital and digital-to-analog conversions), and digital companding.

COMBO CHIPS

A combo chip can provide the analog-to-digital and the digital-to-analog conversions and the transmit and receive filtering necessary to interface a full-duplex (four-wire) voice telephone circuit to the PCM highway of a TDM carrier system. Essentially, a combo chip replaces the older codec and filter chip combination.

Table 16-2 lists several of the combo chips available and their prominent features.

General Operation

The following major functions are provided by a combo chip:

1. Bandpass filtering of the analog signals prior to encoding and after decoding
2. Encoding and decoding of voice and call progress signals
3. Encoding and decoding of signaling and supervision information
4. Digital companding

TABLE 16-2 Features of Several Codec/Filter Combo Chips

2916 (16-Pin)	2917 (16-Pin)	2913 (20-Pin)	2914 (24-Pin)
μ-law companding only	A-law companding only	μ/A-law companding	μ/A-law companding
Master clock, 2.048 MHz only	Master clock, 2.048 MHz only	Master clock, 1.536 MHz, 1.544 MHz, or 2.048 MHz	Master clock, 1.536 MHz, 1.544 MHz, or 2.048 MHz
Fixed data rate	Fixed data rate	Fixed data rate	Fixed data rate
Variable data rate, 64 kbps–2.048 Mbps	Variable data rate, 64 kbps–4.096 Mbps	Variable data rate, 64 kbps–4.096 Mbps	Variable data rate, 64 kbps–4.096 Mbps
78-dB dynamic	78-dB dynamic range	78-dB dynamic range	78-dB dynamic range
ATT D3/4 compatible	ATT D3/4 compatible	ATT D3/4 compatible	ATT D3/4 compatible
Single-ended input	Single-ended input	Differential input	Differential input
Single-ended output	Single-ended output	Differential output	Differential output
Gain adjust transmit only	Gain adjust transmit only	Gain adjust transmit and receive	Gain adjust transmit and receive
Synchronous clocks	Synchronous clocks	Synchronous clocks	Synchronous clocks
			Asynchronous clocks
			Analog loopback
			Signaling

Figure 16-9a shows the block diagram of a typical combo chip. Figure 16-9b shows the frequency response curve for the transmit bandpass filter and Figure 16-9c shows the frequency response for the receive low-pass filter.

Fixed-Data-Rate Mode

In the *fixed-data-rate mode,* the master *transmit* and *receive clocks* on a combo chip (CLKX and CLKR) perform the following functions:

1. Provide the master clock for the on-board switched capacitor filter
2. Provide the clock for the analog-to-digital and digital-to-analog converters
3. Determine the input and output data rates between the codec and the PCM highway

Therefore, in the fixed-data-rate mode, the transmit and receive data rates must be either 1.536 Mbps, 1.544 Mbps, or 2.048 Mbps—the same as the master clock rate.

Transmit and receive frame synchronizing pulses (FSX and FSR) are 8-kHz inputs that set the transmit and receive sampling rates and distinguish between *signaling* and *nonsignaling* frames. $\overline{TSX}$ is a *time-slot strobe buffer enable* output that is used to gate the PCM word onto the PCM highway when an external buffer is used to drive the line. TSX is also used as an external gating pulse for a time-division multiplexer (see Figure 16-10).

Data are transmitted to the PCM highway from DX on the first eight positive transitions of CLKX following the rising edge of FSX. On the receive channel, data are received from the PCM highway from DR on the first eight falling edges of CLKR after the occurrence of FSR. Therefore, the occurrence of FSX and FSR must be synchronized between codecs in a multiple-channel system to ensure that only one codec is transmitting to or receiving from the PCM highway at any given time.

Figure 16-10 shows the block diagram and timing sequence for a single-channel PCM system using a combo chip in the fixed-data-rate mode and operating with a master clock frequency of 1.536 MHz. In the fixed-data-rate mode, data are input and output for a single channel in short bursts. (This mode of operation is sometimes called the *burst*

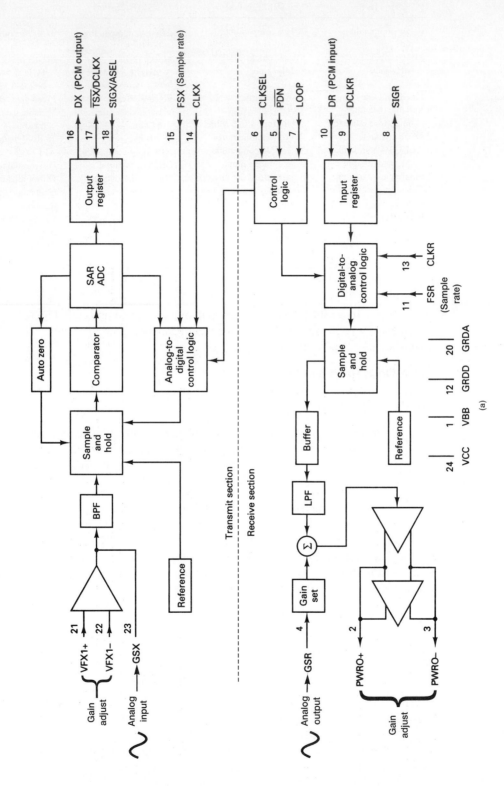

FIGURE 16-9 Combo chip: (a) block diagram; (*Continued*)

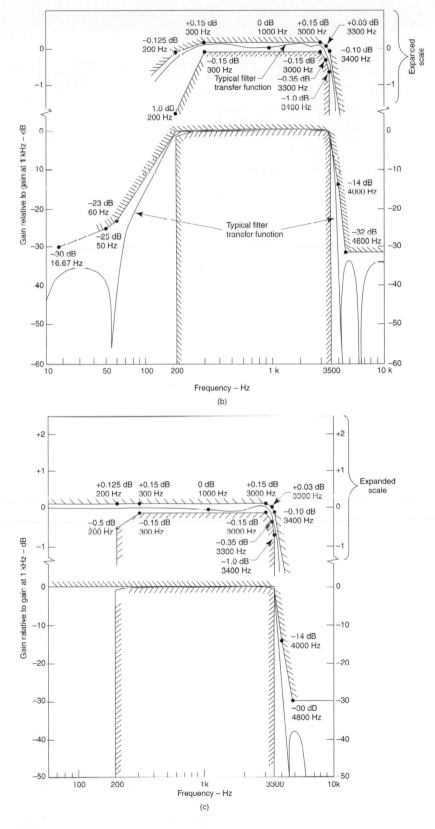

FIGURE 16-9 (Continued) (b) transmit BPF response curve; (c) receive LPF response curve

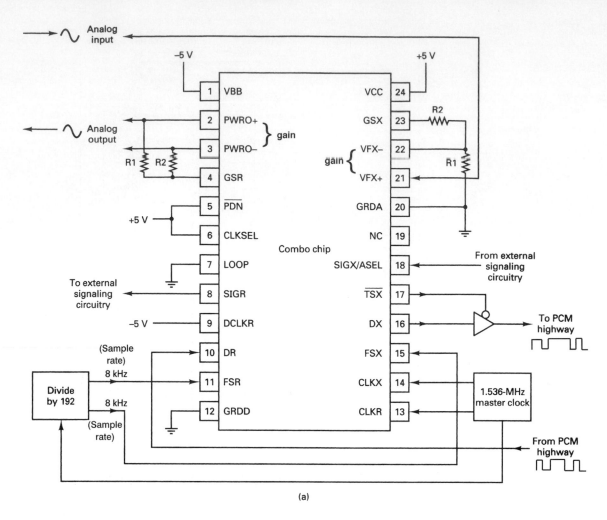

FIGURE 16-10 Single-channel PCM system using a combo chip in the fixed-data-rate mode:
(a) block diagram (*Continued*)

mode.) With only a single channel, the PCM highway is active only 1/24 of the total frame time. Additional channels can be added to the system provided that their transmissions are synchronized so that they do not occur at the same time as transmissions from any other channel.

From Figure 16-10 the following observations can be made:

1. The input and output bit rates from the codec are equal to the master clock frequency, 1.536 Mbps.
2. The codec inputs and outputs 64,000 PCM bits per second.
3. The data output (DX) and data input (DR) are enabled only 1/24 of the total frame time (125 μs).

To add channels to the system shown in Figure 16-10, the occurrence of the FSX, FSR, and $\overline{\text{TSX}}$ signals for each additional channel must be synchronized so that they follow a timely sequence and do not allow more than one codec to transmit or receive at the same time. Figure 16-11 shows the block diagram and timing sequence for a 24-channel PCM-TDM system operating with a master clock frequency of 1.536 MHz.

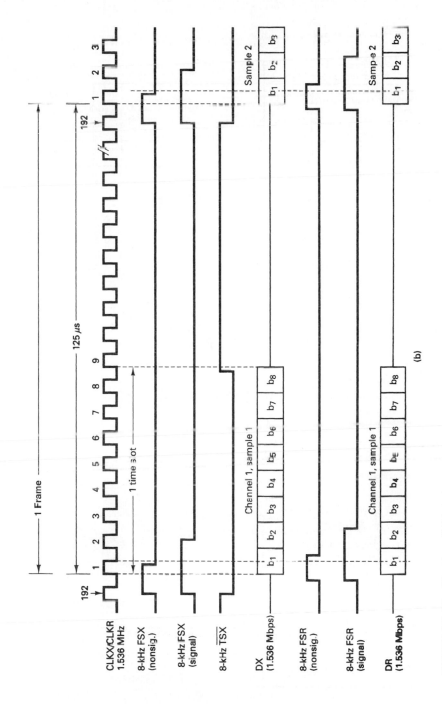

FIGURE 16-10 (Continued) (b) timing sequence

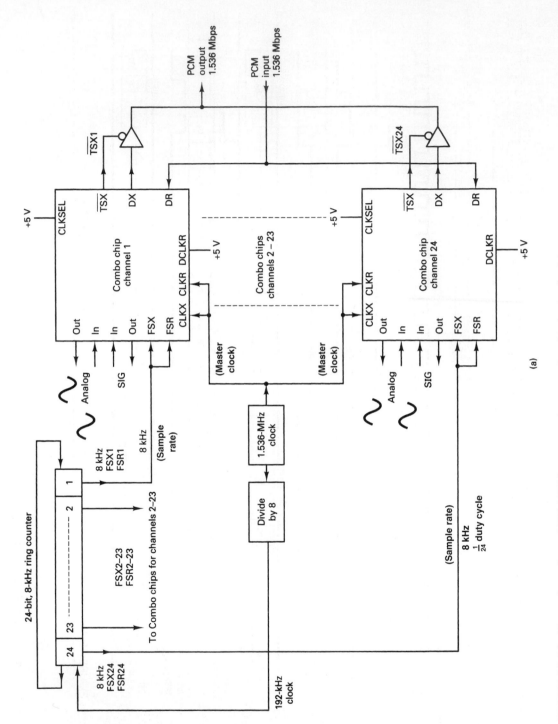

FIGURE 16-11 Twenty-four channel PCM-TDM system using a combo chip in the fixed-data-rate mode and operating with a master clock frequency of 1.536 MHz: (a) block diagram [*Continued*]

(a)

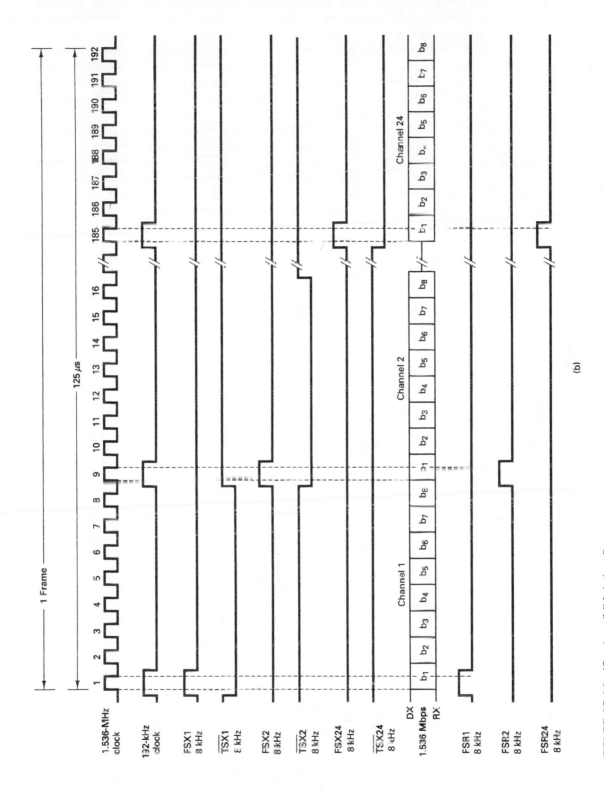

FIGURE 16-11 (Continued) (b) timing diagram

(b)

725

Variable-Data-Rate Mode

The *variable-data-rate mode* allows for a flexible data input and output clock frequency. It provides the ability to vary the frequency of the transmit and receive bit clocks. In the variable-data-rate mode, a master clock frequency of 1.536 MHz, 1.544 MHz, or 2.048 MHz is still required for proper operation of the onboard bandpass filters and the analog-to-digital and digital-to-analog converters. However, in the variable-data-rate mode, DCLKR and DCLKX become the data clocks for the receive and transmit PCM highways, respectively. When FSX is high, data are transmitted onto the PCM highway on the next eight consecutive positive transitions of DCLKX. Similarly, while FSR is high, data from the PCM highway are clocked into the codec on the next eight consecutive negative transitions of DCLKR. This mode of operation is sometimes called the *shift register mode.*

On the transmit channel, the last transmitted PCM word is repeated in all remaining time slots in the 125-μs frame as long as DCLKX is pulsed and FSX is held active high. This feature allows the PCM word to be transmitted to the PCM highway more than once per frame. Signaling is not allowed in the variable-data-rate mode because this mode provides no means to specify a signaling frame.

Figure 16-12 shows the block diagram and timing sequence for a two-channel PCM-TDM system using a combo chip in the variable-data-rate mode with a master clock frequency of 1.536 MHz, a sample rate of 8 kHz, and a transmit and receive data rate of 128 kbps.

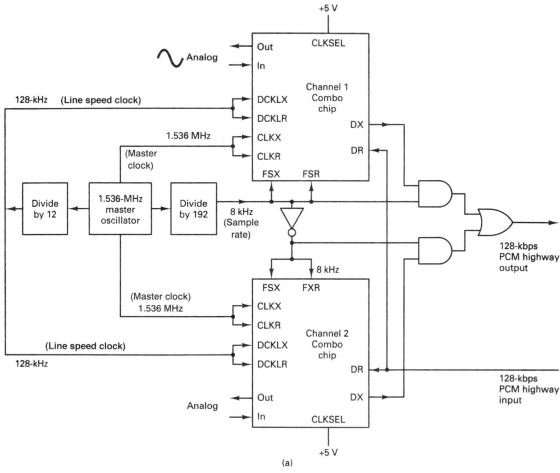

(a)

FIGURE 16-12 Two-channel PCM-TDM system using a combo chip in the variable-data-rate mode with a master clock frequency of 1.536 MHz: (a) block diagram (*Continued*)

With a sample rate of 8 kHz, the frame time is 125 μs. Therefore, one 8-bit PCM word from each channel is transmitted and/or received during each 125-μs frame. For 16 bits to occur in 125 μs, a 128-kHz transmit and receive data clock is required.

$$t_b = \frac{1 \text{ channel}}{8 \text{ bits}} \times \frac{1 \text{ frame}}{2 \text{ channels}} \times \frac{125 \mu s}{\text{frame}} = \frac{125 \text{ } \mu s}{16 \text{ bits}} = \frac{7.8125 \text{ } \mu s}{\text{bit}}$$

$$\text{bit rate} = \frac{1}{t_b} = \frac{1}{7.8125 \text{ } \mu s} = 128 \text{ kbps}$$

or

$$\frac{8 \text{ bits}}{\text{channel}} \times \frac{2 \text{ channels}}{\text{frame}} \times \frac{8000 \text{ frames}}{\text{second}} = 128 \text{ kbps}$$

The transmit and receive enable signals (FSX and FSR) for each codec are active for one-half of the total frame time. Consequently, 8-kHz, 50% duty cycle transmit and receive data enable signals (FSX and FXR) are fed directly to one codec and fed to the other codec 180° out of phase (inverted), thereby, enabling only one codec at a time.

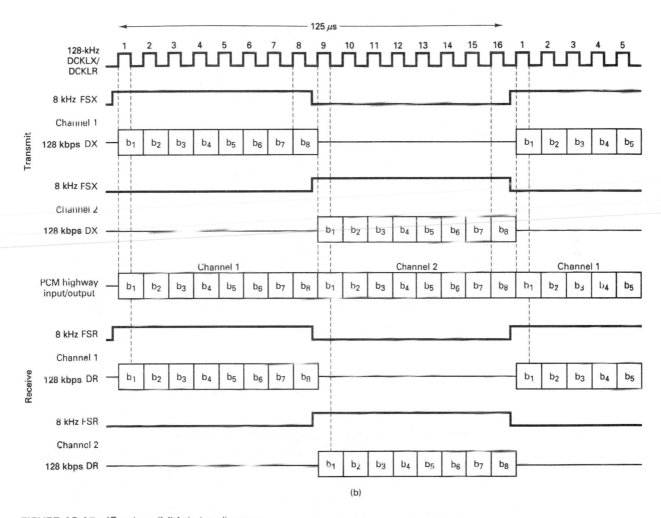

(b)

FIGURE 16-12 (Continued) (b) timing diagram

To expand to a four-channel system, simply increase the transmit and receive data clock rates to 256 kHz and change the enable signals to 8-kHz, 25% duty cycle pulses.

Supervisory Signaling

With a combo chip, *supervisory signaling* can be used only in the fixed-data-rate mode. A transmit signaling frame is identified by making the FSX and FSR pulses twice their normal width. During a transmit signaling frame, the signal present on input SIGX is substituted into the least significant bit position (b_1) of the encoded PCM word. At the receive end, the signaling bit is extracted from the PCM word prior to decoding and placed on output SIGR until updated by reception of another signaling frame.

Asynchronous operation occurs when the master transmit and receive clocks are derived from separate independent sources. A combo chip can be operated in either the synchronous or asynchronous mode using separate digital-to-analog converters and voltage references in the transmit and receive channels, which allows them to be operated completely independent of each other. With either synchronous or asynchronous operation, the master clock, data clock, and time-slot strobe must be synchronized at the beginning of each frame. In the variable-data-rate mode, CLKX and DCLKX must be synchronized once per frame, but may be different frequencies.

NORTH AMERICAN DIGITAL HIERARCHY

Multiplexing signals in digital form lends itself easily to interconnecting digital transmission facilities with different transmission bit rates. Figure 16-13 shows the American Telephone and Telegraph Company's (AT&T) North American Digital Hierarchy for multiplexing digital signals with the same bit rates into a single pulse stream suitable for transmission on the next higher level of the hierarchy. To upgrade from one level in the hierarchy to the next higher level, special devices called *muldems* (*mul*tiplexers/*dem*ultiplexers) are used. Muldems can handle bit-rate conversions in both directions. The muldem designations (M12, M23, and so on) identify the input and output digital signals associated with that muldem. For instance, an M12 muldem interfaces DS-1 and DS-2 *digital signals*. An M23 muldem interfaces DS-2 and DS-3 signals. DS-1 signals may be further multiplexed or line encoded and placed on specially conditioned lines called T1 lines. DS-2, DS-3, DS-4 and DS-5 signals may be placed on T2, T3, T4M, and T5 lines, respectively.

Digital signals are routed at central locations called *digital cross-connects*. A digital cross-connect (DSX) provides a convenient place to make patchable interconnects and to perform routine maintenance and troubleshooting. Each type of digital signal (DS-1, DS-2, and so on) has its own digital switch (DSX-1, DSX-2, and so on). The output from a digital switch may be upgraded to the next higher level or line encoded and placed on its respective T lines (T1, T2, and so on).

Table 16-3 lists the digital signals, their bit rates, channel capacities, and services offered for the line types included in the North American Digital Hierarchy.

When the bandwidth of the signals to be transmitted is such that after digital conversion it occupies the entire capacity of a digital transmission line, a single-channel terminal is provided. Examples of such single-channel terminals are mastergroup, commercial television, and picturephone terminals.

Mastergroup and Commercial Television Terminals

Figure 16-14 shows the block diagram of a mastergroup and commercial television terminal. The mastergroup terminal receives voice-band channels that have already been frequency-division multiplexed (a topic covered later in this chapter) without requiring that each voice-band channel be demultiplexed to voice frequencies. The signal processor provides frequency shifting for the mastergroup signals (shifts it from a 564-kHz to 3084-kHz

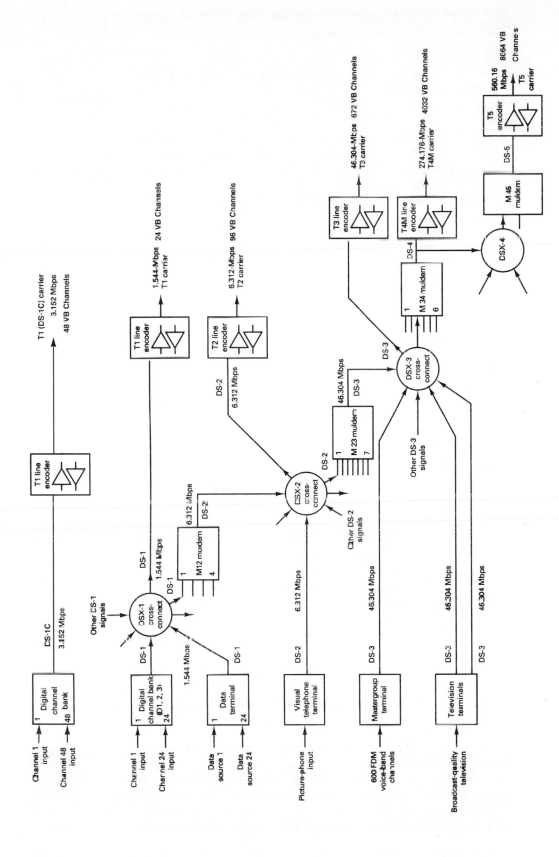

FIGURE 16-13 North American Digital Hierarchy

TABLE 16-3 Summary of the North American Digital Hierarchy

Line Type	Digital Signal	Bit Rate (Mbps)	Channel Capacities	Services Offered
T1	DS-1	1.544	24	Voice-band telephone
T1C	DS-1C	3.152	48	Voice-band telephone
T2	DS-2	6.312	96	Voice-band telephone and picturephone
T3	DS-3	46.304	672	Voice-band telephone, picturephone, and broadcast-quality television
T4M	DS-4	274.176	4032	Same as T3 except more capacity
T5	DS-5	560.160	8064	Same as T4 except more capacity

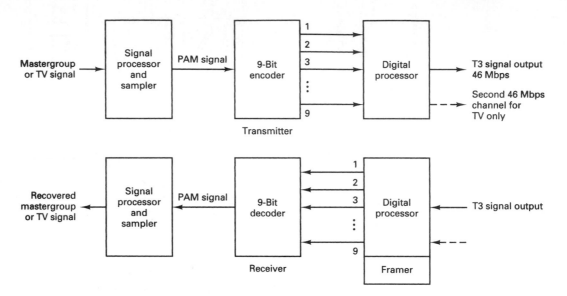

FIGURE 16-14 Block diagram of a mastergroup or commercial television digital terminal

bandwidth to a 0-kHz to 2520-kHz bandwidth) and dc restoration for the television signal. By shifting the mastergroup band, it is possible to sample at a 5.1-MHz rate. Sampling of the commercial television signal is at twice that rate or 10.2 MHz.

To meet the transmission requirements, a nine-bit PCM code is used to digitize each sample of the mastergroup or television signal. The digital output from the terminal is, therefore, approximately 46 Mbps for the mastergroup and twice that much (92 Mbps) for the television signal.

The digital terminal shown in Figure 16-14 has three specific functions: (1) It converts the parallel data from the output of the encoder to serial data; (2) it inserts frame synchronizing bits; and (3) it converts the serial binary signal to a form more suitable for transmission. In addition, for the commercial television terminal, the 92-Mbps digital signal must be split into two 46-Mbps digital signals because there is no 92-Mbps line speed in the digital hierarchy.

Picturephone Terminal

Essentially, *picturephone* is a low-quality video transmission for use between nondedicated subscribers. For economic reasons it is desirable to encode a picturephone signal into the T2 capacity of 6.312 Mbps, which is substantially less than that for commercial network broadcast signals. This substantially reduces the cost and makes the service affordable. At

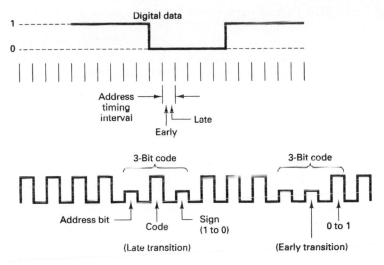

FIGURE 16-15 Data coding format

the same time, it permits the transmission of adequate detail and contrast resolution to satisfy the average picturephone subscriber. Picturephone service is ideally suited to a differential PCM code. Differential PCM is similar to conventional PCM except that the exact magnitude of a sample is not transmitted. Instead, only the difference between that sample and the previous sample is encoded and transmitted. To encode the difference between samples requires substantially fewer bits than encoding the actual sample.

Data Terminal

The portion of communications traffic that involves data (signals other than voice) is increasing exponentially. Also, in most cases the data rates generated by each individual subscriber are substantially less than the data rate capacities of digital lines. Therefore, it seems only logical that terminals be designed that transmit data signals from several sources over the same digital line.

Data signals could be sampled directly; however, this would require excessively high sample rates, resulting in excessively high transmission bit rates, especially for sequences of data with few or no transitions. A more efficient method is one that codes the transition times. Such a method is shown in Figure 16-15. With the coding format shown, a three-bit code is used to identify when transitions occur in the data and whether that transition is from a 1 to a 0, or vice versa. The first bit of the code is called the address bit. When this bit is a logic 1, this indicates that no transition occurred; a logic 0 indicates that a transition did occur. The second bit indicates whether the transition occurred during the first half (0) or during the second half (1) of the sample interval. The third bit indicates the sign or direction of the transition; a 1 for this bit indicates a 0-to-1 transition and a 0 indicates a 1-to-0 transition. Consequently, when there are no transitions in the data, a signal of all 1s is transmitted. Transmission of only the address bit would be sufficient; however, the sign bit provides a degree of error protection and limits error propagation (when one error leads to a second error, and so on). The efficiency of this format is approximately 33%; there are three code bits for each data bit. The advantage of using a coded format rather than the original data is that coded data are more efficiently substituted for voice in analog systems. Without this coding format, transmitting a 250-kbps data signal requires the same bandwidth as would be required to transmit 60 voice channels with analog multiplexing. With this coded format, a 50-kbps data signal displaces three 64-kbps PCM-encoded channels, and a 250-kbps data stream displaces only 12 voice-band channels.

Line encoding involves converting standard logic levels (TTL, CMOS, and the like) to a form more suitable to telephone line transmission. Essentially, six primary factors must be considered when selecting a line-encoding format:

1. Transmission Voltages and DC Component
2. Duty Cycle
3. Bandwidth Considerations
4. Clock Recovery
5. Error Detection
6. East of Detection and Decoding

Transmission Voltages and DC Component

Transmission voltages or levels can be categorized as either *unipolar* (UP) or *bipolar* (BP). Unipolar transmission of binary data involves the transmission of only a single nonzero voltage level (e.g., +V for logic 1 and 0 V or ground for a logic 0). In bipolar transmission, two nonzero voltage levels are involved (e.g., +V for a logic 1 and −V for a logic 0).

Over a digital transmission line, it is more power efficient to encode binary data with voltages that are equal in magnitude but opposite in polarity and symmetrically balanced about 0 V. For example, assuming a 1-Ω resistance and a logic 1 level of + 5 V and a logic 0 level of 0 V, the average power required is 12.5 W (assuming an equal probability of the occurrence of a 1 or a 0). With a logic 1 level of +2.5 V and a logic 0 level of −2.5 V, the average power is only 6.25 W. Thus, by using bipolar symmetrical voltages, the average power is reduced by a factor of 50%.

Duty Cycle

The *duty cycle* of a binary pulse can also be used to categorize the type of transmission. If the binary pulse is maintained for the entire bit time, this is called *nonreturn to zero* (NRZ). If the active time of the binary pulse is less than 100% of the bit time, this is called *return to zero* (RZ).

Unipolar and bipolar transmission voltages and return-to-zero and nonreturn-to-zero encoding can be combined in several ways to achieve a particular line-encoding scheme. Figure 16-16 shows five line-encoding possibilities.

In Figure 16-16a, there is only one nonzero voltage level (+V = logic 1); a zero voltage simply implies a binary 0. Also, each logic 1 maintains the positive voltage for the entire bit time (100% duty cycle). Consequently, Figure 16-16a represents a unipolar nonreturn-to-zero signal (UPNRZ). In Figure 16-16b, there are two nonzero voltages (+V = logic 1 and −V = logic 0) and a 100% duty cycle is used. Figure 16-16b represents a bipolar nonreturn-to-zero signal (BPNRZ). In Figure 16-16c, only one nonzero voltage is used, but each pulse is active for only 50% of the bit time. Consequently, Figure 16-16c represents a unipolar return-to-zero signal (UPRZ). In Figure 16-16d, there are two nonzero voltages (+V = logic 1 and −V = logic 0). Also, each pulse is active only 50% of the total bit time. Consequently, Figure 16-16d represents a bipolar return-to-zero (BPRZ) signal. In Figure 16-16e, there are again two nonzero voltage levels (−V and +V), but here both polarities represent a logic 1 and 0 V represents a logic 0. This method of encoding is called *alternate mark inversion* (AMI). With AMI transmissions, each successive logic 1 is inverted in polarity from the previous logic 1. Because return to zero is used, this encoding technique is called *bipolar-return-to-zero alternate mark inversion* (BPRZ-AMI).

With NRZ encoding, a long string of either 1s or 0s produces a condition in which a receiver may lose its amplitude reference for optimum discrimination between received 1s and 0s. This condition is called *dc wandering*. The problem may also arise when there is a significant imbalance in the number of 1s and 0s transmitted. Figure 16-17 shows how dc

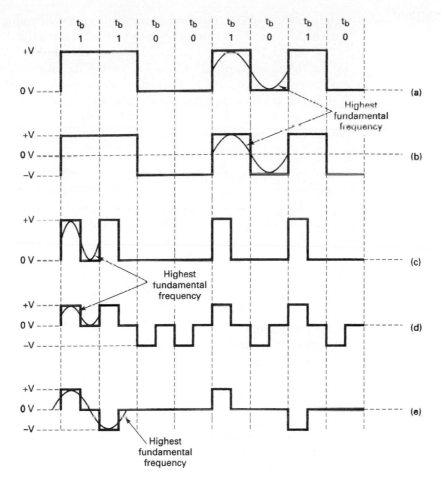

FIGURE 16-16 Line-encoding formats: (a) UPNRZ; (b) BPNRZ; (c) UPRZ;
(d) BPRZ; (e) BPRZ-AMI

FIGURE 16-17 DC wandering

wandering is produced by a long string of successive logic 1s. It can be seen that after a
long string of 1s, 1-to-0 errors are more likely than 0-to-1 errors. Similarly, long strings of
0s increase the probability of a 0-to-1 error.

The method of line encoding used determines the minimum bandwidth required for
transmission, how easily a clock may be extracted from it, how easily it may be decoded,
the average dc level, and whether it offers a convenient means of detecting errors.

Bandwidth Considerations

To determine the minimum bandwidth required to propagate a line-encoded signal, you must
determine the highest fundamental frequency associated with it (see Figure 16-16). The highest fundamental frequency is determined from the worst-case (fastest transition) binary bit

sequence. With UPNRZ, the worst-case condition is an alternating 1/0 sequence; the period of the highest fundamental frequency takes the time of two bits and is, therefore, equal to one-half the bit rate. With BPNRZ, again the worst-case condition is an alternating 1/0 sequence, and the highest fundamental frequency is one-half the bit rate. With UPRZ, the worst-case condition is two successive 1s. The minimum bandwidth is, therefore, equal to the bit rate. With BPRZ, the worst-case condition is either successive 1s or 0s, and the minimum bandwidth is again equal to the bit rate. With BPRZ-AMI, the worst-case condition is two or more consecutive 1s, and the minimum bandwidth is equal to one-half the bit rate.

Clock Recovery

To recover and maintain clocking information from received data, there must be a sufficient number of transitions in the data signal. With UPNRZ and BPNRZ, a long string of consecutive 1s or 0s generates a data signal void of transitions and, therefore, is inadequate for clock synchronization. With UPRZ and BPRZ-AMI, a long string of 0s also generates a data signal void of transitions. With BPRZ, a transition occurs in each bit position regardless of whether the bit is a 1 or a 0. In the clock recovery circuit, the data are simply full-wave rectified to produce a data-independent clock equal to the receive bit rate. Therefore, BPRZ encoding is best suited for clock recovery. If long sequences of 0s are prevented from occurring, BPRZ-AMI encoding is sufficient to ensure clock synchronization.

Error Detection

With UPNRZ, BPNRZ, UPRZ, and BPRZ transmissions, there is no way to determine if the received data have errors. With BPRZ-AMI transmissions, an error in any bit will cause a bipolar violation (the reception of two or more consecutive 1s with the same polarity). Therefore, BPRZ-AMI has a built-in error-detection mechanism.

Ease of Detection and Decoding

Because unipolar transmission involves the transmission of only one polarity voltage, an average dc voltage is associated with the signal equal to $+V/2$. Assuming an equal probability of 1s and 0s occurring, bipolar transmissions have an average dc component of 0 V. A dc component is undesirable because it biases the input to a conventional threshold detector (a biased comparator) and could cause a misinterpretation of the logic condition of the received pulses. Therefore, bipolar transmission is better suited to data detection.

Table 16-4 summarizes the minimum bandwidth, average dc voltage, clock recovery, and error-detection capabilities of the line-encoding formats shown in Figure 16-16. From Table 16-4 it can be seen that BPRZ-AMI encoding has the best overall characteristics; therefore, it is the most commonly used method.

Digital Biphase, Miller, and Dicodes

Digital *biphase* (sometimes called the *Manchester code* or *diphase*) is a popular type of line encoding that produces a strong timing component for clock recovery and does not cause

TABLE 16-4 Line-Encoding Summary

Encoding Format	Minimum BW	Average DC	Clock Recovery	Error Detection
UPNRZ	$f_b/2$*	$+V/2$	Poor	No
BPNRZ	$f_b/2$*	0 V*	Poor	No
UPRZ	f_b	$+V/4$	Good	No
BPRZ	f_b	0 V*	Best*	No
BPRZ-AMI	$f_b/2$*	0 V*	Good	Yes*

*Denotes best performance or quality.

dc wandering. Biphase is a form of BPRZ transmission that uses one cycle of a square wave at 0° phase to represent a logic 1 and one cycle of a square wave at 180° phase to represent a logic 0. Digital biphase encoding is shown in Figure 16-18. Notice that a transition occurs in the center of every signaling element, regardless of its phase. Thus, biphase produces a strong timing component for clock recovery. In addition, assuming an equal probability of 1s and 0s, the average dc voltage is 0 V and there is no dc wandering. A disadvantage of biphase is that it contains no means of error detection.

Biphase encoding schemes have several variations including *biphase M, biphase L,* and *biphase S.* Biphase M is used for encoding SMPTE (Society of Motion Picture and Television Engineers) time-code data for recording on videotapes. Biphase M is well suited for this application because it has no dc component and the code is self-synchronizing (self-clocking). Self-synchronization is an import feature because it allows clock recovery from the data stream even when the speed varies with tape speed, such as when searching through a tape in either the fast or slow modes. Biphase L is commonly called the Manchester code. Biphase L is specified in IEEE standard 802.3 for Ethernet local area networks (Chapter 14).

Miller codes are forms of *delay-modulated codes* where a logic 1 condition produces a transition in the middle of the clock pulse and a logic 0 produces no transition at the end of the clock intervals unless followed by another logic 0.

Dicodes are multilevel binary codes that use more than two voltage levels to represent the data. Bipolar RZ and RZ-AMI are two dicode encoding formats already discussed. Dicode NRZ and dicode RZ are two more commonly used dicode formats.

Figure 16-19 shows several variations of biphase, Miller, and dicode encoding and Table 16-5 summarizes their characteristics.

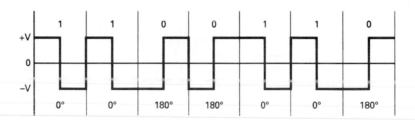

FIGURE 16-18   Digital biphase

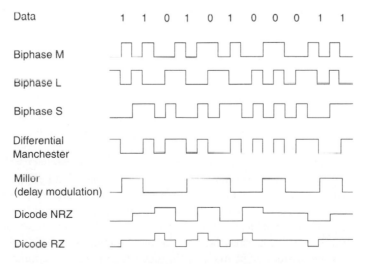

FIGURE 16-19   Biphase, Miller, and dicode encoding formats

TABLE 16-5 Summary of Biphase, Miller, and Dicode Encoding Formats

Biphase M (Biphase-mark)
   1 (Hi)—transition in the middle of the clock interval
   0 (Low)—no transition in the middle of the clock interval
   Note: There is always a transition at the beginning of the clock interval.
Biphase L (Biphase-level/Manchester)
   1 (Hi)—transition from high-to-low in the middle of the clock interval
   0 (Low)—transition from low-to-high in the middle of the clock interval
Biphase S (Biphase-space)
   1 (Hi)—no transition in the middle of the clock interval
   0 (Low)—transition in the middle of the clock interval
   Note: There is always a transition at the beginning of the clock interval.
Differential Manchester
   1 (Hi)—transition in the middle of the clock interval
   0 (Low)—transition at the beginning of the clock interval
Miller/delay modulation
   1 (Hi)—transition in the middle of the clock interval
   0 (Low)—no transition at the end of the clock interval unless followed by a zero
Dicode NRZ
   One-to-zero and zero-to-one data transitions change the signal polarity.
   If the data remain constant, then a zero-voltage level is output.
Dicode RZ
   One-to-zero and zero-to-one data transitions change the signal polarity in half-step voltage increments. If
   the data do not change, then a zero-voltage level is output.

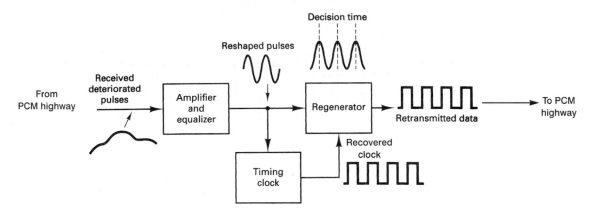

FIGURE 16-20 Regenerative repeater block diagram

T-CARRIERS

T-carriers are used for the transmission of PCM-encoded time-division multiplexed digital signals. In addition, T-carriers utilize special line-encoded signals and metallic cables that have been conditioned to meet the relatively high bandwidths required for high-speed digital transmissions. Digital signals deteriorate as they propagate along a cable due to power loss in the metallic conductors and the low-pass filtering inherent in parallel-wire transmission lines. Consequently, *regenerative repeaters* must be placed at periodic intervals. The distance between repeaters depends on the transmission bit rate and the line-encoding technique used.

Figure 16-20 shows the block diagram of a regenerative repeater. Essentially there are three functional blocks: an amplifier/equalizer, a timing circuit, and the regenerator. The amplifier/equalizer shapes the incoming digital signal and raises its power level so that a pulse/no pulse decision can be made by the regenerator circuit. The timing circuit recovers the clocking information from the received data and provides the proper timing information to the regenerator so that decisions can be made at the optimum time that minimizes the chance of an error occurring. Spacing of the repeaters is designed to maintain an adequate signal-to-noise ratio for error-free performance. The signal-to-noise ratio (S/N) at the output of a regenerator is exactly what it was at the output of the transmit terminal or at the output of the previous regenerator (I.e., the S/N does not deteriorate as a digital signal propagates through a regenerator; in fact, a regenerator reconstructs the original pulses with the original S/N ratio).

T1 and T1C Carrier Systems

The T1 carrier system utilizes PCM and TDM techniques to provide short-haul transmission of 24 voice-band signals. The lengths of T1 carrier systems range from about 5 miles to 50 miles. T1 carriers use BPRZ-AMI encoding with regenerative repeaters placed every 6000 ft; 6000 ft was chosen because telephone company manholes are located at approximately 6000-ft intervals and these same manholes are used for placement of the repeaters, facilitating convenient installation, maintenance, and repair. The transmission medium for T1 carriers is either a 19-gauge or 22-gauge wire pair.

Because T1 carriers use BPRZ-AMI encoding, they are susceptible to losing synchronization on a long string of consecutive 0s. With a folded binary PCM code, the possibility of generating a long string of consecutive 0s is high (whenever a channel is idle it generates a ±0-V code, which is either seven or eight consecutive 0s). If two or more adjacent voice channels are idle, there is a high probability that a long string of consecutive 0s will be transmitted. To reduce this possibility, the PCM code is inverted prior to transmission and inverted again at the receiver prior to decoding. Consequently, the only time a long string of consecutive 0s is transmitted is when two or more adjacent voice-band channels each encode the maximum possible positive sample voltage, which is unlikely to happen.

With T1 and T1C carrier systems, provisions are taken to prevent more than 14 consecutive 0s from occurring. The transmissions from each frame are monitored for the presence of either 15 consecutive 0s or any one PCM sample (eight bits) without at least one nonzero bit. If either of these conditions occurs, a 1 is substituted into the appropriate bit position. The worst-case conditions are as follows:

	MSB		LSB MSB		LSB	
Original	1000	0000	0000	0001		14 consecutive 0s
DS-1 signal						(no substitution)

	MSB		LSB MSB		LSB	
Original	1000	0000	0000	0000		15 consecutive 0s
DS-1 signal						
Substituted	1000	0000	0000	0010		
DS-1 signal				↑		
				substituted bit		

A 1 is substituted into the second least significant bit, which introduces an encoding error equal to twice the amplitude resolution. This bit is selected rather than the least significant bit because, with the superframe format, during every sixth frame the LSB is the signaling bit and to alter it would alter the signaling word.

	MSB		LSB MSB		LSB	MSB	LSB
Original	1010	1000	0000	0000	0000	0001
DS-1 signal						
Substituted	1010	1000	0000	0010	0000	0001
DS-1 signal				↑		
				substituted bit		

The preceding process above is used for older T1 and T1C carrier systems. Also, if at any time 32 consecutive 0s are received, it is assumed that the system is not generating pulses and is, therefore, out of service due to the occurrence of 32 consecutive 0s which is prohibited.

More recent T1 and T1C carrier systems employ a method known as *binary eight zero substitution* (B8ZS) to ensure that sufficient transitions occur in the data to maintain clock synchronization. With B8ZS, whenever eight successive 0s are encountered, one of two special patterns is substituted for the eight 0s, either $+ - 0 - + 0\,0\,0$ or $- + 0 + - 0\,0\,0$. The + and − represent positive and negative logic 1 conditions. A zero simply indicates a logic 0 condition. The eight-bit code substituted for the eight 0s is selected to purposely induce bipolar violations in the fourth and seventh bit positions. Two examples of B8ZS are shown.

	MSB LSB	MSB LSB
Original DS-1 signal	00000000	0+−0+000
	substituted pattern	
Substituted DS-1 signal	+−0−+000	0+−0+000
	bipolar violations	

and

	MSB LSB	MSB LSB
Original DS-1 signal	00000000	0−+0−000
	substituted pattern	
Substituted DS-1 signal	−+0+−000	0−+0−000
	bipolar violations	

T2 Carrier System

The T2 carrier utilizes PCM to time-division multiplex 96 voice-band channels into a single 6.312-Mbps data signal for transmission up to 500 miles over a special LOCAP (low capacitance) cable. A T2 carrier is also used to carry a single picturephone signal. T2 carriers also use BPRZ-AMI encoding; however, because of the higher transmission rate, clock synchronization becomes more critical. A sequence of six consecutive 0s could be sufficient to cause loss of clock synchronization. Therefore, T2 carrier systems use an alternative method of ensuring that ample transitions occur in the data. This method is called *binary six zero substitution* (B6ZS).

With B6ZS, whenever six consecutive 0s occur, one of the following codes is substituted in its place: $0 - + 0 + -$ or $0 + - 0 - +$. Again, the + and − represent positive and negative logic 1s. A zero simply indicates a logic 0 condition. The six-bit code substituted for the six 0s is selected to purposely cause a bipolar violation. If the violation is caught at the receiver and the B6ZS code is detected, the original six 0s can be substituted back into the data signal. The substituted patterns cause a bipolar violation in the second and fifth bits of the substituted pattern. If DS-2 signals are multiplexed to form DS-3 signals, the B6ZS code must be detected and stripped from the DS-2 signal prior to DS-3 multiplexing. An example of B6ZS is as follows:

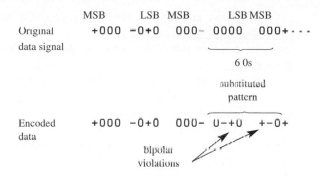

T3 Carrier System

A T3 carrier time-division multiplexes 672 PCM-encoded voice channels for transmission over a single metallic cable. The transmission rate for T3 signals is 46.304 Mbps. The encoding technique used with T3 carriers is *binary three zero substitution* (B3ZS). Substitutions are made for any occurrence of three consecutive 0s. There are four substitution patterns used: $00-$, $-0-$, $00+$, and $+0+$. The pattern chosen should cause a bipolar error in the third substitute bit. An example is as follows:

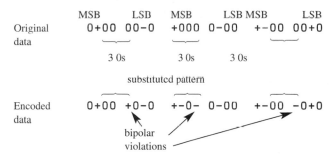

T4M Carrier System

A T4M carrier time-division multiplexes 4032 PCM encoded voice-band channels for transmission over a single coaxial cable up to 500 miles. The transmission rate is sufficiently high that substitute patterns are impractical. Instead, T4M carriers transmit scrambled unipolar NRZ digital signals; the scrambling and descrambling functions are performed in the subscriber's terminal equipment.

T5 Carrier System

A T5 carrier system time-division multiplexes 8064 PCM encoded voice-band channels and transmits them at a 560.16-Mbps rate over a single coaxial cable.

FRAME SYNCHRONIZATION

With TDM systems it is imperative that a frame be identified and that individual time slots (samples) within the frame also be identified. To acquire frame synchronization, a certain amount of overhead must be added to the transmission. Five methods are commonly used to establish frame synchronization: added-digit framing, robbed-digit framing, added-channel framing, statistical framing, and unique-line code framing.

Added-Digit Framing

T1 carriers using D1, D2, or D3 channel banks use *added-digit framing*. A special *framing digit* (framing pulse) is added to each frame. Consequently, for an 8-kHz sample rate

(125-μs frame), 8000 digits are added per second. With T1 carriers, an alternating 1/0 frame synchronizing pattern is used.

To acquire frame synchronization, the receive terminal searches through the incoming data until it finds the alternating 1/0 sequence used for the framing bit pattern. This encompasses testing a bit, counting off 193 bits, and then testing again for the opposite condition. This process continues until an alternating 1/0 sequence is found. Initial frame synchronization depends on the total frame time, the number of bits per frame, and the period of each bit. Searching through all possible bit positions requires N tests, where N is the number of bit positions in the frame. On average, the receiving terminal dwells at a false framing position for two frame periods during a search; therefore, the maximum average synchronization time is

$$\text{synchronization time} = 2NT = 2N^2t$$

where T = frame period of Nt
N = number of bits per frame
t = bit time

For the T1 carrier, $N = 193$, $T = 125$ μs, and $t = 0.648$ μs; therefore, a maximum of 74,498 bits must be tested and the maximum average synchronization time is 48.25 ms.

Robbed-Digit Framing

When a short frame is used, added-digit framing is very inefficient. This occurs in single-channel PCM systems such as those used in television terminals. An alternative solution is to replace the least significant bit of every nth frame with a framing bit. The parameter n is chosen as a compromise between reframe time and signal impairment. For $n = 10$, the SQR is impaired by only 1 dB. *Robbed-digit framing* does not interrupt transmission, but instead periodically replaces information bits with forced data errors to maintain clock synchronization. B6ZS and B3ZS are examples of systems that use robbed-digit techniques.

Added-Channel Framing

Essentially, *added-channel framing* is the same as added-digit framing except that digits are added in groups or words instead of as individual bits. The CCITT multiplexing scheme previously discussed uses added-channel framing. One of the 32 time slots in each frame is dedicated to a unique synchronizing sequence. The average frame synchronization time for added-channel framing is

$$\text{synchronization time (bits)} = \frac{N^2}{2(2^L - 1)}$$

where N = number of bits per frame
L = number of bits in the frame code

For the CCITT 32-channel system, $N = 256$ and $L = 8$. Therefore, the average number of bits needed to acquire frame synchronization is 128.5. At 2.048 Mbps, the synchronization time is approximately 62.7 μs.

Statistical Framing

With *statistical framing,* it is not necessary to either rob or add digits. With the Gray code, the second bit is a 1 in the central half of the code range and 0 at the extremes. Therefore, a signal that has a centrally peaked amplitude distribution generates a high probability of a 1 in the second digit. A mastergroup signal has such a distribution. With a mastergroup encoder, the probability that the second bit will be a 1 is 95%. For any other bit, it is less than 50%. Therefore, the second bit can be used for a framing bit.

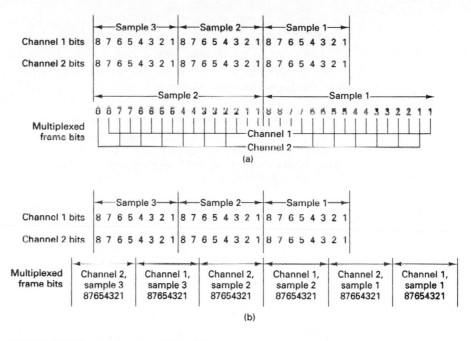

FIGURE 16-21 Interleaving: (a) bit; (b) word

Unique-Line Code Framing

With *unique-line code framing,* the framing bit is different from the information bits. It is either made higher or lower in amplitude or of a different time duration. The earliest PCM-TDM systems used unique-line code framing. D1 channel banks used framing pulses that were twice the amplitude of normal data bits. With unique-line code framing, added-digit or added-word framing can be used or data bits can be used to simultaneously convey information and carry synchronizing signals. The advantage of unique-line code framing is that synchronization is immediate and automatic. The disadvantage is the additional processing requirements required to generate and recognize the unique framing bit.

BIT INTERLEAVING VERSUS WORD INTERLEAVING

When time-division multiplexing two or more PCM systems, it is necessary to interleave the transmissions from the various terminals in the time domain. Figure 16-21 shows two methods of interleaving PCM transmissions: *bit interleaving* and *word interleaving.*

T1 carrier systems use word interleaving; eight-bit samples from each channel are interleaved into a single 24-channel TDM frame. Higher-speed TDM systems and delta modulation systems use bit interleaving. The decision as to which type of interleaving to use is usually determined by the nature of the signals to be multiplexed.

STATISTICAL TIME-DIVISION MULTIPLEXING

Typically, transmissions over a synchronous time-division multiplexing system contain an abundance of time slots within each frame that contain no information (i.e., the channels are idle). For example, TDM is commonly used to link remote data terminals or PCs to a common server or mainframe computer. A majority of the time, however, there are no data being transferred in either direction, even if all the terminals are active. The same is true for

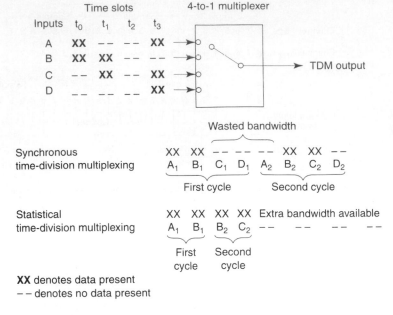

FIGURE 16-22 Comparison between synchronous and statistical TDM

PCM-TDM systems carrying voice-grade telephone conversations. Normal conversation generally involves information being transferred in only one direction at a time with significant pauses embedded in typical speech patterns. Consequently, there is a lot of time within each TDM frame wasted. There is, however, an efficient alternative to synchronous TDM called statistical TDM (sometimes called asynchronous or intelligent TDM).

A statistical TDM multiplexer exploits the natural breaks in transmissions by dynamically allocating time slots on demand. Just as with the multiplexer in a synchronous TDM system, a statistical multiplexer has a finite number of low-speed data input lines and one high-speed multiplexed data output line, and each input line has its own buffer. With the statistical multiplexer, there are n input lines, but only k time slots available within the TDM frame (where $k < n$). The multiplexer scans the input buffers, collecting data until a frame is filled, at which time the frame is transmitted. On the receive end, the same holds true; there are more output lines than time slots within the TDM frame. The demultiplexer removes the data from the time slots and distributes them to their appropriate output buffers.

Statistical TDM takes advantage of the fact that the devices attached to the inputs and outputs are not all transmitting or receiving all the time, and the data rate on the multiplexed line is lower than the combined data rates of the attached devices. In other words, a statistical TDM multiplexer requires a lower data rate than a synchronous multiplexer needs to support the same number of input devices. Alternatively, a statistical TDM multiplexer operating at the same transmission rate as a synchronous TDM multiplexer can support more devices.

Figure 16-22 shows a comparison between statistical and synchronous TDM. Four data sources are shown (A, B, C, and D) and four time slots or epochs (t_0, t_1, t_2, and t_3). The synchronous multiplexer has an output data rate equal to four times the data rate of each of the input channels. During each frame, data are collected from all four sources and transmitted regardless of whether there is any input data. As the figure shows, during time slot t_0 channels C and D had no input data resulting in a transmitted TDM frame void of information in time slots C and D. With a statistical multiplexer, however, the empty time slots are not transmitted. Thus, during the first time slot, only information from channels A and B are transmitted. A disadvantage of the statistical format, however, is that the positional significance of the time slots is lost. There is no way of knowing ahead of time which chan-

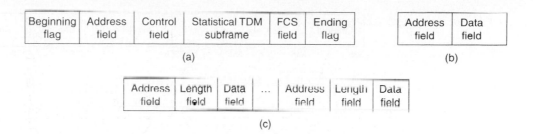

| Beginning flag | Address field | Control field | Statistical TDM subframe | FCS field | Ending flag |

(a)

| Address field | Data field |

(b)

| Address field | Length field | Data field | ... | Address field | Length field | Data field |

(c)

FIGURE 16-23 Statistical TDM frame format: (a) overall statistical TDM frame, (b) one source per frame, (c) multiple sources per frame

nel's data will be in which time slot. Because data arrive and are distributed to receive buffers unpredictably, address information is necessary to ensure proper delivery. This necessitates more overhead per time slot for statistical TDM because each slot must carry an address as well as data.

The frame format used by a statistical multiplexer has a direct impact on system performance. Obviously, it is desirable to minimize overhead to improve data throughput. Normally, a statistical TDM system will use a synchronous protocol such as HDLC. Control bits for multiplexing must be included within the HDLC frame. Figure 16-23a shows the overall frame format for a statistical TDM multiplexer. Figure 16-23b shows the frame when only one data source is transmitting. The transmitting device is identified by an address. The data field length is variable and limited only by the length of the frame. Such a scheme works well in times of light loads but rather inefficiently under heavy loads. Figure 16-23c shows one way to improve the efficiency by allowing more than one data source to be included within a single frame. With multiple sources, however, some means is necessary to specify the length of the data stream from each source. Hence, the statistical frame consists of sequences of data fields labeled with an address and a bit count. There are several techniques that can be used to further improve the efficiency. The address field can be shortened by using a relative addressing scheme where each address specifies the position of the current source relative to the previously transmitted source, modulo the total number of sources. With relative addressing an eight-bit address field can be replaced with a four-bit address field.

Another method of refining the frame is to use a two-bit label with the length field. The binary values 00, 01, 10, and 11 correspond to a data field of 1, 2, or 3 bytes and no length field is necessary. The 11 code means that a length field is included.

FREQUENCY-DIVISION MULTIPLEXING

In *frequency-division multiplexing* (FDM), multiple sources that originally occupied the same frequency spectrum are each converted to a different frequency band and transmitted simultaneously over a single transmission medium. Thus, many relatively narrowband channels can be transmitted over a single wideband transmission system.

FDM is an analog multiplexing scheme; the information entering an FDM system is analog and it remains analog throughout transmission. An example of FDM is the AM commercial broadcast band, which occupies a frequency spectrum from 535 kHz to 1605 kHz. Each station carries an intelligence signal with a bandwidth of 0 kHz to 5 kHz. If the audio from each station were transmitted with the original frequency spectrum, it would be impossible to separate one station from another. Instead, each station amplitude modulates a different carrier frequency and produces a 10-kHz double-sideband signal. Because adjacent stations' carrier frequencies are separated by 10 kHz, the total commercial AM band is divided into 107 10-kHz frequency slots stacked next to each other in the frequency

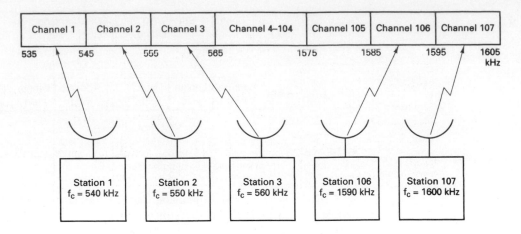

FIGURE 16-24 Frequency-division multiplexing commercial AM broadcast band stations

domain. To receive a particular station, a receiver is simply tuned to the frequency band associated with that station's transmissions. Figure 16-24 shows how commercial AM broadcast station signals are frequency-division multiplexed and transmitted over a single transmission medium (free space).

There are many other applications for FDM, such as commercial FM and television broadcasting and high-volume telecommunications systems. Within any of the commercial broadcast bands, each station's transmissions are independent of all the other stations' transmissions. Consequently, the multiplexing (stacking) process is accomplished without any synchronization between stations. With a high-volume telephone communication system, many voice-band telephone channels may originate from a common source and terminate in a common destination. The source and destination terminal equipment is most likely a high-capacity *electronic switching system* (ESS). Because of the possibility of a large number of narrowband channels originating and terminating at the same location, all multiplexing and demultiplexing operations must be synchronized.

AT&T'S FDM HIERARCHY

Although AT&T is no longer the only long-distance common carrier in the United States, it still provides a vast majority of the long-distance services and, if for no other reason than its overwhelming size, has essentially become the standards organization for the telephone industry in North America.

AT&T's nationwide communications network is subdivided into two classifications: *short haul* (short distance) and *long haul* (long distance). The T1 carrier explained earlier in this chapter is an example of a short-haul communications system.

Long-Haul Communications with FDM
Figure 16-25 shows AT&T's North American FDM hierarchy for long-haul communications. Only a transmit terminal is shown, although a complete set of inverse functions must be performed at the receiving terminal.

Message Channel
The *message channel* is the basic building block of the FDM hierarchy. The basic message channel was originally intended for voice transmission, although it now includes any transmissions that utilize voice-band frequencies (0 kHz to 4 kHz), such as voice-band data circuits. The basic voice-band (VB) circuit is called a 3002 channel and is actually bandlimited

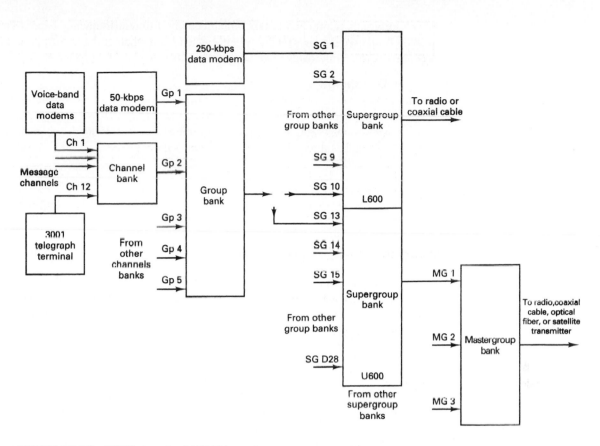

FIGURE 16-25 AT&T's long-haul FDM hierarchy

to a 300-Hz to 3000-Hz band, although for practical considerations it is considered a 4-kHz channel. The basic 3002 channel can be subdivided into 24 narrower 3001 (telegraph) channels that have been frequency-division multiplexed to form a single 3002 channel.

Basic Group

A *group* is the next higher level in the FDM hierarchy above the basic message channel and is, consequently, the first multiplexing step for the message channels. A basic group consists of 12 voice-band channels stacked next to each other in the frequency domain. The 12-channel modulating block is called an *A-type* (analog) channel bank. The 12-channel *group* output of the A-type channel bank is the standard building block for most long-haul *broad-band* communications systems. Additions and deletions in total system capacity are accomplished with a minimum of one group (12 VB channels). The A-type channel bank has progressed generically from the early A1 channel bank to the most recent A6 channel bank.

Basic Supergroup

The next higher level in the FDM hierarchy shown in Figure 16-25 is the combination of five groups into a *supergroup*. The multiplexing of five groups is accomplished in a group bank. A single supergroup can carry information from 60 VB channels or handle high-speed data up to 250 kbps.

Basic Mastergroup

The next higher level in the FDM hierarchy is the basic *mastergroup*. A mastergroup consists of 10 supergroups (10 supergroups of five groups each = 600 VB channels). Supergroups are combined in supergroup banks to form mastergroups. There are two categories of mastergroups (U600 and L600), which occupy different frequency bands. The type of mastergroup used depends on the system capacity and whether the transmission medium is a coaxial cable, a microwave radio, an optical fiber, or a satellite link.

Larger Groupings

Master groups can be further multiplexed in mastergroup banks to form *jumbogroups, multijumbogroups,* and *superjumbogroups.* A basic FDM/FM microwave radio channel carries three mastergroups (1800 VB channels), a jumbogroup has 3600 VB channels, and a superjumbogroup has three jumbogroups (10,800 VB channels).

COMPOSITE BASEBAND SIGNAL

Baseband describes the modulating signal (intelligence) in a communications system. A single message channel is baseband. A group, supergroup, or mastergroup is also baseband. The composite baseband signal is the total intelligence signal prior to modulation of the final carrier. In Figure 16-25 the output of a channel bank is baseband. Also, the output of a group or supergroup bank is baseband. The final output of the FDM multiplexer is the *composite* (total) baseband. The formation of the composite baseband signal can include channel, group, supergroup, and mastergroup banks, depending on the capacity of the system.

Formation of Groups and Supergroups

Figure 16-26a shows how a group is formed with an A-type channel bank. Each voice-band channel is bandlimited with an antialiasing filter prior to modulating the channel carrier. FDM uses single-sideband suppressed-carrier (SSBSC) modulation. The combination of the balanced modulator and the bandpass filter makes up the SSBSC modulator. A balanced modulator is a double-sideband suppressed-carrier modulator, and the bandpass filter is tuned to the difference between the carrier and the input voice-band frequencies (LSB). The ideal input frequency range for a single voice-band channel is 0 kHz to 4 kHz. The carrier frequencies for the channel banks are determined from the following expression:

$$f_c = 112 - 4n \quad \text{kHz}$$

where n is the channel number. Table 16-6 lists the carrier frequencies for channels 1 through 12. Therefore, for channel 1, a 0-kHz to 4-kHz band of frequencies modulates a 108-kHz carrier. Mathematically, the output of a channel bandpass filter is

$$f_{out} = (f_c - 4 \text{ kHz}) \text{ to } f_c$$

where f_c = channel carrier frequency ($112 - 4n$ kHz) and each voice-band channel has a 4-kHz bandwidth.

For channel 1, $f_{out} = 108$ kHz $- 4$ kHz $= 104$ kHz to 108 kHz

For channel 2, $f_{out} = 104$ kHz $- 4$ kHz $= 100$ kHz to 104 kHz

For channel 12, $f_{out} = 64$ kHz $- 4$ kHz $= 60$ kHz to 64 kHz

The outputs from the 12 A-type channel modulators are summed in the *linear* combiner to produce the total group spectrum shown in Figure 16-26b (60 kHz to 108 kHz). Note that the total group bandwidth is equal to 48 kHz (12 channels $\times$ 4 kHz).

Figure 16-27a shows how a supergroup is formed with a group bank and combining network. Five groups are combined to form a supergroup. The frequency spectrum for each group is 60 kHz to 108 kHz. Each group is mixed with a different group carrier frequency in a balanced modulator and then bandlimited with a bandpass filter tuned to the difference frequency band (LSB) to produce a SSBSC signal. The group carrier frequencies are derived from the following expression.

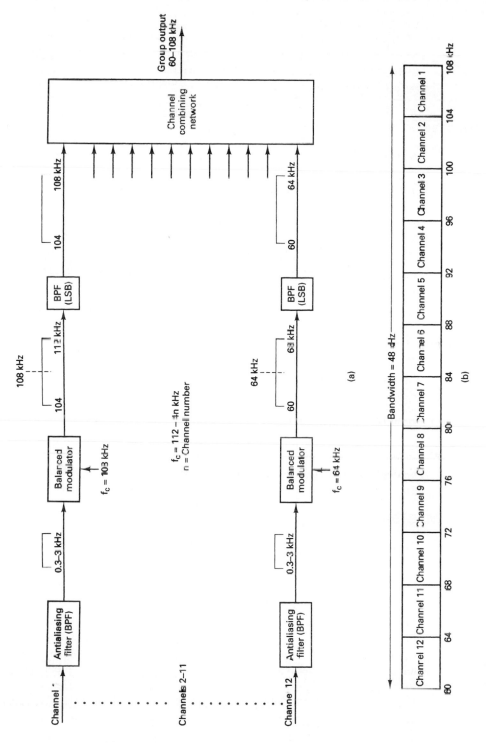

FIGURE 16-26 Formation of a group: (a) A-type channel bank block diagram; (b) output spectrum

TABLE 16-6 Channel Carrier Frequencies	
Channel	Carrier Frequency (kHz)
1	108
2	104
3	100
4	96
5	92
6	88
7	84
8	80
9	76
10	72
11	68
12	64

TABLE 16-7 Group Carrier Frequencies	
Group	Carrier Frequency (kHz)
1	420
2	468
3	516
4	564
5	612

$$f_c = 372 + 48n \text{ kHz}$$

where n is the group number. Table 16-7 lists the carrier frequencies for groups 1 through 5. For group 1, a 60-kHz to 80-kHz group signal modulates a 420-kHz group carrier frequency. Mathematically, the output of a group bandpass filter is

$$f_{out} = (f_c - 108 \text{ kHz}) \text{ to } (f_c - 60 \text{ kHz})$$

where f_c = group carrier frequency ($372 + 48n$ kHz)
 and for a group frequency spectrum of 60 KHz to 108 KHz

Group 1, $f_{out} = 420 \text{ kHz} - (60 \text{ kHz to } 108 \text{ kHz}) = 312 \text{ kHz to } 360 \text{ kHz}$

Group 2, $f_{out} = 468 \text{ kHz} - (60 \text{ kHz to } 108 \text{ kHz}) = 360 \text{ kHz to } 408 \text{ kHz}$

Group 5, $f_{out} = 612 \text{ kHz} - (60 \text{ kHz to } 108 \text{ kHz}) = 504 \text{ kHz to } 552 \text{ kHz}$

The outputs from the five group modulators are summed in the linear combiner to produce the total supergroup spectrum shown in Figure 16-27b (312 kHz to 552 kHz). Note that the total supergroup bandwidth is equal to 240 kHz (60 channels $\times$ 4 kHz).

FORMATION OF A MASTERGROUP

There are two types of mastergroups: L600 and U600 types. The L600 mastergroup is used for low-capacity microwave systems, and the U600 mastergroup may be further multiplexed and used for higher-capacity microwave radio systems.

U600 Mastergroup

Figure 16-28a shows how a U600 mastergroup is formed with a supergroup bank and combining network. Ten supergroups are combined to form a mastergroup. The frequency spectrum for each supergroup is 312 kHz to 552 kHz. Each supergroup is mixed with a different supergroup carrier frequency in a balanced modulator. The output is then bandlimited to the difference frequency band (LSB) to form a SSBSC signal. The 10 supergroup carrier frequencies are listed in Table 16-8. For supergroup 13, a 312-kHz to 552-kHz supergroup band of frequencies modulates a 1116-kHz carrier frequency. Mathematically, the output from a supergroup bandpass filter is

$$f_{out} = f_c - f_s \text{ to } f_c$$

where f_c = supergroup carrier frequency
 f_s = supergroup frequency spectrum (312 kHz to 552 kHz)

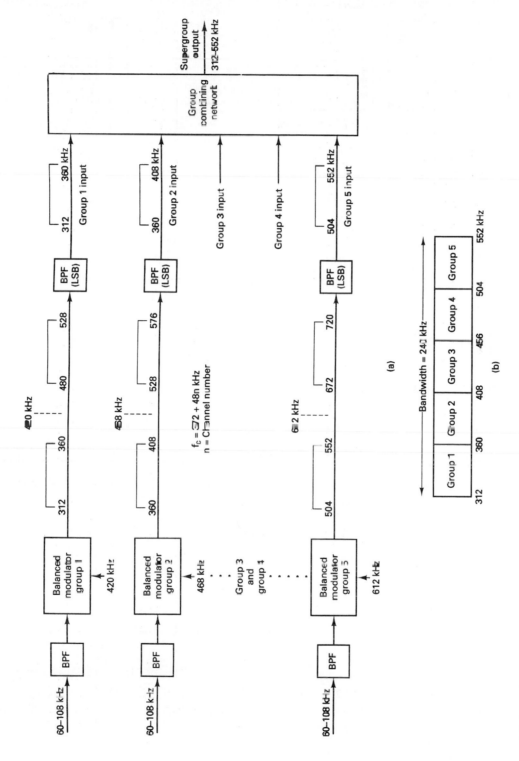

FIGURE 16-27 Formation of a supergroup: (a) group bank and combining network block diagram (b) output spectrum

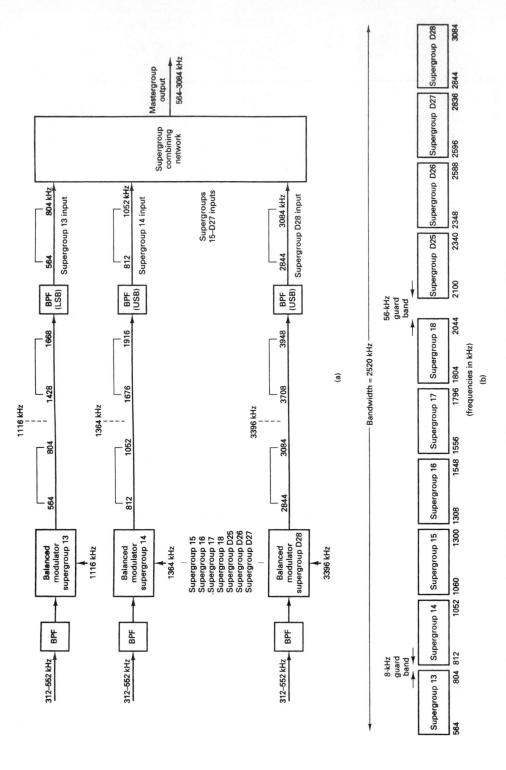

FIGURE 16-28 Formation of a U600 mastergroup: (a) supergroup bank and combining network block diagram; (b) output spectrum

TABLE 16-8 Supergroup
Carrier Frequencies For a
U600 Mastergroup

Supergroup	Carrier Frequency (kHz)
13	1116
14	1364
15	1612
16	1860
17	2108
18	2356
D25	2652
D26	2900
D27	3148
D28	3396

For supergroup 13,

$$f_{out} = 1116 \text{ kHz} - (312 \text{ kHz to } 552 \text{ kHz}) = 564 \text{ kHz to } 804 \text{ kHz}$$

For supergroup 14,

$$f_{out} = 1364 \text{ kHz} - (312 \text{ kHz to } 552 \text{ kHz}) = 812 \text{ kHz to } 1052 \text{ kHz}$$

For supergroup D28,

$$f_{out} = 3396 \text{ kHz} - (312 \text{ kHz to } 552 \text{ kHz}) = 2844 \text{ kHz to } 3084 \text{ kHz}$$

The outputs from the 10 supergroup modulators are summed in the linear summer to produce the total mastergroup spectrum shown in Figure 16-28b (564 kHz to 3084 kHz). Note that between any two adjacent supergroups there is a void band of frequencies that is not included within any supergroup band. These voids are called *guard bands*. The guard bands are necessary because the demultiplexing process is accomplished through filtering and down-converting. Without the guard bands, it would be difficult to separate one supergroup from an adjacent supergroup. The guard bands reduce the *quality factor* (Q) required to perform the necessary filtering. The guard band is 8 kHz between all supergroups except 18 and D25, where it is 56 kHz. Consequently, the bandwidth of a U600 mastergroup is 2520 kHz (564 kHz to 3084 kHz), which is greater than is necessary to stack 600 voice-band channels (600 $\times$ 4 kHz = 2400 kHz).

Guard bands were not necessary between adjacent groups because the group frequencies are sufficiently low and it is relatively easy to build bandpass filters to separate one group from another.

In the channel bank, the antialiasing filter at the channel input passes a 0.3-kHz to 3-kHz band. The separation between adjacent channel carrier frequencies is 4 kHz. Therefore, there is a 1300-Hz guard band between adjacent channels. This is shown in Figure 16-29.

L600 Mastergroup

With an L600 mastergroup, 10 supergroups are combined as with the U600 mastergroup, except that the supergroup carrier frequencies are lower. Table 16-9 lists the supergroup carrier frequencies for an L600 mastergroup. With an L600 mastergroup, the composite baseband spectrum occupies a lower-frequency band than the U-type mastergroup (Figure 16-30). An L600 mastergroup is not further multiplexed. Therefore, the maximum channel capacity for a microwave or coaxial cable system using a single L600 mastergroup is 600 voice-band channels.

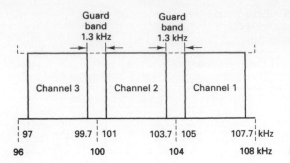

FIGURE 16-29 Channel guard bands

TABLE 16-9 Supergroup Carrier Frequencies for a L600 Mastergroup

Supergroup	Carrier Frequency (kHz)
1	612
2	Direct
3	1116
4	1364
5	1612
6	1860
7	2108
8	2356
9	2724
10	3100

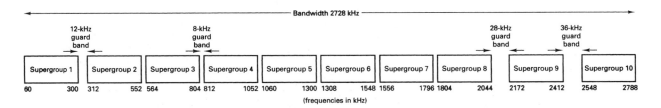

FIGURE 16-30 L600 mastergroup

Formation of a Radio Channel

A *radio channel* comprises either a single L600 mastergroup or up to three U600 mastergroups (1800 voice-band channels). Figure 16-31a shows how an 1800-channel composite FDM baseband signal is formed for transmission over a single microwave radio channel. Mastergroup 1 is transmitted directly as is, while mastergroups 2 and 3 undergo an additional multiplexing step. The three mastergroups are summed in a mastergroup combining network to produce the output spectrum shown in Figure 16-31b. Note the 80-kHz guard band between adjacent mastergroups.

The system shown in Figure 16-31 can be increased from 1800 voice-band channels to 1860 by adding an additional supergroup (supergroup 12) directly to mastergroup 1. The additional 312-kHz to 552-kHz supergroup extends the composite output spectrum to 312 kHz to 8284 kHz.

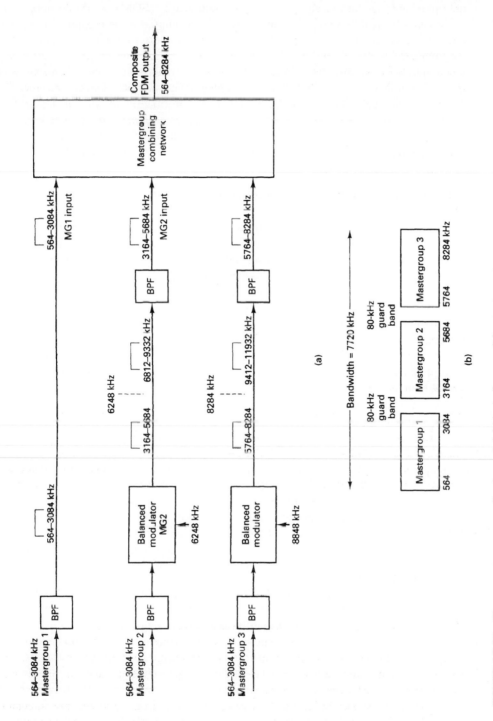

FIGURE 16-31 Three-mastergroup radio channel: (a) block diagram; (b) output spectrum

Wavelength-division multiplexing (WDM) is sometimes referred to as simply *wave-division multiplexing.* Since wavelength and frequency are closely related, wavelength-division multiplexing is similar to frequency-division multiplexing (FDM). WDM resembles FDM in that the idea is to send information signals that occupy the same band of frequencies through the same fiber at the same time without them interfering with each other. This is accomplished by modulating injection laser diodes that are transmitting highly concentrated light waves at different wavelengths (i.e., at different frequencies). Therefore, WDM is coupling light at two or more discrete wavelengths into and out of an optical fiber. Each wavelength is capable of carrying large amounts of information in either analog or digital form and the information can already be time- or frequency-division multiplexed. Although the information used with lasers is almost always time-division multiplexed digital signals, the wavelength separation used with WDM is analogous to analog radio channels operating at different carrier frequencies.

Wavelength-Division Multiplexing versus Frequency-Division Multiplexing

Although frequency- and wavelength-division multiplexing share similar principles, they are not the same. The most obvious difference is that optical frequencies (in THz) are much higher than radio frequencies (in MHz and GHz). Probably the most significant difference, however, is in the way the two signals propagate through their respective transmission media. With FDM, information signals with the same bandwidth from multiple sources modulate different frequencies, with each frequency having its own modulator circuit and each information signal its own modulation rate. FDM signals propagate at the same time, through the same medium, and follow the same transmission path.

The basic principle of WDM, however, is somewhat different. Different wavelengths in a light pulse travel through an optical fiber at different speeds (e.g., blue light propagates slower than red light). In standard optical fiber communications systems, as the light propagates down the cable, wavelength dispersion causes the light waves to spread out and distribute their energy over a longer period of time. Thus, in standard optical fiber systems, wavelength dispersion creates problems which impose limitations on the system's performance. With WDM, however, wavelength dispersion is the essence of how the system operates. With WDM, information signals from multiple sources that occupy the same bandwidth modulate lasers operating at different wavelengths. Hence, the signals enter the fiber at the same time and travel through the same medium. However, they do not take the same path down the fiber. Since each wavelength takes a different transmission path, they each arrive at the receive end at a slightly different time. Thus, data can be encoded sequentially onto the WDM channel using a single data modulator. The result is a series of rainbows made of different colors (wavelengths) each about 20 billionths of a second long, simultaneously propagating down the cable. Figure 16-32 illustrates the basic principles of FDM and WDM signals propagating through their respective transmission media.

D-WDM, Wavelengths, and Wavelength Channels

WDM is generally accomplished at approximate wavelengths of 1550 nm (1.55 μm) with successive frequencies spaced in multiples of 100 GHz (e.g., 100 GHz, 200 GHz, 300 GHz). At 1550-nm and 100-GHz frequency spacing, the wavelength separation is approximately 0.8 nm. For example, three adjacent wavelengths each separated by 100 GHz correspond to wavelengths of 1550.0 nm, 1549.2 nm, and 1548.4 nm. Using a multiplexing technique called *dense-wave-division multiplexing* (D-WDM), the spacing between adjacent frequencies is considerably less. However, there seems to be no standard definition of exactly what D-WDM means, but generally optical systems carrying multiple optical signals spaced more than 200 GHz or 1.6 nm apart in the vicinity of 1550 nm are considered as standard WDM,

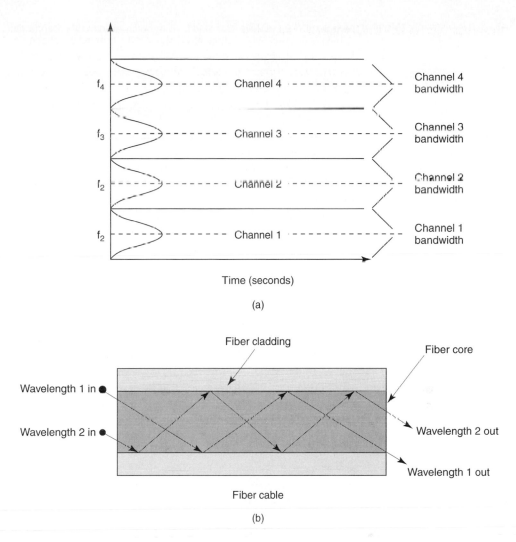

f_4 ---- Channel 4 ---- Channel 4 bandwidth

f_3 ---- Channel 3 ---- Channel 3 bandwidth

f_2 ---- Channel 2 ---- Channel 2 bandwidth

f_2 ---- Channel 1 ---- Channel 1 bandwidth

Time (seconds)

(a)

Fiber cladding

Fiber core

Wavelength 1 in

Wavelength 2 in

Wavelength 2 out

Wavelength 1 out

Fiber cable

(b)

FIGURE 16-32 (a) Frequency-Division Multiplexing and (b) Wavelength-Division Multiplexing

and WDM systems carrying multiple optical signals in the vicinity of 1550 nm with less than 200-GHz separation are considered D-WDM. Obviously, the more wavelengths used in a WDM system, the closer they are to each other and the more dense the wavelength spectrum.

Light waves consist of many frequencies (wavelengths) and each frequency corresponds to a different color. Transmitters and receivers for optical fibers have been developed that transmit and receive only a specific color (i.e., a specific wavelength with a specific frequency and fixed bandwidth). WDM is a process in which different sources of information (channels) are propagated down an optical fiber on different wavelengths where the different wavelengths do not interfere with each other. In essence, each wavelength adds an optical lane to the transmission superhighway; and the more lanes there are, the more traffic (voice, data, video, etc.) that can be carried on a single optical fiber cable. In contrast, conventional optical fiber systems have only one channel per cable which is used to carry information over a relatively narrow bandwidth. A Bell Laboratories research team recently constructed a D-WDM transmitter using a single femtosecond, erbium-doped fiber-ring laser that can simultaneously carry 206 digitally modulated wavelengths of color

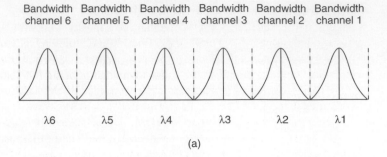

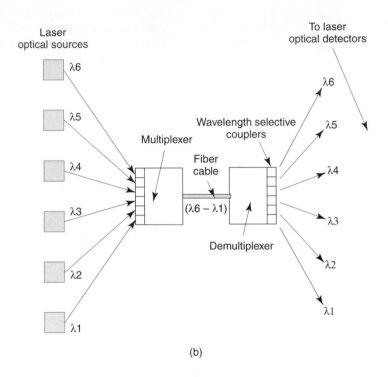

FIGURE 16-33 (a) Wavelength spectrum for a WDM system using six wavelengths and (b) Multiplexing and demultiplexing six lasers.

over a single optical fiber cable. Each wavelength (channel) has a bit rate of 36.7 Mbps with a channel spacing of approximately 36 GHz.

Figure 6-33a shows the wavelength spectrum for a WDM system using six wavelengths, each modulated with equal-bandwidth information signals. Figure 16-33b shows how the output wavelengths from six lasers are combined (multiplexed) then propagated over a single optical cable before being separated (demultiplexed) at the receiver with wavelength selective couplers. Although it has been proven that a single, ultrafast light source can generate hundreds of individual communications channels, standard WDM communications systems are generally limited to between 2 and 16 channels.

Wavelength-division multiplexing enhances optical fiber performance by adding channels to existing cables. Each wavelength added corresponds to adding a different channel with its own information source and transmission bit rate. Thus, WDM can extend the information-carrying capacity of a fiber to hundreds of gigabits per second or higher.

Advantages and Disadvantages of WDM

An obvious advantage of WDM is enhanced capacity; and with WDM, full-duplex transmission is also possible with a single fiber. In addition, optical communications networks use optical components which are simpler, more reliable, and often less costly than their electronic counterparts. WDM has the advantage of being inherently easier to reconfigure (i.e., adding or removing channels). For example, WDM local area networks have been constructed that allow users to access the network by simply tuning to a certain wavelength.

There are also limitations to WDM. Signals cannot be placed so close in the wavelength spectrum that they interfere with each other. Their proximity depends on system design parameters such as whether optical amplification is used and what optical technique is used to combine and separate signals at different wavelengths. The International Telecommunications Union adopted a standard frequency grid for D-WDM with a spacing of 100 GHz or integer multiples of 100 GHz, which at 1550 nm corresponds to a wavelength spacing of approximately 0.8 nm.

With WDM, the overall signal strength should be approximately the same for each wavelength. Signal strength is affected by fiber attenuation characteristics and the degree of amplification, both of which are wavelength dependent. Under normal conditions, the wavelengths chosen for a system are spaced so close to one another that attenuation differs very little among them.

One difference between FDM and WDM is that WDM multiplexing is performed at extremely high optical frequencies, whereas FDM is performed at relatively low radio and baseband frequencies. Therefore, radio signals carrying FDM are not limited to propagating through a contained physical transmission medium such as an optical cable. Radio signals can be propagated through virtually any transmission medium, including free space. Therefore, radio signals can be transmitted simultaneously to many destinations, whereas light waves carrying WDM are limited to a two-point circuit or combination of many two-point circuits that can go only where the cables go.

The information capacity of a single optical fiber can be increased n-fold, where n represents how many different wavelengths the fiber is propagating at the same time. Each wavelength in a WDM system is modulated by information signals from different sources. Therefore, an optical communications system using a single optical cable propagating n separate wavelengths must utilize n modulators and n demodulators.

WDM Circuit Components

The circuit components used with WDM are similar to those used with conventional radio-wave and metallic-wire transmission systems; however, some of the names used for WDM couplers are sometimes confusing.

Wavelength-division multiplexers and demultiplexers. *Multiplexers* or *combiners* mix or combine optical signals with different wavelengths in a way that allows them to all pass through a single optical fiber without interfering with one another. *Demultiplexers* or *splitters* separate signals with different wavelengths in a manner similar to the way filters separate electrical signals of different frequencies. Wavelength demultiplexers have as many outputs as there are wavelengths, with each output (wavelength) going to a different destination. Multiplexers and demultiplexers are at the terminal ends of optical fiber communications systems.

Wavelength-division add/drop multiplexer/demultiplexers. *Add/drop multiplexer/ demultiplexers* are similar to regular multiplexers and demultiplexers except they are located at intermediate points in the system. Add/drop multiplexers and demultiplexers are devices that separate a wavelength from a fiber cable and reroute it on a different fiber going in a different direction. Once a wavelength has been removed, it can be replaced with a new signal at the same wavelength. In essence, add/drop multiplexers and demultiplexers are used to reconfigure optical fiber cables.

Wavelength-division routers. WDM *routers* direct signals of a particular wavelength to a specific destination while not separating all the wavelengths present on the cable. Thus, a router can be used to direct or redirect a particular wavelength (or wavelengths) in a different direction from that followed by the other wavelengths on the fiber.

Wavelength-Division Couplers

WDM *couplers* enable more efficient utilization of the transmission capabilities of optical fibers by permitting different wavelengths to be combined and separated. There are three basic types of WDM couplers: *diffraction grating, prism,* and *dichroic filter.* With diffraction gratings or prisms, specific wavelengths are separated from the other optic signal by reflecting them at different angles. Once a wavelength has been separated, it can be coupled into a different fiber. A dichroic filter is a mirror with a surface that has been coated with a material that permits light of only one wavelength to pass through while reflecting all other wavelengths. Therefore, the dichroic filter can allow two wavelengths to be coupled in different optical fibers.

WDM and the Synchronous Optical Network

The *synchronous optical network* (SONET) is a multiplexing system similar to conventional time-division multiplexing except SONET was developed to be used with optical fibers. The initial SONET standard is OC-1. This level is referred to as *synchronous transport level 1* (STS-1). STS-1 has a 51.84-Mbps synchronous frame structure made of 28 DS-1 signals. Each DS-1 signal is equivalent to a single 24-channel T1 digital carrier system. Thus, one STS-1 system can carry 672 individual voice channels (24 $\times$ 28). With STS-1 it is possible to extract or add individual DS-1 signals without completely disassembling the entire frame.

OC-48 is the second level of SONET multiplexing. It combines 48 OC-1 systems for a total capacity of 32,256 voice channels. OC-48 has a transmission bit rate of 2.48332 Gbps (2.48332 billion bits per second). A single optical fiber can carry an OC-48 system. As many as 16 OC-48 systems can be combined using wave-division multiplexing. The light spectrum is divided into 16 different wavelengths with an OC-48 system attached to each transmitter for a combined capacity of 516,096 voice channels (16 $\times$ 32,256).

QUESTIONS

16-1. Define *multiplexing.*

16-2. Describe time-division multiplexing.

16-3. Describe the Bell System T1 carrier system.

16-4. What is the purpose of the signaling bit?

16-5. What is frame synchronization? How is it achieved in a PCM-TDM system?

16-6. Describe the superframe format. Why is it used?

16-7. What is a codec? A combo chip?

16-8. What is a fixed-data-rate mode?

16-9. What is a variable-data-rate mode?

16-10. What is a DSX? What is it used for?

16-11. Explain *line coding.*

16-12. Briefly explain unipolar and bipolar transmission.

16-13. Briefly explain return-to-zero and nonreturn-to-zero transmission.

16-14. Contrast the bandwidth considerations of return-to-zero and nonreturn-to-zero transmission.

16-15. Contrast the clock recovery capabilities with return-to-zero and nonreturn-to-zero transmission.

16-16. Contrast the error detection and decoding capabilities of return-to-zero and nonreturn-to zero transmission.

16-17. What is a regenerative repeater?

16-18. Explain B6ZS and B3ZS. When or why would you use one rather than the other?

16-19. Briefly explain the following framing techniques: added-digit framing, robbed-digit framing, added-channel framing, statistical framing, and unique-line code framing.

16-20. Contrast bit and word interleaving.

16-21. Describe frequency-division multiplexing.

16-22. Describe a message channel.

16-23. Describe the formation of a group, a supergroup, and a mastergroup.

16-24. Define *baseband* and *composite baseband*.

16-25. What is a guard band? When is a guard band used?

16-26. Describe the basic concepts of wave-division multiplexing.

16-27. What is the difference between WDM and D-WDM?

16-28. List the advantages and disadvantages of WDM.

16-29. Give a brief description of the following components: wavelength-division multiplexer/de-multiplexers, wavelength-division add/drop multiplexers, wavelength-division routers.

16-30. Describe the three types of wavelength-division couplers.

16-31. Briefly describe the SONET standard including OC-1 and OC-48 levels.

PROBLEMS

16-1. A PCM-TDM system multiplexes 24 voice-band channels. Each sample is encoded into 7 bits and a framing bit is added to each frame. The sampling rate is 9000 samples/second. BPRZ-AMI encoding is the line format. Determine the following:
   (a) Line speed in bits per second.
   (b) Minimum Nyquist bandwidth.

16-2. A PCM-TDM system multiplexes 32 voice-band channels each with a bandwidth of 0 kHz to 4 kHz. Each sample is encoded with an 8-bit PCM code. UPNRZ encoding is used. Determine
   (a) Minimum sample rate.
   (b) Line speed in bits per second.
   (c) Minimum Nyquist bandwidth.

16-3. For the following bit sequence, draw the timing diagram for UPRZ, UPNRZ, BPRZ, BPNRZ, and BPRZ-AMI encoding.

   bit stream: 1   1   1   0   0   1   0   1   0   1   1   0   0

16-4. Encode the following BPRZ-AMI data stream with B6ZS and B3ZS.

   + − 0 0 0 0 + − + 0 − 0 0 0 0 0 + − 0 0 +

16-5. Calculate the 12 channel carrier frequencies for the U600 FDM system.

16-6. Calculate the five group carrier frequencies for the U600 FDM system.

16-7. A PCM-TDM system multiplexes 20 voice band channels. Each sample is encoded into 8 bits and a framing bit is added to each frame. The sampling rate is 10,000 samples/second. BPRZ-AMI encoding is the line format. Determine the following:
   (a) The maximum analog input frequency.
   (b) The line speed in bps.
   (c) The minimum Nyquist bandwidth.

16-8. A PCM-TDM system multiplexes 30 voice-band channels each with a bandwidth of 0 kHz to 3 kHz. Each sample is encoded with a 9-bit PCM code. UPNRZ encoding is used. Determine the following:
   (a) The minimum sample rate.
   (b) The line speed in bps.
   (c) The minimum Nyquist bandwidth.

16-9. For the following bit sequence, draw the timing diagram for UPRZ, UPNRZ, BPRZ, BPNRZ, and BPRZ-AMI encoding.

   bit stream: 1   1   0   0   0   1   0   1   0   1

16-10. Encode the following BPRZ-AMI data stream with B6ZS and B3ZS.

$$- \ + \ 0 \ 0 \ 0 \ 0 \ 0 \ 0 \ + \ - \ 0 \ 0 \ 0 \ + \ 0 \ 0 \ -$$

16-11. Calculate the frequency range for a single FDM channel at the output of the channel, group, supergroup, and mastergroup combining networks for the following assignments.

CH	GP	SG	MG
2	2	13	1
6	3	18	2
4	5	D25	2
9	4	D28	3

16-12. Determine the frequency that a single 1-kHz test tone will translate to at the output of the channel, group, supergroup, and mastergroup combining networks for the following assignments.

CH	GP	SG	MG
4	4	13	2
6	4	16	1
1	2	17	3
11	5	D26	3

16-13. Calculate the frequency range at the mastergroup combining network for the following assignments.

GP	SG	MG
3	13	2
5	D25	3
1	15	1
2	17	2

16-14. Calculate the frequency range at the mastergroup combining network for the following assignments.

SG	MG
18	2
13	3
D26	1
14	1

CHAPTER 17

Microwave Radio Communications and System Gain

INTRODUCTION

Microwaves are generally described as electromagnetic waves with frequencies that range from approximately 500 MHz to 300 GHz or more. Therefore, microwave signals, due to their inherently high frequencies, have relatively short wavelengths, hence the name "micro" waves. For example, a 100-GHz microwave signal has a wavelength of 0.3 cm, whereas a 100-MHz commercial broadcast-band FM signal has a wavelength of 3 m. The wavelengths for microwave frequencies fall between 1 cm and 60 cm, slightly longer than infrared energy. Table 17-1 lists some of the microwave radio-frequency bands available in the United States. For full-duplex (two-way) operation as is generally required of microwave communications systems, each frequency band is divided in half with the lower half identified as the *low band* and the upper half as the *high band*. At any given radio station, transmitters are normally operating on either the low or the high band while receivers are operating on the other band.

The vast majority of the communication systems established since the mid-1980s are digital in nature and, thus, carry information in digital form. However, terrestrial (earth based) *microwave radio relay* systems using frequency (FM) or digitally modulated carriers (PSK or QAM) still provide approximately 35% of the total information-carrying circuit mileage in the United States. There are many different types of microwave systems operating over distances that vary from 15 miles to 4000 miles in length. *Intrastate* or *feeder service* microwave systems are generally categorized as *short haul*, because they are used to carry information for relatively short distances, such as between cities within the same state. *Long-haul* microwave systems are those used to carry information for relatively long distances, such as *interstate* and *backbone* route applications. Microwave radio system capacities range from less than 12 voice-band channels to more than 22,000 channels. Early microwave systems carried frequency-division-multiplexed voice-band circuits and used conventional, noncoherent frequency-modulation techniques. More recently developed microwave systems carry pulse-code-modulated time-division-multiplexed voice-band

TABLE 17-1 Microwave Radio-Frequency Assignments

Service	Frequency (MHz)	Band
Military	1710–1850	L
Operational Fixed	1850–1990	L
Studio Transmitter Link	1990–2110	L
Common Carrier	2110–2130	S
Operational Fixed	2130–2150	S
Operational Carrier	2160–2180	S
Operational Fixed	2180–2200	S
Operational Fixed Television	2500–2690	S
Common Carrier and Satellite Down-Link	3700–4200	S
Military	4400–4990	C
Military	5250–5350	C
Common Carrier and Satellite Up-Link	5925–6425	C
Operational Fixed	6575–6875	C
Studio Transmitter Link	6875–7125	C
Common Carrier and Satellite Down-Link	7250–7750	C
Common Carrier and Satellite Up-Link	7900–8400	X
Common Carrier	10700–11700	X
Operational Fixed	12200–12700	X
Cable Television (CATV) Studio Link	12700–12950	Ku
Studio Transmitter Link	12950–13200	Ku
Military	14400–15250	Ka
Common Carrier	17700–19300	Ka
Satellite Up-Link	26000–32000	K
Satellite Down-Link	39000–42000	Q
Satellite Cross-Link	50000–51000	V
Satellite Cross-Link	54000–62000	V

circuits and use more modern digital modulation techniques, such as phase shift keying (PSK) or quadrature amplitude modulation (QAM).

ADVANTAGES OF MICROWAVE RADIO COMMUNICATIONS

Microwave radios propagate signals through Earth's atmosphere between tranmitters and receivers often located on top of towers spaced about 15 miles to 30 miles apart. Therefore, microwave radio systems have the obvious advantage of having the capacity to carry thousands of individual information channels between two points without the need for physical facilities such as coaxial cables or optical fibers. This, of course, avoids the need for acquiring right-of-ways through private property. In addition, radio waves are better suited for spanning large bodies of water, going over high mountains, or going through heavily wooded terrain that impose formidable barriers to cable systems. The advantages of microwave radio include the following:

1. Radio systems do not require a right-of-way acquisition between stations.
2. Each station requires the purchase or lease of only a small area of land.
3. Due to their high operating frequencies, microwave radio systems can carry large quantities of information.
4. High frequencies mean short wavelengths which require relatively small antennas.
5. Radio signals are more easily propagated around physical obstacles such as water and high mountains.
6. Fewer repeaters are necessary for amplification.
7. Distances between switching centers are less.

8. Underground facilities are minimized.
9. Minimum delay times are introduced.
10. Minimal crosstalk exists between voice channels.
11. Increased reliability and less maintenance are important factors.

ANALOG VERSUS DIGITAL MICROWAVE

A vast majority of the existing microwave radio systems are frequency modulation, which of course is analog. Recently, however, systems have been developed that use either phase shift keying or quadrature amplitude modulation, which are forms of digital modulation. This chapter deals primarily with conventional FDM/FM microwave radio systems. Although many of the system concepts are the same, the performance of digital signals are evaluated quite differently. Chapter 19 deals with satellite systems that utilize PCM/PSK. Satellite radio systems are similar to terrestrial microwave radio systems; in fact, the two systems share many of the same frequencies. The primary difference between satellite and terrestrial radio systems is that satellite systems propagate signals outside of Earth's atmosphere and, thus, are capable of carrying signals much farther while utilizing fewer transmitters and receivers.

FREQUENCY VERSUS AMPLITUDE MODULATION

Frequency modulation (FM) is used in microwave radio systems rather than amplitude modulation (AM) because amplitude-modulated signals are more sensitive to amplitude nonlinearities inherent in *wideband microwave amplifiers*. Frequency-modulated signals are relatively insensitive to this type of nonlinear distortion and can be transmitted through amplifiers that have compression or amplitude nonlinearity with little penalty. In addition, FM signals are less sensitive to random noise and can be propagated with lower transmit powers.

Intermodulation noise is a major factor when designing FM radio systems. In AM systems, intermodulation noise is caused by repeater amplitude nonlinearity. In FM systems, intermodulation noise is caused primarily by transmission gain and delay distortion. Consequently, in AM systems, intermodulation noise is a function of signal amplitude, but in FM systems it is a function of signal amplitude and the magnitude of the frequency deviation. Thus, the characteristics of frequency-modulated signals are more suitable than amplitude-modulated signals for microwave transmission.

FREQUENCY-MODULATED MICROWAVE RADIO SYSTEM

Microwave radio systems using frequency modulation (FM) are widely recognized as providing flexible, reliable, and economical point to point communications using Earth's atmosphere for the transmission medium. FM microwave systems used with the appropriate multiplexing equipment are capable of simultaneously carrying from a few narrowband voice circuits up to thousands of voice and data circuits. Microwave radios can also be configured to carry high-speed data, facsimile, broadcast-quality audio, and commercial television signals. Comparative cost studies have proven that FM microwave radio is very often the most economical means for providing communications circuits where there are no existing metallic cables or optical fibers or where severe terrain or weather conditions exist. FM microwave systems are also easily expandable.

A simplified block diagram of an FM microwave radio system is shown in Figure 17-1. The *baseband* is the composite signal that modulates the FM carrier and may comprise one or more of the following:

1. Frequency-division-multiplexed voice-band channels
2. Time-division-multiplexed voice-band channels
3. Broadcast-quality composite video or picturephone
4. Wideband data

FM Microwave Radio Transmitter

In the FM *microwave transmitter* shown in Figure 17-1a, a *preemphasis* network precedes the FM deviator. The preemphasis network provides an artificial boost in amplitude to the higher baseband frequencies. This allows the lower baseband frequencies to frequency modulate the IF carrier and the higher baseband frequencies to phase modulate it. This scheme ensures a more uniform signal-to-noise ratio throughout the entire baseband spectrum. An FM deviator provides the modulation of the IF carrier that eventually becomes the main microwave carrier. Typically, IF carrier frequencies are between 60 MHz and 80 MHz, with 70 MHz the most common. *Low-index* frequency modulation is used in the FM deviator. Typically, modulation indices are kept between 0.5 and 1. This produces a *narrowband* FM signal at the output of the deviator. Consequently, the IF bandwidth resembles conventional AM and, approximately, is equal to twice the highest baseband frequency.

The IF and its associated sidebands are up-converted to the microwave region by the mixer, microwave oscillator, and bandpass filter. Mixing, rather than multiplying, is used to translate the IF frequencies to RF frequencies, because the modulation index is unchanged by the heterodyning process. Multiplying the IF carrier would also multiply the frequency deviation and the modulation index, thus increasing the bandwidth.

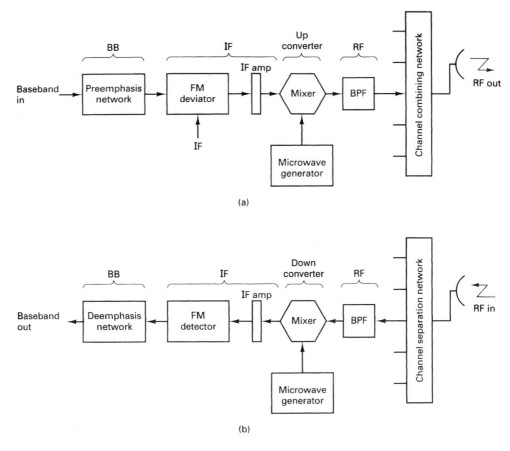

(a)

(b)

FIGURE 17-1 Simplified block diagram of an FM microwave radio system: (a) transmitter; (b) receiver

Microwave generators consist of a crystal oscillator followed by a series of frequency multipliers. For example, a 125-MHz crystal oscillator followed by a series of multipliers with a combined multiplication factor of 48 could be used to a 6-GHz microwave carrier frequency. The channel-combining network provides a means of connecting more than one microwave transmitter to a single transmission line feeding the antenna.

FM Microwave Radio Receiver

In the FM microwave receiver shown in Figure 17-1b, the channel separation network provides the isolation and filtering necessary to separate individual microwave channels and direct them to their respective receivers. The bandpass filter, AM mixer, and microwave oscillator down-convert the RF microwave frequencies to IF frequencies and pass them on to the FM demodulator. The FM demodulator is a conventional, *noncoherent* FM detector (i.e., a discriminator or a PLL demodulator). At the output of the FM detector, a deemphasis network restores the baseband signal to its original amplitude-versus-frequency characteristics.

FM MICROWAVE RADIO REPEATERS

The permissible distance between an FM microwave transmitter and its associated microwave receiver depends on several system variables, such as transmitter output power, receiver noise threshold, terrain, atmospheric conditions, system capacity, reliability objectives, and performance expectations. Typically, this distance is between 15 mi and 40 mi. Long-haul microwave systems span distances considerably longer than this. Consequently, a single-hop microwave system, such as the one shown in Figure 17-1, is inadequate for most practical system applications. With systems that are longer than 40 mi or when geographical obstructions, such as a mountain, block the transmission path, *repeaters* are needed. A microwave repeater is a receiver and a transmitter placed back to back or in tandem with the system. A simplified block diagram of a microwave repeater is shown in Figure 17-2. The repeater station receives a signal, amplifies and reshapes it, then retransmits the signal to the next repeater or terminal station down line from it.

The location of intermediate repeater sites is greatly influenced by the nature of the terrain between and surrounding the sites. Preliminary route planning generally assumes relatively flat areas, and path (hop) lengths will average between 25 miles and 35 miles between stations. In relatively flat terrain, increasing path length will dictate increasing the antenna tower heights. Transmitter output power and antenna gain will similarly enter into the selection process. The exact distance is determined primarily by line-of-site path clearance and received signal strength. For frequencies above 10 GHz, local rainfall patterns could also have a large bearing on path length. In all cases, however, paths should be as level as possible. In addition, the possibility of interference, either internal or external, must be considered.

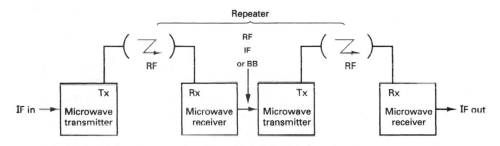

FIGURE 17-2 Microwave repeater

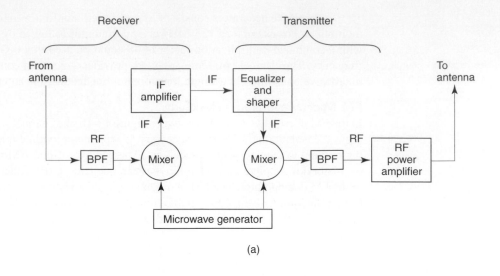

(a)

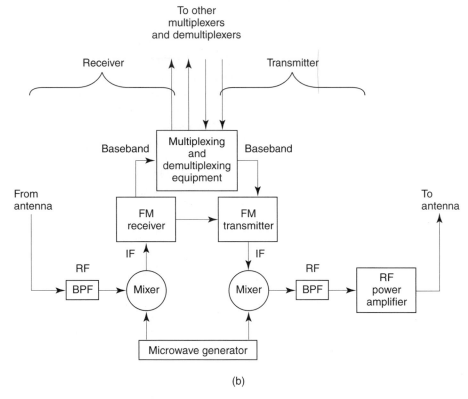

(b)

FIGURE 17-3 Microwave repeaters: (a) IF; (b) baseband; (Continued)

Basically, there are three types of microwave repeaters: IF, baseband, and RF (see Figure 17-3). IF repeaters are also called *heterodyne* repeaters. With an IF repeater (Figure 17-3a), the received RF carrier is down-converted to an IF frequency, amplified, reshaped, up-converted to an RF frequency, and then retransmitted. The signal is never demodulated below IF. Consequently, the baseband intelligence is unmodified by the repeater. With a baseband repeater (Figure 17-3b), the received RF carrier is down-converted to an IF frequency, amplified, filtered, and then further demodulated to baseband. The baseband signal, which is typically frequency-division-multiplexed voice-band channels, is further demodulated to a mastergroup, supergroup, group, or even channel level. This allows the

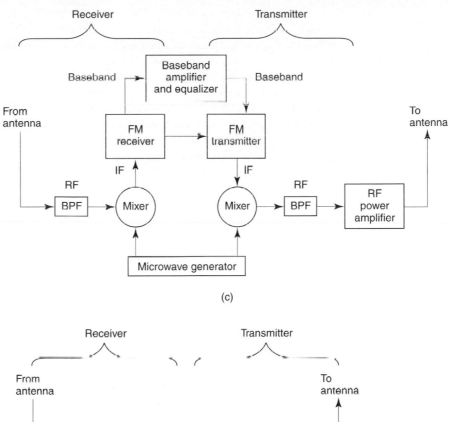

FIGURE 17-3 (Continued) Microwave repeaters: (c) baseband, and (d) RF

baseband signal to be reconfigured to meet the routing needs of the overall communications network. Once the baseband signal has been reconfigured, it FM modulates an IF carrier, which is up-converted to an RF carrier and then retransmitted.

Figure 17-3c shows another baseband repeater configuration. The repeater demodulates the RF to baseband, amplifies and reshapes it, then modulates the FM carrier. With this technique, the baseband is not reconfigured. Essentially, this configuration accomplishes the same thing that an IF repeater accomplishes. The difference is that in a baseband configuration, the amplifier and equalizer act on baseband frequencies rather than IF frequencies. The baseband frequencies are generally less than 9 MHz, whereas the IF frequencies are in the range 60 MHz to 80 MHz. Consequently, the filters and amplifiers necessary for baseband repeaters are simpler to design and less expensive than the ones required for IF repeaters. The disadvantage of a baseband configuration is the addition of the FM terminal equipment.

Figure 17-3d shows an RF-to-RF repeater. With RF-to-RF repeaters, the received microwave signal is not down-converted to IF or baseband; it is simply mixed (heterodyned) with a local oscillator frequency in a nonlinear mixer. The output of the mixer is tuned to either the sum or difference between the incoming RF and the local oscillator frequency, depending on whether frequency up- or down-conversion is desired. The local oscillator is sometimes called a shift oscillator and is considerably lower in frequency than either the received or transmitted radio frequencies. For example, an incoming RF of 6.2 GHz is mixed with a 0.2-GHz local oscillator frequency producing sum and difference frequencies of 6.4 GHz and 6.0 GHz. For frequency up-conversion the output of the mixer would be tuned to 6.4 GHz, and for frequency down-conversion the output of the mixer would be tuned to 6.0 GHz. With RF-to-RF repeaters, the radio signal is simply converted in frequency then re-amplified and transmitted to the next down-line repeater or terminal station. Reconfiguring and reshaping are not possible with RF-to-RF repeaters.

DIVERSITY

Microwave systems use *line-of-site* transmission; therefore a direct signal path must exist between the transmit and the receive antennas. Consequently, if that signal path undergoes a severe degradation, a service interruption will occur. Over time, radio path losses vary with atmospheric conditions which can vary significantly, causing a corresponding reduction in the received signal strength of 20, 30, or 40 or more dB. This reduction in signal strength is temporary and referred to as *radio fade*. Radio fade can last for a few milliseconds (short term) or for several hours or even days (long term). Automatic gain control circuits, built into radio receivers, can compensate for fades of 25 dB to 40 dB, depending on system design; however, fades in excess of 40 dB can cause a total loss of the received signal. When this happens, service continuity is lost.

Diversity suggests that there is more than one transmission path or method of transmission available between a transmitter and a receiver. In a microwave system, the purpose of using diversity is to increase the reliability of the system by increasing its availability. Table 17-2 shows a relatively simple means of translating a given system reliability percentage into terms which are more easily related to experience. For example, a reliability percentage of 99.99% corresponds to about 53 minutes of outage time per year, while a reliability percentage of 99.9999% amounts to only about 32 seconds of outage time per year.

When there is more than one transmission path or method of transmission available, the system can select the path or method that produces the highest-quality received signal. Generally, the highest quality is determined by evaluating the carrier-to-noise (C/N) ratio at the receiver input or by simply measuring the received carrier power. Although there are

TABLE 17-2 Reliability and Outage Time

Reliability (%)	Outage Time (%)	Year (Hours)	Outage Time per Month (Hours)	Day (Hours)
0	100	8760	720	24
50	50	4380	360	12
80	20	1752	144	4.8
90	10	876	72	2.4
95	5	438	36	1.2
98	2	175	14	29 minutes
99	1	88	7	14.4 minutes
99.9	0.1	8.8	43 minutes	1.44 minutes
99.99	0.01	53 minutes	4.3 minutes	8.6 seconds
99.999	0.001	5.3 minutes	26 seconds	0.86 seconds
99.9999	0.0001	32 seconds	2.6 seconds	0.086 seconds

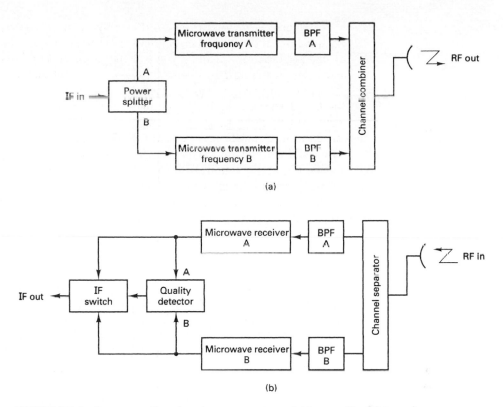

FIGURE 17-4 Frequency-diversity microwave system: (a) transmitter; (b) receiver

many ways of achieving diversity, the most common methods used are frequency, space, polarization, hybrid, or quad.

Frequency Diversity

Frequency diversity is simply modulating two different RF carrier frequencies with the same IF intelligence, then transmitting both RF signals to a given destination. At the destination, both carriers are demodulated, and the one that yields the better-quality IF signal is selected. Figure 17-4 shows a single-channel frequency-diversity microwave system.

In Figure 17-4a, the IF input signal is fed to a power splitter, which directs it to microwave transmitters A and B. The RF outputs from the two transmitters are combined in the channel-combining network and fed to the transmit antenna. At the receive end (Figure 17-4b), the channel separator directs the A and B RF carriers to their respective microwave receivers, where they are down-converted to IF. The quality detector circuit determines which channel, A or B, is the higher quality and directs that channel through the IF switch to be further demodulated to baseband. Many of the temporary, adverse atmospheric conditions that degrade an RF signal are frequency selective; they may degrade one frequency more than another. Therefore, over a given period of time, the IF switch may switch back and forth from receiver A to receiver B, and vice versa, many times.

Frequency-diversity arrangements provide complete and simple equipment redundance and have the additional advantage of providing two complete transmitter-to-receiver electrical paths. Its obvious disadvantage is that it doubles the amount of frequency spectrum and equipment necessary.

Space Diversity

With space diversity, the output of a transmitter is fed to two or more antennas that are physically separated by an appreciable number of wavelengths. Similarly, at the receiving end, there may be more than one antenna providing the input signal to the receiver.

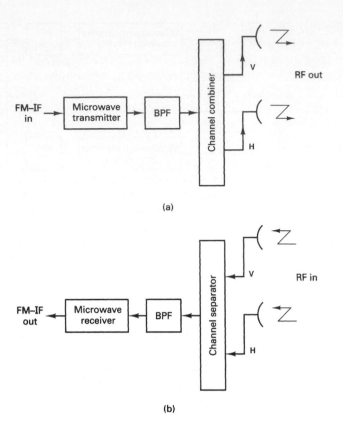

(a)

(b)

FIGURE 17-5 Space-diversity microwave system: (a) transmitter; (b) receiver

If multiple receiving antennas are used, they must also be separated by an appreciable number of wavelengths. Figure 17-5 shows a single-channel space-diversity microwave system.

When space diversity is used, it is important that the electrical distance from a transmitter to each of its antennas and to a receiver from each of its antennas is an equal multiple of wavelengths long. This is to ensure that when two or more signals of the same frequency arrive at the input to a receiver, they are in phase and additive. If received out of phase, they will cancel and, consequently, result in less received signal power than if simply one antenna system were used. Adverse atmospheric conditions are often isolated to a very small geographical area. With space diversity, there is more than one transmission path between a transmitter and a receiver. When adverse atmospheric conditions exist in one of the paths, it is unlikely that the alternate path is experiencing the same degradation. Consequently, the probability of receiving an acceptable signal is higher when space diversity is used than when no diversity is used. An alternate method of space diversity uses a single transmitting antenna and two receiving antennas separated vertically. Depending on the atmospheric conditions at a particular time, one of the receiving antennas should be receiving an adequate signal. Again, there are two transmission paths that are unlikely to be affected simultaneously by fading.

Space-diversity arrangements provide for path redundancy but not equipment redundancy. Space diversity is more expensive than frequency diversity because of the additional antennas and waveguide. Space diversity, however, provides efficient frequency spectrum usage and a substantially greater protection than frequency diversity.

Polarization Diversity

With *polarization diversity,* a single RF carrier is propagated with two different electromagnetic polarizations (vertical and horizontal). Electromagnetic waves of different polarizations do not necessarily experience the same transmission impairments. Polarization diversity is generally used in conjunction with space diversity. One transmit/receive antenna pair is vertically polarized and the other is horizontally polarized. It is also possible to use frequency, space, and polarization diversity simultaneously.

Hybrid Diversity

Hybrid diversity is a somewhat specialized form of diversity, which consists of a standard frequency-diversity path where the two transmitter/receiver pairs at one end of the path are separated from each other and connected to different antennas that are vertically separated as in space diversity. This arrangement provides a space-diversity effect in both directions; in one direction because the receivers are vertically spaced and in the other direction because the transmitters are vertically spaced. This arrangement combines the operational advantages of frequency diversity with the improved diversity protection of space diversity. Hybrid diversity has the disadvantage, however, of requiring two radio frequencies to obtain one working channel.

Quad Diversity

Quad diversity is another form of hybrid diversity and undoubtedly provides the most reliable transmission; however, it is also the most expensive. The basic concept of quad diversity is quite simple: It combines frequency, space, polarization, and receiver diversity into one system. Its obvious disadvantage is providing redundant electronic equipment, frequencies, antennas, and waveguide, which are economical burdens.

PROTECTION SWITCHING ARRANGEMENTS

To avoid a service interruption during periods of deep fades or equipment failures, alternate facilities are temporarily made available in a *protection switching* arrangement. The general concepts of protection switching and diversity are quite similar: They both provide protection against equipment failures and atmospheric fades. The primary difference between them is, simply, diversity systems only provide an alternate transmission path for a single microwave link (i.e., between one transmitter and one receiver) within the overall communications system. Protection switching arrangements, on the other hand, provide protection for a much larger section of the communications system which generally includes several repeaters spanning a distance of 100 mi or more. Diversity systems also generally provide 100% protection to a single radio channel, whereas protection switching arrangements are usually shared between several radio channels.

Essentially, there are two types of protection switching arrangements, *hot standby* and *diversity.* With hot standby protection, each working radio channel has a dedicated backup or spare channel. With diversity protection, a single backup channel is made available to as many as 11 working channels. Hot standby systems offer 100% protection for each working radio channel. A diversity system offers 100% protection only to the first working channel to fail. If two radio channels fail at the same time, a service interruption will occur.

Hot Standby

Figure 17-6a shows a single-channel hot standby protection switching arrangement. At the transmitting end, the IF goes into a *head-end bridge,* which splits the signal power and directs it to the working and the spare (standby) microwave channels simultaneously. Consequently, both the working and standby channels are carrying the same baseband information. At the receiving end, the IF switch passes the IF signal from the working channel to the FM terminal equipment. The IF switch continuously monitors the received signal

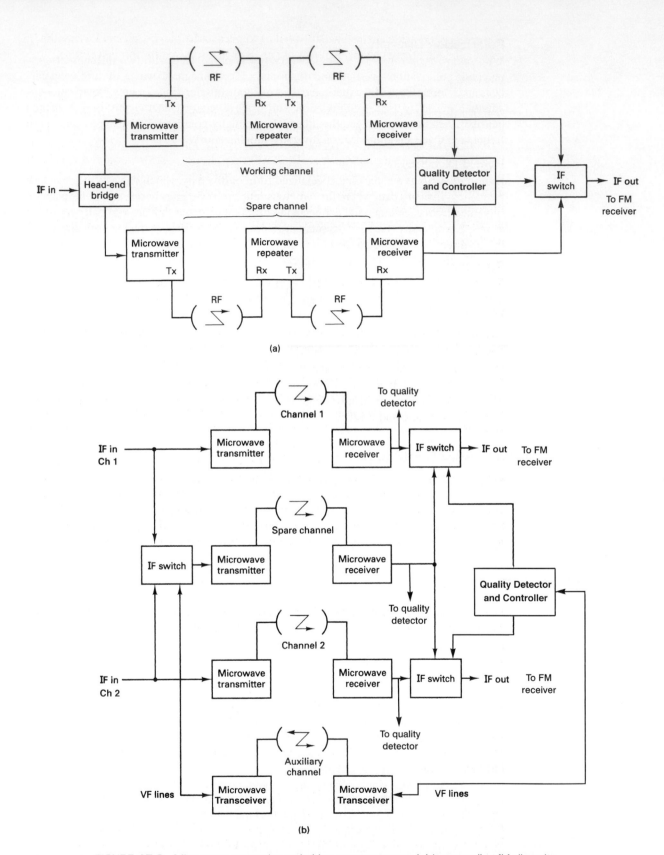

FIGURE 17-6 Microwave protection switching arrangements: (a) hot standby; (b) diversity

power on the working channel and, if it fails, switches to the standby channel. When the IF signal on the working channel is restored, the IF switch resumes its normal position.

Diversity

Figure 17-6b shows a diversity protection switching arrangement. This system has two working channels (channel 1 and channel 2), one spare channel, and an *auxiliary* channel. The IF switch at the receive end continuously monitors the receive signal strength of both working channels. If either one should fail, the IF switch detects a loss of carrier and sends back to the transmitting station IF switch a VF *(voice frequency)* tone-encoded signal that directs it to switch the IF signal from the failed channel onto the spare microwave channel. When the failed channel is restored, the IF switches resume their normal positions. The auxiliary channel simply provides a transmission path between the two IF switches. Typically, the auxiliary channel is a low-capacity low-power microwave radio that is designed to be used for a maintenance channel only.

Reliability

The number of repeater stations between protection switches depends on the *reliability objectives* of the system. Typically, there are between two and six repeaters between switching stations.

As you can see, diversity systems and protection switching arrangements are quite similar. The primary difference between the two is that diversity systems are permanent arrangements and are intended only to compensate for temporary, abnormal atmospheric conditions between only two selected stations in a system. Protection switching arrangements, on the other hand, compensate for both radio fades and equipment failures and may include from six to eight repeater stations between switches. Protection channels also may be used as temporary communication facilities, while routine maintenance is performed on a regular working channel. With a protection switching arrangement, all signal paths and radio equipment are protected. Diversity is used selectively—that is, only between stations that historically experience severe fading a high percentage of the time.

A statistical study of outage time (i.e., service interruptions) caused by radio fades, equipment failures, and maintenance is important in the design of a microwave radio system. From such a study, engineering decisions can be made on which type of diversity system and protection switching arrangement is best suited for a particular application.

FM MICROWAVE RADIO STATIONS

Basically, there are two types of FM microwave stations: terminals and repeaters. *Terminal stations* are points in the system where baseband signals either originate or terminate. *Repeater stations* are points in a system where baseband signals may be reconfigured or where RF carriers are simply "repeated" or amplified.

Terminal Station

Essentially, a terminal station consists of four major sections: the baseband, wire line entrance link (WLEL), FM-IF, and RF sections. Figure 17-7 shows the block diagram of the baseband, WLEL, and FM-IF sections. As mentioned, the baseband may be one of several different types of signals. For our example, frequency-division-multiplexed voice-band channels are used.

Wire line entrance link (WLEL). Often in large communications networks, such as the American Telephone and Telegraph Company (AT&T), the building that houses the radio station is quite large. Consequently, it is desirable that similar equipment be physically placed at a common location (i.e., all FDM equipment in the same room). This simplifies alarm systems, providing dc power to the equipment, maintenance, and

output amplifiers. Typical gains for microwave antennas range from 10 dB to 40 dB, and typical transmitter output powers are between 0.5 W and 10 W.

A *microwave generator* provides the RF carrier input to the up-converter. It is called a microwave generator rather than an oscillator because it is difficult to construct a stable circuit that will oscillate in the gigahertz range. Instead, a crystal-controlled oscillator operating in the range 5 MHz to 25 MHz is used to provide a base frequency that is multiplied up to the desired RF carrier frequency.

An *isolator* is a unidirectional device often made from a ferrite material. The isolator is used in conjunction with a channel-combining network to prevent the output of one transmitter from interfering with the output of another transmitter.

The RF receiver (Figure 17-8b) is essentially the same as the transmitter except that it works in the opposite direction. However, one difference is the presence of an IF amplifier in the receiver. This IF amplifier has an *automatic gain control* (AGC) circuit. Also, very often, there are no RF amplifiers in the receiver. Typically, a highly sensitive, low-noise balanced demodulator is used for the receive demodulator (receive mod). This eliminates the need for an RF amplifier and improves the overall signal-to-noise ratio. When RF amplifiers are required, high-quality, *low-noise amplifiers* (LNAs) are used. Examples of commonly used LNAs are tunnel diodes and parametric amplifiers.

Repeater Station

Figure 17-9 shows the block diagram of a microwave IF repeater station. The received RF signal enters the receiver through the channel separation network and bandpass filter. The receive mod down-converts the RF carrier to IF. The IF AMP/AGC and equalizer circuits amplify and reshape the IF. The equalizer compensates for *gain-versus-frequency nonlinearities* and *envelope delay distortion* introduced in the system. Again, the transmod up-converts the IF to RF for retransmission. However, in a repeater station, the method used to generate the RF microwave carrier frequencies is slightly different from the method used in a terminal station. In the IF repeater, only one microwave generator is required to supply both the transmod and the receive mod with an RF carrier signal. The microwave generator, shift oscillator, and shift modulator allow the repeater to receive one RF carrier frequency, down-convert it to IF, and then up-convert the IF to a different RF carrier frequency. It is possible for station C to receive the transmissions from both station A and station B simultaneously (this is called *multihop interference* and is shown in Figure 17-10a). This can occur only when three stations are placed in a geographical straight line in the system. To prevent this from occurring, the allocated bandwidth for the system is divided in half, creating a low-frequency and a high-frequency band. Each station, in turn, alternates from a low-band to a high-band transmit carrier frequency (Figure 17-10b). If a transmission from station A is received by station C, it will be rejected in the channel separation network and cause no interference. This arrangement is called a high/low microwave repeater system. The rules are simple: If a repeater station receives a low-band RF carrier, then it retransmits a high-band RF carrier, and vice versa. The only time that multiple carriers of the same frequency can be received is when a transmission from one station is received from another station that is three hops away. This is unlikely to happen.

Another reason for using a high/low-frequency scheme is to prevent the power that "leaks" out the back and sides of a transmit antenna from interfering with the signal entering the input of a nearby receive antenna. This is called *ringaround*. All antennas, no matter how high their gain or how directive their radiation pattern, radiate a small percentage of their power out the back and sides; giving a finite *front-to-back* ratio for the antenna. Although the front-to-back ratio of a typical microwave antenna is quite high, the relatively small amount of power that is radiated out the back of the antenna may be quite substantial compared with the normal received carrier power in the system. If the transmit and receive carrier frequencies are different, filters in the receiver separation network will prevent ringaround from occurring.

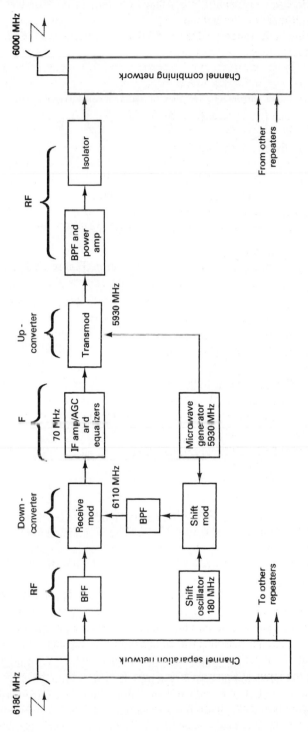

FIGURE 17-9 Microwave IF repeater station

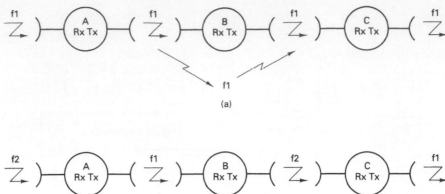

(a)

(b)

FIGURE 17-10   (a) Multihop interference and (b) high/low microwave system

A high/low microwave repeater station (Figure 17-10b) needs two microwave carrier supplies for the down- and up-converting process. Rather than use two microwave generators, a single generator with a shift oscillator, a shift modulator, and a bandpass filter can generate the two required signals. One output from the microwave generator is fed directly into the transmod and another output (from the same microwave generator) is mixed with the shift oscillator signal in the shift modulator to produce a second microwave carrier frequency. The second microwave carrier frequency is offset from the first by the shift oscillator frequency. The second microwave carrier frequency is fed into the receive modulator.

Example 17-1

In Figure 17-9 the received RF carrier frequency is 6180 MHz, and the transmitted RF carrier frequency is 6000 MHz. With a 70-MHz IF frequency, a 5930-MHz microwave generator frequency, and a 180-MHz shift oscillator frequency, the output filter of the shift mod must be tuned to 6110 MHz. This is the sum of the microwave generator and the shift oscillator frequencies (5930 MHz + 180 MHz = 6110 MHz).

This process does not reduce the number of oscillators required, but it is simpler and cheaper to build one microwave generator and one relatively low-frequency shift oscillator than to build two microwave generators. This arrangement also provides a certain degree of synchronization between repeaters. The obvious disadvantage of the high/low scheme is that the number of channels available in a given bandwidth is cut in half.

Figure 17-11 shows a high/low-frequency plan with eight channels (four high band and four low band). Each channel occupies a 29.7-MHz bandwidth. The west terminal transmits the low-band frequencies and receives the high-band frequencies. Channels 1 and 3 (Figure 17-11a) are designated as *V channels*. This means that they are propagated with vertical polarization. Channels 2 and 4 are designated as H or horizontally polarized channels. This is not a polarization diversity system. Channels 1 through 4 are totally independent of each other; they carry different baseband information. The transmission of *orthogonally* polarized carriers (90° out of phase) further enhances the isolation between the transmit and receive signals. In the west-to-east direction, the repeater receives the low-band frequencies and transmits the high-band frequencies. After channel 1 is received and down-converted to IF, it is upconverted to a different RF frequency and a different polarization for retransmission. The low-band channel 1 corresponds to the high-band channel 11, channel 2 to channel 12, and so

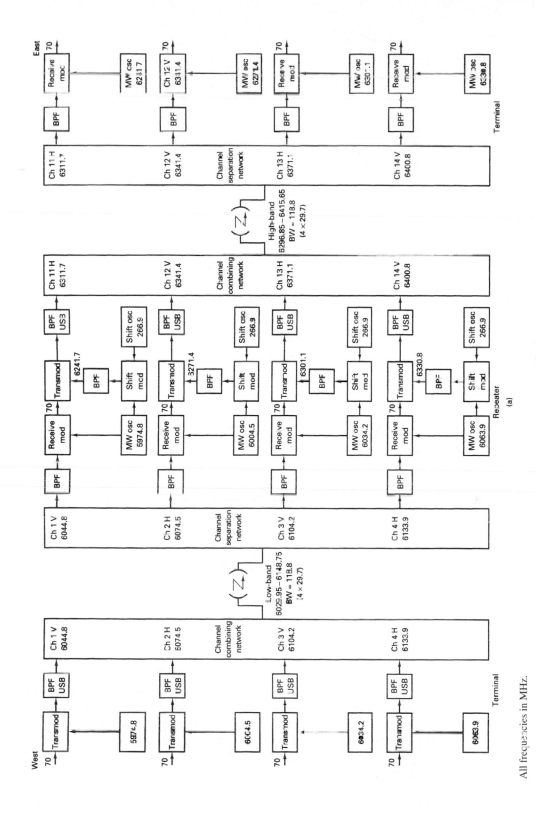

All frequencies in MHz.

FIGURE 17-11 Eight-channel high-/low frequency plan (a) west to east; (Continued)

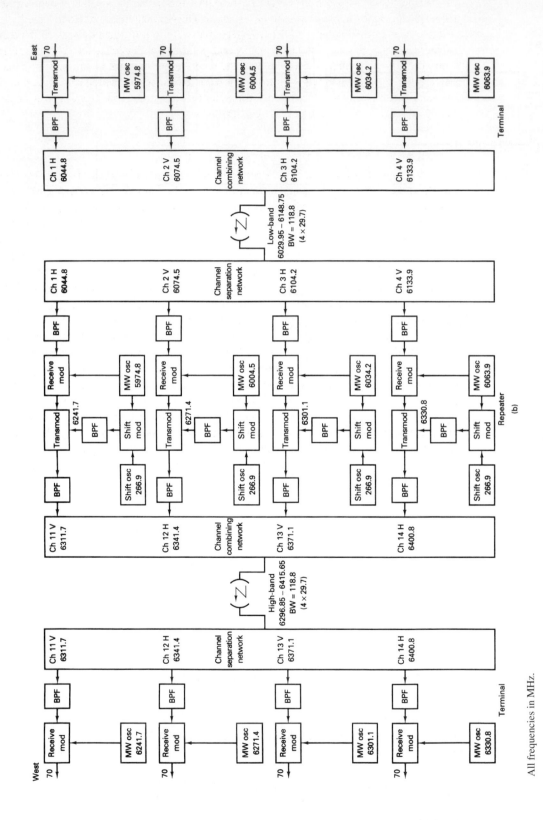

All frequencies in MHz.

FIGURE 17-11 (Continued) (b) east to west.

on. The east-to-west direction (Figure 17-11b) propagates the high- and low-band carriers in the sequence opposite to the west-to-east system. The polarizations are also reversed. If some of the power from channel 1 of the west terminal were to propagate directly to the east terminal receiver, it has a different frequency and polarization than channel 11's transmissions. Consequently, it would not interfere with the reception of channel 11 (no multihop interference). Also, note that none of the transmit or receive channels at the repeater station has both the same frequency and polarization. Consequently, the interference from the transmitters to the receivers due to ringaround is insignificant.

PATH CHARACTERISTICS

The normal *propagation paths* between two radio antennas in a microwave radio system are shown in Figure 17-12. The *free-space path* is the *line-of-sight path* directly between the transmit and receive antennas (this is also called the *direct wave*). The *ground-reflected wave* is the portion of the transmit signal that is reflected off Earth's surface and captured by the receive antenna. The *surface wave* consists of the electric and magnetic fields associated with the currents induced in Earth's surface. The magnitude of the surface wave depends on the characteristics of Earth's surface and the electromagnetic polarization of the wave. The sum of these three paths (taking into account their amplitude and phase) is called the *ground wave*. The *sky wave* is the portion of the transmit signal that is returned (reflected) back to Earth's surface by the ionized layers of Earth's atmosphere.

All paths shown in Figure 17-12 exist in any microwave radio system, but some are negligible in certain frequency ranges. At frequencies below 1.5 MHz, the surface wave provides the primary coverage, and the sky wave helps to extend this coverage at night when the absorption of the ionosphere is at a minimum. For frequencies above about 30 MHz to 50 MHz, the free-space and ground-reflected paths are generally the only paths of importance. The surface wave can also be neglected at these frequencies, provided that the antenna heights are not too low. The sky wave is only a source of occasional long-distance interference and not a reliable signal for microwave communications purposes. In this chapter the surface and sky-wave propagations are neglected, and attention is focused on those phenomena that affect the direct and reflected waves.

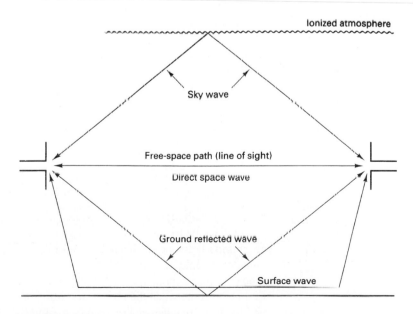

FIGURE 17-12 Propagation paths

Fading

Fading is a general term applied to the reduction in signal strength at the input to a receiver. The term *fading* applies to propagation variables in the physical radio path which affect changes in the path loss between the transmitter at one station and its normal receiver at the other station. The path changes are associated with both atmospheric conditions and the geometry of the path itself (i.e., the relative position of the antenna with respect to the ground and other surrounding terrain). Substandard atmospheric refraction may transform a clear line-of-site path into a highly obstructed one. Fading can occur under conditions of heavy ground fog or when extremely cold air moves over a warm earth. The result in either case is a substantial increase in path loss over a wide frequency band. The magnitude and rapidity of occurrence of this type of slow, flat fading can generally be reduced only by using greater antenna heights.

A more common form of fading is a relatively rapid, frequency selective type of fading caused by interference between two or more rays in the atmosphere. The separate paths between transmitter and receiver are caused by the irregularities in the variations in dielectric permittivity with height. The refraction effect depends on the average slope of the same variation in dielectric permittivity. The transmission margins that must be provided against both types of fading are important considerations in determining overall system parameters and reliability performance.

An interference type of fade may occur to any depth, but fortunately, the deeper the fade the less frequently it is likely to occur and the shorter its duration when it does occur. Both the number of fades and the percentage of time below a given level tend to increase as either the repeater spacing or the frequency of operation increases. Multiple paths are usually overhead, although ground reflections can occasionally be a factor. The effects of multipath fading can be minimized by using either frequency or space diversity.

SYSTEM GAIN

In its simplest form, *system gain* is the difference between the nominal output power of a transmitter and the minimum input power required by a receiver. System gain must be greater than or equal to the sum of all the gains and losses incurred by a signal as it propagates from a transmitter to a receiver. In essence, it represents the net loss of a radio system. System gain is used to predict the reliability of a system for given system parameters. Mathematically, system gain is

$$G_s = P_t - C_{min}$$

where G_s = system gain (dB)
P_t = transmitter output power (dBm)
C_{min} = minimum receiver input power for a given quality objective (dBm)

and where

$$P_t - C_{min} \geq \text{losses} - \text{gains}$$

Gains A_t = transmit antenna gain (dB) relative to an isotropic radiator
A_r = receive antenna gain (dB) relative to an isotropic radiator

Losses L_p = free-space path loss between antennas (dB)
L_f = waveguide feeder loss (dB) between the distribution network (channel-combining network or channel-separation network) and its respective antenna (see Table 17-3)
L_b = total coupling or branching loss (dB) in the circulators, filters, and distribution network between the output of a transmitter or the input to a receiver and its respective waveguide feed (see Table 17-3)
F_m = fade margin for a given reliability objective

TABLE 17-3 System Gain Parameters

Frequency (GHz)	Feeder Loss, L_f Type	Loss (dB/100 m)	Branching Loss, L_b (dB) Diversity Frequency	Space	Antenna Gain, A_t or A_r Size (m)	Gain (dB)
1.8	Air filled coaxial cable	5.4	5	2	1.2	25.2
					2.4	31.2
					3.0	33.2
					3.7	34.7
7.4	EWP 64 eliptical waveguide	4.7	3	2	1.5	38.8
					2.4	43.1
					3.0	44.8
					3.7	46.5
8.0	EWP 69 eliptical waveguide	6.5	3	2	2.4	43.8
					3.0	45.6
					3.7	47.3
					4.8	49.8

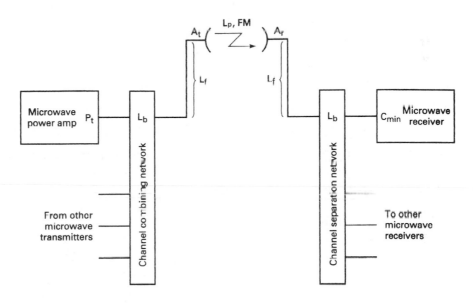

FIGURE 17-13 System gains and losses

Mathematically, system gain is

$$G_s = P_t - C_{min} \geq F_m + L_p + L_f + L_b - A_t - A_r \qquad (17\text{-}1)$$

where all values are expressed in dB or dBm. Because system gain is indicative of a net loss, the losses are represented with positive dB values and the gains are represented with negative dB values. Figure 17-13 shows an overall microwave system diagram and indicates where the respective losses and gains are incurred.

Free-Space Path Loss

Free-space path loss (sometimes called spreading loss) is defined as the loss incurred by an electromagnetic wave as it propagates in a straight line through a vacuum with no absorption or reflection of energy from nearby objects. Free-space path loss is frequency dependent and increases with distance. The expression for free-space path loss is given as

$$L_p = \left(\frac{4\pi D}{\lambda}\right)^2 = \left(\frac{4\pi f D}{c}\right)^2$$

where L_p = free-space path loss (unitless)
D = distance (meters)
f = frequency (hertz)
λ = wavelength (meters)
c = velocity of light in free space (3×10^8 m/s)

Converting to dB yields

$$L_{p(\text{dB})} = 10 \log \left(\frac{4\pi f D}{c}\right)^2$$

$$= 20 \log \frac{4\pi f D}{c}$$

$$= 20 \log \frac{4\pi}{c} + 20 \log f + 20 \log D \qquad (17\text{-}2)$$

When the frequency is given in MHz and the distance in km,

$$L_{p(\text{dB})} = 20 \log \frac{4\pi (10)(10)^3}{3 \times 10^8} + 20 \log f_{(\text{MHz})} + 20 \log D_{(\text{km})} \qquad (17\text{-}3)$$

$$= 32.4 + 20 \log f_{(\text{MHz})} + 20 \log D_{(\text{km})}$$

When the frequency is given in GHz and the distance in km,

$$L_{p(\text{dB})} = 92.4 + 20 \log f_{(\text{GHz})} + 20 \log D_{(\text{km})} \qquad (17\text{-}4)$$

Similar conversions can be made using distance in miles, frequency in kHz, and so on.

Example 17-2

For a carrier frequency of 6 GHz and a distance of 50 km, determine the free-space path loss.

Solution

$$L_p = 32.4 + 20 \log 6000 + 20 \log 50$$
$$= 32.4 + 75.6 + 34 = 142 \text{ dB}$$

or

$$L_p = 92.4 + 20 \log 6 + 20 \log 50$$
$$= 92.4 + 15.6 + 34 = 142 \text{ dB}$$

Fade Margin

Essentially, *fade margin* is a "fudge factor" included in the system gain equation that considers the nonideal and less predictable characteristics of radio-wave propagation, such as *multipath propagation (multipath loss)* and *terrain sensitivity*. These characteristics cause temporary, abnormal atmospheric conditions that alter the free-space path loss and are usually detrimental to the overall system performance. Fade margin also considers system reliability objectives. Thus, fade margin is included in the system gain equation as a loss.

In April 1969, W.T. Barnett of Bell Telephone Laboratories described ways of calculating outage time due to fading on a nondiversity path as a function of terrain, climate, path length, and fade margin. In June 1970, Arvids Vignant (also of Bell Laboratories) derived formulas for calculating the effective improvement achievable by vertical space diversity, as a function of the spacing distance, path length, and frequency.

Solving the Barnett-Vignant reliability equations for a specified annual system availability for an unprotected, nondiversity system yields the following expression:

$$F_m = 30 \log D + 10 \log (6ABf) - 10 \log (1 - R) - 70 \qquad (17\text{-}5)$$

$$\underbrace{}_{\substack{\text{multipath} \\ \text{effect}}} \quad \underbrace{}_{\substack{\text{terrain} \\ \text{sensitivity}}} \quad \underbrace{}_{\substack{\text{reliability} \\ \text{objectives}}} \quad \underbrace{}_{\text{constant}}$$

where F_m = fade margin (dB)

D = distance (kilometers)

f = frequency (gigahertz)

R = reliability expressed as a decimal (i.e., 99.99% = 0.9999 reliability)

$1 - R$ = reliability objective for a one-way 400-km route

A = roughness factor

= 4 over water or a very smooth terrain

= 1 over an average terrain

= 0.25 over a very rough, mountainous terrain

B = factor to convert a worst-month probability to an annual probability

= 1 to convert an annual availability to a worst-month basis

= 0.5 for hot humid areas

= 0.25 for average inland areas

= 0.125 for very dry or mountainous areas

Example 17-3

Consider a space-diversity microwave radio system operating at an RF carrier frequency of 1.8 GHz. Each station has a 2.4-m-diameter parabolic antenna that is fed by 100 m of air-filled coaxial cable. The terrain is smooth and the area has a humid climate. The distance between stations is 40 km. A reliability objective of 99.99% is desired. Determine the system gain.

Solution Substituting into Equation 17-5, we find that the fade margin is

$$F_m = 30 \log 40 + 10 \log [(6)(4)(0.5)(1.8)] - 10 \log (1 - 0.9999) - 70$$

$$= 48.06 + 13.34 - (-40) - 70$$

$$= 48.06 + 13.34 + 40 - 70 = 31.4 \text{ dB}$$

Substituting into Equation 17-4, we obtain path loss

$$L_p = 92.4 + 20 \log 1.8 + 20 \log 40$$

$$= 92.4 + 5.11 + 32.04 = 129.55 \text{ dB}$$

From Table 17-3,

$$L_b = 4 \text{ dB } (2 + 2 = 4)$$

$$L_f = 10.8 \text{ dB } (100 \text{ m} + 100 \text{ m} = 200 \text{ m})$$

$$A_t = A_r = 31.2 \text{ dB}$$

Substituting into Equation 17-3 gives us system gain

$$G_s = 31.4 + 129.55 + 10.8 + 4 - 31.2 - 31.2 = 113.35 \text{ dB}$$

The results indicate that for this system to perform at 99.99% reliability with the given terrain, distribution networks, transmission lines, and antennas, the transmitter output power must be at least 113.35 dB more than the minimum receive signal level.

Receiver Threshold

Carrier-to-noise (C/N) ratio is probably the most important parameter considered when evaluating the performance of a microwave communications system. The minimum wideband carrier power (C_{min}) at the input to a receiver that will provide a usable baseband output is called the receiver *threshold* or, sometimes, receiver *sensitivity*. The receiver threshold is dependent on the wideband noise power present at the input of a receiver, the noise introduced within the receiver, and the noise sensitivity of the baseband detector. Before C_{min} can be calculated, the input noise power must be determined. The input noise power is expressed mathematically as

$$N = KTB$$

where N = noise power (watts)
   K = Boltzmann's constant (1.38×10^{-23} J/K)
   T = equivalent noise temperature of the receiver (kelvin) (room temperature = 290 kelvin)
   B = noise bandwidth (hertz)

Expressed in dBm,

$$N_{(dBm)} = 10 \log \frac{KTB}{0.001} = 10 \log \frac{KT}{0.001} + 10 \log B$$

For a 1-Hz bandwidth at room temperature,

$$N = 10 \log \frac{(1.38 \times 10^{-23})(290)}{0.001} + 10 \log 1$$

$$= -174 \text{ dBm}$$

Thus, $N_{(dBm)} = -174 \text{ dBm} + 10 \log B$ (17-6)

Example 17-4

For an equivalent noise bandwidth of 10 MHz, determine the noise power.

Solution   Substituting into Equation 17-6 yields
$$N = -174 \text{ dBm} + 10 \log (10 \times 10^{6})$$
$$= -174 \text{ dBm} + 70 \text{ dB} = -104 \text{ dBm}$$

If the minimum C/N requirement for a receiver with a 10-MHz noise bandwidth is 24 dB, the minimum receive carrier power is

$$C_{min} = \frac{C}{N} + N = 24 \text{ dB} + (-104 \text{ dBm}) = -80 \text{ dBm}$$

For a system gain of 113.35 dB, it would require a minimum transmit carrier power (P_t) of
$$P_t = G_s + C_{min} = 113.35 \text{ dB} + (-80 \text{ dBm}) = 33.35 \text{ dBm}$$

This indicates that a minimum transmit power of 33.35 dBm (2.16 W) is required to achieve a carrier-to-noise ratio of 24 dB with a system gain of 113.35 dB and a bandwidth of 10 MHz.

Carrier-to-Noise Versus Signal-to-Noise Ratio

Carrier-to-noise (C/N) is the ratio of the wideband "carrier" (actually, not just the carrier, but rather the carrier and its associated sidebands) to the wideband noise power (the noise bandwidth of the receiver). C/N can be determined at an RF or an IF point in the receiver. Essentially, C/N is a *predetection* (before the FM demodulator) signal-to-noise ratio. Signal-to-noise (S/N) is a *postdetection* (after the FM demodulator) ratio. At a baseband point in the receiver, a single voice-band channel can be separated from the rest of the baseband and measured independently. At an RF or IF point in the receiver, it is impossible to separate a single voice-band channel from the composite FM signal. For example, a typical bandwidth for a single microwave channel is 30 MHz. The bandwidth of a voice-band channel is 4 kHz. C/N is the ratio of the power of the composite RF signal to the total noise power in the 30-MHz bandwidth. S/N is the ratio of the signal power of a single voice-band channel to the noise power in a 4-kHz bandwidth.

Noise Factor and Noise Figure

Noise factor (F) and *noise figure* (NF) are figures of merit used to indicate how much the signal-to-noise ratio deteriorates as a signal passes through a circuit or series of circuits. Noise factor is simply a ratio of input signal-to-noise ratio to output signal-to-noise ratio. In other words, a ratio of ratios. Mathematically, noise factor is

$$F = \frac{\text{input signal-to-noise ratio}}{\text{output signal-to-noise ratio}} \text{ (unitless ratio)} \qquad \text{(17-7a)}$$

Noise figure is simply the noise factor stated in dB and is a parameter commonly used to indicate the quality of a receiver. Mathematically, noise figure is

$$NF = 10 \log \frac{\text{input signal-to-noise ratio}}{\text{output signal-to-noise ratio}} \text{ (dB)} \qquad \text{(17-7b)}$$

or
$$NF = 10 \log F \qquad \text{(17-7c)}$$

In essence, noise figure indicates how much the signal to noise ratio deteriorates as a waveform propagates from the input to the output of a circuit. For example, an amplifier with a noise figure of 6 dB means that the signal-to-noise ratio at the output is 6 dB less than it was at the input. If a circuit is perfectly noiseless and adds no additional noise to the signal, the signal-to-noise ratio at the output will equal the signal-to-noise ratio at the input. For a perfect, noiseless circuit the noise factor is 1 and the noise figure is 0 dB.

An electronic circuit amplifies signals and noise within its passband equally well. Therefore, if the amplifier is ideal and noiseless, the input signal and noise are amplified the same, and the signal-to-noise ratio at the output will equal the signal-to-noise ratio at the input. In reality, however, amplifiers are not ideal. Therefore, the amplifier adds internally generated noise to the waveform, reducing the overall signal-to-noise ratio. The most predominant noise is thermal noise, which is generated in all electrical components. Therefore, all networks, amplifiers, and systems add noise to the signal and, thus, reduce the overall signal-to-noise ratio as the signal passes through them.

When two or more amplifiers are cascaded as shown in Figure 17-14, the total noise factor is the accumulation of the individual noise factors. *Friiss' formula* is used to calculate the total noise factor of several cascaded amplifiers. Mathematically, Friiss' formula is

$$F_T = F_1 + \frac{F_2 - 1}{A_1} + \frac{F_3 - 1}{A_1 A_2} + \frac{F_n - 1}{A_1 A_2 A_3} \qquad \text{(17-8)}$$

where F_T = total noise factor for n cascaded amplifiers
F_1 = noise factor, amplifier 1
F_2 = noise factor, amplifier 2
F_3 = noise factor, amplifier 3
F_n = noise factor, amplifier n
A_1 = power gain, amplifier 1
A_2 = power gain, amplifier 2
A_3 = power gain, amplifier 3

Note that to use Friiss' formula, the noise figures must be converted to noise factors. The total noise figure is simply

$$NF_{T(dB)} = 10 \log F_T \qquad \text{(17-9)}$$

It can be seen that the noise factor of the first amplifier (F_1) contributes the most toward the overall noise figure. The noise introduced in the first stage is amplified by each of

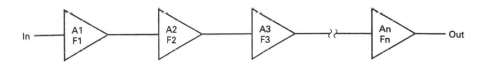

FIGURE 17-14 Total noise figure

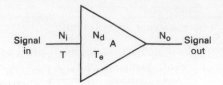

FIGURE 17-15 Noise figure as a function of temperature

the succeeding amplifiers. Therefore, when compared with the noise introduced in the first stage, the noise added by each succeeding amplifier is effectively reduced by a factor equal to the product of the power gains of the preceding amplifiers.

When precise noise calculations (0.1 dB or less) are necessary, it is generally more convenient to express noise figure in terms of noise temperature or equivalent noise temperature rather than as an absolute power. Because noise power (N) is proportional to temperature, the noise present at the input to a device can be expressed as a function of the device's environmental temperature (T) and its equivalent noise temperature (T_e). Noise factor can be converted to a term dependent on temperature only as follows (refer to Figure 17-15).

Let

$$N_d = \text{noise power added by a single amplifier, referred to its input}$$

Then
$$N_d = KT_eB \tag{17-10}$$

where T_e is the equivalent noise temperature. Let

$$N_o = \text{total output noise power of an amplifier (watts)}$$
$$N_i = \text{total input noise power of an amplifier (watts)}$$
$$A = \text{power gain of an amplifier (unitless)}$$

Therefore, N_o may be expressed as

$$N_o = AN_i + AN_d$$

and
$$N_o = AKTB + AKT_eB$$

Simplifying yields
$$N_o = AKB\,(T + T_e)$$

and the overall noise factor (F_T) equals

$$F_T = \frac{(S/N)_{in}}{(S/N)_{out}} = \frac{S/N_i}{AS/N_o} = \frac{N_o}{AN_i} = \frac{AKB\,(T + T_e)}{AKTB} \tag{17-11}$$

$$F_T = \frac{T + T_e}{T} = 1 + \frac{T_e}{T}$$

Example 17-5

In Figure 17-14, let $NF_1 = NF_2 = NF_3 = 3$ dB and $A_1 = A_2 = A_3 = 10$ dB. Solve for the total noise figure.

Solution Substituting into Equation 17-8 (*Note:* All gains and noise factors are given in absolute values.) yields

$$F_T = F_1 + \frac{F_2 - 1}{A_1} + \frac{F_3 - 1}{A_1 A_2}$$

$$F_T = 2 + \frac{2 - 1}{10} + \frac{2 - 1}{10} = 2.11$$

$$NF_T = 10 \log 2.11 = 3.24 \text{ dB}$$

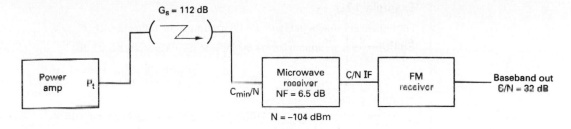

FIGURE 17-16 System gain for Example 17-6

An overall noise figure of 3.24 dB indicates that the S/N ratio at the output of A_3 is 3.24 dB less than the S/N ratio at the input to A_1.

The noise figure of a receiver must be considered when determining C_{min}. The noise figure is included in the system gain equation as an equivalent loss. (Essentially, a gain in the total noise power is equivalent to a corresponding loss in the signal power.)

Example 17-6

Refer to Figure 17-16. For a system gain of 112 dB, a total noise figure of 6.5 dB, an input noise power of -104 dBm, and a minimum $(S/N)_{out}$ of the FM demodulator of 32 dB, determine the minimum receive carrier power and the minimum transmit power.

Solution To achieve a S/N ratio of 32 dB out of the FM demodulator, an input C/N of 15 dB is required (17 dB of improvement due to FM quieting). Solving for the receiver input carrier-to-noise ratio gives

$$\frac{C_{min}}{N} = \frac{C}{N} + NF_t = 15 \text{ dB} + 6.5 \text{ dB} = 21.5 \text{ dB}$$

Thus,

$$C_{min} = \frac{C_{min}}{N} + N = 21.5 \text{ dB} + (-104 \text{ dBm}) = -82.5 \text{ dBm}$$

$$P_t = G_s + C_{min} = 112 \text{ dB} + (-82.5 \text{ dBm}) = 29.5 \text{ dBm}$$

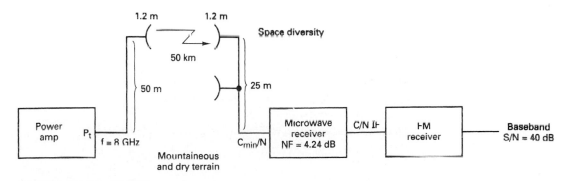

Reliability objective = 99.999%
Bandwidth = 6.3 MHz

FIGURE 17-17 System gain for Example 17-7

Example 17-7

For the system shown in Figure 17-17, determine the following: G_s, C_{min}/N, C_{min}, N, G_s, and P_t.

Solution The minimum C/N at the input to the FM receiver is 23 dB.

$$\frac{C_{min}}{N} = \frac{C}{N} + NF_T = 23 \text{ dB} + 4.24 \text{ dB} = 27.24 \text{ dB}$$

Substituting into Equation 17-6 yields

$$N = -174 \text{ dBm} + 10 \log B = -174 \text{ dBm} + 68 \text{ dB} = -106 \text{ dBm}$$

$$C_{min} = \frac{C_{min}}{N} + N = 27.24 \text{ dB} + (-106 \text{ dBm}) = -78.76 \text{ dBm}$$

Substituting into Equation 17-5 gives us

$$F_m = 30 \log 50 + 10 \log [(6)(0.25)(0.125)(8)]$$
$$-10 \log (1 - 0.99999) - 70 = 32.76 \text{ dB}$$

Substituting into Equation 17-4, we have

$$L_p = 92.4 \text{ dB} + 20 \log 8 + 20 \log 50$$
$$= 92.4 \text{ dB} + 18.06 \text{ dB} + 33.98 \text{ dB} = 144.44 \text{ dB}$$

From Table 17-3,

$$L_b = 4 \text{ dB}$$
$$L_f = 0.75 (6.5 \text{ dB}) = 4.875 \text{ dB}$$
$$A_t = A_r = 37.8 \text{ dB}$$

Note: The gain of an antenna increases or decreases proportional to the square of its diameter (i.e., if its diameter changes by a factor of 2, its gain changes by a factor of 4 which is 6 dB).
Substituting into Equation 17-1 yields

$$G_s = 32.76 + 144.44 + 4.875 + 4 - 37.8 - 37.8 = 110.475 \text{ dB}$$
$$P_t = G_s + C_{min} = 110.475 \text{ dB} + (-78.76 \text{ dBm}) = 31.715 \text{ dBm}$$

QUESTIONS

17-1. What constitutes a short-haul microwave system? A long-haul microwave system?

17-2. Describe the baseband signal for a microwave system.

17-3. Why do FDM/FM microwave systems use low-index FM?

17-4. Describe a microwave repeater. Contrast baseband and IF repeaters.

17-5. Define *diversity*. Describe the three most commonly used diversity schemes.

17-6. Describe a protection switching arrangement. Contrast the two types of protection switching arrangements.

17-7. Briefly describe the four major sections of a microwave terminal station.

17-8. Define *ringaround*.

17-9. Briefly describe a high/low microwave system.

17-10. Define *system gain*.

17-11. Define the following terms: *free-space path loss, branching loss,* and *feeder loss.*

17-12. Define *fade margin*. Describe multipath losses, terrain sensitivity, and reliability objectives and how they affect fade margin.

17-13. Define *receiver threshold*.

17-14. Contrast carrier-to-noise ratio and signal-to-noise ratio.

17-15. Define *noise figure*.

PROBLEMS

17-1. Calculate the noise power at the input to a receiver that has a radio carrier frequency of 4 GHz and a bandwidth of 30 MHz (assume room temperature).

17-2. Determine the path loss for a 3.4-GHz signal propagating 20,000 m.

17-3. Determine the fade margin for a 60-km microwave hop. The RF carrier frequency is 6 GHz, the terrain is very smooth and dry, and the reliability objective is 99.95%.

17-4. Determine the noise power for a 20-MHz bandwidth at the input to a receiver with an input noise temperature of 290°C.

17-5. For a system gain of 120 dB, a minimum input C/N of 30 dB, and an input noise power of -115 dBm, determine the minimum transmit power (P_t).

17-6. Determine the amount of loss attributed to a reliability objective of 99.98%.

17-7. Determine the terrain sensitivity loss for a 4-GHz carrier that is propagating over a very dry, mountainous area.

17-8. A frequency-diversity microwave system operates at an RF carrier frequency of 7.4 GHz. The IF is a low-index frequency-modulated subcarrier. The baseband signal is the 1800-channel FDM system described in Chapter 16 (564 kHz to 8284 kHz). The antennas are 4.8-m-diameter parabolic dishes. The feeder lengths are 150 m at one station and 50 m at the other station. The reliability objective is 99.999%. The system propagates over an average terrain that has a very dry climate. The distance between stations is 50 km. The minimum carrier-to-noise ratio at the receiver input is 30 dB. Determine the following: fade margin, antenna gain, free-space path loss, total branching and feeder losses, receiver input noise power (C_{min}), minimum transmit power, and system gain.

17-9. Determine the overall noise figure for a receiver that has two RF amplifiers each with a noise figure of 6 dB and a gain of 10 dB, a mixer down-converter with a noise figure of 10 dB, and a conversion gain of -6 dB, and 40 dB of IF gain with a noise figure of 6 dB.

17-10. A microwave receiver has a total input noise power of -102 dBm and an overall noise figure of 4 dB. For a minimum C/N ratio of 20 dB at the input to the FM detector, determine the minimum receive carrier power.

17-11. Calculate the noise power at the input to a receiver for the following temperatures and bandwidths.

T (°C)	B (kHz)
0	10
20	40
200	20
500	50

17-12. Determine the path loss for the following frequencies and distances.

f (MHz)	D (km)
200	0.5
800	0.8
3000	5
5000	10
8000	25
18000	10

17-13. Determine the fade margin for a 30-km microwave hop. The RF frequency is 4 GHz, the terrain is water, and the reliability objective is 99.995%.

17-14. Determine the noise power for a 40-MHz bandwidth at the input to a receiver with an input temperature $T = 400$°C.

17-15. For a system gain of 114 dB, a minimum input C/N = 34 dB, and an input noise power of -111 dBm, determine the minimum transmit power (P_t).

17-16. Determine the amount of loss contributed to a reliability objective of 99.9995%.

17-17. Determine the terrain sensitivity loss for an 8-GHz carrier that is propagating over a very smooth and dry terrain.

17-18. A frequency diversity microwave system operates at an RF = 7.4 GHz. The IF is a low-index frequency-modulated subcarrier. The baseband signal is a single mastergroup FDM system. The antennas are 2.4-m parabolic dishes. The feeder lengths are 120 m at one station and 80 m at the other station. The reliability objective is 99.995%. The system propagates over an average terrain that has a very dry climate. The distance between stations is 40 km. The minimum carrier-to-noise ratio at the receiver input is 28 dB. Determine the following: fade margin, antenna gain, free-space path loss, total branching and feeder losses, receiver input power (C_{min}), minimum transmit power, and system gain.

17-19. Determine the overall noise figure for a receiver that has two RF amplifiers each with a noise figure of 8 dB and a gain of 13 dB, a mixer down-converter with a noise figure of 6 dB, and a conversion gain of −6 dB, and 36 dB of IF gain with a noise figure of 10 dB.

17-20. A microwave receiver has a total input noise power of −108 dBm and an overall noise figure of 5 dB. For a minimum C/N ratio of 18 dB at the input to the FM detector, determine the minimum receive carrier power.

CHAPTER 18

Satellite
Communications

INTRODUCTION

In astronomical terms, a *satellite* is a celestial body that orbits around a planet (for example, the moon is a satellite of Earth). In aerospace terms, however, a satellite is a space vehicle launched by humans and orbits Earth or another celestial body. Communications satellites are man-made satellites that orbit Earth providing a multitude of communication functions to a wide variety of consumers including military, governmental, private, and commercial subscribers.

In essence, a *communications satellite* is a microwave repeater in the sky that consists of a diverse combination of one or more of the following: receiver, transmitter, amplifier, regenerator, filter, on-board computer, multiplexer, demultiplexer, antenna, waveguide, and about any other electronic communications circuit ever developed. A satellite radio repeater is called a *transponder*, of which a satellite may have many. A *satellite system* consists of one or more satellite space vehicles, a ground-based station to control the operation of the system, and a user network of earth stations that provides the interface facilities for the transmission and reception of terrestrial communications traffic through the satellite system.

Transmissions to and from satellites are categorized as either *bus* or *payload*. The bus includes control mechanisms that support the payload operation. The payload is the actual user information conveyed through the system. Although in recent years new data services and television broadcasting are more and more in demand, the transmission of conventional speech telephone signals (in analog or digital form) is still the bulk of satellite payloads.

In the early 1960s, AT&T released studies indicating that a few powerful satellites of advanced design could handle more telephone traffic than the entire existing AT&T long-distance communications network. The cost of these satellites was estimated to be only a fraction of the cost of equivalent terrestrial microwave or underground cable facilities. Unfortunately, because AT&T was a utility, and government regulations prevented them from developing the satellite systems, smaller and much less lucrative companies were left to develop the satellite systems and AT&T continued for several more years investing billions of dollars each year in conventional terrestrial microwave and metallic cable systems. Because of this, early developments in satellite technology were slow in coming.

HISTORY OF SATELLITES

The simplest type of satellite is a *passive reflector*, which is a device that simply "bounces" signals from one place to another. A passive satellite reflects signals back to Earth as there are no gain devices on board to amplify or modify the signals. The moon is a natural satellite of Earth, visible by reflection of sunlight and having a slightly elliptical orbit. Consequently, the moon became the first passive satellite in 1954 when the U.S. Navy successfully transmitted the first message over this Earth-to-moon-to-Earth communications system. In 1956, a relay service was established between Washington, D.C., and Hawaii and, until 1962, offered reliable long-distance radio communications service limited only by the availability of the moon. Over time, however, the moon proved to be an inconvenient and unreliable communications satellite as it is above the horizon only half of the time and its position relative to Earth is constantly changing.

An obvious advantage of passive satellites is that they do not require sophisticated electronic equipment on board, although they are not necessarily void of power. Some passive satellites require *radio beacon transmitters* for tracking and ranging purposes. A beacon is a continuously transmitted unmodulated carrier that an earth station can lock on to and use to determine the exact location of a satellite so the earth station can align its antennas. Another disadvantage of passive satellites is their inefficient use of transmitted power. For example, as little as 1 part in every 10^{18} of an earth station's transmitted power is actually returned to earth station receiving antennas.

In 1957, Russia launched *Sputnik I,* the first *active* earth satellite. An active satellite is capable of receiving, amplifying, reshaping, regenerating, and retransmitting information. *Sputnik I* transmitted telemetry information for 21 days. Later in the same year, the United States launched *Explorer I,* which transmitted telemetry information for nearly five months.

In 1958, NASA launched *Score,* a 150-lb conical-shaped satellite. With an on-board tape recording, *Score* rebroadcast President Eisenhower's 1958 Christmas message. *Score* was the first artificial satellite used for relaying terrestrial communications. *Score* was a *delayed repeater* satellite as it received transmissions from earth stations, stored them on magnetic tape, and then rebroadcast them later to ground stations farther along in its orbit.

In 1960, NASA in conjunction with Bell Telephone Laboratories and the Jet Propulsion Laboratory launched *Echo,* a 100-ft-diameter plastic balloon with an aluminum coating. *Echo* passively reflected radio signals it received from large earth station antennas. *Echo* was simple and reliable, but required extremely high-power transmitters at the earth stations. The first transatlantic transmission using a satellite was accomplished using *Echo.* Also in 1960, the Department of Defense launched *Courier,* which was the first transponder-type satellite. *Courier* transmitted 3 W of power and lasted only 17 days.

In 1962, AT&T launched *Telstar I,* the first active satellite to simultaneously receive and transmit radio signals. The electronic equipment in *Telstar I* was damaged by radiation from the newly discovered Van Allen belts and, consequently, lasted for only a few weeks. *Telstar II* was successfully launched in 1963 and was electronically identical to *Telstar I,* except more radiation resistant. *Telstar II* was used for telephone, television, facsimile, and data transmissions and accomplished the first successful transatlantic video transmission.

Syncom I, launched in February 1963, was the first attempt to place a geosynchronous satellite into orbit. Unfortunately, *Syncom I* was lost during orbit injection; however, *Syncom II* and *Syncom III* were successfully launched in February 1963 and August 1964, respectively. The *Syncom III* satellite was used to broadcast the 1964 Olympic Games from Tokyo. The *Syncom* satellites demonstrated the feasibility of using geosynchronous satellites.

Since the *Syncom* projects, a number of nations and private corporations have successfully launched satellites that are currently being used to provide national as well as regional and international global communications. Today, there are several hundred satellite communications systems operating in virtually every corner of the world. These companies provide worldwide, fixed common-carrier telephone and data circuits; point-to-point television broadcasting; network television distribution; music broadcasting; mobile telephone service; navigation service; and private communications networks for large corporations, government agencies, and military applications.

Intelsat I (called *Early Bird*) was the first commercial telecommunications satellite. It was launched from Cape Kennedy in 1965 and used two transponders and a 25-MHz bandwidth to simultaneously carry one television signal and 480 voice channels. Intelsat stands for *In*ternational *Tele*communications *Sat*ellite Organization. Intelsat is a commercial global satellite network that manifested in 1964 from within the United Nations. Intelsat is a consortium of over 120 nations with the commitment to provide worldwide, nondiscriminatory satellite communications using four basic service categories: international public-switched telephony, broadcasting, private line/business networks, and domestic/regional communications. Between 1966 and 1987, Intelsat launched a series of satellites designated *Intelsat II, III, IV, V,* and *VI. Intelsat VI* has a capacity of 80,000 voice channels. Intelsat's most recent satellite launches include the 500, 600, 700, and 800 series space vehicles.

The former Soviet Union launched the first set of *domestic satellites* (Domsats) in 1966 and called them *Molniya,* meaning "lightning." Domsats are satellites that are owned, operated, and used by a single country. In 1972, Canada launched its first commercial satellite designated *Anik,* which is an Inuit word meaning "little brother." Western Union launched their first Westar satellite in 1974 and Radio Corporation of America (RCA) launched its first Satcom (*Sat*ellite *Com*munications) satellites in 1975. In the United States today, a publicly owned company called *Com*munications *Sat*ellite Corporation (Comsat) regulates the use and operation of U.S. satellites and also sets their tariffs. Although a company or government may own a satellite, its utilities are generally made available to anyone willing to pay for them. The United States currently utilizes the largest share of available worldwide satellite time (24%); Great Britain is second with 13%, followed by France with 6%.

KEPLER'S LAWS

A satellite remains in orbit because the centrifugal force caused by its rotation around Earth is counterbalanced by Earth's gravitational pull. In the early seventeenth century while investigating the laws of planetary motion (i.e., motion of planets and their heavenly bodies called moons), German astronomer Johannes Kepler (1571–1630) discovered the laws that govern satellite motion. The laws of planetary motion describe the shape of the orbit, the velocities of the planet, and the distance a planet is with respect to the sun. *Kepler's laws* may be simply stated as (1) the planets move in ellipses with the sun at one focus, (2) the line joining the sun and a planet sweeps out equal areas in equal intervals of time, and (3) the square of the time of revolution of a planet divided by the cube of its mean distance from the sun gives a number that is the same for all planets. Kepler's laws can be applied to any two bodies in space that interact through gravitation. The larger of the two bodies is called the *primary* and the smaller is called the *secondary* or *satellite.*

Kepler's first law states that a satellite will orbit a primary body (like Earth) following an elliptical path. An ellipse has two *focal points (foci)* as shown in Figure 18-1a (F_1 and F_2), and the center of mass (called the barycenter) of a two-body system is always centered on one of the foci. Because the mass of Earth is substantially greater than that of the satellite, the center of mass will always coincide with the center of Earth. The geometric properties of the ellipse are normally referenced to one of the foci which is logically selected to be the one at the center of Earth.

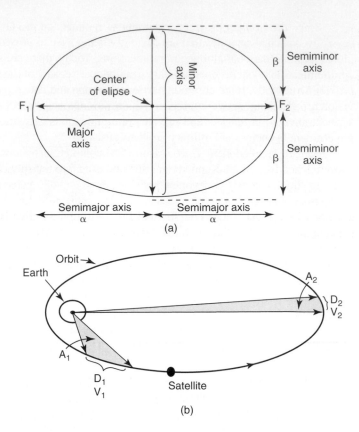

FIGURE 18-1 (a) Focal points F_1 and F_2; semimajor axis a, and semiminor axis b of an ellipse; (b) Kepler's second law.

For the semimajor axis (α) and the semiminor axis (β) shown in Figure 18-1a, the *eccentricity* (abnormality) of the ellipse can be defined as

$$\epsilon = \frac{\sqrt{\alpha^2 - \beta^2}}{\alpha} \tag{18-1}$$

where ϵ is eccentricity

Kepler's second law, enunciated with the first law in 1609, is known as the *law of areas*. Kepler's second law states that for equal intervals of time a satellite will sweep out equal areas in the orbital plane, focused at the barycenter. As shown in Figure 18-1b, for a satellite traveling distances D_1 and D_2 meters in 1 second, areas A_1 and A_2 will be equal. Because of the equal area law, distance D_1 must be greater than distance D_2 and, therefore, velocity V_1 must be greater than velocity V_2. The velocity will be greatest at the point of closest approach to Earth (known as the *perigee*) and the velocity will be least at the farthest point from Earth (known as the *apogee*).

Kepler's third law, announced in 1619, is sometimes known as the *harmonic law*. The third law states that the square of the periodic time of orbit is proportional to the cube of the mean distance between the primary and the satellite. This mean distance is equal to the semimajor axis; thus, Kepler's third law can be stated mathematically as

$$\alpha = AP^{2/3} \tag{18-2}$$

where A = constant (unitless)
         α = semimajor axis (kilometers)
         P = mean solar earth days

and P is the ratio of the time of one sidereal day (t_s = 23 hours and 56 minutes) to the time of one revolution of Earth on its own axis (t_e = 24 hours).

thus,

$$P = \frac{t_s}{t_e}$$

$$= \frac{1436 \text{ minutes}}{1440 \text{ minutes}}$$

$$= 0.9972$$

Rearranging Equation 18-2 and solving the constant A for earth yields

$$A = 42241.0979$$

Equations 18-1 and 18-2 apply for the ideal case when a satellite is orbiting around a perfectly spherical body with no outside forces. In actuality, Earth's equatorial bulge and external disturbing forces result in deviations in the satellite's ideal motion. Fortunately, however, the major deviations can be calculated and compensated for. Satellites orbiting close to Earth will be affected by atmospheric drag and by Earth's magnetic field. For more distant satellites, however, the primary disturbing forces are from the gravitational fields of the sun and moon.

SATELLITE ORBITS

Most of the satellites mentioned thus far are called *orbital* satellites, which are *nonsynchronous*. Nonsynchronous satellites rotate around Earth in an elliptical or circular pattern as shown in Figure 18-2a and b. In a circular orbit, the speed or rotation is constant; however, in elliptical orbits the speed depends on the height the satellite is above Earth. The speed of the satellite is greater when it is close to Earth than when it is farther away.

If the satellite is orbiting in the same direction as Earth's rotation (counterclockwise) and at an angular velocity greater than that of Earth ($\omega_s > \omega_e$), the orbit is called a *prograde* or *posigrade* orbit. If the satellite is orbiting in the opposite direction as Earth's rotation or in the same direction with at an angular velocity less than that of Earth ($\omega_s < \omega_e$), the orbit is called a *retrograde* orbit. Most nonsynchronous satellites revolve around Earth in a prograde orbit. Therefore, the position of satellites in nonsynchronous orbits is continuously changing in respect to a fixed position on Earth. Consequently, nonsynchronous satellites have to be used when available, which may be as little as 15 minutes per orbit. Another disadvantage of orbital satellites is the need for complicated and expensive tracking equipment at the earth stations so they can locate the satellite as it comes into view on each orbit and then lock its antenna onto the satellite and track it as it passes overhead. A major advantage of orbital satellites, however, is that propulsion rockets are not required on board the satellites to keep them in their respective orbits.

Satellite Elevation Categories

Satellites are generally classified as having either a *low earth orbit* (LEO), *medium earth orbit* (MEO), or *geosynchronous earth orbit* (GEO). Most LEO satellites operate in the 1.0-GHz to 2.5-GHz frequency range. Motorola's satellite-based mobile-telephone system, *Iridium,* is a LEO system utilizing a 66-satellite constellation orbiting approximately 480 miles above Earth's surface. The main advantage of LEO satellites is that the path loss between earth stations and space vehicles is much lower than for satellites revolving in medium- or high-altitude orbits. Less path loss equates to lower transmit powers, smaller antennas, and less weight.

MEO satellites operate in the 1.2-GHz to 1.66-GHz frequency band and orbit between 6000 miles and 12,000 miles above Earth. The Department of Defense's satellite-

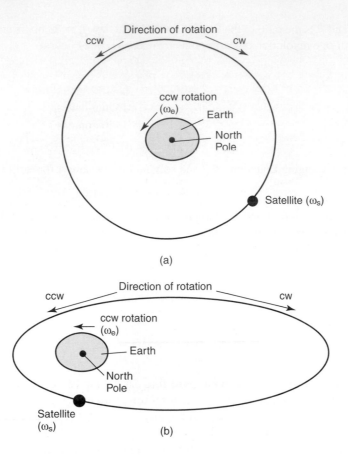

FIGURE 18-2 Satellite orbits: (a) circular; (b) elliptical

based global positioning system, *NAVSTAR*, is a MEO system with a constellation of 21 working satellites and six spares orbiting approximately 9500 miles above Earth.

Geosynchronous satellites are high-altitude earth-orbit satellites operating primarily in the 2-GHz to 18-GHz frequency spectrum with orbits 22,300 miles above Earth's surface. Most commercial communications satellites are in geosynchronous orbit. Geosynchronous or *geostationary* satellites are those that orbit in a circular pattern with an angular velocity equal to that of Earth. Geostationary satellites have an orbital time of approximately 24 hours, the same as Earth; thus, geosynchronous satellites appear to be stationary as they remain in a fixed position in respect to a given point on Earth.

Satellites in high-elevation, nonsynchronous circular orbits between 19,000 miles and 25,000 miles above Earth are said to be in *near-synchronous* orbit. When the near-synchronous orbit is slightly lower than 22,300 miles above Earth, the satellite's orbital time is lower than Earth's rotational period. Therefore, the satellite is moving slowly around Earth in a west-to-east direction. This type of near-synchronous orbit is called *subsynchronous*. If the orbit is higher than 22,300 miles above Earth, the satellite's orbital time is longer than Earth's rotational period and the satellite will appear to have a reverse (retrograde) motion from east to west.

Satellite Orbital Patterns

Before examining satellite orbital paths, a basic understanding of some terms used to describe orbits is necessary. For the following definitions, refer to Figure 18-3.

> *apogee*—the point in an orbit which is located farthest from Earth
>
> *perigee*—the point in an orbit which is located closest to Earth

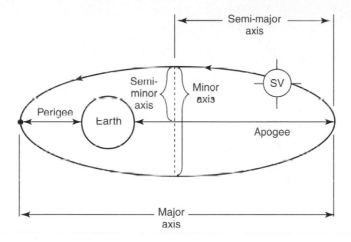

FIGURE 18-3 Satellite orbital terms

major axis—the line joining the perigee and apogee through the center of Earth; sometimes called *line of apsides*

minor axis—the line perpendicular to the major axis and halfway between the perigee and apogee (Half the distance of the minor axis is called the semiminor axis.)

Although there is an infinite number of orbital paths, only three are useful for communications satellites. Figure 18-4 shows three paths that a satellite can follow as it rotates around Earth: inclined, equatorial, or polar. All satellites rotate around Earth in an orbit that forms a plane that passes through the center of gravity of Earth called the *geocenter.*

Inclined orbits are virtually all orbits except those that travel directly above the equator or directly over the North and South Poles. Figure 18-5a shows the *angle of inclination* of a satellite orbit. The angle of inclination is the angle between the Earth's equatorial plane and the orbital plane of a satellite measured counterclockwise at the point in the orbit where it crosses the equatorial plane traveling from south to north. This point is called the *ascending node* and is shown in Figure 18-5b. The point where a polar or inclined orbit crosses the equatorial plane traveling from north to south is called the *descending node,* and the line joining the ascending and descending nodes through the center of Earth is called the *line of nodes.* Angles of inclination vary between 0° and 180°. To provide coverage to regions of high latitudes, inclined orbits are generally elliptical. Kepler's second law shows that the angular velocity of the satellite is slowest at its apogee. Therefore, the satellite remains visible for a longer period of time to the higher latitude regions if the apogee is placed above the high-latitude region.

An *equatorial orbit* is when the satellite rotates in an orbit directly above the equator, usually in a circular path. With an equatorial orbit, the angle of inclination is 0° and there are no ascending or descending nodes and, hence, no line of nodes. All geosynchronous satellites are in equatorial orbits.

A *polar orbit* is when the satellite rotates in a path that takes it over the North and South Poles in an orbit perpendicular to the equatorial plane. Polar orbiting satellites follow a low-altitude path that is close to Earth and passes over and very close to both the North and South Poles. The angle of inclination of a satellite in a polar orbit is nearly 90°. It is interesting to note that 100% of Earth's surface can be covered with a single satellite in a polar orbit. Satellites in polar orbits rotate around Earth in a longitudinal orbit while Earth is rotating on its axis in a latitudinal rotation. Consequently, the satellite's radiation pattern is a diagonal line that forms a spiral around the surface of Earth that resembles a barber pole. As a result, every location on Earth lies within the radiation pattern of a satellite in a polar orbit twice each day.

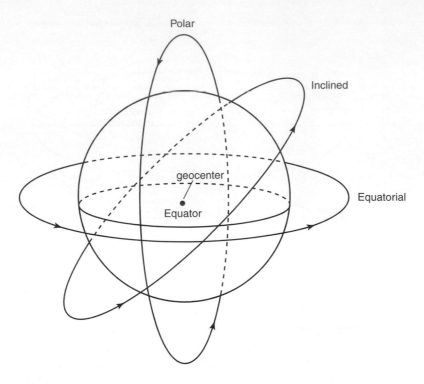

FIGURE 18-4 Satellite orbital patterns

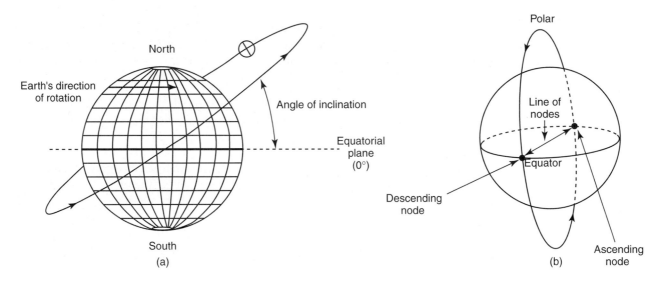

FIGURE 18-5 (a) Angle of inclination; (b) ascending node, descending node, and line of nodes

Earth is not a perfect sphere, as it bulges at the equator. In fact, until the early 1800s, a 20,700-ft mountain in Ecuador called Volcan Chimborazo was erroneously thought to be the highest point on the planet. However, due to equatorial bulge, Volcan Chimborazo proved to be the farthest point from the center of the Earth. An important effect of the Earth's equatorial bulge is causing elliptical orbits to rotate in a manner that causes the apogee and perigee to move around the Earth. This phenomena is called *rotation of the line of apsides;* however, for an angle of inclination of 63.4°, the rotation of the line of apsides

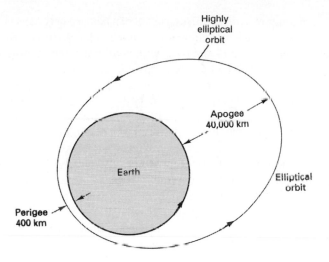

FIGURE 18-6 Soviet *Molniya* satellite orbit

is zero. Thus, satellites required to have an apogee over a particular location are launched into orbit with an angle of inclination of 63.4°, which is referred to as the 63° slot.

One of the more interesting orbital satellite systems currently in use is the Commonwealth of Independent States (CIS) *Molniya* system of satellites, which is shown in Figure 18-6. The CIS is the former Soviet Union. Molniya can also be spelled *Molnya* and *Molnia,* which means "lightning" in Russian (in colloquial Russian, *Molniya* means "news flash"). *Molniya* satellites are used for government communications, telephone, television, and video.

The *Molniya* series of satellites use highly inclined elliptical orbits to provide service to the more northerly regions where antennas would have to be aimed too close to the horizon to detect signals from geostationary space vehicles rotating in an equatorial orbit. *Molniya* satellites have an apogee at about 40,000 km and a perigee at about 400 km. The apogee is reached while over the Northern Hemisphere and the perigee while over the Southern Hemisphere. The size of the ellipse was chosen to make its period exactly one-half of a *sidereal day.* One sidereal day is the time it takes Earth to rotate back to the same constellation. The sidereal day for Earth is 23 hours and 56 minutes, slightly less than the time required for Earth to make one complete rotation around its own axis—24 hours. A sidereal day is sometimes called the *period* or *sidereal period.*

Because of its unique orbital pattern, the *Molniya* satellite is synchronous with the rotation of Earth. During a satellite's 12-hour orbit, it spends about 11 hours over the Northern Hemisphere. Three or more space vehicles follow each other in this orbit and *pass off* communications to each other so that continuous communications is possible while minimal earth station antenna tracking is necessary. Satellites with orbital patterns like *Molniya* are sometimes classified as having a highly elliptical orbit (HEO).

GEOSTATIONARY SATELLITES

As stated, geosynchronous satellites orbit Earth above the equator with the same angular velocity as Earth. Hence, geosynchronous (sometimes called *stationary* or *geostationary*) satellites appear to remain in a fixed location above one spot on Earth's surface. Since a geosynchronous satellite appears to remain in a fixed location, no special antenna tracking equipment is necessary—earth station antennas are simply pointed at the satellite. A single high-altitude geosynchronous satellite can provide reliable communications to approximately 40% of the earth's surface.

Satellites remain in orbit as a result of a balance between centrifugal and gravitational forces. If a satellite is traveling at too high a velocity, its centrifugal force will overcome Earth's gravitational pull and the satellite will break out of orbit and escape into space. At lower velocities, the satellite's centrifugal force is insufficient and gravity tends to pull the vehicle toward Earth. Obviously, there is a delicate balance between acceleration, speed, and distance that will exactly balance the effects of centrifugal and gravitational forces.

The closer to Earth a satellite rotates, the greater the gravitational pull and the greater the velocity required to keep it from being pulled to Earth. Low-altitude satellites orbiting 100 miles above Earth travel at approximately 17,500 mph. At this speed, it takes approximately 1.5 hours to rotate around Earth. Consequently, the time that a satellite is in line of sight of a particular earth station is 0.25 hour or less per orbit. Medium-altitude Earth-orbit satellites have a rotation period of between 5 and 12 hours and remain in line of sight of a particular earth station for between 2 and 4 hours per orbit. High-altitude earth-orbit satellites in geosynchronous orbits travel at approximately 6840 mph and complete one revolution of Earth in approximately 24 hours.

Geosynchronous orbits are circular; therefore, the speed of rotation is constant throughout the orbit. There is only one geosynchronous earth orbit; however, it is occupied by a large number of satellites. In fact, the geosynchronous orbit is the most widely used earth orbit for the obvious reason that satellites in a geosynchronous orbit remain in a fixed position relative to Earth and, therefore, do not have to be tracked by earth station antennas.

Ideally, geosynchronous satellites should remain stationary above a chosen location over the equator in an equatorial orbit; however, the sun and the moon exert gravitational forces, solar winds sweep past Earth, and Earth is not perfectly spherical. Therefore, these unbalanced forces cause geosynchronous satellites to drift slowly away from their assigned locations in a figure-eight excursion with a 24-hour period that follows a wandering path slightly above and below the equatorial plane. In essence, it occurrs in a special type of inclined orbit sometimes called a *stationary inclined orbit*. Ground controllers must periodically adjust satellite positions to counteract these forces. If not, the excursion above and below the equator would build up at a rate of between 0.6° and 0.9° per year. In addition, geosynchronous satellites in an elliptical orbit also rift in an east or west direction as viewed from Earth. The process of maneuvering a satellite within a preassigned window is called *station keeping.*

There are several requirements for satellites in geostationary orbits. The first and most obvious is that geosynchronous satellites must have a 0° angle of inclination (i.e., the satellite vehicle must be orbiting directly above Earth's equatorial plane). The satellite must also be orbiting in the same direction as Earth's rotation (eastward—toward the morning sun) with the same angular (rotational) velocity—one revolution per day.

The semimajor axis of a geosynchronous earth orbit is the distance from a satellite revolving in the geosynchronous orbit to the center of Earth (i.e., the radius of the orbit measured from Earth's geocenter to the satellite vehicle). Using Kepler's third law as stated in Equation 18-2 with $A = 42241.0979$ and $P = 0.9972$, the semimajor axis α is

$$
\begin{aligned}
\alpha &= AP^{2/3} \\
&= (4224.0979)(0.9972)^{2/3} \\
&= 42,164 \text{ km}
\end{aligned}
\tag{18-3}
$$

Hence, geosynchronous earth-orbit satellites revolve around Earth in a circular pattern directly above the equator 42,164 km from the center of Earth. Because Earth's equatorial radius is approximately 6378 km, the height above mean sea level (h) of a satellite in a geosynchronous orbit around Earth is

$$
\begin{aligned}
h &= 42,164 \text{ km} - 6378 \text{ km} \\
&= 35,768 \text{ km}
\end{aligned}
$$

or approximately 22,300 miles above Earth's surface.

Geosynchronous Satellite Orbital Velocity

The circumference (C) of a geosynchronous orbit is

$$C = 2\pi(42{,}164 \text{ km})$$

$$= 264{,}790 \text{ km}$$

Therefore, the velocity (v) of a geosynchronous satellite is

$$v = \frac{264{,}790 \text{ km}}{24 \text{ hr}}$$

$$= 11{,}033 \text{ km/hr}$$

or
$$v \approx 6840 \text{ mph}$$

Round-Trip Time Delay of Geosynchronous Satellites

The round-trip propagation delay between a satellite and an earth station located directly below it is

$$t = \frac{d}{c}$$

$$= \frac{2(35{,}768 \text{ km})}{3 \times 10^5 \text{ km/s}}$$

$$= 238 \text{ ms}$$

Including the time delay within the earth station and satellite equipment, it takes more than a quarter of a second for an electromagnetic wave to travel from an earth station to a satellite and back when the earth station is located at a point on Earth directly below the satellite. For earth stations located at more distant locations, the propagation delay is even more substantial and can be significant with two-way telephone conversations or data transmissions.

Clarke Orbit

A geosynchronous earth orbit is sometimes referred to as the *Clarke orbit* or *Clarke belt,* after Arthur C. Clarke who first suggested its existence in 1945 and proposed its use for communications satellites. Clarke was an engineer, a scientist, and a science fiction author who wrote several books including *2001: A Space Odyssey.* The Clarke orbit meets the concise set of specifications for geosynchronous satellite orbits: (1) be located directly above the equator, (2) travel in the same direction as Earth's rotation at 6840 mph, (3) have an altitude of 22,300 miles above Earth, and (4) complete one revolution in 24 hours. As shown in Figure 18-7, three satellites in Clarke orbits separated by 120° in longitude can provide communications over the entire globe except the polar regions.

An international agreement initially mandated that all satellites placed in the Clarke orbit must be separated by at least 1833 miles. This stipulation equates to an angular separation of 4° or more, which limits the number of satellite vehicles in a geosynchronous earth orbit to less than 100. Today, however, international agreements allow satellites to be placed much closer together. Figure 18-8 shows the locations of several satellites in geosynchronous orbit around Earth.

Advantages and Disadvantages of Geosynchronous Satellites

The advantages and disadvantages of geosynchronous satellites are as follows:

Advantages
1. Geosynchronous satellites remain almost stationary in respect to a given earth station. Consequently, expensive tracking equipment is not required at the earth stations.
2. Geosynchronous satellites are available to all earth stations within their *shadow* 100% of the time. The shadow of a satellite includes all the earth stations that

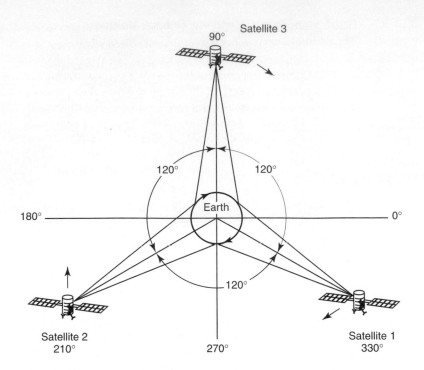

FIGURE 18-7 Three geosynchronous satellites in Clarke orbits

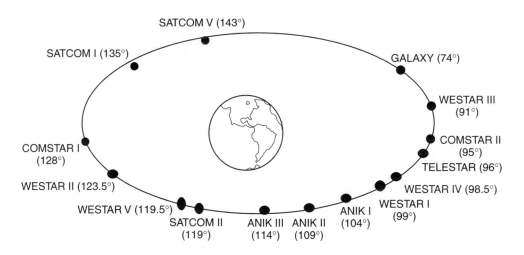

FIGURE 18-8 Satellites in geosynchronous earth orbits

have a line-of-sight path to it and lie within the radiation pattern of the satellite's antennas.

3. There is no need to switch from one geosynchronous satellite to another as they orbit overhead. Consequently, there are no transmission breaks due to switching times.

4. The effects of Doppler shift are negligible

Disadvantages

1. An obvious disadvantage is geosynchronous satellites require sophisticated and heavy propulsion devices on board to keep them in a fixed orbit.

2. High-altitude geosynchronous satellites introduce much longer propagation delays. The round-trip propagation delay between two earth stations through a geosynchronous satellite is between 500 ms and 600 ms.
3. Geosynchronous satellites require higher transmit powers and more sensitive receivers because of the longer distances and greater path loses.
4. High-precision spacemanship is required to place a geosynchronous satellite into orbit and to keep it there. Also, propulsion engines are required on board the satellites to keep them in their respective orbits.

ANTENNA LOOK ANGLES

To optimize the performance of a satellite communications system, the direction of maximum gain of an earth station antenna (sometimes referred to as the *boresight*) must be pointed directly at the satellite. To ensure that the earth station antenna is aligned, two angles must be determined: the *azimuth* and the *elevation angle*. Azimuth angle and elevation angle are jointly referred to as the antenna *look angles*. With geosynchronous satellites, the look angles of earth station antennas only need to be adjusted once as the satellite will remain in a given position permanently, except of occasional minor variations.

The location of a satellite is generally specified in terms of latitude and longitude similar to the way the location of a point on Earth is described; however, because a satellite is orbiting many miles above the Earth's surface, it has no latitude or longitude. Therefore, its location is identified by a point on the surface of earth directly below the satellite. This point is called the *subsatellite point* (SSP) and for geosynchronous satellites the SSP must fall on the equator. Subsatellite points and earth station locations are specified using standard latitude and longitude coordinates. The standard convention specifies angles of longitude between 0° and 180° either east or west of the Greenwich prime meridian. Latitudes in the Northern Hemisphere are angles between 0° and 90° N and latitudes in the Southern Hemisphere are angles between 0° and 90° S. Since geosynchronous satellites are located directly above the equator, they all have a 0° latitude. Hence, geosynchronous satellite locations are normally given in degrees longitude east or west of the Greenwich meridian (for example, 122° W or 78° E). Figure 18-9 shows the position of a hypothetical geosynchronous satellite vehicle (GSV), its respective subsatellite point (SSP), and an arbitrarily selected earth station (ES) all relative to Earth's geocenter. The SSP for the satellite shown in Figure 18-9 is 30° E longitude and 0° latitude. The earth station has a location of 30° W longitude and 20° N latitude.

Angle of Elevation

Angle of elevation (sometimes called *elevation angle*) is the vertical angle formed between the direction of travel of an electromagnetic wave radiated from an earth station antenna pointing directly toward a satellite and the horizontal plane. The smaller the angle of elevation, the greater the distance a propagated wave must pass through Earth's atmosphere. As with any wave propagated through Earth's atmosphere, it suffers absorption and may also be severely contaminated by noise. Consequently, if the angle of elevation is too small and the distance the wave travels through Earth's atmosphere is too long, the wave may deteriorate to the extent that it no longer provides acceptable transmission quality. Generally, 5° is considered as the minimum acceptable angle of elevation. Figure 8-10 shows how the angle of elevation affects the signal strength of a propagated electromagnetic wave due to normal atmospheric absorption, absorption due to thick fog, and absorption due to heavy rainfall. It can be seen that the 14/12-GHz band shown in Figure 18-10b is more severely affected than the 6/4-GHz band shown in Figure 18-10a, due to the smaller wavelengths associated with the higher frequencies. The figure also shows that at elevation angles less than 5°, the amount of signal power lost increases significantly. Figure 18-11a illustrates angle of elevation of an earth station antenna with respect to a horizontal plane.

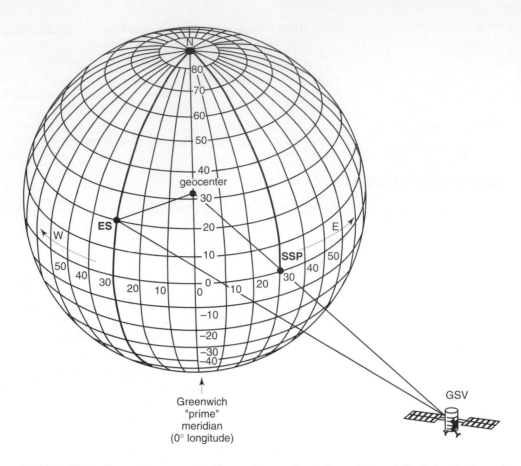

FIGURE 18-9 Geosynchronous satellite position, subsatellite point, and Earth longitude and latitude coordinate system

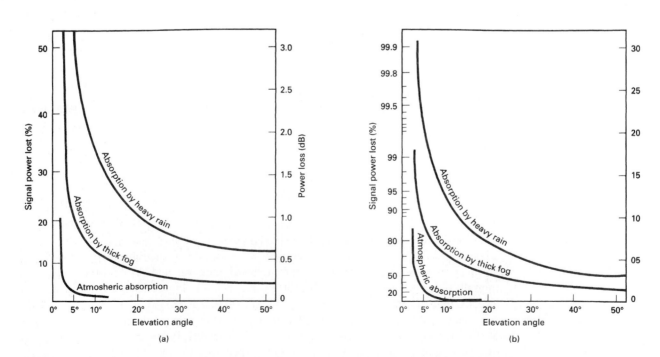

FIGURE 18-10 Attenuation due to atmospheric absorption: (a) 6/4-GHz band; (b) 14/12-GHz band

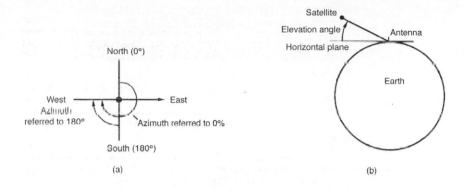

(a)   (b)

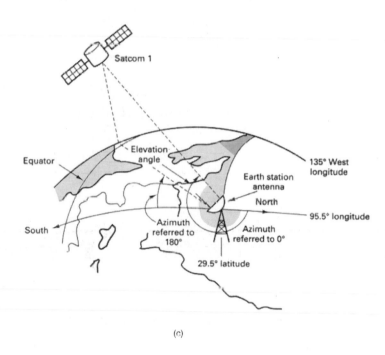

(c)

FIGURE 18-11 Azimuth and angle of elevation, "lookangles"

Azimuth Angle

Azimuth is the horizontal angular distance from a reference direction, either the southern or northern most point of the horizon. *Azimuth angle* is defined as the horizontal pointing angle of an earth station antenna. For navigation purposes, azimuth angle is usually measured in a clockwise direction in degrees form true north. However, for satellite earth stations in the Northern Hemisphere and satellite vehicles in geosynchronous orbits, azimuth angle is generally referenced to true south (i.e., 180°). Figure 18-11b illustrates the azimuth angle referenced to due north (0°) and due south (180°), and Figure 18-11c shows elevation angle and azimuth of an earth station antenna relative to a satellite.

Angle of elevation and azimuth angle both depend on the latitude of the earth station and the longitude of both the earth station and the orbiting satellite. For a geosynchronous satellite in an equatorial orbit, the procedure for determining angle of elevation and azimuth is as follows: From a good map, determine the longitude and latitude of the earth station. From Table 18-1 determine the longitude of the satellite of interest. Calculate the difference, in degrees (ΔL), between the longitude of the satellite and the longitude of the earth station. Then from Figure 18-12 determine the azimuth angle and from Figure 18-13

TABLE 18-1 Longitudinal Position of Several Current Synchronous Satellites Parked in an Equatorial Arc*

Satellite	Longitude (°W)
Satcom I	135
Satcom II	119
Satcom V	143
Satcom C1	137
Satcom C3	131
Anik I	104
Anik 2	109
Anik 3	114
Anik CI	109.25
Anik C2	109.15
Anik C3	114.9
Anik EI	111.1
Anik E2	107.3
Westar I	99
Westar II	123.5
Westar III	91
Westar IV	98.5
Westar V	119.5
Mexico	116.5
Galaxy III	93.5
Galaxy IV	99
Galaxy V	125
Galaxy VI	74
Telstar	96
Comstar I	128
Comstar II	95
Comstar D2	76.6
Comstar D4	75.4
Intelsat 501	268.5
Intelsat 601	27.5
Intelsat 701	186

*0° Latitude

determine the elevation angle. Figures 18-12 and 18-13 are for geosynchronous satellites in equatorial orbits.

Example 18-1

An earth station is located in Houston, Texas, which has a longitude of 95.5° W and a latitude of 29.5° N. The satellite of interest is RCA's *Satcom 1,* which has a longitude of 135° W. Determine the azimuth angle and elevation angle for the earth station.

Solution First determine the difference between the longitude of the earth station and the satellite vehicle.

$$\Delta L = 135° - 95.5°$$
$$= 39.5°$$

Locate the intersection of ΔL and the earth station's latitude on Figure 18-12. From the figure the azimuth angle is approximately 59° west of south (i.e., west of 180°). On Figure 18-13 locate the intersection of ΔL and the earth station's latitude. The angle of elevation is approximately 35°.

Limits of Visibility

For an earth station in any given location, the Earth's curvature establishes the *limits of visibility* (i.e., *line-of-sight limits*) which determine the farthest satellite away that can be seen looking east or west of the earth station's longitude. Theoretically, the maximum line-of-

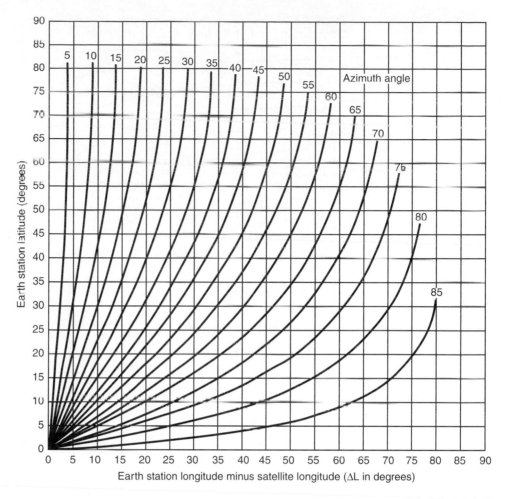

FIGURE 18-12 Azimuth angles for earth stations located in the northern hemisphere referenced to 180 degrees.

sight distance is achieved when the earth station's antenna is pointing along the horizontal (zero elevation angle) plane. In practice, however, the noise picked up from Earth and the signal attenuation from Earth's atmosphere at zero elevation angle is excessive. Therefore, an elevation angle of 5° is generally accepted as being the minimum usable elevation angle. The limits of visibility depend in part on the satellite's elevation and the earth station's longitude and latitude.

SATELLITE CLASSIFICATIONS, SPACING, AND FREQUENCY ALLOCATION

The two primary classifications for communications satellites are *spinners* and *three-axis stabilizer satellites*. A spinner satellite uses the angular momentum of its spinning body to provide roll and yaw stabilization. With a three-axis stabilizer, the body remains fixed relative to Earth's surface while an internal subsystem provides roll and yaw stabilization. Figure 18-14 shows the two main classifications of communications satellites.

Geosynchronous satellites must share a limited space and frequency spectrum within a given arc of a geostationary orbit. Each communications satellite is assigned a longitude in the geostationary arc approximately 22,300 miles above the equator. The position in the

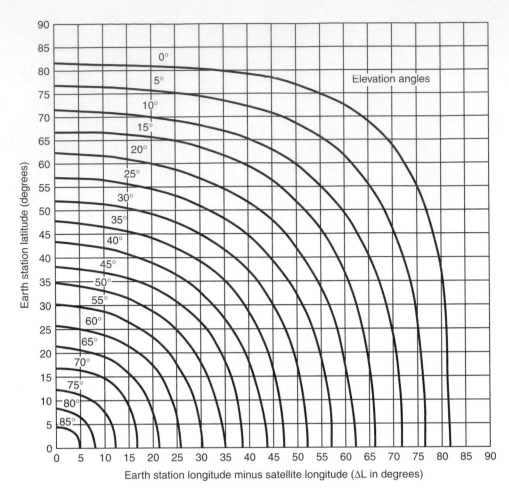

FIGURE 18-13 Elevation angles for earth stations located in the Northern Hemisphere

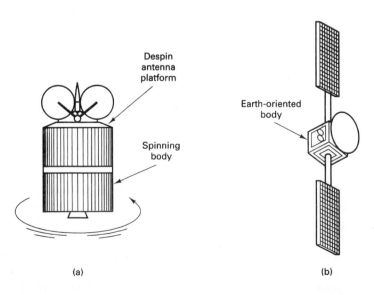

FIGURE 18-14 Satellite classes: (a) spinner; (b) three-axis stabilizer

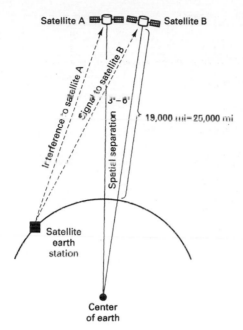

FIGURE 18-15 Spatial separation of satellites in geosynchronous orbit

slot depends on the communications frequency band used. Satellites operating at or near the same frequency must be sufficiently separated in space to avoid interfering with each other (Figure 18-15). There is a realistic limit to the number of satellite structures that can be stationed (*parked*) within a given area in space. The required *spatial separation* is dependent on the following variables.

1. Beamwidths and side lobe radiation of both the earth station and satellite antennas
2. RF carrier frequency
3. Encoding or modulation technique used
4. Acceptable limits of interference
5. Transmit carrier power

Generally, 3° to 6° of spatial separation is required depending on the variables stated above.

The most common carrier frequencies used for satellite communications are the 6/4-GHz and 14/12-GHz bands. The first number is the up-link (earth station-to-transponder) frequency, and the second number is the down-link (transponder-to-earth station) frequency. Different up-link and down-link frequencies are used to prevent ringaround from occurring (Chapter 17). The higher the carrier frequency, the smaller the diameter required of an antenna for a given gain. Most domestic satellites use the 6/4-GHz band. Unfortunately, this band is also used extensively for terrestrial microwave systems. Care must be taken when designing a satellite network to avoid interference from or with established microwave links.

Certain positions in the geosynchronous orbit are in higher demand than the others. For example, the mid-Atlantic position, which is used to interconnect North America and Europe, is in exceptionally high demand; the mid-Pacific position is another.

The frequencies allocated by the World Administrative Radio Conference (WARC) are summarized in Figure 18-16. Table 18-2 shows the bandwidths available for various services in the United States. These services include *fixed-point* (between earth stations located at fixed geographical points on Earth), *broadcast* (wide-area coverage), *mobile* (ground-to-aircraft, ships, or land vehicles), and *intersatellite* (satellite-to-satellite crosslinks).

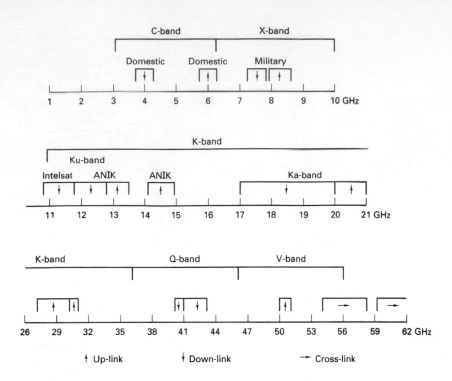

FIGURE 18-16   WARC satellite frequency assignments

TABLE 18-2   Satellite Bandwidths Available in the United States

	Frequency Band (GHz)			
Band	Up-link	Cross-link	Down-link	Bandwidth (MHz)
C	5.9–6.4		3.7–4.2	500
X	7.9–8.4		7.25–7.75	500
Ku	14–14.5		11.7–12.2	500
Ka	27–30		17–20	—
	30–31		20–21	—
Q	—		40–41	1000
	—		41–43	2000
V	50–51		—	1000
(ISL)		54–58		3900
		59–64		5000

SATELLITE ANTENNA RADIATION PATTERNS: FOOTPRINTS

The area on Earth covered by a satellite depends on the location of the satellite in its orbit, its carrier frequency, and the gain of its antenna. Satellite engineers select the antenna and carrier frequency for a particular spacecraft to concentrate the limited transmitted power on a specific area of Earth's surface. The geographical representation of a satellite antenna's radiation pattern is called a *footprint,* or sometimes a *footprint map.* In essence, a footprint of a satellite is the area on Earth's surface that the satellite can receive from or transmit to. The shape of a satellite's footprint depends on the satellite orbital path, height, and the type of antenna used. The higher the satellite, the more of the Earth's surface it can cover. A typical satellite footprint is shown in Figure 18-17. The contour lines represent limits of equal receive power density.

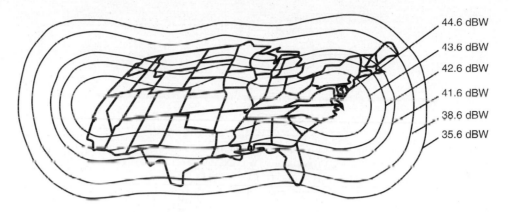

44.6 dBW
43.6 dBW
42.6 dBW
41.6 dBW
38.6 dBW
35.6 dBW

FIGURE 18-17 Satellite antenna radiation patterns (footprints)

Down-link satellite antennas broadcast microwave-frequency signals to a selected geographic region within view (line of sight) of the space craft. The effective power transmitted is called effective isotropic radiated power (EIRP) and is generally expressed in dBm or dBW. A footprint map is constructed by drawing continuous lines between all points on a map with equal EIRPs. A distinctive footprint map is essentially a series of contour lines superimposed upon a geographical map of the region served. A different footprint could exist for each beam from each communications satellite.

The pattern of the contour lines and power levels of a footprint are determined by precise details of the down-link antenna design as well as by the level of microwave power generated by each on-board channel. Although each transponder is a physically separate electronic circuit, signals from multiple transponders are typically down-linked through the same antenna. As might be expected, receive power levels are higher in areas targeted by the down-link antenna boresight and weaker in off-target areas. A receive antenna dish near the edge of a satellite coverage area must be larger than those located at or near the center of the footprint map. Extremely large-diameter earth station antennas are necessary for reception of satellite broadcasts in geographic areas located great distances from the down-link antenna boresight.

Characteristically, there are variations in footprint maps among satellites. For example, European Ku-band spacecraft generally have footprint radiation patterns that are circularly symmetric with power levels that decrease linearly in areas removed progressively further from the center of the satellite's boresight. American C-band satellites typically have relatively flat power levels over the region of coverage with fairly sharp drop-offs in power beyond the edges. Recently launched satellites such as the American DBS-1 (direct-broadcast satellites) have employed more sophisticated beam-shaping down-link antennas that permit designers to shape footprints to reach only specified targeted areas, hence not wasting power in nontargeted areas.

It is possible to design satellite down-link antennas that can broadcast microwave signals to cover areas on Earth ranging in size from extremely small cities to as much as 42% of the Earth's surface. The size, shape, and orientation of a satellite down-link antenna and the power generated by each transponder determine geographic coverage and EIRPs. Radiation patterns from a satellite antenna are generally categorized as either *spot, zonal, hemispherical,* or *earth* (global). The radiation patterns are shown in Figure 18-18.

Spot and Zonal Beams

The smallest beams are *spot beams* followed by *zonal beams.* Spot beams concentrate their power to very small geographical areas and, therefore, typically have proportionately higher EIRPs than those targeting much larger areas because a given output power can be more concentrated. Spot and zonal beams blanket less than 10% of the earth's surface. The

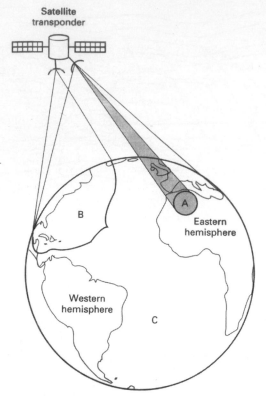

Satellite
transponder

B

A

Eastern
hemisphere

Western
hemisphere

C

FIGURE 18-18 Beams: (a) spot;
(b) zonal; (c) earth

higher the down-link frequency, the more easily a beam can be focused into a smaller spot pattern. For example, the new breed of high-power Ku-band satellites can have multiple spot beams that relay the same frequencies by transmitting different signals to areas within a given country. In general, most Ku-band footprints do not blanket entire continental areas and have a more limited geographic coverage than their C-band counterparts. Therefore, a more detailed knowledge of the local EIRP is important when attempting to receive broadcasts from Ku-band satellite transmissions.

Hemispherical Beams
Hemispherical down-link antennas typically target up to 20% of the Earth's surface and, therefore, have EIRPs that are 3 dB or 50% lower than those transmitted by spot beams that typically cover only 10% of the Earth's surface.

Earth (Global) Beams
The radiation patterns of *earth coverage* antennas have a beamwidth of approximately 17° and are capable of covering approximately 42% of Earth's surface which is the maximum view of any one geosynchronous satellite. Power levels are considerably lower with earth beams than with spot, zonal, or hemispherical beams and large receive dishes are necessary to adequately detect video, audio, and data broadcasts.

Reuse
When an allocated frequency band is filled, additional capacity can be achieved by *reuse* of the frequency spectrum. By increasing the size of an antenna (i.e., increasing the antenna gain) the beamwidth of the antenna is also reduced. Thus, different beams of the same frequency can be directed to different geographical areas of Earth. This is called frequency reuse. Another method of frequency reuse is to use dual polarization. Different information

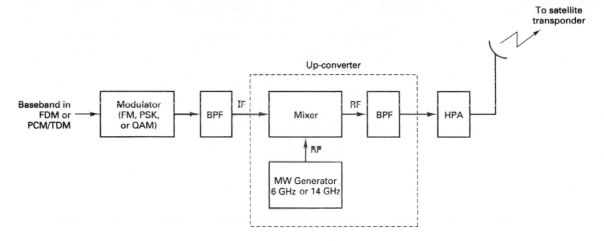

FIGURE 18-19 Satellite up-link model

signals can be transmitted to different earth station receivers using the same band of frequencies simply by orienting their electromagnetic polarizations in an orthogonal manner (90° out of phase). Dual polarization is less effective because Earth's atmosphere has a tendency to reorient or repolarize an electromagnetic wave as it passes through. Reuse is simply another way to increase the capacity of a limited bandwidth.

SATELLITE SYSTEM LINK MODELS

Essentially, a satellite system consists of three basic sections: an up-link, a satellite transponder, and a down-link.

Up-Link Model

The primary component within the *up-link* section of a satellite system is the earth station transmitter. A typical earth station transmitter consists of an IF modulator, an IF-to-RF microwave up-converter, a high-power amplifier (HPA), and some means of bandlimiting the final output spectrum (i.e., an output bandpass filter). Figure 18-19 shows the block diagram of a satellite earth station transmitter. The IF modulator converts the input baseband signals to either an FM, a PSK, or a QAM modulated intermediate frequency. The up-converter (mixer and bandpass filter) converts the IF to an appropriate RF carrier frequency. The HPA provides adequate input sensitivity and output power to propagate the signal to the satellite transponder. HPAs commonly used are klystons and traveling-wave tubes.

Transponder

A typical *satellite transponder* consists of an input bandlimiting device (BPF), an input *low-noise amplifier* (LNA), a *frequency translator,* a low-level power amplifier, and an output bandpass filter. Figure 18-20 shows a simplified block diagram of a satellite transponder. This transponder is an RF-to-RF repeater. Other transponder configurations are IF and baseband repeaters similar to those used in microwave repeaters. In Figure 18-20, the input BPF limits the total noise applied to the input of the LNA. (A common device used as an LNA is a tunnel diode.) The output of the LNA is fed to a frequency translator (a shift oscillator and a BPF), which converts the high-band up-link frequency to the low-band down-link frequency. The low-level power amplifier, which is commonly a traveling-wave tube, amplifies the RF signal for transmission through the down-link to earth station receivers. Each RF satellite channel requires a separate transponder.

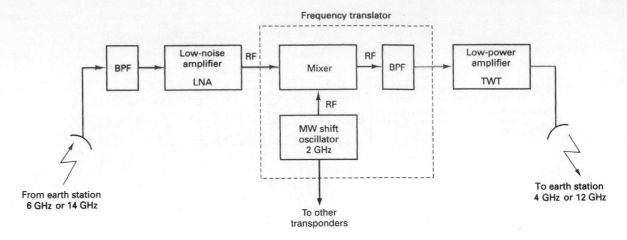

FIGURE 18-20   Satellite transponder

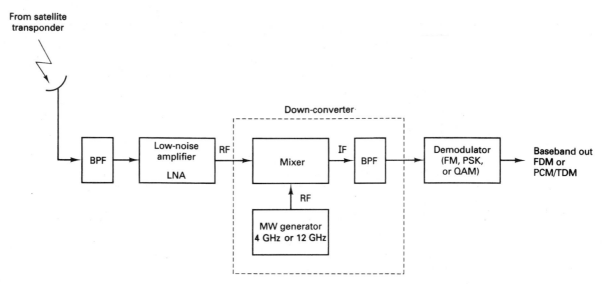

FIGURE 18-21   Satellite down-link model

Down-Link Model

An earth station receiver includes an input BPF, an LNA, and an RF-to-IF down-converter. Figure 18-21 shows a block diagram of a typical earth station receiver. Again, the BPF limits the input noise power to the LNA. The LNA is a highly sensitive, low-noise device such as a tunnel diode amplifier or a parametric amplifier. The RF-to-IF down-converter is a mixer/bandpass filter combination which converts the received RF signal to an IF frequency.

Cross-Links

Occasionally, there is an application where it is necessary to communicate between satellites. This is done using *satellite cross-links* or *intersatellite links* (ISLs), shown in Figure 18-22. A disadvantage of using an ISL is that both the transmitter and receiver are *space bound*. Consequently, both the transmitter's output power and the receiver's input sensitivity are limited.

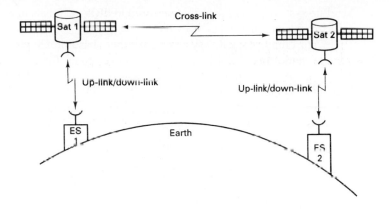

FIGURE 18-22 Intersatellite link

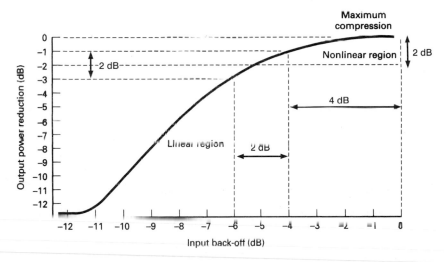

FIGURE 18-23 HPA input/output characteristic curve

SATELLITE SYSTEM PARAMETERS

Back-Off Loss

High-power amplifiers used in earth station transmitters and the traveling-wave tubes typically used in satellite transponders are *nonlinear devices;* their gain (output power versus–input power) is dependent on input signal level. A typical input/output power characteristic curve is shown in Figure 18-23. It can be seen that as the input power is reduced by 4 dB, the output power is reduced by only 1 dB. There is an obvious *power compression.* To reduce the amount of intermodulation distortion caused by the nonlinear amplification of the HPA, the input power must be reduced (*backed off*) by several dB. This allows the HPA to operate in a more *linear* region. The amount the output level is backed off from rated levels is equivalent to a loss and is appropriately called *back-off loss* (L_{bo}).

Transmit Power and Bit Energy

To operate as efficiently as possible, a power amplifier should be operated as close as possible to saturation. The *saturated output power* is designated $P_{o(sat)}$ or simply P_t. The output power of a typical satellite earth station transmitter is much higher than the output power from a terrestrial microwave power amplifier. Consequently, when dealing with satellite systems, P_t is generally expressed in dBW (decibels in respect to 1 W) rather than in dBm (decibels in respect to 1 mW).

Most modern satellite systems use either phase shift keying (PSK) or quadrature amplitude modulation (QAM) rather than conventional frequency modulation (FM). With PSK and QAM, the input baseband is generally a PCM-encoded, time-division-multiplexed signal that is digital in nature. Also, with PSK and QAM, several bits may be encoded in a single transmit signaling element. Consequently, a parameter more meaningful than carrier power is *energy per bit* (E_b). Mathematically, E_b is

$$E_b = P_t T_b \qquad (18\text{-}4)$$

where E_b = energy of a single bit (joules per bit)
$\qquad P_t$ = total saturated output power (watts or joules per second)
$\qquad T_b$ = time of a single bit (seconds)

or because $T_b = 1/f_b$, where f_b is the bit rate in bits per second,

$$E_b = \frac{P_t}{f_b} = \frac{J/s}{b/s} = \frac{Joules}{bit} \qquad (18\text{-}5)$$

Example 18-2

For a total transmit power (P_t) of 1000 W, determine the energy per bit (E_b) for a transmission rate of 50 Mbps.

Solution

$$T_b = \frac{1}{f_b} = \frac{1}{50 \times 10^6 \text{ bps}} = 0.02 \times 10^{-6}\,\text{s}$$

(It appears that the units for T_b should be s/bit but the per bit is implied in the definition of T_b, time of bit.)

Substituting into Equation 18-4 yields
$$E_b = 1000\ \text{J/s}\ (0.02 \times 10^{-6}\ \text{s/bit}) = 20\ \mu\text{J}$$
(Again the units appear to be J/bit, but the per bit is implied in the definition of E_b, energy per bit.)

$$E_b = \frac{1000\ \text{J/s}}{50 \times 10^6\ \text{bps}} = 20\ \mu\text{J}$$

Expressed as a log with 1 joule as the reference,
$$E_b = 10 \log (20 \times 10^{-6}) = -47\ \text{dBJ}$$
It is common to express P_t in dBW and E_b in dBW/bps. Thus,
$$P_t = 10 \log 1000 = 30\ \text{dBW}$$
$$E_b = P_t - 10 \log f_b = P_t - 10 \log (50 \times 10^6)$$
$$= 30\ \text{dBW} - 77\ \text{dB} = -47\ \text{dBW/bps}$$

or simply -47 dBJ.

Effective Isotropic Radiated Power

Effective isotropic radiated power (EIRP) is defined as an equivalent transmit power and is expressed mathematically as

$$\text{EIRP} = P_{in}A_t$$

where EIRP = effective isotropic radiated power (watts)
$\qquad P_{in}$ = antenna input power (watts)
$\qquad A_t$ = transmit antenna gain (unitless ratio)

Expressed as a log,

$$\text{EIRP}_{(dBW)} = P_{in(dBW)} + A_{t(dB)}$$

In respect to the transmitter output,

$$P_{in} = P_t - L_{bo} - L_{bf}$$

Thus,
$$EIRP = P_t - L_{bo} - L_{bf} + A_t \qquad (18\text{-}6)$$

where P_{in} = antenna input power (dBW per watt)
L_{bo} = back-off losses of HPA (decibels)
L_{bf} = total branching and feeder loss (decibels)
A_t = transmit antenna gain (decibels)
P_t = saturated amplifier output power (dBW per watt)

Example 18-3

For an earth station transmitter with an antenna input power of 40 dBW (10,000 W), a back-off loss of 3 dB, a total branching and feeder loss of 3 dB, and a transmit antenna gain of 40 dB, determine the EIRP.

Solution Substituting into Equation 18-6 yields

$$EIRP = P_{in} - L_{bo} - L_{bf} + A_t$$
$$= 40 \text{ dBW} - 3 \text{ dB} - 3 \text{ dB} + 40 \text{ dB} = 74 \text{ dBW}$$

Equivalent Noise Temperature

With terrestrial microwave systems, the noise introduced in a receiver or a component within a receiver was commonly specified by the parameter noise figure. In satellite communications systems, it is often necessary to differentiate or measure noise in increments as small as a tenth or a hundredth of a decibel. Noise figure, in its standard form, is inadequate for such precise calculations. Consequently, it is common to use *environmental temperature* (T) and *equivalent noise temperature* (T_e) when evaluating the performance of a satellite system. In Chapter 17 total noise power was expressed mathematically as

$$N = KTB \qquad (18\text{-}7a)$$

Rearranging and solving for T gives us

$$T = \frac{N}{KB} \qquad (18\text{-}7b)$$

where N = total noise power (watts)
K = Boltzmann's constant (joules per kelvin)
B = bandwidth (hertz)
T = temperature of the environment (kelvins)

Again from Chapter 17,

$$F = 1 + \frac{T_e}{T} \qquad (18\text{-}8a)$$

where T_e = equivalent noise temperature (kelvin)
F = noise factor (unitless)
T = temperature of the environment (kelvin)

Rearranging Equation 18-8a, we have

$$T_e = T(F - 1) \qquad (18\text{-}8b)$$

Typically, equivalent noise temperatures of the receivers used in satellite transponders are about 1000 K. For earth station receivers T_e values are between 20 K and 1000 K. Equivalent noise temperature is generally more useful when expressed logarithmically referenced to 1°K with the unit of dBK, as follows:

$$T_{e(dBK)} = 10 \log T_e \qquad (18\text{-}8c)$$

TABLE 18-3 Noise Unit Comparison

Noise Factor (F) (unitless)	Noise Figure (NF) (dB)	Equivalent Temperature (T_e) (°K)	dBK
1.2	0.79	60	17.78
1.3	1.14	90	19.54
1.4	1.46	120	20.79
2.5	4	450	26.53
10	10	2700	34.31

For an equivalent noise temperature of 100 K, $T_{e(dBK)}$ is

$$T_e = 10 \log 100 \quad \text{or} \quad 20 \text{ dBK}$$

Equivalent noise temperature is a hypothetical value that can be calculated but cannot be measured. Equivalent noise temperature is often used rather than noise figure, because it is a more accurate method of expressing the noise contributed by a device or a receiver when evaluating its performance. Essentially, equivalent noise temperature (T_e) represents the noise power present at the input to a device plus the noise added internally by that device. This allows us to analyze the noise characteristics of a device by simply evaluating an equivalent input noise temperature. As you will see in subsequent discussions, T_e is a very useful parameter when evaluating the performance of a satellite system.

Noise factor, noise figure, equivalent noise temperature, and dBK are summarized in Table 18-3.

Example 18-4

Convert noise figures of 4 dB and 4.1 dB to equivalent noise temperatures. Use 300 K for the environmental temperature.

Solution   Converting the noise figures to noise factors yields,

$$NF = 4 \text{ dB}, F = 2.512$$
$$NF = 4.1 \text{ dB}, F = 2.57$$

Substituting into Equation 18-8b yields

$$T_e = 300(2.512 - 1)$$
$$= 453.6 \text{ K}$$
$$T_e = 300(2.57 - 1)$$
$$= 471 \text{ K}$$

From Example 18-4, it can be seen that a 0.1-dB difference in the two noise figures equated to a 17.4° difference in the two equivalent noise temperatures. Hence, equivalent noise temperature is a more accurate method of comparing the noise performances of two receivers or devices.

Noise Density

Simply stated, *noise density* (N_0) is the noise power normalized to a 1-Hz bandwidth, or the noise power present in a 1-Hz bandwidth. Mathematically, noise density is

$$N_0 = \frac{N}{B} = \frac{KT_eB}{B} = KT_e \tag{18-9}$$

where N_0 = noise density (watts/per hertz) (N_0 is generally expressed as simply watts; the
per hertz is implied in the definition of N_0), 1 W/Hz = $\dfrac{1 \text{ joule/sec}}{1 \text{ cycle/sec}} = \dfrac{1 \text{ joule}}{\text{cycle}}$

N = total noise power (watts)

B = bandwidth (hertz)

K = Boltzmann's constant (joules/per kelvin)

T_e = equivalent noise temperature (kelvin)

Expressed as a log with 1 W/Hz as the reference,

$$N_{0(dBW/Hz)} = 10 \log N - 10 \log B \qquad (18\text{-}10)$$

$$= 10 \log K + 10 \log T_e \qquad (18\text{-}11)$$

Example 18-5

For an equivalent noise bandwidth of 10 MHz and a total noise power of 0.0276 pW, determine the noise density and equivalent noise temperature.

Solution Substituting into Equation 18-9, we have

$$N_0 = \frac{N}{B} = \frac{276 \times 10^{-16}\text{W}}{10 \times 10^6 \text{ Hz}} = 276 \times 10^{-23} \text{ W/Hz}$$

or simply, 276×10^{-23} W.

$$N_0 = 10 \log (276 \times 10^{-23}) = -205.6 \text{ dBW/Hz}$$

or simply -205.6 dBW. Substituting into Equation 18-10 gives us

$$N_0 = 10 \log 276 \times 10^{-16} - 10 \log 10 \text{ MHz}$$

$$= -135.6 \text{ dBW} - 70 \text{ dB} = -205.6 \text{ dBW}$$

Rearranging Equation 18-9 and solving for equivalent noise temperature yields

$$T_e = \frac{N_0}{K}$$

$$= \frac{276 \times 10^{-23} \text{ J/cycle}}{1.38 \times 10^{-23} \text{ J/K}} = 200 \text{ K/cycle}$$

$$= 10 \log 200 = 23 \text{ dBK}$$

$$= N_0 - 10 \log K = N_0 - 10 \log 1.38 \times 10^{-23}$$

$$= -205.6 \text{ dBW} - (-228.6 \text{ dBWK}) = 23 \text{ dBK}$$

Carrier-to-Noise Density Ratio

C/N_0 is the average wideband carrier power-to-noise density ratio. The *wideband carrier power* is the combined power of the carrier and its associated sidebands. The noise density is the thermal noise present in a normalized 1-Hz bandwidth. The carrier-to-noise density ratio may also be written as a function of noise temperature. Mathematically, C/N_0 is

$$\frac{C}{N_0} = \frac{C}{KT_e} \qquad (18\text{-}12)$$

Expressed as a log,

$$\frac{C}{N_0}(\text{dB}) = C_{(dBW)} - N_{0(dBW)} \qquad (18\text{-}13)$$

Energy of Bit-to-Noise Density Ratio

E_b/N_0 is one of the most important and most often used parameters when evaluating a digital radio system. The E_b/N_0 ratio is a convenient way to compare digital systems that use different transmission rates, modulation schemes, or encoding techniques. Mathematically, E_b/N_0 is

$$\frac{E_b}{N_0} = \frac{C/f_b}{N/B} = \frac{CB}{Nf_b} \qquad (18\text{-}14)$$

E_b/N_0 is a convenient term used for digital system calculations and performance comparisons, but in the real world, it is more convenient to measure the wideband carrier power–to–noise density ratio and convert it to E_b/N_0. Rearranging Equation 18-14 yields the following expression:

$$\frac{E_b}{N_0} = \frac{C}{N} \times \frac{B}{f_b}$$

The E_b/N_0 ratio is the product of the carrier-to-noise ratio (C/N) and the noise bandwidth-to-bit rate ratio (B/f_b). Expressed as a log,

$$\frac{E_b}{N_0}(dB) = \frac{C}{N}(dB) + \frac{B}{f_b}(dB) \qquad (18\text{-}15)$$

The energy per bit (E_b) will remain constant as long as the total wideband carrier power (C) and the transmission rate (bps) remain unchanged. Also, the noise density (N_0) will remain constant as long as the noise temperature remains constant. The following conclusion can be made: For a given carrier power, bit rate, and noise temperature, the E_b/N_0 ratio will remain constant regardless of the encoding technique, modulation scheme, or bandwidth used so long as the bandwidth equals the bit rate.

Figure 18-24 graphically illustrates the relationship between an expected probability of error $P(e)$ and the minimum C/N ratio required to achieve the $P(e)$. The C/N specified is for the minimum double-sided Nyquist bandwidth. Figure 18-25 graphically illustrates the relationship between an expected $P(e)$ and the minimum E_b/N_0 ratio required to achieve that $P(e)$.

A $P(e)$ of 10^{-5} ($1/10^5$) indicates a probability that 1 bit will be in error for every 100,000 bits transmitted. $P(e)$ is analogous to the bit error rate (BER).

Example 18-6

A coherent binary phase-shift-keyed (BPSK) transmitter operates at a bit rate of 20 Mbps. For a probability of error $P(e)$ of 10^{-4}:

(a) Determine the minimum theoretical C/N and E_b/N_0 ratios for a receiver bandwidth equal to the minimum double-sided Nyquist bandwidth.

(b) Determine the C/N if the noise is measured at a point prior to the bandpass filter, where the bandwidth is equal to twice the Nyquist bandwidth.

(c) Determine the C/N if the noise is measured at a point prior to the bandpass filter where the bandwidth is equal to three times the Nyquist bandwidth.

Solution (a) With BPSK, the minimum bandwidth is equal to the bit rate, 20 MHz. From Figure 18-24, the minimum C/N is 8.8 dB. Substituting into Equation 18-15 gives us

$$\frac{E_b}{N_0} = \frac{C}{N} + \frac{B}{f_b}$$

$$= 8.8\ dB + 10 \log \frac{20 \times 10^6}{20 \times 10^6}$$

$$= 8.8\ dB + 0\ dB = 8.8\ dB$$

Note: The minimum E_b/N_0 equals the minimum C/N when the receiver noise bandwidth equals the bit rate which for BPSK also equals the minimum Nyquist bandwidth. The minimum E_b/N_0 of 8.8 can be verified from Figure 18-25.

What effect does increasing the noise bandwidth have on the minimum C/N and E_b/N_0 ratios? The wideband carrier power is totally independent of the noise bandwidth. However, an increase in the bandwidth causes a corresponding increase in the noise power. Consequently, a decrease in C/N is realized that is directly proportional to the increase in the noise bandwidth. E_b is dependent on the wideband carrier power and the bit rate only. Therefore, E_b is unaffected by an increase in the noise bandwidth. N_0 is the noise power normalized to a 1-Hz bandwidth and, consequently, is also unaffected by an increase in the noise bandwidth.

(b) Because E_b/N_0 is independent of bandwidth, measuring the C/N at a point in the receiver where the bandwidth is equal to twice the minimum Nyquist bandwidth has absolutely no effect on E_b/N_0. Therefore, E_b/N_0 becomes the constant in Equation 18-15 and is used to solve for the new value of C/N. Rearranging Equation 18-15 and using the calculated E_b/N_0 ratio, we have

$$\frac{C}{N} = \frac{E_b}{N_0} - \frac{B}{f_b}$$

$$= 8.8 \text{ dB} - 10 \log \frac{40 \times 10^6}{20 \times 10^6}$$

$$= 8.8 \text{ dB} - 10 \log 2$$

$$= 8.8 \text{ dB} - 3 \text{ dB} = 5.8 \text{ dB}$$

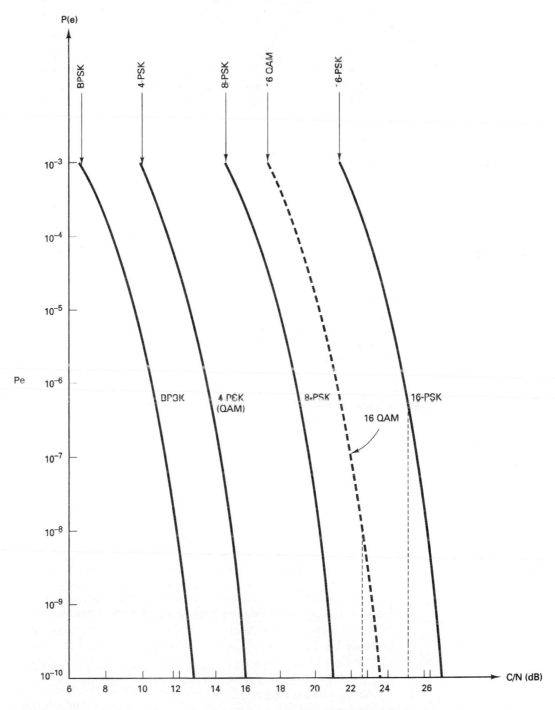

FIGURE 10-24 $P(e)$ performance of M-ary PSK, QAM, QPR, and M-ary APK coherent systems. The rms C/N is specified in the double-sided Nyquist bandwidth

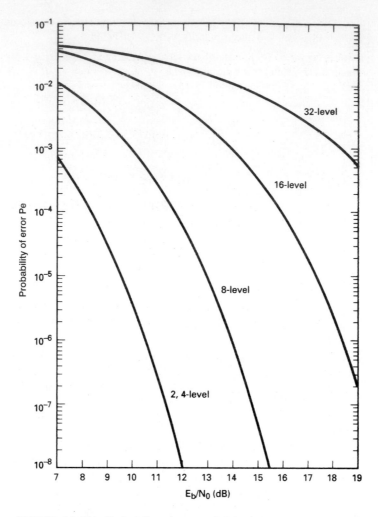

FIGURE 18-25 Probability of error $P(e)$ versus E_b/N_0 ratio for various digital modulation schemes

(c) Measuring the C/N ratio at a point in the receiver where the bandwidth equals three times the minimum bandwidth yields the following results for C/N.

$$\frac{C}{N} = \frac{E_b}{N_0} - 10 \log \frac{60 \times 10^6}{20 \times 10^6}$$

$$= 8.8 \text{ dB} - 10 \log 3 = 4.03 \text{ dB}$$

The C/N ratios of 8.8, 5.8, and 4.03 dB indicate the C/N ratios that could be measured at the three specified points in the receiver and still achieve the desired minimum E_b/N_0 and $P(e)$.

Because E_b/N_0 cannot be directly measured to determine the E_b/N_0 ratio, the wideband carrier-to-noise ratio is measured and, then, substituted into Equation 18-15. Consequently, to accurately determine the E_b/N_0 ratio, the noise bandwidth of the receiver must be known.

Example 18-7

A coherent 8-PSK transmitter operates at a bit rate of 90 Mbps. For a probability of error of 10^{-5}:
(a) Determine the minimum theoretical C/N and E_b/N_0 ratios for a receiver bandwidth equal to the minimum double-sided Nyquist bandwidth.
(b) Determine the C/N if the noise is measured at a point prior to the bandpass filter where the bandwidth is equal to twice the Nyquist bandwidth.

(c) Determine the C/N if the noise is measured at a point prior to the bandpass filter where the bandwidth is equal to three times the Nyquist bandwidth.

Solution (a) 8-PSK has a bandwidth efficiency of 3 bps/Hz and, consequently, requires a minimum bandwidth of one-third the bit rate or 30 MHz. From Figure 18-24, the minimum C/N is 18.5 dB. Substituting into Equation 18-15, we obtain

$$\frac{E_b}{N_0} = 18.5 \text{ dB} + 10 \log \frac{30 \text{ MHz}}{90 \text{ Mbps}}$$

$$= 18.5 \text{ dB} + (-4.8 \text{ dB}) = 13.7 \text{ dB}$$

(b) Rearranging Equation 18-15 and substituting for E_b/N_0 yields

$$\frac{C}{N} = 13.7 \text{ dB} - 10 \log \frac{60 \text{ MHz}}{90 \text{ Mbps}}$$

$$= 13.7 \text{ dB} - (-1.77 \text{ dB}) = 15.47 \text{ dB}$$

(c) Again, rearranging Equation 18-15 and substituting for E_b/N_0 gives us

$$\frac{C}{N} = 13.7 \text{ dB} - 10 \log \frac{90 \text{ MHz}}{90 \text{ Mbps}}$$

$$= 13.7 \text{ dB} - 0 \text{ (dB)} = 13.7 \text{ dB}$$

It should be evident from Examples 18-6 and 18-7 that the E_b/N_0 and C/N ratios are equal only when the noise bandwidth is equal to the bit rate. Also, as the bandwidth at the point of measurement increases, the C/N decreases.

When the modulation scheme, bit rate, bandwidth, and C/N ratios of two digital radio systems are different, it is often difficult to determine which system has the lower probability of error. E_b/N_0 is independent of bandwidth and modulation scheme, so it is a convenient common denominator to use for comparing the probability of error performance of two digital radio systems.

Gain-to-Equivalent Noise Temperature Ratio

Essentially, *gain-to-equivalent noise temperature ratio* (G/T_e) is a figure of merit used to represent the quality of a satellite or an earth station receiver. The G/T_e of a receiver is the ratio of the receive antenna gain to the equivalent noise temperature (T_e) of the receiver. Because of the extremely small receive carrier powers typically experienced with satellite systems, very often an LNA is physically located at the feedpoint of the antenna. When this is the case, G/T_e is a ratio of the gain of the receiving antenna plus the gain of the LNA to the equivalent noise temperature. Mathematically, gain-to-equivalent noise temperature ratio is

$$\frac{G}{T_e} = \frac{A_r + A_{(LNA)}}{T_e} \tag{18-16}$$

Expressed in logs, we have

$$\frac{G}{T_e} (\text{dBK}^{-1}) = A_{r(dB)} + A_{(LNA)(dB)} - T_{e(dBK)} \tag{18-17}$$

G/T_e is a useful parameter for determining the E_b/N_0 and C/N ratios at the satellite transponder and earth station receivers. G/T_e is essentially the only parameter required at a satellite or an earth station receiver when completing a link budget.

Example 18-8

For a satellite transponder with a receiver antenna gain of 12 dB, an LNA gain of 10 dB, and an equivalent noise temperature of 26 dBK, determine the G/T_e figure of merit.

Solution Substituting into Equation 18-17 yields

$$\frac{G}{T_e} = 12 \text{ dB} + 10 \text{ dB} - 26 \text{ dBK} = -4 \text{ dBK}^{-1}$$

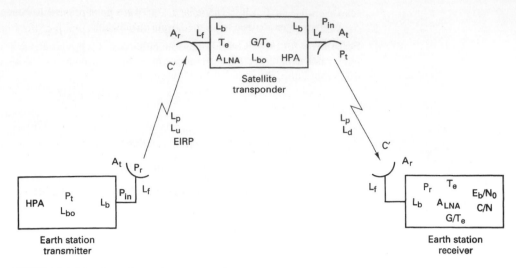

FIGURE 18-26 Overall satellite system showing the gains and losses incurred in both the up-link and down-link sections. HPA, high-power amplifier; P_t, HPA output power; L_{bo}, back-off loss; L_f, feeder loss; L_b, branching loss; A_t, transmit antenna gain; P_r, total radiated power $= P_t - L_{bo} - L_b - L_f$; EIRP, effective isotropic radiated power $P_{in} A_t$; L_u, additional up-link losses due to atmosphere; L_p, path loss; A_r, receive antenna gain; G/T_e, gain-to-equivalent noise ratio; L_d, additional down-link losses due to atmosphere; LNA, low-noise amplifier; C/T_e, carrier-to-equivalent noise ratio; C/N_0, carrier-to-noise density ratio; E_b/N_0, energy of bit-to-noise density ratio; C/N, carrier-to-noise ratio

SATELLITE SYSTEM LINK EQUATIONS

The error performance of a digital satellite system is quite predictable. Figure 18-26 shows a simplified block diagram of a digital satellite system and identifies the various gains and losses that may affect the system performance. When evaluating the performance of a digital satellite system, the up-link and down-link parameters are first considered separately, then the overall performance is determined by combining them in the appropriate manner. Keep in mind, a digital microwave or satellite radio simply means that the original and demodulated baseband signals are digital in nature. The RF portion of the radio is analog, that is, FSK, PSK, QAM, or some other higher-level modulation riding on an analog microwave carrier.

LINK EQUATIONS

The following *link equations* are used to separately analyze the up-link and down-link sections of a single radio-frequency carrier satellite system. These equations consider only the ideal gains and losses and effects of thermal noise associated with the earth station transmitter, earth station receiver, and the satellite transponder.

Up-Link Equation

$$\frac{C}{N_0} = \frac{A_t P_{in}(L_p L_u) A_r}{K T_e} = \frac{A_t P_{in}(L_p L_u)}{K} \times \frac{G}{T_e}$$

where L_d and L_u are the additional up-link and down-link atmospheric losses, respectively. The up-link and down-link signals must pass through Earth's atmosphere, where they are partially absorbed by the moisture, oxygen, and particulates in the air. Depending on the elevation angle, the distance the RF signal travels through the atmosphere varies from one earth station to another. Because L_p, L_u, and L_d represent losses, they are decimal values less than 1. G/T_e is the receive antenna gain plus the gain of the LNA divided by the equivalent input noise temperature.

Expressed as a log,

$$\frac{C}{N_0} = \underbrace{10 \log A_t P_{in}}_{\substack{\text{EIRP} \\ \text{earth} \\ \text{station}}} - \underbrace{20 \log\left(\frac{4\pi D}{\lambda}\right)}_{\substack{\text{free-space} \\ \text{path loss} \\ L_p}} + \underbrace{10 \log\left(\frac{G}{T_e}\right)}_{\substack{\text{satellite} \\ G/T_e}} - \underbrace{10 \log I_u}_{\substack{\text{additional} \\ \text{atmospheric} \\ \text{losses}}} - \underbrace{10 \log K}_{\substack{\text{Boltzmann's} \\ \text{constant}}} \quad (18\text{-}18)$$

$$= \text{EIRP (dBW)} - L_p\,(\text{dB}) + \frac{G}{T_e}\,(\text{dBK}^{-1}) - L_u\,(\text{dB}) - K\,(\text{dBWK}) \quad (18\text{-}19)$$

Down-Link Equation

$$\frac{C}{N_0} - \frac{A_t P_{in}(L_p L_d)A_r}{KT_e} = \frac{A_t P_{in}(L_p L_d)}{K} \times \frac{G}{T_e}$$

Expressed as a log

$$\frac{C}{N_0} = \underbrace{10 \log A_t P_{in}}_{\substack{\text{EIRP} \\ \text{satellite}}} - \underbrace{20 \log\left(\frac{4\pi D}{\lambda}\right)}_{\substack{\text{free-space} \\ \text{path loss} \\ L_p}} + \underbrace{10 \log\left(\frac{G}{T_e}\right)}_{\substack{\text{earth} \\ \text{station} \\ G/T_e}} - \underbrace{10 \log L_d}_{\substack{\text{additional} \\ \text{atmospheric} \\ \text{losses}}} - \underbrace{10 \log K}_{\substack{\text{Boltzmann's} \\ \text{constant}}}$$

$$= \text{EIRP (dBW)} - L_p\,(\text{dB}) + \frac{G}{T_e}\,(\text{dBK}^{-1}) - L_d\,(\text{dB}) - K\,(\text{dBWK})$$

LINK BUDGET

Table 18-4 lists the system parameters for three typical satellite communication systems. The systems and their parameters are not necessarily for an existing or future system; they are hypothetical examples only. The system parameters are used to construct a *link budget*. A link budget identifies the system parameters and is used to determine the projected C/N and E_b/N_0 ratios at both the satellite and earth station receivers for a given modulation scheme and desired $P(e)$.

Example 18-9

Complete the link budget for a satellite system with the following parameters.

Up-link
1. Earth station transmitter output power at saturation, 2000 W	33	dBW
2. Earth station back-off loss	3	dB
3. Earth station branching and feeder losses	4	dB
4. Earth station transmit antenna gain (from Figure 18-27, 15 m at 14 GHz)	64	dB
5. Additional up-link atmospheric losses	0.6	dB
6. Free-space path loss (from Figure 18-28, at 14 GHz)	206.5	dB
7. Satellite receiver G/T_e ratio	−5.3	dBK^{-1}
8. Satellite branching and feeder losses	0	dB
9. Bit rate	120	Mbps
10. Modulation scheme		8-PSK

TABLE 18-4 System Parameters for Three Hypothetical Satellite Systems

	System A: 6/4 GHz, earth coverage QPSK modulation. 60 Mbps	System B: 14/12 GHz, earth coverage 8-PSK modulation, 90 Mbps	System C: 14/12 GHz, earth coverage 8-PSK modulation, 120 Mbps
Up-link			
Transmitter output power (saturation, dBW)	35	25	33
Earth station back-off loss (dB)	2	2	3
Earth station branching and feeder loss (dB)	3	3	4
Additional atmospheric (dB)	0.6	0.4	0.6
Earth station antenna gain (dB)	55	45	64
Free-space path loss (dB)	200	208	206.5
Satellite receive antenna gain (dB)	20	45	23.7
Satellite branching and feeder loss (dB)	1	1	0
Satellite equivalent noise temperature (K)	1000	800	800
Satellite G/T_e (dBK^{-1})	−10	16	−5.3
Down-link			
Transmitter output power (saturation, dBW)	18	20	10
Satellite back-off loss (dB)	0.5	0.2	0.1
Satellite branching and feeder loss (dB)	1	1	0.5
Additional atmospheric loss (dB)	0.8	1.4	0.4
Satellite antenna gain (dB)	16	44	30.8
Free-space path loss (dB)	197	206	205.6
Earth station receive antenna gain (dB)	51	44	62
Earth station branching and feeder loss (dB)	3	3	0
Earth station equivalent noise temperature (K)	250	1000	270
Earth station G/T_e (dBK^{-1})	27	14	37.7

Down-link

1. Satellite transmitter output power at saturation, 10 W   10   dBW
2. Satellite back-off loss   0.1   dB
3. Satellite branching and feeder losses   0.5   dB
4. Satellite transmit antenna gain (from Figure 18-27, 0.37 m at 12 GHz)   30.8   dB
5. Additional down-link atmospheric losses   0.4   dB
6. Free-space path loss (from Figure 18-28, at 12 GHz)   205.6   dB
7. Earth station receive antenna gain (15 m, 12 GHz)   62   dB
8. Earth station branching and feeder losses   0   dB
9. Earth station equivalent noise temperature   270   K
10. Earth station G/T_e ratio   37.7   dBK^{-1}
11. Bit rate   120   Mbps
12. Modulation scheme   8-PSK

Solution   *Up-link budget:* Expressed as a log,

$$\text{EIRP (earth station)} = P_t + A_t - L_{\text{bo}} - L_{bf}$$

$$= 33 \text{ dBW} + 64 \text{ dB} - 3 \text{ dB} - 4 \text{ dB} = 90 \text{ dBW}$$

Carrier power density at the satellite antenna:

$$C^{'} = \text{EIRP (earth station)} - L_p - L_u$$

$$= 90 \text{ dBW} - 206.5 \text{ dB} - 0.6 \text{ dB} = -117.1 \text{ dBW}$$

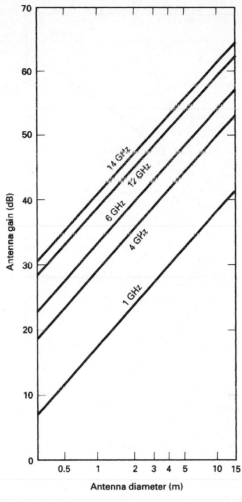

FIGURE 18-27 Antenna gain based on the gain equation for a parabolic antenna:

$$A \text{ (db)} = 10 \log \eta \, (\pi \, D/\lambda)^2$$

where D is the antenna diameter, λ = the wavelength, and η = the antenna efficiency. Here η = 0.55. To correct for a 100% efficient antenna, add 2.66 dB to the value.

C/N_0 at the satellite:

$$\frac{C}{N_0} = \frac{C}{KT_e} = \frac{C}{T_e} \times \frac{1}{K} \qquad \text{where } \frac{C}{T_e} = C' \times \frac{G}{T_e}$$

Thus,

$$\frac{C}{N_0} = C' \times \frac{G}{T_e} \times \frac{1}{K}$$

Expressed as a log,

$$\frac{C}{N_0} = C' + \frac{G}{T_e} - 10 \log (1.38 \times 10^{-23})$$

$$= -117.1 \text{ dBW} + (-5.3 \text{ dBK}^{-1}) - (-228.6 \text{ dBWK}) = 106.2 \text{ dB}$$

Thus,

$$\frac{E_b}{N_0} = \frac{C/f_b}{N_0} = \frac{C}{N_0} - 10 \log f_b$$

$$= 106.2 \text{ dB} - 10 \, (\log 120 \times 10^6) = 25.4 \text{ dB}$$

and for a minimum bandwidth system,

$$\frac{C}{N} = \frac{E_b}{N_0} \frac{B}{f_b} = 25.4 \quad 10 \log \frac{40 \times 10^6}{120 \times 10^6} = 30.2 \text{ dB}$$

Down-link budget: Expressed as a log,

$$\text{EIRP (satellite transponder)} - P_t + A_t - L_{bo} - L_{bf}$$

$$= 10 \text{ dBW} + 30.8 \text{ dB} - 0.1 \text{ dB} - 0.5 \text{ dB}$$

$$= 40.2 \text{ dBW}$$

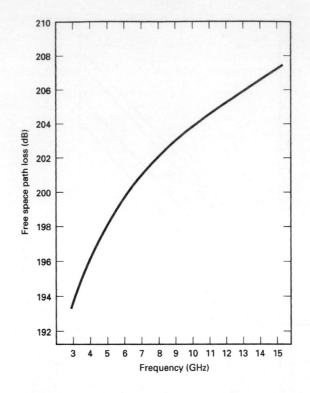

FIGURE 18-28 Free-space path loss (L_p) determined from $L_p = 183.5 + 20 \log f$ (GHz), elevation angle = 90°, and distance = 35,930 km

Carrier power density at earth station antenna:

$$C' = \text{EIRP} - L_p - L_d$$
$$= 40.2 \text{ dBW} - 205.6 \text{ dB} - 0.4 \text{ dB} = -165.8 \text{ dBW}$$

C/N_0 at the earth station receiver:

$$\frac{C}{N_0} = \frac{C}{KT_e} = \frac{C}{T_e} \times \frac{1}{K} \quad \text{where} \quad \frac{C}{T_e} = C' \times \frac{G}{T_e}$$

Thus,
$$\frac{C}{N_0} = C' \times \frac{G}{T_e} \times \frac{1}{K}$$

Expressed as a log,

$$\frac{C}{N_0} = C' + \frac{G}{T_e} - 10 \log (1.38 \times 10^{-23})$$
$$= -165.8 \text{ dBW} + (37.7 \text{ dBK}^{-1}) - (-228.6 \text{ dBWK}) = 100.5 \text{ dB}$$

An alternative method of solving for C/N_0 is

$$\frac{C}{N_0} = C' + A_r - T_e - K$$

$$= -165.8 \text{ dBW} + 62 \text{ dB} - 10 \log 270 - (-228.6 \text{ dBWK})$$
$$= -165.8 \text{ dBW} + 62 \text{ dB} - 24.3 \text{ dBK}^{-1} + 228.6 \text{ dBWK} = 100.5 \text{ dB}$$

$$\frac{E_b}{N_0} = \frac{C}{N_0} - 10 \log f_b$$

$$= 100.5 \text{ dB} - 10 \log (120 \times 10^6)$$
$$= 100.5 \text{ dB} - 80.8 \text{ dB} = 19.7 \text{ dB}$$

TABLE 18-5 Link Budget for Example 18-10

Up-link

1. Earth station transmitter output power at saturation, 2000 W	33 dBW
2. Earth station back-off loss	3 dB
3. Earth station branching and feeder losses	4 dB
4. Earth station transmit antenna gain	64 dB
5. Earth station EIRP	90 dBW
6. Additional up-link atmospheric losses	0.6 dB
7. Free-space path loss	206.5 dB
8. Carrier power density at satellite	−117.1 dBW
9. Satellite branching and feeder losses	0 dB
10. Satellite G/T_e ratio	−5.3 dBK^{-1}
11. Satellite C/T_e ratio	−122.4 dBWK^{-1}
12. Satellite C/N_0 ratio	106.2 dB
13. Satellite C/N ratio	30.2 dB
14. Satellite E_b/N_0 ratio	25.4 dB
15. Bit rate	120 Mbps
16. Modulation scheme	8-PSK

Down-link

1. Satellite transmitter output power at saturation, 10 W	10 dBW
2. Satellite back-off loss	0.1 dB
3. Satellite branching and feeder losses	0.5 dB
4. Satellite transmit antenna gain	30.8 dB
5. Satellite EIRP	40.2 dBW
6. Additional down-link atmospheric losses	0.4 dB
7. Free-space path loss	205.6 dB
8. Earth station receive antenna gain	62 dB
9. Earth station equivalent noise temperature	270 K
10. Earth station branching and feeder losses	0 dB
11. Earth station G/T_e ratio	37.7 dBK^{-1}
12. Carrier power density at earth station	−165.8 dBW
13. Earth station C/T_e ratio	−128.1 dBWK^{-1}
14. Earth station C/N_0 ratio	100.5 dB
15. Earth station C/N ratio	24.5 dB
16. Earth station E_b/N_0 ratio	19.7 dB
17. Bit rate	120 Mbps
18. Modulation scheme	8-PSK

and for a minimum bandwidth system,

$$\frac{C}{N} = \frac{E_b}{N_0} - \frac{B}{f_b} = 19.7 - 10 \log \frac{40 \times 10^6}{120 \times 10^6} = 24.5 \text{ dB}$$

With careful analysis and a little algebra, it can be shown that the overall energy of bit-to-noise density ratio (E_b/N_0), which includes the combined effects of the up-link ratio $(E_b/N_0)_u$ and the down-link ratio $(E_b/N_0)_d$, is a standard product over the sum relationship and is expressed mathematically as

$$\frac{E_b}{N_0} \text{(overall)} = \frac{(E_b/N_0)_u(E_b/N_0)_d}{(E_b/N_0)_u + (E_b/N_0)_d} \qquad (18\text{-}20)$$

where all E_b/N_0 ratios are in absolute values. For Example 18-9, the overall E_b/N_0 ratio is

$$\frac{E_b}{N_0} \text{(overall)} = \frac{(346.7)(93.3)}{346.7 + 93.3} = 73.5$$

$$= 10 \log 73.5 = 18.7 \text{ dB}$$

As with all product-over-sum relationships, the smaller of the two numbers dominates. If one number is substantially smaller than the other, the overall result is approximately equal to the smaller of the two numbers.

The system parameters used for Example 18-9 were taken from system C in Table 18-4. A complete link budget for the system is shown in Table 18-5.

QUESTIONS

18-1. Briefly describe a satellite.

18-2. What is a passive satellite? An active satellite?

18-3. Contrast nonsynchronous and synchronous satellites.

18-4. Define *prograde* and *retrograde*.

18-5. Define *apogee* and *perigee*.

18-6. Briefly explain the characteristics of low-, medium-, and high-altitude satellite orbits.

18-7. Explain equatorial, polar, and inclined orbits.

18-8. Contrast the advantages and disadvantages of geosynchronous satellites.

18-9. Define *look angles, angle of elevation,* and *azimuth.*

18-10. Define *satellite spatial separation* and list its restrictions.

18-11. Describe a "footprint."

18-12. Describe spot, zonal, and earth coverage radiation patterns.

18-13. Explain *reuse.*

18-14. Briefly describe the functional characteristics of an up-link, a transponder, and a down-link model for a satellite system.

18-15. Define *back-off loss* and its relationship to saturated and transmit power.

18-16. Define *bit energy.*

18-17. Define *effective isotropic radiated power.*

18-18. Define *equivalent noise temperature.*

18-19. Define *noise density.*

18-20. Define *carrier-to-noise density ratio* and *energy of bit-to-noise density ratio.*

18-21. Define *gain-to-equivalent noise temperature ratio.*

18-22. Describe what a satellite link budget is and how it is used.

PROBLEMS

18-1. An earth station is located at Houston, Texas, which has a longitude of 99.5° and a latitude of 29.5° north. The satellite of interest is *Satcom V.* Determine the look angles for the earth station antenna.

18-2. A satellite system operates at 14-GHz up-link and 11-GHz down-link and has a projected $P(e)$ of 10^{-7}. The modulation scheme is 8-PSK, and the system will carry 120 Mbps. The equivalent noise temperature of the receiver is 400 K, and the receiver noise bandwidth is equal to the minimum Nyquist frequency. Determine the following parameters: minimum theoretical C/N ratio, minimum theoretical E_b/N_0 ratio, noise density, total receiver input noise, minimum receive carrier power, and the minimum energy per bit at the receiver input.

18-3. A satellite system operates at 6-GHz up-link and 4-GHz down-link and has a projected $P(e)$ of 10^{-6}. The modulation scheme is QPSK and the system will carry 100 Mbps. The equivalent receiver noise temperature is 290 K, and the receiver noise bandwidth is equal to the minimum Nyquist frequency. Determine the *C/N* ratio that would be measured at a point in the receiver prior to the BPF where the bandwidth is equal to (a) 1½ times the minimum Nyquist frequency, and (b) 3 times the minimum Nyquist frequency.

18-4. Which system has the best projected BER?
 (a) 8-QAM, C/N = 15 dB, $B = 2f_N, f_b = 60$ Mbps
 (b) QPSK, C/N = 16 dB, $B = f_N, f_b = 40$ Mbps

18-5. An earth station satellite transmitter has an HPA with a rated saturated output power of 10,000 W. The back-off ratio is 6 dB, the branching loss is 2 dB, the feeder loss is 4 dB, and the antenna gain is 40 dB. Determine the actual radiated power and the EIRP.

18-6. Determine the total noise power for a receiver with an input bandwidth of 20 MHz and an equivalent noise temperature of 600 K.

18-7. Determine the noise density for Problem 18-6.

18-8. Determine the minimum C/N ratio required to achieve a $P(e)$ of 10^{-5} for an 8-PSK receiver with a bandwidth equal to f_N.

18-9. Determine the energy per bit-to-noise density ratio when the receiver input carrier power is -100 dBW, the receiver input noise temperature is 290 K, and a 60-Mbps transmission rate is used.

18-10. Determine the carrier-to-noise density ratio for a receiver with a -70-dBW input carrier power, an equivalent noise temperature of 180 K, and a bandwidth of 20 MHz.

18-11. Determine the minimum C/N ratio for an 8-PSK system when the transmission rate is 60 Mbps, the minimum energy of bit-to-noise density ratio is 15 dB, and the receiver bandwidth is equal to the minimum Nyquist frequency.

18-12. For an earth station receiver with an equivalent input temperature of 200 K, a noise bandwidth of 20 MHz, a receive antenna gain of 50 dB, and a carrier frequency of 12 GHz, determine the following: G/T_e, N_0, and N.

18-13. For a satellite with an up-link E_b/N_0 of 14 dB and a down-link E_b/N_0 of 18 dB, determine the overall E_b/N_0 ratio.

18-14. Complete the following link budget:

Up-link parameters
1. Earth station transmitter output power at saturation, 1 kW
2. Earth station back-off loss, 3 dB
3. Earth station total branching and feeder losses, 3 dB
4. Earth station transmit antenna gain for a 10-m parabolic dish at 14 GHz
5. Free-space path loss for 14 GHz
6. Additional up-link losses due to the Earth's atmosphere, 0.8 dB
7. Satellite transponder G/T_e, -4.6 dBK^{-1}
8. Transmission bit rate, 90 Mbps, 8-PSK

Down-link parameters
1. Satellite transmitter output power at saturation, 10 W
2. Satellite transmit antenna gain for a 0.5-m parabolic dish at 12 GHz
3. Satellite modulation back-off loss, 0.8 dB
4. Free-space path loss for 12 GHz
5. Additional down-link losses due to Earth's atmosphere, 0.6 dB
6. Earth station receive antenna gain for a 10-m parabolic dish at 12 GHz
7. Earth station equivalent noise temperature, 200 K
8. Earth station branching and feeder losses, 0 dB
9. Transmission bit rate, 90 Mbps, 8-PSK

18-15. An earth station is located at Houston, Texas, which has a longitude of 99.5° and a latitude of 29.5° north. The satellite of interest is *Westar III*. Determine the look angles from the earth station antenna.

18-16. A satellite system operates at 14 GHz up-link and 11 GHz down-link and has a projected $P(e)$ of 1 bit error in every 1 million bits transmitted. The modulation scheme is 8-PSK, and the system will carry 90 Mbps. The equivalent noise temperature of the receiver is 350 K, and the receiver noise bandwidth is equal to the minimum Nyquist frequency. Determine the following parameters: minimum theoretical C/N ratio, minimum theoretical E_b/N_0 ratio, noise density, total receiver input noise, minimum receive carrier power, and the minimum energy per bit at the receiver input.

18-17. A satellite system operates a 6-GHz up-link and 4-GHz down-link and has a projected $P(e)$ of 1 bit error in every 100,000 bits transmitted. The modulation scheme is 4-PSK and the system will carry 80 Mbps. The equivalent receiver noise temperature is 120 K, and the receiver noise bandwidth is equal to the minimum Nyquist frequency. Determine the following:
  (a) The C/N ratio that would be measured at a point in the receiver prior to the BPF where the bandwidth is equal to two times the minimum Nyquist frequency.
  (b) The C/N ratio that would be measured at a point in the receiver prior to the BPF where the bandwidth is equal to three times the minimum Nyquist frequency.

18-18. Which system has the best projected BER?

    (a) QPSK, C/N = 16 dB, $B = 2f_N, f_b = 40$ Mbps

    (b) 8-PSK, C/N = 18 dB, $B = f_N, f_b = 60$ Mbps

18-19. An earth station satellite transmitter has an HPA with a rated saturated output power of 12,000 W. The back-off ratio of 4 dB, the branching loss is 1.5 dB, the feeder loss is 5 dB, and the antenna gain is 38 dB. Determine the actual radiated power and the EIRP.

18-20. Determine the total noise power for a receiver with an input bandwidth of 40 MHz and an equivalent noise temperature of 800 K.

18-21. Determine the noise density for Problem 18-20.

18-22. Determine the minimum C/N ratio required to achieve a $P(e)$ of 1 bit error for every 1 million bits transmitted for a QPSK receiver with a bandwidth equal to the minimum Nyquist frequency.

18-23. Determine the energy of bit-to-noise density ratio when the receiver input carrier power is -85 dBW, the receiver input noise temperature is 400 K, and a 50 Mbps transmission rate.

18-24. Determine the carrier-to-noise density ratio for a receiver with a -80 dBW carrier input power, equivalent noise temperature of 240 K, and a bandwidth of 10 MHz.

18-25. Determine the minimum C/N ratio for a QPSK system when the transmission rate is 80 Mbps, the minimum energy of bit-to-noise density ratio is 16 dB, and the receiver bandwidth is equal to the Nyquist frequency.

18-26. For an earth station receiver with an equivalent input temperature of 400 K, a noise bandwidth of 30 MHz, a receive antenna gain of 44 dB, and a carrier frequency of 12 GHz, determine the following: G/T_e, N_0, and N.

18-27. For a satellite with an up-link E_b/N_0 of 16 dB and a down-link E_b/N_0 of 13 dB, determine the overall E_b/N_0.

18-28. Complete the following link budget:

Up-link parameters
1. Earth station output power at saturation, 12 kW
2. Earth station back-off loss, 4 dB
3. Earth station branching and feeder losses, 2 dB
4. Earth station antenna gain for a 10-m parabolic dish at 14 GHz.
5. Free-space path loss for 14 GHz
6. Additional up-link losses due to Earth's atmosphere, 1 dB
7. Satellite transponder G/T_e, -3 dBk
8. Transmission bit rate, 80 Mbps
9. Modulation scheme, 4-PSK

Down-link parameters
1. Satellite transmitter output power at saturation, 5 W
2. Satellite station transmit antenna gain for a 0.5-m parabolic dish at 12 GHz
3. Satellite modulation back-off loss, 1 dB
4. Free-space path loss for 12 GHz
5. Additional down-link losses due to Earth's atmosphere, 1 dB
6. Earth station receive antenna gain for a 10-m parabolic dish at 12 GHz
7. Earth station equivalent noise temperature, 300 K
8. Transmission bit rate, 80 Mbps
9. Modulation scheme, 4-PSK

C H A P T E R 19

Satellite Multiple-Access Arrangements

INTRODUCTION

In Chapter 18 we analyzed the link parameters of *single-channel satellite transponders*. In this chapter, we will extend the discussion of satellite communications to systems designed for *multiple carriers*. Whenever multiple carriers are utilized in satellite communications, it is necessary that a *multiple-accessing format* be established over the system. This format allows for a distinct separation between the up-link and down-link transmissions to and from a multitude of different earth stations. Each format has its own specific characteristics, advantages, and disadvantages.

FDM/FM SATELLITE SYSTEMS

Figure 19-1a shows a single-link (two earth stations) *fixed-frequency* FDM/FM system using a single satellite transponder. With earth coverage antennas and for full-duplex operation, each link requires two RF satellite channels (i.e., four RF carrier frequencies, two up-link and two down-link). In Figure 19-1a, earth station 1 transmits on a high-band carrier (f11, f12, f13, etc.) and receives on a low-band carrier (f1, f2, f3, etc.). To avoid interfering with earth station 1, earth station 2 must transmit and receive on different RF carrier frequencies. The RF carrier frequencies are fixed and the satellite transponder is simply an RF-to-RF repeater that provides the up-link/down-link frequency translation. This arrangement is economically impractical and also extremely inefficient. Additional earth stations can communicate through different transponders within the same satellite structure (Figure 19-1b), but each additional link requires four more RF carrier frequencies. It is unlikely that any two-point link would require the capacity available in an entire RF satellite channel. Consequently, most of the available bandwidth is wasted. Also, with this arrangement, each earth station can communicate with only one other earth station. The RF satellite channels are fixed between any two earth stations; thus, the voice-band channels from each earth station are committed to a single destination.

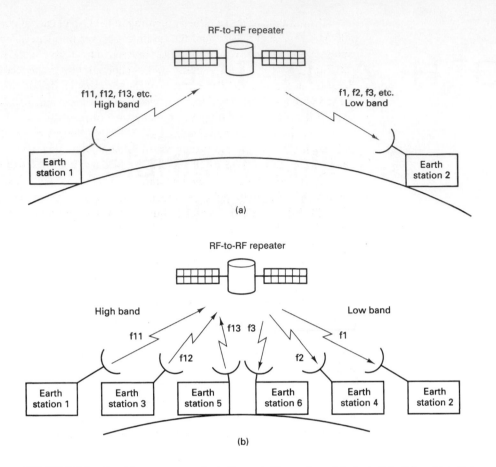

FIGURE 19-1 Fixed-frequency earth station satellite system: (a) single link; (b) multiple link

In a system where three or more earth stations wish to communicate with each other, fixed-frequency or *dedicated-channel* systems such as those shown in Figure 19-1 are inadequate; a method of *multiple accessing* is required. That is, each earth station using the satellite system has a means of communicating with each of the other earth stations in the system through a common satellite transponder. Multiple accessing is sometimes called *multiple destination* because the transmissions from each earth station are received by all the other earth stations in the system. The voice-band channels between any two earth stations may be *preassigned* (*dedicated*) or *demand-assigned* (*switched*). When preassignment is used, a given number of the available voice-band channels from each earth station are assigned a dedicated destination. With demand assignment, voice-band channels are assigned on an as-needed basis. Demand assignment provides more versatility and more efficient use of the available frequency spectrum. On the other hand, demand assignment requires a control mechanism that is common to all the earth stations to keep track of channel routing and the availability of each voice-band channel.

Remember, in an FDM/FM satellite system, each RF channel requires a separate transponder. Also, with FDM/FM transmissions, it is impossible to differentiate (separate) multiple transmissions that occupy the same bandwidth. Fixed-frequency systems may be used in a multiple-access configuration by switching the RF carriers at the satellite, reconfiguring the baseband signals with multiplexing/demultiplexing equipment on board the satellite, or by using multiple spot beam antennas (reuse). All three of these methods require relatively complicated, expensive, and heavy hardware on the spacecraft.

Communications satellites operating in the C-band are allocated a total bandwidth of 500 MHz symmetrical around the satellite's center frequency. This is often referred to as one satellite channel which is further divided into radio channels. Most communications satellites carry 12 transponders (radio channel transmitter/receiver pairs), each with 36 MHz of bandwidth. The carriers of the 12 transponders are frequency-division multiplexed with a 4-MHz guard band between each of them and a 10-MHz guard band on both ends of the 500-MHz assigned frequency spectrum.

If adjacent transponders in the 500-MHz spectrum are fed from a quadrature-polarized antenna, the number of transponders (radio channels) available in one satellite channel can be doubled to 24. Twelve odd-numbered transponders transmit and receive with a vertically polarized antenna and 12 even-numbered transponders transmit and receive on a horizontally polarized antenna. The carrier frequencies of the even channels are offset 20 MHz from the carrier frequencies of the odd-numbered transponders to reduce cross-talk between adjacent transponders. This method of assigning adjacent channels different electromagnetic polarizations is called *frequency reuse* and is possible by using orthogonal polarization and spacing adjacent channels 20 MHz apart. Frequency reuse is a technique for achieving better utilization of the available frequency spectrum.

Anik-E Communications Satellite

Anik is an Eskimo word, meaning "little brother." The Anik-E communications satellites are Domsats (domestic satellites) operated by Telsat Canada. Figure 19-2 shows the frequency and polarization plan for the Anik-E satellite system. One group of 12 radio channels (group A) uses horizontal polarization and one group of 12 radio channels (group B) uses vertical polarization for 24 total radio channels, each with 36 MHz of bandwidth. There is a 4-MHz bandwidth between adjacent radio channels and a 10-MHz bandwidth at each end of the spectrum for a total satellite channel bandwidth of 500 MHz. There are 12 primary radio channels and 12 spare or preemptible radio channels.

MULTIPLE ACCESSING

Satellite *multiple accessing* (sometimes called *multiple destination*) implies that more than one user has access to one or more radio channels (transponders) within a satellite communications channel. Transponders are typically leased by a company or a common carrier for the purpose of providing voice or data transmission to a multitude of users. The method by which a satellite transponder's bandwidth is used or accessed depends on the multiple-accessing method utilized.

Figure 19-3 illustrates the three most commonly used *multiple-accessing arrangements:* frequency-division multiple accessing (FDMA), time-division multiple accessing (TDMA), and code-division multiple accessing (CDMA). With FDMA, each earth station's transmissions are assigned specific up-link and down-link frequency bands within an allotted satellite bandwidth; they may be *preassigned* or *demand assigned*. Consequently, FDMA transmissions are separated in the frequency domain and, therefore, must share the total available transponder bandwidth as well as the total transponder power. With TDMA, each earth station transmits a short burst of information during a specific time slot (*epoch*) within a TDMA frame. The bursts must be synchronized so that each station's burst arrives at the satellite at a different time. Consequently, TDMA transmissions are separated in the time domain, and with TDMA the entire transponder bandwidth and power are used for each transmission but for only a prescribed interval of time. With CDMA, all earth stations transmit within the same frequency band and, for all practical purposes, have no limitations on when they may transmit or on which carrier frequency. Thus, with CDMA, the entire satellite transponder bandwidth is used by all stations on a continuous basis. Signal separation is accomplished with envelope encryption/decryption techniques.

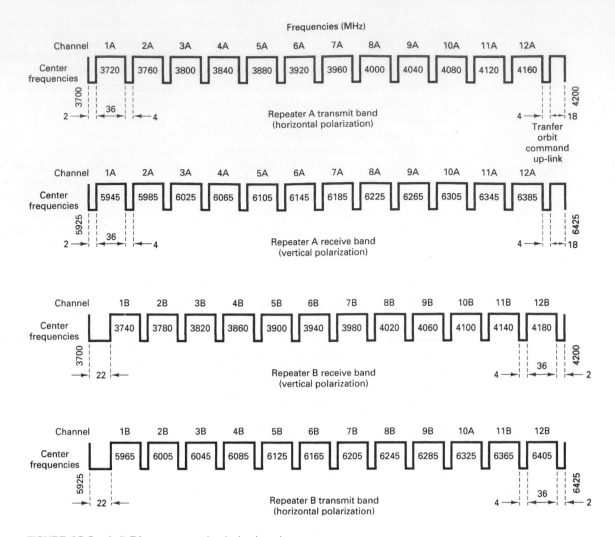

FIGURE 19-2 *Anik-E* frequency and polarization plan

Frequency-Division Multiple Access

Frequency-division multiple access (FDMA) is a method of multiple accessing where a given RF bandwidth is divided into smaller frequency bands called *subdivisions.* Each subdivision has its own IF carrier frequency. A control mechanism is used to ensure that two or more earth stations do not transmit in the same subdivision at the same time. Essentially, the control mechanism designates a receive station for each of the subdivisions. In demand-assignment systems, the control mechanism is also used to establish or terminate the voice-band links between the source and destination earth stations. Consequently, any of the subdivisions may be used by any of the participating earth stations at any given time. If each subdivision carries only one 4-kHz voice-band channel, this is known as a *single-channel per carrier* (SCPC) system. When several voice-band channels are frequency-division multiplexed together to form a composite baseband signal comprised of groups, supergroups, or even mastergroups, a wider subdivision is assigned. This is referred to as *multiple-channel per carrier* (MCPC).

Carrier frequencies and bandwidths for FDM/FM satellite systems using multiple-channel-per-carrier formats are generally assigned and remained fixed for a long period of time. This is referred to as *fixed-assignment, multiple access* (FDM/FM/FAMA). An alter-

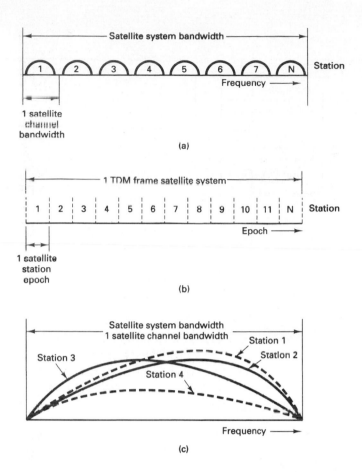

FIGURE 19-3 Multiple-accessing arrangements: (a) FDMA; (b) TDMA; (c) CDMA

nate channel allocation scheme is *demand-assignment, multiple access* (DAMA). Demand assignment allows all users continuous and equal access of the entire transponder bandwidth by assigning carrier frequencies on a temporary basis using a statistical assignment process. The first FDMA demand-assignment system for satellites was developed by Comsat for use on the *Intelsat* series *IVA* and *V* satellites.

SPADE DAMA satellite system. SPADE is an acronym for *single-channel-per-carrier* PCM multiple-*access* *d*emand-assignment *e*quipment. Figures 19-4 and 19-5 show the block diagram and IF frequency assignments, respectively, for SPADE.

With SPADE, 800 PCM-encoded voice-band channels separately QPSK modulate an IF carrier signal (hence, the name *single-carrier per channel,* SCPC). Each 4-kHz voice-band channel is sampled at an 8-kHz rate and converted to an eight-bit PCM code. This produces a 64-kbps PCM code for each voice-band channel. The PCM code from each voice-band channel QPSK modulates a different IF carrier frequency. With QPSK, the minimum required bandwidth is equal to one-half the input bit rate. Consequently, the output of each QPSK modulator requires a minimum bandwidth of 32 kHz. Each channel is allocated a 45-kHz bandwidth, allowing for a 13-kHz guard band between pairs of frequency-division-multiplexed channels. The IF carrier frequencies begin at 52.0225 MHz (low-band channel 1) and increase in 45-kHz steps to 87.9775 MHz (high-band channel 400). The entire 36-MHz band (52 MHz to 88 MHz) is divided in half, producing two 400-channel bands (a low band and a high band). For full-duplex operation, four hundred 45-kHz channels are

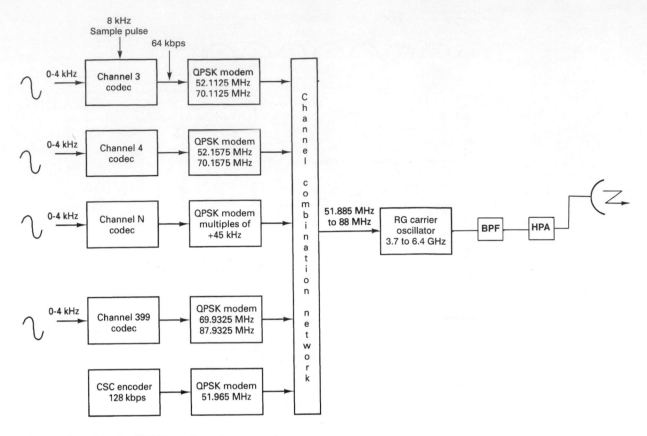

FIGURE 19-4 FDMA, SPADE earth station transmitter

used for one direction of transmission and 400 are used for the opposite direction. Also, channels 1, 2, and 400 from each band are left permanently vacant. This reduces the number of usable full-duplex voice-band channels to 397. The 6-GHz C-band extends from 5.725 GHz to 6.425 GHz (700 MHz). This allows for approximately nineteen 36-MHz RF channels per system. Each RF channel has a capacity of 397 full-duplex voice-band channels.

Each RF channel (Figure 19-5) has a 160-kHz *common signaling channel* (CSC). The CSC is a time-division-multiplexed transmission that is frequency-division multiplexed into the IF spectrum below the QPSK-encoded voice-band channels. Figure 19-6 shows the TDM frame structure for the CSC. The total frame time is 50 ms, which is subdivided into fifty 1-ms epochs. Each earth station transmits on the CSC channel only during its preassigned 1-ms time slot. The CSC signal is a 128-bit binary code. To transmit a 128-bit code in 1 ms, a transmission rate of 128 kbps is required. The CSC code is used for establishing and disconnecting voice-band links between two earth station users when demand-assignment channel allocation is used.

The CSC channel occupies a 160-kHz bandwidth, which includes the 45 kHz for low-band channel 1. Consequently, the CSC channel extends from 51.885 MHz to 52.045 MHz. The 128-kbps CSC binary code QPSK modulates a 51.965-MHz carrier. The minimum bandwidth required for the CSC channel is 64 kHz; this results in a 48-kHz guard band on either side of the CSC signal.

With FDMA, each earth station may transmit simultaneously within the same 36-MHz RF spectrum, but on different voice-band channels. Consequently, simultaneous transmissions of voice-band channels from all earth stations within the satellite network are

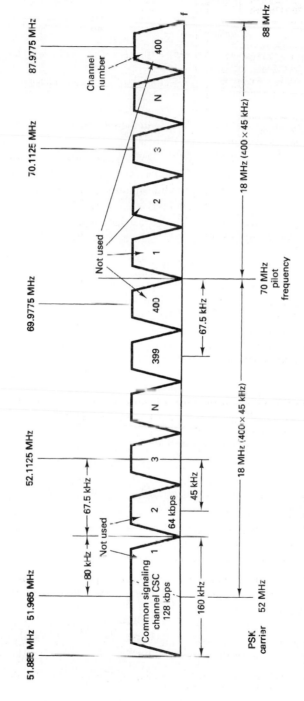

FIGURE 19-5 Carrier frequency assignments for the *Intelsat* single-channel-per-carrier PCM multiple-access demand-assignment equipment (SPADE)

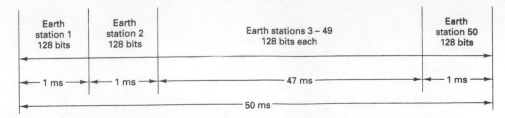

128 bits/1ms × 1000 ms/1s = 128 kbps or 6400 bits/frame × 1 frame/50 ms = 128 kbps

FIGURE 19-6   FDMA, SPADE common signaling channel (CSC)

interleaved in the frequency domain in the satellite transponder. Transmissions of CSC signals are interleaved in the time domain.

An obvious disadvantage of FDMA is that carriers from multiple earth stations may be present in a satellite transponder at the same time. This results in cross-modulation distortion between the various earth station transmissions. This is alleviated somewhat by shutting off the IF subcarriers on all unused 45-kHz voice-band channels. Because balanced modulators are used in the generation of QPSK, carrier suppression is inherent. This also reduces the power load on a system and increases its capacity by reducing the idle channel power.

Time-Division Multiple Access

Time-division multiple access (TDMA) is the predominant multiple-access method used today. It provides the most efficient method of transmitting digitally modulated carriers (PSK). TDMA is a method of time-division multiplexing digitally modulated carriers between participating earth stations within a satellite network through a common satellite transponder. With TDMA, each earth station transmits a short *burst* of a digitally modulated carrier during a precise time slot (epoch) within a TDMA frame. Each station's burst is synchronized so that it arrives at the satellite transponder at a different time. Consequently, only one earth station's carrier is present in the transponder at any given time, thus avoiding a collision with another station's carrier. The transponder is an RF-to-RF repeater that simply receives the earth station transmissions, amplifies them, and then retransmits them in a down-link beam that is received by all the participating earth stations. Each earth station receives the bursts from all other earth stations and must select from them the traffic destined only for itself.

Figure 19-7 shows a basic TDMA frame. Transmissions from all earth stations are synchronized to a *reference burst*. Figure 19-7 shows the reference burst as a separate transmission, but it may be the *preamble* that precedes a reference station's transmission of data. Also, there may be more than one synchronizing reference burst.

The reference burst contains a *carrier recovery sequence* (CRS), from which all receiving stations recover a frequency and phase coherent carrier for PSK demodulation. Also included in the reference burst is a binary sequence for *bit timing recovery* (BTR, i.e., clock recovery). At the end of each reference burst, a *unique word* (UW) is transmitted. The UW sequence is used to establish a precise time reference that each of the earth stations uses to synchronize the transmission of its burst. The UW is typically a string of 20 successive binary 1s terminated with a binary 0. Each earth station receiver demodulates and integrates the UW sequence. Figure 19-8 shows the result of the integration process. The integrator and threshold detector are designed so that the threshold voltage is reached precisely when the last bit of the UW sequence is integrated. This generates a *correlation spike* at the output of the threshold detector at the exact time the UW sequence ends.

Each earth station synchronizes the transmission of its carrier to the occurrence of the UW correlation spike. Each station waits a different length of time before it begins

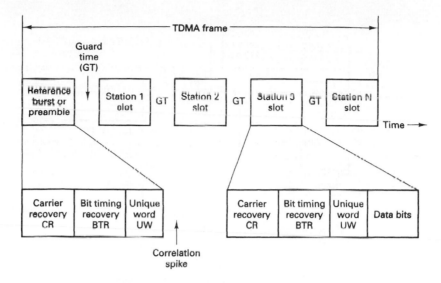

FIGURE 19-7 Basic time-division multiple-accessing (TDMA) frame

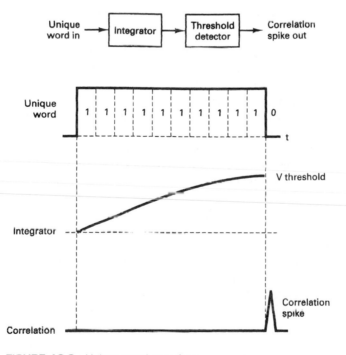

FIGURE 19-8 Unique word correlator

transmitting. Consequently, no two stations will transmit the carrier at the same time. Note the *guard time* (GT) between transmissions from successive stations. This is analogous to a guard band in a frequency-division-multiplexed system. Each station precedes the transmission of data with a *preamble*. The preamble is logically equivalent to the reference burst. Because each station's transmissions must be received by all other earth stations, all stations must recover carrier and clocking information prior to demodulating the data. If demand assignment is used, a common signaling channel also must be included in the preamble.

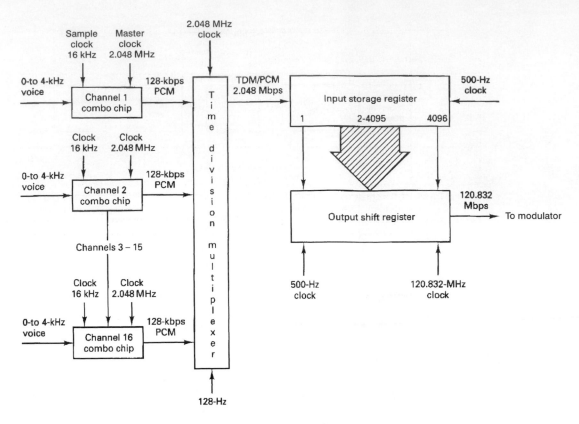

FIGURE 19-9 TDMA, CEPT primary multiplex frame transmitter

CEPT primary multiplex frame. Figures 19-9 and 19-10 show the block diagram and timing sequence, respectively, for the CEPT primary multiplex frame. (CEPT is the Conference of European Postal and Telecommunications Administrations; the CEPT sets many of the European telecommunications standards.) This is a commonly used TDMA frame format for digital satellite systems.

Essentially, TDMA is a *store-and-forward* system. Earth stations can transmit only during their specified time slot, although the incoming voice-band signals are continuous. Consequently, it is necessary to sample and store the voice-band signals prior to transmission. The CEPT frame is made up of 8-bit PCM encoded samples from 16 independent voice-band channels. Each channel has a separate codec that samples the incoming voice signals at a 16-kHz rate and converts those samples to 8-bit binary codes. This results in 128-kbps transmitted at a 2.048-MHz rate from each voice channel codec. The sixteen 128-kbps transmissions are time-division multiplexed into a subframe that contains one 8-bit sample from each of the 16 channels (128 bits). It requires only 62.5 μs to accumulate the 128 bits (2.048-Mbps transmission rate). The CEPT multiplex format specifies a 2-ms frame time. Consequently, each earth station can transmit only once every 2 ms and, therefore, must store the PCM-encoded samples. The 128 bits accumulated during the first sample of each voice-band channel are stored in a holding register while a second sample is taken from each channel and converted into another 128-bit *subframe*. This 128-bit sequence is stored in the holding register behind the first 128 bits. The process continues for 32 subframes (32 × 62.5 μs = 2 ms). After 2 ms, thirty-two 8-bit samples have been taken from each of 16 voice-band channels for a total of 4096 bits (32 × 8 × 16 = 4096). At this time, the 4096 bits are transferred to an output shift register for transmission. Because the total TDMA frame is 2 ms long and during this 2-ms period each of the participating earth

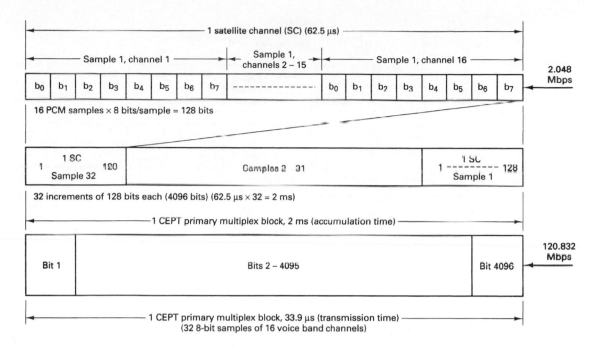

FIGURE 19-10 TDMA, CEPT primary multiplex frame

stations must transmit at different times, the individual transmissions from each station must occur in a significantly shorter time period. In the CEPT frame, a transmission rate of 120.832 Mbps is used. This rate is the fifty-ninth multiple of 2.048 Mbps. Consequently, the actual transmission of the 4096 accumulated bits takes approximately 33.9 μs. At the earth station receivers, the 4096 bits are stored in a holding register and shifted at a 2.048-Mbps rate. Because all the clock rates (500 Hz, 16 kHz, 128 kHz, 2.048 MHz, and 120.832 MHz) are synchronized, the PCM codes are accumulated, stored, transmitted, received, and then decoded in perfect synchronization. To the users, the voice transmission appears to be a continuous process.

There are several advantages of TDMA over FDMA. The first, and probably the most significant, is that with TDMA only the carrier from one earth station is present in the satellite transponder at any given time, thus reducing intermodulation distortion. Second, with FDMA, each earth station must be capable of transmitting and receiving on a multitude of carrier frequencies to achieve multiple-accessing capabilities. Third, TDMA is much better suited to the transmission of digital information than FDMA. Digital signals are more naturally acclimated to storage, rate conversions, and time-domain processing than their analog counterparts.

The primary disadvantage of TDMA as compared with FDMA is that in TDMA precise synchronization is required. Each earth station's transmissions must occur during an exact time slot. Also, bit and frame timing must be achieved and maintained with TDMA.

Code-Division Multiple Access

With FDMA, earth stations are limited to a specific bandwidth within a satellite channel or system but have no restriction on when they can transmit. With TDMA, an earth station's transmissions are restricted to a precise time slot but have no restriction on what frequency or bandwidth it may use within a specified satellite system or channel allocation. With *code division multiple access* (CDMA), there are no restrictions on time or bandwidth. Each earth station transmitter may transmit whenever it wishes and can use any or all of the bandwidth allocated a particular satellite system or channel. Because there is no limitation

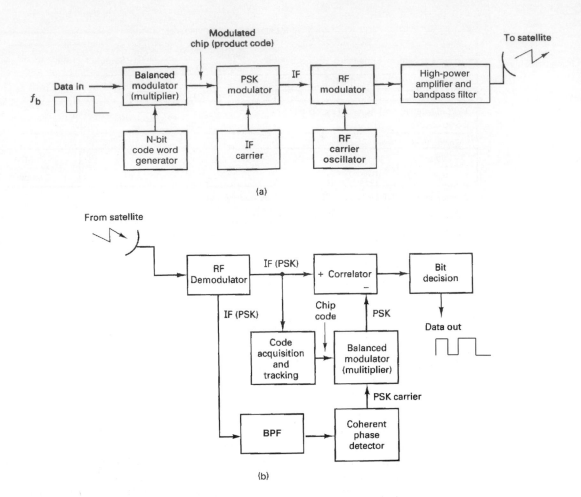

FIGURE 19-11 Code-division multiple access (CDMA): (a) encoder; (b) decoder

on the bandwidth, CDMA is sometimes referred to as *spread-spectrum multiple access;* transmissions can spread throughout the entire allocated bandwidth. Transmissions are separated through envelope encryption/decryption techniques. That is, each earth station's transmissions are encoded with a unique binary word called a *chip code.* Each station has a unique chip code. To receive a particular earth station's transmission, a receive station must know the chip code for that station.

Figure 19-11 shows the block diagram of a CDMA encoder and decoder. In the encoder (Figure 19-11a), the input data (which may be PCM-encoded voice-band signals or raw digital data) is multiplied by a unique chip code. The product code PSK modulates an IF carrier, which is up-converted to RF for transmission. At the receiver (Figure 19-11b), the RF is down-converted to IF. From the IF, a coherent PSK carrier is recovered. Also, the chip code is acquired and used to synchronize the receive station's code generator. Keep in mind, the receiving station knows the chip code but must generate a chip code that is synchronous in time with the receive code. The recovered synchronous chip code multiplies the recovered PSK carrier and generates a PSK-modulated signal that contains the PSK carrier plus the chip code. The received IF signal that contains the chip code, the PSK carrier, and the data information is compared with the received IF signal in the *correlator.* The function of the correlator is to compare the two signals and recover the original data. Essentially, the correlator subtracts the recovered PSK carrier + chip code from the received PSK carrier + chip code + data. The resultant is the data.

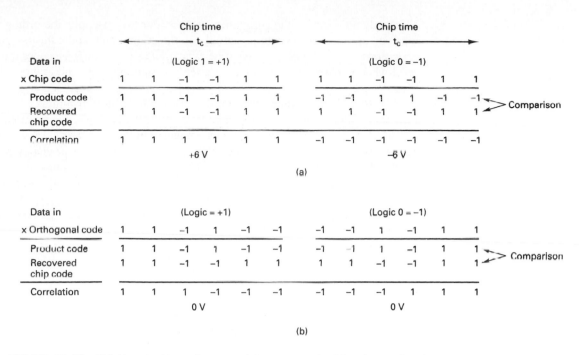

FIGURE 19-12 CDMA code/data alignment: (a) correct code; (b) orthogonal code

The correlation is accomplished on the analog signals. Figure 19-12 shows how the encoding and decoding is accomplished. Figure 19-12a shows the correlation of the correctly received chip code. A $+1$ indicates an in-phase carrier and a -1 indicates an out-of-phase carrier. The chip code is multiplied by the data (either $+1$ or -1). The product is either an in-phase code or one that is $180°$ out of phase with the chip code. In the receiver, the recovered synchronous chip code is compared in the correlator with the received signaling elements. If the phases are the same, a $+1$ is produced; if they are $180°$ out of phase, a -1 is produced. It can be seen that if all the recovered chips correlate favorably with the incoming chip code, the output of the correlator will be a $+6$ (which is the case when a logic 1 is received). If all the code chips correlate $180°$ out of phase, a -6 is generated (which is the case when a logic 0 is received). The bit decision circuit is simply a threshold detector. Depending on whether a $+6$ or -6 is generated, the threshold detector will output a logic 1 or a logic 0, respectively.

As the name implies, the correlator looks for a correlation (similarity) between the incoming coded signal and the recovered chip code. When a correlation occurs, the bit decision circuit generates the corresponding logic condition.

With CDMA, all earth stations within the system may transmit on the same frequency at the same time. Consequently, an earth station receiver may be receiving coded PSK signals simultaneously from more than one transmitter. When this is the case, the job of the correlator becomes considerably more difficult. The correlator must compare the recovered chip code with the entire received spectrum and separate from it only the chip code from the desired earth station transmitter. Consequently, the chip code from one earth station must not correlate with the chip codes from any of the other earth stations.

Figure 19-12b shows how such a coding scheme is achieved. If half of the bits within a code were made the same and half were made exactly the opposite, the resultant would be zero cross correlation between chip codes. Such a code is called an *orthogonal code*. In Figure 19-12b it can be seen that when the orthogonal code is compared with the original chip code, there is no correlation (i.e., the sum of the comparison is zero). Consequently, the orthogonal code, although received simultaneously with the desired chip code, had absolutely no effect on the correlation process. For this example, the orthogonal code is received in exact time synchronization with the desired chip code; this is not always the case. For systems that do not have time-synchronous transmissions, codes must be developed where there is no correlation between one station's code and any phase of another station's code.

The primary difference between spread spectrum PSK transmitters and other types of PSK transmitters is the additional modulator where the code word is multiplied by the incoming data. Because of the pseudorandom nature of the code word, it is often referred to as *pseudorandom noise* (PRN). The PRN must have a high autocorrelation property with itself and a low correlation property with other transmitter's pseudorandom codes. The code word rate (R_{cw}) must exceed the incoming data rate (R_d) by several orders of magnitude. In addition, the code rate must be statistically independent of the data signal. When these two conditions are satisfied, the final output signal spectrum will be increased (spread) by a factor called the *processing gain*. Processing gain is expressed mathematically as

$$G = \frac{R_{cw}}{R_d} \qquad (19\text{-}1)$$

where G is processing gain and $R_{cw} >> R_d$.

A spread-spectrum signal cannot be demodulated accurately if the receiver does not possess a despreading circuit that matches the code word generator in the transmitter. Three of the most popular techniques used to produce the spreading function are *direct sequence, frequency hopping,* and a combination of direct sequence and frequency hopping called *hybrid direct-sequence frequency hopping* (hybrid-DS/FH).

Direct sequence (DS). Direct-sequence spread spectrum (DS-SS) is produced when a bipolar data-modulated signal is linearly multiplied by the spreading signal in a special balanced modulator called a *spreading correlator*. The spreading code rate $R_{cw} = 1/T_c$, where T_c is the duration of a single bipolar pulse (i.e., the chip). Chip rates are 100 to 1000 times faster than the data message, therefore, chip times are 100 to 1000 times shorter in duration than the time of a single data bit. As a result, the transmitted output frequency spectrum using spread spectrum is 100 to 1000 times wider than the bandwidth of the initial PSK data-modulated signal. The block diagram for a direct-sequence spread-spectrum system is shown in Figure 19-13. As the figure shows, the data source directly modulates the carrier signal, which is then further modulated in the spreading correlator by the spreading code word.

The spreading (chip) codes used in spread-spectrum systems are either *maximal-length sequence codes,* sometimes called *m-sequence codes,* or *Gold codes.* Gold codes are combinations of maximal-length codes invented by Magnavox Corporation in 1967 especially for multiple-access CDMA applications. There is a relatively large set of Gold codes available with minimal correlation between chip codes. For a reasonable number of satellite users, it is impossible to achieve perfectly orthogonal codes. You can only design for a minimum cross correlation among chips.

One of the advantages of CDMA was that the entire bandwidth of a satellite channel or system may be used for each transmission from every earth station. For our example, the chip rate was six times the original bit rate. Consequently, the actual transmission rate of information was one-sixth of the PSK modulation rate, and the bandwidth required is six times that required to simply transmit the original data as binary. Because of the coding inefficiency resulting from transmitting chips for bits, the advantage of more bandwidth is partially offset and is, thus, less of an advantage. Also, if the transmission of chips from the various earth stations must be synchronized, precise timing is required for the system to work. Therefore, the disadvantage of requiring time synchronization in TDMA systems is also present with CDMA. In short, CDMA is not all that it is cracked up to be. The most significant advantage of CDMA is immunity to interference (jamming), which makes CDMA ideally suited for military applications.

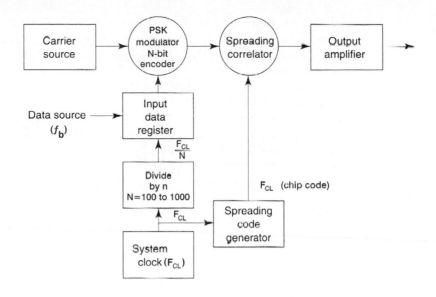

FIGURE 19-13 Simplified block diagram for a direct-sequence spread-spectrum transmitter

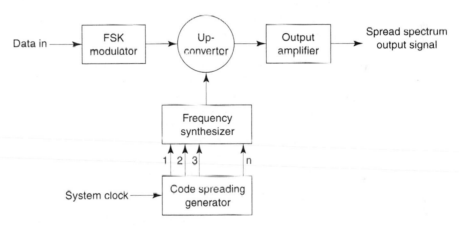

FIGURE 19-14 Simplified block diagram of a frequency-hopping spread-spectrum transmitter

Frequency-hopping spread spectrum (FH-SS).   Frequency hopping is a form of CDMA where a digital code is used to continually change the frequency of the carrier. The carrier is first modulated by the data message and, then, up-converted using a frequency-synthesized local oscillator whose output frequency is determined by an *n*-bit pseudorandom noise code produced in a spreading code generator. The simplified block diagram for a frequency-hopping spread-spectrum transmitter is shown in Figure 19-14.

With frequency hopping, the total available bandwidth is partitioned into smaller frequency bands and the total transmission time is subdivided into smaller time slots. The idea is to transmit within a limited frequency band for only a short time, then switch to another frequency band, and so on. This process continues indefinitely. The frequency-hopping pattern is determined by a binary spreading code. Each station uses a different code sequence. A typical hopping pattern (frequency-time matrix) is shown in Figure 19-15.

With frequency hopping, each earth station within a CDMA network is assigned a different frequency-hopping pattern. Each transmitter switches (hops) from one frequency

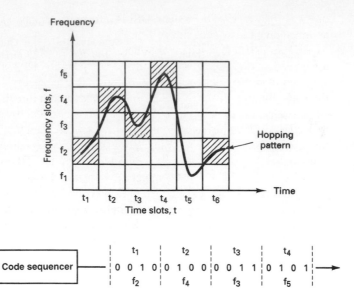

FIGURE 19-15 Frequency time-hopping matrix

band to the next according to their assigned pattern. With frequency hopping, each station uses the entire RF spectrum but never occupies more than a small portion of that spectrum at any one time.

FSK is the modulation scheme most commonly used with frequency hopping. When it is a given station's turn to transmit, it sends one of the two frequencies (either mark or space) for the particular band in which it is transmitting. The number of stations in a given frequency-hopping system is limited by the number of unique hopping patterns that can be generated.

CHANNEL CAPACITY

Essentially, there are two methods used to interface terrestrial voice-band channels with satellite channels: digital noninterpolated interfaces (DNI) and digital speech interpolated interfaces (DSI).

Digital Noninterpolated Interfaces

A *digital noninterpolated interface* assigns an individual terrestrial channel (TC) to a particular satellite channel (SC) for the duration of the call. A DNI system can carry no more traffic than the number of satellite channels it has. Once a TC has been assigned an SC, the SC is unavailable to the other TCs for the duration of the call. DNI is a form of preassignment; each TC has a permanent dedicated SC.

Digital Speech Interpolated Interfaces

A *digital speech interpolated interface* assigns a terrestrial channel to a satellite channel only when speech energy is present on the TC. DSI interfaces have *speech detectors* that are similar to *echo suppressors;* they sense speech energy, then seize an SC. Whenever a speech detector senses energy on a TC, the TC is assigned to an SC. The SC assigned is randomly selected from the idle SCs. On a given TC, each time speech energy is detected, the TC could be assigned to a different SC. Therefore, a single TC can use several SCs for a single call. For demultiplexing purposes, the TC/SC assignment information must be conveyed to the receive terminal. This is done on a common signaling channel similar to the one used on the SPADE system. DSI is a form of demand assignment; SCs are randomly assigned on an as-needed basis.

With DSI it is apparent that there is a *channel compression;* there can be more TCs assigned than there are SCs. Generally, a TC:SC ratio of 2:1 is used. For a full-duplex (two-way simultaneous) communication circuit, there is speech in each direction 40% of the time, and for 20% of the time the circuit is idle in both directions. Therefore, a DSI gain of slightly more than 2 is realized. The DSI gain is affected by a phenomenon called *competitive clipping.* Competitive clipping is when speech energy is detected on a TC and there is no SC to assign it to. During the *wait* time, speech information is lost. Competitive clipping is not noticed by a subscriber if its duration is less than 50 ms.

To further enhance the channel capacity, a technique called *bit stealing* is used. With bit stealing, channels can be added to fully loaded systems by stealing bits from the in-use channels. Generally, an overload channel is generated by stealing the least significant bit from seven other satellite channels. Bit stealing results in eight channels with seven-bit resolution for the time that the *overload channel* is in use. Consequently, bit stealing results in a lower SQR than normal.

Time-Assignment Speech Interpolation

Time-assignment speech interpolation (TASI) is a form of analog channel compression that has been used for suboceanic cables for many years. TASI is very similar to DSI except that the signals interpolated are analog rather than digital. TASI also uses a 2:1 compression ratio. TASI was also the first means used to scramble voice for military security. TASI is similar to a packet data network; the voice message is chopped up into smaller segments made of sounds or portions of sounds. The sounds are sent through the network as separate bundles of energy, then put back together at the receive end to reform the original voice message.

SATELLITE RADIO NAVIGATION

Navigation can be defined as the art or science of plotting, ascertaining, or directing the course of movements; in other words, *knowing where you are and being able to find your way around.* The most ancient and rudimentary method of navigation is *wandering.* Wandering is simply continuing to travel about until you reach your destination, assuming of course that you have one. My good friend and worldwide traveler, Todd Ferguson, once said, "True travel has no destination." Wandering is the popular navigation technique used by many students during their first week of classes at all colleges and universities. Probably the earliest effective or useful means of navigation is *celestial navigation.* With celestial navigation, direction and distance are determined from precisely timed sightings of celestial bodies, including the stars and moon. This is a primitive technique that dates back thousands of years. An obvious disadvantage of celestial navigation is that it works best at night, preferably with clear skies.

Another rather rudimentary method of navigation is *piloting.* Piloting is fixing a position and direction with respect to familiar, significant landmarks such as railroad tracks, water towers, barns, mountain peaks, and bodies of water. Piloting derived its name from early aircraft pilots who used this method of navigation.

Dead (ded) *reckoning* is a navigation technique that determines position by extrapolating a series of measured velocity increments. The term *dead* is derived from the word "*deduced*" and not necessarily from the fate of the people who used the technique. Dead reckoning was used quite successfully by Charles Lindbergh in 1927 during his historic 33-h transatlantic journey and quite unsuccessfully by Amelia Earhart in 1937 during her attempt to make the first round-the-world flight.

Although each of the navigation methods described thus far had its place in time, undoubtedly the most accurate navigation technique to date is *radio* or *electronic navigation.*

With radio navigation, position is determined by measuring the travel time of an electromagnetic wave as it moves from a transmitter to a receiver. There are approximately 100 different types of domestic radio navigation systems currently being used. Some use terrestrial (land-based) broadcast transmitters and others use satellite (space-based) broadcast transmitters. The most accurate and useful radio navigation systems include:

Decca (terrestrial surface broadcast)

Omega (terrestrial surface broadcast)*

Loran (terrestrial surface broadcast)

Navy Transit GPS (low-orbit satellite broadcast)*

Navstar GPS (medium-orbit satellite broadcast)*

Loran and Navstar are the two most often used radio navigation systems today.

Loran Navigation

Until recently, *Loran* (*Lo*ng *Ra*nge *N*avigation) was the most effective, reliable, and accurate means of radio navigation. Loran-A was developed during World War II, and the most recent version, Loran-C, surfaced in 1980. Today, Loran is used primarily for recreational aircraft and ships.

With Loran, receivers acquire specially coded signals from two pairs of high-powered, land-based transmitters whose locations are precisely known. The elapsed time between reception of the coded signals is precisely measured and converted in the receiver to distance using the propagation speed of electromagnetic waves. Using basic geometry and the relationship between distance (d), speed (v), and time (t) ($d = vt$), the location of the receiver can be determined with a high degree of accuracy. There is only one set of coordinates that possess a particular time (distance) relationship from four sources.

Loran is only as accurate as the preciseness of the transmission times of the coded signals. System errors are primarily due to propagation problems, such as the fact that Earth's surface is not smooth nor is it perfectly round. Atmospheric conditions and multiple transmission paths can also adversely affect the performance of Loran. However, probably the most prominent disadvantage of Loran is the fact that it does not provide continuous worldwide coverage. Land-based transmitters can only be located where there is land, which is a relatively small proportion of Earth's surface. Consequently, there are locations where Loran signals simply cannot be received (dead spots). However good or bad Loran may have been or could be is unimportant because a newer, better technique of radio navigation called Navstar GPS has emerged that utilizes satellite-based transmitters.

Navstar GPS

Navstar is an acronym for *Nav*igation *S*ystem with *T*ime *A*nd *R*anging, and *GPS* is an abbreviation of Global Positioning System. Navstar GPS is the newest and most accurate system of radio navigation available. Navstar GPS is a satellite-based open navigation system, which simply means that it is available to anyone equipped with a GPS receiver. The United States Department of Defense (DoD) developed Navstar to provide continuous, highly precise position, velocity, and time information to land-, sea-, air-, and space-based users. In essence, Navstar GPS is a space-based navigation, three-dimensional positioning, and time-distribution system. The intent of the system is to use a combination of ground stations, orbiting satellites, and special receivers to provide navigation capabilities to virtually everyone, at any time, anywhere in the world, regardless of weather conditions. The Navstar Satellite System was completed in 1994 and is maintained by the United States Air Force.

*Provides global coverage

GPS Services

GPS provides two levels of service or accuracy: standard positioning service and precise positioning service.

Standard positioning service (SPS). The *standard positioning service* is a positioning and timing service that is available to all GPS users (military, private, and commercial) on a continuous, worldwide basis with no direct charge. SPS will provide a predictable positioning accuracy that 95% of the time is to within 100 m horizontally, 156 m vertically, and 185 m 3 D, with a time transfer accuracy to UTC (*Universal Transverse Mercator Grid*) within 340 nanoseconds. The accuracy of the SPS service can be downgraded during times of national emergencies. For security reasons, the accuracy of the SPS service is intentionally degraded by the DoD through the use of a technique called *selective availability*. Selective availability (SA) is accomplished by manipulating navigation message orbit data (epsilon) and/or the satellite clock frequency (dither).

Precise positioning service (PPS). The *precise positioning service* is a highly accurate military positioning, velocity, and timing service that is available on a continuous, worldwide basis to users authorized by the DoD. PPS user equipment provides a predictable positioning accuracy 95% of the time of at least 22 m horizontally, 27.7 m vertically, and 35.4 m 3-D, and a time transfer accuracy to UTC within 200 nanoseconds. Only authorized users with cryptographic equipment and keys and specially equipped receivers can use the precise positioning service. PPS was designed primarily to be used by the U.S. and allied military, certain U.S. government agencies, and selected civil users specifically approved by the U.S. government.

Navstar Segments

Navstar GPS consists of three segments: a *space segment,* a *ground control segment,* and a *user segment.*

Satellite segment. The U.S. Air Force Space Command (AFSC) formally declared the Navstar GPS satellite system as being fully operational as of April 27, 1995. The satellite segment, sometimes called the *space segment,* consists of 24 operational satellites revolving around Earth in six orbital planes approximately 60° apart with four satellites in each plane. There are 21 working satellites and 3 satellites reserved as spaces. In the event of a satellite failure, one of the spare space vehicles can be moved into its place. (There are actually more than 24 satellites now as some of the older space vehicles have been replaced with newer satellites with more modern propulsion and guidance systems.) Figure 19-16a shows orbital patterns for the 21 working satellites in the Navstar constellation, and Figure 19 16b shows the relative positions of the 24 satellites in respect to each other.

Navstar satellites are not geosynchronous. The satellites revolve around Earth in a circular pattern with an inclined orbit. The angle of elevation at the ascending node is 55° with respect to the equatorial plane. The average elevation of a Navstar satellite is 9476 statute miles (approximately 20,200 km) above Earth. Navstar satellites take approximately 12 h to orbit Earth. Therefore, their position is approximately the same at the same sidereal time each day (the satellites actually appear four minutes earlier each day). Figure 19-17 shows the orbits of several Navstar satellites superimposed over a Mercator projection of the world. As the figure shows, the satellites spiral around Earth in six planes virtually covering the surface of the entire globe.

The position of the Navstar satellites in orbit is arranged such that between five and eight satellites will be in view of any user at all times, thereby ensuring continuous worldwide coverage. Information from three satellites is needed to calculate a navigational unit's horizontal location on Earth's surface (*two-dimensional reporting*), but information from four satellites enables a receiver to also determine its altitude (*three-dimensional reporting*). Three-

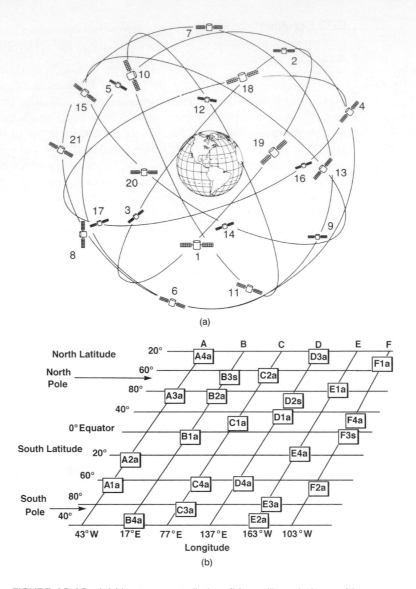

North Latitude 20°

North Pole 60°

80°

40°

0° Equator

South Latitude 20°

60°

South Pole 80°

40°

	A	B	C	D	E	F
A4a				D3a		F1a
		B3s	C2a			
A3a	B2a				E1a	
				D2s		
			C1a	D1a		F4a
	B1a					F3s
A2a					E4a	
A1a		C4a	D4a			F2a
					E3a	
B4a		C3a		E2a		

43°W   17°E   77°E   137°E   163°W   103°W

Longitude

(b)

FIGURE 19-16   (a) Navstar constellation; (b) satellite relative positions

dimensional reporting is obviously more crucial on land because ground surfaces are not constant, whereas the surface of a large body of water is. Navstar satellites broadcast navigation and system data, atmospheric propagation correction data, and satellite clock bias information.

Navstar Satellite Groupings.   There have been three distinct groups plus one subgroup of Navstar satellites. The groups are designated as *blocks*. The 11 block I prototype satellites were intended to be used only for system testing. Block II satellites were the first fully functional satellites that included on-board *cesium atomic clocks* for producing highly accurate timing signals. Block II satellites are capable of detecting certain error conditions, then automatically transmitting a coded message indicating that it is out of service. Block II satellites can operate for approximately 3.5 days between receiving updates and corrections from the control segment of the system. Block IIa satellites are identical to the standard block II versions except they can operate continuously for 180 days between uploads from the ground. The latest satcllites, block IIR versions, can operate for 180 days between uploads and possess autonomous navigation capabilities by generating their own naviga-

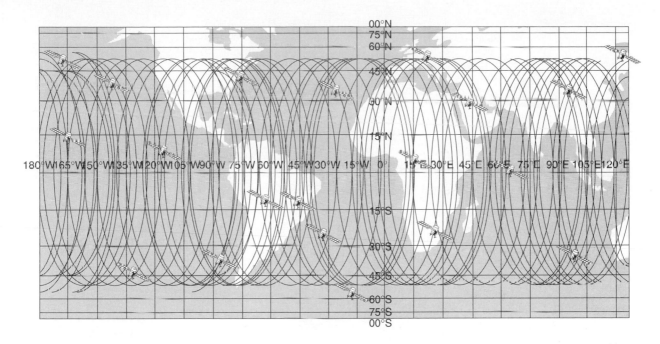

FIGURE 19-17 Mercator projection of Navstar satellite orbits

tion information. Thus, the accuracy of the system using block IIR satellites can be maintained longer between uploads.

Navstar Satellite Identification. Each satellite has three identifying numbers. The first number is the Navstar number that identifies the specific satellite on-board hardware. The second number is the space vehicle (SV) number, which is assigned according to the order of the vehicle's launch. The third number is a *pseudorandom noise* (PRN) *code* number. This unique integer number is used to encrypt the signal from that satellite. Some GPS receivers identify the satellite from which they are receiving transmissions by the SV numbers, others use the PRN number.

Each Navstar satellite continually transmits a daily updated set of digitally coded *ephemeris data* that describes its precise orbit. Ephemeris is a term generally associated with a table showing the position of a heavenly body on a number of dates in a regular sequence, in essence, an astronomical almanac. Ephemeris data can also be computed for a satellite that specifies where on Earth the satellite is directly above at any given instant in terms of latitude and longitude coordinates.

Satellite Ranging. The GPS system works by determining how long it takes a radio signal transmitted from a satellite to reach a land-based receiver and, then, using that time to calculate the distance between the satellite and the earth station receiver. Radio waves travel at approximately the speed of light, 3×10^8 m/s. If a receiver can determine exactly when a satellite began sending a radio message and exactly when the message was received, then it can determine the propagation (delay) time. From the propagation time, the receiver can determine the distance between it and the satellite using the simple mathematical relationship

$$d = v \times t$$

where d = distance between satellite and receiver (meters)
 v = velocity (3×10^8 m/s)
 t = propagation time (seconds)

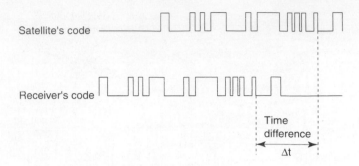

FIGURE 19-18   GPS pseudorandom timing code

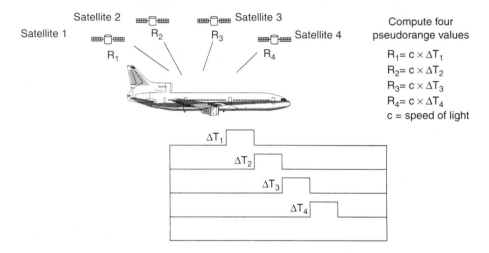

Time signals transmitted by satellites

FIGURE 19-19   GPS ranging solution

The trick, of course, is in determining exactly when the synchronizing signal left the satellite. To determine this, the satellite transmitter and earth station receiver produce identical synchronizing (pseudorandom) codes at exactly the same time, as shown in Figure 19-18. Each satellite continuously transmits its precise synchronizing code. After a synchronizing code is acquired, a receiver simply compares the received code with its own locally produced code to determine the propagation time. The time difference multiplied by the velocity of the radio signal gives the distance to the satellite.

Figure 19-19 illustrates how an aircraft can determine the range (distance) it is from four different satellites by simply measuring the propagation (delay) times and multiplying them by the speed of light. Again, simultaneous equations can be used to determine the aircraft's longitude and latitude.

For a receiver on Earth to determine its longitude and latitude, it must receive signals from three or more satellites identifying the satellite vehicle number or their pseudorandom timing code (PRN) and each satellite's location. The location of a satellite is described using a three-dimensional coordinate relative to Earth's center as shown in Figure 19-20. Earth's center is the reference point with coordinates 0, 0, 0. Thus, each satellite space vehicle has an X_s, Y_s, Z_s coordinate that pinpoints its location in respect to Earth's geocenter. The coordinates of the satellites, however, must be updated continually because

Satellite vehicle
location
(X_s, Y_s, Z_0)

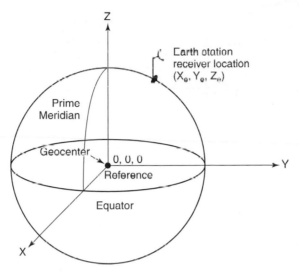

Earth station
receiver location
(X_e, Y_e, Z_e)

FIGURE 19-20 GPS satellite and earth station receiver coordinate system

they vary slightly as the satellite orbits Earth. The location of an earth station also has a three-dimensional coordinate, X_e, Y_e, Z_e, referenced to Earth's center as shown in Figure 19-20.

If an earth station receiver knows the location of a single satellite and the distance the satellite is from the receiver, it knows that it must be located somewhere on an imaginary sphere centered on the satellite with a radius equal to the distance the satellite is from the receiver. This is shown in Figure 19-21a. If the receiver knows the location of two satellites and their distances from the receiver, it can narrow its location to somewhere on the circle formed where the two spheres intersect as shown in Figure 19-21b. If the location and distance to a third satellite is known, a receiver can pinpoint its location to one of two possible locations in space as shown in Figure 19-21c. The GPS receivers can usually determine which point is the correct location as one location is generally a ridiculous value. If the location and distance from a fourth satellite is known, the altitude of the earth station can also be determined.

Figure 19-22 shows there are three unknown position coordinates (x, y, and z). Therefore, three equations from three satellites are required to solve for the three unknown coordinates. A fourth unknown is the error in the receiver's clock, which affects the accuracy of the time-difference measurement. To eliminate the *clock bias error* (C_b), a fourth satellite is needed to produce the fourth equation necessary to solve for four unknowns using simultaneous equations. The solutions to the simultaneous equations for determining latitude and longitude are given in Figure 19-22.

GPS Satellite Signals. All Navstar satellites transmit on the same two *L-band* microwave carrier frequencies: $L_1 = 1575.42$ MHz and $L_2 = 1227.6$ MHz. The L_1 signal carries the navigation message and the standard positioning service (SPS) code signals. The L_2 signal is used by the precise positioning service (PPS) equipped receivers to measure the

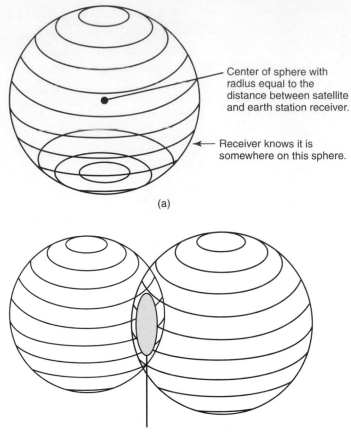

Center of sphere with radius equal to the distance between satellite and earth station receiver.

Receiver knows it is somewhere on this sphere.

(a)

Two measurements put receiver somewhere on this circle.

(b)

Three measurements puts receiver at one of two points.

(c)

FIGURE 19-21 Earth station receiver location relative to the distance from (a) one satellite, (b) two satellites, and (c) three satellites

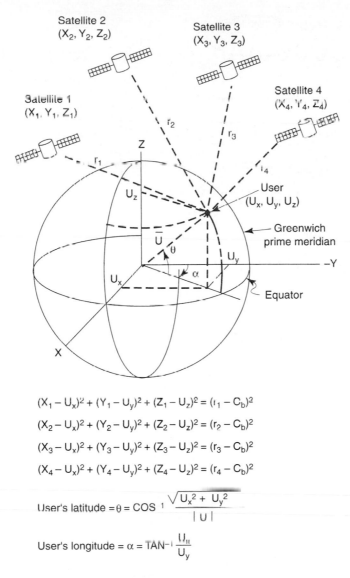

Satellite 2
(X_2, Y_2, Z_2)

Satellite 3
(X_3, Y_3, Z_3)

Satellite 1
(X_1, Y_1, Z_1)

Satellite 4
(X_4, Y_4, Z_4)

r_2

r_3

r_1

r_4

Z

U_z

User
(U_x, U_y, U_z)

$\bar{U}$

θ

Greenwich
prime meridian

U_y

$-Y$

α

U_x

Equator

X

$$(X_1 - U_x)^2 + (Y_1 - U_y)^2 + (Z_1 - U_z)^2 = (r_1 - C_b)^2$$

$$(X_2 - U_x)^2 + (Y_2 - U_y)^2 + (Z_2 - U_z)^2 = (r_2 - C_b)^2$$

$$(X_3 - U_x)^2 + (Y_3 - U_y)^2 + (Z_3 - U_z)^2 = (r_3 - C_b)^2$$

$$(X_4 - U_x)^2 + (Y_4 - U_y)^2 + (Z_4 - U_z)^2 = (r_4 - C_b)^2$$

$$\text{User's latitude} = \theta = \text{COS}^{-1} \frac{\sqrt{U_x^2 + U_y^2}}{|U|}$$

$$\text{User's longitude} = \alpha = \text{TAN}^{-1} \frac{U_x}{U_y}$$

FIGURE 19-22 GPS satellite position calculations

ionospheric delay. GPS satellites use code division multiple accessing (CDMA spread *spectrum*), which allows all 24 satellites to transmit simultaneously on both carriers without interfering with each other. Three pseudorandom binary codes modulate the L_1 and L_2 carriers as shown in Figure 19-23.

1. The coarse/acquisition (C/A) code is a repeating pseudorandom noise (PRN) code with a 1.023-MHz chip rate and a period of 1 ms. This noiselike code modulates the L_1 carrier signal, spreading its spectrum over approximately a 1-MHz bandwidth. Each satellite vehicle has a different C/A PRN code which is used primarily to acquire the P-code. Satellites are often identified by their unique PRN number.

2. The precision (P) code has a 10.23-MHz rate, lasts a period of seven days, and contains the principle navigation ranging code. In the *antispoofing* (AS) mode, the P-code is encrypted into the Y-code which requires a classified AS module in each receiver channel and is used only by authorized users. The P (Y) code is the basis for the precision positioning system.

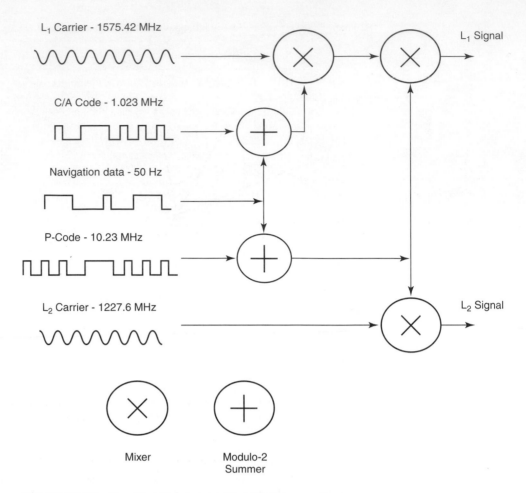

L₁ Carrier - 1575.42 MHz

C/A Code - 1.023 MHz

Navigation data - 50 Hz

P-Code - 10.23 MHz

L₂ Carrier - 1227.6 MHz

L₁ Signal

L₂ Signal

Mixer

Modulo-2
Summer

FIGURE 19-23   Simplified Navstar satellite CDMA transmitter

3. The Y-code is used in place of the P-code whenever the antispoofing (AS) mode of operation is activated. Antispoofing guards against fake transmissions of satellite data by encrypting the P-code to form the Y-code.

Due to the spread-spectrum characteristics of the modulated carriers, the Navstar system provides a large margin of resistance to interference. Each satellite transmits a navigation message containing its orbital elements, clock behavior, system time, and status messages. In addition, an almanac is provided which gives the approximate ephemeris data for each active satellite and, thus, allows the users to find all the satellites once the first one has been acquired.

The navigation message modulates the L_1-C/A code signal as shown in Figure 19-23. The navigation message is a 50-Hz signal made of data bits that describe the GPS satellite orbits, clock corrections, and other system parameters. The data format used for the navigation message is shown in Figure 19-24. The navigation data frame consists of 1500 data bits divided into five 300-bit subframes. A navigation frame is transmitted once every 30 s (6 s for each subframe) for a transmission rate of 50 bps. Each subframe is preceded by a telemetry word (TLM) and a handover word (HOW). The TLM contains an 8-bit preamble, 24 data bits, and six parity bits; the HOW contains a 17-bit code identifying the time of week, seven data bits, and six parity bits.

The first subframe contains satellite vehicle correction data and the second and third subframes contain ephemeris parameter data. The fourth and fifth subframes are used to

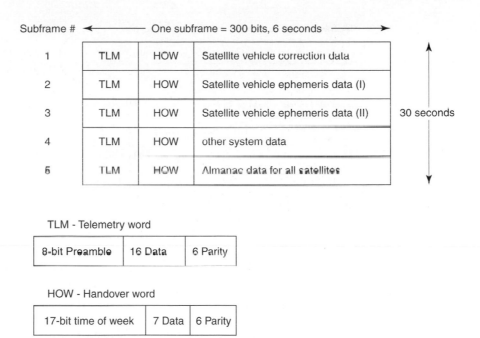

Subframe # ←——————— One subframe = 300 bits, 6 seconds ———————→

1	TLM	HOW	Satellite vehicle correction data
2	TLM	HOW	Satellite vehicle ephemeris data (I)
3	TLM	HOW	Satellite vehicle ephemeris data (II)
4	TLM	HOW	other system data
5	TLM	HOW	Almanac data for all satellites

30 seconds

TLM - Telemetry word

| 8-bit Preamble | 16 Data | 6 Parity |

HOW - Handover word

| 17-bit time of week | 7 Data | 6 Parity |

FIGURE 19-24 Navigation data frame format

transmit different pages of system data including almanac data for all systems. Twenty-five frames (125 subframes) comprise the complete navigation message that is sent over a 12.5-min period.

Control segment.   The Navstar control segment, called the *operational control system* (OCS), includes all the fixed-location ground-based *monitor stations* located throughout the world, a *Master Control Station* (MCS), and up link transmitters. There are passive monitor stations located in California, Hawaii, Alaska, Ascencion Island (off West Africa), Diego Garcia (Indian Ocean), Kwajalein (Pacific Ocean), among others. The monitor stations are simply GPS receivers that track the satellites as they pass overhead and accumulate ranging and ephemeris (orbital) data from them. This information is relayed to the Master Control Station at Falcon Air Force Base, 12 mi east of Colorado Springs, Colorado, where it is processed and determined if the actual satellite position compares with the GPS-computed position. The Master Control Station is managed by the U.S. Air Force's 2nd Space Operations Squadron (2nd SOPS).

The MCS receives data from the monitor stations in real time, 24 hours a day, and uses that information to determine if any satellites are experiencing clock or ephemeris changes and to detect equipment malfunctions. New navigation and ephemeris information is calculated from the monitored signals and uploaded to the satellites once or twice per day. The information calculated by the MCS, along with routine maintenance commands, are relayed to the satellites by ground-based up-link antennas. The ground antennas are located at Ascension Island, Diego Garcia, and Kwajalein. The antenna facilities transmit to the satellites via an *S-band* radio link. In addition to its main function, the MCS maintains a 24-h computer bulletin board system with the latest system news and status.

User segment.   The GPS user segment consists of all the GPS receivers and the user community. GPS receivers convert signals received from space vehicles into position, velocity, and time estimates. Four satellites are required to compute the four dimensions of x, y, z (position) and time. GPS receivers are used for navigation, positioning, time

TABLE 19-1 Summary of GPS Error Sources

Per Satellite Accuracy	Standard GPS	Differential GPS
Satellite clocks	1.5	0
Orbit errors	2.5	0
Ionosphere	5.0	0.4
Troposphere	0.5	0.2
Receiver noise	0.3	0.3
Multipath reception	0.6	0.6
Selective availability	30.	0
Typical Position Accuracy (meters)		
Horizontal	50	1.3
Vertical	78	2.0
3-D	93	2.4

dissemination, mapping, guidance systems, surveying, photogrammetry, public safety, archaeology, geology, geophysics, wildlife, aviation, marine, and numerous other research applications. Navigation in three dimensions, however, is the primary function of GPS.

GPS navigation receivers are made for aircraft, ships, ground vehicles, and handheld units for individuals. GPS navigation precise positioning is possible using GPS receivers at reference locations providing corrections and relative positioning data for remote receivers. Surveying, geodetic control, and plate tectonic studies are examples. Time and frequency dissemination, based on the precise clocks on board the space vehicles and controlled by the monitor stations, is another use for GPS. Astronomical observatories, telecommunications facilities, and laboratory standards can be set to precise time signals or controlled to accurate frequencies by special-purpose GPS receivers.

Differential GPS

Differential GPS makes standard GPS even more accurate. Differential GPS works by canceling out most of the natural and man-made errors that creep into normal GPS measurements. Inaccuracies in GPS signals come from a variety of sources, such as satellite clock drift, imperfect orbits, and variations in Earth's atmosphere. These imperfections are variable and difficult if not impossible to predict. Therefore, what is needed is a means to measure the actual errors as they are occurring.

With differential GPS, a second receiver is placed in a location whose exact position is known. It calculates its position from the satellite data and, then, compares it with its known position. The difference between the calculated and known positions is the error in the GPS signal. Differential GPS is only practical in locations where you can leave a receiver permanently, such as near an airport.

Sources of errors in GPS are satellite clocks, selective availability, ephemeris, atmospheric delays, multipath, receiver clocks, and so on. Table 19-1 summarizes GPS error sources for both standard and differential GPS.

QUESTIONS

19-1. Discuss the drawbacks of using FDM/FM modulation for satellite multiple-accessing systems.

19-2. Contrast *preassignment* and *demand assignment.*

19-3. What are the three most common multiple-accessing arrangements used with satellite systems?

19-4. Briefly describe the multiple-accessing arrangements listed in Question 19-3.

19-5. Briefly describe the operation of Comsat's SPADE system.

19-6. What is meant by *single-carrier per channel?*

19-7. What is a common-signaling channel, and how is it used?

19-8. Describe what a reference burst is for TDMA and explain the following terms: preamble, carrier recovery sequence, bit timing recovery, unique word, and correlation spike.

19-9. Describe guard time.

19-10. Briefly describe the operation of the CEPT primary multiplex frame.

19-11. What is a store-and-forward system?

19-12. What is the primary advantage of TDMA as compared with FDMA?

19-13. What is the primary advantage of FDMA as compared with TDMA?

19-14. Briefly describe the operation of a CDMA multiple-accessing system.

19-15. Describe a chip code.

19-16. Describe what is meant by an orthogonal code.

19-17. Describe cross correlation.

19-18. What are the advantages of CDMA as compared with TDMA and FDMA?

19-19. What are the disadvantages of CDMA?

19-20. What is a Gold code?

19-21. Describe frequency hopping.

19-22. What is a frequency-time matrix?

19-23. Describe digital noninterpolated interfaces.

19-24. Describe digital speech interpolated interfaces.

19-25. What is channel compression, and how is it accomplished with a DSI system?

19-26. Describe competitive clipping.

19-27. What is meant by *bit stealing?*

19-28. Describe time-assignment speech interpolation.

PROBLEMS

19-1. How many satellite transponders are required to interlink six earth stations with FDM/FM modulation?

19-2. For the SPADE system, what are the carrier frequencies for channel 7? What are the allocated passbands for channel 7? What are the actual passband frequencies (excluding guard bands) required?

19-3. If a 512-bit preamble precedes each CEPT station's transmission, what is the maximum number of earth stations that can be linked together with a single satellite transponder?

19-4. Determine an orthogonal code for the following chip code (101010). Prove that your selection will not produce any cross correlation for an in-phase comparison. Determine the cross correlation for each out-of-phase condition that is possible.

19-5. How many satellite transponders are required to interlink five earth stations with FDM/FM modulation?

19-6. For the SPADE system, what are the carrier frequencies for channel 9? What are the allocated passbands for channel 10? What are the actual passband frequencies for channel 12 (excluding the guard bands)?

19-7. If a 256-bit preamble precedes each CEPT station's transmission, what is the maximum number of earth stations that can be linked together with a single satellite transponder?

19-8. Determine an orthogonal code for the following chip code (010101). Prove that your selection will not produce any cross correlation for an in-phase comparison. Determine the cross correlation for each out-of-phase condition that is possible.

CHAPTER 20

Mobile Telephone Service

INTRODUCTION

Although the basic concepts of two-way radio telephone communications are quite simple, *mobile telephone service* has evolved into a communications monster that is a rather complicated issue. Mobile telephone involves intricate and somewhat complex communications networks consisting of both analog and digital communications methodologies, sophisticated computer-controlled switching centers and procedures, and several methods of multiple accessing. The purpose of this chapter is to present the fundamental concepts of mobile telephone service and introduce the reader to several systems currently in use to provide the service including standard *cellular telephone services* (CTS), *personal communications systems* (PCS), and *personal communications satellite systems* (PCSS). Mobile telephone service began in the early 1940s, but due to its high cost, limited availability, and narrow frequency allocation, the early systems were not widely used. In recent years, however, technological advancements, a wider frequency spectrum, increased availability, and improved reliability have provoked a phenomenal increase in people's desire to talk on the telephone, anywhere, at any time, regardless of whether it is necessary or productive.

The mobile station is usually a small handset these days. In early radio terminology, the term *mobile* originally suggested any radio transmitter, receiver, or transceiver that could be moved while in operation. The term *portable,* on the other hand, described a relatively small radio transceiver that was handheld, battery powered, and easily carried by a person traveling at walking speed. The contemporary definition of *mobile,* however, has come to mean moving at high speed such as in a boat or an automobile or at low speed such as in the pocket of a pedestrian. Hence, the modern, all-inclusive definition of *mobile telephone* is any radio telephone that is capable of operating while moving at any speed, battery powered, and small enough to be easily carried by a person.

Mobile telephone is similar to two-way mobile radio in that most communication occurs between a base station and a mobile unit or between two or more mobile units. Mobile telephone, however, is best described by pointing out the primary differences between it and two-way mobile radio. As explained in Chapter 7, two-way mobile radio systems are half-duplex, push-to-talk communications networks where all transmissions (unless scrambled) can be heard by any listener with a receiver tuned to that channel. Hence, two-way mobile radio is a *one-to-many* communications system. The most commonly used mobile radio systems are *citizens band* (CB) radio, which is an AM system, and *public land mobile radio,* which is a two-way FM system such as is used by municipal agencies (e.g., police and fire departments). Most two-way mobile radio systems can only access the public telephone network through a special arrangement called an *autopatch,* and then they are generally limited to half-duplex operation where neither party can interrupt the other. An autopatch is a remote controlled device used to connect a two-way radio transceiver to the public telephone network; however, if both parties talked at the same time through a mobile radio system, there would be no communications. Another limitation of two-way mobile radio is their transmissions are limited to relatively small geographic areas without utilizing complicated and rather limited repeater networks.

Mobile telephone, on the other hand, offers full-duplex transmissions and operates much the same way as the standard *wireline telephone service* provided to homes and businesses by local telephone companies. Mobile telephone is a *one-to-one* system that permits two-way simultaneous transmissions and, for privacy, each mobile telephone unit is assigned a unique number (i.e., a telephone number). Coded transmissions from the base station activate only the intended receiver. With mobile telephone, a person can call virtually anyone with a telephone number, whether it be through a mobile or a wireline service.

EVOLUTION OF MOBILE TELEPHONE

Analog mobile telephone services in the United States were first introduced in 1946 with service provided to 25 major cities. Each utilized one base station consisting of a high-powered transmitter and a sensitive receiver that were centrally located on top of a hill or tower and that covered approximately a 30-mile radius of the base station. The first half-duplex, push-to-talk FM mobile telephone systems were introduced in the late 1940s and required 120 kHz of bandwidth per channel. In the early 1950s the FCC doubled the number of mobile telephone channels by reducing the bandwidth to 60 kHz per channel. In 1960 AT&T introduced direct-dialing, full-duplex service with other performance enhancements, and in 1968 proposed the concept of a cellular mobile system to the FCC. By the mid-1970s, cellular mobile telephone systems were developed and miniature integrated circuits enabled management of the necessarily complex algorithms needed to control network switching and control operations. The bandwidth was again halved to 30 kHz, again increasing the number of mobile telephone channels available by twofold.

In 1974 the FCC allocated an additional 40 MHz of bandwidth for cellular radio service (825 MHz to 845 MHz and 870 MHz to 890 MHz). These frequency bands were previously allocated to UHF television channels 70 to 83. In 1975, the FCC granted AT&T the first license to operate a developmental cellular radio service in Chicago. The following year the FCC granted authorization to the American Radio Telephone Service (ARTS) to install a second developmental system in the Baltimore–Washington, D.C., area. In 1983, the FCC allocated 666, 30-kHz half-duplex mobile telephone channels to AT&T to form the first U.S. cellular telephone system called Advanced Mobile Phone System (AMPS). The AMPS system originally occupied a 40 MHz bandwidth in the 800-MHz band, but in 1989 the FCC granted an additional 166 half-duplex channels.

In 1991 the first digital cellular services were introduced in several major U.S. cities enabling a more efficient utilization of the available bandwidth using voice compression. The capacity specified in the U.S. Digital Cellular (USDC) standard (EIA IS-54) accommodates three times the capacity of AMPS which used conventional FM and frequency-division multiple accessing (FDMA). The USDC standard specifies digital modulation, speech coding, and time-division multiple accessing (TDMA). Qualcomm developed the first cellular telephone system based on code-division multiple accessing (CDMA). Qualcomm's system was standardized by the Telecommunications Industry Association (TIA) as an Interim Standard (IS-95). On November 17, 1998, a subsidiary of Motorola Corporation went live with Iridium, a satellite-based wireless personal communications network, beginning a new era of personal communications services. Iridium is designed to permit a wide range of mobile telephone services including voice, data, facsimile, and paging.

TWO-WAY MOBILE COMMUNICATIONS SERVICES

There are many types of two-way radio communications systems that offer a wide variety of services including the following:

1. Two-way mobile radio. Half-duplex, one-to-many radio communications with no dial tone.
   a. Class D citizens band (CB) radio. Provides 26.96 to 27.41 MHz (40, 10-kHz shared channels) public, noncommercial radio service for either personal or business use utilizing push-to-talk AM DSBFC and AM SSBFC. There are three other lesser known CB classifications (A, B, and C).
   b. Amateur (ham) radio. Covers a broad-frequency band from 1.8 MHz to above 300 MHz. Designed for personal use without pecuniary interest. Amateur radio offers a broad range of classes including CW, AM, FM, radio teleprinter (RTTY), HF slow scan still-picture TV (SSTV), VHF or UHF slow- or fast-scan television and facsimile, and audio FSK (AFSK).
   c. Aeronautical Broadcasting Service (ABS). Provides 2.8 MHz to 457 MHz. ABS disseminates information for the purposes of air navigation and air-to-ground communications utilizing conventional AM and various forms of AM SSB in the HF, MF, and VHF frequency bands.
   d. Private land mobile radio services.
      i. Public safety radio including two-way UHF and VHF push-to-talk FM systems typically used by police and fire departments, highway maintenance, forestry conservation, and local government radio services.
      ii. Special emergency radio including medical, rescue disaster relief, school bus, veterinarian, beach patrol, and paging radio services.
      iii. Industrial radio including power company, petroleum company, forest product, business, manufacturer, motion picture, press relay, and telephone maintenance radio service.
2. Mobile telephone service. Full-duplex, one-to-one radio telephone communications.
   a. Analog cellular radio. FM transmission using FDMA or TDMA.
   b. Digital cellular radio. Personal communications system (PCS). PSK transmission of PCM-encoded voice signals using TDMA, FDMA, and CDMA.
   c. Personal communications satellite service (PCSS). Provides worldwide telecommunications service using handheld telephones that communicate with each other through low earth-orbit satellite repeaters incorporating QPSK modulation and both FDMA and TDMA.

CELLULAR TELEPHONE

Cellular telephone (sometimes called *cellular radio*) corrects many of the problems of traditional two-way mobile telephone service and creates a totally new environment for both mobile and traditional wireline telephone service. The key concepts of cellular radio were uncovered in 1947 by researchers at Bell Telephone Laboratories and other telecommunications companies throughout the world when they developed the basic concepts and theory of cellular telephone. It was determined that by subdividing a relatively large geographical market area, called a *coverage zone*, into smaller sections, called *cells*, the concept of *frequency reuse* could be employed to dramatically increase the capacity of a mobile telephone channel. Frequency reuse is described later in this chapter. In essence, cellular telephone systems allow a large number of users to share a limited number of *common usage* channels available in a region. In addition, integrated-circuit technology and microprocessors and microcontroller chips have recently enabled complex radio and logic circuits to be used in electronic switching machines to store programs that provide faster and more efficient call processing.

Basic Cellular Telephone Concepts

The basic concept of cellular telephone is quite simple. The FCC originally defined geographic cellular radio coverage areas based on modified 1980 census figures. With the cellular concept, each area is further divided into hexagonal-shaped cells that fit together to form a *honeycomb* pattern as shown in Figure 20-1. The hexagon shape was chosen because it provides the most effective transmission by approximating a circular pattern, while eliminating gaps inherently present between adjacent circles. A cell is defined by its physical size and, more importantly, by the size of its population and traffic patterns. The number of cells per system is not specifically defined by the FCC and has been left to the provider to establish in accordance with anticipated traffic patterns. Each geographical area is allocated a fixed number of cellular voice channels. The physical size of a cell varies depending on the user density. For example, *macrocells* typically have a radius of between 1 mile and 15 miles with output power levels of between 1 watt and 20 watts. Microcells typically have

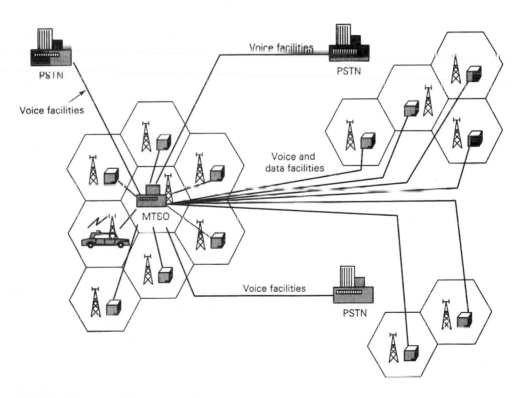

FIGURE 20-1 Simplified cellular telephone system

a radius of between a few feet and several hundred feet with output power levels of between 0.1 watt and 1 watt. *Microcells* are used most often in cities, where they can appear on the streets and inside buildings. By virtue of their low effective working radius, microcells exhibit milder propagation impairments such as reflections and signal delays. Macrocells may overlay microcell clusters with slow-moving mobile units using the microcells and faster moving units using macrocells. The mobile unit will be able to identify itself as either fast or slow moving, thus allowing it to do fewer cell transfers and location updates. Cell transfer algorithms can be modified to allow for the small distances between a mobile unit and its microcellular base station. Figure 20-2 shows what a hexagonal cell grid might look like when it is superimposed over a metropolitan area.

Cellular telephone is an intriguing mobile radio concept that calls for replacing a single, high-powered fixed base station transmitter located high above the center of a city with multiple, low-powered duplicates of the fixed infrastructure distributed over the coverage area on sites placed closer to the ground. The cellular concept adds a spatial dimension to the simple cable-trunking model of typical wireline telephone systems.

Frequency Reuse

Frequency reuse is the process in which the same set of frequencies (channels) can be allocated to more than one cell, provided the cells are a certain distance apart. Reducing each cell's coverage area invites frequency reuse. Cells using the same set of radio channels can avoid mutual interference providing they are a sufficient distance apart. Each cell base station is allocated a group of channel frequencies that are different from those of neighboring cells, and base station antennas are chosen to achieve a desired coverage pattern (footprint) within its cell. However, so long as a coverage area is limited to within a cell's boundaries, the same group of channel frequencies may be used in a different cell providing the two cells are sufficiently separated from one another.

Figure 20-3 illustrates the concept of cellular frequency reuse. Cells with the same letter use the same set of channel frequencies. When designing a system using hexagonal-shaped cells, base station transmitters can be shown in the center of the cell (*center-excited cells*) or on three of the cells six vertices (*edge-* or *corner-excited cells*). Omnidirectional antennas are normally used in center-excited cells and sectored directional antennas are used in edge-excited cells.

The frequency reuse concept can be illustrated mathematically by considering a system with the certain number of full-duplex channels available. Each geographic area is allocated a group of channels which is divided among N cells in a unique and disjoint channel grouping where each cell has the same number of channels. Thus, the total number of radio channels available can be expressed mathematically as

$$F = GN \tag{20-1}$$

where N = number of cells in a cluster
  G = number of channels in a cell
  F = number of full-duplex channels available in a cluster

and $G < F$

The cells that collectively use the complete set of available channel frequencies are called a *cluster*. When a cluster is duplicated m times within a system, the total number of full-duplex channels can be expressed mathematically as

$$C = mGN \tag{20-2a}$$

or
$$= mF \tag{20-2b}$$

where C = channel capacity
  m = number of clusters

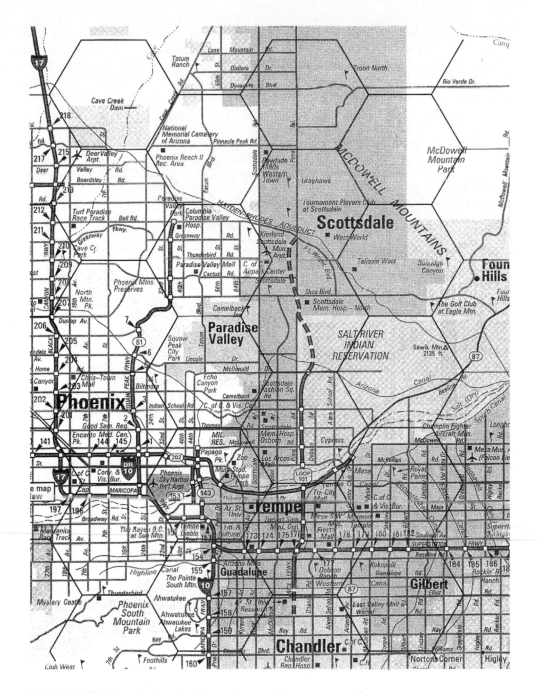

FIGURE 20-2 Hexagonal cell grid superimposed over a metropolitan area

From Equations 20-2a and b, it can be seen that the channel capacity of a cellular telephone system is directly proportional to the number of times a cluster is duplicated in a given service area. The factor N is called the cluster size and is typically equal to 3, 7, or 12. When the cluster size is reduced and the cell size held constant, more clusters are required to cover a given area and, hence, the capacity is higher. The frequency reuse factor of a cellular telephone system is inversely proportional to the number of cells in a cluster (i.e., 1/N). Hence, each cell within a cluster is assigned 1/N th of the total available channels in the cluster.

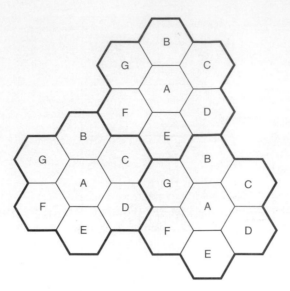

FIGURE 20-3 Cellular frequency reuse concept

Cells use a hexagonal shape which provides exactly six equidistant neighboring cells, and the lines joining the centers of any cell with its neighboring cell are separated by multiples of 60°. Therefore, a limited number of cluster sizes and cell layouts are possible. To connect cells without gaps in between (tessellate), the geometry of a hexagon is such that the number of cells per cluster can only have values that satisfy the equation

$$N = i^2 + ij + j^2 \qquad (20\text{-}3)$$

where N = number of cells per cluster
          i and j = nonnegative integer values

The process of finding the tier with nearest co-channel cells is as follows:

1. Move i cells through the center of successive cells.
2. Turn 60° in a counterclockwise direction.
3. Move j cells forward through the center of successive cells.

Example 20-1

Determine the number of cells in a cluster and locate the co-channel cells for the following values:

$$j = 2 \text{ and } i = 3$$

Solution   The number of cells in the cluster is determined from Equation 20-3.

$$N = 3^2 + (2)(3) + 2^2$$
$$= 19$$

Figure 20-4 shows the six nearest tier 1 co-channel cells for cell A.

Interference

The two major kinds of interferences produced within a cellular telephone system are *co-channel interference* and *adjacent channel interference*.

   Co-channel interference.   With frequency reuse, several cells within a given coverage area use the same set of frequencies. Two cells using the same set of frequencies are called *co-channel cells* and the interference between them is called *co-channel interference*. Unlike thermal noise, co-channel interference cannot be reduced by simply increasing transmit powers, because increasing the transmit power in one cell increases the likelihood of that cell's transmission interfering with another cell's trans-

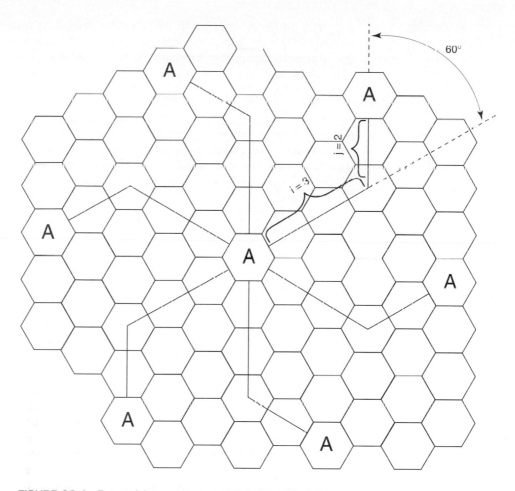

FIGURE 20-4 Determining co-channel cells for Example 20-1

mission. To reduce co-channel interference, co-channels must be separated by a certain minimum distance.

Interference between cells is not proportional to the distance between the two cells but rather to the ratio of the distance to the cell's radius. Since a cell's radius is proportional to the transmit power, more radio channels can be added to a system simply by decreasing the transmit power per cell, by making cells smaller, and by filling in vacated coverage areas with new cells. In a cellular system where all cells are approximately the same size, co-channel interference is dependent on the radius (R) of the cells and the distance to the center of the nearest co-channel cell. Increasing the D/R ratio (sometimes called the *co-channel reuse ratio*) increases the spatial separation between co-channel cells relative to the coverage distance. Therefore, co-channel interference can be reduced by increasing the co channel reuse ratio. For hexagonal geometry,

$$Q = \frac{D}{R} \qquad (20\text{-}4a)$$

$$= \sqrt{3N} \qquad (20\text{-}4b)$$

where Q = co-channel reuse ratio (unitless)
         D = distance to the center of the nearest co-channel cell (kilometers)
         R = cell radius (kilometers)
         N = cluster size (number of cells)

The smaller the value of Q, the larger the channel capacity since the cluster size is also small. However, a large value of Q improves the co-channel interference and, thus, the overall transmission quality. Obviously, in actual cellular system design, a trade-off must be made between the two objectives.

Adjacent channel interference. *Adjacent channel interference* occurs when transmissions from adjacent channels interfere with each other. Adjacent channel interference results from imperfect filters in receivers that allow nearby frequencies to enter the receiver. Adjacent channel interference is most prevalent when an adjacent channel is transmitting very close to a mobile unit's receiver at the same time the mobile unit is trying to receive transmissions from the base station on an adjacent frequency. This is called the *near–far effect* and is most prevalent when a mobile unit is receiving a weak signal from the base station.

Adjacent channel interference can be minimized by using precise filtering in receivers and making careful channel assignments. Adjacent channel interference can also be reduced by maintaining a reasonable frequency separation between channels in a given cell. However, if the reuse factor is small, the separation between adjacent channels may not be sufficient to maintain an adequate adjacent channel interference level.

Cell Splitting

Cellular telephone systems were proposed by the Bell System in the early 1960s as a means of alleviating congested frequency spectrums indigenous to wide-area mobile telephone systems using line-of-site, high-powered transmitters. These early systems offered reasonable coverage over a large area; however, the available channels were rapidly used up. For example, in the early 1970s the Bell System could only handle 12 simultaneous mobile telephone calls at a time in New York City. Cellular telephone systems use low-power transmitters and serve a much smaller geographical area.

The purpose of *cell splitting* is to increase the channel capacity and improve the availability and reliability of a cellular telephone network. Increases in demand for cellular service in a given area rapidly consume the cellular channels assigned the area. Several methods, such as *cell splitting* and *sectoring,* expand the capacity of a cellular network. Cell splitting provides for an orderly growth of a cellular system whereas sectoring utilizes directional antennas to reduce interference and allow channel frequencies to be reassigned (reused).

Producing wide-area coverage with small cells is indeed a costly operation. Therefore, cells are initially set up to cover relatively large areas and, then, the cells are divided into smaller areas when the need arises. This resizing or redistribution of cell areas is called cell splitting. In essence, cell splitting is the process of subdividing highly congested cells into smaller cells each with their own base station and set of channel frequencies. With cell splitting, a larger number of low-power transmitters take over an area previously served by a single, higher-powered transmitter. Cell splitting occurs when traffic levels in a cell reach the point where channel availability is jeopardized. If a new call is initiated in an area where all available channels are in use, a condition called *blocking* occurs. A high occurrence of blocking indicates a system overload.

The area of a circle is proportional to its radius squared. Therefore, if the radius of all the cells shown in Figure 20-1 were divided in half, four times as many smaller cells would be needed to provide service to the same coverage area. Cell splitting allows a system's capacity to increase by replacing large cells, while not disturbing the channel allocation scheme required to prevent interference between cells.

Figure 20-5 illustrates the concept of cell splitting. Macrocells are divided into minicells, which are then further divided into microcells as traffic density increases. Each time a cell is split, its transmit power is reduced. As Figure 20-5 shows, cell splitting increases the channel capacity of a cellular telephone system by rescaling the system and increasing

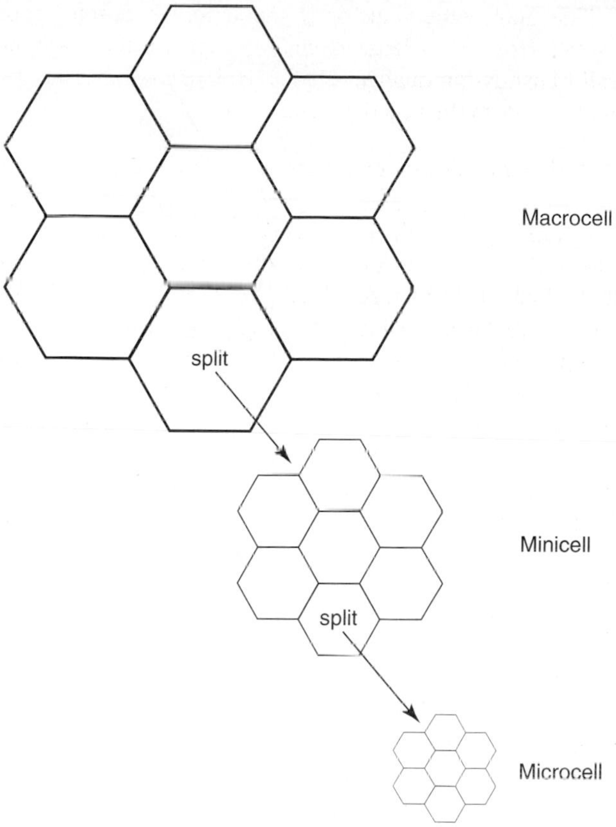

FIGURE 20-5 Cell splitting

the number of channels per unit area (channel density). Hence, cell splitting decreases the cell radius while maintaining the same co-channel reuse ratio (*D/R*).

Sectoring

Another means of increasing channel capacity is to decrease the *D/R* ratio while maintaining the same cell radius. Capacity improvement can be achieved by reducing the number of cells in a cluster, thus increasing the frequency reuse. To accomplish this the relative interference must be reduced without decreasing transmit power.

In a cellular telephone system, co-channel interference can be decreased by replacing a single omnidirectional antenna with several directional antennas, each radiating within a specific area. These areas are called sectors and decreasing co-channel interference while increasing capacity by using directional antennas is called *sectoring*. The degree in which co-channel interference is reduced is dependent on the amount of sectoring used. A cell is normally partitioned either into three 120° sectors or six 60° sectors as shown in Figure 20-6.

When sectoring is used, the channels utilized in a particular sector are broken down into sectored groups that are used only within a particular sector. With seven-cell reuse and 120° sectors, the number of interfering cells in the closest tier is reduced from six to two. Sectoring improves the signal-to-interference ratio and, thus, increases the capacity.

Segmentation and Dualisation

Segmentation and *dualisation* are techniques incorporated when additional cells are required within the reuse distance. Segmentation divides a group of channels into smaller

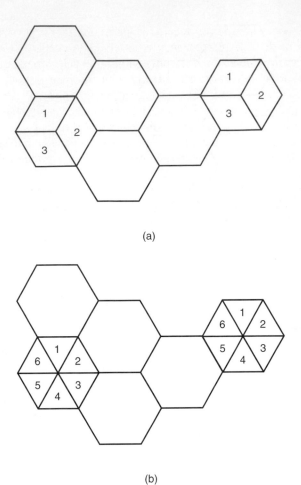

(a)

(b)

FIGURE 20-6 Sectoring: (a) 120-degree sectors; and (b) 60-degree sectors

groupings or segments of mutually exclusive frequencies; and cell sites, which are within the reuse distance, are assigned their own segment of the channel group. Segmentation is a means of avoiding co-channel interference, although it lowers the capacity of a cell by enabling reuse inside the reuse distance which is normally prohibited.

Dualisation is a means of avoiding full-cell splitting where the entire area would otherwise need to be segmented into smaller cells. When a new cell is set up requiring the same channel group as an existing cell (cell 1) and a second cell (cell 2) is not sufficiently far from cell 1 for normal reuse, the busy part of cell 1 (the center) is converted to a primary cell and the same channel frequencies can be assigned to the new competing cell (cell 2). If all available channels need to be used in cell 2, a problem would arise, because the larger secondary cell in cell 1 uses some of these and there would be interference. In practice, however, cells are assigned different channels so this is generally not a problem. A drawback of dualisation is it requires an extra base station in the middle of cell 1. There are now two base stations in cell 1: one a high-power station that covers the entire secondary cell and one a low-power station that covers the smaller primary cell.

Cell System Layout

Figure 20-1 shows a simplified cellular telephone system that includes all the basic components necessary for cellular telephone communications. There is a radio network covering a set of geographical areas (cells) inside of which mobile two-way radio units, such as cellular or PCS telephones, can communicate. The radio network is defined by a set of radio-frequency transceivers located at approximately the physical center of each cell. The locations of these radio-frequency transceivers are called *base stations*. A base station serves as central control for all users within that cell. Mobile units (such as automobiles and pedestrians) communicate directly with the base station, and the base station re-broadcasts those transmissions at a higher power. The base station can improve the transmission quality, but it cannot increase the channel capacity within the fixed bandwidth of the network. Base stations are distributed over the area of system coverage and are managed and controlled by a computerized *cell-site controller* that handles all cell-site control and switching functions. The switch itself is called a *Mobile Telephone Switching Office* (MTSO).

A base station consists of a low-power radio transceiver, power amplifiers, a control unit, and other hardware depending on the system configuration. Cellular and PCS telephones use several moderately powered transceivers over a relatively wide service area, as opposed to a mobile two-way radio which uses a single, high-power transceiver at a high elevation. The function of the base station is to interface between mobile telephone sets and the MTSO. Base stations communicate with the MTSO over dedicated data links, both metallic and nonmetallic facilities, and with mobile units over the airwaves using a control channel. The MTSO controls call processing, call setup, and call termination which includes signaling, supervision, switching, and allocating RF channels. The MTSO also provides a centralized administration and maintenance point for the entire network, and it interfaces with the public switched telephone network (PSTN) over wireline voice facilities to honor services from conventional wireline telephone subscribers.

To complicate the issue, an MTSO is known by several different names depending on the manufacturer and system configuration. *Mobile Telephone Switching Office* (MTSO) is the name given by Bell Laboratories, *Electronic Mobile Xchange* (EMX) by Motorola, *AEX* by Ericcson, *NEAX* by NEC, and *Switching Mobile Center* (SMC) and *Master Mobile Center* (MMC) by Novatel.

Each geographical area or cell can generally accommodate many different user channels simultaneously. How many users depends on the multiple-accessing technique used. Within a cell, each channel can support up to 20 mobile telephone users at a time. Channels are dynamically assigned and dedicated to one or more user for the duration of a call, and any user may be assigned any user channel.

As a car moves away from the base station transceiver, the received signal begins to decrease. The output power of the mobile unit is controlled by the base station through the transmission of up/down commands, which depends on the signal strength it is currently receiving from the base station. When the signal strength drops below a predetermined threshold level, the electronic switching center locates the cell in the honeycomb that is receiving the strongest signal from the particular mobile unit and transfers the mobile unit to the transceiver in the new cell. Moving from one cell to another cell is called *roaming*.

The base station transfer includes converting the call to an available channel within the new cell's allocated frequency subset. This transfer from one cell's base station to another is called a *handoff* (or *handover*) and should be completely transparent to the subscriber (i.e., the subscriber does not know that his or her facility has been switched). A flawless handoff (i.e., no interruption) is called a *soft handover* and normally takes approximately 0.2 s, which is imperceptible to voice telephone users, although the delay may be disruptive to data communications. A connection that is momentarily broken during a cell-to-cell transfer is called a *hard handoff*. Handoffs can be initiated when the signal strength (or signal-to-interference ratio), measured by either the transmitter or the receiver, falls below a predetermined threshold level or when network resource management needs to force a handoff to free resources to place an emergency call. During a handoff, information about the user stored in the first base station is transferred to the new base station.

The six primary components of a cellular telephone system are (1) the electronic switching center, (2) the cell-site controller, (3) radio transceivers, (4) system interconnections, (5) mobile telephone units, and (6) a common communications protocol.

Electronic switching center. The *electronic switching center* is a digital telephone exchange and is the heart of a cellular telephone system. The switch performs two essential functions: (1) It controls switching between the public telephone network and the cell sites for wireline-to-mobile, mobile-to-wireline, and mobile-to-mobile calls; and (2) it processes data received from the cell-site controllers concerning mobile unit status, diagnostic data, and bill-compiling information. The electronic switch communicates with the cell-site controllers with a data link using the X.25 protocol and a transmission rate of 9.6 kbps full duplex.

Cell-site controller. Each cell contains one *cell-site controller* that operates under the direction of the switching center. The cell-site controller manages each of the radio channels at each site, supervises calls, turns the radio transmitter and receiver on and off, injects data onto the control and user channels, and performs diagnostic tests on the cell-site equipment.

Radio transceiver. The *radio transceivers* used for cellular radio are narrowband FM for analog systems and QPSK for digital systems with an audio-frequency band from approximately 300 Hz to 3 kHz. Each cell base station typically contains one radio transmitter and two radio receivers tuned to the same frequency. Whichever radio receiver detects the strongest signal is selected. This is called receiver diversity.

System interconnects. Four-wire leased telephone lines are generally used to connect the switching centers to each of the cell sites. There is one dedicated four-wire trunk circuit for each of the cell's user channels. Also, there must be at least one four-wire trunk circuit to connect the switch to the cell-site controller as a control channel.

Mobile and portable telephone units. Mobile and portable telephone units are essentially identical. The only differences are the portable units have a lower output power, a less efficient antenna, and operate exclusively on a battery. Each mobile telephone unit consists of a control unit, a radio transceiver, a logic unit, and a mobile antenna. The control unit houses all the user interfaces, including a handset. The transceiver uses a frequency synthesizer to tune into any designated cellular system channel. The logic unit interrupts subscriber actions and system commands and manages the transceiver and control units.

Communications protocol. The last constituent of a cellular system is the communications protocol that governs the way a telephone call is established. Cellular protocols differ between countries. In the United States, the Advanced Mobile Phone Service (AMPS) standard is used, while in Canada the AURORA 800 system is used. Each country in Europe has its own standard: Total Access Communications System (TACS) in the United Kingdom, NMT or Nordic System in the Scandinavian countries, RC2000 in France, and NETZ C-450 in Germany. NTT is the Japanese standard for cellular telephone.

Call Processing

A telephone call over a cellular network requires using two full-duplex voice channels simultaneously, one called the *user channel* and one called the *control channel*. The base station transmits and receives on what is called the *forward control channel* and the *forward voice channel,* and the mobile unit transmits and receives on the *reverse* control and voice channels.

Completing a call within a cellular radio system is quite similar to the public switched telephone network. When a mobile unit is first turned on, it performs a series of start-up procedures and then samples the received signal strength on all prescribed user channels. The unit automatically tunes to the channel with the strongest receive signal strength and synchronizes to the control data transmitted by the cell-site controller. The mobile unit interprets the data and continues monitoring the control channel(s). The mobile unit automatically rescans periodically to ensure that it is using the best control channel.

Within a cellular system, calls can take place between a wireline party and a mobile telephone or between two mobile telephones.

Wireline-to-mobile calls.   The cellular system's switching center receives a call from a wireline party through a dedicated interconnect line from the public switched telephone network. The switch translates the received dialing digits and determines whether the mobile unit to which the call is destined is on or off hook (busy). If the mobile unit is available, the switch *pages* the mobile subscriber. Following a *page response* from the mobile unit, the switch assigns an idle channel and instructs the mobile unit to tune in to that channel. The mobile unit sends a verification of channel tuning via the controller in the cell site which responds with an audible *call progress tone* to the subscriber's mobile telephone, causing it to ring. The switch terminates the call progress tones when it receives positive indication that the subscriber has answered the phone and the conversation between the two parties has begun.

Mobile-to-wireline calls.   A mobile subscriber who desires to call a wireline party first enters the called number into the unit's memory using Touch-Tone buttons or a dial on the telephone unit. The subscriber then presses a *send key,* which transmits the called number as well as the mobile subscriber's identification number to the switch. If the identification number is valid, the switch routes the call over a leased wireline interconnection to the public telephone network, which completes the connection to the wireline party. Using the cell-site controller, the switch assigns the mobile unit a nonbusy user channel and instructs the mobile unit to tune into that channel. After the switch receives verification that the mobile unit is tuned to the assigned channel, the mobile subscriber receives an audible *call progress tone* from the switch. After the called party picks up the phone, the switch terminates the call progress tones and the conversation can begin.

Mobile-to-mobile calls.   Calls between two mobile units are also possible in the cellular radio system. To originate a call to another mobile unit, the calling party enters the called number into the unit's memory via the touchpad on the telephone set and then presses the send key. The switch receives the caller's identification number and the called number and then determines if the called unit is free to receive a call. The switch sends a *page command* to all cell-site controllers, and the called party (who may be anywhere in the service area) receives a page. Following a positive page from the called party, the switch assigns each party an idle user channel and instructs each party to tune into their respective user channel. Then the called party's phone rings. When the system receives notice that the called party has answered the phone, the switch terminates the call progress tone, and the conversation may begin between the two mobile units.

If a mobile subscriber wishes to initiate a call and all user channels are busy, the switch sends a *directed retry command,* instructing the subscriber to reattempt the call through a neighboring cell. If the system cannot allocate a user channel through the neighboring cell, the switch transmits an *intercept message* to the calling mobile unit over the control channel. Whenever the called party is *off hook,* the calling party receives a busy signal. Also, if the called number is invalid, the system either sends a reorder message via the control channel or provides an announcement that the call cannot be processed.

Handoff feature.   One of the most important features of a cellular system is its ability to transfer calls that are already in progress from one cell site controller to another as mobile units move from cell to cell within the cellular network. This transfer process is called a *handoff*. Computers at the cell-site controller stations transfer calls from cell to cell with minimal disruption and no degradation in the quality of transmission. The *handoff decision algorithm* is based on variations in signal strength. When a call is in progress, the switching center monitors the received signal strength of each user channel. If the signal level on an occupied channel drops below some predetermined threshold level for more than a given time interval, the switch performs a handoff, provided there is a vacant channel. The handoff operation reroutes the call through a new cell site.

The handoff process takes approximately 200 ms. Handoff parameters allow for optimized transfer based on cell-site traffic load and the surrounding terrain. *Blocking* occurs when the signal level drops below a usable level and there are no usable channels available to switch to. To help avoid blocking or loss of a call during the handoff process, the system employs a load-balancing scheme that frees channels for handoff and sets handoff priorities. Programmers at the central switch site continually update the switching algorithm to amend the system to accommodate changing traffic loads.

ANALOG CELLULAR TELEPHONE

Bell Telephone Laboratories in Murry Hill, New Jersey, proposed the cellular telephone concept as the Advanced Mobile Telephone System (AMPS) in 1971. The cellular telephone concept was an intriguing idea that added a depth or spatial dimension to the conventional wireline trunking model used by the public telephone network at the time. The cellular plan called for low-profile, low-power cell sites linked through a central switching and control center. AMPS was initially put into operation in 1983 by Ameritech and incorporated large cell areas to cover approximately 2100 square miles in the Chicago area. The original system used omnidirectional antennas to minimize initial equipment costs. The radio transceivers used with AMPS cellular telephones use narrowband frequency modulation (NBFM) with an audio-frequency band of 300 Hz to 3 kHz and a maximum frequency deviation of ±12 kHz for 100% modulation. This corresponds to a bandwidth of 30 kHz using Carson's rule. Empirical information determined that an AMPS 30-kHz telephone channel requires a minimum single-to-interference ratio (SIR) of 18 dB for satisfactory performance. The smallest reuse factor that satisfied this requirement utilizing 120° directional antennas was 7. Consequently, the AMPS system uses a seven-cell reuse pattern with provisions for cell splitting and sectoring to increase channel capacity when needed.

AMPS Frequency Allocation

In 1980, the FCC decided to license two common carriers per cellular service area. The idea was to eliminate the possibility of a monopoly and provide the advantages that generally accompany a competitive environment. Subsequently, two frequency allocation systems emerged, system A and system B, each with its own group of channels that shared the allocated frequency spectrum. System A is defined for the nonwireline companies, and system B for wireline companies.

Figure 20-7 shows the frequency management system for the AMPS cellular telephone system. The FCC originally assigned the AMPS system a 40-MHz frequency band consisting of 666 full duplex channels per service area with 30-kHz spacing between adjacent channels. The A channels are designated 1 to 333 and the B channels are designated 334 to 666. For mobile units, channel 1 has a transmit frequency of 825.03 MHz and channel 666 has a transmit frequency of 844.98 MHz. In cellular telephone systems, it is often necessary or desirable for transmissions to occur from base station–to–mobile unit and mobile unit–to–base station simultaneously. Simultaneous transmission in both directions is a transmission mode called *full duplex* or, simply, *duplexing*. Duplexing can be accomplished using frequency or time-domain methods. *Frequency-division duplexing* (FDD) occurs

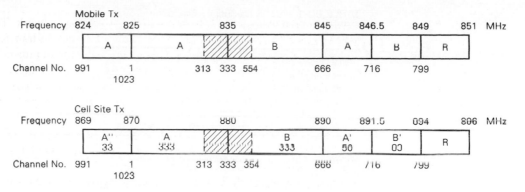

FIGURE 20-7 Advanced Mobile Phone Service (AMPS) frequency spectrum

when two distinct frequency bands are provided to each user. In FDD, each duplex channel actually consists of two simplex (one-way) channels. A special device called a *duplexer* is used in each mobile unit and base station to allow simultaneous transmission and reception on a duplex channel.

Transmissions from base stations to mobile units are called *forward links* and transmissions from mobile units to base stations are called *reverse links*. The receiver for each channel operates 45 MHz above the transmitter; therefore, channel 1 receives at 870.03 MHz and channel 666 at 889.98 MHz. Consequently, every two-way radio channel consists of a pair of simplex (one-way) channels separated by 45 MHz. The 45-MHz separation between transmit and receive frequencies was chosen to make use of inexpensive but highly selective duplexers in the mobile units. An additional 5-MHz frequency spectrum was subsequently added to the original 20-MHz band, which increased the total number of simplex channels available to 832 (416 full duplex).

The AMPS channel spectrums are divided into two basic sets or groups. One set of channels is dedicated for control information exchange between mobile units and the cell site and are appropriately termed *control channels* (shaded areas on Figure 20-7). The second group, termed *voice* or *user channels*, is made up from the remaining channels and used for actual voice conversations and user data exchanges. Figure 20-7 includes the frequency spectrum for the 166 additional AMPS channels. The added frequencies are called the *expanded spectrum* and include channels 667 to 799 and 991 to 1023. The mobile-unit transmit center frequency in MHz for any channel can be determined as follows:

$$0.03\ N + 825.000 \qquad \text{for } 1 \le N \le 866$$

and
$$0.03\ (N - 1023) + 825.000 \qquad \text{for } 990 \le N \le 1023$$

where N is the channel number.

The receive center frequency is obtained by simply adding 45 MHz to the transmit center frequency. For example, the transmit and receive center frequencies for channel 3 are

transmit $0.03\ (3) + 825 = 825.09$ MHz
receive 825.09 MHz $+ 45$ MHz $= 870.09$ MHz

and for channel 991

transmit $0.03\ (991 - 1023) + 825 = 824.04$ MHz
receive 824.04 MHz $+ 45$ MHz $= 869.04$ MHz

Table 20-1 summarizes the frequency assignments for AMPS. The set of control channels may be split by the system operator into subsets of dedicated control channels,

TABLE 20-1   AMPS Frequency Allocation

	AMPS
Channel spacing	30 kHz
Spectrum allocation	40 MHz
Additional spectrum	10 MHz
Total number of channels	832

System A Frequency Allocation

AMPS

Channel Number	Mobile TX, MHz	Mobile RX, MHz
1	825.030	870.030
313[a]	834.390	879.390
333[b]	843.990	879.990
667	845.010	890.010
716	846.480	891.480
991	824.040	869.040
1023	825.000	870.000

System B Frequency Allocation		
334[c]	835.020	880.020
354[d]	835.620	880.620
666	844.980	890.000
717	846.510	891.000
799	848.970	894.000

[a]Last dedicated control channel for system A
[b]First dedicated control channel for system A
[c]Last dedicated control channel for system B
[d]First dedicated control channel for system B

paging channels, and access channels. Note that the channel-1 transmit and receive frequencies do not start from the low end of the frequency set (824 MHz and 869 MHz), because the original 40-MHz allocation started at 825 MHz. When the FCC allocated additional frequencies to the service, some of the new frequencies were added above the original range and some were added below.

AMPS Classification of Cellular Telephones

There are several types of cellular telephones: mobiles (car mount), portables (pocket phones), and handhelds (transportable phones). There are three classes of cellular telephones. The class a particular radio falls into is determined by the type of telephone and how much transmit power it is capable of producing. Mobiles (class 1) radiate the most power and then transportables (class 2); pocket phones (class 3) have the lowest power output capabilities. Table 20-2 shows the classes of cellular phones and their power levels for AMPS.

AMPS Control Channel

Control channels are used in cellular telephone systems to allow mobile units to communicate with the cellular network through the base stations. Control channels are used for call origination, call termination, and to obtain system information. With AMPS, there are 21 control channels in the A system and 21 control channels in the B system. The control channels are located on each side of the A and B system border with the A-system control channels occupying channels 313 and 333 and B-system control channels occupying channels 334 thru 354. Since 21 of the 416 full-duplex channels are used for control, only 395 chan-

TABLE 20-2 AMPS Mobile Phone Power Levels

	AMPS Mobile Station Power Class					
	I		II		III	
Power Level	dBW	mW	dBW	mW	dBW	mW
0	6	4000	2	1600	−2	630
1	2	1600	2	1600	−2	630
2	2	630	−2	630	−2	630
3	−6	250	−6	250	−6	250
4	−10	100	−10	100	10	100
5	−14	40	−14	40	14	40
6	−19	15	−18	15	−18	15
7	−22	6	−22	6	−22	6

nels are available for voice transmission. Control channels cannot carry voice information; they are used exclusively to carry service information. With AMPS, the base station broadcasts on the *forward control channel* (FCC) and listens (receives) on the *reverse control channel* (RCC). The control channels are sometimes called *setup* or *paging* channels. All base stations continuously transmit frequency-shift-keyed (FSK) data on the FCC so that idle cellular telephone units can maintain lock on the strongest FCC regardless of their location. A subscriber unit must be *locked* (sometimes called *camped*) on an FCC before they can originate or receive calls.

Each base station uses a control channel to simultaneously page mobile units to alert them of the presence of incoming calls and to move established calls to a vacant voice channel. The forward control channel continuously transmits 10-kbps data using binary FSK. Forward control channel transmissions may contain *overhead information, mobile station control information,* or *control file information.* The format for the forward control channel is shown in Figure 20-8a. As the figure shows, the control channel message is preceded by a *dotting scheme* which is an alternating sequence of 1s and 0s. The 10-bit dotting scheme is followed by an 11-bit synchronization word with a unique sequence of 1s and 0s that enables a receiver to instantly acquire synchronization. The sync word is immediately followed by the message repeated five times. The redundancy helps to compensate for the ill effects of fading. If three of the five words are identical, the receiver assumes that as the message.

Forward control channel data formats consist of three discrete information streams: stream A, stream B, and the busy-idle stream. The three data streams are multiplexed together. Messages to the mobile unit with the least significant bit of their 32-bit *mobile identification number* (MIN) equal to 0 are transmitted on stream A and MINs with the least significant bit equal to 1 are transmitted on stream B. The busy-idle data stream contains *busy-idle bits* which are used to indicate the current status of the reverse control channel (0 = busy and 1 = idle). There is a busy-idle bit at the beginning of each dotting sequence, at the beginning of each synchronization word, at the beginning of the first repeat of word A, and after every 10 message bits thereafter. Each message word contains 40 bits, and forward control channels can contain one or more words.

The types of messages transmitted over the FCC are the *mobile station control message* and the *overhead message train.* Mobile station control messages control or command mobile units to do a particular task when the mobile unit has not been assigned a voice channel. Overhead message trains contain *system parameter overhead messages, global action overhead messages,* and *control filler messages.* Typical mobile-unit control messages are *initial voice channel designation messages, directed retry messages, alert messages,* and *change power messages.*

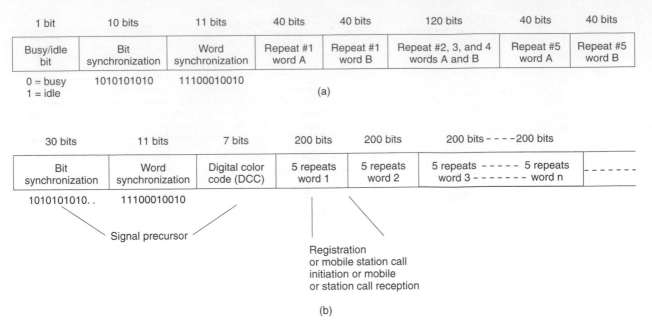

1 bit	10 bits	11 bits	40 bits	40 bits	120 bits	40 bits	40 bits
Busy/idle bit	Bit synchronization	Word synchronization	Repeat #1 word A	Repeat #1 word B	Repeat #2, 3, and 4 words A and B	Repeat #5 word A	Repeat #5 word B

0 = busy   1010101010   11100010010
1 = idle

(a)

30 bits	11 bits	7 bits	200 bits	200 bits	200 bits – – – –200 bits	
Bit synchronization	Word synchronization	Digital color code (DCC)	5 repeats word 1	5 repeats word 2	5 repeats – – – – – 5 repeats word 3 – – – – – – – word n	– – – – – –

1010101010. .   11100010010

Signal precursor

Registration
or mobile station call
initiation or mobile
or station call reception

(b)

FIGURE 20-8 Control channel format: (a) forward control channel; and (b) reverse control channel

Figure 20-8b shows the format for the reverse control channel which is transmitted from the mobile unit to the base station. The control data are transmitted at a 10-kbps rate and include *page responses, access requests,* and *registration requests.* All RCC messages begin with the RCC seizure precursor which consists of a 30-bit *dotting sequence,* an 11-bit *synchronization word,* and the coded *digital color code* (DCC) which is added so the control channel is not confused with a control channel from a nonadjacent cell that is reusing the same frequency. The mobile telephone reads the base station's DCC then returns a coded version of it, verifying that the unit is locked onto the correct signal. When the call is finished, a 1.8-second *signaling timeout signal* is transmitted. Each message word contains 40 bits and is repeated five times for a total of 200 bits.

Voice-Channel Signaling

Analog cellular channels carry both voice using FM and digital signaling information using binary FSK. When transmitting digital signaling information, voice transmissions are inhibited. This is called *blank-and-burst:* The voice is blanked and the data are transmitted in a short burst. The bit rate of the digital information is 10 kbps. Figure 20-9a shows the voice-channel signaling format for a forward voice channel, and Figure 20-9b shows the format for the reverse channel. The digital signaling sequence begins with a 101-bit dotting sequence which readies the receiver to receive digital information. After the dotting sequence, a synchronization word is sent to indicate the start of the message. On the forward voice channel, digital signaling messages are repeated 11 times to ensure the integrity of the message and on the receive channel they are repeated 5 times. The forward channel uses 40-bit words and the reverse channel uses 48-bit words.

Supervisory Audio and Signaling Tones

While voice channels are being used, two additional signaling procedures are used to maintain supervision between the mobile unit and the base station: the *supervisory audio tone* (SAT) and the *signaling tone* (ST). SATs are used to ensure reliable voice communications. The SATs are transmitted by the base station then looped back by the mobile unit. If the return SAT matches the transmit SAT, then the mobile unit knows it is tuned to the correct

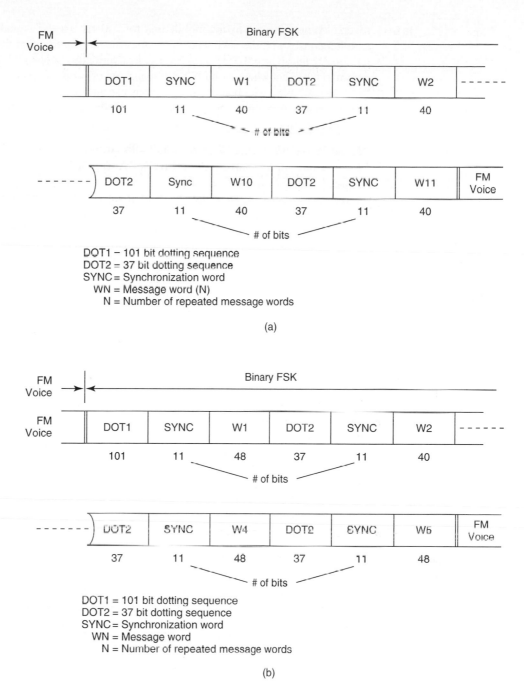

DOT1 = 101 bit dotting sequence
DOT2 = 37 bit dotting sequence
SYNC = Synchronization word
WN = Message word (N)
N = Number of repeated message words

(a)

DOT1 = 101 bit dotting sequence
DOT2 = 37 bit dotting sequence
SYNC = Synchronization word
WN = Message word
N = Number of repeated message words

(b)

FIGURE 20-9 Voice channel format: (a) forward channel; and (b) reverse channel

base station. SAT signals are analog tones of 5970 Hz, 6000 Hz, or 6030 Hz. The base station continuously transmits one of the three SATs on each active voice channel. SATs are superimposed onto the voice signal on both the forward and reverse links. In cells containing more than one base station, the SATs identify the specific base station location for a given channel and are assigned by the switching center for each call.

The signaling tone is a 10-kbps data burst which initiates a call termination by the mobile unit. The ST *end-of-call message* consists of alternating logic 1s and 0s sent on the reverse control channel by the mobile unit for 200 ms. The ST signal must be transmitted simultaneously with the SAT. The ST notifies the base station that the mobile unit has intentionally terminated the call and was not inadvertently dropped by the system. The ST is automatically sent when the mobile unit hangs up or is turned off.

In addition, a wideband *data* signal may use one of the voice channels to provide brief data messages that allow the user and the base station to adjust the mobile units output power or to initiate a handoff.

N-AMPS—Frequency-Division Multiple Accessing

Motorola developed a narrowband AMPS (N-AMPS) to increase the capacity of the AMPS in large cellular markets. N-AMPS allows as many as three mobile units to use a single, 30-kHz bandwidth at the same time by using frequency-division multiple accessing (FDMA) and 10-kHz voice channels. The SAT and ST signaling used with N-AMPS is identical to AMPS except the signaling is accomplished using FSK and subaudible data streams.

With N-AMPS, the maximum frequency deviation is reduced, which lowers the signal to interference ratio, somewhat degrading the audio quality. The degradation is compensated for by using voice companding to provide a *synthetic* voice channel quieting. N-AMPS incorporates a 300-Hz highpass filter in each voice channel so that SAT and ST data do not interfere with voice signals. The SAT and ST data are transmitted in a continuous 200-bps NRZ data stream.

ETACS Cellular Telephone

In Europe, the European Total Access Communications System (ETACS) evolved in the mid-1980s. ETACS is virtually identical to AMPS except ETACS is limited to a 25-kHz bandwidth. ETACS also uses a different method of formatting subscriber telephone numbers (called the mobile identification number or MIN) because of the need to accommodate different-country codes throughout Europe and area codes in the United States.

Analog Cellular Telephone Block Diagram

Figure 20-10 shows the block diagram for a typical cellular telephone transceiver. Note that a cellular radio transceiver is very similar to a standard FM transceiver except for the addition of several stages. Because a cellular telephone must be capable of full-duplex transmissions, it must be designed such that the transmitter and receiver can be on at the same time.

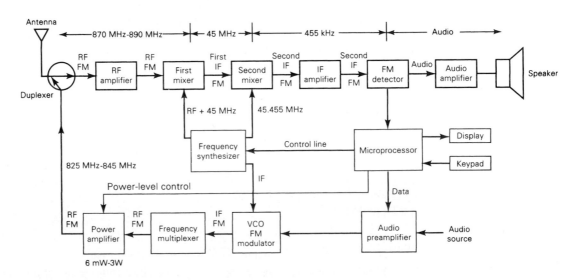

FIGURE 20-10 Block diagram for a typical cellular transceiver

The receiver shown in Figure 20-10 is a double-conversion superheterodyne type. The receiver uses high-side injection and a local oscillator circuit consisting of a single-chip frequency synthesizer with an onboard prescaler and loop filter and a 915-MHz to 937-MHz VCO (45 MHz above the incoming RF). The first IF (45 MHz) is sufficiently high to push the image frequency well beyond the passband of the preamplifier filter, and the second IF (455 kHz) is low enough to be sufficiently amplified to drive the FM detector. In the transmitter, the modulating signal is applied directly to the transmit VCO to produce a low-index, relatively low-frequency direct FM carrier signal that is multiplied and then amplified significantly before reaching the transmit antenna.

Note that the microprocessor has control lines to every major functional block of the transceiver. The microprocessor determines the frequencies at the outputs of the frequency synthesizer. It also monitors the output from the FM detector to determine received signal quality and to detect received setup information. The microprocessor also supplies setup information to the transmitter and controls the gain of the final power amplifier.

DIGITAL CELLULAR TELEPHONE

Cellular telephone companies are faced with the problem of a customer base that is rapidly expanding while at the same time the allocated frequency spectrum remains unchanged. As described, user capacity can be expanded by subdividing existing cells into smaller subcells (i.e., cell splitting) and by modifying antenna radiation patterns (i.e., sectoring). However, the degree of subdivision and redirection is limited by the complexity and amount of overhead required to process handoffs between cells. Another serious restriction is the cost of purchasing property for cell sites in the highest density traffic areas.

AMPS was a first-generation analog cellular telephone system that was not designed to support the high-capacity demands of the modern world, especially in high-density metropolitan areas. In the late 1980s, several major manufacturers of cellular equipment determined that digital cellular telephone systems could provide substantial improvements in both capacity and performance. Consequently, the *United States Digital Cellular* (USDC) system was designed and developed with the intent of supporting a higher user density within a fixed-frequency spectrum.

The USDC cellular telephone system is backward compatible with the AMPS frequency allocation scheme. USDC was designed to use the same carrier frequencies, frequency reuse plan, and base stations. Therefore, base stations and mobile units can be equipped with both AMPS and USDC channels within the same telephone equipment. In supporting both systems, cellular carriers are able to provide new customers with USDC telephones while still providing service to existing customers with AMPS telephones. The USDC system maintains compatibility with the AMPS system in several ways. Therefore, USDC is also known as Digital AMPS (D-AMPS).

USDC uses time-division multiple accessing (TDMA) which, like FDMA, divides the total available radio-frequency spectrum into individual channels. However, TDMA further divides each radio channel into time slots, one for each user. With FDMA systems, subscribers are assigned a channel for the duration of their call; however, with TDMA, mobile-unit subscribers can only "hold" a channel while they are using it. During pauses or other normal breaks in a conversation, other mobile units can use the channel. This technique of *time-sharing* channels significantly increases the capacity of a system, allowing more mobile-unit subscribers to use a system within a given geographical area.

The advantages of TDMA digital multiple-accessing systems over standard FDMA multiple-accessing systems are as follows:

1. Interleaving samples in the time domain allows for a threefold increase in the number of subscribers using a single channel. Time-sharing is realized due to

digital compression techniques, which produce bit rates approximately one-tenth that of the initial digital sample rate and about one-fifth the initial rate when error-detection correction (EDC) bits are included.

2. Digital signals are much easier to process than analog signals. Many of the more advanced modulation schemes and information processing techniques were developed for use in a digital environment.

3. Digital signals (bits) can be easily encrypted and decrypted safeguarding against eavesdropping.

4. The entire telephone system is compatible with other digital formats, such as those used in computers and computer networks.

5. Digital systems inherently provide a quieter (less noisy) environment than their analog counterparts.

A USDC TDMA frame consists of six equal time slots enabling each 30-kHz AMPS channel to support three full-rate users or six half-rate users. Hence, USDC offers as much as six times the channel capacity as AMPS. The USDC standard also utilizes the same 50-MHz frequency spectrum and frequency-division duplexing scheme as AMPS.

In 1990, the Electronic Industries Association and Telecommunications Industry Association (EIA/TIA) standardized the *dual-mode* USDC/AMPS system as Interim Standard 54 (IS-54). Dual mode indicates that a mobile station complying with this standard can operate in either the analog (AMPS) or digital (USDC) mode for voice transmissions. The key criteria for achieving dual-mode operation is that IS-54 channels cannot interfere with transmission from existing AMPS base and mobile stations. This goal is achieved with IS-54 by providing digital control channels and both analog and digital voice channels. Dual-mode mobile units can operate in either the digital or analog mode for voice, and access the system with the standard AMPS digital control channel. When a dual-mode mobile unit transmits an access request, it indicates that it is capable of operating in the digital mode; then the base station will allocate a digital voice channel if one is available. The allocation procedure indicates the channel number (frequency) and the specific time slot within that particular channel's TDMA frame. IS-54 specifies a 48.6-kbps bit rate per 30-kHz voice channel divided among three simultaneous users. Each user is allocated 13 kbps and the remaining 9.6 kbps is used for timing and control overhead.

In many rural areas of the United States, analog cellular telephone systems use only the original 666 AMPS channels. In these areas, USDC channels can be added in the extended frequency spectrum (channels 667 to 832) to support USDC telephones that roam into the system from other areas. In high-density urban areas, selected frequency bands are gradually being converted one at a time to the USDC digital standard to help alleviate traffic congestion. Unfortunately, this gradual changeover from AMPS to USDC often results in an increase in interference and number of dropped calls experienced by subscribers of the AMPS system.

The successful and graceful transition from analog cellular systems to digital cellular systems using the same frequency band was a primary consideration in the development of the USDC standard. The introduction of N-AMPS and a new digital spread-spectrum standard has delayed the widespread deployment of the USDC standard throughout the United States.

USDC Control Channels

The IS-54 USDC standard specifies the same 42 *primary control channels* as AMPS and 42 additional control channels called *secondary control channels*. Thus, USDC offers twice as many control channels as AMPS and is, therefore, capable of providing twice the capacity of control channel traffic within a given market area. Carriers are allowed to dedicate the secondary control channels for USDC-only use since AMPS mobile users do not monitor and cannot decode the new secondary control channels. In addition, to maintain compatibility with existing AMPS cellular telephone systems, the primary forward and reverse control channels in USDC cellular systems use the same signaling techniques and modulation scheme (binary FSK) as AMPS. However, a new standard, IS-136 (formerly IS-54 Rev. C), replaces binary FSK with π/4 DQPSK modulation for the 42 dedicated USDC secondary control channels allowing digital mobile units to operate entirely in the digital domain. IS-54 Rev. C was introduced to provide 4-ary modulation rather than FSK on dedicated USDC control channels to increase the control channel data rates and provide additional specialized services such as paging and short messaging between private mobile user groups.

USDC Digital Voice Channel

Like AMPS, each USDC voice channel is assigned a 30-kHz bandwidth on both the forward and reverse links. With USDC, however, each voice channel can support as many as three mobile users simultaneously by using digital modulation and a time-division multiple-accessing (TDMA) system called North American Digital Cellular (NADC). Each radio-frequency voice channel consists of one 40-ms TDMA frame made of six time slots containing 324 bits each, as shown in Figure 20-11. For full speech rate, three users share the six time slots in an equally spaced manner. For example, mobile user 1 occupies time slots 1 and 4, mobile user 2 occupies time slots 2 and 5, and mobile user 3 occupies time slots 3 and 6. For half-rate speech, each user occupies one time slot per frame.

Each time slot in every USDC voice-channel frame contains four data channels—three for control and one for digitized voice and user data. The full duplex *digital traffic channel* (DTC) carries digitized voice information and consists of a *reverse digital traffic channel* (RDTC) and a *forward digital traffic channel* (FDTC) that carry digitized speech information or user data. The RDTC carries speech data from the mobile unit to the base station, and the FDTC carries user speech data from the base station to the mobile unit. The three supervisory channels are the *coded digital verification color code* (CDVCC), the *slow associated control channel* (SACCH), and the *fast associated control channel* (FACCH).

Coded digital verification color code. The purpose of the CDVCC color code is to provide co-channel identification similar to the SAT signal transmitted in the AMPS

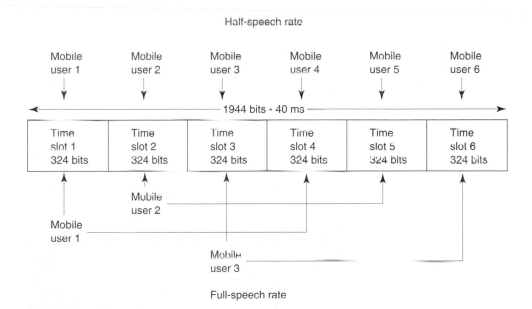

FIGURE 20-11 North American Digital Cellular TDMA frame format

system. The CDVCC is a 12-bit message transmitted in every time slot. The CDVCC consists of an 8-bit digital voice color code number between 1 and 255 appended with 4 additional coding bits derived from a shortened Hamming code. The base station transmits a CDVCC number on the forward voice channel and each mobile unit using the TDMA channel must receive, decode, and retransmit the same CDVCC code (handshake) back to the base station on the reverse voice channel. If the two CDVCC values are not the same, the time slot is relinquished for other users and the mobile unit's transmitter will be automatically turned off.

Slow associated control channel. The SACCH is a signaling channel for transmission of control and supervision messages between the digital mobile unit and the base station while the mobile unit is involved with a call. The SACCH uses 12 coded bits per TDMA burst and is transmitted in every time slot, thus providing a signaling channel in parallel with the digitized speech information. Therefore, SACCH messages can be transmitted without interfering with the processing of digitized speech signals. Because the SACCH consists of only 12 bits per frame, it can take up to 22 frames for a single SACCH message to be transmitted. The SACCH carries various control and supervisory information between the mobile unit and the base station, such as communicating power-level changes and handoff requests. The SACCH is also used by the mobile unit to report signal-strength measurements of neighboring base stations so, when necessary, the base station can initiate a *mobile-assisted handoff* (MAHO).

Fast associated control channel. The FACCH is a second signaling channel for transmission of control and specialized supervision and traffic messages between the base station and the mobile units. Unlike the CDVCC and SACCH, the FACCH does not have a dedicated time slot. The FACCH is a *blank-and-burst*-type transmission that, when transmitted, replaces digitized speech information with control and supervision messages within a subscriber's time slot. There is no limit on the number of speech frames that can be replaced with FACCH data. However, the digitized voice information is somewhat protected by preventing an entire digitized voice transmission from being replaced by FACCH data. The 13-kbps net digitized voice transmission rate cannot be reduced below 3250 bps in any given time slot. There are no fields within a standard time slot to identify it as digitized speech or an FACCH message. To determine if an FACCH message is being received, the mobile unit must attempt to decode the data as speech. If it decodes in error, it then decodes the data as an FACCH message. If the cyclic redundancy character (CRC) calculates correctly, the message is assumed to be an FACCH message. The FACCH supports transmission of dual-tone multiple-frequency (DTMF) Touch Tones, call release instruction, flash hook instructions, and mobile-assisted handoff or mobile-unit status requests. The FACCH data are packaged and interleaved to fit in a time slot similar to the way digitized speech is handled.

Speech Coding

Figure 20-12 shows the block diagram for a USDC digital voice-channel speech encoder. Channel error control for the digitized speech data uses three mechanisms for minimizing channel errors: (1) A rate one-half convolutional code is used to protect the more vulnerable bits of the speech coder data stream; (2) transmitted data are interleaved for each speech coder frame over two time slots to reduce the effects of Rayleigh fading; and (3) a cyclic redundancy check is performed on the most perceptually significant bits of the digitized speech data.

With USDC, incoming analog voice signals are sampled first then converted to a binary PCM in a special *speech coder* (*vocoder*) called a *vector sum exciter linear predictive* (VSELP) *coder* or a *stochastically excited linear predictive* (SELP) *coder*. Linear predictive coders are time-domain type vocoders that attempt to extract the most significant char-

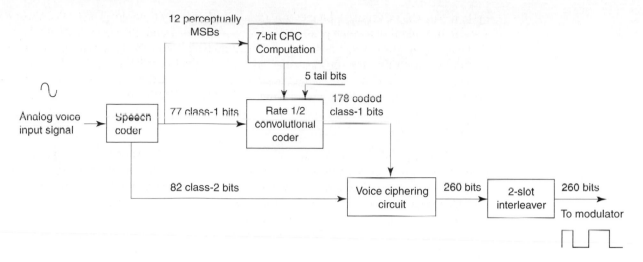

FIGURE 20-12 USDC digital voice-channel speech coder

acteristics from the time-varying speech waveform. With linear predictive coders it is possible to transmit good-quality voice at 4.8 kbps and acceptable, although poorer-quality voice, at lower bit rates.

Because there are many predictable orders in spoken word patterns, it is possible, using advanced algorithms, to compress the binary samples and transmit the resulting bit stream at a 13-kbps rate. A consortium of companies including Motorola developed the VSELP algorithm which was subsequently adopted for the IS-54 standard. Error-detection and correction (EDC) bits are added to the digitally compressed voice signals to reduce the effects of interference, bringing the final voice data rate to 48.6 kbps. Compression/expansion and error-detection/correction functions are implemented in the telephone handset by a special microprocessor called a digital signal processor (DSP).

The VSELP coders output 7950 bps and produce a speech frame every 20 ms, or

$$\frac{7950 \text{ bits}}{\text{second}} \times \frac{20 \text{ ms}}{\text{frame}} = 159 \text{ bits per frame}$$

Fifty speech frames are outputted each second containing 159 bits each, or

$$\frac{50 \text{ frames}}{\text{second}} \times \frac{159 \text{ bits}}{\text{frame}} = 7950 \text{ bps}$$

The 159 bits included in each speech coder frame are divided into two classes according to the significance in which they are perceived. There are 77 class-1 bits and 82 class-2 bits. The class-1 bits are the most significant and are, therefore, error protected. The 12 most significant class-1 bits are block coded using a 7-bit CRC error-detection code to ensure that the most significant speech coder bits are decoded with a low probability of error. The less significant class-2 bits have no means of error protection.

After coding the 159 bits, each speech code frame is converted in a 1/2 convolution coder to 260 channel-coded bits per frame and 50 frames are transmitted each second. Hence, the transmission bit rate is increased from 7950 bps for each digital voice channel to 13 kbps.

$$\frac{260 \text{ bits}}{\text{frame}} \times \frac{50 \text{ frames}}{\text{second}} = 13 \text{ kbps}$$

Figure 20-13 shows the time slot and frame format for the forward (base station–to–mobile unit) and reverse (mobile unit–to–base station) links of a USDC digital

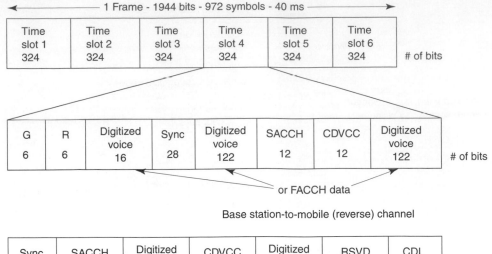

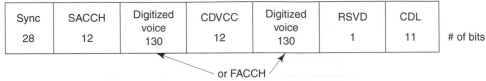

FIGURE 20-13 USDC digital voice channel slot and frame format

voice channel. USDC voice channels use frequency-division duplexing; thus, forward and reverse channel time slots operate on different frequencies at the same time. Each time slot carries interleaved digital voice data from the two adjacent frames outputted from the speech coder.

In the reverse channel, each time slot contains two bursts of 122 digitized voice bits each and one burst of 16 bits for a total of 260 digitized voice bits per frame. In addition, each time slot contains 28 synchronization bits, 12 bits of SACCH data, 12 bits of CDVCC bits, and six guard bits to compensate for differences in the distances between mobile units and base stations. The guard time is present in only the reverse channel time slots to prevent overlapping of received bursts due to radio signal transit time. The ramp-up time consists of 6 bits that allow gradual rising and falling of the RF signal energy within the time slot. Thus, a reverse channel time slot consists of 324 bits. If an FACCH is sent instead of speech data, one time slot of speech coding data is replaced with a 260-bit block of FACCH data.

In the forward channel, each time slot contains two 130-bit bursts of digitized voice data (or FACCH data if digitized speech is not being sent) for a total of 260 bits per frame. In addition, each forward channel frame contains 28 synchronization bits, 12 bits of SACCH data, 12 CDVCC bits, and 12 reserved bits for a total of 324 bits per time slot. Therefore, both forward and reverse voice channels have a data transmission rate of

$$\frac{324 \text{ bits}}{\text{time slot}} \; 3 \; \frac{6 \text{ time slot}}{40 \text{ ms}} \; 5 \; 48.6 \text{ kbps}$$

or

A third frame format, called a *shortened burst,* is shown in Figure 20-14. Shortened bursts are transmitted when a mobile unit begins operating in a larger-diameter cell, because the propagation time between the mobile and base is unknown. A mobile unit transmits shortened burst slots until the base station determines the required time offset. The default delay

| G1 | RSDSDVSDWSDXSDYS | G2 |

Where
- G1 = 6-bit guard time
- R = 6-bit length ramp time
- S = 28-bit synchronization word
- D = 12-bit CDVCC code
- G2 = 44-bit guard time
- V = 0000
- W = 00000000
- X = 000000000000
- Y = 0000000000000000

FIGURE 20-14 USDC shortened burst digital voice channel format

between the receive and transmit slots in the mobile is 44 symbols, which results in a maximum distance at which a mobile station can operate in a cell to 72 mi for an IS-54 cell.

USDC Digital Modulation Scheme

To achieve a transmission bit rate of 48.6 kbps in a 30-kHz AMPS voice channel, a *bandwidth* (*spectral*) *efficiency* of 1.62 bps/Hz is required which is well beyond the capabilities of binary FSK. The spectral efficiency requirements can be met by using conventional pulse-shaped, 4-phase modulation schemes such as QPSK and OQPSK. However, USDC voice and control channels use a *symmetrical differential, phase shift keying* technique known as $\pi/4$ DQPSK or $\pi/4$ *differential quadriphase shift keying* (DQPSK) which offers several advantages in a mobile radio environment, such as improved co-channel rejection and bandwidth efficiency.

A 48.6-kbps data rate requires a symbol (baud) rate of 24.3 ksps (24.3 kilobaud per second) with a symbol duration of 41.1523 μs. The use of pulse shaping and $\pi/4$ DQPSK supports the transmission of three different 48.6-kbps digitized speech signals in a 30-kHz bandwidth with as much as 50-dB of adjacent-channel isolation. Thus, the bandwidth efficiency using $\pi/4$ DQPSK is

$$\eta = \frac{3 \times 48.6 \text{ kbps}}{30 \text{ kHz}}$$
$$= 4.86 \text{ bps/Hz}$$

where η is the bandwidth efficiency.

In a $\pi/4$ DQPSK modulator, data bits are split into two parallel channels that produce a specific phase shift in the analog carrier and, since there are four possible bit pairs, there are four possible phase shifts using a quadrature I/Q modulator. The four possible differential phase changes, $\pi/4$, $-\pi/4$, $3\pi/4$, and $-3\pi/4$, define eight possible carrier phases. Pulse shaping is used to minimize the bandwidth while limiting the intersymbol interference. In the transmitter, the PSK signal is filtered using a square-root raised cosine filter with a roll-off factor of 0.35. PSK signals, after pulse shaping, become a linear modulation technique, requiring linear amplification to preserve the pulse shape. Using pulse shaping with $\pi/4$ DQPSK allows for the simultaneous transmission of three separate 48.6-kbps speech signals in a 30-kHz bandwidth.

USDC Digital Control Channel

The digital control channel is necessarily complex and a complete description is beyond the scope of this book. Therefore, the following discussion is meant to present a general overview of the operation of a USDC digital control channel.

As previously stated, the IS-54 standard specifies three types of channels—analog control channels, analog voice channels, and a 10-kbps binary FSK digital control channel (DCCH). The IS-54 Rev.C standard (IS-136) provides for the same three types of channels plus a fourth—a digital control channel with a signaling rate of 48.6 kbps on USDC-only control channels. The new digital control channel is meant to eventually replace the analog control channel. With the addition of a digital control channel, a mobile unit is able to operate entirely in the digital domain—use the digital control channel for system and cell selection and channel accessing and the digital voice channel for digitized voice transmissions.

IS-136 details the exact functionality of the USDC digital control channel. The initial version of IS-136 was version 0 which has since been updated by revision A. Version 0 added numerous new services and features to the USDC digital cellular telephone system including enhanced user services, such as short messaging and displaying the telephone number of the incoming call; sleep mode which gives the telephone set a longer battery life when in the standby mode; private or residential system service; and enhanced security and validation against fraud. The newest version of IS-136, revision A, was developed to provide numerous new features and services by introducing an enhanced vocoder, over-the-air activation where the network operators are allowed to program information into telephones directly over the air, calling name and number ID, enhanced hands-off and priority access to control channels.

IS-136 specifies several private user group features making it well adapted for wireless PBX and paging applications. However, IS-136 user terminals operate at 48.6 kbps and are, therefore, not compatible with IS-54 FSK terminals. Thus, IS-136 modems are more cost effective as it is necessary to include only the 48.6-kbps modem in the terminal equipment.

Logical channels. The new digital control channel includes several *logical channels* with different functions including the *random access channel* (RACH); the *SMS point-to-point, paging, and access response channel* (SPACH); the *broadcast control channel* (BCCH); and the *shared channel feedback* (SCF) channel. Figure 20-15 shows the logical control channels for the IS-136 standard.

Random Access Channel (RACH). RACH is used by mobile units to request access to the cellular telephone system. RACH is a unidirectional channel specified for transmissions from mobile-to-base units only. Access messages such as origination, registration, page responses, audit confirmation, serial number, and message confirmation are transmitted on the RACH. It also transmits messages that provide information on authentication, security parameter updates, and ***short message service*** (SMS) point-to-point messages. RACH is ca-

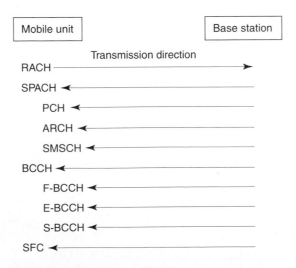

FIGURE 20-15 USDC IS-136 digital control channel—logical channel and logical subchannels

pable of operating in two modes using contention resolution similar to voice channels. RACH can also operate in a ***reservation mode*** for replying to a base-station command.

   SMS Point-to-Point, Paging, and Access Response Channel (SPACH).   SPACH is used to transmit information from base stations to specific mobile stations. RACH is a unidirectional channel specified for transmission from base stations–to–mobile units only and is shared by all mobile units. Information transmitted on the SPACH channel includes three separate logical subchannels: ***SMS point-to-point messages, paging messages,*** and ***access response messages.*** SPACH can carry messages related to a single mobile unit or to a small group of mobile units and allows larger messages to be broken down into smaller blocks for transmission.

   The paging channel (PCH) is a subchannel of the logical channel of SPACH. PCH is dedicated to delivering pages and orders. The PCH transmits *paging messages, message-waiting messages,* and *user-alerting messages.* Each PCH message can carry up to five mobile identifiers. Page messages are always transmitted then repeated a second time. Messages such as *call history count updates* and *shared secret data updates* used for the authentication and encryption process also are sent on the PCH.

   The access response channel (ARCH) is also a logical subchannel of SPACH. A mobile unit automatically moves to an ARCH immediately after successful completion of contention- or reservation-based access on a RACH. ARCH can be used to carry assignments to another resource or other responses to the mobile station's access attempt. Messages assigning a mobile unit to an analog voice channel or a digital voice channel, or redirecting the mobile to a different cell, are also sent on the ARCH along with registration access (accept, reject, or release) messages.

   The SMS channel (SMSCH) is used to deliver short point-to-point messages to a specific mobile station. Each message is limited to a maximum of 200 characters of text. Mobile originated SMS is also supported, however, SMS where a base station can broadcast a short message designated for several mobile units is not supported in IS-136.

   Broadcast Control Channel (BCCH).   BCCH is an acronym referring to the F-BCCH, E-BCCH, and S-BCCH logical subchannels. These channels are used to carry generic, system related information. BCCH is a unidirectional base station–to–mobile unit transmission shared by all mobile units.

   The *fast broadcast control channel* (F-BCCH) broadcasts digital control channel (DCCH) structure parameters including information about the number of F-BCCH, E-BCCH, and S-BCCH time slots in the DCCH frame. Mobile units use F-BCCH information when initially accessing the system to determine the beginning and ending of each logical channel in the DCCH frame. F-BCCH also includes information pertaining to access parameters, including information necessary for authentication and encryptions, and information for mobile access attempts such as the number of access retries, access burst size, initial access power level, and indication of whether the cell is barred or not. Information addressing the different types of registration, registration periods, and system identification information including network type, mobile country code, and protocol revision is also provided by the F-BCCH channel.

   The *extended broadcast control channel* (E-BCCH) carries less-critical broadcast information than F-BCCH intended for the mobile units. E-BCCH carries information about neighboring analog and TDMA cells and optional messages such as emergency information, time and date messaging, and the types of services supported by neighboring cells.

   The *SMS broadcast control channel* (S-BCCH) is a logical channel used for sending short messages to individual mobile units.

   Shared Channel Feedback (SCF) Channel.   SCF is used to support random access channel operation by providing information about which time slots the mobile unit can use for access attempts and also if a mobile unit's previous RACH transmission was successfully received.

Frequency-division multiple accessing (FDMA) is the access method used with AMPS, and both frequency- and time-division multiple accessing (TDMA) are used with D-AMPS. Both FDMA and TDMA use a frequency channelization approach to spectrum management and TDMA also utilizes a time-division approach. With FDMA and TDMA cellular telephone systems, the entire available cellular radio-frequency spectrum is subdivided into narrowband radio channels to be used for one-way communications links between cellular mobile units and base stations.

A totally digital cellular telephone system has recently been made available in the United States based on code-division multiple accessing (CDMA). The CDMA system was recently standardized by the U.S. Telecommunications Industry Association as Interim Standard 95 (IS-95). A cellular telephone system using CDMA is commonly referred to as a *personal communications system* (PCS). CDMA allows users to differentiate from one another by a unique code rather than a frequency or time assignment and, therefore, offers several advantages over cellular telephone systems using TDMA and FDMA multiple-accessing techniques, such as increased capacity and improved performance and reliability. IS-95, like IS-54, was designed to be compatible with the existing analog cellular telephone system (AMPS) frequency band; therefore, mobile units and base stations can easily be designed for dual-mode operation. Pilot CDMA systems developed by Qualcomm were first made available in 1994. The purpose of this section is to introduce the reader to the general concepts and basic operation of CDMA.

Code-Division Multiple Accessing

With IS-95, each mobile user within a given cell, and mobile subscribers in adjacent cells, use the same radio-frequency channels. In essence, frequency reuse is available in all cells. This is made possible because IS-95 is a direct sequence, spread-spectrum CDMA system and does not follow the channelization principles of traditional cellular radio communications systems. Rather than dividing the allocated frequency spectrum into narrowbandwidth channels, one for each user, information is transmitted (spread) over a very wide frequency spectrum with as many as 20 subscribers simultaneously using the same carrier frequency and frequency band. Interference is incorporated into the system so there is no limit to the number of subscribers that CDMA can support. As more mobile subscribers are added to the system, there is a graceful degradation of communications quality.

With CDMA, unlike other cellular telephone standards, subscriber data change in real time, depending on the voice activity and requirements of the network and other users of the network. IS-95 also uses a different modulation and spreading techniques for the forward and reverse channels. On the forward channel, the base station simultaneously transmits user data from all current mobile units in that cell by using different spreading sequence codes for each user's transmissions. A pilot code is transmitted with the user data at a higher power level, thus allowing all mobile units to use coherent carrier detection. On the reverse link, all mobile units respond in an asynchronous manner with a constant signal level controlled by the base station. The speech coder used with IS-95 is the Qualcomm 9600-bps *Code-Excited Linear Predictive* (QCELP) coder. The vocoder converts an 8-kbps compressed-data stream to a 9.6-kbps data stream. The vocoder's original design detects voice activity and automatically reduces the data rate to 1200 bps during silent periods. Intermediate mobile user data rates of 2400 bps and 4800 bps are also used for special purposes. In 1995, Qualcomm introduced a 14,400-bps vocoder that transmits 13.4 kbps of compressed digital voice information.

CDMA frequency and channel allocations. CDMA totally eliminates the need for frequency planning within a given cellular market. The AMPS U.S. cellular telephone system is allocated a 25-MHz frequency spectrum and each service provider is assigned half of the available spectrum (12.5 MHz). AMPS common carriers must provide a 270-kHz guard band (approximately nine AMPS channels) on either side of the CDMA frequency spectrum. To facilitate a graceful transition from AMPS to CDMA, each IS-95 channel is allocated a 1.25-MHz frequency spectrum for each one-way CDMA communications channel. This equates to 10% of the total available frequency spectrum of each U.S. cellular telephone provider. CDMA channels can coexist within the AMPS frequency spectrum by having a wireless operator clear a 1.25-MHz band of frequencies to accommodate transmissions on the CDMA channel. A single CDMA radio channel takes up the same bandwidth as approximately 42, 30-kHz voice channels. However, due to the frequency reuse advantage of CDMA, CDMA offers approximately a 10-to-1 channel advantage over standard analog AMPS and a 3-to-1 advantage over USDC.

For down-link (reverse) channel operation, IS-95 specifies the 824-MHz to 849-MHz band and up-link (forward) channels the 869-MHz to 894-MHz band. CDMA cellular systems also use a modified PCS frequency allocation in the 1900-MHz band. As with AMPS, the transmit and receive carrier frequencies used by CDMA are separated by 45 MHz. Figure 20-16 shows the frequency spacing for two adjacent CDMA channels in the AMPS frequency band. As the figure shows, each CDMA channel is 1.23 MHz wide with a 1.25-MHz frequency separation of the carriers, producing a 200-kHz guard band between CDMA channels. Guard bands are necessary to ensure that the CDMA carriers do not

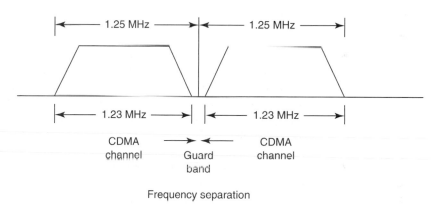

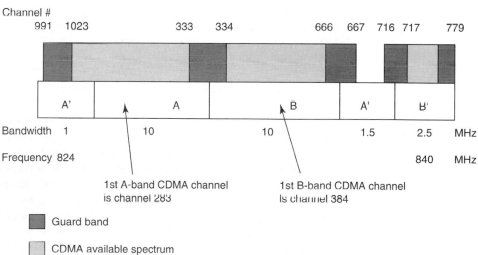

FIGURE 20-16   CDMA channel location, guard band, and frequency separation

interfere with other users. The lowest CDMA channel in the A-band is at AMPS channel 283, and the lowest CDMA carrier in the B-band is at AMPS channel 384. Because the band available between channels 667 and 716 is only 1.5 MHz in the A-band, A-band operators have to acquire permission from B-band carriers to use a CDMA carrier in that portion of the frequency spectrum. When a CDMA carrier is being used next to a non-CDMA carrier, the carrier spacing must be 1.77 MHz. There are as many as nine CDMA carriers available for the A- and B-band operator in the AMPS frequency spectrum. However, the A- and B-band operators have 30-MHz bandwidth in the 1900-MHz PCS frequency band where they can facilitate up to 11 CDMA channels.

With CDMA, many users can share common transmit and receive channels with a transmission data rate of 9.6 kbps. Using several techniques, however, subscriber information is spread by a factor of 128 to a channel chip rate of 1.2288 Mchips/s, and transmit and receive channels use different spreading processes.

In the up-link channel, subscriber data are encoded using a rate 1/2 convolutional code, interleaved, and spread by 1 of 64 orthogonal spreading sequences using Walsh functions. Orthogonality among all up-link cellular channel subscribers within a given cell is maintained because all the cell signals are scrambled synchronously.

Down-link channels use a different spreading strategy since each mobile unit's received signal takes a different transmission path and, therefore, arrives at the base station at a different time. Down-link channel data streams are first convolutional encoded with a rate 1/3 convolution code. After interleaving, each block of six encoded symbols is mapped to one of the available orthogonal Walsh functions ensuring 64-ary orthogonal signaling. An additional fourfold spreading is performed by subscriber-specified and base station–specific codes having periods of $2^{42}-1$ chips and 2^{15} chips, respectively, increasing the transmission rate to 1.2288 Mchips/s. Stringent requirements are enforced in the down-link channel's transmit power to avoid the near–far problem caused by varied receive power levels.

Each mobile unit in a given cell is assigned a unique spreading sequence, which ensures near perfect separation among the signals from different subscriber units and allows transmission differentiation between users. All signals in a particular cell are scrambled using a pseudorandom sequence of length 2^{15} chips. This reduces radio-frequency interference between mobiles in neighboring cells that may be using the same spreading sequence and provides the desired wideband spectral characteristics even though all Walsh codes do not yield a wideband power spectrum.

Two commonly used techniques for spreading the spectrum are *frequency hopping* and *direct sequencing*. Both of these techniques are characteristic of transmissions over a bandwidth much wider than that normally used in narrowband FDMA/TDMA cellular telephone systems such as AMPS and USDC. For a more detailed description of frequency hopping and direct sequencing, refer to Chapter 19.

Frequency-hopping spread spectrum.   Frequency-hopping spread spectrum was first used by the military to ensure reliable antijam and secure communications in a battlefield environment. The fundamental concept of frequency hopping is to break a message into fixed-size blocks of data with each block transmitted in sequence except on a different carrier frequency. With frequency hopping, a pseudorandom code is used to generate a unique frequency-hopping sequence. The sequence in which the frequencies are selected must be known by both the transmitter and receiver prior to the beginning of the transmission. The transmitter sends one block on a radio-frequency carrier then switches (hops) to the next frequency in the sequence, and so on. After reception of a block of data on one frequency, the receiver switches to the next frequency in the sequence. Each transmitter in the system has a different hopping sequence to prevent one subscriber from interfering with transmissions from other subscribers using the same radio channel frequency.

Direct-sequence spread spectrum. In direct-sequence systems, a high-bit-rate pseudorandom code is added to a low-bit-rate information signal to generate a high-bit-rate pseudorandom signal closely resembling noise that contains both the original data signal and the pseudorandom code. Again, before successful transmission, the pseudorandom code must be known to both the transmitter and the intended receiver. When a receiver detects a direct-sequence transmission, it simply subtracts the pseudorandom signal from the composite receive signal to extract the information data. In CDMA cellular telephone systems, the total radio-frequency bandwidth is divided into a few broadband radio channels that have a much higher bandwidth than the digitized voice signal. The digitized voice signal is added to the generated high-bit-rate signal and transmitted in such a way that it occupies the entire broadband radio channel. Adding a high-bit-rate pseudorandom signal to the voice information makes the signal more dominant and less susceptible to interference, allowing lower-power transmission and, hence, a lower number of transmitters and less-expensive receivers.

CDMA Traffic Channels

CDMA traffic channels consist of a down-link (base station–to–mobile unit) channel and an up-link (mobile station–to–base station) channel. A CDMA down-link traffic channel is shown in Figure 20-17a. As the figure shows, the down-link traffic channel consists of up to 64 channels including a broadcast channel used for control and traffic channels used to carry subscriber information. The broadcast channel consists of a pilot channel, a synchronization channel, up to seven paging channels, and up to 63 traffic channels. All these channels share the same 1.25-MHz CDMA frequency assignment. The traffic channel is identified by a distinct user-specific long-code sequence and each access channel is identified by a distinct access channel long-code sequence.

The pilot channel is included in every cell with the purpose of providing a signal for the receiver to use to acquire timing and provide a phase reference for coherent demodulation. The pilot channel is also used by mobile units to compare signal strengths between base stations to determine when a handoff should be initiated. The synchronization channel uses a Walsh W32 code and the same pseudorandom sequence and phase offset as the pilot channel, allowing it to be demodulated by any receiver that can acquire the pilot signal. The synchronization channel broadcasts synchronization messages to mobile units and operates at 1200 bps. Paging channels convey information from the base station to the mobile station such as system parameter messages, access parameter messages, CDMA channel list messages, and channel assignment messages. Paging channels are optional and can

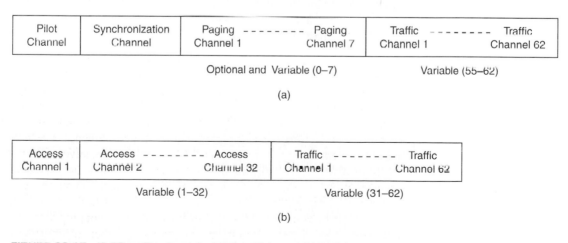

FIGURE 20-17 IS-95 traffic channels. (a) down-link; and (b) up-link

range in number between 0 and 7. The paging channel is used to transmit control information and paging messages from the base station to the mobile units and operates at either 9600 bps, 4800 bps, or 2400 bps. A single 9600-bps pilot channel can typically support about 180 pages per second for a total capacity of 1260 pages per second.

Data on the down-link traffic channel are grouped into 20-ms frames. The data are first convolutionally coded then formatted and interleaved to compensate for differences in the actual user data rates, which varies. The resulting signal is spread with a Walsh code and a long pseudorandom sequence at a rate of 1.2288 Mchips/s.

The up-link radio channel transmitter is shown in Figure 20-17b and consists of access channels and up to 62 up-link traffic channels. The access and up-link traffic channels use the same frequency assignment using direct-sequence CDMA techniques. The access channels are up-link only, shared, point-to-point channels that provide communications from mobile units to base stations when the mobile unit is not using a traffic channel. Access channels are used by the mobile unit to initiate communications with a base station and to respond to paging channel messages. Typical access channel messages include acknowledgments and sequence number, mobile identification parameter messages, and authentication parameters. The access channel is a random access channel with each channel subscriber uniquely identified by their pseudorandom codes. The up-link CDMA channel can contain up to a maximum of 32 access channels per supported paging channel. The up-link traffic channel operates at a variable data rate mode and the access channels operate at a fixed 4800 bps rate. Access channel messages consist of registration, order, data burst, origination, page response, authentication challenge response, status response, and assignment completion messages.

Subscriber data on the up-link radio channel transmitter are also grouped into 20-ms frames, convolutionally encoded, block interleaved, modulated by a 64-ary orthogonal modulation, and spread prior to transmission.

GLOBAL SYSTEM FOR MOBILE COMMUNICATIONS

In the early 1980s, analog cellular telephone systems were experiencing a period of rapid growth in western Europe, particularly in Scandinavia and the United Kingdom, and to a lesser extent in France and Germany. Each country subsequently developed their own cellular system which was incompatible with everyone else's system from both an equipment and an operational standpoint. Most of the existing systems operated at different frequencies and all were analog. In 1982 the *Conference of European Posts and Telegraphs* (CEPT) formed a study group called *Groupe Spécial Mobile* (GSM) to study and develop a pan-European public land mobile telephone system. In 1989 the responsibility of GSM was transferred to the *European Telecommunication Standards Institute* (ETSI) and phase I of the GSM specifications was published in 1990. GSM had the advantage of being designed from scratch with little or no concern for being backward compatible with any existing analog cellular telephone systems.

Commercial GSM service began in 1991 and by 1993 there were 36 GSM networks in 22 countries. GSM networks are now either operational or planned in over 80 countries around the world. North America made a late entry into the GSM market with a derivative of GSM called PCS 1900. GSM systems now exist on every continent and the acronym GSM now stands for *Global System for Mobile Communications*.

GSM is a second-generation cellular telephone system initially developed to solve the fragmentation problems inherent in the first-generation cellular telephone systems in Europe. Prior to GSM, all European countries used different cellular telephone standards; thus, it was impossible for a subscriber in any country to use a single telephone set throughout Europe. GSM was the world's first totally digital cellular telephone system designed to use the services of ISDN to provide a wide range of network services. With between 20 and

50 million subscribers, GSM is now the world's most popular standard for new cellular telephone and personal communications equipment.

GSM Services

The original intention was to make GSM compatible with ISDN in terms of services offered and control signaling formats. Unfortunately, radio channel bandwidth limitations and cost prohibit GSM from operating at the 64-kbps ISDN basic data rate.

GSM telephone services can be broadly classified into three categories: *bearer services, teleservices,* and *supplementary services.* Probably the most basic bearer service (*teleservice*) provided by GSM is telephony. With GSM, analog speech signals are digitally encoded then transmitted through the network as a digital data stream. There is also an emergency service where the closest emergency-service provider is notified by dialing three digits similar to 911 services in the United States. A wide variety of data services is offered through GSM where users can send and receive data at rates up to 9600 bps to subscribers in POTS (*plain old telephone service*), ISDN, Packet Switched Public Data Network (PSPDN), and Circuit Switched Public Data Network (CSPDN) using a wide variety of access methods and protocols such as X.25. Also, since GSM is a digital network, a modem is not required between the user and the GSM network.

Other GSM data services include Group 3 facsimile per ITU-T recommendation T.30. One unique feature of GSM that is not found in older analog systems is the *Short Message Service* (SMS) which is a bidirectional service for sending alphanumeric messages up to 160 bytes in length. SMS messages are transported through the system in a store-and-forward fashion. SMS can also be used in a cell-broadcast mode for sending messages to multiple receivers. Several supplemental services such as *call forwarding* and *call barring* are also offered with GSM.

GSM System Architecture

The system architecture for GSM as shown in Figure 20-18 consists of three major interconnected subsystems that interact among one another and with subscribers through

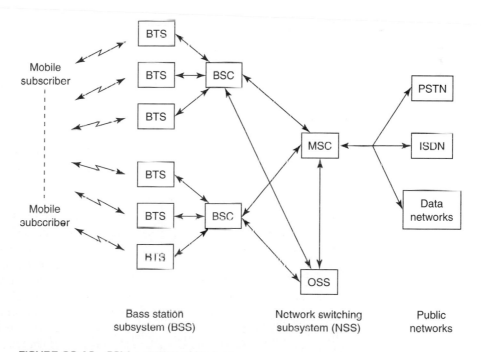

FIGURE 20-18 GSM system architecture

specified network interfaces. The three primary subsystems of GSM are *Base Station Subsystem* (BSS), *Network and Switching Subsystem* (NSS), and the *Operational Support Subsystem* (OSS). Although the mobile station is technically another subsystem, it is generally considered to be part of the base station subsystem.

The BSS is sometimes known as the *radio subsystem,* because it provides and manages radio-frequency transmission paths between mobile units and the *mobile switching center* (MSC). The BSS also manages the radio interface between mobile stations and all other GSM subsystems. Each BSS consists of many base station controllers (BSC) which are used to connect the MS to the NSS through one or more MSCs. The NSS manages switching functions for the system and allows the MSCs to communicate with other telephone networks such as the public switched telephone service and ISDN. The OSS supports operation and maintenance of the system and allows engineers to monitor, diagnose, and troubleshoot every aspect of the GSM network.

GSM Radio Subsystem

GSM was originally designed for 200 full-duplex channels per cell with transmission frequencies in the 900-MHz band; however, frequencies were later allocated at 1800 MHz. A second system, called DSC 1800, was established that closely resembles GSM. GSM uses two 25-MHz frequency bands that have been set aside for system use in all member companies. The 890-MHz to 915-MHz band is used for mobile unit–to–base station transmissions (reverse-link transmissions), and the 935-MHz to 960-MHz frequency band is used for base station–to–mobile unit transmission (forward-link transmissions). GSM uses frequency-division duplexing and a combination of TDMA and FDMA techniques to provide base stations simultaneous access to multiple mobile units. The available forward and reverse frequency bands are subdivided into 200-kHz-wide voice channels called absolute radio-frequency channel numbers (ARFCN). The ARFCN number designates a forward/reverse channel pair with 45-MHz separation between them. Each voice channel is shared among as many as eight mobile units using TDMA.

Each of the ARFCN channel subscribers occupy a unique time slot within the TDMA frame. Radio transmission in both directions is at a 270.833-kbps rate using binary *Gaussian minimum shift keying* (GMSK) modulation with an effective channel transmission rate of 33.833 kbps per user.

PERSONAL COMMUNICATIONS SATELLITE SYSTEM

Mobile Satellite Systems (MSS) provide the vehicle for a new generation of wireless telephone services called *personal communications satellite systems* (PCSS). Universal wireless telephone coverage is a developing MSS service that promises to deliver mobile subscribers both traditional and enhanced telephone features while providing wide-area global coverage.

MSS satellites are, in essence, radio repeaters in the sky and their usefulness for mobile communications depends on several factors, such as the space-vehicle altitude, orbital pattern, transmit power, receiver sensitivity, modulation technique, antenna radiation pattern (i.e., footprints), and several other factors. Satellite communications systems have traditionally provided both narrowband and wideband voice, data, video, facsimile, and networking services using large and very expensive, high-powered earth station transmitters communicating via high-altitude, geosynchronous earth-orbit (GEO) satellites. Personal communications satellite services, however, use low earth-orbit (LEO) and medium earth-orbit (MEO) satellites that communicate directly with small, low-power mobile telephone units. The intention of PCSS mobile telephone is to provide the same features and services offered by traditional, terrestrial cellular telephone providers. PCSS telephones, however, will be able to make or receive calls at anytime, anywhere in the world.

Projected PCSS Market

Industrial surveys indicate that for a PCSS system to be successful it must provide both regional and global coverage since most of its subscribers want to use only one system as they travel in and out of countries or regions with noncompatible operating systems. In addition, PCSS telephone subscribers want coverage 24 hours a day, virtually everywhere including high-density metropolitan areas, rural areas, isolated areas, subterrestrial areas, waterways, highways, airways, unpopulated areas, remote areas, wilderness areas, combat areas, and where there are limited or no services provided by the public telephone company. Subscribers also want small handheld, portable telephone sets with features such as universal ubiquitousness, integrated message services, voice, data, facsimile, vehicle navigation, telemetry, and universal roaming. In essence, everything!

PCSS Industry Requirements

PCSS mobile telephone systems require transparent interfaces and feature sets among the multitude of terrestrial networks currently providing mobile and wireline telephone services. In addition, the interfaces must be capable of operating with both ANSI and CCITT network constraints and be able to provide interpretability with AMPS, E-TACS, USDC, GSM, and PCS cellular telephone systems. PCSS must also be capable of operating in dual mode with *air-access protocols,* such as FDMA, TDMA, or CDMA. PCSS should also provide unique MSS feature sets and characteristics such as inter-/intra-satellite handoffs, land-based to satellite handoffs, and land-base/PCSS dual registration.

PCSS Advantages and Disadvantages

The primary and probably most obvious advantage of PCSS mobile telephone is that it provides mobile telephone coverage and a host of other integrated services virtually anywhere in the world to a truly global customer base. PCSS can fill the vacancies between land-based cellular and PCS telephone systems and provide wide-area coverage on a regional or global basis.

PCSS is ideally suited to fixed cellular telephone applications as it can provide a full complement of telephone services to places where cables can never go due to economical, technical, or physical constraints. PCSS can also provide complementary and backup telephone services to large companies and organizations with multiple operations in diverse locations, such as retail, manufacturing, finance, transportation, government, military, and insurance.

Most of the disadvantages of PCSS are closely related to economics with the primary disadvantage being the high risk associated with the high costs of designing, building, and launching satellites. There is also a high cost for the terrestrial-based networking and interface infrastructure necessary to maintain, coordinate, and manage the network once it is in operation. In addition, the intricate low-power, dual-mode transceivers are more cumbersome and expensive than most telephone units used with conventional terrestrial cellular telephone systems.

PCSS Providers

The top players in the PCSS market include the American Mobile Satellite Corporation (AMSC), Celsat, Comsat, Constellation Communications (Aries), Ellipsat (Ellipso), INMARSAT, LEOSAT, Loral/Qualcomm (Globalstar), TMI Communications, TWR (Odyssey), and Iridium LLC.

Iridium Satellite System

Iridium LLC is an international consortium owned by a host of prominent companies, agencies, and governments including the following: Motorola, General Electric, Lockheed, Raytheon, McDonnell Douglas, Scientific Atlanta, Sony, Kyocera, Mitsubishi, DDI, Kruchinew Enterprises, Mawarid Group of Saudi Arabia, STET of Italy, Nippon Iridium Corporation of Japan, the government of Brazil, Muidiri Investments BVI, LTD of

Venezuela, Great Wall Industry of China, United Communications of Thailand, the U.S. Department of Defense, Sprint, and BCE Siemens.

The *Iridium project,* which even sounds like something out of *Star Wars,* is undoubtedly the largest commercial venture undertaken in the history of the world. It is the system with the most satellites, the highest price tag, the largest public relations team, and the most peculiar design. The $5-billion, gold-plated *Iridium* mobile telephone system is undoubtedly (or at least intended to be) the Cadillac of mobile telephone systems. Unfortunately (and somewhat ironically), on August 1999, on Friday the 13th, Iridium LLC, the beleaguered satellite-telephone system spawned by Motorola's Satellite Communications Group in Chandler, Arizona, filed for bankruptcy under protection of Chapter 11. However, Motorola Inc., the largest stockholder in Iridium, says it will continue to support the company and its customers and does not expect any interruption in service while reorganization is underway.

Iridium is a satellite-based wireless personal communications network designed to permit a wide range of mobile telephone services including voice, data, networking, facsimile, and paging. The system is called Iridium after the element on the periodic table with the atomic number 77, because Iridium's original design called for 77 satellites. The final design, however, requires only 66 satellites. Apparently, someone decided that element 66, dysprosium, did not have the same charismatic appeal as Iridium, and the root meaning of the word is "bad approach." The 66-vehicle low earth-orbit (LEO) interlinked satellite constellation can track the location of a subscriber's telephone handset, determine the best routing through a network of ground-based gateways and intersatellite links, establish the best path for the telephone call, initiate all the necessary connections, and terminate the call upon completion. The system also provides applicable revenue tracking.

With Iridium, two-way global communications is possible even when the destination subscriber's location is unknown to the caller. In essence, the intent of the Iridium system is to provide the best service in the telephone world, allowing telecommunication anywhere, anytime, and any place. The FCC granted the Iridium program a full license in January 1995 for construction and operation in the United States.

Iridium uses a GSM-based telephony architecture to provide a digitally switched telephone network and global dial tone to call and receive calls from any place in the world. This global roaming feature is designed into the system. Each subscriber is assigned a personal phone number and will receive only one bill, no matter in what country or area they use the telephone.

The Iridium project has a satellite network control facility in Landsdowne, Virginia, with a backup facility in Italy. A third engineering control complex is located at Motorola's SATCOM location in Chandler, Arizona.

System layout. Figure 20-19 shows an overview of the Iridium system. Subscriber telephone sets used in the Iridium system transmit and receive L-band frequencies and utilize both frequency- and time-division multiplexing to make the most efficient use of a limited frequency spectrum. Other communications links used in Iridium include EHF and SHF bands between satellites for telemetry, command, and control, as well as routing digital voice packets to and from gateways. An Iridium telephone enables the subscriber to connect either to the local cellular telephone infrastructure or to the space constellation using its *dual-mode* feature.

Iridium gateways are prime examples of the advances in satellite infrastructures that are responsible for the delivery of a host of new satellite services. The purpose of the gateways is to support and manage roaming subscribers as well as to interconnect Iridium subscribers to the public switched telephone network. Gateway functions include the following:

1. Set up and maintain basic and supplementary telephony services.
2. Provide an interface for two-way telephone communications between two Iridium subscribers and Iridium subscribers to subscribers of the public switched telephone network.

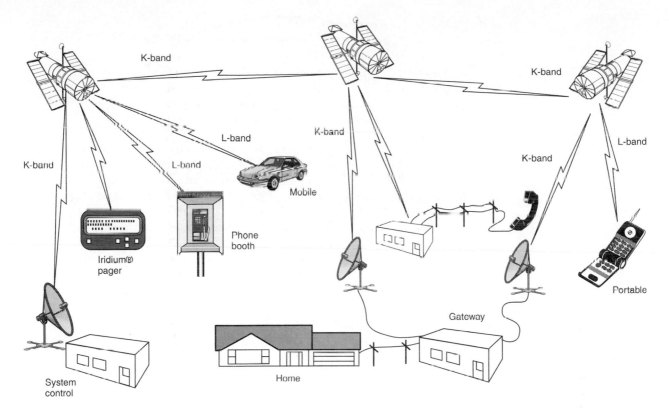

FIGURE 20-19 Overview of Iridium PCSS mobile telephone system

3. Provide Iridium subscribers with messaging, facsimile, and data services.

4. Facilitate the business activities of the Iridium system through a set of cooperative mutual agreements.

Satellite constellation. Providing full-earth coverage is the underlying basis of the Iridium satellite system. Iridium uses 66 operational satellites (there are also some spares) configured at a mean elevation of 420 mi above Earth in six nearly-polar orbital planes (86.4° tilt), in which 11 satellites revolve around Earth in each orbit with an orbital time of 100 min 28 s. This allows Iridium to cover the entire surface area of Earth and whenever one satellite goes out of view of a subscriber a different one replaces it. The satellites are phased appropriately in north–south necklaces forming *co-rotating planes* up one side of Earth, across the poles, and down the other side. The first and last planes rotate in opposite directions, creating a virtual *seam*. The co-rotating planes are separated by 31.6° and the seam planes are 22° apart.

Each satellite is equipped with three L-band antennas forming a honeycomb pattern that consists of 48 individual spot beams with a total of 1628 cells aimed directly below the satellite, as shown in Figure 20-20. As the satellite moves in its orbit, the footprints move across Earth's surface and subscriber signals are switched from one beam to the next or from one satellite to the next in a handoff process. When satellites approach the North or South Pole, their footprints converge and the beams overlap. Outer beams are then turned off to eliminate this overlap and conserve power on the spacecraft. Each cell has 174 full-duplex voice channels for a total of 283,272 channels worldwide.

Using satellite *cross-links* is the unique key to the Iridium system and the primary differentiation between Iridium and the traditional satellite *bent-pipe system* where all transmissions follow a path from Earth-to-satellite-to-Earth. Iridium is the first mobile satellite

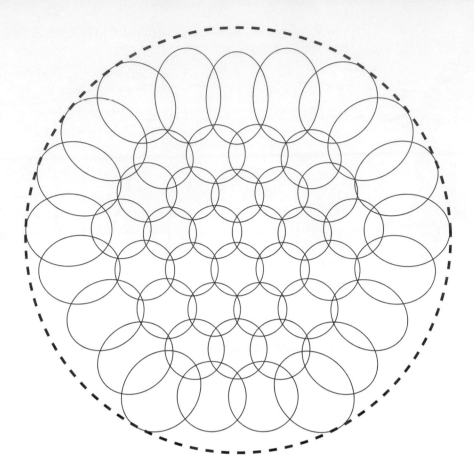

FIGURE 20-20 Iridium system spot beam footprint pattern

to incorporate sophisticated, onboard digital processing on each satellite and cross-link capability between satellites.

Each satellite is equipped with four satellite-to-satellite cross-links to relay digital information around the globe. The cross-link antennas point toward the closest spacecraft orbiting in the same plane and the two adjacent co-rotating planes. *Feeder link* antennas relay information to the terrestrial gateways and the system control segment located at the earth stations.

Frequency plan and modulation.   On October 14, 1994, the Federal Communication Commission issued a report and order Dockett #92-166 defining L-band frequency sharing for subscriber units in the 1616-MHz to 1626.5-MHz band. Mobile satellite system cellular communications is assigned 5.15 MHz at the upper end of this spectrum for TDMA/FDMA service. CDMA access is assigned the remaining 11.35 MHz for their service up-links and a proportionate amount of the S-band frequency spectrum at 2483.5 MHz to 2500 MHz for their down-links. When a CDMA system is placed into operation, the CDMA L-band frequency spectrum will be reduced to 8.25 MHz. The remaining 3.1 MHz of the frequency spectrum will then be assigned to either the Iridium system or another TDMA/FDMA system.

All Ka-band up-links, down-links, and cross-links are packetized TDM/FDMA using quadrature phase shift keying (QPSK) and FEC 1/2 rate convolutional coding with Viterbi decoding. Coded data rates are 6.25 Mbps for gateways and satellite control facility links and 25 Mbps for satellite cross-links. Both up-link and down-link transmissions occupy

100 MHz of bandwidth and intersatellite links use 200 MHz of bandwidth. The frequency bands are as follows:

L-band subscriber-to-satellite voice links = 1.616 GHz to 1.6265 GHz

Ka-band gateway down-links = 19.4 GHz to 19.6 GHz

Ka-band gateway up-links = 29.1 GHz to 29.3 GHz

Ka-intersatellite cross-links = 23.18 GHz to 23.38 GHz

QUESTIONS

20-1. Briefly explain the difference between a *mobile* and a *portable* telephone set.

20-2. Briefly explain the difference between *two-way mobile radio* and *two-way mobile telephone*.

20-3. What is meant by the term *wireline* telephone system?

20-4. When did the FCC grant the first license to operate a developmental cellular radio service?

20-5. What was the first U.S. cellular telephone system?

20-6. List the most common two-way radio communications systems and give a brief description of each.

20-7. Describe the difference between a *coverage zone* and a *cell*.

20-8. Explain why hexagonal cells are used rather than circular cells.

20-9. Describe the differences between a *macrocell* and a *microcell*.

20-10. Explain the basic concept of *frequency reuse*.

20-11. What is the difference between an *edge-excited* and a *center-excited* cell?

20-12. What are the two most predominant forms of interference in cellular telephone systems?

20-13. Briefly describe the two forms of interference listed in Question 20-12.

20-14. Describe the advantage and disadvantage of having a high *co-channel reuse* factor.

20-15. What is meant by the *near–far effect* and how does it affect cellular telephone performance?

20-16. Briefly describe the term *cell splitting*.

20-17. What is the primary purpose of cell splitting?

20-18. What is meant by the term *blocking*?

20-19. Briefly describe the concepts of *sectoring, segmentation,* and *dualisation*.

20-20. Briefly describe the functions of a *mobile telephone switching office* (MTSO).

20-21. What is a *handoff*?

20-22. Explain the difference between a *soft* and a *hard handoff*.

20-23. List and outline the functions of the six major components of a cellular telephone system.

20-24. Briefly describe the procedures for *wireline-to-mobile* calls, *mobile-to-wireline* calls, and *mobile-to-mobile* calls.

20-25. What is meant by the terms *frequency-division multiple accessing* and *frequency-division duplexing*?

20-26. Explain *forward links* and *reverse links*.

20-27. Briefly describe the format for the AMPS *control channel*.

20-28. What is meant by the term *blank-and-burst*? When is it used?

20-29. Briefly describe the functions of the *supervisory audio tone* (SAT) and the *signaling tone* (ST).

20-30. Briefly describe the differences between AMPS and N-AMPS.

20-31. What is ETACS?

20-32. List the advantages of TDMA over FDMA.

20-33. What is the difference between AMPS and D-AMPS?

20-34. What is meant by the term *dual mode*?

20-35. What is the transmission bit rate specified by IS-54 for digitized voice transmissions?

20-36. What is the difference between the *standard* and the *extended frequency* spectrum in USDC cellular systems?

20-37. How many control channels are specified for AMPS systems? USDC systems?

20-38. What type of modulation is used for AMPS control channels? USDC control channels?

20-39. What is the bandwidth of an AMPS voice channel? USDC voice channel?

20-40. What *channel compression ratio* is achieved with USDC systems?

20-41. Briefly describe the functions of the following terms: *coded digital verification color code, slow associated control channel,* and *fast association control channel.*

20-42. When would a *shortened burst* frame format be used?

20-43. What type of modulation is used with USDC voice and control channels?

20-44. What is the bandwidth efficiency of the voice channel with USDC?

20-45. Briefly describe the functions of the following channels: *logical channel; random access channel; SMS point-to-point, paging, and access response channel; broadcast control channel;* and *shared channel feedback channel.*

20-46. What standard specifies CDMA digital cellular systems?

20-47. What is meant by the term PCS?

20-48. Name and briefly describe two *spread-spectrum* techniques.

20-49. What is meant by *up-link* channel? *Down-link* channel?

20-50. What is the bandwidth of a CDMA *traffic* channel?

20-51. What components comprise the CDMA traffic channel?

20-52. Where are GSM systems used?

20-53. Name the three broad *classifications* of GSM telephone services.

20-54. List and briefly describe the three *primary subsystems* of GSM.

20-55. What is the bandwidth of a GSM voice channel?

20-56. What is the frequency separation between GSM transmit and receive carrier frequencies?

20-57. Describe the term PCSS.

20-58. What is the primary disadvantage of PCSS systems?

20-59. List some of the advantages of PCSS systems.

20-60. How many satellites are used in the *Iridium* constellation?

20-61. On which *telephone architecture* is Iridium based?

20-62. Briefly describe the Iridium satellite constellation.

PROBLEMS

20-1. Determine the number of full-duplex channels available in a cluster and the total capacity for a cellular system where there are 10 clusters, each consisting of 20 cells with 18 channels in each cell.

20-2. How many full-duplex channels are required in each cell for a cellular system with 12 clusters, 15 cells per cluster, and a total capacity of 3960 full-duplex channels?

20-3. Determine the number of cells in a cluster for the following values: $j = 3$ and $i = 4$.

20-4. Determine the co-channel reuse ratio for a cluster with 20 cells.

20-5. Determine the co-channel reuse ratio for a cluster when the distance to the center of the nearest co-channel cell is 4 km and the cell radius is 1.2 km.

20-6. Determine the transmit and receive carrier frequencies for the following AMPS channels: 33, 156, 680, 991, and 1008.

A P P E N D I X   A

The Smith Chart

INTRODUCTION

Mathematical solutions for transmission-line impedances are laborious. Therefore, it is common practice to use charts to graphically solve transmission-line impedance problems. Equation A-1 is the formula for determining the impedance at a given point on a transmission line.

$$Z = Z_O\left[\frac{Z_L + jZ_O \tan \beta S}{Z_O + jZ_L \tan \beta S}\right] \tag{A-1}$$

where Z = line impedance at a given point
   Z_L = load impedance
   Z_O = line characteristic impedance
   βS = distance from the load to the point where the impedance value
       is to be calculated

Several charts are available on which the properties of transmission lines are graphically presented. However, the most useful graphical representations are those that give the impedance relations that exist along a lossless transmission line for varying load conditions. The *Smith chart* is the most widely used transmission-line calculator of this type. The Smith chart is a special kind of impedance coordinate system that portrays the relationship of impedance at any point along a uniform transmission line to the impedance at any other point on the line.

The Smith chart was developed by Philip H. Smith at Bell Telephone Laboratories and was originally described in an article entitled "Transmission Line Calculator" (*Electronics*, January 1939). A Smith chart is shown in Figure A-1. This chart is based on two sets of *orthogonal* circles. One set represents the ratio of the resistive component of the line impedance (R) to the characteristic impedance of the line (Z_O), which for a lossless line is also purely resistive. The second set of circles represents the ratio of the reactive component of

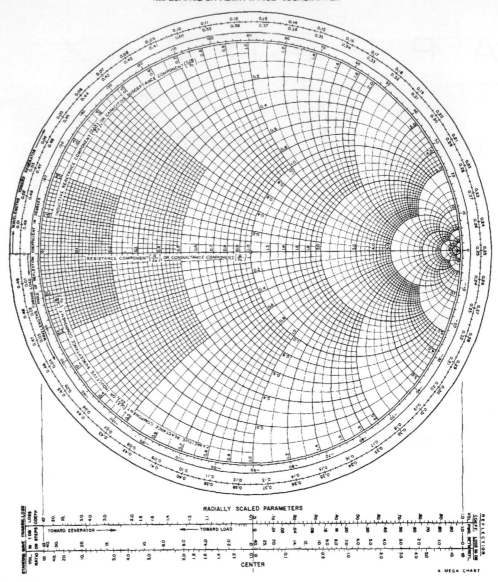

FIGURE A-1 Smith chart, transmission-line calculator

the line impedance ($\pm jX$) to the characteristic impedance of the line (Z_O). Parameters plotted on the Smith chart include the following:

1. Impedance (or admittance) at any point along a transmission line
    a. Reflection coefficient magnitude (Γ)
    b. Reflection coefficient angle in degrees
2. Length of transmission line between any two points in wavelengths
3. Attenuation between any two points
    a. Standing-wave loss coefficient
    b. Reflection loss

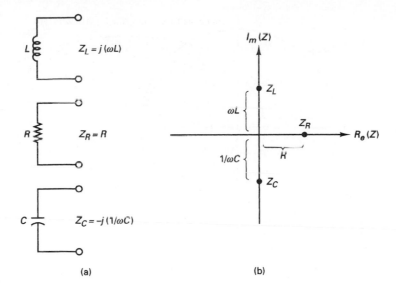

FIGURE A-2   (a) Typical circuit elements; (b) impedances graphed on rectangular coordinate plane. (Note: ω is the angular frequency at which Z is measured.)

4. Voltage or current standing-wave ratio
  a. Standing-wave ratio
  b. Limits of voltage and current due to standing waves

SMITH CHART DERIVATION

The impedance of a transmission line, Z, is made up of both *real* and *imaginary* components of either sign ($Z = R \pm jX$). Figure A-2a shows three typical circuit elements, and Figure A-2b shows their impedance graphed on a *rectangular* coordinate plane. All values of Z that correspond to passive networks must be plotted on or to the right of the imaginary axis of the Z plane (this is because a negative real component implies that the network is capable of supplying energy). To display the impedance of all possible passive networks on a rectangular plot, the plot must extend to infinity in three directions ($+R$, $+jX$, and $-jX$). The Smith chart overcomes this limitation by plotting the complex *reflection coefficient*,

$$\Gamma = \frac{z - 1}{z + 1} \qquad \text{(A-2)}$$

where z equals the impedance normalized to the characteristic impedance (i.e., $z = Z/Z_O$).

Equation A-2 shows that for all passive impedance values, z, the magnitude of Γ is between 0 and 1. Also, because $|\Gamma| \leq 1$, the entire right side of the z plane can be mapped onto a circular area on the Γ plane. The resulting circle has a radius $r = 1$ and a center at $\Gamma = 0$, which corresponds to $z = 1$ or $Z = Z_O$.

Lines of Constant $R_e(z)$
Figure A-3a shows the rectangular plot of four lines of constant resistance $R_e(z) = 0$, 0.5, 1, and 2. For example, any impedance with a real part $R_e = 1$ will lie on the $R = 1$ line. Impedances with a positive reactive component (X_L) will fall above the real axis,

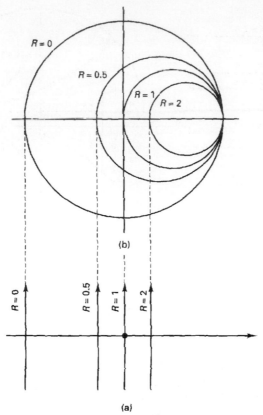

(b)

R = 0
R = 0.5
R = 1
R = 2

(b)

R = 0
R = 0.5
R = 1
R = 2

(a)

FIGURE A-3 (a) Rectangular plot; (b) Γ plane

whereas impedances with a negative reactive component (X_C) will fall below the real axis. Figure A-3b shows the same four values of R mapped onto the Γ plane. $R_e(z)$ are now circles of $R_e(\Gamma)$. However, inductive impedances are still transferred to the area above the horizontal axis, and capacitive impedances are transferred to the area below the horizontal axis. The primary difference between the two graphs is that with the circular plot the lines no longer extend to infinity. The infinity points all meet on the plane at a distance of 1 to the right of the origin. This implies that for $z = \infty$ (whether real, inductive, or capacitive) $\Gamma = 1$.

Lines of Constant *X(z)*

Figure A-4a shows the rectangular plot of three lines of constant inductive reactance ($X = 0.5$, 1, and 2), three lines of constant capacitive reactance ($X = -0.5$, -1, and -2), and a line of zero reactance ($X = 0$). Figure A-4b shows the same seven values of jX plotted onto the Γ plane. It can be seen that all values of infinite magnitude again meet at $\Gamma = 1$. The entire rectangular z plane curls to the right, and its three axes (which previously extended infinitely) meet at the intersection of the $\Gamma = 1$ circle and the horizontal axis.

Impedance Inversion (Admittance)

Admittance (Y) is the mathematical inverse of Z (i.e., $Y = 1/Z$). Y, or for that matter any complex number, can be found graphically using the Smith chart by simply plotting z on the complex Γ plane and then rotating this point 180° about $\Gamma = 0$. By rotating every point on the chart by 180°, a second set of coordinates (the y coordinates) can be developed that is an inverted mirror image of the original chart. See Figure A-5a. Occasionally, the admittance coordinates are superimposed on the same chart as the impedance coordinates. See Figure A-5b. Using the combination chart, both impedance and admittance values can be read directly by using the proper set of coordinates.

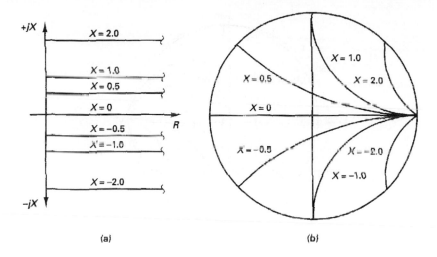

FIGURE A-4 (a) Rectangular plot; (b) Γ plane

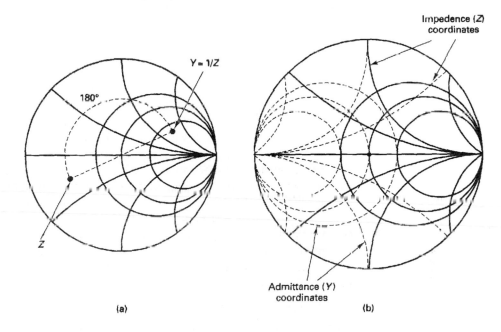

FIGURE A-5 Impedance inversion

Complex Conjugate

The *complex conjugate* can be determined easily using the Smith chart by simply reversing the sign of the angle of Γ. On the Smith chart, Γ is usually written in polar form and angles become more negative (phase lagging) when rotated in a clockwise direction around the chart. Hence, 0° is on the right end of the real axis and ±180° is on the left end. For example, let Γ = 0.5 /+150°. The complex conjugate, Γ*, is 0.5 /−150°. In Figure A-6, it is shown that Γ* is found by mirroring Γ about the real axis.

PLOTTING IMPEDANCE, ADMITTANCE, AND SWR ON THE SMITH CHART

Any impedance Z can be plotted on the Smith chart by simply *normalizing* the impedance value to the characteristic impedance (i.e., $z = Z/Z_O$) and plotting the real and imaginary

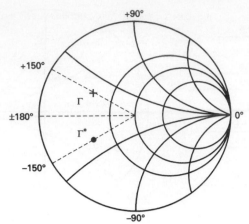

FIGURE A-6 Complex conjugate

parts. For example, for a characteristic impedance $Z_O = 50 \ \Omega$ and an impedance $Z = 25 \ \Omega$ resistive, the normalized impedance z is determined as follows:

$$z \ 5 \ \frac{Z}{Z_O} \ 5 \ \frac{25}{50} \ 5 \ 0.5$$

Because z is purely resistive, its plot must fall directly on the horizontal axis $(\pm jX = 0)$. $Z = 25$ is plotted on Figure A-7 at point A (i.e., $z = 0.5$). Rotating $180°$ around the chart gives a normalized admittance value $y = 2$ (where $y = Y/Y_O$). y is plotted on Figure A-7 at point B.

As previously stated, a very important characteristic of the Smith chart is that any lossless line can be represented by a circle having its origin at $1 \pm j0$ (the center of the chart) and radius equal to the distance between the origin and the impedance plot. Therefore, the *standing-wave ratio* (SWR) corresponding to any particular circle is equal to the value of Z/Z_O at which the circle crosses the horizontal axis on the right side of the chart. Therefore, for this example, SWR = 0.5 ($Z/Z_O = 25/50 = 0.5$). It should also be noted that any impedance or admittance point can be rotated $180°$ by simply drawing a straight line from the point through the center of the chart to where the line intersects the circle on the opposite side.

For a characteristic impedance $Z_O = 50$ and an inductive load $Z = +j25$, the normalized impedance z is determined as follows:

$$z \ 5 \ \frac{Z}{Z_O} \ 5 \ \frac{1 \ jX}{Z_O} \ 5 \ \frac{1 \ j25}{50} \ 5 \ 1 \ j0.5$$

Because z is purely inductive, its plot must fall on the $R = 0$ axis, which is the outer circle on the chart. $z = +j0.5$ is plotted on Figure A-8 at point A, and its admittance $y = -j2$ is graphically found by simply rotating $180°$ around the chart (point B). SWR for this example must lie on the far right end of the horizontal axis, which is plotted at point C and corresponds to SWR $= \infty$, which is inevitable for a purely reactive load. SWR is plotted at point C.

For a complex impedance $Z = 25 + j25$, z is determined as follows:

$$z \ 5 \ \frac{25 \ 1 \ j25}{50} \ 5 \ 0.5 \ 1 \ j0.5$$

$$= 0.707 \ \underline{/45°}$$

Therefore,
$$Z = 0.707 \ \underline{/45°} \times 50 = 35.35 \ \underline{/45°}$$

and
$$Y = \frac{1}{35.35 \ \underline{/45°}} = 0.02829 \ \underline{/45°}$$

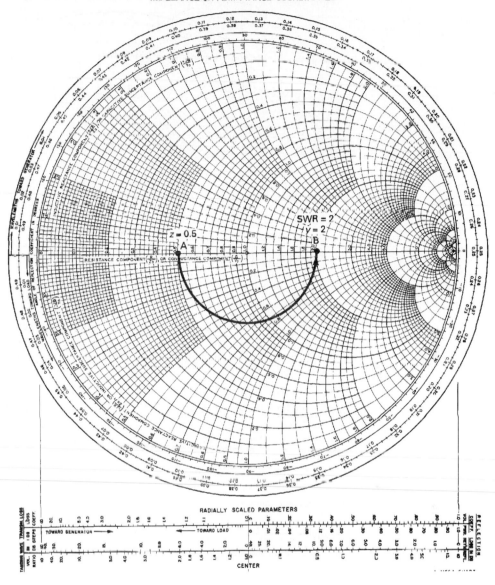

FIGURE A-7 Resistive impedance

Thus,

$$y = \frac{Y}{Y_O} = \frac{0.02829}{0.02} = 1.414$$

and

$$y = 1 - j1$$

z is plotted on the Smith chart by locating the point where the $R = 0.5$ arc intersects the $X = 0.5$ arc on the top half of the chart. $z = 0.5 + j0.5$ is plotted on Figure A-9 at point A, and y is plotted at point B $(1 - j1)$. From the chart, SWR is approximately 2.6 (point C).

INPUT IMPEDANCE AND THE SMITH CHART

The Smith chart can be used to determine the input impedance of a transmission line at any distance from the load. The two outermost scales on the Smith chart indicate distance in

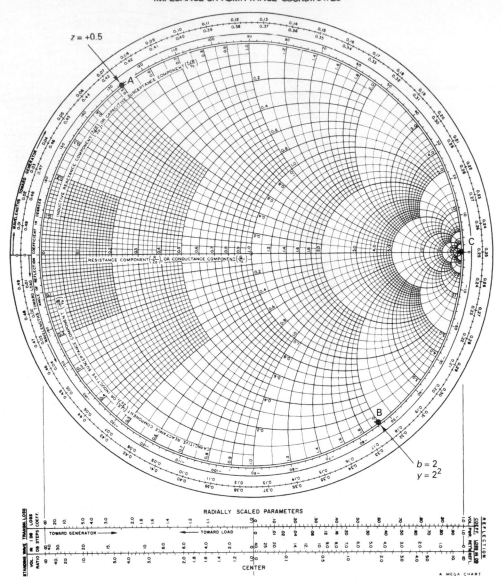

FIGURE A-8 Inductive load

wavelengths (see Figure A-1). The outside scale gives distance from the load toward the generator and increases in a clockwise direction, and the second scale gives distance from the source toward the load and increases in a counterclockwise direction. However, neither scale necessarily indicates the position of either the source or the load. One complete revolution (360°) represents a distance of one-half wavelength (0.5λ), half of a revolution (180°) represents a distance of one-quarter wavelength (0.25λ), and so on.

A transmission line that is terminated in an open circuit has an impedance at the open end that is purely resistive and equal to infinity (Chapter 8). On the Smith chart, this point is plotted on the right end of the $X = 0$ line (point *A* on Figure A-10). As you move toward the source (generator), the input impedance is found by rotating around the chart in a clockwise direction. It can be seen that input impedance immediately becomes capacitive and maximum. As you rotate farther around the circle (move toward the generator), the ca-

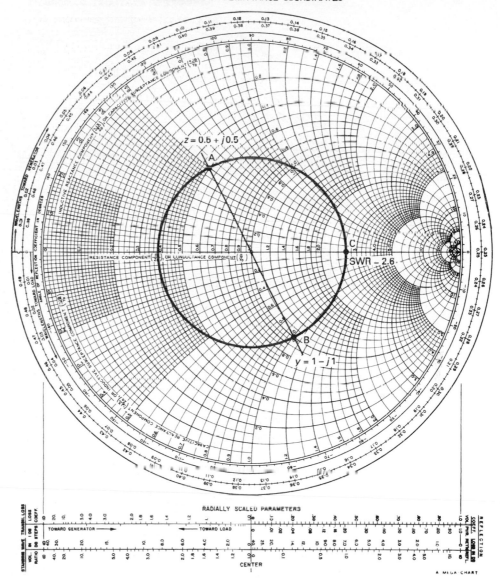

FIGURE A-9 Complex impedance

pacitance decreases to a normalized value of unity (i.e., $z = -j1$) at a distance of one-eighth wavelength from the load (point C on Figure A-10) and a minimum value just short of one-quarter wavelength. At a distance of one-quarter wavelength, the input impedance is purely resistive and equal to 0 Ω (point B on Figure A-10). As described in Chapter 8, there is an impedance inversion every one-quarter wavelength on a transmission line. Moving just past one-quarter wavelength, the impedance becomes inductive and minimum; then the inductance increases to a normalized value of unity (i.e., $z = +j1$) at a distance of three-eighths wavelength from the load (point D on Figure A-10) and a maximum value just short of one-half wavelength. At a distance of one-half wavelength, the input impedance is again purely resistive and equal to infinity (return to point A on Figure A-10). The results of the preceding analysis are identical to those achieved with phasor analysis in Chapter 8 and plotted in Figure 8-20.

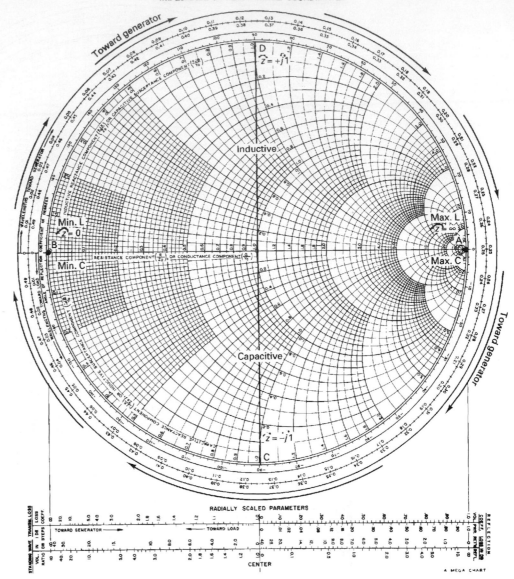

FIGURE A-10 Transmission-line input impedance for shorted and open line

A similar analysis can be done with a transmission line that is terminated in a short circuit, although the opposite impedance variations are achieved as with an open load. At the load, the input impedance is purely resistive and equal to 0. Therefore, the load is located at point *B* on Figure A-10, and point *A* represents a distance one-quarter wavelength from the load. Point *D* is a distance of one-eighth wavelength from the load and point *C*, a distance of three-eighths wavelength. The results of such an analysis are identical to those achieved with phasors in Chapter 8 and plotted in Figure 8-21.

For a transmission line terminated in a purely resistive load not equal to Z_O, Smith chart analysis is very similar to the process described in the preceding section. For example, for a load impedance $Z_L = 37.5 \ \Omega$ resistive and a transmission-line characteristic impedance $Z_O = 75 \ \Omega$, the input impedance at various distances from the load is determined as follows:

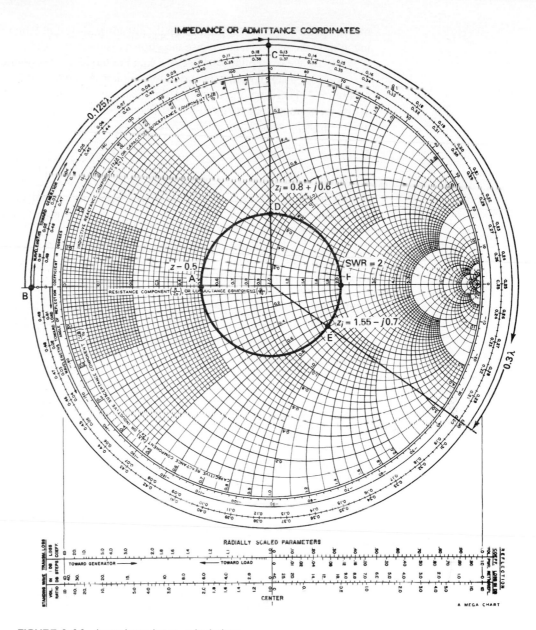

$z_i = 0.8 + j0.6$

$z = 0.5$

SWR = 2

$z_i = 1.55 - j0.7$

RADIALLY SCALED PARAMETERS

A MEGA CHART

FIGURE A-11 Input impedance calculations

1. The normalized load impedance z is

$$z = \frac{Z_L}{Z_O} = \frac{37.5}{75} = 0.5$$

2. $z = 0.5$ is plotted on the Smith chart (point A on Figure A-11). A circle is drawn that passes through point A with its center located at the intersection of the $R = 1$ circle and the $x = 0$ arc.

3. SWR is read directly from the intersection of the $z = 0.5$ circle and the $X = 0$ line on the right side (point F), SWR = 2. The impedance circle can be used to describe all impedances along the transmission line. Therefore, the input impedance (Z_i) at a distance of 0.125λ from the load is determined by extending the z circle to the outside of the chart, moving point A to a similar position on the outside scale (point B on Figure A-11) and moving around the scale in a clockwise direction a distance of 0.125λ.

4. Rotate from point B a distance equal to the length of the transmission line (point C on Figure A-11). Transfer this point to a similar position on the $z = 0.5$ circle (point D on Figure A-11). The normalized input impedance is located at point D $(0.8 + j0.6)$. The actual input impedance is found by multiplying the normalized impedance by the characteristic impedance of the line. Therefore, the input impedance Z_i is

$$Z_i = (0.8 + j0.6)75 = 60 + j45$$

Input impedances for other distances from the load are determined in the same way. Simply rotate in a clockwise direction from the initial point a distance equal to the length of the transmission line. At a distance of 0.3λ from the load, the normalized input impedance is found at point E $(z = 1.55 - j0.7$ and $Z_i = 116.25 - j52.5)$. For distances greater than 0.5λ, simply continue rotating around the circle, with each complete rotation accounting for 0.5λ. A length of 1.125λ is found by rotating around the circle two complete revolutions and an additional 0.125λ.

Example A-1

Determine the input impedance and SWR for a transmission line 1.25λ long with a characteristic impedance $Z_O = 50\ \Omega$ and a load impedance $Z_L = 30 + j40\ \Omega$.

Solution   The normalized load impedance z is

$$z = \frac{30 + j40}{50} = 0.6 + j0.8$$

z is plotted on Figure A-12 at point A and the impedance circle is drawn. SWR is read off the Smith chart from point B.

$$SWR = 2.9$$

The input impedance 1.25λ from the load is determined by rotating from point C 1.25λ in a clockwise direction. Two complete revolutions account for 1λ. Therefore, the additional 0.25λ is simply added to point C.

$$0.12\lambda + 0.25\lambda = 0.37\lambda \text{ (point } D)$$

Point D is moved to a similar position on the $z = 0.6 + j0.8$ circle (point E), and the input impedance is read directly from the chart.

$$z_i = 0.63 - j0.77$$
$$Z_i = 50(0.63 - j0.77) = 31.5 - j38.5$$

Quarter-Wave Transformer Matching with the Smith Chart

As described in Chapter 8, a length of transmission line acts as a transformer (i.e., there is an impedance inversion every one-quarter wavelength). Therefore, a transmission line with the proper length located the correct distance from the load can be used to match a load to the impedance of the transmission line. The procedure for matching a load to a transmission line with a quarter-wave transformer using the Smith chart is outlined in the following steps.

1. A load $Z_L = 75 + j50\ \Omega$ can be matched to a 50-Ω source with a quarter-wave transformer. The normalized load impedance z is

$$z = \frac{75 + j50}{50} = 1.5 + j1$$

2. $z = 1.5 + j1$ is plotted on the Smith chart (point A, Figure A-13) and the impedance circle is drawn.

3. Extend point A to the outermost scale (point B). The characteristic impedance of an ideal transmission line is purely resistive. Therefore, if a quarter-wave transformer is lo-

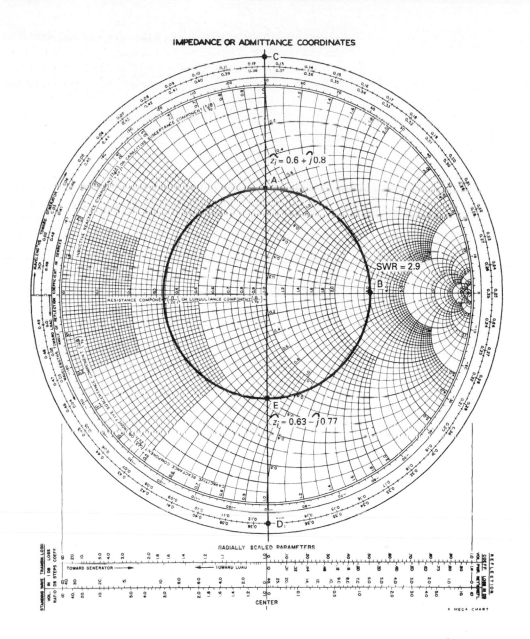

FIGURE A-12 Smith chart for Example A-1

cated at a distance from the load where the input impedance is purely resistive, the transformer can match the transmission line to the load. There are two points on the impedance circle where the input impedance is purely resistive: where the circle intersects the $X = 0$ line (points C and D on Figure A-13). Therefore, the distance from the load to a point where the input impedance is purely resistive is determined by simply calculating the distance in wavelengths from point B on Figure A-13 to either point C or D, whichever is the shortest. The distance from point B to point C is

point C	0.250λ
$-$point B	-0.192λ
distance	0.058λ

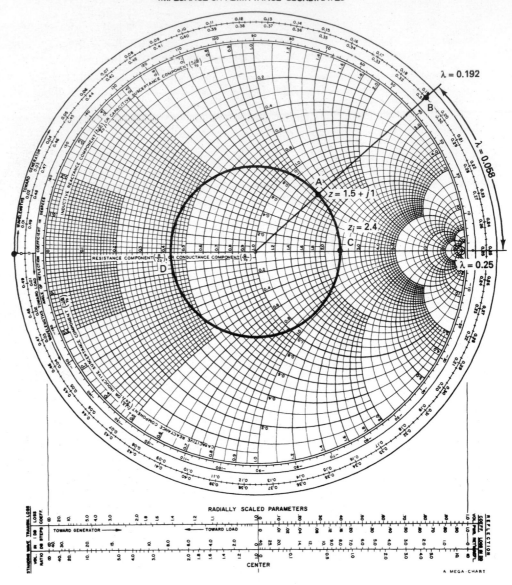

FIGURE A-13 Smith chart, quarter-wave transformer

If a quarter-wave transformer is placed 0.058λ from the load, the input impedance is read directly from Figure A-13, $z_i = 2.4$ (point C).

4. Note that 2.4 is also the SWR of the mismatched line and is read directly from the chart.

5. The actual input impedance $Z_i = 50(2.4) = 120\ \Omega$. The characteristic impedance of the quarter-wave transformer is determined from Equation 8-32.

$$Z_O' = \sqrt{Z_O Z_1} = \sqrt{50 \times 120} = 77.5\ \Omega$$

Thus, if a quarter-wavelength of a 77.5-Ω transmission line is inserted 0.058λ from the load, the line is matched. It should be noted that a quarter-wave transformer does not totally eliminate standing waves on the transmission line. It simply eliminates them from

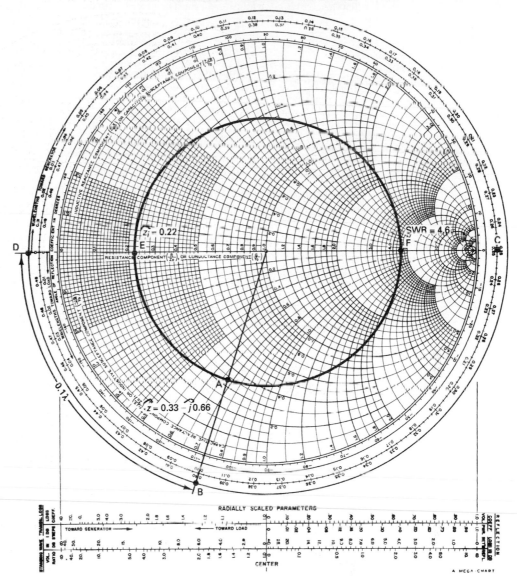

FIGURE A-14 Smith chart for Example A-2

the transformer back to the source. Standing waves are still present on the line between the transformer and the load.

Example A-2

Determine the SWR, characteristic impedance of a quarter-wave transformer, and the distance the transformer must be placed from the load to match a 75-Ω transmission line to a load $Z_L = 25 - j50$.

Solution   The normalized load impedance z is

$$z = \frac{25 - j50}{75} = 0.33 - j0.66$$

z is plotted at point A on Figure A-14 and the corresponding impedance circle is drawn. The SWR is read directly from point F:

$$SWR = 4.6$$

The Smith Chart

The closest point on the Smith chart where Z_i is purely resistive is point D. Therefore, the distance that the quarter-wave transformer must be placed from the load is

$$
\begin{array}{ll}
\text{point } D & 0.5\lambda \\
\underline{-\text{point } B \quad 0.4\lambda} \\
\text{distance} & 0.1\lambda
\end{array}
$$

The normalized input impedance is found by moving point D to a similar point on the z circle (point E), $z_i = 0.22$. The actual input impedance is

$$Z_i = 0.22(75) = 16.5 \ \Omega$$

The characteristic impedance of the quarter-wavelength transformer is again found from Equation 8-32.

$$Z'_O = \sqrt{75 \times 16.5} = 35.2 \ \Omega$$

Stub Matching with the Smith Chart

As described in Chapter 8, shorted and open stubs can be used to cancel the reactive portion of a complex load impedance and, thus, match the load to the transmission line. Shorted stubs are preferred because open stubs have a greater tendency to radiate.

Matching a complex load $Z_L = 50 - j100$ to a 75-Ω transmission line using a shorted stub is accomplished quite simply with the aid of a Smith chart. The procedure is outlined in the following steps:

1. The normalized load impedance z is

$$z = \frac{50 - j100}{75} = 0.67 - j1.33$$

2. $z = 0.67 - j1.33$ is plotted on the Smith chart shown in Figure A-15 at point A and the impedance circle is drawn in. Because stubs are shunted across the load (i.e., placed in parallel with the load), admittances are used rather than impedances to simplify the calculations, and the circles and arcs on the Smith chart are now used for conductance and susceptance.

3. The normalized admittance y is determined from the Smith chart by simply rotating the impedance plot, z, 180°. This is done on the Smith chart by simply drawing a line from point A through the center of the chart to the opposite side of the circle (point B).

4. Rotate the admittance point clockwise to a point on the impedance circle where it intersects the $R = 1$ circle (point C). The real component of the input impedance at this point is equal to the characteristic impedance Z_O, $Z_{in} = R \pm jX$, where $R = Z_O$. At point C, the admittance $y = 1 + j1.7$.

5. The distance from point B to point C is how far from the load the stub must be placed. For this example, the distance is $0.18\lambda - 0.09\lambda = 0.09\lambda$. The stub must have an impedance with a zero resistive component and a susceptance that has the opposite polarity (i.e., $y_s = 0 - j1.7$).

6. To find the length of the stub with an admittance $y_s = 0 - j1.7$, move around the outside circle of the Smith chart (the circle where $R = 0$), having a wavelength identified at point D, until an admittance $y = 1.7$ is found (wavelength value identified at point E). You begin at point D because a shorted stub has minimum resistance ($R = 0$) and, consequently, a susceptance $B = \infty$. Point D is such a point. (If an open stub were used, you would begin your rotation at the opposite side of the $X = 0$ line, point F.)

7. The distance from point D to point E is the length of the stub. For this example, the length of the stub is $0.334\lambda - 0.25\lambda = 0.084\lambda$.

Example A-3

For a transmission line with a characteristic impedance $Z_O = 300 \ \Omega$ and a load with a complex impedance $Z_L = 450 + j600$, determine SWR, the distance a shorted stub must be placed from the load to match the load to the line, and the length of the stub.

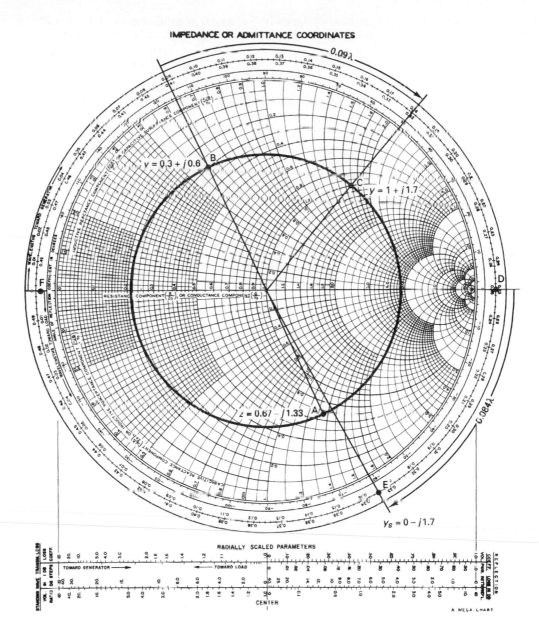

RADIALLY SCALED PARAMETERS

FIGURE A-15 Stub matching, Smith chart

Solution The normalized load impedance z is

$$z = \frac{450 + j600}{300} = 1.5 + j2$$

$z = 1.5 + j2$ is plotted on Figure A-16 at point A and the corresponding impedance circle is drawn. SWR is read directly from the chart at point B.

$$SWR = 4.7$$

Rotate point A 180° around the impedance circle to determine the normalized admittance.

$$y = 0.24 - j0.325 \quad \text{(point } C\text{)}$$

To determine the distance from the load to the stub, rotate clockwise around the outer scale beginning from point C until the circle intersects the $R = 1$ circle (point D).

$$y = 1 + j1.7$$

The Smith Chart

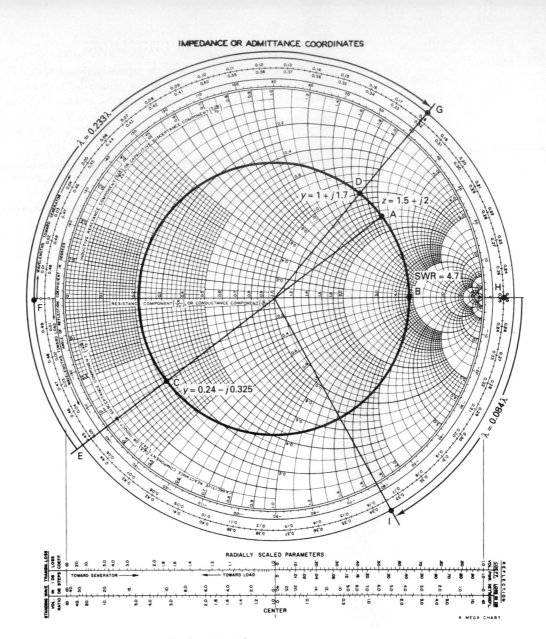

FIGURE A-16 Smith chart for Example A-3

The distance from point C to point D is the sum of the distances from point E to point F and point F to point G.

$$E \text{ to } F = 0.5\lambda - 0.449\lambda = 0.051\lambda$$
$$+F \text{ to } G = \underline{0.18\lambda - 0\lambda} = \underline{0.18\lambda}$$
$$\text{total distance} = 0.231\lambda$$

To determine the length of the shorted stub, calculate the distance from the $y = \infty$ point (point H) to the $y_s = 0 - j1.7$ point (point I).

$$\text{stub length} = 0.334\lambda - 0.25\lambda = 0.084\lambda$$

PROBLEMS

A-1. For a coaxial transmission line with the following characteristics: $Z_O = 72$ ohms, $\epsilon_r = 2.02$, $f = 4.2$ GHz, and $Z_L = 30 - j60$ ohms; determine the following: (a) VSWR, (b) impedance 6.6 inches from load, and (c) minimum purely resistive impedance on the line (Z_{min}).

A-2. For a terminated twin-lead transmission line with the following characteristics: $Z_O = 300$ ohms, $\epsilon_r = 2.56$, $f = 48$ MHz, and $Z_L = 73$ ohms; determine the following: (a) length of the stub and (b) shortest distance from the load that the stub can be placed.

A-3. For a terminated coaxial transmission line with the following characteristics: VSWR $= 3.0$, $f = 1.6$ GHz, $\epsilon_r = 2.02$, $Z_O = 50$ ohms, and distance from a VSWR null (minimum) to the load of 11.0 inches; determine the load impedance (Z_L).

A-4. For a terminated coaxial transmission line with the following characteristics: $Z_O = 80 - j120$ ohms, $Z_O = 50$ ohms, $\epsilon_r = 1.0$, $f = 9.6$ GHz; determine the following: (a) the shortest distance from the load to the transformer, (b) transformer length, and (c) transformer impedance.

A-5. For a shorted coaxial transmission line with the following characteristics: $Z_O = 50$ ohms, $\epsilon_r = 1.0$, $f = 3.2$ GHz, and $Z_{in} = -j80$ ohms; determine the length of the transmission line.

Answers to Selected Problems

CHAPTER 1

1-1. a. VLF **b.** MF **c.** SHF

1-3. Information capacity doubles; information capacity triples

1-5. a. 290 K **b.** 300 K **c.** 256 K **d.** 223 K

1-7. a. 10^{-18} **b.** 10^{-13} **c.** 10^{-15} **d.** 4×10^{-21}

1-9. a. $f_1 = 500$ Hz, $f_2 = 1000$ Hz, $f_3 = 1500$ Hz, $f_4 = 2000$ Hz, $f_5 = 2500$ Hz
$V_1 = 10.19\ V_p$, $V_2 = 0$ V, $V_3 = 3.4\ V_p$, $V_4 = 0$ V, $V_5 = 2.04\ V_p$

b.

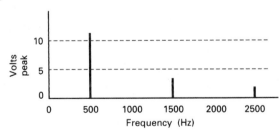

c.

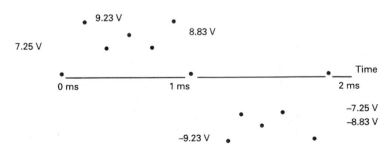

1-11. The frequency spectrum shows five harmonically related frequency components beginning with a fundamental frequency of 1 kHz and four significant higher harmonics. This output spectrum would be typical for a nonlinear amplifier with a single input frequency of 1 kHz and four significant higher harmonics.

1-13. a. 7 kHz, 14 kHz, and 21 kHz; 4 kHz, 8 kHz, and 12 kHz

b.

m	n	Cross Products
1	1	7 ± 4 kHz = 11 and 3 kHz
1	2	7 ± 8 kHz = 15 and 1 kHz
2	1	$14 + 4$ kHz = 18 and 10 kHz
2	2	14 ± 8 kHz = 22 and 6 kHz

c.

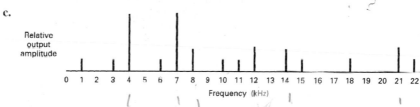

1-15. 20 kHz

1-17. 2nd = 5 kHz   5th = 12.5 kHz   15th = 37.5 kHz

1-19. 2 and 8 kHz, $m = 1$ and $n = 1$

1 and 11 kHz, $m = 1$ and $n = 2$

7 and 13 kHz, $m = 2$ and $n = 1$

4 and 16 kHz, $m = 2$ and $n = 2$

1-21. a. 20 dB   **b.** 26 dB   **c.** -6 dB   **d.** 12 dB

1-23. $F_T = 11.725$, $NF_T = 10.7$ dB

1-25. a. 8.28×10^{-17} W and -130.8 dBm   **b.** 1.287×10^{-7}

1-27. 6.48 dB

1-29. 3 dB

1-31. 21.4 dB

CHAPTER 2

2-1. a. 19.9984 MHz   **b.** 19.9968 MHz   **c.** 20.0032 MHz

2-3. 100 μH

2-5. 0.0022 μF

2-7. a. 1.5 V   **b.** 0.5 V   **c.** 1.85 V   **d.** 0.49 V/rad

2-9. $KV = 86$ dB

2-11. 0.373 V

2-13. 0.25 rad

2-15. 647,126 Hz

2-17. a. -2.4 kHz   **b.** $+2.4$ kHz   **c.** -1.2 kHz

2-19. $+26°$ to $-26°$

2-21. 65 kHz

2-23. a. 80 kHz   **b.** 40 kHz   **c.** 20 kHz/V

2-25. a. 12 kHz/rad   **b.** 5 kHz   **c.** 0.0833 V   **d.** 0.4167 V

e. 0.4167 rad   **f.** 18.84 kHz

2-27. 4.8 kHz

2-29. 39,271 Hz

CHAPTER 3

3-1. a. 95 kHz – 100 kHz and 100 kHz – 105 kHz   **b.** 10 kHz   **c.** 103 kHz and 97 kHz

3-3. 25 V_p and 15 V_p,   0.25 and 25%

3-5. 15 V_p

3-9. 6.4 V_p

3-11. a. 4 V_p **b.** 12 V_p **c.** 8 V_p **d.** 0.667   **e.** 66.7%

3-13. a. 20 W   **b.** 10 W   **c.** 1000 W   **d.** 1020 W

3-15. 3000 W

3-17. a. 112, 32   **b.** 0.224 V, 0.064 V

3-21. a. $m = 0.4$ **b.** $M = 40\%$

3-23. a. 20 V_p **b.** 20 V_p **c.** 10 V_p **d.** 0.5   **e.** 50%

3-25. a. 50%   **b.** 12 V_p and 3 V_p **c.** 18 V_p **d.** 6 V_p

3-27. a. 36.8%   **b.** 38 V_p and 7 V_p

3-29. a. 64 W   **b.** 464 W

3-31. a. 162 and 18   **b.** 1.62 V and 0.18 V

CHAPTER 4

4-1. 8 kHz

4-3. 900 K

4-5. 596 kHz and 604 kHz

4-7. a. 1810 kHz   **b.** 122 or 20.9 dB

4-9. a. 20 kHz   **b.** 14,276 Hz

4-11. 6 dB

4-13. 9 kHz and 26.7 kHz

4-15. 13.6 kHz

4-17. a. 37.685 MHz   **b.** 48.33 MHz

4-19. 40.539 kHz and 23.405 kHz

4-21. 82 dB

4-23. 81.5 dB

CHAPTER 5

5-1. a. 400 kHz to 404 kHz   **b.** 397.2 kHz and 402.8 kHz

5-3. a. 34.1 MHz to 34.104 MHz   **b.** 34.1015 MHz

5-5. a. 28 MHz to 28.003 MHz   **b.** 28.0022 MHz

5-7. a. 496 kHz to 500 kHz   **b.** 497 kHz

5-9. a. 36.196 MHz to 36.204 MHz and 36.2 MHz   **b.** 36.1975, 36.2, and 36.203 MHz

5-11. 10.602 MHz and 10.6 MHz

5-13. a. 202 kHz and 203 kHz   **b.** 5.57 W and 2.278 W

5-15. a. 294 kHz to 306 kHz   **b.** 295.5 kHz to 304.5 kHz

5-17. a. 31.5 MHz to 31.505 MHz   **b.** 31.5025 MHz

5-19. a. 27.0004 MHz to 27.004 MHz   **b.** 27.0018 MHz

5-21. a. 594 kHz to 599.7 kHz   **b.** 597.5 kHz

5-23. a. 594 kHz to 599.7 kHz   **b.** 597.5 kHz

5-25. 19 MHz and 400 kHz

CHAPTER 6

6-1. 0.5 kHz/V and 1 kHz

6-3. a. 40 kHz   **b.** 80 kHz   **c.** 20

6-5. 80%

6-7. a. 4 sets

b.

J_n	V	f
0.22	1.76	carrier
0.58	4.64	1st set
0.35	2.80	2nd set
0.13	1.04	3rd set
0.03	0.24	4th set

d. 16 kHz   **e.** 32 kHz

6-9. 50 kHz

6-11. 2

6-13. 11.858 W, 3.87 W, 0.247 W, 0.008 W

6-15. 0.0377 radians

6-17. a. 7.2 rad   **b.** 14.14 kHz   **c.** 90 MHz

6-19. 0.3 rad/V

6-21. 8 rad

6-23. 1, 2, 3, 4, 8, 14

6-25. 40 kHz and 10 kHz

6-27. 20 kHz

6-29. 144 kHz and 116 kHz

6-31. a. 15 kHz   **b.** 0.03535 rad   **c.** 20 dB

CHAPTER 7

7-1. 18 dB and 22 dB

7-3. 114.15 MHz, 103.45 MHz

7-5. 20.4665 MHz and 20.3335 MHz

7-7. 0.4 V

7-9. 13.3 dB

7-11. −88.97 dBm

7-13. 1 V

7-15. 1.2 V

7-17. 50 dB

CHAPTER 8

8-1.

f	l
1 kHz	300 km
100 kHz	3 km
1 MHz	300 m
1 GHz	0.3 m

8-3. 261 ohms

8-5. 111.8 ohms

8-7. 0.05

8-9. 12

8-11. 1.5

8-13. 252 meters

8-15. 0.8

8-17.

λ	f
5 cm	6 GHz
50 m	600 MHz
5 m	60 MHz
50 m	6 MHz

8-19. 107.4 ohms

8-21. 2.9276×10^8 m/s and 0.976

8-23. 1.01

8-25. 0.833

8-27. 54.77 ohms

CHAPTER 9

9-1. 0.2 μW/m^2

9-3. The power density is inversely proportional to the distance squared. Therefore, the power density would decrease by a factory of 3^2 or 9.

9-5. 14.14 MHz

9-7. 0.0057 V/m

9-9. The power density is inversely proportional to the square of the distance from the source. Therefore, if the distance increases by a factor of 4, the power density decreases by a factor of 4^2 or 16.

9-11. 20 dB

9-13. 8.94 mi

9-15. 17.89 mi

9-17. 0.0095 μW/m^2

9-19. 34.14 mi, 96.57 km

9-21. 3.79 m V/m

9-23. 64

9-25. 16

9-27. 50.58°

9-29. 100.8 mi

CHAPTER 10

10-1. **a.** 25 ohms   **b.** 92.6%   **c.** 926 watts

10-3. 38.13 dB

10-5. 163,611.5 W or 82.1 dBm

10-7. 0.106 μW/m^2

10-9. 16 dB

10-11. 97.9%

10-13. 98.2%

10-15. 5.35 dB and 108.7°

10-17. **a.** 6 GHz   **b.** 5 cm   **c.** 1.54×10^8 m/s   **d.** 5.82×10^8 m/s

10-19. 10 dB

10-21. 82 dBm

10-23. 9.5 μW/m^2

10-25. 9.947 μW

10-27. 87.78 dBm

10-29. 39.5 dB

CHAPTER 11

11-1. **a.** 869 nm, 8690 A°   **b.** 828 nm, 8280 A°   **c.** 935 nm, 9350 A°

11-3. 38.57°

11-5. 36°

11-7. **a.** RZ = 1 Mbps, NRZ = 500 kbps

    b. RZ = 50 kbps, NRZ = 25 kbps

    c. RZ = 250 kbps, NRZ = 125 kbps

11-9. **a.** 789 nm or 7890 A°

    b. 937 nm or 9370 A°

    c. 857 nm or 8570 A°

11-11. 42°

11-13. 36°

11-15. **a.** RZ = 357,143 bps, NRZ = 178,571 bps

    b. RZ = 2 Mbps, NRZ = 1 Mbps

    c. RZ = 250 kbps, NRZ = 125 kbps

CHAPTER 12

12-1. 16 kHz, 4000 baud

12-3. 22 kHz, 10,000 baud

12-5. 5 MHz, 5 Mbaud

12-7. I = 1, Q = 0

12-9.

Q	I	C	phase
0	0	0	+112.5°
0	0	1	+157.5°
0	1	0	+67°
0	1	1	+22°
1	0	0	−112.5°
1	0	1	−157.5°
1	1	0	−67.5°
1	1	1	−22.5°

12-11.

Q	Q'	I	I'	phase
0	0	0	0	−45°
1	1	1	1	+135°
1	0	1	0	+135°
0	1	0	1	−45°

12-13. Input   0 0 1 1 0 0 1 1 0 1 0 1 0 1

     XNOR 1 0 1 1 1 0 1 1 1 0 0 1 1 0 0

12-15. 40 MHz

12-17.

I	Q	phase
0	0	−135°
0	1	+135°
1	0	−45°
1	1	+45°

12-19. 3.333 MHz, 3.333 Mbaud

12-21. 2.5 Mbaud, 2.5 MHz

12-23. **a.** 2 bps/Hz

    b. 3 bps/Hz

    c. 4 bps/Hz

CHAPTER 13

13-1. BCS = 10100000

13-3. 4 Hamming bits

13-5. BCS = 01111111

13-7. 4 Hamming bits

13-9. 44, 4500, 16

13-11. 8 ms and 16 dBm

13-13. greater

13-15. a. harmonic   **b.** intermodulation

13-17. a. -16 dBmO   **b.** 23 dBrncO   **c.** -36 dBm   **d.** 67 dBm

CHAPTER 14

14-1. B8 hex

14-3. 1110001000011111 1110011111 010011101011111 11111 1001011
inserted 0s   0   0   0   0

14-5. 8A hex

14-7. 011011111 110110000011111 00101110001011111 111011111 001
inserted 0s   0   0   0   0

CHAPTER 15

15-1. a. ≥ 8 kHz   **b.** ≥ 20 kHz

15-3. 10 kHz or less

15-5. 54 dB

15-7. a. -2.12 V   **b.** -0.12 V   **c.** $+0.04$ V   **d.** -2.52 **e.** 0 V

15-9. 0.01 V, 0.005 V

15-11. a. $+0.01$ to $+0.03$ **b.** -0.01 to 0   **c.** $+10.23$ to $+10.25$
d. -10.23 to -10.25 **e.** $+5.13$ to $+5.15$ **f.** $+13.63$ to $+13.65$

15-13.

Input	f_s
2 kHz	4 kHz
5 kHz	10 kHz
12 kHz	24 kHz
20 kHz	40 kHz

15-15.

f_s	input
2.5 kHz	1.25 kHz
4 kHz	2 kHz
9 kHz	4.5 kHz
11 kHz	5.5 kHz

15-17.

N	DR	dB
7	63	36
8	127	42
12	2047	66
14	8191	78

15-19.

mμ	V_{max}	V_{in}	Gain
255	1	0.75	0.948
100	1	0.75	0.938
255	2	0.5	1.504

15-21. 50.8 dB, 50.8 dB, 60.34 dB, 36.82 dB

15-23.

V_{in}	12-bit code	8-bit code
−6.592	100110011100	11011001
+12.992	001100101100	01100010
−3.36	100011010010	11001010

12-bit decode	decoded V	% error
100110011000	−6.528	0.98%
001100101000	+12.928	0.495%
100011010100	−3.392	0.94%

15-25. 11001110
00110000
01011111
11111111
00100000

CHAPTER 16

16-1. **a.** 1.521 Mbps   **b.** 760.5 kHz

16-5.

Channel	Frequency (kHz)
1	108
2	104
3	100
4	96
5	92
6	88
7	84
8	80
9	76
10	72
11	68
12	64

16-7. **a.** 5 kHz   **b.** 1.61 Mbps   **c.** 805 kHz

16-10. −+<u>000000</u>+−000+00−   −+<u>000000</u>+−<u>000</u>+00−
0+−0−+   00+00+ 00−
B6ZS   B3ZS

16-11.

CH	GP	SG	MG	CH$_{out}$	GP$_{out}$	SG$_{out}$	MG$_{out}$
2	2	13	1	100–104	364–370	746–750	746–750
6	3	18	2	84–88	428–432	1924–1928	4320–4324
4	5	D25	2	92–96	516–520	2132–2136	4112–4116
9	4	D28	3	72–76	488–492	2904–2908	5940–5944

16-13.

GP	SG	MG	MG$_{out}$
3	13	2	5540–55988
5	D25	3	6704–6752
1	15	1	1248–1296
2	17	2	4504–4552

CHAPTER 17

17-1. −99.23 dBm

17-3. 28.9 dB

17-5. 35 dBm

17-7. −1.25 dB

17-9. 6.39 dB

17-11. −134.2 dBm, −127.9 dBm, −128.8 dBm, −122.7 dBm

17-13. 37.1 dB

17-15. −77 dBm, 37 dBm

17-17. 13.8 dB

17-19. 8.23 dB

CHAPTER 18

18-1. Elevation angle = 51°, azimuth = 33° west of south

18-3. **a.** 11.74 dB   **b.** 8.75 dB

18-5. 68 dBW

18-7. −200.8 dBW

18-9. 26.18 dB

18-11. 19.77 dB

18-13. 12.5 dB overall

CHAPTER 19

19-1. 15 transponders

19-3. 44 stations

19-5. 10 transponders

19-7. 57.44 channels

CHAPTER 20

20-1. 360, 3600

20-3. 37

20-5. 3.33

Index

Antenna polarization, 382
Antenna top loading, 390
Antialiasing, 674
Antifoldover filter, 674
Antipodal signaling, 512
APD, 460
Aperture distortion, 671
Aperture efficiency, 405
Aperture error, 670
Aperture number, 405
Aperture ratio, 403
Aperture time, 670
Apogee, 798
ARCH, 893
ARM, 625
Armstrong, Edwin Howard, 1, 228
Armstrong indirect FM transmitter, 266–269
ARQ, 541
ARQ exact-count code, 536
Array, 391
ASCII, 531–533
Asynchronous data format, 543, 544
Asynchronous modems, 589, 590
Asynchronous protocols, 608–610
Asynchronous receivers, 145
Asynchronous transfer mode (ATM),
    631–634, 643
AT command mode, 596
AT command set, 595, 596
AT on-line mode, 596
AT&T's FDM hierarchy, 744–746
ATM, 631–634, 643
Atmospheric noise, 34
Attenuation, 351, 352, 442
Attenuation distortion, 574–578
Audio detector, 149
Automatic desensing, 178
Automatic frequency control, 264
Automatic gain control (AGC), 54
Automatic gain control (AGC) circuits,
    176–178
Autopatch, 865
Avalanche photodiode (APD), 460
Azimuth, 807
Azimuth angle, 807

B3ZS, 739
B6ZS, 738
B8ZS, 738
Back-off loss, 817
Back-to-back coupling, 401
Baird, J. L., 423
Balanced bridge modulator, 201–203
Balanced diode mixer, 163–165
Balanced interface, 557
Balanced modulators, 163, 197
Balanced ring modulator, 197–199
Balanced slope detector, 278, 279
Balanced transmission line, 557
Balanced transmission system, 313
Baluns, 557
Bandlimiting, 27

Bandpass limiter/amplifier (BPL), 287
Bandwidth, 8–10, 383
Bandwidth distance product (BDP), 446
Bandwidth efficiency, 504
Bandwidth improvement, 142
Bandwidth length product (BLP), 446
Bandwidth utilization ratio, 422
Bar codes, 533–535
Barkhausen criterion, 52
Barnett, W. T., 784
Barnett-Vignant reliability equations, 784
Base stations, 875
Baseband, 746, 763
Baseband repeater, 766, 767
Baseband transmission formats, 649, 650
Basic rate interface (BRI), 638
Baud, 472
Baudot, Emile, 525, 530
Baudot, J. M. E., 472
Baudot code, 530, 531
Bazooka, 315
BCCH, 893
BCS, 539
BDP, 446
BDT, 644
Beacon test, 622
Beamwidth, 382, 383
Beat frequency, 80, 91
Beat frequency oscillator (BFO), 214
Bell, Alexander Graham, 1, 422, 525
Bell system modems, 592
BER, 509
Bessel function identities, 238
Bessel function of the first kind, 238–240
BFO, 214
Binary exponential back-off algorithm, 659
Binary FSK, 471, 472
Binary phase-shift keying (BPSK), 478–484
Biphase, 735
Biphase modulation, 478
Bipolar-return-to-zero alternate mark
    inversion (BPRZ-AMI), 732
Bipolar transistor RF amplifier, 160
Bipolar transmission, 732
BISDN, 643–645
Bisync, 610–614
Bit energy, 818
Bit error rate (BER), 509
Bit interleaving, 741
Bit rate, 472
Bit stealing, 851
Bit timing recovery (BTR), 842
Black-body noise, 35
Blank-and-burst, 882
Blanking circuit, 181
Blinding character, 610
Block check character (BCC), 539
Block check sequence (BCS), 539
Block mode of data transmission, 608
Blocking, 626, 872, 878
BLP, 446
Bockham, G. A., 423

BPL, 287
BPRZ-AMI, 732
BPSK, 478–484
BPSK receiver, 483, 484
BPSK transmitter, 478–482
Braid, 316
Branching loss, 782
BRI, 638
Broadband aspects of ISDN, 643
Broadband distant terminal (BDT), 644
Broadband ISDN (BISDN), 643–645
Broadband mode, 643
Broadband network termination (BNT), 643
Broadband terminal interface (BTI), 643
Broadband transmission formats, 649, 650
Broadcast address, 609
Broadcast control channel (BCCH), 893
Broadside antenna, 391, 392
Brown, Robert, 35
Brownian noise, 35
Buffer amplifier, 127
Bulk acoustic waves (BAWs), 60
Burrus etched-well LED, 454
Burst mode, 719
Bus, 793
Bus topology, 647–649
Byte-interleaved multiplexing, 636

C-message filters, 581
C-message noise, 581
C-message weighting curve, 580
C-notched noise measurements, 582
C-type conditioning, 574–578
CA3028A, 171, 172
Cable bends, 463
Cable losses, 462
Cable-to-light detector interface loss, 463
Capture area, 380, 404, 405
Capture effect, 270, 287
Capture range, 74, 83, 89
Capture ratio, 288
Captured power, 381
Captured power density, 380
Carrier, 2
Carrier-amplitude fading, 196
Carrier leak, 199
Carrier oscillator, 127
Carrier recovery, 505–507
Carrier recovery circuit, 217
Carrier recovery sequence (CRS), 842
Carrier rests frequency, 231
Carrier shift, 131, 132
Carrier swing, 235
Carrier-to-noise (C/N), 785, 786
Carrier-to-noise density ratio, 821
Carrier-to-noise power ratio, 510
Carson, J. R., 241
Carson's rule, 242, 243
Carterfone decision, 525
Cascoded amplifier, 159, 160
Cassegrain-feed parabolic antenna, 407, 409
Cassegrain subreflector, 407

dB, 586
dBm, 586
dBmO, 587
DBPSK receiver, 508, 509
DBPSK transmitter, 507, 508
dBrn, 588
dBrnc, 587
dBrncO, 588
DC wandering, 732, 733
DDD network, 566–571
Dead reckoning, 851
Dead time, 544
Deemphasis, 251, 252
Deep-space noise, 34
DeForest, Lee, 1
Degenerative feedback, 52
Delay lines, 211, 324, 325
Delayed AGC, 176, 178
Delimiting sequence, 615
Delta modulation PCM, 695–697
Delta modulation receiver, 696, 697
Delta modulation transmitter, 695, 696
Demand assignment, 836
Demand assignment, multiple access (DAMA), 839
Demodulation, 3, 100, 140. *See also* Amplitude modulation reception
Demodulator, 3
DEMOS-FET RF amplifier, 159, 160
Demultiplexers, 757
Dense-wave-division multiplexing (D-WDM), 754, 755
Descending node, 799, 800
Descrambler, 593–595
Destructive interference, 211
Detector distortion, 175, 176
Deviation ratio, 244
Deviation sensitivity, 232, 235
Diagonal clipping, 175
Dial switch, 566, 567
Dibits, 484
Dichroic filter, 758
Dicode, 735
Dicode NRZ, 736
Dicode RZ, 736
Dielectric constant, 323
Dielectric heating loss, 326
Differential gain, 574
Differential GPS, 862
Differential Manchester, 736
Differential PCM, 698, 731
Differential phase shift, 144
Differential phase-shift keying (DPSK), 507–509
Differential pulse code modulation (DPCM), 698
Differential transmission system, 313
Diffraction, 357
Diffraction grating, 758
Digit-at-a-time coding, 683
Digital amplitude modulation, 470, 471
Digital biphase, 734, 735

Digital carrier system, 710
Digital cellular telephone, 885–893
Digital communications, 2, 467–523
Digital companding, 686–693
Digital cross-connect (DSX), 728
Digital noninterpolated interface (DNI), 850
Digital radio, 3, 468–470
Digital signal processing (DSP), 667
Digital speech interpolated interface (DSI), 850, 851
Digital-to-analog converter (DAC), 669
Digital transmission, 2, 468, 667–707
Diode detector, 173
Diode mixer, 163, 165
Diplexer, 373
Dipole, 371
Direct FM modulators, 253–258
Direct FM transmitters, 262–266
Direct frequency modulation, 229
Direct frequency synthesizers, 89–91
Direct phase modulation, 229
Direct PM modulators, 258, 259
Direct sequence (DS), 848
Direct-sequence spread spectrum (DS-SS), 848, 849, 897
Direct waves, 361, 781
Directive gain, 377
Directivity, 377
Director, 391
Discrete Fourier transform, 27
Discrete Pierce oscillator, 64, 65
Dish antennas, 401
Distributed parameters, 317, 572
Distribution services, 643
Diversity, 768–771
Diversity protection, 771–773
Double-conversion AM receiver, 183, 184
Double-conversion FM receiver, 277
Double limiting, 288
Double peaking, 168
Double-sideband suppressed-carrier (DSBSC) modulators, 197
Double spotting, 158
Double-tuned transformers, 168
Down-conversion, 4
Down-link equation, 827
Down-link model, 816
Down-link traffic channel, 897, 898
Downward modulation, 131
DPCM, 698
DPSK, 507–509
Driven elements, 391
Driver, 552
Droop, 672
Dropout, 584
DSBSC modulators, 197
DSBSC AM system, 221–223
DSI, 850, 851
DSX, 728
Dual attach, 660
Dual mode, 886
Dualisation, 874

Duct propagation, 362
Dudley, Homer, 694
DuHamel, R. H., 396
Dumb modems, 595
Duplexer, 879
Duty cycle, 22, 732
Dynamic range, 143, 677–679
Dyson, J. D., 396

E-BCCH, 893
E layer, 363, 364
Earhart, Amelia, 851
Early token release mechanism, 651
Earth (global) beams, 814
Earth coverage radiation patterns, 814
EBCDIC, 533
Echo, 341
Echo cancellation, 598
Echo suppressors, 13
Echoplex, 535, 536
EDD, 579
Edge emitters, 454
Edge-emitting LED, 456
Edge-excited cell, 868
Effective isotropic radiated power (EIRP), 378, 379, 818, 819
Effective radiated power (ERP), 378
EIA, 526
EIA RS-232 pin functions, 553–556
Eight-phase PSK (8-PSK), 490–496
8-PSK, 490–496
8-PSK TCM constellations, 519
8-PSK transmitter, 490–492
(8-QAM), 496–500
EIRP, 378, 379, 818, 819
Electrical length (transmission lines), 324
Electrical noise, 34. *See also* Noise analysis
Electrical oscillation, 51
Electrical power, 26
Electromagnetic frequency spectrum, 5
Electromagnetic induction, 1
Electromagnetic polarization, 348
Electromagnetic radiation, 348, 349
Electromagnetic spectrum, 4–8, 425
Electromagnetic wave interference, 357, 359
Electromagnetic wave propagation, 347–370
Electromagnetic wavelength spectrum, 7
Electromagnetic waves, 310–313
Electronic communications system, 1, 2
Electronic Industries Association (EIA), 526
Electronic push-to-talk, 305, 306
Electronic switching center, 876
Electronic switching system (ESS), 570, 744
Elementary dipole, 383
Elementary doublet, 383, 384
Elevation angle, 805
Elliptical polarization, 348
Emission classification, 7
Emitter modulation, 116–118
End-fire antenna, 392
End-fire helical antenna, 399
End separation, 449